The Yale Edition of the Complete Works of St. Thomas More

VOLUME 15

In Defense Of Humanism
LETTER TO MARTIN DORP
LETTER TO THE UNIVERSITY OF OXFORD
LETTER TO EDWARD LEE
LETTER TO A MONK

with
A New Text and Translation of
HISTORIA RICHARDI TERTII

Published by the St. Thomas More Project, Yale University,
under the auspices of Gerard L. Carroll and Joseph B. Murray,
Trustees of the Michael P. Grace, II, Trust,
and with the support of the Editing Program of the
National Endowment for the Humanities
and the Knights of Columbus

NOVVM IN

ſtrumentũ omne, diligenter ab ERASMO ROTERODA MO
recognitum & emendatum, nõ ſolum ad græcam ueritatem, ue-
rumetiam ad multorum utriuſcɧ linguæ codicum, eorumcɧ ueterum ſimul & emendatorum fidem, poſtremo ad pro-
batiſſimorum autorum citationem, emendationem
& interpretationem, præcipue, Origenis, Chry-
ſoſtomi, Cyrilli, Vulgarij, Hieronymi, Cy-
priani, Ambroſij, Hilarij, Auguſti/
ni, una cũ Annotationibus, quæ
lectorem doceant, quid qua
ratione mutatum ſit.
Quiſquis igitur
amas ue-
rath
Theolo/
giam, lege, cogno
ſce, ac deinde iudica,
Necɧ ſtatim offendere, ſi
quid mutatum offenderis, ſed
expende, num in melius mutatum ſit.

APVD INCLYTAM
GERMANIAE BASILEAM.

CVM PRIVILEGIO
MAXIMILIANI CAESARIS AVGVSTI,
NE QVIS ALIVS IN SACRA ROMA-
NI IMPERII DITIONE, INTRA QVATV
OR ANNOS EXCVDAT, AVT ALIBI
EXCVSVM IMPORTET.

Joan. Frobenij

Title-page, *Novum Instrumentum*, Basel, 1516 (reduced)

The Complete Works of
ST. THOMAS MORE

VOLUME 15

Edited by

DANIEL KINNEY

Yale University Press, New Haven and London

Published with assistance from

Copyright © 1986 by Yale University.
All rights reserved.
This book may not be reproduced, in whole
or in part, in any form (beyond that
copying permitted by Sections 107 and 108
of the U.S. Copyright Law and except by
reviewers for the public press), without
written permission from the publishers.

Set in Baskerville type.
Printed in the United States of America by
Murray Printing Company, Westford, Mass.

Library of Congress catalogue number: 63–7949
International standard book number: 0–300–03161–0

The paper in this book meets
the guidelines for permanence and durability
of the Committee on Production Guidelines
for Book Longevity of the Council on
Library Resources.

10   9   8   7   6   5   4   3   2   1

For Clare

tu tamen ingenio clara ferere tuo

ACKNOWLEDGMENTS

This edition owes most to the tireless and expert attentions of Clarence H. Miller, the executive editor of the More Project, whose keen insights, objectives, and answers inform every page of the book. Special thanks also go to Ralph Keen and Kathleen Perry, who have helped research textual cruxes and clear up numerous questions of factual detail. I should also like to thank Louis L. Martz, whose support helped to launch my edition, James K. McConica, who examined the manuscript for Yale University Press, Ann Hawthorne, whose fine copyediting has helped make it a book to be proud of, and my instructors and critics at Yale, in particular Margaret W. Ferguson, A. Bartlett Giamatti, and Thomas M. Greene. I am especially grateful to the following libraries for permission to study and reproduce manuscript materials: the texts of the *Historia Richardi Tertii* and the *Letter to Dorp* are based upon the Paris manuscripts by kind permission of Bibliothèque Nationale, Paris (MS fr. 4996 (Ancien fonds), MS lat. 8703); variants in the text of the *Letter to Dorp* have been recorded from the Sélestat manuscript by kind permission of Bibliothèque Humaniste Sélestat (France) and Conservator Hubert Meyer (MS 345); the text of the *Letter to Oxford,* by kind permission of the Bodleian Library, is based upon an Oxford manuscript (Bodleian MS Top. Oxon. e. 5). I am also grateful to the staff of the Beinecke Library at Yale for their constant and cheerful assistance. Finally, I should like to acknowledge a good deal of help and advice from the rest of the More Project Staff, in particular Stephen M. Foley and Michele Margetts; a supremely well-timed personal grant from the Mrs. Giles Whiting Foundation; and the generous ongoing support of the Knights of Columbus.

J. D. K.

Charlottesville, Virginia

CONTENTS

ILLUSTRATIONS

INTRODUCTION

In both bulk and importance the four letter-essays which make up the first part of this volume bear comparison with More's best-known humanist writings, *Utopia* (1516), *Epigrammata* (1518), and *Historia Richardi Tertii*, an unfinished effort which probably dates from about the same period. The *Letter to Dorp* and book 2 of *Utopia* were written in 1515 during More's first diplomatic mission to Flanders; the *Letter to Oxford* was written in 1518 shortly after More formally entered the service of Henry VIII; and the *Letter to Lee* and the *Letter to a Monk* were both written in 1519, when the Lutheran crisis had already begun. The intellectual and religious concerns which the four letters share with *Utopia* on the one hand and with More's later polemical works on the other make these bold and ambitious Erasmian defenses a singularly valuable resource for any reader who seeks to gain a balanced and reasonably complete understanding of More's life and works.

Earlier scholars have made skillful use of this resource to illuminate particular passages in *Utopia* or to clarify More's ultimate positions on the Church and the meaning of scripture.[1] Nonetheless, there have been surprisingly few efforts to evaluate the early defenses as works with a purpose and form of their own.[2] They are too often treated as casual by-products of *Utopia* or crude anticipations of certain arguments used in the later polemics; since they fail to conform to our notions of what letters should be, they are too readily dismissed as "hasty, rambling composition[s]" permeated with ominous "heat and

---

[1]See especially Edward L. Surtz, S. J., *The Praise of Pleasure: Philosophy, Education, and Communism in More's Utopia* (Cambridge, Mass., 1957; hereafter cited as "Surtz, *Praise of Pleasure*"), and *The Praise of Wisdom: A Commentary on the Religious and Moral Problems and Backgrounds of St. Thomas More's Utopia* (Chicago, 1957; hereafter cited as "Surtz, *Praise of Wisdom*").

[2]For pre-1981 editions and translations of More's humanistic defenses see below, pp. cxix–cxxx. For a full bibliography of previous critical scholarship on the *Letter to Dorp* see Daniel Kinney, "More's *Letter to Dorp*: Remapping the Trivium," *Renaissance Quarterly, 34* (1981), 179, n. 1 (hereafter cited as "Kinney, 'More's *Letter to Dorp*'"); for a more recent study see Uwe Baumann, "Dorp, Erasmus, More: Humanistische Aspekten einer literarischen Kontroverse," *Thomas-Morus-Gesellschaft: Jahrbuch 1982*, ed. Hermann Boventer (Düsseldorf, 1983), pp. 141–59. Mr. Baumann's *Die Antike in den Epigrammen und Briefen Sir Thomas Mores* (Paderborn, Munich, and Vienna, 1984) was published after this edition was already in press. The other defenses have received much less critical attention; see Henri Gibaud, "Thomas More: Réponse à un moine anti-Erasmien," unpublished Mémoire pour le diplome d'études supérieures, University of Tours, 1967 (hereafter cited as "Gibaud, 'Réponse'"), pp. i–xxxvi; Richard J. Schoeck, "More's Letters and the Epistolary Defense of Erasmian Humanism," chapter 1 of *The Achievement of Thomas More: Aspects of His Life and Works* (Victoria, British Columbia, 1976; hereafter cited as "Schoeck"), pp. 25–38; and Clare M. Murphy, "An Epistolary Defense of Erasmus: Thomas More and an English Carthusian," in *Acta Conventus Neo-Latini Turonensis*, ed. J.-C. Margolin (Paris, 1980), pp. 329–47.

confusion."[1] Recent attempts to explain how the genial ambivalence of the Utopian More could give way to the rigid imperiousness of the later polemical More have paid too little attention to the tactfully vehement More of the humanist defenses.[2] Once we see how the program of indirect, gradual persuasion through dialogue which determines the very design of the *Letter to Dorp* complements the suggestive ambivalence of the various reforming initiatives proposed in *Utopia*, we begin to see how More's defenses of Erasmian humanism can help to explain his own practice and aims as a humanist author.[3]

More shows steadily growing impatience and reluctance to compromise with the partisan enemies of Erasmian dialogue in his later humanistic defenses: though Erasmus is able to sustain an increasingly hopeless commitment to reform and persuasion through dialogue in an age of increasingly violent factional strife, More the activist is not. But before he abandons the freedom and tolerance of dialogue entirely, he produces one of the most lucid and forceful apologies for Erasmian values ever written, the astonishing *Letter to a Monk*. Even though More instinctively sides with the Church against partisan dogmatists like Luther and Tyndale, his secular creed is consistently Erasmian, the creed of the humanist defenses.

---

[1] For these assessments of the *Letter to Dorp* see J. H. Hexter, "*Utopia* and Its Historical Milieu," in St. Thomas More, *Utopia*, ed. Edward L. Surtz, S. J., and J. H. Hexter, *The Yale Edition of the Complete Works of St. Thomas More* (New Haven and London, 1963–; hereafter cited as *CW*), *4*, lxvii; and H. A. Mason, *Poetry and Humanism in the Early Tudor Period* (London, 1959), p. 93.

[2] The humanist defenses figure scarcely at all in two otherwise very valuable studies of More's writings, Stephen Greenblatt, *Renaissance Self-Fashioning from More to Shakespeare* (Chicago and London, 1980; hereafter cited as "Greenblatt"), pp. 11–73; and Alistair Fox, *Thomas More: History and Providence* (New Haven and London, 1982; hereafter cited as "Fox, *Thomas More*").

[3] For earlier studies of More's place in the humanist intellectual tradition see especially William Nelson, "Thomas More: Grammarian and Orator," in *Essential Articles for the Study of Thomas More*, ed. Richard S. Sylvester and Germain P. Marc'hadour (Hamden, Conn., 1977; hereafter cited as "*Essential Articles*"), pp. 150–60; Craig R. Thompson, "The Humanism of More Reappraised," *Thought*, *52* (1977), 231–48 (hereafter cited as "Thompson"; and P. O. Kristeller, "Thomas More as a Renaissance Humanist," *Moreana*, *65–66* (1980), 5–22. For a good general treatment of humanist origins in relation to modern-day "humanisms" see Vito R. Giustiniani, "Homo, Humanus, and the Meanings of 'Humanism,'" *Journal of the History of Ideas*, *46* (1985), 167–95.

HISTORICAL CONTEXTS

Letter to Dorp

From 1514 to 1520 probably the principal center of resistance to Erasmian ideas was the University of Louvain, an academy with which Erasmus himself had particularly intimate ties.[1] Though the conservative theologians of Louvain were unusually suspicious of Erasmian innovations, we should probably beware of regarding the Louvain theologians en masse as implacably hostile to the rhetorical and literary pursuits generally stressed by the humanists: humanist grammar and rhetoric had coexisted more or less peacefully with traditional dialectic and theology in the Louvain curriculum for some years before 1514.[2] A less simplistic way of explaining the conflict is to note that traditionally the study of grammar and rhetoric was strictly preliminary to the pursuit of higher studies in which dialectical method prevailed, while according to Erasmus even the loftiest of disciplines, theology itself, was in need of material renewal and methodical reorganization on the basis of humanist rhetoric and grammar.[3] Just as Erasmus' *Praise of Folly* had assailed the quite basic traditionalist assumption that the methods of Aristotelian dialectic afforded the most cogent and

---

[1]For the history of Erasmus' relations with the University of Louvain see Henry De Vocht, *Monumenta Humanistica Lovaniensia: Texts and Studies about Louvain Humanists in the First Half of the Sixteenth Century* (Louvain, 1934; hereafter cited as "De Vocht, *Monumenta*"), pp. 138–253, and *History of the Foundation and Rise of the Collegium Trilingue Lovaniense 1517–1550*, 4 vols. (Louvain, 1951–55). For a more recent, closely related study see Jerry H. Bentley, "New Testament Scholarship at Louvain in the Early Sixteenth Century," *Studies in Medieval and Renaissance History*, New Series, 2 (1979), 51–79. See also Jozef IJsewijn, "The Coming of Humanism to the Low Countries," in *Itinerarium Italicum: The Profile of the Italian Renaissance in the Mirror of its European Transformations*, ed. Heiko A. Obermann with Thomas A. Brady, Jr. (Leiden, 1975), pp. 193–301.

[2]See De Vocht, *Monumenta*, pp. 125–30, 303–08.

[3]For Erasmus' attempt to reorganize the study of theology on the basis of humanist rhetoric and grammar see Charles E. Trinkaus, "Erasmus, Augustine, and the Nominalists," *Archiv für Reformationsgeschichte*, 67 (1976), 5–32; Marjorie O'Rourke Boyle, *Erasmus on Language and Method in Theology* (Toronto and Buffalo, 1977; hereafter cited as "Boyle"); and Salvatore I. Camporeale, "Da Lorenzo Valla a Tommaso Moro: Lo statuto umanistico della teologia," *Memorie domenicane*, New Series, 4 (1973), 9–102; hereafter cited as "Camporeale, 'Da Lorenzo Valla a Tommaso Moro.'" For an indispensable general study of Erasmus' grammatical and rhetorical interests see Jacques

straightforward means of expounding the teachings of Christ, so his project of noting discrepancies between the Vulgate translation of the New Testament and the original Greek challenged the even more basic assumption that the literal sense of Christ's teachings was readily accessible without frequent recourse to the lessons of grammar.[1] By 1514 it seemed clear that Erasmus was mounting a general challenge to traditional curricular priorities in the name of the humanists' own favorite pursuits; he appeared to be merely renewing the insolent assault of the radical rhetorician Lorenzo Valla on the time-honored intellectual privileges of the dialecticians.[2] Not all humanists shared Valla's radicalism, and at least some, like Poggio, evidently believed that the best way to guard humanist studies against the reproach of the dialecticians was to accept the peripheral but relatively uncontroversial role which was assigned to such studies in the established medieval curriculum.[3] A similar attitude toward the most daring claims of rhetorical humanism was initially also characteristic of Maarten van Dorp,

---

Chomarat, *Grammaire et rhétorique chez Erasme*, 2 vols. (Paris, 1981; hereafter cited as "Chomarat"). The following comment by Camporeale (p. 40) is especially pertinent:

> [For Erasmus and More, as for Valla,] la teologia . . . una volta accettato quale modello scientifico la "litterarum scientia," doveva assumere, sempre mediante una trasposizione analogica, i propri strumenti operativi di ricerca dalla "grammatica" o "litteratura" ([Quintilian,] *Inst. orat.* II.14.3) e configurarsi alla Retorica nella propria struttura scientifica di argomentazione dimostrativa.

[1] For Folly's critique of scholastic theology see Erasmus, *Moriae encomium*, ed. Clarence H. Miller, in *Opera omnia Desiderii Erasmi Roterodami*, ed. J. H. Waszink et al., 10 vols. (Amsterdam, 1969–; hereafter cited as *ASD*), 4/3, 144–58. For early references to Erasmus' intention of "correcting" the Vulgate according to the original Greek see *Opus epistolarum Des. Erasmi Roterodami*, ed. P. S. Allen et al., 12 vols. (Oxford, 1906–58; hereafter cited as "Allen"), *1*, 570, lines 155–57; 2, 4–5, lines 31–33; 14, lines 86–88; 78, lines 164–67. See also Allen, *1*, 14, lines 5–16; 64, lines 278–85; and the other references given in Allen, 2, 182–83.

[2] For Valla's assault on the dialecticians see especially Jerrold E. Seigel, *Rhetoric and Philosophy in Renaissance Humanism: The Union of Eloquence and Wisdom, Petrarch to Valla* (Princeton, 1968; hereafter cited as "Seigel"), pp. 137–69; and Camporeale, *Lorenzo Valla: Umanesimo e teologia* (Florence, 1972; hereafter cited as "Camporeale, *Lorenzo Valla*"). For Erasmus' indebtedness to Valla see especially Camporeale, "Da Lorenzo Valla a Tommaso Moro," pp. 9–102; Jerry H. Bentley, *Humanists and Holy Writ: New Testament Scholarship in the Renaissance* (Princeton, 1983), especially pp. 137–67; and Chomarat, *1*, 227–65. For Dorp's 1510 attack on Valla's *De dialectica disputatione* in the name of the Louvain conservatives see De Vocht, *Monumenta*, pp. 131 and 317–18; and note on 98/12–13 below. In Allen, 2, 14, 15, 128, and 135, Dorp also disparages Valla's *Annotationes* on the New Testament and his *Elegantiae linguae latinae*.

[3] For Poggio's opposition to Valla's extreme exaltation of grammar and rhetoric see Camporeale, *Lorenzo Valla*, pp. 33–36, 89–100, 105–08, 350–403.

Louvain humanist-turned-theologian, the first of Erasmus' many critics.[1]

Maarten van Dorp (1485–May 31, 1525), born in Naaldwijk, Holland, took his M.A. in the Collège du Lis of the University of Louvain on April 4, 1504.[2] It is likely that he first met Erasmus in 1502–03 while the latter was visiting Louvain.[3] By 1504 Dorp was probably already established as a teacher of Latin, and by 1505 he was also installed as a lecturer (*legens*) in philosophy.[4] He was personally responsible for organizing performances of two Plautine plays in his college in 1508–09, and in 1509 the city officials of Louvain offered him a fairly lucrative post as a lecturer in Latin poetry.[5] For some time, however, he had also been attending university lectures in theology, and with the encouragement of Meinard Man, abbot of Egmond Abbey, and John Briart of Ath (*Athensis*), Louvain professor of theology, he eventually decided against a traditional humanist career and devoted himself to scholastic theology.[6] He became a bachelor of theology in January 1510, a licentiate in late 1513, and a doctor of theology in August 1515.[7] Meanwhile he continued to pursue various humanist interests and to cultivate humanist friendships. Peter Giles dedicated an edition of Rodolphus Agricola's *Opuscula* to Dorp in 1511; Dorp met with Erasmus in 1514 and supervised publication of various minor works edited by Erasmus along with one minor translation edited by Dorp himself; and in January 1515 he produced the *editio princeps* of Agricola's renowned *De inventione dialectica*.[8] His own minor publications include a supplement

---

[1]Dorp's theoretical affinity with Poggio is emphasized in Camporeale, "Da Lorenzo Valla a Tommaso Moro," p. 44. In a long public letter of 1523 to John Botzheim (Allen, *1*, 22, lines 5–10), Erasmus calls Dorp his first critic; Dorp was almost undoubtedly the first to distribute a written critique of Erasmus.

[2]By far the most thorough biographical study of Dorp is that of De Vocht, *Monumenta*, pp. 63–348; now see also P. Bietenholz, ed., *Contemporaries of Erasmus, A–E* (Toronto, 1985), pp. 398–404. De Vocht's miscellaneous offering includes first editions of an important apology by Dorp (pp. 75–93) and a life of Dorp written by one of his students, Gerard Morinck (pp. 258–81). For Dorp's M.A. degree see De Vocht, *Monumenta*, p. 298.

[3]De Vocht, *Monumenta*, p. 138.

[4]De Vocht, *Monumenta*, pp. 128, 298, 332.

[5]De Vocht, *Monumenta*, pp. 128–29, 133.

[6]De Vocht, *Monumenta*, pp. 132–33.

[7]De Vocht, *Monumenta*, pp. 134, 312–13.

[8]For these three editions see W. Nijhoff and M. E. Kronenberg, *Nederlandsche Bibliographie van 1500 tot 1540*, 3 vols. (The Hague, 1923–42; reprint, 1965; hereafter cited as "Nijhoff–Kronenberg"), *1*, nos. 46, 45, 2, no. 2603. For the volume of minor works edited by Erasmus and primarily devoted to the *Disticha Catonis* see Allen, 2, 1, and 16, lines 156–60. The volume also includes one work Dorp edited alone, the *Parainesis* of Isocrates in the Latin translation of Rodolphus Agricola.

to Plautus' *Aulularia*, prologues for the *Aulularia* and the *Miles gloriosus*, a fairly conventional humanist *Dialogus* on the Choice of Hercules, a dedicatory letter condemning the vices of worldly abbots, and a remarkably liberal *Oratio de laudibus disciplinarum* recommending the study of humanist grammar and rhetoric as well as theology; all these works were published some years after Dorp had begun to refer to himself as a *theologus*.[1] Clearly it would be wrong to view Dorp as an unwavering convert to rigid scholasticism.

After his meeting with Erasmus in mid-1514, Dorp wrote him a letter purporting to state the objections of other Louvain theologians to the levity of the *Praise of Folly* and to the temerity of Erasmus' intention to publicize all the discrepancies between the Vulgate translation of the New Testament and the original Greek.[2] According to Erasmus, the letter was never delivered; he first saw it months later in Antwerp, where a friend had gotten a copy by chance.[3] Erasmus drafted a hasty response in late May 1515, and expanded and altered it slightly for quick publication with *Damiani Senensis elegeia* (Basel, August 1515).[4] Dorp answered the first version of this letter by reiterating

---

[1]According to De Vocht, *Monumenta*, pp. 326–29, Dorp's Plautine additions and his *Dialogus in quo Venus et Cupido omnes adhibent versutias* were originally published as two separate pamphlets in 1513; no copies of these first editions are known to survive. The Plautine additions are printed after the *Dialogus* in the earliest extant edition, that of 1514; see note on 116/6–118/2, below; De Vocht, *Monumenta*, p. 333; and Nijhoff–Kronenberg, *1*, no. 737, and *3*, no. 372. The *Dialogus* is available in a modern edition by J. IJsewijn, "Martinus Dorpius, *Dialogus* (ca. 1508?)," in *Charisterium H. de Vocht 1878–1978*, ed. J. IJsewijn and J. Roegiers, Supplementa Humanistica Lovaniensia 2 (Louvain, 1979), pp. 74–101. Dorp's dedicatory letter condemning worldly abbots, which More cites at 42/4–6 and 108/19, first appeared in the *Quaestiones quodlibeticae* of Adrian of Utrecht, the future Pope Adrian VI (Louvain, T. Martens, March 1515; Nijhoff–Kronenberg, *1*, no. 9); Dorp's letter is reprinted in De Vocht, *Monumenta*, pp. 112–20. For Dorp's *Oratio de laudibus disciplinarum* (Louvain, T. Martens, October 1513) see De Vocht, *Monumenta*, pp. 136–37, 318–23; Nijhoff–Kronenberg, *1*, no. 738, and *3*, no. 0373. Therein Dorp praises humanist grammar and rhetoric but opposes Lefèvre d'Etaples' reformed dialectic and the suspect rhetorical methods of humanist philology (cf. Allen, 2, 15, where Dorp disapprovingly links Lefèvre d'Etaples with Valla). Ortwin Gratius, the enemy of Reuchlin, also couched an apology for moderate humanism in a scholastic rhetorical form; see note on 120/3–4, below. For Dorp's other significant early writings see notes on 98/11–12 and 106/24–25, below. He was also responsible for an important collection of Aesopica; see Paul Thoen, "Aesopus Dorpii: Essai sur l'Esope latin des temps modernes," *Humanistica Lovaniensia, 19* (1970), 241–316.

[2]Allen, 2, 10–16, probably written in September 1514.

[3]Allen, 2, 91, lines 1–2.

[4]Allen, 2, 90–114, probably written in late May 1515. For an early edition of this letter not reported by Allen see Nijhoff–Kronenberg, 2, no. 2938. It exhibits no substantive variants from the first edition noted by Allen.

Anno falu-
tis 1520.

chio Brandenburgenſis,Stetinenſium,Pomeraniæ, Caſſuborum, Scla-
uorumcp dux,Burgrauius Nurenburgenſis,ac Rugiẹ princeps. Vir om
ni uirtutum genere abſolutiſsimus,Dei cultor,utriuſcp imperij guberna
cula conferens,humana in diuina incredibili ſtudio commutauit. Sedit
ann.31.menſ.6.dies 8.obijt anno Domini 1545. die 24.menſ.Septemb.ſuæ
uerò ætatis anno 55.   Anon.in Archiep.Mogunt.Ioan.Sleid.

MARTINVS DORPIVS THEOLOGVS.

1520

Martinus apud Belgas in Hollandia honeſtis
parentibus natus,& in omni genere ſtudio-
rum optimè educatus eſt. Cum is in patria rudimẽ
ta literarũ percepiſſet,ſeſe ad Louanienſem Acade
miam cõtulit,atcp linguarum puritati & S.Theolo
giæ præclaram operam nauauit. Eius enim tẽpore
bonæ literæ in Germaniam reuocatæ, atcp Alexan
der,Petrus Hiſpanus,Tartaretus & ſimiles ex ſcho
lis celebrioribus eiectæ. Itacp cum Martinus feliciter pergeret, atcp inter Theologos magnũ ſibi nomen ſua eruditione comparaſſet, S.literarũ profeſ-
ſor Louanij conſtitutus eſt.Eam profeſsionẽ is ma
gna laude ſuſcepit,atcp in prẹlectione epiſtolarum
D.Pauli præclaram orationem habuit,& edidit 1520. In ea tractat de Pauli lau
dibus,de literis ſacris ediſcendis,de eloquentia,de pernitiæ ſophiſtices, de ſa-
crorum codicũ ad Græcos caſtigatiõe,& de linguarum peritia.Poſtea quocp
Iſocratis Paræneſin recognouit, atcpingenij ſui dexteritatem omnibus pate-
fecit. Itacp Eraſmus Roterodamus hunc Martinũ plurimũm dilexit,& aliquo
ties familiares epiſtolas ei ſcripſit. Cum hac ratione Martinus ſibi multorũ a-
micitiam conciliaſſet, tandem anno 1525 immatura morte obijt, & honorificè
ſepultus fuit. Huic Martino Eraſmus Roterodamus tale epitaphium ſcripſit:

Martinus ubi terras reliquit Dorpſius,
Suum orba partum flet parens Hollandia,
Theologus ordo luget extinctum decus,
Triſtes Camœnæ candidis cum Gratijs
Tantum patronum lachrymis deſiderant,
Louanienſis omnis opplorans ſchola
Sidus ſuum requirit:O mors,inquiens,
Crudelis,atrox,ſæua,iniqua,& inuida
Itan'ante tempus,floridam arborem ſecans,
Tot dotibus,tot ſpebus orbas omnium
Suſpenſa uota?Premite uoces impias.
Non perijt ille,uiuit,ac dotes ſuas
Nunc tutò habet,ſubductus æuo peſsimo.
Sors noſtra flenda eſt,gratulandum eſt Dorpio,
Hæc terra ſeruat mentis hoſpitium piæ
Corpuſculum,quod ad canoræ buccinæ
Vocem,reſignans optima reddet fide,
Eraſ.lib,19.Epiſtolarum.

Martin van Dorp, in Heinrich Pantaleon, *Prosopographiae heroum atque
illustrium virorum totius Germaniae*, 3 vols. Basel, 1565–66, 3, sig. FF$_4$v
(reduced)

and sharpening most of his earlier criticisms and introducing a number of new ones in a letter dated August 27, 1515.[1] This letter, too, was apparently never delivered; Erasmus first read it in a copy provided by More.[2] Dorp personally supervised the publication of his earlier letter and Erasmus' response with the second printing of Erasmus' *Enarratio in primum psalmum* (Louvain, October 1515).[3]

More's *Letter to Dorp*, like book 2 of *Utopia*, was composed during the last half of More's "Utopian embassy" (May 12–October 24, 1515).[4] August 27, the date of Dorp's second letter, provides a firm *terminus a quo* for More's answer, which he was still writing when he received his summons home.[5] Though More states in his letter that his ambassadorial duties detained him in Bruges, he undoubtedly made two excursions to Antwerp and Mechelin to make the acquaintance of Erasmus' admirers Peter Giles and Jerome Busleyden; one of them probably furnished the manuscript letters of Dorp and Erasmus as well as the copies of Dorp's published works which More cites in his own letter.[6] Though he offers his letter as a friendly admonition with a primary bearing on the intemperate language of Dorp's second letter, More also provides a quite thorough rebuttal of Dorp's arguments in both letters; admonition and formal defense alternate throughout. Four months after returning to England More sent a transcript of the letter to Antwerp to be passed on by Peter Giles when Erasmus next visited Antwerp in June 1516; this transcript is the likeliest source for a number of changes and variant readings attested in one of the two extant forms of the *Letter to Dorp*.[7]

---

[1]Allen, 2, 126–36.

[2]Allen, 2, 243, lines 48–50; 496, lines 6–8.

[3]Allen, 2, 60, 91, and 197, lines 152–55.

[4]Allen, 2, commentary at line 94; and *CW 4*, 573–76.

[5]See 122/14–19, below.

[6] For More's visits to Antwerp and Mechelin see *CW 4*, xxix–xxxv. In his letter More cites virtually all of Dorp's published early works; see p. xxii, n. 1, above. This fact suggests More had access to a personal collection which included the whole of Dorp's oeuvre and not only his letters to Erasmus. Busleyden definitely owned one such collection; Giles may well have owned another. But since Erasmus obtained his own copy of Dorp's second letter through More, not through Giles, and since Busleyden seems to have taken a very active role in responding to Dorp's first attacks on Erasmus, Busleyden, not Giles, is the likeliest source of More's knowledge about Dorp's various writings, including the letters to Erasmus (see Allen, 2, 243, lines 48–50; 496, lines 6–8; and note on 4/16 below).

[7]More jestingly refers to the letter as an "epistolium" or "brief note" in a letter to Erasmus of February 1516 (Allen, 2, 197, lines 154–61). Erasmus acknowledges both these letters in a single paragraph of a letter from Antwerp conjecturally dated June 3, 1516 (Allen, 2, 243). In his response to this letter More eagerly solicits Erasmus' opinion

More's letter apparently sufficed to prevent Dorp from publishing his second letter and to forestall any further attacks in the first half of 1516.[1] The Louvain Erasmian Alard of Amsterdam makes an honorable mention of Dorp in a letter of July 1 which suggests that Erasmus and Dorp were on reasonably good terms at that time.[2] Early in July, Dorp delivered an introductory lecture for a course on the Pauline epistles in which he acknowledged the value of linguistic skills in theology and condemned the supplanting of serious theological concerns by sophistical quibbles; in the published version of this recantation, which did not appear until 1519, Dorp gave most of the credit for his own change of outlook to More.[3] Erasmus himself heartily welcomed the news of Dorp's lecture in a letter of July 1516,[4] later printed along with the lecture itself; for a short time, the new understanding between the two humanists seemed perfect. In early October, however, after the conservative Louvain theologians had denied him permission to

---

of the *Letter to Dorp*, again designated an "epistolium" (Allen, 2, 261, lines 81–82). The close association between More's February letter and the *Letter to Dorp* in Erasmus' acknowledgment and More's own response to it makes it likely that Erasmus received his own transcript of the *Letter to Dorp* along with More's letter of February by way of their mutual friend Giles in Antwerp (Allen, 2, 243, lines 32–33). More apparently included a virtually illegible transcript of Dorp's second letter; Erasmus requested a more legible copy in March 1517 (Allen, 2, 243, lines 48–49; 496, lines 6–8).

[1] See note on 176/11–13 below.

[2] Allen, 2, 270, lines 13–15.

[3] De Vocht, *Monumenta*, pp. 160–63, 323–24. The lecture was reprinted by Froben in January and March 1520. For a later edition see Hermann von der Hardt, *Studiosus Graecus*, 2nd ed. (Helmstadt, 1705), pp. 61–128 (described by De Vocht, *Monumenta*, p. 324). For Dorp's tribute to More see *Martini Dorpii . . . Oratio in praelectionem epistolarum Diui Pauli. De laudibus Pauli, de literis sacris ediscendis, de eloquentia, de pernicie sophistices, de sacrorum codicum ad graecos castigatione: et linguarum peritia* ([Antwerp,] M. H[illen], September 1519; Nijhoff–Kronenberg, *1*, no. 739); sig. d₂:

> Atqui inquiet aliquis mihi, Tu non meministi, quid olim in epistola quadam, Eruditissimo domino Erasmo Roterodamo scripseris, quam sedulo nisus fueris alteram sententiam defensare? Memini probe, sed ne longos logos, neue me vertam huc aut illuc, paucis recanto suffragium, tum sic sentiebam, nunc nihil minus. Nam qui potui aliter, quam didiceram[?] verum simul atque veteres theologos accuratius denuo percurri, et ea item legi, quae doctissimi quique huius tempestatis scripserunt, praecipue longe eruditissimus vir Thomas Morus perpetuum suae Britanniae decus in epistola quadam ad me continuo mutaui sententiam. . . .

But an even more powerful though implicit tribute to the persuasive effect of More's letter occurs in Dorp's 1521 apology for his lectures on Paul; therein Dorp borrows several of his arguments directly from More. The apology was first printed in 1934 by De Vocht, *Monumenta*, pp. 75–93. See further p. cxviii, below.

[4] Allen, 2, 277–78.

lecture, Dorp apparently began a new round of attacks on Erasmus.[1]
Though the references in contemporary letters to these new attacks
are exceedingly vague, it seems likely that Dorp singled out various
faults in Erasmus' New Testament of early 1516 and used Erasmus'
July letter as a pretext for writing another conservative critique in the
form of a personal missive.[2] In a letter to Andrew Ammonius in England dated November 9, 1516, Erasmus reported that he had answered Dorp's most recent criticisms with two "rather harsh letters"
after perceiving that his previous moderation had merely made Dorp
grow fiercer.[3] Soon after, another Louvain Erasmian, Gerard Geldenhouwer, indicated to Erasmus that Dorp had no intention of circulating his written critiques and that he wished to settle his differences with
Erasmus in a personal interview.[4] Probably on the basis of Geldenhouwer's report, Erasmus promptly wrote letters to Giles and to More
indicating that Dorp had "returned to his senses" (resipuisse); the letter
to More, which is now lost, probably also contained a remark to the
effect that Erasmus' severity had succeeded in placating Dorp where
his earlier mildness had failed.[5] Near the end of November Dorp wrote
to Erasmus and once again claimed to desire nothing more than an
amicable personal interview to settle their differences; the tone of
Dorp's letter, however, was not altogether conciliatory.[6] Erasmus again
wrote disparagingly of Dorp in a letter to Ammonio dated December
29.[7] Though the two men did meet in Louvain in mid-January, their
full reconciliation was delayed till mid-February, when Dorp wrote a
letter (now lost) to Erasmus reasserting his loyal and friendly intentions
and requesting Erasmus to notify More that the breach had been men-

---

[1]Dorp was denied permission to lecture September 30, 1516, but was apparently
reconciled with his colleagues by October 6 (De Vocht, Monumenta, pp. 165–66; Allen, 2,
355).

[2]See Allen, 2, 354, lines 17–18; 355, lines 18–30; 359, lines 12–15; 360, lines 23–27;
374, lines 24–25; 378, lines 55–66; 380, lines 8–12; 385, line 12; 408, lines 18–25; 409–
10; 420, lines 3–8; 424, lines 14–16; 426–27; 481–82. For strong evidence that the first
edition of Erasmus' New Testament was the occasion for Dorp's new criticisms see Allen,
2, 410, lines 18–22. This second controversy was probably the occulta simultas to which
More refers at 176/2 below.

[3]Allen, 2, 374, lines 24–25.

[4]Allen, 2, 380, lines 8–12.

[5]Allen, 2, 385, line 12; 420, lines 6–8; 482, lines 14–18.

[6]Allen, 2, 409–10. In the first lines of this letter it seems likely that Dorp is deliberately
harking back to Erasmus' remarks in Allen, 2, 278, lines 1–5, in an effort to regain his
confidence.

[7]Allen, 2, 424, lines 14–16.

ded.[1] From two later reports it seems likely that Dorp wished to make quite sure that More would not publish his own letter and that this was a tacit condition of Dorp's final accord with Erasmus, who may well have brought up the possibility of publishing More's letter at his interview with Dorp in mid-January.[2] It would seem that More's own harsh tactics in dealing with Dorp proved to be the decisive ones.

Other humanists continued to suspect Dorp of treachery even after he formally made peace with Erasmus in 1517.[3] When he published his lecture on the Pauline epistles in September 1519, it was partly to vindicate himself in the eyes of his humanist critics; as additional confirmations of his loyalty to the humanist cause he requested Erasmus to solicit commendatory letters for the lecture from his own most distinguished supporters and friends.[4] Two short excerpts from More's laudatory response to Dorp's published oration are preserved in the pages of More's biographer Thomas Stapleton.[5] Dorp's outspoken endorsement of the Erasmian approach to theology and his short-lived and very halfhearted flirtation with Lutheranism probably limited his ultimate effectiveness in the conservative milieu of the Louvain theology faculty.[6] Weakened by overwork and immoderate fasting, he died on May 31, 1525; a whole chorus of Erasmians mourned his passing.[7]

Though the humanists eventually acknowledged the sincerity of Dorp's recantation, it was not without many backward glances at the inconstancy, vanity, and opportunism that were supposed to have gov-

---

[1]For Dorp's meeting with Erasmus see Allen, 2, 426–27. The contents of Dorp's lost conciliatory letter may be inferred from Erasmus' response (Allen, 2, 481–82).

[2]For the two later reports see note on 176/11–13 and Allen, 9, 35.

[3]For later humanist attacks on Dorp see note on 120/3–4, below. Though Erasmus was forced to expostulate with Dorp in late 1517 for composing a work against Reuchlin at the urging of Louvain conservatives (Allen, 3, 350; cf. 2, 381, and De Vocht, *Monumenta*, p. 180, n. 1), Dorp apparently remained reasonably loyal to Erasmus himself; see Allen, 2, 577; 3, 59, 92, 350; and De Vocht, *Monumenta*, pp. 192–200.

[4]For Dorp's published oration see p. xxiv, n. 3, above. For Dorp's request to Erasmus see Allen, 4, 127, commentary at line 49.

[5]Stapleton's excerpts are reprinted in *The Correspondence of Sir Thomas More*, ed. Elizabeth F. Rogers (Princeton, 1947; hereafter cited as "Rogers"), no. 82, pp. 164–66. The phrase "edita . . . oratione" in Rogers, p. 164, line 3, makes it virtually certain that More is referring to Dorp's published oration.

[6]De Vocht, *Monumenta*, pp. 234–43, and 253, n. 2. For Dorp's lost later works, see De Vocht, *Monumenta*, pp. 271–72, 338.

[7]See Morinck's life of Dorp in De Vocht, *Monumenta*, p. 277. For Dorp's humanist mourners see De Vocht, *Monumenta*, p. 253, and the collection of eulogies printed with the first edition of Erasmus' *Ciceronianus* (Basel, Froben, 1528).

erned his conduct before 1519.[1] Dorp's early suggestion that in criticizing Erasmus he was simply expressing the views of the other Louvain theologians gave Dorp's humanist critics a pretext for treating him as if he were merely a conservative hireling who had consciously betrayed his own humanist convictions.[2] Other humanists repeatedly threatened to load him down with the same sort of infamy that satirical tracts like the *Epistolae obscurorum virorum* had heaped on another supposed turncoat humanist, Ortwin Gratius.[3] Dorp's conservative masters were consistently depicted as envious bigots and obscurantists.[4] There was rarely the slightest acknowledgment that Dorp might have sincere reservations about the importance attributed to grammar and rhetoric in Erasmus' new model for theology or that the best way to ensure the acceptance of Erasmian theology might well be to concede that traditional methods should still have a significant place in a reformed theological curriculum. The subsequent history of Erasmus' relations with the Louvain conservatives suggests that except in a few cases their initial resistance to Erasmian ideas merely indicated a strong need for reassurance and clarification about Erasmus' primary intentions.[5] When he moved to Louvain in mid-1517 he was able to provide the required reassurance through his daily involvement in the intellectual life of the university; it was only after his departure to Basel in mid-1518 that the Louvain obscurantists began to regain their ascendancy.[6] The 1517 decision of the Louvain theologians to make Erasmus an official member of the faculty bears comparison with the official encouragement earlier given to Dorp in his own theological studies: the theology faculty was ready to tolerate even progressive humanist viewpoints as long as it could easily monitor their effects on the Louvain curriculum.[7] In the *Letter to Dorp* More himself invoked many of the stereotypes of humanist polemic, but by encouraging Dorp to resolve theoretical differences with Erasmus through personal interviews and not through continued polemical exchanges More also

---

[1]De Vocht, *Monumenta,* pp. 166, 214, 220, 253.

[2]Allen, 2, 12; cf. Erasmus in Allen, 2, 91, lines 23–25; 113, lines 875–82; and More at 96/13–16, 96/21–23 and 116/1–5 below.

[3]See De Vocht, *Monumenta,* p. 220, and note on 120/3–4 below.

[4]See Erasmus in Allen, 2, 98–99, lines 307–34; 100, lines 348–50, 359–64, 373–78; More at 6/13–18, 106/6–10, 116/1–5, below; and De Vocht, *Monumenta,* pp. 207–11.

[5]Even John Briart of Ath, whom Erasmus suspected of having provoked Dorp's original attacks, welcomed him in mid-1517; see De Vocht, *Monumenta,* pp. 179, 188–91.

[6]De Vocht, *Monumenta,* pp. 192–200.

[7]For the decision to make Erasmus an official member of the faculty of theology see De Vocht, *Monumenta,* pp. 191–92.

suggested a promising means of transcending such stereotypes.[1] Personal interviews arranged by Dorp between Erasmus and the Louvain conservatives played a primary role in securing the general accord of mid-1517.[2] Had it not been for the new mood of suspicion aroused by the Lutheran disturbance in 1519, Erasmus might well have retained the support of most Louvain theologians.[3]

Letter to the University of Oxford

Before 1520 Erasmus had numerous powerful protectors in England and few dedicated detractors.[4] John Fisher, the bishop of Rochester, had taken a very active role in promoting the new humanistic studies at Cambridge, where he had been university chancellor since 1504.[5] By 1516 Erasmus was able to report that only one Cambridge college rejected his biblical scholarship.[6] Oxford, too, had a chancellor extremely sympathetic to Erasmus, William Warham, archbishop of Canterbury, one of Erasmus' most loyal and most cherished patrons.[7] Although Warham's university chancellorship was by no means as active as Fisher's, the Erasmians might well have anticipated as little resistance at Oxford as they actually encountered at Cambridge. As early as 1514, however, Erasmus had had his first clash with a conservative English theologian, almost certainly an Oxford alumnus, Henry Standish, the vocal and powerful Franciscan who had earlier challenged John Colet.[8] Standish characteristically objected to Erasmus'

---

[1] See the *Letter to Dorp*, 6/19–8/3.

[2] See De Vocht, *Monumenta*, pp. 175–76. In his letters of this period Dorp repeatedly urges Erasmus to strengthen his personal ties with the other Louvain theologians.

[3] For Louvain attacks linking Erasmus with Luther see Allen, *3*, 523, *4*, 100–02, 119, 121. For Erasmus' short-lived reconciliation with the conservatives in 1519 after he had returned from Basel see De Vocht, *Monumenta*, p. 222.

[4] See Allen, *1*, 433–34, and notes on 146/1–3, 146/7–8, 208/10–13 and 268/27.

[5] See Allen, *1*, 469, and notes on 154/17–18 and 268/21–22 below. For a well researched study of faculty reorganization and academic reform at both Cambridge and Oxford in this period, see Damian R. Leader, "Professorships and Academic Reform at Cambridge: 1488–1520," *The Sixteenth Century Journal*, *14* (1983), 215–27; hereafter cited as "Leader."

[6] Allen, 2, 321.

[7] See note on 146/1–3, below; and cf. the work cited on p. lxxii, n. 2. More and Erasmus both spent time at Oxford; see notes on 20/26–29 and 130/25–27.

[8] See Allen, 2, 108, line 678; 371, line 42; *3*, 21, line 14; 296, line 30 and commentary. For Standish's connection with Oxford see A. G. Little, *The Grey Friars in Oxford*, Publications of the Oxford Historical Society 20 (Oxford, 1892), pp. 271–74. Standish's campaign against Erasmus' New Testament is also described in J. Rendel Harris, *The Origin of the Leicester Codex of the New Testament* (London, 1887), pp. 46–53. For the conservative

intention of emending and elucidating the letters of Jerome: how could he possibly improve on the work of the medieval commentators? Shortly after the publication of Erasmus' New Testament in 1516, More sent Erasmus a half-serious warning about a conspiracy apparently fostered by Standish to seek out and attack every objectionable or questionable passage in all that Erasmus had written.[1] Standish continued to do all he could to discredit Erasmus for many years to come, and not many of the English attacks on Erasmus appear to have been carried out without Standish's personal involvement.

Disappointingly little is known about the particular disturbance which occasioned More's *Letter to Oxford.* The most detailed report occurs in a letter from Erasmus to Peter Mosellanus dated April 22, 1519:

> England possesses two universities by no means obscure, Cambridge and Oxford. Greek is taught in both, and in Cambridge without disturbance, because the head of the institution is Father John Fisher, the bishop of Rochester, whose learning and life are alike worthy of a divine. But at Oxford, where a young man of more than common learning was publicly teaching Greek with some success, some barbarian or other in a public sermon began to inveigh against Greek studies with monstrous great falsehoods. The king, who being quite a scholar himself is a supporter of the humanities, happened to be in the neighborhood, and hearing about this from More and Pace, he declared that those who wished should be welcome to follow Greek. And so those rascals were put to silence.[2]

This account is immediately followed by two other anecdotes; in the first, a court preacher attempting to discredit Greek learning is shamefully refuted by More; in the second, Queen Catherine's confessor is discovered to have appropriated Standish's objections to Erasmus' edition of Jerome.[3] The first anecdote is in some ways remarkably similar to an anecdote of mid-1520 in which More's hapless conservative oppo-

---

attack on John Colet see Erasmus in Allen, 4, 523–26. A favorite court preacher since 1511, Standish was made bishop of St. Asaph in 1518. Despite his theological conservatism he consistently supported the King's interests against those of the clergy. See further the note on 204/28–206/6, below.

[1]Allen 2, 371–72.

[2]Allen, 3, 546–47; the translation is from *The Collected Works of Erasmus*, trans. R. A. B. Mynors and D. F. S. Thomson and annot. Peter G. Bietenholz, Wallace K. Ferguson, and James K. McConica, 8 vols. (Toronto, 1974–; hereafter cited as *CWE*), 6, 316–17.

[3]Allen, 3, 547–48.

nent is definitely Standish; the two stories may even refer to one incident.[1] In a later reference to the incident at Oxford Erasmus describes the troublemakers as *monachi*, a term he sometimes uses disparagingly for his enemies in mendicant as well as monastic orders.[2] It is at least plausible to suggest that the troublemakers at Oxford included a number of Standish's fellow Franciscans.

From Erasmus' remarks it seems likely that More's letter had the backing of Henry's authority. Given that More drafted his letter in Abingdon on March 29 and that Henry was certainly in the vicinity of Abingdon in March 1518, it seems reasonable to assume that the letter was written in 1518 from the king's itinerant court.[3] On the other hand, the earliest of Erasmus' tightly clustered allusions to the incident dates from April 22, 1519, which might suggest that the incident took place in March 1519.[4] If this date were accepted, the Greek lecturer to whom Erasmus refers might conceivably be John Clement, More's highly gifted former protégé who was shortly to become his son-in-law.[5] Since the court was based in Richmond west of London at the

---

[1]Compare Allen, *3*, 547, and *4*, 311–13. The latter anecdote is repeated in a 1520 letter to Luther (Allen, *8*, xlv–xlvi) in which More is explicitly named as Erasmus' defender. In both anecdotes the final discomfiture of Erasmus' attacker involves a display of rank ignorance about the actual relation of the biblical languages Hebrew and Greek. But if Erasmus is writing about Standish in Allen, *3*, 547, he is doubtless exaggerating when he claims that the slanderous preacher was permanently banned from the court.

[2]Allen, *4*, 281, lines 33–36. For a particularly pertinent example of this imprecise use of *monachus* see Allen, *1*, 23, lines 8–14, where Erasmus recalls his 1520 response to the *monachi* in London, Paris, and Brussels who had delivered public sermons attacking his rendering of the first verse of John, "In principio erat sermo." Erasmus' response actually mentions only one English critic of this rendering, the Franciscan preacher Henry Standish; see Allen, *4*, 158, 194–95, 310.

[3]See note on 134/5, below.

[4]For Erasmus' allusions see Allen, *3*, 546–47; 588, lines 26–28; 594, lines 12–14; 595, line 10; 596, lines 13–15; 620, lines 9–14; *4*, 184, lines 127–32; 281, lines 33–36. For a possible echo of More's letter see the note on 134/31–136/6, below. More's *Letter to Oxford* (and conceivably the *Letter to Dorp*) may also have helped to inspire a near-contemporary defense of Greek studies at Cambridge; see Richard Croke, *Orationes duae* (Paris, 1520), sigs. a₄v-a₅ (cf. 130/20–24 below); a₅v, a₇ (cf. 142/16–18); a₇ (cf. 104/5–6); c₂ (cf. 142/22–24); c₃v (cf. 144/18–23); c₄-c₄v (cf. 130/24–28). Croke himself was the Cambridge Greek lecturer when he wrote his defense; as we might expect, he uses more strictly literary arguments for the value of Greek and less theological arguments than More does. More and others had previously attempted to get Croke to teach Greek at Oxford; see *Orationes duae*, sig. c₇v, and cf. sig. c₄, where Croke praises More's "candida et eloquentissima urbanitas." For a more extended discussion of Croke's career see Rogers, no. 81, introd.

[5]For Clement and his teaching of the *studia humanitatis* at Oxford see Allen, 2, 198, commentary at line 173, and W. T. Mitchell, ed., *Epistolae Academicae, 1508–1596*, Oxford Historical Society, New Series 26 (1980), pp. 83–84. The *studia humanitatis* would

beginning of April 1519, perhaps More's letter indicates a brief regal visit to Abingdon in March 1519.[1]

Erasmus' exultant remarks on the outcome of the incident suggest that More's letter was totally successful and that Erasmus' detractors in Oxford were silenced completely.[2] More himself, it would seem, was unusually proud of the letter, which he gave to his daughters as a Latin translation exercise: More's biographer Stapleton reports that he saw an English translation of the letter by one of More's daughters and a new Latin version by another.[3] Some years later, upon offering More the position of university high steward, the administrators of the university gratefully acknowledged More's devotion to Oxford in terms reminiscent of his own remarks in this letter; even if his first letter to Oxford was not the main gesture which endeared him to Oxford authorities it clearly did not serve to antagonize or bully them in the way that an earlier translator of the letter suggests.[4] More's close official relationship with the University of Oxford lasted throughout his public career.[5]

Letter to Edward Lee

Erasmus' most acrimonious controversy in the years 1514–20 was with a wellborn and comparatively well-educated conservative from England, the future archbishop of York, Edward Lee (ca. 1482–1544).[6]

---

not necessarily include the study of Greek, but Edward Wotton, the first official Greek lecturer in Foxe's humanistically oriented Corpus Christi College, is not mentioned in the college accounts before 1520–21. For the teaching of Greek at Oxford and Cambridge in this period, see the references in Leader, p. 216, n. 8, and p. 225, n. 65.

[1]For the court's location in April 1519, see Allen, *3*, 526, commentary at line 46.

[2]For the striking popularity of Erasmus' writings in Oxford only months after the anti-Greek faction was silenced see James K. McConica, *English Humanists and Reformation Politics under Henry VIII and Edward VI* (Oxford, 1965; hereafter cited as "McConica, *English Humanists*"), pp. 88–89. Among the Erasmian best-sellers in Oxford were the *Apologia de In principio erat sermo* and the *Epistolae aliquot eruditorum* against Edward Lee.

[3]Thomas Stapleton, *Tres Thomae . . .* (Douai, 1588; hereafter cited as "Stapleton"), sigs. h₅v–h₆.

[4]For the Oxford officials' acknowledgment see Rogers, p. 305; for the suggestion that More meant to bully the Oxford officials see T. S. K. Scott-Craig, "Thomas More's 1518 Letter to the University of Oxford," *Renaissance News*, *1* (1948), 17–24.

[5]For additional correspondence between More and Oxford see Rogers, nos. 114, 133, 134, 150, 151, 157, 158, 167, 177, 181.

[6]For Lee's biography see the *Dictionary of National Biography*, 63 vols. (London, 1885–1900; hereafter cited as *DNB*), *32*, 347–49; and A. B. Emden, *A Biographical Register of the University of Oxford to A.D. 1500 [and] A.D. 1501 to 1540*, 4 vols. (Oxford, 1957–74), *2*, 1122–23; for his ancestry see also Sylvia L. Thrupp, *The Merchant Class of Medieval London 1300–1500* (Chicago, 1948), p. 353. More's remark on Lee's relative age at 160/12

Lee's grandfather, Sir Richard Lee, had been lord mayor of London, and his immediate family retained its close ties with the mid-London parish of St. Stephen's in Walbrook, where it seems that his parents and More's became intimate friends.[1] Lee studied at both Oxford and

---

suggests that Lee's birthdate was actually closer to 1487. Lee became archbishop of York in December 1531 and reluctantly supported the Act of Supremacy. Rogers (p. 9) repeats a traditional error in making Edward Lee the brother of the Minoress Joyce Lee to whom More is thought to have dedicated his translation of the *Life of John Picus*. This Joyce Lee was almost certainly the daughter of Ralph Lee of Stockwell and Lambeth in Surrey (see John Tanswell, *History and Antiquities of Lambeth*, London, 1858, pp. 40–42); Edward Lee was the son of Richard Lee, Esq., of Lee Magna in Kent. Though there may have been some distant kinship between the two families, the sources which I have consulted do not make this clear. The name of Edward Lee's mother is given in one source as Letuce (*Laetitia;* see the following note); it may be that this name is there used as a Latinate synonym for Joyeuce (*Joyeuse*) and that Edward Lee's mother, instead of the Lambeth Joyce Lee, is the real addressee of More's *Pico.* Edward Lee had two brothers, Richard Lee, Esq., and "Galfredus" (Wilfred or Geoffrey, sometimes misdesignated as William); see 152/3 and Robert Hovenden, ed., *The Visitation of Kent Taken in the Years 1619–1621*, Publications of the Harleian Society 42 (London, 1898), pp. 55–56. For the wills of Lee's grandfather (d. 1472), father (d. ca. 1498), and brother Richard (d. 1526), all parishioners of St. Stephen's in Walbrook, London, see J. Challenor C. Smith, ed., *Index of Wills Proved in the Prerogative Court of Canterbury*, 2 vols., The Index Library 10–11 (London, 1893–95), 2, 330, which also lists wills for the Minoress Joyce Lee (d. 1507) and her relatives Ralph Lee (d. 1509) and Sir John Lee (d. 1523). For prior accounts of Lee's controversy with Erasmus see A. Bludau, *Die beiden ersten Erasmus-Ausgaben des Neuen Testaments und ihre Gegner*, Biblische Studien 7/5 (Freiburg im Breisgau, 1902), pp. 86–125; Allen, *3*, 203; *4*, 108–11, 210; and Wallace K. Ferguson, "Apologia qua respondet duabus invectivis Eduardi Lei: Introduction" (hereafter cited as *Apologia qua respondet), in Erasmi Opuscula: A Supplement to the Opera Omnia* (The Hague, 1933; hereafter cited as "Ferguson"), pp. 225–35. All of these accounts are marred by a confusion between the first version of Lee's annotations and the two pamphlets to which Erasmus responds in Allen, *3*, nos. 750 and 843, 184–87, 312–30. Lee almost certainly helped to instigate the second of these pamphlets (see p. xxxix, n. 2, below) but wrote neither.

[1] For More's connection with St. Stephen's in Walbrook, which included part of Bucklersbury, see Allen, *4*, 17, commentary at line 133; William Roper, *The Lyfe of Sir Thomas Moore, knighte*, ed. E. V. Hitchcock, EETS, Original Series no. 197 (London, 1935; hereafter cited as "Roper"), pp. 6–7; and *CW 6*, 79/1–2, and Commentary. For the Lee family's connection with this parish see the preceding note and Thomas Milbourn, "Church of St. Stephen Walbrook," *Transactions of the London and Middlesex Archeological Society*, 5 (1881), 345, 355, 385–86, 388, 393, 395. On p. 355 Milbourn cites churchwardens' records which mention a 1510 obit for "Master Richarde Lee, and Dame Letuce hys wyfe," probably Edward Lee's parents. For the friendship between More's family and Lee's see 160/10–13 below. More's suggestion that Lee was a very young boy when they met indicates that the relationship between the two families was established long before More himself moved to St. Stephen's parish in approximately 1514. For the More family's previous residences in London see Nicholas Harpsfield, *The Life and Death of Sir Thomas Moore*, ed. E. V. Hitchcock and R. W. Chambers, EETS, Original Series no. 186 (London, 1932, hereafter cited as "Harpsfield"), commentary on p. 9.

Cambridge; he received his M.A. from the latter in 1504 and his B.D. in 1511–12. After several more years spent in Cambridge preparing for the doctorate, Lee migrated to Louvain in mid-1516 to study Greek and Hebrew.[1] It seems that one of his principal aims was to gain enough linguistic competence to discredit Erasmus' New Testament, which he had disparaged informally even before he left England.[2] Nonetheless, after moving to Louvain in mid-1517, Erasmus himself took an amicable interest in advancing Lee's studies; evidently he thought that once Lee had the requisite linguistic skills he could scarcely avoid recognizing the worth of Erasmus' edition.[3] Not long after their first meeting Erasmus may have casually invited him to note any deficiencies in the first version of Erasmus' New Testament; Lee made several notes, which Erasmus rejected as "hairsplitting trifles"; and shortly before Erasmus left for Basel in May 1518, Lee grew openly hostile.[4]

While Erasmus was in Basel completing the notes for the second edition of the New Testament, Lee completed and started to circulate in Louvain and England a manuscript volume of highly abusive annotations. The tone of this version may be gauged from the one note by Lee that Erasmus procured on returning to Louvain through a mutual acquaintance, Martin Lypsius.[5] At an interview with Erasmus in October Lee apparently boasted that he had discovered and annotated at least three hundred faults in Erasmus' first edition.[6] In a letter to

---

[1]See note on 176/16–17 below.

[2]See note on 176/20–21.

[3]See 160/6–8; Allen, *4*, 198, lines 21–26; and Erasmus, *Apologia qua respondet*, Ferguson, p. 242. For other indications that Erasmus' relations with Lee in Louvain were originally quite friendly see Allen, *3*, 20, line 15; 111, line 23; 424, lines 58–59; *4*, 141, lines 83–85, 147, lines 325–28; and the following note. Erasmus sent Lee a quite cordial letter in January 1518, simply stating that he could not use a particular collection of Lee's annotations because Lee's scribe had not let him have them; see Allen, *3*, 203–04.

[4]Lee suggests that Erasmus initially sought him out very soon after Charles V left for Spain (or in mid-1517; see Allen, *3*, 3) and at that point requested him to note any flaws in the first edition of Erasmus' New Testament; see Edward Lee, *Annotationes in Annotationes Novi Testamenti Desiderii Erasmi* (Paris, [1520]; hereafter cited as "Lee, *Annotationes*"), sig. AA₂. Erasmus denied that he ever made such a request (*Apologia qua respondet*, Ferguson, p. 242). For Erasmus' rejection of Lee's first notes as "hairsplitting trifles" see 154/7, below; Allen, *3*, 424 and 471; Lee, *Annotationes*, sig. AA₄; and Erasmus, *Apologia qua respondet*, Ferguson, pp. 246–47. For Erasmus' last confrontation with Lee before leaving for Basel in May 1518, see Allen, *3*, 424–25, and *4*, 199; and *Apologia qua respondet*, Ferguson, p. 243.

[5]See Allen, *3*, 439–42, and p. xxxviii, n. 1, below. For a biographical sketch of Lypsius see Allen, *3*, 185–86.

[6]See Erasmus, *Apologia qua respondet*, Ferguson, p. 245, and commentary.

Lypsius he labeled Erasmus a slanderer of holy scripture and appointed himself its defender.[1] From an early date he maintained that Erasmus was too proud to accept good advice; he also maintained that Erasmus had plagiarized all his corrections from Lee's manuscript notes, and when Erasmus confronted him with the abusive remarks he had written to Lypsius he began to insist that Erasmus must have obtained a complete copy of Lee's manuscript from Lypsius, the "traitor," before leaving for Basel.[2] At his October interview with Erasmus he turned down three fairly equitable proposals for bringing the quarrel to a rapid conclusion and demanded instead that his work and Erasmus' New Testament be submitted for formal arbitration requiring at least several months; Erasmus was shortly compelled to send off the last portions of his text to the printer in Basel, and the planned arbitration fell through.[3] Erasmus fretted about the impending attack on his most cherished work while Lee sharpened his criticisms at leisure.

Erasmus repeatedly sought to make Lee either quit spreading rumors about how many disgraceful mistakes he had noted or else publish his notes and be done with them.[4] At the same time, he attempted to gain access to a manuscript copy of Lee's notes so that he could refute them without more delay.[5] Lee continued to stall, and in late 1518 Erasmus began to complain to a number of his English friends in an effort to make them press Lee to behave more straightforwardly.[6] Though Erasmus became more and more certain that Lee's vanity would never be satisfied with a quiet private settlement and that the safest recourse was to goad him into publishing his volume at once, Fisher, More, Pace, and Colet all wished to avoid the embarrassment of

---

[1]See Lee in Allen, *4*, 169, lines 398–407; and Erasmus in *Apologia qua respondet*, Ferguson, pp. 277, 288, and commentary. Erasmus' first reference to Lee's charge occurs in a letter of April 22, 1519 (Allen, *3*, 546).

[2]See 154/6–10; 182/26–27; Lee, *Annotationes*, sig. BB₁; and Allen, *4*, 160–61, lines 72–78; 169, lines 401–07; 179, lines 795–97; answered by Erasmus in *Apologia qua respondet*, Ferguson, pp. 262–63; and Allen, *4*, 200, lines 102–09. For Erasmus' confrontation with Lee about his written comments to Lypsius see Allen, *4*, 169, lines 398–407. Although Lypsius did possess a complete copy of Lee's annotations before Erasmus' departure for Basel, he apparently concealed the fact from him; see p. xxxviii, n. 1, below. Lypsius' motives are puzzling; perhaps he enjoyed the excitement of spying for Erasmus but shrank from an outright betrayal of Lee.

[3]Erasmus, *Apologia qua respondet*, Ferguson, pp. 247–49. The first arbitrator selected was John Briart of Ath. For the printing of the second edition of Erasmus' New Testament see Allen, *3*, 387.

[4]See Erasmus in *Apologia qua respondet*, Ferguson, pp. 249, 251.

[5]See p. xl, n. 1, below.

[6]See Erasmus in Allen, *3*, 424–25, and 464, commentary at line 21.

an open dispute between Lee and Erasmus, and all four wrote to Lee in the first half of 1519 urging him not to publish.[1] According to Lee, More's long letter of May 1 did the most to deter him at that point.[2] Though he had already published one passage which was probably meant to goad Lee into publishing immediately, Erasmus reluctantly accepted his friends' plan to let Fisher arbitrate; he apparently hoped that if Fisher could not actually settle the quarrel he would at least let Erasmus see Lee's notes.[3] Lee continued to spread rumors about all the disgraceful mistakes he had noted, and Erasmus returned to provoking him in print.[4] Fisher proposed yet another amicable solution in late 1519, but the proposal came too late to do any good.[5] After one more delay while Lee searched for a suitable printer, his volume was printed in Paris in February 1520.[6]

Erasmus' first response to Lee's book was the preface to his *Apologia de In principio erat sermo* (Louvain, late February 1520), where he announced that a full-length rebuttal of Lee would appear very shortly.[7] Between March and May he wrote and published three answers in all, the *Apologia qua respondet invectivis Lei* and two lengthy *Responsiones* to Lee's substantive criticisms.[8] At the same time, he encouraged his Ger-

---

[1]See Erasmus in *Apologia qua respondet*, Ferguson, pp. 250–51 and commentary.

[2]Allen, *4*, 175, lines 603–04; cf. Rogers, p. 207, lines 32–34, and p. 209, lines 14–15.

[3]For his English friends' plan, which was repeatedly urged upon Lee between April and July 1519, see note on 154/17–18, below; Erasmus *Apologia qua respondet*, Ferguson, p. 267; and Allen, *4*, 89, 91–92. When he sent Fisher his notes to examine, Lee apparently required him to promise that he would not pass them on to Erasmus; see *Apologia qua respondet*, Ferguson, p. 267; and Allen, *4*, 93–94, 192. The latter passage, which also suggests that as of October 17, 1519, More could not have transcribed Lee's notes except from the copy in Fisher's possession, makes it reasonably certain that More never possessed his own copy of Lee's notes in manuscript (cf. Allen, *4*, 148, variant at line 361, and *4*, 88, commentary at line 14). It seems likelier that More earlier had access to a few notes transcribed from a copy of the book which was shown to Hugh Latimer; cf. 168/11–20, below, and Allen, *4*, 160, line 61. For Erasmus' first published provocation of Lee see note on 156/9–10, below.

[4]For the rumors Lee was spreading in May 1519, see Allen, *3*, 597–600. For Erasmus' provocations see Allen, *4*, 9–12, 139–52, 166–79.

[5]See Erasmus in Allen, *4*, 191–92; and *Apologia qua respondet*, Ferguson, pp. 258–59, 269.

[6]See Allen, *4*, 110; for the full title and contents of Lee's work see above, p. xxxiii, n. 4, and p. xxxviii, n. 4 below. Lee repeatedly charged that Erasmus had tried to prevent Louvain printers from publishing the volume; Erasmus responded quite convincingly that what chiefly deterred Lee from publishing in Louvain or Antwerp was the fear that Erasmus would be able to respond to the book almost as soon as it came off the press (*Apologia qua respondet*, Ferguson, pp. 251–58; cf. Allen, *4*, 142–48, 200).

[7]Allen, *4*, 194–95; cf. *4*, 378, commentary at line 6. For this work's popularity in Oxford see p. xxxi, n. 2, above.

[8]Allen, *4*, 110.

man supporters to write letters attacking Lee; some of these letters were entrusted to William Nesen, who combined them with letters from Erasmus' supporters in England, including More's *Letter to Lee* and his *Letter to a Monk,* to produce *Epistolae aliquot eruditorum* (Antwerp, May 1520).[1] This volume was reprinted three months later in Basel with several additional letters, including More's two 1520 epistles to Lee.[2] Erasmus arranged for the publication of Lee's substantive criticisms along with his own restrained *Responsiones* in a volume of May 1520; the omission of Lee's two invectives and the irate *apologia* refuting them may be viewed as a tentative peace gesture. He formally made peace with Lee at Calais in July 1520, in the presence of their English friends.[3] Allen associates these two events with a number of statements by Erasmus suggesting that he actually suppressed German letters against Lee and concludes that Erasmus may not have been party to the August reprinting of the *Epistolae aliquot eruditorum* in Basel.[4] But a later report clearly suggests that Erasmus' remarks must refer to a large manuscript volume of letters surrendered to More, probably at Calais in mid-1520; since Erasmus' July reconciliation with Lee was unstable at best, he probably never had any intention of suppressing the letters which were already printed.[5] In the last half of 1520 Lee

---

[1]See Allen, *4,* 216, lines 10–12; 233, lines 7–10; 244. See also *4,* 23, lines 315–21. The letters from Erasmus' English supporters were forwarded to Nesen by Thomas Lupset: see the following note.

[2]See p. cxxvii, below; for More's two 1520 epistles to Lee see Rogers, nos. 84–85, pp. 206–12. For the likelihood that More himself furnished the copies of the three letters to Lee and the *Letter to a Monk* which Lupset transmitted to Nesen see 194/24–31 and Lupset's letter to Nesen in *Epistolae aliquot eruditorum uirorum* (Basel, Froben, August 1520), sig. G₃:

> Mitto ad te epistolas aliquot Thomae mori, et Ricardi Pacaei, quo certius persuadeas Germaniae tuae, quam praeter horum uoluntatem Leus negocium hoc aggressus sit, adieci prolixam epistolam, qua Morus refellit monachi cuiusdam plusquam insani conuitia. Tales histriones subornant isti, ut per tales obscuros agant, quod ipsos pudet facere, Imo potius quia nihil pudet, quod uident se non impune facturos. Non est opus ut prodam hominem, ipse se prodet breui, adeo insanit gloriae, siti, famaeque, cum sit mundo mortuus, et cum angelis tantum colloquatur.

Lupset's comment already appears in the Antwerp edition of May. By rebuking Lee gently and rebuking Lee's allies severely in a published collection of letters More was able to repudiate Lee's notes in a very decisive way without ever betraying his friendship.

[3]Allen, *4,* 110, 259, 296, 325, commentary at line 18.

[4]Allen, *4,* 111, 210. For Erasmus' remarks on the suppressed German letters see Allen, *4,* 337, lines 99–101; 375, lines 1–4; 387, lines 142–46; 477, lines 603–05.

[5]For the volume of letters surrendered to More see Erasmus in Allen, *9,* 35. It would be easier to surrender a large volume of letters in person, and More's only personal meet-

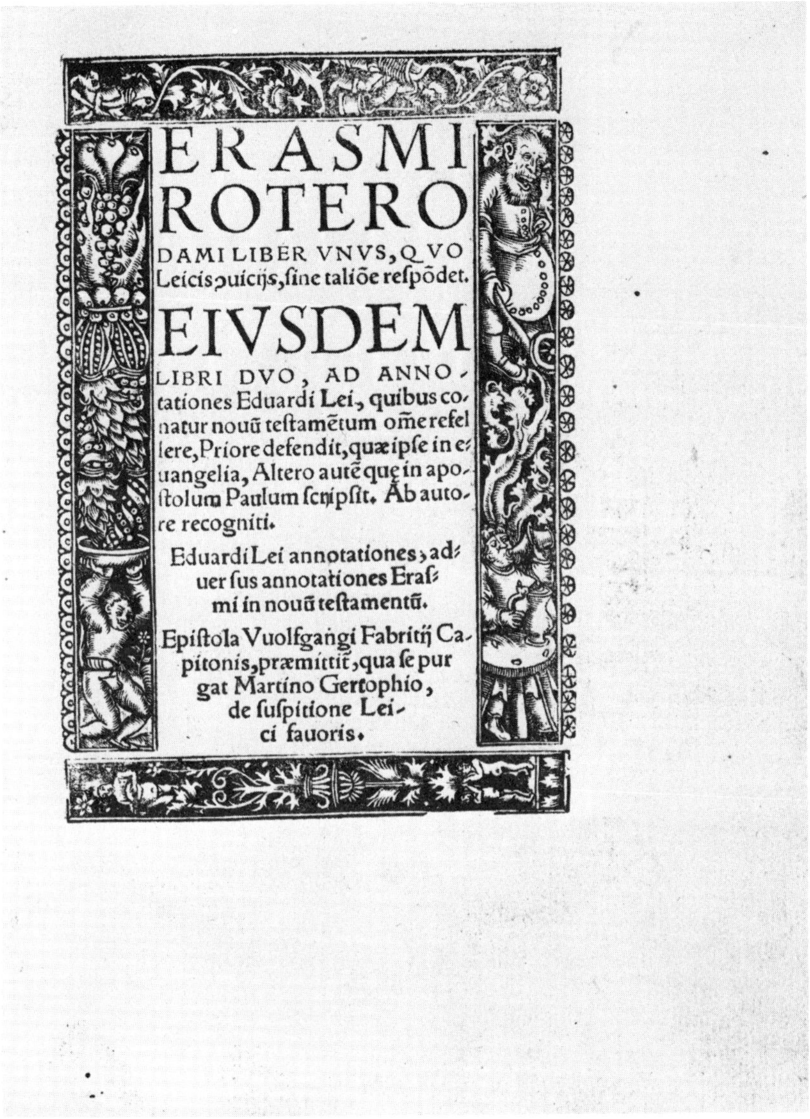
ERASMI
ROTERO
DAMI LIBER VNVS, QVO
Leicis ꝯuiciis, ſine taliõe reſpõdet.
EIVSDEM
LIBRI DVO, AD ANNO-
tationes Eduardi Lei, quibus conatur nouũ teſtamẽtum omẽ refel
lere, Priore defendit, quæ ipſe in e-
uangelia, Altero autẽ quę in apo-
ſtolum Paulum ſcripſit. Ab auto-
re recogniti.
Eduardi Lei annotationes, ad-
uer ſus annotationes Eraſ-
mi in nouũ teſtamentũ.
Epiſtola Vuolfgangi Fabritii Ca-
pitonis, præmittit, qua ſe pur
gat Martino Gertophio,
de ſuſpitione Lei-
ci fauoris.

Title page, Edward Lee, *Annotationes,* Mainz, 1520 (reduced)

returned to England, where he was installed as one of Henry VIII's chaplains by December.[1] Two much later attacks on Erasmus suggest that Lee never forgave his old adversary.[2]

Two confusions have needlessly complicated previous accounts of the Lee controversy. The first confusion is relatively simple: a long excerpt from one of More's 1520 letters to Lee, cited out of context by Stapleton, has been printed as if it represented a quite distinct earlier letter in which More seems to be offering Lee his support should a further dispute with Erasmus arise.[3] There are actually only three known extant letters from More to Edward Lee, and the one printed here is the earliest. All three are intended to make Lee give up his attacks on Erasmus.

The second confusion is somewhat more serious. P. S. Allen and others have held that a lengthy epistolary defense by Erasmus dated May 7, 1518, is a response to a bundle of Lee's annotations passed on to Erasmus by Lypsius.[4] As Ferguson remarks, "this is the only known basis for Lee's charge of treachery":[5] if this letter is not a response to a bundle of Lee's annotations, then Lypsius is innocent of having divulged them to Erasmus before he departed for Basel; if the letter does

---

ings with Erasmus in 1520 were connected with the royal conference at Calais. When he refers to the same volume of letters in the *Spongia* (*ASD 9/1*, 160, lines 915–19), Erasmus states that he never showed it to anyone besides Dorp and More. For Erasmus' continuing troubles with Lee in the latter half of 1520 and immediately thereafter see Allen, *4*, 296, commentary at line 6, as well as Erasmus' *Letter to Botzheim* (1523), Allen, *1*, 24, variant at lines 21–35.

[1]See Allen, *4*, 338, commentary at line 17.

[2]For a pseudonymous 1525 attack on Erasmus which was dedicated to Lee see Allen, *4*, 463; and Rogers, p. 317, commentary at line 6. In 1526 Erasmus maintained that an unpublished work by Lee was the basis for an abusive *libellus* by Erasmus' monastic detractors in Spain, where Lee himself was then serving on an embassy; see Allen, *6*, 403.

[3]Rogers, no. 48, pp. 100–01, conjecturally dated autumn 1517, is actually an excerpt from More's defensive letter to Lee dated February 29, 1520 (Rogers, no. 85, pp. 211–12, lines 112–33). Stapleton's citation of this letter to establish More's sympathy with Lee seems deliberately misleading. If this excerpt is taken from the printed version of More's letter, which appeared along with his first letter to Lee and the *Letter to a Monk* in *1520ᵃ*, Stapleton's silence regarding these two major Erasmian statements is surely suggestive.

[4]Allen, *3*, 312–20, no. 843.

[5]See *Apologia qua respondet*, Ferguson, p. 262, commentary at line 600. It appears that Lee himself had a different, conjectural basis for making the charge: Lypsius behaved somewhat treacherously after Erasmus returned to Louvain; Lypsius owned a manuscript of Lee's annotations before Erasmus departed for Basel; therefore Lypsius must have betrayed the entire contents of the manuscript to Erasmus before his departure (see 182/26–27 below; Lee, *Annotationes*, sig. BB₁; and Allen, *4*, 161, lines 76–78; 169, lines 401–07; 179, lines 795–97; answered by Erasmus in *Apologia qua respondet*, Ferguson, pp. 262–63; and Allen, *4*, 200, lines 102–08).

answer Lee's notes, then Erasmus is perjuring himself when he maintains that Lypsius showed him only one of Lee's notes and a few of Lee's letters, all after Erasmus returned to Louvain in September 1518.[1] In the *Letter to Botzheim* (1523) Erasmus refers to no. 843 in a way which suggests that the critic to whom he responds there is definitely not Lee.[2] Erasmus wrote no. 843 on his way to Basel in May 1518, whereas Lee himself states that Erasmus' first letters attacking him were written after Erasmus' return to Louvain in September.[3] Furthermore, though both Lee and Erasmus profess to provide a complete history of the major events in the controversy, neither of them makes any mention of no. 843 or the pamphlet it answers.[4] While Lee's *Annotationes* are exclusively concerned with Erasmus' New Testament, the lost pamphlet to which Erasmus is responding in no. 843 was a general attack on the whole of his *oeuvre* like the one planned by Standish or the one which More counters in the *Letter to a Monk*.[5] The most conclusive argument

---

[1]See Erasmus in *Apologia qua respondet*, Ferguson, pp. 262–63, and Allen, *4*, 200, lines 102–08. Erasmus' reaction to the one note that Lypsius did give him confirms that Erasmus had not seen the rest (Allen, *3*, 442, lines 5–6; cf. *4*, 471). Erasmus is writing under oath in the narrative sections of *Apologia qua respondet* (Ferguson, pp. 237, 259–60). For the date of Erasmus' return see Allen, *3*, 392.

[2]See Allen, *1*, 23, lines 15–17: "Primus omnium scripserat aduersus Nouum Testamentum obscurus quidam a nobis versum, cui satis habuimus epistola responderemus suppresso nomine." Allen's own note identifies this response with no. 843 (= "Lond. iii.1, LB. 375"). Erasmus has already listed his responses to Lee on the preceding page: "Nec ita multo post [*sc.* post Fabrum] prosiliit Eduardus Leus . . . cui respondimus tribus libellis, tametsi secunda aeditione primum omisimus, quod is tantum ad virulentias illius et plus quam muliebres rixas responderet . . ." (Allen, *1*, 22, lines 15–20). The first response is *Apologia qua respondet;* the second and third are Erasmus' two *Responsiones.* See Allen, *4*, 110, 259. For a similar reference to no. 843 see the polemical preface which was added to Erasmus' New Testament in 1519, "Capita argumentorum adversus indoctos quosdam atque morosos," (*Opera omnia*, ed. Jean LeClerc, 10 vols. Leiden, 1703–06, *6*, **3v; hereafter cited as "*Opera omnia*").

[3]Lee, *Annotationes*, sig. BB$_2$.

[4]Lee's history of the controversy appears in "Apologia Edouardi Leei contra quorundam calumnias," *Annotationes*, sigs. AA–DD, and in his long letter to Erasmus, *Annotationes*, sigs. K$_4$–O$_5$v, reprinted in Allen, *4*, 159–79; see Allen, *4*, 108–09. Erasmus' version appears in the *Letter to Lupset*, Allen, *4*, 139–52, and in *Apologia qua respondet*, Ferguson, pp. 236–71. The manuscript *responsiones* Lee mentions in Allen, *4*, 160, line 74, were mere marginal comments by Erasmus on notes Lee had given him; see Erasmus in *Apologia qua respondet*, Ferguson, pp. 243, 260, 262, 265. Besides his two lengthy *apologiae* and his actual annotations, Lee's volume includes a long index of purportedly dangerous mistakes in Erasmus' New Testament; see *Apologia qua respondet*, Ferguson, pp. 280–81 and commentary.

[5]For the attack planned by Standish see p. xxix, above. The anonymous critic answered by no. 843 attacked not only Erasmus' New Testament but also the adage-essay

of all for distinguishing between Lee and the anonymous critic refuted in no. 843 is Erasmus' repeated assertion that this critic condemns Erasmus' New Testament without even having examined it: Lee had certainly examined Erasmus' New Testament by May 1518.[1] The sole plausible reason for the identifying the pamphlet with a bundle of Lee's annotations is that Lypsius passed on the pamphlet to Erasmus in the same way that he later passed on one of Lee's annotations, but there can be no doubt that Erasmus used Lypsius' services in tracking down other attacks besides those personally authored by Lee.[2] The traditional description of no. 843 as a response to Lee's notes is erroneous.

Largely on the assumption that no. 843 was directed at Lee, Allen connected a number of other letters with Lee which are principally concerned with Erasmus' anonymous critic; once we restore them to their proper context and order, it becomes easier to trace the development of the Lee controversy as a whole.[3] Lee was apparently mistaken

---

"Sileni Alcibiadis," Erasmus' edition of Jerome, Erasmus' open letter to Dorp, the *Praise of Folly*, and the *Enchiridion;* see Allen, *3*, 316–17, 326–29. The anonymous critic even presented his own work as a general challenge and not as a casual collection of notes; see Allen, *3*, 330, and contrast Lee's own description of the manuscript *Annotationes* as reported by More at 154/21–27.

[1] For Erasmus' assertions see Allen, *3*, 325, lines 484–90. Lee had definitely begun his annotations by January 1518; see Allen, *3*, 203.

[2] Erasmus requests Lypsius' help under similar circumstances in Allen, *4*, 136–37, 139 (cf. 216). There Erasmus refers to an anonymous pamphlet which was probably prompted (though not actually written) by Lee; for the likelihood that Lee had a similar role in instigating the pamphlet refuted by no. 843 see note on 176/20–21. Erasmus' disparaging reference to his critic as a "Scotus" in Allen, *3*, 314, line 80, somewhat strengthens the likelihood that the pamphlet was prompted by Lee, whom Erasmus repeatedly describes thus (see *Apologia qua respondet*, Ferguson, p. 289, commentary at line 1320); so does the anonymous critic's defense of Lee's own ally, Standish (Allen, *3*, 326–27; for Lee's alliance with Standish see Allen, *4*, 286–87, 310, and p. xliv, n. 6, below). On the assumption that Lee was the actual author of the pamphlet, others have identified the instigator or "paraclete" as John Briart of Ath; see *CWE 6*, 20, commentary at line 538.

[3] If our characterization of no. 843 is correct, then the following letters exchanged between Erasmus and Lypsius refer not to Lee but to Erasmus' anonymous critic: Allen, *3*, nos. 750, 843, 897, and 898. Furthermore, Allen, *3*, no. 912, should precede Allen, *3*, nos. 899–901; these four letters as well as no. 922 introduce Lee by name. As Allen acknowledges, it is impossible to date these four letters securely according to internal evidence; thus, it is rather surprising that Allen prints no. 912 last of the four when it appears first in both of Lypsius' manuscript letter-books. (For a description of each of these manuscripts see Allen, *1*, 564, and *4*, xxvii–xxviii.) Two other letters nos. 921–22, intervene between nos. 898 and 912 in the manuscripts; there is no really compelling reason for shifting them to a later date, either. In one of the letter-books no. 912 is accompanied by an elaborate *argumentum* including a brief biographical sketch of Lee and a short history of the first stages of the controversy; it is hard to see why Lypsius

in claiming that Erasmus had used devious means to obtain a complete copy of Lee's annotations before May 1518. On the other hand, Erasmus did manage to secure and refute a brief pamphlet which was probably prompted by Lee, and in the last months of 1518 Erasmus did attempt to gain access to Lee's notes by fair means or foul.[1] He apparently had only limited success, and it is very unlikely that the manuscript version of Lee's *Annotationes* contributed significantly to the long list of corrections and refinements introduced in the second edition of Erasmus' New Testament.

From the very beginning, Erasmus' response to Lee's criticisms was far more intemperate than any response he had made to the strictures of Dorp.[2] We can best explain his immoderate reaction by stressing that Lee, unlike Dorp, had a penchant for spreading particularly invidious rumors in a particularly invidious way.[3] Erasmus' letters in this period are full of complaints about critics who would rather spread slanderous gossip than expose their own errors in print.[4] In particular, Lee's many connections with Erasmus' own friends and patrons in

---

should have inserted these comments at this point in the manuscript if Lee were the subject of so many preceding letters. It is also remarkable that Erasmus and Lypsius both avoid mentioning the name of the critic in nos. 750, 843, 897, and 898, whereas neither is hesitant to mention Lee's name in nos. 922, 912, 899–901, or in their later correspondence. Finally, the *argumentum* of no. 750 suggests that Erasmus' anonymous critic began his "sycophantic" attack no later than September 1517 (see Allen, *3*, 64, line 11; 73, lines 10–14; and 185), whereas the *argumentum* of no. 912 suggests that Lee first began stirring up serious trouble after Erasmus' departure for Basel in May 1518. One other letter, no. 1019, is apparently misdated in Allen; Lypsius' *argumentum* refers to the first English letter campaign to dissuade Lee from publishing (Lee in Allen, *4*, 175, lines 603–04; Erasmus in *Apologia qua respondet*, Ferguson, pp. 250–51), so that this letter should probably be dated slightly later than no. 955, now conjecturally assigned to late April 1519. Allen's misdating of no. 912 has already been noted and corrected in *CWE 6*, 182–83.

[1] See Lypsius in Allen, *3*, 471, 572–73, as well as Ferguson's introduction to *Apologia qua respondet*, p. 228. Erasmus later made no secret of his schemes to gain access to Lee's annotations, but took care to stress how completely his efforts had failed; see *Apologia qua respondet*, Ferguson, pp. 250, 263, 265.

[2] Erasmus himself seems to contrast his restraint in deferring to Dorp with his impetuousness in responding to Lee (Allen, *4*, 557).

[3] As Erasmus points out in *Apologia qua respondet*, Ferguson, pp. 277–78, even Lee's written charges are far more abusive than Dorp's; see, for example, Allen, *4*, 165, 173. Nor did Dorp ever claim that Erasmus could never have edited the New Testament successfully without his advice.

[4] See Allen, *3*, 574, 589; *4*, 149–50, and 248/17–22 below. Contradictions which might well go unnoticed in a series of rumors are easily exposed in a book; see Erasmus in *Apologia qua respondet*, Ferguson, p. 301, and 210/14–15, below.

England threatened one of his principal sources of moderate support at a time when he may well have felt most in need of it.[1] Under the circumstances it is hardly surprising that for a brief time Erasmus was tempted to make common cause with such hotheaded Germans as Ulrich von Hutten against Lee and his fellow obscurantists.[2]

Letter to a Monk

More's *Letter to a Monk,* almost certainly composed between March and September of 1519, is a forceful rebuttal of a virulent general attack on Erasmus' life and works which was coyly addressed as a personal re-monstrance to More.[3] More reports that the man he is answering is a young, poorly educated member of one of the stricter religious orders whose personal acquaintance with More is of fairly long standing.[4] The identity of More's correspondent has at last been established quite firmly by Dom David Knowles, who points out that in letters of this period Erasmus complains about only one young monkish critic from England, the London Carthusian John Batmanson.[5] A list of Batman-

---

[1]Lee's vehement allegations temporarily confused and alienated a number of Eras-mus' English friends; see Allen, *4,* 335, lines 30–31; and cf. 234, lines 19–21. In mid-1519 Erasmus was thinking of moving to England to escape his detractors in the Low Countries; see Allen, *3,* 578–79.

[2]For the somewhat uneasy alliance between Erasmus and the German radicals at the time of the Lee controversy see Allen, *4,* 23, 210, 286–87; *8,* xlv–xlvii.

[3]The monk's letter was largely concerned with the second edition of Erasmus' New Testament, which appeared in March 1519 (Allen, *3,* 387; see note on 236/3–6 below). As late as April 20 Lee still had not seen the edition in Louvain; see 152/3–6, 182/27–29. More's letter mentions John Colet and William Grocyn among living defenders of Eras-mus; Colet died September 16, 1519, and Grocyn died in October. See 208/10–21 and notes, as well as Allen, *1,* 242. The monk's letter, which circulated openly in manuscript among anti-Erasmians, was apparently meant to be published; see 304/11–25 and p. xxxvi, n. 2. For the likelihood that the monk's attack on Erasmus was presented as a personal remonstrance to More see 198/8–200/7.

[4]See 202/18–22, 262/28–31, 270/8–13; 270/20–29. More's acquaintance with the monk perhaps dates from More's four years of residence as a lay brother in the Charterhouse of London (1499–1503); see Roper, p. 6.

[5]See Dom David Knowles, *The Religious Orders in England,* 3 vols. (Cambridge, 1948–59; hereafter cited as "Knowles"), *3,* 469. Knowles refers to the following passages in the letters of Erasmus (Allen, *4,* 258–59, 287, May 5 and June 21, 1520):

Subornauit [*sc.* Leus] Londini Cartusiensem quendam, opinor nomine Ioannem Batmanson, iuuenem, vt e scriptis apparet, prorsus indoctum, sed ad insaniam vsque gloriosum.

Habet in Anglia [*sc.* Leus] duos stolidos Abbates et Minoritam Standicium, nunc episcopum, cuius mencio fit in Prouerbiis meis. Hii subornarunt Cartusiensem

son's works which was compiled by John Bale on the basis of statements by one of Batmanson's fellow Carthusians makes it clear that the young monk was in fact a quite active conservative polemicist.[1] He wrote pamphlets attacking not only Erasmus but also Luther and Lefèvre

---

quendam, iuuenem simpliciter indoctum, sed dyabolicum hypocritam et prorsus alterum Leum. Is scribit ἐξ ἁμαξῶν in me, in Fabrum insaniora Horeste.

Erasmus' phrase ἐξ ἁμαξῶν recalls More's "conuicia velut e plaustro" (202/11). By confusing John Batmanson the Carthusian with an older John Batmanson who was probably his father, Allen obscured the connection between these two passages and More's *Letter to a Monk.* As Knowles points out, the elder Batmanson was remarried in 1511, while the younger was ordained as a deacon by Bishop Fitzjames of London on March 31, 1510. Batmanson may have been as young as twenty-two at the time. He was prior of Hinton from 1523 until 1529 and of the London Charterhouse from 1529 until his death in 1531. The identity of More's correspondent with the Batmanson mentioned in Erasmus' letters may have been suspected by one reader as early as 1524, when a complete stranger conjectured in a letter to Erasmus that More's correspondent was probably a Carthusian (Allen, 5, 488). For a judgment condemning More's vehement response to Erasmus' monkish critic see Knowles, 3, 154.

[1]The following list of Batmanson's works appears in John Bale, *Scriptorum illustrium Maioris Brytanniae* . . . 2 vols. in 1 (Basel, 1557–59), 2, sig. k₂ (cf. *1*, sig. Vu₃):

De unica Magdalena, contra Fabrum, lib. I
Contra annotationes Erasmi, lib. I
Contra quaedam scripta Lutheri, lib. I
In prouerbia salomonis, lib. I
In Cantica canticorum, lib. I
Instructiones nouiciorum, lib. I
De contemptu mundi, lib. I
De Christo duodenni [*sic*], Hom. I. Cum factus esset annorum
     duodecim [Luke 2:42]
Super Missus est [Luke 1:26], Hom. I
Et retractiones tandem edidit, quod tam precipitanter
in Erasmum et Lutherum scripsisset.
     Petrus Wattes . . . Ex relatione.

Bale goes on to report that Peter Watts was at one point a member of the same Carthusian community ("eiusdem Carthusianae sodalitatis") but that he accepted the closing of the monasteries and eventually became vicar of Winterton by regal appointment. A shorter list of Batmanson's works which omits both his tract against Lefèvre d'Etaples and his work on the Song of Songs is attributed to Watts in an earlier version of Bale's work; see John Bale, *Index Britanniae scriptorum,* ed. R. L. Poole and M. Bateson (Oxford, 1902), pp. 181–82. John Pits copies Bale's longer list in his *Relationum historicarum de rebus Anglicis tomus primus* . . . (Paris, 1619), sigs. VVuu₃v–VVuu₄, adding that Batmanson's writings are praised for their learning and piety by Nicolaus Brigamus and Theodorus Petreius, two earlier historians.

d'Etaples.[1] More's vexation at Batmanson's personal assault on Erasmus and at his general disregard for the spirit of his Carthusian vows was expressed in a detailed attack on monastic abuses which is probably as forceful as anything written by Erasmus and which may well be More's own most thoroughly Erasmian work.

More's *Letter to a Monk* is the longest and most substantive contribution to the *Epistolae aliquot eruditorum* of May 1520, a volume of letters in which English and German Erasmians denounced Edward Lee for attacking Erasmus' New Testament.[2] The inclusion of More's letter in in a volume of letters defending Erasmus against Lee may be topically justified by the way in which Batmanson's general attack on Erasmus complements Lee's more limited attack on Erasmus' most prestigious work.[3] Lee himself in collusion with Standish actually instigated the

---

[1] It is interesting that Batmanson was apparently attacking Erasmus and supporting John Fisher's polemic against Lefèvre d'Etaples and his writings *De tribus magdalenis* at about the same time; see Allen, *3,* 205, 522; *4,* 92–93, 287; and Eugene F. Rice, Jr., ed., *The Prefatory Epistles of Jacques Lefèvre d'Etaples and Related Texts* (New York and London, 1972; hereafter cited as "Rice"), p. 400. Meanwhile one of Erasmus' most stubborn opponents in Louvain, the Carmelite Nicholas Egmondanus, launched a verbal attack on Erasmus, Lefèvre d'Etaples, and Luther which probably had much in common with Batmanson's written attacks; see Allen, *4,* 348, commentary at line 32, and Erasmus in *Apologia qua respondet,* Ferguson, p. 292. Batmanson certainly attacked Luther as well as Erasmus in his letter to More (see 262/17–23 below), so that his two tracts against Erasmus and Luther may well have been one and the same tract. If this was so, his retraction of what he had written against Luther would probably have formed part of the "palinode" for his pamphlet attacking Erasmus, and More's vehement denunciation of his unchristian conduct in slandering his "brother" would probably have been instrumental in eliciting both recantations. More's response may have been all that stopped Batmanson from publishing his attack on Erasmus; see p. xxxvi, n. 2 above. More appears to be citing the *incipit* of Batmanson's lost letter at 306/10–11; see note.

[2] See pp. xxxvi and cxxvii of this Introduction. The long title of the letter in both editions of this volume draws attention to its special significance; see 198/1–7 and note.

[3] Batmanson's tract actually combined three different types of anti-Erasmian polemic. Batmanson alleged that Erasmus had privately espoused heretical notions in the presence of an unnamed informant (see 204/28–212/2). He also mounted a general attack on a variety of Erasmus' writings (212/3–262/23). Finally, he attacked Erasmus' life-style as that of a vagabond monk (see 274/25–29 and 294/14–30). The unnamed informant was probably Standish (see note on 204/28–206/6), and Batmanson's general attack on Erasmus' writings almost certainly had much in common with a general attack planned by Standish in 1516 (see pp. xxix and xxxviii, above). The attack on Erasmus' vagabond lifestyle was probably suggested by Lee among others (see *Apologia qua respondet,* Ferguson, pp. 294–96, Allen, *3,* 439–42; and note on 294/14–298/8, below). In connection with the first type of polemic Batmanson also alleged that a divine revelation had identified Erasmus as a herald of Antichrist; for other instances of this charge see the note on 202/24–26.

parallel attack on Erasmus by Batmanson, and a rebuttal of Lee without any rebuttal of Standish or Batmanson would have been inconclusive at best.[1] Beyond that, More's vehement rebuttal of Batmanson includes a large number of striking rhetorical and thematic parallels with More's much gentler *Letter to Lee,* published in the same volume;[2] these parallels hint strongly that Lee, who shared so many biographical and intellectual characteristics with Batmanson, probably shared his intolerable arrogance, as well. In this way, without openly repudiating Lee's friendship, the most prestigious English Erasmian was able to repudiate Lee's actions completely.[3]

The conclusion of More's letter is quite different in tone from the text which precedes it; this suggests that More may have rewritten at least part of the letter when he decided to let it be published.[4] More's long apology for Erasmus' translation of John 1:1 (236/3–248/28) bears a striking resemblance to Erasmus' *Apologia de In principio erat sermo,* the original version of which was published in February 1520, and it might be supposed that More also rewrote and expanded this section of the letter after reading Erasmus' defense.[5] But Erasmus had already published a briefer defense of this rendering in the notes which accompanied the second edition of his New Testament (March 1519), and More was perfectly capable of building his own detailed argument on that earlier and simpler foundation. Erasmus also reports that in mid-1519 More defended this rendering successfully in an oral disputation with Standish.[6] More is likelier to have contributed a few

---

[1]See p. xli, n. 5, above.

[2]Not to mention the paternal concern More expresses for each of his younger compatriots, see the other parallels cited in the notes on 162/6–12, 166/24–168/6, 174/2–3, 200/21, and the obvious parallel between 172/21–32 and 270/20–26.

[3]See p. xxxvi, n. 2, above.

[4]See 304/11–310/9.

[5]For Erasmus' *Apologia* see Allen, *4,* 194–95, 210, 378, commentary at line 6; and Boyle, pp. 3–31.

[6]See Allen, *4,* 310–11; *8,* xlv–xlvi. Standish is the English preacher refuted in the *Apologia de In principio erat sermo;* see p. xxx, n. 6, above. The Louvain conservative there linked with Standish is a younger disciple of the Carmelite Nicholas Egmondanus ("Camelita"); see Erasmus, *Apologia de In principio erat sermo, Opera omnia, 9,* 112CD, and contrast Boyle, pp. 151–52. In Erasmus' writings the insulting nickname "Camelita" seems invariably to refer to Egmondanus himself; see Allen, *4,* 394, commentary at line 12. For another possible indication of collusion between Egmondanus and the English conservatives in this period see p. xliii, n. 1, above. Remarkably, Lee himself did not openly challenge Erasmus' translation of John 1:1, leaving this task to his allies in England. Erasmus associates Lee with the critics of "In principio erat sermo" in *Apologia qua respondet,* Ferguson, p. 275.

arguments to Erasmus' *Apologia* than to have used it himself as a source.[1]

---

[1]Boyle (p. 14) notes one instance in which Erasmus may have borrowed an argument from a lost written summary of More's oral defense against Standish, but she does not consider the possibility that Erasmus is directly indebted to the *Letter to a Monk*. The second version of the *Apologia de In principio erat sermo* (August 1520) introduces several new authorities and arguments which may have been borrowed from the *Letter to a Monk*, namely Cyprian, *Adversus Iudaeos* 2.5 (Erasmus, *Opera omnia, 9,* 114C; cf. 246/9–11 below); Ambrose [?], *De fide orthodoxa contra Arianos* 2 (*Opera omnia, 9,* 117C; cf. 240/22– 242/3 below); Lactantius, *Divinae institutiones* 4.8, 9 (*Opera omnia, 9,* 117F–118A; cf. 242/6–11 below); the claim ". . . ita praeferam sermonem, ut verbum non reijciam" (*Opera omnia, 9,* 113E; cf. 246/23 below); and a long refutation of the argument against *sermo* which is based on Augustine's assertion that the primary meaning of *verbum* is a *conceptus mentis tacitus* (*Opera omnia, 9,* 119A–120E; cf. 238/19–240/4 and 244/23–30 below). In Allen, *8,* xlv, Erasmus attributes this argument to an unidentified Spanish Minorite who was working with Standish in England; it is likely that Batmanson borrowed this argument from the Spaniard and that Erasmus first learned about it from More. Even in the first version of his *Apologia* (Louvain, February 1520, sig. a₄) Erasmus cites one biblical verse (Sap. 18:15) to which More had already appealed in his oral disputation with Standish (Allen, *4,* 311, lines 74–75; cf. 240/15–20 below). Erasmus introduces one further argument in later editions of his annotations on John which may also owe something to the *Letter to a Monk:* ". . . in hoc meo proposito [*sc.* Evangelii denuo vertendi in usum studiosorum], quo maior est varietas, hoc plus est fructus . . ." (*Annotationes in Novum Testamentum, Opera omnia, 6,* 336D; cf. 238/1–4 below). On Erasmus' defense of *varietas* in translating see further Boyle, pp. 11–12, and p. lxxx, n. 1, below.

CHRISTIAN WISDOM AND SECULAR LEARNING

The relation between Christian wisdom and secular learning has always been rich in perplexities.[1] Christ warned that none would be saved without being born again into childlike simplicity.[2] St. Paul added that God had chosen the foolish things of the world to confound the wise and that knowledge "puffs up" whereas charity edifies.[3] On the other hand, even St. Paul freely and skillfully cited pagan authors.[4] His suggestion that "to the pure all things are pure" could be used to defend the same secular learning that he seemed to condemn in his contrast of knowledge and charity.[5] Christ himself bade the faithful to put on the wisdom of serpents along with the innocence of doves.[6] The possibility if not the necessity of a tentative compromise between Christian wisdom and secular learning is also suggested by Paul's counsel to "prove all things" but "hold fast that which is good."[7] Jerome and Augustine both appealed to Old Testament precedents for cautiously

---

[1]For earlier studies with an immediate bearing on the relation between Christian wisdom and secular learning see E. Harris Harbison, *The Christian Scholar in the Age of the Reformation* (New York, 1956), especially pp. 1–67; Harald Hagendahl, *Latin Fathers and the Classics* (Göteborg, 1958); Jean Leclercq, O.S.B., *The Love of Learning and the Desire for God: A Study of Monastic Culture*, trans. Catharine Misrahi (New York, 1961; hereafter cited as "Leclercq, *Love of Learning*"); Anthony Levi, *Pagan Virtue and the Humanism of the Northern Renaissance*, The Society for Renaissance Studies Occasional Papers 2 (London, 1974; hereafter cited as "Levi"); Marjorie O. Boyle, *Christening Pagan Mysteries: Erasmus in Pursuit of Wisdom* (Toronto, 1981); and Daniel Kinney, "Erasmus' *Adagia:* Midwife to the Rebirth of Learning," *Journal of Medieval and Renaissance Studies, 11* (1981), 169–92, hereafter cited as "Kinney, 'Erasmus' *Adagia*.'"

[2]Matt. 18:3–4, 19:14, Mark 10:13–15, Luke 9:46–48, 18:15–17; John 3:3–8; cf. Matt. 11:25. For the more general principle that the last shall be first in the kingdom of heaven see Matt. 20:26–27, 23:10–12; Mark 9:35; Luke 14:8–11.

[3]Rom. 1:20–25; 1 Cor. 1:17–29, 3:18–21, 8:1.

[4]Acts 17:23, 28; 1 Cor. 15:33; Phil. 1:12.

[5]Titus 1:15; cf. Rom. 8:28 and 1 Cor. 3:22–23. Erasmus adduces the first of these proof-texts in *Antibarbari, ASD 1/1*, 85, line 14. For the use of Rom. 8:28 in defense of secular learning see Leclercq, *Love of Learning*, p. 158; and cf. 298/28–300/4 below.

[6]Matt. 10:16 (cf. 1 Cor. 14:20); see 260/5–6 and 274/21–22 and notes; cf. also Matt. 22:21, Mark 12:17, and Luke 20:25.

[7]1 Thess. 5:21.

appropriating the servants and goods of an alien culture: secular learning should be used with discretion for the service and honor of Christ.[1]

As the Church assumed more and more of the functions of the decaying Roman secular government, the need for a practical compromise between Christian wisdom and secular learning became more acute. The official position on secular learning, as on secular things generally, was *uti non frui*, "Use but do not enjoy"; Colet expressed the same qualified receptiveness in his admonition "Use well temporal things. Desire eternal things."[2] But while the formal distinction between use and enjoyment might satisfy some tender consciences, the practical question of what constitutes immoderate reliance on secular learning was never completely resolved.[3] Different notions of human psychology could generate quite different answers to this basic question. Those who believed in the natural primacy of the intellect characteristically associated immoderate reliance on secular learning with the serious study of subjects like poetry and rhetoric which were concerned with arousing the passions; those who believed in the natural primacy of the will characteristically associated this fault with the serious study of subjects like logic and metaphysics which seemed especially likely to produce intellectual arrogance. Renaissance humanists tended to champion the latter conception of human psychology while medieval scholastics characteristically (if not always openly) championed the former.[4] Pauline texts could be cited which seemed to

---

[1]See Jerome, *Epistòlae* 70.2, in *Patrologiae Cursus Completus: Series Latina*, ed. J. P. Migne, 221 vols. (Paris, 1844–1903; hereafter cited as *PL*), 22, 665–66; and Augustine, *De doctrina christiana* 2.40.60 (*PL 34*, 63; cf. 140/1–2 below and note).

[2]John Colet, *A Right Fruitful Monition*, in J. H. Lupton, *A Life of John Colet . . .* , 2nd ed. (London, 1909; reprint, Hamden, Conn., 1961), p. 310. On the commonplace principle *uti non frui* see Augustine, *De doctrina christiana* 1.3.3–1.4.4, 1.33.37 (*PL 34*, 20–21, 33), and D. W. Robertson, Jr., *A Preface to Chaucer: Studies in Medieval Perspectives* (Princeton, 1962), especially pp. 65–69. Thompson (p. 248) cites Colet's maxim to sum up More's own attitude toward secular learning.

[3]For two opposing conceptions of moderation (*mediocritas*) see 140/25–142/1 and 220/25–26; cf. also 270/13–15.

[4]Naturally not all the humanists were voluntarists, and the same humanists can seem to be voluntarists in some of their statements and intellectualists in others. Chomarat (*1*, 61) notes that Erasmus espouses an intellectualist dualism when he is writing against sensual indulgence; when his purpose is Christian persuasion he tends to exalt the emotions and distinguish their promptings from those of the flesh. But it does seem quite clear that a voluntarist tendency prevailed in rhetorical humanism, as it did in the preaching theology of certain scholastics; see p. lxxxvi, n. 1, below. For a similar conclusion linking this rhetorical tendency with one aspect of Renaissance Augustinianism see William J. Bouwsma, "The Two Faces of Humanism: Stoicism and Augustinianism in Renaissance Thought," in *Itinerarium Italicum: The Profile of the Italian Renaissance in the Mirror of Its*

oppose both the rhetorical emphasis of the humanists and the speculative emphasis of the scholastics.[1] Thus the ancient debate between rhetoric and philosophy was revived at the end of the Christian Middle Ages, with both sides hurling charges of paganism.[2]

Closely related to Augustine's rather ambiguous distinction between "use" and "enjoyment" was his seemingly clearer distinction between the "science [or "knowledge"] of things," which is edifying, and the "science of signs," which inflates.[3] The context of Augustine's opposition between the two "sciences" is a discussion of how much importance should be given to good Latin grammar. The pointed allusion in this passage to Paul's opposition between the knowledge which inflates and the charity which edifies made it easy for scholastic polemicists like Dorp to suggest that Augustine and Paul were both sanctioning philosophy, the traditional "science of things," and disparaging rhetoric and grammar, the traditional "science of signs."[4] Augustine's general suspicion of secular "custom," the very foundation of the "science of

---

European Transformations . . . , ed. H. A. Oberman and T. A. Brady, Jr. (Leiden, 1975), pp. 3–60. For More's longest discussion of the relation between will and intellect see *CW 8*, 497–509.

[1] For a dismissive allusion to rhetoric see 2 Cor. 11:6. For disapproving remarks on contentious speculation see 1 Tim. 1:4, 6:3–5, 20–21; 2 Tim. 2:23; Titus 3:9. Erasmus refers to such passages in *Moriae encomium, ASD 4/3*, 154, lines 451–56, and in *Ratio verae theologiae*, in *Ausgewählte Werke*, ed. Hajo Holborn and Annemarie Holborn (Munich, 1933; hereafter cited as "Holborn"), p. 187, lines 17–20. Paul also disparages human wisdom and eloquence together; see 1 Cor. 1:17, 2:1–13. Christ had already admonished the faithful to acknowledge only one teacher (*magister*), Christ himself (Matt. 23:10); this exclusion encouraged the humanists in their assault on the pride of scholastic professors, who styled themselves *magistri nostri* (see 224/4–6 below and note).

[2] See Chomarat, *1*, 447–49. For the ancient debate between rhetoric and philosophy see Seigel, especially pp. vii–xvii and 1–30.

[3] Augustine, *De doctrina christiana* 2.13.20 (*PL 34*, 44–45), clearly alluding to 1 Cor. 8:1. The equation of vainglorious knowledge with the "science of signs" may owe something to Rom. 1:23–25: "Et mutauerunt gloriam incorruptibilis Dei in similitudinem imaginis corruptibilis hominis. . . . commutauerunt ueritatem Dei in mendacio, et coluerunt et seruierunt creaturae potius quam Creatori, qui est benedictus in saecula." Cf. also 2 Cor. 3:6: "littera enim occidit, Spiritus autem uiuificat."

[4] Augustine's statement is cited by Dorp in Allen, 2, 133, lines 246–53. Cf. the monk's opposition between *veritas scripturarum* and *flosculi sermonum* at 222/6–9 below. The opposition between a science of things and a science of signs was exploited in a similar way by Giovanni Pico della Mirandola in his "Epistola de barbaro dicendi genere philosophorum," reprinted in Eugenio Garin, ed., *Prosatori latini del Quattrocento* (Milan, 1952; hereafter cited as "Garin"), pp. 804–23. For Erasmus' response to Pico's letter see Kinney, "Erasmus' *Adagia*," pp. 178–88, and Erasmus, *Apologia in dialogum Jacobi Latomi* (Opera omnia, 9, 102E).

signs," made it easier still to enlist him as a patron of *ratio* against *oratio* or of speculation against rhetoric.[1]

The humanists employed various strategies in an effort to discount Augustine's disparaging attitude toward the "science of signs." On occasion they simply denied that Augustine himself was infallible: "Being a man, he could make a mistake."[2] With a similar motive they often drew attention to Augustine's long quarrel with Jerome and implicitly or explicitly challenged Augustine's intellectual priorities by championing those of Jerome.[3] On other occasions they either stressed that Augustine himself was a master of eloquence (he had once been a teacher of rhetoric) or maintained that he actually sanctioned the study of grammar and rhetoric no less than he sanctioned dialectic.[4] If grammar and rhetoric were potentially useful to Christians, then the ar-

---

[1]Augustine, *Confessiones* 1.16.25–1.18.29 (*PL* 32, 672–74); *De doctrina christiana* 2.13.19–20 (*PL 34*, 44–45). Cf. Dorp in Allen, 2, 127, lines 38–42; 128–29, lines 85–92; 129–30, lines 116–45; 133, lines 246–56; and Erasmus in Allen, 3, 336, lines 219–28. See also 238/20–30 and note, below, for Augustine's attempt to give *verbum* the primary meaning *tacitus mentis conceptus*. For a provocative discussion of the radical reformers' Augustinian assault on convention and More's response in his later polemics see Lawrence Manley, *Convention, 1500–1750* (Cambridge, Mass., and London, 1980), pp. 67–86.

[2]More, *Letter to Dorp*, 68/1–4 below. Cf. 214/12–17; *CW 3/1*, 4/21–28; and Erasmus' *Antibarbari, ASD 1/1*, 114, lines 7–10. More is probably thinking of Augustine's own statement that no mortal's opinions should be taken as gospel; see 216/10–13 below.

[3]See the notes on 6/27–29, 212/20–21, 212/22–24, 212/24–214/1, 214/2–4, 214/4–5, 214/6–7 and 224/23–24. Cf. also Allen, 2, 15, lines 138–40, where Dorp borrows an argument which Augustine had used against Jerome. For a good recent account of the quarrel see Robert J. O'Connell, "When Saintly Fathers Feuded: The Correspondence between Augustine and Jerome," *Thought, 54* (1979), 344–68. Implicit and explicit challenges to Augustine's intellectual priorities in comparison with those of Jerome may be found in Erasmus, *Antibarbari, ASD 1/1*, 82, 92, 112–13; *Vita Hieronymi*, Ferguson, pp. 167–68, 180–81; and Allen, 3, 334–37. For two passages strongly suggesting that Jerome, not Augustine, was More's favorite patristic authority before 1520 see 68/3–5 and 254/19–21 below. These passages should be used to qualify the traditional view that More took Augustine as his principal patristic model; see Germain Marc'hadour, *Thomas More et la Bible: La place des livres saints dans son apologétique et sa spiritualité* (Paris, 1969), pp. 531, 537, and *The Bible in the Works of St. Thomas More: A Repertory*, 5 vols. (Nieuwkoop, 1969–72; hereafter cited as "Marc'hadour, *The Bible*"), *4, 9*.

[4]On Augustine as a master of eloquence see Erasmus, *Antibarbari, ASD 1/1*, 78, lines 13–15. For Erasmus' defensive use of Augustine's *De doctrina christiana* see Chomarat, *1*, 171–73. For Augustine's insistence on the value of grammatical instruction see *De doctrina christiana, prologus* (*PL 34*, 15–20). Erasmus refers to Augustine's recommendation of rhetoric (*De doctrina christiana* 4.2.3–4.30.63; *PL 34*, 89–120) in *Antibarbari, ASD 1/1*, 115, lines 20–22; cf. notes on 222/14–17 and 222/20–22 below. Even when More cites Augustine against Dorp, he does so in a way which suggests that Augustine was often allied with scholastic conservatives in their opposition to the humanists; see 80/17–18.

rogant intolerance of those who condemned them completely was as bad as the arrogant self-indulgence of those who esteemed nothing else.[1] This defense of the "science of signs" merely offset the traditional argument for the primacy of things over signs with another traditional argument for shunning contentious, reductive extremes. Since the medieval curriculum had never excluded traditional grammar and rhetoric completely, the real basis for the humanists' charges of reckless obscurantism remained to be seen. What was chiefly at issue was the primacy of speculation over practical learning in general, and in order to challenge this primacy the humanists would have to displace the prevailing conception of a secular "science of things."

One of the humanists' favorite techniques for combating the speculative prejudice was to subject the scholastics' intellectual pretensions to the same psychological inversion that Paul had applied to the claims of the pagan philosophers. "Professing themselves to be wise, they became fools, and changed the glory of the incorruptible God into an image made like to corruptible man. . . ."[2] Pagans worshiped false gods fashioned in their own image; the secret pagans of the scholastic establishment did much the same thing in exalting a spurious ideal of intellectual self-sufficiency. Folly's only half-playful critique of scholastic philosophy and theology achieves some of its most memorable effects through precisely this sort of inversion.[3] Humanist thinkers habitually wrote secular variations on Paul's admonition "If any man among you seemeth to be wise in this world, let him become a fool that he may be wise."[4] In this dialectic of inversion the counsel of Paul against trusting in secular wisdom could be assimilated—for polemical purposes, at least—to the doctrine of the skeptical Academy that no earthly knowledge is certain.[5] Thus the Ciceronian convention linking rhetoric with Academic skepticism made it possible to represent rhetoric as a modest alternative to the vainglorious "science" the scholastics professed: to

---

[1] See 136/29–138/7, 258/19–20, and notes, as well as *CW* 3/2, no. 260: "In pinguem quendam patrem cui frequens erat in ore[,] scientia inflat."

[2] Rom. 1:22–23.

[3] On the hubristic delusions of the Stoics and their imitators among the scholastics see Erasmus, *Moriae encomium, ASD* 4/3, 80, line 150; 106, lines 631–46; 144, lines 369–74, 148, lines 408–13. Cf. also *CW 4*, 158/25–29.

[4] 1 Cor. 3:18; cf. Seigel, pp. 57, 74–75; Erasmus, *Moriae encomium, ASD* 4/3 186, lines 71–72; and 130/17–19 and note, below.

[5] For the "dialectic of the Silenus" see Pierre Mesnard, *Erasme ou le christianisme critique* (Paris, 1969), pp. 43–52; Jean-Claude Margolin, "Erasme et le verbe: De la rhétorique à l'hermèneutique," in *Erasme, l'Alsace, et son temps . . .* (Strasbourg, 1971), pp. 87–110 and especially pp. 109–10; and Kinney, "Erasmus' *Adagia*," pp. 184–92.

the extent that the scholastics mistook arbitrary intellectual constructs for ultimate realities, they themselves could be charged with professing a "science of signs" as a "science of things."[1] After all, the traditional wisdom of grouping *dialectica* with *grammatica* and *rhetorica* as the three "language arts" of the trivium implied that all three were primarily sciences of signs; what entitled scholastics to claim that the first furnished more direct access to "things" than did the second or third?[2] It is worth noting, however, that without a more durable foundation in human experience, rhetoric itself would be vulnerable to the same dialectic of inversion once it took the place of scholastic speculation as a governing "science."[3] The only definite polemical value of this humanistic response to the speculative prejudice was to show that Augustine's distinction between a "science of things" and a "science of signs" was as ambiguous as the parallel distinction between "use" and "enjoyment."

For this reason More's *Letter to Dorp* represents an especially important contribution to the defense of the humanist program with its emphasis on grammar and rhetoric. We might suppose that this emphasis was sufficiently vindicated by the humanists' practical achievements in the areas of biblical philology and literary scholarship of every variety, but if we did so we would simply be assuming what needs to be proved; were the humanists really better equipped than their scholastic rivals to make sense of a cultural heritage which was common to both? The humanist program affected not only the way in which advanced scholars chose to attack this or that particular intellectual problem, but

---

[1] For the Ciceronian convention linking rhetoric and Academic skepticism see Seigel, pp. 16–17, 57, 74–75, 188; and cf. Erasmus, *Antibarbari, ASD* 1/1, 89, lines 12–15; 90, line 16–91, line 7; *Moriae encomium, ASD* 4/3, 130, lines 98–100; *Ratio verae theologiae,* Holborn, p. 297. For the relation between rhetoric and fideism in the thought of Erasmus and Valla see Chomarat, *1*, 32–34, and Seigel, p. 158. For an important indication of the limits of Ciceronian skepticism see Cicero, *De officiis* 2.2.7–8. More represents some speculative theologians as inflated or "distended" with trifling dialectical questions at 54/13–17 below; cf. Erasmus, *Antibarbari, ASD* 1/1, 88, line 5.

[2] See Juan Luis Vives, *Epistola in pseudodialecticos* (1519), in *Juan Luis Vives against the Pseudodialecticians: A Humanist Attack on Medieval Logic,* ed. and trans. Rita Guerlac (Dordrecht, Boston, and London, 1979; hereafter cited as "Vives, *Epistola*"), p. 52: "Tum dialecticam quis non videt scientiam esse de sermone? quod ostendit ipsa Graeca nominis ratio διαλεκτικὴ καὶ λογικὴ uti est rhetorice uti et grammatice. . . ." Cf. 16/4–26 below. Aristotle's restriction of dialectic to inference based on merely probable premises seems to have been largely ignored in the late Middle Ages, so that "dialectic" and "logic" were frequently treated as synonyms; see Aristotle, *Topica* 1.1–2; and 24/9–11, 24/19–26/4, and 28/2–6 below.

[3] For this contest between humanist rhetoric and scholastic dialectic for the status of governing "science" see p. xix, n. 3, above.

also the way in which the recipients of even a rudimentary education
were brought to conceive systematically of all human knowledge. Scholastic dialectic provided, or professed to provide, an indispensable
principle of organization for every variety of inquiry. It was, in the
words of Peter of Spain, its most widely known exponent, "the art of
arts and the science of sciences, comprising the way to the principles of
all methods."[1] The "new philosophy" of the humanist program set out
to dispense with this organizational principle, and thus threatened to
"cast all in doubt":

> In terms of the established pattern, humanism forced a crisis by
> proposing a program which in effect challenged the primacy of
> dialectic and, in so doing, impugned the whole curricular organi-
> zation and the teaching profession as such, and thereby threat-
> ened the intelligibility of the whole universe.[2]

Even if the humanist movement originally lacked any pretensions to
philosophical rigor, the consequences of its challenge to the traditional
order in education were philosophically so disturbing that humanist
theoreticians eventually had to rise to the occasion, even endeavoring
to supplant the dialectic of the scholastics with humanist "dialectic," a
more or less arbitrary system for conveniently marshaling one's arguments.[3] The history of humanist apologetics is above all the history of
an endeavor to discredit scholastic dialectic as the organizational principle of all disciplines and to set forth a sounder alternative, an endeav-

---

[1]*Tractatus, called afterwards Summule Logicales,* ed. L. M. de Rijk (Assen, 1972; hereafter
cited as *"Tractatus"*), p. 1 (*Tractatus* 1.1); I have translated the commonest reading of
More's day. Peter's statement is an expansion of Aristotle, *Topica* 1.2 (101b3–4). Cf. the
humanist's parallel definition of grammar which is cited by W. Keith Percival, "Grammar
and Rhetoric in the Renaissance," in *Renaissance Eloquence: Studies in the Theory and Practice of Renaissance Rhetoric,* ed. James J. Murphy (Berkeley, Los Angeles, and London,
1983), pp. 303–04: "Grammatica est scientia recte loquendi recteque scribendi, origo et
fundamentum liberalium artium."

[2]Walter J. Ong, *Ramus: Method and the Decay of Dialogue* (Cambridge, Mass., 1958;
hereafter cited as "Ong"), p. 166. See also Terrence Heath, "Logical Grammar, Grammatical Logic, and Humanism in Three German Universities," *Studies in the Renaissance,
18* (1971), 9–64 (hereafter cited as "Heath"), and N. W. Gilbert, *Renaissance Concepts of
Method* (New York, 1960). On medieval curricular organization see Anthony Kenney and
Jan Pinborg, "Medieval Philosophical Literature" in *Cambridge History of Later Medieval
Philosophy, from the Rediscovery of Aristotle to the Disintegration of Scholasticism, 1100–1600,*
ed. Norman Kretzman et al. (Cambridge, 1982), pp. 11–42; hereafter cited as *CHLMP.*

[3]Ong, pp. 92–130. See also Lisa Jardine, "Humanism and the Sixteenth-Century
Cambridge Arts Course," *History of Education, 4/1* (1975), 16–31, and "Humanism and
the Teaching of Logic," *CHLMP,* pp. 797–807; cf. James H. Overfield, *Humanism and
Scholasticism in Late Medieval Germany* (Princeton, 1984) esp. chaps. 2–3, 6, 8.

or which finds one of its most effective expressions in More's systematic rebuttal of Dorp.

More's elaborate attack on scholastic dialectic (26/25–36/18) is one of the most striking innovations in the letter. Though this passage provides a rhetorical foundation for a critique of scholastic theology which is largely inspired by Erasmus' own antischolastic remarks in his letter to Dorp and the *Moriae encomium,* More himself seems to stress that the groundwork he lays is his own (78/16–20). Other humanists, most notably Valla, had also condemned the scholastics for elaborating their logical vocabulary and theories of inference with virtually complete disregard for traditional Latin usage, but More appears to surpass even Valla in convincingly linking the scholastics' transgressions against common usage with their transgressions against common sense.[1]

More begins by suggesting that the new logic of the scholastics is actually sophistic, not logic at all; their first mistake is to think that a doctrine so cluttered with mystifications could provide any essential assistance in clarifying the logical relations between actual statements (26/25–26; cf. 36/10–14). He proceeds with a bitter pun on the name of a treatise called the *Parva logicalia* ("Little Logic"), "so called probably because it contains little logic" (28/9–10). While this treatise is indeed, as earlier interpreters have noted, identical with the last half of the *Summulae logicales* of Peter of Spain, the principal textbook of medieval logic, More mentions it here only as the prime expression among many of the depraved dialectical interests prevailing among the scholastics.[2] Only about half of the sophisms More goes on to cite are

---

[1]For the history of humanist apologetics before More see Hanna H. Gray, "Valla's Encomium of St. Thomas Aquinas and the Humanist Conception of Christian Antiquity," in *Essays in History and Literature Presented . . . to Stanley Pargellis,* ed. Heinz Bluhm (Chicago, 1965; hereafter cited as "Gray"), pp. 37–51; Seigel, passim; Cesare Vasoli, "Intorno al Petrarca ed ai logici 'moderni,'" in *Antiqui und Moderni: Traditionsbewusstsein und Fortschrittsbewusstsein im späten Mittelalter,* Miscellanea Medievalia 9 (Berlin and New York, 1974), pp. 142–54, and "La première querelle des 'anciens' et des 'modernes' aux origines de la Renaissance," in *Classical Influences on European Culture, A.D. 1500–1700,* ed. R. R. Bolgar, pp. 67–80; Rita Guerlac's introduction to Vives, *Epistola,* pp. 9–43; Letizia A. Panizza, "Lorenzo Valla's *De vero falsoque bono:* Lactantius and Oratorical Skepticism," *Journal of the Warburg and Courtauld Institutes, 41* (1978), 76–107; and James D. Tracy, "Against the 'Barbarians': The Young Erasmus and his Humanist Contemporaries," *Sixteenth-Century Journal, 11/1* (1980), 3–22. See also the works cited on p. xvii, n. 2, above.

[2]See note on 28/3. More's reference contradicts the assertion of de Rijk (*Tractatus,* p. xcvii; see also p. xcix) that Peter's treatise "never seems to have enjoyed a great vogue in England." Cf. Allen, 2, 328, line 229, where Erasmus states that the *Parva logicalia* formed a mainstay of the Cambridge curriculum near the end of the fifteenth century.

liv   INTRODUCTION

straightforwardly traceable to Peter of Spain; the other half, associated
with one sort of ambiguity which does not trouble Peter, derive from
the sophism collections of such later dialecticians as the Parisian *magister* John Buridan. The best way to deal with these sophisms is to group
them according to the four "neoteric" expressions which More himself
borrows from Peter at 28/11–13: "so-called suppositions . . . ampliations, restrictions, and appellations."

The term supposition is fundamental to the innovative logical system
presented in the second half of the *Summulae logicales*. While the first
half of this textbook (treatises 1–5) confines its attention to the problems first handled by Aristotle, the second half introduces a whole
range of new problems based on ambiguities of "supposition." Supposition is defined as "the acceptance of a substantive term [which is
already significant] as denoting something."[1] Suppositions always figure as elements in complete sentences. The sort of problem here indicated by ambiguities of supposition is the sort in which one attempts to
make *man* in the sentence "Man is a species" function the same way as
man in the sentence "A man shut the door." The scholastic dialecticians
attempted to distinguish meticulously between a number of different
types of supposition, dissolving the meaning of each substantive term
into a variety of virtually unrelated meanings. They were apparently so
fascinated with this proliferation of meanings that they never approxi-
mated the strictly functional analysis of modern symbolic logic.[2] At
least equally telling, once the scholastics dissected a noun in this way, it
would often retain only the slightest resemblance to its counterpart in
everyday discourse.

Restriction is defined as "the contraction of a general term from a
greater supposition to a lesser," for example by means of an adjectival
qualifier. Ampliation, the opposition of restriction, is defined as "the
extension of a general term from a lesser supposition to a greater," for
example by means of a verb of potential. Appellation or connotation,
finally, is defined as "the acceptance of a term for an existing thing,"

---

[1]This and the following definitions are taken from *The Summulae Logicales of Peter of
Spain*, trans. J. P. Mullally (Notre Dame, 1945), pp. 3, 47, 39, and 45. The first three are
quoted by Surtz in his useful discussion of the parallel passage in *Utopia, CW 4*, 159 (*Praise
of Pleasure*, pp. 91–93). For the further development of supposition-theory in the late
Renaissance see E. J. Ashworth, *Language and Logic in the Post-Medieval Period* (Dordrecht,
1974), pp. 77–100, and the article cited in the following note. For the relation of Peter of
Spain to the humanist dialecticians, see Ong, pp. 53–91.

[2]See E. J. Ashworth, "The Doctrine of Supposition in the Sixteenth and Seventeenth
Centuries," *Archiv für Geschichte der Philosophie, 51* (1969), 263: ". . . one basic criticism
can be made, namely that the [supposition-]logicians concentrated on the meaning of
individual words rather than the meaning of sentences."

and differs from supposition in that the latter includes terms accepted for things which do not exist—centaurs, for instance.

Half of More's sophisms (28/13–30/5) are appellation-sophisms while the other half (30/14–32/25) are ampliation-sophisms. In between (30/6–13) there are three sophisms apparently based on an ambiguity of relative supposition.[1] We thus get a pattern in which the last of the four terms cited by More prompts the first sampling of sophisms; the first, most general term prompts three rather unspecialized transitional examples; and the second and third terms prompt the second sampling of sophisms. In this light it is easy to see why More here supplements the list "suppositions, ampliations, and restrictions" which appears in the contemporaneous book 2 of *Utopia:* "appellations" helps balance his treatment and clarify its intent.[2]

It is also worth noting why More selects these two types of sophism as principal targets. In his selection of ampliation-sophisms More contrives to let scholastic dialectic provide its own *reductio ad absurdum.* If we mix verbs in the past, present, and future tenses indiscriminately, virtually any statement may be defended as true. But then language stops being functional, and the whole game must cease. As More himself notes, "indeed neither Antichrist nor the final day of judgment itself could upset nature's order as thoroughly as this dialectic . . ." (32/8–10). Consider, for instance, Peter of Spain's prime example: "It will be impossible that Antichrist has not been. But it may be [*potest esse*] the case that Antichrist has not been. Therefore the impossible may be the case.[3] This set of sophisms illustrates the extreme theoretical consequences of scholastic disregard for common sense, while the appellation-sophisms illustrate the extent to which practical disregard for common usage vitiates the scholastics' analysis of even quite simple everyday statements. The two types of exemplary fallacy are equally apt for More's argument.

More's sampling of appellation-sophisms enables him to set the scho-

---

[1] See Peter of Spain, *Tractatus* 8.7, "De relativis," p. 187 ("The man sees an ass, who is rational," or "The man, who is rational, sees an ass"). Of course, puzzles like these can present more than one sort of logical difficulty; for a lucid discussion of one good example, see E. J. Ashworth, "I promise you a horse: A Second Problem of Meaning and Reference in Late Fifteenth and Early Sixteenth-Century Logic (I)," *Vivarium, 14* (1976), 62–79.

[2] See *CW 4,* 159.

[3] *Tractatus* 9.4, p. 195. For More's ampliation-sophisms see also John Buridan, *Sophisms on Meaning and Truth,* trans. T. K. Scott (New York, 1966, hereafter cited as "Buridan"), pp. 144, 146, 153; and Juan Luis Vives, *De causis corruptarum artium* (1531) 3.6, *Opera omnia,* ed. Gregorius Majansius, 8 vols. (Valencia, 1745; reprint, London, 1964; hereafter cited as "Vives, *Opera omnia*"), 6, 143.

lastics' arbitrary distortions of traditional Latin syntax in sharp contrast to the humanists' method of explaining ambiguous expressions by appealing to grammatical precedent or rhetorical context. John Buridan devotes a whole chapter in his treatise on sophisms to "resolving" ambiguities of this sort by performing a trick of syntactic inversion. In particular, the sophism "You ate raw meat today" prompts the following explanation:

> . . . in the minor proposition "Something raw you bought," the term "raw" connotes rawness indifferently and disjunctively for present or past time, while in the conclusion "I eat something raw" the term "raw" connotes rawness only for the present. Hence it does not stand for that to which rawness is related before, unless it is still so related at present.[1]

The scholastics contended that a term employed after a verb or some other syntactic determinant is "distributed" differently from the same term placed before the verb: if I simply announce, "I ate raw meat today," I imply that I ate it "under the aspect of *raw*," whereas if I say "Raw meat I ate today," I imply only that this meat at some point in time was not cooked yet. The philosophical problem which these sophisms treat is a real one, and Buridan's efforts toward solving it have received some respectful attention of late from historians of logic.[2] What is at issue in this section of More's letter, however, is not the factitious nature of the problem itself so much as the factitious nature of the syntactic "solutions" advanced by the scholastics: everyday language cannot sustain the distinctions which Buridan strives to impose on it. Indeed, the effort to impose such distinctions distracts the investigator from applying more trustworthy standards of meaning to such a routine imprecision of phrasing, namely the standards of common linguistic custom and simple common sense.[3] In certain contexts there

[1]Cf. 28/19–23 below. This "solution" comes from Buridan, p. 118. For More's other appellation-sophisms cf. Buridan, pp. 137–43, and Vives, *De causis corruptarum artium*, *Opera omnia*, 6, 143.

[2]On the sophism "I owe you a horse" see Peter Geach, "A Medieval Discussion of Intentionality," in *Inquiries into Medieval Philosophy*, ed. J. F. Ross (Westport, Conn., 1971), pp. 23–34; and the introduction to Vincent Ferrer, *Tractatus de suppositionibus*, ed. J. A. Trentman (Stuttgart, 1977), pp. 41–49.

[3]For the humanists' understanding of *sensus communis* as a diplomatic and quasi-rhetorical faculty whose work is to settle disputes between vying perceptions, perspectives, or ethical impulses see Kinney, "Erasmus' *Adagia*," pp. 188–90. The humanist *exemplum* had a similar diplomatic function, mediating as it did between personal practice and general precept; see John M. Wallace, "'Examples Are Best Precepts': Readers and Meanings in

might be nothing remarkable about the assertion "I ate raw meat to-day"; in others, a sense of rhetorical context or a sense of outlandish assertions like this one as strongly "performative" uses of language would generally suffice to clear up any actual confusion.[1]

More begins and concludes his critique of scholastic dialectic with pointed references to the way that its "supersophistical trifles" have invaded both grammar and theology (26/10–26, 36/19–27). The windy debates of sophistical thinkers who scorn all material and factual constraints are "expansive"; "they extend their domain far and wide beyond nature's own bounds" (30/15–16). The boundlessness of these sophists' pretensions is matched only by the vacuousness of their actual attainments; their false sense of being knowledgeable about everything puffs them up more grotesquely than knowledge itself ever could.[2] Images of windy expansion and sudden deflation and dispersion abound in the first half of More's letter; it is as if Paul's opposition between the knowledge which "puffs up" and the charity which "edifies" had been literalized in the contrast between the "distended" scholastics on the one hand and the real builders like Varro, Aristarchus, Augustine, and Jerome on the other.[3]

What lends special point to this grotesque development of Paul's opposition in a critique of scholastic dialectic and its effects on both grammar and theology is that scholastic dialectic actually did tend to crowd out or impoverish the traditional subject matter of other fields of study without furnishing new matter in its place, so that vast "webs of learning" were spun to disguise gross deficiencies of historical and factual substance.[4] Since he wishes to emphasize precisely this sort of deficiency, More's attack on medieval grammarians exempts those who fall short of the humanists' stylistic criteria and singles out instead

---

Seventeenth-Century Poetry," *Critical Inquiry, 1* (1974), 273–90. The "public" faculty of *sensus communis* also bears an intriguing relation to the Freudian concept of ego; see Margaret W. Ferguson, *Trials of Desire: Renaissance Defences of Poetry* (New Haven and London, 1983), especially pp. 138–42.

[1]On "performative" statements see J. L. Austin, *How to Do Things with Words*, 2nd ed. (Cambridge, Mass., 1975).

[2]Cf. 48/13–24 and Erasmus, *Antibarbari, ASD 1/1*, 86–88.

[3]For these themes see especially 8/22–24, 10/4–8, 12/27–14/11, 18/25–20/4, 26/10–22, 26/25–26, 30/14–16, 34/9–11, 36/23–25, 48/13–24, 54/10–17, 56/10–15, 58/2–5, 72/10–74/3, 76/8–9.

[4]The phrase "webs of learning" is taken from Francis Bacon, *The Advancement of Learning*, in *Works*, ed. James Spedding et al., 14 vols. (London, 1857–74), *1*, 285; cf. 72/10–20, below. Among humanist critics of scholasticism the most important intermediary between More and Bacon is Juan Luis Vives.

"speculative grammarians" who have wholly lost sight of the practical rules of expression which it is their duty to teach.[1] In this, More displays a capacity to discriminate between form and substance which is usually lacking in those fifteenth-century polemicists who mount similar attacks on medieval grammarians. Erasmus in general exhibits a similar failing.[2]

The system of Modist or "speculative" grammar, representing an attempt to impose rigid dialectical distinctions between various "modes of signifying," constitutes a near-perfect example of the scholastic disdain for the precepts of common sense which More taxes so frequently elsewhere in this letter. According to the Modists, each mode of signifying corresponds strictly to a mode of being; hence, the passive participant in any action, construed as an action, will have to be signified by a noun in an objective case. As Juan Luis Vives intimates in a later criticism of the Modists (1531), this means that the same action cannot be described with the same degree of propriety using a nominative-case noun and a verb in the passive voice: "John is beaten by Richard" cannot serve as well for describing an action as "Richard beats John."[3] But then language used "properly" has nothing to do with the language of common sense: nothing "properly" means what we think it does. More does not need to criticize the form of the scholastic grammars: their substance is generally faulty enough to be damned in its own right. He will deal in a similar way with sophistic theologians.

Having examined the primary objects of More's attacks on medieval dialectic and grammar, we can now offer a fuller description of his design for remapping the complex of *artes sermocinales* (rhetoric, dialec-

---

[1]See 26/15–22 and note. For the speculative bias of the Modist grammarians see G. L. Bursill-Hall, *Speculative Grammars of the Middle Ages: The Doctrine of Partes Orationis of the Modistae* (The Hague and Paris, 1971), p. 38:

> . . . [the] association with logic and other non-linguistic disciplines had a profound effect on Modistic grammatical theories. Their conception of reality and of human reason led them to maintain that grammar must be "one," and therefore Robert Kilwardby, one of the immediate predecessors of the Modistae, could argue that grammar can only be a science if it is one for all men; as a result of the intimacy between the reality of things and their conceptualization by the mind, grammar becomes the study of the formulation of these concepts, their actual expression being accidental, and therefore incidental to Modistic grammatical theory.

While the relation between "speculative" grammar and some types of modern linguistics is clear, its relation to any historical language is less so.

[2]See note on 26/13–14.

[3]Vives, *De causis corruptarum artium, Opera omnia, 6,* 92; cf. Thomas of Erfurt, *Grammatica speculativa,* ed. and trans. G. L. Bursill-Hall (London, 1972), §§ 4, 25, 26, pp. 136–38, 208–19.

tic or logic, and grammar) which, officially at least, constituted the
medieval trivium. In practice the majority of scholastics virtually discarded the distinction between grammar and rhetoric and made both
subordinate to their dialectic, which alone was esteemed more or less
on a par with the rest of philosophy.[1] This downgrading of rhetoric
was linked to a particular theory of how language works; it is this
theory which More systematically strives to discredit.

To begin with, More, unlike Erasmus, distinctly perceives the chief
threat which Dorp's challenges pose to the humanist program: the
threat to discredit the pursuit of *eloquentia* itself as a passion for words,
for mere "signs," which can only distract its most serious votaries from
the dialectical "science of things." More combats this threat by denying
the existence of the transcendent paradigm for workaday signification
which Dorp's own distinction between signs and things presupposes:
temporal language, along with the three disciplines chiefly concerned
with it, has its origin in temporal *utilitas*, not in some unearthly fixed
correlation between things and our signs for them. In advancing this
pragmatic or instrumentalist notion of signification, More capitalizes
on the fact that Aristotle's own logical writings were traditionally known
as the *Organon* ("Tool" or "Instrument," 24/27). Even dialectic itself,
the most abstract of the three "language arts," was contrived with a
straightforward view to supplying a practical need in particular historical circumstances:

> For what else are the very precepts of dialectic but a particular
> product of intelligence, that is, the particular formulas of rational
> conjecture which reason perceives to be useful in learning about
> the real world? (16/21–24)

If More's argument sometimes seems to do violence to the Aristotelian
conviction that speculative inquiry is worthwhile for its own sake and
not merely for its temporal utility, this is perhaps because More's personal notion of temporal utility is considerably more generous than

[1]See Ong, p. 139:

Ramus [*Scholae in liberales artes* (1569), cols. 1075, 1022] says that students who were
in their first three years of philosophy . . . were commonly styled *summulistae* (after
Peter of Spain's work), *logici*, and *physici* respectively. . . . All these philosophy students, Ramus further explains, were lumped together as *philosophi*, while the arts
students not yet *philosophi*, that is, those studying grammar or rhetoric, were lumped
together as *grammatici*. . . . dialectic or logic has migrated from the trivium to become
associated with "physics" and the rest of "philosophy" . . .

See also P. O. Kristeller, *Renaissance Thought and Its Sources* (New York, 1979), pp. 117,
231–32, 244.

Aristotle's: the good to be gained by speculation, no less than the good to be gained by any other intellectual activity, is a public and temporal good, not a private and abstract one.[1] But this cavil affects only More's broadest argument respecting theology. Where it treats dialectic, More's text seems to reflect Aristotle's priorities quite fairly: dialectic is merely a "serving science," useful only for exercising men's intellects with a view to more serious disciplines (74/23). The precepts of dialectic itself are arrived at inductively, a fact which Aristotle himself concedes readily enough, though he may resist its implications for the structure of science in general.[2] Any theory of signification which claims a foundation in a clear a priori distinction between signs and things, losing sight of the actual workings of everyday speech, has only a very limited application to real human discourse in particular historical circumstances. One sure way to miss capturing the "substance" of useful disciplines is to deal with the language of their exposition the way Dorp, the despiser of "signs," does.

Following Quintilian, More distinguishes between two standards of correctness in speech, namely *ratio* and *proprietas;* while More seems ready to preserve the standard of *ratio* as the province of dialectic, leaving only *proprietas* to the grammarians, he tellingly stresses the interrelation between them by his use of the term *sensus communis* to refer both to the precepts of *ratio* and to the precepts of plain common usage.[3] The dialecticians who produce quasi-rhetorical "solutions" to appellation-sophisms by means of inverted word order cause themselves to lose sight of *proprietas* by imposing hypersubtle semantic distinctions where ordinary syntax rejects them; the dialecticians who generate ampliation-sophisms defy even the most basic, commonsensical precepts of *ratio* in making so much of chimerical linguistic constructs which only appear to have meaning. While it is doubtless worthwhile to distinguish between these two sophistic abuses, both similarly

---

[1]Cf. Aristotle, *Ethica Nicomachea* 10, *Metaphysica* 12.9. In his general insistence that even disciplines without obvious practical applications must possess either moral or propaedeutic utility More is obviously closer to Cicero than to Aristotle; see note on 296/11–13.

[2]On induction (*epagōgē*) as establishing the principles of science see Aristotle, *Analytica posteriora* 1.18 (81a38–b9); 2.19 (100b3–5); *Topica* 1.12 (105a10–19).

[3]For these two senses of *sensus communis* see 36/17–18 and 48/15. Quintilian's distinction runs as follows: "Sermo constat ratione vel vetustate, auctoritate, consuetudine" (1.6.1), where the latter three terms correspond to More's *proprietas sermonis* 34/21–36/11. Quintilian's *ratio* comprises "analogy in particular and sometimes etymology"; More uses both methods rhetorically (for a striking example see 76/15–19 and notes).

betoken a rash disregard for the boundary between grammar and dialectic. The grammarian "teaches the right way to speak, and yet [he] invents no laws of speech in defiance of custom; instead, [he] simply sees which constructions appear the most often in speech and points these out to those who are unschooled in speech so that their speech will not flout common usage" (34/11–14). The "sane" dialectician, on the other hand, makes it his business "to press us along with true reasoning, to any conclusion, by using the same language we do . . ." (36/11–13).[1] The two tasks are distinct but related, and the integrity of the dialectician's own province depends on how well he respects that of grammar.

More takes up the relation between dialectic and rhetoric in a passage which begins with the familiar comparison of dialectic to a closed fist and rhetoric to an open palm, a comparison which may suggest that the two disciplines are essentially one and the same (16/5–10). He remembers, however, that closed fists and open palms themselves have distinct uses, and accordingly retains a distinct role for dialectic in the trivium *ad ingenia exercenda* (74/23).[2] Indeed, he wants to retain "purified" dialectic as Aristotle himself taught it (22/16–17, 24/24–26/9) and explicitly recommends Lefèvre d'Etaples' new rendering of the *Organon* for use in university curricula (22/23–27). Further, at a number of points More acknowledges that the problems so dear to the "neoteric" dialecticians have their own kind of limited usefulness (62/5–6, 66/2–5, 74/11–76/2). Far from wishing to collapse the trivium into either grammar or rhetoric or both, More intends to restore its three disciplines to some understandable order, with rhetoric again at the apex.

The relation between rhetoric and grammar in More's scheme is such that the former emerges as what might be called a general "science" of human culture, while the latter provides detailed empirical information about how facts, methods, opinions, and values are passed on and revised in a variety of disciplines and historical circumstances. Rhetoric coordinates the precepts of both dialectic and grammar and applies them in every variety of cultural inquiry. The preeminence of rhetoric in More's reformed scheme for the trivium stands assured

---

[1]More here may have in mind the medieval mnemonic "Gram. loquitur; Dia. vera docet; Rhe. verba ministrat." (see E. R. Curtius, *European Literature and the Latin Middle Ages*, trans. Willard Trask, Princeton, 1973, p. 37).

[2]More uses virtually the same terms in a later defense of scholastic disputation; see the *Letter to Bugenhagen*, Rogers, p. 335, line 360.

despite two facts which seem to imply that More values not rhetoric but grammar most highly among the three disciplines.[1] Indeed, these same facts can be used to confirm the preeminence of rhetoric. To begin with, More presents his ideal humanist in the guise of a perfect *grammaticus,* not an *orator:* ". . . 'grammarian' means precisely the same thing as 'man of letters,' whose area of study extends across every discipline. . . . no one, in my opinion, at least, may be styled a man of letters who has not pored through each and every one of the sciences" (12/19–21, 24–25).[2] Although More seems to insist on the primacy of grammar, a science which even scholastics invest with some measure of honor, what he actually does is to elevate rhetoric to primacy without mentioning its much-abused name, readily linked with the "science of signs which inflates."[3] The names Aristarchus and Varro (14/11–13) here stand for the most generally honored achievements of a program which is essentially rhetorical: ". . . indeed, no one can be an orator complete in all points of merit, who has not attained a knowledge of all important subjects and arts" (Cicero, *De oratore* 1.6.20). More also twice uses grammar, not rhetoric, as his paradigm for the *artes sermocinales* in general (24/21–28, 34/11–15). But he does so because grammar is the empirical discipline par excellence in the complex of "language arts." He consistently wishes to argue, against the scholastics, that every science of signification must perforce be empirical and "positive," in large part dependent on temporal *consuetudo.* In dialectic and, to a lesser degree, in rhetoric, the synthetic and partly autonomous working of *ratio* somewhat obscures the empirical origins of the data at hand; in grammar, which is essentially nothing more than a body of rules drawn from everyday usage (34/11–14), empirical method stands fully revealed and accessible. Nevertheless, the same simplicity which makes grammar a useful paradigm for the purposes of *ad hominem* argument in the *Letter to Dorp* makes it a quite unsatisfactory paradigm for the purposes of general inquiry: grammar gets us no further than learning

---

[1]The preeminence of rhetoric in More's hierarchy of secular disciplines was previously noted by Martin Fleisher, *Radical Reform and Political Persuasion in the Life and Writings of Thomas More* (Geneva, 1973), pp. 97–98.

[2]More's description of the ideal *grammaticus* has an important precedent in the writings of Angelo Poliziano. See note on 12/19–21 and Aldo Scaglione, "The Humanist as Scholar and Politian's Conception of the *Grammaticus," Studies in the Renaissance, 8* (1964), 61–62.

[3]Dorp considers that humanist rhetoric and grammar are fine in their place, but his distrust of humanist philology suggests that in his view their place is at best quite a lowly one. See p. xxii, n. 1, above; and cf. Dorp's dismissal of rhetorical argument in Allen, 2, 127, lines 10–16.

to speak and read passably (24/21–24; cf. 20/19–23, 34/11–14). An adequate general understanding of historical process in language and an adequate systematic appreciation of the affective, performative, and political elements in speech of all sorts belong rather to rhetoric.

Though More's claims for the wide-ranging competence of a true "man of letters" are remarkably similar to Cicero's claims for the general knowledge of a well-rounded orator, it should still give us pause when More hints that the well-rounded orator and the well-rounded *grammaticus* or scholar are actually one and the same. There can be little doubt that this hint is intentional, since More promptly refers to Erasmus as a consummate master in each of these roles (14/11–16, 16/3–4). On the other hand, we are not in the habit of treating serious scholarly discourse on essentially the same level as oratory. Furthermore, several modern historians contend that rhetorical and scholarly or philological tendencies were actually at odds with each other in Renaissance humanism and that the rise of professional philologists like Angelo Poliziano betokened a growing disenchantment with humanist rhetoric as an instrument for change and reform.[1] Finally, as early as 1513 Dorp himself condemned "garrulous" humanist philology even as he praised humanist orators like Rodolphus Agricola; from Dorp's words, which include an allusion to Erasmus' unflattering sketch of punctilious grammarians in *Moriae encomium*, it would seem that the contrast between the rhetorical and philological tendencies in Renaissance humanism was marked from the very beginning.[2] But before we assume that Dorp's critical attitude toward humanist philology has any straightforward affinity with that of some modern historians, it is worth noting that Dorp's favorite targets among humanist philologists are not insignificant pedants but rather such prominent and controversial figures as Valla, Lefèvre d'Etaples, Reuchlin, and Erasmus himself, whose contributions to biblical philology were regarded as serious threats to the theological status quo.[3] In comparison with this sort of aggressively encyclopedic philology the rhetorical writ-

---

[1] See, for example, William J. Bouwsma, "Changing Assumptions in Later Renaissance Culture," *Viator*, 7 (1976), 431; and Ronald Witt, "Medieval 'Ars Dictaminis' and the Beginnings of Humanism: A New Construction of the Problem," *Renaissance Quarterly*, 35 (1982), 34; hereafter cited as "Witt."

[2] Dorp's description of philology as a caricature of sound rhetoric occurs in his *Oratio de laudibus disciplinarum* (1513); see p. xxii, n. 1, above. The passage cited by De Vocht (*Monumenta*, p. 137, n. 1) from sig. B₂v of the *Oratio* is an allusion to Erasmus, *Moriae encomium*, ASD 4/3, 138, lines 260–64.

[3] See p. xx, n. 2; p. xxii, n. 1; and p. xxvi, n. 3.

ings of a less daring humanist like Agricola might well appear posi-
tively innocuous to someone like Dorp.[1] It is probably worthwhile to
distinguish at least three different tendencies in Renaissance humanism, one narrowly rhetorical, one narrowly philological, and one
broadly critical and investigative. The third tendency, highly rhetorical
in its own right, is best represented by Erasmus and More's model
philologist-orator, whose tongue is his pen.[2]

The empirical and contingent foundation of the discipline which
More here sets forth as a governing science of human culture necessi-
tates a challenge to the scholastic conception of every scientific discipline as founded on a priori principles; More provides this challenge in
his attack on the substance of a priori, speculative grammar and the
impoverished dialectical model of language which it presupposes. The
scholastics, ignoring Aristotle's admonition in *Ethica Nicomachea* 1.3 not
to seek perfect precision in any science of human culture, strove to
impose Aristotle's a priori criteria for *epistēmē* or "science" in the full
sense on the science of grammar.[3] The scholastics distinguished this
"regular" or "speculative" grammar from "positive" or empirical
grammar, which they generally scorned as a kind of half-knowledge
(*empeiria*). This distinction explains how the exemplary grammarians
introduced at 12/10–14/19 can provoke Dorp's most stinging contempt, whereas at 26/15–16 "a certain Albert," who also sets himself
up as a teacher of grammar, can hold sway among many scholastics as
an intellectual cult-hero: the two types of grammar are actually two
quite different disciplines. One attempt to articulate this distinction
makes especially clear the dependence of "regular" grammar on the
order of dialectic:

---

[1] It seems that not even Agricola's handbook of humanist argumentation, *De inventione dialectica*, upset very many conservatives. One effect of Agricola's "rhetorical" emphasis on the marshaling of commonplace arguments was to trivialize his logic *qua* logic: it was possible to maintain a fundamentally scholastic attitude toward the substance of the trivium and still welcome Agricola's new protocol for debating. Thus, Dorp himself had no qualms about overseeing and introducing the *editio princeps* of this work (January 1515) in the same year that he mounted his second attack on Erasmus. See De Vocht, *Monumenta*, pp. 405–06, and p. xxi, above.

[2] See notes on 16/24 and 296/11–13 and *CW* 3/2, Commentary at 620/6.

[3] The science of grammar itself is post-Aristotelian in origin. For a good recent study see Michael Frede, "Principles of Stoic Grammar," in *The Stoics*, ed. J. M. Rist (Berkeley, 1978), pp. 27–76. A good starting-point for a general study of grammatical speculation in the Middle Ages is R. W. Hunt, in *Collected Papers on the History of Grammar in the Middle Ages*, ed. G. L. Bursill-Hall, Amsterdam Studies in the History of Linguistics 5 (Amsterdam, 1980).

Grammar is twofold—positive and regular. Positive is knowledge of the significations of terms and the rules of grammar (but not knowledge of their causes). . . . It is not a science properly called, but a certain imperfect knowledge. Regular grammar is knowledge of the grounds of grammatical rules, by which they are known demonstrably and through causes, and such knowledge is certainly a science, and cannot be acquired before logic except imperfectly, for it is acquired through argumentation which is known through logic.[1]

But the ultimate result of the attempt to substitute the order of dialectic for the order of linguistic custom, as we see in the case of More's ampliation-sophisms, is to turn nature's order upside down (32/9–10), whence it follows that grammatical disciplines cannot themselves be "epistemic." But if the empirical alternative to the dialectical study of language fails to qualify as a science, there can be no "scientific" solutions whatever to the sophisms More mentions at 28/14–32/25; we will never be able to tell whether X has been bereft of all the cash in the world or only a bit of it based on the allegation that Y has robbed X of (certain unspecified) cash (28/22–30/1). To avoid this perplexing conclusion, most people, including most dialecticians, will probably concede that the empirical exposition and scrutiny of *sensus communis* should be classed as a substantive science in its own right. Thus More helps to lay the foundations for a rhetorical, "positive," and historical science of language and culture.[2]

---

[1]Quoted by Heath, p. 48, from Johannes Versor's commentary on the *Summulae logicales*. For a similar formulation see Noam Chomsky, *Essays on Form and Interpretation* (New York, Amsterdam, and Oxford, 1977), p. 16: "The more abstract are the principles, the more deeply embedded in a particular theoretical structure and remote from the presented phenomena, the more interesting and significant is the study of language." Purged of many of its absurdities, modist theory lives on, one might say, in the theory of Chomsky.

[2]I would suggest that More's sketch of this rhetorical and "positive" science of culture is closely related to the new models for science which were later expounded by Vives and Vico. A similar conception of history and culture is refracted in Erasmus' *Adagia*. Perhaps the most characteristic feature of all these "scientific" developments of literary rhetoric is the way they exploit the rhetorical system of *topoi* or commonplace arguments not primarily as a speaker's resource for the ready retrieval of plausible claims and rejoinders but instead as a framework for cultural analysis. For modern theoretical ventures along similar lines see Ernesto Grassi, *Rhetoric as Philosophy: The Humanist Tradition* (University Park, Pa., and London, 1980); Paulo Valesio, *Novantiqua: Rhetorics as a Contemporary Theory* (Bloomington, Ind., 1980); Gerald L. Bruns, *Inventions: Writing, Textuality, and Understanding in Literary History* (New Haven and London, 1982); and James L. Kinneavy, "Contemporary Rhetoric" in *The Present State of Scholarship in Historical and Contemporary*

Implicit in More's vindication of rhetoric as a new governing science is a strong intimation that a secular "science of signs," recognized as just that, may well have more affinity with a transcendent "science of things" than a secular science which pretends to be dealing with ultimate realities. More could offset Augustine's suspicion of secular custom, and thus of the "science of signs" which expounds it, with the scholarly precedent set by Augustine himself in composing the *City of God,* "a book whose recurrent theme is 'our business within this common mortal life.'"[1] If revelation is the form of a Christian existence, the matter is history; but the matter of history itself is primarily secular custom.

More enlists the historical scrutiny of secular custom in the service of prudent simplicity. He repeatedly suggests that without the capacity to distinguish the providential from the contrived or the merely fortuitous on the basis of secular precedent, few believers' simplicity will spare them from botching the business of life.[2] Like Erasmus, More frequently seems to suggest that the true Christian's existence on earth may be best understood as an unceasing struggle to coordinate the provisional with the providential and the historical with the eternal. Revelation is out of our hands; we must deal with those things which are left up to us. Though it is at least possible to treat this anti-speculative and secular bias in Erasmus as an expression of simple indifference toward the entire ceremonial and dogmatic edifice of the medieval Church,[3] it seems clear that for More the continuity of the institutional and visible Church was precisely what made virtually all speculation redundant. Apostolic succession ensured that revealed

---

Rhetoric, ed. Winifred B. Horner (Columbia and London 1983), especially pp. 174–84. What appears to be lacking as yet is a coherent theory of persuasion which can distinguish it clearly from mere enticement or intimidation on the one hand and the communication of uncontroversial "facts" on the other. For most Renaissance humanists, persuasion was strictly contractual, and the very perception that none of the terms of the contract were naturally fixed was enough to establish the need for some transcendent warrant of equity. See *CW 4,* 220/24–29, and *CW 3/2,* 580–82.

[1]Peter Brown, *Augustine of Hippo: A Biography* (Berkeley and Los Angeles, 1969), p. 324, quoting *De civitate dei* 15.21.15. For Augustine, of course, "things" themselves could be viewed as God's own "signs" or "figures." As a young man More gave public lectures on the *City of God;* see Erasmus in Allen, *4,* 17. At least one scholar claims that Augustine is the primary intellectual authority for the historical and secular emphases of rhetorical humanism; see the article cited on p. xlvii, n. 4, above.

[2]See, for example, 202/18–204/5, 216/13–19, 260/4–6, 276/17–21, and 278/25–27. See also *CW 3/1,* 4/17–6/20; and 82/10–16, below.

[3]For Erasmus' supposed indifference to Church institutions see Eugene F. Rice, Jr., "Erasmus and the Religious Tradition, 1495–1499," *Journal of the History of Ideas, 11* (1950), 387–411.

Christian truth would be preached and perpetuated; there remained only the business of learning the best way to live in the world.[1] In their responses to Dorp both More and Erasmus distinguished between the episcopal or pastoral hierarchy and the university theological establishment to the distinct disadvantage of the latter: far from providing an essential support for the Church's dogmatic authority, sophistic theologians and casuists often threatened the moral integrity of Christians in general.[2] Their dogmatic pronouncements on questions of practical piety did not lessen but rather augmented the number of snares which awaited an unwary conscience in earthly existence; they did not ease responsible choice but denied the intrinsic importance of choosing.[3] For More, their procedural failings suggested the need to distinguish between a perpetually vital dogmatic tradition and a Christianized cultural tradition which (like all historical growths) must be subject to gradual decay and dependent on constant renewal; in his opinion, the secular science best equipped to direct this renewal was not formal logic but encyclopedic philology.[4] He never goes quite so far as to claim with Erasmus that learning per se is a product of secular culture, but he does quite deliberately conflate the material bases of Christian and secular learning under one meaningful heading: *bonae litterae*.[5] A responsible Christian existence will often depend at least partly on a

---

[1]See 64/24–66/5, 86/24–88/12, and 112/11–16 below.

[2]For passages discriminating between bishops and university theologians see Erasmus in Allen, 2, 100, lines 355–70, and 112/11–16 below. For a few passages stressing the ambivalent or harmful effect of sophistic theologians and casuists on practical piety see Erasmus in Allen, 3, 367; and 50/25–52/7, 64/8–23, 70/20–27, and 74/11–16 and notes below.

[3]See Levi, especially pp. 3–6.

[4]See the passages cited in n. 1, above. Also pertinent is *CW 3/1*, 6/15–20. Though More's later polemical efforts were largely devoted to upholding the "oral" or institutional tradition against those who placed exclusive stress on the written tradition, he still cited at least one authority in *The Confutation of Tyndale's Answer* (*CW 8*, 369) for the position that the two traditions were of equal importance. See further *CW 5*, 242/5–6; *CW 6*, 254/21–26; E. Flesseman-Van Leer, "The Controversy about Scripture and Tradition between Thomas More and William Tyndale," *Nederlands Archief voor Kerkgeschiedenis*, n. s. *43* (1959), 143–64 (hereafter cited as "Flesseman-Van Leer"); *CW 8*, 1285–94; and Richard C. Marius, "Thomas More and the Early Church Fathers," *Traditio, 24* (1968), 395–97 (hereafter cited as "Marius").

[5]For the claim that all learning per se is a product of secular culture see Erasmus, *Antibarbari, ASD 1/1*, 80, 84. Valla argues very similarly in *Elegantiae 4, praefatio* (*Opera omnia*, Basel, 1540; reprinted as vol. 1, Turin, 1962; hereafter cited as "Valla, *Opera omnia*"), sigs. H3v–H4v. For More's conflation of *bonae litterae* with *litterae sacrae* see especially 14/15–16, and 62/7–9, below. A similar conflation occurs at 98/1–8 in an argument claiming that Greek *litterae* are eminently worth studying, or *optimae*.

sense of historical perspective, and the task of imparting historical perspective is that of the true *litteratus*, the well-rounded Christian philologist.

It may seem that the humanists are guilty of inflating the scope and importance of grammar and rhetoric as preposterously as the scholastics inflated the scope and importance of logic, but the analogy is actually deceptive. First of all, humanist theorists like More never viewed the humanities as merely a substitute for the speculative disciplines which dominated the medieval curriculum. The humanities were taught propaedeutically, as a preparation for responsible life in the world of affairs, while the speculative disciplines of the medieval curriculum were taught magisterially, as if their explanations represented an end in themselves. No traditional thinker in the late Middle Ages could have thought lowly grammar a serious pursuit in its own right; by ingenuously appropriating St. Paul's dialectic of inversion, the humanists were able to turn even the traditionalists' scorn to advantage: "If any man among you seemeth to be wise in this world, let him become a fool, that he may be wise."[1] The traditional association of grammar with "elementary" education allowed the humanists to associate the rebirth of learning with Christ's affirmation of childlike simplicity at the expense of the "infantile old men" who had grown gray in sophistry without ever acquiring the rudiments of Christian discretion.[2] More and Erasmus both hinted that the humanist program was at least partially a program of "unlearning," of dismantling mistaken conceptions of human potential and purpose so that genuine human

---

[1] 1 Cor. 3:18. Cf. Erasmus' preface to Valla's *Annotationes* (March 1505), Allen, *1*, 410, lines 132–37:

> Ac ne ipsa quidem, opinor, disciplinarum omnium regina theologia ducet indignum admoueri sibi manus, ac debitum exhiberi obsequium a pedissequa grammatica; quae tametsi nonnullis est dignitate posterior, nullius certe opera magis necessaria. In minimis versatur, sed sine quibus nemo euasit maximus; nugas agitat, sed quae seria ducant.

The last line contains an allusion to Horace, *Ars poetica* 451. For Erasmus' defensive employment of the commonplace "multum in parvo" see Kinney, "Erasmus' *Adagia*," pp. 173–74, 177–78, 188; and cf. Rosalie L. Colie, *The Resources of Kind: Genre Theory in the Renaissance* (Berkeley, Los Angeles, and London, 1973), pp. 32–75.

[2] For two passages describing a return to grammatical studies as "rejuvenescence" see Erasmus in Allen, 2, 166, line 21; 216, line 174; and cf. 76/13–14, below. For the association of the rebirth of learning with Christian rebirth see Erasmus, *Paraclesis*, Holborn, p. 145, lines 5–7; and the discussion in Levi, pp. 12–14. For "infantile old men" see 6/16–17 and note.

potential might be better realized.[1] To the extent that it championed the text of experience against untested secular certainties and philological research against a regimen of virtually pure speculation, the humanist emphasis on grammar and rhetoric did not halt the advancement of learning outside those two fields but provided a context which hastened it.

A more conventional defense of rhetorical culture is elaborated with equal finesse in More's *Letter to Oxford*. Although More often seems to be borrowing themes fairly directly from Erasmus' *Antibarbari*, the main theme of the letter may be traced back to Seneca and beyond: liberal arts prepare the soul for virtue.[2] There is nothing distinctively Christian about this "ethical" defense of rhetorical culture; indeed, fundamentalist Christians distrustful of secular custom might reject this defense altogether, whereas other traditionalists might consider it valid for logic alone or insist that the rest of the liberal arts play only a minor supporting role in preparing the soul for true virtue. In order to make a really rigorous case for rhetorical culture on the basis of this borrowed ethical defense one would have to establish, as More does in the *Letter to Dorp,* that a broad education in secular custom is a better foundation for responsible Christian behavior than a training in pure speculation, but an elaborate argument of this sort would be out of place in the *Letter to Oxford*. Accordingly, More finds an indirect way to

---

[1]See, for example, Erasmus, *Antibarbari, ASD 1/1,* 59–61; and More, letter to Gonnell, Rogers, p. 123, lines 95–99:

> Neque aliam causam puto, cur hoc malum [*sc.* superbia] tam ineluctabile pectoribus nostris inhaereat, quam quod prope simul ac nati sumus, mollibus animulis puerorum a nutricibus inseritur, fouetur a magistris, a parentibus alitur atque perficitur. . . .

For the typically Erasmian notion that "men are made, not born," see Chomarat, *1,* 67–71. More's endorsement of this notion in the passage just cited suggests that his views on the power of mankind to ameliorate its own lot here on earth were originally more similar to those of Erasmus than some scholars claim; see most notably James McConica, "The Patrimony of Thomas More," in *History and Imagination: Essays in Honour of Hugh Trevor-Roper,* ed. H. Lloyd-Jones et al. (London, 1981; hereafter cited as "McConica, 'Patrimony'"), p. 65.

[2]See 138/10–11 and note. The many close parallels between the *Letter to Oxford* and Erasmus' *Antibarbari* suggest that More studied it closely in manuscript; it was not printed until 1520. In 1517 Erasmus was considering introducing More as a character in a revised version of the dialogue; see More in Allen, *3,* 133; and Kazimierz Kumaniecki's introduction to the *Antibarbari, ASD 1/1,* 11–13. An interesting variation of More's ethical defense of rhetorical culture appears in his personal letter to William Gonnell, his children's tutor (Rogers, pp. 120–23).

support his most far-reaching claim for the ethical worth of the science
of secular custom: he makes several more tentative claims which he
knows his readers are bound to accept, and the cumulative force of
these claims is to suggest that the ethical worth of the science of secular
custom has been conceded in practice all along.

More's first claim is that since they are learned, his readers will not be
so arrogant as to scorn his advice out of hand (130/16–19). This claim
is more than a conventional *captatio benevolentiae:* it emphasizes that the
object of learning is as much to eliminate unjustified self-assurance as it
is to instill actual knowledge.[1] More's next pertinent claim is that
whether or not liberal arts actually do prepare the soul for virtue, the
study of *litterae* ("letters") has always been the sole obvious reason for
frequenting Oxford (138/11–13). He then appeals once again to Oxo-
nian usage: there are Oxford-trained lawyers as well as divines
(138/15–17). Could so many Oxonians have been quite mistaken with
regard to the value of *litterae?* He then moves on to make three modest
claims for the value of secular studies to theology: humanities provide
a good schooling in human psychology and rhetorical tact for the
preacher-to-be; earthly studies can furnish a basis for gradual ascent to
the "contemplation of higher realities"; and a good training in the
biblical languages constitutes an essential prerequisite for the serious
study of scripture and positive theology (138/17–140/20). Taken together, these claims suggest that it would be quite absurd to sequester
theology from the other varieties of *litterae* on which it in large part
depends: if theology can claim ethical value, its adjuncts can claim it, as
well. In this way More succinctly accredits his Erasmian ethical defense
of rhetorical culture.

Our discussion of the *Letter to Dorp* has established that More's own
argumentative resources were not limited to the tactful *ad hominem*
arguments he employs in the *Letter to Oxford.* Nonetheless, at least one
scholar has suggested that even in the *Letter to Dorp* More relies almost
totally on "*ad hominem* argumentation," and in all of the humanist
defenses he resorts to *ad hominem* arguments no less freely than to
other, more rigorous proofs.[2] Indeed, the *Letter to Lee* contains virtually no rigorous, impersonal arguments at all; More reserves his own
strongest formal objections to Lee's mode of biblical scholarship for the

---

[1]See note on 130/17–19 and cf. More's letter to Gonnell, Rogers, p. 121, lines 28–31:
"At inter egregia illa beneficia, quae doctrina confert hominibus, haud aliud hercle duco
praestabilius, quam quod ex literis docemur, in perdiscendis literis non laudem spectare
sed vsum."
[2]See De Vocht, *Monumenta,* p. 158.

long middle section of the *Letter to a Monk*. More's *ad hominem* arguments are generally not so much captious alternatives to rigorous
proofs as Socratic experiments in exposing the hidden inconsistencies
in the statements and actions of others. Even in book 3 of *The Confutation of Tyndale's Answer* (1532), where More generally claims all the rigor
he can for his arguments, he concedes that *ad hominem* arguments are
merely preparatory for any truly conclusive proof:

> And then for some lykelyhed towarde a profe of the contrary / I
> wyll lay forth for authorite agaynst wyllyam Tyndale, the wordes
> of one man whom Tyndale wold were moste byleued of all men /
> that is to wytte the wordes of wyllyam Tyndale him selfe.[1]

Since the humanist program was at least partly a program of "unlearning" mistaken conceptions of human potential and purpose, Socratic
techniques of *ad hominem* rebuttal and demystification could play a
legitimate role in accrediting this program at the expense of the pompous scholastic *magistri* who rashly condemned it. Thus, for example,
the argument that the traditionalists' own wanton conceits and stylistic
extravagances rivaled those of the poets and orators might not settle
the question of the value of poetry or oratory, but at least it established
that the question remained open despite the traditionalists' prejudices.[2] The fairly trivial observation that the traditionalists' own knowledge of Aristotle was limited by their ignorance of Greek might not
prove that the study of Greek is essential for all advanced scholars, but
at least it suggested that Aristotelian traditionalists themselves should
not be overquick to condemn language study in general.[3] Like the
satirical reflections he prizes so highly before 1520 in the works of
Jerome and Erasmus, the *ad hominem* arguments of More's humanist
defenses draw attention to commonplace self-contradictions and
failures of judgment and thus help to "make us see ourselves as we
really are."[4] Satire, irony, and *ad hominem* argument, the most suspect
constituents of rhetorical culture, all play major roles in the fostering
of prudent simplicity.

---

[1]*CW 8*, 330/9–13. More also discusses his later polemical practice in the preface and
first chapter of *The Debellation of Salem and Bizance;* see also *CW 3/2*, 584, note 1.
[2]See especially 32/18–28, 40/12–15, 114/2–23, 170/23–27, 218/6–10, 218/23–27,
and 222/4–12.
[3]See especially 96/23–100/18, 104/5–12, 142/16–21, and notes.
[4]See 290/7–21 and cf. 106/11–108/15, 120/14–20, 272/24–28, and 274/21–29. See
also Robert A. Kantra, "Jerome and Erasmus: Holy Orders, Literary Talent, and Intellectual Revolution" in *The Papin Festschrift: Essays in Honour of Joseph Papin*, ed. Joseph
Armenti, 2 vols. (Villanova, 1976), 2, 425–37.

POSITIVE THEOLOGY AND ERASMIAN REFORM

In the humanist defenses More not only challenges the dialectical foundation of late medieval theology; he also defends an alternative approach to theology based on the writings of the Greek and Latin fathers and on the text of the Bible itself. He twice uses the term *positiva* (48/3, 140/15) to refer to the works of the fathers; in both cases the context suggests that the epithet was already current in the schools as a disparaging way of referring to old-fashioned, nondialectical treatises on various subjects.[1] Germain Marc'hadour rightly relates More's use of the term to

> the pre-scholastic, patristic approach [to theology] in which Christian doctrine
> —was still an immediate, almost homiletic echo of its biblical sources;
> —spoke the language of secular literature, the *communis sermo* [34/5] which More opposes to academic jargon;
> —was never divorced from a purpose of exhortation and edification.[2]

While it is clear that More means to associate the term with patristic theology above everything else, his careful use of the neuter plural adjective *positiva* at both 48/3 and 140/15 suggests that he also has in mind the whole gamut of nondialectical studies which could be slightingly described with the same adjective.[3] The term naturally suggests a developmental, historical, and mainly practical understanding

---

[1] For an earlier use of the term *positiva* in connection with a historical form of theology see note on 48/3 and Tharcisse Tshibangu, *Théologie positive and théologie spéculative: Position traditionelle et nouvelle problématique* (Louvain and Paris, 1965; hereafter cited as "Tshibangu"), pp. 195–99.

[2] Marc'hadour, *The Bible, 4*, 23. Not all the scholastics consistently scorned *positiva*, as More is the first to concede; see the elegant revisionist study by A. J. Minnis, *Medieval Theory of Authorship* (London, 1984; hereafter cited as "Minnis"), esp. pp. 119–30, 154–59, and cf. Guy F. Lytle, "The Church Fathers and Oxford Professors . . ." in *Acta Conventus Neo-Latini Bononiensis*, ed. R. J. Schoeck (Binghamton, 1985), pp. 101–15.

[3] For "positive" as distinguished from "regular" and "speculative" grammar see p. lxv, above. For "positive" or "manmade" as distinguished from natural or divine law see Marc'hadour, *The Bible, 4*, 23.

of a particular subject as opposed to a rigorously scientific one; what
the scholastics regard as a deficiency in patristic theology More wishes
to stress as a virtue.

In both passages More draws attention to one other trait which
distinguishes patristic theology from the "disputatious theology" professed by the dialecticians: patristic theology, like poetry and rhetoric,
is stylistically complex enough to require a good grounding in languages.[1] The association of "positive" theology and stylistic complexity
suggests that the disparaging force of the term *positiva* is quite similar
to that of a term sometimes used by scholastics to scoff at Jerome's
works: *grammatica*.[2] Jerome's name was associated with rhetorical elab-
orateness and with the lowly "historical" or grammatical exegesis of
scripture; Augustinians could view him as wholly immersed in the
"science of signs."[3] For Erasmus, on the other hand, Jerome was the
greatest of Latin theologians precisely because he, like the Greek fathers generally, made such brilliant use of the "science of signs" to
illuminate "our business within this common mortal life."[4] The scholastics regarded methodical exposition of dogma as the primary task of
theology; most of the Latin fathers divided their energies between this
task and that of expounding and preaching the practical meaning of
the gospel, although even Augustine placed somewhat more stress on
the latter task.[5] More's particular use of the term *positiva* emphasizes
this practical exegetical element of patristic theology so dramatically as
to suggest that he means to associate the rest of the fathers with the
heavily rhetorical, grammatical, and ethical bias of Jerome; indeed,
before 1520 Jerome seems to dominate More's view of the fathers
almost as much as he dominates that of Erasmus.[6] Other fathers who
receive special praise in More's humanist defenses are generally the
ones whose own literary and intellectual characteristics are most like
Jerome's; thus More recommends the Greek fathers in general above

---

[1]See also 46/16–18 and 222/26–224/13 below.

[2]See Erasmus in Allen, 2, 99, lines 319–20; *Antibarbari, ASD I/1*, 118, lines 14–16; and
Vita Hieronymi, Ferguson, 179, lines 1215–30.

[3]See note on 254/14–258/4 and Erasmus, *Vita Hieronymi*, Ferguson, p. 180, lines
1234–35. For Augustine's distinction between the "science of signs" and the "science of
things" see pp. xlviii–li, above. In *Apologia qua respondet*, Ferguson, p. 287, line 1247,
Erasmus himself speaks of grammar as the lowest part of theology.

[4]See Erasmus in Allen, 2, 86, lines 220–31. For "our business within this common
mortal life" see p. lxvi, above.

[5]For Augustine's prestige as a methodological theologian and dialectician see Dorp in
Allen, 2, 133, line 246; Erasmus in Allen, 3, 334, lines 141–65; 336, lines 219–28; and in
Vita Hieronymi, Ferguson, p. 180, lines 1256–57; and note on 254/14–258/4, below.

[6]See p. xlix, n. 3, above.

any of the Latins, extols the great stylist St. Cyprian, and guardedly but generously praises the great moral interpreter Origen.[1] Hence it seems that in More's usage the term *positiva* is not simply synonymous with "patristic": it connotes a specific philological and practical orientation which could just as well be called "Erasmian."

Patristic theology was invoked in the Renaissance both as a means of aligning a given religious tendency with a venerable Christian tradition and as a means of defending the new emphasis placed on secular literature by pious and less pious humanists alike.[2] The discussion in the preceding chapter suggested that it would be wrong to insist on a clear-cut distinction between Christian and secular motives for this turn to "positive" learning of all sorts.[3] The secular grammarians' favorite interpretative techniques of *collatio locorum*, contextual analysis, and figurative exegesis were also favorite techniques of the fathers; for Erasmus, at any rate, the application of these same techniques in a "positive" attempt to make Christianized secular custom conform in a less casual way with the teachings of Christ was a principal duty of any authentic theologian.[4] Thus the fathers' "grammatical" exegesis was a model of pious instruction as well as sound scholarship.[5]

---

[1]For More's praise of the Greek fathers in general see 142/16–18, 220/11–12, and notes. In Allen, *2*, 86, lines 220–31, Erasmus suggests that among Latin fathers Jerome alone rivals the Greeks in his general erudition. In Allen, *3*, 334, lines 164–65, Erasmus further suggests that Jerome, like the Greek fathers, was not only more learned than most of the Latins but also less quick to define his positions dogmatically; cf. 174/1–3 below. For More's praise of Cyprian see 246/12–13; in Allen, *4*, 26–27, Erasmus sets him on a par with Jerome as a stylist. For More's circumspect praise of Origen see 58/21–25 below; More is obliquely responding to Dorp's statement cited at 54/18–22.

[2]For primarily religious appeals to the works of the fathers during the Renaissance and Reformation see Tshibangu, pp. 169–86; Marius, pp. 379–407; S. L. Greenslade, "The Morean Renaissance," *Journal of Ecclesiastical History,* 24 (1973), 395–403; William P. Haugaard, "Renaissance Patristic Scholarship and Theology in Sixteenth-Century England," *Sixteenth-Century Journal, 10/3* (1979), 37–60; and the work cited in the note on 142/26–27 below. For the less strictly religious appeals see Gray, pp. 37–51; August Buck, "Die Rückgriff des Renaissance-Humanismus auf die Patristik," in *Festschrift Walter von Wartburg,* ed. Kurt Baldinger, 2 vols. (Tübingen, 1968), *1,* 153–85; and the works cited above, p. lxxii, n. 2, and below in the notes on 138/10–11 and 142/22–24.

[3]Cf. Boyle, p. 108: "Distinguishing Erasmus' Renaissance from what will emerge as modern secularism is a convergence of orders, the sacralization of the secular through the presence of the incarnate *Logos.*"

[4]For *collatio locorum,* contextual analysis, and figurative interpretation see notes on 82/19–21, 48/22–24 and 58/6–60/23. Erasmus elaborates these teachings in his *Ratio verae theologiae* (1518). For "collating" secular custom with the teachings of Christ see especially the passages in Holborn, pp. 156–57, 192–93, 295.

[5]Erasmus explicitly proposes the fathers as models of learning for Christians to imitate in *Antibarbari, ASD 1/1,* 128–30.

POSITIVE THEOLOGY AND ERASMIAN REFORM

One can argue, however, that even at this early date More considered the fathers exemplary Christians in a way that Erasmus did not. More did not share Erasmus' belief in the capacity of every individual Christian to distinguish the presence of Christ in the world for himself by applying the standard of scripture directly to secular custom.[1] For More, the "inflexible standard of truth" was not the written gospel per se but "that living gospel of faith which has been infused into the hearts of the faithful throughout the whole Church . . ." (88/2–6). The fathers as a group were essential intermediaries in relaying at least some of the precepts and customs appointed by Christ to the faithful in general (62/21–66/5). For this reason, the convergence of sacred and secular orders in More never threatens to become a conflation as some feel that it does in Erasmus. The institutional consensus of the fathers is authoritative in a way that no one father's teaching can be and in a way that not even the literal authority of scripture can rival, since the living "Gospel of faith" must take precedence over the dead letter.[2] In the humanist defenses More already associates the fathers with a transcendent principle of Church unity; this connection is wanting in Erasmus.[3]

For More, patristic theology as distinct from immediate revelation is provisional or "positive" in method but not in results:

> Sometyme [God] sheweth [His truth] leysourly, suffrying his flokke to comen and dyspute theruppon / and in theyr treatynge of the mater, suffreth them wyth good mynde & scrypture and naturall wisedome, with inuocacyon of his spiritual helpe, to serche and seke for the treuth, and to vary for a whyle in their opynyons, tyll that he rewarde theyr vertuouse dylygence with ledying them secretely in to the consent and concorde and bylyef of the trouth by his holy spirite *qui facit vnanimes in domo,* whyche maketh his flokke of one mynde in hys house, that is to wyt his chyrche.[4]

---

[1]See especially Erasmus, *Methodus,* Holborn, pp. 156–57, 160. Slightly modified forms of these passages appear in *Ratio verae theologiae,* Holborn, pp. 192–93, 295.

[2]See Marius, pp. 399–400, 405; and *CW 8,* 714/32–715/4, 1293.

[3]Cf. Marius, p. 400, on More's later polemical use of the fathers: "What More did was to make the passion for ecclesiastical unity the most important single element in patristic theology."

[4]*CW 8,* 248/15–24. More is answering Tyndale's assertion that the fathers are often in basic disagreement. For a broader discussion of More and *consensus fidelium* see *CW 6,* 498–501, and Brian Gogan, *The Common Corps of Christendom: Ecclesiological Themes in the Writings of Sir Thomas More* (Leiden, 1982), pp. 298–302, 354–70; hereafter cited as "Gogan."

The fathers are exemplary not only individually for their "vertuouse dylygence" but also collectively for their ultimate deference to the unity of Christian tradition, an inspired deference which progressively clarified the actual substance of Christian tradition. For Erasmus before 1520, the fathers were exemplary mainly as pious and learned—though fallible—men, but for More they were also exemplary en masse as sustaining doctrinal authorities of a unified Church.[1] The careers of the fathers provided one pattern for prudent simplicity and another for faith: for the attainment of prudent simplicity, the fathers' historical disagreements and personal errors were actually instructive; for cultivating the faith, these shortcomings were simply irrelevant.[2]

By appealing to this suprapersonal patristic consensus as an exemplary learned expression of Christian consensus in general, More could dispose of the charge that the humanists were simply dissolving theology into "positive" disciplines like grammar even as he defended the "positive" methods preferred by the fathers themselves, who assuredly owed none of their own privileged insights to the "scientific" models established by Peter Lombard or Peter of Spain.[3] Erasmus' insistence on the primacy of the gospel per se meant that in applying the "positive" methods of humanist philology to editing and interpreting the New Testament he would be torn between a theoretical inclination toward nostalgic primitivism in his own formulation of doctrine and a practical need to defer to the readings preferred by his own age.[4] Without a firm theological basis for challenging the current under-

---

[1]More draws a sharp distinction between the personal and suprapersonal or historical and suprahistorical roles of the fathers in the *Letter to a Monk;* see 216/1–19.

[2]See 210/24–212/2, 216/9–18, and 250/22–27.

[3]See 26/25–28/13, 32/26–28, and 62/21–64/23.

[4]For Erasmus' insistence on the primacy of the gospel see especially *Paraclesis,* Holborn, p. 146, and the discussion in *CW 8,* 1192–93. Erasmus suggests that Christ's promise in Matt. 28:20 to abide with the faithful refers to his presence in scripture; More believes that the promise refers to the Church. Erasmus shared a certain propensity toward nostalgic primitivism with many other humanists and reformers; see Chomarat, *1,* 103–06; and cf. John W. O'Malley, S. J., "Historical Thought and the Reform Crisis of the Early Sixteenth Century," *Theological Studies, 28* (1967), 537–48. For a study contrasting More's attitude toward historical development with that of Erasmus see Alistair Fox, "Thomas More's Controversial Writings and His View of the Renaissance," *Parergon, 11* (April 1975), 41–48. Chomarat (*1,* 483–86) notes a tendency in Erasmus to treat *vetus* and *emendatus* as virtual synonyms; this meant that his logic for changing a reading might be strictly circular, not a very satisfactory basis for biblical emendation, at least. See further Kinney, "Erasmus' *Adagia,*" pp. 174–75; and the section entitled "Teorie umanistiche sulla genesis delle corruttele" in Silvia Rizzo, *Il lessico filologico degli umanisti* (Rome, 1973), pp. 226–35. For Erasmus' sense of the practical need to preserve current readings wherever possible see especially Allen, 2, 167, lines 54–61.

standing of a particular scriptural text by adopting a variant reading, he had no satisfactory answer for Dorp's allegation that such challenges would weaken people's faith in the providential authority of the visible Church as a whole; he could only oppose philological common sense to the theological scruples of the conservatives.[1] He apparently never thought through the quite serious objection that as long as he assigned doctrinal primacy to a historical document which had descended to his generation through a very considerable number of manuscript copies, philological common sense would inevitably suggest that the Church of his own day was less competent to interpret scripture than the primitive Church and that even his own interpretations of scripture might incorporate serious textual errors and impressionistic anachronisms. More's appeal to patristic consensus construed as a steady historical clarification of a suprahistorical "gospel of faith" meant that he could uphold the providential authority of the visible Church even as he asserted the still quite provisional character of its text of the gospel per se; he could even suggest that divergences between various texts and translations were "useful" in the same way that divergences between various patristic interpretations could often be useful in providing a basis for more precise judgments by readers to come.[2] In effect, he transformed a paradoxical Erasmian manifesto for retrograde progress—"return to the sources"—into a truly progressive prescription for the continual renewal and refinement of the "living gospel of faith."[3] Since the Holy Spirit consistently seconds the "vertuouse dylygence" of the faithful in their "positive" search for the truth, there can really be no contradiction between philological com-

---

[1] This point is well argued by Giovanni Santinello, "Teologia e linguaggio in Tommaso Moro," *Studia Patavina: Rivista di scienze religiose, 24* (1977), 621, 626–28; hereafter cited as "Santinello." For Dorp's allegation see especially Allen, 2, 15, lines 108–10; 131, lines 179–89; and 132, lines 226–28. For Erasmus' appeal to philological common sense see especially Allen, 2, 111–12, lines 817–24. Cf. Lee, *Annotationes*, sig. DD₁v: "Egregia vero his [*sc.* Erasmicis] ea laus fuerit, mihi exprobrare grammatica disputanti de theologicis." Dorp found More's theological argument convincing in a way that Erasmus' grammatical argument could not be; see p. xxiv, n. 3, above.

[2] See 82/10–26; 236/16–238/4, and 250/14–27; cf. also 82/1–9.

[3] One might describe More's own program for cultural renewal as a dextrous conflation of distinctively "Renaissance" themes with a far more traditional theme of continuous "reform." For the former, see 18/13, 194/24, and *CW 3/2*, no. 21 and commentary; on the latter, and on the distinction itself, see most notably Gerhart B. Ladner, *The Idea of Reform: Its Impact on Christian Thought and Action in the Age of the Fathers*, Rev. ed. (New York, Evanston, and London, 1967), pp. 137–39, and "Terms and Ideas of Renewal," in *Renaissance and Renewal in the Twelfth Century*, ed. Robert L. Benson *et al.* (Cambridge, Mass., 1982), pp. 37–67. Cf. also p. lxxxviii, below.

mon sense and the belief that the visible Church, once distinguished
from merely historical and personal accretions, has final authority.
Thus the same suprapersonal consensus to which More will later appeal in defense of the visible Church and of its providential traditions
here supplies an essential support for the basic Erasmian thesis that
"positive" review of provisional traditions is eminently good for the
Church.

More never condemns "disputatious theology" outright in favor of
positive theology.[1] What he does condemn is the arrogant sloth of
sophistic theologians who imagine that their dialectic alone gives them
privileged access to the meaning of scripture and everything else.[2]
This arrogant sloth, which is almost the perfect antithesis of the "vertuouse dylygence" of the fathers, can result from a dialectician's bad
habit of valuing argumentative technique over hard factual evidence;
far from constituting a privileged "science of things," dialectic can
readily degenerate into a "science" which discounts hard facts altogether and prefers to impress with mere "signs."[3] "Vertuouse
dylygence" in More's view involves working humbly and patiently to
make sense of intractable facts, just as arrogant sloth involves making
precipitate statements and calling them certainties.[4] A scholastic who
exhibited the same modesty and industriousness that More found in
Erasmus as well as in the fathers would deserve and receive the same
honor that More gave to them, but a scholastic who humbled himself to
the factual evidence in this way would thereby acknowledge that his
method, too, was in large part dependent on "positive" inquiries.[5]
Though More never revises his slighting opinion of Johannes Duns
Scotus, he can later hail St. Thomas Aquinas as "the very floure of
theology"; this is not necessarily a reversal of More's earlier theological
priorities, since Aquinas' own modest industriousness had sufficed to
make even Erasmus treat him on a par with the fathers.[6] On the other

---

[1]For the expression *theologia disputatrix* see 46/26 and note. More does suggest that this
type of theology is simply expendable; see 46/16–22 and 66/2–5.

[2]See especially 48/16–24, 72/17–20, 136/29–138/7, and 224/11–12.

[3]See especially 36/14–18, 44/24–26, 46/23–48/8, 54/15–16, 72/17–20, and 76/7–9;
for the "science of things" and the "science of signs" see pp. xlviii–li, above.

[4]See especially 56/25–58/5, 130/18–19, 260/17–19, and *CW 3/2*, Commentary at
620/6. In the *Letter to Lee* More credits Erasmus with "unsurpassed industriousness" and
immediately adds that no one could be further from the arrogance of which Lee has
accused him (172/24–25, 174/1).

[5]For the fathers' *modestia* see especially 58/12–16.

[6]For More's attitude toward Scotus see 286/12–15 and note; for his ultimate attitude
toward Aquinas see *CW 8*, 713/24, *CW 6*, 533–34, and José Morales, "La formación
espiritual e intelectual de Tomás Moro y sus contactos con la doctrina y obras de Santo

hand, Scotus and other impetuous definers of dogma among the scholastics seemed to More to lose track of authentic theology entirely.[1]

One of the principal issues on which More cites the fathers against Dorp is the issue of *claritas scripturae*, the "clarity of scripture." Dorp has asserted that the scholastics' *quaestiones* were not only more difficult but also more useful than a thorough understanding of scripture; More devotes a good deal of attention to the question of relative difficulty even though he suggests that the question of relative usefulness is really more basic.[2] The main purpose of More's argument here for the obscurity of scripture is to link the profession of theology more closely than ever with *sacrarum litterarum peritia*, conceived as the objective of a cooperative and continuous labor in sacred philology.[3] Dorp's scholastics imagine that nothing could be simpler than to fathom the meaning of scripture; here, too, they reveal how incautiously boastful they are in comparison with the fathers, none of whom dared to claim he himself understood it.[4] Like the fathers themselves, More conceives of the infinite mystery embedded in scripture as a lure to entice slothful, self-satisfied minds "with the promise of buried and hard-to-reach treasure," and thus as the perfect incentive to "vertuouse dylygence"; in refusing to acknowledge the mystery at all, Dorp's scholastics are not only shunning essential hard work but are also opposing an insolent private conception of scripture to that of a pious consensus.[5] Just as further along in the letter More invokes the "inflexible standard" of living consensus or a "living gospel of faith" to authorize closer critical scrutiny of the text of the gospel per se, so he here emphasizes the mysterious ambiguity of scripture to suggest that without divine aid of the sort that rewarded the modest industriousness of the fathers, the meaning of scripture can never be clarified at all.

Tomás de Aquino," *Scripta Theologica*, 6 (Pamplona: University of Navarra, 1974), 439–89. He does not mention Aquinas in the humanist defenses despite Dorp's partisan reference to him in Allen, 2, 129, lines 94–99. In his 1516 *Apologia* (Holborn, p. 171, lines 21–27) Erasmus carefully distinguishes Aquinas and the fathers from the majority of the moderns, who are characterized by their "impudens temeritas et insolens inscitia." I would suggest that Erasmus and More both regarded Aquinas as an illustrious exception among the scholastics; see 184/12–15 below, where More declares that Erasmus gives the moderns in general as much credit as they deserve.

[1]For More's swipes at impetuous definers of dogma see 32/23, 174/2–3, and 286/12–15; cf. also 64/14–19, 200/22–28, and 216/10–19.

[2]See 54/18–56/8 and 62/2–6.

[3]More pointedly equates theology proper with *sacrarum litterarum peritia* at 14/15–16.

[4]See 48/18–24, 54/18–56/8, and 58/12–15.

[5]For the mystery embedded in scripture as a "buried and hard-to-reach treasure" see 58/14–20.

More insists on the edifying but daunting complexity of both the text
and the meaning of scripture in a way that Erasmus does not in his
writings before 1520.[1] Erasmus' insistence on the primacy of the gospel per se means that he must maintain that the authentic meaning and
text are directly accessible to anyone with the same fervent longing to
learn and the same philological skills that distinguished the fathers; he
never suggests that traditional consensus itself has to mediate a personal response to the gospel.[2] More paraphrases his own argument concerning the pregnant obscurity of scripture again and again in his
writings against the radical reformers, who repeat the contentious
scholastics' mistake in believing that their private reading of scripture
must be the definitive one.[3] Erasmus himself finally follows More's
lead in suggesting that *claritas scripturae* is a postulate naturally linked
to a habit of wrangling intransigence, but by that time Erasmus' polemical comments are addressed not to Dorp but to Luther.[4] Until he must
choose between Luther and Catholic tradition, he resists More's suggestion that the historically simplistic postulate of *claritas scripturae* is
actually at odds with a "positive" approach to theology.

Both More and Erasmus consider the fathers to be exemplary sacred
philologists as well as exemplary theologians; on the other hand, both
of them stress that the fathers can also make mistakes. More agrees
with Erasmus that it is possible to improve on the works of the fathers
considered as fallible individuals; he differs with Erasmus in suggesting that it is virtually impossible to improve on the fathers' consensus,
regarded as one of the most vital manifestations of that "living gospel
of faith" which he calls "the inflexible standard of truth." Nonetheless,
at least once More suggests that not even patristic consensus may be
altogether "inflexible," since the fathers in general doubted the
Blessed Virgin's immaculate conception while virtually all More's contemporaries accept it.[5] It may always be necessary to distinguish be-

---

[1]Marius (pp. 388–89) notes the high value More places on variant readings and interpretations as stimulants for thought (see especially 82/16–26, 236/16–238/4, and
250/14–252/2) and goes on to suggest that More's attitude toward variants was very
different from that of Erasmus. For one instance in which More's arguments defending
varietas may have influenced Erasmus see p. xlv, n. 1, above.

[2]See especially Erasmus, *Paraclesis,* Holborn, p. 141, lines 29–33; and *Methodus,*
Holborn, p. 160, lines 11–17.

[3]See note on 60/12–23.

[4]For the likelihood that Erasmus actually had More's *Letter to Dorp* in mind when he
wrote about wrangling intransigence and *claritas scripturae* in *De libero arbitrio* and *Hyperaspistes diatribes* see notes on 16/25, 60/4–10, and 60/22–23.

[5]See 214/17–21 and note. For other passages obliquely suggesting that progressive
revelation might occasionally entail the *abandonment* of some generally held Christian
belief, see *CW 6,* 140/35–141/8 and 146/30–147/7.

tween casual traditionalism on the part of past Christians and a binding
resolve to perpetuate a given tradition as a proper extension of central
Christian dogmas.

This cautious attitude toward casual traditionalism is especially
marked in More's discussion of how much authority one is rationally
obliged to concede to the Vulgate translation of scripture. Much of
More's argument is an elaboration of points which Erasmus had already made in his letter to Dorp, but More carefully handles one point
which Erasmus had simply avoided: how can one establish (*except* by
appealing to philological common sense) that an informal Catholic
consensus approving the Vulgate need not make the Vulgate fundamentally more authoritative than its Greek original?[1] Dorp had emphasized that the whole Latin Church had relied on the Vulgate for
centuries but had allowed many other translations to perish; in Dorp's
view the unique popularity and tenacity of the Vulgate translation
implied that past Christians had deliberately resolved to establish this
version of scripture as definitive in order to safeguard against variant
texts which might weaken the faith.[2] More points out that the Vulgate
itself represents Jerome's modified version of a text which was already
widely accepted; if a purely informal consensus somehow makes the
Vulgate definitive, then why did Jerome feel entitled to alter a text
which could claim the same kind of authority?[3] Jerome's own modifications were based on the premise that the same philological common

---

[1] Erasmus' most substantive responses to Dorp's traditionalist defense of the Vulgate
occur in Allen, 2, 109–11, lines 713–92. Like More, he rejects Dorp's conjectural argument that the Greeks have neglected or even intentionally corrupted their texts since
Jerome's day, and like More, he insists on the abundant philological evidence that scribal
corruptions have crept into the text of the Vulgate whereas many of Jerome's emendations have not been retained. Unlike More, Erasmus here never directly disputes the
suggestion that an authoritative edition of Jerome's revised text would provide a completely definitive version of scripture. A traditionalist could easily consent to the correction of any obvious errors in the Vulgate which were exposed by a simple collation of
Latin authorities; after all, the corrections themselves would derive from the Vulgate's
own textual tradition. But the result of this cautious restorative review of the Vulgate
would be a recension which had more in common with the Clementine Vulgate than with
the *Novum Instrumentum* of Erasmus. For Erasmus' repeated attempt to defend his own
version as nothing more than a restorative recension see the passages cited in Werner
Schwarz, *Principles and Problems of Biblical Translation: Some Reformation Controversies and
Their Background* (Cambridge, 1955; hereafter cited as "Schwarz"), p. 154, n. 2. More's
comparatively daring rationale for revising the Vulgate was anticipated in certain respects by an early (1515) defense of Lefèvre d'Etaples by Josse Clichtove; this defense was
first published and analyzed by Jean-Pierre Massaut, *Critique et tradition à la veille de la
Réforme en France* (Paris, 1974), pp. 49–52, 125–30.

[2] See 80/1–10 and note.

[3] See 80/11–18.

sense which applied to assessing any other translation also applied to assessing even the most current Latin translation of scripture: deviations in the Latin from the meaning of the Greek were not providential refinements but simply mistakes of the translator.[1] Jerome's unchallenged procedural precedent suggests that the same philological common sense should apply to assessing his own revised text: like any other normal translation, it is still only a human, provisional approximation of an authoritative original.[2] Thus until the Church formally rules otherwise More feels entitled to assume that the Church itself grants the validity of arguments which philological common sense would ordinarily treat as self-evident.[3] He similarly maintains that the loss of other ancient translations of scripture was a matter of simple neglect, not of pious solicitude: philological common sense indicates that "the carelessness of the times, which indeed allowed much else besides those translations to perish," should not be mistaken for a model expression of Christian selectiveness.[4] More appeals to patristic tradition in order to prove that not every informal consensus can vindicate casual traditions as dogmatic certainties; simple habit is not an "inflexible standard of truth."

In the *Letter to Dorp* More's intention is not to determine how many traditions are firmly established according to this rigid standard of truth; his intention is rather to identify the standard in principle so that biblical philology need no longer be viewed as a threat to tradition per se. In his growing impatience with a wide range of human traditions which the visible Church had attracted, Erasmus had failed to appreciate that the legitimacy of his own philological program was directly dependent on the legitimacy which Catholic tradition assigned to the sacred philology of the fathers. More saw that Erasmian reform could be vindicated as a way of renewing the fathers' own "positive" scrutiny of provisional traditions in the name of divine ones; he also saw that in order to make this vindication convincing, Erasmus would have to

---

[1] See 80/18–24 and note.

[2] See 82/1–9. Augustine challenged Jerome's deviations from the Septuagint translation of the Old Testament but approved of his altering the Latin translation of the New Testament; see note on 80/17–18.

[3] See 86/9–15; cf. 228/15–20. The Vulgate, "quae longo tot saeculorum usu in ipsa ecclesia probata est," was declared the authoritative Latin version of scripture in the second decree of the Fourth Session of the Council of Trent (April 8, 1546); see Giuseppe Alberigo et al., eds., *Conciliorum oecumenicorum decreta*, 3rd ed. (Bologna, 1973; hereafter cited as "Alberigo"), p. 664. In the Eighth Session of the Second Vatican Council (November 18, 1965) the Vulgate was simply described as the most honored Latin translation of scripture; see Alberigo, p. 979.

[4] See 82/13–16.

define his own program more clearly as a continuation of the work of
the fathers and not as a new, rival scheme for immediate return to the
sources. One can plausibly claim that the *Letter to Dorp* contains more
than a little strategic advice for Erasmus himself.[1]

More may have hoped that the *Letter to Dorp* would make Erasnius
himself more aware of the need to defer to patristic consensus as a
matter of explicit principle and to acknowledge the pregnant obscurity
of scripture itself as nothing less than the permanent raison d'être of
sacred philology, but if Erasmus eventually accepted More's second
oblique admonition he never unambiguously accepted the first. Even
after rejecting the radical biblicism of reformers like Luther, Erasmus
was cautious and slow in acknowledging the doctrinal force of patristic
consensus, whereas More was perhaps overemphatic or rash in asserting the doctrinal force of patristic consensus for theses which some of
the fathers might well have rejected.[2] The two attitudes toward Christian tradition are not easily reconciled, but More's final energetic defense of Erasmus' constructive intentions invites us to look for a way.[3]
Perhaps the humanist in More wished to make one last gesture promoting the peaceable union of caution and zeal in the virtue of prudent
simplicity.

If More and Erasmus disagreed on the principle that patristic consensus could be invoked as a virtually absolute doctrinal standard, they
agreed on preferring the fathers' primarily exegetic and pastoral, gos-
pel-centered theology to the speculative theology of the moderns. The
scholastics enjoyed representing theology as the "queen of all disciplines," as if theological knowledge belonged to an utterly distinct
higher order.[4] More preferred to describe sacred scripture as the

[1]For this claim see Santinello, p. 628.

[2]For Erasmus' rather hesitant acknowledgments of the doctrinal force of *consensus
fidelium* see James K. McConica, "Erasmus and the Grammar of Consent," in *Scrinium
Erasmianum*, ed. Joseph Coppens, 2 vols. (Leiden, 1969; hereafter cited as "McConica,
'Erasmus'"), 2, 77–99, and Gogan, pp. 365–70. For More's selectiveness in reporting the
views of Augustine see Marius, p. 403.

[3]For More's final defense of Erasmus' constructive intentions see especially *CW 8*, 177,
lines 12–23; and Allen, *10*, 32–33; the latter passage is strangely reminiscent of the *Letter
to a Monk*.

[4]For this commonplace description of theology see 138/24–140/1 and commentary.
For the general prestige of theology in the Middle Ages see R. Guelluy, "La place des
théologiens dans l'Eglise et la société médiévales," in *Miscellanea Historica in Honorem
Alberti de Meyer*, 2 vols. (Louvain and Brussels, 1946), *1*, 571–89; for the traditional
uneasy relation between theology and grammar see M.-D. Chenu, O.P., "Grammaire et
théologie aux XIIᵉ et XIIIᵉ siècles," *Archives d'histoire doctrinale et littéraire du Moyen Age*,
10/11 (1936), 5–28. See also Gregorius Magnus, *Moralia in Job, praefatio, PL* 75, 516B, on
the inappropriateness of subjecting the words of celestial truth to the rules of Donatus.

"queen of all *litterae*" and to represent sacred letters in general as *litterae* par excellence, so that the true theologian's material claim to preeminence was actually no different from that of the true *litteratus,* More's model philologist-orator.[1] More accepts the Erasmian conception of theologians as essentially "doctors of the gospels" and explicitly compares the importance of scripture and its ancient interpreters in the training of a theologian to the importance of ancient Latin authors in the training of a competent Latinist.[2] In the humanist defenses he characteristically espouses the Erasmian view that correct theological method is fundamentally grammatical and rhetorical.

In accordance with the view that theologians are essentially "doctors of the gospels" More suggests that their two most material concerns are sustaining the faith and encouraging virtue (*fidei pietas* and *morum probitas,* 48/7–8).[3] He goes on to ask himself what useful service sophistical problems equip theologians to perform for the Church and then takes two such services as test cases.[4] The first test case, debating with heretics, corresponds to sustaining the faith, while the second, vernacular preaching, corresponds in an obvious way to encouraging virtue. More maintains that sophistical subtleties can be exploited as well by the heretics as by orthodox Christians and that "one little bundle of faggots" will generally do more to silence a heretic than "many large bundles of syllogisms"; this assertion is probably not so much an endorsement of physical coercion per se as an expression of the typically Erasmian sentiment that even coercion is a more natural method of silencing heretics than trying to surpass them in sophistry.[5] In any event, More's main emphasis falls on the sophists' shortcomings as preachers: they have nothing instructive to say and no notion at all of the right way to say it.[6] Once again More associates the primary function of theology with the study and preaching of scripture on the methodological basis of grammar and rhetoric.

The quite obvious grammatical and rhetorical stress of Erasmian

---

[1]See 14/12–16 and 62/8–9.

[2]See 68/17–70/5 and 76/6–7.

[3]For the suggestion that the principal objects of study in scripture may be divided into *praecepta vivendi* and *regulae credendi* see Augustine, *De doctrina christiana* 2.9.14 (*PL 34,* 42).

[4]See 70/4–72/12.

[5]See 70/29–31 and note.

[6]See 72/1–9, 138/17–21, 140/1–20, and cf. the related contrast between casuistic acuity and evangelical fervor at 64/8–23.

theology has led some to describe it as a *theologia rhetorica,* a theology in which rhetoric itself becomes formally essential.[1] Others have objected that it is less useful to speak of this composite discipline as "rhetorical theology" than as "theological rhetoric," at least partly, I think, because it seems to them that a rhetorical orientation would tend to trivialize theology whereas a theological orientation would tend to dignify rhetoric.[2] Erasmus himself felt defensive about the suggestion that he had conflated theology with rhetoric: "Who in the world is foolish enough to make theology and rhetoric one and the same?"[3] Nonetheless it seems clear that Erasmus did emphasize the rhetorical and pedagogical concerns of the theologian to the virtual exclusion of speculative theology; it remains to be shown why Erasmus and More among others believed that this radical reversal of traditional theological priorities was not only legitimate but also long overdue.

Erasmus and More both assert more than once that sophistic theologians are simply impostors: they cannot be called theologians at all.[4] At one point More uses the term *theologistae* to distinguish these sham theologians from real theologians, the ones who have actually gone to the trouble of studying the gospels and reading the works of the fathers. More borrows this term from a pamphlet by Johann Reuchlin in which he attacks the "theologists'" notion of the meaning of *theologia.* According to Reuchlin, who cites one of the Greek fathers to back up his own definition, the true meaning of *theologia* is "talking with God."[5] In fact many Greek fathers and some prescholastic Latin authors accepted this meaning of the term, whereas others defined it as "talking

---

[1]See Charles E. Trinkaus, "Erasmus, Augustine, and the Nominalists," *Archiv für Reformationsgeschichte,* 67 (1976), 31; and Boyle, especially p. 199, n. 132.

[2]See Georges Chantraine, S. J., *Erasme et Luther: Libre et serf arbitre, étude historique et théologique* (Paris and Naumur, 1981), p. 263, n. 45, and the clarification in *Moreana,* 77 (1983), 89–90, where Prof. Chantraine prefers to speak of Erasmus' "theological rhetoric" precisely because he acknowledges the pedagogical and devotional emphasis of Erasmus' religious thought; in other words, he prefers not to acknowledge the basis of a genuine theology in Erasmus' own unifying rhetorical concept of Christ's ministry. Those who hold (with Erasmus?) that the methods of theology may well in large part coincide with the methods of rhetoric will not make the same subtle distinction between *theologia rhetorica* and *rhetorica theologica* that Prof. Chantraine does, even granted that the adjective in such pairings generally refers to the "formal point of view of a discipline."

[3]Erasmus, *Apologia in dialogum Jacobi Latomi, Opera omnia,* 9, 104B: "Quis autem tam insanus est usquam, ut Theologiam eandem faciat cum Rhetorica?"

[4]See 18/12–20, 54/14–17, 76/17–18, and 76/28–78/1; for Erasmus' assertions, see Allen, 2, 99, line 333; 111, line 797; and cf. 100, lines 354–55.

[5]See 106/16 and note.

about God"; both these meanings suggest that theology proper is more a matter of fervent devotional utterance than of dispassionate theoretical inquiry.[1] Even a scholastic theologian like Scotus would admit that theology is not purely a matter of "reasoning about God"; humanists like Erasmus and More chose to stress that pure "reasoning about God" is essentially peripheral to everyday Christian experience and in consequence tended to discount this variant meaning entirely.[2] The centrality of scripture in Erasmian theology is explained at least partly by its function as a "promptuary" of devotional utterance, as the divine Word which administers an endless supply of devotional responses to any reader whose heart is receptive.[3] On fairly obvious stylistic grounds, many humanists found it easier to view scripture as a natural sourcebook for a *theologia rhetorica* than as a methodical compendium of subtle theological propositions; this suitability in itself was enough to persuade them that authentic Christian theology was likely to be not so much an abstruse and sequestered department of scientific speculation as a devotional elevation of everyday human discourse.

One of the most remarkable passages in the humanist defenses is a climactic statement in the *Letter to Dorp* about how people ought to behave toward the sham theologians who now occupy places of some academic distinction.[4] Dorp had implied that an affront offered to any professional theologian is an affront to the profession in general. More responds that the sham theologians themselves are the ones who disgrace their profession; they ought to be thrown out of office in the same way that bad secular magistrates were dealt with in Rome. These are very strong words for a layman to use in a semipublic letter addressed to a foreign theologian, words that someone was cautious enough to delete from one manuscript of the *Letter to Dorp*. More himself later claims that incompetent magistrates ought to be suffered

---

[1]See Jean Leclercq and Jean-Paul Bonnes, *Un maître de la vie spirituelle au XIe siècle: Jean de Fécamp* (Paris, 1946), pp. 76–78; and Leclercq, *Love of Learning*, pp. 127, 282. For scholastic survivals of this older, "affective" model of theology see Minnis, pp. 119–30.

[2]See Tshibangu, p. 147: "Scote la definit en général à la manière traditionelle: 'Theologia est sermo vel ratio de Deo.'" For passages stressing the very marginal value of pure "reasoning about God" see especially 70/20–27 and 138/17–21 below. For a direct appeal to the devotional definition of *theologia* see Erasmus, *Paraclesis*, Holborn, 142/36–143/1: "Vereor enim, ne inter theologos reperire liceat, qui multum absint a suo titulo, hoc est, qui terrena loquantur, non divina. . . ."

[3]For scripture as a "promptuary" see 166/8 and 210/24 and cf. Erasmus, *Paraclesis*, Holborn, p. 146.

[4]See 76/15–19; cf. 38/18–40/6, 76/21–78/4 and note.

in silence except by their peers and superiors.[1] What induced him to think that he had any business attacking unfit theologians in 1515?

When the humanists challenged the prevailing understanding of *theologia* as primarily a scientific discipline they also made it possible to speak seriously of any learned and devout common citizen as a "lay theologian."[2] It seems clear that Erasmus enjoyed viewing More as a lay theologian, though More's repeated involvement in theological controversy made him more than a little uneasy.[3] When Erasmus spoke of a "lay theologian" approvingly he was generally thinking of a layman who centered his own spiritual life on the gospel to the point of being able to dispense with the mediating activity of professional theologians altogether: the true lay theologian was an erudite moral and rhetorical imitator of Christ.[4] Although More, too, gave enormous importance to the diligent imitation of Christ, he was not as convinced as Erasmus that scripture alone could be trusted to furnish an objective view of the model which ought to be imitated; for More, *imitatio Christi* naturally involved *imitatio patrum*.[5] More's lay theologian was not automatically excluded from imitating the fathers' public teaching and controversial writing any more than from imitating their private devotions, since the fathers themselves showed exemplary modesty in their reluctance to state novel theses dogmatically on their own initiative. Though he might be less qualified than they were to pronounce on abstruse and complex theological issues, he was surely as competent to remind theologians like Dorp of the "positive" facts and to remonstrate with sham theologians for shirking their most basic duties. Even so, More may have attributed more importance to professional theologians as a group than Erasmus himself did, since the professional

---

[1]See especially *CW 8*, 590–92.

[2]See Erasmus, *Paraclesis*, Holborn, p. 143, lines 13–16; p. 145, line 3; *Methodus*, Holborn, p. 155, line 27; *Ratio verae theologiae*, Holborn, p. 192, lines 5–6; 193, lines 18–22; cf. *Antibarbari, ASD 1/1*, 96, lines 7–23.

[3]See Erasmus in Allen, *4*, 21, lines 265–67. In a 1526 letter to More (Allen, *7*, 12) Erasmus pointedly criticized laymen who wish to be taken for controversial theologians; in a late letter lamenting More's death (Allen, *11*, 216) Erasmus expressed a wish that More had left theological disputes to professionals.

[4]See Albert Rabil, Jr., *Erasmus and the New Testament: The Mind of a Christian Humanist* (San Antonio, Texas, 1972), pp. 152–53; and Boyle, pp. 232–33, n. 243.

[5]For More's traditionalist understanding of *imitatio Christi* see McConica, "Patrimony," p. 60; for More's praise of Erasmus as an imitator of the apostles and fathers see especially 294/14–300/4. Also pertinent and stimulating is Peter Brown's "The Saint as Exemplar in Late Antiquity," *Representations, 3* (1983), 1–25.

theologians had inherited the essential exemplary role he assigned to the fathers. He writes as a proprietary admirer.

More's criticism of professional theologians in the *Letter to Dorp* has a good deal in common with his criticism of contemporary religious orders in the *Letter to a Monk*. In both cases he writes as a proprietary admirer;[1] in both cases he draws a sharp contrast between the humble devotion of the ancients and the self-flattering elitism of many of the moderns; and in both he suggests that Erasmus succeeds as an imitator of primitive Christians whereas many of the moderns are disgraceful failures.[2] Erasmus' rhetorical theology bears many resemblances to the "monastic theology" which gave way to the speculative discipline of Peter Lombard and the other scholastics, and if More had restricted his criticisms to the ignorance and wrangling intransigence of Erasmus' monkish critics it would be easy to take his remarks as a call for the general renewal of authentic monastic erudition as well as authentic theology.[3] But in fact More suggests something quite different.

---

[1]For More's personal devotion to monasticism see 274/31–276/6 and note on 202/18. Cf. also Walter J. Gordon, "The Monastic Achievement and More's Utopian Dream," *Medievalia et Humanistica*, New Series, 9 (1979), 199–214. There is some need to qualify McConica's statement ("Patrimony," p. 64) that "even here [*sc.* in the *Letter to a Monk*] More acknowledged the superiority of the life of vows in ways that Erasmus would have found uncongenial": More acknowledges the theoretical superiority of the life of vows in conventional terms (274/31–276/11, 300/9–13, 300/23–24) but suggests that Erasmus' evangelical activity is more fruitful than cloistered monastic devotions (296/8–13). Only a monk who was utterly "dead to the world" (see p. xxxvi, n. 2) would present a true "pattern of angelic life" (300/9–22), but such a pattern would profit the faithful no differently than the literary patterns of angelic life left behind in the works of the fathers and later restored by Erasmus (cf. Rogers, p. 123). More's attraction to monastic existence is perhaps un-Erasmian, but his understanding of its practical value is not.

[2]For More's contrasts between ancients and moderns see especially 58/6–20 and 264/5–17; for his remarks about proper and improper imitation of the fathers and apostles see 32/26–28, 46/11–22, 68/17–70/5, 204/20–22, 216/13–19, 272/3–28, 294/14–30, and cf. Marc'hadour, *The Bible*, 4, 153–54.

[3]For "monastic theology" see Leclercq, *Love of Learning*, especially pp. 1–9, 127–29, and 233–86; for the similarities between the humanist educational ideal and the early medieval ideal of monastic erudition see also Georges Chantraine, *"Mystère" et "Philosophie du Christ" selon Erasme* (Namur and Gembloux, 1971), pp. 372–74; and Noel L. Brann, *The Abbot Trithemius (1462–1516): The Renaissance of Monastic Humanism* (Leiden, 1981; hereafter cited as "Brann"), especially pp. xvi–xvii and 204–28. Erasmus' own universalist stress on the need to disseminate Christian erudition as widely as possible was one element of his educational program which distinguished it sharply from the rather elitist ideal of monastic erudition; for the monastic position and a typical humanist response to it see Brann, pp. 258–66. McConica (*English Humanists*, p. 37) describes More as a monastic layman and Erasmus as a laicized monk; both men's attitudes represented a challenge to the traditional sharp opposition between "religious" and "secular" voca-

Though he does seem to perceive some affinity in principle between Erasmus' religious activity and that of the various preaching orders, he insists on the absolute discontinuity between Erasmus' scholarly pursuits and the proper concerns of contemplatives like Batmanson, whom he actually attacks for his interest in Erasmian learning.[1] In his rejoinder to Batmanson More occasionally seems to apply his own principle of *imitatio patrum* in a tendentious way, as if he had forgotten that Jerome himself managed to combine the vocations of hermit and pilgrim, *solitarius* and wide-ranging scholar. More's theoretical sense of a radical and total dichotomy between the life of withdrawal and the life of engagement reflects not so much a unanimous patristic consensus as an unresolved tension in More's own mind between a powerful activist impulse and an equally powerful impulse toward retiring asceticism.[2]

There is one very telling discrepancy between precept and practice in the *Letter to a Monk:* More condemns Batmanson's tendentious and facile appeals to patristic and scriptural authorities, but he often invokes them himself in a similarly uncritical way. More and Erasmus repeatedly suggest that haphazard citation of a prestigious model out of context is a primary token of crude and inept imitation.[3] Batmanson's naive denial that the fathers ever made a mistake, like his "patchwork" citation of scripture, simply discounts the historical and contextual substance of the works of the fathers and of scripture itself.[4] He

---

tions. For Erasmus' characteristic suggestion that Christian society as a whole may be viewed as one vast monastery see Allen, *1,* 568, line 86, and *3,* 376; cf. 278/14–16 ; nd note, below.

[1]For the affinity between Erasmus and the Franciscans see 294/14–30 and note on 294/20–23; for More's criticism of Batmanson's learning see 218/20–27, 262/10–13, and 262/24–264/12.

[2]Cf. Greenblatt, p. 16: "It is as if, in the midst of intensely valued attachments to family and friends, he carried within himself the perspective of the London Charterhouse in which he had lived, without vow, for four years. . . ." If More sensed that the dichotomy between the life of withdrawal and the life of engagement should be total and absolute, why did he himself make a habit of straddling the boundary between them? Was his ambivalence a matter of commonplace irresolution, or was it an expression of the same salutary uncertainty about one's own religious vocation which More recommends to the monk Batmanson at 300/13–22? Doubtless each explanation is partly correct, though it should be observed that the very notion of prudent simplicity involves much the same sort of ambivalence as More's "double life." One can regard the irrepressible disorderliness of provisional existence as either a threat or a challenge; the Erasmian More perceived mainly the challenge, the retiring More mainly the threat. But at least in provisional terms, these perceptions are not incompatible.

[3]See especially *CW* 3/2, 612/15–19, and Commentary.

[4]See 214/22–24 and 272/3–28.

pretends to be using these texts as his models but actually avoids ever
coming to terms with them; instead, he sets out to buffer himself
against any basic challenge to his own preconceptions and prejudices
with snippets of text which he treats as if they meant whatever he wants
them to mean.[1] From the *Letter to Dorp* it would seem that in More's
view the reassertion of sound authentic Christian tradition is closely
linked to a reassertion of sound imitative procedure based on diligent
contextual study of scripture as well as the works of the fathers.[2] His
own arguments for biblical philology in the *Letter to Dorp* rest on precisely this sort of intelligent contextual analysis: without simply echoing
Jerome, he distills and refines on Jerome's basic principles as they may
be gleaned from Jerome's philological prefaces. In the *Letter to a Monk*,
on the other hand, the exigencies of an all-out polemic induce More to
seize on patristic and scriptural citations and use them as weapons
almost as impulsively as Batmanson himself does. Even in his impressive defense of Erasmus' translation "In principio erat sermo"
More simply amasses an imposing assembly of testimonies without ever
attempting a careful analysis of any of them; in this complex and
invidious argument More, like Erasmus, prefers to suggest that the
facts ought to speak for themselves.[3] The *Letter to a Monk* could be

---

[1]See especially 202/26–27, 204/20–22, 222/12, 254/13–258/4, 270/13–17, and notes.
Cf. also Rogers, p. 326, lines 33–35: ". . . fecisse modestius videreris, si mores Apostoli
potius esses imitatus, quam si tibi arrogasses Apostolicum stylum."
[2]See especially 46/11–48/24 and 68/17–70/5.
[3]For More's defense of "In principio erat sermo" see 236/3–248/28 and notes; for the
relation between More's defense and the two versions of Erasmus' *Apologia de In principio
erat sermo* see p. xlv, n. 1. To avoid aggravating conservative suspicions of this unfamiliar
translation, both More and Erasmus preferred simple compilation of authorities to any
detailed account of the doctrinal advantages to be gained by translating the Johannine
λόγος as *sermo* or discursive utterance (cf. Boyle, p. 13), though both clearly appreciated
the predominantly rhetorical character of this interpretation as opposed to the metaphysical character of the more traditional rendering *verbum* (see Erasmus, *Annotationes in
Novum Testamentum, Opera omnia*, 6, 335C, and note on 238/20–30). Since More fails to
provide any detailed account of the doctrinal advantages of *sermo*, he must merely shrug
off the monk's claim that, while *sermo* may be an adequate rendering of λόγος in analo-
gous scriptural contexts, it is less adequate than the traditional *verbum* in the first verse of
John (244/14–246/4; cf. 248/6–8). In the absence of a painstaking contextual analysis of
what John and his commentators were actually trying to say it is hard to exclude the
theoretical possibility that More's strongest patristic authorities were simply mistaken in
assuming that *sermo* as well as *verbum* is an acceptable rendering of λόγος in the first verse
of John, but in the midst of a heated polemic a painstaking contextual analysis of this
verse would probably arouse more suspicions than it would dispel. More preferred
simply to silence the personal adversary; cf. 246/8–11.
   More's remarkable array of scriptural and patristic testimonies for *sermo* must have
impressed even his earliest editors, who titled the letter "eruditissima" ("most learned,"

viewed as a scriptural "patchwork" in its own right.[1]

It is never easy to combine polemical vehemence and critical cir-
cumspection, and it may never have been harder than in the first
years of the Reformation. Even so, from a modern perspective More's
vehemence on behalf of Erasmian reform in the *Letter to a Monk* somewhat offsets and tempers his vehemence on behalf of traditionalism in
polemical works still to come, thus inviting the modern reader, at
least, to reassert More's own central ideal of judicious restraint in the
midst of polemical excess. By beginning the *Letter to a Monk* with a
pointed allusion to a similar work by Jerome, More apparently means
to remind us that on occasion the judicious fathers themselves felt no
qualms about answering vehemence with vehemence.[2] Even in its polemical impetuousness the *Letter to a Monk* is a highly suggestive expression of More's *imitatio patrum*.

Though More never explicitly repudiated his Erasmian writings
any more than he ever repudiated Erasmus himself, he did finally
retrench or abandon a number of Erasmian positions upheld in the
humanist defenses. His energetic defense of monasticism in the *Letter
to Bugenhagen* and of Christian ceremonies in *A Dialogue Concerning
Heresies* makes it hard to believe he could ever have written a tren-
chant critique like the *Letter to a Monk*. By 1526 he begins to sound
considerably more tolerant of the *quaestio* method in theology, and by
1532 he appears to have altered his earlier, somewhat deprecatory
view of Nicolas de Lyra.[3] He also effectively repudiates satire and
critical comments directed at unworthy magistrates, and he defends

---

198/1–2); this list of authorities is the most concentrated display of learning in the entire
work. I have not located any *catena* of scriptural interpreters from which More could
have drawn the majority of his references, though his reference to Sap. 18:15 at 240/15–
18 could be partly inspired by Aquinas, *Super epistolas Sancti Pauli lectura: in Epistolam ad
Hebraeos* 4.2 on Heb. 4:12, a commentary which Erasmus cites explictly in *Apologia de In
principio erat sermo, Opera omnia, 9,* 116B. Erasmus may have furnished at least some of the
references in a letter to More which has not been preserved, and More may have received
some assistance in gathering the rest from the Erasmian theologian John Stokesley; for
his assistance in More's oral defense of Erasmus' translation see Allen, *4,* 310–13. More
could not have drawn most of his references from the first version of Erasmus' *Apologia;*
see p. xlv, n. 1, above.

[1]More's intention often seems to be merely to "drown out" Batmanson's scriptural
citations with others of his own; see especially 204/14–22, 264/17–24, 300/15–302/10,
and notes. He also repeatedly tries to hoist Batmanson on his own scriptural petard; see
especially 224/13–18, 270/13–18, and 272/24–28. Despite the obvious rhetorical effectiveness of most of More's scriptural citations, it is rather disturbing that he shows so little
regard for alternative contextually plausible ways of construing them.

[2]See note on 198/8–12; for another allusion to the same work see 270/26–29 and note.

[3]See Rogers, p. 335, and note on 216/10 below.

at great length the same heresy-trial procedure that he seems to be challenging implicitly in the first several pages of the *Letter to a Monk*.[1] At least equally telling, he abandons the thesis that scripture is virtually invulnerable to deliberate heretical tampering and flatly repudiates Tyndale's grammatical paradigm for the restoration of authentic Christian tradition in general.[2] It would be hard to explain all these changes as simple expressions of embattled loyalty to the same governing ideal of Church unity that More had been serving in less direct ways all along: in his latest works More effectively denies himself both the right and the critical means to distinguish between casual and providential traditionalism even as he appears to reserve the same right for Erasmus.[3] Though some may find the notion surprising, even in his last years More apparently saw in Erasmus an exemplary scholar-ascetic and felt that in violent times, among private individuals, only an exemplary scholar-ascetic could be trusted to draw such precarious yet vital distinctions without actually harming the Church.[4] More may have expressed his own form of asceticism in a contrary effort to "captyue" his own understanding, to overcome his own impulse to challenge traditions which struck him as arbitrary, but as a matter of principle he never forgot or renounced the Erasmian alternative.[5]

---

[1]See notes on 76/15–19 and 206/27–29. More further elaborates his defense of traditional heresy-trial procedure in *The Apology* and *The Debellation of Salem and Bizance*.

[2]See notes on 88/22–90/22 and 68/17–70/3; for a similar reversal see the note on 224/23–24.

[3]For the traditional Catholic explanation of the differences between More's humanist writings and his later polemics see especially Surtz, *Praise of Wisdom*, pp. 16–17. For More's equation between providential tradition in general and the whole range of particular Catholic traditions, see Flesseman-Van Leer, pp. 146–50, 161. More appears to make an exception for Erasmus' ongoing review of ecclesiastical tradition in *CW 8*, 177/12–13, and Allen, *10*, 32–33. Cf. McConica, *English Humanists*, pp. 287–94.

[4]For Erasmus as an exemplary scholar-ascetic see 292/11–300/4 and Allen, *10*, 32.

[5]For the meritorious endeavor to "captyue our vnderstandynge" see 2 Cor. 10:5; *CW 6*, 167/34, 254/28–29; *CW 8*, 121/11, 127/17, 240/8, 242/17–18, 464/16 and 503/18–19; *CW 9*, 33/31, 35/17; and Rogers, p. 450, line 349.

STRUCTURE, STYLE, AND MORE'S READERS

Although much has been written on the Renaissance familiar epistle, the Renaissance "open letter" or letter-essay has scarcely been studied at all.[1] Scholars generally tend to assume that long letters are actually speeches or books in disguise and that the personal addressees of such letters have more in common with the ceremonial dedicatees of conventional treatises than they do with the true addressees of familiar epistles. Since medieval epistolary convention prescribed that all letters should be written in a highly rhetorical style, there is also some tendency to look down on rhetorical letters by Renaissance authors as old-fashioned, as if there were no suitable styles for the literary middle ground between the total intimacy of the familiar epistle and the total reserve of the formal public petition or well-rehearsed speech. Since Erasmus himself puts a great deal of stress on just these intermediate styles in his treatise on letter-writing (*De conscribendis epistolis,*), it is hardly surprising that More should employ them quite freely in the humanist defenses. In their structure and style all the defenses but the *Letter to Lee* are distinctly rhetorical; in their constant attentiveness to a personal addressee all the humanist defenses are clearly epistolary.

The rhetorical structure of the *Letter to Dorp* is a good deal less casual than that of a standard familiar epistle. More adapts the traditional design of a public defensive oration to the more relaxed etiquette of a

---

[1]On the Renaissance familiar epistle see especially E. Catherine Dunn, "Lipsius and the Art of Letter-Writing," *Studies in the Renaissance, 3* (1956), 145–56: Cecil H. Clough, "The Cult of Antiquity: Letters and Letter Collections," in *Cultural Aspects of the Italian Renaissance: Essays in Honor of P. O. Kristeller* (Manchester and New York, 1976), pp. 33–67; and Marc Fumaroli, "Genèse de l'epistolographie classique: Rhétorique humaniste de la lettre, de Pétrarque à Juste Lipse," *Revue d'histoire littéraire de la France, 78* (1978), 886–905. On the relations between familiar and public epistles in the Renaissance see Witt, especially pp. 8, 14, and 32; and Judith Rice Henderson, "Defining the Genre of the Letter: Juan Luis Vives' *De Conscribendis Epistolis,*" *Renaissance and Reformation,* new series 7 (1983), 90–97, 100–01. For specialized studies of long letter-essays and public epistles see Martin L. Stirewalt, "The Form and Function of the Greek Letter-Essay," in *The Romans Debate,* ed. Karl P. Donfried (Minneapolis, 1977), pp. 177–206; and James J. Fernandes, "The Public Letters of Cicero," *Communication Quarterly, 26/1* (1976), 21–26. Also pertinent and provocative is a recent study of the epistolary novel, Janet G. Altman, *Epistolarity: Approaches to a Form* (Columbus, Ohio, 1982).

personal letter; what appears to be casual digressiveness actually serves a coherent, though complex, rhetorical purpose. If its long salutation and flattering proem are taken as forming a single introductory unit, the *Letter to Dorp* shares a seven-part structural scheme with a large number of frankly rhetorical public defenses, including More's open *Letter to Brixius*. Like them, the *Letter to Dorp* consists of an introduction (*exordium*), a review of the principal facts of the case (*narratio*), an outline of the actual issues at stake and the positive arguments which bear on them (*divisio*), a statement of principal theses and aims (*propositio*), the positive argumentation itself (*confirmatio*), a rebuttal of contrary arguments (*refutatio*), and an elaborate conclusion (*peroratio*).[1] But unlike such traditional defenses, the *Letter to Dorp* is addressed at least technically as a personal letter of friendly advice to a basically sympathetic recipient. Dorp had claimed to be offering Erasmus nothing more than well-meaning advice; More repays him in kind.[2] The avowed purpose of the *Letter to Dorp* is to make Dorp live up to his own professed humanist principles. It purports to be pure admonition, not a formal apology at all;[3] in a letter of this sort, it seems that the author could safely take most of his own general theses for granted and simply dispense with the thankless additional chore of composing a formal rebuttal. What More actually does in the *Letter to Dorp* is to intersperse passages of pure admonition with passages of formal rebuttal, artfully introducing the latter as lengthy asides or digressions.[4] If Dorp wished to confirm his essential agreement and sympathy with Erasmus, he could simply refer these apparent digressions to More's conversational expansiveness;[5] if he had merely been feigning such sympathy when he wrote his own letters of dubiously friendly advice to Erasmus, he

---

[1]For the rhetorical structure of the *Letter to Brixius* see *CW* 3/2, 553–57. In *De oratore* 2.19.79–80 Cicero outlines a six-part rhetorical scheme as a more or less standard one but does so in a way which suggests that two parts he considers as one, namely *divisio* and *propositio*, might well be counted separately. On the distinction between *divisio* and *propositio* see further pseudo-Cicero, *Rhetorica ad Herennium* 1.3.4 and 1.10.17. For the close relation between *salutatio* and *exordium* see Witt, p. 13. This rhetorical analysis of the *Letter to Dorp* is intended as a refinement on the analysis in Kinney, "More's *Letter to Dorp*," pp. 195–96.

[2]See 6/10–11 and note.

[3]See 10/16–24 and 48/11–13 below and cf. the *Letter to Oxford*, 142/13–16, 144/4–6, and 144/24–26. See also Erasmus, *De conscribendis epistolis*, *ASD* 1/2, 489, on the *genus monitorium* of epistles.

[4]For the rhetorical figure of *revocatio* ("recalling oneself to the business at hand") see Quintilian 9.1.42; for examples in the *Letter to Dorp* see 4/15–16, 6/19–20, 12/8, 14/17, 38/5; for an example in the *Letter to Lee*, see 186/25. One effect of excusing apparent digressions in this way is to give an impression of colloquial casualness.

[5]For More's colloquial expansiveness see 122/17–19 and note.

would then have to reckon with a formal rebuttal as well as a similar bounty of dubiously friendly advice. The ambivalence of Dorp's own remarks to Erasmus helps to account for More's disarming admission at the end of the letter that at a number of points he has rather been answering Erasmus' detractors through Dorp than addressing him personally.[1] Dorp himself claimed to be writing as a friend but repeatedly wrote more like an enemy. If he actually wrote as a friend, More's advice should provoke him to answer Erasmus' detractors himself, passing on More's elaborate rebuttals; if he actually wrote as an enemy, More could still answer Erasmus' detractors through Dorp by releasing the letter to the public. By nonchalantly conflating the hortatory and personal *confirmatio* of his letter with the more general arguments of a formal *refutatio* More was able to address a presumably friendly private correspondent and a less friendly public at once.

More begins with a brief introduction (2/6-4/14) in which he assures Dorp of his friendly intentions and explains how Erasmus has given all his friends such a flattering impression of Dorp that his name is as highly esteemed among English men of letters as it is in Louvain. He proceeds with a tactful review of the principal facts of the case (4/15-8/24), concentrating on Dorp's two critical letters addressed to Erasmus and on Erasmus' provisional response to the first. By presenting this review of the facts in the form of a dialogue between More himself and a number of Erasmian strangers he contrives to shift the responsibility for the most incriminating allegations against Dorp onto a nameless third party.

In his outline of the actual issues at stake and of the positive arguments which bear on them (8/25-10/15) More first puts aside as too trivial for extended comment Dorp's attacks on *The Praise of Folly,* poets, grammarians, Erasmus' *Annotations,* and Greek erudition, although each of these arguments will eventually receive a rebuttal; this stratagem of emphasizing a particular topic under pretext of simply dismissing it is the rhetorical figure of *praeteritio* or "bypassing." He then goes on to outline what he here represents as more serious issues, Dorp's intemperate polemical style and his inflammatory distortions of Erasmus' own statements. In his *propositio* (10/16–24) More suggests that he has no intention of defending Erasmus, since he lacks the appropriate skills and since there is no need for a defense in any case; he is writing to warn Dorp against giving his own detractors good reason to see him as envious and arrogant in attacking Erasmus.

More begins the *confirmatio/refutatio* (10/25-122/13) with an elabo-

---

[1]See 124/19–22.

rate figurative apology for frank admonition, which can provide the
same kind of self-insight that a writer could gain by looking on unobserved as his readers respond to his works. As an example of an especially annoying rhetorical flourish More cites Dorp's repeated suggestion that he speaks for all theologians while Erasmus himself
represents mere grammarians. This suggestion provokes More's first
apparent digression, introduced with a "quanquam" ("although" or
"and yet," 12/16-14/16), in which he formally discredits the sharp
opposition between *theologia* and *grammatica* that he simply dismissed
without argument in the preceding paragraph.[1] The same sequence of
admonition and formal rebuttal by way of digression recurs in More's
treatment of Dorp's slighting references to Erasmus' competence as a
dialectician (14/17-16/26). More then (18/1–10) makes a point of recalling himself to the principal business at hand and reiterates the
charges of stylistic intemperateness and inflammatory contextual distortions which he already stressed in the *divisio*. His first example of
inflammatory contextual distortion is a passage in which Dorp insinu-
ates that Erasmus is basically hostile to medieval universities in general
and the whole intellectual establishment. Once again More begins with
advice (18/11-20/18) and continues with formal rebuttal by way of
digression, one of the longest "digressions" in the letter (20/18-38/4).
In his lengthy response to Dorp's inflammatory distortions of Erasmus'
remarks on scholastic theologians (38/5-78/15), More begins with a
lengthy *ad hominem* lesson in rhetorical tact and proceeds with a formal
rebuttal of scholastic theologians' pretensions to omniscience. In his
defense of Erasmus' projected New Testament (78/16-94/24) he never
pretends to be offering Dorp simple friendly advice, but in the
following section, a passionate exhortation to the study of Greek
(96/1-104/12), Dorp's own scholarly welfare appears to be More's main
concern once again. He seems aware that not every Erasmian sympathizer was obliged to think well of Erasmus' intention to challenge
the Vulgate; consequently he answers Dorp's arguments concerning
this one point without stressing Dorp's own dereliction of humanist
principles. In the following section, however, where More mounts an
amusing defense of *The Praise of Folly* and satirical fiction in general
(104/13-122/13), *ad hominem* lessons in rhetorical tact and theoretical
claims for the general value of satire as a spur to self-knowledge rein-

---

[1]For More's use of *quanquam* to introduce a new sentence or new thought see R.
Monsuez, "Le Latin de Thomas More dans Utopia," *Annales publiées par la Faculté des
lettres et sciences humaines de Toulouse*, New Series, 2/1 (1966), *Caliban 3*, 36 (hereafter cited
as "Monsuez"): "Il [sc. More] aime *quanquam* dans le sens de *cependant*."

force one another so thoroughly that it is useless to try to distinguish between friendly admonition and formal rebuttal. "Know thyself" is the burden of the friendly advice; it is also the basis of the formal apology, satirically elaborated, for satire itself. The letter concludes with an elaborate protestation of goodwill and modesty which is also an invitation to Dorp to answer More's letter in a similar spirit and cultivate the same qualities in himself (122/14-126/8); Dorp the humanist can no longer mistake the definitive personal style of Erasmian *humanitas.* Monologue opens the way for a less partial and less partisan dialogue.

The design of the *Letter to Oxford,* a frankly rhetorical public defense, is considerably simpler than that of the *Letter to Dorp.*[1] More begins with a brief introduction (130/5-132/9) representing his confidence in the tolerance of his erudite hearers and his loyalty to his Oxford alma mater as his primary motives for writing a letter of humble instruction and counsel about what he describes as an issue of crucial importance to Oxford, the issue of whether anyone there should be allowed to deride any branch of the liberal arts with impunity. In his *narratio* (132/10-136/6) he describes how the obscurantist opponents of Greek learning in Oxford have harassed Greek scholars at home and in public and have even abused the occasion of a Lenten sermon to rail at the liberal arts generally. He then advances directly to substantive argumentation, in which *ad hominem* reflections on the obscurantists' conduct alternate with defenses of secular learning in general and Greek learning in particular (136/7-146/30). In the *Letter to Oxford,* as in the *Letter to Dorp,* More's avowed aim is merely to advise his own readers and not to persuade them; consequently the actual defense of Erasmian humanism is once again technically supplementary to the proffered advice.[2] In the *Letter to Dorp,* this defense was elaborated in a series of seemingly casual digressions; in the *Letter to Oxford,* it is summarized in a pair of reassuringly practical and conventional arguments purporting to state what is probably already obvious to such prudent

---

[1]Stapleton (sig. d₄) twice refers to the *Letter to Oxford* as an *oratio;* elsewhere (sig. h₅v) he describes it as an *apologia.* For a formal analysis of the letter in terms of the epistolary models established by the medieval *ars dictaminis* see Schoeck, pp. 28–29. Since *ars dictaminis* was itself a derivative of classical rhetoric and since More's letter is not formulaic in the way that most *artes dictaminis* appear to prescribe, I would suggest that the *artes dictaminis* may have exerted only a very limited influence on the structure and phrasing of the *Letter to Oxford.* On the other hand, the *etiquette* of formal epistles addressed to a body of dignified readers appears to have changed very little between the twelfth century and More's day; see Witt, pp. 12–15, on the "rhetoric of harmony."

[2]See 142/13–15, 144/4–8, and 144/24–31.

observers as the Oxford vice-regent and Masters' Guild (138/8-140/20, 142/13-146/30). More's ceremonial reluctance to avow his own defensive arguments as such does very little to disguise the straightforwardly defensive character of the tract as a whole; the decorum of a formal persuasive epistle addressed to a body of especially dignified readers differs scarcely at all from the decorum of a formal persuasive oration delivered to an especially dignified audience.[1] Indeed, by laying so much stress on his own efforts not to seem tactless and on the obscurantists' stolid indifference to tact he even seems to invite us to interpret his letter as a decorous counterpart to the highly indecorous Lenten address of the obscurantists' ringleader.[2] More concludes with a promise to remember the generous attentiveness of the Oxford authorities and with a prayer that God will see fit to grant Oxford "perpetual increase of all honest learning and virtue" (148/1–15).

In the *Letter to Lee* More avoids the conspicuous rhetorical framework employed in the rest of the humanist defenses. Lee had charged More with partisanship and Erasmus with mystification through rhetoric;[3] in the *Letter to Lee* More endeavors to parry both charges by cultivating a style of austere objectivity and by representing the rhetorical structure of his own letter as strictly dependent on that of the two letters to which it responds. Though he answers Lee's claims in a slightly different order from the one in which they were originally presented, he can and does plead that the seeming confusion in Lee's own pronouncements really leaves him no choice but to do so.[4]

The letter begins with a perfunctory salutation and with virtually no introduction at all.[5] More plunges directly *in medias res,* summarizing the contents of Lee's earlier letter (152/6-154/27). In this letter Lee claimed that More could not possibly condemn his annotations on Erasmus' New Testament before even reading them unless he wished to seem shamefully biased and disloyal to Lee. He went on to lay all of the blame for the quarrel on Erasmus. Finally, he announced his intention of sending his manuscript volume of annotations to Bishop

---

[1] See Witt, pp. 8, 14, and 32; and Erasmus, *De conscribendis epistolis, ASD* I/2, 224–25.

[2] For More's insistence on the obscurantists' *inepta oratio* see 132/29-134/1, 134/6–7, 136/4–6, 138/19-20, 140/21, and 144/7.

[3] See 152/6–23 and the note on 170/24–25.

[4] See 154/28–30 and 158/1–3.

[5] In the only vestige of a conventional *exordium* in the *Letter to Lee* More pointedly praises not Lee himself but his brother Galfridus or Wilfred, an Erasmian sympathizer; see 152/3–4 and note. In *De conscribendis epistolis, ASD* I/2, 323, Erasmus recommends abrupt beginnings to create an effect of colloquial immediacy.

John Fisher and letting him arbitrate the dispute. More then summarizes the contents of Lee's second letter, which suggested that Lee must have "gone through a sudden and complete transformation" (154/28-156/26). In this letter Lee stated that the time had come for More to demonstrate his own fairness and impartiality. He went on to assert that, despite all his own conciliatory efforts, Erasmus had suddenly and wantonly libeled him by including an unflattering sketch of an unnamed detractor in his *Apology against Latomus*. Lee then declared that because of this unflattering sketch he felt he had no choice but to vindicate himself by publishing his annotations, a plan he felt that no fair or sensible judge could oppose. Finally he reiterated his urgent petition to More to stand firm in his friendship.

More begins his response with a glance at Lee's willfulness in scorning all cautious advice and then takes up Lee's indirect charge of disloyalty (156/17-170/20). Even though he has read very few of Lee's annotations he would rather seem unfair to Lee than prove grossly unfair to the numerous learned readers who are sure that Erasmus' New Testament is valuable and basically sound despite Lee's claims that it is pernicious and useless; there is a limit to how far respect for one friend should countervail the opinion of everyone else. Next he takes up the claim that Erasmus' ingratitude and arrogance are exclusively to blame for the quarrel and suggests that on balance Lee seems a good deal more inclined than Erasmus himself to claim credit and personal prestige which are not actually due to him (170/21-178/4). He then praises Lee's earlier intention of letting Fisher arbitrate the dispute and regrets Lee's abrupt change of heart; can he blame the change solely on Erasmus (178/5-180/9)? More then proceeds directly to Lee's ill-supported contention that Erasmus had libeled him: how could he possibly take offense at Erasmus' anonymous sketch while denying that it actually bore any resemblance at all to him (180/10-182/14)? In his answer to Lee's claim that he has no choice but to vindicate himself by publishing his volume, More argues that even if Lee actually needed to vindicate himself he could not hope to do so by publishing a volume of notes that he supposed Erasmus had already seen (182/15-192/10). Finally, in response to Lee's urgent request to stand firm in his friendship More states that the friendliest gesture of which he is capable for Lee's benefit is an offering of heartfelt advice to "dispense with these odious reproaches" and to find some other way of making a name for himself (192/11-194/31). The numerous obvious distortions and inconsistencies in Lee's version of the facts of the quarrel make it easy for More to repudiate his project as a whole even as he holds open the possibility that at a number of points Lee may be able to suggest real improvements on Erasmus' edition of the New Testament (194/6–14). In the face of such manifest self-contradiction, a purely *ad hominem* rejoinder can reasonably be couched in a style of austere objectivity; it does not take a partisan reader to recognize fundamental deficiences in Lee's rationale for attacking Erasmus.

The design of the *Letter to a Monk* is essentially that of an elaborate and frankly rhetorical public defense. In the *Letter to Lee* More was forced to restrain his own rhetoric; in its lengthy companion piece he gives free rein to his anger with Lee's pharisaical supporters in an impetuous but lucid Erasmian rhetoric which makes the *Letter to a Monk* one of his most powerful humanist compositions.[1] The letter begins with a curt, formulaic *salutatio/exordium* (198/8–9) and a sarcastically worded *narratio* in which More sums up the rhetorical excesses of the monk's open letter to him as a primary justification for his outraged response (198/8-200/2).[2] In a figurative and sarcastic *propositio/divisio* he suggests that since the monk has expressed such immoderate concern for More's spiritual welfare, it would he highly ungracious for More to look on without comment as the monk blithely imperils his own soul; consequently he plans to begin by confirming that the values and outlooks he happens to share with Erasmus are no danger at all to his spiritual welfare and then to reveal for the monk how his arrogant certainties threaten to lead to disaster (200/3–13). In a subsidiary rhetorical division (200/14–28) More introduces the principal themes of the long *confirmatio* (202/1-262/31): there is no danger in believing that Erasmus has translated many New Testament passages better than the old translator; there is no danger in reading Erasmian works, which the most learned and pious people are virtually unanimous in praising; there is little danger of absorbing dangerous doctrines from the works of a man who never states anything definitively and who acknowledges himself to be fallible; even if Erasmus did claim to be making definitive statements, they could pose little danger for anyone who knew how to use his own judgment as More does. More first develops a sharp contrast between the sort of

---

[1] For the close relation between the *Letter to Lee* and the *Letter to a Monk* see pp. xliii–xliv; for More's charge of pharisaism see especially 292/7–10. More's lucid Erasmian rhetoric in this letter is well suited to the limited capacities of its main addressee: see 218/2–5. Though More suggests at 262/24–28 that virtually all men of learning take the style of Erasmus as their primary model, he also has very high praise for the distinctly unErasmian styles of Budé (Rogers, pp. 124–25) and the French historian Paulus Aemilius (*CW* 3/2, 620/3–4, and Commentary).

[2] Erasmus uses the same salutation in Allen, 3, 605.

people who have helped the monk elaborate his outrageous accusations and the sort of people who vouch for Erasmus' good character
(202/1-212/2). He then vindicates Erasmian scholarship against the
monk's charges of "blatant impiety," showing that Erasmus consistently follows the precedent of the fathers even in his repeated
suggestion that not even the fathers were infallible (212/3-224/27).
Next he mounts a defense of Erasmus' New Testament, showing that
the Vulgate need not be regarded as wholly authoritative and that
Erasmus' departures from the Vulgate are generally well founded
(226/1-258/7). Finally he sets out to defend some of Erasmus' most
problematic and vulnerable works, his satirical writings and his correspondence with Luther; at this point More implicitly appeals to the
thesis that the judicious reader will always be able to discern a constructive intention in the works of Erasmus even when they appear most
subversive (258/8-262/31). By withholding the defense of Erasmus'
New Testament and his other most vulnerable works until he has
completely refuted the monk's most preposterous charges, More is
able to make his apology appear more consistently cogent than it actually is; from the quite uncontroversial thesis that Erasmus' distinguished supporters in England outnumber his enemies More gradually proceeds to the much more debatable thesis that there is more
genuine piety in Erasmian satire than in some of the monk's favorite
ceremonies (258/21-260/6).

More's *ad hominem* remarks near the end of the *confirmatio* on the
proper employment of monastic leisure lead naturally into the long
refutatio (264/1-304/10), in which More challenges the monk's pharisaical misunderstanding of the monastic vocation in general. More
traces most of the monk's insupportable actions to partisan pride and
self-righteousness and introduces three deliberately shocking accounts of religious abuses in order to show where the monk's extreme
form of complacency is likely to lead. In a long laudatory excursus
(294/11-300/4) More turns on its head the monk's charge that Erasmus is merely a vagabond: Erasmus does more for the Christian
religion in a month of wandering than the monk and his peers generally do in a year of sitting still.[1] More concludes by explaining his

---

[1] More himself represents this long laudatory passage as an excursus, albeit a functional one, at 294/11-14. The preceding paragraph of more temperate praise (292/11-
294/10) is a modest rebuttal of the monk's pharisaical insults reported at 292/6. Cicero
(*De oratore* 2.19.80) notes that some rhetoricians actually prescribe that a well-made
oration should include a digression near the end of the *refutatio* and before the conclusion; cf. Cicero, *De inventione* 1.51.97.

motives for publishing the letter and by mocking the monk's foolish closing remark that he would be perfectly willing to make up with Erasmus if he would correct his "minor mistakes" (304/11-310/8). Since the monk himself seems to admit that he trumped up his most serious charges out of nothing, he should let them recede into nothing again, concentrate on his proper vocation of monastic repose, and leave Christian philology and the other more onerous labors of learned devotion to scholar-ascetics like Erasmus.

The style of More's humanist defenses is remarkably varied to accommodate particular readers and particular formal or thematic demands.[1] In addressing the "most eminent scholar," Martin Dorp, More begins with a dignified but relaxed periodic construction four units in length:[2]

> Si mihi ad te uenire tam esset liberum,
> quam uehementer mi Dorpi cupio,
> tum ista, quae nunc parum commode committo litteris,
>   commodius tecum coram ipse tractarem,
> tum (quo nihil mihi iucundius potuisset accidere)
>   teipso interea praesens praesente perfruerer . . . (2/6–10)

---

[1] Scattered comments on the style of the humanist defenses may be found in the works cited on p. xvii, n. 2. For more detailed discussions of More's style in his other Latin writings see CW 14, 754–63, 769–74, and the works cited in CW 14, 754, n. 2. Also pertinent are D. F. S. Thomson, "The Latinity of Erasmus," in Erasmus, ed. T. A. Dorey (London, 1970; hereafter cited as "Thomson"), pp. 115–37; and Alain Jolidon, "Thomas More et Erasme traducteurs du 'Tyrannicide' (1506)," in Thomas More 1477–1977 Travaux de l'Institut Interuniversitaire pour l'étude de la Renaissance et de l'Humanisme 6 (Brussels, 1980), pp. 39–69.

[2] For a particularly lucid discussion of periodic composition see Aldo Scaglione, The Classical Theory of Composition from Its Origins to the Present: A Historical Survey (Chapel Hill, 1972), pp. 27–37. The following principles are especially pertinent to my own discussion of More's periods: periodicity is largely a matter of balance and suspense; to enhance the rhetorical suspense, the last units of a period will often be longer than the first ones; in the interests of balance as well as suspense, periods are generally composed of four units, most often a protasis and an apodosis consisting of two units each (certain cumulative periods are notable exceptions to this general rule); the main units or cola of a period may be longer or shorter than a single full clause; to avoid tedium, the lengthiest periods are frequently offset with much shorter sentences. The first period in the Letter to Dorp creates little rhetorical suspense but preserves a high level of balance; in its way it is clearly periodic. The following syllable-counts for More's first seven periods, resolved into four units each, show a general conformity with the usual practice of lengthening the last units of a period and of offsetting long periods with shorter sentences: 14, 11, 29, 34 (2/6–10); 14, 18, 11, 13 (2/10–12); 19, 18, 42, 33 (2/13–18); 11, 13, 15, 21 (2/18–21); 15, 8, 9, 16 (2/21–23); 13, 14, 26, 13 (2/23–26); 14, 34, 11, 16 (2/26-4/3).

The two massive units which finish the period together with the cohesive force of the pairings "tam" / "quam," "tum" / "tum," "parum commode" / "commodius," and "praesens" / "praesente," give the period a palpable character of roundness and fullness in spite of the incomplete closure of the actual sense. More proceeds with another relaxed four-unit period, somewhat shorter than the first, in which the principal theme of the introduction is insinuated through a pun linking Erasmus' own *praenomen* ("Desiderius," "subject of longing") with the generative essence of unselfish friendship:

> cuius uidendi, cognoscendi, complectendique,
> mirum pectori meo desyderium inseuit Erasmus,
> utriusque nostrum amantissimus,
> tum utrique, uti spero, ex aequo charus. (2/10–12)

The tricolon crescendo of the first unit is answered by the sequence "desyderium . . . amantissimus . . . charus" in which More sets out to complete the unfolding of the meanings implicit in the Latinized Greek name "Erasm[i]us" ("Dear one").[1] More continues to elaborate complementary aspects of the Erasmian genius for friendship in the following period, where the rhyming construction "suauissimorumque morum" further complements the evocative sequence of near-cognates "gratia charissimus" to suggest that the same sort of affinity which links friendly intentions and winning behavior links "Morus" or More and "Erasm[i]us" ("Dear one," "Gratus," or "Charus"):

> Nihil est enim quod ille maiore cum uoluptate faciat,
> quam ut apud presentes amicos suos, absentes predicet,
> Siquidem quum sit ipse plurimis,
>   idque in diuersis orbis terrarum partibus,
>   doctrinae, suauissimorumque morum gratia charissimus,
> conatur sedulo
>   ut quo in unum se, omnes animo sunt,
>   eodem etiam inter se omnes conglutinet. (2/13–18)

---

[1] More directly alludes to the Greek meaning of Erasmus in a letter of October 7, 1517 ("Erasme mi ἐρασμιότατε," Allen, *3*, 104, line 13). Elsewhere he prefers Latin near-equivalents of this Greek epithet, especially "charissimus" and "dulcissimus." For a wide range of puns based on More's name and those of his friends see Germain Marc'hadour, "A Name for All Seasons," in *Essential Articles*, pp. 539–62; for Erasmus in particular, see Marjorie O'Rourke Boyle's fine article, "The Eponyms of 'Desiderius Erasmus,'" *Renaissance Quarterly, 30* (1977), 12–23.

More offsets this long period with a pair of considerably shorter ones. In the first, an elaborate pattern of parallelism and antithesis combines with an etymological figure of varied repetition (three different derivatives of *amor*) to give unity and point to the whole:

> Non cessat ergo apud uniuersos,
> singulatim amicorum quemque referre,
> et quo in cunctorum amicitias insinuet,
> omnes cuiusque dotes, quibus amari promereatur, exponere.
> (2/18–21)

In the second of these shorter periods, More exploits a tricolon crescendo enhanced by anaphora to lay special stress on Erasmus' obliging behavior toward Dorp:

> Quod quum ille assidue faciat de omnibus,
> de nullo tamen saepius,
> de nullo faciat effusius,
> de nullo quam de te charissime Dorpi libentius. . . . (2/21–23)

More concludes his ceremonial opening paragraph with two more relaxed periods of moderate length held together somewhat less obtrusively by the pairings "ita" / "ut," "Anglia" / "Louaniensibus," "nemo" / "cui non," "celebreque" / "celeberrimum," "ipsis" / "quibus," "ita" / "ut," "depinxit" / "eluxit," "iam olim" / "postea," "pulcherrimam" / "elegantissimis," and "eandem" / "quae":

> quem ita dudum celebrauit in Anglia,
> ut nemo sit ibi litteratorum uirorum,
> cui non Dorpij nomen aeque notum celebreque sit,
>   atque Louaniensibus ipsis,
> quibus est, (ut esse debet) celeberrimum.
> Seorsum uero ita te depinxit apud me,
> ut iam olim pulcherrimam animi tui ymaginem,
>   planeque eandem apud animum meum praesumpserim,
> quae mihi postea quam huc appuli,
> ex elegantissimis opusculis tuis eluxit. (2/23-4/3)

More's attempt to do justice stylistically to Dorp's erudition and public prestige while preserving at least some of the relaxed manner usually displayed in familiar epistles makes the first paragraph of the *Letter to Dorp* an impressive experiment in varied periodic construction.

Even though More habitually exploits periodic effects of rhetorical balance and suspense in the *Letter to Dorp,* there are some passages in which he deliberately cultivates an opposite effect of abrupt or impetuous unevenness, often called *inconcinnitas*. In his narrative passages he often abandons the period for disjointed clauses of curt exposition;[1] in a number of playful or satirical passages he exploits an effect of vernacular spontaneity;[2] and in two passages reporting characteristic remarks by unlearned scholastics he resorts to the crudest kind of parataxis or coordinate sentence structure with an obvious parodic intent.[3] At one point he employs nonperiodic style very ingeniously as a means of dramatic characterization: Dorp's anonymous accuser, whose comments are cited verbatim in More's long *narratio*, bursts out with a series of charges which he is at first too irate to present one by one as the elements of a disciplined period; once he has vented the worst of his anger, he is able to summarize his thoughts in a period almost as well organized as any of More's own.[4] Through the vividness or *enargeia* of this dramatic characterization More compels Dorp to "see" for himself how most readers respond to his letters (12/8–10). More relies on a fairly complex periodic style throughout most of the *Letter to Dorp;* nonetheless, he occasionally resorts to a number of quite different styles in a skillful endeavor to offset the cumbersome gravity of periodic composition in general.

The *Letter to Oxford* is more formal than the *Letter to Dorp;* it is also more purely periodic in style. It begins with a very majestic but ponderous period ten clauses in length:

> Dubitaui nonnihil,
>   Eruditissimi viri,
>   liceretne mihi
>   de quibus nunc decreui rebus
>   ad vos scribere:

---

[1]See especially 4/15-6/4, 50/19–28, and 66/24-68/11. Classical rhetoricians frequently prescribe a curt and concise style for the narrative sections of speeches; see pseudo-Cicero, *Rhetorica ad Herennium* 1.9.14; Cicero, *De inventione* 1.20.28; and Quintilian 4.2.31. In *De oratore* 2.19.80–83 and 2.80.326, Cicero insists that brevity for its own sake is no more desirable in narrative passages than in any other part of a speech.

[2]See especially 28/9-32/25, 110/8–19, and 122/5–13.

[3]See 28/2–6 and 68/13–16.

[4]See 6/12-8/3. In the accuser's single fairly well-organized periodic statement (6/29-8/3), introduced by the clause "Qua in re uide quam sincere faciat," the four major units are "primum . . . accusat," "eum . . . simulat," "Deinde . . . audiat," and "quae . . . omnes." The structure of this rather convoluted period bears especially close comparison with that of the anxious and overwrought period in which More states how he had to subdue his own impulse to criticize Dorp's letters before the anonymous accuser (6/5–11).

nec id usque adeo stili respectu mei dubitaui
    (quanquam eum ipsum quoque pudet in coetum prodire viro-
                         rum tam eloquentium),
quam ne videri nimium superbus possim,
    si homuncio non magna prudentia,
    minore rerum vsu,
    doctrina vero minus quam mediocri,
      tantum mihi arrogem,
        vt ulla in re, sed praecipue literaria,
          consilium dare vnus audeam vobis omnibus,
quorum quiuis ob eximiam eruditionem prudentiamque sit
                   idoneus,
qui multis hominum milibus consulat. (130/5–14)

More reinforces the connection between the first and second units of
the period through chiastic repetition ("Dubitaui nonnihil" / "nec
id . . . dubitaui"), using the first half of the period to emphasize his
purely subjective reservations about drafting the letter and then stressing more serious, objective constraints in the second half. He enhances
rhetorical suspense in a variety of ways. The verbs "liceret" and "decreui" share the single verbal object "scribere," which is deferred to the
end of the first unit of the period through a combination of zeugma
and hyperbaton. In the second unit the clause answering "nec id usque
adeo . . . dubitaui" is delayed by a lengthy parenthesis, while the verb
governed by "si" in the third unit is postponed for an intricate tricolon
and the related phrase "ulla in re, sed praecipue litteraria." Even in the
fourth unit the crucial verb "consulat" is initially displaced by an almost
superfluous verbal construction ("sit idoneus qui . . .").[1] The whole
period is centered on the polar distinction established in the first unit
between More's private *mihi* and the *vos* of the Oxford authorities.
There is no room in this introduction for the exuberant etymological
figures deployed in the opening paragraph of the *Letter to Dorp;* here
the scrupulously dignified proem sets the tone for the letter as a whole.
Though More somewhat relaxes his style in the narrative section of the
letter, periodic complexity tends to dominate throughout.[2] It is a re-

---

    [1]More could have shortened the construction "sit idoneus qui . . . consulat" to some-
thing like "posset . . . sapienter consulere."
    [2]The other periods of the introductory paragraph are also fairly conventional exam-
ples consisting of four units each. I distinguish the units as follows: "Verum . . . deterruit," "tantum . . . recreauit," "cum . . . audire," "ita . . . consilium"
(130/14–19);   "Sed . . . estis,"   "etiamsi . . . videatur,"   "sed . . . consilium,"
"quod . . . pectore" (130/19–24); "Postremo . . . considero," "quod . . . retuli," "vide-

markable tribute to More's mastery of tonal decorum that despite the insistently periodic sentence structure and the highly conventional humanist themes of the *Letter to Oxford,* few readers have ever dismissed it as simply a mass of rhetorical clichés; like a good Elizabethan sonnet, it is a quite unabashed tour de force in enlivening a standard rhetorical form which has already lost much of its freshness.[1]

The style of the *Letter to Lee,* like the form, is conspicuously different from that of More's other humanistic defenses.[2] More appears to avoid uniform periodic sentence structure in the *Letter to Lee* for the same reason that he avoids using a standard rhetorical famework for the letter as a whole: since Lee links Erasmian argumentation with mystification through rhetoric, More simply shuns most conventional rhetorical ploys in disposing of Lee's rationale for attacking Erasmus. One could also explain the peculiar unevenness of the *Letter to Lee* more prosaically as a natural characteristic of a rushed composition in which a deliberate effort to write with the utmost concision conflicts with an urge to forestall every possible objection or cavil by providing a detailed analysis of the pertinent facts; at one point, More himself actually seems to invite us to interpret the letter in this way.[3] Nonetheless it seems clear that the *Letter to Lee* is a good deal less artless than More makes it out to be. On the level of local rhetorical effects it is possibly even more complex than the *Letter to Dorp;* it is full of elaborate wordplay and startling experiments with word order.[4] More's own remarks on the specific character of the *Letter to Lee* are completely consistent with the conscious cultivation of what merely purports to be an unpremeditated deliberative style. For a particular rhetorical purpose,

---

tur . . . exigere," "ne . . . censeam" (130/24–29); "Quamobrem . . . dicerent," "contraque . . . posse," "malui . . . praedicarent," "quam . . . sentiam" (130/29-132/6); "maxime . . . tanta," "quanta . . . obtigit," "quae . . . vultis)," "exactius . . . animaduertenda" (132/6–9). Though not all of the sentences in the rest of the letter conform to this four-unit pattern, virtually all of them clearly exploit periodic effects of rhetorical balance and suspense.

[1]More himself seems to have taken considerable pride in the *Letter to Oxford* as a study in tactful persuasion; see p. xxxi, above.

[2]Even More's English writings are more evenly periodic in style than the *Letter to Lee.* The style of More's two shorter letters responding to the actual publication of Lec's *Annotationes* is certainly closer to the style of the other humanist defenses than to the style of the *Letter to Lee;* see Rogers, pp. 206–12.

[3]See 158/1–6.

[4]For More's wordplay see 158/4–5, 158/14–15, 160/18, 162/21–22, 164/23–24, 166/5, 166/6–7, 168/8, 172/23–24, 172/28–29, 174/22–24, 176/12, 176/33, 186/18, 188/22, 190/21–22, 190/23, 192/22, 192/23–24, 192/26–27, and 194/29–30. For particularly striking deviations from predictable word order see 152/3–4, 160/2–5, 168/12–17, 172/17–19, 176/27–30 and 190/18–19.

More resorts to the same sort of idiosyncratic and uneven sentence structure which later distinguishes the "loose style" of professedly anti-rhetorical writers like Browne and Montaigne.[1]

More begins the *Letter to Lee* with a summary account of the two letters to which he is responding. One effect of More's avowedly selective condensation is to bring Lee's incompatible statements and tenuous conjectural arguments into sharper relief while preserving enough of his pompous, long-winded phrasing to show that his rhetoric is at least as extravagant as anyone else's.[2] In the following sentence, More exploits an unwieldy periodic arrangement to make Lee's incompatible statements about his attachment to More appear even less convincing than they would if each one were read separately:

Quam rem si exploratam haberes,
    aut tecum libere (si quidem posset animus ferre) decerneres,
        vt ne flocci quidem talem amicum faceres,
    aut (si tibi imperare id non posses),
        quippe qui nihil aeque dolenter atque ingratitudinem feras,
            habenas dolori permitteres,
    vt cui ipsa mors quam tanti amici iactura foret optatior,
        quem non vulgariter amaueris,
            ac pro virili semper in astra laudibus vexeris. . . . (152/11–18)

The two parenthetical clauses are intrusive, pretentious embellishments which do nothing to enhance our respect for Lee's grief at More's putative treachery. In the second unit of the period, Lee seems to suggest that his continued esteem for More is completely contingent on how he reacts to Lee's feud with Erasmus; in the third unit he hints that at the slightest provocation he is ready to charge More with ingratitude; in the fourth unit he insists that he has always loved More with an uncommon fervor and praised him with the utmost devotion. The insinuations comprised in the previous units belie both the as-

---

[1] On the "loose style" and the "trailing period" of anti-Ciceronian writers like Browne and Montaigne see especially Morris W. Croll, "The Baroque Style in Prose," in *Studies in English Philology in Honor of Frederick Klaeber,* ed. Kemp Malone and Martin B. Ruud (Minneapolis, 1929), pp. 427–56. One of the most striking characteristics of the "loose style" is the avoidance or highly unorthodox use of subordinating connectives; this unorthodox usage is also characteristic of More's sprawling sentences in the *Letter to Lee.* For More's usual care in employing connectives of this sort see *CW 14,* 758. On More's "baroque" syntax see *CW 14,* 769–71.

[2] For More's acknowledgment that he is condensing selectively see 152/6. For Lee's disavowal of rhetorical embellishment see 154/20–23. More directly accuses Lee of "playing the orator" at 170/23-172/2.

surances comprised in the last unit; More's own method of "condensing" Lee's rhetoric shows it to be totally empty. Turning the tables on
Lee, More represents him as merely a bombastic orator with nothing of
any importance to say, whereas More casts himself as a cautious, impartial observer who may not be able to say all that needs to be said. His
meticulous deliberative analysis is appropriately couched in the "loose
style," whereas Lee's rash assertions are typically summed up in gran-
diose periods.

The conspicuous *inconcinnitas* or unevenness of More's style in the
Letter to Lee is produced by a frequent avoidance of neat parallelism and
by the discursive expansion of particular units of a sentence in ways
which suggest that the writer is still in the process of shaping his
thoughts. Such expansion may occur either in the middle or at the end
of what might have been written more tersely as a single well-organized
period; either type of expansion suggests that the writer is less interested in cultivating rhetorical balance and suspense than in treating
every nuance of a particular problem exhaustively as it occurs to him.
One good example of the "trailing period" which is characteristic of
works in the "loose style" occurs in the first paragraph of More's actual
response to Lee's arguments:

> Verum istud ausim affirmare maxime,
> si eos ante consulere maluisses quam ipse constituere,
> perquam hercle paucos repperisses hic,
> qui non annotationes istas tibi abdendas potius perpetuo
>   quam aedendas esse vnquam censuissent,
> quos ipsos tamen deierare liquet
>   (quod te quoque Lee certe credo credere)
>   non minus ex animo vereque esse tuos,
> aliquot item
>   (quod spero)
>   non minus sapientes,
> qui te ab isto satagant proposito retinere,
> quam sit istorum quisquis est isthic prudentissimus,
>   qui te in aeditionem istam tam importune protrudant atque
>   praecipitant. (158/12–21)

What begins as an afterthought ("quos ipsos tamen") lengthens into a
complex assertion sufficient to form a new period. Yet the syntax
remains problematic even if we begin a new period after "censuissent"
with a phrase like "Et tamen eos ipsos." More introduces the phrase
"aliquot item . . . non minus sapientes" ("several of them . . . no less
wise") to preclude one objection allowed by the preceding clause, in

which More sets out to assert that all those who want Lee to suppress his
volume are no less devoted to his interests than anyone who encour-
ages him to publish it; if this clause stood alone, Lee could always retort
that devoted advisers are not always wise ones. Thus the phrase "aliquot item . . . non minus sapientes" considerably enriches the deliberative content of the passage, but at the expense of rhetorical balance:
the Latin syntax of this phrase is not at all parallel to that of the clause
with which More juxtaposes it. The two parenthetical clauses in this
passage permit further refinement of deliberative content even as they
impede any steady progressive development of rhetorical suspense.
Though the *Letter to Lee* includes more than a few unobtrusive conventional periods, it also includes many "trailing periods" a good deal
more diffuse and expansive than the one just discussed.[1] When contrasted with the elegant periodic complexity of the *Letter to Oxford,* the
imposing deliberative complexity of More's nonperiodic style in the
Letter to Lee shows a level of functional versatility in his Latin style which
few humanists could rival.[2]

   The *Letter to a Monk* is composed in a fluent and generally lucid
Erasmian style which derives its coherence primarily from simple parallelism and sententious antithesis. Though the letter intermittently
exploits virtually all the stylistic effects emphasized in the earlier humanist defenses, it generally relies on a succession of much more colloquial forms of expression, namely simple paratactic assertions or rhetorical questions, antithetical periods two to four units in length, and
rather informal cumulative periods comprising a whole range of
loosely related remarks on a single broad theme. More begins with a
four-unit scheme which appears to be purely paratactic:

> Perlatae sunt ad me litterae tuae,
> frater in Christo charissime,
> longae quidem illae,
> et mira quaedam signa prae se ferentes amoris erga me tui.
>
> (198/8–10)

---

[1]For other "trailing periods" see 160/8–24, 160/27-162/12, 164/20-166/10,
166/11-168/4, 168/11–20, 170/12–20, 172/2–19, 176/10–32, 184/17–23, 184/26-186/7,
186/15–24, 188/17-190/8, 190/9–25, 192/1–10, and 192/11–24. Vaguely similar rhetorical effects are produced by the spontaneous digressiveness of the unnamed accuser in
the *Letter to Dorp* and by Hythloday's seemingly interminable deliberative periods in
Utopia; see 6/12-8/3 below and *CW 4,* 86/22–90/22 and 90/22–96/31.
[2]More's best-known experiment in nonperiodic or at any rate non-Ciceronian style is
the *Historia Richardi Tertii* (reprinted on pp. 314–484, below), a fairly free imitation of
Sallust.

Though the third and fourth units both technically modify "litterae" in the first unit, the fourth unit also constitutes an ironic gloss on the epithet "charissime" of the second unit, while the long first and fourth units balance each other chiastically. The introduction continues with a three-unit rhetorical question in which the second and third units balance the emphatic "vehementior" of the first:

> Quis enim possit affectus esse vehementior,
> quam qui te tam impense reddit de mea salute sollicitum,
> vt etiam tuta pertimescas? (198/10–13)

More proceeds with a stilted antithetical period in which he appears to be parodying the monk's own preciosity:

> Times enim ne sic Erasmum diligam,
> vt eius contagio corrumpar,
> ne sic hominis adamem litteras,
> vt noua eius peregrinaque doctrina
>   (sic enim scribis)
>   inficiar. (198/13–15)

He then includes a more intricate period in which a colloquial freedom of word order is used to disguise an elaborate tricolon crescendo:

> Quod ne accidat,
> postquam aliquot paginis in hominis et eruditionem et mores
>   totis (quod aiunt) habenis inuectus es,
> oras tandem
>   atque obsecras perquam sancte
>   ac per ipsam dei misericordiam tantum non adiuras
> vt diligenter ab illo caueam. (198/15–19)

After three sentences of curt narrative parataxis and another antithetical period, More introduces the following exuberant *propositio:*

> Quamobrem,
>   nisi tam grati erga me animi gratia,
>   gratias immensas agerem,
> merito viderer ingratus,
> ingratior adhuc futurus,
> si posteaquam tu me gradientem videns in planicie,
>   feruido quopiam amoris aestu,
>   pertimuisti ne caderem,
>   ego te per praecipitia currentem intrepidus ac securus
>   aspiciam,
>   neque ad te clamitem,

vt tibi caute prospicias,
    sensimque inde ac circumspecte referas pedem,
        vnde sit periculum ne corruas. (200/3–9)

What begins as a sententious antithetical period contrasting two types
of ingratitude expands into a cumulative period emphasizing the
shocking completeness of the monk's self-deception. The dense and
emphatic construction "ego te per praecipitia currentem intrepidus ac
securus aspiciam" confirms and completes the transition begun by the
metaphors of the fourth unit from the theme of ingratitude to the
more central theme of the monk's perilous self-assurance. The sober-
ing sarcasm of the last sub-units offsets the more frivolous sarcasm of
the opening wordplay and suggests that this is one familiar letter in
which the usual polite formulas of friendly approval and deference
would be quite out of place. In this way More's colloquial cumulative
period forestalls the reproach of ingratitude a good deal more effectively than the well-balanced antithetical period which he seemed to be
planning at the outset; it also performs the same function as any routine *propositio* without seeming punctilious or perfunctory. In a similar
way he disguises the schematic character of his terse *divisio:*

Itaque primo collustrabo locum,
    in quo versor ipse,
in quo quum tuta omnia docuero,
tum denique commonstrabo tibi,
arcem istam tuam,
    e qua Erasmum velut e sublimi tutoque despicis,
        periculose nutare. (200/9–13)

While the *Letter to Lee* stresses deliberative thoroughness at the expense
of elaborate periodic effects, the *Letter to a Monk* shortens and varies the
period colloquially to create an effect of sententious incisiveness. It is as
if More were writing the *Letter to a Monk* to spell out more distinctly and
forcefully the conclusions he reached so painstakingly in the *Letter to
Lee.*

    Although More's periodic sentence structure in some of the human-
ist defenses can reasonably be called Ciceronian, his eclectic, adventurous diction and syntax cannot.[1] In his diction and syntax he proves

---

[1]For "Ciceronian" hypotaxis and periodic balance as typical features of More's Latin
style in *De tristitia Christi*, the Lucianic translations, and *Utopia* see CW *14*, 755 and 758,
and Thomson, pp. 117–118. For a brief discussion linking More's style in *Utopia* to the
"anti-Ciceronianism" of the late-sixteenth-century Latinist Justus Lipsius see Monsuez,
p. 77. There is actually no contradiction between these two accounts of More's style:
More is generally Ciceronian in his use of rhetorical periods but not at all Ciceronian in

to be staunchly Erasmian; the emphatic application of the occasional rare word or neologism, the proverbial use of allusions, colloquial turns of expression, and technical formulae, and the casual employment of loose and elliptical syntax are as characteristic of More as they are of Erasmus. Indeed, though both More and Erasmus exhibit some taste for unclassical diminutives and other rare words and late coinages, More's taste for emphatic odd words generally seems more developed than that of Erasmus.[1] Like Erasmus, More uses proverbial expressions to anchor his arguments in common experience and to stress that all specialized discourse owes its authority if not its validity to its common acceptance as a useful extension and complement of everyday discourse.[2] He generally avoids any allusion which is merely orna-

---

his choice of words and his somewhat irregular syntax. More's different styles in the humanist defenses can be treated as subtle variations on the *proverbiale dicendi genus* popularized by Erasmus and condemned by the strict Ciceronian, Dolet; see Kinney, "Erasmus' *Adagia*," p. 173, n. 6. Although More has high praise for Erasmian lucidity, he also esteems the more challenging style of the French humanist Budé; see p. c, n. 1, above.

[1] For emphatic diminutives, generally contemptuous, see 12/12, 28/13, 134/8–9, 146/11, 190/21, 224/19, 270/11–12, 278/5–6, 280/20, 282/10, 282/13, 306/20, and notes. This list does not include diminutives well-attested in classical authors. More's use of diminutives is especially frequent in the *Letter to a Monk*. For Erasmus' use of diminutives see note on 224/19 and Thomson, pp. 125–126. For other emphatic odd words in the humanist defenses see 8/19–20, 42/12, 58/17, 60/27, 68/13, 82/23, 102/20–24, 116/25, 122/15, 154/7, 164/13–14, 164/25, 166/8, 170/26, 186/11, 208/23, 210/16–17, 224/13, 230/3, 264/20, 272/27, 296/13, 298/28, 308/9, 308/15, and notes. More consistently avoids such expressions in the *Letter to Oxford* (for one exception see 134/11, "politiem," where "politionem" is what we expect). Two other classes of neologisms deserve mention here, namely those which More uses in their simple technical senses and those which he invokes chiefly to expose the pretensions of the people who normally use them. For the former class of neologisms see 10/15, 36/7; 48/3, the variant at 50/8, 60/1, 66/27, 140/15, 238/18, 244/12 and notes; for the latter see 28/2–6, 28/10-32/25, 68/15, 218/9–10, 218/19, 224/14–17, 230/27–28 and cf. the polemical coinages patterned on scholastic jargon at 28/19, 46/26, 96/17, and 106/16. More also uses many other words in unusual or clearly unclassical senses; see, for example 18/2, 56/27, 162/11–12 and notes. But the frequency with which other humanists used these words in a similar way seems to indicate that very few of More's contemporaries would have thought them remarkable or objectionable.

[2] In Erasmus' opinion, proverbial expressions can serve both as positive arguments and as heuristic tools; they can either anchor a particular thesis in common experience or test the limits of common experience by proposing provocatively tenuous links between abstract conceptions and workaday phrases and images. See Kinney, "Erasmus' *Adagia*," pp. 188–90; for an excellent discussion of how proverbs function as positive arguments see Karla Taylor, "Proverbs and the Authentication of Convention in *Troilus and Criseyde*," in *Chaucer's Troilus: Essays in Criticism*, ed. Stephen Barney, Hamden, Conn., 1980, pp. 277–96; and for More's own appeals to the oral authority of proverbs see John R. Cavanaugh, C.S.B., "The Use of Proverbs and 'Sententiae' for Rhetorical Amplifica-

mental: one long section of the *Letter to Dorp* in which proverbial arguments would be inappropriate contains only two minor conventional
allusions.[1] Though he often cites phrases from classical authors without seeming particularly interested in their original context, he shows
far more regard for the context of phrases he cites from Erasmus'
Praise of Folly and the works of the Roman comedians; evidently the
humanist defenses have a basic conceptual affinity with the comic defense of *humanitas*, so that the context of a comic allusion is as pertinent
for More as its substance.[2] A good deal of his loose and elliptical syntax
is also inspired by the Roman comedians, whom he viewed as models of
colloquial Latinity.[3] In the humanist defenses More writes as a versatile
and skilled Latin stylist whose interest in argumentation and tonal
variety often distracts him from trying to maintain rigorous classical
standards of grammatical purity and consistency.[4]

---

tion in the Writings of Saint Thomas More," Ph.D. dissertation, St. Louis University,
1969. When such workaday phrases and images are drawn from a specialized discourse
like that of philosophy or law, they immediately become public property; thus the humanists' proverbial usage emphasizes the central authority of everyday discourse and
counteracts the scholastic tendency to withdraw common words from the domain of
semantic consensus (34/3–5, 36/17–18 and notes). For More's proverbial use of technical formulae see especially 68/9, 204/27, 206/22, 222/12, 252/24, and notes; for his
proverbial use of colloquial turns of expression see note on 208/20. Though the primary
effect of his learned proverbial allusions is to anchor his arguments in common experience, they also perform an important heuristic function by challenging one form of
conventional wisdom with another, more venerable one.

[1]See the long section (78/16-94/3) in which More sets out to provide a purely theological rationale for Erasmus' philological scrutiny of the Vulgate. More's allusions
occur at 84/3–4 and 88/10. For a striking contrast see 56/14-76/19, where More uses a
wide range of proverbial allusions to deflate the immoderate pretensions of pompous
scholastics.

[2]Citations of *The Praise of Folly* and the Roman comedians are particularly frequent in
the *Letter to Dorp*, a defense of the *Folly* against the aspersions of a former disciple of
Plautus; for a primary thematic connection between the *Letter to Dorp* and the *Folly* see
note on 36/17–18. The *Letter to Oxford* owes almost as much to Erasmus' *Antibarbari* as the
Letter to Dorp owes to the *Folly;* for his more dignified defense of *humanitas*, More resorts
to a slightly more dignified Erasmian model. Though the *Letter to a Monk* seems to owe
more to Erasmus' *Enchiridion* than it owes to the *Folly*, comic citations and casual allusions
to the *Folly* counterpoint More's religious discussion throughout; see especially 290/15,
290/23, 306/20 and 310/4. Erasmus himself claimed that the *Folly* and the *Enchiridion*
present the same message in two different guises; see Allen, 2, 93, lines 91–92.

[3]For More's high assessment of Plautus' Latinity see 114/20–24 and Allen, 4, 224, lines
313–18. More generally appears to be even fonder of Terence than of Plautus.

[4]For a detailed account of the syntactical irregularities in *Utopia* see Monsuez, especially pp. 70–76. Similar irregularities are common in the humanist defenses; the most
striking examples are discussed in the Commentary. A few seriously misleading blunders
in the use of indicative forms where subjunctive forms are needed have been corrected in
this edition; see p. cxxxi, below.

This brief comparative study permits us to distinguish between the middle style of the *Letter to Dorp*, the high style of the *Letter to Oxford*, and the two relatively down-to-earth styles of the *Letter to Lee* and the *Letter to a Monk*.[1] The mixed style of the *Letter to Brixius*, which is almost contemporary with the *Letter to a Monk*, represents a distinct combination of unusually elaborate periodic effects and unusually blunt phrasing intended to contrast with Brixius' style of ill-mannered refinement. Though its relatively colloquial style makes the *Letter to a Monk* more immediately accessible to most readers than More's other extended defense of Erasmian humanism, the *Letter to Dorp*, it would probably be wrong to account for the stylistic difference between them as simply a token of More's growing facility and skill as a Latinist: though both works have the form of extended open letters, in the *Letter to a Monk* he deliberately generalizes and simplifies the specifically epistolary decorum which accounts at least partially for the unique stylistic complexity of the *Letter to Dorp*. He addresses the monk in almost the same way he would address an especially shameless opponent in court: even though he is technically intent on convincing the monk to abandon his impudent charges, his main goal is to convince a jury of general readers that they should dismiss all such charges as impudent whether or not the monk actually withdraws them. The accessible style of the *Letter to a Monk* is a style of direct public persuasion: by addressing the letter to a correspondent who is neither learned nor particularly sympathetic to More's way of thinking, he neatly collapses epistolary decorum into that of a standard polemical pamphlet. Though he addresses a somewhat more limited erudite public in the *Letter to Oxford* and the *Letter to Brixius*, in these two open letters, as well, he is chiefly concerned with a project of quite direct public persuasion. Even the *Letter to Lee* can be viewed as an essentially public document, as a persuasive record of how hard More tried to deter Lee and his colleagues with sensible private advice before denouncing them publicly in the *Letter to a Monk*. None of the styles More employs in the later defenses seems meant to create a distinctive and private rapport between More and his prime addressee: he gives up conversation for more standard rhetoric.

In the *Letter to Dorp*, on the other hand, More exploits the decorum of

---

[1]For a humanist discussion which More must have read about the three *genera dicendi* or levels of style and their appropriateness in various types of letter see Niccolo Perotti, *Elementa grammatices* (Venice, 1486), f. CXXV, excerpted by Helene Harth, "Poggio Bracciolini und die Brieftheorie des 15. Jahrhunderts: Zur Gattungsform des humanistischen Briefs," in *Der Brief im Zeitalter der Renaissance*, ed. Franz J. Worstbrock (Bonn, 1983), p. 90, n. 20 (see also p. 94, n. 30). In his Latin poem on at the end of Holt's *Lac puerorum*, More recommends Perotti's grammar for advanced students (*CW* 3/2, Commentary at 274/16).

a personal letter to develop adventurous theses with a freedom denied by the mode of direct public persuasion. The challengingly varied style of the letter is well suited to an uninhibited intellectual debate between two learned equals or near-equals: the dignified style which is More's discreet tribute to Dorp's solid intellectual attainments offsets the irreverent style in which he treats a few of Dorp's actions and arguments, while the very diversity of styles in the letter gives an air of refined spontaneity to the whole. More consistently stresses Dorp's learning, intelligence, and essential good character in a way which is virtually unparalleled in his later polemics. Even his oblique strictures are frequently compliments to Dorp's critical intelligence, since a good deal of More's irony would be lost on an insensitive reader; through his subtle manipulation of nuance and context he is reminding Dorp how to apply his own humanist interpretive skills and not only his humanist principles. For example, More hints that Dorp's "elegant minor works" are no match for the "more massive fieldworks" with which Erasmus could easily counter them (4/1–3, 10/8). Dorp's anonymous accusers know Erasmus "from his writings and reputation," but they know Dorp "in other ways, as well" (4/18–19). A prime reason for thinking that Dorp did not mean to disseminate his second letter is that he would in that case have marshaled his taunts "either somewhat more sparingly or at any rate, my dear Drop, more wittily" (8/23–24). More caps a long sampling of Dorp's own rather heavy-handed sarcasm with an excruciatingly polite retort borrowed in large part from Terence: "But if you have finished your joking, now, Dorp, it is your turn to listen" (20/12–13). More also progresses very slowly and tactfully from the cautious suggestion that Dorp actually feels none too friendly toward Erasmus to the blunt allegation that Dorp alone is responsible for misapplying to all theologians Erasmus' unflattering comments directed at only a few (4/19–20, 40/21–23; cf. 6/5–8, 6/12–13, 6/29-8/1, 8/13–24, 10/9–15, 18/3–11, and 38/18–21). While the *Letter to Dorp* is by no means a gentle or flattering letter, its criticism along with its praise is an eloquent tribute to Dorp's personal stature as an adversary.

As a further indication of the open-ended, dialogic character of his personal interchange with Dorp, More takes pains to establish that Dorp must decide how More's arguments will be further disseminated, and indeed whether they will be further disseminated at all.[1] Dorp has various options: he can either borrow More's arguments selectively to answer Erasmus' detractors himself, write a private rebuttal to dispose of More's arguments completely, or else abandon the pose of well-

---

[1]See 78/9–14 and 124/11–126/2 and cf. 36/27–38/4. For another remark stressing the dialogic character of the *Letter to Dorp* see 122/17–19 and note.

meaning devil's advocate and thus give More the option of publishing them. By making Dorp personally responsible for screening the arguments of the *Letter to Dorp,* More allows himself to be quite uninhibited in elaborating his own theoretical position: he enlists Dorp and his least biased colleagues to mediate between the daring ideas of the *Letter to Dorp* and the general reader in much the same way that "Morus" and his correspondents mediate between Hythloday's daring ideas and the general reader of *Utopia.* The qualified familiarity of More's style in the *Letter to Dorp* permits formal discussion with no loss of informal candor; in this letter, as in *Utopia,* conversation is once again elevated into a speculative work of art.

The general development of More's Latin style in the humanist defenses away from the dignified intimacy of the *Letter to Dorp* may be linked to a gradual change in More's own sense of purpose as a writer. In the increasingly heated polemical atmosphere of the years just before 1520, More apparently began to lose faith in the Utopian notion of indirect, gradual persuasion and thus to abandon the exploratory, dialogic rhetoric of works like *Utopia* and the *Letter to Dorp* for the more forceful rhetoric of direct public persuasion.[1] His own taste for systematic coherence made it difficult for him to combine forceful rhetoric and cautious deliberate ambiguity in the same unremittingly circumspect way that Erasmus combined them. While the sententious style of the *Letter to a Monk* is Erasmian, its unguarded outspokenness is not; the main weakness of More's manifesto in comparison with those of Erasmus is also its primary strength. On the other hand, More's bitter frustration with the enemies of Erasmian dialogue has already begun to express itself with a violence which may not be justified by their actual offenses: even if no one criticized Erasmian dialogue, it obviously would not change the world overnight. In the later humanist defenses More emerges as a highly skilled public persuader who appears to share little of Hythloday's skepticism about public persuasion in general. In defense of Erasmian dialogue he begins to sound almost

---

[1]Fox (*Thomas More,* pp. 111, 123, 199) notes a further "deterioration" of dialogue into one-sided polemic in More's later controversial writings. For the Utopian notion of gradual, indirect persuasion see *CW 4,* 86/13–16 and 100/12–17: through the medium of More's written word, Hythloday the recluse makes his "speech" universally audible to all who are ready to hear it. As this distinctively relaxed literary mode of persuasion came to seem increasingly peripheral to the chief controversies of More's day, he apparently lost at least some of his humanist faith in the book as a primary agent of progress and change and in secular learning in general; see Marc'hadour, *The Bible,* 5, 35–36; and Fox, *Thomas More,* p. 101. But he continued to hold that the works of Erasmus and the fathers could edify their readers in a much subtler way than ephemeral works of direct public persuasion; see above, p. lxxxviii, n. 1.

as peremptory as those who condemn it: epistolary discussion begins to give way to one-sided polemic.

Although none of More's Erasmian defenses had a particularly widespread literary influence, the *Letter to Dorp* was an important source for at least three works by other noted humanists. The letter not only provoked Dorp's *Praelectio,* in which he recanted his earlier conservative arguments; it also provided the basis for a formal apology in which Dorp defended the *Praelectio* and its vehement attack on sophistic theology.[1] The letter also furnished the primary source for Juan Luis Vives' *Epistola in pseudodialecticos,* one of the most famous humanist attacks on scholastic dialectic.[2] Finally, the letter almost certainly contributed several important details to Erasmus' *De libero arbitrio* opposing the Lutheran doctrine of *claritas scripturae.*[3] Erasmus may briefly echo the *Letter to Oxford* in one of his own open letters, and he may have borrowed a few of the proof-texts in his *Apologia de In principio erat sermo* from the *Letter to a Monk.*[4] It is also possible that the particularly fervent defense of Erasmus in the *Letter to a Monk* prompted Etienne Dolet to assign More a prominent role in his *Erasmianus sive Ciceronianus* (1535) as a servile defender of Erasmus. Otherwise none of the letters appears to have been widely read, let alone widely imitated: the Lutheran upheaval made many earlier humanist apologies for moderate reform obsolete.[5] The *Letter to Dorp* was proscribed by a Catholic inquisitor in a Madrid *Index librorum expurgatorum* of 1584.[6]

---

[1]On Dorp's *Praelectio* see pp. xxiv and xxvi, above. Dorp's apology was first published, with an extensive commentary, by De Vocht, *Monumenta,* pp. 63–112. Dorp's most obvious modified borrowing from the *Letter to Dorp* (22/23–27 and 24/24-26/4) may be found in De Vocht, *Monumenta,* p. 88.

[2]For a detailed account of Vives' borrowings from More see Kinney, "More's *Letter to Dorp,*" pp. 201–05, 208–10. For More's subsequent relations with Vives see Foster Watson, "A Friend of Sir Thomas More," *Nineteenth Century, 83* (1918), 540–52, and Juan Luis Vives, *Epistolario,* ed. Jose J. Delgado (Madrid, 1978), pp. 46–47.

[3]See p. lxxx, n. 4.

[4]See note on 134/31-136/6 and p. xlv, n. 1.

[5]The volume including the *Letter to Lee* and the *Letter to a Monk* did enjoy a brief vogue in Oxford; see p. xxxi, n. 2. More himself often echoes the letters; see "More" in the Index.

[6]For the proscription of the *Letter to Dorp* see *Index librorum expurgatorum illustrissimi . . . Gasparis Quiroga . . . iussu editus . . . iuxta exemplar, quod typis mandatum est Madriti . . . M.LXXXIIII* [i.e., 1584] (Saumur, T. Portau, 1601), sig. V$_8$. For the circumstances of the 1601 reprint, see *CW 3/2,* Commentary at 255/5–10. This work, originally published in Madrid in 1584, also strikes out a number of passages from *Utopia* (*CW 4,* 8/28–10/1, 82/8–9, 18–20, and the sidenote at 230/7–9). See also F. H. Reusch, *Der Index der verbotenen Bücher: Ein Beitrag zur Kirchen- und Literaturgeschichte,* 2 vols. (Bonn, 1883–85), *1,* 489–90. Reusch indicates that the *Letter to Dorp* was also banned in Quiroga's *Index et catalogus librorum prohibitorum* of 1583.

THE HISTORY OF THE TEXTS

Each of More's humanistic defenses has its own unique textual history, though the *Letter to Lee* and the *Letter to a Monk* have consistently been published together until very recently. The *Letter to Dorp* is preserved in two significantly different recensions. The first of these is best represented by a freestanding manuscript in the Bibliothèque nationale in Paris, MS lat. 8703, written in an elegant sixteenth-century Italic hand. This manuscript (*P*), previously MS regius 5936, entered the royal library in 1700 along with many other manuscript volumes which had previously belonged to the great book-collector Archbishop Charles-Maurice Le Tellier of Rheims; it was then duly entered in the hand-written catalogue of manuscripts begun in 1682 by the royal librarian Nicholas Clément (Bibliothèque nationale MS nouv. acq. fr. 5402).[1] Probably on the basis of the multiple salutations in this manuscript, the first of which could have served as the letter's address, P. S. Allen conjectured that this manuscript was the copy More actually sent to Dorp.[2] The other recension of the letter is imperfectly represented by a manuscript from the collection of the humanist Beatus Rhenanus, currently catalogued as MS 345, fols. 6–30, in the Bibliothèque munici-pale of Sélestat, Alsace (France), and by the *editio princeps* of the letter in *Thomae Mori Lucubrationes* (Basel, 1563).[3] The Sélestat manuscript (*S*),

---

[1]This catalogue has been published in Henri Omont, *Anciens inventaires et catalogues de la Bibliothèque nationale*, 5 vols. (Paris, 1908–21), *3*, 165–514, and *4*, 1–186. The Dorp manuscript is listed as a small folio (Omont, *3*, 477). A copy of this catalogue executed before 1700 and thus lacking entries for MSS regii 5932–38 is still preserved in the Bibliothèque nationale (MS lat. 9359). I owe the clarification of several bibliographical and chronological details to the courtesy of Jacqueline Sclafer, Keeper of Manuscripts at the Bibliothèque nationale.

[2]Allen, 2, 197, commentary at line 157. De Vocht, *Monumenta*, p. 159, n. 3, also stresses the presence of a date at the end of this copy as an argument for considering it the copy which was actually sent. Laetitia Yeandle of the Folger Shakespeare Library and Paul O. Kristeller of Columbia University have both graciously seconded the traditional dating of *P* to the first half (or first quarter) of the sixteenth century. Though John Clement, More's personal secretary at the time the letter was written, seemed a promising candidate as the scribe of *P*, the handwriting of *P* bears little resemblance to Clement's Latin script as preserved in a number of later documents.

[3]There has been some confusion in previous bibliographical references to the Sélestat manuscript of the *Letter to Dorp*. Rogers (p. 27) designates it "Sélestat MS. Cat. Rhen. 174

CXX   INTRODUCTION

bound with Erasmus' *Farrago nova epistolarum* (Basel, 1519) and *Hyper-aspistes II* (Basel, 1527), is accompanied by the unique sixteenth-century copy of Dorp's second letter to Erasmus (MS 345, fols. 1–5v; Allen, 2, 126–36); this text, transcribed in the same hand as the *Letter to Dorp* (possibly by Beatus Rhenanus himself), bears the colophon "Exscrip: Basileae 1518" ("Copied in Basel 1518"). The Basel *editio princeps* of More's letter, which bears the sidenote "Haec epistola nunquam antehac edita" ("This epistle has never been published before"), may derive from one of the manuscripts left by Erasmus to Boniface Amorbach of Basel; in any case the connection of both *S* and the *editio princeps* (*1563*) with the city of Basel suggests that a copy of the letter originally belonging to Erasmus in Basel may have provided the source-text for both.[1] These two texts of the letter share a number of readings substantially different from those of *P* as well as a number of additions and one significant omission (76/15–19). Several casual omissions peculiar to *S* make it clear that *1563* cannot be derived from this text as De Vocht has suggested.[2]

Before listing the most noteworthy differences between the two major recensions of the *Letter to Dorp* we will do well to consider the provenance of the second edition of the text, *Thomae Mori Dissertatio epistolica* . . . (Leiden, Elzevir, 1625; reissued Leiden, "Sambix" [Elzevir], 1654).[3] This edition (*1625*) was not only published by one of

---

fin."; De Vocht (*Monumenta*, p. 159, n. 4) speaks of it as "forming with the *Institutio Christiani Matrimonii* (Basle, 1526) and other manuscripts, the nº 176 of the Beatus Rhenanus books in the Schlettstadt Library" (cf. Allen, 2, 126). According to yet another cataloguing system the manuscript of Dorp's second letter and More's *Letter to Dorp* has been designated K 1103 c. For several of these details I am indebted to the curator of the Sélestat Bibliothèque municipale. For More's *Lucubrationes* (Basel, 1563) see R. W. Gibson and J. Max Patrick, *St. Thomas More: A Preliminary Bibliography of His Works and of Moreana to the Year 1750* (New Haven and London, 1961; hereafter cited as "Gibson"), no. 74. Gibson (p. 158) wrongly reports that the *Letter to Dorp* is also found in *Erasmi operum tomus tertius epistolas complectens* (Basel, 1538; reprints, 1541 and 1558).

[1]For the sidenote see the variants at 2/6; for Erasmus' last will and testament see Allen, *11*, app. xxv. Since Dorp himself apparently suppressed his second letter to Erasmus (see note on 176/11–13) and since More definitely sent Erasmus a transcript of both Dorp's second letter and the *Letter to Dorp* itself (Allen, 2, 126, 197, 243, 261, 496), their copresence in the Sélestat manuscript is another argument for the dependence of this manuscript on a manuscript owned by Erasmus. See also p. xxiii, above.

[2]See the variants at 56/24–25, 62/8, 78/26, 94/10–12, 112/23–25; and De Vocht, *Monumenta*, p. 159, n. 3.

[3]See Alphonse Willems, *Les Elzevier: Histoire et annales typographiques* (Brussels, Paris, and The Hague, 1880), no. 240, pp. 65–66. In the Elzevier edition the *Letter to Dorp* is preceded by Erasmus' letter to More (Allen, *4*, no. 1162) about a later confrontation between Erasmus and the Louvain theologians; a few leaves of this letter have been reset in *1654*, but otherwise the two issues are made up of the same sheets.

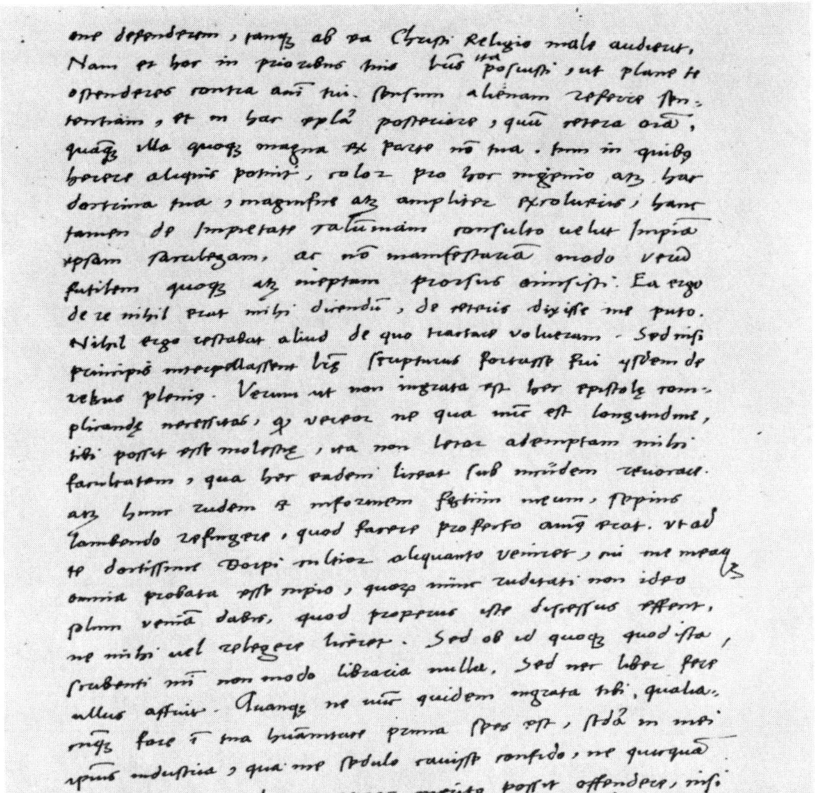

Letter to Dorp, Séléstat MS. 345 (K1103), fol. 28 (reduced)

ad suū pduxerint, quū neꝗ in re cōsiliū sit, neꝗ i uerbis
uenus, sit nimirū uti tota illa momilisatio quā uocant
sine ulla grū spiruenꝗ frigescat. Sed tñ ut dixi omittam.

At certꝗ ipsū literalē sensū tātū cōtinere difficultatis puto, quātū nescio an quisꝗ, oīm cōprehēdere possit.

Neꝗ oīm cuiꝗ censeo literalē hōrū uerbōrū sensū cōprehe-
sū esse, Dixit dñs dño meo sede a dexteris meis. nisi
ei qui ea prophetā de ipo Christo uaticinatū intellegat.

Quod exceptis prophetis nec iudeorū quisꝗ, ꝗꝗ in hos libros
uniuersam operā stam collocabat, intellexit priusꝗ Christus ēius eis huo eiꝰ literē sensū aperuit. Qui tāetsi apostolis, ac discipulis suis interpretatus est scripturas, neꝗ
eम̄ ꝗ scium questiunculas istas cū eis disputauit magna?

Hō ausim tñ affirmare uniuersū scripturꝗ sensū, eis
ipis, aut presente tradidisse, aut ꝑ spiritū sanctū eā

the most renowned presses of northern Europe but was also prepared
with the collaboration of two noted seventeenth-century Latinists,
Daniel Heinsius and Erycius Puteanus. Two letters from Puteanus
dated July 26 and December 15, 1623, make it clear that Puteanus was
responsible for borrowing a prized, unique text of More's letter from
its unnamed owner and submitting it to the Elzevirs in the first place,
while Heinsius was expected to approve the text for publication, ex-
pedite preparation of a printer's copy, and provide editorial guidance
(*directio*).[1] The readings of *1625* are remarkably close to the readings
of *P*.[2] The two texts share precisely the same notable omissions in
comparison with the Basel recension, and they both include the
rather daring passage at 76/15–19 which both texts of the Basel recension omit. Furthermore, in most of the places where *1625* diverges
even slightly from *P*, a conspicuous dash in the margin of *P* marks the
place; these marks prove that *P* was collated quite carefully at some
point with *1625* or its actual copy-text. Finally, in at least one passage
it would be very difficult to explain the reading of *1625* without reference to the reading of *P*.[3] At 58/28-60/1, where the correct reading is
"illa moralisatio quam uocant," the scribe of *P* originally spelled the
noun "morilisatio" and then clumsily corrected the first *i* to an *a* in
such a manner that the new stroke of the *a* touches the preceding *r*
while the vertical stroke of the *a* still appears to be dotted. At this

---

[1] See Erycius Puteanus, *Ad Constantinum Hugenium et Danielem Heinsium . . . epistolae*,
ed. M. Z. Boxhorn (Leiden, F. Hack, 1647), sigs. E₇, E₇v–E₈:

> Est nunc etiam quod peculiariter te rogem. Scribunt ad me Elzevirii, scriptum illud
> Mori pro Erasmo, ut legeres, traditum tibi esse: ego hic ut reddam vehementer
> urgeor, et ab eo qui instar thesauri illud aestimat, et a maioribus suis accepit. Si liber
> placet, describi subito exemplar poterit et excudi. Et quomodo non placeat? Tua jam
> humanitate opus, ne male de me meriti Elzevirii videantur. Tibi autem universum
> libri pretium debebo. Hic nunc etiam amorem tuum ostende, et Vale, verum lit-
> terarum decus et lumen. Lovanii, in Arce, VII. Kalend, Sextil. MDCXXIII. . . .
>
> Illa Mori si scias quam avide exspectem, praecipitare cupias. Omnino dignum
> luce, dignum directione tua scriptum est. Vale . . . Lovanii, in Arce, III. Eid. De-
> cemb. MDCXXIII.

[2] Two one-word additions in *1625* and one apparently deliberate departure from the
reading of *P* (simul *1625*, sola *P*) make it very unlikely that *1625* derives directly from *P*,
since the two added words and the odd reading *simul* are not actually written in the
manuscript (see the variants at 4/13–14, 30/6, and 90/17). Even with the dashes in the
margin of *P* it would have been difficult for the most learned printer to make all the
minor corrections which these dashes apparently call for and which are incorporated in
1625.

[3] There are several other instances in which an abbreviation in *P* may explain an odd
reading in *1625*. See the variants at 16/20, 36/7, 60/13, 62/24, 74/26, 102/15, 104/13,
104/25, and 124/20.

point *1625* has the meaningless reading "monilisatio"; it appears that
the copyist or editor misread the correction in *P* and admitted the
meaningless "monilisatio" on the strength of "quam vocant" ("as they
call it"), a phrase frequently used to apologize for an improper term
borrowed from elsewhere. If we assume that *1625* actually is derived
at one remove from *P*, Puteanus' remarks on the source-text of *1625*
reinforce the hypothesis that *P* is the actual copy that More sent to
Dorp; for according to Puteanus, the source-text he lent to the
Elzevirs was an heirloom belonging to a resident of Louvain, Dorp's
own home. Although a number of More's friends and relatives could
conceivably have brought such a manuscript with them when they
settled in Louvain as exiles, it is worth noting that when Stapleton
quotes the *Letter to Dorp* he draws not on a manuscript text but on
1563 even though he had privileged access to the most complete collection of More's letters brought over by the exiles.[1] It is plausible to
conclude that *P* at least closely resembles the letter as actually sent.

Though we may simply discount most of the word-order variants in
the *Letter to Dorp* given the ease with which casual inversions of this sort
occur, we must still reckon with the numerous lexical variants in both *S*
and *1563* which could not have arisen except through a process of
conscious revision. At 118/19 *P* attributes a saying to Jerome which
Jerome himself borrowed from Sallust; *S* and *1563* substitute Sallust's
name for Jerome's. At 74/10 *P* has the pastiche hexameter "personae
mutae truncoque simillimus Hermae"; *S* and *1563* here read "Mercurij
statuae truncoque simillimus Hermae," also an acceptable hexameter.
Nor are these the only suggestive examples.[2] There are also a number
of telling additions in both *S* and *1563*.[3]

While a number of the lexical changes in *S* and *1563* are improvements on the readings in *P* and while the additions in *S* and *1563* are
undoubtedly important in their own right, we must beware of assuming that *S* and *1563* at their best represent a definitive state of More's
text. First of all, there is evidence that some of the changes in *S* and

---

[1] In his *Tres Thomae . . .* (Gibson, nos. 121–23) Stapleton cites many of More's letters
from a unique collection he personally received from the widow of John Harris, More's
secretary. He explicitly states on p. 260 that he is citing the *Letter to Dorp* from the Basel
edition. Stapleton's papers apparently were dispersed when he died; see Allen, *3*, 338;
and Charles W. Crawford, "Thomas Stapleton and More's *Letter to Bugenhagen*," *Moreana*, *19/20* (1968), 106, and *26* (1970), 5.

[2] Other interesting lexical variants occur at 4/27, 16/7–8, 24/5, 24/24, 28/3, 28/9,
34/23–24, 44/13, 44/20, 44/25, 48/25, 52/23, 54/6–7, 64/19, 74/13, 78/1, 86/7, 86/24–
25, 108/11, and 118/4–5.

[3] See the minor additions at 6/29, 16/25, 50/8, 78/11, 82/24, 104/12, 108/10, 114/4,
114/17, and the somewhat more significant additions at 16/24, 20/24, 62/12–13, 118/3–
4, and 122/19; neither list is exhaustive.

1563 are not really corrections at all: the barbarous diction at 28/3,
28/4–5, 68/13, and 68/13–14 seems to have been regularized in the
source-text of *S* and *1563* by someone who failed to appreciate the
satiric intent of the barbarisms, and the daring passage omitted at
76/15–19 leaves an important rhetorical development without any real
conclusion in *S* and *1563*, a deficiency More would have remedied if he
had omitted this passage himself (see note). Furthermore, although
several of the extended additions in *S* and *1563* actually enhance the
argument, the longest of them all (see the variants at 122/19) interferes
with the sense of the paragraph in which it is interpolated. One extended addition in *S* and *1563* actually seems to derive from redundant
material in More's archetype which the scribe of *P* started to copy and
then quickly abandoned; see the variants at 98/20.[1] These additions in
the source-text of *S* and *1563* may correspond on a larger scale to the
interlineated authorial variants or "doublets" which abound in the
manuscripts of More's Latin *Richard III;* and as More himself notes in
the *Letter to Brixius* with regard to such variants, his scribe or his reader
may take them or leave them.[2] Several vestigial doublets of this sort are
apparent in both *P* and *S*.[3] Given the uncertain authority of many of
the changes in *S* and *1563* and the provisional character of the phrasing in general, the best policy is probably to use *P* as the basis of a
critical text which makes no claim to rigid finality.

All the other known texts of the *Letter to Dorp* before Rogers' edition
of 1947 are directly or indirectly dependent on *1563* or *1625* or a
casual collection of both. Oxford MS Wood F. 22, fols. 50–79 (*O*), and
the version of the letter included in an appendix to *Erasmi Epistolarum
libri xxxi* (London, 1642) are both directly dependent on *1563*, and both
texts reproduce the casual omissions in *1563* found at 72/20–21,
86/16–17, 118/23, and 120/15–16.[4] The *Letter to Dorp* was also printed
five times between 1629 and 1676 with Erasmus' *Praise of Folly;* all these
texts are dependent on *1625*, and they all reproduce that text's casual
omission of an essential short clause from the sizable passage preserved
only in *P* and *1625* (76/15–19).[5] The versions of the letter in *Thomae*

---

[1]Similarly, the word order in *S* and *1563* at 28/18 is the word order finally rejected in
P.

[2]See the *Letter to Brixius, CW* 3/2, 626/21–27.

[3]See the variants at 8/23, 8/26, 10/18, 12/5, 34/11, 34/18, 52/23, 60/27, and 100/5.

[4]For *1642* see Gibson, no. 147.

[5]The *Letter to Dorp* is included in the following editions of the *Praise of Folly: Erasmi
Moriae encomium* (Amsterdam, G. Blaeuw, 1629); *Erasmi Moriae encomium* (Leiden, J.
Maire, 1648); *Erasmi Moriae encomium* (Oxford, W. Hall for F. Oxlad, 1663 [misdated
1633]); *Erasmi Moriae encomium* (Oxford, W. Hall for S. Bolton, 1668); *Erasmi Moriae
encomium*, ed. C. Patin (Basel, Typis Genethianis, 1676). Only *1676* is noted in Gibson (no.
130).

Mori Opera omnia (Frankfurt, 1689) and *Erasmi Opera omnia,* ed. Jean Leclerc (Leiden, 1703–06), 3/2, are both composite texts; both restore 76/15–19 and incorporate several superior readings attested in *1625* but reproduce the additions and many of the inferior readings and casual omissions in *1563*.[1] Where *1625* omits the essential short clause "ut laudem" at 76/15, *1689* supplies the words "ut probem" on the basis of "probo" at 76/3; *1703* here incorporates the reading of *1689*. It would undoubtedly make little sense to record every reading of texts which are clearly derivative.

On the basis of all the available evidence, a tentative textual stemma for the *Letter to Dorp* may be outlined as follows:

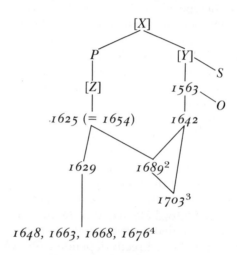

Rogers' 1947 text of the letter is based on a collation of *P, S, 1563, 1642,* and *1703;* although I have examined all fourteen of the extant early versions, I have based my own text on a somewhat more thorough collation of *P, S, 1563,* and *1625*.[5]

---

[1]For *1689* and *1703* see Gibson, nos. 77 and 149.

[2]It is uncertain whether *1689* is dependent on *1563* or *1642*, though the fact that *1689* includes several other letters found in *1642* but not in *1563* makes dependence on *1642* appear somewhat more likely.

[3]Once again it is unclear whether *1703* is dependent on *1563* or *1642*, though Leclerc surely knew of the 1642 London edition of Erasmus' letters. He mentions an *alia editio.*

[4]All these editions share many corruptions with *1629*. I have not tried to determine whether any of the four is an intermediate source for one or more of the others.

[5]For the readings of *1563* I have relied on the copy in the Beinecke Rare Book Library of Yale University; for those of *1625* I have relied on a microfilm of the copy owned by the British Library.

Thomas Morus Reuerendis patribus, Commissario,
Procuratoribus, ac Reliquo Senatui Scholasticorum
Oxoniensium Salutem Plurimam Dicit.

Erasmus epla quadam libro 6.to
elarum ad Petrum Moscellanu
occasionem huius epistola (vt
puto) ne rrat, ad istum modum.

[A]nglia (inquit) duas habet Academias haud quanquam incelebres, Canta-
brigiam et Oxoniam: in vtraq traduntur graca litera, sed Cantabrigia
tranquille, quod eius Schola princeps sit Joannes Fisherus Epus Roffen.
non eruditione tantum sed et vita theologica. Verum Oxonia, cum
iuuenis quidam non vulgariter doctus, satis faliciter graca profiteretur,
barbarus quispiam in populari concione magnis et atrocibus conuitijs
debacchari cepit in gracas tras. At Rex, vt non indoctus ipse, ita bonis
literis fauens, qui tum forte in propinquo erat (re per Morum et Pacæu
cognita) denunciauit, vt volentes ac lubentes Græcanicam Iraturam
amplecterentur. Ita rabulis illis impositum est silentium. A.o Dm. 1519.

Sequitur Epistola.

[D]ubitaui nonnihil (Eruditissimi Viri) liceretne mihi de quibus nunc decreui rebus ad vos scribere; nec id vsq adeo stili respectu mei dubitaui, (quanquam
cun istum queq pudet in catum prodire virorum tam eloquentium) quàm ne videri nimium superbus possim, si homuncio non magnâ prudentiâ, minore rerum
vsu, doctrinâ verò minus quàm mediocri, tantum mihi arrogem, vt vllâ in re, sed
precipuè literariâ, consilium dare vnus audeam vobis omnibus; quorum quiuis
ob eximiam eruditionem, prudentiamq, sit idoneus qui multis hominu millibus
consulat. Verùm contra (venerandi patres) quantum me primo conspectu
singularis ista sapientia vestra deterruit; tantum me penitius inspecta recreauit; cun subyt animum, sicuti stulta atq arrogans inscitia neminem dignatur
audire; ita quo quisq est sapientior, doctiorq, eo minus sibijpsi confidere aut cuiusquam aspernari consilium. Sed, et hoc me vehementer animauit, quòd nemini vnquam fraudi fuit apud æquos iudices, quales vos imprimis estis, etiamsi quis
in consulendo non satis prospexisse videatur; sed laudem semper gratiamq meru-
isse consilium, quod quanquam non prudentissimum, fidum tamen fuerit, et amico
profectum pectore. Postremò, cùm apud me considero, quòd hanc quantulamcunq
doctrinam meam, secundum Deum, vestra isti Academia acceptam ferre debeo, vnde eius initia retuli; videtur à me officium meum fidesq in vos exigere, ne quidquam
silentio transeam, quod vos audire vtile esse censeam. Quamobrem cùm in scribendo
totum periculum in eo viderem situm, si me quidam nimis arrogantem licerent;
contraq intelligerem silentium meum à multis damnari ingratitudinis posse: malui
innes vt me mortales audaculum prædicarent, quàm quisquam ingratum iudicaret,
in vestra

Letter to Oxford, MS. Rawlinson D. 399, fol. 98 (reduced)

Tho. Morus Reuerendis patribus,
Commissario, Procuratoribus, ac
reliquo Senatui Scholasticorum
Oxoniensium. Salutem. P. D.

Dubitaui nonnihil, Eruditissimi viri, liceretne mihi, de
quibus nunc decreui rebus ad vos scribere: nec id usq adeo
stili respectu mei dubitaui: (quanquam cu ipsu quoque
pudet in coetum prodire virorum tam eloquentium) quam
ne videri nimiu superbus possim, si homuncio non magna
prudentiâ, minore rerum usu, doctrinâ vero minus qu
mediocri, tantum mihi arrogem, Vt ulla in re, sed praecipue lraria, consiliu dare vnus audeam vobis omnibus.
quoru quiuis ob eximiam eruditionem prudentiamq, sit
idoneus qui multis hominu millibus consulat. Verum
contra (Venerandi patres) singularis ista sapientia
vra quantum me primo conspectu deterruit; tantum
me penitius inspecta recreauit, cu subijt animu, sicuti
stulta atq arrogans inscitia neminem dignat audire,
ita quo quisq est sapientior doctiorq, eo minus sibi ipsi
confidere aut cuiusquam aspernari consilium: Sed
et hoc me vehementer animauit, quod nemini vnq fraudi fuit apud aequos iudices, quales vos imprimis estis, e-
tiamsi quis in consulendo non satis prospexisse videatur; sed laudem semper gratiamq meriusse consiliu, quod quanq non prudentissimu fidum tamen
fuerit, et amico profecto pectore. Postremo, quum
apud me considero quod hanc quantulamcunq doctrinam
meam secundu Deu, vra isti Academiae acceptam ferre
debeo,

Letter to Oxford, MS. Top. Oxon. e.5, fol. 292 (reduced)

The *Letter to Oxford* is preserved in two manuscript miscellanies, both in Oxford, Bodleian MS Top. Oxon. e. 5 (*T*) and MS Rawlinson D. 399 (*R*). The *editio princeps* of the letter, *Epistola Thomae Mori ad Academiam Oxoniensem,* ed. Richard James (Oxford, 1633), was the basis of two other early editions: one in *Guilelmi Roperi Vita Thomae Mori,* ed. Thomas Hearne (Oxford, 1716), and another in John Jortin, *The Life of Erasmus* (London, 1758–60; reprint, 1808).[1] A long excerpt from the letter (138/8–140/20) is also included in Stapleton's *Tres Thomae . . .* (Douai, 1588). Although Stapleton himself may have introduced several of the variant readings in this excerpt, at least two of them add new material in a way which suggests that the text used by Stapleton was a different and possibly earlier draft of More's letter; see the variants at 140/13 and 140/16–17.[2] *T, R,* and *1633* are all accompanied by the following note: "Erasmus Epistola quadam lib. 6 Epistolarum ad Petrum Mosellanum occasionem huius epistolae vt puto narrat ad istum modum."[3] (A short excerpt follows from Allen, *3,* 546–47, lines 183–94: "Anglia . . . silentium.") In each of the manuscripts Twyne's note is transcribed in the same hand as the main body of the letter, a fact which suggests that neither of these two very similar manuscripts was copied before 1600.[4] The presence of this note in *T, R,* and *1633* makes it likely that all three are derived either directly or indirectly from a single manuscript of the letter to which Twyne's note was joined. Two substantial if casual omissions peculiar to *1633* (140/11, 142/21–23) make it clear that neither manuscript is a copy of the printed text; one substantial omission peculiar to *R* and *1633* (146/26) makes it clear that *T* is not a copy of *R;* two one-word omissions peculiar to *T* (142/8, 146/22) make it rather unlikely that *R* is a copy of *T;* and the numerous points at which *1633* agrees with one of these manuscripts against the other in minor details of phrasing or word order make it rather unlikely that *1633* is derived even indirectly from either.[5] Thus, in spite of the many corruptions and rather inept editorial

---

[1]For *1633* and *1716* see Gibson, nos. 59 and 118. Both *1716* and *1760* reproduce unique readings from the *editio princeps,* for example at 132/9 and 138/21. Jortin explicitly names the *editio princeps* as his source in *The Life of Erasmus,* 2 vols. (London, 1758–60), 2, 662.

[2]For Stapleton's collection of More's letters see p. cxxii, n. 1, above.

[3]Preceded in *1633* by the heading: "Nota Magistri Briani Twyne."

[4]Brian Twyne (ca. 1579–1644), celebrated Oxford antiquary, did most of his Oxford historical work after 1600; see *DNB* 57, 401–02.

[5]Though it is conceivable that the copy-text of *1633* was a scribal conflation of *T* and *R,* the readings of *1633* could be explained just as well by the hypothesis that *T, R* and *1633* all derived from one source-text.

changes in *1633*, it seems reasonably likely that *T*, *R*, and *1633* all derive independently from a single Oxford manuscript.[1] On the other hand, it would probably be wrong to assume in this case that the agreement of any two texts must authenticate their reading against that of the third, since at least one significant change was apparently made in their source-text sometime after the copying of *T* and before the preparation of *R* or *1633*. At 146/26, where *T* reads "conferri aut comparari," *R* and *1633* both read merely "conferri"; the second verb has apparently been deleted from the source as redundant. More, however, is fond of the doublet "confer and compare," which he uses at least once in Latin and three times in English; it seems that the source-text of *R* and *1633* has been edited away from More's wording.[2] On the basis of this instance I am inclined to uphold *T* against *R* and *1633* in a few other passages, most notably 140/24, 146/19, 146/21–22, 146/22, and 148/4. Finally, More suggests at 148/9–10 that the letter he is sending to Oxford is written in his own hand, but the ungrammatical and virtually meaningless reading "detonauit" found in *T* and *R* at 142/5 is not the sort of mistake one would expect to find in a formal autograph text of a letter.[3] These conclusions lend support to the following textual stemma, the simplest one which can explain all the facts:[4]

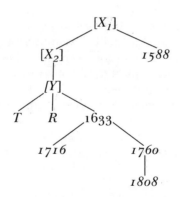

---

[1]The readings of *1633* are markedly inferior to the manuscript readings at 130/16, 130/19, 132/12, 132/24, 132/25, 134/11, 134/25, 134/26–27, 136/22, 138/5–6, 138/21, 138/23, 140/6, 142/15, 144/21, and 146/5.

[2]For "conferre et comparare" see *CW 14*, 265/6; for "confer and compare" see *CW 8*, 997/11; *The Supplication of Souls*, EW, sig. v₈; *The Debellation of Salem and Bizance*, EW, sig. N₅v.

[3]At this point *1633* has the elegant but obvious correction "denotauit."

[4]On the assumption that Stapleton's copy of the letter represented an earlier draft than the one actually sent (see the variants at 140/13 and 140/16–17) it is necessary to indicate two physically distinct autograph forms of the letter in the stemma ([X_1] and [X_2]), since More suggests at 148/9 that the letter he is sending to Oxford is written in his

Rogers' 1947 text is based on a very imperfect collation of all extant versions of the letter except *1808;* my own text is based on a complete collation of *T, R, 1588,* and *1633.*[1]

The *Letter to Lee* and the *Letter to a Monk* were both printed twice in 1520 and not printed again until 1760, when Jortin included them in the second volume of his *Life of Erasmus.* The two 1520 editions are found in the following works:[2]

Epistolae aliquot eruditorum, nunquam antehac excusae, multis nominibus dignae quae legantur a bonis omnibus, quo magis liqueat quanta sit insignis cuiusdam sycophantae virulentia (Antwerp, M. Hillen [May 1520]), here designated *1520*[m]

Epistolae aliquot eruditorum uirorum, ex quibus perspicuum quanta sit Eduardi Lei uirulentia (Basel, Froben, August 1520), here designated *1520*[a]

It appears that no manuscript texts of these letters survive. There is little point in tracing a stemma for the five printed versions of the letters: Jortin states very clearly that the two 1520 editions form the basis of his own texts, first printed in 1760 and reprinted in 1808, whereas Rogers constructed her 1947 text on the basis of *1760* and *1520*[a].[3] Rogers made no direct use at all of *1520*[m], the *editio princeps,* and her description of the source-texts on which she relied for the *Letter to a Monk* is misleading.[4] The two 1520 editions exhibit a

---

own hand. The scribal error repeated in both *T* and *R* makes it useful to distinguish between their source-text ([*Y*]) and the autograph ([X_2]) from which it was probably copied.

[1]For the readings of *1588* and *1625* I have relied on the copies in the Beinecke Rare Book Library of Yale University.

[2]Gibson (nos. 152–53) gives a very confused and confusing description of these two editions. For the dating of the Antwerp edition see Allen, *4,* 210. This edition was reissued in June with four additional letters appended; see Nijhoff–Kronenberg, *1,* nos. 128, 765. The Basel edition of the *Epistolae* was included in the same volume as a revised and much-expanded version of Erasmus' *Apologia de In Principio erat sermo* (see Allen, *4,* 194–95). Though the two works are given separate title pages, the pagination and signatures are continuous; Erasmus' *Apologia* occupies sigs. A_2–C_4v.

[3]Gibaud ("Réponse," pp. iii–iv) includes a Latin text of the *Letter to a Monk* which is based on Rogers and a thorough collation of the 1808 reprint of Jortin.

[4]Rogers (p. 165) lists the following sources for the *Letter to a Monk:* "Epistolae Aliquot Eruditorum 1520 fol. G. iii; Jortin II, p. 670." By "Epistolae Aliquot Eruditorum" she undoubtedly means *1520*[m]; see Rogers, p. 137. Remarkably, though she does not even mention *1520*[a] as a source for the *Letter to a Monk,* the majority of the readings she here assigns to *1520*[m] actually derive from *1520*[a] rather than *1520*[m], so that she frequently cites *1520*[m] as an authority against its own reading. But a considerable number of the readings she attributes to *1520*[m] do not seem to occur in either of the 1520 editions. Rogers' text of the *Letter to Lee* owes as little to *1520*[m] as does her text of the *Letter to a Monk.*

number of interesting divergences that make it hard to decide which edition is closer to what More actually wrote; probably the best policy is to accept all the obvious corrections included in *1520*[a] but to recognize that *1520*[m] may in general be closer to More's manuscript.[1]

The text of the *Letter to Lee* given in *1520*[a] introduces many distinct improvements on the text given in *1520*[m].[2] *1520*[a] also introduces several inferior readings.[3] Other acceptable or even attractive changes which do not really count as corrections are introduced in *1520*[a] at 152/7, 158/11–12, 158/16, 164/13–14, and 194/22. At 188/22 we find an attempted emendation which seemingly misses the point of More's phrasing; this false correction suggests that More himself may not have planned all the more striking changes we find in this version of the text. On the other hand, who else but More would have altered the date of the letter from May 1 to May 20 at 194/31? Even if we assume that "20 die Maij" is a mere mistranscription of "2° die Maij" ("the second day of May"), we must still ask who but More would have had any interest in changing the date of the letter at all. Perhaps More passed on a short list of corrections to William Nesen, the editor of *1520*[m], and these corrections and a number of other unauthorized changes were then introduced into the copy of *1520*[m] which was used as a copy-text for *1520*[a].[4]

Similar changes appear in the *1520*[a] edition of the *Letter to a Monk*.[5]

---

[1]For evidence that More personally provided the manuscript on which *1520*[m] was based see p. xxxvi, n. 2. Certain peculiarities in *1520*[m] and *1520*[a] make it seem very likely that the second is substantially dependent on the first; see the variants at 176/27, 210/8, 218/3, 220/27–28, 234/10, 236/23, 266/3, 268/27, 286/7–8, and 306/6. It would certainly be rather unusual for the second edition of a miscellaneous collection like the *Epistolae* to be printed entirely from manuscripts.

[2]For only the most notable instances see the variants at 152/12, 154/11, 156/10, 166/19, 166/21, 166/23, 166/24, 166/25, 168/2, 168/5, 178/22, 182/23, 186/22–23, 186/29, 188/23, 190/27, 192/15, and 192/16.

[3]See the variants at 154/31, 156/7, 158/1, 166/5, 166/8, 166/17, 170/18, 172/1, 172/12, 172/31, 178/3, 180/21, and 194/10.

[4]For Nesen's role in compiling and editing *1520*[m] see Allen, *4*, 210. Erasmus may have helped edit the volume; see Allen, *4*, 233, lines 7–10. For More's friendly relations with Nesen at this time see Allen, *4*, 232, line 621.

[5]Improved readings appear at 198/8–9, 198/20, 202/16, 204/22, 208/17, 210/18, 212/6, 212/13–14, 216/16, 222/1, 222/17, 224/10–11, 240/20, 240/25, 242/11, 252/11, 254/3, 258/28, 262/15, 272/18, 278/12, 280/9, 282/5, 292/25, 294/28, 296/13–14, 300/13, 302/15, 306/1, and 306/20, not to mention the more trivial instances. Inferior readings are introduced at 198/12, 198/14, 204/18, 206/12, 208/28, 210/5, 210/19, 210/26, 212/8, 212/22, 216/9, 216/25, 218/9, 222/2, 226/19, 228/4, 228/18–19, 228/26, 234/6, 234/31, 240/1–2, 240/22, 244/12, 246/2, 246/26, 248/16, 252/16, 254/1, 256/3, 258/4, 258/18, 260/22, 262/18, 268/3,4,28, 270/27, 274/13, 276/31, 278/5–6, 278/23,

EPISTOLAE
ALIQVOT
ERVDITORVM,
nunc̄ antehac excusæ, multis nominibus di
gnæ quæ legantur a bonis omnibus, quo
magis liqueat, quanta sit insi
gnis cuiusdam sycophan
tæ virulentia.

Title page, *Epistolae aliquot eruditorum*, Antwerp, May 1520 (reduced)

Title page, *Epistolae aliquot eruditorum virorum*, Basel, August 1520 (reduced)

Here, too, there are several examples of what seem to be unauthorized and inept emendations, most notably at 250/12, 264/5, 268/3–4, 286/7–8, 288/8, and 304/10. Finally there is an interesting omission at 306/9–11, where 1520^m seems to cite the first line of the letter from the monk to which More is responding. The changed title of the *Letter to a Monk* in 1520^a merely reflects a revised editorial strategy: since Erasmus' own *Apologia de In principio erat sermo* is included in the same volume it is no longer necessary to stress that the *Letter to a Monk* is in part a defense of Erasmus' translation of John 1:1. Once again, it is likely that More is responsible for some but by no means all of the revisions in 1520^a; neither 1520 text is definitive.[1]

TRANSLATIONS

There are already five full-length translations of the *Letter to Dorp*, one in English, three in French, and another in Russian. All five translations are relatively recent, and all are dependent on Rogers' edition of the Latin.[2] There are two complete English translations of the *Letter to Oxford;* one of these two translations is based on the inferior Latin of *1633*, and the second is highly dependent on the first.[3] There is only an

---

280/22, 282/23–24, 284/12, 286/1, 286/13, 304/13, 304/19, 306/11, and 310/3–4, again leaving aside ordinary typographical errors. Attractive but unnecessary changes are introduced at 212/17, 216/26, 218/19–20, 220/8, 224/7, 234/10, 246/10, 248/12, 252/14–15, 262/22, 266/11–12, 278/16, 280/30–31, 282/28, 286/10, and 286/27.

[1]For the readings of 1520^m and 1520^a I have relied on microfilms of the copies in the Bodleian Library, Oxford, and the Bayerische Staatsbibliothek, Munich. For the readings of *1760* I have relied on a copy in the Sterling Library of Yale University.

[2]The first English translation of the *Letter to Dorp* (by Marcus Haworth, S.J.) appears in St. Thomas More, *Selected Letters*, ed. E. F. Rogers (New Haven and London, 1961; hereafter cited as *SL*). French translations appear in St. Thomas More, *Lettre à Dorp / La Supplication des âmes*, trans Germain Marc'hadour (Namur, 1962); and *La correspondance d'Erasme*, ed. Alois Gerlo and Paul Forier, 10 vols. (Paris and Brussels, 1967–81), 2 (Trans. M. A. Nauwelaerts). I have also been able to examine an unpublished translation by Roland Galibois through the courtesy of Germain Marc'hadour. For J. M. Kagan's Russian translation see Томас Мор 1478-1978: Коммунистическне Идеалы и История Культуры (Moscow, 1981), pp. 323–74. Partial English translations of the letter have also appeared in James J. Greene and John P. Dolan, eds., *The Essential Thomas More* (New York, 1967; hereafter cited as *"The Essential Thomas More"*); and with Vives, *Epistola in Pseudodialecticos*, ed. and trans. Rita Guerlac. Guerlac's partial translation is accurate and eloquent.

[3]The first complete English translation of the *Letter to Oxford*, by T. S. K. Scott-Craig, first appeared as "Thomas More's 1518 Letter to the University of Oxford," *Renaissance News*, *1* (1948), 17–24: it has also been printed in *SL* and elsewhere. The second English translation is included in *The Essential Thomas More*.

unpublished English translation of the *Letter to Lee*.[1] The *Letter to a Monk* has been translated once into English and once into French, but only the French and one section of the English are available in print.[2] All of these translations are based almost exclusively on the Latin of Rogers' edition. If there is room for improvement in Rogers' edition of the Latin there must also be room for improvement in even the most expert translation. Furthermore, an elaborate but versatile rhetoric like More's in these letters works by nuance as much as by simple assertion, so that modern vernacular translations must not only make sense of his Latin; they must also try to suggest how the discursive sense is conditioned and tempered by More's sense of style. The translator must try to preserve More's own suppleness of tone even as he preserves what he can of More's knotty Latin syntax; to do justice to that element of meaning which is most easily preserved in translation, he must furthermore try to do justice to those elements which are most easily lost. The successes of all who interpret or translate a work of rewarding complexity are apt to be partial but cumulative; "indeed, even average translators who come along after their betters will now and then find something on which they can make useful refinements" (*Letter to Dorp*, 82/4–5).

A NOTE ON THE TEXTS

Each of the Latin texts in this volume represents a moderately conservative transcription of the most authoritative available source-text. Thus, the copy-text for the *Letter to Dorp* is the manuscript *P*, for the *Letter to Oxford* the manuscript *T*, and for the *Letter to Lee* and the *Letter to a Monk* the *editio princeps* (1520^m). In each case, however, simple and necessary corrections attested in other versions of the texts have been adopted without hesitation on the assumption that not every slip of the pen in the copy-texts corresponds to a telling deviation in the phrasing of More's own lost autograph versions. More himself strongly endorses

---

[1]This unpublished translation is by Marcus Haworth, S.J.

[2]Half of Marcus Haworth's English translation of the *Letter to a Monk* is included in *SL*. A French version with a facing Latin text is included in Gibaud, *Réponse;* the translation alone has been published in *Moreana*, 27–28 (1970), 31–82. A partial translation (284/12–288/25) was included in John Day, *Day's Descant on Davids Psalmes . . .* (Oxford, 1620), sigs. D₃v–D₄v; this translation has been reprinted twice, once in *Bibliotheca Topograhica Britanniae*, 4/8, no. 17 (1783), 40–42; and once in A. W. Reed, *Early Tudor Drama* (London, 1926), app. VII, pp. 226–29. The earlier reprint is based on a manuscript copy of Day's excerpt (Lambeth Palace MS 595, p. 7) which was apparently the work of an archbishop of Canterbury, William Sancroft.

this working assumption in at least two discussions of editing; see the *Letter to a Monk,* 308/8–13, and the *Letter to Brixius.*[1] In a few other instances minor corrections have been introduced into the text; in particular, a few lingering indicative verb forms governed by *ut, ne, quin,* or *ut ne* in clauses of purpose or result have been changed to subjunctive forms in the interest of clarity. All such corrections, as well as all other substantive variants in the textual authorities, are recorded in the variant readings.[2]

The punctuation of the other main textual authorities is noted only where the punctuation of the present edition diverges from that of the copy-text. There are no paragraph divisions in the copy-texts for the *Letter to Dorp* and the *Letter to Oxford;* here the variant readings record only the two or three paragraph divisions found in the other textual authorities for these letters, and my own paragraph divisions have been introduced silently. There are only two paragraph divisions in either 1520 text of the *Letter to Lee,* both in *1520*[m] (156/17, 156/22); here, too, paragraph divisions have been introduced silently. There are numerous paragraph divisions in the 1520 texts of the *Letter to a Monk,* and here every departure from the paragraph division of these early texts is recorded in the variant readings. Even minor adjustments of capitalization or spelling have been faithfully recorded except in the *Letter to Oxford,* which includes so many adjustments of an intrusive uppercase *V* or *L* in the copy-text that it would be pointless to note all the instances. Except in the salutations and concluding dates, abbreviations in all four letters have been silently expanded.[3] Quotation marks have been silently inserted wherever appropriate. Square brackets in the text indicate an editorial addition; in the variant readings for the *Letter to Dorp,* they occasionally indicate a minor internal variant within one of the extended additions found in *S* and *1563.* Pointed brackets in the variants indicate letters or words which were written and then canceled in a manuscript.

The following major sigla have been used:

Letter to Dorp

P Paris, Bibliothèque nationale MS lat. 8703
S Sélestat, Bibliothèque municipale MS 345, fols. 6–30

---

[1]*CW* 3/2, 624/26-626/2.

[2]Words are frequently divided without hyphens in *1520*[m] and *1520*[a]; not all these casual divisions have been noted.

[3]Fairly often in P "ȩ" appears where it seems fairly clear that the scribe intended not "æ" but "e," for example in adverbial endings. In these cases, too, "ȩ" has been presented as "æ" in the variants.

1563 *Thomae Mori Lucubrationes*, Basel, 1563, sigs. z_7–D_6v.

1625 *Thomae Mori Dissertatio epistolica*, Leiden, 1625

Letter to Oxford

T Oxford, Bodleian MS Top. Oxon. e. 5

R Oxford, Bodleian MS Rawlinson D. 399

1588 Excerpt in Thomas Stapleton, *Tres Thomae . . .* , Douai, 1588, sigs. d_4–d_4v

1633 *Epistola Thomae Mori ad Academiam Oxoniensem*, ed. Richard James, Oxford, 1633

Letter to Lee, Letter to a Monk

1520[m] *Epistolae aliquot eruditorum . . .* , Antwerp, [May 1520], sigs. B_4–F_1, G_3–O_6

1520[a] *Epistolae aliquot eruditorum virorum . . .* , Basel, August 1520 sigs. G_4v–K_2, M_2v–S_1v

1520 Agreement of readings in *1520*[m] and *1520*[a]

1760 John Jortin, *The Life of Erasmus*, London, 1758–60, 2, 646–58, 670–99; reprint, 1808, 3, 342–53

HISTORIA RICHARDI TERTII

Textual History

Despite the invaluable editorial contribution of Richard Sylvester to the study of More's Latin history of Richard III, neither of the two Latin texts reproduced in *CW* 2 constitutes an entirely reliable guide to what More actually wrote. On the most rudimentary level both texts are replete with opaque, ungrammatical phrases which give the misleading impression that More left his Latin history not merely unpolished but barely half-formed. Although a judicious composite text would have resolved a large number of these textual cruxes,[1] the two principal source-texts Sylvester was able to turn to are both so imperfect that frequently neither affords more than a dubious hint of a really acceptable reading. Since the title page of the *editio princeps* (*1565*) explicitly states that More never found leisure to polish the style of the history in Latin, it would have been risky and virtually pointless to try to "restore" the whole text to a more refined form through conjecture.[2] Furthermore, since the two principal source-texts available to him represent two significantly different forms of the text, it is not at all strange that Sylvester decided to print both texts substantially unaltered instead of conflating acceptable readings from both at the cost of fidelity to either; but in consequence we have been left with a pair of corrupt Latin texts where at worst we expected one unpolished one.

Through an understandable oversight the most valuable textual authority for More's Latin history, catalogued as a manuscript in French, has gone unnoticed by students of More for the last several centuries. I discovered the text quite by accident while searching through a variety of manuscript catalogues for additional texts of More's letters. Along with a collection of Anglo-French treaties, the most recent of which dates from 1547, the new manuscript (*P*) is part of MS fr. 4996 (Ancien

---

[1] Jozef IJsewijn offered many improved readings of the Latin text as it appears in *CW* 2 ("Textverbesserungen zum 'Ricardus Tertius' des Thomas Morus," *Wolfenbütteler Renaissance Mitteilungen, 9/1* [1985], 8–10).

[2] For the text of the title-page notice in the *editio princeps* see the variants at 314/1–2.

fonds) of the Bibliothèque nationale in Paris.[1] Though the history now occupies folios 208–252 in the volume, the first two folia of the history were originally numbered "Fo. 1" and "Fo. 2"; thus the history has not always been bound along with the treaties. This new manuscript, an elegant and meticulous fair copy in an early- to mid-sixteenth-century hand,[2] contains a somewhat fuller version of the *Historia Richardi Tertii* than either of those reproduced in *CW 2*. Although *P* displays almost none of the treacherous vagaries of spelling which characterize the Arundel manuscript (*A*) transcribed in *CW 2*, *A* and *P* (together with the Harleian fragment *H*) almost certainly stem from a single working copy (*Y*) in which numerous but basically minor adjustments were made between the time when *A* was copied and the time when *P* and *H* were copied. *P* not only includes almost all of the remarkable interlineated or superscript variants that Sylvester has noted in *A* but also introduces a large number of others; *P* has fully 230 variants of this

---

[1]The small-folio volume passed into the manuscript collection of the Bibliothèque nationale in 1706 from the collection of the French bibliophiles Jean, Nicolas, and Emery Bigot, and in the inventories of the Bibliothèque nationale it is also described as Bigot MS 236. See also Leopold Delisle's reprint of the 1706 Bigot catalogue, *Bibliotheca Bigotiana Manuscripta* (Rouen, 1877), p. 64. According to L. E. Doucette, *Emery Bigot: Seventeenth-Century French Humanist* (Toronto, 1970), p. 5, Jean Bigot, father of Emery (1626–1689), was particularly interested in manuscripts bearing on French regional history; he may have acquired MS fr. 4996 to form part of his historical collection.

Incidentally, there is a false report of another manuscript of More's history (excerpts only) in the *Index to the Additional Manuscripts . . . Preserved in the British Museum and Acquired in the Years 1783–1835* (London, 1849), p. 318. British Library Add. MS 5482, fol. 4, actually contains nothing but the abdication speech of Richard II taken from a portion of Hall's *Chronicle* with which More's own history has nothing to do. Though the word "moore" does appear at the end of the excerpt, the page reference accompanying the name makes it clear that the excerpt was taken from Hall's printed text. Probably whoever copied the passage first noticed More's name in the list of authors prefixed to the *Chronicle* and then jumped to the baseless conclusion that More wrote the history of Richard II which the *Chronicle* includes. See *Hall's Chronicle* (London, 1809), pp. [viii] and 11.

[2]Laetitia Yeandle has graciously ventured to date the hand to "the first half of the sixteenth century"; P. O. Kristeller has tentatively assigned it to the "very early sixteenth century, or even very late fifteenth century if that is at all possible." Even though topical references establish that the *Historia* as it appears here cannot have been finished before 1514 (*CW 2*, lxiii-lxv), it also seems certain that *P* was completed not very many years after that date. Kathleen Perry has examined the manuscript's watermarks and found two different marks very similar to a French form of 1537; see C. M. Briquet, *Les filigranes*, Jubilee-Edition (Amsterdam, 1968), no. 12661. But since small variations in this very popular pattern may stand for quite different producers and dates, it would be rash to argue as if we had a definite date for either one of these variant watermarks, which simply bear out other probable evidence that the manuscript in question was copied before 1540.

sort, whereas *A* has no more than 80.[1] Many of the alternative readings in *P*, including a few which appear in *A* and a few which resurface in *1565*, are written in two italic hands (*P*^a and *P*^b) quite distinct from the main hand in this manuscript.[2] A variety of evidence, above all the distinctive array of omissions in *1565* as compared with omissions in *A*, *P*, and *H* and in excerpts translated from Latin in Rastell's edition of More's English history (*1557*^L), makes it clear that the excerpts in Rastell are based on a still earlier manuscript, probably autograph (*X*); the same evidence also supports the unsettling conclusion that the source-text for *1565* was in fact nothing more than a whimsically edited copy (*Z*) of the earliest stage of *Y*. Therefore *P* is not only the least garbled transcript of More's Latin history; it also provides, along with

---

[1]Since there are multiple internal variants at some points in *P* and *A*, and since certain consecutive variants are syntactically interdependent (and thus must be taken or left as a unit), it may be more informative to speak about internal variant *sites*. By my reckoning there are 204 such sites in *P* and 73 in *A* (most of them, in both manuscripts, to be found in the second half of the history). All but one of the sites in *A* (340/15) coincide with locations of internal variants in *P*, for a total of 205 sites; only once (at 426/7) does *A* furnish a variant incorporated in *1565* but omitted from *P*. At all but 31 of the 205 sites the reading of *1565* at least approximates one of the readings attested in the manuscripts. Since *1565* then turns out to agree with one of the readings in *P* at 173 out of 174 sites but with (one of) the readings in *A* at only 114 sites, it initially seems that *1565* must have a closer connection with *P* than with *A*; this appearance is actually misleading. If we count main readings as well as interlineated variants, *A* provides a total of approximately 260 readings at the first 182 variant sites (no *A* readings at all are available beyond 474/15, where *A* ends); of these readings, 44 percent are incorporated in *1565*, as opposed to about 39 percent of the 435 readings provided by *P* (42 percent even if we count each group of multiple variants as one unit). Most of the instances in which *A* lacks a reading attested in *P* and *1565* may result from the copyist's negligence; for two cases in which the scribe of *A* almost certainly disregarded an interlineated addition or supplement because he thought that it was a variant, see the variants at 450/11–13 and 464/13. At more than 80 percent of the variant sites for which the readings of *A* are available, the main reading of *A* agrees with the main reading of *P* and if *A* has a variant it agrees with a variant in *P*. In these instances, at least, it seems likely that *P* and *A* have refrained from reversing main readings and variants as found in their copy-text (for More's personal treatment of such readings see *CW 14*, 759, n. 4), so that the superscript reading in each case may well be the later one—not necessarily the better one, or else More simply would have discarded the first; where alternative readings are kept in a manuscript, it would be rash to ignore any one of them.

[2]It is hard to explain why a reading which must have already been present in *Y* at the time *A* was copied from *Y* should have had to be added to *P* by *P*^a or *P*^b if we hold that *P* was copied considerably later than *A*. I suspect that the main scribe of *P* could not always decipher the variant readings of *Y* and that many of the variants supplied by *P*^a (*P*^b generally merely corrects faulty readings in *P*) were supplied on the basis of variant readings already attested in *Y* which the main scribe of *P* either simply neglected or failed to decipher.

the Harleian fragment, the most final known form of a text which we know More never finished completely.[1] After sketching the evidence for the textual stemma I have already described, I will go on to argue that More himself probably had nothing to do with the radical alterations introduced in the source-text of *1565*. I will then turn to the implications of this new genealogical account of More's text for the relation between More's Latin history of Richard III and the parallel history in English.

The textual stemma that I am proposing is best represented as follows:

$$
\begin{array}{c}
[X] \\
\diagup \qquad \diagdown 1557^{\mathrm{L}} \\
[Y_1 - Y_2 - Y_3] \\
| \quad | \quad | \diagdown \\
[Z] \quad A \quad P \quad H \\
| \\
1565 \\
\diagup \qquad \diagdown \\
T \qquad 1689
\end{array}
$$

Sylvester's Tanner manuscript (*T*) and the edition of More's Latin history in the Frankfurt *Opera omnia* of 1689 are uncritical copies of

---

[1]Besides the apologetic title page of *1565* which informs us that More never finished or emended his history in Latin, there is also the evidence of two blank spaces in our manuscript texts of the Latin which correspond to blank spaces in Rastell's own almost certainly autograph texts of the Latin and English (see p. cxlvi). More apparently never quite finished either the Latin or the English version of the history; for further discussion of this topic see *CW* 2, xxvii, xxx.

As for the tenacious suspicion that the Latin history is essentially John Morton's work, not More's at all, see A. N. Kincaid's especially thorough presentation of the arguments for the existence in 1595 of a historical pamphlet attributed to Morton ("Sir Edward Hoby and 'K. Richard': Shakespeare Play or Morton Tract?" *Notes and Queries*, 226 [1981], 124–26). The chief "witness" for Morton is Sir Edward Hoby, who may well have examined a Latin tract very similar to More's English history around 1595 and who may well have heard from its owner, More's grandson Thomas Roper, that it was not More's work but Morton's. As Kincaid suggests, only a close correspondence between English and Latin could have justified Hoby's apparent conviction that More's English was merely derivative; since the extant versions of the Latin do not in fact correspond page-for-page with More's English, it seems highly unlikely that Hoby is referring to a still more distant *Urtext* of some sort which displayed few or none of the minor distinguishing features that are shared by More's English and all extant versions of the Latin. Thus the

Historia Richardi Tertii, Bibliothèque Nationale MS. fr. 4996 (*ancien fonds*), fol. 230ᵛ (reduced)

Effigy of Cardinal Morton in Canterbury Cathedral (reduced)

1565 without any real textual importance. The first step in defending this stemma is to establish the primitive character of the source-text of *1557*^{L}.[1] For this task it will not do simply to appeal to the evidence of omissions peculiar to *1557*^{L}, since it seems that occasional abridgment was one of the very few liberties that Rastell did claim as a translator. On the other hand, more certain evidence is not far to seek. We have the following sentence at 400/15–21 of *P, A,* and *1565:*

> Ceterum Protector ac Dux / vbi Cardinalem atque Cancellarium cum Eboracensi Archiepiscopo Comiteque Darabiae atque Eliensi presule nec non Hastyngo Camerario multisque alijs nobilibus collocauerant de ordine ritu ac solemnibus insigniendi Regis cere- monijs locuturos / ipsi interim subducentes sese . . . alio in loco longe diuersa tractabant.

> But when the Protector and the Duke had assembled the cardinal and the chancellor along with the archbishop of York, the Earl of Derby, the prelate of Ely, Hastings the lord chamberlain, and many other noblemen to talk over the program, the ritual, and the solemnities of the king's coronation, they themselves meanwhile slipped off . . . to discuss very different things elsewhere.[2]

The corresponding sentence in *1557*^{L} (*CW* 2, 44/15–18) begins in the following way:

> But the protectour and the duke, after y^t, that they had set the lord Cardinall, the Archebishoppe of Yorke than lorde Chancellour,

---

Latin text that Hoby had in mind must have been very much like our versions; but all of our versions are full of reports and allusions that could not have been made before 1513– 17 or by anyone but More. We may trust Hoby's conceivably eyewitness-account of the manuscript without accepting his hearsay account of its provenance according to More's grandson Roper, who may simply have gotten two manuscripts confused or else made far too much of an old family rumor that More's work was based on a document by Morton; nor would Roper have felt much regret at transferring authorial rights to a work as ill- written and even as shortsighted as the Louvain edition of the Latin *Richardus* made it seem. In any case we can safely assume that the Latin history that we have is More's, whether or not he had access to any notes about Richard by Morton.

[1]For earlier attempts to establish the relation between *1557*^{L} and surviving texts of More's Latin see *CW* 2, xliv–xlvii; and Hanham, pp. 198–99, 106–07.

[2]Unless otherwise noted, translations in this introduction are mine. In citing More's Latin I give only my own text and page references except for extended verbatim citations from *A* or *1565,* for which I give a page reference to *CW* 2 followed by a page reference to my text unless it has been given previously. Page references to More's English in *CW* 2 are accompanied by a page reference to my Latin text unless I have already referred to the parallel passage in Latin.

the Bishoppe of Ely, the lord Stanley and the lord Hastinges than lord chamberleine, w^t many other noble men. . . .

By this point we have already read in both the English and the Latin histories that the archbishop of York was deprived of the chancellorship immediately after the Prince of Wales first came to London (*CW* 2, 25/3–4 [358/26–27]). Apparently More did not know this when he prepared the first version of the Latin; by the time that the second was copied he had already made the correction. In the autograph text of More's English on which Rastell based the rest of *1557* there was another confusion regarding the archbishop of York which suggests that there, too, More originally thought the archbishop remained in good standing as chancellor even after the Prince's arrival.[1] Since the error in *1557*^{L} is not present in *P, A,* or *1565,* it is clear that all three must derive from a more advanced form of More's history in Latin.

Another indication that *1557*^{L} probably stems from an earlier form

---

[1] In the English of *CW* 2, 27/24–25 and 28/9, the archbishop of York is twice named instead of the lord cardinal (archbishop of Canterbury) as the very man whom Richard of Gloucester, the future Richard III, wants to send to the queen to persuade her to let her second son out of sanctuary. It seems very unlikely that More would have ever had Richard address the strong flattery of *CW* 2, 26/26–31, to the same man that Richard and his supporters had "greatlye reproued" and deprived of his office at a council described on the preceding page (*CW* 2, 25/3–4). More presumably inserted the reference to the removal of the archbishop of York from the chancellorship at the same time that he altered the reference at *CW* 2, 26/26–31, from the archbishop of York to the cardinal, while the next two erroneous references in his English manuscript escaped his attention. This account of the textual confusions at *CW* 2, 27/23–25, 28/9, and 44/15–18 seems a good deal more plausible to me than Sylvester's hypothesis, according to which More was at some point misled into thinking that Thomas, lord cardinal, archbishop of Canterbury, was actually the same person as Thomas, archbishop of York (*CW* 2, 194). For one thing, it would certainly have been easier for More to get two minor details wrong in his research, the details of which cleric Richard sent to the queen and of when the archbishop of York lost the chancellorship, than the more basic facts that Thomas, archbishop of York, was no cardinal and that Thomas, archbishop of Canterbury, was no chancellor. For another thing, the Latin of *P, A,* and *1565,* where it differs from Rastell's translation at *CW* 2, 44/15–18, does not have to be translated the way Sylvester translates it, as if More were explicitly claiming that the cardinal himself was lord chancellor: "Cardinalem atque Cancellarium cum Eboracensi archiepiscopo" does not necessarily mean "the cardinal and chancellor with the archbishop of York" (*CW* 2, 211) if by "cardinal and chancellor" we mean the same person (cf. Hanham, p. 207, n. 7). But Sylvester, who wishes to argue that the source-text of *1557*^{L} was a more advanced form of the history than the source-text of *A* so that he can explain an omission appearing in both *1557*^{L} and *1565* as a deliberate authorial deletion (*CW* 2, xlvii), contends that "the lord Cardinall, the Archebishoppe of Yorke th[e]n lorde Chancellour," and so on, is actually an improvement on the reading preserved in the extant Latin texts; to do so, he has to interpret the Latin in this rather unlikely way.

of the text and indeed a more primitive manuscript than either *P* or *1565* is an omission which disrupts the sense of the Latin in both of these texts (*A* and *H* have already broken off) where the sense was apparently complete in the source-text of *1557*ᴸ. The omission presumably occurred when the working copy *Y* was being made from the autograph *X*. At 484/16–18 of the history, where More is describing Richard's return from accepting the kingship at Westminister, *P* reads as follows:

> Inter remigrandum vt quemque habuit in via obuium ita semper ad seruilem prope adulationem animus iacet admissi conscius. . . .

At this point *1565* has the following (*CW* 2, 81/31–82/2):

> Inter remigrandum vt quemque habuit in via obuium, ita semper illis ad seruilem prope adulationem se demisit, admissi conscius. . . .

The reading in *1557*ᴸ (*CW* 2, 82/3–5) makes considerably more sense:

> In his returne homeward, whom so euer he met he saluted. For a mind that knoweth it self giltye, is in a maner deiected to a seruile flattery.

From the last several words of the English, a literal rendering of "semper ad seruilem prope adulationem animus iacet admissi conscius," it is clear that the source-text of *1557*ᴸ was substantially in agreement at this point with the source-text of *P*; the reading in *1565*, on the other hand, seems to incorporate a rather inept emendation. As we shall see, alterations of this sort are common in *1565*. What concerns us for now is not how the editors of *1565* tried to repair the omission but rather the fact that this omission is evident in both *P* and *1565*. There is no equivalent in either of these Latin texts for the words "he saluted" and "For" that we find in *1557*ᴸ. What constitutes a freestanding *sententia* in the English has been muddled up with the syntax of a larger historical-infinitive construction in the Latin of both *P* and *1565*.[1] It would seem

---

[1] For More's *sententia* cf. Plautus, *Bacchides* 1024: "qui deliquit supplex est ultro omnibus." More's historical-infinitive construction includes the verbs and verb phrases "securus esse . . . confidere . . . referre . . . circumspectare vndique velut repercussurus" (484/19–21). For the syntax of the historical or descriptive infinitive in Latin see Kühner–Stegmann, 2/1, 135–38. For other examples in More's *Historia* see 324/8–13, 354/17–20, 402/7–10, 420/21-422/2, 438/14–19, and 472/6–8. I have conjecturally identified the missing infinitive at 484/17 as *adblandiri* on the basis of *blandiebatur* at 484/19 and the visual resemblance between *semper adblandiri* and *semper ad seruilem* at 484/17.

that the scribe of a manuscript which lies behind both *P* and *1565* overlooked a few words of More's Latin through simple haplography (for example, "ita [semper adblandiri / nam] semper ad seruilem prope adulationem") and thus generated the problem in both later texts.

Since the three translated excerpts which constitute *1557*[L] occupy only about four complete pages of *CW* 2, it is fortunate that they include even two such good clues about their source-text in Latin. There is one other clue in these excerpts which is equally important for establishing the relation of the source-text of *1565* to both earlier and later ones. At 400/8–10, after describing the unsought largesse which Richard added to the favors requested by Buckingham as the price of his joining Richard's conspiracy, More appends an important qualification which is present in both *A* and *P* but omitted in both *1557*[L] and *1565:*

> . . . nisi falsa discordanti post exprobrauit velut tantis ipsius beneficijs ingrato.
> . . . unless Gloucester falsely reproached him with this, as if he were ungrateful for such immense favors, when he opposed him later on.

There is nothing thematically or stylistically objectionable about this qualification; there is certainly no reason why both Rastell and the editors of *1565* should deliberately omit it. Furthermore, it is probably an afterthought, precisely the sort of passage we would expect to see introduced here and there in the more advanced stages of a text; nor is this the only such afterthought which is present in *A* and *P* but omitted in *1565*.[1] Even though *1565* almost certainly stems from a more advanced manuscript than the source-text of *1557*[L], it is clear that the source-text of *1565* was in some ways more primitive than the source-text behind *A* and *P*.

There is some evidence of kinship between the source-text of *1565* and the source-text of *A*. At *CW* 2, 13/15–19 (336/4–8), *1565* and *A* read as follows:

> Verum si vos in pueri regno discordia occupet, multi nimirum viri boni atque egregij videntur ante perituri, vt [et *A*] pariter ipsi nec

---

[1] For other extended omissions in *1565* see the variants at 316/9, 320/8, 366/19, 392/15, 412/8, 412/12–14, 414/3–5, 418/12–13, 418/25, 426/17-428/11, 428/29-430/2, 430/24–25, 462/2–3, 468/17, 472/14, 478/3–6, 480/17–18, 480/22, and 482/20–24. The following deletions, unlike most of the omissions I have already mentioned, appear to be cases of straightforward censorship; 424/8–10, 428/19–21, 428/22–23, 434/4–6.

> Principe interim tuto, & vobis ipsis in primis [impunis *A*] periculo obnoxijs, quam populus intestina semel seditione soeuiens in pacem rursus ac [et *A*] concordiam redeat.

> But if you fall at variance in the reign of a child, many good and excellent men are likely to perish and you yourselves also, with the prince threatened and you in the most danger of all, before a nation which has once broken out in internal sedition will be restored to tranquility and harmony.

The redundant words "et pariter ipsi" ("and you yourselves also") are almost certainly a kind of false start, inadvertently left in a form of the text from which both *1565* and *A* derive. There is no trace of them in *P* or *H*, or for that matter in the parallel passage of More's English history. Once again *1565* appears to incorporate a rather ineffectual emendation: "vt pariter ipsi" is as redundant as "et pariter ipsi." These words were presumably canceled in *Y* between the time that *A* was copied and the time that *P* and *H* were copied. Another feature that *1565* and *A* have in common is the omission of a whole summary clause (given in *P* and More's English) at 468/17. Once again there is nothing thematically or stylistically objectionable about what is omitted; indeed, the clause helps to elucidate the lines it succeeds. This omission is yet another indication of how *Y* was gradually altered after giving rise to *Z*: in its second state *Y* was the source-text of *A*, in its third state the source-text of *P*.

There is a witty anecdote in both *A* and *P* (and also in More's English) which is lacking in *1565*. In this one instance, *A* has a clause which is absent in *P*; I believe that in this case More simply omitted a clause which, while not quite redundant, detracts from the pungency of the quip. At *CW* 2, 131/21–26 (422/20–26), after describing the way Richard and Buckingham defeated their own rhetorical purposes by issuing an edict which must have taken many hours to compose in order to denounce a conspiracy which they had supposedly discovered only two hours before, *A* continues as follows:

> Itaque magister ludi quidam / nisi quod res attrocior erat quam que ioculares facetias admitteret / haud irridicule tam solertem edicti stulticiam illuserat nam vt turbe immixtus auscultabat legentem / temporis angustiam cum longitudinem [*sic*] scriptorum et cura comparans protinus theretiani [*sic*] dicti admonitus haud satis commode diuisa sunt temporibus daue hec tibi inquit.

> And so, if the matter were not too atrocious to be a fit subject for witticisms, the joke that a certain schoolmaster directed at the

crafty stupidity of the edict would certainly have been not unamusing. For as he stood in the crowd listening to the man who was
reading the edict and as he compared the shortness of the time
with the length and laboriousness of the writing, he was promptly
reminded of a saying from Terence and commented, "You have
not spaced these episodes very well, Davus."

Since the clause "temporis . . . comparans" ("and as he compared the
shortness of the time with the length and laboriousness of the writing")
merely recapitulates what has been said in the preceding lines, it would
make sense for More to delete it. Thus this instance does not contradict
the hypothesis that the source-text of P was a more advanced form of
the source-text of A.

We must also consider the provenance of the Harleian manuscript
(H). This mid-sixteenth-century fragment is too short to include many
clues of the sort we have so far considered, but peculiarities of spelling
make it reasonably likely that the fragment derives either directly or
indirectly from the same manuscript that gave rise to A and P.[1] The
high quality of the text makes it likely that H is directly dependent on Y;
it is out of the question that H has been copied from A as Sylvester
suggests.[2] Meanwhile one constructive omission (at 336/5) that is evident in both P and H makes it likely, at least, that the fragment was
copied from the most advanced stage of Y, and of course if the fragment does date from the mid-sixteenth century, that is, after More's
death, it must either have been copied directly from the most advanced
stage of Y or else not have been copied directly from Y at all. On the
other hand, there are a number of superior readings in H which do not
appear in either of the other two manuscripts, and at one point where
1565, A, and P read "sapientior" H substitutes "prudentior";[3] thus it is
at least possible that the source-text of H was a still more advanced
stage of Y which we might call Y_4. H generally incorporates either the
interlineated variant or the main reading found at a given point in the
other two manuscripts but virtually never gives both readings. I suspect this is merely an instance of scribal selection; the fact that the
manuscript ends in mid-page at a logical stopping-place suggests that it

---

[1]For a detailed and careful collation of A and H see *CW* 2, 96–107. P, A, and H all have
the following odd spellings corrected in *1565:* "sanxiretur" for "sanciretur" (328/23),
"consiliandos" for "conciliandos" (334/7), and "sanctiendae" for "sanciendae" (344/1).
[2]For Sylvester's suggestion see *CW* 2, xl; for two features of H with no precedent in A
see p. cxli above, and the variants at 332/24.
[3]For superior readings in H see the variants at 318/7, 318/29, and 322/15; for "prudentior" see the variants at 320/21.

was never intended as a complete and exhaustively detailed reproduction of its own original, and scribal selection between variants is a sufficiently common phenomenon for More to describe it at one point as almost a matter of course.[1] Therefore *H* does not necessarily exclude the same variants that More himself would have excluded in a final revision; contrary to Sylvester's account of how More's Latin history developed, there is really no manuscript evidence that a final revision occurred.[2]

Though I think it is now fairly clear that the main textual source of *1565* was a cruder form of the text than the ones from which *A, P,* and *H* were derived, we must still deal with the possibility that More turned aside to the source-text of *1565* and there introduced radical changes which somehow escaped being transferred to the rest of the manuscript tradition. Sylvester acknowledges the possibility that these changes were not made by More and acutely remarks on the difference between the quite minor lexical changes suggested by variant readings in *A* and the sweeping syntactical changes imposed by rewriting in *Z*, the source-text of *1565*.[3] Now that the additional variant readings attested in *P* show how uncharacteristic the sweeping syntactical changes of *Z* actually are when compared with the tentative lexical changes accompanying each new stage of *Y*, it is harder than ever to see why an author content to revise his own wording in a more complete manuscript of a work would have turned back to overhaul much of his syntax in a cruder and less complete manuscript. Though there is nothing particularly embarrassing about the Latinity of More's history, at least in its most advanced form, it is clear from the apologetic title page of *1565* that the editors of that text did consider the Latin of More's history embarrassing—embarrassing enough, I believe, to provoke them to garble More's Latin again and again in a clumsy attempt to improve it. Since the Arundel manuscript is both corrupt and incomplete it was natural enough for Sylvester to hope that the text of *1565* embodied a more correct version of More's Latin history; in fact it does not. Though it does introduce a few obvious corrections, it generally worsens real textual problems wherever it seeks to resolve them.

---

[1] In the *Letter to Brixius, CW 3/2,* 626/21–30, More mentions scribal selection between variants as one of the three likeliest reasons for unauthorized readings in Froben's edition of More's Latin poetry.

[2] For Sylvester's account see *CW 2,* xl–xli.

[3] See *CW 2,* xxxiv; "The possibility that they [*sc.* the editors of *1565*] themselves indulged in some effort to smooth out the text will haunt the remainder of this discussion"; and *CW 2,* xxxix.

Sylvester's best arguments for the greater correctness of *1565* rely on omissions of something essential in *A* where the author, it seems, has repaired the omission in *1565*.[1] The first argument is based on the fact that while the manuscripts describe only three of Edward IV's daughters at the beginning of the history and then leave a gap in the text, *1565* concurs with More's English history in describing all five daughters. Here is how the passage runs in *1565* (*CW* 2, 3/1–17 [314/6–23]):

> EDVARDVS Rex, eius nominis quartus . . . concessit fatis . . . super-stitibus masculi sexus liberis duobus, foeminei quatuor: Eduardo videlicet Rege designato, annorum circiter tredecim: Richardo Eboraci Duce, qui biennio minor erat: Elisabetha, quae postea ducentibus fatis Henrici septimi coniunx fuit, et octaui mater, regina forma atque indole egregia. Cecilia, non perinde fortunata ac formosa. Et Brigitta, virtutem eius cuius nominis erat reprae-sentante, professa, et vitam religiosam ducente in monasterio monialium inclusarum apud Dertfordiam. Anna, postea honor-ifice nupta Thomae, tunc temporis domino Havvardo, et postea Comiti de Surre. Et Catherina, quae sortem subinde variam experta, interdum secundam, saepius aduersam. Postremo si haec postrema est, (nam adhuc viuit) pietate, beneficentiaque nepotis Henrici octaui prosperrimam, ac se plane dignam consecuta est.

All the manuscripts omit the words "Et Brigitta . . . Surre. Et." Two things are remarkable about this addition: it is an unusually close Latin equivalent of the corresponding passage in More's English history, and it clumsily disrupts the asyndeton of the rest of the Latin by beginning and ending with "Et" (the description of Brigitte does not start with "And" in the English). I believe that the passage was translated from *1557* by the editors of *1565* to fill up an obvious sense-gap in their Latin source-text.[2] This view gains support from the fact that while *1565* catalogues all five daughters, it mentions just "quatuor," or "four," at

---

[1] *CW* 2, xxxv–xxxvi.

[2] The editors of *1565* were undoubtedly aware of *1557;* see *CW* 2, 2. It is strange that More left such an obvious lacuna in the Latin at a point where the sense of the English is fairly complete; perhaps he wished to make it quite clear that the Latin was still in an unfinished and unpolished state, not yet ready for publishing. A humanist's prestige could suffer very considerable harm from the publication of any Latin work showing any stylistic "rough edges" at all; see More's comments in the *Letter to Brixius, CW* 3/2, 626/3–5. Until the editors of *1565* turned to *1557* and obtained an appropriate stopgap, the lacuna near the very beginning of More's Latin history must have protected it very effectively against being published without More's consent and assistance.

the start of the catalogue; at this point in the catalogue the manuscripts all mention "quinque," or "five," though the reading in *P* is corrected from "quatuor."[1] This discrepancy suggests once again that the source-text of *1565* was a copy of the crude, *less* complete stage of *Y*. The passage in *1565* includes one other quite minor correction which could also have come from the English: while the manuscripts all give the age of Prince Edward as "vndecim," *1565* rightly reads "tredecim." I do not find it likely that More would have made this correction and taken the trouble to translate descriptions of King Edward's other two daughters without also correcting the overall tally of daughters in this text the same way that he did in Y_2. This is probably just one more example of careless revision by the editors of *1565*.

Sylvester's three other main arguments (apart from those based on two lengthy omissions peculiar to *A*) bear on three short omissions apparent in both *A* and *P* where it looks as if *1565* has corrected the textual problem.[2] In these instances, however, *P* enables us to see that *1565* simply tries to conceal the problem and that the omissions in More's text should stand. The first text (338/26-340/3) reads as follows in *P*, *A*, and *H*:

---

[1]The fact that the number of Edward IV's daughters is once again wrongly given as four later on in the Latin (352/3) indicates that this error is probably primitive and does not result from a transcription error in the source-text of *1565* as Sylvester suggests. As in the case of More's incorrect reference to the archbishop of York in the English (see p. cxxxviii above), More here apparently corrected the first instance of the numerical error in *Y* but neglected the second. Interestingly, More correctly names all *five* of Edward IV's daughters who lived past early infancy in his "Rueful Lamentation" for the death of the eldest, Elizabeth, in 1503 (*The History of King Richard III and Selections from the English and Latin Poems*, ed. R. S. Sylvester, New Haven and London, 1976, p. 122); either the correct tally of Edward IV's children had simply slipped More's mind by the time that he started to write the first draft of the history (traditionally assigned to the year 1513), or else the first draft of the history antedates More's poem on Elizabeth. Neither possibility provides any new support for the old claim that More's Latin history was substantially the work of his patron, John Morton (see Sir George Buck, *The History of King Richard III* [1619], ed. Arthur N. Kincaid, Gloucester, 1979, pp. ciii–cvi, 121): Morton was considerably less likely than More to mistake the true tally of Edward IV's children, just as the former councillor of Edward IV was less likely than More to exaggerate that king's age at the time of his death by a margin of nearly thirteen years (see *CW* 2, Commentary at 3/1). Morton's contribution to More's history was probably limited to a disjointed series of anecdotes, some true, others merely defamatory.

[2]For the lengthy omissions peculiar to *A* see the variants at 386/21, 400/3, and 474/15. Since the final words preceding the first omission are written as catchwords in *A* at the bottom of a page, the likeliest explanation for this omission is that one gathering of leaves has been lost from the manuscript. The second passage omitted consists of the last four and a half pages of the history.

"Meminisse vos" (inquit) "opinor patrem eius . . . eius factionis suasu impulsuque quouis circumactum / longe profecto magis quam aut ex ipsius honore aut re cuiusquam fuerit preterquam illorum immoderatam   qui suane bona an mala nostra auidius appetierunt in incerto est."

The corresponding passage in More's English (*CW* 2, 15/3–9) runs as follows:

Ye remember I trow king Edward himself . . . was . . . in manye thynges ruled by ye bende, more then stode either with his honour, or our profite, or with the commoditie of any man els, except onely the immoderate aduauncement of them selfe. Whiche whither they sorer thirsted after their own weale, or our woe, it wer hard I wene to gesse.

The English word "auauncement" is written in the margin alongside the blank space in *P;* clearly More wished to convey the same sense in the Latin that is given by the English phrase "except onely the immoderate aduancement of them selfe." *1565* here reads simply "praeterquam illorum qui" and thus loses the force of the English entirely. The next of Sylvester's omissions occurs in a passage which *A* gives as follows (*CW* 2, 107/26–29 [344/10–13]):

. . . forte accidit vt vodiuilus reginae frater quem diximus ibidem restiterit postero mane iturus ad regem vbi eam noctem transegit   ab hamptona millibus / igitur vodeuilus officiose ducibus concurrens . . .

1565 omits "millibus" and begins a new sentence with "ab," thus distorting the sense of the passage. The blank space in *A*, which is clearly intended for a numeral to modify "millibus," corresponds to a blank space in the autograph of More's English history from which Rastell printed *1557* (*CW* 2, variant at 17/14): More did not know how many miles separate Northhampton from Stony Stratford when he wrote the two histories, and for this reason he left a blank space in both texts to be filled if he ever found out. There is a similar blank in both *P* and *1557*^L near the end of the text (*CW* 2, variant at 82/8 [484/22]) which *1565* once again roughly tries to conceal with unfortunate results for the sense. The next omission noted by Sylvester occurs at 344/20: More left a short blank in the source-text of *A* and *P* for the names of some fellow conspirators of Richard and Buckingham. At this point *1565* reads "alios"; *1557* (*CW* 2, 17/21) has the equally vague "a few of their moste priuye frendes." "Alios" here is simply a stopgap, and in this case the text would read almost as well with no stopgap at all.

Thus, many of the corruptions in *1565* have the look of misguided corrections, though some are undoubtedly simple mistakes of transcription. A few fairly clear cases of tampering will suffice to show that the editors of *1565* were quite capable of radically changing their source-text. At 332/2–4, *P*, *A*, and *H* read as follows:

> Virilis etatis robori vestra fortasse sufficiat fides / at puerilis authoritate regenda est / adolescens fulcienda consilijs. . .

More's English is reasonably similar (*CW* 2, 11/20–21):

> If they wer menne, your faithfulnesse happelye woulde suffise. But childehood must be maintained by mens authoritye, and slipper youth vnderpropped with elder counsayle. . . .

At this point *1565* turns a compliment into a slur (*CW* 2, 11/23–25):

> Quod si viri essent, minus fortasse desideraretur fides. At vero pueritia autoritate regenda est, adolescentia fulcienda consilijs. . .

While the manuscript version agrees with the English in suggesting that all of the courtiers King Edward addresses are faithful if less than judicious, *1565* clearly hints that the courtiers are neither. Edward never impugns the fidelity of either court faction with regard to the young princes themselves, and in a speech of reconciliation it would make no sense for him to do so. The editors of *1565* thought that "vestra fortasse sufficiat fides" implied that the courtiers did not have much *fides* to offer, and on this assumption the editors rewrote More's own words in a way which confused the true sense.[1] The next corruption is easier to deal with because it results from an obvious verbal misreading of the manuscript text. At 342/15–19 *P*, *A*, and *H* read as follows:

> . . . si amici Reginae cogant multitudinem / iniecturos haud dubie metum his quibus aliquando simultas cum illis intercesserat / ne

---

[1]Of course it is just barely conceivable that "minus fortasse desideraretur fides" is an earlier and cruder version of what More thought that Edward should say here. At two points in the history the source-text of *1565* may well have included material which was canceled in the two later stages of *Y;* see the variants at 404/9–14 and 420/1–8, where the reading of *1565* actually says nothing new but does stay rather closer to More's English than does the comparable passage in *P* and *A* (for a similar survival of canceled material in manuscript copies of More's *De Tristitia* see *CW 14,* 725–26). Even so, I find it hard to believe that More would ever have adopted such a roundabout way of expressing the notion that "faithfulness" in a young monarch's counsellors will not be enough if clear judgment is lacking.

> non tutandi Regis causa / cui nemo discrimen intentet / sed inua-
> dendi sui congregetur / recrudescente discordia. . . .

Now here is the same passage in *1565* (*CW* 2, 16/13–16):

> . . . si amici reginae cogant multitudinem, iniecturos haud dubie
> metum hijs quibus aliquando simultas cum illis intercesserat, ne
> non tantummodo regis causa, cui nemo discrimen intentet, inua-
> dendi: sin congregetur, discordia.

A simple confusion between "sui" and "sin" has led the editors of *1565* to change "tutandi" into "tantummodo," to omit the essential words "sed" and "recrudescente," and to treat the ablative "discordia" as a nominative, all in a futile attempt to make better sense of a passage with which nothing was basically wrong in the first place. Three other clear cases in which someone has either deleted a number of words or rewritten a whole phrase in response to a trivial difficulty in the copy-text occur in *1565* at 368/5, 444/17, and 446/6–7 (see the variants). In another amusing instance it would seem that the editors of *1565* altered each of two adjacent words in an effort to make More's Latin more elegant, but while More's words make sense as they stand, the words in *1565* must be rearranged before they make any real sense at all ("perquam rem gratam facturam" for "egregie gratificaturum" at 378/19). There is no reason to think that these editors showed any greater respect for their copy-text at the other places where their own printed version diverges from *P, A,* and *H*.

This new genealogical account of More's history in Latin suggests several significant modifications in Sylvester's schema relating More's history in Latin to his history in English.[1] On the basis of all the available evidence, a complete family tree of More's histories in English and Latin should look something like the chart given on the opposite page. Broken lines represent routes of textual *contaminatio* or cross-pollination. In the formative stages, this cross-pollination may well have produced some impressive stylistic effects in both languages; on the other hand, non-authorial *contaminatio* in the later diffusion-stages has (as usual) produced sheer confusion.[2] As the diagram shows, I am not convinced that the differently-organized Hardyng-Hall versions of the English (*1543, 1548*) are derived from a deviant form of the text for

---

[1] *CW* 2, l–lix.

[2] For cross-pollination between English and Latin in the formative stages of the history see p. cl, n. 1: for *contaminatio* in *1565* see pp. cxliv–cxlv above; for *contaminatio* in *1568* see *CW* 2, xxiv and lii. Since Rastell marked his own translated excerpts from More's Latin in *1557*, his conflation is not *contaminatio* in the usual sense of the word.

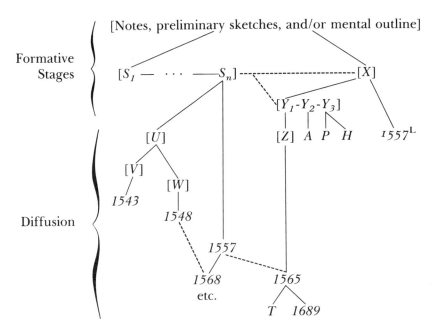

which More was responsible, though a few minor variants in those versions may derive from a slightly earlier stage in the development of the author's own manuscript (S) than the stage which eventually gave rise to *1557*.[1]

A detailed comparison of *1557* with the most final known version of More's history in Latin reveals that each text includes valuable if minor additions to the history as it probably appeared in the copy-text of *1565* but that these two sets of additions are not coextensive: More's working texts of the Latin and English were both revised rather haphazardly in many details after the copy-text of *1565* was transcribed from a form of the Latin text more closely related to a lost earlier form of the English.[2] Hence syntactical and lexical comparison

---

[1]The assumption that *S* went through more than one stage appears justified by the factual inconsistency discussed on p. cxxxviii above: More apparently corrected some instances of one factual error in *S* (also present in *X*) but overlooked several other instances of the same error.

[2]We have seen that the wording of *1565* includes many unauthorized departures from the wording of More's Latin manuscripts; thus a simple comparison of the Latin wording in *1565* and the English wording in *1557* is rather unlikely to reveal any close connection between the copy-text of *1565* and any form of the history in English. On the other hand, quite a few extended omissions which are not improvements are com-

between the advanced English version of *1557* and the corrupt Latin version of *1565* or the advanced version of *P* is unlikely to show us which primitive parallel version of More's history, whether English or Latin, was actually prior, since we do not have either one to compare.[1] Though the case might be altered significantly if we could accept the assumption that the differently-organized Hardyng-Hall versions (*1543, 1548*) preserve an authentically primitive text of More's history in English, this strictly conjectural assumption now seems quite unlikely.[2] Even granted that the verbal differences between *1543* (Richard Grafton's editorial supplement to John Hardyng's metrical chronicle) and *1548* (Grafton's edition of Edward Hall's chronicle, which incorporates More's history) strictly rule out the possibility that both texts are directly derived from the same manuscript, it is still perfectly possible that both are derived indirectly from one manuscript (*U*) in which some reader tampered extensively with More's organization and phrasing.[3] *1543* and *1548* share the same omissions as *1557* with

---

mon to *1565* and *1557* (see the variants at 320/8, 412/7–8, 412/12–14, 414/3–5, 426/17-428/11, 428/19–21, 462/2–3, 472/14, 480/17–18, 480/22, and the English of *1557* in *CW* 2); these omissions suggest that in terms of its content the source-text of *1565* bore considerably more resemblance to a primitive form of the English than the copy-texts of *P*, *A*, or *H* (*1557* also concurs with the reading of *P* at a number of other points where *1565* has omissions; compare this list with the one given on p. cxl, n. 1, above). For two instances in which the wording of *1565* does stay considerably closer to that of the English than that of the manuscript Latin see p. cxlvii, n. 1, above.

[1] It may well be essentially misleading to speculate about which form of the history, the Latin or the English, is actually prior, since there is evidence of considerable cross-pollination in either direction between extant versions in each language. At one point in the Latin More was definitely at a loss for the right word to translate the English "a-vauncement" (see the variants at 340/1–2); on the other hand, in King Edward's deathbed oration (330/16-336/16), an elaborate rearrangement and paraphrase of a deathbed oration in Sallust (*Bellum Iugurthinum* 9.4–11.1), it seems likely that More's Latin provided an intermediate source for his English. Though the stylistic advice that More gives to his children in Rogers, pp. 256–57 (quoted in *CW* 2, xli), according to which it is generally good policy to write out a rough draft in English before working a text up in Latin, might appear to suggest that he must have begun the *Historia* with a rough draft in English, it is doubtful that he himself generally wrote out an English rough draft when composing such works as *Utopia*. The circular or spiraling processes of "double translation" (see p. xxxi above) may well furnish a better analogy for the composition of More's double history than the straightforward process which he recommends to his children.

[2] For this assumption see *CW* 2, xx–xxix.

[3] Sylvester has already suggested (*CW* 2, 276) that Edward Hall may have furnished the manuscript (*V*) which Grafton used as a copy-text for *1543;* Hall was perfectly capable of "improving" on More's text, as the many bizarre verbal flourishes found only in *1548* very amply establish. It may be that Hall introduced various changes into *U* before the copy-text (*V*) of *1543* was copied and then made further changes in pre-

the Latin of *1565*, and like *1557* they concur with the reading of the extant Latin manuscripts at a number of other points where *1565* has omissions (see p. cxlix, n. 2, above); hence it seems that the copy-text of *1543* and *1548*, like the copy-text of *1557*, was affected by a good deal of textual cross-pollination with the advanced stages of More's Latin (Y_2 and Y_3). From the placement of one of Rastell's translated excerpts (*CW* 2, 42/24-44/18 [396/21-400/20]) it is clear that the organization of even the primitive Latin text X resembled that of the extant Latin versions and not that of *1543* and *1548* (see *CW* 2, xxvi); it seems highly unlikely that More would have retained an alternative and even more primitive organization in one form of his English while revising its contents along with a more advanced form of his Latin. Other considerations make it equally unlikely that the Hardyng-Hall texts represent a still more *advanced* form of More's English.[1] We are left with two somewhat divergent authorial versions of the history in English and Latin (best represented by *1557* and *P*) and two heavily and capriciously "edited" versions (the Hardyng-Hall texts and *1565*).

Quite apart from mere verbal discrepancies, a comparison of *1557* and the manuscript Latin text reveals structural differences between the English and Latin that may be as important as any detailed sim-

---

paring the copy (*W*) from which *1548* was derived. Neither Grafton nor Hall seems to have felt any qualms about "editing" More's history away from the incomplete state in which they must have found it: even Hanham (pp. 203, 216–17), who defends the authority of the Hardyng-Hall versions, appears to acknowledge that one of the editors is responsible for several significant (and jarring) interpolations and changes in More's English (cf. *CW* 2, xxiii–xxiv). Though Hanham (p. 210) suggests that "there was no obvious reason for an editor to disturb the order" of More's English history, Hall had very good reason to rearrange More's text, since in Hall's scheme it forms a transitional "history of Edward V," while in More's standard versions the drama of Richard's usurpation forms a self-contained whole. As another large-scale compiler, Richard Grafton may well have been similarly tempted to rearrange More's text.

[1] For a vigorous effort to vindicate the Hardyng-Hall text as a more advanced draft of More's history see Hanham, pp. 202–19. One interpolated speech (*CW* 2, 58/3 variant) which Hanham (pp. 181, 205) describes as an authorial improvement is assigned to a character of whom More has just written that he was beheaded before he could speak and declare his own innocence (*CW* 2, 57/28-58/1); More could scarcely have admitted this blatant contradiction into a *more* advanced draft (cf. Hanham, p. 208). And as Hanham herself concedes (p. 188), the fragmentary continuation of the history beyond Richard's coronation which appears in both *1557* and the Hardyng-Hall text seems to be inconsistent with the artistic pattern of the rest of the work as we have it; in a considerably more advanced draft than the one which gave rise to *1557*, this continuation would surely have been somewhat reworked or omitted entirely. Only the Latin substitutes other material for this ragged ending; it seems likely that the Latin of *P* is the most advanced draft of More's history.

ilarity. While the English version devotes relatively little attention to the grotesque theatrics which prelude the crowning of Richard III, it is clear that these very theatrics provide the grand climax of More's Latin history.[1] Contrary to Richard Sylvester's tentative thesis that one intermediate stage of More's Latin proceeded and ended the same way that More's English ends, with the troubles that plagued Richard's first year of rule, both the copy-text of *1557*[L] and the copy-text of *1565* and *P* must have ended with the splendidly empty rhetorical flourishes that accompanied Richard's accession.[2] Whereas More's English history takes on the appearance at last of a disjointed and incomplete chronicle, his Latin achieves an unusual compactness by restricting its scope to the play of mendacious and partisan rhetoric that leads up to Richard's success in usurping the throne. This is not the place for a detailed analysis of the rhetoric of More's Latin history, but at least we should mention that well over half of the history in Latin is made up of speeches, direct and reported, and that all three of the sizeable excerpts that Rastell transferred to the English from Latin are further refinements of this same rhetorical interplay.[3] According to the title-page of *1565*, More wrote his Latin history strictly *exercitationis gratia*, as a stylistic exercise. While I think that the work has a serious historical purpose, as well, it is safe to assume on the basis of the elaborate rhetorical structure revealed in the most final form of the work that in much of it More is engaged in the stylistic exercise *par excellence*, the declaimer's endeavor to make the best case *pro* and *contra* for theses where one or the other position could normally be taken for granted.[4]

---

[1] The autograph English manuscript from which Rastell printed *1557* apparently lacked any equivalent for the entire conclusion of the Latin, beginning at 482/25.

[2] For this thesis see *CW* 2, xxxv, lii. *1557*[L], *1565*, and *P* all conclude with the same reference to Richard's coronation. More's original plan for the Latin history may well have been considerably more ambitious, but the conclusion of the Latin as we have it produces a considerable impression of dramatic completeness.

[3] *1557*[L] consists of the following three passages in English translation: 388/28-390/10 ("Quod si . . . fuit"); 396/21-400/18 ("Igitur . . . nobilibus"); and 482/25-484/4 ("Sequente . . . destinatus"). I do not understand why Sylvester alleges (*CW* 2, xxxi, 210) that the second of these insertions duplicates material to be found in the English at *CW* 2, 87/21-88/19: it is Buckingham who is wooing Richard in that English passage, while in the Latin Richard forcefully woos Buckingham. Since More's Latin explicitly dismisses the theory that Buckingham wooed Richard and even suggests that this theory was made up by Richard's defenders ("Protectoris amici," 396/24-398/1), it would seem that More's Latin expresses a more carefully considered historical viewpoint in this case, at least. Hanham (pp. 207–08) also notes that the two passages are incompatible but explains the discrepancy differently.

[4] For More's keen interest in declamation see Allen, *4*, 21, where Erasmus reports that More was especially fond of defending such problematic and challenging propositions as the sharing of wives which is advocated in Plato's *Republic*.

With unusual acuteness More saw that the factional rhetoric of the era of Richard III had a great deal in common with the radically and intentionally problematic rhetoric of pure declamation. His history is not only a study of Richard's own crudely coercive rhetorical tactics; it is also a study in how a divided society gradually loses the ability to distinguish between biased, potentially coercive rhetoric and honorable counsel.[1]

A Note on the Text

This edition of the *Historia Richardi Tertii* is primarily based on the newly discovered Paris manuscript (*P*). I have noted all substantive variants (but not obvious scribal mistakes) in the other two manuscripts; since I believe that most of the numerous unique variants in *1565* have no basis in More's own Latin text, I have cited here only the ones which I think are especially noteworthy. In the rare places where *P*, *A*, and *H* all appear to be missing one word or more, I have inserted the addition in square brackets whether it comes from *1565* or from some other source; when *P* alone seems to be missing a word I have made the addition without brackets. All such cases are noted in the variants. I have silently divided the text into paragraphs, inserted quotation marks, expanded abbreviations, and standardized capitalization. Otherwise I have tried to record every revision of either the punctuation or the spelling of *P;* I have also noted the few paragraph-divisions that *P* does contain.[2]

The frequency of superscript (that is, interlineated) variants in both *A* and *P* and the presence of two hands in *P* besides that of the principal scribe call for special notation. The three hands in *P* have been noted as *P*, *P*^{a}, and *P*^{b}; superscript variants have been noted as *P*^{s} and *A*^{s}. A superscript variant by the second or third hand in *P* is noted as *P*^{sa} or *P*^{sb}; in the rare instances when it is necessary to distinguish between two superscript variants for the same word in *P*, as when *A* or *A*^{s} agrees with one of these variants, they are noted as *P*^{s1} and *P*^{s2} or occasionally *P*^{sa1} and *P*^{sa2}. Wherever a substantive variant occurs in *P*, *A*, or *H*, I report every available reading for that particular point in the text.[3] I also

---

[1]For a more detailed treatment of More's Latin history along these same lines see my article, "King's Tragicomedies: Generic Misrule in More's *History of Richard III*," *Moreana*, 86 (1985), 128–50.

[2]Since the punctuation marks are much fainter than the letters in *P*, I may have guessed wrongly in recording some punctuation marks.

[3]Since eccentric, intractable syntax in *1565* often provides no precise counterpart for the manuscript readings, I do not always note the readings of *1565;* they may easily be checked in *CW* 2.

report every available reading (except for completely intractable readings in *1565*) when the one I adopt in the text is substantially different
from the one found in *P*. But where I have simply adjusted the spelling
or punctuation of *P*, I give only the reading of *P* in the variants. *P*
employs many virgules and few commas; for the sake of consistency I
have changed commas to virgules throughout. Where *P* uses a virgule
followed by a period as the equivalent of a period alone, I have let the
text stand as it is; when *P* uses a virgule followed by a period as the
equivalent of a virgule alone, I give only the virgule.

The following sigla have been adopted in the textual apparatus:

P MS fr. 4996 (Ancien fonds), Bibliothèque nationale
A MS Arundel 43
H MS Harley 902, British Library
1565 *Opera omnia*, Louvain, 1565
1557[L] *Workes*, London, 1557 (excerpts translated from Latin in More's
      English history)
1557 *Workes*, London, 1557 (More's English history)

LETTER TO MARTIN DORP
TEXT AND TRANSLATION

[1] Viro undecunque doctissimo Martino
Dorpio Theologo. Louanij [2]

Morus Dorpio suo salutem dicit [3]

Thomas Morus Martino Dorpio
S P D

5

Sɪ ᴍɪʜɪ ad te uenire tam esset liberum, quam uehementer mi
Dorpi cupio, tum ista, quae nunc parum commode committo
litteris, commodius tecum coram ipse tractarem, tum (quo nihil
mihi iucundius potuisset accidere) teipso interea praesens prae-
10 sente perfruerer, cuius uidendi, cognoscendi, complectendique,
mirum pectori meo desyderium inseuit Erasmus, utriusque
nostrum amantissimus, tum utrique, uti spero, ex aequo charus.
Nihil est enim quod ille maiore cum uoluptate faciat, quam ut
apud presentes amicos suos, absentes predicet, Siquidem quum
15 sit ipse plurimis, idque in diuersis orbis terrarum partibus, doctrinae, suauissimorumque morum gratia charissimus, conatur
sedulo [3v] ut quo in unum se, omnes animo sunt, eodem etiam
inter se omnes conglutinet. Non cessat ergo apud uniuersos,
singulatim amicorum quemque referre, et quo in cunctorum
20 amicitias insinuet, omnes cuiusque dotes, quibus amari pro-
mereatur, exponere. Quod quum ille assidue faciat de omnibus,
de nullo tamen saepius, de nullo facit effusius, de nullo quam de
te charissime Dorpi libentius, quem ita dudum celebrauit in Anglia, ut nemo sit ibi litteratorum uirorum, cui non Dorpij nomen
25 aeque notum celebreque sit, atque Louaniensibus ipsis, quibus
est, (ut esse debet) celeberrimum. Seorsum uero ita te depinxit

---

1–2 Viro . . . Louanij] *P 1625, om. S 1563; preceded by what are probably late editorial titles in P
1563 1625 (see commentary)*   3 Morus . . . dicit] *P, om. S 1563 1625; written in P in an
elegant hand which appears only here and at 126/8*   5 S P D] *P 1625,* S D *1563, om. S*   6
sidenote in 1563 Haec epistola nunquam antehac edita   8–9 nihil mihi] *P 1563 1625,*
mihi nihil *S*   11 desyderium] *S 1563 1625,* desyderium, *P*   21 assidue] *S 1563 1625,*
assiduae *P*   24–25 nomen aeque] *1563 1625,* nomen, aequae *P,* nomen, aeque
S   25 celebreque sit] *P S 1563,* celebreque *1625*   26 esse debet] *P 1625,* debet esse *S
1563*

2

To the most eminent scholar Martin Dorp, Theologian. Louvain.

More sends his greetings to Dorp

Thomas More sends his heartiest greetings to Martin Dorp

I F I were at liberty to visit you, my dear Dorp, as I very much wish that I could, first of all I would discuss with you personally in a more fitting way all that I now entrust in a less fitting way to a letter. I would also have liked nothing better than to get to know you face to face, since Erasmus, who feels great affection for both of us, and who is, I hope, equally dear to us both, has instilled in my heart a remarkable longing to see you, to make your acquaintance, and to show you my love. In fact nothing gives him more pleasure than to praise absent friends to friends present, and since his learning and his delightful disposition have endeared him to so many people in various parts of the world, he is constantly trying to make all of them share with each other the same special attachment which binds them to him. Thus he never stops mentioning each of his friends one by one to the rest or describing the gifts for which each merits love, so that each gains a share in the friendship of all. Though he regularly commends all his friends in this way, he commends none more often, more lavishly, or more heartily than he commends you, my dear Dorp, whom he has been celebrating for so long in England that there is no learned man in that country who does not know and honor the name Dorp the same way that the scholars of Louvain themselves do; and they, as they should, honor it very greatly indeed. He has portrayed you so well to me

apud me, ut iam olim pulcherrimam animi tui ymaginem, plane-
que eandem apud animum meum presumpserim, quae mihi
postea quam huc appuli, ex elegantissimis opusculis tuis eluxit.

Itaque quum me primum scirem ab inuictissimo [4] rege
5   nostro, in has partes legatione functurum, crede mi Dorpi mihi,
non pro minimo itineris tanti precio ducebam, quod oblata mihi
uidebatur occasio, qua tecum quoquo pacto congrederer. Verum istam conueniendi tui facultatem, quam prebitam esse spe-
raueram, negotij nobis demandati ratio praeripuit, quae me
10 Brugis, ubi cum magnificis illustrissimi principis uestri oratoribus, res ut nobis tractaretur, conuenerat, alligauit. Quo fit ut
uehementer doleam, quum haec legatio mihi multis alioqui
nominibus arrideat, qua tamen in re optaueram maxime fortunam affuisse propiciam, ea me maxime ab illa destitui.

15 Verum (ut ad id tandem ueniam quod me coegit inpresente
scribere) dum hic uersor, incidi forte in quosdam, qui non alieni
a litteris uidebantur. Apud hos de Erasmo, et de te item sermonem ingero. illum ex litteris ac [4v] fama, te uero etiam alias
nouerant. Narrant mihi rem ut parum laetam, ita neutiquam
20 credibilem, te uidelicet in Erasmum animo esse parum amico,
idque ex litteris ad eum tuis liquere, quas (quoniam ad credendum aegre me adduci uidebant) postero die allaturos sese
pollicebantur.

Redierunt postridie: tum litteras ad me ternas apportarunt,
25 unas abs te ad Erasmum scriptas, quas ille (quod ex eius responsione colligo) non acceperat, sed earum exemplar (id quod mihi
nunc euenit) nescio quo monstrante, legerat. In his Moriam insimulas, et ad sapientiae laudem inuitas. Institutum eius de
emendando nouo testamento ex graecis codicibus, tam parum
30 probas, tam angustis limitibus ut coartet suades, ut pene in uniuersum dissuadeas. Alterae fuerunt ipsius, quibus tibi breuiter,

---

2 eandem] eandem ⟨esse⟩ P   3 postea quam] P 1563 1625, posteaque S   9 deman-
dati] S 1563 1625, demandati, P   10 uestri] P 1625, nostri S 1563   11 2nd ut] P
1625, ut nunc S 1563   12–13 mihi multis alioqui nominibus] P 1563 1625, multis
alioqui nominibus mihi S   13 maxime] 1563 1625, maximae P, om. S   13–14 for-
tunam] P S 1563, fortunam mihi 1625   14 maxime] S 1563 1625, maximae, P   15
inpresente] P, in presenti S 1563, in praesens 1625   16 qui] P 1625, qui mihi S
1563   17 uidebantur.] 1625, uidebantur, P S 1563; hos] interl. P; te] interl. P   22
aegre] S 1563 1625, aegrae P; sese] P S 1625, se esse 1563   24 postridie:] postridie, P S
1563, postridie; 1625   25 abs te] S 1563 1625, abste P   27 legerat] P 1625,
perlegerat S 1563

personally that my mind's eye has long since conceived a most flattering image of your mind, the same image, in fact, that I found to illuminate your elegant minor works after I arrived here.

For this reason, as soon as I learned from our most invincible king that I was to serve on an embassy here, believe me, my Dorp, one of the main compensations to which I looked forward in making so lengthy a journey was that I thought it would offer me some opportunity to meet with you. But the nature of the business assigned to us has detained me in Bruges and prevented me from visiting you as I had hoped, for it had previously been agreed that our negotiations with your magnificent prince's most distinguished ambassadors would be conducted here. Thus I deeply regret that though I have enjoyed many other aspects of this embassy I have been disappointed by fortune precisely where I had most hoped for her favor.

But let me finally get down to the issue that has induced me to write this letter. During my stay here I happened to meet several people who to me seemed no strangers to literature. I started a conversation with them about Erasmus and also about you. They knew him from his writings and reputation, but they knew you in other ways as well. They told me something that was as unpleasant as it was incredible, namely that you do not feel any too friendly toward Erasmus and that your letters to him confirm the fact. They promised to bring me the letters the next day, since they saw I was hardly convinced.

They came back the next day, bringing three letters with them. One of these you had written to Erasmus, even though I infer from his answer that he had not received the original of your letter, but rather, like me, he had read it when someone else showed him a copy. In this letter you criticize the *Folly* and exhort him to a *Praise of Wisdom*. You show so little approval and advise such repressive constraints for his project of emending the New Testament from Greek that you virtually oppose the whole enterprise. The second of these letters was written by

utpote fessus ex itinere, [5] atque adeo in eodem adhuc itinere
occupatus, satisfacit, copiosius idem se facturum professus,
quum Basileam delatus esset. Denique tertiae litterae tuae
fuerunt, quibus rursus ad hanc Erasmi respondes epistolam.

5   Has ego quum presentibus illis perlegissem, quanquam erant
aliqua, non quae mihi quidem inimicum esse te illi persuaderent,
(quid enim posset esse tale ut hoc persuadeat mihi?) sed animo
tamen aliquanto magis turbido, quam expectaram, tamen quia
hanc opinionem illis ex animo eradi potius, quam confirmari
10   cupiebam, asserui nihil ibi legisse me, quod non ab amicissimo
pectore profectum uideatur.

"At" inquit eorum unus, "non estimo quae scripserit, sed meo
iudicio neutiquam amice fecit, omnino quod scripserit. Nam si
Moria quenquam tam uehementer offendit, quod ego nusquam
15   ne Louanij [5v] quidem quanquam ibi post editam Moriam saepe
multumque uersatus, audiui, preterquam ab uno aut altero, morosissimis atque infantissimis senibus, et quos ibi pueri quoque
rident, quum alioquin et hic et ibi tam grata fuerit omnibus, ut
multi, multas eius partes, memoriter ediscant etiam: Verum
20   quod coepi dicere, si Moria quenquam tam uehementer offendit, ut Erasmus ad palinodiam quoque uideretur inuitandus,
tamen quum Dorpius non ita pridem accersitus ad Erasmum
esset, idque ut ipse scribit solus, quid attinebat scribere; si quid
monendum putauit, cur non praesentem, praesens admonuit;
25   cur non (ut apud Therentium est) coram quae facto opus essent,
imperabat, potius quam quum exisset clamaret de uia, idque
Erasmo tam longe semoto, ut quae eum aut primum, aut etiam
solum [6] audire oportuerat, ea et solus aliquamdiu nesciuerit, et
postremo non nisi per alios acceperit? Qua in re uide quam
30   sincere faciat: primum quem nemo accusat, eum apud omnes

---

2 satisfacit, copiosius] *P*, satisfacit copiosius, *S 1563*, satisfacit; copiosius *1625*   3
tertiae] *S 1563 1625*, tertie *P*   6 persuaderent] *P 1563 1625*, persuadeant *S*   7
posset] *P 1625*, possit *S 1563*   13 amice] *S 1563 1625*, amicae *P*   14 quenquam] *P
1563 1625*, quemque *S;* nusquam] *P 1563 1625*, nusque *S*   15 Louanij] *P 1563 1625*,
Louonij *S*   16 audiui,] *1563 1625*, audiui: *P*, audiui *S*   16–17 morosissimis] morosissimis ⟨senibus⟩ *P*   19 etiam:] *S 1625*, etiam. *P 1563*   20 dicere,] *1563 1625*,
dicere *P*, dicere: *S;* quenquam] *1563 1625*, quemque *S*   28 aliquamdiu] diu *interl.
after* aliquñ *P*   29 acceperit?] *1563 1625*, acceperit. *P S;* uide] *P 1625*, uide (inquit) *S
1563*   30 faciat:] faciat, *P*, faciat. *S 1563 1625*

Erasmus while he was still weary with traveling, and indeed still engaged in his journey, as a cursory response to your criticisms; he also promised to write a fuller response when he had reached Basel. Then there was the third letter, your answer to that of Erasmus.

When I read these letters in the presence of those men, although none of your statements convinced me, at any rate, that you were an enemy to Erasmus (for what would suffice to convince me of that?), there were nonetheless some which convinced me that you were somewhat more agitated than I had expected. But as I wished rather to banish this thought from their minds than to reinforce it, I asserted that I had read nothing in your letters which did not seem to me to be written with the friendliest intentions.

"But," said one of them, "even discounting what he wrote, it was no friendly gesture on his part to write in the first place. For suppose that anyone was so terribly upset by the *Folly*—and I have never heard anyone anywhere say so, not even in Louvain, a place where I have spent many long periods of time since the *Folly* was published, apart from one or two infantile old grumblers that even the boys there make fun of, whereas otherwise both here and there everybody takes such delight in the *Folly* that many people have learned many passages from it by heart—but as I started to say, suppose that anyone was so terribly upset by the *Folly* that it actually seemed necessary to ask for a palinode from Erasmus. Even so, since, as Dorp himself writes, he had recently been summoned for a private visit with Erasmus, what was the purpose of writing to him? If he thought that some matter required his advice, why not give the advice face to face? As the scene goes in Terence, why not give his instructions in person instead of waiting to step out the door and then shouting them up from the street, when Erasmus was so far away that, though he should have been either the first or even the only person to hear the advice, he was not only the last to find out about it but he learned of it only through others? Consider how candidly Dorp is conducting this business: first of all he pretends that he is defending against everyone a person whom no one

defendere sese simulat. Deinde quibus eum rationibus tuetur, quum nescio an quisquam audiat, quae contra eum obijcit, (preter eum solum qui solus debet) publice legunt omnes."

5 Hec quum ille dixisset, alijque eorum alia, quae nunc necesse non habeo commemorare, ita respondi, atque ita a me dimisi, ut facile intelligerent, nihil sinistri me de te libenter audire, animoque esse in te propemodum aeque propenso, atque in Erasmum ipsum, in quem tam propenso sum, ut esse propensiore non possim. Nam quod scribere ad eum, quam coram rem tractare

10 maluisti, quocunque tu id consilio feceris, certe non fecisse malo, et ego mi Dorpi mihi pro mea de te opinione persuadeo, [6v] et ille certus animi erga se tui non dubitat.

At secundas istas litteras tuas, quae iam passim parum secunde leguntur, nullo omnino consilio tuo, sed plane casu quopiam in

15 publicum emanasse crediderim. In quam sententiam, uel eo imprimis impellor, quod in his nonnulla sunt huiusmodi, ut plane mihi persuadeam, te si uelles emittere, fuisse mutaturum, utpote non satis idonea quae uel ad eum scriberentur, uel abs te. Neque enim quaedam tam acerbe ad amicum tantum, neque tam nec-

20 lectim ad hominem tam doctum, Immo sat scio et pro modestissimo ingenio tuo, clementius, et pro eximia doctrina tua scripsisses accuratius. Porro iocis scommatibusque, quibus plusquam modice scriptio tota scatet, non dubito quin usurus fueris aut aliquanto parcius, aut certe mi Dorpi salsius. [7]

25 Nam quod Moriam insectaris, quod in Poetas inueheris, Grammaticos omnes subsannas, Annotationes in scripturam parum probas, graecarum litterarum peritiam non admodum ad rem pertinere censes, hec inquam omnia non magni facio, ut

3 publice] S 1563 1625, publicae P   4 alia] interl. S   4–5 necesse non] P 1625, non necesse S 1563   7 aeque] 1563 1625, aequae P, om. S   8 ut esse] P 1563 1625, ut S   12 tui] S 1563, tui, P 1625; dubitat.] S 1563 1625, dubitat P   13 passim] interl. S; secunde] 1563, corr. from secundae S, secundae P 1625   16 huiusmodi] P 1563 1625, eiusmodi S; plane] S 1563 1625, planae P   19 acerbe] S 1563 1625, acerbae P   19–20 neclectim] changed from neglectim P, neglectim S 1563 1625   23 modice] S 1563 1625, modicae P; usurus] usurus ⟨sis⟩ P; fueris] S 1563, fueras P 1625   24 parcius] S 1563 1625, partius P; certe] S 1563 1625, certae P   25 Nam] P 1625, Namque S 1563; insectaris] P 1563 1625, insimulas S   26 subsannas] P 1563 1625, uel insectaris uel subsannas S; in scripturam] P 1625, in sacram scripturam S 1563   27 peritiam] S 1563 1625, peritiam, P

accuses, and then, though I am not sure that anyone listens to the arguments that he offers in Erasmus' defense, everyone is reading publicly (except for the one man who ought to) the things Dorp alleges against him."

After he had said this and the others had said various other things which I think it as well to omit here, I answered them and then I dismissed them in such a way as to make it quite clear that I do not want to hear any slighting remarks about you and that I am almost as fond of you as I am of Erasmus, of whom I am so fond that I could not be fonder of anyone. Indeed, whatever motives you had for writing to Erasmus when you could have talked over the matter in person, they were certainly not bad ones; of this, my dear Dorp, my esteem for you makes me quite sure, while Erasmus, secure in his notion of your feelings toward him, has no doubt about it.

But as for that second letter of yours, a very poor second, which is being read everywhere, I could easily believe that you had no intention at all of releasing it to the public but that it got out completely by accident. The main reason that drives me to think so is that there are some passages in your letter which I am convinced you would have changed had you chosen to publish it, passages unworthy of being written either to him or by you. For you would not have written in certain passages so acerbically to such a great friend or so shoddily to such a great scholar; indeed I am sure that you would have written more mercifully in accordance with your modest character and more carefully in accordance with your uncommon learning. Furthermore, as for the jokes and the taunts that are too much in evidence throughout your composition, I have no doubt that you would have introduced them either somewhat more sparingly or at any rate, my dear Dorp, more wittily.

I am not particularly troubled by the way that you carp at the *Folly*, inveigh at the poets, snarl at all the grammarians, disapprove of his annotations on scripture, or judge that a training in Greek literature is simply irrelevant. In these matters, without

in quibus citra cuiusquam offensam, liberum cuiuis est, sentire
quod uelit, et ita abs te sunt adhuc disputata, ut non dubitem,
quin inter legendum, multa cuique succurrant, quae responderi
ex aduerso debeant: porro tantum abest, ut in horum quoquam
5 nimium abs te dictum existimem, ut in quibusdam etiam multa
desyderem, quibus optassem hoc scriptum tuum ad Erasmum
prodijsse instructius, quo maior ei preberetur occasio sua ex
aduerso castra maioribus operibus communiendi.

    At istud me nonnihil certe commouit, quod Erasmum in eo
10 libello tuo, uideris aliquanto secus quam te atque illo est dignum
attingere, quippe quem ita tractas, tanquam modo contemnas,
modo [7v] uelut e sublimi derideas, interdum quasi non admoneas, sed tanquam patruus, aut tristis censor obiurges,
Postremo uerbis eius aliorsum detortis, Theologos omnes, atque
15 adeo uniuersitates (quas uocant) in eum concites.

    Nec in eam partem accipi hec mea scripta uolo, quasi aduersus
te, quem plane credo nihil horum ulla in eum malignitate fecisse,
ego, cui nimirum ipsi patrono opus sit, in patrocinium suscipiam
illum, quem certe maiorem et haberi, apud omnes, et esse scio,
20 quam ut in reorum ordinem redigi debeat. Sed quoniam te amo,
famaeque tuae bene cupio, idcirco admonere te eorum uolui,
unde ansam apprehendunt hi, (quibus modestia tua, et uere
cycneus animi tui candor non satis exploratus est) qua famae te,
et tuae nimis auidum, et alienae insidiantem putant.

25 Vtinam quemadmodum Aeneas sese apud Vergilium [8] circumseptus nebula, Carthaginensibus immiscuit, ac se suaque
facta in tapetibus depicta spectauit, sic utinam non uisus ipse
uidere posses, quo uultu posterior hec epistola tua legatur. Sat

---

1 offensam] P S 1563, offensum 1625; cuiuis est] P 1625, cuique sit S 1563   2 quod] S
1563, quid P 1625   4 debeant:] S, debeant, P, debeant. 1563 1625; quoquam] P S,
quoque 1625, quenquam 1563   8 aduerso] P 1625, diuerso S 1563; operibus] P 1625,
opibus S 1563   9 istud] P S 1625, istuc 1563; me nonnihil certe] P 1625, certe me
nonnihil S 1563; certe] S 1563 1625, certae P   10 illo] corr. from illum S   17 plane] S
1563 1625, planae P   18 cui nimirum] P 1563 1625, nimirum cui S; opus] opus ⟨est⟩
P   19 maiorem et] P 1563 1625, et maiorem S   20 reorum] P 1625, eorum S
1563   21 admonere te] P 1563 1625, te admonere S   24 auidum] auidum ⟨putant⟩
S   25 Vtinam] P 1625, Vtinam Dorpi S 1563

offending anyone, everyone has a right to his own point of view. Besides, you have so far presented your case on these topics in such a way that I have no doubt that many arguments occur to everyone while reading your letter which ought to be stated for the opposite viewpoint. In fact, far from considering that you have said too much on any of these topics, on a number I find a good deal left unsaid, with which I would have liked to see your composition come forth better armed so that Erasmus would have had greater occasion to fortify his opposing position with more massive fieldworks.

On the other hand, it certainly disturbed me a good deal that you seem to handle Erasmus in a way that is worthy of neither of you. You treat him sometimes as if you despise him, sometimes as if you regard him with haughty derision, sometimes as if you are not so much offering advice as chastising him like a stern uncle or humorless censor, and lastly as if you are deliberately twisting the meaning of his words to get all the theologians and even all the universities, as they are called, up in arms against him.

I do not want you to regard this composition of mine as if it were directed against you, for I do not believe you have done any of this out of ill will toward him, or as if I, who could use a defender myself, plan to mount a defense for a man whom I know to be too great in all men's esteem and in actual fact to be relegated to the ranks of the accused. But since I love you and cherish your fame, I did want to advise you about certain things which those persons who fail to appreciate fully the modesty and the veritably swanlike candor of your nature are making a pretext for thinking that you are too keen to enhance your own fame and are treacherously attacking another's.

Would that, just as Aeneas in Vergil stood hidden by a cloud in the midst of the Carthaginians and there looked at himself and his deeds represented in tapestries, would that you too could stand by unobserved and observe the expressions with which people read this last letter of yours. I am sure you would con-

scio longe maiores mihi gratias habendas duceres, qui te sincere
admoneam, ut mutare possis (potes nanque mutando efficere,
ut hanc omnes id quod ipse facio non emissam tibi sed elapsam
iudicent) quam eis, qui quae te coram adulati laudant, eadem
5 clam etiam ipsi detractant.

Quanquam profecto miror, si quisquam usque adeo adulari
in animum induxit suum, ut ista uel te praesente collaudet,
quae ut coepi dicere, utinam per cancellos transpicere possis,
quo uultu, qua uoce, quo affectu, legantur, quum apud Eras-
10 mum non semel inculcas, "Thcologos nostros Erasme, et grammaticos uestros," quasi quum ipse sublimis in Theologorum ordine consedeas, illum deorsum inter grammaticulos detrudas.
[8v] Et sedes tu quidem inter Theologos merito, nec sedes
modo, sed praesides quoque. Nec ille tamen e theologorum sol-
15 ijs in grammaticorum subsellia depellendus.

Quanquam Grammatici nomen quod tu frequentius, quam
facetius irrides, Erasmus opinor haud aspernabitur: imo (ut est
modestus) quanquam meretur maxime, fortasse nec agnoscet
tamen, quippe quum sciat, Grammaticum idem omnino sig-
20 nificare, quod Litteratus, cuius officium per omnes litterarum
species, hoc est, per omnes sese disciplinas effundit, Quo fit, ut
qui dialecticen imbiberit, Dialecticus, qui Arithmeticen, Arith-
meticus uocari possit, tum in caeteris artibus ad eundem
modum. At litteratus mea certe sententia, nisi qui omnes omnino
25 scientias excusserit, appellari nemo debet, alioquin et infantibus
licet grammaticorum nomen attribuas, quicunque ex alpha Beta
ipsas [9] litterarum formas edidicere. Quod si tu eos tantum
grammaticos esse uis, quos ais ferulas sceptrorum uice gestantes

---

1 mihi] *interl.* P; sincere] S *1563 1625*, sincerae P   4 qui] *interl.* P, qui ⟨te⟩ S   5
detractant] P *1625*, lacerant detractant S, lacerant *1563*   7 induxit] P *1625*, inducat S
1563   10–11 Theologos . . . uestros] *ital. 1625*   10 Erasme] P S *1625*, Erasmum
1563   12 consedeas] P *1625*, con *written over* subsideas S, consideas *1563;* detrudas.] S
1563 1625 detrudas, P   13 tu] *interl.* P   17 aspernabitur:] aspernabitur, P S *1563,*
aspernabitur; *1625*   18 maxime, fortasse] *1625*, maximae, fortasse P, maxime fortassis, S *1563;* agnoscet] P *1625*, agnoscit S *1563*   19 idem omnino] P *1563 1625,*
omnino idem S   20 Litteratus] P *1625*, litteratum S *1563;* officium] S *1563 1625,*
officium, P   22 Dialecticus,] S *1563*, Dialecticus. P, Dialecticus; *1625*   23 possit,] S,
possit. P *1625*, possit: *1563*   24 certe] S *1563 1625*, certae P   25 scientias] S *1563*
1625, scientias, P   26 alpha] P S *1625*, Alpha et *1563*   27 ipsas litterarum] P *1625*,
litterarum S *1563*

clude that you owe me a good deal more gratitude for advising you to change what you wrote (for by changing it you can make everyone judge, as I do, that you did not issue this letter but let it slip forth) than you owe to your flatterers, since even they themselves criticize in your absence the very things that they praise to your face.

Yet I wonder indeed if anyone is so bent on flattery that he can praise some of your flourishes even in your presence; as I started to say, would that you could observe through a lattice the faces, the voices, the feelings with which people read your expressions as you harp away more than once at Erasmus, "Our theologians, Erasmus, and your grammarians," as if you yourself, sitting on high in the ranks of the theologians, cast him down among grammar-school tyros. You do indeed rightfully sit among the theologians, nor do you merely sit; you preside. Nonetheless he is not to be banished from the theologian's throne to the grammarian's footstool.

Yet I suspect that Erasmus will by no means spurn the title "grammarian" which you ridicule more frequently than cleverly. Or rather, modest as he is, even though he deserves it more than anyone, he may still hesitate to accept it, since he knows that "grammarian" means precisely the same thing as "man of letters," whose area of study extends across every variety of literature, that is, every discipline. For this reason, though anyone who has studied dialectic may be called a dialectician, anyone who has studied arithmetic may be called an arithmetician, and so on in the rest of the arts, no one, in my opinion at least, may be styled a man of letters who has not pored through each and every one of the sciences; otherwise you could confer the title of grammarian even upon infants who know merely the letters of the alphabet. But if you claim that there are no grammarians besides the ones who, as you put it, play king in low dives where the air rings with blows, wielding hickory sticks for their

in antro plagoso regnare, tum philautia, ac Moria stultiores,
arbitrari se omnes nosse disciplinas, quod uoculas intelligunt
ipsas, et orationum structuram, ego mediusfidius mi Dorpi,
etiam eos, quanquam procul ab disciplinis esse concesserim,
5 tamen aliquanto propius accessisse puto, quam Theologos illos,
qui et structuram orationum, et uoculas ipsas ignorant, ex quo
genere, et ego aliquot, et tu (ut opinor) plures, quanquam uterque sedulo dissimulamus, agnoscimus. Erasmus certe neque illis
ex grammaticis est, qui tantum uoculas didicerunt, neque ex his
10 Theologis quibus preter perplexum questiuncularum labyrinthum nihil omnino cognitum est, sed ex illo grammaticorum
genere, quo Varro atque Aristarchus, ex illo Theologorum quo
ipse tu, mi Dorpi, hoc est, ex optimo, [9v] ut qui nec illas questiunculas ignoret, et quod tu quoque abunde fecisti, longe uti-
15 liorem bonarum litterarum, id est sacrarum maxime, tum
caeterarum quoque peritiam adiunxerit.

Sed pergo in Epistola tua, in qua illud quoque eiusdem ferme
notae est, "Si unquam Decretales Erasme uideris," quasi Decretales epistolas quas tu uidisse te significas, ille uidelicet nus-
20 quam uidere potuerit. Iam illud quale est, quod in eum objicis,
"Aquam ardeae perturbatam esse, et imperitis item omnia perturbata, quoties in disceptandi palestram descenditur," Et illud
preterea, "Non enim potes Erasme diiudicare, inter Dialec-
ticum, et Sophistam quid intersit, si utranque artem ignores." Et
25 paulo post, "Nisi forte tibi Sophistae sunt omnes, quibus disputatione uidearis inferior, hoc est omnes dialectici." Itane queso
Dorpi putas, perturbata Erasmo omnia disputanti fore, neque

2 intelligunt] *P 1563 1625*, intelligant *S*   3 structuram] *corr. from* structuras *P*   8
certe] *S 1563 1625*, certae *P*   10 questiuncularum] *P 1563 1625*, questionum *S*   11
illo] *P S 1563*, illorum *1625*   13 mi] mi ⟨Mi⟩ *S;* optimo,] *S 1563*, optimo *P*, optimo;
1625   14 abunde] *S 1563 1625*, abundae *P*   14–15 utiliorem] *P 1563 1625*, abunde
S   15 maxime] *S 1563 1625*, maximae *P*   17 Sed pergo in] *P S 1625*, Sed pergo. In
1563; illud] illud ⟨ferme⟩ *P*   18 est,] *1563*, est. *P S*, est: *1625;* Si . . . uideris] *ital.*
1625   20 objicis,] *S 1563 1625*, objicis *P*   21–22 Aquam . . . descenditur] *ital.*
1625   22 descenditur,] *1563*, descenditur. *P 1625*, descenditur *S*   23 preterea,]
preterea *P*, praeterea. *S*, praeterea: *1563 1625*   23–24 Non . . . ignores] *ital.*
1625   25 post,] *S 1563*, post. *P*, post: *1625*   25–26 Nisi . . . dialectici] *ital. 1625*

scepters, and who, even though they are more foolish than Self-Love and Folly, suppose that they know every science just because they have mastered the mere words and syntax, on my honor, my dear Dorp, though I admit that grammarians of that sort are far from being learned, I believe even they come considerably closer to learning than those theologians who have not even mastered the syntax and mere words. I myself know of several who fit this description, and you know (I suspect) of still more, though we each do our best to conceal the fact. Erasmus is certainly not one of those grammarians who have mastered no more than mere words, nor is he one of those theologians who know nothing at all outside a tangled labyrinth of petty problems. He is a grammarian of the same stamp as Varro and Aristarchus and a theologian of the same stamp as you, Dorp, that is, of the best. For he is not ignorant of those petty problems, and he has gone on to do what you too have done in such depth; he has gained something vastly more useful, a general command of sound literature, which means sacred letters especially but not at the expense of the rest.

But I will proceed with your letter, in which this innuendo is pretty much more of the same, "If you should ever see the *Decretals,* Erasmus," as if he might never get a glimpse of the decretal epistles which you indicate you have seen. So is this slur against him: "Herons muddy the water wherever they go, and beginners too muddle up everything whenever they enter the arena of debate." So is this one: "You cannot figure out what distinguishes a dialectician from a sophist if you know nothing about either of those arts." And then a little later, "Unless you think that everyone is a sophist who shows more skill in disputing than you do, that is, every dialectician." Do you honestly think, Dorp, that Erasmus muddles up everything whenever he dis-

aut quid dialectice sit, aut quid sit omnino sophista nouisse? et
eum nescire solum, quae ferme pueri sciunt omnes? [10]

   At Rhetoricam opinor uel tu propriam ei, ac quodammodo
peculiarem esse concedes, quam si tribuas, nescio qui possis Di-
5 alecticen tam prorsus adimere, Si quidem recte senserunt non
infimi philosophorum, qui tantum censuerunt inter dialecticam
Rhetoricamque differre, quantum pugnus distat a palma, quod,
quae dialectice colligit astrictius, eadem omnia Rhetorice copiosius explicat, utque illa mucrone pungit, ita hec ipsa mole pe-
10 nitus prosternit, obruitque.

   Sed age nihil sit Dialecticae cum Rhetorica commune. Ergo
quia non in scholis disputat, quia non in puerorum corona rixa-
tur, quia iam (quod tu quoque postea facies) questiunculas illas
ualere sinit, nunquam eum putas illas didicisse? sed existimas in
15 disputando inferiorem esse dialecticis omnibus? At hic uide
quam oppido abs te dissentiam. Ego nec illiteratum quidem
quempiam, mediocri ingenio preditum, longo tamen interuallo
minore, quam sit Erasmicum, hunc inquam ego non omni di-
alectico reor inferiorem in disputando fore, modo res de qua
20 disceptatur utrique sit nota, [10v] quum quod arti deest ingenium suppleat. Nam et ipsa dialectices praecepta, quid aliud,
quam quaedam ingenij foetura sunt? ratiocinationum uidelicet
formae quaedam, quas ratio fore ad rerum disquisitionem utiles
animaduertit? Tantum abest ut Erasmus, cuius et ingenium, et
25 doctrinam mirantur omnes, futurus sit in disputando omnibus
prorsus dialecticis, hoc est etiam pueris inferior.

---

1 dialectice] *P S 1625*, Dialecticus *1563*   2 omnes?] *S 1563 1625*, omnes; *P*   5
adimere,] adimere. *P 1563 1625*, adimere: *S;* senserunt] *P S 1625*, censuerunt *1563*   6
philosophorum,] *S 1563*, philosophorum *P*, philosophorum; *1625;* censuerunt] *1563*
1625, censuerunt, *P S*   6–7 inter dialecticam Rhetoricamque] *P 1625*, Dialecticam ab
Rhetorica *S 1563*   11 Sed . . . commune] *inserted in margin P*   13 facies] *P S 1625*,
facis *1563;* illas] *P 1625*, istas *S 1563*   14 didicisse] *P S 1625*, decidisse *1563*   15
omnibus?] *1625*, omnibus; *P*, omnibus: *S*, omnibus. *1563*   18 minore] *P 1565*, mi-
noreque *S 1563*   20 disceptatur] *S 1563*, disceptāt *P*, disceptant *1625;* utrique] *P S*
1563, utcumque *1625;* nota,] *S 1563*, nota. *P 1625*   20–21 ingenium] ingenium
⟨deest⟩ *P*   23 fore] *P S 1625*, fere *1563*   24 animaduertit?] *1563 1625*, animaduertit. *P S;* animaduertit? Tantum] *P 1625*, animaduertit? Neque enim quenquam
[quemque *S*] esse puto, qui dubitet, quin has ipsas quoque si uolet questiunculas non in
rixosis illis concertationibus ubi rationem clamor uincit, Vnde conspuentes inuicem
consputique discedunt, a quibus moribus modestia eius pudorque abhorret, sed aut
calamo aut graui ac seria disputatione ita tractabit, ut non solum non omnibus inferior,
sed supremis etiam aut par aut superior sit futurus. Tantum *S 1563*   25 omnes] *P*
1625, omnes, unus *S 1563*

putes, that he has not an inkling of what dialectic is or even what a sophist is, or that he alone is ignorant of something that is known to almost every schoolboy?

But I believe that even you grant him an uncommon and virtually unique skill in rhetoric. If you do give him that, then I fail to see how you can deny him any dialectical skill whatsoever. After all, not the least of philosophers had reason to think dialectic and rhetoric as closely akin as a fist and a palm, since dialectic infers more concisely what rhetoric sets out more elaborately, and where dialectic strikes home with its daggerlike point rhetoric throws down and overwhelms the opponent with its very weight.

But suppose dialectic has nothing in common with rhetoric. Just because he does not dispute in the schools, just because he does not brawl for an audience of boys, just because he now dispenses with those petty problems (as you too will hereafter), do you think that he never learned them, and do you imagine that he has less skill in disputing than any dialectician? On this point see how thoroughly we differ: by my reckoning not even a typical illiterate of average intelligence, but far less intelligent than Erasmus, not even an illiterate, I say, will prove less skilled than every dialectician in any dispute where both parties are familiar with the subject of the argument and where intelligence can make up for what is lacking in artifice. For what else are the very precepts of dialectic but a particular product of intelligence, that is, the particular formulas of rational conjecture which reason perceives to be useful in learning about the real world? So unlikely it is that Erasmus, whose intellect and learning are admired by everyone, should prove less skilled at disputing than every dialectician, mere schoolboys included.

Sed mitto ista omnia, nempe minoris momenti, ut in quibus litterarum duntaxat estimatio uentiletur. At illud certe odiosius est, quod Hieronymi Hussitae, Cresconijque grammatici, utriusque uidelicet heretici, mentio abs te non satis temperanter iniec
5 ta est, quippe quos quibusdam ita referre uideris, tanquam conferre uelis. Quid quod nonnulla tam acerbe tractas, tanquam nihil agas aliud, quam ut in eum primo Louanienses Theologos, deinde quotquot ubique sunt omnes, postremo achademias uniuersas extimules, inque eam rem quibusdam uerbis illius, lon
10 gissime [11] a proposito detortis abutaris?

Nam (ut a postremo incipiam) quum ille dixisset non omnes theologos damnare Moriam, sed eos solos has excitare Tragoedias, qui dolent bonas renasci litteras, foreque ut nec Hieronymianam aeditionem (quam tu theologis placere scripseras)
15 comprobarent hi, qui moriam damnauerant, ibi tu protinus arrepta lepida iocandi materia, "Noua" inquis "gloria, si aedas quod pauci probabunt," quasi uero relinquantur pauci qui probent, si ex tanto dignissimorum Theologorum coetu, unus aut alter morosissimi senes, nec ullo minus digni quam quod
20 profitentur nomen, eximantur. et tu tamen Dorpi, longius eundem tam festiuum iocum prosequeris. Ais enim, "Age non probabunt Theologi" (sic ille dixit scilicet): "qui queso probabunt ergo; Iurisconsulti; an medici; an Philosophi denique, ut falcem immittant alienae messi? Sed grammaticis eam paras. Sedeant
25 itaque [11v] grammatici in solio censores omnium disciplinarum, et nouam nobis Theologiam parturiant, nascituram tandem aliquando cum ridiculo mure. Verum nec metus est ne

---

2 uentiletur.] *1563 1625*, uentiletur, *P S;* certe] *S 1563 1625*, certae *P*   6 acerbe] *S 1563 1625*, acerbae *P*   9 uerbis illius] *P 1625*, illius verbis *S 1563*   9–10 longissime] *S 1563 1625*, longissimae *P*   10 proposito] *P 1563 1625*, preposito *S;* abutaris?] abuteris, *P S 1563*, abutaris. *1625*   15 hi] *P S 1625*, ij *1563*   15–16 arrepta] *S 1563 1625*, arrepta, *P*   16 lepida] *P 1563 1625*, lepide *S;* materia] *P 1625*, ansa *S 1563*   16–17 Noua . . . probabunt] *ital. except* inquis *1625*   18 coetu] *1563 1625*, cetu *P S*   20 profitentur] *S 1563 1625*, profitentur, *P;* nomen] *P 1625*, nomine *S 1563*   21 prosequeris] *P 1625*, persequeris *S 1563;* enim,] enim *P S*, enim: *1563 1625*   21–20/10 Age . . . graece] *ital. except words in parentheses 1625*   22 scilicet):] scilicet) *P S 1563*, scilicet!) *1625*   23 falcem] *corr. from* fascem *P*   23–24 falcem immittant] *P 1625*, saltem immittant falcem *S*, saltem falcem immittant *1563;* messi?] *S 1563 1625*, messi; *P*   25 solio censores] *P 1563 1625*, solio *S*

But I will leave these points alone; they are relatively minor affairs, since they merely involve disagreement about the importance of literature. But that other slur is certainly much more offensive, where you recklessly drag in the names of the Hussite Jerome and the grammarian Cresconius, both heretics, of course; for you seem to be trying to link them with those in whose company you name them. What of this, that you treat several points so invidiously that it seems you would like nothing more than to turn first the Louvain theologians, then all the other theologians in the world, and finally all the universities against him by twisting the meaning of some of his words in the most irresponsible way?

To begin with the last point: he said that not all theologians find fault with the *Folly,* but only the ones who resent the rebirth of sound learning, and then, since you had written that his new edition of Jerome pleased the theologians, he said that the ones who found fault with the *Folly* would dislike the edition as well. Here you snatch up this elegant theme for a joke and exclaim, "What a novel achievement, to edit a text few will like," as if there remain only a few who will like it once we eliminate from the great crowd of legitimate theologians one or two grumbling old men who have not the slightest legitimate claim to the title they profess. And yet, pressing ahead with the same charming joke, you say, "Well, then, theologians will not like it" (doubtless those were his words); "then please tell us, who will? lawyers, or doctors, or even philosophers, so that they can encroach on an alien field? No, you are preparing that text for grammarians. Then make ready a throne for the grammarians to be arbiters of all the sciences; let them breed us a new kind of theology which will finally be born like a ludicrous mouse. Nor do we need to worry

nolint studiosi illorum se sceptris inclinare. Sceptra enim sunt
ferulae, quibus plagoso regnant in antro, et philautia, et Moria
stultiores, arbitrantur se omnes nosse disciplinas, quod uoculas
intelligunt ipsas et orationum structuram. Ergo non est opus
5   achademijs. Schola Zoulensis aut dauentriana suffecerit, et certe
hec est sententia magni uiri Hieronimi Hussitae, Vniuersitates
tam prodesse ecclesiae dei, quam diabolum. Nec grammaticos
uel tantillum commouet, quod damnata fuerit ea sententia in
concilio Constantiensi, quippe in quo certum sit neminem fuisse
10 non amusum, aut qui non ignorauerit graece." Iniurius tibi Dorpi sim, si iocum saepius interpellem tuum, in quo iamdiu, mirum
quam te suauiter oblectasti. Sed si satis iocatus es, audi nunc iam
Dorpi.
    Nemini obscurum esse [12] potest tua ipsius uerba legenti, te
15 ad hanc uniuersitatum mentionem, sine ulla prorsus occasione
descendisse, totumque hunc locum tibi copiose, ac perquam diserte sane, sed extra controuersiam tamen esse declamatum, nec
esse ulla responsione opus. Neque tamen ambigendum puto quo
in uniuersitates affectu Erasmus sit, in quibus et didicit, et do-
20 cuit, non ea modo quae tu grammatica uocas, sed cum alia multa,
multo magis Christianis omnibus utilia, tum eas etiam ipsas,
(quas tu nunc tam magnifacis quam posthac parui facturus es)
questiunculas. Quis nescit quamdiu parisijs ille, quantoque in
pretio fuit, Tum Bononiae preterea ut nihil interim de Rhoma
25 dicam, quam ego tamen uel principem Achademiarum esse omnium duco? Iam Oxonia, Cantabrigiaque tam charum habent
Erasmum, quam habere debent eum, qui in utraque diu, cum
ingente scholasticorum fruge, nec minore sua laude, uersatus
est. Vtraque eum ad se inuitat, [12v] Vtraque eum in suorum
30 Theologorum numerum (quoniam eo honore alibi est insignitus) transplantare conatur.

---

2 plagoso] S 1563 1625, plagloso P   3 omnes nosse] P 1625, nosse omnes S 1563   4
structuram] corr. from structuras P   5 Zoulensis] S, Nolensis P 1625, Zuollensis 1563;
certe] S 1563 1625, certae P   9 Constantiensi] P S 1625, Constantinensi 1563   12 te
suauiter] P S 1625, suauiter te 1563; oblectasti] corr. from oblectes P; satis] S 1563 1625, sa
tis P   15 uniuersitatum] P 1563 1625, vniuersitatem S   16 copiose] S 1563 1625, copiosae P   16–17 diserte] S 1563 1625, disertae P   21 tum] tum ⟨etiam⟩ P   23
parisijs ille] P 1563 1625, ille Parisijs S   24 fuit, Tum] P 1625, fuit, tum Patauij, tum S,
fuit, tum Patauij, cum 1563   26 duco?] duco. P S 1625, duco.) 1563; charum] P S
1563, clarum 1625   29 ad se] S 1563 1625, adse P   30 quoniam eo] P 1563 1625,
quoniam S

lest scholars refuse to bow down to their scepters. For scepters they have hickory sticks, and with these they play king in low dives where the air rings with blows, and though they are more foolish than Self-Love and Folly, they suppose that they know every science just because they have mastered the mere words and syntax. And so there is no need for universities: schools like Zwolle and Deventer will suffice us. And certainly this is the opinion of that great man, the Hussite Jerome, that God's church derives as much benefit from universities as it does from the devil; nor does it worry the grammarians in the least that this opinion was condemned in the Council of Constance, since it was surely attended by no one who was not quite uncultured and ignorant of Greek." It would be wrong of me, Dorp, to break in on your joking too often, although it is amazing how long it has kept you so very amused. But if you have finished your joking, now, Dorp, it is your turn to listen.

No one reading your own words could fail to perceive that you had no occasion at all for this tangential comment about universities or that no matter how copiously or eloquently you declaimed your set-piece it has nothing to do with the argument and does not require any answer. Nonetheless I think there should be no room for doubt as to how Erasmus feels about universities, in which he has both studied and taught, and not only what you label grammar, but also (along with much else of considerably more use to all Christians) even those petty problems you presently value so much and will ultimately value so little. Everyone knows how long and how highly regarded he was at Paris, and then later at Bologna as well, to say nothing of Rome for the moment, even though I consider it the foremost of all universities. Oxford and Cambridge now cherish Erasmus, as they clearly should, for he was active for long periods in both, winning praise for himself as immense as the good he conferred on their scholars. They both urge him to join them, and since he was awarded his doctorate in theology elsewhere, they both seek to adopt him as one of their own theologians.

Sed tu quanti nostras uniuersitates facis haud scio, qui tantum
Louanio, Parisijsque tribuis, ut caeteris uideare mortalibus, presertim ex dialectica, nihil omnino relinquere. Ais enim nisi Louanienses, ac Parisienses Theologi essent dialectici, fieri uidelicet,
5 ut dialectica toto exulet orbe, exulaueritque multis iam seculis.
Ego in utraque Achademia fui abhinc septennium, non diu
quidem, sed interim tamen dedi operam, quae in utraque traduntur, quisque sit utrobique tradendi modus, ut scirem. Et
profecto (quanquam utranque suspicio) quantum tamen quiui
10 uel presens audiendo, uel absens inquirendo, cognoscere, nihil
hactenus unquam accepi causae, quamobrem uel in dialectica,
meos liberos, quibus optime consultum cupio, in alterutra earum edoceri potius, quam Oxoniae, aut Cantabrigiae uelim.
Non negabo tamen (neque enim libenter quenquam sua [13]
15 gloria fraudauerim) nostros permultum Iacobo Fabro Parisiensi
debere, quem ut instauratorem uerae dialecticae, ueraeque philosophiae, presertim Aristotelicae, foeliciora passim apud nos
ingenia, sanioraque iudicia consectantur, ut per eum uirum
Lutecia gratiam nobis referre quodammodo accepti olim bene-
20 ficij uideatur, quum per eum apud nos disciplinas restaurent,
quas ipsi a nobis initio acceperunt, quod usque adeo in confesso
est, ut id Gaguinus quoque nec detractator gallicae laudis, nec
buccinator nostrae, in Annales suos retulerit. Atque utinam et
Louanienses, et Parisienses quoque scholastici omnes, Fabri
25 commentarios in Aristotelicam Dialecticen reciperent: Esset ea
disciplina (ni fallor) et minus utrisque rixosa, et paulo repurga-
tior.

---

2 mortalibus] *P 1563 1625*, natalibus *S*   3 omnino] *interl. S*   3–5 nisi . . . seculis]
ital. 1625   5 exulet] *1563*, exulat *P S 1625;* seculis] *corr. from* saeculis *P*   8 quisque] *P
1625*, quique *S 1563;* tradendi] *corr. from* tradendus *P*   11 uel in] *P S 1625*, uel
1563   12 optime] *S 1563 1625*, optimae *P*   14 libenter quenquam] *P 1563 1625*,
quemque libenter *S*   15 nostros] *P S 1563*, nostras *1625;* permultum] *corr. from*
permultus *S*   16 ueraeque] *P 1563 1625*, uerae *S*   18 sanioraque] *P 1563 1625*,
saniora *S*   20 uideatur] *S 1563 1625*, uiuideatur *P;* restaurent] restaurēt *P*,
restauraret *1625*, instaurent *S 1563*   22 detractator] *1563*, detractor *P 1565*,
detrectator *S (see commentary)*   25 reciperent:] *S 1625*, reciperent, *P*, reciperent.
1563   26 fallor)] *1563 1625*, fallor, *P S;* utrisque] *S 1563, interl. P*, utriusque *1625*

Yet I am not at all sure that you have much respect for our universities, since you confer so much importance on Louvain and Paris that it seems you leave nothing at all for the rest of mankind, especially in dialectic. You say, after all, that if the theologians of Louvain and Paris were not dialecticians there would be no dialectic on earth nor would there have been any for these many centuries. I was in both universities seven years ago; not long, to be sure, but while there I tried hard to learn what things are taught in each university and what method of teaching is used there. And indeed, though I honor them both, I have so far discovered no reason, either in what I heard while I was there or in what I have learned since I left, why, even for dialectic, I ought to prefer either one of them to Oxford or Cambridge for the education of my own children, for whom I want strictly the best.

And yet I will admit (for I would not like to deny anyone his fair share of praise) that we Englishmen owe a great debt to the Parisian, Jacques Lefèvre d'Etaples. All of our better minds and sounder judgments acknowledge in him a restorer of true dialectic and true philosophy, especially Aristotelian. Through this man it seems Paris is paying us back, in a way, for a benefit received long ago, since through him they restore to our country the same sciences we originally taught them. This last point is so generally acknowledged that even Gaguin, no belittler of France's prestige and no patron of England's, includes it in his *Annals*. And would that the scholars of Louvain and Paris alike would accept Lefèvre's commentaries on Aristotle's dialectic. Unless I am mistaken, in both universities that science would then be less contentious and not quite so corrupt.

Miror tamen cur Louanienses, ac parisienses, in Dialectices
commemoratione coniunxeris, qui usque adeo inter se discor-
dant, ut ne nomine quidem conueniant, quum alteri realium,
alteri nominalium nomen affectent. Quanquam si Ari[13v]
5 stotelem recipiunt, si utrique interpretantur, si non alia de re
quam de eius mente, tot inter se rixas excitant, iam quum Parisienses aliter, aliter eum Louanienses interpretantur, nec aliter modo, sed contra quoque, qui scire possis, utris potius
accedendum censeas? Sin ad dialecticen pertinent huiusmodi
10 lites, sed nihil ad Aristotelem tamen, iam non Aristotelicam tantum logicam (quod tu ais) sed aliam preterea, aut alteri, aut
utrique profitentur. Sin autem, quae in tanta controuersia sunt,
nec ad ipsam dialecticam attineant, (nec attinent certe si ad eum
non attinent modo is dialecticam perfecte tradiderit) iam hoc
15 aegregie fuerit absurdum, ut discatur Dialectica, de rebus ad
eam rem neutiquam spectantibus tot annos digladiari.

Et profecto Dorpi propemodum adducor ut credam, magnam
illam opinionum partem de quibus tam diu tanta contentione,
uelut pro aris focisque dimica[14]tur, aut ad logicam parum
20 pertinere, aut ad eam perdiscendam non admodum conferre.
Nam ut in grammatica suffecerit, eas obseruationes didicisse,
quibus possis et ipse latine loqui, et quae ab alijs latine scripta
sunt intelligere, non autem anxie innumeras loquendi regulas
aucupari, litterasque inter, ac syllabas insenescere, itidem in di-
25 alectica satis esse crediderim, dictionum naturam, enunciationum uires, tum ex his collectionum formulas edoctum, Dialecticam protinus, uelut instrumentum ad caeteras disciplinas
accommodare. Atque hoc nimirum ipsum spectauit Aristoteles
quum dialecticam suam decem illis summis, siue rerum, siue

---

2 qui] *P 1563 1625*, quod *S*   3 quidem] *P 1563 1625*, quidem inter se *S*   4
affectent.] *1563 1625*, affectent, *P S*   4–5 Aristotelem] *P 1625*, Aristotelem utrique *S*
1563   5 interpretantur] *P 1625*, tradunt *S 1563*   6 mente] mente, ⟨rixantur⟩ *S*
9 pertinent] *P 1563 1625*, pertinet *S*   13 certe] *S 1563 1625*, certae *P*   14 perfecte]
S 1563 1625, perfectae *P*   15 aegregie] *S 1563 1625*, aegregiae *P; Dialectica,] S 1563*,
Dialectica *P 1625*   19 uelut] *corr. from* uelit *P;* dimicatur] dimica⟨n⟩tur *S*   22 possis]
1563 1625, possis, *P S;* latine . . . latine] *S 1563 1625*, latinae . . . latinae *P*   23 anxie]
S 1563 1625, anxiae *P* ¹   24 insenescere] *P 1625*, consenescere *S 1563; sidenote in P* Quid
satis in dialectica   27 *sidenote in P* logica Aristotelis

But I wonder why you linked the scholars of Louvain and Paris in your comment about dialectic: they are so thoroughly at odds with each other that they do not even agree on a name, since the former affect the name "realists," the latter the name "nominalists." But suppose that they both accept Aristotle, that both are engaged in interpreting him, and that all their contentions concern nothing else but his meaning; since the scholars of Louvain and Paris interpret him in two different, or rather in two contradictory senses, how do you know which party you ought to join? On the other hand, if this sort of quarrel is actually relevant to dialectic but not at all relevant to Aristotle, either one party or both are professing not only the logic of Aristotle, as you say they do, but some other, as well. But if the points which give rise to such controversy are not even relevant to dialectic (which they certainly are not, if you hold that he taught dialectic perfectly and if they have no relevance to him), it would be highly absurd to endeavor to learn dialectic by feuding for so many years over things which have nothing to do with it.

Indeed, Dorp, I am tempted to think that many of the theories over which battles are constantly raging as if home and hearth were at stake either have little to do with logic or are not very useful for learning it well. In the study of grammar, for instance, it should be enough to learn those empirical precepts which prepare you to speak Latin yourself and to read it intelligently, but not anxiously to seek out innumerable rules of speech or to squander your life over letters and syllables. In dialectic, by the same token, I should have thought it sufficient to master the nature of words, the force of propositions, and the forms of syllogisms, and at once to apply dialectic as a tool to the other branches of learning. With this very thing in mind Aristotle restricted his own dialectic to the ten ultimate classes of real

nominum generibus, deinde enunciationum tractatu, adiunctis postremo collectionum formulis, et quae necessario demonstrant, et quae suadent probabiliter, et quae callide cauillantur, absoluit. Ad haec tanquam aditum, introitumque quendam Porphirius [14v] quinque illas uniuersa complectentes seu res seu uoces appellari malis adiecit. Porro eiusmodi questiones, quibus rudia adhuc, et aptioribus imbuenda, detinentur potius quam promouentur ingenia, neuter eorum proposuit: Porphirius etiam ex professo abstinuit.

At nunc absurda quaedam portenta, ad certam bonarum artium nata perniciem, et luculenter ab antiquis distincta commiscuerunt et ad ueterum purissimas traditiones suis adiectis sordibus infecerunt omnia. Nam in grammatica (ut omittam Alexandrum, atque id genus alios qui quanquam imperite tamen grammaticam utcunque docuerunt) Albertus quidam grammaticam se traditurum professus, logicam nobis quandam, aut metaphysicam, imo neutram, sed mera somnia, mera deliria, grammaticae loco substituit. Et tamen hae nugacissimae nugae in publicas achademias, non tantum receptae sunt, sed etiam plerisque tam impense placue[15]runt, ut is propemodum solus aliquid in grammatica ualere censeatur, quisquis fuerit Albertistae nomen assequutus. Tantum authoritatis habet, ad peruertenda bonorum quoque ingeniorum iudicia, semel ab ineptis tradita magistris, deinde tempore corroborata, persuasio.

Quo fit ut minus mirer ad eundem modum in dialecticae locum, nugas plusquam sophisticas irrepsisse, quae cultoribus suis argutiarum nomine, tam uehementer arrident, ut mihi nuper his de rebus obiter loquenti, quidam Dialecticus (ut ferebatur, doctissimus) asseruerit Aristotelem (referam ipsius uer-

---

1–2 tractatu, adiunctis postremo] *P S*, tractatu adiunctis, postremo *1563*, tractatu; adiunctis postremo *1625*   3 callide] *S 1563 1625*, callidae *P*   5 complectentes] *P 1625*, amplectentes *S 1563*   6 appellari] *1625, corr. from* appellare *P*, appellare *S 1563*   8 promouentur] *S 1563 1625*, promouentur, *P; proposuit:*] proposuit. *P 1625*, proposuit *S*, proposuit, *1563*   10 portenta,] *S*, portenta *P 1563 1625*   11–12 distincta commiscuerunt] distincta, commiscuerunt, *P*, distincta commiscuerunt, *S 1563*, distincta, commiscuerunt; *1625*   12 traditiones] *1625*, traditiones, *P S 1563*   13 sordibus] *S 1563*, sordibus, *P 1625*   14 imperite] *S 1563 1625*, imperitae *P*   20 impense] *S 1563 1625*, impensae *P*   25 mirer] *P 1563 1625*, mireris *S*   26 quae] *1563 1625*, que *P S*   28–29 ferebatur,] ferebatur *P S 1563*, ferebatur) *1625*   29–28/6 Aristotelem . . . sua] *ital. except words in parentheses 1625*

entities or of predicables, to a treatise on propositions, and to the forms of the syllogism, the demonstrative, the probable, and the captious. To these Porphyry added a kind of entrance or introduction in his five universals, which may be construed either as entities or as words. Certainly neither propounded, and Porphyry flatly refused to propound, those sophistical problems that do more to stunt than to foster young intellects in need of more wholesome instruction.

But there have sprung up of late certain monstrous absurdities, the bane of sound learning in general, which have muddled up subjects which were clearly distinguished by the ancients and have corrupted all subjects by sullying the oldest and purest traditions with their foul accretions. In grammar, for instance, to say nothing of Alexander and others like him (for they did teach grammar somehow, no matter how crudely), a certain Albert, professing to expound grammar, has presented us instead with some sort of logic or metaphysics, or rather with out-and-out drivel and nonsense; yet this unsurpassed trifling is not only accepted in the universities but is even admired so much by some that according to them no one who has not earned the title of Albertist is worth anything as a grammarian. So great is the power of a conviction to pervert even sound minds and judgments once it has been planted by incompetent teachers and reinforced by the passage of time.

For this reason I am not so astonished that the same kind of supersophistical trifling has crept in to supplant dialectic; this trifling affords such delight to its votaries, because of its "subtlety," that in a talk which I recently had on this topic with a certain dialectician who passes for very learned, he claimed (I

ba neque enim aliter possum tam nitidum eloquentiae florem
assequi) "nisi grosso modo scripsisse," et "nunc sunt" (inquit)
"pueri in paruis Logicalibus suis tam mirabiliter fundati quod
bene credo certe quod si Aristoteles a sepulchro suo resurrex-
5 eret et argueret cum eis illi bene concluderent eum non solum in
sophistria [15v] sed etiam in logica sua." Reliqui hominem oppido quam inuitus nisi quod aliquanto (ut tum res erat) oc-
cupatior fui, quam ut uacaret ludere.

Sed liber ille paruorum logicalium (quem ideo sic appellatum
10 puto quod parum habeat logices) opereprecium est uidere, In
suppositionibus quas uocant, In ampliationibus, restrictionibus,
apellationibus, et ubi non? quam ineptas, quam etiam falsas
praeceptiunculas habet, ut ex quibus adiguntur inter has atque
huiuscemodi enunciationes distinguere, "Leo animali est for-
15 tior," et "Leo est fortior animali," quasi non idem significent, et
profecto tam sunt ineptae, ut utraque propemodum nihil significet, quanquam si quicquam, haud dubie idem. Tantundem-
que inter se differunt "Vinum bibi bis," et "bis uinum bibi," hoc
est secundum hos Logistas multum, sed reuera nihil. Iam si quis
20 non assas modo, sed adustas quoque carnes ederit, eum uolunt
uerum dicere si sic enunciet, "Ego crudas carnes comedi," non
[16] autem si sic, "ego comedi crudas carnes." tum si quis parte
relicta mihi, partem sibi pecuniae meae sustulerit, mentiar
uidelicet si dixero, "spoliauit me denarijs," sed ne desint mihi
25 uerba quibus apud iudicem querar, licebit dicere, "denarijs

1 neque enim aliter possum] *P S 1625*, nequeo enim aliter *1563*   2–6 nisi . . . sua]
gothic script P   2 scripsisse,] scripsisse *P*, scripsisse: *S 1563*, scripsisse. *1625*   3 mira-
biliter] *P 1625*, substantialiter *S 1563*   4–5 resurrexeret] *P 1625*, resurrexerit *S
1563*, distinguere. *P*, distinguere: *S 1625*   14–15 Leo . . . animali] *ital. except* et *1625;*
Sed] *P 1625*, Ceterum *S 1563; sidenote in P* sophisticam taxat merito   12 non? quam] *P
S 1625*, inquam tam *1563*   14 huiuscemodi] *P 1625*, eiusmodi *S 1563;* distinguere,]
1563, distinguere. *P*, distinguere: *S 1625*   14–15 Leo . . . animali] *ital. except* et *1625;*
fortior,] *S 1563*, fortior. *P*, fortior: *1625*   16 ineptae] *P 1563 1625*, inepte *S*
16–17 significet] *corr. from* significent *P*   17 dubie] *S 1563 1625*, dubiae *P*   18
differunt] differunt. *P S*, differunt, *1563*, differunt: *1625;* Vinum . . . bibi] *ital. except* et
1625; bibi bis,] ⟨bis⟩ bibi bis / *P*, bis bibi. *S*, bis bibi, *1563*, bibi bis: *1625;* bibi,] *S*, bibi. *P
1625*, bibi: *1563*   19 reuera] *P 1625*, re vera *S 1563*   21 enunciet,] *1563*, enunciet.
P S, enunciet: *1625*   21 Ego . . . comedi] *ital. 1625;* comedi,] *S*, comedi. *P*, comedi:
1563 comedi; *1625*   22 ego . . . carnes] *ital. 1625*   24 dixero,] *1563*, dixero. *P*,
dixero: *S 1625;* spoliauit . . . denarijs] *ital. 1625;* desint mihi] *P 1563 1625*, desint *S*
25–30/ denarijs . . . me] *ital. 1625*

will use his own words; I cannot see how else to achieve the same brilliant perfection of eloquence) that "how Aristotle wrote was real vulgar," and "these days," he said, "schoolboys get so wonderfully grounded in their *Little Logic* that I am pretty well certain that if Aristotle rose again out of his grave and picked an argument with them they would shut him up good, not only in sophistry but in his logic, too." I was as sorry as I could be to take leave of the fellow, but as things stood just then I was rather too busy for play.

But as for that book, *Little Logic,* so called probably because it contains little logic, it is worth having a look at its chapters on so-called suppositions, on ampliations, restrictions, and appellations, and everywhere else, to see all of the pointless and even false little precepts it does contain, such as those which oblige one to draw a distinction between these propositions (and other ones like them): "The lion than an animal is stronger" and "The lion is stronger than an animal," as if they did not mean the same thing; and admittedly both are so pointless that each of them means almost nothing, though if anything, then doubtless the same. There is just as much difference between "Wine I drank twice" and "Twice I drank wine"; that is to say, a great difference according to those logic-choppers, but in actual fact none at all. Now if anyone eats meat which is not just well-done, but half-charred, they insist he is telling the truth if he asserts, "Raw meat I ate"; not, however, if he asserts, "I ate raw meat." Then if someone leaves one part for me but appropriates the rest of my money for himself, I will supposedly be lying if I say, "He has robbed me of cash," but lest I should lack words to file my accusation in court I can say, "Of cash he has robbed me." And in one

spoliauit me." Et in aliquo casu (ut aiunt) "possibili posito," hec erit uera, "Papam uerberaui," quum eodem manente casu hec erit falsa, "uerberaui papam," Nempe si is qui nunc papa sit, puer olim a me uapulauerit. Digni Hercle qui talia iam senes
5 docent, ut quoties pueros docent, toties ipsi uapulent.

Quid quod hanc falsam aiunt, "Omnis homo est pater, qui habet filium," nisi omnes prorsus homines iam habeant filios, quoniam uidelicet huic equipollet, "omnis homo est pater, et omnis homo habet filium"? At hanc interim ueram affirmant,
10 "Pater erit Sortes quando Sortes non erit pater," et hanc, "Pater manebit Ioannes, quando Ioannes non manebit pater," Quod quis sic audire potest [16v] ut sibi non interim credat enigma proponi?

At hec uerba "SVM" et "POSSVM" regnant plane, et quoniam
15 (ut aiunt) "ampliatiua" sunt, pomeria sua ultra ipsas naturae fines longe lateque proferunt. Nam hanc ueram astruunt, "Omne quod erit, est," sed eam tamen callide interpretantur. Aiunt enim, "omne quod erit est," significare, "omne quod est quod erit est." atque hoc pacto cauent ne Antichristus qui olim
20 erit iam sit. nam quanquam "omne quod erit est," et quanquam "Antichristus erit," tamen non sequitur, "Antichristus est," propterea scilicet quod "Antichristus non est ens quod erit."

---

2 uera,] *1563*, uera P, vera: S *1625;* Papam uerberaui] *ital. 1625;* uerberaui,] S *1563*, uerberaui P, verberavi; *1625*   3 uerberaui papam] *ital. 1625;* papam,] papam. P S *1563 1625*   3–4 sit, puer] P *1563 1625*, sit, S   6 Quid] P S *1563*, Quid, quaeso *1625;* aiunt,] S *1563*, aiunt. P, aiunt? *1625;* est pater] P *1625*, pater est S *1563*   6–7 Omnis . . . filium] *ital. 1625*   7 homines iam] P *1563 1625*, iam homines S; filios,] S *1625*, filios. P, filios: *1563*   8 equipollet,] *1563*, equipollet. P, equipollet S, aequipollet: *1625*   8–9 omnis . . . filium] *ital. except* et *1625*   8 pater, et] P S *1625*, pater *1563*   9 filium"?] filium P S, filium. *1563 1625;* affirmant,] *1563*, affirmant. P, affirmant: S *1625*   10–11 Pater . . . pater] *ital. except* et *1625*   10 Sortes . . . Sortes] P S *1563*, Socrates . . . Socrates *1625;* hanc,] *1563*, hanc. P, hanc S, hanc: *1625*   11 *2nd* manebit] P *1625*, manet S *1563*; pater,] pater. P S *1563 1625*   13 proponi?] *1563 1625*, proponi. P, proponi S   14 plane] S *1563 1625*, planae P; *sidenote in* P pulchre   15 ipsas] P *1625*, ipsos S *1563*   16 longe lateque] S *1563 1625*, longae lataeque P; astruunt,] *1563*, astruunt. P S, astruunt: *1625*   17 Omne . . . est] *ital. 1625;* est,] est. P S *1625*, est: *1563;* tamen] S *1563*, tum P *1625;* callide] S *1563 1625*, callidae P   18 enim,] *1563 1625*, enim P S; *1st* omne] P S *1563*, omnes *1625;* omne . . . est] *ital. 1625;* est,] *1625*, est P S *1563;* significare,] *1563 1625*, significare P, significare. S   18–19 omne . . . est] *ital. 1625;* erit] erit, ⟨erit⟩ S   21 sequitur,] *1563 1625*, sequitur P S; Antichristus est] *ital. 1625*   22 erit.] *1563 1625*, erit, P S

hypothetical instance, which they call a "posited possible," the statement "The pope I have beaten" will be true, while the statement "I have beaten the pope" will be false for the same hypothetical instance, namely, given that whoever is now pope long ago as a boy took a beating from me. By Jove, those who teach this sort of thing as old men should be given a beating themselves for every lesson that they teach to boys.

What about this? They say that the statement "Every man is a father who has a son" is false unless all men already have sons, since of course it amounts to the same thing as saying "Every man is a father, and every man has a son." But at the same time, they affirm that this statement is true, "A father will Socrates be when Socrates will not be a father," and this one, "A father will John go on being when John will not go on being a father." Who can listen to that without thinking that what he is hearing is a riddle?

But the words "AM" and "CAN" simply rule the world, and because, as the saying goes, they are "expansive," they extend their domain far and wide beyond nature's own bounds. Indeed, those men maintain that this statement is true: "Everything which will be, is." But, of course, they interpret it shrewdly. For according to them, "Everything that will be, is," means "Everything that is something that will be, is"; and in this way they see to it that Antichrist, who will be eventually, may not be just yet. For even though "Everything that will be, is," and even though "Antichrist will be," it still does not follow that "Antichrist is," since of course "Antichrist is not a being-that-will-be." And had

Quod nisi hanc plusquam subtilem propositionis huius exposi-
tionem circumspexissent acuti in Dialecticis argutijs Theologi,
Rempublicam christianam haud dubie iam olim Antichristus in-
uasisset non sine magno caeterorum omnium periculo. Nam
5 ipsis non uideo quid possit imminere discriminis, quippe quum
fateantur has etiam ueras esse, "Anti[17]christus est amabilis," et
"Antichristus est amatiuus."
   Quanquam profecto nec Antichristus, nec supremus ipse
iudicij dies rerum naturam magis poterit quam hec dialectica
10 subuertere, quae docet has enunciationes esse ueras, "Viuum
fuit mortuum," "Futurum fuit preteritum," quibus nimirum fit,
ut mortuorum resurrectio, non ut ipsi loquuntur "in fieri," sed
"in facto" esse uideatur. Iam istae non minus mirandae, sed sunt
amenae quoque, ac plausibiles quum sint uerae scilicet, "Virgo
15 fuit meretrix," Et "Meretrix erit uirgo," et "Meretrix Possibiliter
est uirgo." Non facile dictu est dialecticis tam benignis utrae
magis, uirginesne, an meretrices debeant. debent certe utraeque
plurimum. Poetae ergo nugas, dialectici seria tractant. Poetae
fingunt, ac mentiuntur, Dialectici nunquam nisi uera loquuntur,
20 ne tum quidem quum hanc esse uerissimam affirmant, "Homo
mortuus potest celebrare missam," quod quanquam non audeo
asserentibus eis, ac propemodum etiam iurantibus non credere
[17v] (neque enim tot doctoribus tam irrefragabilibus fas est
refragari) hactenus tamen (quantum memini) neminem un-
25 quam repperi, qui se narraret mortuo celebranti ministrasse.
Hanccine dialecticam docet Aristoteles? Hanc Hyeronymus
laudat? Hanc probat Augustinus? quam (ut ait Persius) "Non
sani esse hominis non sanus iuret Orestes"?

---

1 Quod] P S 1563, Qui 1625; propositionis] propositionis ⟨eius⟩ P   3 dubie] S 1563
1625, dubiae P   6 esse,] esse. P S, esse: 1563 1625   6–7 Antichristus . . . amatiuus]
ital. except et 1625   10 subuertere,] S 1563, subuertere. P, subuertere; 1625; ueras,]
ueras. P S, ueras: 1563 1625   11 mortuum,] 1563, mortuum. P S, mortuum: 1625
13–14 sunt amenae . . . plausibiles] P 1563 1625, amenae . . . plausibiles sunt S   14
amenae quoque] S 1563 1625, amenaequoque P; scilicet,] 1563, scilicet. P, scilicet S,
scilicet: 1625   14–16 Virgo fuit . . . est uirgo] ital. except et 1625   15 meretrix,] S
1563, meretrix. P, meretrix; 1625; 2nd Meretrix] insert in margin P   16 facile] corr.
from faciles P   17 certe] S 1563 1625, certae P   18 Poetae] P S 1563, Poeta 1625
20 affirmant,] 1563, affirmant. P, affirmant: S 1625   20–21 Homo . . . missam] ital.
1625   21 missam,] S, missam. P 1563 1625   27 Persius] P 1563 1625, Parsius S
27–28 Non . . . Orestes] ital. 1625   28 Orestes] corr. from Horestes P; Orestes"?]
Orestes. P S 1625, Orestes? 1563

we not been furnished with this hyperacute exposition of that proposition by theologians adept in dialectical subtleties, Antichrist would doubtless have invaded Christendom long ago, not without immense danger for everyone else. For I fail to see how the theologians themselves could feel threatened at all, since they hold that these too are true statements: "Antichrist is lovable" and "Antichrist is receptive to love."

But indeed neither Antichrist nor the final day of judgment itself could upset nature's order as thoroughly as this dialectic, which teaches that these propositions are true: "The living was dead"; "The future was past"; whence of course it results that the resurrection of the dead seems to be (as they themselves say) not just "in progress," but rather "in fact." And there are others which are no less remarkable, but these are delightful, besides, and appealing as well as undoubtedly true: "The virgin was a whore" and "The whore will be a virgin" and "The whore is potentially a virgin." It is hard to say which of the two, virgins or whores, owe more thanks to such generous dialecticians; certainly both of them owe a great deal. So the poets are busy with trifles, dialecticians with serious affairs. Poets feign and tell lies; dialecticians speak only the truth, even when they affirm this proposition to be indisputably true: "A dead man is able to celebrate mass." But although I dare not disbelieve this when the dialecticians assert it, and indeed almost swear to it, for to controvert such an assembly of incontrovertible doctors is out of the question, nonetheless to this day, to the best of my memory, I have never met anyone who professed to have served a mass said by a dead celebrant. Is this really the same dialectic that Aristotle teaches? That Jerome recommends? That Augustine esteems? Dialectic that even "mad Orestes," in Persius' phrasing, "would swear was the work of a madman"?

Miror hercle homines acutuli, quonam pacto senserunt illas
enunciationes sic intelligendas esse, quomodo nemo in toto orbe
preter eos intelligit. Nec sunt artis illa uocabula, ut sint eis quasi
in peculio, et ab eis, si quis uolet uti, sumenda mutuo, communis
5 nimirum sermo est, nisi quod quaedam deterius reddunt, quam
a cerdonibus eadem acceperunt. A uulgo sumpserunt, uulga-
ribus abutuntur.

At regula quam uocant logices in eos sensus tales propositiones docet interpretandas. Quae (malum) regula in angulo
10 quopiam ab his composita, qui uix loqui sciant, uniuerso terrarum orbi, nouas loquendi leges imponet? [18] Grammatica
recte loqui docet, nec ea tamen insuetas loquendi regulas com-
miniscitur, sed quae plurimum in loquendo uidet obseruari,
eorum loquendi rudes, ne contra morem loquantur, admonet.
15 Nec aliter quicquam dialectica facit quae sana est. Nempe hic
syllogismus, "Omne animal currit, omnis homo est animal, ergo
omnis homo currit," non ideo syllogismus est quia rite secundum
dialecticae normam colligitur, ac formatur in barbara, sed quia
postremam orationem ad praemissa consequi docet ratio, quae
20 regulam ob id ipsum talem fecit. Alioquin aliter eam factura,
quaqua uersus ab ipsa rerum natura flecteretur. Ipsi quoque
eodem modo hanc propositionem "Meretrix erit uirgo," ne di-
cant sic interpretandam, "Meretrix quae est uel fuit," quia sic
iubet regula, sed rationem afferant ab ipsa re quare fieri deberet
25 talis regula. Nam si recta est ea interpretatio, necesse est eam aut
ab ipsa re, quae enunciatur, aut ex proprietate sermonis emer-
gere.

---

1 hercle] *P S 1625*, hercule *1563;* acutuli] *S 1563 1625*, acutili *P*   3 eis,] *1625*, eis *P S*
1563   11 loquendi] loquendi ⟨regulas⟩ *P*   12 recte] *S 1563 1625*, rectae *P*   12
insuetas loquendi] *P 1563 1625*, insuetas *S*   13–14 obseruari, eorum] *1563 1625*,
obseruari eorum, *P*, obseruari eorum *S*   14 loquantur] *S 1563 1625*, loquuntur *P*
15 quae] *1563 1625*, que *P S*   15–16 hic syllogismus *S 1563 1625*, hunc syllogismum
P   16–17 Omne . . . currit] *P 1563, ital. 1625*, Oē animal currit, Oīs hō est al'. go Oē
hō crt *S*   17 rite] *S 1563 1625*, ritae *P*   18 barbara] *ital. 1625;* barbara, sed] *P 1563
1625*, barbara, uel caterua, sed *S*   21 Ipsi] *P 1563 1625*, Ipse *S*   22 hanc proposi-
tionem] *1625*, in hac propositione *P S 1563;* Meretrix . . . uirgo] *ital. 1625*   23
Meretrix . . . fuit] *ital. 1625;* quae] *1563 1625*, que *P S;* uel fuit] *P 1625*, uel que erit *S*
1563   24 deberet] *P 1625*, debeat *S 1563*   25 est ea] *P 1625*, est *S 1563*   26 quae]
1563 1625, que *P S*

I wonder, by Jove, how these petty adepts ever reached the conclusion that those propositions should be understood in a way that no one on earth but themselves understands them. Those words are not technical terms on which these men can claim a monopoly, as it were, so that anyone wishing to use them must go and ask them for a loan. Such expressions are actually common language, though these men do return some of them in a worse state than they were in when they were appropriated from ordinary craftsmen. They have borrowed their words from the public domain; they abuse public property.

But the so-called rule of logic teaches that this is the right way to construe propositions like those. Damn it, since when can some rule slapped together in some corner by men who themselves barely know how to speak impose new laws of speech on the entire world? Grammar teaches the right way to speak, and yet it invents no laws of speech in defiance of custom; instead, it simply sees which constructions appear the most often in speech and points these out to those who are unschooled in speech so that their speech will not flout common usage. Nor does sane dialectic, at least, do its work any differently. For example, this syllogism, "Every animal runs; man is an animal; therefore man runs," is a syllogism not because it is duly set up in accordance with the norm of dialectic and constructed in the figure of "barbara," but because reason teaches that the last statement follows from the premises; and this is precisely why reason made the rule as it did. Otherwise, should it set out to make that rule differently, it would swerve off in every direction from the structure of nature itself. By the same token, let those men also stop insisting that we must interpret the proposition "The whore will be a virgin" as "The whore (who is still or was once a virgin) . . ." just because a rule orders that it should be so; let them bring us a reason from the fact of the matter why such a rule should have been made. For if that interpretation is right then it must emerge either from the fact of the matter being stated or from the particular force of the idiom employed.

Ergo quum tam multis eorum [18v] qui latine iam olim loquuti
sunt, neque ingenium defuerit, neque eruditio, nec sermonis
proprij fuerit minor quam istis est (uti credo) peritia, quomodo
euenit ut ex illis nemo potuerit intelligere hanc ueram esse,
5   "Meretrix erit uirgo," aut inter has distinguere, "Nummum non
habeo," et "Non habeo nummum"? Quanquam nemo negauerit
transpositiones uocabulorum diuersum saepe sensum gignere,
Neque enim idem est, "Bibas priusquam eas," et "Eas priusquam
bibas." Sed hoc affirmo, quando ita sensus uariatur, omnes in
10 idem mortales assentire, trahente uidelicet ratione, non dialecticorum iubente potius quam persuadente regula, quorum officium est ut more nostro loquentes, quouis nos ueris rationibus
impellant, Sophistarum uero, ut insidiosis eo prestigijs addu-
cant, quo nos peruenisse miremur. Nam hoc hebetissimum acu-
15 men est, et stultissima solertia, se disputando pronunciare uic-
tores, et triumphum sibi decernere, quia nos nescimus in quem
sensum ipsi clanculum pacti sunt, sermones nostros [19] contra
communem omnium sensum accipere.

At hec quum nec sophistica dici mereantur, tamen non pro
20 sophisticis nugis ducuntur, sed inter abstrusissimos dialecticae
thesauros numerantur, nec a pueris tanquam dediscenda dis-
cuntur, sed a senibus quoque, in ipsa theologiae penetralia susci-
piuntur. His quidam theologicas perplexitates infarciunt, ex his
propositiones tam ridiculas effingunt, ut ridendi materia nus-
25 quam oriri possit uberior, nisi quod multo malim, eos qui sic
ineptiunt, ad sanitatem conuerti, quam ipse ex insanorum deli-
rijs capere uoluptatem. Quanquam quid hec dico tibi Dorpi, cui

---

1 latine] S 1563 1625, latinae P   5 Meretrix . . . uirgo] ital. 1625   5–6
Nummum . . . nummum] ital. except et 1625   6 habeo,] S 1563, habeo. P, habeo;
1625   7 transpositiones] S 1563 1625, traspositiones P; diuersum] S 1563, diūsum P,
diuisum 1625   8 est,] 1563, est. P, est: S 1625   8–9 Bibas . . . bibas] ital. except et
1625   8 eas . . . Eas] P 1625, edas . . . Edas S 1563   11 iubente] P 1563 1625,
lubente S; potius] S 1563 1625, potius, P   14–15 acumen est] P 1625, est acumen S
1563   16 nescimus] S 1563, nescimus, P 1625   19 nec] P S 1563, non 1625   20
ducuntur] P 1625, changed to dicuntur S, dicuntur 1563; abstrusissimos dialecticae] P
1563 1625, Dialecticae abstrusissimos S   22–23 suscipiuntur] P 1625,
suspiciuntur S 1563   24 ridendi] P 1625, ridenda S 1563; materia] S 1563 1625,
materia, P   26 ipse] interl. P   26–27 ipse ex . . . capere] P 1625, ex . . . ipse capere
S 1563

Now, then, since so many of those who spoke Latin long ago
lacked neither intelligence nor erudition, nor were they, I think,
any less versed in their idiom than these fellows are, how does it
happen that none of the ancients could understand this statement to be true, "The whore will be a virgin,"or distinguish
between these two, "Not a penny have I" and "I have not a
penny"? Although no one would deny that transpositions of
words often produce different meanings, nor does "Drink before you go" mean the same thing as "Go before you drink." But
I do affirm this, that when meanings do vary in this way, all
mortals agree on the fact; for they are guided to do so by reason
and not coerced rather than persuaded by the rule of the dialecticians, whose real task is to press us along with true reasoning, to
any conclusion, by using the same language we do; to lure us
along with insidious trumpery to the point that we wonder how
we ever got there is a task, not for them, but for sophists. For this
is the dullest kind of acumen and the most foolish finesse in the
world, for these men to declare themselves champion debaters
and crown themselves victors just because we do not know in
what sense, against all common sense, they have secretly agreed
to construe our own words.

Yet these quibbles, which do not even merit the label "sophistic," are not seen as sophistical trifles; instead, they are numbered among the most recondite treasures of dialectic. They are
not learned by boys as things to be unlearned later on; instead,
they are introduced even by old men into the innermost shrine
of theology. Some of them use these quibbles to pad out perplexed theological inquiries; from these quibbles they contrive such
ridiculous propositions that nowhere on earth could you find
such a rich crop of laughing matter, although I would much
rather see those who talk this sort of drivel converted to sanity
than take pleasure myself in the drivel they talk while insane.
And yet why am I saying this to you, Dorp, since I know you

non dubito has naenias non minus displicere, quam mihi, si posses mutare? et fortasse poteris, adiutus a tui similibus, modo ne statuas tecum illorum obsequi ineptijs, quos multo magis par est, tuo parere iudicio.

5   Sed ad epistolam tuam reuertor, ut ostendam nullam ex Erasmi uerbis ansam tibi datam, [19v] qua eum (id quod facis) diceres, Louanienses Theologos multoque adhuc minus caeteros omnes imperitiae damnare, Si quidem quum ille dixisset se ualere sinere, non omnes quidem Theologos, ut qui prius in
10   eadem epistola multos dixerit esse prestantissimos, sed eos tantum (si qui tales sunt, ut certe sunt) qui preter sophisticas nugas nihil didicerunt, Hic tu statim, "theologos istos puto" (inquis) "Louanienses designari." Quid ita Dorpi? quasi uero difficile sit, huius farinae, immo istius furfuris, aliquos ubique reperire?
15   Belle profecto sentis de Louaniensibus, si eos, et solos, et omnes, putas eiusmodi descriptione cognobiles, quod ille neque sentit, neque dicit.

     Paulo post tamen sic dictum accipis, tanquam non in Louanienses modo, sed in omnes quotcunque sunt ubique gentium
20   Theologi, diceretur, quod ille nec in alios omnes, nec in Louanienses ipsos est loquutus. Tu tamen perinde ac si neque illum, neque temet audias, uideris in hec uerba non descen[20]dere, sed uelut abreptus impetu animi efferuescentis erumpere, "Nonne uidemus abiectissimos opifices, imo uilissima mancipia
25   clarissimis esse predita ingenijs? Quid ergo sibi uolunt hec in Theologos omnes detorta uocabula, pingues, rudes, pestilentes, et qui nihil habent mentis? Nullius est artis probra dicere in

---

1 displicere] S 1563 1625, displacere changed from placere P   2 mutare?] mutare. P 1625, mutare S, mutare, 1563; fortasse] P 1563 1625, forte S   5 reuertor,] 1563, reuertor. P, reuertor S, reuertor; 1625; nullam] interl. S   7 minus] P S 1563, magis 1625   8 damnare,] 1563, damnare. P S 1625   10 epistola] S 1563 1625, epistola, P; dixerit] S 1563, dixit P 1625   11 si qui] P S 1625, qui 1563; certe] S 1563 1625, certae P   12 didicerunt,] didicerunt. P S 1563 1625; statim] P 1625, statim per S 1563 12–13 theologos . . . designari] ital. 1625   15 Belle] S 1563 1625, Bellae P   18 post tamen] P 1625, tamen post S 1563   20 ille] P S 1563, om. 1625   22 audias] corr. from audisse P   23 erumpere,] erumpere. P 1563, erumpere: S 1625   24–40/6 Nonne . . . religionem] ital. 1625   27 habent] P 1625, habeant S 1563; mentis?] 1625, mentis; P, mentis. S 1563

would approve of this nonsense as little as I do if you were able to change it? And with the help of men like you, perhaps you can do so, unless you have resolved to be ruled by the driveling of people who should in all fairness defer to your judgment.

But I will return to your letter to show that Erasmus' words gave you no pretext for saying (as you do say) that he charges the Louvain theologians with ignorance, much less all the other theologians in the world. He said he could dispense, not with all theologians, of course—he had already said in the same letter that many of them were outstandingly qualified—but only with those theologians (if some happen to fit the description, and some certainly do) who have never learned anything but sophistical trifles. Here you interject, "I think 'those theologians' refers to the ones in Louvain." Why so, Dorp? As if it were hard to find some theologians of this stamp, or rather this stripe, anywhere in the world? You certainly do have a pretty impression of those in Louvain if you think that they all, and they alone, fit this sort of description, whereas he neither says so nor thinks so.

But a bit further along you construe what he said as if it were said not just against those in Louvain but against all the theologians found anywhere in the world, whereas he spoke it neither against all the rest nor against the Louvain theologians themselves. And yet then, as if you were not listening to him, or even to yourself, you seem not so much to proceed to the following words as to burst out with them, carried away in a violent explosion of feeling: "Do we not see the humblest artisans, or even the basest servants, endowed with the most splendid intellects? Then what is the meaning of those epithets you misapply to all theologians, 'stupid,' 'ignorant,' 'pestilential,' and 'senseless'? It takes no skill to throw insults at whomever you please,

quosuis, sed neque honestum est, aut boni uiri officium, si
seueram saluatoris nostri sententiam perpendamus, 'qui dixerit
fratri suo "racha" reus erit concilio: Qui autem dixerit "fatue,"
reus erit gehennae ignis.' Vbi Hieronymus, 'Si de ocioso ser-
5   mone reddituri sumus rationem, quanto magis de contumelia?
qui in deum credenti, dicit "fatue," impius est in religionem.'"

     Sunt ista quidem uerba tua Dorpi, non grauitatis modo, sed
sanctitatis quoque plena, uereque seuero Theologo digna, quae
utinam in loco dicerentur suo. Sunt enim meliora, quam ut per-
10 ire debeant. Quod si desuper e suggestu librarentur in populum,
nunquam ita errare possent, [20v] ut non in aliquem, in quo
herere uiderentur, inciderent. At nunc me miseret, in unum
Erasmum quod declamas omnia, in quem unum, eorum quae
declamas omnium, nihil quicquam competit. Nam quod affers
15 ex Euangelio, "Qui dixerit fratri suo, 'fatue,' reus erit gehennae," nihil ad eum spectat qui nominato nemine, uelit asserere,
esse unum, alterumue, in magno hominum numero fatuum.
Alioquin decem gehennae non suffecerint ei qui dixit, "Stultorum infinitus est numerus."

20   Porro quod queris, "quid sibi uolunt hec in Theologos omnes
detorta uocabula," hoc mihi de te Dorpi querendum est. Nam
quae ille dixit in paucos, tu solus in omnes detorsisti, quod te
instituisse facere, uehementer admiror: Si quidem ut nullius est
artis (ueluti tu dicis) probrosa in quosuis dicere, ita nullius est
25 artis, quod tu facis, bene dicta male narrando corrumpere,
quippe quae non male scripta sunt in merentes, ea tu conaris,
quo male scripta uiderentur, [21] ad immerentes inflectere,
quod in quauis re, quam facile factu sit, ipse facile uides.

---

2 nostri] *interl. P*   3 concilio:] consilio. *P S 1625,* concilio. *1563;* fatue] *corr. from* fatuae
P   5 contumelia?] *1625,* contumelia, *P S 1563*   8 uereque] *S 1563 1625,* ueraeque
P   15 Euangelio,] Euangelio. *P,* Euango *S,* Euangelio: *1563 1625*   15–16
Qui . . . gehennae] *ital. 1625*   18 suffecerint] *P 1563 1625,* sufficient *S*   18–19
Stultorum . . . numerus] *ital. 1625*   20–21 quid . . . uocabula] *ital. 1625*   22
paucos] *P 1625,* paucos, ea *S 1563*   23 admiror:] *S,* admiror. *P 1563 1625*   24
ueluti] *P 1625,* sicuti *S 1563;* probrosa] *corr. from* probosa *P;* quosuis] *corr. from* quod uis
S   25 bene dicta] *1625, corr. from* benedicta *P,* benedicta *S 1563*   28 uides] *P 1625,*
uides. Nam *S 1563*

but it is neither an honorable practice nor something a good man would do, if we take careful note of our Savior's stern sentence: 'A man who says "Racha" to his brother will be liable to the Council, but a man who says "fool" will be liable to the fire of Gehenna.' Here Jerome writes, 'If we are to give an accounting for each idle word, how much more must we give for an insult! A man who says "fool" to a believer in God shows contempt for religion.'"

Here, at any rate, your words are replete with both gravity and sanctity, and truly worthy of a stern theologian; if only they were spoken in their proper place! They are certainly too good to waste, and if they were hurled down at the people from high in the pulpit, they would never go so far astray as to fail to hit someone or other in whom their points might seem to stick. As things are, though, it pains me to see you declaim all these things at Erasmus alone when he alone is a quite inappropriate target for each of the things you declaim. For the verse that you cite from the gospel, "A man who says 'fool' to his brother will be liable to Gehenna," has nothing to do with a man who names no names but merely asserts that in a great number of men there are one or two fools. Otherwise, ten hells would not be enough for the man who said, "Infinite is the number of fools."

Furthermore, as for your asking him, "What is the meaning of these epithets that you misapply to all theologians?" I am going to have to ask you the same question, Dorp. For you alone have misapplied to them all what he said about only a few. But I find it completely amazing that you sought to do so, for if—as you say—it takes no skill to throw insults at whomever you please, it certainly requires no skill to pervert things well said by reporting them badly, as you yourself do when you try to make fair criticism seem unfair by deflecting it from those who deserve it to those who do not. Just how easy it is to do this in any circumstances at all you can easily see for yourself.

   Profecto si quis ea quae tu scripsisti ad hunc excuciat modum,
nihil tam circumspecte scriptum est (quanquam omnia circum-
spectissime) ut non alicunde possit obnoxium esse calumniae,
ueluti illa ipsa epistola, quae est abs te ut nouissime, ita ac-
5 curatissime scripta in aeditionem quodlibetorum Dignissimi uiri
Adriani Florentini de traiecto in qua, quum et opus magnifice, et
authorem copiose laudaueris, utrumque (ut ego certe puto) tam
ex animo, quam uere, Tamen si quis incideret interpres paulo
malignior, uideri possis, altera manu panem, altera lapidem por-
10 rexisse, Primo, quod ut eius operis aeditionem curares, nullo tuo
in eum librum studio, nec nisi aliorum precibus, atque adeo
opplorationibus adduci potuisti, quasi in rem, quam ipse non
magnifeceris, aliorum affectibus operam tuam indulseris, Deinde quod te scribis seria studia tan[21v]tisper seposuisse, dum
15 quodlibetica illa corrigeres, perinde ac si illa serijs non essent in
studijs numeranda, Quum tamen magister Ioannes Athensis,
uir tantae, et doctrinae pariter, et iudicij non grauabatur operam
in eam rem suam, uel intempesta nocte frequenter (ut ais) accommodare, tanquam uelut obstetrices excitari de nocte solent,
20 quum mulieres parturiunt, ita hoc opus emendari non potuerit
interdiu. Quid quod eiusdem Adriani dum aequitatem laudas,
aequitatem ei Lesbiam uideris attribuere, ad Lesbiam nimirum
regulam alludens, quam plumbeam fuisse meminit Aristoteles,
non aequam semper, sed ad rerum inaequalitates flexibilem?
25 Nec me mi Dorpi putes hec eo dicere, quod te putem tale quicquam sensisse, aut sic denique uel in tanto uiro, uel tali opere,

---

2 nihil] *P 1625*, nihil abs te *S 1563*; circumspecte] *S 1563 1625*, circumspectae *changed
from* circumscriptae *P*   2–3 circumspectissime] *S 1563 1625*, circumspectissimae
P   4 quae est] *P 1625*, quae *S 1563*; abs te] *S 1563 1625*, abste *P*; nouissime] *S 1563
1625*, nouissimae *P*   4–5 accuratissime] *S 1563 1625*, acuratissimae *P*   5
quodlibetorum] *P 1625*, quodlibeticorum *S 1563*   6 magnifice] *S 1563 1625*,
magnificae *P*   7 copiose] *S 1563 1625*, copiosae *P*; certe] *S 1563 1625*, certae *P*   8
uere] *S 1563 1625*, uerae *P*   9–10 porrexisse,] *S*, porrexisse. *P 1625*, porrexisse:
1563   14 studia] *P 1625*, studia tua *S 1563*; tantisper seposuisse] *P 1625*, seposuisse
tantisper *S 1563*   15 illa corrigeres] *P 1625*, corrigeres illa *S 1563*; ac si] *S 1563 1625*,
acsi *P*   15–16 non essent in studijs] *P 1625*, in studijs non essent *S 1563*   16
Athensis] *1563*, Athen *P S 1625*   19 excitari de nocte] *P 1563 1625*, de nocte excitari *S*
21 dum aequitatem] *P 1563 1625*, equitatem dum *S*   24 flexibilem?] flexibilem. *P S
1563 1625*   26 tanto] tanto ⟨opere⟩ *P*; tanto uiro] *P 1625*, uiro tanto *S 1563*

Honestly, suppose someone subjected your writings to this kind of scrutiny; not a one of your written productions, meticulous as they all are, is meticulous enough to be wholly immune to misrepresentation, not even your latest, most polished epistle, written as an editor's preface for the *Quodlibetica* of that most worthy man, Adriaan Floriszoon of Utrecht. Even though your epistle confers fine and copious praise on that work and its author, praise which I, at least, think to be equally earnest and truthful, nonetheless if a slightly more unsympathetic interpreter came along he might feel you were holding out bread in one hand and a stone in the other. First of all, no enthusiasm on your part, indeed nothing but the prayers and the tearful entreaties of others could induce you to take on the project of editing that work, as if you yourself did not think much of it and accepted the task just to gratify others who liked it. Secondly, you write that you set aside your serious studies for the short time it took you to correct those *Quodlibetica,* as if they had no place among serious studies, even though Master John of Ath, a man as learned as he is judicious, freely lavished his attention on that work, often, as you say, even in the dead of night; for as midwives are commonly summoned by night to help women give birth, it seems that that work could not be emended by day. And then what about this? You praise Adriaan for being unbiased, yet you seem to suggest he is no more unbiased than a Lesbian rule, a rule made out of lead which, as Aristotle reminds us, is not always unbiased, since it bends to fit uneven shapes. My dear Dorp, you must not think that I say these things because I think you meant anything of the sort or were actually joking around in this way when you praised

famae commendando lusisse: Nam et uirum multis modis audio
multum eximiae laudis assequutum, et opus ipsum censeo in suo
certe genere perfectum. Sed hec omnia eo dico ut ostendam,
nihil tam minutum esse, in quo locum sibi [22] non possit in-
5 uenire calumnia, quando tuis etiam scriptis tam accurate, tam
circumspecte limatis, tamen impetrandum est ut cum fauore
legantur.

Quanquam Erasmus, ne quisquam prorsus ullam occasionem
posset arripere, qua dicat eum in omnes ea quae tu obijcis ei
10 dixisse Theologos, uel eo cauisse uidetur, quod ait, "cottidie re
ipsa experior, quam nihil habeant mentis, qui preter sophisticas
nugas, nihil addidicerunt." Non dicit "quam nihil habent mentis
omnes Theologi," sed neque, "qui sophisticam didicerunt," sed
"qui nihil preterea." Quamobrem quum sic scribis, "Porro quod
15 hypothesim facias Erasme nostros Theologos solis sophismatum
meditationibus esse occupatos, tota erras uia," Hic tu mi Dorpi
tota erras uia, quum hypothesim facis, Erasmum talem hypothesim fecisse de omnibus Theologis uestris quam ille de uno
tantum facit, aut altero, neque quicquam dicit quo sit necesse
20 omnes theologos includi.

Quare nec id quidem ad rem facit quod protinus adiecisti,
"Dic age quidnam eos quamuis sane [22v] poeseos ignaros ar-
cebit ab Euangelijs paulinis epistolis totaque Biblia euoluenda?"
Nihil sane Dorpi, modo ipsi non arcerent sese, quod aliqui fa-
25 ciunt, qui uitam uniuersam questiunculis impendentes, Bibliam
certe, ueluti nihil ad rem pertineat, nunquam dignantur in-

---

1 lusisse:] S, lusisse. P 1563 1625   2 eximiae] S 1563 1625, eximie P   3 certe] S 1563
1625, certae P   4 minutum] P 1625, munitum S 1563; quo] S 1563 1625, quo, P; sibi]
sibi ⟨calumnia⟩ P   5 accurate] S 1563 1625, acuratae P   6 circumspecte S 1563
1625, circumspectae P   9 posset] S 1563, potest P, possit 1625; ea quae] P 1563 1625,
quae S; ei] ei, P S 1563 1625   10 ait,] 1563, ait. P, ait S, ait: 1625   10–12
cottidie . . . addidicerunt] ital. 1625   11 quam] P 1563 1625, que S   12
addidicerunt] P 1625, didicerunt S 1563; quam] S 1563, quod P 1625   13
sophisticam] P 1625, sophisticas nugas S 1563   14 scribis,] scribis. P, scribis: S 1563
1625   14–16 Porro . . . uia] ital. 1625   16 uia,] uia. P S 1563, via: 1625   19
altero,] altero. P S, altero: 1563, altero; 1625; dicit] P 1625, dicit in S 1563   20
theologos] P 1625, theologos uestros S 1563   21 adiecisti,] 1563, adiecisti. P S,
adiecisti: 1625   22–23 Dic . . . euoluenda] ital. 1625   22 sane] sane ⟨per⟩ P   23
euoluenda?] S 1563 1625, euoluenda; P   25 impendentes] P 1625, consecrantes S
1563   26 certe] S 1563 1625, certae P

such a man and such a work. For I hear that the man has won much splendid praise for his manifold accomplishments, and I judge that, at least in its genre, the work is a masterpiece. I say all these things merely to prove that not even sheer trifles are immune to misrepresentation, since even your own meticulous and carefully polished writings require that we read them indulgently.

But it seems that Erasmus took care to give no one the slightest excuse to say he spoke of all theologians when he said the things you hold against him, even when he declares, "Every day I find out by experience just how senseless those men are who have never learned anything else but sophistical trifles." He does not say "how senseless all theologians are," or even "those who have learned sophistry," but "those who have learned nothing else." And so when you write, "Moreover, Erasmus, when you make the assumption that our theologians are busy with nothing but studying sophisms you are far off the mark," here you are the one, my dear Dorp, who is far off the mark, since you make the assumption that Erasmus made such an assumption about all of your theologians when he actually makes it about only one or two, and says nothing which has to be taken to include all theologians.

Thus the next point you added is equally irrelevant: "So tell me then—what is to prevent even those who know nothing at all about poetry from perusing the gospels, the letters of Paul, and the whole of the Bible?" Nothing at all, Dorp, if they did not prevent themselves, as some do who devote their whole lives to those petty problems but certainly never deign to examine the Bible, as if it were simply irrelevant. And Erasmus thinks some to

spicere. Atque ille aliquos huiusmodi putat esse, non omnes, ut
intelligas id quoque te sine causa ulla subnectere, "Proferam ego
multos hinc qui reiectis libris sola memoriae ui cum quouis de
textu scripturae certabunt. Caue credas Endimionis somnum
5 dormire Theologos, quo tempore uos litteris inuigilatis, aut ingenio carere, quicunque non poetantur, aut rhetorissant."
   Nemo Dorpi negat esse qui reiectis libris de scripturae textu
certare possint. Imo plus satis ubique reperias eorum qui libris
non reiectis modo, sed etiam nunquam inspectis, cum quouis in
10 scripturis exercitatissimo sint parati de quouis scripturae textu
non memoriae sed Moriae ui certare pertinacissime. Neque
negabo [23] tamen, et apud uos et ubique esse, qui e scripturis
multa memoriter teneant, ex quibus eos qui non in hoc solum
collocarunt operam, ut memoriae mandent, quod illiterati etiam
15 monachi, fratresque faciunt, sed uel multo magis ut intelligant,
qui tantam sermonis facultatem parauerunt sibi, ut pernoscen-
dis Hieronimi, Augustini, Ambrosij, caeterorumque id genus
lucubrationibus pares esse possint, eos inquam ego in Theologorum albo meritissimo iure collocandos puto, etiam si uer-
20 sus nunquam fecerint, tam hercle quam si disputatiunculis istis
non totos centum annos insumpserint, ut ne dicam, si in uniuersum neglexerint.
   Sed tu quoque, si uera uis fateri, non inficias ibis, ex Theologorum, qui uocantur numero esse rursus aliquos, qui scrip-
25 turae libros, ita reijciant, ut reiectos nunquam resumant, qui ita
sese totos Theologiae huic disputatrici deuoueant, ut non solum
non poetentur, neque rhetorissent, uerum etiam sanctissimos
patres, antiquissimos quosque scripturarum interpretes propemodum floccifaciant, [23v] certe quod satis constat eorum in
30 sacras litteras enarrationes negligant, unaque ipsarum sacrarum

---

2 subnectere,] subnectere. *P. S*, subnectere: *1563*, subnectere? *1625*   2–6
Proferam . . . rhetorissant] *ital. 1625*   4 certabunt.] *S 1563 1625*, certabunt, *P;*
somnum] *P 1625*, somnium *S 1563*   9 sed] sed ⟨certa⟩ *P*   11 pertinacissime] *S 1563*
1625, pertinacissimae *P*   12 uos] uos ⟨esse⟩ *P*   14 ut memoriae] *P 1625*, memoriae
ut *S 1563;* mandent] *P 1625*, mandarent *S 1563*   16 ut] *corr. from* quod *S*   19 puto,]
1563 1625, puto. *P S*   26 deuoueant] *corr. from* deuouerint *S*   27 neque] *P 1625*, ac
S 1563   28 quosque] *P 1625*, quoque *S 1563*   29 certe] *S 1563 1625*, certae *P*   30
negligant] ne⟨c⟩gligant *P;* ipsarum] *S 1563*, ipm̄ *P*, ipsum *1625*

be like this, not all. Thus, you see, you had no cause to tack on that other point, either: "I can produce many theologians from here who will put aside their books and then, strictly from memory, debate with whomever you please on the text of scripture. Do not make the mistake of believing that theologians are sleeping the sleep of Endymion while you are awake studying literature or that all are deficient in intellect who do not play the poet or orator."

No one denies, Dorp, that there are some who can put aside their books and debate on the text of scripture. Indeed, you can everywhere find all too many who not only have put aside their books but have never examined them, men prepared to debate very stubbornly with true scripture scholars on any text from scripture at all, not from memory but rather from folly. Neither will I deny that there are some in Louvain, as indeed there are everywhere, who have memorized many passages from scripture, and of these men whoever has focused his energies not only on memorizing—even illiterate monks and friars do as much—but far more on absorbing the meaning, and has gained sufficient linguistic ability to measure up to the challenge of fully understanding the works of Jerome, Augustine, Ambrose, and other men like them, such a man, in my view, has an unsurpassed right to be registered among theologians, even if he has never written a verse; yes, and even if he has not spent a whole century on those petty disputes or has even ignored them completely.

But you, too, if you wish to acknowledge the truth, will admit that among those who are called theologians there are also some men who put aside the books of scripture in such a way that they never take them up again; men who give themselves up so completely to this disputatious theology that not only do they not "play the poet or orator," they apparently care next to nothing about all the holiest fathers and most ancient interpreters of scripture, and (this much is quite obvious) they definitely neglect both the fathers' expositions of scripture and the study of scrip-

litterarum studium, postremo quaecunque sunt optima, pijs-
sima, maxime christiana, uerisque Theologis dignissima, ea inquam omnia quod sint ut ipsi uocant "positiua" contemnant,
neque eorum quicquam dignum putent, ubi ipsi neruos
5 intendant suos, homines ad questiunculas nati, res tanto
uidelicet interuallo maiores, ex quibus ipsis tamen maxime questiones consectantur eiusmodi, quae uel ad fidei pietatem, uel ad
morum cultum minime omnium pertineant.

   Ego itaque ut prius illud Theologorum genus ueneror, ac
10 suspicio, ita hoc posterius hercle non admodum magnipendo:
aduersus quos tamen non est consilium poesim, aut rhetoricam
defendere, quippe qui a poesi, rhetoricaque, tam longe propemodum absim, quam illi ipsi. absunt autem ipsi tam longe
fere, quam ab ipsa Theologia, a qua tam longe absunt, ut ab nulla
15 re absint, preterquam a communi hominum sensu, longius, [24]
uel ideo maxime, quod ad insignem rerum omnium inscitiam,
accessit omnigenae scientiae peruersa persuasio, qua sibi adeo
blandiuntur, ut omnium hominum scripta, ac ipsas etiam sacras
litteras, ut quicquam audierint quapiam occasione prolatum, qui
20 locum nunquam uiderint, nunquam librum inspexerint, quid ea
uerba praecedat, quid sequatur nesciant, imo id ipsum quod
citatur, sitne, an non sit ibi unde citatur ignorent, se tamen solos
arbitrentur idoneos, qui protinus in quencunque libeat sensum
interpretentur. Ex quo genere quum in multos inciderim, unum
25 saltem, ex quo caeterorum indoles agnosci possint, non pigebit,
uelut speciminis loco referre.

2 maxime] S 1563 1625, maximae P   4 putent] 1625, putant P S 1563   5 intendant]
P 1563 1625, intendunt S; nati] corr. from natos P   6 ipsis] P S 1563, ipsi 1625; maxime]
S 1563 1625, maximae P   9 Ego itaque] S 1563 1625, Ego S; genus] S 1563 1625,
genus, P   10 magnipendo:] 1563, magnipendo, P S, magnipendo. 1625   13 absim]
S 1563, corr. from absum P, absunt 1625; longe] S 1563 1625, longae P   14 quam ab] P
S 1625, quam 1563; longe] S 1563 1625, longae P   16 maxime] S 1563 1625, maximae
P   17 omnigenae] S 1563 1625, omnigene P   18 omnium hominum] S 1563,
omnium P 1625   21 sequatur] S 1563, sequatur, P 1625; nesciant] P S 1563, nesciunt
1625   22 sitne] 1563 1625, sit ne P S; sit ibi] P 1625, sit S 1563; ignorent,] ignorent. P
1625, ignorant: S 1563   23 arbitrentur] arbitrantur P S 1563 1625   24
interpretentur] S 1563 1625, inter pretentur P   25 possint] P 1625, possit S 1563;
pigebit] P 1625, pigebit hercle S 1563; sidenote in 1563 Lepida historia

ture itself; finally, men who shrug off as mere "positive" doctrine whatever is most valuable, most pious, most Christian, and most worthy of true theologians, although these men think none of it worthy of any exertion on their part; they are born to debate petty problems, as matters of much greater import, though the problems that these men pursue most of all are the ones that pertain least of all to sustaining the faith or encouraging virtue.

Now then, just as I revere and admire that first kind of theologian, even so I have really very little respect for the second, against whom, nonetheless, I myself do not plan to defend either poetry or rhetoric, since I am almost as far removed from poetry and rhetoric as they are themselves. But they are almost as far removed from those arts as they are from theology proper; and from nothing, apart from ordinary common sense, are they further removed than from that. The main reason for this is precisely that on top of their blatant and general ignorance they are perversely convinced of their total omniscience, on which they flatter themselves to the point that whatever they hear being cited, in whatever context, without ever reading the passage or seeing the book it appears in, without knowing what has preceded or what is to follow the words of the quotation, and without even knowing whether or not the text quoted appears in the quoted location, they think they alone can interpret the writings of all men, and even sacred scripture itself, in whatever sense happens to suit them. Having run across many of this kind, I will not hesitate to describe at least one, using him as a sample to show what we can expect from the rest.

   Cenaui olim apud Italum quendam mercatorem, non minus
doctum, quam diuitem (erat autem ditissimus). forte aderat in
cena religiosus quidam Theologus, disputator egregius, qui recens e continente uenerat, ut questiones aliquot quas pre-
5 meditatas aduexerat, Londini disputaret, experturus uidelicet,
in ea disceptandi palestra, quid Angli prestare possent, simul
nomen suum iam apud [24v] suos celebre, apud nostros quoque
propagaturus. Is quas conclusiones affixerit, tum quam belle
disputatio processerit homini, quanquam longum esset, non
10 grauarer profecto narrare, si tam ad hanc rem pertinens foret,
quam festiuum fuit. Caeterum in cena nihil a quoquam dici tam
bene munitum, aut libratum tam circumspecte potuit, quod non
ille uix prolatum aliquo statim syllogismo conuelleret, quantumuis res de qua sermo erat, nihil ad Theologiam pertinens, ad
15 philosophiam tantundem, quantumuis denique ab uniuersa eius
professione esset alienum, nisi quod initio cenae fecerat, ne alienum esse quicquam ab eius professione posset. professus est
enim se, in utramque partem, de re quacunque disputaturum.
   Paulatim coepit mercator, ad questiones magis Theologicas
20 descendere. De usura proponebat, de decimis, quaedam de con-
fessionibus, quae in aliena parochia fratribus essent factae. In
omnibus nihil erat Theologo pensi utram sustineret partem, sed
utramcunque aliquis asseruisset, illam oppugnabat, ac uicissim
quamcunque alius negauerat, [25] hanc ille protinus astruebat.
25   Tandem per iocum Mercator sermonem de concubinis iniecit,
coepitque defendere minus mali esse, unam quampiam domi
habere, quam foris per multas discurrere. Ibi rursus Theologus
instare, oppugnare ferociter, non quod usque adeo concubinam
uideretur odisse, sed ne cum quoquam ei quidquam conueniret,

---

3 quidam Theologus] *P 1563 1625*, quidam *S*   4 continente] *corr. from* continenti
P   4–5 premeditatas] *P 1625*, praemeditatus *S 1563*   8 conclusiones] *P 1625*,
conclusiones ut uocant *S 1563;* tum] *1563 1625*, tū *P*, tamen *S;* quam] *P S 1625*,
quanquam *1563;* belle] *S 1563 1625*, bellae *P*   9 disputatio] disputatio⟨nes⟩ *P*   11 a
quoquam] *S 1563 1625*, aquoquam *P*   12 circumspecte] *S 1563 1625*, circumspectae
P   18 se] *P 1625*, sese *S 1563*   20 quaedam] *1563 1625*, quedam *P S*   24
quamcunque] *P 1563 1625*, quantumuis *S*   26 mali esse] *P 1625*, mali *S 1563*   28
ferociter,] *S 1563*, ferociter *P*, ferociter; *1625;* non] *P S 1563*, nec *1625*   29 quoquam]
P 1563 1625, quoque *S*

I recently dined with a certain Italian merchant as learned as he is rich (and he certainly is rich). There also happened to be a theologian at dinner, a member of a religious order; a distinguished disputant, he had recently come from the Continent to London in order to dispute various problems which he had prepared and brought with him. In that arena of disputation he intended to test at first hand what the English could show for themselves and to make his name generally acclaimed among our theologians as it was already renowned among those at home. Though it would take a while, I would certainly not hesitate to tell you what theses he posted and how smartly the whole disputation came off for the fellow if it were as pertinent as it was amusing. Anyway, nothing anyone said at that dinner was guarded well enough or supported meticulously enough to keep that man from toppling it over with one of his syllogisms as soon as the speaker had uttered it, even when the topic of the discussion had nothing to do with theology and as little to do with philosophy, indeed even when it had not the slightest connection with that man's profession. At the start of the dinner, however, he had made it clear that nothing could lack a connection with his profession, for he professed he was ready to dispute *pro* and *contra* upon any topic at all.

Gradually the merchant began to get down to more theological problems. He stated some views about usury, about tithes, and about friars hearing confessions in parishes where they were not authorized. It never made a bit of difference to the theologian which side he was defending, but whatever anyone asserted he himself took to task, and whatever anyone else denied he immediately defended.

Finally, as a joke, the merchant brought up the subject of mistresses. He began to defend the position that it was not so evil to have one woman at home as to run through a number away from home. Here again the theologian closed in and ferociously took him to task, not that he appeared to have any real grudge against mistresses but that he hated agreeing with anyone on

siue quod hominem fortasse uarietas oblectabat. Caeterum asserebat esse conclusionem famosam cuiusdam limpidissimi Doctoris qui fecit illum singularissimum librum, qui intitulatur Directorium concubinariorum, plus eum peccare qui unam domi
5 concubinam quam qui decem foris meretrices haberet, idque cum ob malum exemplum, tum ob occasionem saepius peccandi cum ea quae domi sit.

Respondit Mercator docte mehercle et acute, quae et longum recitare fuerit, et apud te superuacaneum. At quum olfecisset
10 Theologum, non perinde in scripturis, atque in questiunculis illis exercitatum, coepit hominem ludere, argumentarique interdum per locos ab Authoritate. [25v] Effingebat enim ex tempore sententiolas quasdam breues, suae parti quae uiderentur astipulari, Quumque ipse omnes nusquam ante auditas pro libito
15 fuisset commentus, hanc tamen ex Epistola quapiam Diui Pauli, illam ex Petri, aliam rursus ex medio citabat euangelio, idque tam diligenter ut neque capitulum unquam dum citabat omitteret, nisi quod si quis liber in sexdecim capitula distinguebatur, ille data opera citabat ex uicesimo.

20 Quid ille bonus Theologus interim? Ad caetera certe strenuus, et tanquam herinacius spinis sese suis obuoluit. At personatas illas authoritates uix hercle huc atque illuc uitabundus euasit, Sed euasit tamen. tantum ualet ars, et exercitatio disserendi. Nam quum ille quid in sacris continebatur litteris omnino
25 nesciret, neque dubitaret quin quod inde citaretur ibi esset, non deferre uero, cedereque authoritati scripturae, nephas duceret, at loco depelli [26] uincique turpissimum, Tantis circumseptus angustijs, uide obsecro, qua astutia tamen proteus ille e medijs

---

1 fortasse] *P 1625*, fortassis *S 1563*   4 concubinariorum] *corr. from* concubinarum
P   4–5 plus . . . haberet] *S 1563, om. P 1625*   8 docte] *S 1563 1625*, doctae *P;*
mehercle] *S 1563 1625*, meherclae *P;* acute] *S 1563 1625*, acutae *P*   9 fuerit] *corr. from*
fuit *S;* superuacaneum] *P 1563 1625*, supervacuum *S*   13–14 astipulari,] *S*, astipulari.
P 1625, astipulari: *1563*   16 aliam rursus] *P 1625*, rursus aliam *S 1563*   17 neque]
P 1625, ne *S 1563*   18 sexdecim] *1625*, sex decim *P*, sedecim *S 1563;* capitula] *P 1625*,
capita *S 1563*   20 certe] *S 1563 1625*, certae *P;* strenuus,] strenuus. *P*, strenue *S*,
strenue, *1563*, strenuus; *1625*   21 herinacius] *corr. from* hericius *P;* herinacius spinis . . . obuoluit] *P 1625*, spinis . . . obuoluit eritius *S*, spinis . . . obuoluit *1563*   23 et]
interl. P; et exercitatio] *P 1625*, exercitatioque *S 1563*   24 quum ille] *P 1625*, quum *S*
1563   26 duceret,] *S 1563*, duceret. *P*, duceret; *1625*   27 at] *P 1625*, ac *S 1563*
28 tamen] *P 1625*, tandem *S 1563*

anything, or perhaps the man just liked variety. Anyway, he asserted that it was the conclusion of a certain Most Translucent Doctor, who wrote that most singular book entitled *A Directory for Men Who Keep Mistresses,* that a man who has one mistress at home is more sinful than a man who has ten whores away from home, not only because of the evil example it sets but also because there are more opportunities to sin with a woman at home.

Though the merchant's responses were certainly learned and acute, it would be time-consuming and idle to list them for you. But as soon as he noticed that the theologian was not such an expert in scripture as in those petty problems, he started to play with the fellow and draw various arguments from authority. As he went along, he made up various brief texts which appeared to support his position, and even though he had arbitrarily contrived them all out of thin air he would quote one as if from some epistle of St. Paul, another as if it were from an epistle of Peter, and still another as if it were straight from the gospel. Indeed he was so diligent in doing so that he always included a chapter citation for what he was quoting, except that if a book was divided into sixteen chapters he would purposely quote from the twentieth.

Meanwhile what of that good theologian? He made brisk work of the other points, certainly, and wrapped himself up like a hedgehog in prickly retorts, but on my word, for all his evasions he barely escaped those fictitious authorities. Yet he did escape; such is the efficacy of art and experience in discourse. For even though he knew nothing at all about the contents of sacred scripture, and though he did not doubt that the words being quoted from scripture were actually there, and though he thought it wrong to oppose or defy the authority of scripture but at the same time considered it shameful to give up the field in defeat, even when he was caught in such desperate straits, please observe with what cunning that Proteus slipped out of the net. As

Drectoriũ cõ-
cubinarioꝛũ saluberrimũ quo
quedã stupẽda et quasi iaudita

pericula ꝙaꝑtissime resoluũtur nedũ clericis aut etiaꝫ laicis hoc
crimiue pollutis necessariũ. sed ꝫ ꝯmuni populo pꝛesertim erga sa-
cerdotes ꝛcubinarios ꝙvtilissimũ. ob infinitos laqueos quibꝫ taꝫ
ipsi ꝙ indoctũ vulgus ꝓpter ipsos irretiũtur

Therentius
Veritas odium parit
Esdras
Sed iusto sub iudice vincit

Title page, *Directorium concubinariorum saluberrimum*, Cologne, 1509
(reduced)

Gramatiris qnq̃; genera
qnq̃; casus, et qnq̃; deuo-
tiones.

τε χὖκ,πέντε π̄ώσαις
και πέντε κατάραις.i.

quincᵽ genera, qncᵽ
casus,& qncᵽ deuoti
ones, ob quincᵽ pri-
mos uersus Homeri
cos,quorum primus
incipit a μῖνῖν, quod
iram significat. Secū-
dus,οὐλομῖλίλω,qᵈᵖ p
niciē significat,habet
& μυρία ἄλγεα.i. in-
nūcros dolores. Ter-
tius, anīas mittit ad
inferos. Quartus,ca
nū laniationē,Quin
tus, auium,& iram
Iouis. Atcᵽ his auspi
cijs ingrediuntur sui
um munus. Epigrā-
ma autem est libro prim[o]

Tyrānis lu-
di magistro-
rum.

τευτάσϊχός ὅσι κατάρα
τὰ δ' οὐλομῖλίλω,δ'ανα ῶ,
δημκατάγει τωι δ'επται
χόλⲉ ὅσι διὸς πῶς οὐ
τε π̄ώσοⲛ,μὴ μέγα πένθ[
bus contenta,est deuotio
perniciosam, Græcorum

Drawings by Holbein the younger in Myconius' copy of *Moriae encomium*,
Basel, 1515: a. Tyrannis ludi magistrorum (sig. M₄v). b. Erasmus (sig. S₃).
c. Atlas (sig. P₁v). d. Theological dispute (sig. T₂v). (all reduced)

Dum ad hunc locum perue-
niebat Erasmus, subridens
sic videns exclamauit, ohe
ohe, si Erasmus adhuc ta-
lis esset, duceret profecto
uxorem.

es, triſte i fere habui
ſē exitū, idignatus
ripſit, Σωκράτlω ὁ
ὅσμ⊕ πεποίηκε σο,
ὸμ εἶναι καὶ κακῶς,
ἕλε τὸμ σοκράτlω ὁ
ὅσμ⊕ Εμ τῆ φυλα
κώνειομ ὅτι πιὼμ τέ
ηκεμ πυλύποδα φα
ὼμ ὁ διογύης ὠμὸμ
θνηκεμ Αἰχύλω γρά,
ὐτῖ ἐπιπέπῆωκε χε
ὐκ Σοφοκλῆς, ρᾶσα
γὼμ ϛαφυλῆς πυι/
ις τέθνηκε καὐες οἳ
Τὰ βράκlω, εὑριπῖ/
μ ἔζωγμ τὸμ θεῖομ
ſapientem eſſe. Et
ā bibens mortuus
Aeſchylo ſcriben
atus perijt. Canes
es confecit. Timo
tiſſimus, de q̃ Sui
ὑμωνομ καὶ τὰϛ πί

·ERASMVS·

Quid Theologum in primis deceat (marginal note)

ter, simile est illis, & vſ
ηϲιοις ποϲιν & ανſ
ηϲιοις χεραιν. i. illotis
pedib°, & illotis ma/
nibus. Vt Euãgeliũ
aũt Paulinas episto/
las.) Ex hoc loco paſ
lam est, nõ reprehen
di theologos doctos,
& pios, sed eos qui to
tã uitã, in hmõi conſ
sumunt quæstiuncu/
lis, cũ in primis opor
tet theologum ipsos
imbibiſſe fõtes, & in
lege domini, noctes
ac dies meditatũ esse,
ut aſſiduitas uertat
in naturam, ut nõ ſo/
lum intelligat huma/
no more, sed etiam af
ficiatur & rapiat. Ne
mo ѱe itelligit Chri/
stũ, niſi tractº a Chri
sto. Tantum abest, ut
ab his comprehẽda/
tur, q impij ppter ſo/
phisticas nænias, ni/
hil omnino uel sciũt,
uel legunt. Noui per

Vt probe intelligere
ſacras literas, non velim
ad illos, q hic taxantur
recurras, imo vero
ad Origenem, Basiliũ, (marginal note)

....

ſtruiter auter

iuramentun

culæ. Trilin

Tres linguæ

ca, Latina, &

ca, qbus trac

omnes ſcien

humanæ, q̃

Quas adeo

as ueteres a

literas iudica

etiám decreti

ficijs cautũ ſi

guarũ noticia

lis publice tr

quód ſine his

literaꝝ myſte

intelligi poſſe

rent. Cæterun

Theologi ade

faleċticis argu

diti, ut ne latiɿ

dem linguam

curent. Græ

los) Feſtiua ꝫ

....

retibus elapsus est. Statim ut aliqua sententia, quae nusquam
erat, tanquam e sacris litteris aduersus eum citabatur, "Bene
citas" (inquit) "Domine, sed illum textum ego sic intellego." et
iam interpretabatur, non sine aliqua distinctione bimembri,
5 quorum alterum pro aduersario stare diceret, altero ipse
effugeret. Quod si quando Mercator instabat molestius, contenditque eius textus non illum uerum esse sensum, quem Theologus afferebat, iurabat homo tam sancte ut quiuis posset credere, Nicholaum de Lyra eundem textum sic interpretari.
10 Profecto mi Dorpi in illa una caena plusquam uiginti poculenti
textus totidemque poculenta glossemata inter pocula, at adeo ex
poculis, tanquam e serpentis dentibus terrigenae illi fratres, et
nati sunt, et periere.
    Quid tu [26v] ais ergo Dorpi? Tu istiusmodi homines sacra-
15 rum inanes litterarum, questionibus illis Theologicis quantun-
cunque distentos theologorum censes insigniendos uocabulo?
Non opinor. Quanquam hercle ut uere dicam, animi ambiguum
tui, hec tua me uerba faciunt, "Non persuadeas Erasme tibi eum
demum absolutum esse Theologum, qui Bibliae seriem ad lit-
20 teram intelligat, nec eum item qui morales sensus, aeque atque
alter Origenes nouit eruere. Multa restant discenda, ut intellectu
difficiliora, ita et utiliora gregi pro quo mortuus est Christus.
Alioqui qui sciemus, ut Sacramenta sint administranda,
quaenam sint eorum formae, quando absoluendus peccator,

1 sententia,] *1625*, sententia *P S 1563*   2 erat,] *S 1563 1625*, erat *P;* litteris] *S 1563*,
litteris, *P 1625;* citabatur,] *S*, citabatur. *P*, citabatur: *1563 1625*   2–3
Bene . . . intellego] *ital. 1625*   6 effugeret] *S 1563 1625*, effugeret *changed to* effugere
P   6–7 contenditque eius] *P 1625*, contendere, eiusque *S 1563*   7 sensum,] *S 1625*,
sensum. *P*, sensum *1563*   8 afferebat] *P 1625*, affirmabat *S 1563;* sancte] *S 1563 1625*,
sanctae *P;* posset] *S 1563 1625*, possit *P*   8–9 credere,] *1563 1625*, credere *P S*   9
eundem] *P 1625*, eum *S 1563*   10 plusquam] *P 1563 1625*, plusque *S*   11 at] *P*, et
1625, atque *S 1563;* adeo ex] *P S 1625*, ex *1563*   12 serpentis] *corr. from* serpentibus
P   13 periere] *P 1625*, perierunt *S 1563*   15 Theologicis] *corr. from* Theologis
P   16 insigniendos uocabulo] *P 1625*, uocabulo insigniendos *S 1563*   17 uere] *S*
1563 1625, uerae *P*   18 faciunt,] *S*, faciunt. *P 1563*, faciunt: *1625*   18–56/8
Non . . . periclitari] *ital. 1625*   18 Erasme] *P S 1625*, Erasmo *1563*   19 demum
absolutum] *P 1625*, demum *S 1563*   20 aeque] *S 1563 1625*, aequae *P;* atque] *P 1563*
1625, ac *S*   21 eruere] *P S 1563*, erigere *1625*   22 difficiliora] *P 1563 1625*,
difficilia *S;* utiliora] *P 1563 1625*, utilior *S*   23 sint] *1625*, sunt *P S 1563*

soon as some supposedly scriptural text was quoted against him right out of thin air, "You quote well, sir," he said, "but I understand that text as follows." And then he would interpret it, not without some bipartite distinction in which he would first say that one meaning supported his opponent and then he would evade it by finding another. But whenever the merchant closed in too intently and claimed that the theologian was not giving the true sense of the text, then the fellow would swear so devoutly that anyone could have believed him that Nicolas de Lyra interpreted that text the same way. Honestly, my dear Dorp, at that one dinner, over the drinks, and indeed from the drinks, just like those earthborn brothers who sprang from the teeth of the serpent, more than twenty of these drunken texts and as many drunken glosses sprang up and at once passed away.

Now, Dorp, what do you say? Do you really think fellows of this sort with their meager knowledge of sacred scripture, however puffed up they may be with those theological problems, deserve to be called theologians? I suppose not, but I must say that these comments of yours leave me not at all sure what you think: "Do not let yourself be persuaded, Erasmus, that anyone with a literal understanding of the text of the Bible or even someone with Origen's knack for discovering a moral significance is already a perfect theologian. There are many things yet to be learned which are not only more difficult to understand but also more useful to the flock for whom Christ died. How else are we to know how we ought to administer the sacraments, what their forms are, when we ought to absolve and when we ought to

quando sit reijciendus, quid praeceptum sit restitui, quid seruari possit, et innumera eiusmodi? Multum nisi erro longe minori opera bonam Bibliae partem edisceres, priusquam uel unius perplexitatis nodum discas dissoluere cuiusmodi plurimi cot-
5 tidie occurrunt, ubi uel in quattuor uerbis diutissime herendum est. [27] nisi tu has etiam uoces Theologorum naenias, quaecun-que ad sacramenta pertineant, sine quibus tamen sancta dei ec-clesia catholica profitetur salutem hominis periclitari."

   Crede mihi Dorpi nisi hec tute scriberes, nunquam adduci
10 possem, hec te sentire ut crederem. Scilicet istae neotericorum questiunculae (nam de his agitur) non intellectu tantum dif-ficiliores, sed gregi quoque pro quo mortuus est Christus uti-liores sint quam exactissima cognitio sacrarum litterarum om-nium? Hui ex quantula culice, quam ingentem Elephantem
15 facis. Nam eam rem primum tam difficilem putas, ut Erasmus minore opera bonam Bibliae partem posset edisceret, quam uel unius perplexitatis nodum discat dissoluere, cuiusmodi plu-rimos cottidie in scirpo querunt, ubi tam diu in tenaci ne dicam sordido quattuor uerborum luto herendum est, dum posses
20 amoenissimum, ac saluberrimum totius Bibliae pratum, a capite pene ad calcem sensim perambulare. Hactenus ergo periculum erat, ne questiunculas istas non didi[27v]cisset. nunc ut uideo maius quippiam timendum est, ne tam longe supra captum eius sint, ut apprehendere ne sufficiat quidem. Quid ille possit omit-
25 to querere. Verum hoc scio, quosdam nouisse me, ad caetera plane stipites, ingenio certe pistillo quouis obtusiore, qui in eiusmodi tamen argutijs non modo breui promouerint, sed

---

1 quid praeceptum] *P 1563 1625*, quia praeceptum *S*   2 eiusmodi] *P 1625*, huiusmodi *S 1563;* longe minori] *P 1625*, longeque minore *S 1563*   3 edisceres] *P 1563 1625*, ediscere *S;* priusquam] *P 1563 1625*, priusque *S*   5 diutissime] *S 1563 1625*, diutissimae *P;* herendum] *P 1563 1625*, hesitandum *S*   6 Theologorum] *corr. from* Theologicas *P*   6–7 quaecunque] *1563 1625*, quecunque *P S*   9 hec tute] *P 1625*, tute hec *S 1563*   10 te] *interl. P*   11 his] *P 1625*, ijs *S 1563*   13 sint] *P 1625*, sunt *S 1563*   14 quantula] *P 1625*, quantulo *S 1563*   16 minore] *changed from* minori *P*   19 sordido] sordido ⟨in⟩ *P*   20 Bibliae] *S 1563 1625*, Biblie *P*   23 longe] *S 1563 1625*, longae *P*   24–25 ut apprehendere . . . hoc scio] *P 1563 1625*, ut scio *S* 25 scio,] *1563 1625*, scio *P S;* nouisse] *S 1563 1625*, nouissae *P*   26 plane] *S 1563 1625*, planae *P;* certe] *S 1563 1625*, certae *P;* obtusiore] *P 1625*, obtusiores *S 1563*   27 eiusmodi] *P 1625*, huiusmodi *S 1563;* modo breui] *P S 1625*, modo *1563*

refuse absolution to a sinner, how much restitution we must make and how much we can keep, and innumerable things of that sort? Unless I am very mistaken you can learn a good deal of the Bible by heart much more easily than you can learn to unravel even one of those perplexities which crop up by the score every day, in which even four words can detain one indefinitely—unless what you call theological trifles includes all that pertains to the sacraments, though without them, according to God's holy catholic church, man's salvation is endangered."

Believe me, Dorp, if you had not written this yourself nothing in the world could have made me believe that you held this opinion. So those problems made up by the moderns (for those are the real issue) are not only more difficult to understand but also more useful to the flock for whom Christ died? My word, what a huge elephant you make out of such a small gnat! For at first you consider that subject so difficult that Erasmus could learn a good deal of the Bible by heart more easily than he could learn to unravel even one of those perplexities they contrive by the score every day, in which four words as sticky and squalid as mud can detain you so long that in the same length of time you could have read the whole Bible and strolled through its delightful and life-giving meadows step by step from one side to the other. So then, the danger thus far was that he had not learned those problems. Now I see there is something still worse to be feared, that they may so transcend his capacity that he will not even be able to grasp them. I do not raise the question of what he can do. But of this I am sure: I know some who in other matters are absolute blockheads, as dull as the dullest of pestles, while in this sort of subtlety they have not only been quick to progress but

sodales suos quoque multo melioris ingenij, nec minoris industriae, equis (ut aiunt) albis in disputando precesserint, Ita quouis
importune prorumpit audax et inuerecunda stultitia, quum in-
genuam animi indolem et sanum plerunque iudicium nugandi
remoratur pudor.

Est profecto Dorpi quod merito gaudere debes, nec tuis
uiribus acceptum, sed bonorum omnium Largitori deo referre,
cuius eximia in te benignitate profluxit hec tam rara foelicitas, ut
in sacris litteris omnia tibi tam facilia uideantur, Neque enim in
hoc libro, quem signacula septem clauserunt, cuncta reperires
aperta, nisi ille tibi agnus librum resignasset, qui [28] "aperit, et
nemo claudit, claudit et nemo aperit." Sed hic ipse liber Dorpi,
qui tam facilis tibi uidetur, Hieronimo certe uisus est dif-
ficillimus. Augustinus putauit impenetrabilem. Neque quisquam est antiquorum omnium, qui se fateri est ausus intelligere,
ut cuius intellectum putant altissimo dei consilio, uel ob id ipsum
profundius obstrusum esse, ut curiosos oculos prouocaret, et
semotis, ac labore eruendis opibus, segnia excitaret ingenia,
quae alioquin ad obuios, expositosque thesauros ipsa securitate
torpescerent.

Iam ut omittam interim quam non sit uulgaris eruditionis
opus, quam non cuiuslibet ingenij, quae a moribus interdum
primo aspectu abhorreant, ea tam commode ad mores, ac tam
foeliciter appellere, ut non aliunde eo tracta, sed ad id ipsum
nata uideantur. Quam rem nonnulli nunc tam inepte moliuntur,
ut quum hactenus sint progressi, ut rem ab ipsius magis loco
detraxerint quam [28v] ad suum perduxerint, quum neque in re
consilium sit, neque in uerbis uenus, fiat nimirum uti tota illa

2 precesserint] P 1563 1625, processerint S   3 importune] S 1563 1625, importunae
P   4 sanum] sanum ⟨et insanum⟩ P   5 pudor.] P 1625, pudor. Sed S 1563   6
debes,] S 1563 1625, debes P   7 deo] S 1563, deo, P 1625; referre] corr. from referas
P   9 tibi] interl. S   10 reperires] 1563 1625, corr. from reperies P, reperies S   13
certe] S 1563 1625, certae P   17 obstrusum esse] P 1625, esse abstrusum S, abstrusum
esse 1563   18 opibus] P S 1625, obicibus 1563   19 alioquin ad] P S 1625, alioquin
1563   21 non] non ⟨sit⟩ P   23 1st tam] P 1625, tamen S 1563; commode] S 1563
1625, commodae P   24 eo] corr. from ea S; ad id] P 1625, ad S 1563   25 inepte] S
1563 1625, ineptae P   27 quum neque] P 1563 1625, quum neque neque S   28 fiat]
fit P S 1563 1625

have also outstripped—at a gallop, as they say—their own far more intelligent and no less industrious comrades in the art of disputing. Indeed, reckless and impudent folly will always leap in where good character and sound judgment will generally hold back out of shame at the prospect of trifling.

Dorp, you honestly ought to rejoice in this rare gift of yours, which you owe not to your personal powers but to God, the bestower of every good thing; for it is through his unusual kindness to you that everything in scripture should strike you as so easy. For you would scarcely have found everything openly expressed in this book, which has been closed by seven seals, if it had not been unsealed for you by that same Lamb who "opens the book, and none closes it, who closes the book, and none opens it." Mind you, Dorp, this same book which strikes you as so easy struck Jerome as exceedingly difficult. Augustine considered it impenetrable. Not one of the ancients, indeed, dared to claim that he understood it, for they thought that God, in his unfathomable wisdom, deliberately hid its meaning far from the surface precisely in order to challenge the sharpest eye and to stimulate minds with the promise of buried and hard-to-reach treasure which their very assurance might otherwise render indifferent to riches set plainly in view.

I will not dwell just now on what uncommon learning and what rare intelligence are needed to take texts which at first may seem quite incompatible with morality and to reconcile them with morality so neatly and skillfully that they seem to be made for the purpose and not dragged in from elsewhere to serve it. Some now practice this art so ineptly that since they get no further than dragging a text from its previous context without fitting it into their own and since there is no sense in their matter or charm in their words, it naturally turns out that their moraliza-

moralisatio quam uocant sine ulla gratia spirituque frigescat.
Sed haec ut dixi omittam. At certe ipsum litteralem sensum tantum continere difficultatis puto, quantum nescio an quisquam
omnium comprehendere possit. Neque enim cuiquam censeo
5 litteralem horum uerborum sensum comprehensum esse, "Dixit
dominus domino meo 'sede a dexteris meis,'" nisi ei qui ea
Prophetam de ipso Christo uaticinatum intelligat. Quod exceptis
prophetis nec Iudeorum quisquam, quanquam in hos libros uniuersam operam suam collocabant, intellexit priusquam Christus
10 eis hunc eius litterae sensum aperuit. Qui tametsi apostolis, ac
discipulis suis interpretatus est scripturas, (neque enim quod
sciam questiunculas istas cum eis disputauit unquam), Non ausim tamen affirmare uniuersae scripturae sensus, eis ipsis, aut
presentem tradidisse, aut per spiritum sanctum postquam [29]
15 ascendit infudisse. Nam ut multa sunt ibi quae de Christo prophetae cecinerant, quorum alios omnes subterfugit intellectus,
quousque ea omnia ipsius uita, passio, resurrectioque de-
clarauerunt, ita mortalium impares esse uires puto ad indagan-
dum, utrum adhuc in eisdem lateant, aut de finali iudicio aut
20 alijs de rebus, nobis incogitabilibus, neque ulli hominum aut
hactenus cognita, aut ante cognoscenda mysteria, quam euentus
eadem temporibus ac momentis soli preuisis inscrutabili dei prouidentiae patefecerit.

Sed esto Dorpi. sit scriptura facilis, difficiles questiunculae,
25 nihil impedit tamen, quin illius cognitio, harum possit esse disciplina fructuosior. Quanquam enim saltare, atque in girum se
colligere, quod saltatriculi quidam ac circulatores faciunt, dif-
ficilius est quam ambulare, et dentibus panem facilius est, quam
testacea fragmenta conterere, neminem tamen esse puto qui

---

1 moralisatio] S *1563*, *corr. from* morilisatio P, monilisatio *1625*   2 certe] S *1563 1625*,
certae P   3 quisquam] P *1563 1625*, quisque S   4 censeo] P *1625*, sentio S *1563*
5 comprehensum] P *1625*, intellectum S *1563*   6 dexteris] P *1625*, dextris S *1563;*
meis,] S, meis. P, meis: *1563*, meis; *1625;* ea] P *1563 1625*, eam S   7 uaticinatum]
uaticinatum ⟨ne⟩ S   9 priusquam] P *1563 1625*, priusque S; Christus] Christus ⟨eius⟩
P   12 unquam),] unquam). P, vnquam:) S *1625*, unquam) *1563*   13 ipsis] S *1563*,
ipīs P, ipsum *1625*   17 passio] P *1563 1625*, passioque S   17–18 declarauerunt] P
1625, declarauerant S *1563*   24 difficiles] P *1625*, difficilesque S *1563;* questiunculae]
P S *1625*, quaestiones *1563*   26 atque] P *1563 1625*, aut S   27 saltatriculi quidam
ac] saltatriculi quidam P *1625*, saltatriculae quidem ac S *1563* (*see commentary*)

tion (as they call it), devoid of all spirit and grace, leaves us perfectly cold. I will not dwell on this, as I said. But in any case, even the literal sense is in my view a matter of such immense difficulty that I am not sure any mortal can quite comprehend it. For example, I think no one comprehends the literal sense of the words, "The Lord said to my Lord, 'Sit at my right hand,'" unless he understands that in these words the prophet is making a mystical prediction about Christ himself. And apart from the prophets, not one of the Jews, even though they were constantly studying these books, understood those words thus before Christ revealed this as their literal meaning. And even if he did interpret the scriptures for his apostles and disciples (for so far as I know he never disputed those petty problems with them), I would still hesitate to affirm that he either taught them the whole meaning of scripture in person or conveyed it to them by the Holy Spirit after his ascension. For just as the meaning of many of the things that the prophets had foretold about Christ escaped everyone else until all was made plain by Christ's life, passion, and resurrection, even so I think that the powers of mortals are not equal to settling the question of whether there may still lie hidden in scripture mysterious truths about either the Last Judgment or other things we cannot even imagine, mysterious truths none has discerned before now or will ever discern before they are unfolded in actual events at a date and a time foreseen only by God in his inscrutable providence.

But so be it, Dorp: scripture is easy, petty problems are difficult. That by no means keeps a knowledge of scripture from being more worthwhile than a training in problems. So, too, vaulting and tying one's body in knots the way certain acrobats and mountebanks do are more difficult feats than to walk, and it is easier to chew bread than to grind up potsherds with your teeth, but I think no one would be willing to trade these normal

rectos illos, uulgaresque naturae usus uelit huiusmodi inanibus
ostentis permutare. Quamobrem utra res sit [29v] difficilior non
admodum magnifacio. At quod utiliores etiam sacrarum litterarum cognitione questiunculas istas esse uis gregi pro quo
5 mortuus est Christus, ferre profecto non possum: quas si cog-
noscendas assereres, haud refragarer. Si ueterum lucubrationibus exaequares, non tolerarem. Nunc uero quum ancillas
istas coquinarias, ipsi Bibliae sacrosanctae litterarum omnium
reginae non confers modo, sed prefers etiam, dabis mihi mi
10 Dorpi ueniam, continere me hercle non possum quin illo
Therentiano procul eas omnes abigam, "Abite hinc in malam
rem cum isthac magnificentia fugitiuae."
    Neque profecto satis admirari queo, quum ea uerba lego
quibus eas ita magnifice attollis, tanquam, uti apud Poetas in
15 Atlantis humeros coelum, ita in perplexas huiuscemodi questiunculas, hoc est arundinem, uniuersa prorsus inclinata incumbat ecclesia, alioqui uidelicet periclitatura, ne tota semel collaberetur in cineres. Ais enim, "alioqui qui sciemus quomodo sint
sacramenta administranda, quaenam sint eorum formae, quan-
20 do absol[30]uendus peccator, quando reijciendus, quid praeceptum sit restitui, quid seruari possit?" Itane putas Dorpi ista, quae
tu nusquam alibi quam apud neotericos questionistas inueniri
uis, antiquos omnes sanctissimos patres nec minus etiam doctos
ignorasse omnia? Hieronymus, Ambrosius, Augustinus ad sac-

1 uelit] S 1563 1625, uelit, P   3–4 sacrarum litterarum cognitione] 1625, sacrarum
litterarum cognitione, P, sacrarum cognitione litterarum, S, quam sacrarum cognitionem literarum, 1563   4 uis] S 1563 1625, uis, P   5 possum:] possum, P S,
possum. 1563 1625   8 coquinarias, ipsi . . . sacrosanctae litterarum] P 1563 1625,
coquinarias litterarum S   9 mi] P 1625, om. S 1563   10 hercle] interl. P   11
abigam,] 1563, abigam. P S, abigam: 1625   11–12 Abite . . . fugitiuae] ital. 1625
12 fugitiuae] P S 1563, fugitiue 1625   12–13 fugitiuae." Neque] P 1625, fugitiuae.
Adeo putatis uos aut uestra facta ignorarier? Neque S 1563   14 magnifice] S 1563
1625, magnificae P   16 uniuersa] P 1625, in uniuersa S, in uniuersum 1563; prorsus]
prorsus ⟨ecclesia⟩ P   18–21 alioqui . . . possit] ital. 1625   21 Itane] 1625, Ita ne P S
1563   22 nusquam] P 1563 1625, nusque S; apud] apud ⟨poetas⟩ P   23 omnes] S
1563, omnes, P 1625; sanctissimos] 1563, scīssimos P, sctīssimos S, scientissimos 1625;
patres] S 1563, patres, P 1625

and commonplace functions for such vain displays. Hence it does not matter much to me which of the two is more difficult. But that you should pretend that those problems are even more useful than a knowledge of scripture to the flock for whom Christ died, this I honestly cannot endure. For if you claimed that those problems were worth knowing, I would certainly not disagree; if you set them alongside the works of the ancients, I would say you were going too far; since in fact you rank those kitchenmaids of yours not just as high as but indeed even higher than the Bible itself, holy queen of all genres of literature, you must pardon me, Dorp, but by Jove I cannot keep from sending them packing with that line from Terence, "Get lost, you tramps, and take those grand airs with you!"

Indeed, I am dumbfounded when I read the passage where you make such grand claims for those problems, as if the whole weight of the Church were sustained by perplexed problems of this sort—that is, by a reed—just as the poets say heaven is sustained on the shoulders of Atlas, as if the Church would be in immediate danger of collapsing into a heap of ashes if it lacked such a prop. For you ask, "How else are we to know how we ought to administer the sacraments, what their forms are, when we ought to absolve and when we ought to refuse absolution to a sinner, how much restitution we must make and how much we can keep?" Dorp, do you really think all the old holy fathers, who were as learned as they were devout, were completely ignorant of all those points which you suppose to be found only in modern compilers of problems? Were Jerome, Ambrose, and Augustine

ramentorum formas, ac materias cecutiebant? Ergo tota ecclesia
plusquam mille annos, (nam plusquam mille anni a passione
Christi numerantur ad Petri Lombardi tempora, e cuius sententijs, uelut ex equo Troiano, uniuersum istud questionum agmen
5 erupit), Tot annos ergo, immo tot saecula, uniuersa Christi ecclesia, aut sacramentis caruit; aut ista non habuit; quando recipi-
endus peccator, quando reijciendus, tam diu fuit incognitum; et
item quid praeceptum esset restitui, nesciebant? Nam quid
seruari posset, concesserim apud ueteres non fuisse tam acute,
10 quam apud istos disputatum. Sed ut Zacheus ueritus [30v] ne
male parta parce redderet, quadruplum sese redditurum professus est, ita ueteres illi patres ut uel plus satis quisque res-
titueret hortabantur. Non erant illi fateor hac in re quam isti
sunt, tam in diffiniendo ac distinguendo curiosi. Sed ego tamen
15 illorum (ut Therentius ait) emulari malo negligentiam, potius
quam istorum obscuram diligentiam, apud quos anxie res disputatur, et queritur, non tam quid restitui debeat, quam quid
seruari possit, non quam procul a peccato sit abscedendum, sed
quam prope ad peccatum sine peccato liceat accedere, et qui
20 consilium conuasatori dat, nimirum tanquam alienae pecuniae
frugi dispensator, obseruat ut in reddendo citra subsistat potius
uel mille passus, quam ultra latum (ut aiunt) unguem promoueat.
    Ego certe mi Dorpi nec te (puto) refragante contenderim,
25 quaecunque sunt ad salutem necessaria, id est sine quibus salui
esse non possumus, ea [31] primum ab ipsis sacris litteris, deinde
priscis earum interpretibus, ad hec communi ab antiquis pa-

1 formas, ac materias] P 1625, formas S 1563   2 plusquam . . . plusquam] P 1563
1625, plusque . . . plusque S; anni] P 1563 1625, annis S; sidenote in 1563 Petri Lombardi
Sententiae   4 uelut] S 1563 1625, uelud P; questionum] corr. from quaestionarum
S   5 erupit),] erupit] P 1563, erupit.) S, erupit,) 1625   9 posset] P 1563 1625, possit
S   9 acute] S 1563 1625, acutae P   11 parce] S 1563 1625, parcae P; sese] P 1625, se
S 1563   15 negligentiam] S 1563 1565, necgligentiam P   16 anxie] S 1563 1625,
anxiae P   19 peccatum] S 1563 1625, peccatum, P; liceat accedere, et] licet accedere,
et P, liceat accedere. Et 1625, possit accedi. Iam S 1563   21 dispensator] corr. from
dispensatori S; potius] S 1563 1625, potius, P   24 certe] S 1563 1625, certae P; (puto)
refragante] puto refragante, P, (ut puto refragante:) S, (ut puto) refragante 1563, puto,
refragante, 1625   25 quaecunque] 1563 1625, quecunque P S; necessaria] S 1563
1625, nenecessaria P; salui] corr. from saluiss P   27 earum] P 1625, eorum S 1563; ad
hec] S 1563 1625, adhec P

stark blind when it came to the form and matter of the sacraments? And so for more than a thousand years—note that more
than a thousand years separate the passion of Christ and the
time of Peter Lombard, whose *Sentences,* like the Trojan horse,
poured forth this entire army of problems—for so many years,
no, for so many centuries, was the Church without sacraments?
Did it not have the same ones? Was it so long unknown when we
ought to absolve a sinner and when we ought to refuse absolution? Were they ignorant, too, of how much restitution we are
taught to make? For I will concede that the ancients were not so
acute as those men in disputing how much we can keep. Rather,
just as Zaccheus, afraid of returning too little of his ill-gotten
gains, publicly promised to make a fourfold restitution, just so
those ancient fathers urged everyone to repay even more than
enough. In this area they were not, I confess, as precise as the
moderns in defining and hair-splitting. Still, as Terence puts it, I
would rather emulate the negligence of the former than the
pedantic diligence of the latter, who dispute the case over-intent-
ly and ask rather what we can keep than what we should give
back, rather how close we can get to a sin without sinning than
how wide a berth we should give it. And indeed, when one of
them gives a thief advice about restitution, like a careful steward
of someone else's money, he takes more care to prevent him
from going a finger's breadth too far, as they say, than from
stopping too short by a mile.

I myself would contend, as I think even you would concede,
my dear Dorp, that whatever is necessary for salvation—that is,
the things without which we cannot be saved—have been abun-
dantly transmitted to us, first of all through sacred scriptures
themselves, then through their first interpreters, then too by the

tribus, quasi per manus tradita consuetudine, postremo sacris
ecclesiae sanctionibus abunde nobis tradita. Quod si quid supra
quam in his est, homines isti acuti curiosius addiderunt, ut multa
concedam commoda esse, atque utilia, ita plane eius esse generis
5 puto omnia, ut sine eis uiui possit.

At fortasse dices, non omnia apud ueteres tam inuentu
prompta, tamque in numerato esse, quam apud istos recentiores, qui omnia cognata, quasique similia, in capita quaedam
uelut in suam quodque tribum descripserunt. In hac re Dorpi
10 fortasse accedo tibi, fateorque non nihil esse commodi, uelut in
domestica supellectile, sic in re litteraria quoque ita seorsum
habere singula quaeque distincta, ut ad quodcunque uelis illico
manum possis absque errore porrigere. Est istud quidem (ut
dixi) commodum. Verum hoc [31v] tanto commodo quidam tam
15 abutuntur incommode ut propemodum prestitisse uideatur,
hoc ipso etiam commodo caruisse. Neque enim aliud quicquam
magis in causa fuisse puto, quare uetustissimus quisque sacrarum litterarum interpres a tam multis tam diu neclectui
habeatur, quam quod infoelicium ingeniorum corrupta iudicia,
20 primum sibi, deinde alijs quoque, persuasere nihil usquam esse
mellis quod non in illos summularum alueos congestum sit, ideoque fit ut illis contenti solis, caetera omnia per incuriam
contemnant.

In cuius animi quendam etiam ipse iam olim in quadam Bibli-
25 opolae taberna incidi, erat enim senex, qui alterum (ut aiunt)
pedem habebat in sepulchro, et certe non multo post utrumque.
Iam doctoratus (ut uocant) honore plus quam annos triginta
fuerat insignitus. Dico forte apud eum, beatum Augustinum
aliquando putasse Daemones omneis substantias esse corporeas.

1 tradita consuetudine] S 1563 1625, traditaconsuetudine P   2 ecclesiae] S 1563 1625,
ecclesie P; abunde] S 1563 1625, abundae P   7–8 recentiores] corr. from recensiores
P   11 quoque] P S 1563, quaque 1625   13 manum] P 1563 1625, man ī S   15
abutuntur] P 1625, utuntur S 1563; incommode] S 1563 1625, incommodae P   16
ipso] interl. P; Neque enim] P 1563 1625, Neque S   17 magis in causa fuisse] P 1563
1625, in causa fuisse magis S   18 neclectui] P (g added in margin), neglectui 1563 1625,
neglectim S (see commentary)   23–24 contemnant. In] S 1563 1625, contemnant, in
P   24 cuius] P S 1625, eius 1563; quendam] S 1563 1625, quendam, P   25 senex] P
1625, senex et S 1563   26 certe] S 1563 1625, certae P; utrumque.] S 1625, utrumque,
P, utrumque: 1563   27 ut] P 1625, quem S 1563; plus quam] P 1563 1625, plusque S;
sidenote in 1563 Mori cum sene theologo disceptatio   29 Daemones] P 1625, demonas
S, daemonas 1563

customs transmitted to us from hand to hand, as it were, by the ancient fathers, and finally through the sacred decrees of the Church. And if those acute moderns have subjoined any more precise precepts to those which make up this tradition, I will grant that a number of these innovations are advantageous and useful, but I certainly think not a one is so vital that people cannot live without it.

But perhaps you will say that not everything in the works of the ancients is as easy to find or as neatly classified as it is in the works of these moderns, who have assembled all sorts of related and seemingly parallel passages into chapters as if splitting them up into their proper clans. On this point, Dorp, perhaps I concur with you, and I grant that there is some advantage in having the contents of written works, like domestic supplies, thoroughly sorted and clearly distinguished so that you can immediately put your hand on whatever you want without any mistake. This is indeed, as I said, an advantage. But some use this considerable advantage to such disadvantage that it almost appears that, advantage or not, we would be better off without it. For I think that the principal reason that all of the most ancient interpreters of scripture have been neglected for so long by so many is simply that the corrupt judgments of less gifted intellects persuaded first themselves and then others as well that no honey remains to be found beyond what is amassed in the beehives of those compilations, and therefore, content with the hives alone, they neglect and scorn everything else.

Long ago I myself met a man with this attitude in a certain bookseller's shop. He was an old man, with one foot in the grave, as they say, and both feet before long, I am certain. He had been awarded the distinction of a doctorate, as they call it, more than thirty years before. I happened to say in his presence that St. Augustine once thought that all demons were corporeal sub-

Ibi ille statim supercilium contrahere, et temeritatem meam
rugosa fronte compescere. Tum ego, "non dico" [32] inquam
"hoc ipse, pater, nec Augustinum in ea re defendo. Homo erat.
errare potuit. Credo ei quantum cui plurima, sed nemini uni
5 omnia." Iam uero cepit homo excandescere uel ob id precipue,
quod tanto patri calumniam tantam intenderem. Nam "putas
me" (inquit) "non legisse Augustinum? imo" (inquit) "priusquam tu nascereris." Me iam suis seuis dictis protelasset, nisi
commode fuisset paratus elenchus. Nam ut erat in taberna,
10 sumo in manus libellum Augustini de diuinatione Demonum.
uerto ad locum, atque ostendo. ubi locum semel atque iterum
legit, ac tercia demum lectione (me adiuuante) coepisset intellegere, tandem admirabundus "Certe" (inquit) "ego ualde miror
de hoc quod Augustinus dicit sic in isto libro quia certe non dicit
15 sic in magistro sententiarum qui est liber magis magistralis quam
iste."

Qui sunt ex hac farragine, qui neque [32v] ueterum quenquam neque scripturarum quicquam legunt nisi in sententijs, et
earum commentarijs, hi perinde mihi uidentur facere, ac si quis
20 Authoribus omnibus, qui latine scripserunt omissis, construc-
tionum praeceptis ab Alexandro petitis, reliquum latinae linguae, ex Perotti Cornucopia, et Calepino conetur ediscere, quod
persuasum habeat in his omnia latinae linguae uocabula sese
reperturum, et profecto reperiet plurima, eademque elec-
25 tissima, Vtque apud recentiores Theologos priorum dicta authoritatis loco leguntur inserta, ita hic quoque ueteres poetae

5 precipue] S 1563 1625, precipuae P   6–8 putas . . . nascereris] ital. except inquit
1625   9 commode] S 1563 1625, commodae P; fuisset paratus elenchus] P 1625,
paratus fuisset ἐλέγχος S, fuisset paratus *ελ 1563   12 tercia] tercia ⟨diuinatione⟩
P   13 admirabundus] admirabundus. P, admirabundus: S 1563, admirabundus,
1625   13–16 Certe . . . iste] ital. except inquit 1625, gothic script except inquit P   13
ego ualde] P 1625, ualde S 1563   13–14 miror de hoc] P 1625, miror S 1563   14
quia] P S 1563, quod 1625   20 latine] S 1563 1625, latinae P   21–22 reliquum
latinae linguae] P 1625, reliquum S 1563   22 conetur] P 1625, conentur S 1563   23
habeat] habeat, ⟨ac si⟩ S   25 Vtque] P 1625, Nempe ut S 1563; priorum] S 1563, p̄orū
P, patrum 1625   26 quoque ueteres] P 1563 1625 quoque S; poetae] corr. from poetas
P

stances, whereupon he at once wrinkled his forehead and checked my temerity with his furrowed brow. Then I said, "I myself do not say this is so, father, nor do I defend Augustine for saying so. Being a man, he could make a mistake. I take his word as seriously as anyone's, but I take no one man's word unconditionally." Now the man really started to seethe, most of all because I had tried to foist so great a misrepresentation on so great a father. For "You think," he exclaimed, "I have not read Augustine? Quite the contrary," he said, "before you were born." His sharp words would have put me to flight had there not been a counterproof ready and waiting. For since all this occurred in a bookshop, I picked up Augustine's tract *On the Divination of Demons,* turned to the passage, and showed it to him. When he had read the passage once, and then once more, and at last, on the third reading, with me to assist him, he had begun to understand what he read, he finally said in bewilderment, "I certainly am amazed that Augustine puts it that way in this book when he certainly does not put it that way in the *Master of the Sentences,* which is a more masterly book than this one."

Men of this motley crew, men who never read any of the ancients or anything out of the scriptures except in the *Sentences* and their commentaries, seem to me to be acting like someone who neglects all the authors who actually wrote Latin, takes his syntactical precepts from Alexander, and then tries to learn the rest of the Latin language from Perotti's *Cornucopia* and Calepino since he thinks he will find all the words of that language contained in their books. And indeed he will find a great many, and choice ones, at that; and just as one can read sayings of earlier theologians introduced as authorities in the works of more recent ones, so too in these glossaries one can read various

atque Oratores aliquot, etiam qui nunc nec extant quidem. Sed
neque hec unquam facient latinum, nec illa mi Dorpi Theologum, si sola sint, etiam si decem millibus spinosissimarum
questionum fuerit instructus, quibus miror, quum sit talis, qua in
5 re possit ecclesiae esse usui.

Disputando fortasse aduersus hereticos, (nam hoc nomine
praecipue sese solent [33] uenditare.) At hi aut docti sunt aut
indocti. Si indocti (ut est multo maxima pars) neque acumina
ista, quibus iste solis ualet, neque uerba tam insueta, quibus iste
10 solis assueuit, intelligerent. Necesse est ergo talem disputa-
tionem tantum fructus consequi, quantum si quis Turcam
quempiam patriae duntaxat linguae peritum, composita oratione, sermone gallico (nam eum solum elegantem galli putant)
exhortetur ad fidem. Sin docti sint heretici idque in illis ipsis
15 questionibus (neque enim fere accidit ut alias sint heretici) quando iam redarguentur? Quis erit disputandi finis? quum ex illis
ipsis questionibus, quibus oppugnantur, ipsis quoque referiendi
ministratur inexhausta materia, ut propemodum eis accidere
uideatur, quod nudis inter aceruos lapidum pugnantibus, ut quo
20 feriat neutri desit, quo se defendat, neuter habeat. Nempe
quidam, qui in scholis inter primos leguntur, et sunt non minus,
quam habentur acuti, ut omittam interim, quod quasdam questiones de deo tam ridiculas [33v] excogitarunt, ut putes ridere,
propositiones tam blasphemas ut censeas irridere: Certe contra
25 fidem tam gnauiter obijciunt, tam segniter obiecta dissoluunt, ut
preuaricatores agere, et fidem ioco tueri, serio oppugnare uideantur. Heretici ergo cum talibus compositi, quales ante dixi
Theologos, quum sint in eodem docti ludo, quando succum-
bent? non cito hercle opinor, si non unum magis lignorum fas-
30 ciculum uererentur, quam multos syllogismorum fasces pertimescerent.

3 sola] *corr. from* solat P; spinosissimarum] P 1563 1625, spinosarum S   4 miror, quum
sit talis,] 1625, miror quum sit talis P S, miror cum sit talis, 1563   5 ecclesiae esse usui]
P 1625, usui esse S 1563   7 praecipue] S 1563 1625, praecipuae P   9 iste solis] P
1625, iste solus S, solus 1563   10 solis] P 1625, solus S 1563; intelligerent] P 1625,
intelliget S 1563   14 docti sint] P 1625, docti S 1563   17 ipsis quoque referiendi] P
1625, eisdem quoque referendi S 1563   19 pugnantibus,] 1563, pugnantibus P,
pugnantibus. S, pugnantibus; 1625   21 primos] P S 1563, primas 1625   24
irridere:] 1625, irridere. P 1563, ridere. S; Certe] S 1563 1625, Certae P   30
uererentur] P 1563 1625, uenerentur S

ancient poets and orators, including a few who are not even extant today. But these scraps can no more make a Latin-speaker than those alone can make a theologian, not even if he is armed with ten thousand of the prickliest problems on earth; and when I see a theologian of this sort, I wonder just what useful service such problems can ever equip him to do for the Church.

Perhaps to dispute against heretics; for this is their principal selling point. But the heretics are either learned or unlearned. If they are unlearned, as the great majority of them are, then they would understand neither those subtleties which are his only weapon nor the outlandish words which are his only means of expression. Necessarily, then, this sort of disputation would be just as productive as if someone delivered an elaborate oration in French (for the French think no other tongue elegant) exhorting some Turk versed in no other language but Turkish to convert to our faith. But if the heretics are learned, indeed learned in those very problems (for they are almost never heretics with reference to anything else), when will they be refuted? Will there be any end to disputing? For the very problems with which they are assaulted afford them no end of material with which to strike back, so that the plight of both parties is very much like that of men fighting naked between heaps of stones: neither one lacks the means to strike out; neither one has the means to defend himself. Indeed, some of the principal authors they read in the schools—authors fully as subtle as they are reported to be—not to mention that they have dreamt up certain problems about God so ridiculous you might think they were raising a laugh and so blasphemous you might feel they were laughing directly at him, they are certainly so zealous in raising objections to the faith and so backward in answering them that they seem to be in collusion with the opposition, defending the faith in jest and assaulting it in earnest. Now then, pitted against the sort of theologians I have mentioned, how soon are the heretics going to succumb, since they have been trained in the same school of tactics? Not very soon, to be sure, in my view, were they not more intimidated by one little bundle of faggots than daunted by many large bundles of syllogisms.

Sed idoneus erit saltem qui concionetur ad populum. Hercules hoc ipsum est quod aiunt Bouem ad ceroma. Nam quum nihil didicerit, preter questiones, quae sunt ad aures populi perquam insolentes, minimeque omnium idoneae, ediscendus est ei
5 nimirum sermo quispiam, ex Sermonibus Discipuli, aut VENI MECVM, aut DORMI SECVRE: res per se ineptae, quas dum homo tractat ineptior, utpote nec ad id munus assuetus, et qui totam [34] illam uerborum congeriem ex alieno stomacho declamet, necesse est ut contio tota frigescat.
10 Quamobrem plane non uideo, questiones istae quid faciunt ei quem solae possident, nisi quod eum ad caetera omnia reddunt inutilem, ut cui si quid ex his proponatur subtilibus magis, quam solidis disputationibus, in quibus se ante millies exercuit, iam domi suae est, iam cristas erigit uelut gallus qui in suo ster-
15 quilinio superbit. At extra illa septa si paulo producatur longius, illico ignota rerum omnium facies tenebras ac uertiginem offundit. Nec iam dialectica rerum cecitate labanti, quantumuis fortis, quantumuis acuta succurrit, quae ut cognita rerum natura, uarias inde species, multasque argumentorum formas elicit, ita
20 rebus ignoratis ipsis, necesse est sine ullo usu obmutescat. Adde quod illas ipsas questiones, quas et penitus, et solas per tot annos imbibit, quum sese iam senex scholasticorum contubernio, ubi eadem assidue uentilantur, quapiam occasione subduxerit, iam intra biennium, acumina illa [34v] uniuersa, numerosa nimium
25 uidelicet, euanida, nullo rerum subnixa pondere, tanquam nebula, fumusque, disparent, iamque ei nimirum ipsi usu uenit,

---

1 erit] erit ⟨certae⟩ P   4 minimeque] S 1563 1625, minimaeque corr. from minimamque P   5 Discipuli,] S 1563 1625, Discipuli. P; aut] S 1563 1625, AVT, P   6 MECVM,] 1563 1625, MECVM. P S; SECVRE:] SECVRAE, P, SECVRE, S 1563, SECVRE. 1625   7 assuetus] 1625, corr. from assuetum P, asuetus S, assuetum 1563   7–8 qui totam] P S 1563, quo tam 1625   10 faciunt] P S 1625, faciant 1625   13 exercuit,] S 1563, exercuit P, exercuit; 1625   15 superbit.] superbit, P S 1563, superbit: 1625   16 ignota] P 1563 1625, ignorata S; facies] 1563 1625, facies, P S   17 Nec] corr. from Nam P; labanti] P 1563 1625, labenti S   19 multasque] P 1625, multas S 1563   20–21 ipsis, necesse . . . illas ipsas] P S 1625, ipsis ipsas 1563   21 questiones] P 1625, captiunculas S 1563; solas] P S 1563, solos 1625   22 sese] corr. from esse P; senex] P 1625, senex e S 1563   23 eadem] P 1563 1625, ea S; assidue] S 1563 1625, assiduae P; uentilantur,] 1563 1625, uentilantur P, uentilatur S; subduxerit] S 1563, subduxerat P 1625   24 acumina illa uniuersa] P 1625, uniuersa illa acumina S 1563; numerosa nimium] S 1563, nimium P 1625   25 uidelicet,] 1563, uidelicet P S 1625   26 iamque ei] P 1625, idemque S 1563; ipsi usu uenit] P 1625, usu uenit ipsi S 1563

But he will at least be well suited to preach to the people. Good lord, talk about drafting an ox as a boxer! For since the man has learned nothing but problems which are totally unfamiliar and extremely ill suited to the ears of the people, naturally he must learn some sermon by heart out of *The Disciple's Sermons, The Preacher's Companion,* or *The Sleep-Well;* those sermons are silly affairs in themselves, and when the man who delivers them is sillier still, having never prepared for that task and declaiming that whole mass of words from another man's stomach, the whole sermon perforce leaves us cold.

Therefore I simply fail to see what those problems can do for a man who knows nothing besides but to render him useless for everything else, since if someone advances some topic from those disputations, more subtle than solid, which he has already practiced a thousand times, now he feels right at home, now he ruffles his feathers like a cock riding high on his dunghill, but if he is led a bit further away from his native preserve, all at once the unknown look of everything buries him in confusion and darkness. Nor does dialectic, no matter how powerful and acute, rescue him as he stumbles about in his blindness to actual things: just as dialectic elicits various species and numerous patterns of arguments from the nature of things once it is known, even so when the things themselves remain a mystery dialectic necessarily falls silent, of no use at all. Furthermore, once this fellow, by now an old man, has for whatever reason made off from the camp of the schoolmen, where those problems are constantly being argued, within two years the same problems which he has explored both intensively and exclusively for so many years, all those subtleties, too many to keep track of, slip easily away into nothing, unrestrained by connections with actual things, and disappear like a cloud of smoke, and predictably he himself

quod de anima pueri ex Aristotele subinde citari solet, ut ipsius
anima fiat denique uelut tabula rasa in qua nihil omnino de-
pingitur, et mirum in modum uersa rerum uice, contingit, ut qui
prius omnes sapientiae numeros in argumentosa loquacitate
5 posuerat, iam senex infantissimus omnibus risui foret, nisi stul-
titiae suae superciliosum silentium sapientiae loco pretexeret,
imo potius hoc ipso ridiculus, quod qui fuerat Stentore modo
clamosior, nunc uicio tam longe diuerso, taciturnior pisce red-
datur, et inter loquentes sedeat ueluti caput sine lingua, atque
10 (ut aiunt) "personae mutae, truncoque simillimus Hermae."
   Denique ut quid ego de hac tota re sentio semel intellegas,
neque Theologos omnes taxo, neque neotericorum questiones
omnes condemno, sed eas quae nihil ad rem pertinent, quae sunt
huiusmodi, ut neque quidquam eruditioni conferant, et multum
15 [35] pietati detrahant, eas non improbandas modo, sed despuen-
das quoque censeo, ceteras uero quae tractant, aut humana
grauiter, aut diuina reuerenter, tum utrisque adhibita modestia,
qua ueritatem sese inuestigare magis, quam altercari probent,
modo ne quenquam sibi totum uendicent, ne quenquam nimis
20 diu detineant, et suo se pede metiantur, neque se melioribus
conferant, nedum non anteferant, has inquam sic institutas, admodum libenter amplector, hactenus tamen ut eas tales esse
fatear, quibus non inutiliter exerceantur ingenia, tales esse per-
negem, in quas salus uniuersae procumbat atque innitatur
25 ecclesiae.
   Iam Theologos non eos uitupero qui has degustarunt, imo
laudo etiam, qui ad altiorem sacrarum litterarum peritiam, ad
meliorem priscorum et sanctissimorum, et doctissimorum pa-

2 denique] S 1563 1625, denique, P   3 modum] S 1563 1625, modum, P; rerum uice]
P 1563 1625, uice rerum S   5–6 stultitiae] S 1563 1625, stultitie P   8 longe] S 1563
1625, longae P   9 sedeat] 1563, sedeat, P S 1625   9–10 sedeat . . . truncoque] P
1625, sedeat, Mercurij statuae truncoque S 1563   11 de hac tota re] P 1625, tota interl.
after hac de re S, hac de re tota 1563   12 neotericorum] P 1625, Imperitorum S
1563   13 sed] P 1625, uerum S 1563   15 pietati] P S 1625, impietati 1563; eas]
1625, eas ⟨eruditioni conferant⟩ P, eas (inquam) S 1563   17 utrisque] P 1625,
utrumque S 1563   18 sese inuestigare] P 1625, inuestigare sese S 1563   19 2nd ne]
P 1625, neque S 1563   20 et] interl. P   21 nedum non] P 1625, nedum S 1563
22 libenter] S 1563 1625, libentur P   24 procumbat] S 1625, procumbat, P, recumbat
1563   26 qui] S 1563 qⁱ P, quod 1625   27 altiorem] P S 1563, altiorum 1625

suffers in practice what Aristotle is frequently quoted as saying holds true for the soul of a child, namely that his soul finally becomes, as it were, a clean slate, on which nothing at all is depicted, and it turns out, through a wondrous reversal, that he who once thought the sum total of wisdom consisted of argumentative loquacity has become an old man with the tongue of an infant, a man all would laugh at if he did not use haughty silence in place of wisdom to cloak his own folly; but in fact he is all the more laughable precisely because the same man who was lately more clamorous than Stentor has now, by the opposite defect, been rendered more dumb than a fish, and now sits among speakers as if he himself had not a tongue in his head, like "a player without any lines," as they say, and "a truncated statue of Hermes."

Finally, so that you may understand once and for all how I feel about this whole affair, I neither criticize all theologians nor condemn all the problems of the moderns; but the kind that are wholly irrelevant, the sort that contribute nothing to erudition and detract a good deal from piety, this sort I believe should be not merely censured but thrown out entirely. As for those that remain, those that treat human concerns seriously or divine concerns reverently, always using a modest approach which will show that their goal is the truth and not winning a quarrel, given that they must not monopolize anyone's attention or take up too much of anyone's time, given that they must acknowledge their own limitations and not rank themselves as high as their betters (let alone even higher), these problems, presented like this, I repeat, I am perfectly glad to embrace, although only so far as to grant that such inquiries do have their use as a method of intellectual exercise even as I deny that they furnish an essential and central support for the salvation of the Church as a whole.

Now then, I do not castigate those theologians who have had a good taste of these problems; indeed, I even praise those who have complemented a loftier training in sacred scripture and a nobler education in the earliest, holiest, and most learned fa-

trum eruditionem, has quoque non abijciendas accessiones
adiecerint. Verum huiusmodi [35v] Theologos (ut ex animo dicam) non probo, qui questionibus cuiusque generis non insenes-
cunt modo, sed immoriuntur quoque, qui seu ingenij sterilitate
5 quadam impediti, seu puerili scholasticorum incitati plausu, ne-
glectis antiquorum omnium litteris, posthabitis etiam ipsis,
quorum se doctores profitentur, euangelijs, nihil omnino preter
questiunculas didicerunt, partim per se inanes, partim inanes
his, qui caeterarum rerum omnium inancs ipsi sunt, idque iam
10 senes, atque ideo deplorati, quod neque scripturas commode
tractare, incognitis ueterum scriptis, queunt, neque ad ea cognoscenda, qua nunc sunt latinae linguae penuria, pares esse
possunt: Redire uero ad grammaticam, atque inter pueros, imo
uero a pueris etiam discere, hoc non solum dispudet, sed etiam
15 serum est. Istos ego mi Dorpi tantum abest ut laudem, ut etiam
quomodo apud Rhomanos, mali magistratus publicis sese coge-
bantur abdicare muneribus [36] ita istos quoque non tam re
quam uocabulo Theologos, adigendos censeam, ad hunc magistratum, quo tam immerito funguntur, eiurandum.
20   Neque mirum est tamen esse aliquos in tanto Theologorum
numero tales. Nam quis ordo obsepiri tam diligenter potest, ut
non ambitione, precio, gratia, aut alijs malis artibus, aliquis indignus irrepat, qui quum sit in editum receptus, quam potest
plurimos sui similes in eundem locum suo suffragio subleuat?
25 Ita fit ut nullus ordo sit, qui non indignis abundet. Nam ut in
Senatu Rhomano fuerunt, quorum maiestatem nulli reges aequabant, ita rursus erant quidam adeo tenues, atque inglorij, ut
misere inter spectacula uulgi compressu elisi perierint. Quanquam ut nec illorum fulgori, istorum humilitas obfuit, nec isto-
30 rum tenuitatem senatorium nomen exemit contemptui, ita nec

---

2 adiecerint] *P 1563 1625*, adiecerunt *S;* huiusmodi] huiusmodi ⟨accessioni⟩ *P*   5
incitati plausu] *P 1625*, plausu incitati *S 1563*   8 inanes, partim inanes] *P S 1625*,
inanes *1563*   10 quod] *P 1625*, qui *S 1563;* commode] *S 1563 1625*, commodae *P*
11 queunt] *P 1625*, queant *S 1563*   11–12 ea cognoscenda] *P S 1625*, eas cognoscen-
das *1563*   13 possunt:] *1625*, possunt. *P*, possint, *S*, possint: *1563*   15–20 est.
Istos . . . eiurandum. Neque] *P 1625*, est. Neque *S 1563*   15 abest ut laudem] *P*, abest
1625, abest ut probem *1689 1703*   21–22 ut non] *P 1563 1625*, ut *S*   23 irrepat,] *S
1563*, irrepat; *P*, irrepat: *1625*   24 subleuat?] *1563*, subleuat. *P 1625*, subleuat, *S*
25 non indignis] *P 1563 1625*, indignis non *S*   28 perierint] *P 1563 1625*, perierunt
S   28–29 Quanquam] *P 1563 1625*, Quanque *S*   30 nomen exemit] *P 1563 1625*,
exemit nomen *S*

thers with these not contemptible accessory studies. But in all honesty I do not praise the sort of theologians who do not merely squander their youth over problems of every variety, but even expire over them; who, hampered by some intellectual deficiency or spurred on by the childish applause of the schoolmen, have neglected the writings of all of the ancients, slighted even the very gospels of which they profess themselves doctors, and learned nothing at all except those petty problems, which are partly barren in their own right and partly barren for those who are barren of everything else; who, still worse, are already old men, given up for dead losses, since they cannot treat scripture aptly without knowing the works of the ancients, and they cannot come to know those with the poor Latin that they now possess, while to go back to grammar and learn among boys, indeed from boys, is not merely a disgraceful proposal but also comes too late to do any good. My dear Dorp, I am so far from praising such men that I even think these theologians in name, not in fact, should be forced, as the Romans compelled bad officials to give up their public employments, to resign from the office they occupy so undeservingly.

And yet it is no wonder that there are some like this among so great a number of theologians. For what order of men can be cordoned off so strictly that not even one unworthy person may ambitiously worm his way in with a bribe or a favor or other machinations and then, once he has gained a high standing, raise as many like himself as he can into the same high position by giving them his support? This is why there is no order of men that is not rife with unworthy members. For just as there were men in the Roman senate whose majesty no kings could equal, even so there were several so base and inglorious that they died a miserable death in the course of a festival, crushed by the press of the crowd. And yet even as the lowliness of some senators did not lessen the brilliance of the rest, nor did the senatorial title rescue the baseness of the unworthy from being exposed to contempt, so their title does not exempt unworthy theologians

indignos Theologos nomen eripit contumelijs, nec eorum con-
temptus aut erga sin[36v]gulos, qui uere sunt, honoris quicquam
adimit, aut erga uniuersos quicquam reuerentiae, ac maiestatis
imminuit, cuius ego certe tam conseruandae, atque ampliandae
5 sum cupidus, quam quisquis uiuit usquam cupidissimus. Nam de
Erasmo stultum fuerit idem polliceri, quum nemo nesciat, in
sacrum Theologorum ordinem nihil perperam aut dici aut fingi
posse, ut non proprie ac peculiariter ipsius agatur negocium.
   Habes igitur hac in re animum mi Dorpi meum, nec dubito
10 hercle quin etiam (si tu is es quem ego mecum fingo) tuum, quem
si probas etiam Erasmi puta, sin minus, nec meum diutius, quam
tu uoles, futurum. Neque enim quicquam animo est unquam
tam obstinate obfirmatum meo, ut non paratus sim eo iubente
mutare, quem sciam nunquam quidquam sine ratione iussurum.
15 Sed hec hactenus.
   Ad reliquas epistolae tuae partes ero tanto breuior, quanto in
hac fui uel aequo uerbosior. [37] Vtrunque etiam merito. Nam
ut ea, de quibus ante disserui, Erasmus nunquam uidit, ita de
quibus deinceps sum dicturus, et scripsit ipse, et se diligentius
20 pollicetur scripturum, tum quaedam uero sunt huiusmodi, ut in
his Diuus etiam Hieronimus non suo solum exemplo quasi preiudicio, Erasmi partem tueatur, sed totam litem quoque tanquam edita in scriptis sententia secundum eum pronunciauerit.
Neque enim quicquam est quo tu, ne quicquam in scriptura
25 mutetur e graecorum fide codicum prohibes, quod non olim
aduersus Beatum Hieronimum et obiectum sit, et ab eo

1 indignos Theologos] *P 1625*, indignis Theologis istorum nomen *S 1563;* contumelijs] *P
1625*, contumeliae *S 1563*   2 sunt,] *1563 1625*, sunt *P S*   2–3 quicquam adimit] *P S
1563*, adimit quicquam *1625*   4 certe] *S 1563 1625*, certae *P*   5 sum] *interl. P;*
quisquis] *P 1625*, quisquam *S 1563;* uiuit] *P S 1563*, iuuit *1625;* usquam] *P S 1625*, etiam
1563   8 proprie] *S 1563 1625*, propriae *P*   9 Habes] *Para. 1625*   10 ego] *P 1563
1625, om. S*   11 probas] *corr. from* probes *S;* etiam] *P S 1625*, esse *1563;* minus, nec] *P
1625*, minus tantum meum, immo nec *S 1563*   13 obstinate] *S 1563 1625*, obstinatae
P; meo] *P 1563 1625*, meum *S*   19 scripsit ipse] *P 1625*, ipse scripsit *S 1563*   20
quaedam uero] *P 1625*, quaedam *S 1563*   21 etiam] *interl. P;* suo solum] *P 1563 1625*,
solum suo *S*   24 Neque] *P 1625*, Nec *S 1563;* quicquam] *P 1563 1625*, quicque *S;* quo]
P S 1625, quod *1563;* ne] *corr. from* neque *S;* quicquam in] *P 1563 1625*, quicquam *S
25* e] *S 1563 1625*, ae *P*   26 aduersus Beatum] *P 1563 1625*, aduersus *S*

from being reviled, nor does any contempt they provoke dero-
gate in the slightest degree from the honor of true theologians or
impair in the slightest the reverend majesty of theologians in
general, something which I myself am as keen to protect and
enhance as any man that has ever lived. For it would be foolish to
make the same claim for Erasmus, since everyone knows that
whatever is said or imagined unjustly against the sacred order of
theologians is Erasmus' own special and personal concern.

There you have my opinion about this affair, my dear Dorp,
and by heaven I am convinced that (if you are the man I imagine
you are) there you have your opinion, as well; if it meets your
approval, consider it that of Erasmus, as well as my own, but if
not, then not even my own any longer than you would so have it.
For I do not hold any opinion so stubbornly that I am not ready
to change it at the command of a person who will never, I know,
command anything without a good reason. But so much for that.

Concerning the rest of your letter I will be just as brief as,
regarding this part, I have been disproportionately verbose—
rightly so, on both counts. For Erasmus, who never saw what you
have written concerning the points I have so far discussed, has
both written and promised to write more precisely concerning
the points I am planning to talk about next. Moreover, a number
of these bear on issues in which St. Jerome himself not only sides
with Erasmus by way of his personal example, as if in a judicial
precedent, but has also in effect published his verdict in writing
and ruled on Erasmus' behalf. For everything that you say to
prevent any changes in scripture on the basis of Greek textual
authorities was urged long ago against St. Jerome and very pow-

ualidissime confutatum: nisi hoc uideri nouum uis, quod translationibus, (ut ais) quae multae olim fuerant, eiectis omnibus ne
uarietate codicum fideles uacillarent, Hanc unam a sanctis patribus acceptam, ab Hieronimo castigatam, atque ad nos usque
5 transmissam comprobauit ecclesia, non uno aliquo concilio sed
perpetua consuetudine ad eam recurrendi, quoties in ullo concilio de fide nodus incidisset: Neque enim alioquin fieri potuisse
ut [37v] caeterae omnes interierint atque hec ad nos sola per-
uenerit, nisi id non sorte accidisset, sed adhibita a maioribus
10 nostris industria fuisset curatum.

Primum mi Dorpi nemini dubium esse puto, quin hec ipsa
editio ante Hieronimi tempora (neque enim alioquin ipse hanc
potissimum castigasset) et recepta sit ab ecclesia et assiduo citan-
di usu comprobata, quod ego uel solum in causa fuisse puto
15 quod ad nos usque sola durauerit. Cur ergo Hieronimus ausus
est mutare quicquam? idque non alijs modo et optimis et sanctissimis uiris approbantibus factum, sed ipso quoque Augustino
adhortante ut fieret? Mutauit uero Hieronimus (ut ipse fatetur)
si quid in sensu fuit, quo latinus codex discreparet a graeco. Hoc
20 ille putauit utilius quam ea quae tu Erasmo suades ut faciat:
uidelicet, ut ea tantum adnotet, quae commodius ac signifi-
cantius interpres uertere potuisset, sensum uero, si quando discrepent, manere patiatur, nec mendae manifestae Latinos admoneat. Quod Diuus Hieronimus non [38] usque adeo
25 curandum censuit, eius tu precipuam curam habendam putas.
Quod ille iudicauit potissimum, ab eo tu potissimum deterres.

Sed hic occurris ac fateris id ab Hieronimo recte factum quod
uidelicet tunc opus erat, dum adhuc uulgata hec editio non satis
esset emendata, At nunc repurgatis uicijs superuacaneum
30 iterum purgandi laborem fore. Nam si opus tam nunc esset,
quam tunc erat non est ratio cur minus bene mereretur a quo
nunc idem denuo fieret, quod tunc Hieronimus fecit.

---

1 ualidissime] *S 1563 1625*, ualidissimae *P*; confutatum:] confutatum. *P 1563 1625*,
confutatum, *S*   2 (ut ais)] *interl. P*   3 uacillarent,] *1563*, uacillarent. *P S*, vacillarent;
1625   5 concilio] *1629*, consilio *P S 1563 1625*   6–7 concilio] *1629*, consilio *P S*
1563 1625   7 incidisset:] *S*, incidisset. *P 1563 1625*   9 sorte] *P 1625*, forte *S*
1563   15 quod] *P 1625*, quare *S 1563*; duraruerit] *corr. from* durauerat *P*   18
fieret?] *1563 1625*, fieret. *P S*   22 sensum] *P 1563 1625*, sensu *S*; uero,] *1625*, uero *P S*
1563   22–23 discrepent] *P 1625*, discrepet *S 1563*   23–24 admoneat.] *S 1563*
1625, admoneat, *P*   27 recte] *S 1563 1625*, rectae *P*   29 emendata,] *S*, emendata. *P*,
emendata: *1563 1625*

erfully refuted by him, unless you claim to be making a new point when you say that long ago there were many translations, but that all of these were rejected so that textual variations would not cause the faithful to waver, whereas this one, the same one adopted by the holy fathers, emended by Jerome, and passed on all the way down to us, is the only translation the Church has approved, not in some single council but through an unvarying custom of referring to this text whenever any council has faced some perplexity concerning the faith. For it could not have happened that all the rest should have vanished while this one alone has come down to us unless that was the work, not of chance, but of our forefathers' deliberate planning.

First of all, my dear Dorp, I think everyone knows that this very edition, even before Jerome's time—for why else would he have emended this one in particular?—was both accepted by the Church and approved through the regular practice of quoting its text, which I think was indeed the sole reason why it is the only one that has come down to us. Now then, why did Jerome dare to make any changes? But not only did other most virtuous and holy men give their approval to what he had done; even Augustine himself urged him to do it. And Jerome himself states that the changes he made were at points where the sense of the Latin text differed from that of the Greek. He thought this more useful than that which you counsel Erasmus to do, namely to annotate only those points where the translator could have rendered the meaning more aptly and pointedly, but to leave the sense just as it is, if the texts ever differ, and not point out an obvious corruption to readers of Latin. What Jerome felt to be barely worth troubling about you think ought to get more attention than anything else; what he judged most important you declare to be most ill advised.

But responding to this, you concede that Jerome was right to do what he did, since there was still a need for such work when the Vulgate had not yet been completely corrected, but now that it has been emended it is pointless to try to emend it again. For if the need were as great now as it was then, there is no reason why anyone who did again now what Jerome did then should get any less credit than he did.

Primum neminem esse omnium puto (dicam enim audacius)
nec Hieronimum quidem ipsum qui profiteri ausus sit esse se
tam certum sui ut in uertendo nihil eum omnino possit subterfugere, Vsque adeo non deerit uel mediocribus interdum post
5 meliores etiam in quo uersentur utiliter. "Ergo quis uertendi
finis erit?" inquis: facillimus, si euenerit ut quisquam tam commode uerterit, aut ab alio non optime uersum alius ita correxerit, ut his manentibus integris, non inueniant posteri quod im-
mutandum censeant.

10   At periculum est [38v] interim ne uariae translationes dubios
faciant animos fidelium, utram credere debeant ueriorem, quod
ipsum in causa fuisse censes, ut reliquae omnes de industria
reiectae sint, hac una seruata, ne fideles uacillarent, qua in re
usque adeo ego abs te dissentio ut quod tu maiorum curae tri-
15 buis, ego temporum assignem incuriae, qua nimirum non illae
tantum translationes, sed multa etiam alia periere. Alioquin
etiam si unam in ecclesijs canendam recepissent, reliquas tamen
quid necesse fuit abijcere, ex quibus non erat periculum ne
fideles uacillarent, sed quemadmodum nunc euangelistarum
20 uaria narratione series rerum in luculentiorem peruenit
notitiam, ita in diuersorum collatione interpretum, studioso lectori daretur occasio, si quem, aut uerbum fefellit aequiuocum,
aut orationis Amphibologia decepit, aut sermonis proprietas imposuit, ex reliquis conijciendi quid uerum sit? Quod utilissimum
25 esse, et Augustinus sentit, et Origenes experimento didicit, et
Iacobus Faber Psalterij Quintuplicis editione docuit. [39]

1 dicam enim] *P 1563 1625*, dicam *S*   2 sit esse] *P 1625*, sit *S 1563;* se] *interl. P*   3
omnino possit] *P 1625*, possit omnino *S 1563*   6 finis erit?] *1625*, finis erit, *P 1563*, erit
finis *S;* inquis:] inquis? *P S 1563*, inquis. *1625*   6–7 commode] *S 1563 1625*,
commodae *P*   7 optime] *S 1563 1625*, optimae *P;* uersum] *1625*, uersum, *P S
1625*   8–9 immutandum] *P 1625*, mutandum *S 1563*   10 At] *corr. from* Ac *P*   14
ego] *P S 1563, om. 1625*   15 assignem] *S 1563 1625*, assigno *P;* illae] *S 1563 1625*, ille
P   17 canendam] *P S,* tenendam *1563*, cavendam *1625;* recepissent] *P 1563 1625*,
recepisset *S;* reliquas] *P S 1563*, reliquos *1625*   18 abijcere,] *1563*, abijcere *P*, abijcere.
S, abijcere? *1625*   19 sed] *P 1625*, imo *S 1563*   21 notitiam,] *S 1563*, notitiam *P*,
notitiam; *1625;* ita in] *P 1625*, ita tum ex *S 1563*   22 fefellit] *P 1625*, fefellisset *S
1563*   23 Amphibologia decepit] *P*, decepisset Amphibologia *S 1563*, amphibolia
decepit *1625*   23–24 imposuit] *P 1625*, imposuisset *S 1563*   24 sit?] sit. *P S 1563
1625;* Quod] *P 1625*, quod sane *S 1563*

First of all, to speak boldly, I think no human being, not even Jerome, has been so bold or so self-assured as to claim that he never missed anything at all as he translated; indeed, even average translators who come along after their betters will now and then find something on which they can make useful refinements. "Then will there be any end to translating?" you ask; yes, the easiest of ends, once it turns out that someone has translated so aptly or corrected another's imperfect translation so well that as long as his work stays intact no one later will find anything he thinks should be changed.

But meanwhile there is a risk that these differing translations may render the minds of the faithful unsure about which they ought to believe the most trustworthy, and you think that this is precisely why all the rest were deliberately rejected, while this one was saved, so that they would not cause the faithful to waver. On this point I disagree with you so completely that what you attribute to the care of our forefathers I assign to the carelessness of the times, which indeed allowed much else besides those translations to perish. Otherwise, even if our forefathers had required that only one be chanted in the churches, still, why was it necessary to throw out the others? There was no risk that these might cause the faithful to waver; indeed, just as now, through the differing accounts of the evangelists, the real sequence of events comes to be understood more distinctly, even so by comparing various translations the studious reader would be given the chance to note points where equivocal words or ambivalent syntax or the particular force of an idiom had misled some translator, and then, by consulting the others, to grasp the true sense by conjecture. What a useful procedure this is has been noted by Augustine, learned through personal experience by Origen, and confirmed by Jacques Lefèvre d'Etaples, the editor of the *Quincuplex Psalter.*

Atque hec ideo dixi ut ostenderem etiam si Diui Hieronimi
labor adhuc maneret integer, non illum tamen reprehenden-
dum esse, quisquis, si quid ab illo quoque preteritum inuenisset,
hoc ipse uelut relictas a messore spicas, colligeret. Nunc uero
5 quis non putet codices latinos nihilo minus atque olim e graecis
esse corrigendos, quum ita sint rursus infecti mendis, ut ne
uestigia quidem Hieronimianae emendationis appareant? Quod
usque adeo in confesso est, ut ipse tu qui maxime negas, fatearis
tamen. Nam quum ideo maxime contendas corrigendi laborem
10 frustra sumi quod Hieronimi castigationes asseris magna patrum diligentia seruatas esse integras, tamen in proximo fere
uersu subdidisti, "Responde iam Erasme utram probet aeditionem ecclesia? graecamne qua non utitur, an latinam quam
solam citat, quoties ex sacra scriptura aliquid definiendum est,
15 uel preterito Hieronimo, siquando aliter legat, quod quidem
non raro contingit?" Imo tu nunc [39v] responde Dorpi, si (ut
ipse dicis et uere dicis) non raro legat aliter Hieronimus, quam
uulgaris habet aeditio, quomodo potest esse uerum quod ante
dixisti, eandem editionem ita manere correctam, ut ille correx-
20 erat? Neque enim quenquam arbitror esse crediturum, illum
quicquam contra suam ipsius correctionem proposuisse legendum. Tam ergo nunc opus correctione est, quam olim fuit. An
tantundem liceat, hoc restat inquirendum. Quanquam nec inquirendum hoc nec dubitandum uidetur, quin emendati codices
25 tam nunc sint ecclesiae utiles, quam olim fuerunt.
   Sed "ecclesia nunc" inquis "istam editionem comprobauit."
Atqui eadem ecclesia eodem etiam modo eandem editionem,
ante Hieronimi correctiones approbauerat, id quod iam ante
respondi. Quanquam non pigebit eandem rationem tuam quam

---

5 olim] *interl. P*   7 appareant?] *1563*, appareant. *P S 1625*   8 tu qui maxime negas,
fatearis] *P 1625*, tu quoque qui id maxime negas, idem fatearis *S 1563;* maxime] *S 1563*
1625, maximae *P*   9 maxime] *S 1563 1625*, maximae *P*   11 tamen] *P 1625*, tum *S*
1563   12 subdidisti,] *1563*, subdidisti. *P*, subdidisti *S*, subdidisti: *1625*   12–16
Responde . . . contingit] *ital. 1625*   13 graecamne] *1563 1625*, graecam ne *P S*   14
est,] *1563 1625*, est *P*, est. *S*   16 contingit?] *1563 1625*, contingit. *P S;* ut] *P 1563 1625*,
tu *S*   17 legat aliter] *P 1563 1625*, legat *S*   20 illum] *S 1563 1625*, illum, *P*   22
An] *P 1625*, An uero *S 1563*   27 eodem etiam] *P 1625*, eodem *S 1563*   29
rationem] *P 1625*, orationem *S 1563*

I have said this much in order to show that even if St. Jerome's work were intact to this day there would still be no reason to censure whoever found something Jerome overlooked and then gathered it up like the ears left behind by a reaper. But as things actually stand, who can doubt that the need to correct Latin texts from the Greek is as great as it was in Jerome's day, since those texts are so choked with corruptions again that not even the traces of Jerome's emendation are still to be found? This is so generally acknowledged that even you, who deny it most stoutly, admit it yourself. For though your stoutest argument for claiming that there is no point in attempting to correct what we have is that the great diligence of our forefathers has kept Jerome's emendations intact, in the next line, almost, you go on to say: "Tell me this, now, Erasmus, which edition has the Church's approval, the Greek, which it does not use, or the Latin, which is the only text it quotes every time that it has to resolve some point according to holy scripture, not even deferring to Jerome if at times he has a different reading, which indeed often happens?" Rather you tell me this now, Dorp: if, as you rightly say, Jerome often has readings different from those of the Vulgate edition, how can what you said before be right, namely that this edition is still as correct as it was after he had corrected it? For I think no one is going to believe that he would have proposed any reading against his own correction. Thus the need for correction is just as great now as it was in his day. Whether it should still be as permissible has yet to be argued, even though it appears there is no room for argument or doubt as to whether emended texts are as useful today to the Church as they formerly were.

But you say, "Now the Church has approved this edition." But the same Church, as I already said, had approved the same edition in the same way even before Jerome's corrections. But I will not hesitate to examine your reasoning again, which you

tu tam inuictam censes denuo excutere, ne me praeteruehi quicquam dissimulanter putes. Videris ergo mihi sic colligere. Augustinus nec euangelio duxit esse credendum nisi ecclesiae compelleret Authoritas. At ecclesia comprobauit in hac [40]
5 translatione uerum esse euangelium, Consequitur ergo si quid
sit in graecis codicibus diuersum, ut uerum in illis euangelium
esse non possit. Hec est (uti mihi uidetur) argumentationis tuae
summa, quae mihi uidetur eiusmodi, quam non sit difficile soluere. Nam primum Ecclesia sic in latinis codicibus contineri
10 credit euangelium, ut fateatur tamen e graeco translatum. Credit ergo translationi, sed magis tamen archetypo. Credit euangelium in graecis esse uerum, in latinis uerum esse credit eatenus, quatenus fidit interpreti, in quo (ut opinor) nunquam
tantam habet fiduciam, quin eum labi cognoscat humana fragili
15 tate potuisse.

At in concilijs citatur ex latino codice, non ex graeco; Mirum
uero si latini ex latino citent codice, quasi ideo fecerint, ut de
industria fidem graecis archetypis abrogent. Apostoli nonne citabant ex prophetis secundum translationem septuaginta in
20 terpretum, omissa interim hebreici textus ueritate, dum graecis
scriberent? Nec ideo tamen Hieronimus [40v] factum putauit
esse preiudicium quasi graeca translatio quam Hebreica littera
apostolorum censeatur authoritate sincerior.

Ego certe hoc persuadeo mihi, idque (ut opinor) uere, quic
25 quid ad fidem astruendam faciat non esse a quouis melius uersum quam ab ipsis Apostolis perscriptum. Ideoque fit ut quotiens in latinis codicibus occurrat quicquam, quod aut contra
fidem aut mores facere uideatur, scripturarum interpretes, aut

7 uti mihi uidetur] P 1625, quantum perspicio S 1563   11 magis tamen] P 1625, magis
S 1563   16 concilijs] S 1563 1625, consilijs P   16–17 codice, non . . . codice, quasi]
P S 1625 codice, quasi 1563   18 graecis archetypis abrogent] P 1625, archetypis
abrogent graecis S 1563   21 scriberent] P 1563 1625, scribent S   23 censeatur] P
1625, censeretur S 1563   24 certe] S 1563 1625, certae P; uere] S 1563 1625, uerae
P   24–25 quicquid ad fidem astruendam faciat non esse] P 1625, quicquid ab apostolis nobis traditum est, non esse iam S 1563   25 esse] S 1563 1625, esse, P   25–26
uersum] S 1563 1625, uersam P   26 perscriptum] S 1625, perscriptam P,
praescriptum 1563   26–27 quotiens] P 1563 1625, quoties S

find so invincible, lest you think I am glossing over anything. Now then, you seem to be making the following inference: Augustine maintained that the gospel itself would not merit belief if the Church's authority did not decree that it must be believed. But the Church has approved the position that the true gospel is in this translation. Thus it follows that if the Greek texts ever differ from ours the true gospel cannot be in them. As it seems to me, this is the gist of your argument, which to me seems the sort that is not going to be hard to refute. For first of all, the Church believes that the gospel is contained in the Latin rendering—in such a way, however, that it grants that the Gospel was translated from Greek. Therefore it believes in the translation, but even more in the archetype. It believes that the true Gospel is in the Greek texts; it believes that the Gospel in the Latin texts is actually the true one to the same extent that it has faith in the translator, in whom I suppose it will never have so much blind faith that it forgets that he could have erred through human frailty.

But in councils they quote from the Latin text, not from the Greek. Well, how strange that Latin-speakers should quote from a Latin text, as if they did so in order to lessen our confidence in its Greek archetype! Did not the apostles occasionally set aside the authentic Hebrew text and cite passages from the prophets according to the Septuagint translation while writing for Greeks? Yet Jerome did not think that this set any precedent, as if the Greek translation ought to be judged more reliable than the letter of the Hebrew on the basis of the apostles' authority.

I for one am persuaded (and rightly, I think) that whatever contributes to building the faith has not been translated better by anyone than it was written by the apostles themselves. This is why every time a passage crops up in the Latin that apparently undermines faith or morality, the interpreters of scripture ei-

ex alijs alibi uerbis quid illud sibi uelit dubium expiscentur, aut
ad uiuum euangelium fidei, quod per uniuersam ecclesiam in
corda fidelium infusum est, quod etiam priusquam scriberetur a
quoquam, apostolis a christo, ab Apostolis uniuerso mundo
5 predicatum est, dubios eiusmodi sermones applicent, atque ad
inflexibilem ueritatis regulam examinent, ad quam si non satis
adaptare queunt, aut sese non intelligere, aut mendosum esse
codicem non dubitant, cuius morbi medelam censent aut a diuersis interpretationibus tanquam medicis implorandam (quod
10 tibi tam periculosum uidebatur) [41] aut uelut a fonte quodam,
ab ea lingua repetendam, unde ea scriptura in latinum profluxit
eloquium.

Verum tu mi Dorpi concedis, olim recte fecisse eos, qui latinos,
quanquam ab ecclesia receptos, atque approbatos codices e
15 graecis emendauerint, sed idem tamen negas nunc recte fieri,
propterea quod sit uerisimile ipsorum libros graecorum, aut de
industria fuisse deprauatos ab ipsis iam olim ab ecclesia Rho-
mana desciscentibus, aut postea saltem per incuriam uiciatos,
neque enim esse credibile, si latinorum, quibus perpetua fidei
20 cura fuit, codices paulatim tamen labefactati sunt, incorruptos
adhuc restare graecorum, apud quos ipsa iam olim fides corrupta sit. Hec ratio Dorpi non flexit Hieronimum, quo minus
instrumentum uetus ex Hebraeo sermone transferret, quanquam, si quid hic ualere debet, ibi multo magis debuit, quum
25 nemo nesciat Iudeos ex professo infestiores fuisse hostes Christianis omnibus, ut [41v] quibus in uniuerso repugnabant, quam

---

1 expiscentur] *1625*, expiscantur *P S 1563*   1–2 aut ad uiuum] *P 1625*, ad unius *S
1563*   3 priusquam] *P 1563 1625*, priusque priusque *S*   5 applicent] *1625*,
applicant *P S 1563*   6 examinent] *1625*, examinant *P S 1563*   8 censent] *1563 1625*,
censent, *P S*   9 interpretationibus] *S*, interpretationibus, *P 1563 1625*   10 tam] *P
1625*, iam *S 1563*   11 profluxit] *P 1625*, fluxit *S 1563*   13 recte] *S 1563 1625*, rectae
P   14 e] *S 1563 1625*, ae *P*   15 tamen] *S 1563*, tum *P*, tu *1625*   15 recte] *S 1563
1625*, rectae *P*   16 sit uerisimile] *P 1625*, uerisimile sit *S 1563*   16–17 de industria
fuisse] *S 1563*, de industria *P 1625*   19–20 fidei cura] *P 1625*, fides *S 1563*   20
paulatim tamen] *P 1563 1625*, tamen paulatim *S*   24 ibi multo] *P 1625*, ibi *S 1563;*
debuit] *P 1625*, debuisset *S 1563*   25–26 Christianis omnibus] *P 1625*, Christianis *S
1563*   26 repugnabant,] *S 1563*, repugnabant *P*, repugnabant: *1625*

ther tease out the meaning of the dubious passage from various statements found elsewhere or evaluate such dubious phrases according to that living gospel of faith which has been infused into the hearts of the faithful throughout the whole Church, the same gospel which, even before it was written by anyone, was preached to the apostles by Christ and by them to the whole of mankind; and then if these interpreters, bringing to bear on such phrases the inflexible standard of truth, cannot make them conform to it properly, they readily grant they have either mistaken the sense or the text is corrupt, for which they think it best (though you think it so dangerous) to solicit a cure from several different translations, like doctors, or else to obtain one direct from the source, so to speak, from the language whence all Latin texts of the scriptures derive.

But, my dear Dorp, you grant that back then men were right to emend, from the Greek, Latin texts which the Church had already received and approved, yet you claim it is not right to do so today on account of the likelihood that the Greeks' own books were either deliberately tampered with when the Greeks broke away from the Roman church many years ago or have at any rate grown faulty since then out of negligence, since you say it is hard to believe that the texts of the Latins have gradually deteriorated, even though they have never stopped caring for the faith, while the texts of the Greeks still remain uncorrupted though they let their faith itself grow corrupt many years ago. This argument, Dorp, did not keep Jerome from translating the Old Testament from Hebrew, though if it ought to have any weight with Erasmus it should have had much more weight with Jerome, since everyone knows that the Jews are avowedly more bitter enemies to all Christians, with whom they are thoroughly

graecos latinis, quibuscum communi Christianorum nomine
conuenerant, licet in quibusdam dissenserint. Et profecto (ut
uere dicam) uidetur mihi neutiquam credibile, ullam gentem in
deprauandos libros unquam conspirare uoluisse, ut ne dicam
5 nec potuisse quidem. Quae enim spes esse potuisset neminem ab
ea re alieno animo fore? aut clam id fore consilium, quod si
resciceretur (ut erat necesse, quum a Iudeis ad Christum, a
grecis ad latinos aliqui nullo non die perfugerent) nonne pre-
uidebant fore, quum nihil assequerentur, suae preterea parti
10 sese praeiudicium allaturos, si se faterentur eam fouere causam
quam sibi conscij essent non aliter posse se, quam codicum deprauatione defendere? Sed de Iudeis Hieronimus uiderit.
Graecos certe ab hac falsitatis suspitione liberat, uel istud, quod
in his de quibus eis nobiscum fuit controuersia, eorum libri cum
15 nostris consentiunt, [42] nec de littera unquam, sed de intellectu
litterae questio fuit. Quanquam nemini potest esse dubium, eos
si mutare uoluissent quicquam, non ea primum modo, sed sola
quoque fuisse mutaturos, quae pro nobis contra eos faciunt,
quae si falsassent, non fuisset causa tamen cur in alijs idem fac-
20 turi putarentur. Nunc uero quid comminisci quisquam possit,
cur alia falsare uelint, quum hec ipsa reliquerunt integra, quae
uel sola falsare uoluissent?

Sed incuria saltem uitiatos esse credi potest, praesertim si hoc
nostris contigit, quibus uerisimile est, libros fidei sicut fidem
25 ipsam maiori semper curae fuisse. Possem hic opponere non
Hieronimum modo, sed Augustinum quoque, quorum uterque

---

1 quibuscum] quibus cum, P quibus cum S 1563, quibuscum, 1625   2 dissenserint] S
1563, dissenserant P 1625   3 uere] S 1563, uerae P, uera 1625   4 uoluisse, ut ne
dicam] S, uoluisse (ut ne dicam) P, uoluisse, ut ne dicam, 1563 1625   5 nec] P S 1563,
ne 1625; quidem.] S 1625, quidem, P, quidem 1563   8 perfugerent] P 1625,
profugerent S 1563   9 fore,] S 1625, fore P 1563   10 allaturos,] allaturos? P S
1563, allaturos; 1625; si se] P 1563 1625, sese S   12 defendere?] 1625, defendere. P S
1563   13 certe] S 1563 1625, certae P; istud,] S 1563, istud. P, istud; 1625   16
litterae] S 1563 1625, littere P   17 sola] P S 1563, simul 1625   18 eos] P S 1625, eos
tamen 1563; faciunt] ⟨faciunt⟩ S   19 causa tamen] 1625, causa tñ P, cã S, causa 1563;
idem] corr. from ijsdem P   21 uelint] P 1625, uoluissent S 1563; reliquerunt] P 1625,
reliquerint S 1563; quae] 1563 1625, que P S   22 uoluissent?] 1625, uoluissent. P S
1563   26 Hieronimum modo] S 1563, Hieronimum P 1625

at odds, than the Greeks are to the Latins, with whom they agree in the shared name of Christians even though on some points they think differently. And indeed, in all honesty, I find it simply impossible to believe that any people has ever purposely conspired to tamper with its own books, not to mention that none could have done so. For could they have hoped that no one at all would object to the scheme, or that their plan would go undetected? Could they not all foresee that if it were revealed (and it would be, perforce, since every day some deserted the Jews to join Christ or the Greeks to join the Latins) they would not only not gain by the scheme, they would also discredit their own faction if they showed they supported a cause which they knew they could defend only by tampering with texts? But let Jerome deal with the Jews. The Greeks at least have this to clear them from that charge of falsehood: in the texts which gave rise to their controversy with us their books are consistent with ours; there was never any question about the text, but only about what the text means. Although no one can doubt that if they had wanted to change anything they would have changed first— indeed, only—those passages which support our position against theirs, and that if they had falsified those passages there would still be no reason to think they would do the same to others. But in actual fact can you imagine any reason why they might want to falsify others, since they left intact the very passages which are actually the only ones they would have wanted to change?

But one may still believe that their texts have at any rate grown faulty through negligence, especially if our own texts have done so, since it is plausible to assume that we have always devoted more care to the books of the faith just as we have to the faith itself. I could cite for the opposite viewpoint not only Jerome, but Augustine as well, who both think that Greek texts are not as

censet emendatiores esse graecos codices, quam latinos. Sed ego
ratione malo, quam authoritate contendere. Hoc certe assero
neminem esse tam cuiusquam libri incuriosum, ut ita transcri-
bendum locet, tanquam pensi sit habiturus nihil uiciosumne an
5 emendatum [42v] referat, quum alioqui possit operae et impen-
sis parcere, si omnino ne scribatur curet. Persuadeo ergo mihi
graecos etiam curasse ut diligentia in transcribendis ipsorum
libris adhiberetur, quod nemo dubitauerit qui libros eorum diligenter inspexerit. Hoc preterea rursus affirmo, apiculos, dis-
10 tinctiones, et accentuum notas in causa esse, quo minus facile
apud eos scribendo erretur, nec ab hoc affirmando deterreor,
quod tu hoc argumentum in aduersam partem retorsisti, propterea quod (ut ais) "facilius erratur, ubi multa sunt obseruanda."
Verum ego contra censeo, ibi minus facile errari, ubi facile er-
15 ratur, ut ego quoque Dialecticorum more aenigma proponam.
Verum sic opinor tamen imo sic experior, quemadmodum in
planicie dum festinamus intrepide, ubi nemo casum expectat,
sepe labimur, cum a precipicio salui sensim, nec nisi certo atque
explorato gressu descendamus, haud aliter euenire scribendo,
20 ut [43] ad exemplar perplexum, scriptor eo transcribat uerius,
quo uidelicet attentius, quum ex pulchro codice ipsa securitate
labatur. Quanquam et nostros uiciatos esse, et eos remansisse
sinceros, uel hinc elucescit, quod in nostris eadem nunc uicia
deprehendantur, quae Hieronimus olim censuit emendanda, In
25 illis eadem adhuc uidebis uerba, ex quibus ea Hieronimum constat emendasse. Ergo quas ille mendas olim eiecit, nunc non
licebit ex ijsdem codicibus rursus eijcere? Et quum relligiones

---

1 Sed ego] P 1625, Sed S 1563   2 certe] S 1563 1625, certae P   3 cuiusquam] P 1563
1625, cuiusque S; incuriosum] S 1563 1625, in curiosum P   4 pensi] pensi non P S
1563 1625; nihil] 1625, interl. P, om. S 1563; uiciosumne] 1625, uiciosum ne P S 1563
5 emendatum] S 1563 1625, emendatum, P; quum] P 1563 1625, quin S; operae] P 1563,
opere S 1625   5–6 impensis] corr. from impensae P   6 scribatur] S 1563, scribatur,
P 1625   7 diligentia] diligentia⟨m⟩ P; ipsorum] P 1563 1625, eorum S   9
inspexerit] P 1625, inspexit S 1563; apiculos] S 1563, apiculas P 1625   11 eos] P 1625,
eos in S 1563   14–15 erratur, ut] erratur ⟨Vbi multa sunt obseruanda.⟩ Vt S   17
intrepide] S 1563 1625, intrepidae P   18 sepe] S 1563 1625, sepae P   19
descendamus] S 1563, descendimus P 1625   23 eadem nunc] P 1563 1625 nunc
eadem S   24 deprehendantur] P 1625, deprehendimus S 1563   25–26
Hieronimum constat] P 1563 1625, constat Hieronimum S   27 ijsdem] S 1563 1625,
isdem P; eijcere] P 1625, expungere S 1563

corrupt as the Latin. But I wish to argue my case from reason and not from authority. I certainly maintain that no one cares so little about any book as to order a copy without feeling any concern about whether the copy he gets is a faulty or a sound one, since otherwise he could save himself time and expense by not ordering a copy at all. Therefore I am persuaded that the Greeks, too, took care to have their books copied diligently— which no one will doubt who inspects their books diligently. Furthermore, I assert that their vowel markings, punctuation, and accents make it harder for them to make scribal mistakes, and I will not be deterred from asserting this by the fact that you twisted this argument around for the contrary thesis, since you say it is easier to make a mistake where many things need attention. But I think, to the contrary, that it is harder to make a mistake where it is easy to make a mistake, if I too, like the dialecticians, may here pose a riddle. But I have the impression, or rather I know by experience, that just as we often fall down when we are hastening boldly along level ground, where no one expects to fall, whereas we do not fall when we climb down a slope very slowly, carefully weighing our steps, even so when a scribe has to copy from a difficult original he copies more accurately because he must copy more carefully, whereas he falls into error from sheer overconfidence when the text he is copying is neat. Another fact also makes it clear that our texts have grown faulty, whereas theirs have remained reliable: in ours one can now find the same faults that Jerome thought required emendation long ago, but in theirs you will still see the same words on which Jerome's emendations were obviously based. Thus, shall we be forbidden today to expel from the same texts the very corruptions Jerome expelled then, and though it is accepted

(quas uocant) omnes fas erit sepius, renascentibus uicijs refor-
mare, libros semel purgatos repullulantibus mendis nephas re-
purgare ducemus?

    Iam quod quaeris quid sit quod latinos codices non sinat incor-
5 ruptos, deinde tibi ipse respondes, "quid nisi Calcographorum
incuria pariter, et imperitia?" et illico subiungis, "uide iam utros
inuenies rariores; Qui graecis imprimendis sint idonei, an qui
latinis; et scies utros codices censere debeas castigatiores": Quid
tu his [43v] uerbis Dorpi uelis non intellego, neque enim te
10 uereri puto ne in adnotationibus in scripturas Erasmus impressis
utatur libris, cum neque scriptorum codicum desit copia, neque
in eam rem impressis uti etiam si uelit possit, quum nouum
testamentum, in quod eius desudat labor, nunquam hactenus
quod sciam graece calcographorum typis excusum sit. Quod si
15 hoc uoluisti dicere, quum calcographi graecas imprimant litteras
quam latinas deprauatius, idem in ueteribus etiam utriusque
linguae scriptoribus accidere, semoueamus istos Dorpi qui litteras sic latinas imprimunt, ut graecae magis quam latinae, sic
uicissim grecas ut arabicae magis quam graecae uideantur. Com-
20 paremus in utroque genere, qui utrumque possunt, cuiusmodi
Aldus Manutius Rhomanus erat in primis, et nunc quoque
Ioannes Frobenius Basiliensis. Hos atque huiusmodi calco-
graphos audeo affirmare, quod ipse cottidie experimentis comperio, uerius ac sincerius graeca, quam ipsa latina referre. [44]

1 erit] P 1625, sit S 1563; renascentibus] P S 1563, renasentibus 1625   3 ducemus] P
1563 1625, dicemus S   4 quaeris] P S 1563, quaevis 1625   5 ipse] P 1625 ipsi S
1563   5–6 quid . . . imperitia] ital. 1625   6 incuria] S 1563 1625, incuria, P;
imperitia?] 1563 1625, imperitia, P, imperitia S   6–8 uide . . . castigatiores] ital.
1625   7 rariores;] ra⟨tione⟩riores? P, rariores? S 1563 1625   8 castigatiores":] castigatiores. P S 1563 1625   9 his] P 1563 1625, is S   10 ne] S 1563 1625, nae P
10–12 impressis utatur . . . impressis uti] P 1563 1625, impressis, vti S   11 libris,]
libris P, libris: 1563 1625   13 labor,] S 1563 1625, labor P   14 graece] S 1563 1625,
graecae P; calcographorum] S 1563 1625, calographorum P   15 graecas] P 1563
1625, graecos S   17 accidere] P 1625, accidisse S 1563   18 latinas] P 1563 1625,
latinos S; graecae] P 1563 1625, grece S; latinae] P 1563 1625, latine S   19 graecae] P
1563 1625, grecae corr. from grecas S   21 in primis] S 1563, imprimis P 1625; nunc
quoque] P 1625, nunc S 1563   23–24 comperio,] 1563 1625, comperio P S   24
referre.] S 1563 1625, referre P

procedure to reform all religious orders (as they are called) as often as vices reappear in them, if corruptions reappear in books which have been corrected once before, shall we think it improper to correct them again?

Next you ask why it is that Latin texts grow corrupt, and you answer yourself, "Is it not the combined negligence and ignorance of the printers?" Then at once you proceed, "Look and see which are rarer, those fit to print Greek or those fit to print Latin, and then you will know which texts you ought to think sounder." I do not understand what you mean by these words, Dorp; I do not believe you can suspect that Erasmus may use printed books in his scriptural annotations, for there is no shortage of manuscript texts, nor in what he is doing could he use printed texts even if he wanted to, since (so far as I know) the New Testament, on which he is working so hard, has never yet been printed by any press in Greek. But if you meant to say that since printers print Greek worse than Latin, ancient scribes of both languages did likewise, Dorp, let us forget about those who print Latin so that it looks more like Greek and print Greek so that it looks more like Arabic; in both areas let us compare those who are competent in both, among whom Aldus Manutius the Roman was one of the greatest, as Johann Froben of Basel is today. I venture to assure you of what I myself know through daily experience: these printers and others like them reproduce Greek more accurately and reliably than they do even Latin.

Quod ipsum, multaque itidem alia ad hanc rem facientia
multo certius ipse legendo quam audiendo intelliges, si te quoque aliquando ad graecam linguam pernoscendam conuerteris,
id quod ualde opto, nam suasurus frustra sim, quod nec Eras-
5 mus persuasit, aduersus quem, imo temet aduersus ipsum, sedulo te defendis, ne cogare uidelicet ex graecarum litterarum
cognitione proficere. Quam ob rem ut ad eas te litteras pro
animo isthoc tuo tam aduersus eas obfirmato hortari super-
sedeo, ita pro meo in te amore optare tibi non desino, nec spem
10 tamen unquam depono, fore aliquando nec id quidem ita multo
post, ut cessantibus hac de re disputationibus, in quibus assidua
tua illa in Scholis uictoria non patitur te libenter cedere, quod (ut
uideo) iam nemo potest alius, ipse nimirum persuadeas tibi,
quum istos imperatores tuos quibus nunc militas, quorumque
15 interim gratiam tam magnae eruditionis parti praefers, aut ma-
turiore iudicio neglexeris, aut certe etiam [44v] illis ipsis, utile et
tibi et eorum consilijs fore persuaseris, quo uidelicet graecistas
istos suis ipsorum gladijs confodias, maioreque aduersus eos
authoritate disseras, quam nunc de re tibi tam in totum ignorata
20 disputes.

Qua de re tamen quum perinde scribas ac si superuacaneam
putes operam, quae in graecas litteras impenditur, mihi profecto
non persuades ea te sentire, quae scribis. Neque enim simile ueri
fit, te uel ea prudentia, commoditates eius linguae non uidere,
25 uel eo in bonas arteis omnes studio, non concupiscere, presertim
quum abs te quoque dum negligendam disputas, propemodum
afferantur causae, quibus incitari maxime ad eam consequen-

---

1 ipsum,] S, ipsum P 1563 1625   2 legendo] S 1563, legendo, P 1625   5 persuasit] P
S 1625, persuauit 1563; aduersus quem] P 1625, aduersum quem S 1563; aduersus
ipsum] P 1563 1625, aduersum ipsum S   6–7 graecarum litterarum cognitione] P
1625, graecarum cognitione litterarum S 1563   8 obfirmato] P 1563 1625, affirmato
S   9 desino] P 1625, desinam S 1563   10 depono,] S 1563 1625, depono P; nec id
quidem ita] nec id quidem haud ita P 1625, nec id quidem haud S 1563   14 tuos] P
1563 1625, tuo S; quorumque] P S 1625, quorumcunque 1563   16 certe] S 1563 1625,
certae P   17 tibi] 1563 1625, tibi, P S; fore] P 1563 1625, forte S   19 nunc] P 1625,
nunc quum S 1563   20 disputes] P 1625, disputas S 1563   21 ac si] S 1563 1625, acsi
P   23 ueri] ueri ⟨est⟩ P   24 fit] P 1563 1625, sit S   27 maxime] S 1563 1625,
maximae P

Your own reading would give you a much better understanding of this fact than hearsay does now, and indeed of much else
that pertains to this topic, if someday, of your own accord, you
would turn to the serious study of Greek. This is something I
very much long for, but I can scarcely hope to persuade you to
do so where Erasmus himself has failed, against whom—or
rather, against your own interests—you so earnestly defend
yourself against having to benefit from the knowledge of Greek.
Accordingly, even though, since you have such a stubborn aversion to Greek, it is pointless for me to exhort you to learn it, I
continue to long, indeed still dare to hope, for the day, none too
far in the future, when the debates on this topic have ceased,
when your long winning-streak in the schools has stopped making you loath to give way on this point, and when you will do what
I see no one else can do, namely, persuade yourself to learn
Greek. For by then you will either use your better judgment and
ignore those same generals whose cause you now serve, and
whose favor you prize more than such an important department
of learning, or else you will persuade even them that your Greek
will prove useful for their ends as well as to you, in that it will
enable you to rout those Grecophiles with their own weapons
and to argue against them with greater authority than you now
do by debating an issue about which you know nothing at all.

Even so, when you write on this issue as if you think it is quite
pointless to spend time on Greek, you do not persuade me, at
least, that you mean what you write. For it is not likely that you,
with your good sense, should not see the advantages of that
language, or that you, with your zeal for all forms of sound
learning, should not wish to acquire it, especially since you yourself all but advance the most excellent reasons for wanting to
learn it even as you are arguing that we ought to ignore it. For

dam possis. Nam si (ut tute uerissime certe ac sapientissime dixisti) unaquaeque lingua ea precipue dote prestat atque excellit
alias, si contingat ei ut maiorem bonarum disciplinarum thesaurum in suis litteris uelut arculis contineat, [45] Quis hac una
ratione tua, nesciat graecam esse eam quae summopere sit cum
uniuersis mortalibus, tum uero seorsum a Christianis amplec-
tenda, utpote a qua et omnes disciplinae reliquis, et nouum testamentum fere totum nobis foelicissime successit? nisi tu illam hoc
translationum cottidiano prouentu, uclut assiduo partu, effoe-
tam nunc tandem, atque exhaustam putas.

At primum ex his ipsis commentatoribus Aristotelis, quos tu in
illa oratione commemoras, quam siue ut Laurentium uituperes,
siue ut laudes Aristotelem (nam utrumque acriter et ex aequo
facis) elegantissime certe scripsisti, Alexandro iñquam, Themistio, Ammonio, Simplicio, Philopono, Olimpiodoro, Quotusquisque ex his inquam est, excepto uno Themistio, qui non adhuc sua tantum lingua legatur, nisi quod Alexandri Problemata
in latinum uenere sermonem? Ex reliquis si quid latine legitur
(neque enim ignoro haberi et Alexandri et Simplicij fra[45v]g-
menta) id totum tam est parum latinum ut a latinis propemodum
minus quam graeca intelligatur. Neque iam aut de poetis, aut
oratoribus dico quicquam, sed neque de alijs philosophis aut alijs
etiam eiusdem Aristotelis commentatoribus uerbum facio ul-

1 tute uerissime certe ac sapientissime] S 1563 1625, tutae uerissimae certae ac sapien-
tissimae P 2 unaquaeque] 1563 1625, unaqueque P S 3 maiorem bonarum] S
1563 1625, maiorembonarum P 5 cum] P 1625, cum ab S 1563 7 reliquis] P S
1625, reliquae 1563 8 foelicissime] S 1563 1625, foelicissimae P; successit?] successit.
P 1625, successit, S, successit: 1563; hoc] P 1563 1625, hac S 9 partu,] 1563 1625,
partu P S 12 quam] P 1625, quem S, quae 1563 13 acriter et] P 1625, acriter S
1563 14 elegantissime] S 1563 1625, elegantissimae P; scripsisti,] S 1563, scripsisti. P,
scripsisti,) 1625; inquam,] 1563 1625, inquam P S 15 Olimpiodoro] changed from
Olympiodoro P 17 sua tantum] P 1563 1625, sua S 18 sermonem?] 1625,
sermonem. P S, sermonem 1563; latine] S 1563 1625, latinae P 19 haberi et] et interl.
after haberi P 20 totum] totum ⟨eius⟩ P; totum tam est parum] P 1625, totum eius
generis est, ac tam parum S 1563; propemodum] S 1563 1625, pro pemodum P 21
quam] P 1625, quam ipsa S 1563; intelligatur] P 1625, intelligantur S 1563; iam aut] P
1625, iam S 1563 22 philosophis] S 1563 1625, philoso phis P

you said, very truly and wisely indeed, that any language excels and takes precedence over others primarily according to how great a treasure of sound learning it keeps housed in the vaults of its literature. Is not this by itself quite enough to convince anyone that all mortals, and especially Christians, should eagerly embrace Greek, since it is from Greek that the rest of mankind has received every variety of knowledge and that we have been fortunate enough to receive nearly all the books of the New Testament? Unless you think that Greek is worn out and exhausted at last by this steady outpouring of translations as if by continuous childbearing.

First of all, among those very commentators on Aristotle whom you mentioned in that elegant speech which you wrote to praise Aristotle (or was it to castigate Valla? you are equally vehement about both), among these very commentators, Alexander, I mean, Themistius, Ammonius, Simplicius, Philoponus, and Olympiodorus, how many of them (I say) apart from Themistius and the *Problems* of Alexander (for these have made their way into Latin) are yet read in any language but Greek? Anything by the rest of these authors that can be read in Latin (for I know that we do have some fragments of Alexander and Simplicius) is in such poor Latin that it is almost more obscure to Latin readers than the Greek is. I will say nothing here about poets or orators, nor will I say a word about other philosophers, or even about other commentators on Aristotle, although John

lum, quanquam uel unus Ioannes Grammaticus tantum habet
acuminis, tantum eruditionis, presertim Aristotelicae, ut si cum
eo posses ipsius lingua loqui, reduceret te satis scio unus ille
Grammaticus cum Grammaticis omnibus, quibus nunc parum
5 propicius uideris, in gratiam. At ex antiquis Christianae doctrinae scriptoribus, cum multo maximam partem graece constet
scripsisse, perpauci pro tanto numero uersi sunt, quidam uero
ita uersi, ut potius uideantur subuersi. Ad Aristotelem ipsum
uenio quem et ego ut supra multos, ita cum multis amo, quem tu
10 in memorata oratione tua uideris non supra multos modo, sed
pro multis quoque atque adeo pro omnibus [46] amplecti. Hic
ergo ipse non poterit totus tibi sine graecarum peritia litterarum
innotescere. Nam ut omittam illud quod nihil eius tam commode
uersum est, ut non idem suis ipsius uerbis acceptum in pectus
15 influat potentius, Et illud item quod quaedam opera eius adhuc
graeca feruntur, quorum titulos nescio an Latini habeant, Certe
ex his ipsis operibus, quae nunc habent, sic habent quaedam, ut
etiam non habeant.

E qua sorte ipsum etiam Metheorologicorum opus tam constat
20 esse, quam dolendum est, quum nescio an ullus ex tam multis
eius uiri laboribus dignior scitu sit, aut ipsa rerum natura ab ulla
sui parte mirabilior, quam ab ea, quae ut nobis proxima circum-
fusaque undique, ita magis ignorata atque incerta est quam as-
trorum positio, motusque siderum, quae tam porro semota sunt.
25 Sed hoc opus tamen, spero propediem fore ut a Thoma Linacro
nostrate, illustrissimi regis nostri medico latinis donetur auribus,
utpote cuius iam nunc duos libros absol[46v]uit, perfecissetque
nimirum opus, atque aedidisset uniuersum, nisi Galenus eum

---

2 Aristotelicae,] S 1563, Aristotelicae P, Aristotelicae; 1625   3 posses] P 1625, possis S
1563   3–4 ille Grammaticus] ille Grammaticus, P 1625, ille S 1563   5 Christianae]
Christianae ⟨ecclesiae⟩ P   6 graece] S 1563 1625, graecae P   11 pro . . . pro] P 1563
1565, pre . . . pre S   13 illud quod] P 1625, illud S 1563; commode] S 1563 1625,
commodae P   14 idem] P S 1625, idem ipsum 1563   15 potentius,] potentius. P S
1563, potentius: 1625; quaedam] 1563 1625, quedam P S   16 habeant] P 1563 1625,
habeunt S; Certe] S 1563 1625, Certae P   17 habent,] S 1563 1625, habent P   18
habeant.] 1563 1625, habeant, P S   19 E qua] S 1625, Ae qua P, aequa 1563; Methe-
orologicorum] 1625, MetheoroLogicorum P, Metereologicorum S, Meteorologicorum
1563   23 est] S, est, P 1563 1625   24 siderum,] 1563 1625, siderum P S   26 regis
nostri] P 1563 1625, regis S

the Grammarian, all by himself, displays so much subtlety and learning, particularly in Aristotle, that I know that if you could converse with him in his own language that single grammarian would reconcile you with all the grammarians, toward whom you now seem ill disposed. But then, even among ancient writers of Christian doctrine, the great majority of whom certainly wrote their works in Greek, only a very small fraction of these have been translated, while some have been translated so badly that it seems they have rather been travestied. I will come straight to Aristotle himself, whom I too esteem more than many but along with many others, whereas in the speech I have mentioned you seem to cherish him not only more than many but instead of many, and even instead of all. Now then, not even he will be totally accessible to you if you have not learned Greek. I will overlook the fact that none of his works has been translated so well that it does not make a greater impression when couched in his own words, and also the fact that even today there are Greek works believed to be his of which I do not think that the Latins have even the titles; but certainly out of those very works that they do have today they have some as if they did not have them at all.

It is as certain as it is regrettable that even the *Meteorologica* of Aristotle belongs to this category, though I do not think that any of his labors can yield more valuable knowledge or that any province of nature itself is more admirable than that which is closest to us and surrounds us, though about it we know so much less than about the position of the stars and the motions of heavenly bodies which are so far away from us. But I hope that this work will be made available shortly in Latin by my countryman Thomas Linacre, physician to our most illustrious king, for he has recently finished two books of it and would already have completed and published the work as a whole had not Galen, as

exorasset, ut quum ipse dux atque imperator medicae rei sit, uel
seposito interim Aristotele, Latinus, eius opera, prius ipse redderetur. Prodibit ergo Aristoteles aliquanto serius, sed prodibit
tamen nihil incultior, preterea nec incomitatus. Nam Alexandri
5 Aphrodisei commentarios in idem opus una uertit, initurus
apud Latinos omnes immortalem gratiam, in quorum non
uulgarem utilitatem philosophi prestantissimi operi tam egregio, prestantissimum interpretem sic adiunxerit, ut eius labore
demum ab Latinis possit intellegi, quod hactenus a nemine (ut
10 ego certe suspicor) qui graece nescierit intellectum est. Nam
quum ipse iam olim idem Aristotelis opus audirem graece,
eodem mihi prelegente, atque interpretante Linacro, libuit interdum experiundi gratia uulgatam etiam translationem inspicere, e cuius lectione mentem [47] illico subijt eiusdem philo-
15 sophi de physicis suis dictum. Nam ut illa sic ait aedita, ut tamen
aedita non sint, ita hec quoque sic uersa uidebantur, ut nullo
pacto uersa uiderentur, usqueadeo ut quae graece callebam
probe, eadem ipsa uersa non intelligerem.

   Neque est quod a latinis interpretibus sperari possit auxilium,
20 quum albertus quoque quem ad emulationem Alexandri magni
magnum uocant, quique se periphrasten Aristotelis profitetur,
paraphrastes uerius in eo opere iudicari debeat, ita, quum eius
officium sit Aristotelis sensum alijs uerbis referre, affert prorsus
(ut aiunt) ex diametro diuersa. At Gaitanus (nam is quoque facit
25 commentarios) describit nobis unus terrae pugillus, in quot pu-

---

1 quum ipse] *P 1625*, quum *S 1563*   2 Latinus,] Latinus *P S 1563 1625*; prius] *P 1625*,
prior *S 1563*   4 nihil] *P 1625*, nihilo *S 1563*; incultior,] *S*, incultior *P*, incultior: *1563*
1625; nec incomitatus] *P 1563 1625*, incontaminatus *S*; Alexandri] *corr. from*
Alexandrum *P*   7 prestantissimi] *S 1563 1625*, prestantissimi, *P*   10 graece] *S 1563*
1625, graecae *P*; nescierit] *P 1563 1625*, nesciuerit *S*   11 graece] *S 1563 1625*, graecae
P   12 prelegente] *P S 1625*, perlegente *1563*   13 experiundi] *P 1625*, experiendi *S*
1563   14 e cuius] *S 1563 1625*, ecuius *P*   15 tamen] *S 1563*, tñ *P*, tum *1625*   17
graece] *S 1563 1625*, graecae *P*   18 probe] *S 1563 1625*, probae *P*; eadem] *S 1563*
1625, eaadem *P*   20 *sidenote in 1563* Albertus Magnus   21 periphrasten] *corr. from*
perifrasten *P*; Aristotelis] Aristotelis ⟨uerius⟩ *S*; profitetur,] profitetur. *P*, ⟨vocat⟩ profitetur *S*, profitetur: *1563*, profitetur; *1625*   22 uerius in eo opere iudicari] *P 1625*,
uerius uero, in eo iudicare *S*, uerius uero, in eo opere iudicari *1563*   22–23 eius
officium sit] *P 1625*, sit eius officium *S 1563*   23 sit] *interl. P*   24 Gaitanus] *P S 1563*,
Cajeanus *1625*; *sidenote in 1563* Gaitanus

leader and prince of physicians, prevailed on him to put Aristotle aside for a while and to teach him to speak Latin first. Thus Aristotle will appear somewhat later, but by no means less polished; furthermore, he will not be alone. For Linacre is also translating the commentary on that work by Alexander of Aphrodisias; for all this he will earn lasting thanks from all readers of Latin, whom he will have done no common service by issuing this excellent work by that brilliant philosopher, along with this brilliant interpreter, so that his efforts will at last make it possible for readers of Latin to understand what I personally suspect no one has understood so far without knowing Greek. For some time ago, while I was studying the Greek text of that work by Aristotle under the tutelage of Linacre, I myself felt an urge to examine the common translation, as well, to see what it was like. What I read instantly made me recall that philosopher's saying about his own *Physics:* he said that work had been made public, but in such a way that it was not in fact public, whereas this work, it seemed, had been translated in such a way that it was not actually translated at all, to the point that the very ideas I grasped easily in Greek I could not understand in the translation.

Nor is there any help to be had from the Latin interpreters, since even Albert, whom they call "the Great" in emulation of Alexander the Great, and who claims to be giving us a paraphrase of Aristotle, might more truly be said to have given us a parody of this work, for though it is his job to express Aristotle's meaning in different words, what he actually does is to introduce meanings which are (as they say) diametrically opposed to it. And Gaetano (for he too wrote a commentary) tells us how many

gillos aquae liquescit, et aquae item pugillus unus in quot pugil-
los aeris dissoluitur, et quo non ulterius ad eundem modum
progreditur? Sed dum has tam immensurabiles mensuras
metitur, ad Aristotelis interim sensum ne Gry quidem. [47v]
5   Infinitum mi Dorpi fuerit explicare, quam multa desunt ei cui
greca desunt. Neque tamen ignoro, et alios multos, et te imprimis ipsum sine graecis litteris, ipsam doctrinae arcem uersus
eousque prouectum, quo multi non possint, etiam graece docti,
sudantes atque anhelantes ascendere. Sed hoc unum tamen au-
10 sim affirmare, si caeteris disciplinis tuis litteras preterea graecas
adieceris, quantum nunc alios etiam graece peritos exsuperas,
tantum tunc te etiam ipsum superabis.
    De Moria quoniam Erasmus qui eam olim meo patrocinio
commendauit, eandem rursus tuendam suscepit sibi, non est
15 necesse multa dissereŕe, quum res per se facilis reddita sit partito
labore facilior. Itaque ut non dubito quin ille sit ea dicturus, imo
in illa breui epistola iam nunc dixit, quae sufficere apud omnes
debent, ita ego quae dicam, quantulumcunque apud alios
ualitura sint, apud te (ut opinor) inualida esse non possunt. Et
20 primum miror quid hec sibi tua uerba uelint, "Ecce repente
in[48]fausta Moria tanquam Dauus interturbat omnia." At
quomodo nunc "repente"? quasi nunc primum Moria repente
prodierit, quae iam plus annis septem septies interim nouis ex-
cusa formis in clarissima luce uersata, in omnium sinus recepta
25 sit? Aut quamobrem quaeso "infausta," quae quam foelicibus
auspicijs processerit, nonne hoc abunde demonstrat, quod non

1 *1st* aquae] aquae ⟨aquae⟩ *P*   3 Sed] *P 1625*, Sed tamen *S 1563*   8 possint,] *S 1625*,
possint *P 1563;* graece] *1563 1625*, graecae *P*, graeci *S*   10 tuis] *P 1625*, tuis tu *S 1563;*
litteras preterea graecas] *P 1625*, graecas preterea litteras *S 1563*   11 etiam] *1625*, eī
P, et *S 1563;* graece] *S 1563 1625*, graecae *P*   11 exsuperas] *1625*, exuperas *P S*
1563   12 te etiam ipsum] *P 1563 1625*, etiam teipsum *S*   12–13 superabis. De] *P*
1625, superabis. Sed de his hactenus. De *S 1563*, Superabis. Sed de litteris hactenus. De
1947   13 quoniam] *S 1563*, quñ *P*, quum *1625*   14 sibi] *P 1625*, tibi *S 1563*   15
res] *P 1625*, res alioqui *S 1563;* facilis] *S 1563*, facilis, *P 1625*   16 Itaque ut] *P 1625*,
Itaque *S 1563*   20 uelint,] uelint. *P*, uolunt: *S*, uolunt, *1563*, uelint: *1625*   20–21
Ecce . . . omnia] *ital. 1625*   21 infausta] *S 1563 1625*, in fausta *P;* interturbat] *S 1625*,
interbat *P*, interturbabat *1563*   22 quomodo] *P 1563 1625*, quō *S*   25 sit?] sit. *P*
1563 1625, sit, *S;* quam] *S 1563*, q̃ *changed from* qᵃ *P*, quum *1625*   26 nonne] *P 1625*,
nonne uel *S 1563;* abunde] *S 1563 1625*, abundae *P*

handfuls of water we get when we liquefy one handful of earth, and how many handfuls of air when we evaporate one handful of water, and so on, with no end in sight; yet these measureless measures he measures do not add one iota to our understanding of Aristotle.

My dear Dorp, it would take me forever to list all that anyone lacks who lacks Greek. Nonetheless I am not unaware that without any Greek many others, and you above all, have advanced even higher toward the very citadel of learning than many can climb who do know Greek, however hard they strain and pant. Even so, I would dare to say this much is certain: if you would add Greek to the rest of your attainments you would then surpass even yourself by as much as you now surpass others regardless of their skill in Greek.

Since Erasmus, who once put me in charge of defending the *Folly*, has now undertaken to defend it himself, I do not need to argue its merits at length, for that task, which was already easy, is easier still now that we have divided the work. Thus, while I have no doubt that what he will say, indeed what he has already said in that short letter of his, ought to satisfy everyone, I also believe that what I have to say, which may not carry much weight with others, must carry at least some weight with you. And first, I wonder what you mean by saying, "And now all of a sudden, like Davus, this inopportune *Folly* is upsetting everything." But in what sense "now all of a sudden," as if the *Folly* had just now appeared, when in fact it has been circulating openly for more than seven years, known and cherished by all, going through seven new editions already? Or how is it "inopportune"? Is this not quite enough to show what an auspicious appearance it

debuisset totiens in tot exemplaria diffundi, nisi tam multos inuenisset, quibus impense placuerit, nec hos ex fece uulgi (neque
enim eas merces facile distractas esse mirarer, quae placerent
indoctis, quorum ubique turba scaturit) sed ex doctissimis? Nam
5 eam non nisi doctis placere, uel hoc indicio est, quod non nisi
docti intellegant, quod ipsum fortasse fuit in causa, ut hi quoque
duo aut tres Theologi, quos Moria commouit, irascerentur,
quod ab alijs persuasi credunt plus ab ea dictum, quam dictum
sit, alioquin fors non succensuri, si ea ipsa quae dicuntur, ipsi
10 intelligerent.

Sed tu mi Dorpi putas [48v] nullos rideri debuisse Theologos,
quanquam tales esse, quales Moria ioco descripsit, ipse propemodum serio fateris, quum ais, "Asperae facetiae, quibus
multum ueri admixtum est, acrem sui memoriam relinquunt."
15 Verum est hercle quod dicis, Non tam acriter has tulissent facetias isti Theologistae, nisi quam erant asperae, tam etiam uerae
fuissent. Ergo cum tales sint, quales ipse fateris esse, probas?
Non opinor. Vituperas ergo? apud te certe scio facis, faceresque
palam, nisi in animum induxisses tuum, nemini esse aduersus, et
20 ita te comparare statuisses, ut te omnes prorsus cuiuscunque
modi sint, docti indocti, boni malique laudent, cui (ut ais) uolupe
sit si uel catelli cauda uelut amicitiae symbolo blandiantur.

Facis tu profecto mi Dorpi cautius, sed nec ille tamen deterius,
qui in malos aperte, ac simpliciter, (quod Gerarduš facit
25 Nouiomagus) inuehitur, quanto minus qui quod Erasmus facit,
sumpta Moriae persona, et pudenter magis, et minus licenter
[49] iocatur, cuius quum iocos salesque non feras, et Palinodiam

1 totiens] P 1625, toties S 1563   2 placuerit] P 1625, placuisset S 1563   4 sed ex] P
1625, sed S 1563; doctissimis?] doctissimis. P 1563 1625, doctissimis S   5 1st non]
1625, ñ inserted P, om. S 1563; indicio] 1563 1625, inditio P S   6 intellegant] P 1625,
intelligunt S 1563; hi quoque] P 1625, hi S 1563   9 succensuri] P 1563 1625,
successuri S   11 debuisse] P S 1625, potuisse 1563   12 tales] P 1625, tales eos S
1563; descripsit] P 1625, describit S 1563   13–14 Asperae . . . relinquunt] ital.
1625   15 dicis,] S 1563, dicis. P 1625   17 tales] interl. P; fateris] P 1625, fatearis S
1563   18 certe] S 1563 1625, certae interl. P   20 1st te] te ⟨commodas⟩ P   21 sint]
P 1563 1625, sunt S   23 ille] P 1563 1625, illo S   24 aperte] S 1563 1625, apertae
P   24–25 sidenote in 1563 Gerardus Nouiomagus   26 pudenter] 1625, corr. from
prudenter P, prudenter S 1563   27 Palinodiam] P 1625, Palinodia S, παλινωδεῖν 1563

made, that it could not have been issued so often in so many copies had it not found so many whom it could delight? Nor did these readers come from the common herd of humanity (for I would not be surprised to see wares easily sold which pleased ignorant people, since there is a crowd of these everywhere) but rather from among the most learned. For one proof that Folly pleases only the learned is simply that only the learned understand her, which indeed was perhaps why those two or three theologians that Folly upset became angry: on the basis of what others told them, they thought she said more than she did, while perhaps if they themselves understood what was actually said they would not feel provoked.

But, my dear Dorp, you think she should not have laughed at any theologians, though you all but acknowledge in earnest that some are as Folly described them in jest when you say, "Biting quips which contain a large element of truth leave a bitter memory behind them." By heaven, what you say is true: those sham theologians would not be so embittered by those quips if they were not as true as they are biting. Now then, if those theologians are what you acknowledge them to be, do you prize them? I think not. Well, then, do you castigate them? I am sure that you do so in private, at least, and would do so in public if you had not made up your mind never to cross anyone and to behave in such a way as to make everyone praise you, of whatever character, learned and unlearned, good men and bad, since you say that you like even puppies to signal their friendship by wagging their tails at you.

Though I grant you are acting more cautiously, Dorp, that does not make it any less just to attack bad men simply and openly, the way Gerard of Nijmegen does, let alone to do what Erasmus does when he jokes about them both more decorously and less violently by assuming the character of Folly. Yet though you cannot tolerate his jokes and witticisms and you want him to

cani uelis, in Satyris Nouiomagi, ut scribis, nihil inuenisti quod
mutari uelles, quum tamen illae Satyrae sint mordaciores, ubi
sunt lenissimae, quam Moria, ubi mordet maxime, meritoque.
Nam id poeseos natura poscit, quae nisi sit acerba non est Satyra.
5   Itaque operae precium est uidere, quam Satirice in Monachos
ubique ac fratres inuehitur, ut illorum superbiam, luxum, inscitiam, compotationes, ingluuiem, Libidines, Hypocrisimque
describit, non minus eleganter quam acerbe, nec minus etiam
merito, quum, licet multi illis sint opprobrijs indigni non desint
10 tamen in quos uniuersa competant. Quamobrem non miror
quod nihil in eis repperisti, quod uelles mutari, sic uti nec ego
certe. Sed hoc miror, cur abs te non possit impetrare Moria ut
impune iocaretur in Theologos, quum illae abs te optineant Satyrae ut tam acriter obiurgent religiosos, atque in his Theologos
15 etiam.
        Sed omitto Gerardi satyras, si quis tuas [49v] mi Dorpi excutiat
epistolas, nihilne reperiri possit quo tu ullum hominum genus
aliquo mordaci dicto perstrinxeris? An illud edentulum prorsus
esse putas, quo in memorata epistola tua ad Dominum Menar-
20 dum Abbatem respergis antistites, qui dum illum laudas, alios
hoc pacto deploras? "Heu me heu miseros eos qui non religiosos
agunt. caballis stipati Caesaris triumphos nobis referunt, quos

1 cani] P S 1625, eum 1563; Nouiomagi] P 1625, Nouiomagi, tamen S 1563; scribis,]
1625, scribis P, scribis:) S, scribis) 1563   2 Satyrae] S 1563 1625, Satyre P;
mordaciores] 1563 1625, mordatiores P S   3 lenissimae] P S 1563, leuissimae 1625;
maxime] S 1563 1625, maximae P   5 uidere] P 1625, audire S 1563; Satirice] S 1563
1625, Satiricae P   7 Hypocrisimque] corr. from Hipocrisimque P   8 eleganter] S
1563, eleganter, P 1625; acerbe] S 1563 1625, acerbae P   9 quum, licet
multi . . . desint] P 1625, Nam multi licet . . . desunt S 1563   10 tamen in . . . compe-
tant] P 1625, tamen aliqui, in quos singula quadrent [quadrant 1563], quidam etiam
in . . . concurrant S 1563   11 quod nihil in eis repperisti] P 1625, nihil in eis repperisse
te S 1563; uelles mutari] P 1625, mutari uelles S 1563   12 certe.] S 1563 1625, certae,
P; miror,] 1563 1625, miror P S; non] interl. S   13 impune] S 1563, 1625, impunae P;
illae] P 1563 1625, ille S; abs te] S 1563 1625, abste P   14 obiurgent] S 1563 1625,
obiurgent, P   17 reperiri] P 1625, reperire S 1563   18 An] P 1563 1625, At S
19 memorata] corr. from memorta P; tua] P 1625, om. S 1563; ad Dominum] ad .D. P
1625, ad S 1563   20 qui dum] S 1563, qui P 1625   21 deploras?] deploras. P S,
deploras, 1563, deploras: 1625   21–110/2 Heu . . . peruenire] ital. 1625   22
agunt.] P 1625, agunt, sed S 1563

issue a palinode, you write that you found nothing in Nijmegen's
satires you would want him to change, even though those satires
are more cutting at their gentlest than Folly is at her most cutting; and so they might well be. For that is prescribed by the
nature of the poetry itself, which is not satire if it is not acerbic.
And so it is worth seeing how satirically he always attacks monks
and friars and how he describes their pride, luxury, ignorance,
drinking bouts, gluttony, lust, and hypocrisy, in a manner as
elegant, and indeed as appropriate, as it is acerbic. For though
many may not have deserved those reproaches, there are still
some who are open to all of them. Therefore I do not wonder
that you found nothing in his satires you would want him to
change; in fact, neither did I. But I do wonder why Folly could
not get your permission to joke freely about theologians when
those satires have your permission to aim such harsh reproaches
at members of religious orders and even at the theologians
among them.

But, putting aside Gerard's satires, if anyone pored through
your letters, my dear Dorp, could he not find any passage in
which you score some class of people with some cutting word?
Do you think there is no bite at all in the passage from your letter,
which I have mentioned already, to the lord abbot Menard, in
which you heap scorn on religious superiors? While you praise
him, you lament the rest thus: "Oh, alas, alas, for those miserable
monks who do not live like monks. Surrounded by horses, they
re-stage the triumphs of Caesar, though they would do better to

satius foret humi repere, quam ad inferos equites properare, ni
pedites timeant serius illuc peruenire." Hec mi Dorpi tam mor-
dax facetia usque adeo tibi blandita uidetur, ut ideo de equis
potissimum locutus uideare, ne tam bonum dictum perderes,
5 alioquin opinor uides non usque͏̀adeo magnum facinus esse si
abbates equitent, et bestijs in quos creati sunt usus utantur. Audiui etiam nec alios antistites equitare semper, et illum tuum
interdum, ut in illum ipsum pene iocus tuus recidat, a quo eum
cupis in alios auertere. Sed ita sua cuique blanditur ratio, tam
10 bene suus cuique crepitus olet, ut quum ad aliorum iocos frontem contrahimus, et uelut [50] asperos non patimur, nostros
neque magis festiuos, et magis mordaces amplectamur.

Sed hec in religiosos antistites iocatum te negabis, uerum deplorasse te dices potius, presertim quum ab illa inauspicata inter-
15 iectione auspicaris, "Heu." Ego certe quacunque figura proferatur, iocum puto, quod ita dicitur, ut nemo sine risu audiat.
quanquam quid refert ioco an serio mordeas? imo refert adeo
quum nemo fere sit qui iocoso in se dicto non arrideat, serium
nemo sit qui ferat. Alioqui si deplorare licitum, iocari uetitum
20 putas, facile Moriae fuerit toti orationi iocosae, interiectionem
dolendi preponere, et mutata figura Theologos eosdem quos
ante derisit ijsdem uerbis denuo deplorare, neque enim facile
discernas utrum deplorandi magis an ridendi sint.

Sed in Antistites fortasse quiduis licere debet etiam mediocres,
25 at in Theologos utut sint, licere debet nihil. Nam eo fere tendunt
quae in hac nouissima ad Erasmum scribis epistola. Ais enim,

8 interdum] *P 1625*, interim *S 1563;* illum] *P 1625*, illum etiam *S 1563*   11
contrahimus] *corr. from* conthrahimus *P;* et] *P S 1625*, ut *1563*   12 amplectamur] *S*
1563 1625, amplectimur *P*   13 antistites iocatum te] *P 1563 1625*, te antistites iocatum
S   13–14 deplorasse te dices] *P 1625*, deplorasse *S 1563*   15 auspicaris,] *1563*
1625, auspicaris *P S;* Heu] *ital. 1625;* certe] *S 1563 1625*, certae *P;* quacunque] *P S 1563*,
quaecunque *1625*   15–16 proferatur,] *1625*, proferatur *P S 1563*   16 audiat.] *S*
1563 1625, audiat, *P*   17 quanquam] *P 1563 1625*, Quanque *S;* mordeas?] *1563 1625*,
mordeas, *P S*   18–19 serium nemo] *P 1625*, serium qui nemo *S*, nemo *1563*   20
iocosae *P S 1625*, iocose *1563*   21 preponere] *P S 1625*, proponere *1563*   22
ijsdem] *S 1563 1625*, isdem *P;* neque] *S 1563 1625*, (neque *P*   25 utut] *1563*, ut ut *P S*
1625   26 ad] *S 1563 1625*, Ad *P;* enim,] *1563*, enim *P S*, enim: *1625*

creep on the ground than to gallop on horseback to hell, unless they are afraid they cannot get there as quickly on foot." Cutting as it is, my dear Dorp, this quip seems to have charmed you so much that you seem to have brought up the subject of horses expressly in order to keep that fine saying from going to waste. Otherwise, I think you are aware that it is not such a terrible outrage for abbots to ride and use animals as they were designed to be used. Besides, I have heard that not all other religious superiors ride about all the time, and that Abbot Menard rides occasionally, so that your joke very nearly recoils on the very man you wish to spare when you aim it at others. But so charming does everyone find his own notions, so fragrant does everyone find his own farts, that while we wrinkle our foreheads at other men's jokes and condemn them as bitter we cherish our own even when they are not as amusing and more bitter still.

But you will deny you were joking about religious superiors and will say you were rather lamenting them, especially since you start out under the auspices of that inauspicious interjection, "Alas." I personally regard anything as a joke—in whatever figure of speech it is couched—which is said in such a way that no one can help laughing who hears it. Although what difference does it make if you are being cutting in jest or in earnest? Or rather, it does make a difference: virtually no one refuses to laugh at a jocular saying aimed at him; no one stands for a serious one. Otherwise, if you think it all right to lament, but forbidden to joke, it will be easy for Folly to preface her whole joking discourse with one interjection of woe and thus, changing the figure of speech, use the same words again to lament the very theologians that she originally ridiculed. Nor indeed could you easily tell whether they are more lamentable or laughable.

But perhaps we should think it permissible to say anything we like against religious superiors, even average ones, but forbidden to say even a word against any theologians, no matter how bad. After all, you write words to almost that effect in your most recent letter to Erasmus. For you say, "You are surprised that

112   LETTER TO DORP

[50v] "Miraris tantos conciuisse motus tuam Moriam quae plurimis placet, non Theologis modo sed episcopis etiam. Atqui ego
te demiror Erasme qui pluris facias Episcoporum in hac re
iudicium, quam Theologorum, Si quidem Episcoporum nostri
5 saeculi uitam, mores, eruditionem dicam an inscitiam? noueris,
quorum ut sunt certe nonnulli tanto digni fastigio, ita mira est
paucitas." Hic tu Dorpi quum Theologos egre leuissimo ioco
patiaris aspergi, Episcopos apertis opprobrijs magna cum Authoritate perfundis, ut in quibus non tantum eruditionem re-
10 quiris, et carpis inscitiam, sed uitam quoque ac mores con-
tumeliose condemnas. Sed Theologos plurimum refert (ut ais)
integrae apud populum authoritatis esse, quasi nihil referat
apud populum quales estimentur episcopi, qui quem locum teneant in ecclesia Christi, quam longe supra Theologos tuos, non
15 est ignotum tibi, qui pontifices liquidissime nouisti in Apostolorum successisse locum. Neque cautius prospexisse te putes
[51] tibi quod nonnullos fateris episcopos tanto dignos esse fastigio, quum nec ipse Moriam credas indignorum uicia dignis
imputare Theologis, quae tamen uel hoc te uincit, quod nihil
20 impedit per eam multos dignos esse Theologos, at episcoporum
per te bonorum non modo paucitas est, sed etiam mira paucitas.

Sed donemus hoc tibi nihil esse mali, pontifices uel ridere
dicterijs, uel maledictis incessere, modo ne sacrosanctos Theologorum magistratus attingas. Quid ad hoc dices quod illos
25 ipsos Theologos non nomine quidem sed descriptione tam eui-
dente, ut non ullo nomine designari potuissent expressius, ita

1–7 Miraris . . . paucitas] *ital. 1625*   1 motus] *S 1563 1625*, motus, *P;* quae] *1563 1625*,
que *P S*   1–2 plurimis] *P 1625*, pluribus *S 1563*   3 te] *interl. P S*   4
Theologorum,] Theologorum. *P S 1563 1625*   5 noueris,] *S*, noueris. *P*, noveris: *1563*
1625   6 certe] *S 1563 1625*, certae *P*   7 egre] *S 1563 1625*, egrae *P*   9
perfundis,] *S 1563*, perfundis *P*, perfundis: *1625*   10–11 contumeliose] *S 1563 1625*,
contumeliosae *P*   12 authoritatis esse] *P 1625*, esse authoritatis *S 1563*   14 Christi,]
1563 1625, Christi *P S;* longe] *S 1563 1625*, longae *P*   15 liquidissime] *S 1563 1625*,
liquidissimae *P*   16 prospexisse] *P S 1563*, perspexisse *1625;* te putes] *P 1625*, putes *S*
1563   17 fateris] *P 1625*, feceris *S 1563*   17–18 fastigio,] *S*, fastigio *P*, fastigio:
1563, fastigio; *1625*   18 Moriam credas] *P 1563 1625*, credas Moriam *S*   19 quae]
1563 1625, que *P S*   20 Theologos,] *S*, Theologos. *P 1563 1625;* at] *interl. P*   20–21
episcoporum per te] *P 1563 1625*, per te episcoporum *S*   21 paucitas est] *1625*, est
interl. after paucitas *P*, paucitas *S 1563*   23–25 sacrosanctos Theologorum . . . ipsos
Theologos] *P 1563 1625*, sacrosanctos Theologos *S*   24 ad hoc] *1563 1625*, adhoc *P*

your Folly, who pleases so many, not only theologians but also bishops, has provoked such an angry reaction. But Erasmus, I myself am amazed that you value the judgment of bishops in this regard more highly than that of theologians, since you are well acquainted with the life-style, the character, and the learning (or should I call it the ignorance?) of the bishops of today; for although there are certainly some who are worthy of such a high place there are actually amazingly few." Here, Dorp, even as you refuse to let theologians be touched with the most harmless joke, you yourself pour down open abuse on the bishops, with all your authority; for you not only find them deficient in learning and carp at their ignorance, but you furthermore savagely criticize their life-style and character. But you say it is very important that the authority of theologians should not be impaired in the eyes of the people, as if it is not at all important how bishops are looked on by the people, even though you are not unaware what position they hold in Christ's church or how much higher than your theologians they stand, since you know very well that bishops are the successors of the apostles themselves. Nor should you think you have made yourself any safer just because you acknowledge that there are some bishops who are worthy of such a high station, since not even you believe that Folly is imputing the defects of unworthy theologians to worthy ones. Indeed, Folly outdoes you in tact: nothing she says denies that there are many worthy theologians, whereas you say not merely that there are few good bishops but even that there are amazingly few.

But suppose that we grant you that there is no harm in attacking bishops with either mockery or slander provided that you do not aim one word at the sacrosanct office of theologians. How will you answer this, that you yourself treat those very theologians so cuttingly that you practically tear them apart—not by name, I concede, but by describing them so plainly that, even by name, they could not have been indicated more clearly—in the

mordes, ut pene laceres, in prohoemio quod in Pyrgopolinicen Plauti fabulam lepidissime conscripsisti?

Verum interim Plauti me nomen admonuit eorum quae tu sparsim per epistolam tuam in Poetas ex Beati Augustini uerbis
5 congeris, quae res longiorem disquisitionem flagitat, quam ut a me in hac disputetur epistola. Sed hoc tamen abs te quero utrum tibi illis uerbis [51v] hoc uoluisse uidetur Augustinus, Christianis uidelicet non esse legendum Therentium? quod si ab eo perdiscendo non deterreat, nihil aduersus poetarum lectiones facit ille
10 locus. sin Augustinum id egisse putas, ut a poeseωs studio Christianos auerteret, rursus abs te percontor, Ipsene Therentium adhuc docendum censeas? quod si censes, quid attinet id tam citare diligenter, cui non putas esse parendum? Sin docendum neges, ab Augustino uidelicet persuasus, miror profecto quo
15 pacto acciderit, ut tandem nunc primum tam sero persuaserit ille, quem te non dubito tam diu ante legisse, nec interea tamen abstinuisse a Plauto legendo, docendo, exhibendo, agendoque publice, Poeta nihil quam Therentius est castiore, imo nec tam casto quidem. Quid quod militem gloriosum facetissimo prologo
20 locupletasti, Aululariae, non prohoemium modo, sed qui comediae defuerat, finem adiecisti, qui mihi seu sermonis elegantia spectetur, seu sa[52]les uere Plautini, nulla parte totius comediae uidetur inferior?

---

1 quod] P 1563 1625, quid S; Pyrgopolinicen] 1625, changed from Pyrgopolynicen P, Pyrgopolim S, Pyrgopolinicem 1563   2 lepidissime] S 1563 1625, lepidissimae P   4 tuam in Poetas] P 1625, tuam, cum in [tu S] ceteros poetas, tum in Terentium nominatim S 1563; ex Beati] P 1625, ex S 1563; uerbis] S 1563 1625, uerbis, P   5 congeris,] S, congeris. P 1625, congeris: 1563   6 disputetur] corr. from disputatur P; epistola.] S 1563 1625, epistola P; abs te] S 1563 1625, abste P; utrum] corr. from utrumque P   7 tibi] P 1625, ibi S 1563; illis uerbis] P S 1625, illis 1563   8 non] interl. P   9 deterreat] corr. from perterreat S   10 locus.] S 1563 1625, locus, P; egisse] P 1563 1625, legisse S; putas,] S 1563 1625, putas P; poeseωs] P, poeseos S 1563 1625   11 abs te] S 1563 1625, abste P; percontor,] 1625, percontor. P, percunctor: S, percunctor, 1563   12 censeas?] 1563, censeas, P S, censeas. 1625   13 putas] P 1625, putes S 1563   14 neges,] S 1563 1625, neges P   16 ante] P 1625, antea S 1563; interea] corr. from poeta P   17 Plauto legendo, docendo] P 1625, legendo Plauto, nec a legendo tantum, sed nec a docendo S 1563   18 publice,] S 1563 1625, publicae P   19 quod] P 1625, quod eiusdem S 1563   20 locupletasti,] locupletasti P S, locupletasti? 1563 1625; Aululariae] P 1625, Aululariae uero S 1563   20–21 comediae] corr. from commediae P   22 spectetur] P 1563 1625, spectatur S; seu] P 1625, siue S 1563; sales] P S 1625, sales, sales 1563; uere] S 1563 1625, uerae P   23 inferior?] inferior. P 1563 1625, inferior, S

elegant prologue you wrote for Plautus' play, the *Pyrgopolynices?*

But meanwhile Plautus' name has reminded me of the words you excerpt from Saint Augustine and turn against poets a number of times in your letter. This subject calls for a more thorough discussion, and I will not debate it in this letter. Still, I will ask you this: does it seem to you that by these words Augustine himself meant that Christians ought not to read Terence? For if he is not warning us against making a thorough study of Terence, then that passage affords no support for an argument against reading poets. But if you think that Augustine was trying to make Christians abandon the study of poetry, my next question is this: do you personally feel that Terence still ought to be taught? If you feel that he should, why keep quoting a warning which you do not think we ought to obey? But if, following Augustine's advice, of course, you maintain that Terence ought not to be taught, then I certainly do wonder why it took you so long to accept his advice, which you doubtless had read long before, even though in the meantime you did not refrain from the reading, the teaching, or the public production and staging of Plautus, a poet no chaster than Terence, or rather, not even as chaste. What of this, that you furnished the *Miles gloriosus* with a most charming prologue and supplied for the *Aulularia* not only a prologue but also that comedy's missing ending, a supplement which seems to me not inferior to any other part of the comedy for either its elegant language or its true Plautine wit?

Cuius rei uel isti ipsi uersus erunt indicio, quibus (ut dixi)
Theologos istos amusos, quos nunc tueris, ita belle describis, ut
nemo derideat salsius, nemo insectetur uehementius. Nam quid
his carminibus (referam enim) uel magis facetum possit esse uel
5   magis elegans?

> Primum omnium, qui sint amusi, et litteris
> Non proletarijs male inaugurati, eos
> Ablegat hinc in maximam malam crucem
> Siquidcm stomachabundi oblatratores facere
> 10 Pergant etiamdum, quod nunquam non factitant,
> Clamoribus ampullosis infremere, et
> Venena liuoris effunditare sui,
> Et obloqui, et oggannire, et dentibus omnia
> Arrodere carniuoracibus, et sicut canes
> 15 Solent, quibuslibet allatrare sibi obuijs. [52v]
> Eos homines (si quidem sint et ipsi homines
> Quum illiterati sint, quum sint agrarij),
> Mihi sedulo iussit Plautus hinc abigere.
> Sin forte sint presto, nisi comprimant sibi os
> 20 Nihilque graxint, minatust fore ulmeos
> Vbi hospitio excipientur acherontico.

En mi Dorpi quam neque poetis abstinendum putasti, et amusos
illos Theologos quam bene suis coloribus depinxisti. Quod si te
neges tunc fuisse Theologum, siquidem scripta sunt abhinc sep-
25 tennium, certe uix sesquiannus elapsus est, quod eadem recol-
lecta aedidisti, iam certe Theologus quadriennio post habitam

---

1 isti] *P 1625*, hi *S 1563*   2 tueris,] *1563 1625*, tueris *P S;* belle] *S 1563 1625*, bellae
P   6 sint] *P 1625*, sunt *S 1563*   9 stomachabundi] *1563*, stomachabundi, *P S
1625*   10 factitant,] *1563*, factitant *P S*, factitant; *1625*   12 sui,] *S 1563 1625*, sui
P   15 obuijs.] *1563 1625*, obuijs *P S*   16 Eos] Eos ⟨os⟩ *P;* sint et] *P 1625*, et *S 1563;*
homines] homines) *P S 1563 1625*   17 agrarij),] agrarij. *P*, agrarij *S*, agrarij, *1563
1625*   18 abigere.] *1563*, abigere *P S*, abigere: *1625*   20 Nihilque] *P 1625*, Nihil
quique *S*, Nihil quoque *1563;* minatust] *P 1625*, minatus est *S 1563*   22 quam] *P 1563
1625*, quod *S*   25 certe] *S 1563 1625*, certae *P;* elapsus est] *P 1625*, est elapsus *S
1563*   26 certe] *S 1563 1625*, certae *P*

What I mean may be illustrated by those very verses in which, as I said, you provide such a handsome description of those uncultured theologians, whom now you defend, that no one could mock them more wittily and no one could attack them more forcefully. For what could be more charming or elegant than the verses which I shall now quote?

> To start with, all of those uncultured louts
> Whose erudition ends with uncouth books
> Can beat it, Plautus says, and go to hell
> Should they, malicious snarlers that they are,
> Do any more of what they do continually,
> Bellowing out their windy disapproval,
> Venting the poison of their chronic envy,
> Bad-mouthing, snapping, sinking grisly fangs
> In everything, and, just the way that dogs do,
> Barking like mad at everyone they meet.
> This sort of men (if they are really men,
> Illiterates and bumpkins that they are)
> Plautus told me to drive away on sight;
> Should any stay to hoot and interfere,
> He promised them a beating for a greeting
> When they become his fellow guests in Hades.

Observe, my dear Dorp, just how little you thought about shunning the poets and just how well you painted those uncultured theologians in their natural colors. But if you deny that you were a theologian yourself then, since you wrote these lines seven years ago, certainly no more than a year and a half has elapsed since you published them in a new collection; and by then you were certainly a theologian, four years after you gave your bril-

luculentissimam orationem tuam de Assumptione Deiparae Virginis. Quid ergo refert an Theologus effeceris, an prius facta Theologus aedendo comprobaueris?

Ergo mi Dorpi dum e dentatis Gerardi Satyris, quibus re-
5 ligiosorum spurcissima [53] describit uicia, nihil mutandum censes, dum ipse religiosorum antistitum sic misereris ut rideas, sic rides, ut mordeas, caeterorum episcoporum, preterquam mire paucorum, inscitiam, uitam, ac mores acerbe uituperas, dum Theologos istos ipsos in quorum moriam, Moriam iocari
10 nephas ducis, ipse amusos uocas, oblatratores, stomachabundos, litteris non proletarijs male inauguratos, ampullosis infrementes clamoribus, uenena liuida effundentes, obloquentes, obgannientes, dentibus omnia carniuoracibus arrodentes, in obuios quosque sicut canes solent allatrantes, illiteratos, agrarios,
15 postremo uix homines in maximam malam crucem censes ablegandos, Dum haec mi Dorpi facis, quomodo tibi non uenerunt in mentem tua tam bene consulta consilia, quibus Erasmum nunc tam amice ac tam prudenter admones? Vbi tunc illud Hieronimi? "Extremae dementiae nihil aliud quam odium se
20 fatigando querere." [53v] Vbi tunc illud Cornelij Taciti? "Asperae facetiae quibus multum ueri admixtum est acrem sui memoriam relinquere." Quo tunc fugerat illud Epicteti? "Ne putes omnibus iucunda auditu, quae tibi sunt iucunda dictu."

---

1 Deiparae] S *1563 1625*, Deipare *P*   1–2 Virginis] *P 1563 1625*, Virginis Mariae *S*   3 comprobaueris?] *1563 1625*, comprobaueris. *P*, comprobaueris, *S*   3–4 comprobaueris? Ergo] *P 1625*, comprobaueris, imo refert adeo. Nam ad scribendum impetu plerunque trahimur, intermissa quum retractamus certum adhibetur iudicium. Ergo *S 1563*   4 e] S *1563 1625*, ae *P*   4–5 religiosorum] *P 1625*, Monachorum *S 1563*   6 censes,] *S,* censes *P*, censes: *1563 1625;* ipse] ipse ⟨studiosorum⟩ *P*   7 rides] *corr. from* rideas *P*   8 mire paucorum,] *1563 1625*, mirae paucorum *P*, mire paucorum *S;* acerbe] *S 1563 1625*, acerbae *P;* uituperas,] *S,* uituperas *P*, uituperas: *1563 1625*   9 in quorum moriam, Moriam] *P 1625*, quorum in Moriam *S*, quorum in moriam, Moriam *1563*   12 effundentes] *P 1563 1625*, effunditantes *S*   12–13 obgannientes,] *S 1563 1625*, obgannientes *P*   16 ablegandos,] ablegandos. *P 1563*, ablegandos: *S 1625*   17 tua] *P 1625*, tua illa *S 1563*   18 amice] *S 1563 1625*, amicae *P;* admones?] *1563 1625*, admones. *P*, admones: *S*   19 Hieronimi] *P 1625*, Sallustij *S 1563;* Extremae] *P 1625*, extremae esse *S 1563*   20 Taciti?] *1625*, Taciti. *P*, Taciti *S*, Taciti, *1563*   22 relinquere.] *1625*, relinquere *P*, relinquunt. *S*, relinquunt? *1563;* fugerat] *P 1625*, fuget *S*, fugiat *1563;* Epicteti?] *1625*, Epicteti. *P S*, Epicteti, *1563*   23 iucunda] iucunda ⟨esse⟩ *P*   23–120/1 auditu, quae . . . dictu." Profecto] *P S 1625*, auditu? Profecto *1563*

liant speech on the assumption of the Virgin Mother of God. Now, then, what difference does it make if you wrote these lines as a theologian or if, having become one, you gave your blessing to lines written earlier by choosing to publish them?

Well, then, my dear Dorp, when you found nothing you thought should be changed in Gerard's mordant satires describing the filthiest vices of the religious orders, when you yourself mocked as you pitied religious superiors and mocked in a way that would wound, when you acerbically castigated the ignorance, life-style, and character of all but "amazingly few" bishops, when you yourself called the very theologians whose folly you think it improper for Folly to joke about "uncultured louts," "malicious snarlers," men "whose erudition ends with uncouth books," who "bellow out their windy disapproval," who "vent the livid poisons of their envy," who "bad-mouth, snap, and sink their grisly fangs in everything," who "bark like dogs at everyone they meet," and who, "illiterate bumpkins," barely men, at last you said should simply go to hell, when you did all this, my dear Dorp, just how was it that you never thought of the same cautious counsels on which you now base your most friendly and prudent advice to Erasmus? What had become of that saying from Jerome, "It is totally insane to work hard just to make people hate you"? What had become of the one from Cornelius Tacitus, "Biting quips which contain a good deal of truth leave a bitter memory behind them"? What had happened to the one from Epictetus, "Do not suppose everyone will enjoy hearing what you enjoy saying"?

Profecto mi Dorpi charissime sic est a natura comparatum, ut modum semper ab alijs exigamus, libertatem omnes indulgeamus nobis. Noui ego qui Reuclinum (Deus bone, quem uirum?) non satis aequo animo ferrent quod in emulos suos
5 uidelicet imperitissimos doctissimus, in stupidissimos uir prudentissimus, in uanissimos nebulones homo integerrimus, ab ijsdem tam immani lacessitus iniuria, ut si manu se uindicasset, ignoscendum ei uideretur, Noui tamen inquam qui non ferrent (quanquam eius etiam studiosi) quod stilo contra illos libere, nec
10 magis libere tamen quam uere, affectus suos effunderet. Noui itidem eos ipsos, qui non ferebant, paulo post in rebus et minoris momenti, neque ad se tam proprie pertinentibus [54] multo etiam atrocius excandescere. Tanto nimirum procliuius est alienis affectibus quenquam temperare, quam suis. "Ergo non lic-
15 uit" inquis "mihi uel satyras Gerardi probare, uel in Theologos amusos, adde antistites atque episcopos quoque uel ioco uel serio dicere, modo uera, neque nominato quoquam?" Imo uero mi Dorpi usque adeo licuisse tibi censeo quod fecisti facere, ut mihi nihil unquam in uita melius fecisse uidearis, modo ea ne desit
20 aequitas qua tibi quod laudi ducis, idem in alio non uicio uerteris.
     Istud ergo totum de Moria, mea mi Dorpi sententia, et sine causa mones, quum nihil sit quod moneri debeat, et si quid esset,

---

1 comparatum] *P S 1563*, comparatum *1625*   2 exigamus,] *S 1563 1625*, exigamus *P;* libertatem] *P 1563 1625*, liber tatem *S*   2–3 indulgeamus] *P 1563 1625*, indulgemus *S*   3–4 (Deus bone, quem uirum?)] *1625* Deus bone. quem uirum? *P S*, Deus bone quem uirum? *1563; sidenote in 1563* Ioannes Reuchlinus   7 ijsdem] *1563 1625*, isdem *P S;* tam immani] *P 1625*, immani *S*, in tantum *1563;* uindicasset,] *S 1563 1625*, uindicasset *P*   8 Noui tamen] *P 1625* Noui *S 1563*   9 (quanquam . . . studiosi)] quanquam . . . studiosi *P*, quanquam . . . studiosi, *S 1563*, (quanquam . . . studiosi,) *1625;* etiam] *interl. S;* quod] quod ⟨co⟩ *P;* libere] *S 1563 1625*, liberae *P;* nec] *P S 1625*, ac *1563*   10 libere] *S 1563 1625*, liberae *P;* uere] *S 1563 1625*, uerae *P*   11 qui] *P 1625*, qui hec *S 1563;* post] *P 1625*, post tamen *S 1563*   12 proprie] *S 1563 1625*, propriae *P*   14 quenquam] *P 1563 1625*, quemque *S*   15–16 satyras Gerardi . . . antistites atque] *P S 1625*, satyras atque *1563*   16 serio] serio, ⟨modo⟩ *P*   17 quoquam] *P 1563 1625*, quoque *S*   20 non] *S 1563*, ne *P 1625*   22 et si] *P 1563 1625*, etsi *S;* esset,] *S 1563 1625*, esset *P*

Indeed, my dearest Dorp, we are naturally prone to require self-restraint from other people as a matter of course while we give ourselves license to do as we please. I myself know of some who could simply not stand it when Reuchlin (good lord, what a man he is!), confronting his personal detractors, that is, a most learned, most prudent, most honorable person confronting the most ignorant, most fatuous, most worthless wretches alive, who had done him so great an injustice that not even a physical act of revenge on his part would have seemed altogether excessive, I know of some, I repeat, who though they actually favored his cause could not stand it when freely, but still no more freely than truthfully, he vented his anger against his detractors in writing. I know, too, that before long the same men who could not stand for Reuchlin's response themselves grew much more violently irate over things which both had less intrinsic importance and did not affect them so directly. So much easier it is to prescribe self-control for the anger of others than it is for our own. "Did I not have the right, then," you ask, "either to approve of Gerard's satires or to speak against uncultured theologians, and religious superiors and bishops, too, either in jest or in earnest, provided that I spoke the truth and did not mention anyone's name?" Quite the contrary, my dear Dorp, I think that you had so much right to do what you did that it seems to me you have never done anything better in your life, provided that you will also be fair enough not to find fault with others for something you praise in yourself.

To conclude, my dear Dorp, in my view none of all your advice on the *Folly* has any real point: no advice is in order, and even if it

post tot annos etiam sero mones. Nam quod in calce prioris
epistolae tuae posuisti, reconciliatum iri Theologis istis Erasmum, quos Moria commouit, si Moriae laudibus sapientiae
laudem opponeret, mediocrem mihi risum mediusfidius exci-
5 tauit. Sapiunt scilicet si hoc Moriae Encomio Moriam sic putant
esse laudatam, ut laudari cupiant eadem figura sapientiam.
Quod si censent, [54v] Quid irascuntur, quum sint ipsi quoque a
tam laudata moria, tam abunde laudati? Preterea non uideo quo
pacto ueris sapientiae laudibus istorum in se inuidiam Erasmus
10 lenire possit, quin potius uelit nolit multo acerbiorem redderet,
quippe quum eos tam ex sapientiae contubernio cogeretur eijcere, quam nunc coactus est inter penitissimos Moriae mystas
asciscere.

Hec scribenti mihi superuenerunt litterae quibus ad se meus
15 me princeps reuocat. hae me adhuc scripturientem coegerunt ut
sisterem aliquando, atque istam finirem uel inuitus epistolam,
quae quum tam longa sit, ut breuior fortasse fuerit "scriptus et in
tergo necdum finitus Orestes," Nescio tamen quo tecum colloquendi studio adhuc cupiebat increscere. Verum ut non ingrata

---

1 sero] *P S 1563*, serio *1625*   3 laudibus] *1563 1625*, laudibus, *P S*   4–5 excitauit] *P
1625*, excussit *S 1563*   7 censent,] *1563*, censent *P S*, censent: *1625;* irascuntur,] *S*
irascuntur *P*, irascuntur? *1563 1625*   8 abunde] *S 1563 1625*, abundae *P;* laudati?]
laudati. *P 1563 1625*, laudati, *S*   8–9 quo pacto] *S 1563 1625*, quopacto *P*   12
coactus est] *P S 1625*, coactus *1563;* penitissimos] *P 1625*, peritissimos *S 1563*   13
asciscere] *P 1625*, asscribere *S 1563*   15 reuocat.] *S 1563 1625*, reuocat, *P;* hae] *S 1563
1625*, he *corr. from* hec *P*   17 fuerit] *S 1625*, fuerit, *P 1563*   17–18
scriptus . . . Orestes] *ital. 1625*   18 quo] *interl. P*   19 increscere. Verum] *P 1625*,
increscere. Quanquam iam nunc opinor nihil intactum reliquimus, certe quod sciam
nihil per dissimulationem pretermissus. Neque enim istud reor expectaturum quenquam ut Moriam a βλασφemiarum, atque impietatis etiam suspitione defenderem,
tanque ab ea Christi Religio male audierit, Nam et hoc in prioribus tuis litteris ita posuisti,
ut plane te ostenderes contra animi tui sensum alienam referre sententiam, et in hac
epistola posteriore, quum cetera omnia, quanquam illa quoque magna ex parte non tua,
tum in quibus herere aliquis potuit, color pro hoc ingenio atque hac doctrina tua, magnifice atque ampliter excoluris, hanc tamen de Impietate calumniam consulto uelut Impiam ipsam sacrilegam, ac non manifestariam modo verum futilem quoque atque ineptam prorsus omisisti. Ea ergo de re nihil erat mihi dicendum, de ceteris dixisse me puto.
Nihil ergo restabat aliud de quo tractare volueram. Sed nisi principis interpellassent
litterae scripturus fortasse fui ijsdem de rebus plenius. Verum *S*, increscere. Quanquam
iam nunc nihil intactum reliquimus, certe, quod sciam, nihil per dissimulationem
praetermisimus. Neque enim istud reor expectaturum quenquam, ut Moriam a blas-

were, after so many years your advice comes too late. For honestly, I could not keep from chuckling when I read what you wrote at the end of your earlier letter to the effect that Erasmus could pacify those theologians whom the *Folly* upset if he would counter his praises of Folly with a praise of Wisdom. They certainly are wise if they think this encomium of Folly by Folly affords her such exemplary praise that they want Wisdom also to be praised in this mode of address. If this is how they feel, why are they so aroused, since they themselves have been praised at such length by this Folly who gets so much praise? Furthermore, I do not see how Erasmus could ease their resentment against him by writing true praises of Wisdom or how he could even avoid making them resent him all the more, whether he wanted to or not, since he would then feel just as compelled to exclude them from the company of Wisdom as he now does to give them a place in the first rank of Folly's initiates.

As I was writing these last words a letter arrived from my prince summoning me to return to him. His letter has forced me to stop writing at last, though I do not want to stop, and makes me finish this letter, however unwillingly; even though it is already so long that an "interminable *Orestes*, spilling off the page," might well be shorter, I was somehow so eager to speak with you that it wanted to keep right on growing. But though I

est hec epistolae complicandae necessitas, quod uereor ne qua
nunc est longitudine, tibi possit esse molestiae, ita non laetor
ademptam mihi facultatem, qua hec eadem liceat sub incudem
reuocare, atque hunc rudem et informem foetum meum saepius
5 lambendo refingere. [55] Quod facere profecto decreueram, ut
ad te doctissime Dorpi, cultior aliquanto ueniret, cui me meaque
omnia probata esse cupio. Quorum ruditati non ideo solum
ueniam dabis, quod properus iste discessus effecit ne mihi uel
relegere liceret, sed ob id quoque quod ista scribenti mihi non
10 modo libraria nulla, sed nec liber fere ullus fuit.

Quanquam ne nunc quidem ingrata tibi hec qualiacunque
fore in tua humanitate prima spes est, secunda in mea ipsius
industria, qua me sedulo cauisse confido, ne quicquam in his
esset quod tuas aures merito posset offendere, nisi mihi, ut
15 homo sum, meorum amor imposuit. Quod si usquam incidat,
culpam admonitus agnoscam ingenue, nec tuebor meam.
Nempe ut quos amo siquid eorum intersit, non grauatim ad-
moneo, sic ab amicis ipse admoneri, ualde mediusfidius gaudeo.
Neque hoc me fugit tamen, Erasmo quaedam ex stomacho te
20 non obiecisse tuo, sed ab alijs accepta potius pertulisse, ut tu
uicissim intellegas, me multa his in litteris, illis per te potius
respondisse, quam tibi, quem ego non solum ut [55v] aman-

---

phemiarum atque impietatis etiam suspicione defenderem, tanquam ea Christi religio
male audierit. Nam hoc et in prioribus literis tuis ita posuisti, ut plane te ostenderes
contra animi tui sensum alienam referre sententiam: et in hac epistola posteriore, cum
caetera omnia, quanquam illa quoque magna ex parte non tua, tum in quibus haerere
aliquis potuit color pro hoc ingenio atque hac doctrina tua, magnifice atque ampliter
excolueris: hanc tamen de impietate calumniam consulto, uelut impiam ipsam sacri-
legamque, ac non manifestariam modo, uerum futilem quoque atque ineptam prorsus
omisisti. Ea ergo de re nihil erat mihi dicendum, de caeteris dixisse me puto. Nihil ergo
restabat aliud de quo tractare uolueram. Sed nisi Principis me interpellassent literae,
scripturus fortasse fui ijsdem de rebus plenius. Verum *1563 For a restored text see commentary*   1 est] *S 1563 1625*, est, *P*   5 decreueram] *P 1625*, animus erat *S 1563*   5–6
ut ad te . . . cultior] *P S 1625*, ad te . . . ut cultior *1563*   7 Quorum] *P 1625*, quorum
nunc *S 1563*   10 fuit] *P 1625*, affuit *S 1563*   11 Quanquam] *P 1563 1625*, Quanque
S; tibi hec] P 1625, tibi *S 1563*   12 mea] mei *P S 1563 1625*   14 posset] *P 1625*,
possit *S 1563*   14–15 mihi, ut homo sum,] *1625*, mihi ut homo sum *P*, mihi (ut homo
sum) *S 1563*   16 ingenue] *S 1563 1625*, ingenuae *P*   18 mediusfidius] *interl. P*
19 quaedam] *1563 1625*, quedam *P S*   20 pertulisse] *S 1563*, p̱tulisse *P*, protulisse
1625   22 tibi,] *S 1563*, tibi. *P 1625*

do not find it unpleasant to have to fold up my letter at this point, since I am afraid it is already so long that you may find it tedious, even so it does not make me happy that I will not have any chance to refine it or to lick this ungainly and amorphous offspring of mine into shape by degrees. I was certainly planning to do so in order to make it seem somewhat more polished when it got to you, learned Dorp, since I want you to look with approval on me and on all that is mine. You will pardon my letter's ungainliness not only because in my haste to depart I could not even stop to reread it, but also because I had no store of books, indeed virtually no books at all, to consult as I wrote it.

Still, I hope, even such as it is, you will not find my letter displeasing, for although I rely first of all on your humane indulgence I also rely on the thoroughness of my own effort to guard against writing one word in this letter that might give you just cause for offense, unless through human weakness esteem for my own works misleads me. If this does ever happen, and I am advised of it, I will freely acknowledge my fault and not try to defend it. Indeed, just as I am not slow to advise those I love, should it be in their interest, so too, on my honor, I am delighted to have my friends advise me. Nor am I unaware that on a number of points you are not leveling your own charges at Erasmus but rather reporting what you heard from others, so that you too should understand that at a number of points in this letter I have rather been answering those men through you than addressing you personally, whom I not only prize as an excellent

tissimum diligo, ut doctissimum suspicio, uerum etiam ut op-
timum uirum reuereor. Vale charissime Dorpi, uereque tibi persuade neminem esse tui magis uel in Hollandia tua studiosum
quam sit Morus apud toto diuisos orbe Britannos, ut cui non
5 minus charus es quam ipsi es Erasmo. Nam charior esse non
potes, ne mihi quidem. Iterum Vale. Brugis Vicesimo primo
Octobres.

Vale Brugis uicesimo primo Octobres Iterum uale.

---

1 diligo, ut] *P S 1625*, diligo, et *1563*   2 uereque] *S 1563 1625*, ueraeque *P*   4
Morus] *corr. from* morus *S;* diuisos] *P S 1625*, diuisos ab *1563*   6–8 Vicesimo . . . uale]
P, Vicesimo primo Octobris *1625, om. S 1563*   8 Vale . . . uale] *only in P; written in the
same elegant hand as 2/3*

friend and respect as an excellent scholar but also revere as an excellent man. Farewell, my dearest Dorp, and be assured that no one, not even in your own Holland, regards you more highly than More does in the land of the faraway Britons, since you are no less dear to him than you are to Erasmus. Than that you can never be dearer, not even to me. Once more, farewell. Bruges, 21 October.

Farewell. Bruges, 21 October. Once more, farewell.

LETTER TO THE UNIVERSITY OF OXFORD
TEXT AND TRANSLATION

Tho. Morus Reuerendis patribus,
Commissario, Procuratoribus, ac
reliquo Senatui Scholasticorum
Oxoniensium. Salutem. P. D.

5 DVBITAVI nonnihil, Eruditissimi viri, liceretne mihi de
quibus nunc decreui rebus ad vos scribere: nec id usque adeo stili
respectu mei dubitaui (quanquam eum ipsum quoque pudet in
coetum prodire virorum tam eloquentium), quam ne videri nimium superbus possim, si homuncio non magna prudentia, mi-
10 nore rerum vsu, doctrina vero minus quam mediocri, tantum
mihi arrogem, vt ulla in re, sed praecipue literaria, consilium
dare vnus audeam vobis omnibus, quorum quiuis ob eximiam
eruditionem prudentiamque sit idoneus qui multis hominum
millibus consulat. Verum contra (venerandi patres) singularis
15 ista sapientia vestra, quantum me primo conspectu deterruit,
tantum me penitius inspecta recreauit, cum subijt animum,
sicuti stulta atque arrogans inscitia neminem dignatur audire, ita
quo quisque est sapientior doctiorque, eo minus sibi ipsi confidere aut cuiusquam aspernari consilium. Sed et hoc me vehe-
20 menter animauit, quod nemini vnquam fraudi fuit apud aequos
iudices, quales vos imprimis estis, etiamsi quis in consulendo non
satis prospexisse videatur, sed laudem semper gratiamque me-
ruisse consilium, quod quanquam non prudentissimum fidum
tamen fuerit, et amico profectum pectore. Postremo, quum
25 apud me considero quod hanc quantulamcunque doctrinam
meam secundum Deum, vestrae isti Academiae acceptam ferre
[293] debeo, vnde eius initia retuli, videtur a me officium meum
fidesque in vos exigere, ne quidquam silentio transeam, quod
vos audire vtile esse censeam. Quamobrem quum in scribendo

---

1 Reuerendis] *T R*, Reuerendissimis *1633*   5 mihi] *R 1633*, mihi, *T*   7 dubitaui]
1633, dubitaui: *T*, dubitaui, *R*   8 eloquentium),] eloquentium) *T R 1633*   12
omnibus,] *1633*, omnibus. *T*, omnibus; *R*   14–15 singularis . . . quantum me primo
conspectu deterruit] *T 1633*, quantum me primo conspectu singularis . . . deterruit
R   15 vestra,] vestra *T R 1633*; deterruit,] *R 1633*, deterruit; *T*   16 penitius inspec-
ta] *T R*, penitus inspectu *1633*   17 audire,] *1633*, audire; *T R*   19 aspernari] *T R*,
aspernari solet *1633*; consilium.] *R 1633*, consilium: *T*   21 etiamsi] *T R*, etsi si
1633   22 videatur,] *1633*, videatur; *T R*   24 pectore.] *R 1633*, pectore: *T*

Thomas More sends his heartiest greetings
to the Reverend Fathers, the Vice-Chancellor,
the Proctors, and the other members of the
Masters' Guild of the University of Oxford.

LEARNED gentlemen, I felt some misgivings about whether it
would be proper for me to address you concerning the issues I
presently mean to discuss. My misgivings arose not so much
from concern about my style (although I am embarrassed about
that, too, in the face of so eloquent an assembly) as from fear of
appearing presumptuous if an insignificant person like myself,
with little prudence, less experience, and only a modicum of
learning, were so brash and so bold as to offer my personal
advice about anything, but especially about anything literary, to
a group of men each of whom is sufficiently learned and prudent to advise many thousands of men. But on the other hand,
reverend fathers, this same singular wisdom of yours, which
intimidated me so at first glance, reassured me on closer exam-
ination, for it occurred to me that whereas foolish and arrogant
ignorance refuses to listen to anyone, the wisest and most
learned men are the least self-assured and the least prone to
scorn anyone's advice. Something else that encouraged me
greatly was the thought that fair judges like you never think any
less of a man, and indeed always honor and thank him, for
offering even imprudent advice which is heartfelt and friendly.
Finally, when I consider that next after God this university of
yours should be given the credit for whatever learning I do have,
since it was there that I came by its rudiments, I seem bound by
my duty and loyalty to you not to pass over anything in silence
that I think you would do well to hear. And so when I saw that

totum periculum in eo viderem situm, si me quidam nimis arrogantem dicerent, contraque intelligerem, silentium meum a
multis damnari ingratitudinis posse, malui omnes vt me mortales audaculum praedicarent, quam quisquam ingratum iudica-
5 ret, in vestram praesertim scholam, cuius honori tuendo vehementer ipse me deuinctum sentiam; maxime cum res sit tanta,
quanta profecto, vt mea fert opinio, nulla multis iam annis obtigit quae (si honori commodoque gymnasij vestri bene consultum vultis) exactius fuerit vestra grauitate animaduertenda.
10   Ea res cuiusmodi sit accipite. Ego quum Londini essem, audiui
iam nuper saepius, quosdam scholasticos Academiae vestrae,
siue graecarum odio literarum, seu prauo quopiam aliarum studio, seu quod opinor verius, improba ludendi nugandique libidine, de composito conspirasse inter sese, vt se Troianos ap-
15 pellent. Eorum quidam (senior quam sapientior vt ferunt)
Priami sibi nomen adoptauit, Hectoris alius, alius item Paridis,
aut aliorum cuiuspiam veterum Troianorum, caeterique ad eundem modum, non alio consilio, quam vti per ludum iocumque
velut factio Graecis aduersa graecarum studiosis literarum il-
20 luderent. Itaque hac ratione factum aiunt, ne quisquam eius
linguae quidquam qui degustasset, aut domi suae, aut in publico
possit consistere, quin digito notetur, cachinno rideatur, et ap-
petatur scommatibus, ab [294] aliquo ridiculorum illorum
Troianorum; qui nihil rident aliud nisi (quas solas nesciunt)
25 omnes bonas literas; vsque adeo vt in Troianos istos aptissime
quadrare videatur uetus illud adagium, "Sero sapiunt Phryges."
    Hac de re quum assidue multos audirem multa referentes,
quanquam et displiceret omnibus, et mihi in primis esset acer-
bum, scolasticos esse aliquot apud uos, qui talibus ineptijs, et otio

---

3 damnari] R *1633*, damnari, *T;* posse,] *1633*, posse; *T*, posse: R   4–5 ingratum
iudicaret] *T R*, iudicaret ingratum *1633*   7 profecto,] *R*, profecto *T 1633*   9 vestra
grauitate] *T R*, vestrae grauitati *1633;* animaduertenda.] *R 1633*, animaduertenda;
T   10 Ego] *Para. R*   12 seu] *T R*, ceu *1633*   12–13 studio,] *R 1633*, studio; *T*
15 senior . . . ferunt] *T R*, senior (ut ferunt) quam sapientior *1633;* ferunt)] *1633*,
ferunt;) *T*, ferunt, *R*   17 cuiuspiam] cuiuspiam, *T*, cuiuscuam *R 1633;* Troianorum,]
R 1633, Trioianorum. *T*   19 studiosis literarum] *R*, studiosis literarum, *T*, literarum
studiosis *1633*   23–24 ridiculorum illorum Troianorum] *T R*, Troianorum illorum
ridiculorum *1633*   24 (quas solas nesciunt)] quas solas nesciunt *T*, quas solas nesciunt,
R, quod solas nesciunt *1633*   25 vsque adeo vt] *T R*, vsque adeo *1633*   29 aliquot] *T
R*, aliquos *1633*

the only risk in my writing was that some people might think me
arrogant, whereas my silence could make many people condemn
my ingratitude, I was more willing to let all mortals call me a little
too bold than to let anyone call me ungrateful, especially toward
this school of yours—for I feel very strongly obliged to stand up
for its honor—and particularly since I believe that the matter at
hand is so crucial that no other problem has arisen in quite a long
time which deserves more of your serious attention than this one
if you wish to safeguard the honor and welfare of your
university.

Let me tell you what matter I mean. I have recently heard it
reported by a number of people in London that certain scholars
of your university, prompted either by hatred of Greek learning,
by a misguided devotion to some other sort, or (as I think more
likely) by a shameless addiction to joking and trifling, have
formed a deliberate conspiracy to call themselves Trojans. One
of them, who is said to be riper in years than in wisdom, has
assumed the name "Priam," another the name "Hector," another the name "Paris" or else that of some other ancient Trojan,
and the rest have been doing the same, for the sole purpose of
jokingly setting themselves up as a faction opposed to the Greeks
to make fun of the students of Greek learning. And so, they say,
these men have seen to it that no one who has even a passing
acquaintance with that language is allowed to appear either at
home or in public without being pointed at, laughed at, and
scoffed at by one of those laughable Trojans, who are not laughing at anything but what they know nothing about, namely
sound learning in general. Thus it seems that these Trojans are
eminent witnesses to the aptness of that ancient adage, "Trojans
grow wise too late."

Though I continually heard many different reports on this
matter from many different people, and although it irked everyone and upset me especially that some of your scholars were

abuterentur suo, et bonis aliorum studijs essent molesti, tamen
quoniam videbam nunquam vndique sic posse prospici, vt e tanta hominum turba, omnes et saperent, et frugi modestique essent, caeperam apud me rem pro leui ducere. Caeterum postea-
5   quam huc Abingdoniam inuictissimum Regem sum comitatus,
accepi rursus, ineptias illas in rabiem demum caepisse procedere, Nempe nescio quem e Troianis illis, hominem, ut ipse
sentit, sapientem; vt fautores eius excusant, hilarem atque di-
caculum; ut alij iudicant, qui facta eius considerant, insanum;
10 hoc sacro ieiunij tempore, concionibus publicis, non modo contra graecas literas, et latinarum politiem, sed ualde liberaliter
aduersus omnes liberales artes blaterasse; Tum quo sibi tota res
congrueret, neu tam stolidum sermonis corpus vteretur sano
capite, neque integrum vllum Scripturae caput tractauit, quae
15 res in vsu fuit veteribus, neque dictum aliquod breuius e sacris
literis, qui mos apud nuperos inoleuit, sed thematum loco dele-
git brytannica quaedam anilia prouerbia; Itaque non dubito sermonem illum tam nugacem vehementer offendisse eos qui in-
tererant, quum eos videam omnes tam iniquis auribus rem
20 accipere, qui vel frustatim inde quidquam audiunt; quorum
quotusquisque est, qui modo vel scintillam habet Christianae
mentis in pectore, qui non lamentatur Maiestatem [295] sacro-
sancti concionatoris officij, quod mundum Christo lucrifacit,
nunc ab his violari potissimum, quorum officio potissimum in-
25 cumbit, eius muneris autoritatem tueri? In quod concionandi
officium, quae potuit excogitari contumelia insignior, quam, qui
concionatoris nomen profitetur, eum in sacratissimo anni tempore, magna Christianorum frequentia, in ipso Dei templo, in
altissimo pulpito velut ipsius Christi solio, in venerabilis Christi
30 corporis conspectu, quadragesimalem sermonem in bacchanales
conuertisse naenias? Quo vultu credimus auditores eius stetisse,

---

1 molesti,] *1633*, molesti; *T*, molesti: *R*   3–4 essent,] *1633*, essent; *T*, essent: *R*   6–7
procedere,] *1633*, procedere. *T*, procedere: *R*   7 hominem,] hominem *T R 1633*   8
sapientem;] sapientem, *T R 1633;* excusant,] *R 1633*, excusant *T*   9 insanum;] *R*,
insanum, *T 1633*   11 latinarum] *T R*, Latinam *1633*   12 blaterasse;] blaterasse. *T
1633*, blaterasse: *R;* sibi] *T R*, siue *1633*   14 capite,] *1633*, capite; *T R*   19 quum eos]
T R, quum *1633*   20 qui] *interl. T*   25 autoritatem] *T R*, autoritate *1633*   26–27
qui . . . profitetur, eum] *T*, eum, qui . . . profitetur *R*, sic qui . . . profitetur *1633*   27
sacratissimo] *T R*, sacratissimo totius *1633*

wasting their time and disrupting the sound studies of others
with this sort of impertinence, nonetheless, since I saw that no
measures, however elaborate, could ever ensure that every
member of such a large group of people would sensibly mind his
own business I began to think light of the matter. But after I
arrived here in Abingdon in the company of our invincible king,
I was further informed that this impertinence had started to
turn into sheer lunacy. For I learned that one of those Trojans,
to show off what he views as his wisdom, what his partisans
excuse as his humor and wit, and what others who look at his
actions condemn as his madness, chose this holy season of fasting
and the medium of a public sermon to blather all too liberally not
only against Greek learning and stylistic refinement in Latin but
also against all the liberal arts. To avoid any inconsistency in his
performance and to make sure that the heading of his sermon
was as mad as its body was stolid, he did not expound either a
whole chapter of scripture, as the ancients used to do, or a single
short passage from sacred scripture, which is the prevalent practice among moderns. Instead, he took as his text various old
wives' proverbs in English. And so I have no doubt that so trifling a sermon was very offensive to those who were actually
present, since I see how it outrages everyone who has heard even
a scrap of it. For could anyone with the least spark of Christian devotion in his heart not lament how the majesty of the sacrosanct
office of preaching, which won the world over to Christ, is now
being violated by the very men who are officially most responsible for upholding the authority of that function? Could anyone
imagine a more blatant affront to the office of preaching than
for a person who styles himself a preacher to step forth in the
holiest season of the year and before a large audience of Christians, in the very temple of God, in the loftiest pulpit—in Christ's
very throne, as it were—and in sight of Christ's venerable body,
to turn his Lenten sermon into a bacchanalian travesty? How do
you think those who stood listening received it when they saw

quum illum, a quo spiritalem sapientiam venerant audituri, gesticulantem, et ridentem, cachinnosque edentem e pulpito simij
in morem cernerent, et quum pia mente verba vitae expectas-
sent, abeuntes nihil audisse recordarentur, praeter oppugnatas
5 literas, et praedicandi officium ineptia praedicatoris infamatum?

At quod seculares disciplinas omnes insectatur, si bonus ille vir
mundo se procul subducens diu vitam traduxisset in heremo,
atque inde repente prodiens isthac oratione vteretur; Insisten-
10 dum esse vigilijs, orationi, ieiunijs; hac via gradiendum, si qui
caelum petant; caetera nugas esse; quin ipsarum etiam studium
literarum compedum vice esse; rusticos atque indoctos expedi-
tius ad caelum prouolare; ferri vtcunque fortassis haec oratio a
tali persona posset, et veniam mereretur simplicitas; quam qui
15 audirent benigni, interpretarentur sanctimoniam; qui vero
grauissime, piam saltem atque deuotam inscitiam. At nunc
quum vident in suggestum scandere hominem paenulatum,
humeros instratum velleribus, habitu qui profiteatur literatum,
atque inde in medio Academiae, quo nemo nisi literarum causa
20 venit, palam contra [296] omnes ferme literas debacchari, istud
profecto nemo videt, qui non caecam putet atque insignem malitiam, superbamque aduersus meliores inuidiam. Quin demi-
rantur multi vehementer, quid homini in mentem venerit, cur
putaret sibi praedicandum, aut de latina lingua, de qua non
25 multum intelligit, aut de scientijs liberalibus, e quibus adhuc
minus intelligit, aut postremo de graeca lingua, cuius οὐδὲ γρῦ
intelligit; quum ei tam vberem suppeditare materiam potuissent, septem peccata mortalia, res nimirum concionibus idonea,
tum cuius creditur ipse neutiquam imperitus; qui quum sic in-
30 stitutus sit, uti quicquid nescit, id reprehendere malit quam discere, quid est si haec inertia non est? Ad haec quum palam

---

1 spiritalem] *T R*, spiritualem *1633*   3 cernerent,] *1633*, cernerent; *T R*   5
officium] *R 1633*, officium, *T*   5–6 infamatum?] *1633*, infamatum. *T R*   7 At] *T R*,
Atque *1633*   14 posset,] *1633*, posset; *T R*   15 benigni] *T R*, benigne *1633*   17
scandere] *1633*, scandere, *T R*   18 velleribus,] *R 1633*, velleribus *T*; literatum,] *1633*,
literatum; *T*, literatum: *R*   22 meliores] *T R*, meliores artes *1633*   26 intelligit,] *R*
1633, intelligit; *T*   27 intelligit;] *1633*, intelligit, *T R*   27–28 materiam potuissent]
materiam potuissent, *T*, materiam possent, *R*, potuissent materiam *1633*   28
mortalia,] *R 1633*, mortalia; *T*   29 imperitus;] *1633*, imperitus: *T R*

their preacher, from whom they had come to hear lessons of spiritual wisdom, cavorting, guffawing, and monkeying around in the pulpit, and when those who had gathered there piously expecting to hear the words of life went away not recalling that they had heard anything but slurs against literature and impertinent preaching which had dishonored the office of preacher?

But as for his tirade against all types of secular learning, if that good man had withdrawn from the world altogether and had lived many years as a hermit, and if he then abruptly stepped forth and declared that we ought to concentrate on vigils, prayer, and fasting, that this is the right way to get to heaven, and that all other things are mere trifles, or even that study and learning are actually a hindrance, since simple and unlearned people have an easier time rising heavenward, such a sermon might perhaps have been tolerated from a person like this, whose simplicity would earn him indulgence; for his generous hearers would construe it as saintliness and even the most critical hearers as an ignorance which was at any rate pious and devout. But as it is, when they see a man climb to the pulpit clad in an academic gown, with a furred hood on his shoulders—dressed, that is, as a man of learning—and there, in the middle of the university, a place no one frequents except for the sake of learning, they see him rage openly against virtually all branches of learning, certainly no one who sees this considers it anything but blind and egregious malice and proud envy directed at his betters. In fact many are utterly amazed how the man got it into his head that he ought to be preaching either about the Latin language, of which he understands only a little, or about liberal studies, of which he understands even less, or especially about the Greek language, of which he understands not one iota, when he had such a rich, handy store of material in the seven deadly sins, an appropriate topic for sermons and one with which he seems to be not at all unfamiliar. For he feels more inclined to condemn anything he knows nothing about than to learn it; if this is not sloth, then what is? And he openly slanders anyone he

infamat quoscunque scire quidquam deprehenderit, quod ipse
quo minus addiscat segnities aut ingenij desperatio prohibet,
annon haec inuidia est? Denique quum nullum scientiae genus
in precio vellet esse, nisi quod ipse scire se falso sibi persuaserit,
5   atque ab ignorantia maiorem sibi laudem arroget, quam ab scientia quorundam fert modestia; numnam haec suprema est
superbia?

Itaque quod ad seculares literas pertinet, quanquam nemo
negat saluum esse quemquam sine literis non illis modo, sed
10 prorsus vllis posse, doctrina tamen, etiam secularis vt ille vocat,
animam ad virtutem praeparat; quae res utut sese habeat, nemo
saltem dubitat, literas vnam prope, atque vnicam esse rem, propter quam frequentatur Oxonia: quandoquidem rudem illam et
illiteratam virtutem quaeuis bona mulier liberos suos ipsa docere
15 non pessime posset domi: praeterea non quisquis ad vos venit,
protinus ad perdiscendam theologiam venit: oportet sint qui et
leges perdiscant. Noscenda est [297] et rerum humanarum prudentia, res adeo non inutilis theologo ut absque hac sibi fortassis
intus non insuauiter possit canere, at certe ad populum inepte sit
20 cantaturus: Quae peritia haud scio an alicunde vberius, quam e
poetis, oratoribus atque historijs hauriatur. Quin sunt nonnulli
qui cognitionem rerum naturalium, velut viam sibi, qua trans-
cendant in supernarum contemplationem, praestruunt, iterque
per philosophiam, et liberales artes, (quas omnes iste saecularis
25 nomine literaturae damnat) faciunt ad theologiam, spoliatis vid-

1 infamat] R 1633, infamat, T   5 arroget,] R arroget; T, arrogat 1633   5–6 scientia]
T R scientia, sicut 1633   6 numnam] T R, nonne 1633   8 quanquam] first word in
1588   9 literis] 1588 1633, literis, T R   10 prorsus] T 1633, interl. R, vel 1588;
posse,] 1588 1633, posse; T, posse: R; etiam] T R 1633, eaque 1588   11 animam] T R
1588, animum 1633   11–12 quae . . . rem] T R 1633, Neque quisquam est qui dubitet
doctrinam hanc vnam prope atque vnicam esse 1588   13 frequentatur] T 1588 1633,
frequentetur R; Oxonia] T R 1633, Oxonium 1588; et] T R 1633, atque 1588   14
docere] 1588 1633, docere, T R   15–16 non quisquis . . . protinus] T R 1588,
quisquis . . . non protinus 1633   16 oportet] T R 1633, oportet vt 1588   16–17
qui . . . perdiscant] T R 1633, qui leges calleant 1588   17 est] R 1588 1633, est, T
18 absque] T R 1633, sine 1588   20 e] T R 1588, a 1633   21 historijs] T R 1588,
historicis 1633   23 supernarum] T R 1588, supernam 1633; contemplationem,] R
1588, contemplationem T 1633; praestruunt,] praestruunt: T R 1588, praestruant, 1633;
iterque] T R 1633, et 1588   25 nomine literaturae] T R 1633, literaturae nomine 1588;
damnat)] damnat,) iter T, damnat) xxx R, damnat) iter 1588, damnat 1633; theologiam,]
1633, theologiam: T 1588, Theologiam; R

has found to know anything he himself has omitted to learn, whether through laziness or through sheer despair of his own intellectual powers; is this not clearly envy? Finally, he tries to deny any value to any aspect of knowledge but the one he is falsely convinced he has mastered, and he arrogantly lays claim to more praise for his ignorance than the modesty of some will accept for their knowledge; is this not the summit of pride?

Now then, as for secular learning, no one denies that a person can be saved without it, and indeed without learning of any sort. But even secular learning, as he calls it, prepares the soul for virtue. And however that may be, certainly no one disputes that learning is virtually the one and only incentive that draws people to Oxford, inasmuch as that rude and illiterate virtue is something which any good woman can teach well enough to her children at home. Furthermore, not everyone who comes to Oxford comes just to learn theology; some must also learn law. They must also learn prudence in human affairs, something which is so far from being useless to a theologian that without it he may be able to sing well enough for his own pleasure, but his singing will certainly be ill suited for the people. And I doubt that any study contributes as richly to this practical skill as the study of poets, orators, and histories. Indeed, some plot their course, as it were, to the contemplation of celestial realities through the study of nature, and progress to theology by way of philosophy and the liberal arts (all of which he condemns under the name "secular literature"), thus despoiling the women of Egypt to grace their

elicet Aegypti mulieribus in reginae cultum. Quam theologiam
(quoniam hanc solam videtur admittere, si vel hanc admittat)
non video tamen quo pacto possit attingere, citra linguae peritiam, vel Hebraeae uel Graecae uel Latinae: nisi forte sibi per-
5 suasit homo suauis, satis in id librorum scriptum esse Britannice:
aut totam prorsus theologiam putat intra septum illarum claudi
quaestionum, de quibus tam assidue disputant: in quas pernoscendas, pars exigua fateor linguae latinae suffecerit; verum
enimuero intra has angustias, augustam illam coeli reginam the-
10 ologiam, sic coerceri pernego, ut non praeterea sacras incolat
atque inhabitet scripturas, indeque per omnes antiquissimorum
ac sanctissimorum patrum cellas peregrinetur, Augustini dico,
Hieronymi, Ambrosij, Cipriani, Chrysostomi, Gregorij, Basilij,
atque id genus aliorum, quibus (ut nunc contemptim vocant)
15 positiua scribentibus, theologiae studium stetit, a Christo passo,
plus annis mille, priusquam argutae istae nascerentur, quae iam
prope solae uentilantur, quaestiunculae. Quorum opera patrum
quisquis a se iactat intelligi, sine suae cuiusque eorum linguae
non vulgari peritia, diu id iactabit imperitus, prius quam ei [298]
20 periti credant.
   At si nunc velamen ineptiae suae concionator ille praetexat,
non saeculares ab se damnatas literas, sed immoderata earum
studia, non uideo in eam partem tam passim peccari, vt opus
fuerit, publica concione corripi ac reuocari velut in praeceps
25 ruentem populum. Neque enim valde multos audio in hoc literarum genere eousque peruasisse, quin paulo adhuc progressi

1 Quam] T R 1633, Ad quam 1588   2 videtur] T R 1588, videatur 1633; admittat)] R,
admittat:) T, admittit) 1588, admittat, 1633   3 possit] T R 1633, queat 1588; attingere]
T 1588 1633, pertingere R   4–5 sibi persuasit] T R, persuasit sibi 1588, sibi persuaserit
1633   5 satis in] T R 1633, satis 1588   6 putat] R 1588 1633, putat, T; illarum] T R
1588, illum 1633   7 tam assidue] T R 1633, assidue 1588   7–8 pernoscendas] T R
1633, noscendas 1588   10 coerceri pernego] T R 1633, coerceri 1588; praeterea
sacras] T R 1633, sacras praeterea 1588   11–12 omnes antiquissimorum ac] T R 1588,
omnes 1633   13 Gregorij, Basilij] T R 1633, Cyrilli, Gregorij 1588   14–15
quibus . . . scribentibus] T R 1633, per quos 1588   16–17 priusquam . . . quaestiun-
culae] T R 1633, priusquam istae nascerentur questiunculae, foret periniquum, addo
etiam impium 1588   17 uentilantur,] uentilantur T R 1633   18 sine suae] T R 1633,
sine 1588   20 credant] last word in 1588   23 studia,] 1633, studia; T R; peccari,] R,
peccari; T, peccari 1633   24 corripi] T, corrigi R 1633

own queen. But since theology is the only subject he seems to allow (if he actually allows even this), I do not see how he can pursue it without any skill in either Hebrew or Greek or Latin, unless perhaps the fine fellow has convinced himself that there are enough books on that subject in English, or unless he thinks that all of theology falls within the confines of those problems which they dispute about so assiduously, for I grant that one needs little Latin to learn those. But I certainly deny that theology, that venerable heavenly queen, is so pent up in those narrow limits that she does not also inhabit and dwell in holy scripture as her proper home, from which she makes her pilgrimage through all the cells of the oldest and holiest fathers, Augustine, I mean, Jerome, Ambrose, Cyprian, Chrysostom, Gregory, Basil, and other men like them, whose "positive" writings, as they are now called with contempt, were the mainstay of theological studies for more than a thousand years after the passion of Christ, before those subtle problems which now command almost exclusive attention were even invented. But whoever boasts of understanding the works of the fathers without considerable skill in the language of each of them will be making that unskillful boast a long time before those who are skilled will believe him.

But if that preacher now tries to cover up for his impertinence by pretending that what he condemned was not secular learning but rather the immoderate study thereof, I do not see that that vice is so widespread that the whole populace needed to be chided or warned about it in a public sermon as if they were all falling head-over-heels over the brink. For I do not see that many have made so much progress in this branch of learning that they might not advance somewhat further while still stop-

longius aliquanto tamen citra medium subsisterent. Caeterum
ille bonus vir, ut facile declararet, quam longe ab ea sermonis
moderatione abesset, quicunque graecas appeterent literas, a-
perte vocauit haereticos: ad haec lectores earum diabolos max-
5 imos denotauit, auditores vero, diabolos etiam illos, sed modestius, et ut ipsi uidebatur, facete, minutulos. Itaque hoc impetu,
imo ista furia, sanctus iste vir, diaboli uocabulo notauit, virum
quendam, quem omnes talem sciunt, qualem is qui vere diabolus
est, perquam aegre ferret concionatorem fieri; quanquam haud
10 nominatim citauit hominem, uerum tam aperte tamen hominem
designauit, ut omnes tam intelligerent quem notaret, quam ipsum qui sic notasset, notarent amentiae.

   Haud ita, viri literatissimi, desipio, ut in me sumam grecarum
patrocinium literarum, apud Prudentias vestras; quibus facile
15 intelligo, earum utilitatem perspectam esse prorsus et cognitam:
etenim cui non perspicuum est, cum in caeteris artibus omnibus,
tum in ipsa quoque theologia, qui vel optima quaeque inuenere,
vel inuenta tradiderunt accuratissime fuisse Graecos? Nam in
philosophia, exceptis duntaxat his, quae Cicero reliquit et Sene-
20 ca, nihil habent latinorum scholae, nisi vel graecum, uel quod e
graeca lingua traductum est. Taceo nouum testamentum, totum
fere primo scriptum graece. Taceo [299] vetustissimos quosque
atque peritissimos sacrarum literarum interpretes fuisse
Graecos, graeceque scripsisse; hoc certe non sine eruditorum
25 omnium consensu dicam: quanquam iam olim quaedam trans-
lata sint, et multa iam nuper melius, tamen neque dimidium
graecorum voluminum, latio donatum est, neque quicquam fere
sic a quoquam versum, vt non idem adhuc in sua lingua legatur
aut emendatius aut certe efficacius, eamque ob causam veterum
30 quisque doctorum latinae Ecclesiae, Hieronymus, Augustinus,
Beda, multique itidem alij, sedulo se dederunt perdiscendo
graecorum sermoni; idque pluribus libris iam tum traductis,

---

2 ille bonus] *T R*, bonus ille *1633*   3 abesset,] *1633*, abesset; *T R*   5 denotauit,] *1633*,
detonauit; *T*, detonauit: *R;* illos,] *1633*, illos *T*, illos; *R*   8 talem] *T*, talem esse *R*
1633   9 ferret] *R 1633*, ferret, *T*   14 patrocinium literarum] *T R*, literarum patrocinium *1633*   15 earum] *T R*, eam *1633*   16 artibus omnibus] *T 1633*, omnibus
artibus *R*   21–23 testamentum, totum . . . quosque atque] *T R*, Testamentum atque
1633   26 sint] *T R*, sunt *1633;* melius,] *1633*, melius; *T*, melius: *R*   27 latio] *T R*,
Latio adhuc *1633;* quicquam fere] *T 1633*, fere quicquam *R*   30 Ecclesiae,] *R*,
Ecclesiae *T 1633*   32 sermoni] *T R*, sermonem *1633*

ping short of the mean. Furthermore, that fine fellow made it perfectly clear he was far from conveying such a moderate message: he openly called everyone a heretic who wished to pursue Greek learning, and he went on to brand lecturers in Greek as "archdevils," and students of Greek (in a more modest and wittier vein, as he thought) as "underdevils." And in the heat of this passion, or rather this frenzy, that holy man used the term "devil" to label a man who, as everyone knows, is the sort of man who would cause the real devil a great deal of grief by becoming a preacher; and though he did not actually name the man, he referred to him in such an obvious way that everyone was as quick to discern who was meant by that label as they were to label the man who had labeled him that way a madman.

Learned gentlemen, I am hardly so foolish as to take it upon myself to defend Greek learning before prudent judges like yourselves, since I am well aware that you must have already perceived and acknowledged its usefulness. For can anyone fail to perceive that not only in all other arts, but in theology as well, the most original thinkers and the most diligent interpreters of their thoughts were Greek? For in philosophy, apart from the works left by Cicero and Seneca, the schools of the Latins have nothing to offer that is not either Greek or translated from Greek. I will say nothing about the New Testament, which was first written almost entirely in Greek. I will say nothing of the fact that all the most ancient and most skilled interpreters of sacred scripture were Greeks and wrote in Greek. But I will say this much, not without the agreement of all learned men: though some works were translated long ago, and though many have recently been translated better, not even half of the volumes in Greek have been translated into Latin, and virtually none has been translated so well that the Greek text is not less corrupt or at least more expressive. And for this reason all the ancient doctors of the Latin church, Jerome, Augustine, Bede, and many others besides, made a strenuous effort to learn the Greek language, doing so at a time when more books had al-

quam multi nunc qui sibi impendio videntur eruditi solent legere: Nec didicere solum, sed posteris consuluerunt etiam, his in
primis qui vellent esse theologi, idem ipsi ut facerent.

Quamobrem, non est, ut dixi, consilium apud Prudentias ves-
5 tras Graecae linguae studium defendere, sed pro meo in vos
officio potius inhortari, ne quenquam permittatis, aut publicis
concionibus, aut priuatis ineptijs a graecarum studio literarum
deterreri apud Academiam vestram, quam linguam vniuersa
sanxit ecclesia in omni schola docendam esse. Itaque pro pru-
10 dentia vestra facile videtis, non omnes prorsus esse stupidos, qui
ex vestris graecae sese linguae dediderunt, verum aliquot ex his
esse eiusmodi, ut vestra schola, non in hoc regno tantum, sed per
exteras etiam gentes, eorum fama doctrinae, multum verae
gloriae sit consecuta: praeterea multos iam caepisse videtis,
15 quorum exempla sequentur alij, multum boni vestro conferre
gymnasio, quo et omnigenam literaturam promoueant, et modo
nominatim graecam, quorum nunc [300] feruidus in vos adfectus, mirum ni frigescat, si tam pium propositum suum lubibrio
isthic haberi sentiant; praesertim quum Cantabrigiae, cui vos
20 praelucere semper consueuistis, illi quoque qui non discunt
graece tamen communi scholae suae studio ducti, in stipendium
eius qui alijs graeca praelegit, viritim, quam honeste contribuunt. Haec inquam vos videtis, multaque item alia, quibus inue-
niendis ingenioli mei paruitas non sufficit, cui propositum est
25 potius eorum vos commonefacere, quae alij dicunt ac sentiunt,
quam quid vos facere deceat consulere, qui multo acutius quam
ego facio perspicitis, nisi tales improbe suborientes factiones mature comprimatis, fore ut pluribus paulatim contagio infectis
peior pars in maiorem tandem possit excrescere, atque ita futu-
30 rum, alij vt cogantur in vestrum, qui boni ac sapientes estis, auxilium manus apponere; nam ego certe neminem esse reor, qui
vllo tempore vnquam fuit e vobis, quin academiae vestrae statum
tam ad se pertinere ducat, quam ad ipsos vos qui nunc ibi viuitis.

---

4 est,] R, est T 1633   5 defendere,] 1633, defendere; T R   8 deterreri] 1633,
deterreri, T R   11 vestris] 1633, vestris, T R   17 nominatim] T 1633, nominatam
R   18 suum] T R, summo 1633   19 isthic] T R, isthinc 1633; sidenote in R Nota
21 graece] graece, T 1633, graece; R; tamen] T R, tam 1633; scholae suae] T R, suae
scholae 1633   22 quam] T R, perquam 1633   28 infectis] 1633, infectis, T R   29
excrescere,] 1633, excrescere: T R   30 estis,] R, estis T 1633   32 vobis,] 1633, vobis
T R; statum] 1633, statum, T R   33 ibi viuitis] T R, viuitis ibi 1633

ready been translated than many men of today who consider themselves very learned would normally read; nor did they merely learn it, they also advised later scholars, especially those who were going to become theologians, to do the same thing.

Therefore, as I have said, my intention is not to defend the study of Greek before prudent judges like yourselves, but rather to do as my own sense of duty directs me: to urge you to let none be deterred from the pursuit of Greek learning in your university whether by public sermons or by private impertinence, since that language is one which the Church has decreed should be taught in all universities. Hence men of your prudence will easily discern that not everyone in your community who has devoted his energies to Greek is completely obtuse; indeed, some of these men have distinguished themselves so highly that their own fame for learning has won a good deal of real glory for your school not only in this realm but also abroad. You will also discern that a large number of people, whose precedent others will follow, have lately begun to make large contributions to your university with the aim of promoting both literary studies in general and, most recently, Greek in particular. But their present enthusiasm for you will undoubtedly wane if they find that their pious intentions are mocked there in Oxford, particularly since in Cambridge, which you have always been wont to outshine, even those who are not learning Greek are each moved by a common devotion to their school to make a handsome personal contribution for the salary of a lecturer to teach others Greek. You will discern all these arguments, I repeat, and a number of others, as well, which my own humble intellect is too weak to discover. But my purpose is rather to tell you what others are saying and thinking than to give you advice about what you should do. You perceive much more sharply than I do that unless you suppress such unsavory factions at once as they arise, more and more will contract this disease until the worse party may grow to outnumber the better, so that others will be forced to step in and help those of you who are virtuous and sensible. For I certainly think that no one who has ever belonged to your number feels any less personal concern for the status of your university than you yourselves do who live there today.

Corpus Christi College, Oxford, in David Loggan, *Oxonia Illustrata*, Oxford, 1675 (reduced)

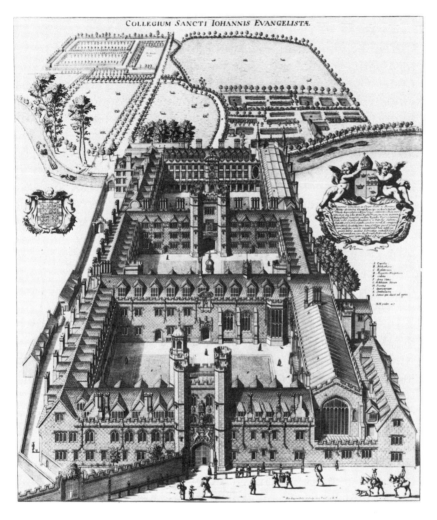

St. John's College, Cambridge, in David Loggan, *Cantabrigia Illustrata*,
Cambridge, [1690?] (reduced)

   Neque dubitandum est, quin Reuerendissimus in Christo pater Cantuariensis Antistes, qui et cleri totius nostri primas est et
uester Cancellarius, non erit hac in re vlla ex parte remissus,
idque vel cleri causa vel vestra: quorum vtriusque valde sentit
5   interesse, ne studia isthic intercidant; intercident autem, si con-
tentionibus laborante gymnasio, a stultis passim atque inertibus
artes bonae permittantur impune punederideri. Quid autem reuerendissimus in Christo pater Cardinalis Eboracensis, qui et
literarum promotor, et ipse literatissimus Antistes est? an is bo-
10 narum artium et linguarum studium impune apud vos ludibrio
haberi pa[301]tienter ferat? ac non potius aduersus sciolos istos,
contemptores earum, et doctrinae et virtutis et authoritatis suae
aculeos est exerturus? Denique christianissimus princeps noster,
cuius sacra Maiestas bonas artes omnes tanto fauore prose-
15 quitur, quanto Principum vnquam quisquam, et qui praeterea
tantum habet eruditionis ac iudicij, quantum hactenus Principum habuit nemo, nunquam haud dubie pro immensa prudentia sua tantaque in Deum pietate patietur bonarum artium
studia malorum atque inertium studijs hominum in eo dilabi
20 loco, in quo maiores eius clarissimi, clarissimum gymnasium statuerunt, quod non solum sit ex vetustissimis, vnde multi tantae
eruditionis exorti sunt, vt non Angliam solum, sed et totam il-
lustrarint Ecclesiam, verumetiam quod pluribus Collegijs or-
natum est, quibus perpetui prouentus assignantur ad alendos
25 studiosos, quam vt sit extra suum regnum Academia vlla, quae
cum isto gymnasio vestro in ea vna re conferri aut comparari
possit: quorum omnium Collegiorum hic scopus est, et tantum
isthic apud vos prouentuum non aliam ob causam collatum est,
quam vt magnus scholasticorum numerus, liber a parandi victus
30 sollicitudine, bonas ibi artes perdisceret.

2 Antistes,] R, Antistes T 1633; est] 1633, est, T R   5 isthic] T R, isthac 1633   11
istos,] R, istos T 1633   12 doctrinae et virtutis] 1633, doctrinae, et virtutis, T, doctrinae
et virtutis, R   16–17 Principum habuit] T R, habuit principum 1633   18 sua] 1633,
sua, T R   19 studia] 1633, studia, T R; studijs hominum] T, studijs R 1633   20–21
statuerunt,] 1633, statuerunt; T R   21–22 tantae eruditionis] T, tanta eruditione R
1633   22 totam] T, totam etiam R 1633   23 Ecclesiam,] 1633, Ecclesiam; T,
Ecclesiam) R; sidenote in R Nota   26 conferri aut comparari] T, conferri R 1633   30
sollicitudine,] sollicitudine T R 1633; perdisceret.] R 1633, perdisceret: T

There is no room for doubt that the most reverend father in Christ, the archbishop of Canterbury, who is the primate of all our clergy as well as your chancellor, will do all that he can in this matter, both for the clergy's sake and for your own, since he realizes how important it is both for the clergy and for you that your system of studies should not go to ruin. But it will go to ruin if the university is racked by contention and if the foolish and slothful are allowed to flout sound learning everywhere with impunity. And what about the most reverend father in Christ, the cardinal of York, both a patron of learning and a most learned bishop in his own right? Is he going to stand by and permit sound learning and the study of languages to be mocked among you with impunity? Or is he not more likely to launch all the darts of his learning, his virtue, and his authority to punish those witlings who are treating sound learning with contempt? Finally, what of our most Christian prince? His sacred majesty has shown as much favor for all sound learning as any prince ever did, while in erudition and judgment he is more than a match for any previous prince. With his limitless prudence and great piety toward God he will undoubtedly never permit the endeavors of wicked and slothful individuals to abolish the pursuit of sound learning in a place where his own most illustrious forebears established a most illustrious university, which is not only one of the oldest, with a long roll of learned alumni who have been ornaments not only to England but to the entire Church, but can also boast so many colleges with perpetual endowments for the support of students that in this one respect there is no foreign university which can compete or compare with your own. And the sole purpose of all of these colleges and the one reason for which you have all those endowments is so that a great number of scholars, free from having to worry about earning a living, can study the liberal arts there.

Verum ego nihil dubito Prudentias vestras facile rationem
inituras, qua contentiones istas et ineptissimas factiones ipsi
compescatis, curaturasque ut omne genus bonarum literarum,
non modo vacet irrisu atque ludibrio, sed in precio quoque atque
5   honore habeatur. Qua vestra diligentia, et multum bonis studijs
apud vos proderitis et illustrissimum Principem nostrum dictos-
que Reuerendissimos in Christo patres vix dici potest quantum
demerebimini: me vero ipsum, qui haec omnia ob ingentem
amorem meum erga vos, hoc tempore, hac manu mea [302]
10   scribenda esse duxi, mirabiliter profecto deuincietis; cuius studium et operam in vestram vtilitatem paratissima non vniuersi
modo, sed singuli quoque vestrum praesto sibi fore intelligent.
Deus clarissimam istam Academiam vestram seruet incolumem
reddatque indies magis magisque bonis literis omnibus et virtute
15   florentem. Abingdoniae quarto Kal. April.

                                                    Thomas Morus

---

4 irrisu] *T*, irrisione *R 1633*   9 vos,] *R*, vos *T 1633*   10 deuincietis;] deuincietis *T*,
deuincietis: *R*, deuincietis. *1633*

But I have no doubt that prudent men like yourselves will easily devise your own plan to suppress those disturbances and impertinent factions and that you will make sure that all types of sound learning will not only be safe from derision and mockery but will also be valued and honored. By your diligence in this regard you will do a great service to sound studies at Oxford, and it is hard to express how much thanks you will earn both from our most illustrious prince and from those reverend fathers in Christ I have named. And although the great love that I bear you already is what led me to write all these things at this time, and with this my own hand, you will also endear yourselves more intensely than ever to me personally, whose devotion and energies your whole assembly and each of its members will perceive to be always at your service. May God keep and preserve this illustrious university of yours and may he grant it perpetual increase of all honest learning and virtue. Abingdon. 29 March.

Thomas More

LETTER TO EDWARD LEE
TEXT AND TRANSLATION

Thomas Morvs
Eduardo Leo S. P. D.

Accepi, mi charissime Lee, binas e fratre tuo Galfrido, et
optimo simul et humanissimo adolescente, litteras, vtrasque
5 Louanij scriptas: alteras quidem decimo, alteras vero xx. Aprilis
die. In superioribus tria potissimum haec continentur: Primum
videlicet tibi esse allatum, ac id etiam per Erasmicos quosdam
passim [B₄v] esse sparsum, me non parum iniquo animo tulisse
te contra Erasmum nonnihil esse molitum, atque ob id me abs te
10 vsque adeo alienatum, vt non modo ex amicorum numero ex-
emerim, sed quippiam etiam aduersus te mali machiner. Quam
rem si exploratam haberes, aut tecum libere (si quidem posset
animus ferre) decerneres, vt ne flocci quidem talem amicum
faceres, aut (si tibi imperare id non posses), quippe qui nihil
15 aeque dolenter atque ingratitudinem feras, habenas dolori permitteres, vt cui ipsa mors quam tanti amici iactura foret optatior,
quem non vulgariter amaueris, ac pro virili semper in astra
laudibus vexeris: Quo minus mirum sit si tibi iam videatur non
ferenda molestia, si ipse contra tam ingratus atque adeo iniquus
20 sim, vt contra amicum velim necdum auditum praeposteram
ferre sententiam. Quare id a me esse factum nec posse te scribis
nec velle credere, quantumuis id constanter Erasmici confir-
ment, antequam eius rei ex meis litteris ipsius fias certior.

---

3 Accepi, mi charissime Lee,] Accepi mi charissime Lee *1520;* Galfrido] Gal frido *1520*ᵐ,
Golfrido *1520*ᵃ   4 simul] *1520*ᵃ simul, *1520*ᵐ; adolescente,] adolescente *1520*   5
Louanij] *1520*ᵐ, Louan *1520*ᵃ; xx.] *1520*ᵐ, vicjmo *1520*ᵃ   6 continentur:] continentur. *1520*ᵐ, continentur *1520*ᵃ   7 id] *1520*ᵐ, iam *1520*ᵃ   8 tulisse] tulisse, *1520*
9–10 me . . . adeo] *1520*ᵐ, usque adeo me abs te *1520*ᵃ   12–13 libere (si . . . ferre)]
*1520*ᵃ, libere, si . . . ferre, *1520*ᵐ   12 posset] *1520*ᵃ, possit *1520*ᵐ   14 aut
(si . . . posses),] aut si . . . posses, *1520*   16 mors] mors, *1520*   18 vexeris:] vexeris.
1520   19 ingratus] *1520*ᵃ, ingratus, *1520*ᵐ   20 necdum] *1520*ᵃ, nec dum *1520*ᵐ
21 scribis] scribis, *1520*   22 credere,] *1520*ᵃ, credere *1520*ᵐ   23 litteris ipsius]
*1520*ᵐ, ipsius literis *1520*ᵃ

THOMAS MORE sends his heartiest
greetings to Edward Lee.

M Y DEAREST Lee, I have received two letters through your
brother Wilfred, a most virtuous and amiable young man; both
were written in Louvain, one on the tenth day of April and the
other on the twentieth. The first one contains three main points,
which are these. First of all, you have heard a report which is
being spread everywhere by certain Erasmians to the effect that
I was more than a little upset by your having prepared a work
challenging Erasmus, and that this had turned me against you to
the point that I had not only struck you from my list of friends
but was also preparing to do you a bad turn. And if you were
quite certain of this you would either resolve, if your feelings
would bear it, to spurn such a friend altogether, or if you could
not bring yourself to do that you would freely indulge your own
grief, since nothing grieves you as much as ingratitude, while to
you death itself would be preferable to the loss of so great a
friend, whom you have loved with an uncommon fervor and
constantly praised to the skies with your utmost devotion; thus, it
is not surprising that you would consider it an intolerable hardship if I were in turn so ungrateful and even so unfair as to pass
hasty judgment on my friend before even hearing him out.
Therefore you write that you neither can nor will believe that I
have done so, even though the Erasmians steadily insist that I
have, before you receive definite news of the fact in a letter
directly from me.

Secundo loco, conatus apud me probare, nihil in toto isto
negocio tua culpa commissum, sed totam istam tragoediam Erasmo deberi, fusius explicatiusque rem omnem ab origine re-
petens, totius litis et ortae simul et auctae semina declaras: Pri-
5 mum quod istam annotandi operam nunquam fueras obiturus,
nisi et amore et precibus eius pertinacibus superatus: Deinde
quod ille tuas annotationes vt minutias ac nugamenta reiecerit,
ac nihilo minus a scriba tuo clanculum sibi curauerit exscriben-
das, indeque excerpsisse si quid forte in secun[C₁]da aeditione
10 mutauit in melius, Nec tamen his contentus, tuum nomen per
Europam totam infame reddiderit quasi minuta collegeris,
quasique eadem neotericorum decretis munieris, negaerisque
ipsi facere videndi copiam, quo vel errata corrigat, vel defendat
sese.
15 Tercio subijcis quod cum annotationes tuas in eius dedecus
emittere licuisset, eas tamen hactenus suppresseris, nihil adhuc
in eo negocio vltra progredi decernens, nisi prius eas ad reuerendum in Christo patrem episcopum Roffensem expendendas excutiendasque dedisses, qui (si id cuperem) mihi quo-
20 que videndi faceret potestatem. Hic oras vt rem aequa lance exa-
minem, perspecturus si id fecero quam simpliciter cum eo agas,
quam citra fucum, citra lenocinium, citra morsum, tantum annotans quid ille scribat quidque ipse contra sentias. Quod si qua
tamen eum acrius liberiusque taxas, rogas vt aeque id quoque
25 perpendam, videlicet an sic ille mereatur. Iam fore asseris (nisi
longe te tua fallat opinio) vt et grauiter eum et foede lapsum esse
comperiam.
Haec vt arbitror superioris epistolae tuae summa est. Iam ad
secundas litteras, quae decimo post priores die scriptae te totum
30 subito mutatum indicant. In his enim scribis iam adesse tempus
quo me eum declarem, quem tu me semper apud animum tuum

---

1 loco,] loco *1520*   4 auctae] *1520*ᵃ, auctae, *1520*ᵐ; declaras:] declaras. *1520*   6
superatus:] superatus. *1520*   9 excerpsisse] *See commentary.*   10 melius,] melius.
1520   11 infame] *1520*ᵃ, infamem *1520*ᵐ   18–19 expendendas] *1520*ᵃ,
expendendas, *1520*ᵐ   22 fucum,] *1520*ᵃ, fucum *1520*ᵐ   22–23 annotans] *1520*ᵃ,
annotans, *1520*ᵐ   23 scribat] scribat, *1520*   29 scriptae] scriptae, *1520*   31 me
eum] *1520*ᵐ, me *1520*ᵃ; tu me] *1520*ᵐ, tu *1520*ᵃ

Secondly, you try to prove to me that you are not to blame for anything that has happened in this controversy and that all the credit for this tragedy should go to Erasmus. You rehearse the whole course of events more completely and circumstantially and you detail the origins of the entire quarrel from birth to full growth, claiming first that you would never have undertaken that project of annotation if you had not been prevailed upon by your love and his persistent requests, that he then rejected your annotations as hairsplitting trifles, that he nonetheless had your scribe copy them out for him secretly and took from them any corrections he made in his second edition, and that now, not content with this, he has made your name infamous throughout Europe as if you gathered nothing but trifles and as if you supported them with the doctrines of modern thinkers and refused to let him see your work so that he could either retract any errors or defend himself.

Thirdly, you add that even though you could have disgraced him by publishing your annotations you have so far suppressed them, having resolved not to go any further in this controversy until you had delivered them to the reverend father in Christ, the bishop of Rochester, to weigh and examine, who would allow me to see them too, if I wanted to do so. Here you beg me to give your behavior a fair, balanced assessment, confident that if I do so I will see how straightforwardly you are dealing with him, how unaffectedly, how unobsequiously, how inoffensively, only noting what he writes and in what respect you disagree. But if you ever criticize him more sharply and freely, you ask me also to be fair in weighing the question of whether he deserves it. You assert that (unless your opinion completely misleads you) I will then find that he has made serious and shameful mistakes.

I think this is the gist of your first letter; now on to your second, written just ten days later, which suggests you have gone through a sudden and complete transformation. For in this one you write that now is the time for me to prove myself the sort of

praesumpseris, hoc est aequum, et cui nullus vnquam affectus
(vt tuis verbis vtar) imposuerit. Nam cum male ab Erasmo habitus, communibus tamen amicis rem integram componendam,
donec famae tuae consultum esse posset, permisisses, libellum-
5   que iam tum reueren[C₁v]do patri Roffensi cuius tu iudicio
standum censueras transmisisses, cui rei etiam Erasmus ipse,
cum id ei significasses, subscripserat, is tamen, longe aliter quam
prae se ferebat cogitans, intra paucos quibus haec pactus esset
dies repente in sua contra Latomum apologia, temere et loco
10 alieno, tum nec abs te lesus, plusquam insana vomuerit, cuius etsi
nomine abstinebat, non ita tamen id tecte, quin statim clamarent
omnes, illud telum in tuum caput esse contortum. Itaque etsi nec
tuum nomen ibi legebatur, neque res quicquam in tuos mores
competeret, tamen cum tota Europa sic interpretaretur, perinde
15 ac palam te nominatimque designatum accipis, maxime quod is
tuo rogatu, Apologia quapiam, hac te suspicione liberare
noluerit. Quare cum ille hoc pacto se gesserit, atque negocium
ipsum tam longe iam euectum sit, iniuriam mihi te facturum
putas, nisi me tam aequum existimares, vt non modo sinam ver-
20 umetiam suadeam id vt agas sedulo, quo fama tua in tuto col-
locetur, cui cum nullo alio modo quam aeditis annotationibus
consulere possis, hac tibi necessario esse grassandum: Denique
hoc tam infixum animo tuo persuasumque esse, vt neque bonum
quemquam nec prudentem putes dissuasurum. Qua in re me vt
25 amicus perstem, quemadmodum tu mihi semper fueris, semper-
que futurus sis, etiam atque etiam oras.

---

4 posset,] posset *1520*   7 significasses,] significasses *1520*ᵐ, significas *1520*ᵃ   7–8
tamen, longe . . . cogitans,] tamen longe . . . cogitans *1520*   10 tum] *1520*ᵃ, tamen
*1520*ᵐ; nec]*1520*ᵐ, naec *1520*ᵃ; lesus,] lesus *1520*   15 accipis, maxime] *1520*ᵃ, accipis:
maxime, *1520*ᵐ   17 Quare] *Para. 1520*ᵐ   18 ipsum] *1520*ᵃ, ipsum, *1520*ᵐ   20
sedulo] *1520*ᵃ, saedulo *1520*ᵐ   22 grassandum:] grassandum. *1520;* Denique] *Para.*
*1520*ᵐ   26 sis,] *1520*ᵃ, sis *1520*ᵐ

man you always supposed I was, namely a fair one, a man whom, in your words, "no partisan feelings have ever deceived." For though you—even after Erasmus had treated you badly—had left it to your common friends to remedy the situation for as long as that policy might safeguard your honor, and though you had already sent the book to the reverend father of Rochester, whose judgment you had decided to stand by, and though even Erasmus himself had approved of this plan when you mentioned it to him, his actual intentions were totally different from those he professed, and within a few days of agreeing to your plan he suddenly spewed out a barrage of utterly insane abuse, wantonly and inappropriately and with no provocation from you, in his *Apology against Latomus,* in which even if he did avoid mentioning your name he was still not discreet enough to keep everyone from shouting immediately that that shot had been aimed straight at you. And so even if your name does not appear in the passage, and even if what he said there does not match your character at all, nevertheless, since all of Europe has been interpreting it this way, you take it as if you had been mentioned expressly by name, especially since he refused your request to relieve you of this suspicion with any apology. Thus, since he has behaved in this way and the business has now gone so far, you feel you would be doing me an injustice if you did not think me fair enough that I would not merely allow you but actually urge you to make every effort to protect your own honor; and since you cannot safeguard it except by publishing your annotations, this is the way you will have to proceed. Finally, you are so firmly persuaded of this that you feel no good or prudent person will try to dissuade you. And you beg me again and again to be your steadfast friend in this matter as you have always been and will always be mine.

Tametsi mi Lee tuarum litterarum materia tam varia sit ac multiplex, vt breuibus respondere non possim, respondebo tamen quam [C₂] breuissime possum, quando neque tui temporis multum libet occupare, nec mei tantum superest, vt inde
5 multum liceat decerpere quod in scribendas huiusmodi litteras impartiar. Quod ipsum alioquin vt nunc res habet videri possim nullo cum fructu facturus, quandoquidem tute tecum quid sequi velis tanquam iurata styge sanxisti, neque moratus quicquam reditum fratris et praecisis omnibus omnium amicorum consi-
10 lijs. Qui quid nunc dicturi sint haud scio. Sequentur fortasse quidam vetus illud consilium, "feras, non culpes, quod mutari non potest." Verum istud ausim affirmare maxime, si eos ante consulere maluisses quam ipse constituere, perquam hercle paucos repperisses hic, qui non annotationes istas tibi abdendas
15 potius perpetuo quam aedendas esse vnquam censuissent, quos ipsos tamen deierare liquet (quod te quoque Lee certe credo credere) non minus ex animo vereque esse tuos, aliquot item (quod spero) non minus sapientes, qui te ab isto satagant proposito retinere, quam sit istorum quisquis est isthic prudentissimus,
20 qui te in aeditionem istam tam importune protrudunt atque praecipitant.

Certe quod ad me attinet quemadmodum litteris ac prudentia cuique fere tuorum amicorum cesserim, sic beneuolentia et fide nullum non fidenter prouocauerim, ne tu me putes ea parte
25 superari, qua sic amari me abs te atque honorifice scribis praedicari. Qua in re vicem rettulisse me, cum summates aliquot viros [C₂v] testes habeo, tum quos neque potes reijcere, neque ab ijsdem potes iam saepe non audisse, fratrem vtrumque charissimum. Quanquam ne fratribus quidem tuis tametsi fratres
30 sint istud concesserim, tibi magis vt ex animo bene velint, quam ipse cupiam. Erasmum fateor vehementer diligo, nec id ob aliam

---

1 materia] *1520*ᵐ, mateira *1520*ᵃ; tam] *1520*ᵐ, iam *1520*ᵃ   9 fratris] fratris, *1520*
9–10 consilijs.] *1520*ᵃ, consilijs *1520*ᵐ   11–12 mutari non potest] *1520*ᵐ, mutare non
potes *1520*ᵃ   14 abdendas] *1520*ᵃ, abdendas, *1520*ᵐ   15 perpetuo] perpetuo, *1520*
16 quoque] *1520*ᵐ, quoque mi *1520*ᵃ   17 animo] *1520*ᵃ, animo, *1520*ᵐ   18 (quod
spero)] *1520*ᵃ, quod spero *1520*ᵐ   23 cesserim,] cesserim: *1520*ᵐ, cesserim. *1520*ᵃ
26 rettulisse me,] *1520*ᵃ, rettulisse, me *1520*ᵐ   28 audisse,] audisse *1520*   30
magis vt] *1520*ᵐ, ut magis *1520*ᵃ   31 diligo,] *1520*ᵃ, diligo *1520*ᵐ

Even though, my dear Lee, the subject matter of your letters is
so varied and complex that I can make no brief response, I will
still respond as briefly as I possibly can, since I do not wish to
occupy much of your time and I myself have too little to spare to
spend much of it writing a letter of this sort. And besides, as the
matter now stands, there might seem to be no point at all in my
doing so, since you have already fixed on your own plan of action
with Stygian finality, not delaying at all for your brother's return
and thus forestalling all the advice of every one of your friends. I
do not know what they are going to say now; perhaps some of
them will take the old advice, "Make the most of what cannot be
changed." But I would venture to give you my strongest assurance that, if you had asked their advice beforehand instead of
deciding the point by yourself, you would have found very few
here who would not have thought you would do better to put
away those annotations forever than ever to publish them. And
yet these men, who are anxious to stop you from putting your
plan into action, can swear with a clear conscience (and I certainly believe, Lee, that you too believe it) that they are no less
sincerely and truly yours, just as several of them are (I hope) no
less wise, than the most prudent of those over there who are
goading you on so insistently to rush into publication.

As for myself, though I would defer to almost any of your
friends in a contest of learning and prudence, when it comes to
goodwill and good faith there is none with whom I would not
confidently compete, so that you will not think I am thrown for a
loss at the point where you write about how much you love and
extol me. I can name various eminent men who will testify that I
have responded in kind, and two others whose testimony you
cannot reject and must have already heard frequently, namely
each of your very dear brothers. And yet even if they are your
brothers, I would not concede even to them that they feel more
sincere goodwill for you than I myself do. I confess that I am
very fond of Erasmus, for practically no other reason than that

ferme causam quam eam de qua totus eum Christianus orbis
amplectitur, Nempe quod inexhaustis eius vnius laboribus
omnes vndique bonarum studiosi litterarum, quantum non alterius fere cuiusquam aliquot ante saeculis, eruditione cum pro-
5 phana tum etiam sacra promouerint. Qua de re non mihi tamen
tam charus debet esse, quam tibi, qui (quod tuae luculenter os-
tendunt litterae) haudquaquam paulo plus fructus ab illo retulisti. Contra non vnam esse causam video, quae seorsum tibi mi
Lee me studio non vulgari deuinciat, vel ipsius, vt reliquas omit-
10 tam, patriae communis gratia, vel parentum inter se nostrorum
tam amica, tam diuturna coniunctio, quae res effecerunt, vt ego
te olim puerulum certe scitissimum annis ipse decem prouectior
exosculatus, iam illam inde perpetuo deamarim indolem, Sed
amicus magis interim quam familiaris, futurus profecto, quoad
15 per me liceret, familiarissimus, nisi nos diuersa vitae conditio
atque institutum longe disiunxisset, nec tam longe tamen dis-
iunxit vnquam, vt non ob oculos interim versaretur meos eximium illud tam probe eductum atque educatum ad litteras ingenium, doctrinae sitis inextincta, tam feruens in disciplinas
20 impetus, tam instans et indefessa contentio, Quae me res in se
libenter intentum magis indies magis[C₃]que in amorem tui
rapiebant, vel ea spe maxime quod magno cum gaudio pol-
licebar mihi tempus aliquando fore, quum nostra haec Britannia
totum per orbem reliquum tua celebraretur industria.
25   Ego quidem hactenus erga te non aliter ac dixi sum affectus,
qui ne nunc quidem aut amorem retraho, aut spem abijcio: tantum abest, vt machiner aut miner male. Sed tamen profecto mi
Lee, quo te vehementius adamaui, quo maiorem de te nobis
promisi gloriam, eo nunc vror impensius, cum ea te videam
30 animo tam obfirmato moliri, vnde non solus animo praesagiam,
neque tibi commodum neque patriae nostrae decus accessurum,
quando res inuidiosa videbitur, vnum te potissimum opus illud

---

2 amplectitur,] amplectitur. *1520*   4 saeculis,] saeculis *1520*   4–5 prophana] pro-
phana, *1520*   6–7 (quod . . . litterae)] quod . . . litterae, *1520*   7 litterae] littere
1520ᵐ, literae *1520ᵃ*   10 nostrorum] *1520ᵃ*, nostrorum, *1520ᵐ*   11 quae] *1520ᵃ*,
que *1520ᵐ*   13 indolem,] indolem. *1520*   15 liceret,] liceret *1520;* conditio] *1520ᵃ*,
conditio, *1520ᵐ*   18 eductum] *1520ᵃ*, eductum, *1520ᵐ*   20 contentio,] contentio
1520ᵐ, contentio. *1520ᵃ*   26 abijcio:] *1520ᵃ*, abijcio, *1520ᵐ*   32 videbitur,]*1520ᵃ*,
videbitur *1520ᵐ*

for which all of Christendom cherishes him, namely that this one man's unceasing exertions have done more to advance all students of sound intellectual disciplines everywhere in both secular and sacred learning than virtually anyone else's exertions for the last several centuries, though on this basis he should be less dear to me than to you, who have derived not a little more profit from him, as your letters show clearly. On the other hand, Lee, I see more than one reason why I should be linked to you personally by a bond of uncommon affection; not to mention the rest, there is devotion to our common fatherland and the friendly, enduring connection between our respective parents, through which I first came to embrace you many years ago, a precocious boy ten years my junior; and I have remained an admirer of yours ever since. Yet meanwhile I have been more of a friend than an intimate colleague, though I would certainly have been happy to be as intimate as possible if our separate professions and stations in life had not drawn us widely apart. And yet they never drew us so widely apart that I ever lost sight of that fine intellect, so well trained and well cultivated for learning, that insatiable thirst for knowledge, that fervent passion for studies, or that intense and unwearying drive, traits which easily held my attention and led me to love you more and more by the day, most of all in the hope that, as I very joyfully promised myself, a time would eventually come when your endeavors would make this Britain of ours famous throughout the rest of the world.

My own feelings for you until now have been just as I have described them, and not even now will I take back my love or abandon my hope; that is how far I am from designing or threatening to harm you. But assuredly, my dear Lee, the more vehemently I have loved you, and the greater the glory I thought you would bring us, the more deeply it hurts me to see you so stubbornly set on a plan which I am not alone in expecting will neither advance your own interests nor add to our country's prestige, since it will be seen as an invidious action on your

tam hostiliter oppugnare, quod alius haud absque magno fortunae salutisque suae dispendio communibus mortalium omnium commodis elaborauit: quin periculum est, si quo coepisti
perrexeris, ne animo te omnes communiter in se hostili esse
5 potius quam in Erasmum iudicent, quorum commoda studeas
corrumpere, quum huius auertere commoda non possis, quippe
qui suo nequit praemio fraudari apud benefactorum re-
muneratorem deum, etiamsi apud mortales opus eius vel reij-
ceretur, vel penitus interiret, quorum vel inuidia vel incuria iam
10 ante numerosa perierunt et perquam fructuosa volumina,
quorum nihilo minus autores fructum, quem terris afferre
studuerunt, ipsi retulerunt in coelo.

Verum hic mihi video respondendum esse ad eam epistolae
tuae particulam, qua tibi cum ingratus esse videar, tum iniurius,
15 si de labore tuo, quem nondum perlegi, tam praeceps ac mal-
i[C_3v]gne praeiudicem. Ego profecto mi Lee deiectioris animi
sum, quam vt mihi de cuiusquam operibus iudicium arrogem,
satis esse semper ratus ad arcendam temeritatis calumniam, si
aliorum accessissem calculis, praesertim talium quorum nec vir-
20 tus obscura sit et indubitata doctrina. Quam apud classem quum
velut vno celeumate sensissem plus huic vni, cui tu reclamas,
operi succlamatum, quam reliquis eius ipsius operibus omnibus,
cuius nulli mirifice non applauditur, mihi certe videbar nec
praecipitis accusandus iudicij, nec ingrati erga te animi censen-
25 dus, si ne lecto quidem vllo tui libelli versiculo tamen illis
putarem omnibus magis fidendum esse quam tibi. Cui si tam
aequus esse debuissem, vt te versionem Erasmi damnasse non
nisi exacto et irrefragabili iudicio praesumerem, in illos necesse
est omnes grauissimam atque iniquissimam censuram exer-
30 cuissem, quos aut tam socordes existimassem vt rem tantam
quantam tu hanc vis videri neglexerint, aut tam stupidos, vt
quod tibi fuit tam obuium non intellexerint, aut denique tam

1–2 fortunae] *1520*ᵃ, fortunae, *1520*ᵐ   2 suae] *1520*ᵃ, sue *1520*ᵐ; dispendio] dispendio, *1520*   3 elaborauit:] elaborauit, *1520*ᵐ, elaborauit. *1520*ᵃ   9 incuria] *1520*ᵃ,
incuria, *1520*ᵐ   10 perierunt] perierunt, *1520*   14 iniurius,] *1520*ᵃ, iniurius
*1520*ᵐ   15 perlegi,] *1520*ᵃ, perlegi *1520*ᵐ   20 sit] sit, *1520*; et indubitata] nec indubitata *1520*, nec dubitata *conj. 1760;* doctrina.] *1520*ᵃ, doctrina *1520*ᵐ   21 celeumate]
1520, celeusmate *conj. 1760;* reclamas,] reclamas *1520*   25 versiculo] *1520*ᵃ, versiculo,
*1520*ᵐ   27 damnasse] damnasse, *1520*   28 praesumerem,] *1520*ᵃ, praesumerem:
*1520*ᵐ

part when you alone make such a hostile attack on the very work that another man elaborated for the common benefit of all mortals at no small expense to his personal fortunes and health. Indeed, there is a danger that if you go on as you have begun, all will judge that you harbor a general hostility toward all of mankind, and not just toward Erasmus, since it is their interests that you will be trying to hurt; you cannot obstruct his. He is not to be cheated of his due reward at God's hand, who requites all good deeds, even if mortal men should either reject his work or allow it to perish completely as their envy or carelessness has allowed many very profitable volumes to perish before now, though their authors have still reaped the same profit in heaven that they tried to bestow on the earth.

But I see that I must now respond to that part of your letter in which you see me as both ungrateful and unjust if I pass a hasty and dispararaging judgment on your labor before reading it through. My dear Lee, I certainly do not have so high an opinion of myself as to presume to pass judgment on anyone's works; I have always thought it a sure enough way to avoid accusations of temerity if I voted the way other men vote, particularly if they were men of manifest virtue and undoubted learning. And when I observed that this class of men was unanimous in acclaiming this one work—the one you assail—more than all of his other works combined, although there is not one of his works they do not applaud enthusiastically, I certainly did not think that I would be charged with precipitate judgment or found guilty of ingratitude toward you if before reading even one line of your book I felt I ought to place more trust in all of those men than in you. For if I should have been so fair for your sake as to assume that your judgment in condemning Erasmus' translation was rigorous and irrefutable, I would have had to deliver a very severe and very unfair verdict on all of those men, whom I must have supposed to be either so lazy that they had neglected an issue as important as you contend this one to be, or so stupid that they had not understood something which was so obvious to you,

impios, vt pro Christo ei recusarint resistere, cui tu velut Dauid
contra Goliath pro Israhel opposuisti temet, in ea demum re
quam recta scirent in magnam ecclesiae perniciem (sic enim
scribis) tendere. Dabis hanc mihi mi Lee veniam, si tuo malui
5 iudicio timidius aliquanto credere, quam apud animum meum
cogerer acerbe condemnare tam multos, eosdemque tantos, vt
tibi sat scio videretur abunde magnum consecutus honorem,
quisquis ad viros eiusmodi virtute [C₄] putetur ac litteris aliquanto propius, quanquam ad aliquot adhuc parasangas distet,
10 accedere.

Quod si contra doctos esse dicas qui tecum sentiant, ea res mihi
fraudi esse non debet, quum ipse vix vnum audiam aut alterum
qui non sit indoctissimus: quos si tu hic audires suas obblaterantes ineptias, puderet te, certe mi Lee scio, talibus te lixis
15 potius quam militibus ducem deligi, nisi te (quod non spero)
Caesareus ille spiritus afflauerit, vt malis primus esse Mutinae
(nisi nomen excidit) quam secundus Romae. Quanquam vt est
eruditorum ciuilitas et indoctorum superbia, primum tibi locum
opinor citius cedant illi, quam hi vel secundum vel tercium.
20 Quod si tibi forte quidam animum faciunt istic, sunt nimirum hi
propter quos minus audeo hac in re credere tibi, cui haud paulo
plus credidissem soli, si non huiusmodi testes accessissent: Non
quod illis eruditionem vel auferam magnopere, vel tribuam
(nam sunt opinor ex his qui adhuc albine sint an atri nescimus)
25 sed quod in ERASMVM nimisquam feruntur iniqui, siue eos vt
homines sumus omnes humana titillet aemulatio, siue (quod
opinor verius) daemon aliquis eius pestis parens excitauit, vt

1 ei recusarint] *1520*ᵐ, recusarint ei *1520*ᵃ   2 temet,] *1520*ᵃ, temet. *1520*ᵐ   3
perniciem] *1520*ᵐ, pernicem *1520*ᵃ   5 quam] *See commentary.*   6 multos,] multos
1520; tantos,] *1520*ᵃ, tantos: *1520*ᵐ   8 quisquis ad] *1520*ᵐ, quisquis *1520*ᵃ; eiusmodi]
*1520*ᵃ, eiusmodi: *1520*ᵐ   9 propius,] *1520*ᵃ, propius: *1520*ᵐ; distet,] *1520*ᵃ, distet:
*1520*ᵐ   11 sentiant,] *1520*ᵃ, sentiant: *1520*ᵐ   12 debet,] *1520*ᵃ, debet: *1520*ᵐ
13–14 obblaterantes] oblatrantes *1520*ᵐ, oblaterantes *1520*ᵃ (*see commentary*)   14 te,]
te *1520*   15 deligi] *1520*ᵃ, delegi *1520*ᵐ; (quod non spero)] *1520*ᵃ, quod non spero
*1520*ᵐ   18 ciuilitas] ciuilitas, *1520*   22 accessissent:] accessissent. *1520*   24
albine] albi ne *1520*   25 nimisquam] *1520*ᵃ, nimis quam *1520*ᵐ   26–27 (quod opin-
or verius)] quod opinor verius *1520*ᵐ, quod opinor uerius, *1520*ᵃ

or finally so impious that they had refused to resist for Christ's
sake the same man against whom you have pitted yourself, like a
David opposing Goliath for Israel's sake, on an issue they knew
would contribute directly to what you describe as "the ruin of the
church." My dear Lee, you will have to forgive me for preferring
to be somewhat tentative in the way I accepted your judgment so
that I would not be driven to the ruthless condemnation of so
many others in my heart, especially when they are such great
men that I am sure you would consider it an ample distinction
for anyone if he were believed even to approximate the virtue
and learning of men such as these, though he might still fall
several leagues short of them.

You may answer that some learned men side with you. That
should not be considered to weigh against me, since I have heard
of barely one or two who are not altogether unlearned; and if
you heard them blathering their nonsense over here, I am sure,
my dear Lee, you would be quite ashamed to be chosen to lead
camp followers of this sort instead of real soldiers, unless
Caesar's ambition inspires you, which I hope it does not, to prefer the first rank in Mutina (unless that is not the right name) to
the second in Rome. But learned civility and unlearned arrogance being what they are, I suspect that the learned will grant
you the first rank before the unlearned will grant you the second
or third. But if you are actually being encouraged by certain men
over there, they are the very ones who make me still more reluctant to trust you regarding this issue, since I would have trusted
you singly considerably more than I do now that witnesses like
these have joined you. It is not that I particularly doubt or, for
that matter, acknowledge their learning, since I suspect they are
the sort of men who could be black or white for all we know; it is
rather that these men are reported to be unequivocally unfair to
Erasmus, whether they are egged on by plain human jealousy
(for we are all human) or whether, as I think more likely, some
demon gave rise to this plague by inciting them, secretly instigat-

quem nullis ipse rerum damnis, nullis corpusculi vel morbis vel
periculis, potuit a bonis vnquam studijs et toti terrarum pro-
futuris orbi reuellere, eum nunc submissis ac subornatis suis istis
satellitibus abducat, qui personata sanctimonia, [C₄v] Christi
5 negocium praetexentes, Christi negocium praepediant, dum ei
qui Christi negocium vere agit suis Sycophantijs moleste
negocium exhibent, atque a sacrarum tractatu literarum (vnde
velut ex inexhausto promptuario, profectui studiorum quotidie
fere depromebat aliquid) nunc ad apologias non perinde nobis
10 vtiles atque ipsi necessarias in transuersum agunt.

Hi semper (vt fertur) adornant aliquos, qui te inter atque Erasmum cursitent, et consutis vtrinque mendacijs, dum tibi ab illo
falsa atque illi vicissim abs te referunt, vos scelerate committant,
vt tuo periculo suis obsequantur affectibus, ipsi multo dig-
15 nissimi, qui illud potius odium subeant, quod perquam aegre
vitauerit quisquis id instituet, quod illi iam suadent tibi, non vt
vnum atque alterum decerpas locum in quibus aut illum labi,
quod fieri potest, ostendas, aut hallucinari te, quod et ipsum
possit accidere, Sed in totum opus adeo contorqueas machinam,
20 vt verti prorsus non debuisse contendas, neque, si quid a latinis
graeci discrepent codices, eius nos admoneri, vel si maxime deceat id fieri, tamen illum minime idoneum esse qui faceret, contra vel hic vel ibi sentientibus non omnibus tantum vndecunque
doctis sed ipso quoque doctorum omnium calculis anteponendo
25 pontifice, non maximo solum sed etiam optimo, cuius ad pium

1 corpusculi] *1520*ᵃ, corpusculi, *1520*ᵐ   2 studijs] studijs, *1520*   3 orbi reuellere,]
*1520*ᵃ, orbi, reuellere: *1520*ᵐ   4 satellitibus abducat,] satellitibus, abducat *1520*ᵐ,
satellitibus abducat *1520*ᵃ; personata] *conj. 1760*, personati *1520*   5 praepediant]
*1520*ᵐ, praedicant *1520*ᵃ   8 ex] *om. 1520*ᵃ; studiorum] *1520*ᵐ, studiosorum *1520*ᵃ;
quotidie] *1520*ᵃ, coditie *1520*ᵐ   10 vtiles] *1520*ᵃ, vtiles, *1520*ᵐ   11 (vt fertur)] vt
fertur *1520*   17 locum] *1520*ᵃ, locum, *1520*ᵐ; illum] *1520*ᵐ, illud *1520*ᵃ   18
potest,] potest *1520;* te,] te: *1520*ᵐ, te *1520*ᵃ   19 possit] *1520*ᵃ, posset *1520*ᵐ;
accidere,] *1520*ᵃ, accidere. *1520*ᵐ; Sed] *See commentary.*   20 prorsus] *1520*, potius
1760   20–21 neque, si . . . codices,] neque si . . . codices *1520*   21 nos] *1520*ᵃ, non
*1520*ᵐ   23 omnibus] *1520*ᵃ, omnibus, *1520*ᵐ   24 sed ipso quoque] *1520*ᵃ, et ipso-
que *1520*ᵐ   25 solum] *1520*ᵃ, solo, *1520*ᵐ

ing those minions of his to deter the man whom no material expense and no physical illness or danger could tear from the virtuous labors which he was performing for the good of the entire world. With a pretense of holiness they claim to be furthering Christ's work, but they are actually hindering Christ's work as they create work with their irksome slanders for the man who is really pursuing Christ's work and divert him from writing about sacred scripture, out of which, as if out of an inexhaustible storehouse, he used to bring something new almost daily for the advancement of scholarship, to writing apologies which are not so much useful to us as compulsory for him.

It is reported that these men get others to run back and forth between you and Erasmus, patching together lies and reporting falsely what each of you has been saying about the other, so that this vile deception will set you at odds and those fellows can serve their own partisan feelings at your peril. They themselves deserve to endure all the hatred which will inevitably be directed against anyone who sets out to do what these men are now urging you to do, not to select just a passage or two in which you can show either that he has made a mistake (which is certainly possible) or that you miss the point (which is also quite possible), but rather to launch an all-out attack on his project by claiming that he ought not to have made the translation at all and ought not to have told us about the discrepancies between the Greek texts and the Latin, and that even if this were worth doing he was not at all competent to do it. Not only do all learned men both in Louvain and here disagree with you on each of these points, but the pope, best and greatest of primates, who ought to take precedence over all learned men's votes, disagrees with you, too. For at his

suasum Erasmus eum laborem obedienter aggressus, rem bis
iam feliciter adiuuante deo perfecit: Bis a pontifice, quod eius
declarant veneranda diplomata, gratiam laudemque non vul-
garem promeruit.

5   Quamobrem si de libro qui Christi continet doctrinam, Christi
vicario [D₁] credidi, qui eum librum bis iam pronunciauit vtilem,
huic inquam si te reclamante credidi, qui librum scribis esse
perniciosum, neque temere me fecisse, neque te iniuria affecisse
iudico, etiam si mihi liber tuus omnino esset ignotus. At nec is
10   tam prorsus est ignotus mihi, vt non aliquid inde saltem de-
gustarim, ex quo reliqua liceat conijcere. Nam etsi ad me non
peruenerat, peruenit tamen ad quosdam, amica tuorum sollicitudine, aliorum iudicia ne nimium tibi fideres explorantium,
qui cum legissent ac perpendissent secum, tum de re tota sic
15   iudicassent, vt his a quibus acceperant librum suaderent, vti ad te
scriberent, si tuo vellent honori consultum, huic labori supersederes (Quam rem non dubito, quin ijdem amici tui pro sua in
te fide significarint), Mihi quoque velut speciminis loco indica-
runt quaedam, sed non nisi praecipua, quibus potissimum vide-
20   baris tibi spondere victoriam. Non mihi mi Lee, quod dixi, tantum sumo, vt in Theologicarum rerum controuersijs feram
sententiam, ne quis mihi merito possit ingerere, "Ne sutor vltra
crepidam." Sed tamen profecto, quas mihi communicabant,
quas certe tanquam primarias communicabant, pleraeque
25   omnes erant eiusmodi, quas ipse quoque videor mihi sine magno
posse negocio dissoluere. Quamobrem ex praecipuis cum
plerasque repperissem tales, merito videbar ex illis reliquas quoque, velut ex vngue, quod aiunt, leonem posse existimare. Nam
cuius vngues non laeserint, eius non est quod pilos valde
30   pertime[D₁v]scas.
    Certe illa contentio de vocabulo "proprij," quam litteris tuis ad
nos inseruisti, quae tam firma videtur tibi, vt non vnis litteris
mirari te testeris Erasmi impudentiam, quem non pudeat in re

1 rem] *perhaps we should read* cum rem   2 perfecit:] perfecerit, *1520ᵐ*, perfecit, *1520ᵃ*
(*see commentary*)   5 continet] *1520ᵃ*, continent *1520ᵐ*   11 etsi] et si *1520*   12
quosdam,] quosdam *1520*   13 iudicia] iudicia, *1520*   16 consultum,] *1520ᵃ*,
consultum *1520ᵐ*   16–17 supersederes] supersederes. *1520*   18 significarint),]
significarint) *1520ᵐ*, significarint *1520ᵃ*   20 Lee,] Lee *1520*   22 quis] *1520ᵐ*, quis
illud *1520ᵃ*   25 videor] *1520ᵃ*, videar *1520ᵐ*   33 mirari te] *1520ᵐ*, mirari *1520ᵃ*

pious urging Erasmus obediently undertook this task, which with God's help he has now performed twice with success, and thereby he has twice earned the pope's special thanks and approval, as his solemn missives acknowledge.

Therefore, given that this book contains the teaching of Christ, if I trusted the vicar of Christ to assess it, who has twice now declared the book useful, if I trusted the pope, I repeat, even though you oppose him and write that the book is pernicious, I judge that I have done nothing rash or unjust to you, even if your own book were completely unknown to me. But in fact it is not so totally unknown to me that I have not at least sampled enough of it to guess what the rest is like. For though it never reached me, it did reach certain people through the friendly solicitude of your close associates when they were surveying the judgments of others lest you might be placing inordinate trust in your own. When these people had read and considered the book thoroughly, and had judged the whole matter in such a way that they urged those who had submitted it that, if they wished to protect your reputation, they should write to you, urging you to abandon this task (and no doubt those same friends faithfully relayed this message to you), they then indicated a few of your principal points to me, too, as examples, the very points on which you seemed to feel that your victory was certain. As I said, my dear Lee, I am not presumptuous enough to hand down a verdict in disputes about theological topics lest anyone should rightly admonish me, "Let the cobbler stick to his last." But even so, the notes which they showed me, which they clearly did as if these were the best ones, were mostly the kind that I feel even I can refute without any great effort. Consequently, when I found most of your principal notes were of this sort, I thought that I could fairly size up the rest on the basis of these, like a lion from his claw, as the saying goes. For if a lion's claws do you no harm, there is no point in fearing his whiskers.

Certainly that argument about the term "proprium" ["one's own"] which you included in your letter to me, and which seems so substantial to you that in more than one letter you testify that you are amazed at Erasmus' impudence in daring to defend his

tam aperta suam tueri partem, non mihi modo, sed reliquis quoque, ad quos eadem de re scripsisti, tam tenuis videtur argutia, vt
contra valde miremur, sustinuisse te, vt eam rem ei vicio ver-
teres. Nam si mortales omnes tam adamantinis vinculis ad Por-
5   phyrij constringas Εἰσαγωγήν, vt quando ille "proprium" id de-
finiat, quod ita sit meum, vt nulli sit mecum commune, fas idcirco non sit eodem vocabulo sic vti quo modo publicitus omnes
vbique gentes vtuntur, piaculum profecto sit si quis posthac propriam dicat patriam in qua natus est, aut propriam vocet pa-
10   rochiam in qua versatur, aut denique patrem, a quo genitus est,
appellet proprium, si modo fratres habeat, quibus sit pater cum
illo communis, Quanquam nec Porphyrius tam difficilis est hac
in parte, quam tu, qui plures tradit modos citra vicium eius
vsurpandi vocabuli, de quo vocabulo, nihil ego in praesentiarum
15   fueram dicturus omnino, nisi quod in epistolis istud tuis ipse
commemorasti, quandoquidem de re tota quid haberem animi
quum fratribus tuis, tum amicorum tuorum penitissimis olim
indicaui, per quos iam diu ad te (id quod volebam) peruenisse
scio, ne nunc primum esset opus id rumore demum te per Eras-
20   meos disperso didicisse.

    Venio nunc ad expositionem tuam, qua rem a principio
repetis, id videlicet agens, vt ostendas Erasmi tantum culpa
to[D₂]tam hanc et natam et altam esse tragoediam. Quanquam
hac in parte profecto operaeprecium est videre, vt id quod vnum
25   sic Erasmo tribuis, vt praeterea nihil, ipse tibi desumas, et rhetoris hic agas partes, res videlicet per se exiles cumulatim verbis
exaggerans. Quorum tamen, si quis detracta mole nudas in
vnum res collegerit, opinor non inueniet, cur tibi videri debeas
ab illo tam capitaliter offensus, vt, dum illum contingat laedere,
30   ne communibus quidem omnium bonis euertendis abstineas
manum. Etenim si quis omnia congerat, quae in tuis litteris vel ad
me vel ad alium quempiam memorasti, quibus illius in te con-

---

4 omnes tam . . . vinculis] omnes, tam . . . vinculis, *1520*   5 Εἰσαγωγήν] εἰσαγωγήν
1520; quando] *1520*ᵃ, qñ *1520*ᵐ   7 vti] vti, *1520*   13 modos] *1520*ᵃ, modos, *1520*ᵐ
16 commemorasti,] *1520*ᵃ, commemorasti. *1520*ᵐ   18 indicaui] *1520*ᵐ, iudicaui
*1520*ᵃ; te (id . . . volebam)] te id . . . volebam *1520*ᵐ, te, id . . . uolebam, *1520*ᵃ   19
scio,] scio *1520;* demum] *1520*ᵃ, demum, *1520*ᵐ   23 natam] *1520*ᵃ, natam, *1520*ᵐ;
altam] *1520*ᵐ, alitam *1520*ᵃ   25 nihil,] nihil *1520*   26 exiles] *1520*ᵃ, exiles,
*1520*ᵐ   29 vt,] vt *1520*   31 litteris] litteris, *1520*

own views when the truth is so obvious, seems to me, and to others as well, to be such a tenuous bit of sophistry that we on the contrary are thoroughly amazed at your willingness to use it against him. For if you hold all mortals to Porphyry's *Eisagōgē* with such adamantine strictness that, just because he defines "proprium" as that which is exclusively mine and not common to anyone else, therefore no one should use the same word in the way that all peoples everywhere openly do use it, it will then be a crime every time someone calls the country in which he was born his own country, or the parish in which he resides his own parish, or the father by whom he was sired his own father if he happens to have any brothers who have the same father in common with him. Although not even Porphyry is as troublesome on this point as you are, since he mentions many acceptable ways of employing that term. Nor would I have said anything at all about that term in the present letter if you yourself had not mentioned it in yours, since I indicated some time ago how I felt about this entire matter to your brothers and your closest friends, and I know that they passed on my feelings to you long ago, as I meant for them to, so that there would be no need for you to find out about my feelings now, for the first time, through a rumor being spread by Erasmians.

Now I come to your exposition, in which you rehearse the affair from the outset in an effort to show that Erasmus is wholly to blame for the birth and growth of this tragedy. But when it comes to this topic it is certainly worth seeing how you yourself show off the one and only kind of skill you concede to Erasmus and how you play the orator here, heaping up many words to exaggerate things which are basically petty. If anyone removed that mass of words and assembled the things by themselves, I think he would find nothing which ought to make you feel so mortally offended by Erasmus that for a chance to hurt him you would not even balk at subverting the common good of all men. For if anyone gathered up everything you have mentioned in your letters to me or to anyone else in which you magnify his

tumelias amplificas, summa tamen huc rerum redit tandem,
quod tuas annotationes neglexerit. Quae (vt tibi verum fatear)
non satis vehemens causa multis visa est, cur homo Christiana
modestia tam hostiliter opus illud impeteres, quod alioqui te
5 fateris fuisse promoturum, si laus videlicet (nam sic accipiunt)
expectationi respondisset tuae, quae nunc maligna videbatur,
quod se tam paucis in locis a te fatebatur edoctum, cum tamen
contra videri debuerat honorificum, si vel vnum quidpiam sese
vir omnibus in litteris tantus a te didicisse fateretur, Siue illud
10 vere siue ciuilitatis causa fassus, cui tu tamen, parum ciuiliter,
mirum est, quod ad sacras attinet litteras, quam nihil omnino
tribuas, cum tibi tamen sumas tantum, vt aperte praedicas in
secunda quoque aeditione (in quam denuo tantum studij [D₂v]
ac laboris, collatis etiam tot codicibus, euolutis tot autoribus, tot
15 praeterea consultis litteratissimis viris exhausit) Errores tamen
eum multos magnosque reliquisse, si non ad tuas annotationes
correxerit, quasi quae tu deprehenderis, ille neque sua videlicet
neque alterius cuiusquam opera peruestigare potuerit quam so-
lius tua.

20 Ego mi Lee ingenium ac doctrinam tuam tam valde probo
quam quisquis probat maxime, nec de te raro glorior. Caeterum
quando non dubito quin satis tuo tributum ingenio censeas, si
quis illud Erasmico tantum conferat, nec expectes opinor vt
praeferat, Industria vero atque assiduitate studendi Erasmum a
25 puero semper fuisse constat insuperabili, magnifice profecto de
te sentire videor mihi, si te posthac aliquando talem, qualis nunc
est Erasmus, non desperem futurum, Sed tum videlicet demum,
quum ad annos hos quos nunc habet ille perueneris, nec iure tibi
videbor iniurius, si te interim ab illo censeam eruditione tantum
30 a tergo relinqui, quantum te annis ille praecesserit, quos in vnam
Theologiam profecto non pauciores insumpsit, quam tu in
omnes pene quas a puero didicisti litteras.

---

1 redit] *1520*ᵐ, reddit *1520*ᵃ   2 Quae (vt . . . fatear)] Quae vt . . . fatear *1520*ᵐ, Quae,
ut . . . fatear, *1520*ᵃ   8 debuerat] *1520*ᵃ, debuerit *1520*ᵐ   9 fateretur,] *1520*ᵃ,
fateretur. *1520*ᵐ   10 vere] vere, *1520;* tamen, parum ciuiliter,] tamen parum, ciuiliter
*1520*ᵐ, tamen parum ciuiliter, *1520*ᵃ   12 praedicas] *1520*ᵐ, praedices *1520*ᵃ   13–
14 studij ac laboris,] studij, ac laboris *1520*ᵐ, studij ac laboris *1520*ᵃ   17 videlicet]
videlicet, *1520*   26 posthac] post hac *1520*   27 Erasmus,] Erasmus *1520;* futurum,]
*1520*ᵃ, futurum. *1520*ᵐ   29 eruditione] *1520*ᵐ, aeruditione *1520*ᵃ   31 quam tu]
*1520*ᵐ, quantum *1520*ᵃ

affronts to you, the upshot of these things amounts to the fact that he has neglected your annotations. And to tell you the truth, many feel that this is not a sufficiently compelling reason for you, a man of Christian modesty, to make such a hostile attack on a work that you grant that you would have promoted if—this is the way they interpret your conduct—his praise of you had met your expectations, though in fact you considered it stingy because of the small number of passages he granted that you had explained to him. But you actually should have considered it an honor for such a great man in all fields of learning to grant he had learned anything at all from you, whether he was telling the truth or simply granted it out of politeness. And yet it is amazing how uncivil you are in denying him any competence at all in sacred scripture, whereas you claim a great deal for yourself: you go so far as to predict openly that even in his second edition, on which once again he lavished so much study and effort and for which he compared so many manuscripts, pored through so many authors, and also consulted so many great scholars, he would still have left many glaring errors if he had not corrected it according to your annotations, as if he could not have tracked down for himself, or with anyone else's assistance but yours, the things which you discovered.

My dear Lee, I value your intellect and learning as highly as anyone does; indeed I not infrequently boast of you. But I am sure you consider it a fine enough tribute to your intelligence if anyone merely compares it to that of Erasmus, and I think you do not expect anyone to prefer it to his, whereas it is well known that Erasmus' industriousness and devotion to study since boyhood have been unsurpassed. Thus I think my opinion of you is remarkably high if I do not despair of your one day hereafter becoming a man of the sort that Erasmus is now, but not before you have lived as many years as he has already, nor will I justly be thought to be doing you any injustice if meanwhile I think that he excels you as much in learning as he does in years, since indeed he has spent almost as many years on theology alone as you have spent on your entire literary education since boyhood.

Nec tamen quisquam longius ab ea distat arrogantia, quam
obijcis. Quis enim aut parcius definit, aut affirmat timidius,
quod plaerique nimis faciunt fortiter? Ille tantum quid habeant
libri commonet: suo quemque iudicio relinquens, non vt sibi
5   stetur postulat: qui sicubi, dum animum aperit suum, attingat
eos a quibus ipse dissentiat, quid facit aliud, quam quod omnibus
aetatum omnium scriptoribus et vsitatum est et concessum? [D₃]
et se tamen vbique submittit ecclesiae iudicio, subinde fassus
hominem esse se, quem in eo possint opere multa subterfugere,
10 quo in opere tu tamen qui desideras in illo modestiam magna
cum autoritate profiteris perfecisse te, quod quidem ad Theologiam attinet, nam ea est opinor quam vocas harenam tuam,
ne quis illic possit quicquam inuenire postea, iure quod queat
impetere, modo correxerit Erasmus quicquid tu annotasti. Qua
15 professione plus vni sumpsisti tibi, quam aut Erasmi pudor vltro
delatum admiserit, aut ego ambobus certe vobis etiam coniunctis
tribuerim, quum tibi tamen tribuam plurimum, illi omnes propemodum tribuant omnia. Qui quum is sit qui omnium minime
egeat admonitu, nemo tamen magis gaudet admoneri: quae res
20 liquet ex ipsis epistolis, quas ille tum in Angliam tum alio qua-
quauersus emisit ad eos quorum iudicio potissimum confidebat,
quorum nonnulli quid sibi videretur ostenderunt: omnibus egit
gratias, quorundam admisit monitus, quidam errasse se ipso
rescribente senserunt, eiusque rei gratia et ipsi egerunt gratias
25 quod quum docere conarentur didicissent. Certe nullius recor-
dor, qui tragoedias mouerit, quod non omnia consilia sua Euan-
geliorum vice suscepta sint. Nam quid illud sibi velit non intelligo, quod eum scribis ne Morum quidem monitorem ferre.
Neque enim vnquam me pro tanto viro gessi, a quo vel in aliquo
30 litterarum genere, vel in rerum perpensione communium, Erasmus admonendus esse videretur.

---

3 fortiter?] fortiter. *1520*   4 commonet:] commonet, *1520*   5 postulat:] postulat,
1520; sicubi,] sicubi *1520;* aperit suum,] *1520*ᵃ, aperit, suum *1520*ᵐ   7 scriptoribus]
scriptoribus, *1520*   11 te,] *1520*ᵃ, te *1520*ᵐ   13 postea,] postea *1520*   14
impetere,] *1520*ᵃ, impetere *1520*ᵐ   20 ille] *1520*ᵃ, ille: *1520*ᵐ   22 ostenderunt:]
ostenderunt, *1520*ᵐ, ostenderunt. *1520*ᵃ

And yet no one is further from the arrogance of which you accuse him. Who makes fewer definitive claims? Who makes rigid assertions more timidly, something many men do all too boldly? He merely points out what the books say. Letting everyone judge for himself, he does not require anyone to agree with him. And if he ever reveals his own views and takes issue with those who hold different ones, is he doing anything but what writers of all eras have been free to do as a matter of course? And yet he submits all of his views to the judgment of the church. He repeatedly grants that, being human, he may misconstrue many points in that work; whereas you, who fault him for immodesty, profess with a tone of great authority that you have perfected that work, with regard to theology at least (for I think that is what you mean by "your own province"), to the point that no one could find anything else in it that deserved to be criticized if only Erasmus corrected whatever you note. But when you profess this, you claim more for yourself alone than Erasmus' own modesty would let him accept, even if others freely bestowed it on him, or than I personally would concede to you both put together, even though I concede you a great deal and everyone concedes him almost everything. And though he needs advice less than anyone, no one appreciates advice more than he does. This is quite clear even in the letters he wrote, both to England and to many other countries, to the people whose judgment he trusted the most, some of whom told him what they themselves thought. He thanked them all and accepted the advice some had given, while his written responses led others to see their mistakes so that they themselves thanked him for teaching them even as they were trying to teach him. Certainly I recall no one who created an uproar because not all his counsels were accepted as if they were gospel. For I have no idea what you mean when you write that he would not even let More advise him, since I have never considered myself such a great man that Erasmus should need my advice, whether about any aspect of learning or in his decisions about matters of general importance.

    Iam quod Dorpium scribis ab illo male dum admoneret accep-
tum, Ego num quid [D₃v] occultae simultatis intercesserit haud
intelligo: certe in ea Apologia qua Dorpio respondit palam,
quanquam ab eo prouocatus, ac propemodum obiurgatus as-
5 pere, tamen adeo modeste respondit, imo reuerenter potius, vt
non aliud vnquam quicquam tantundem honoris conciliarit Dorpio quam quod tantum autoritatis Erasmus ei praesertim lacessitus attribuit. Quae res vna facit, ne facile adducar vt credam
eius beneficij oblitum Dorpium amicum in se tam candidum
10 denuo velle lacessere. Qua in sententia vel eo confirmor, quod
illam epistolam quam calore quodam dictarat acerbius, de-
feruescente impetu, consilio censuit consultiore supprimendam,
qua de re ego quoque vicissim pressi meam, qui contentiones
huiusmodi, quibus vt nihil fructus, ita multum damni possit ori-
15 ri, sopire atque obruere libentius quam fouere studeam, qui ab
eo tempore sic amaui Dorpium ac magni semper feci, vt tibi
quoque Louanium petituro suaserim, eum praecipue ex Louaniensibus omnibus esse adiungendum, quod nunquam certe
fecissem, nisi eum plane apud animum meum praesumpsissem
20 talem a quo tu, quem (vt vere mi Lee dicam) etiam olim non
admodum aequum in Erasmum cognouimus, in Erasmi pel-
licereris amorem, quum sit Erasmus illius amantissimus, natura
certe tam placabilis, vt nescio an vsquam possis inuenire quemquam, qui tam multas ac tam insignes in se contumelias tam
25 patienter tulerit, qui quidem potens sit tam valide retorquere,
nec dolori suo morem interim regestis in maledicos maledictis
gesserit, Nempe qui nec in eos, qui locis aliquot ex opusculis eius
ad calumniam delectis, ne [D₄] dubitari possit quem impeterent,
quidlibet in famam eius impudenter euomuerint, conuicia ipsis
30 digna regesserit, sed eorum dissimulata malicia satis habuit, si
sua tueretur scripta, eorum honori adeo indulgenter parcens, vt
non modo nihil inde detriuerit, verum etiam nonnihil astruxerit.
Quanquam haec illius tam immodesta modestia maxime profec-

1–2 acceptum,] acceptum. *1520*   3 intelligo:] *1520ᵃ*, intelligo *1520ᵐ*   10
confirmor,] confirmor *1520*   13 meam,] meam *1520*   14 huiusmodi,] huiusmodi
1520   20 tu,] tu *1520*   24 multas] *1520ᵃ*, multas, *1520ᵐ*; contumelias] *1520ᵃ*,
contumelias, *1520ᵐ*   25 tam] *om. 1520ᵃ*   26 morem] *1520ᵃ*, morem, *1520ᵐ*   27
gesserit,] gesserit. *1520;* in eos] *conj. 1760*, eos *1520*   28 delectis,] delectis *1520*

Now as for what you write about the ungracious way he received Dorp's advice, I have no idea whether there might have been some secret feuding between them, but certainly in the apology in which he replied to Dorp publicly he replied with such modesty and indeed with such reverence, despite being provoked and to some extent rudely berated, that nothing else will ever win so much honor for Dorp as the fact that, even after being offended by him, Erasmus conceded him so much authority. This in itself makes it difficult to convince me that Dorp, having forgotten that favor, would wish to injure once more a friend so honorably disposed toward him. I am confirmed in that opinion by this in particular: that when his feelings cooled down he decided to suppress that harsh letter which he had dictated in the heat of the moment; and on this basis I, too, suppressed mine in turn, since I am always more eager to silence and bury such quarrels, which can do little good and a great deal of harm, than to foster them. Since that time I have loved and esteemed Dorp so much that when you were about to depart for Louvain I urged you to form an especially close tie with him out of all the Louvain academics. I would certainly never have done so if I had not assumed that he was definitely the right man to make you start loving Erasmus (for to be truthful with you, my dear Lee, we knew you were not any too fair in your view of Erasmus even then), since Erasmus has such love for him. And by nature Erasmus is certainly so quick to forgive that I doubt you could find anyone anywhere who would have shown so much patience in bearing so many conspicuous affronts if he had had the same power to retaliate or who would have refrained from indulging his grief now and then by repaying abuse with abuse. For not even when some selected various passages from his minor works as a basis for slander, so that there could be no doubt about whom they were attacking, and then slandered his reputation with all sorts of shameless abuse, not even then did Erasmus repay them with the insults that such men deserve, but dissembling their malice he thought it enough to defend his own writings. He was so generous in sparing their honor that he not only left it unimpaired but to some extent actually enhanced it. And yet this same immoderate modesty of

to fuit in causa, cur tot amputatis huius hydrae capitibus noua
subinde repullulent: alioqui non dubito, quin aliquot eum minus
petulanter incessissent, si sui similes vidissent durius aliquanto
reiectos.

5   Venio nunc ad prioris epistolae calcem, quo te significas Erasmo quoque vel adsentiente vel simulante litem hanc totam re-
uerendi patris episcopi Roffensis permisisse iudicio, atque ad
eum tuarum annotationum transmisisse volumen. Quod factum
certe, siue vtriusque vestrum siue vnius tuum, mirifice laudant
10   omnes, quum quod animos adieceritis ad pacem, tum quod eum
delegeritis pacificatorem, qui non modo propter eruditionem
singularem, cuius nunc mundum testem habet, maxime sit idoneus qui iudicet, verumetiam propter eximiam pietatem non sit
passurus quicquid in alterutro boni sit interire: Porro qui sic
15   amet vtrumque, vt toto pectore sit ad concordiam incubiturus:
homo tam solers ac dexter, vt viam inueniat facile, qua sibi censeat vterque satisfactum.

Verum enimuero (vt posteriores tandem litteras attingam)
hoc tam salubre propositum, seu vestrum fuerit siue (quod
20   scribis) tuum, quo sanctius excogitatum est, eo nimirum magis
est incusandus vtriuscunque culpa contigit vt deficerétur effectu. [D$_4$v] Ego hanc in culpam neutrum vel impingo, vel ex-
imo, caeterum quid alijs videatur exponam, qui primum id considerant, quod vt solus videri vis episcopi delegisse iudicium, ita
25   primus videris denuo declinasse, atque ita primus vt propemodum etiam solus. Nam Erasmum ne adhuc quidem constat
reiecisse, vt qui prior miserit librum, et nullis litteris appellarit a
iudice, Quem nec potuit iudicem refugere, qui aedito libro
omnes fecerat iudices. Tu contra cum librum huc ad alios iam
30   olim transmiseris clanculum, episcopum rem celasti maxime,

---

1 capitibus] *1520*ᵃ, capitibus, *1520*ᵐ   2 repullulent:] *1520*ᵃ, repullulent, *1520*ᵐ   3
sui] *1520*ᵐ, tui *1520*ᵃ   6 adsentiente] *1520*ᵃ, adsentiente, *1520*ᵐ   9 certe,] certe
1520; vestrum] vestrum, *1520*   12 habet,] *1520*ᵃ, habet: *1520*ᵐ   13 iudicet,]
*1520*ᵃ, iudicet: *1520*ᵐ   14 passurus] *1520*ᵃ, passurus, *1520*ᵐ; interire:] interire.
1520   15 vtrumque,] *1520*ᵃ, vtrumque: *1520*ᵐ; incubiturus:] incubiturus *1520*ᵐ,
incubiturus, *1520*ᵃ   16 dexter,] *1520*ᵃ, dexter: *1520*ᵐ   19 propositum,] *1520*ᵃ,
propositum *1520*ᵐ; fuerit] fuerit: *1520*ᵐ, fuit, *1520*ᵃ   20 tuum,] *1520*ᵃ, tuum: *1520*ᵐ;
est,] *1520*ᵃ, est: *1520*ᵐ   21–22 effectu.] *1520*ᵃ, effectu *1520*ᵐ   22 neutrum] *1520*ᵃ,
neutram *1520*ᵐ   28 iudice,] iudice. *1520*

his is undoubtedly the main reason that this hydra is constantly growing new heads after losing so many already. Otherwise I am sure some would not have attacked him so wantonly if they had seen others like them repulsed now and then with a bit more asperity.

Now I come to the end of your first letter, where you indicate that, with the agreement or professed agreement of Erasmus, you have submitted this entire quarrel to the judgment of the reverend father, the bishop of Rochester, to whom you have forwarded the volume of your annotations. This is one action that everyone praises greatly, whether you acted with Erasmus or alone, both because you have turned your attention to peace and because you have chosen a peacemaker who is not only a particularly well-qualified judge because of his singular learning, which he now has the world to attest, but is also unlikely, because of his extraordinary piety, to let anything good in either book go to waste; a man who moreover loves both of you so much that he will devote all his energies to concord, and a man of such skill and resourcefulness that he will easily find a way to satisfy both of you.

But indeed (to move on to your second letter) to the extent that this wholesome proposal of yours was a holy idea in the first place, whether it was a mutual plan or—as you write—entirely your own, to this same extent whichever of you is to blame for subverting the plan deserves serious reproach. I myself neither blame nor exonerate either one of you. I will merely state how the affair looks to others, who begin by observing that while you want it to look as if you were alone in soliciting the bishop's judgment it looks as if you were the first to decline it again, indeed first to the point of being virtually alone in declining it. For it is still unconfirmed that Erasmus has rejected it, since he sent his book first and has written no letter recalling it from a judge he could not shun in any case, since by publishing the book he had made everyone his judge. On the other hand, some time ago you sent the book over here secretly to others, but you completely concealed the affair from the bishop; and only now,

nunc vero demum, paterno quodam affectu consulentem tibi,
ne huic te operi immisceas, videlicet statuis iudicem: sed ita statuis, vt non ante sibi tributum hunc magistratum, quam rursus
ademptum cognouerit. Nam neque liber tuus ad eum venit, ne-
5 que litterae, quae iudicem illum facerent, nisi simul traditis al-
teris, quae iudicandi munus eriperent, ac denunciarent aeditionem tecum te nullius expectato iudicio decreuisse. Haec atque
alia conferentibus oboritur certe suspitio, nunquam istud syn-
cere tibi de iudice deligendo cogitatum.
10   Quam suspitionem praeter alia confirmat tua certe, quae multis videtur perquam infirma, defensio, qua te videri vis eo loco ex
Apologia notatum, quem locum non quisquam censet quicquam
ad te pertinere. Nam neque nomen tuum ibi legis, neque mores
qui describuntur agnoscis, et alij sunt, qui de illo male sunt meri-
15 ti, ijdemque magis Latomo familiares, Porro quidam non multo
melioribus ab his depicti coloribus, qui istinc huc indies com-
migrant, quam eo loco quisquis est ille describitur. Quam ob
rem, vt nulla praebetur [E₁] ansa, qua locus haereat in te, sic non
desunt fortasse vestigia, quibus ad eorum quempiam per-
20 ueniatur, qui callide rem dissimulant, et tua credulitate freti, quo
longius ab sese auertant, ea te persona volentem ornant, atque
ita producunt in proscenium, suoque plausu traducunt publice
miserantibus amicis tuis, inimicis ridentibus, maxime sibi placen-
tibus ijs, qui te circumuentum suis versutijs vicarium sibi his-
25 trionem gaudent supposuisse.
    "Sed teneo," inquis, "manifestarium. Nam cum per fratrem
expostulassem de iniuria, atque is negasset ea scripsisse de me,
tamen recusauit me petente aliqua saltem illud apologia testari."
    Rem profecto mi Lee neque illi facilem, neque tibi vtilem
30 flagitasti. Nam ad hunc modum alio super alium idem pos-

---

1 demum,] demum *1520*   2 iudicem:] iudicem, *1520*ᵐ, iudicem. *1520*ᵃ   5 quae]
conj. 1760, qui *1520*   6 denunciarent] *1520*ᵐ, denunciaret *1520*ᵃ   11 infirma,]
infirma *1520*   13 mores] *1520*ᵃ, mores, *1520*ᵐ   15 familiares,] familiares. *1520*
20 callide] *1520*ᵐ, calide *1520*ᵃ   21 auertant] *1520*ᵐ, uertant *1520*ᵃ   23 ridentibus,
maxime] *1520*ᵃ, ridentibus maxime, *1520*ᵐ   24 ijs] *1520*ᵐ, his *1520*ᵃ; qui . . . suis]
*1520*ᵃ, qui te circumuentum ijs, qui te circumuentum suis *1520*ᵐ; versutijs] *1520*ᵃ,
versutijs, *1520*ᵐ   28 petente] *1520*ᵃ, petente, *1520*ᵐ

when he offers you fatherly advice not to get involved with this work, you appoint him your judge. But you do so in such a way that he did not learn that he had been given this office before learning that it had been taken away. For your book did not reach him, and neither did your letter declaring him judge, before another letter arrived to deprive him of his judgeship and to announce your independent decision to publish without waiting for anyone's judgment. When people compare these and other observations, they certainly begin to suspect you were never sincere about that plan of choosing a judge.

This suspicion is certainly strengthened by your own defense, among other things, a defense many view as exceedingly weak, in which you want to make it appear that you were the target of a passage in Erasmus' *Apology* which no one considers has anything to do with you. For you do not find your name in the passage, nor do you acknowledge the characteristics described there. Furthermore, there are many other people who have done him some wrong and who are more intimate colleagues of Latomus; indeed there are some whom those who frequently travel here from there describe in a hardly more flattering light than the person in that passage, whoever he may be. Thus though there is no pretext for linking the passage to you, there may be certain traces which might lead the reader to any of those men who are cunningly dissembling the matter and exploiting your own credulity to dissociate themselves from that role by conferring it on you, who so gladly accept it. And in this mask they lead you onstage and dishonor you publicly with their applause while your friends pity you, your enemies laugh, and these men feel especially pleased with themselves and rejoice in having been wily enough to trick you into acting their part as a stand-in.

"But," you say, "I have caught him red-handed. For when I complained to him through my brother about this injury, even though he denied he had written those statements against me, he refused when I asked him to testify to that effect with at least an apology." My dear Lee, what you demanded would not have been easy for him or beneficial to you. For then when one person after another made such a demand of him, he would either have

tulante, aut ille necesse fuisset aliquem negando perdere, atque
ex occulta simultate aperte bellum in se recipere, aut cum suae
causae praeiudicio quempiam laudare publice, quem paulo fortasse post palam cogeretur incessere. Tibi vero censes honeste
5   consulturum, si scripto testetur, se non illorum quae scripsit
quicquam scripsisse de te, quasi ea videri possint alioqui in te
competere. An non belle te purgasset scilicet, si protinus ei loco
subiunxisset, "monitos omnes volo, ne quis nimium suspicax
haec me suspicetur vel dicere vel cogitare de Leo"? Quanto tibi
10 fuisset consultius, eam rem, quae nihil ad te attinebat, in te non
admittere, et si quis in te torquere niteretur, velut malum atque
inuidum interpretem reijcere, quam sic rem tibi sumere, vt vel
quae scripta sunt videaris agnoscere, vel quod possis expostulare
non habeas?
15   Ego profecto mi Lee [E₁v] quanquam te viam video sententiae
meae praecludere, cum aut famae tuae parum fauentem censeas
aut certe non satis prouidentem, quisquis tibi non suaserit annotationes istas protinus emittendas, tamen non dubitabo committere, vt vtrobique apud te existimationis meae pericliter, po-
20 tius quam vt quae tuae putem conductura, non consulam, Id est
in primis, vt ab huius aeditione voluminis abstineas, quod tibi
nihil boni, multum conciliabit inuidiae. Nam quod nunc tute
tecum reputas fore, vt omnes cognoscant vel tibi deberi gratiam,
si quid errati correxerit, vel suae dandum pertinaciae, si nec
25 monitus quidem correxerit, id vt video pro confesso sumis, cuius
fidem aegre fortasse obtineas, vt tuis videlicet corruptis scribis ex
te quicquid est erratum credatur didicisse. Nam eius ipsius quod
affers fidem ipse nimirum vel hoc argumento minuis, quod nec
visa adhuc secunda aeditione librum tuum tamen statuas aedere,
30 Quod multi credant nunquam te fuisse facturum, nisi spem con-

---

3 praeiudicio] *1520*ᵃ, praeiudicio, *1520*ᵐ   5 scripsit] scripsit, *1520*   9 dicere] dicere, *1520*   14 habeas?] habeas. *1520*   16 praecludere,] *1520*ᵃ, praecludere:
*1520*ᵐ; censeas] censeas, *1520*   19–20 periclíter, potius] *1520*ᵃ, periclíter potius,
*1520*ᵐ   23 cognoscant] cognoscant, *1520;* deberi] *1520*ᵃ, debere *1520*ᵐ   26 scribis]
*1520*ᵃ, scribis, *1520*ᵐ   29 aedere,] aedere. *1520*   30 credant] *1520*ᵃ, credent,
*1520*ᵐ

had to hurt someone by turning him down and provoke open hostility against himself in the place of a secret feud, or else he would have had to damage his own cause by praising someone publicly whom he might soon be forced to attack in an explicit way. But you think it will safeguard your honor if he testifies in writing that not one of those statements he wrote was directed against you, as if otherwise they might seem to fit you. Would it not be a fine way to clear you indeed if he promptly appended a note to that passage saying, "I hereby admonish everyone not to let undue suspicion cause him to suspect that these statements were written or intended against Lee"? How much better you would have safeguarded yourself by not applying to yourself statements that had nothing to do with you, and by rejecting as a malicious and spiteful interpreter anyone who attempted to transfer them to you, than by taking the matter upon yourself in such a way that you either appear to confess to the statements he wrote or you lack anything to complain about!

Even though, my dear Lee, I see you shutting out my opinion before it is offered, since you think that whoever does not urge the immediate release of those annotations of yours either has scant concern for your honor or certainly does not watch out for it well enough, I myself will not hesitate to endanger my own reputation in your eyes on both counts before I would withhold the advice that I think most expedient for your reputation, and that means, above all, the advice to refrain from the publication of this volume, which will do you no good and earn you much ill will. For when you yourself suppose that this step will make everyone recognize either that you deserve all the credit if Erasmus has corrected any errors or that his stubbornness is to blame if he failed to correct them even after you warned him, you are taking something for granted that you will probably have a hard time making others believe, namely that he bought off your scribes and thus found out about all his errors from you. For you undercut your own assertion by deciding to publish your book before you have even seen his second edition; this is something that many believe you would never have done unless you had

cepisses aliquam, fieri vt ignoratione tuarum annotationum aliquot adhuc errata sua non deprehenderit. Nam si cogitares annotationes tuas omnes ei factas esse palam, non posses profecto
dubitare, quin aut omnes illos locos emendauerit, aut certe vi-
5   deat quo pacto queat defendere, qui si hoc videat, non est quod
magnam posses expectare gloriam: sin illud fecerit, appetitae
perperam gloriae vix declinares infamiam, quasi praepostero
laudis aucupio nullo iam fructu sis admoniturus, non quid nunc
viciosum sit, sed quid olim fuerit.
10   "At famam" inquis "purgare debeo, quam ille [E_2] de-
populatus est, qui non minuta modo me annotasse clamitat, sed
et neotericorum decretis ea communire." Hic interim mi Lee,
non video qui tecum constes, qui tanquam facinus capitale obijcis
Erasmo, quod parum neotericis tribuit, quibus ille certe tribuit
15   satis, cum nescio an ijsdem quisquam plus ademerit quam tute,
qui tibi ducis infamiae si neotericorum decretis tua dicaris an-
notamenta munire. Verum si fama tibi sic esset aspersa maculis
vt necessario purganda sit, nec alia via possit perlui quam si
confestim iste liber tuus aedatur, quanquam vel nominis potius
20   aliquam iacturam sustinere deceat quam vt, dum nostro bono
nimium studemus, multorum bonis cogamur obficere, tamen vt
nunc sunt mores ignoscam facile si tibi bene malis esse quam
alteri. Sed mihi neque famae tuae tam valde detractum videtur,
et si maxime detractum sit, hac aeditione tamen minime posse
25   restitui. Nam locus ille ex apologia nihil ad te quicquam prorsus
pertinet. Tum si quas huc scripsit epistolas, nihil minus egisse

1 aliquam, fieri] aliquam fieri, *1520;* annotationum] *1520*ᵃ, annotationum, *1520*ᵐ   2–
3 annotationes tuas] *1520*ᵐ, tuas annotationes *1520*ᵃ   4–5 videat] videat, *1520*ᵐ,
uiderit *1520*ᵃ   6 gloriam:] gloriam, *1520;* fecerit,] *1520*ᵃ, fecerit *1520*ᵐ   7 gloriae]
gloriae, *1520*   12–13 mi . . . video] *1520*ᵐ, non uideo mi Lee *1520*ᵃ   15 ademerit]
ademerit, *1520;* tute,] *1520*ᵃ, tute: *1520*ᵐ   16 infamiae] infamiae: *1520*ᵐ, infamiae,
*1520*ᵃ   17 maculis] maculis: *1520*ᵐ, maculis, *1520*ᵃ   18 sit,] *1520*ᵃ, sit: *1520*ᵐ;
perlui] perlui: *1520*ᵐ, perlui, *1520*ᵃ   19 iste liber] *1520*ᵐ, liber ille *1520*ᵃ; aedatur,]
*1520*ᵃ, aedatur: *1520*ᵐ   20 deceat] *1520*ᵃ, deceat: *1520*ᵐ; vt,] vt *1520*   21
studemus,] *1520*ᵃ, studemus: *1520*ᵐ; obficere,] *1520*ᵃ, obficere: *1520*ᵐ   22 facile]
facile: *1520*ᵐ, facile, *1520*ᵃ   23 videtur,] *1520*ᵃ, videtur: *1520*ᵐ   24 sit,] *1520*ᵃ, sit.
*1520*ᵐ   26 epistolas,] *1520*ᵃ, epistolas: *1520*ᵐ; minus] *1520*ᵐ minus uel *1520*ᵃ

some hope that he might still have overlooked some of his errors through his ignorance of your annotations. For if you thought that he had already gained access to your annotations, you could have no doubt that either he would already have emended those passages or at least he would see a good way to defend himself: if he does see one, there would be no reason for you to anticipate winning much glory; on the other hand, if he has emended, you could scarcely avoid disrepute for attempting to win glory perversely, as if, backwardly angling for praise, you were uselessly going to point out not the book's present faults but its past ones.

"But," you say, "I must vindicate my honor, which he has damaged severely by claiming not only that my annotations are trifles but that I support them with the pronouncements of the moderns." By the way, my dear Lee, I do not see how this is consistent with your other views, since you indict Erasmus—as if it were a capital crime—for conceding the moderns too little authority, though he certainly concedes them enough, whereas I doubt that anyone detracts from them more than you do in considering that it dishonors you if he says you support your annotations with the pronouncements of moderns. But if your honor had been sullied so thoroughly that it had to be vindicated, and if there were no other way to cleanse it but to publish this book of yours at once, even though it is more respectable to bear even some loss of renown than to show such an inordinate regard for our own welfare that it drives us to injure the welfare of many, even so I can easily forgive you, today's morals being what they are, if you care more about your own good than about anyone else's. But in my view your honor has not been so terribly slighted, and even if it had, it could scarcely be salvaged with this publication. For that passage in his *Apology* has nothing at all to do with you, and in the letters he has written to England the last

videtur vel cogitasse, quam vt tuo noceret nomini: contra vero
annum hic fere totum de tuis in eum scriptis susurratum est,
quum nec interim bonorum quenquam viderim tuo gaudere
proposito, nec animi erga te offensi vllum ab illo signum de-
5 prehenderim, nisi quod modo visus est aliquid de tuo contra se
facto conqueri, de te tamen ipso scribens multo certe quam tu de
illo temperantius. Quorum si quis vtriusque narrationem perpendat, vereor profecto, ne te potius condemnet iniuriae, nisi
quis [E₂v] ea credat esse mendacia, quae sunt ad illum delata de
10 te, quod ego certe tam libenter credo, quam tu quoque debes
libenter vana credere, quae ijdem rumigeruli de illo detulerunt
ad te, quos si mendaces esse credes, vt si vis absolui credes, illum
pariter ab hac iniuria, cuius nunc accusas, absolues.
    Sed nescio quas litteras loqueris quibus ille te sit grauiter insec-
15 tatus, quales an proferre posses haud scio. Verum hoc vnum
scio, extare mi Lee tuas, et quo minus inficiari possis, αὐτογράφους, e quibus conijci potest, ad istas annotationes longe alio
animo et accessisse te, et processisse, quam nunc toties in testem
citata conscientia prae te feras, tum sic accessisse, vt praeiu-
20 dicium domo (quod aiunt) attuleris tecum, quo sementem
totam, cuius adhuc nec herbam videras, damnandam esse
praesumeres, quum inde passim omnes boni, qui quidem nos-
sent agricolam, optimam et pulcherrimam sibi messem promitterent.
25 Verum quod coepi dicere, si maxime famam tuam purgari
oporteat, hac aeditione tamen censeo minime posse procedere,
qua dum eam depurgare laboras, vereor ne limo densius lutoque
permisceas. Nam primum in quibusdam video te plane falli, nec
absimile veri est, idem tibi in aliquot aeque locis, quos ipse non

---

1 cogitasse,] *1520*ᵃ, cogitasse: *1520*ᵐ   2 annum] *1520*ᵐ, animum *1520*ᵃ; est,] est:
*1520*ᵐ, est. *1520*ᵃ   4 proposito,] *1520*ᵃ, proposito: *1520*ᵐ   4–5 deprehenderim,]
*1520*ᵃ, deprehenderim: *1520*ᵐ   6 conqueri,] *1520*ᵃ, conqueri: *1520*ᵐ   7–8 perpendat,] *1520*ᵃ, perpendat: *1520*ᵐ   9 ea credat] *1520*ᵃ, ea credat ea *1520*ᵐ   13
accusas,] *1520*ᵃ, accusas *1520*ᵐ   15 posses] *1520*ᵐ, possis *1520*ᵃ   16 scio,] scio
1520; tuas,] *1520*ᵃ, tuas *1520*ᵐ; possis,] *1520*ᵃ, possis *1520*ᵐ   16–17 αὐτογράφους,]
*1520*ᵃ, αὐτογράφους *1520*ᵐ   22–23 nossent] *1520*ᵃ, noscent *1520*ᵐ   27 densius]
*1520*ᵃ, densius, *1520*ᵐ   29 absimile] *1520*ᵃ, absimili *1520*ᵐ

thing he appeared to be doing, or indeed even thinking of doing, was injuring your reputation. On the other hand, people here have been whispering for almost a whole year about what you have written against him, though I have not yet seen any good man who is pleased with your plan, nor have I yet perceived any signs of his feeling offended with you, unless we count his recent expressions of some grief at your actions against him, though he certainly writes much more temperately about you than you do about him. And if anyone weighs both your stories I am certainly afraid he will convict you rather than Erasmus of being unjust, unless anyone thinks that the tales he has heard about you are untrue. I myself am as eager to think so as you should be to think that those tales which the same scandalmongers tell you about him are untrue, for if you think that these men are liars, which you will if you want other men to absolve you, you will likewise absolve him of the injustice with which you now charge him.

But you talk about some letter or other in which he has attacked you severely. I do not know if you can produce it, but one thing I do know, my dear Lee, is that there is a letter from you— and an autograph letter, at that, which you cannot disclaim— from which one may deduce that you yourself both entered upon and proceeded with those annotations in a far different spirit from the one you profess now, calling on your own conscience so often to vouch for it, and that you actually entered upon them in such a way that before you set out, as they say, you had already come to a verdict, prejudging the whole crop to be worthless before you had even seen the shoots, even though all good men everywhere who knew anything of the farmer were confident that it would come to an excellent and beautiful harvest.

But as I started to say, even if you were called on to vindicate your honor I scarcely think you will achieve that objective with this publication, and I fear that while trying to cleanse it in this way you will actually cover it with more mire and filth. For first of all, I see that you are simply mistaken in a number of passages, and it is not unlikely that you are equally mistaken in several

vidi, contingere. Iam quaedam sunt, quod nec ipse diffiteris,
non admodum magni momenti: quaedam certe, vt non aperte
contra te militent, ita pro te non valde multum faciunt: bona pars
iam diu controuersa, de quibus adhuc sub iudice lis, quae si de
5 summa subduxeris, reliquum rationis erit pauxillulum, nec sane
satis dig[E₃]num vnde tu nouas conficias tabulas, Vt praeteream
interim, quod alij non praetereunt, qui perquam intempestiuum
censent de mendis admonere iam emendatis.

Atque is quidem tuae rei status fuerit, etiamsi mutum nactus
10 esses aduersarium, qualem non esse tuum, tute probe pernosti,
nunc vero cum contra te rem tractabit cuiusuis tractandae rei
mirificus artifex, tum qui hanc in rem vnam plus propemodum
laboris ac studij quam in reliquas, quas vnquam egit omnes,
impenderit, certe mi Lee non credas quam multa sis quae nun-
15 quam credidisses auditurus, quae si animo posses iam ante concipere, dubio procul abstinendum duceres ab inauspicatis istis
laboribus, quos vtinam tantum possis perdere. Nam ille quicquid
annotasti minutulum, prorsus in nihil comminuet: quicquid te
nunc parum iuuat, sic tractabit vt etiam noceat: quod hactenus
20 videbatur ambiguum, id contra te reddet dilucidum: tum si quid
mutauit in melius, eius non modo nullam tibi habebit gratiam,
sed reum etiam aget insolentiae, eiusque rei valde ridicule tanquam non glorieris modo velut Ἐπιμηθεὺς μετὰ τὰ πράγματα
eorum nos admonere quorum tempus praeterijt, dum salebras
25 mones ac lacunas esse vitandas quae iam sint complanatae, sed
alienae praeterea laudem captes industriae, qui quicquid aut
ipsum notauisse comperisses aut alios, id in tuas totum annota-

1 vidi,] vidi *1520;* sunt,] 1520ᵃ, sunt *1520*ᵐ   2 momenti:] momenti *1520*ᵐ, momenti,
*1520*ᵃ; quaedam certe,] *1520*ᵃ, quaedam, certe *1520*ᵐ, quaedam quae certe *or* quaedam
certe quae *conj. 1760*   3 faciunt:] faciunt, *1520*   3–4 bona pars iam] *1520*ᵐ, iam
pars bona *1520*ᵃ   6 tabulas,] tabulas *1520*   7 interim,] interim *1520*   11
tractabit] *1520*ᵃ, tractabit, *1520*ᵐ   13 studij] studij, *1520;* omnes,] omnes *1520*   15
animo posses] *1520*ᵐ posses animo *1520*ᵃ   16 inauspicatis] *1520*ᵃ, in auspicatis
*1520*ᵐ   18 comminuet:] comminuet, *1520*   19 noceat:] noceat, *1520*   20 dilucidum:] dilucidum, *1520*   22 ridicule] *1520*ᵐ, ridiculae *1520*ᵃ   23 Ἐπιμηθεὺς]
ἐπιμεθεὺς *1520*ᵐ, ἐπιμηθεὺς *1520*ᵃ   24 praeterijt,] *1520*ᵃ, praeterijt *1520*ᵐ   25 vi-
tandas] vitandas, *1520*   27 alios,] *1520*ᵃ, alios *1520*ᵐ

which I have not seen. Furthermore, a number of your points are not very important, as not even you will deny; a number of points, even if they do not openly contradict you, certainly do not afford you much support; and a sizable number are points which have long been controversial and on which the judge has yet to rule. And if you subtract these from your total, the rest of the reckoning will be minuscule, and at any rate not large enough to justify your drawing up a new ledger—not to mention one thing which other people are mentioning, who consider it very untimely to point out mistakes which have already been emended.

This is how your case would stand even if you had found a mute adversary, which you know very well yours is not. As it is, since the case against you will be argued by a consummate master in arguing all kinds of cases, who has also devoted more labor and study to this case than to all the others he has ever prepared, certainly, my dear Lee, you will not believe how many things you will hear that you never expected, and if you could have conceived of them before now you would undoubtedly have chosen to have nothing to do with those ill-omened labors of yours— would that you could simply dispense with them! For any trifles you note he will reduce altogether to nothing; anything that is not very helpful to you he will treat in a way that will even make it hurt you; anything that has so far seemed ambiguous he will clearly resolve against you; and if he has altered anything for the better he will not only not thank you on that account, he will even arraign you for insolence, and a thoroughly ludicrous specimen of it at that, as if you not only glory in playing Epimetheus after the fact and in giving us warnings we no longer need, warning us to shun rough spots and holes which have already been evened out, but you also seek praise which should go to the diligence of others, copying whole in your own annotations every note you

tiones referens aliorum partus aedas pro tuis, quorum adhuc
quidam belli videntur tibi, quos qui genuerant, ijdem velut informes ac monstrosos fetus abiecerint: Iam vero cum ad ea venerit, quibus errare te manifeste coar[E₃v]guat, non est quod ex-
5 pectes illam qua semper hactenus pepercit alijs humanitatem,
qua quia multorum in se audaciam videt prouocasse sese, vertet
haud dubie vela, atque ita (vereor) tractabit te, alijs vt sis exemplo, ne quis ei negocium denuo solitae spe ciuilitatis exhibeat.
   Qua in re veniam vel temet iudice debet obtinere, Qui si tibi
10 causam putes esse cur illum inuadas acriter, vel quod tacere
nefas ducis, si quid adhuc reliquit incorrectum, vel, si nihil reliquit, tamen vt tuam repares ac sartias famam, quae tibi tota
funditus interierit Si toti credaris Europae (nam id populus curat scilicet) annotasse minutias, quanto aequius illi debes igno-
15 scere, si tuam in se libertatem pari libertate retaliet, siue, vt nunc
est eius opus recognitum, nihil eorum retineat quae tu repre-
henderis, siue tu velut errata redarguas quae sua sibi conscientia
dictet esse rectissima, qui sibi non minus certe quam tibi citra
vllam potest arrogantiae culpam fidere, vt non illud addam in-
20 terim, quod totus iste tumultus tuus huc tendit denique, ne per
illum putareris reculas quaspiam, vel parum recte vel paulo
minus magnas annotasse, Quum illi contra te sit enitendum, ne,
si tu recte magna notaueris, ipse magna carere nota non possit,
quasi (quod nefas nemo non ducit) sancta parum sancte trac-
25 tauerit. Haec cum ita sese habeant, non est mihi crede quod
speres quin, si illum aeditis istis annotationibus attingas, suetae
sibi suae lenitatis oblitus, su[E₄]um ius summa vi persequatur.

---

1 referens] *1520*ᵃ referens, *1520*ᵐ   3 abiecerint:] abiecerint, *1520*ᵐ, abiecerant.
*1520*ᵃ   4–5 expectes] *1520*ᵃ, expectes, *1520*ᵐ   7–8 exemplo,] *1520*ᵃ, exemplo
*1520*ᵐ   9 obtinere,] obtinere. *1520*   10 causam putes] *1520*ᵐ, putes causam
*1520*ᵃ; esse] esse, *1520*   11 vel,] vel *1520*   11–12 reliquit,] *1520*ᵃ, reliquit *1520*ᵐ
13 interierit] interierit. *1520*   15 libertatem] *1520*ᵃ, libertatem, *1520*ᵐ; siue,] siue
1520   17 redarguas] redarguas, *1520*   18 certe] *1520*ᵃ, certe, *1520*ᵐ   22 annotasse,] annotasse. *1520*; ne,] ne *1520*   24 sancte] *1520*ᵃ, sanctae *1520*ᵐ   26
speres quin,] speres, quin *1520*; attingas,] *1520*ᵃ, attingas *1520*ᵐ   27 sibi] *See commentary;* oblitus,] oblitus *1520*; persequatur] *1520*ᵃ, persequetur *1520*ᵐ

could find made by him or by others and presenting the off-spring of these other men as if they were your own, some of which you continue to find handsome even though their true parents have thrown them away as amorphous and misbegotten monstrosities. But when he finally comes to the points about which he can clearly prove you are mistaken, you have no cause to expect the same sort of kindness he has always displayed until now in sparing others. Since he sees that this trait has provoked many men to be bold in attacking him, he will undoubtedly alter his tactics, and I fear he will make an example of you so that others will not make more trouble for him in the hope of en-countering his usual politeness.

Such a reaction is one for which even your judgment should pardon him. For you feel you have cause for a bitter attack on him, whether because you think it wrong to keep silent about anything he left uncorrected or because, even if he left nothing of the sort, you still need to redeem and restore your own honor, which would be totally ruined if all of Europe—as if common folk care for such things—thought that your annotations were trifles. How much more justly you ought to forgive him for answering your freedom with similar freedom, whether his work as it has now been revised retains none of the things that you criticized or the things you reprove as his errors are things that his conscience assures him are perfectly correct (and with-out any lapse into arrogance he can trust his own judgment no less surely than you can trust yours). Not to mention that all of this agitation on your part is intended to keep him from making people think that any minor points you had annotated were either not right or not very significant, whereas he has to con-tend against you to escape major notoriety, which he could not escape if your notes on major points were correct, as if he had done something that everyone thinks to be wrong, namely han-dled holy matters in an unholy way. This being the case, believe me, if you rouse him by publishing those annotations, you can only expect him to forget his customary gentleness and to de-fend his own rights with all possible rigor.

Itaque vehementer metuo ne famam tuam, quantum ego video, adhuc per illum integram, tute videri possis importuna
purgatione polluere, quod quibusdam ante video contigisse, qui
an minus tuti fuerint quam tu, id quidem necesse est euentus
5 iudicet: certe non minus fuerant securi quam tu, quoad ille quid
respondisset audiuissent. Tum vero demum senserunt suae
cenae sumptus absque hospite (quod aiunt) frustra secum depu-
tasse, quod qui faciunt, denuo oportet computent, cum hospes
plerumque in rationem adferat, quod illi vel non recordabantur
10 vel sibi parcentes omiserant.

Quamobrem, mi charissime Lee, etiam te atque etiam rogo, ne
tecum statuas nimium tuae spei fidere, qui quum me sis obtestatus per sanctissimum mihi nomen amicitiae, vt me hac in re
tibi aequum praebeam, Sic mihi mi Lee contingat te vt per-
15 petuum amicum habeam, vt ego nullo mihi pacto videor in te
futurus aequior, quam si te contra (quod obnixe facio) per si
quid est amicicia sanctius obtester, vt odiosis huiusmodi excussis
iurgijs in amiciciam cum Erasmo redeas, quod illum non recusaturum ausim profecto meam tibi fidem obstringere, neu
20 velis eam prouinciam suscipere, quam semel ingressus nunquam
possis deponere, in qua perpetuo tumultu, rixa, contentione,
molestijs tunica molesta molestioribus aetatem reliquam, cuius
adhuc spero tibi multum [E$_4$v] supra mediam superest, arsurus
sis verius, mi Lee, quam victurus. Quin tu Christianae te charitati
25 restituens, animo serenato, laetus hanc vitam et tranquillus ex-
ige, contemptaque vnius inauspicati libelli iactura, qui futuris
etiam foeturis tuis nonnihil offundat inuidiae, feliciorem ali-

---

1 tuam,] tuam *1520*   1–2 video,] video *1520*   2 integram,] *1520*ª, integram *1520*ᵐ
5 iudicet:] iudicet, *1520;* securi quam tu,] *1520*ª, securi, quam tu 1520ᵐ   6 de-
mum] *1520*ª, demun *1520*ᵐ   7 sumptus] *1520*ª, sumptus, *1520*ᵐ   8 faciunt,]
faciunt *1520*   9 recordabantur] recordabantur, *1520*   11 Quamobrem,] Quamobrem *1520*   12–13 obtestatus] *1520*ª, obtestatus, *1520*ᵐ   14 praebeam,] praebeam.
1520   15 videor] *1520*ª, videar *1520*ᵐ   16 futurus] *1520*ª, facturus *1520*ᵐ   21–
22 tumultu, rixa, contentione, molestijs] *1520*ª, tumultu rixa contentione molestijs,
*1520*ᵐ   24 sis . . . Lee] *1520*ᵐ, mi Lee sis uerius *1520*ª   25 restituens, animo
serenato,] restituens animo serenato *1520;* laetus] *1520*ª, laetus, laetus *1520*ᵐ; vitam]
*1520*ª, vitam, *1520*ᵐ

And so I am very afraid you may seem to impair your own honor in a tactless endeavor to vindicate it at a point when, as far as I can see, he has not yet impugned it. I have seen others suffer the same fate before. Though the outcome must tell whether they were less safe than you are, they were certainly no less convinced of their safety than you are until they had heard his response. Only then did they find out that without the host, as it is said, they had reckoned the cost of their dinner in vain, since whoever does this has to reckon again; for the host generally adds some expense to the bill that they either forgot or conveniently omitted in order to spare themselves.

Therefore, my dearest Lee, I implore you again and again not to stake too much on your self-confidence. Since you implored me in the name of friendship, a name I hold especially sacred, to be fair to you in this episode, may I be as assured, my dear Lee, of retaining your friendship forever as I am convinced that I have no way of showing more fairness than by imploring you in return, as I fervently do, by whatever is even more sacred than friendship, to dispense with these odious reproaches, to resume friendly relations with Erasmus (for I would venture to give you my word that he would not reject them), and to give up the idea of accepting a province which you could not resign once you had entered it, and in which for the rest of your life—which I hope is much less than half finished—amid tumult, reviling, contention, and vexations more vexing than vestments of pitch, my dear Lee, you will feel more as if you are burning than actually living. Recover your own Christian charity instead, and retrieve your serenity. Live this life in contentment and peace. Scorn the loss of one ill-omened book which would even draw down some ill will on your offspring to come, and seek out a more promising

quam materiam tibi circumspice quam eleganter expolias, quae
cum prodierit aliquando, prosit et probetur omnibus, quae tuam
famam et praesentibus reddat amabilem et magno cum fauore
transmittat posteris, quae denique sit eiusmodi, vt eius praemium potissimum sperare possis a deo, quod genus mercedis
multo est omnibus mortalium bonis vberius. In qua ego materia
non veto si quid fors inciderit, in quo vel Erasmus aliquid, vel
quisquis alius quicquam scripsit vnquam, sit ita lapsus insigniter,
vt admonendus magnopere videatur orbis, ad eundem ne quis
rursus impingat lapidem, non inquam veto, quo minus tu quoque denuncies quae declinari profuerint offendicula. Nec id abs
te fieri aequus quisquam potest inique ferre, modo res tractetur
ea modestia, quae fidem faciat oblatam potius monendi necessi-
tatem, quam carpendi ansam esse quaesitam, a quo limite quis
non videt sulcus iste quam longe deliret, cum ex professo liber
cum libro velut hostis cum hoste committitur? Quod ne tu velis
committere, rursus mi Lee te per tuam famam, mea mihi propemodum chariorem, per meas de te spes, qui de nullo
nostratium vnquam concepi grandiores, per charitatem patriae,
cui debitum ex te splendorem nubecula pergis obducere, per
amicorum tuorum sollicitudinem, qui mecum trepidi [F₁] suas
quisque preces adiungunt, Obsecro atque obtestor quam possum maxime, vt et tibi parcas et patriae, ne vel Leus dicatur vel
Anglus augescentibus orbis Christiani commodis inuidere. Sin
tibi penitus insederit tam generosus ardor gloriae, vt potius
quam cum illo non dimices, malis genuinum frangere, tuam
quidem vicem amplius quam dolere non possum, patriae certe
pro mea virili connitar, vt hoc tuum factum, quod tantis
bonorum doctorumque omnium odijs exponi video, Britanni
potius esse, quam Britanniae censeatur, salua mihi tecum semper quoad per te licebit amicitia. Vale. Cal. Mai. An. M. D. XIX.

1 circumspice] circumspice, *1520*   3 amabilem] *1520ª* amabilem, *1520ᵐ*   5 a deo]
1520ᵐ, adeo *1520ª*   9 videatur orbis,] *1520ª*, videatur, orbis *1520ᵐ*   10 impingat]
1520ᵐ, impingant *1520ª*   11 denuncies] *1520ª*, denuncies, *1520ᵐ*; profuerint] *1520*,
profuerit *conj. 1760*   16 libro] *1520ª*, libro, *1520ᵐ*; committitur?] committitur.
1520   19 per] *1520ᵐ*, et per *1520ª*   22 adiungunt,] adiungunt. *1520ᵐ*, adiungunt
1520ª; Obsecro] *1520ᵐ*, Obsecro te *1520ª*   23 parcas] *1520ª*, parcas, *1520ᵐ*; dicatur]
1520ª, dicatur, *1520ᵐ*   24 inuidere.] *1520ª*, inuidere, *1520ᵐ*   25 insederit] *1520ª*,
insederit, *1520ᵐ*   30 censeatur,] *1520ª*, censeatur: *1520ᵐ*   31 Cal. Mai.] *1520ᵐ*, 20
die Maij *1520ª*

theme for yourself to write up in an elegant way, so that when it eventually appears it will benefit and please everyone, it will both endear your fame to your contemporaries and commend it very favorably to posterity, and above all it will be the sort of work for which you can hope God will provide the supreme recompense, for that kind of reward is much richer than all mortal goods. I have no objection, if there happens to be some point germane to that theme where Erasmus or any other writer has made a particularly serious mistake, and it seems clear that the world should be warned of it so that no one else will trip up over the same obstacle—I have no objection, I repeat, if you too let us know of the stumbling blocks we should avoid; nor could any fair person object to it, provided that the point was discussed with enough moderation to prove that the need for a warning had simply presented itself and that you had not sought out a pretext for faultfinding. But who does not see how that other course deviates from this limitation when book is deliberately pitted against book like enemy against enemy? To deter you from starting a fight of this sort, my dear Lee, once again I beseech and implore you with all the force I can muster, by your honor, which is practically dearer to me than my own; by my hopes for you, which are as great as I have ever conceived for any of my countrymen; by your love for your country, which you are about to embarrass by clouding the bright reputation you owe it; and by the solicitude of your friends, who are all apprehensively joining their own prayers to mine: spare yourself and your country alike, and let no one say either that Lee or that anyone English envies Christendom its present advances. But if you are completely obsessed with so noble a passion for glory that you would rather break your own jaw-tooth than pass up a fight with Erasmus, I can do nothing but pity your plight, but for my country's sake I will do everything in my power to establish that this action of yours, which I see invites so much ill will from all virtuous and learned men, is the act of a Briton, not of Britain, though I will always maintain our friendship to whatever extent you permit me to do so. Farewell. 1 May 1519.

LETTER TO A MONK
TEXT AND TRANSLATION

ERVDITISSI-
MA EPISTOLA CLARISSIMI VIRI DOMINI
Thomae Mori, qua respondet indoctis ac virulentis
litteris monachi cuiusdam, qui inter alia, etiam illud insectatus est stolidissime quod Erasmus verterit, "In principio erat sermo, etc."

PERLATAE sunt ad me litterae tuae, frater in Christo charissime, longae quidem illae, et mira quaedam signa prae se ferentes amoris erga me tui. Quis enim possit affectus esse vehementior, quam qui te tam impense reddit de mea salute
sollicitum, vt etiam tuta pertimescas? Times enim ne sic Erasmum diligam, vt eius contagio corrumpar, ne sic hominis ada-
mem litteras, vt noua eius peregrinaque doctrina (sic enim
scribis) inficiar. Quod ne accidat, postquam aliquot paginis in
hominis et eruditionem et mores totis (quod aiunt) habe[G₃v]nis
inuectus es, oras tandem atque obsecras perquam sancte scilicet
ac per ipsam dei misericordiam tantum non adiuras vt diligenter
ab illo caueam. Nam primum iuxta apostolum inquis "Corrumpunt bonos mores consortia praua." Deinde citas ex illius pro-
uerbijs, quod "qui iuxta claudum habitat, discet subclaudicare."
Denique adfers e poeta quoque testimonium (vt facias opinor
triadem), "dum spectant oculi lesos, leduntur et ipsi." Hijs atque
alijs huiusmodi, quanquam nihil est eius periculi quod tu per-

---

1–7 ERVDITISSIMA . . . etc.] _1520_ᵐ, EPISTOLA CLARISSIMI VIRI THO | mae
Mori, qua refellit rabiosam maledicentiam | monachi cuiusdam iuxta indocti atque |
arrogantis. _1520_ᵃ   6 verterit,] verterit. _1520_ᵐ   8 tuae,] tuae _1520_   8–9 charissime,] _1520_ᵃ, charissimae _1520_ᵐ   10 tui.] _1520_ᵃ, tui _1520_ᵐ   12 pertimescas]
_1520_ᵐ, pertimeas _1520_ᵃ   14 vt] _1520_ᵐ, ne _1520_ᵃ   16 hominis et] _1520_ᵐ, hominis
_1520_ᵃ   17 scilicet] scilicet, _1520_   18 misericordiam] _1520_ᵃ, misericordiam, _1520_ᵐ
20 ex illius] _1520_ᵃ, ex _1520_ᵐ   22 testimonium] _1520_ᵃ, testimonium, _1520_ᵐ   23
triadem),] triadem) _1520;_ Hijs] _Para. 1520_ᵃ

A learned epistle from a man of renown,
Master Thomas More, in response to a certain
monk's ignorant and virulent letter,
a senseless invective, belaboring,
among other issues, Erasmus' translation,
"In the beginning was Speech, etc."

D EAREST brother in Christ, I have received your long letter, fraught with various remarkable tokens of how much you love me. For could any affection be stronger than the one which makes you so inordinately concerned for my well-being as to fear even imaginary dangers? For you fear that I cherish Erasmus so much that his contact is going to corrupt me, that I adore the man's writings so much that (in your words) his new and unorthodox teaching is going to infect me. And lest this should happen, first you fill up a number of pages with an all-out polemic, one might say, against the man's learning and character, and then at length, in the holiest of tones, you pray, plead, and indeed all but conjure me in the name of God's mercy to take care to shun him. First you quote the apostle's reminder that "Bad company corrupts a good character." Then you cite, from Erasmus' *Adagia*, "A person who lives with a lame man will learn how to limp." Finally you draw on the testimony of a poet as well, doubtless so as to make up a triad: "When we look on another's affliction, our eyes are afflicted, as well." With these arguments and others like them, although there is no danger of the sort that

timescis, sedulo tamen abs te curatum est, vt ego ab eo loco in quo
tu periculum esse putas (si modo putas) auerterer.

   Quamobrem, nisi tam grati erga me animi gratia, gratias im-
mensas agerem, merito viderer ingratus, ingratior adhuc futu-
5 rus, si posteaquam tu me gradientem videns in planicie, feruido
quopiam amoris aestu, pertimuisti ne caderem, ego te per pre-
cipitia currentem intrepidus ac securus aspiciam, neque ad te
clamitem, vt tibi caute prospicias, sensimque inde ac circumspecte referas pedem, vnde sit periculum ne corruas. Itaque
10 primo collustrabo locum, in quo versor ipse, in quo quum tuta
omnia esse docuero, tum denique commonstrabo tibi, arcem
istam tuam, e qua Erasmum nostrum velut e sublimi tutoque
despicis, periculose nutare.

   Nam primum quid mihi periculi est si Erasmum credam in
15 nouo testamento rectius multa vertisse quam interpretem veterem, si credam graecis ac latinis litteris Erasmum illo pe-
ritiorem? id quod non credo tantum, sed etiam pla[G₄]ne video,
scioque. Nec potest id cuiquam esse ambiguum, cui vel exigua
fuerit vtriusque linguae noticia. Quid periculi est, si eorum lib-
20 rorum lectione delecter, quos doctissimi quique maximeque pij
velut vna voce collaudant, quos pontifex maximus pariter et
optimus bis iam pronunciauit vtiles esse studiosis? Quomodo
tam periculosa possim illo docente discere, qui nihil ipse definit,
qui vel aliena vel sua sic proponit in medium, vt iudicium re-
25 seruet integrum lectori? Qui si maxime falsa assereret, non tamen vsque adeo sum stupidus, vt non olfaciam quid verae fidei,
quid morum probitati congruat, nec sic in cuiusquam verba
iuratus, vt non libere ab illo sicubi subsit causa dissentiam.

---

3 Quamobrem,] Quamobrem *1520; no para. 1520*   5 planicie,] *1520ᵃ*, planicie:
1520ᵐ   6 aestu,] aestu *1520*   7 currentem] *1520ᵃ*, currentem, *1520ᵐ*; aspiciam,]
1520ᵃ, aspiciam *1520ᵐ*   8 prospicias,] *1520ᵃ*, prospicias *1520ᵐ*   10 ipse,] *1520ᵃ*,
ipse *1520ᵐ*   12 tuam,] *1520ᵃ*, tuam *1520ᵐ*; nostrum] *1520ᵃ*, nostrum, *1520ᵐ*   13
despicis,] *1520ᵃ*, despicis *1520ᵐ*   14 Nam] *No para. 1520*   15 vertisse] vertisse,
1520   21 pariter] *1520ᵃ*, pariter, *1520ᵐ*   22 studiosis?] *1520ᵃ*, studiosis. *1520ᵐ*

you fear, you have tried hard to drive me away from the place where you think (or at least claim to think) that the danger resides.

Thus, of course, I could rightly be seen as an ingrate for failing to greet such a gracious concern for my welfare with unbounded gratitude. I would be even more of an ingrate, in view of the way that your own fervid transports of love made you fear I would stumble when you saw me walking on even terrain, if I looked on without the least qualm as you ran on the rim of a precipice or if I did not shout you a warning that you ought to watch your own step and begin your own wary and cautious descent from where you are in danger of falling. Thus I will start by going over my own position, showing everything here to be safe, and then I will go on to show you that that lofty stronghold of yours from which, smug and secure, you look down upon our friend Erasmus is dangerously shaky.

For, first of all, how is it dangerous for me to believe that Erasmus has translated many New Testament passages better than the old translator, or for me to believe that Erasmus knows more about Greek and Latin literature than he did? Nor do I just believe it, I see it and know it for a fact; nor could anyone doubt it who has any command of both languages. How is it dangerous for me to enjoy reading those books which the most learned and most pious people are virtually unanimous in praising, and which the pope, best and greatest of primates, has twice now declared to be useful to scholars? How can I learn such dangerous doctrines from a teacher who himself never takes a definitive position, who presents both his own views and those of others in such a way that the reader remains free to judge them? And even if he made assertions which were utterly false, I am not so stupid that I cannot tell what will square with true faith or with soundness of morals, nor am I so committed to anyone's opinions that I will not freely disagree with him where I have good cause.

Quamobrem ab illo, quod dixi, nihil discriminis imminet mihi,
etiamsi (quod tu scribis) quaedam forent parum sana quae
scriberet. At tibi contra, quod doleo, nescio qua mala sorte contigisse video, vt cum ille tam numerosa volumina, tam plena non
5   eruditionis modo, sed verae quoque pietatis aediderit, quam non
alius quisquam multis iam retro saeculis: tu nobis in periculum
venias, vt quod alijs salubre sit remedium, id tibi praestigiator
aliquis verterit in venenum. Non potui (mihi crede) pro meo in te
amore sine graui dolore legere, quae nescio quo tu calore scrip-
10   sisti, cum in hominem nihil male meritum de te, publice vero de
omnibus meritum bene, conuicia velut e plaustro tam intem-
peranter euomeres, dum eruditioni detrahis, debaccharis in vitam, vagabundum dicis et pseudotheologum, Sycophantam
[G₄v] clamitas, haereseos crimen impingis et schismatis, eo vsque
15   progressus petulantiae, vt praeconem etiam voces Antichristi,
Etiamsi eam rem videlicet perbelle praemollias, quod cum id
improbissime dixeris, dicas te nolle dicere.

Quis versipellis et callidus daemon, amice iam diu charissime,
strophas huiusmodi veteratoriasque versutias in tuum pectus
20   tam simplex olim, vereque candidum, cum adhuc prophanus
esses, nunc tandem tot annos monachi, quodque multo sanctius
esse debet, etiam sacerdotis, inuexit, vt dicas, "haereticum non
voco, sed ea facit quae qui fecerit est haereticus, non appello
schismaticum, sed ea facit quae qui facit schismaticus est. Anti-
25   christi praeconem ego non nomino, sed quid si deus hoc ipsum
de Erasmo asseruerit? Parco tamen ne forte existimes aliquid de
me supra id quod vides, aut audis de me"? Proh deum atque
hominum fidem, quid ego ex te audio? Testor hoc in loco tuam

---

1 Quamobrem] *No para. 1520;* illo,] illo *1520*   3 contra,] contra *1520*   9 amore]
1520ᵃ, amore, *1520ᵐ*   11 plaustro] *1520ᵃ,* plaustro, *1520ᵐ*   12–13 vitam,] *1520ᵃ,*
vitam: *1520ᵐ*   13   dicis] dicis: *1520ᵐ,* dicis, *1520ᵃ;* pseudotheologum,]
pseudotheologum: *1520ᵐ,* pseudotheologum. *1520ᵃ*   14 impingis] impingis, *1520;*
et] *1520ᵐ,* ac *1520ᵃ*   16 perbelle praemollias] *1520ᵃ,* belle permollias *1520ᵐ*   17
dixeris,] *1520ᵃ,* dixeris: *1520ᵐ*   18 Quis] *No para. 1520ᵃ;* charissime,] charissime
1520   19 huiusmodi] huiusmodi, *1520*   22 debet,] *1520ᵃ,* debet *1520ᵐ;*
sacerdotis,] sacerdotis *1520*   24 qui facit] *1520ᵐ,* qui fecerit *1520ᵃ*   27 audis de]
1520ᵐ, audis in *1520ᵃ;* me"?] me. *1520*   28 ex] *1520ᵐ,* de *1520ᵃ*

As I said, then, Erasmus' opinions are no threat to me, even if (as you write) there were some unsound opinions in what he has written. But you, on the other hand, as I see to my sorrow, are sadly in danger, through some trick of fortune, of having his numerous volumes, replete with both learning and true piety, more such volumes than anyone else has produced for the last several centuries, transformed by some wily magician from a health-giving cure to a poison. Believe me, for the love that I bear you I was unable to read without profound sorrow your shockingly heated attack, in which you so intemperately vomit abuse by the wagonload onto a man who has done you no wrong and has publicly done all a service, whereas you belittle his learning, rave against his life-style, call him "vagrant" and "pseudo-theologian," cry "slanderer" at him, and brand him with charges of heresy and schism, going so far in your scurrility that you even proclaim him a "herald of Antichrist," even though you do hedge that insult very tactfully indeed: as you make such an outrageous accusation, you say you do not want to make it.

My old, dear friend, tell me, what sly, crafty demon has managed to plant so much guile and insidious subterfuge in a heart as sincere and as candid as yours was while you were still a layman, in the heart of a monk and (a word which deserves much more reverence) a priest of so many years' standing, to the point where you are able to say, "I do not call him a heretic, but whoever acts thus is a heretic. I do not proclaim him schismatic, but whoever acts thus is schismatic. I do not pronounce him a herald of Antichrist, but what if this very assertion concerning Erasmus had come straight from God? But I will forbear, lest your hopes for me should surpass what you see me or hear me to be." By all that is sacred in this world and the next, what do I hear you saying? At this point I appeal to your conscience: does it not

conscientiam, non erubescis? non totus intremescis, dum rem
tam impiam talibus adornas prodigijs? Dum quod homuncio
quispiam scelerate mentitur, id tu tam sancte nobis veluti e coe-
lesti vaticinio decantas? dum alienae famae detrectationem,
5 opus plane diaboli, ad deum refers autorem? Nam quod tanquam modestiae causa parcere te dicis, ne magnum aliquid de te
existimem, ita, deum precor, vterque nostrum de se sentiat hu-
militer, vt ego de te nihil existimassem sublimius etiamsi id a-
perte narrasses tibi reuelatum ipsi, etiam si nomen expressisses
10 vel angeli vel daemonis, qui hoc ad te detulisset, Quippe quam
rem ne iurato quidem [H₁] credidissem, sed suasissem potius, ne
omni spiritui crederes, praesertim ei, qui quantumuis falsa luce
praefulserit, angelum tamen tenebrarum sese detractionis et calumniae susurro, peculiari satanae signo, prodidisset. Malu-
15 issem tibi occinere illud Pauli, "In nouissimis temporibus disce-
dent quidam a fide, attendentes spiritibus erroris, et doctrinis
daemoniorum in hypocrisi loquentium mendacium, et cau-
teriatam habentium conscientiam." Item illud eiusdem, "Nemo
vos seducat volens in humilitate et religione angelorum, quae
20 non vidit inambulans frustra, inflatus sensu suae carnis." Haec
nimirum magis congruebant, quam illud quod tu tibi stulte ap-
plicas ex apostolo. Nunc vero, quando significas non reuelatum
tibi sed alij nescio cui, multo minus etiam commoueor. Etenim
quanquam non dubitem deum interdum quaedam reuelare
25 mortalibus, non tamen vsqueadeo stulte sum credulus, vt trepidus expauescam, quicquid aut delirus quispiam somniet, aut
confingat impostor, aut energumeno malus inspiret genius.
    Non dubito quin similibus afflatus sit orgijs, is etiam quem
scribis his verbis admonuisse te: "Noueris pro certo, quod Eras-
30 mus iste, quem tanta sequitur pompa verborum, non recte sentit

---

4 decantas?] decantas, *1520;* detrectationem,] detrectationem *1520*ᵐ, detractionem,
*1520*ᵃ   7 ita,] ita *1520*   8 sublimius] sublimius, *1520*   9 ipsi,] *1520*ᵃ, ipsi *1520*ᵐ
9–10 expressisses vel] *1520*ᵐ, expressisses *1520*ᵃ   10 detulisset,] detulisset.
1520   13 detractionis] detractionis, *1520*   17 daemoniorum] *1520*ᵐ, daemonum
*1520*ᵃ   18 Item] *1520*ᵐ, Idem *1520*ᵃ   20 inambulans] *1520*ᵐ, ambulans *1520*ᵃ
22 vero,] vero *1520;* reuelatum] *1520*ᵃ, relatum *1520*ᵐ   23 tibi] tibi, *1520;* minus
etiam] *1520*ᵐ, etiam minus *1520*ᵃ   28 Non] *No para. 1520*   29 te:] te. *1520*

make you blush, does it not make you tremble all over, when you trick out such an impious charge with such monstrous extravagance, when you take up some nobody's criminal lie and recite it to us with such sanctimony, as if by divine revelation, and when you take defamation of character, the manifest work of the devil, and call God its author? Now as for your saying, as if out of modesty, that you would forbear lest I look for great things from you, would to God it were as certain that each of us felt truly humble as it is that your tale would not have raised my opinion of you in the least, even if you had openly stated that it was your own revelation, even if you had mentioned the name of the angel or demon who brought you the message, it being one I would not have believed even from a sworn witness. Rather, I would have warned you against being too quick to believe every spirit, especially that one, for however brightly he had shone with false light he would still have betrayed himself as an angel of darkness by his buzz of detraction and slander, a sure mark of Satan. I would rather have countered by echoing that verse from Paul, "In the latter times some shall depart from the faith, hearkening unto spirits of error and the doctrines of devils who speak lies in hypocrisy and have consciences seared with a hot iron," and also that other verse of his, "Let no man lead you astray in a voluntary humility and worshiping of angels, intruding vainly into things he has not seen, puffed up by his carnal conceit." For these verses would be more to the point than the one which you foolishly transfer to yourself from the apostle. As it is, though, since you indicate that this revelation was not yours but some other fellow's, I am even less impressed. For though I do not doubt that God does now and then bestow some revelations on mortals, I am nonetheless not so foolishly credulous as to be frightened out of my wits by whatever some madman dreams up, some impostor invents, or else some evil spirit suggests to the man he possesses.

I do not doubt that your other informant owes his inspiration to similar unholy rituals, the one who you write warned you as follows: "Be assured that Erasmus, who has such a fine train of words to attend him, has unorthodox opinions regarding the

de fide catholica aut sacra scriptura. hoc multociens ostendit, vbi
secretam possit habere audientiam. Expertus sum quod dico, et
hoc saepius." Hactenus illius boni viri de Erasmo apud te praeconium, quem dicis etiam, quisquis est, egregiam excogitasse
5 aduersus Erasmum apologiam, quem tamen admones ne sus-
pi[H₁v]cer esse Leum. Noli vereri, non suspicor. Nam de Leo
satis persuasum habeo, quanquam nescio quo impetu eo sit ingressus, vnde nunc pudet regredi, ea tamen virtutis indole
praeditum, his artibus adformatum ingenium esse, vt etiam si de
10 litteris obstrepat, non prorupturus sit in conuicia. Tuum vero
hunc praedicant quidam longe Laeo dissimilem. Nam quem tu
fide dignum dicis, virum plane grauem atque, vt tuis vtar
flosculis, morigeratum, secundum saeculi dignitatem honorabilem, nec minus integritate vitae quam praeclara eruditione
15 conspicuum, eum qui nouere penitus longe depingunt aliter,
non dignum fide, non valde moratis moribus, vere morosum,
honoratum tamen alicubi magis quam honorabilem. Eruditionem vero, apologia quam laudas ostendit, quam qui videre
quidam, et non indocti et qui bene consultum cupiunt homini,
20 eoque suaserunt vt vel exureret vel abderet perpetuo, constanter
asserunt hominem ferme ad insaniam vsque delirum, nisi quod
quibusdam gaudet lucidis interuallis. Quem cum talem delini-
arent, impetrare non potui, vti quis esset edicerent, ne per ipsos
nominatim traduci posset, priusquam egregium ingenij ac doc-
25 trinae specimen in lucem prodiens praeclara illa apologia
prodidisset.

Sed excutiamus obsecro paululum quam fide dignus sit iste
perfidus, cui tu fidem habes, Erasmum non recte sentire de fide:
qua de re, ne fidem infido non habeas, ait Erasmum id saepius
30 ostendere, vbi secretam possit habere audientiam, seque ipsum
id non expertum tantum, sed etiam [H₂] saepius expertum, vt
non ab alijs, sed ab ipso Erasmo istud eum frequenter audisse

1 scriptura.] scriptura, *1520;* multociens] *1520*ᵐ, multoties *1520*ᵃ   4 etiam,] etiam
1520   6 vereri,] *1520*ᵃ, vereri *1520*ᵐ   7 nescio] *1520*ᵃ, nescio, *1520*ᵐ   12 dicis,
virum] dicis virum, *1520;* plane] *1520*ᵐ, plene *1520*ᵃ; grauem atque,] grauem, atque
1520   14 vitae] *1520*ᵃ, vitae, *1520*ᵐ   15 penitus] *1520*ᵃ, penitus, 1520ᵐ   17
alicubi] *1520*ᵃ, alicubi, *1520*ᵐ   18 vero, apologia] vero apologia, *1520*ᵐ, uero Apologia *1520*ᵃ   19 indocti] indocti, *1520*   20 exureret] exureret, *1520*   25 prodiens]
prodiens, *1520*   27 Sed] *No para.* *1520*   28 fide:] fide *1520*ᵐ, fide, *1520*ᵃ

Catholic faith and holy scripture. He frequently shows this is so whenever he can get a private hearing. I speak from repeated experience." So much for that fine fellow's report to you about Erasmus, though you say that, whoever he is, he has also thought up a distinguished apology against Erasmus; then you warn me not to suspect that the fellow is Lee. Rest assured, I do not suspect Lee, since I feel quite convinced that though he has been carried away by some passion or other to the point that he now feels ashamed to retreat, his own mind is endowed with such virtue and shaped with such learning that even though he may quarrel about scholarly issues he will not break out into abuse. But some people describe this informant of yours as a man very different from Lee. For though you call him a man of good faith, a man clearly both serious and (using your own pretty phrase) genial-mannered, honorable by the standards of secular dignity, and as conspicuous for personal integrity as for his illustrious learning, he is drawn in a quite different light by the people who know him the best: not a man of good faith, far from genial in character, and actually churlish, though honored by some— honored rather than honorable. But the extent of his learning is shown in the apology you praise, whereas some learned men who have seen it and wish the man well, and for that reason urged him to burn it or suppress it forever, insist that the man is deranged to the point of sheer lunacy, though he does have a few lucid intervals. And as they were sketching him thus I could not get them to say who he was; they themselves did not want to disgrace him by name before that illustrious apology came forth to provide a definitive sample of his wit and learning.

But if you please, let us ponder a little just how much good faith that perfidious fellow can claim whose good faith makes you think that Erasmus' opinions regarding the faith are unorthodox, a fellow who goes on to say (lest you doubt the good faith of so faithless a man) that Erasmus repeatedly shows this is so, whenever he can get a private hearing, and that he himself speaks from experience, and repeated experience at that, so that you could be sure that he heard the fact frequently from none

intelligeres. Vt semper veritas exerit sese? vt concinnantes mendacia vel casus aliquis arguit, vel rei natura destituit, vel ipsi sese
tanquam sorices produnt? Quid enim veri possit esse similius
quam, si de fide perperam sentiebat Erasmus, homo tam stu-
5   pidus, vt non sentiret simul quid ex ea re discriminis esset futurum, quid inquam veri fuerit similius, quam aliquos ambire semper solitum [eum] aut precibus impetrare, vt sibi liceret apud eos
narrare secreto sese esse haereticum? Nec enim requirebat aliud, vt ait iste tuus fide dignus testis, quam secretam audientiam.
10   At quam diu vixit apud Coletum, quam diu apud Reuerendum patrem Roffensem episcopum, quam diu apud Reuerendissimum Cantuariensis ecclesiae pontificem, vt omittam interim Monioium, Tunstallum, Paceum, Grocinum, quibuscum
saepe diuque versatus est, de quorum virorum laudibus, si quid
15   conarer exponere, merito viderer ineptus, quum horum nemo
sit, quem non omnes intelligant, a nemine satis laudari posse?
Quis istorum non centies cum illo colloquutus est secretissime?
Quis eorum vel semel audiuit aliquid, vnde vel suspicio possit
oboriri, non illum rectissime sentire de fide? Nam si quid tale
20   fuissent vel subodorati, meliores certe sunt, quam vt rem tam
atrocem dissimulare potuerint. At quis est eorum omnium, qui
non ita perpetuo dilexit illum, vt quo diutius eum nouerit, ac
pernorit intimius, eo semper magis magisque deamarit?
      Sed illis [H₂v] opinor non ausus est credere, talium virorum
25   veritus pietatem. Recte sane, quaerebat ergo aliquem cuius neque conscientiam vereretur, neque proditionem metueret,
Nempe quem ex vultu, verbis, vita, probe perpendisset eiusdem
sacri mysten esse. Talis igitur necesse est fuerit ille tibi tam impense laudatus, Ille, inquam, fide dignus, grauis, morigeratus,

---

1 sese?] sese, *1520*   1–2 mendacia] mendacia, *1520*   2 ipsi] *1520*ᵐ, ipse *1520*ᵃ   3
produnt?] produnt   *1520*ᵐ, produnt. *1520*ᵃ   3–4 similius quam,] similius? quam
*1520*ᵐ, similius, quam *1520*ᵃ   5 simul] simul, *1520*   7 solitum eum] solitum, *1520*
(see commentary); aut] *1520*ᵐ, ac *1520*ᵃ   10 At] *No para.* 1520   16 posse?] posse.
1520   17 centies] *1520*ᵃ, senties *1520*ᵐ   24 Sed] *No para.* 1520   26 metueret,]
metueret. *1520*   28 mysten esse] *1520*ᵐ, mysterij *1520*ᵃ; est] est, *1520*   29
laudatus,] *1520*ᵃ, laudatus. *1520*ᵐ; Ille, inquam,] Ille inquam *1520*

other than Erasmus himself. How the truth never fails to assert itself! How contrivers of falsehoods are either exposed through some chance event, balked by the facts of the matter, or given away by their own indiscretion, like shrew-mice! For supposing Erasmus did have wrong opinions regarding the faith, how likely is it that he would be too stupid to see how dangerous this would be for him, and how likely is it that he would always be looking for people, or begging them even, to let him inform them in private that he was a heretic? For as that good-faith witness attests, a private hearing was all the inducement he needed.

But how long did Erasmus live with Colet? How long with the reverend father, the bishop of Rochester? How long with the most reverend primate of Canterbury? Not to mention Mountjoy, Tunstall, Pace, and Grocyn, with whom he has associated long and often. I would rightly look silly if I tried to put into words any part of the praise that is due to these men, since everyone knows that no one can praise any one of them richly enough. Which of them has not spoken with him in the most perfect privacy a hundred times? Which of them, even once, has heard anything which could foster the slightest suspicion that Erasmus' opinions regarding the faith are not perfectly orthodox? For if they had detected the least indication of any such fault, they are certainly too good to have concealed such a monstrous discovery. But which one of them all has not always cherished Erasmus and yet come to love him all the more upon longer and deeper acquaintance?

But I suppose he did not dare trust men such as these, having too much respect for their piety. Naturally, then, he was looking for someone whose conscience he need not respect, and from whom he need not fear betrayal, a person whose face, words, and life-style plainly showed him to be an initiate of the same cult. Such a one must your much-praised informant have been— yes, that man of good faith, serious, genial, honorable, learned,

honorabilis, eruditus, integer, cui (vt vides) nunquam illud secretum toties commisisset Erasmus, nisi praeter tot egregias abs te
commemoratas dotes etiam fuisset haereticus. Si queramus ab
illo, quum se tam saepe dicat expertum, quomodo se probet
5   expertum vel semel, fatebitur, opinor, probari non posse. Nam
rem sibi negat nisi secreto creditam. At quisquis eius arguit criminis quenquam, quod ipse fatetur se docere non posse, Certe si
Sycophanta non est, perquam affinis est Sycophantae. Sed age
quaeramus, cum tam saepe sit expertus, vbinam de suis
10 haeresibus collocuti sunt, aut quando tractarunt inuicem? Necesse est olim fuerit, nam Erasmus iam diu abfuit. Cur igitur illo
praesente conticuit, Quando non paulo magis ad rem pertinebat
vt proderet, quo vitaretur noxius, quam nunc, vbi eo absente
non tantundem imminet periculi? Nam in libris nihil potest la-
15 tere secretum quod non oculi perspicaces eruerint. Sed longior
sum quam par est in reijciendis ἀποκαλύψεως illius praestigiaturis, et arguendo singulari isto non teste modo sed accusatore
quoque, atque etiam suopte indicio reo, qui fictus est (vt vides) et
scelerate mendax, et, nisi mentiretur, sceleratior, nem[H₃]pe
20 diu conscius, et serus proditor, Denique, seu vera seu falsa referat, vtrobique perfidus. certe neque ERASMI fides obscura
esse potest, quam tot labores, tot vigiliae, tot pericula, tot rerum,
tot salutis incommoda ob sacras suscepta litteras, ipsum fidei
promptuarium, illustrant, Nec noua est ista aduersus optimos
25 quosque haereseos excogitata calumnia, sed in sanctissimos iam
olim viros a satanae satellitio tam valida contorta machina, vt

---

1 (vt vides)] vt vides *1520*   3 dotes] dotes, *1520*   5 expertum vel semel,] expertum,
vel semel *1520*ᵐ, expertum, uel semel, *1520*ᵃ; fatebitur, opinor,] fatebitur opinor *1520;*
probari] *1520*ᵐ, probare *1520*ᵃ   6 negat] *1520*ᵃ, negat, *1520*ᵐ   7 posse,] *1520*ᵃ
posse: *1520*ᵐ   8 Sycophantae] *conj. 1760,* Sycophantiae *1520*   9 expertus,] *1520*ᵃ,
expertus *1520*ᵐ; vbinam] vbi nam *1520;* suis] *1520*ᵐ, *om. 1520*ᵃ   12 conticuit,] *1520*ᵃ,
conticuit? *1520*ᵐ   14 periculi?] periculi. *1520*ᵐ, periculi, *1520*ᵃ   17 isto] *1520*ᵃ,
isto, *1520*ᵐ   18 indicio] *1520*ᵃ, iudicio *1520*ᵐ   18 est (vt vides)] est, vt vides *1520*ᵐ,
est ut uides *1520*ᵃ   19 et, nisi mentiretur,] et nisi mentiretur *1520;* sceleratior,]
sceleratior *1520*ᵐ, scelerator, *1520*ᵃ   20 proditor, Denique,] proditor. Denique
1520   20–21 referat,] *1520*ᵃ, referat *1520*ᵐ   21 perfidus.] *1520*ᵃ, perfidus,
*1520*ᵐ   23 incommoda] incommoda, *1520*   24 promptuarium,] promptuarium
1520; illustrant,] *1520*ᵃ, illustrant. *1520*ᵐ   26 viros] viros, *1520;* tam] *1520,* iam *1760;*
valida] *1520*ᵐ, ualide *1520*ᵃ

and full of integrity, to whom you now see that Erasmus would never have confided his secret so often unless, besides all the remarkable gifts you assign him, he were also a heretic. Though he says that he speaks from repeated experience, if we ask him to prove that he had even one such experience I think he will confess that it cannot be proved, since he maintains that the secret was vouchsafed him only in private. But whoever accuses a man of a crime yet confesses that he cannot prove it is undoubtedly either a slanderer or something close to it. But then too, since he speaks from repeated experience, let us ask where they talked over their heresies or when they had any dealings with each other at all. It must have been some time ago, since Erasmus has long been away. Now then, why did the man hold his tongue when Erasmus was here and when it would have done much more good to expose him, so that we would have shunned the offender, than it can do now, when Erasmus is gone and when we are not in as much danger? For in books no secret is buried too deep for sharp eyes to uncover it. But I am taking more time than I should in refuting this sham revelation and exposing this singular witness, accuser, and self-declared suspect all rolled into one, who you now see is either a fraud and a criminal liar or, if he were telling the truth, a still worse sort of criminal, namely a long-standing partner in crime and a tardy informant—in sum, whether lying or telling the truth, a man wholly perfidious. There can certainly be nothing obscure about Erasmus' own faith, which has been brightly illuminated by the many exertions and vigils, the many dangers and material and physical hardships that he has sustained for sacred scripture, the very supply-house of faith, nor indeed is there anything new in fabricating a charge of heresy, something that can be done against every good man. Long ago Satan's followers launched the same charge at the saintliest of men with such violence and craft that the same

quorum laboribus vndique fides effloruit, ipsi coacti sint aeditis in id symbolis fidei suae rationem reddere.

Nunc ad ea veniam, quibus praeter illius fide digni testimonium, praeterque per corneam illam homeri portam coelitus emissa somnia, ansam ex illius libellis arripuisti, qua teneres hominem manifestae videlicet impietatis reum. E quibus illud grauissimum caput est, quod "non veritus est," vt ais, "audaculus iste ERASMVS pluries inter scribendum adserere, id quod nefas est, ipsos sanctissimos pariter atque doctissimos patres, illa inquam praeclarissima spiritus sancti organa Hieronymum, Ambrosium, Hilarium, Augustinum et alios huiusmodi, qui vniuersam dei ecclesiam ita suo illustrarunt lumine, vt nihil iam indigeat istiusmodi obscuri hominis tenebrositate nouiter colorari, lapsos esse alicubi." Obsecro nefas tibi videtur esse, si quis dicat illos ipsos, quos commemorasti, lapsos alicubi? Quid si illi ipsi, quibus defendendis aduocatus non vocatus aduenis, attestentur ERASMO? An non tum [H₃v] ridicule eorum causam qui tuum recusant patrocinium peroraueris?

Age ergo negas vnquam eorum quemquam esse lapsum. Rogo te, cum Augustinus Hieronymum censet male vertisse quaedam scripturae loca, Hieronymus suum tuetur factum, neuter labitur? Quum Augustinus asserat indubitatam habendam esse fidem translationi septuaginta interpretum, Hieronymus neget, et eos errasse contendat, neuter labitur? Cum Augustinus consensum illum ex spiritu sancto, ex diuersis cellulis eadem proferentium, adstruat, Hieronymus contra ineptum illud com-

---

3 Nunc] *No para. 1520*   4 portam] *1520ᵃ*, portam, *1520ᵐ*   5 illius] *1520ᵐ*, ipsius *1520ᵃ*   6 manifestae] *1520ᵃ*, manifeste *1520ᵐ*   7 est, vt ais,] est: vt ais *1520ᵐ*, est, ut ais *1520ᵃ*   8 adserere] *1520ᵐ*, adferre *1520ᵃ*   9 est,] est *1520*   11 Hilarium,] *1520ᵃ*, Hilarium: *1520ᵐ*; huiusmodi,] *1520ᵃ*, huiusmodi: *1520ᵐ*   12 lumine,] *1520ᵃ*, lumine: *1520ᵐ*   13–14 colorari . . . alicubi] *1520ᵃ*, colorari etc. *1520ᵐ*   14 Obsecro] *Para. 1520ᵐ*; esse,] esse: *1520ᵐ*, esse *1520ᵃ*   15 ipsos,] *1520ᵃ*, ipsos: *1520ᵐ*; commemorasti,] commemorasti *1520*   16 ipsi,] ipsi: *1520ᵐ*, ipsi *1520ᵃ*; aduenis,] aduenis: *1520*   17 causam] *1520ᵐ*, causam tu *1520ᵃ*   19 Age] *No para. 1520*; lapsum.] *1520ᵃ*, lapsum? *1520ᵐ*   21 loca,] *1520ᵃ*, loca: *1520ᵐ*   22 asserat] *1520ᵐ*, adferat *1520ᵃ*   23 interpretum,] interpretum: *1520*   24 errasse] *1520ᵃ*, errasse, *1520ᵐ*   25 sancto,] sancto *1520*; cellulis] *1520ᵃ* cellulis, *1520ᵃ*   25–26 proferentium,] proferentium *1520*

men whose labors had made the faith flourish were compelled to give an account of their faith by publishing their own creeds.

Now I will turn away from the testimony of that good-faith witness of yours, and from those dreams which were sent down from heaven through the gate of horn mentioned by Homer, and I will proceed to the points in Erasmus' own books which you use as a pretext to charge him with blatant impiety. The most serious of your indictments is this, that "That impudent fellow Erasmus does not hesitate to make the outrageous assertion in many places in his writings that even the holiest and most learned fathers, those illustrious instruments of the Holy Spirit, Jerome, Ambrose, Hilary, Augustine, and others like them, whose light has illuminated the Catholic church well enough that it has no need of this obscure fellow to darken and stain it anew, were occasionally wrong." Does it really strike you as outrageous for anyone to say that the very men you singled out were occasionally wrong? What if those very men, whose unbidden defender you are, should agree with Erasmus? Will it not make a joke of your vehemence on their behalf if they scorn your support?

Now then, you deny that any of these men was ever wrong. Tell me this: when Augustine maintains that Jerome has mistranslated some places in scripture, while Jerome vindicates his performance, is neither one wrong? When Augustine asserts that the fidelity of the Septuagint version should not be impugned, while Jerome denies this and contends that the Septuagint translators made mistakes, is neither one wrong? When Augustine adduces that tale of their perfect consensus according to which all of them were guided by the Holy Spirit to produce the same version in their separate cells, while Jerome derides

mentum derideat, neuter labitur, quum sentiant ex diametro
diuersa? Quum Hieronymus epistolam ad Galatas sic interpretetur vt dicat Petrum simulate reprehensum a Paulo, Augustinus neget, neuter labitur? Quum Hieronymo displiceant
5 Augustini labores in psalmos, Augustino placeant, neuter labitur? Quum Augustino quodcunque mendacium peccatum sit,
Hieronymus mendacium in loco laudet, neuter labitur? Quum
Augustinus vxore ob fornicationem dimissa neget illa viua alteram duci posse, Ambrosius licere confirmet, neuter labitur?
o Hieronymus censuit vxorem ante baptismum habitam, alteram
item post baptismum, non imputari ad digamiam: ecclesia nunc
censet errasse. Augustinus daemones asserit atque angelos item
omnes substantias esse corporeas: non dubito quin tu neges.
Asserit infantes sine baptis[H$_4$]mo defunctos aeterna sensus
5 poena torquendos, quod nunc quotus est quisque qui credat, nisi
quod Lutherus fertur, Augustini doctrinam mordicus tenens,
antiquatam sententiam rursus instaurare? Quotus est quisque
sanctorum veterum, qui non crediderit diuam virginem in origi-
nali peccato conceptam? At nuper exorti sunt qui negent, ad
?o quos propemodum Christianus orbis a veteribus omnibus
desciuit.
   Nullus erit finis si cuncta coner persequi, in quibus doctissimos
illos et sanctissimos viros liquido constet errasse, quorum libros si
legis, errata nescire non potes, nisi quae legas non intelligas.
25 Ergo qui illum vocas audaculum ipse multo deprehenderis au-
dacior, qui audes illos affirmare nunquam lapsos esse, quod si
velis tueri necesse est eorum libros vel non legisse te, vel non

---

−2 labitur, quum . . . diuersa?] *1520*^{m}, labitur? quum . . . diuersa, *1520*^{a} 6 sit,]
1520^a, sit: *1520*^{m} 7 mendacium] *1520*^{a}, mendacium, *1520*^{m} 8 fornicationem]
1520^a, formicationem *1520*^{m} 9 confirmet,] confirmet: *1520*^{m}, confirmat, *1520*^{a}
13 corporeas:] corporeas, *1520*   14 defunctos] defunctos, *1520*   16 fertur,] fertur
1520   17 instaurare?] instaurare. *1520*   18 veterum,] veterum: *1520*^{m}, ueterum
1520^a; virginem] *1520*^{a}, virginem, *1520*^{m} 20 orbis] *1520*^{a}, orbis, *1520*^{m} 22
Nullus] *No para.* *1520;* persequi] *1520*^{m}, prosequi *1520*^{a} 23 illos] *1520*^{a}, illos, *1520*^{m}
24 legis,] legis: *1520*^{m}, legas, *1520*^{a}; legas] *1520*^{m}, legis *1520*^{a} 27 libros] libros,
1520

that silly fiction, is neither one wrong, though their viewpoints are diametrically opposed? When Jerome interprets the letter to the Galatians as if Paul were only pretending to rebuke Peter, while Augustine denies this, is neither one wrong? When Jerome disapproves of Augustine's work on the Psalms, while Augustine approves of it, is neither one wrong? When Augustine regards every lie as a sin, while Jerome praises an opportune lie, is neither one wrong? When Augustine denies that a man who divorced his first wife for fornication can marry again in her lifetime, while Ambrose affirms he can do so, is neither one wrong? Jerome maintained that to marry one wife before baptism and another thereafter does not count as two marriages; the Church now maintains he was mistaken. Augustine asserts that all demons, and all angels too, are corporeal substances; no doubt you deny it. He asserts that infants who die without baptism are condemned to an eternity of physical suffering; how many believe that today besides Luther, who they say clings fast to the teachings of Augustine, and is reviving this obsolete notion? Did not most of the ancient saints believe that the Blessed Virgin was conceived in original sin? But some recent writers sprang up to deny it, and most of Christendom has sided with these men against all the ancients.

There would be no end to it if I tried to list all the points on which it is quite clear that the most learned and holiest men had mistaken ideas, and if you read their books you could not overlook their mistakes if you understood what you were reading. Thus though you call him impudent, you prove to be not a little more reckless than he is when you make the reckless assertion that those men were never wrong, an assertion you cannot defend without showing that you either did not read their books or

intellexisse fatearis. Imo qua fronte potes eum reprehendere,
qui idem dicat quod tu? Nam lapsum Augustinum in asserendis
daemonum corporibus, In damnandis infantibus, Hieronymum
in digamia, omnes prope veteres in conceptu virginis, non du-
5 bito quin tute dicas, et tamen haec ita cum sint, et cum in sacrarum interpretatione litterarum sancti illi patres inter se tam
saepe dissenserint, idque magis perspicuum sit, quam vt possit
negari, mirum est tamen, vt tu pueriliter exclamas, et coelum
terrae permisces, sicubi quis [H₄v] vel Carrensem conuincat er-
10 rasse, vel delirasse Lyranum. Augustinus non veritus est dicere,
nemini se post Apostolos tantum autoritatis tribuere, vt eius
dictis indubitatam habeat fidem, nisi quatenus aut ex scripturis
aut ratione liquido possit docere. Tu diuos omnes putas tibi
demereri perpetuo, si vocifereris eos nunquam esse lapsos. At illi
15 vel inscitiam tuam derident, vel importunum istud studium
tuum detestantur. Neque talem expetunt patronum, quorum
charitas magis eorum fauet industriae, qui si quid illi lapsi sint
ammoneant alios, quam eorum superstitiosae pietati, qui inutili
patrocinio eorum lapsus in aliorum ruinam propagent.
20   Iam vero quum etiam in stilum eius stilum intendas tuum,
dabis mihi hanc veniam, non possum profecto me continere
quin rideam. Nam cum desideras in illo eam sermonis facilitatem, quam quiuis lector intelligat, dum in illo damnas ac rides,
quod latinis interdum graeca permiscet, tam circumspectus es, vt
25 non videas eadem opera te taxare Hieronymum, in quem etiam,
velis nolis, praeclara illa tua recidunt scommata, qui et ipse Latinis interserat graeca, et quaedam scripserit eruditiora virginibus, quam quae nunc Theologiae plerique professores intelligant. Quid si aliquem tractatum integrum graece perscripsisset
30 Erasmus, an non tum eum multo magis cum ratione posses irridere, quam nunc quum non nisi quaedam interspargat? Atqui

---

2 tu?] tu. *1520*   4 veteres] *1520*ᵃ, veteres, *1520*ᵐ   6 litterarum] *1520*ᵃ, litterarum,
*1520*ᵐ; se] *1520*ᵃ, se, *1520*ᵐ   9 Carrensem] *1520*ᵐ, Corrensem *1520*ᵃ   10
Lyranum.] *1520*ᵃ, Lyranum, *1520*ᵐ   13 Tu] *Para. 1520*ᵐ   16 patronum] *1520*ᵃ,
patronem *1520*ᵐ   20 Iam] *No para. 1520*   22 desideras] *1520*ᵐ, desideres *1520*ᵃ
25 videas] *1520*ᵐ, videras *1520*ᵃ   25–26 etiam, velis nolis,] etiam velis nolis *1520*
26 ipse] *1520*ᵐ, saepe *1520*ᵃ   27 interserat] *1520*ᵐ, interserit *1520*ᵃ   30 posses]
*1520*ᵃ, possis *1520*ᵐ   31 quam] *1520*ᵐ, quod *1520*ᵃ

did not understand them. Worse yet, how can you be so brazen as to rebuke him for saying just what you say? For no doubt you yourself say Augustine was wrong in asserting that demons have bodies and in damning infants, Jerome was wrong about double marriages, and almost all the ancients were wrong about the Virgin's conception. And yet, even though this is so, and though those holy fathers disagreed with each other so often in interpreting sacred scripture, and though this is too obvious for anyone to deny it, it is amazing how childishly you storm and turn heaven and earth upside down every time someone detects either error in Hugh of St. Cher or delirium in Nicolas de Lyra. Augustine was not afraid to say he granted no man besides the apostles so much authority that he would accord an unquestioning faith to what he said except insofar as he could prove it clearly either from scripture or from reason. You think you put all the saints forever in your debt by protesting that they were never wrong. But they either laugh at your ignorance or deplore your misguided devotion. Nor do they want defenders like you, since their charity has more regard for the diligence of those who warn others about it if the saints ever made a mistake than it does for the superstitious piety of those whose misguided defensiveness propagates such mistakes to the peril of others.

But when you go so far as to pit your style against his, you will have to forgive me, I simply cannot keep from laughing. For when you say he lacks that facility of speech which is intelligible to any reader and you censure and mock him for the way he at times mixes Greek words with Latin, you are so very clever that you never notice that this stricture of yours applies equally well to Jerome, on whom, whether you like it or not, those fine quips of yours also reflect, since he too intersperses Greek words in his Latin, while some of what he wrote for virgins is too learned for many theology professors to understand it today. What if Erasmus had written some treatise entirely in Greek? Would you not then have much better reason to mock him than now, when he merely throws in some Greek words here and there? But our women could give the same reason for mocking all those who

eadem ratione nostrae mulieres eos irriserint omnes, quicunque
scripsere latine. Quid quod [I₁] nec magis aperte, nec stilo magis
facili quisquam scripsit vnquam, qui quidem latine scripserit,
vsqueadeo vt nimiam stili facilitatem Budaeus in illo, vir alioqui
5   doctissimus, non sit veritus reprehendere? Nemo diligentius vitat (quod tu illi vicium obijcis) insuetiora vocabula, cum isti tamen, quos tu ais vti modestiore stilo, fere tertium quodque verbum effingant nouum, ex quibus te quoque puto sermonis istas
delibasse delitias, "morigeratus," "vagabunda conuersatio,"
10 "tenebrositas," "identitas," aliasque id genus gemmulas.

Verum cum praeter affectatam eloquentiam multa sint alia,
eaque indigna, quae obiectas Erasmo, Age fatebitur omnia, si is
in integro aliquo volumine tantum affectauerit eloquentiae,
quantum tute interdum in vno affectas versiculo, velut exempli
15 causa cum quaeritas, "quid ergo dicent ad haec qui totos annos in
huiusmodi expendunt perituris, et illico marcessuris rhetorum
depictis flosculis?" Profer ex omnibus quae te significas in Erasmo legisse, si quid vnquam legisti tam turgidum, quam sit hic
vnus versiculus tuus, cum tamen sit male grammaticus. Nec ta-
20 men istud eo dico, quod soloecismum in te vituperandum
putem, a quo sermonis puritatem nec expecto nec exigo, cum
non ignorem, neque tibi vacasse vnquam vt posses discere, nec si
vacasset maxime, praeceptores contigisse, qui traderent. Sed
haec eo dico vt cum tibi decorum putes tam anxie eloquentiam
25 affectare, cum ne grammaticam quidem possis consequi, ne vicio
vertas Erasmo, quod olim partam et nunc vltro offerentem sese
non aspernatur elegantiam.

Cum aduersus linguarum studium disseris, illud non iniucun-
dum est, quod doles, [I₁v] dum graeca lingua discitur et

---

1 irriserint] *1520ᵃ*, iiriserint *1520ᵐ*   3 scripserit] scripserīt *1520ᵐ*, scripserint *1520ᵃ*
5   doctissimus,] *1520ᵃ*, doctissimus *1520ᵐ*; reprehendere?] reprehendere. *1520*
5–6 vitat] vitat, *1520*   9 morigeratus] *1520ᵐ*, morigeratus et *1520ᵃ*   11 Verum]
No para. 1520   12 Erasmo,] Erasmo. *1520*   13 affectuauerit] *1520ᵃ*, affect-
auit *1520ᵐ*   17 flosculis?] *1520ᵃ*, flosculis. *1520ᵐ*; Profer] *Para. 1520ᵐ*   19
grammaticus.] *1520ᵃ*, grammaticus? *1520ᵐ*   19–20 tamen istud] *1520ᵐ*, istuc tamen
1520ᵃ   21 puritatem nec expecto] puritatem, nec expecto, *1520ᵐ*, puritatem nec
expecto, *1520ᵃ*   28 Cum] *No para. 1520*   28–29 non iniucundum] *1520ᵐ*, iucun-
dum *1520ᵃ*   29 est,] est *1520*

have written in Latin. What of this, that of all those who have in fact written in Latin, not one has ever written more plainly than he or perfected an easier style, to the point that Budé, a most learned man with regard to most things, did not hesitate to criticize Erasmus for an excessively easy style? No one is more careful to shun farfetched terms, though you charge he affects them, whereas those men who you say use a more modest style make up virtually every third word, men from whom I imagine you yourself must have learned those pet phrases of yours, "genial-mannered," "vagabond life-style," "tenebrosity," "identity," and other such gems.

But look here, though you make many other unjustified charges against Erasmus besides affectation of eloquence, he will confess to them all if he has ever affected as much eloquence in an entire volume as you sometimes affect in one line, when you ask, for example, "Then how will they answer these points, they who spend all their years on such short-lived, quick-withering, prettified flowerlets of rhetoric?" Out of all you profess to have read in the works of Erasmus, produce anything you have read as pretentious as this line of yours, which is ungrammatical as well. Nor am I mentioning this because I think you ought to be blamed for a solecism. I neither expect nor demand pure speech from you; I am not unaware that you never had free time to learn it, and even if you had had the time, you would still have lacked teachers to instruct you in it. I am mentioning these points to show that, since you think it is seemly for you to engage in such a strained affectation of eloquence before you even master your grammar, you should not take Erasmus to task for refusing to spurn the refinement which he made his own long ago and which waits on him now uninvited.

When you argue against studying languages it is not unamusing to hear you lament that in learning Greek and Hebrew we

haebraica, aliquid interim de latinae linguae puritate deperire,
in cuius venustatem paulo ante tam atrociter exclamaueras,
quasi tantum terrarum inter puritatem sermonis intersit ac venustatem, cum tamen Hieronymus eo loco quem citas queratur
5   defloratam esse venustatem, nec id ob aliud, quam vt vehementius suum commendet studium, quod in hebraeas litteras in-
sumpserat, quas dignas censuit, quae vel cum latinae linguae
detrimento discerentur, quum graecae sint multo adhuc magis
vtiles, vel ob nouum testamentum, quod tam longe praestat ve-
10   teri quam corpus vmbram aut veritas figuram antecellit, vel
propter sacrarum litterarum interpretes, quorum optimus quisque ac sanctissimus ferme scripsit graece, vel denique propter
artes, quas liberales vocant, ac philosophiam, quibus de rebus
Latini scripsere propemodum nihil. Quid quod negare non
15   potes, vt quisque Latinorum maxime sciuit graece, ita eundem in
sua quoque lingua fuisse disertissimum, idque non olim tantum,
sed nunc quoque passim vsu venire? Nec Hieronymus ipse post
imbibitas haebraicas litteras, minus venuste scripsit, quam prius,
id quod opera eius posteriora declarant, quanquam illi placuit
20   excusare stilum suum, vel qua de causa memoraui, vel quod
vbique id agit, vt eloquentia quam adfert comes accessisse videatur inaccersita.

Illud certe pulcherrimum est, quod eo rem deducis tandem, vt
mediocrem linguarum notitiam laudes, nimium tantum stu-
25   dium damnes: quasi longe vltra mediocritatem iam pro[I₂]mo-
tum sit, citra quam adhuc longo interuallo subsistitur. Sermonis
puritatem obuijs (quod aiunt) vlnis fateris amplectendam, at in
lepidae orationis venustatem tragicis clamoribus intonas, defles-
que admodum lamentabiliter, quod in eius sinum, qui olim tan-
30   tum patebat ethnicis, nunc tandem bona Christianismi pars de-
flexerit miserabiliter, Quasi vetustissimi quique sacrorum

---

3 intersit] *1520*ᵃ, intersit, *1520*ᵐ   8 sint multo] *1520*ᵐ, sint *1520*ᵃ   9–10 veteri]
veteri, *1520*   10 vmbram] vmbram, *1520;* antecellit,] *1520*ᵃ, antecellit: *1520*ᵐ   12
graece,] graece: *1520*ᵐ, graece. *1520*ᵃ   17 venire?] *1520*ᵃ, venire. *1520*ᵐ   18
prius,] *1520*ᵃ, prius: *1520*ᵐ   19 declarant,] *1520*ᵃ, declarant: *1520*ᵐ   21 adfert]
*1520*ᵃ, adfert, *1520*ᵐ   23 Illud] *No para. 1520*   24 linguarum notitiam] *1520*ᵐ,
noticiam linguarum *1520*ᵃ   27 vlnis] *1520*ᵃ, vlnis, *1520*ᵐ   27–28 in lepidae] in-
lepidae *1520*   29 sinum,] *1520*ᵃ, sinum *1520*ᵐ   31 miserabiliter,] miserabiliter.
1520

tend to lose the purity of our Latin, when you have just finished
your merciless tirade against graceful Latin, as if there were such
a vast difference between pure and graceful speech. Besides, in
the passage you cite, Jerome really complains of the harm done
to the gracefulness of his speech, and he does so with no other
aim than to recommend even more strongly his own study of
Hebrew writings, since he thought them worth mastering even
at the expense of Latin. But Greek writings are patently more
useful still, whether we consider the New Testament (for it takes
the same precedence over the Old that a substance has over a
shadow or a reality over a figure), or the interpreters of sacred
scripture (for almost all the finest and holiest of them wrote in
Greek), or finally those arts we call liberal, as well as philosophy
(for on these topics speakers of Latin wrote practically nothing).
Furthermore you can scarcely deny that those Latins who knew
the most Greek were also the most fluent in their own tongue,
and that this was not only the general rule in the past but is still so
today. Nor did Jerome himself write less gracefully after he
mastered Hebrew than he did before, as his later works prove,
even though he saw fit to apologize for his own style, whether for
the reason I mentioned or else because he continually strives to
sustain the impression that he never courted the eloquence
which now attends him.

   This is surely your most splendid touch: you finally come to
the point of saying that you approve of a moderate acquaintance
with languages and merely condemn too much study of them, as
if the study of them had already been pushed well past the mean,
while in fact it is still stopped well short of it. You profess that we
ought to embrace pure speech with open arms, as they say, yet
you thunder with tragic extravagance against a graceful and
elegant style, and you lament most pathetically that now a large
portion of Christendom has been pitifully ensnared by its
charms, though they once appealed only to heathens, as if all of

patrum non venustate claruerint, cum qui hodie sacras tractant
litteras, augustam illam tantae rei maiestatem impuro sermone
fere contaminent.

   At hac in parte tam belle videris tibi dicere, vt postea quoque,
5 cum pro eadem sententia depugnasti fortiter, tandem velut victor insultes, et quaeras: "quorsum igitur attinet diuinarum veritatem scripturarum flosculis adornare sermonum, quod et
Apostoli, caeterique doctores vt rem absurdissimam prorsum
euitabant, maxime quod exiguitati parum eruditorum penitus
10 aduersari videbantur?" Denique ad hunc modum mirifice rhe-
toricatus epilogum totum facete scilicet sumpto ex euangelijs
epiphonemate concludis, "Vetus melius est." (Quibus in verbis
istud perpulchrum est, quod Apostolos et sanctos illos nascentis
ecclesiae patres ita copulas, tanquam eodem stilo sint vsi.) Au-
15 gustinus Apostolis etiam eloquentiam tribuere non dubitat, ita
illis propriam, vt nec alios illa decere possit, nec illos alia, sed
quae rhetorum tamen figuris omnibus abundet etiam. Certe
sancti illi patres, Hieronymum dico, Cyprianum, Ambrosium,
caeteros eius aetatis disertissimos oratores aequabant.

20   Eloquentia adeo non officit orationis [I₂v] luci vt etiam non sit
eloquens quisquis est obscurus, quum sit hoc in primis oratorum
praeceptis, vt sermo sit dilucidus. Si apostoli sermonis elegantiam ideo declinabant maxime, quod (vt tu ais) exiguitati parum
eruditorum maxime aduersari videbatur, cur adhuc adeo sunt
25 obscuri, vt neque parum eruditi, neque multum sine multo labore intelligant, sed ne sic quidem vbilibet? Vetustissimi patres
ijdemque sanctissimi sicuti scripserunt eloquenter, ita scripserunt etiam luculenter, et tamen hodie plerisque Theologiae
professoribus illucescere non possunt: quid ita? Nempe quod

---

1 venustate] *1520*ᵃ, vetustate *1520*ᵐ   2 tantae] *1520*ᵐ, tanti *1520*ᵃ   4 At] *No para.*
1520   6 insultes, et quaeras] *conj. 1760,* insultas, et quaeris *1520*   8 caeterique]
*1520*ᵐ, caeterique sancti *1520*ᵃ; vt] *1520*ᵃ, (vt *1520*ᵐ; absurdissimam] *1520*ᵃ,
absurdissimam: *1520*ᵐ   9 euitabant, maxime] *1520*ᵃ, euitabant maxime, *1520*ᵐ
10 videbantur?] videbantur. *1520*   11 euangelijs] *1520*ᵃ, euangelijs, *1520*ᵐ   12–
14 (Quibus . . . vsi.)] Quibus . . . vsi. *1520*   14 patres] *1520*ᵃ, patres, *1520*ᵐ   15
Apostolis etiam] *1520*ᵐ, etiam apostolis *1520*ᵃ   17 tamen] *1520*ᵃ, tum *1520*ᵐ   18
Ambrosium] *1520*ᵐ, Ambrosium, et *1520*ᵃ   20 Eloquentia] *No para. 1520*ᵐ   22
dilucidus.] *1520*ᵃ, dilucidus *1520*ᵐ; Si] *Para. 1520*ᵐ   23 (vt tu ais)] vt tu ais *1520*
26 vbilibet?] vbilibet. *1520*   29 possunt:] possunt, *1520*

the most ancient holy fathers had not been illustrious for their graceful style, whereas those who discuss sacred scripture today virtually desecrate the venerable majesty of that noble office with their impure speech.

But you think you have spoken so well on this topic that even later on, having bravely concluded the fight for that viewpoint, you crow like a victor, demanding, "So what is the point of adorning the verity of sacred scripture with flowerlets of speech, which both the apostles and the other doctors completely avoided as wholly absurd, especially since such ornaments seemed to be altogether at odds with the humble capacities of the modestly learned?" Finally, after staging this marvelous display of your rhetoric, you tie up your whole epilogue, ever so wittily, by borrowing a tag from the gospels: "Older is better." (One touch in these words is especially splendid: you link the apostles and those fathers of the early Church as if both groups employed the same style.) Augustine ventured to attribute eloquence also to the apostles—an eloquence so proper to them that it cannot suit anyone else, nor can anyone else's suit them, though their own eloquence also teems with all sorts of rhetorical figures. Certainly those holy fathers—Jerome, I mean, Cyprian, and Ambrose—were a match for the most fluent speakers of their times.

Nor is eloquence an obstacle to lucidity of style. To the contrary, no obscure speaker is eloquent: one of the cardinal precepts of rhetoric is that we should express ourselves clearly. If the apostles avoided refined speech especially because, as you put it, it seemed to be especially at odds with the humble capacities of the modestly learned, why are they still so obscure that neither the modestly learned nor the very learned understand them without making a great effort, and occasionally not even then? The most ancient and holiest fathers wrote both eloquently and clearly, and yet they are not clear to many theology

nulla lux tam potest esse lucida, vt luceat etiam caecis. Sunt enim
isti non, vt dicis, parum eruditi, sed prorsus ineruditi. Nam quod
sanctos patres non intelligunt, suam caecitatem in causa esse,
non illorum tenebras, vel hinc euidenter liquet, quod quae nunc
5 isti magistri nostri non intelligunt, olim intelligebant virgunculae.

Scribebant illi, quod dixi, disertissime, sed ijdem apertissime si
quis linguam latinam calleat. Etenim rati sunt fore vt quisquis eos
cuperet intelligere, is aut latine disceret aut curaret vertendos in
10 linguam vernaculam, neque enim diuinare poterant talia vnquam portenta conscensura cathedras, quae in suae segniciei
patrocinium cuncta velut obscura condemnarent, quaecunque
scripta non essent lingua latinogotthica. Quamobrem quum
Euangelica illa centona, nam hoc tuum est verbum, concludas,
15 "vetus melius esse," confiteor meliorem esse priscorum patrum
eloquentiam, quam neotericorum balbutiem: ita vides hanc centonam tuam, qua te mire video placuisse tibi, pro Erasmo facere
maxime, et in tuum caput esse retortam.

Eiusdem farinae est quo tibi videre facetulus quum [I₃] la-
20 bores eius in Hieronymum perstringis inquiens, "perdidisti
nobis vinum infusa aqua." Quum tot mendis eius libros purgat,
tot locis veram lectionem restituit, perdidit tibi vinum infusa
aqua? Cur igitur dilutum bibis, quando vetus illud acetum tuum,
quod febrienti palato merum sapit, adhuc sit integrum? Verum
25 de discernendis eius autoris operibus, quando res nonnihil a
phrasi dependet, ignosco tibi certe, si digito quoque monstratas
eius censurae causas tamen videre non potes.

---

2 non,] non *1520*   4 liquet,] *1520*ᵃ, liquet *1520*ᵐ   7 Scribebant] *No para. 1520;* illi,
quod dixi,] illi quod dixi *1520*ᵐ, illi, quod dixi *1520*ᵃ; ijdem] *1520*ᵐ, quidem etiam *1520*ᵃ
10–11 vnquam] *1520*ᵃ, nunquam *1520*ᵐ   11 segniciei] *1520*ᵐ, segnitiae *1520*ᵃ
13 Quamobrem] *Para. 1520*ᵐ   14 centona,] centona *1520;* verbum, concludas,] verbum concludas *1520*   16 balbutiem:] balbutiem *1520*ᵐ, balbutiem, *1520*ᵃ   17
tuam,] *1520*ᵃ, tuam *1520*ᵐ; tibi,] *1520*ᵃ, tibi: *1520*ᵐ   19 Eiusdem] *No para. 1520;* quo]
*1520*ᵐ, quod *1520*ᵃ; facetulus] facetulus, *1520*   23 bibis,] *1520*ᵃ, bibis? *1520*ᵐ   24
sapit,] *1520*ᵃ, sapit *1520*ᵐ; Verum] *Para. 1520*ᵃ

professors today. Why is this so? Because no light, of course, can shine brightly enough to illuminate even the blind. For those fellows are not (as you put it) modestly learned, but rather, not learned at all. For one fact makes it quite clear that what keeps them from understanding the holy fathers is blindness on their part and not any darkness in what they are reading: young girls once understood what today's proud professors cannot.

I have already said that the style of the fathers is very refined; it is perfectly open, as well, to whoever knows Latin. For they reasonably thought that whoever wanted to understand them would either learn Latin or have their works translated into the vernacular, nor indeed could they guess that such monsters would ever ascend to the chairs of theology, men who to cover up for their own sloth would condemn as obscure every text not in Latino-Gothic. Now then, since you tie up your "stitchwork" from the gospel (for that is your word for it) with "older is better," I admit that the eloquence of the earliest fathers is better than the stammering of the moderns; so you see that this "stitch-work" of yours, which I see you were marvelously proud of, emphatically strengthens Erasmus' position and recoils on you.

Of the same stripe is what you regard as a cute little joke aimed at his work on Jerome: "You have spoiled the wine for us by watering it down." When he purifies Jerome's works of so many corruptions, when he restores the true reading in so many passages, is this spoiling the wine for you by watering it down? Then why drink it diluted, since you can still get your old vinegar which, to a sick palate, tastes like pure wine? But as for determining what is genuine in that author's works, since the matter depends largely on considerations of style, I will certainly not hold it against you if you fail to see the reasons for Erasmus' verdict even when he points them out with his finger.

Iam vero, quum tibi visum esset ostendere graecam linguam
non tam necessariam esse ad veram scripturarum intelligentiam,
quam quidam censent, et superuacaneos esse labores Erasmi
nouum testamentum rursus vertentis e graeco, tanquam firmam
5 subijcis basim, quod "sancti illi patres" (nam tua verba recen-
sebo) "Hillarius et Augustinus satis nobis fuisse asserebant interpretationem septuaginta interpretum ad omnem sacrae
scripturae veritatem. Habemus nempe," inquis, "si id sat non
esset, Hieronymianam quoque aeditionem, omnium linguis
10 merito praedicandam, habemus et alias tum praeclaras, tum
etiam iuxta eruditas, et tamen nescio quo pacto haec omnia nihil
conferre videntur, nisi istiusmodi noui interpretis addatur
translatio."
        Iam vide, ab initio, cum te viderem hanc suscepisse prouin-
15 ciam, neque nescius essem, vix potuisse fieri, vt quae ad causam
facerent vnquam didicisses, nihil dubitabam, etiam si quaedam
effutire posses in genere, tamen si quando speciatim ad ea de-
scensurus esses, ex quibus vel constabilire tua deberes vel aliena
reuellere, tum demum proditurum te quam tenuiter venires
20 instructus ad negotium. Obsecro te per tu[I_3v]am fidem, tu qui
tot habes aeditiones tot translationes in nouum testamentum,
tum praeclaras tum eruditas, vt nunc non sit opus Erasmica: cur
inestimabilem thesaurum vni seruas tibi? Ego certe quanquam
non sum nescius olim fuisse multas, eamque rem fateatur Au-
25 gustinus multum fuisse vtilem, tamen hodie non reperio quenquam qui praeter hanc vulgatam sese fateatur vnquam vidisse
aliam. Adnotauit Valla vtiliter quaedam, non transtulit: eas annotationes Erasmus edidit: alius fortasse non fecisset qui quidem
statuisset idem tractare argumentum. Faber stapulensis paulinas
30 vertit epistolas, non totum testamentum. tibi igitur ostendendae
sunt praeter translationem septuaginta interpretum, ac praeter

---

1 Iam] *No para.* *1520*ᵐ; vero,] vero *1520*   8 veritatem.] veritatem, *1520; nempe,]*
nempe *1520*   9 quoque aeditionem] *1520*ᵐ, aeditionem quoque *1520*ᵃ   14 vide,
ab initio,] vide ab initio *1520*ᵐ, vide ab initio, *1520*ᵃ   15 essem,] essem *1520*   16
didicisses,] *1520*ᵃ, didicisses: *1520*ᵐ; dubitabam, etiam] *1520*ᵃ, dubitabam etiam,
*1520*ᵐ   18 deberes] deberes, *1520*   19 tum] *1520*ᵐ, tam *1520*ᵃ   22 tum . . .
tum] *1520*, tam . . . tam *conj. 1760*   27 quaedam,] *1520*ᵃ, quaedam *1520*ᵐ   27–28
annotationes] *1520*ᵃ, annotationes, *1520*ᵐ   28 edidit:] edidit, *1520*ᵐ, aedidit.
*1520*ᵃ   30 epistolas,] *1520*ᵃ, epistolas *1520*ᵐ; testamentum.] *1520*ᵃ, testamentum,
*1520*ᵐ

But then, since you wanted to show that Greek learning is not as necessary for the true understanding of scripture as some think it is and that there was no need for the work that Erasmus devoted to retranslating the New Testament from Greek, you propose as a solid foundation the thesis that "those holy fathers," in your words, "Hilary and Augustine, asserted that the Septuagint version was sufficient according to every criterion of scriptural truth; and indeed, if that were not sufficient," you say, "we also have the edition of Jerome, which all tongues rightly ought to acclaim, and we have many others which are both famous and likewise learned, and yet for some reason all these are supposed to be useless unless we add such a rendering as this one by an upstart translator."

See here, from the moment I saw you take up this particular task, since I knew you could never have learned what you needed to know to support your own case, I had no doubt that, even if you could blurt out a few general arguments, just as soon as you got down to the specific ones that you ought to use to defend your own claims and refute the opposing ones, you would show how inadequately prepared you were for the business at hand. In the name of your faith I beseech you: since you have so many both famous and learned editions and so many translations of the New Testament that there is no need for the one by Erasmus, why are you keeping this priceless treasure all to yourself? I for one am not unaware that there were many of them long ago, and that Augustine professes that they were most useful, and yet I do not find anyone today who professes to have ever seen any apart from the Vulgate. Valla made useful notes on some passages, but he did not translate. Erasmus published those notes; someone else who himself had decided to discuss the same subject might well not have done so. Lefèvre d'Etaples has translated the Pauline epistles and not the whole Testament. Thus you have yet to exhibit those other translations besides the

Hieronymianam quoque, aliae illae quae tam praeclarae sunt
atque eruditae, vt prolatis his abijcere oporteat Erasmicam.
    Iam Hieronymus, cuius translationem habere te dicis, si cre-
das ipsi, non transtulit, sed quam tunc praecipue receptam vidit,
5 eam ad graecorum codicum fidem emendauit, id quod illa satis
declarat epistola, "nouum opus me facere cogis ex vetere," si
quis eam epistolam satis intelligat. Hieronymi labores per-
diderunt eaedem pestes, quae nunc inuadunt Erasmicos, inscitia
atque inuidia eorum quibus ille prodesse studuerat. Certum est
10 in hac aeditione quae nunc in templis canitur nullum extare
propemodum Hieronymiani laboris vestigium, Imo illas ipsas
adhuc extare mendas, quas ille censuerat emendandas, ex
quibus aliquot Erasmus obiter annotauit: Quam rem demiror
non aduertisse te, nam alioqui potu[I₄]isses hac de re aliquanto
15 iudicare sanius. Ne clamites totam ecclesiam tot aetates hanc
probasse translationem. legit enim vt vel optimam quam habuit,
vel (quod ego verius opinor) primam, quamque semel receptam
atque imbibitam non erat certe facile vel oblata meliore com-
mutare, approbauit vero nunquam (neque enim idem est legere,
20 quod approbare), Quum contra constet nunquam fere fuisse
quemquam sacrarum litterarum studiosum, qui quidem aliquam sibi compararit vtriusque linguae facultatem, quin is in illo
interprete multa desiderarit. At is, quod non praestitit quae non
potuit, dignus est venia, quod vero quae potuit praestitit, dignus
25 est etiam gratia, quam et hij merentur, qui vel quod illi defuerat
adferunt, vel quod ab alijs deprauatum est sartiunt. Sed interim
vides aeditionem Hieronymianam, quam habere te dicis, "omnium linguis merito praedicandam," nulla iam lingua legi.

1 quoque,] *1520ª*, quoque *1520ᵐ*   3 Iam] *No para. 1520;* Hieronymus,] *1520ª*,
Hieronymus *1520ᵐ*   4 ipsi,] ipsi *1520ᵐ*, ipse *1520ª*   6 epistola,] epistola *1520*
8 Erasmicos,] *1520ª*, Erasmicos *1520ᵐ*   11 vestigium,] vestigium. *1520*   12
emendandas,] *1520ª*, emendandas *1520ᵐ*   13 annotauit:] *1520ª*, annotauit, *1520ᵐ*
15 ecclesiam] *1520ª*, ecclesiam, *1520ᵐ*   16 translationem.] *1520ª*, translationem,
1520ᵐ   17 quamque] *1520ᵐ*, quanque *1520ª*   18 imbibitam] imbibitam, *1520*
18–19 commutare] *1520ᵐ*, communicare *1520ª*   19–20 (neque . . . approbare),] neque . . . approbare. *1520*   23 is,] is *1520;* praestitit] *1520ª*, praestitit, *1520ᵐ*   24
potuit,] *1520ª*, potuit *1520ᵐ*   26 adferunt] *1520ᵐ*, asserunt *1520ª*   27
Hieronymianam,] *1520ª*, Hieronymianam *1520ᵐ*; dicis,] dicis *1520*

Septuagint and that of Jerome which are so famous and learned that we should accept them and throw away that of Erasmus.

Now Jerome, whose translation you say that you have, never made one, if you take his word for it; rather, he took what he saw was at that time the most current version and emended it according to trustworthy Greek texts. This is adequately established by his letter, "You compel me to make a new work out of an old one," for whoever can understand that letter adequately. Jerome's work was spoiled by the same agents of blight that now threaten that of Erasmus, the ignorance and the envy of those he endeavored to benefit. Certainly in the edition which is now chanted in churches there is hardly a trace of Jerome's work; indeed, you can still see the very corruptions that he thought should be emended, some of which Erasmus has mentioned in passing in his notes. I am very surprised you never noticed this fact; if you had, then your judgment concerning these facts might have been somewhat sounder. Do not cry out about how the whole Church has sanctioned this translation for so many centuries. It read this one only because this was either the best one it had or (which I think more likely) the first—once this version was generally adopted it would certainly not have been easy to replace it even if someone submitted a better one—but the Church never sanctioned this version: to read and to sanction are not the same thing. On the other hand, it is quite certain that virtually every student of sacred scripture who has achieved any competence in both Latin and Greek has found many inadequacies in that translator. And yet he deserves pardon for failing to do what he could not do, even as he deserves thanks for doing all that he could, the same thanks that we owe to whoever adds something that this translator lacks or restores something that someone else garbled. But meanwhile you see that the edition prepared by Jerome which you say that you have, the edition "which all tongues rightly ought to acclaim," is a version which no tongue reads today.

At interpretatio septuaginta interpretum ea saltem sufficit, sic
enim scribis, ad omnem scripturae veritatem: quod ne quis audeat oppugnare, propugnatrices obijcis sanctorum patrum Hilarij atque Augustini sententias. Quid hic faciam, quo me ver-
5 tam? negare non audeo, quod sanctissimi patres adfirmant. At si
concessero, quicquid nunc vertit ERASMVS, id iam olim ab interpretibus illis septuaginta sufficienter esse versum, necesse est
fatear simul, multo minore cum fructu idem [I₄v] hunc vertisse
denuo. Quid si sic interea tempus differam, vt negem sanctos
10 illos patres istud asserere, quod tu ab his adsertum asseris? et
certe sic faciam quoad tu ostenderis. Vide igitur, vt locum proferas in quo dicunt illi, septuaginta interpretes testamentum
nouum sufficienter in linguam vertisse latinam. Interea vero
dum tu illum locum quaeris, mihi licebit quod ad hanc rem
15 attinet per te quietum esse. At eum haudquaquam inuentu facilem credo, cum eos omnes audiam non nisi graece vertisse.
Quod si verum est, quomodo potest eorum versio Latinis esse
sufficiens? Quin et illud tibi simul quaerendum est, quo pacto
potuerint septuaginta interpretes sufficienter vertere testamen-
20 tum nouum, cum eos omnes mortuos esse constet annis plus
minus ducentis ante Christum natum. Non dubito, quin cum
haec ita habere comperies, pariter etiam comperias, eos quibus
hactenus his de rebus credidisti, nihil ipsos hactenus comperisse
veri.
25 Venio nunc ad ea, quae tu minutula vocas ac nihili, quae velut
eximie nugacia speciminis loco descripsisti, quibus facias omnibus perspicuum meris ineptijs illum macerare sese, et "totos
quaternos" (vt tuis verbis vtar) implere. Primum reprehendis
quod displiceat ei "sagenae" vocabulum Matthaei xiij. ac "ver-
30 riculum" legi velit, cum tamen (vt ais) "eandem rem significent
'sagena,' et 'verriculum.'" Non dubito, quin videare tibi dixisse

---

1 At] *No para. 1520*ᵃ   3 oppugnare,] *1520*ᵃ, oppugnare: *1520*ᵐ   4–5 vertam?]
*1520*ᵃ, vertam *1520*ᵐ   6 concessero,] concessero *1520;* ERASMVS] *1520*ᵃ,
ERASNVS *1520*ᵐ   7 versum,] *1520*ᵃ, versum: *1520*ᵐ; necesse] *1520*ᵐ, nacesse
*1520*ᵃ   10 asseris?] asseris, *1520*   12 illi,] illi *1520*   22 comperies . . . comperias]
comperies . . . comperies *1520*ᵐ, comperias . . . comperies *1520*ᵃ   25 Venio] *No
para. 1520;* vocas] *1520*ᵃ, vocas, *1520*ᵐ; nihili,] *1520*ᵃ, nihili: *1520*ᵐ   26 descripsisti,]
descripsisti: *1520*ᵐ, descripsisti *1520*ᵃ   29 Matthaei] .M. *1520*

But you write that the Septuagint version, at least, is sufficient according to every criterion of scriptural truth, and lest anyone should dare to oppose that assertion you bring in as its champions the opinions of the holy fathers Hilary and Augustine. What shall I do? Where shall I turn? I dare not deny what the holiest fathers affirm, but as soon as I grant that whatever Erasmus has recently translated was translated well enough long ago by the Septuagint translators, I must also confess that it was far less useful for Erasmus to translate it again. What if I stall for the time being by denying that those fathers make the assertion you assert that they made? And I will certainly do so until you show me where they have made it. Look to it, then: bring me a passage where they say that the Septuagint translators produced a satisfactory Latin version of the New Testament. But for the time being, while you look around for that passage, I can assume that on this point, at least, you will leave me in peace. And that passage, I think, will not be at all easy to find, since I hear that the Septuagint translators made only one version—in Greek. Now if that is the case, how can their version be sufficient for Latin speakers? And indeed you must also look around for an explanation of how the Septuagint translators could produce a sufficient version of the New Testament when we know that they all died approximately two hundred years before the birth of Christ. When you discover that these are the facts, I am sure you will also discover that the people whose word you have taken up to now concerning these issues have not, up to now, discovered one bit of the truth.

Now I come to what you call his petty and futile remarks, those you thought were uncommonly trifling and therefore transcribed as examples to make it clear to everyone that Erasmus is wasting his energies and filling "whole sheaves," in your words, with sheer nonsense. First you criticize his objection to the reading "sagena" ["fishnet"] in Matthew 13, where he would prefer to read "verriculum," even though, as you put it, " 'sagena' and 'verriculum' signify the same thing." I am sure you think you

praeclare, sed primum doce displicuisse ei "sagenae" vocabulum, quod ille vocabulum non reprehendit, quanquam
praefert alterum: tantum dicit interpretem reliquisse vocem
graecam. "At idem significat" inquis [K₁] " 'verriculum' et 'sagena' ": quis hoc aut negat, aut nescit? Sed tamen vt eius annotatio
te docere potuit, "sagena" vox est graeca, cum "verriculum"
latina sit, quemadmodum "decretum" ac "psephisma." Et tibi
continuo nugari videtur quisquis e graeca transferens in latinam, latinis vocabulis malit vti quam graecis? At fortasse asseres
"sagenae" vocabulum apud latinos etiam autores haberi. Quid
tum postea? Si Latinus quispiam vocabulum graecum medijs
latinis interserat, neque desinit tamen esse graecum, neque protinus efficitur latinum. Neque enim cuiquam in manu est omnia
vocabula Romana ciuitate donare, nihilo magis hercule quam
omnes homines. Neque enim "psephisma" latinum verbum est,
quanquam Cicero quoque semel atque iterum vsus est, neque
"energia" graecum esse desinit, etiamsi Hieronymus latine
scribens vsus est interdum vel apud eos, quos graece doctos intelligebat, vel non reperiens fortasse latinam vocem, quae commode satis explicaret, vt ita dicam, τὴν τῆς ἐνεργείας ἐνέργειαν.
At tu parum feliciter imitatus Hieronymum, eo verbo passim
aliter quam significat abuteris. Vides ergo, dum immissa "sagena" conaris expiscari quod reprehendas attracto "verriculo," nihil neque verris, neque prendis.

   Rursum carpis quod parum latine dici putat, "Nuptiae impletae sunt discumbentium," sed asserat dici oportere "discumbentibus," Et tu, si superis placet, Erasmum docebis gramm-
maticam. Tum Calepinum ingeris, quasi in sermone latino non
sit amplius vni ERASMO fidendum, quam Calepinis decem.
Tum id egregie ridiculum, quod Calepino citato nihil aliud adfers tamen quam [K₁v] quod ab ipso mutueris Erasmo. Vnum

1–2 vocabulum, quod] *1520*ᵃ, vocabulum: quod *1520*ᵐ   2 reprehendit,] *1520*ᵃ, reprehendit: *1520*ᵐ   4 inquis] *1520*ᵃ, inquis: *1520*ᵐ   4–5 sagena' ":] sagena, *1520*   8
graeca] *1520*ᵐ, graeca lingua *1520*ᵃ; transferens] *1520*ᵃ, transferans *1520*ᵐ   14 magis
hercule] *1520*ᵐ, hercle magis *1520*ᵃ   18 scribens] *1520*ᵃ, scribens, *1520*ᵐ   22
ergo,] ergo *1520*   25 Rursum] *No para.* *1520*   26–27 discumbentibus," Et tu,] discumbentibus. Et tu *1520*   30–31 adfers tamen] *1520*ᵃ, adfers, tamen, *1520*ᵐ   31
mutueris] *1520*ᵐ, mutuaris *1520*ᵃ

have said something very impressive, but first prove that Erasmus objected to the term "sagena." He does not criticize this term, though he prefers the other one; he merely says that the translator left the Greek expression. "But 'verriculum' and 'sagena' mean the same thing," you say. Who denies it? Who needs to be told? But as you could have learned from Erasmus' note, "sagena" is a Greek expression while "verriculum" is Latin; they are as distinct as "decretum" and "psephisma" ["decree"]. Even you cannot automatically think that whoever prefers to use Latin terms rather than Greek in a Latin translation from Greek is just trifling. But perhaps you will assert that the term "sagena" is also found in Latin authors. What of it? A Greek term does not stop being Greek and immediately start being Latin as soon as some speaker of Latin employs it among Latin terms. No one has the power to confer Roman citizenship on all terms, by Jove, any more than on all human beings. Nor is "psephisma" a Latin word, even though Cicero himself employed it once or twice, nor does "energia" ["force" or "import"] stop being Greek even if Jerome did employ it occasionally in Latin, whether because he was writing to people he knew to have been trained in Greek or perhaps because he could find no Latin expression that conveyed well enough (if I may say so) τὴν τῆς ἐνεργείας ἐνέργειαν ["the import of 'import'"]. But in clumsy imitation of Jerome you repeatedly employ that word with an incorrect meaning. So you see that when you try to fish up something to criticize as you haul in "sagena" and seize on "verriculum," this sweep of the net nets you nothing at all.

You go on to find fault with his opinion that "Nuptiae impletae sunt discumbentium" ["The wedding feast was full of guests"] is not very good Latin, where he asserts we should read "discumbentibus" ["filled with guests"], and then (by all that is holy!) you set out to lecture Erasmus on grammar. Then you drag in Calepino, as if Erasmus were not ten times as trustworthy as Calepino on matters of good Latin speech. And then it is especially funny that after citing Calepino you produce nothing but what you have borrowed from Erasmus himself. You left out

tantum reliquisti, quo vno didicisse debueras, omnia nihil esse
quae dixeras. Nam cum breuiter ostendisset "Impleor" et gene-
tiuo copulari et ablatiuo, eademque protulisset exempla, quae
tu, sic rem concludit, vt dicat, quanquam latine dici possit, "im-
5 plentur vini," tamen hanc orationem non esse latinum: "domus
impletur hominum." I nunc et quaeras exempla, quibus istud
conuincas.

Iam quod Matthaei vi. in oratione dominica potius vertendum
censuit, "remitte nobis debita nostra," quam "dimitte," tu censes
10 illum tam manifeste nugari, vt vel nemo negare queat, atque id
videris tibi ex ipsius verbis colligere. Nam "si ἄφες," inquis,
"πολύσημον est, vt Erasmus annotauit ipse, quis negare potest
eum manifestissime nugari, qui 'remitte' potius verti velit, quam
'dimitte,' cum vox illa graeca vtrisque deseruiat, quum 'dimitto'
15 etiam, quod secundum priscos autores significat 'do,' vel 'dono,'
satis bene quadret eidem sensui?" Hic tu proferas oportet priscos illos autores, apud quos reperisti "dimittere" idem esse quod
"dare." Nam ni hos proferas, quos opinor non proferes, tute
manifeste nugaris. Ego certe non puto latine dici, "dimitte mihi
20 vestem," pro eo quod est "da mihi vestem." Praeterea si "dimittere" idem significaret quod "dare," non concedam tamen hanc
orationem latinam esse, "dimitte nobis debita nostra," sicuti nec
hanc ipsam, cuius exemplo tueris eam, "da nobis debita nostra":
si tuis auribus idem sonat, "dare debita," et "remittere debita,"
25 non possum [K₂] tuo morbo mederi. "At quid refert?" inquis,
"nam sensus ex illius 'dimitte,' non minus liquet, quam ex huius
'remitte.'" quis negat diuinari posse quid ille sentiat? nec sequitur tamen orationem eius satis latinam esse, nec si quis admoneat quid erret ille, nugatur: sed qui vera monentem re-
30 darguit, ille nugatur. Et si nugatur Erasmus, certe hoc honestius
nugatur, quod socium habet Cyprianum, tam sacrum ecclesiae

---

3 copulari] copulari, *1520*   4 tu,] *1520*ᵃ, tu: *1520*ᵐ; quanquam] *1520*ᵃ, quanquam
*1520*ᵐ; latine] *1520*ᵐ, latiue *1520*ᵃ   6 I nunc] *1520*ᵐ, nunc *1520*ᵃ   8 Iam] *No para.*
1520; Matthaei] Matthaei. *1520*ᵐ, Matth. *1520*ᵃ   9 dimitte,] *1520*ᵃ, dimitte: *1520*ᵐ
10 vel] *1520*ᵐ, id *1520*ᵃ; negare] negari *1520*   13 potius] *1520*ᵃ, potins *1520*ᵐ
16 sensui?] sensui. *1520*ᵐ, sensui *1520*ᵃ; oportet] *1520*ᵃ, oportet, *1520*ᵐ   21
significaret] *1520*ᵐ, significat *1520*ᵃ   23 nostra":] nostra, *1520*   25 refert?] refert
1520   27 remitte.] *1520*ᵃ, remitte, *1520*ᵐ; sentiat?] sentiat, *1520*   28 esse,] esse.
1520   31 Cyprianum,] *1520*ᵃ, Cyprianum *1520*ᵐ; sacrum] *1520*ᵐ, sacrae *1520*ᵃ

just one point, though that one should have taught you that all you had said comes to nothing at all. For after he briefly indicated that "impleor" is used with both the genitive and the ablative and provided the same examples that you do, he sums up the matter by saying that though it is possible to say in good Latin "implentur vini" ["They are full of wine"], this phrase is not good Latin: "domus impletur hominum" ["The house is full of people"]. Now go out and look for examples which contradict that.

Now when he judged that the translation of the Lord's prayer in Matthew 6 should read "remitte nobis debita nostra" ["forgive us our debts"] instead of "dimitte" ["pardon"], you judge this to be such an obvious instance of trifling that none can deny it, and you think you infer this from Erasmus' own words. For "if ἄφες ["pardon"] has multiple meanings, as Erasmus himself noted," you say, "how can he prefer the translation 'remitte' to 'dimitte' when that Greek expression serves for both, while indeed 'dimitto,' which according to ancient authors means 'do' or 'dono' ["I give" or "I present"], conveys well enough the same meaning?" Here you ought to produce those ancient authors according to whom you found that "dimittere" is the same thing as "dare." For unless you produce them, and I think you will not, you yourself are obviously trifling. I for one do not think it is good Latin to say "dimitte mihi vestem" ["pardon me a coat"] for "da mihi vestem" ["give me a coat"]. Further, even if "dimittere" did mean the same thing as "dare," I still do not concede that the phrase "dimitte nobis debita nostra" is good Latin, any more than this other one on the basis of which you defend it: "da nobis debita nostra" ["give us our debts"]. If to your ears "dare debita" sounds the same as "remittere debita," your disease is one I cannot cure. "But," you say, "what difference does it make? For the sense is as clear with that translator's 'dimitte' as with this one's 'remitte.'" Who denies we can guess what sense he has in mind? Even so, it does not follow that his phrasing is sufficiently good Latin, nor is it trifling for someone to indicate what he got wrong; but it *is* trifling to contradict someone who is indicating the truth. And if Erasmus is trifling, he is certainly trifling in a more decent way since he does so in the company of Cyprian,

doctorem, qui maluit dicere "remitte nobis debita" quam
"dimitte."

"Ingens" inquis "ac periculosa temeritas hominis, quod contra
omnium antiquorum patrum iudicium in primo capite Ioannis
5 tam solenne mutarit vocabulum, 'sermo' pro 'verbum' apponens." Iam id pro confesso sumis, quod est falsissimum, veterum neminem ausum pro "verbo" "sermonem" dicere. At tu
interim fateris, Hieronymum testari, quod λόγος alia significet
praeter "verbum" quae satis apte competant in filium dei: id
10 quod adeo confirmat diuus Gregorius Nazanzenus, vt filium dei
λόγον appellatum sentiat, non solum quod sermo sit aut verbum,
sed quod ratio quoque sit et sapientia, praeter alia significata τοῦ
λόγου, tanquam Euangelista, diuino prorsus consilio, id deli-
gente vocabulum, quod multa complecteretur, quorum quoduis
15 idoneum sit ad significandum omnipotentis dei filium: adeo vt
mihi certe, si vlli vocabulo id reuerentiae debebatur, vt integrum
atque immutabile seruaretur, quod in κύριε ἐλέησον, "Alleluia,"
"Amen," et "Osanna" seruatum est, id me[K₂v]ritissimo iure
videatur huic dictioni "logos" oportuisse tribui, quae quum sanc-
20 tarum significationum mire foecunda sit, e quibus quam cui
praeferas, haud procliue sit statuere, fuisset non incautum,
eadem seruata voce nullum fecisse praeiudicium, imo vnico verbo, eoque disyllabo, multa pariter Christi vocabula complecti.

1 doctorem,] 1520ᵃ, doctorem: 1520ᵐ; debita] 1520ᵃ, debita: 1520ᵐ   3 hominis,]
1520ᵃ, hominis: 1520ᵐ   5 vocabulum,] 1520ᵃ, vocabulum 1520ᵐ   6 sumis,] 1520ᵃ,
sumis: 1520ᵐ; falsissimum,] 1520ᵃ, falsissimum: 1520ᵐ   8 testari,] testari: 1520ᵐ,
testari 1520ᵃ   9 verbum] verbum: 1520ᵐ, uerbum, 1520ᵃ   10 Nazanzenus,]
Nazanzenus: 1520ᵐ, Nazienzenus, 1520ᵃ   11 sentiat,] 1520ᵃ, sentiat: 1520ᵐ;
verbum,] 1520ᵃ, verbum 1520ᵐ   12 sapientia,] sapientia: 1520ᵐ, sapientia 1520ᵃ
13 λόγου,] λόγου: 1520ᵐ, λόγου 1520ᵃ; Euangelista,] Euangelista 1520   13–14
deligente] 1520ᵐ, delegente 1520ᵃ   14 vocabulum,] 1520ᵃ, vocabulum: 1520ᵐ;
complecteretur,] 1520ᵃ, complecteretur: 1520ᵐ   16 certe,] 1520ᵃ, certe: 1520ᵐ;
debebatur,] 1520ᵃ, debebatur: 1520ᵐ; integrum] 1520ᵃ, integrum, 1520ᵐ   17 ἐλέησον,] 1520ᵃ, ἐλέησον. 1520ᵐ   18 est,] 1520ᵃ, est: 1520ᵐ; iure] 1520ᵃ, iure, 1520ᵐ
19 logos] 1520ᵐ, λόγος 1520ᵃ   20 e] 1520ᵐ, a 1520ᵃ   22 praeiudicium,]
praeiudicium 1520ᵐ, praeiudicium. 1520ᵃ   23 disyllabo,] dyssilabo 1520ᵐ, dissylabo
1520ᵃ

one of the holiest doctors of the Church, who preferred to say "remitte nobis debita" instead of "dimitte."

You say, "It showed enormous and dangerous temerity for this fellow to go against the judgment of all the ancient fathers in changing such a well-established word in the first chapter of John, where he puts 'sermo' ["Speech"] in place of 'verbum' ["the Word"]." Here you assume, as if it could be taken for granted, the utterly false thesis that none of the ancients dared to say "sermo" in place of "verbum." But meanwhile you admit that, according to Jerome, λόγος has other meanings besides "verbum" which are quite appropriate for the Son of God, testimony confirmed by Gregory of Nazianzus, who goes so far as to assert that the Son of God was called λόγος not only because he is Speech and the Word but also because he is Reason and Wisdom, not to mention the other meanings of λόγος, as if the evangelist, according to God's own intention, chose that word because it embraced many meanings each of which can appropriately be applied to the Son of almighty God. I myself would go so far as to say that if any word should be so revered as to be kept in its original form, as we have done with κύριε ἐλέησον, "Alleluia," "Amen," and "Osanna," words which we have retained in their original unaltered form, then this utterance "logos" would seem to have had the best possible claim to such reverence. And since it is wonderfully rich in holy meanings, out of which it is not at all easy to choose which you ought to prefer to the others, it would have been not imprudent to retain that very word, without setting a tendentious precedent, and indeed to include many of

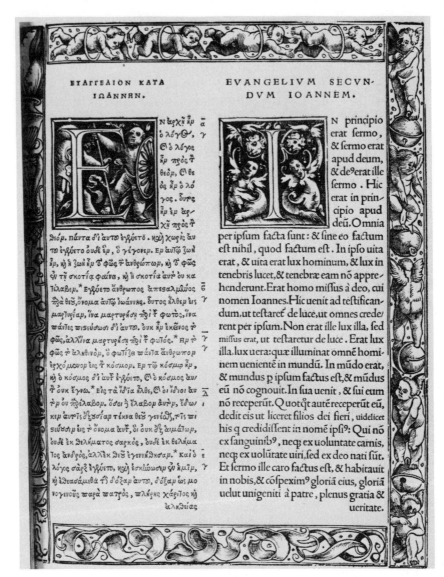

Novum Testamentum, Basel, 1519, sig. q₅ (reduced)

IN EVANGELIVM IOANNIS ANNOTA-
TIONES DES. ERASMI ROTERODAMI.

Orbis cōdi-
ti & redēpti
ſimile initiū.

λόγος mul-
ta declarat
Græcis.

Articulus
græc° quan-
tam uim ha-
beat.
Exēpla e phi-
loſophis.

E literis ſa-
cris.

Auguſtini
exemplū.

Filius homi-
nis.i.Adæ.
Agnus dei.
Lux mundi.
Bon°paſtor.

Oſtium.
Meſſias.
Rex.
Spiritus.

N PRINCIPIO erat uerbum.) Illud in primis anno-
tandum,quod indicauit & Chryſoſtomus, Ioannem neq̀
Matthæi,aut Marci more ſumere exordiū, neq̀ ad exemplum Lucæ,ſed ijſdem uerbis ingreſſus eſt hiſtoriā Euan-
gelicā,quibus Moſes ingreſſus geneſim mundi. Sed quod
illic quidā interpretantur,in principio,id eſt in filio,hic certe locum non habet.   Erat uerbum.) λόγος græcis uaria
ſignificat,uerbū,orationē,ſermonem,rationē,modum, ſup-
putationem,nōnunq̀ & pro libro uſurpatur,à uerbo λέγω
quod eſt dico ſiue colligo. Horum pleraq̀ diuus Hieronymus putat competere in filium dei. Miror autē cur uerbū,
magis placuerit latinis q̀ ſermo,in quo genus cōueniſſet,& ſermo magis exprimit græcā
uoce q̀ uerbū,quod græcis ῥῆμά ſeu λέξις potius diceret. Certe Cyprianus & Hilarius nō
uerētur dei filiū ſermonē patris uocare. Verū id quoniā uſqͥadeo receptū erat,nō ſumus
auſi mutare,protinus ne quem offenderemus infirmū. Cæterū illud propius ad hoc inſti-
tutum pertinet,nō ſimpliciter poſitum λόγος,ſed additū articulum ὁ λόγος.ut non poſſit
de quouis accipi uerbo,ſed de certo quopiā & inſigni. Habet em̄ hāc uim articulus,quem
latine utcūq̀ reddimus adiecto pronomine ille,ueluti cū Ariſtoteles, in genere de quoli-
bet agit bono, ἀγαθόμ uocat. Cæterū cum unicū illud ac ſummū bonū intelligi uult,addit
articulū τ᾽ἀγαθόμ.Item καλόμ appellant philoſophi,quod quouis modo pulchrū ſit. τὸ καὶ
λόμ eximiū illud ac uere pulchrū ſiue honeſtū,quod à uirtute proficiſcitur. Itē πᾶμ appellant,quod quocunq̀ modo totū eſt.uerū abſolutum illud uniuerſum,quod uere comple-
ctitur omnia,nō ſimpliciter πᾶμ,ſed τ᾽ πᾶμ appellant.Itidē in diuinis literis,cū deos uocat
amicos dei,nō apponitur articulus, ſed tantū θεοί ἐϲε,id eſt,dij eſtis.aut cū intelligitur dij
gentiū,quale eſt apud Paulū in epiſtola ad Corinthios prima cap.viij.Et ſi ſunt q dicūt
dij,ſiue in cœlo ſiue in terra, queadmodū ſunt dij multi, & domini multi. Nullus em̄ hic
appoſit° eſt græcus articulus.Auguſtinus in quæſtionib° quas ſcripſit in geneſim libro primo,adducit & alterū exēplū ex geneſeos cap.xxxiij.in quo Iacob ait ſe uidiſſe faciē Elau,
ac ſi quis uideat faciē dei,negás in græcis exēplaribus eſſe ſcriptū,πρόϲωπομ τὸ θεῶ appo-
ſito articulo,ſed πρόϲωπομ θεοῦ,citra articulū.At quoties ſignificat uerus ille & ſolus deus,
ſemper additur articulus ὁ θεός.Et quoties ſe uult intelligi Chriſtū,nō quouis modo dei
filiū,ſed natura ac uere filiū, ὁ ὑὸς τῶ θεοῦ dicit.Rurſus ubi diuinitate diſſimulans,ſe filiū
hom̄inis appellat,ſed utriq̀ nomini ſuo præpoſito articulo, ὁ ὑὸς τῶ ἀνθϟώπου,ceu nō quili-
bet Adæ fili°,ſed eximius ille filius hominis,humani generis reſtitutor. Rurſum ὁ ἀμνὸϲ
cū multi ſint agni,unicus ille agnus intelligitur,cuius immolatione tollunt peccata mūdi.
Et ὁ προφήτηϲ,unicus ille ,ppheta per Moſen promiſſus. Et cū lux illa deſignat unde lux
omnis nobis fluit,τὸ φῶϲ dicit,addito articulo.Et cum paſtor bonus dicitur,unicus ille paſtor Chriſtus,ἐγώ ἐιμι ὁ ποιμὴμ ὁ καλόϲ,congeminato articulo, Et, ἐγώ ἐιμι ἡ θύρα,ego ſum
oſtium,cum nō quoduis oſtium,ſed unicū illud denotatur.Et paulo inferius inuenimus
Meſſiā,τὸμ μεσϲίαμ,unicū illum Meſſiā,Et tu es rex Iſrael,ὁ βασιλεὺϲ. Didymus libro de ſpi-
ritu,quem latinū fecit Hieronymus,diligenter & hoc adnotauit,quoties in diuinis literis
mentio ſit ſpiritus diuini,articulū apponi, τὸ πνεῦμα, idq̀ confirmat compluribus arcanæ
ſcripturæ locis in hoc adductis.Atq̀ hoc potiſſimum argumento docet eundē fuiſſe ſpi-
ritum,qui afflauit prophetas,& quem hauſerūt Apoſtoli. Annotauit idem Athanaſius libro de ſpirituſancto ad Serapionem, & hic ſuam ſententiā compluribus ſcripturarū teſti-
monijs

Nunc vero quoniam aliter visum est vertentibus, mihi certe videtur proximus esse fructus, vt vertant varie, quo nulla sig-
nificatio τοῦ λόγου, quae quidem in Christum competat, aut
ignoretur aut obsolescat.

5   At Hieronymus "verbum" mutare non ausus est: mirum certe
quod non mutauit, quum non esset occasio. Nam queso cur mu-
taret, quum non verteret denuo, sed id quod versum est recen-
seret? At si vertendum sibi de integro sumpsisset Euangelium,
non adeo se putasset veteris interpretis obstrictum praeiudicio,
10   quin sibi liberum arbitraretur aliter vertere, modo verteret bene,
etiamsi prior interpres non vertit male. Neque enim alia de causa
admonuit λόγον alia quoque significare quam "verbum" quae
recte de filio dei dicerentur, quam vt id quod tu negas ostenderet, λόγον aliter quoque quam "verbum" recte verti potuisse.
15   Nam "sermo" et "verbum" vbique fere promiscue vertitur in
scripturis vbicunque λόγον habet codex graecus, quanquam
nemo est qui nesciat, qui quidem vel tantillum sciat graece, "sermonem" multo tritius λόγου significatum esse quam "verbum."
At tu rationem adfers (deus bone qualem) quare filius dei
20   "verbum" rectius dicatur quam "sermo." Nam "'sermo,'" inquis, "proprie loquendo, illud est magis quod voce profertur,
'verbum' vero quod intus mente concipitur, videlicet cogitatio
quae intra animi silentium adhuc conscientiae [K₃] secreto reti-
netur, et si quando foris exierit, sic tamen prodit in publicum, vt
25   intus etiam iugiter teneatur clausum." Rogo te quis hoc discrimen te docuit inter "sermonem" et "verbum"? Nam is, e cuius
verbis ista quae de "verbo" adfers excerpsisti, non negat idem
etiam posse de "sermone" dici, neque quisquam est, qui non
videat eadem ratione interiorem esse mentis sermonem qua ver-
30   bum, et "verbum" proprie significare quod voce profertur, sicut
et "sermonem," quum sentiant, qui verborum scrutantur origines, ab aere verberando "verbum" esse deductum. Quod si

---

1 vertentibus,] *1520*ᵃ, vertentibus: *1520*ᵐ   2 fructus,] *1520*ᵃ, fructus *1520*ᵐ   5 At]
No para. 1520; est:] est, *1520*ᵐ, est. *1520*ᵃ   8 Euangelium,] *1520*ᵃ, Euangelium *1520*ᵐ
13–14 ostenderet,] ostenderet *1520*   16 scripturis] scripturis, *1520*   17 nesciat,] *1520*ᵃ, nesciat *1520*ᵐ; graece,] *1520*ᵃ, graece *1520*ᵐ   18 λόγου] *1520*ᵃ, λόγομυ *1520*ᵐ *(see commentary)*   19 At] *No para. 1520;* (deus bone qualem)] deus bone
qualem *1520*ᵐ, deus bone qualem, *1520*ᵃ   20–21 sermo,'" inquis,] sermo inquis
1520   22 concipitur,] *1520*ᵃ, concipitur *1520*ᵐ   25 Rogo] *Para. 1520*ᵐ   31
sermonem,] *1520*ᵃ, sermonem: *1520*ᵐ; sentiant,] *1520*ᵃ, sentiant *1520*ᵐ   31–32
origines,] *1520*ᵃ, origines *1520*ᵐ

Christ's epithets in one two-syllable word. But since translators have actually thought it best to do otherwise, I for one think that the next-best procedure is for them to translate it variously so that none of the meanings of λόγος appropriate for Christ goes unknown or falls into disuse.

But Jerome did not dare to change "verbum": how very surprising that he did not change it when he had no occasion to do so! For I ask you, why would he have changed it, since he was not making an entirely new translation but correcting one that already existed? But if he had taken it upon himself to translate the gospel all over again, he would not have felt so constrained by the precedent of the ancient translator as to think he could not take the liberty of translating differently, provided that he translated well, even if his predecessor did not translate badly. It was for this very reason that he indicated that λόγος has other meanings besides "verbum" which could rightly be referred to the Son of God: he wanted to demonstrate just what you deny, namely that λόγος could rightly have been translated in other ways than "verbum." For the translations "sermo" and "verbum" are used almost interchangeably in scripture wherever the Greek text has λόγος, although no one who knows any Greek does not know that "sermo" is the meaning of λόγος much more often than "verbum."

But you bring up a reason (good lord, what a reason!) for saying that the Son of God is more rightly called "verbum" than "sermo." For "'sermo,'" you say, "properly speaking, is rather that which is expressed with the voice, whereas 'verbum' is that which is inwardly conceived by the mind, namely the thought which is still confined in the silence of the soul, in the privacy of personal knowledge; and if it is ever released to the world, it still becomes public in such a way as to remain permanently closed up within." I ask you, who taught you this distinction between "sermo" and "verbum"? For the author from whom you have excerpted the remarks you adduce about "verbum" does not deny that the same may be said about "sermo," and no one fails to see that there is internal mental speech by the same reasoning according to which there is an internal word, or that "verbum" properly means that which is expressed with the voice, just as "sermo" does, since those who examine the origins of words hold

tam "sermo" quam "verbum" significet animi conceptum tacitum, rursusque tam "verbum" quam "sermo" conceptus ex-
pressos voce, vides vt egregia illa ratio, qua mire fultus tibi videbare, collabitur.

5   Quanquam ego non multum certe his in rebus rationi tribuo,
quae cognosci nisi deo reuelante non possunt. Certus sum dei
filium recte λόγον dici, seuque "verbum" intelligatur, seuque
"sermo," seuque "ratio," seuque "causa," seuque aliud eorum
quippiam, quae significat λόγος, seuque omnia: certus sum in-
10 quam recte λόγον dici, namque id me docet ille qui supra pectus
domini in coena recubuit, Scioque quod filius dei "sermo" recte
dicitur ac "verbum," nam his nominibus tota illum appellat ecclesia catholica, docti aliquot ac sancti patres etiam "rationem,"
Sed tota ecclesia Romana "verbum" et sine vlla exceptione "ser-
15 monem." Etenim dum Christi natale hoc solemni cantu concelebrat, "Quum medium silentium tenerent omnia, et nox in
suo cursu medium iter perageret, omnipotens sermo tuus domine exsiliens e coelo a regalibus sedibus venit," non est ambiguum, "sermonem" dici filium dei, quum vbi nos legimus
20 [K₃v] in psalmo, "verbo dei coeli firmati sunt": Alij legunt, atque
in his Augustinus, "sermone dei coeli solidati sunt": dubium non
est vtrobique significari filium dei. Nam tibi contradicit Ambrosius, quum dicit, "Non enim dixit Euangelista, 'In principio
factum est verbum,' sed 'in principio' (inquit) 'erat verbum.'
25 Quicunque principium verbi assignare volueris, praeiudicatum

---

1–2 tacitum] *1520ᵐ*, tantum *1520ᵃ*   3 ratio,] ratio *1520*   3–4 videbare,] videbare
1520   5 Quanquam] *No para. 1520*   6 cognosci] *1520ᵐ*, congnosci *1520ᵃ*   7
dici,] *1520ᵃ*, dici: *1520ᵐ*   7–8 seuque "verbum" . . . seuque "sermo," seuque] *1520ᵐ*,
seu verbum . . . seu sermo, seu *1520ᵃ* (*perhaps we should read* seu qua *throughout*)   9
λόγος,] *1520ᵃ*, λόγος *1520ᵐ*; omnia:] omnia, *1520*   10 namque id] nam id quod
1520ᵐ, nam id *1520ᵃ* (*perhaps More actually wrote* nam id quidem)   11 recubuit,] recubuit. *1520;* Scioque] *Para. 1520ᵃ*   15–16 concelebrat,] concelebrat. *1520*   18
exsiliens] exiliens *1520;* e] *1520ᵐ*, de *1520ᵃ*; venit,] *1520ᵃ*, venit: *1520ᵐ*   20 sunt":]
sunt. *1520;* legunt,] *1520ᵃ*, legant *1520ᵐ*   21 sunt":] sunt, *1520*   22 Nam] *1520ᵐ*,
Num *1520ᵃ*   23 dicit,] dicit. *1520*   24 (inquit)] inquit *1520ᵐ*, inquit, *1520ᵃ*   25
volueris] *1520ᵃ*, nolueris *1520ᵐ*

that "verbum" is derived from "aere verberando" ["striking the air"]. But if "sermo" as well as "verbum" can mean an unspoken conception of the mind, whereas "verbum" as well as "sermo" can mean conceptions expressed with the voice, you see how that remarkable reasoning collapses which you thought gave you such fine support.

And yet I myself certainly do not assign much importance to reasoning in these matters, which cannot be known except by divine revelation. I am certain that the Son of God is rightly called λόγος, whether it is understood to mean "verbum" or "sermo" or "ratio" or "causa" or anything else λόγος means, or indeed all it means. Once again, I am certain that he is rightly called λόγος, for I learned this from him who reclined on the breast of the Lord at the Supper, and I know that the Son of God is rightly called "sermo" and "verbum," for the whole Catholic church addresses him by these names. Several learned and holy fathers call him "ratio," as well, but the whole Roman church calls him "verbum" and "sermo," without any exception. For when it celebrates the birth of Christ with this solemn chant, "When all things dwelt in the midst of silence and the night was in the midst of her course, your almighty Speech, O Lord, leapt forth from heaven and came from its royal throne," the Son of God is unambiguously called "Speech"; and where we read in the psalm, "By the Word of God the heavens were made firm," whereas others read, and among them Augustine, "By the Speech of God the heavens were made solid," the Son of God is undoubtedly what is meant by both readings. For Ambrose contradicts you when he says, "For the evangelist did not say, 'In the beginning the Word came to be,' but 'In the beginning,' he said, 'was the Word.' Anyone who would attempt to assign a beginning to the Word will be checked by this precedent, since he said,

habebis, quia 'in principio' (inquit) 'erat,' non quod duo prin-
cipia ex rerum diuersitate dicamus, Sed quod sermo filius semper cum patre est, et de patre natus est." Ad idem facit Hilarius,
quum dicit, "Hoc verbum in principio apud deum erat, quia
5 sermo cogitationis aeternus est, quum qui cogitat sit aeternus."
Ad idem facit Lactantius, cuius haec verba sunt: "Quomodo
igitur procreauit? primum nec sciri a quoquam possunt, nec
enarrari opera diuina, sed tamen sanctae litterae docent, in
quibus cautum est illum dei filium dei esse sermonem." Item
10 alibi, "sed melius graeci λόγον dicunt, quam nos 'verbum' siue
'sermonem.' λόγος enim et 'sermonem' significat et 'rationem.'"
Ad idem Cyprianus, cuius haec verba sunt in eo capite, cui tit-
ulum fecit, "Quod Christus idem sit sermo dei," quod sequen-
tibus verbis probat: "In psalmo xliiij, 'Eructauit cor meum ser-
15 monem bonum, dico ego opera mea regi.' Item in psalmo,
'Sermone dei coeli firmati sunt, et spiritu oris eius omnis virtus
eorum.' Item apud Esaiam, 'Verbum consummans et breuians
in iusticia quoniam sermonem breuiatum faciet deus, in to[K₄]to
orbe terrae.' Item in psalmo, 'Misit sermonem suum, et curauit
20 illos.' Item in Euangelio secundum Ioannem, 'In principio erat
verbum, et verbum erat apud deum, et deus erat verbum, hoc
erat in principio apud deum, omnia per ipsum facta sunt, et sine
ipso factum est nihil quod factum est, in ipso vita erat, et vita erat
lux hominum, et lux lucet in tenebris, et tenebrae illum non
25 comprehenderunt.' Item in Apocalypsi, 'Et vidi coelum aper-
tum, et ecce equus albus, et qui sedebat super eum vocabatur
fidelis et verus, aequum iustumque iudicans et praeliaturus,
eratque coopertus veste conspersa sanguine, et dicitur nomen
eius sermo dei.'" Ad idem facit Augustinus, quum eam sibi

---

1 (inquit)] inquit *1520*ᵐ, inquit, *1520*ᵃ   2 dicamus,] *1520*ᵃ, dicamus. *1520*ᵐ   4
dicit,] *1520*ᵃ, dicit. *1520*ᵐ   6 sunt:] sunt. *1520*   7 procreauit?] *1520*ᵃ, procreauit,
*1520*ᵐ   11 enim et] *1520*ᵃ, enim, *1520*ᵐ   12 idem] *1520*ᵐ, idem facit *1520*ᵃ; sunt]
*1520*ᵃ, sunt, *1520*ᵐ   13 fecit,] *1520*ᵃ, fecit. *1520*ᵐ   14 probat:] probat *1520*ᵐ,
probat. *1520*ᵃ; In] in *1520*ᵐ, In in *1520*ᵃ; psalmo xliiij,] psalmo. xliiij. *1520*ᵐ, psal. xliiij
*1520*ᵃ   15 psalmo,] *1520*ᵃ, psalmo. *1520*ᵐ   20 Ioannem,] Ioannem. *1520*   21
deum,] *1520*ᵃ, deum *1520*ᵐ   23–25 factum est nihil . . . comprehenderunt] *1520*ᵐ,
etc. *1520*ᵃ   25 Apocalypsi,] *1520*ᵃ, Apocalypsi *1520*ᵐ

'In the beginning it was'; not that we should speak of two principles arising from a difference of substance, but because Speech
the Son is always with the Father and was born of the Father."
Hilary makes the same point when he says, "This Word was in
the beginning with God, because the speech of thought is eternal
when the thinker is eternal." Lactantius makes the same point in
these words: "Then how did he beget him? First of all, no man
can either understand or explain the works of God. Nonetheless
sacred scripture teaches us this much; in them it is explicitly
stated that that Son of God is the Speech of God." He also says
elsewhere, "But the Greek term λόγος is more suitable than our
'word' or 'speech.' For λόγος means both 'speech' and 'reason.'"
Cyprian makes the same point in these words from the chapter
he entitled "That this same Christ is the Speech of God," which
he proves with the following words: "In psalm 44, 'My heart has
brought forth a good Speech; I will tell of my works to the King.'
Likewise in the psalm, 'By the Speech of God the heavens were
made firm, and all their strength by the breath of his mouth.'
Likewise in Isaiah, 'ratifying and consummating his Word in
justice, for God will consummate his Speech throughout the
earth.' Likewise in the psalm, 'He sent forth his Speech and it
healed them.' Likewise in the gospel according to John, 'In the
beginning was the Word, and the Word was with God, and God
was the Word; this was in the beginning with God. All things
were made by him, and of the things that were made nothing was
made without him. In him was life, and the life was the light of
men, and the light shines in the darkness, and the darkness
comprehended it not.' Likewise in the Apocalypse, 'And I saw
heaven opened, and behold! a white horse; and he that sat upon
him was called faithful and true, in fairness and justice judging
and making war. And he was clothed in a garment besprinkled
with blood, and his name is called the Speech of God.'" Au-

sumat psalterij translationem commentandam potissimum, qua
legitur "Sermone dei coeli solidati sunt," quam lectionem non
improbat, sed asserit idem valere, quod valet nostra, qua legitur,
"Verbo dei coeli firmati sunt," quum et hic "verbum" et illic
5 "sermonem" apertissime censeat esse filium dei. Praeterea ad
Hebraeos quarto, "Viuus est enim sermo dei," quo in loco glossa
non interliniaris modo, sed ordinaria quoque, sermonem aperte
declarat esse filium. Quin Lyranus quoque, cui studium fuit
litteralem scripturae sensum explicare, docet euidenter "ser-
10 monem" idem significare, quod "verbum," atque hoc loco sermonem non aliud esse, quam filium dei, atque ad eum modum
locum ipse non ad allegoriam vllam, Sed plane litteraliter (vt
vocant) exponit. [K$_4$v]
   At operaeprecium est videre, cum ista fateri cogaris, soluere
15 vero non possis, quam pulchre coneris elabi. Nam "plurimum"
inquis "interest inter locorum congruentias, vt quod ibi apte
positum est, hic minus conueniat, Sed nolo hac in re longius
demorari, ne codicem potius quam epistolam excudere videar."
Belle profecto subducis te, cum breuitatis praetextu recuses dicti
20 tui causam reddere, eius praesertim dicti, vnde totius causae
summa dependet, idque cum nec ibi finias epistolam, sed tam
multum chartae consumas postea in his quae nihil ad rem attinent. Hoc certe scio, si te torseris annum, aliam causam non
inuenies vnquam, praeter eam quam et commemorasti, et velut
25 inefficacem timide tetigisti, Nempe quod "sermo" potius significat id quod profertur voce, quam tacitum mentis conceptum,
quam causam si satis sapuisses, penitus non debebas attingere, vt
quae tam contra "verbum" militat, quam "sermonem": nam et
"verbum" proprie conceptum significat prolatum voce. At alia
30 causa nulla potest esse. Nam si tam "sermo" quam "verbum"
significet filium dei, non modo qualis erat postquam ex matre

---

3 valet nostra] *1520*^{m}, nostra ualet *1520*^{a} 4 verbum] verbum, *1520*   6 quarto,]
quarto. *1520*^{m}, iiij. *1520*^{a} 8 filium.] *1520*^{m}, filium dei, *1520*^{a}; quoque,] quoque
1520   11 modum] *1520*^{a}, modum, *1520*^{m} 12 ipse] *1520*^{m}, ipsum *1520*^{a}; vllam,]
1520^a, vllam. *1520*^{m} 14 At] *No para.* *1520*^{a} 15 elabi.] *1520*^{a}, elabi, *1520*^{m} 16
interest] *1520*^{a}, interest, *1520*^{m} 23 annum,] *1520*^{a}, annum *1520*^{m} 25 tetigisti,]
1520^a, tetigisti. *1520*^{m} 25–26 significat] *1520*^{a}, significat, *1520*^{m} 31 dei,] *1520*^{a},
dei: *1520*^{m}

gustine makes the same point when he takes as the principal basis for his commentary that translation of the Psalter which reads, "By the Speech of God the heavens were made solid." Nor does he disapprove of that reading; instead, he asserts that it has the same import as our reading, "By the Word of God the heavens were made firm," while he manifestly thinks that both "verbum" in this translation and "sermo" in that one are the Son of God. There is also, in the fourth chapter of Hebrews, "For the Speech of God is alive," a passage in which not only the *Glossa interlinearis* but also the *Glossa ordinaria* declare plainly that Speech is the Son. Indeed, even de Lyra, who proposed to explain the literal sense of scripture, clearly teaches that "sermo" means the same thing as "verbum" and that in this passage Speech is nothing else but the Son of God, and in this way he himself expounds the passage not according to any allegory but quite "literally" as we use that term.

But since you must acknowledge those proof-texts, and you cannot refute them, it is worth seeing the fine way you attempt to evade them. For you say, "There is a great deal of difference between what is fitting in various contexts: what is suitable in one is less appropriate in another. But I do not want to spend too much time on this subject lest you think I am drafting a book, not a letter." What a graceful retreat! Under pretext of brevity you refuse to support your own statement, indeed that very statement on which your whole argument depends, and yet not even then do you actually finish your letter. Instead, you go on to waste more paper still on matters that are not at all to the point. I am certain about this much: even if you rack your brains for a year you will never find any support for your case besides that single point you have already mentioned—indeed, barely touched on, as if you yourself found it flimsy—namely, that "sermo" means that which is expressed with the voice and not an unspoken conception of the mind. But if you had any sense you would not have touched this point at all, since it is just as inimical to "verbum" as it is to "sermo." For "verbum," too, properly speaking, means a concept expressed with the voice. But there can be no other support for your case. For if both "sermo" and "verbum" can mean the Son of God not only as he was after his

natus est, sed etiam qualis erat in sinu patris ante susceptam
carnem: antequam creatus est orbis: quid comminisci potes, cur
ob vllam (vt tu vocas) locorum conuenientiam non possit filius
dei tam in illo loco "sermo" dici, quam in alijs dicitur? Cum
5 Cyprianus probet aduersus Iudaeos, filium dei esse sermonem
dei, non solum ex alijs locis, verum ex illo ipso quoque "In principio erat verbum," an non vides nihil eum probare prorsus, nisi
etiam illo [L₁] ipso loco idem esset sermo quod verbum? At vt tibi
penitus os obstrueret, non solum ita citat locum Cyprianus, ve-
10 rum paulo post his ipsis citat, "In principio fuit sermo, et sermo
erat apud deum, et deus erat sermo." I nunc et Erasmum clama
nouatorem esse verborum, quum audias doctissimum patrem ac
sanctissimum athletam Christi, verbum dei, pro quo fudit sanguinem, et legisse et appellasse "sermonem" plus annis mille
15 priusquam nasceretur Erasmus. Qua in re beato Cypriano diuus
Augustinus in commentarijs suis super Ioannem apertissime
subscribit.

Iam quod ais ad tuae causae stabilimentum sufficere, quod
sancta mater ecclesia, ex omnium sanctorum consensu, per tot
20 saecula tam sacrato sit vsa vocabulo "verbi," istud quomodo tuas
partes stabiliat ipse videris. Erasmo certe non modo non nocet
verum etiam factum eius in primis tuetur atque defendit. Nam
quum ille "sermonem" vertit, "verbum" non reprehendit, nec
vetus interpres, cum "verbum" vertit, "sermonem" reicit atque
25 refellit, Sed ne ecclesia quidem cum "verbum" haberet in vsu
reiecit "sermonem" quem itidem habebat et habet in vsu. Erasmus igitur cum "sermonem" vertit neque contradicit ecclesiae,
nec veterem taxat interpretem. Rursus cum "sermonem" vertit
pro Christo, cur non illi quoque debet ad stabilimentum suae
30 causae sufficere, quod vt ipse scripsisti de "verbo," ita quoque
sancta mater ecclesia ex omnium doctorum et sanctorum con-

---

1 erat] *1520*ᵃ, erat, *1520*ᵐ   2 potes,] potes: *1520*ᵐ, potest, *1520*ᵃ   4 dici,] *1520*ᵃ,
dici: *1520*ᵐ   6 dei,] *1520*ᵃ, dei: *1520*ᵐ   10 his ipsis citat,] his ipsis citat. *1520*ᵐ, his
citat uerbis. *1520*ᵃ; fuit] *1520*ᵐ, erat *1520*ᵃ   13 Christi,] Christi *1520*   13–14
sanguinem,] *1520*ᵃ, sanguinem *1520*ᵐ   14 sermonem] *1520*ᵃ, sermonem, *1520*ᵐ
18 Iam] *No para. 1520;* ais] *1520*ᵃ, ais, *1520*ᵐ; stabilimentum] *1520*ᵃ, stabilimentum,
*1520*ᵐ; sufficere,] sufficere *1520*ᵐ, sufficere. *1520*ᵃ   21 videris.] *1520*ᵃ, videris *1520*ᵐ
23 vertit,] *1520*ᵃ, vertit *1520*ᵐ   24 reicit] reicit, *1520*ᵐ, reijcit *1520*ᵃ   26 reiecit]
*1520*ᵐ, reijcit *1520*ᵃ   29 debet] *1520*ᵃ, debet, *1520*ᵐ

mother gave birth to him but also as he was in the bosom of the Father before he took on fleshly form, before the world was even created, what rationale can you make up for saying that any consideration of what you call contextual appropriateness prevents us from calling the Son of God "sermo" in this passage as well as in others? When Cyprian proves against the Jews that the Son of God is the Speech of God, not only from other texts but also from that very text "In the beginning was the Word," do you not see that he would not be proving anything at all unless Speech and the Word were the same thing in that very passage? But to silence you once and for all, Cyprian not only cites the passage in this way; a bit later he cites it in these very words: "In the beginning was Speech, and Speech was with God, and God was Speech." Now go on and call Erasmus an innovator of words, since you hear that a most learned father and a most holy champion of Christ read and used the name "sermo" for the Word of God, for whom he shed his blood, more than a thousand years before Erasmus was born. And on this point St. Augustine in his commentary on John very plainly concurs with St. Cyprian.

Now you say it suffices to confirm your own case that for so many centuries, with the consensus of all the saints, holy mother church has religiously used the term "verbum," but you must figure out for yourself how that fact can confirm your position. It certainly does not hurt Erasmus; more than that, it even supports and defends what he has done. For he is not criticizing "verbum" when he translates "sermo," any more than the old translator is condemning and censuring "sermo" when he translates "verbum," or indeed any more than the Church condemned "sermo" when it retained "verbum" in regular usage, in which it retained and still does retain "sermo," as well. Thus when he translates "sermo" Erasmus neither contradicts the Church nor finds fault with the old translator. Then again, when he translates "sermo" as a way of referring to Christ, why should it not also suffice to confirm his case that—as you yourself wrote about "verbum"—for so many centuries, with the consensus of all the saints and doctors, holy mother church has religiously

sensu, per tot saecula tam sacrato sit vsa vocabulo "sermonis"?
Quis vetabit interpretem e duobus eiusdem rei vocabulis sumere, quod sibi libet? Quis iure in ius vocabit translatorem
nouum, [L₁v] quod "vxorem" verterit, quam prior appellarit
5 "coniugem"?

   "Imo vero" inquis, "nam turbat insuetiore vocabulo simplicem
plebeculam. Itaque cernis, quorsum Erasmi istius tendit labor,
nempe vt schisma oriatur, vanitas introducatur." Ille obsecro
turbat simplicem plebeculam, quae quid ille scribat nunquam sit
10 cogitatura, nisi quosdam instigaret inuidia? qui, velut alter
Chain, quandoquidem e fraterno sacrificio fumum vident ascendere, suum vero deorsum ferri, concidentes vultu, quod in ipsis
est, innocentem conantur occidere, impijs obtrectationibus ob-
pugnantes agnitam veritatem, populumque simplicem seditiosis
15 excitantes clamoribus, quos vel tacendo quiescere permisissent,
vel certe, quos falsa narrando commouerant, eosdem debuerant
rursus vera monendo compescere. Alioqui si quod Erasmus
elaborat doctis, id isti, cum tueri se suas partes non posse apud
sapientes intelligant, apud indoctum vulgus oblatrent, et im-
20 portune res litterarias auriculis ingerant illiteratis, ac stultum
vulgi plausum captent, quia prudentibus placere non possunt,
Ipsi nimirum schisma commouent. Alioqui si vel his de rebus
tacerent apud vulgus, vel saltem vera loquerentur, nihil esset
schismatis. Nam cur oriretur ex eo schisma, quod diuersi diuersa
25 verba transtulerint, cum significata sint eadem? qua in re tuum
tibi dictum licebit opponere, quod tute nuper Erasmo obieceras
ex Ambrosio, qui dicit, "Mihi non distat in verbo, quicquid non
distat in sensu."

   At vereris ne hoc pacto accidat, vt breui innumerabiles
30 habeamus aeditiones, cum "haud pau[L₂]cos" (vt ais) "habeat

---

3 libet?] *1520*ᵃ, libet, *1520*ᵐ; translatorem] *1520*ᵃ, traslatorem *1520*ᵐ   5 coniugem"?]
coniugem. *1520*   6 Imo] *No para. 1520*   10 inuidia?] inuidia, *1520;* qui,] qui
1520   12 concidentes] *1520*ᵐ, concidente *1520*ᵃ   16 vel certe,] vel certe *1520*ᵐ, uel
*1520*ᵃ   18 isti,] isti *1520*   21 possunt,] possunt. *1520*ᵐ, possunt *1520*ᵃ   22
nimirum] *1520*ᵐ, nimium *1520*ᵃ; commouent] *1520*ᵐ, mouent *1520*ᵃ   24 oriretur]
*1520*ᵐ, orietur *1520*ᵃ   25 eadem?] eadem, *1520*   27 dicit,] dicit. *1520*ᵐ, dicit
*1520*ᵃ   29 At] *No para. 1520;* breui] *1520*ᵃ, breue *1520*ᵐ

used the term "sermo"? Will anyone forbid a translator to employ whichever he likes of two terms which denote the same thing? Can anyone justly indict a new translator for rendering as "wife" what the previous one called a "spouse"?

"Yes indeed," you say, "since he disturbs the simple common folk with the less familiar term. And so you see where the work of this fellow Erasmus is headed—at starting a schism and fostering vain quarrels." Pray tell, is it really he who disturbs the simple common folk, who would never give a thought to what he writes if it were not for the envy inciting a few? For like another Cain, these men, their countenances falling when they see how the smoke from their brother's burnt offering rises while theirs is brought low, try their hardest to murder a man who is innocent. They use impious slanders to combat the recognized truth and seditious outcries to provoke simple people, whom they either could have kept calm just by not speaking out or at least should have soothed with the truth after stirring them up with their falsehoods. Otherwise, if those fellows see that they cannot defend their position to intelligent people and so cry out to the unlearned crowd against works that Erasmus addressed to the learned, if they tactlessly force literary debates on illiterate hearers and court the applause of the crowd because they cannot please the discerning, it is they who are stirring up schism. Otherwise, had they either said nothing of these matters to the crowd or at any rate spoken the truth, there would be no schism. For why should it start a schism if different translators employ different words when the words mean the same? On this point I can use against you the very saying you borrowed from Ambrose to hurl at Erasmus: "In my view there is no difference in wording where there is no difference in sense."

But you are afraid that on this basis we will soon have innumerable editions, since you say that "the world contains not a few

mundus, qui in graecanicae linguae scientia Erasmo aut pares
sunt, aut certe superiores." Nescio qui numerus apud te superet
paucitatem, sed si numerare nominatim coeperis, non dubito,
quin pares illos infra paucitatem reperias, superiores fortassis
5   infra vnitatem. Si sacrarum litterarum studium adiunxeris, sine
qua quantalibet etiam linguae peritia impar huic prouinciae futura sit, Ego certe non dubito Erasmi labores facile effecturos, ne
posthac existant multi, qui eadem vertant denuo. Nam vt poterunt exoriri facile, qui fortassis vno atque altero loco confisuri
10 sint aliquid sese peruidisse certius, ita neque tam doctum expecto, neque tam audacem quenquam, qui speret aliquando sese
toto rursus vertendo opere, quod Erasmus ante transtulerit, facturum operaeprecium.
     Quanquam si plurimae forent aeditiones, quid id nocuerit?
15 Diuus Augustinus id quod tu times censet in primis esse vtile,
dum etiam si pares omnes esse non possent, alius tamen alibi
vertit commodius. "At interim lector" inquis "reddetur incertus,
e tam multis, cui potissimum possit credere." Istud quidem verum est, si lector plane sit stipes, qui nec ingenium adferat se-
20 cum, nec iudicium. Alioqui si mentem habeat, e varijs trans-
ferentium versionibus facilius multo possit, vt Augustinus ait,
verum quid sit elicere. Quaeso te cur tantum periculi metuis e
diuersis atque inter se varijs translatorum versionibus, qui nihil
offenderis quum tam multiplices legas enarrationes interpre-
25 tum, qui nihil variante littera, nihil ipsi inter sese de litterae
sensu consentiunt? et tamen saepe dissentiunt vtiliter, quod studiosis [L₂v] et cogitandi et iudicandi prebent occasionem. Denique quantum prosint aeditiones variae neque quicquam confun-
dant ecclesiam, psalmi saltem tam varie versi lectique declarant,
30 neque enim alia res magis adiuuerit eum, qui in eos pernoscen-

---

1 scientia] *1520*ᵃ, scientia, *1520*ᵐ   4 reperias] *1520*ᵃ, reperies *1520*ᵐ   6 prouin-
ciae] *1520*ᵃ, prouinciae, *1520*ᵐ   12 transtulerit] *1520*ᵐ, transtulerit se *1520*ᵃ   14
Quanquam] *No para. 1520*   15 Augustinus] *1520*ᵃ, Augustinus, *1520*ᵐ   22 metuis]
*1520*ᵃ, metuis, *1520*ᵐ   24 offenderis] *1520*ᵃ, offenderis: *1520*ᵐ   24–25
interpretum,] interpretum: *1520*ᵐ, interpretum *1520*ᵃ   25 littera,] *1520*ᵃ, littera:
*1520*ᵐ   26 consentiunt?] consentiunt: *1520*ᵐ, consentiunt *1520*ᵃ; tamen] *1520*ᵐ, tum
*1520*ᵃ; vtiliter,] vtiliter: *1520*ᵐ, utiliter *1520*ᵃ

people who are equal or indeed superior to Erasmus in their knowledge of Greek." I do not know what number makes more than a few by your reckoning, but I have no doubt that if you start to count them by name you will find that his equals number less than a few and his superiors perhaps less than one. If you add the study of sacred scripture, without which even the greatest linguistic expertise will be unequal to this undertaking, I for one have no doubt that the work of Erasmus will easily ensure that not many hereafter will translate the same texts again. For though some people may well appear who believe that in one or two passages, perhaps, they have understood something more clearly than he did, I do not expect that there will ever be anyone either learned or reckless enough to hope he could do something worthwhile by retranslating a whole work that Erasmus had already translated.

But suppose that there were many editions; what harm would there be in that? Saint Augustine regards as exceedingly useful the very thing you are afraid of, for though not all of the translators could be equally good, there are places where each of them translates more aptly. "But meanwhile," you say, "the reader will be rendered uncertain as to which one of so many translations he ought to trust most." That is undoubtedly true if the reader is simply a blockhead without any intelligence or judgment of his own. Otherwise, if he does have a mind, he will find it much easier to elicit the true sense out of a variety of translations, as Augustine says. I ask you, why do you fear so much danger from variety and diversity of translations when you do not take any offense as you read such a heterogeneous assortment of commentators who can reach no consensus at all on the sense of the letter where the letter does not vary at all? And yet their disagreements are frequently useful, since they offer the studious a good opportunity to exercise their thought and judgment. Finally, the extent to which various versions are actually a help to the Church, and by no means a source of confusion, is established at least by the Psalms, which are read in translations that vary considerably, nor does anything else prove as helpful to those who endeavor to study them thoroughly, unless anyone is senseless

dos operam nauare decreuerit, nisi quis adeo desipiat vti satis
esse putet viennensis legisse commenta.

Omiseram pene quiddam, quod tibi videtur fortissimum, mihi
vero tam imbecille, atque infirmum, vt vel vno flatu possit euerti.
5 Sed quoniam id perspicio velut omnium munitissimum in tuis
haberi praesidijs, tua ipsius verba statui recensere, ne me queri
posses rationes tuas deprauare narrando. Ais igitur, "plane mirari non desino multorum caecitatem, qui bene actum fuisse
putant, quicquid ad graeca vel hebraica adducitur exemplaria,
10 quum omnibus perspicuum sit (ex Iudaeorum perfidia, graecorum varijs erroribus) ipsa eorum exemplaria, mirum in modum
fore deprauata, ac multiplicium erratuum fecibus plena. adde
quod ex nimia diurnitate, necesse est eadem exemplaria de-
prauatiora esse, quam nostra, vt taceam interim quod diuus Hi-
15 eronymus etiam suo aeuo testatus sit latina exemplaria emendatiora fuisse quam graeca, graeca quam hebraea." Quod tu
haec mirari non desinis ego plane demiror quum facile possis
intelligere diuo Hieronymo haec olim omnia et obiecta esse, et
confutata plenissime. Nam primum stultum esse censet, si quis
20 credat gentem aliquam totam conspirare in omnes omnium cor-
rumpendos libros. Qua in re, vt alia praetereantur incommoda,
neque spem vllam poterant concipere, fore vt celaretur perpetuo quod facerent, neque dubitare [L₃] quin reuelata re, suis
ipsi indicijs cecidisse causa viderentur, quum constaret eos eam
25 fouisse litem quam faterentur aliter non posse sese quam codicum deprauatione defendere. Clam vero non potuisse fieri,
quod publicitus a toto fieret populo, tu quoque opinor vides:
quin et illud opinor vides, quum quoque die descisscerent ab

3 Omiseram] *No para. 1520;* fortissimum,] *1520*ᵃ, fortissimum *1520*ᵐ   5 perspicio]
*1520*ᵃ, perspicio, *1520*ᵐ; munitissimum] *1520*ᵃ, munitissimum, *1520*ᵐ   7 posses]
*1520*ᵐ, possis *1520*ᵃ   10–11 graecorum] *1520*ᵐ, Graecorumque *1520*ᵃ   11 in mo-
dum] *1520*ᵃ, immodum *1520*ᵐ   12 plena.] *1520*ᵃ, plena, *1520*ᵐ   14–15 Hiero-
nymus] *1520*ᵐ, Hieronymus interim *1520*ᵃ   16 graeca, graeca] *1520*ᵐ, Graeca *1520*ᵃ;
hebraea] *1520*ᵐ, Hebraica *1520*ᵃ   17 desinis] *1520*ᵐ, desinas *1520*ᵃ   19 ple-
nissime] *1520*ᵐ, planissime *1520*ᵃ   20 conspirare] *1520*ᵃ, conspirare, *1520*ᵐ   21
re,] re *1520*   22 concipere,] concipere *1520*   26 defendere.] *1520*ᵃ, defendere
*1520*ᵐ   27 vides:] vides *1520*ᵐ, uides. *1520*ᵃ   28 vides,] *1520*ᵃ, vides *1520*ᵐ

enough to suppose that the commentary of Vienne is sufficient.

I had almost omitted one argument which you think is your strongest, though I think it so flimsy and weak that just one breath could blow it down. But since I see that you regard it as the best fortified of all your defenses, I have decided to quote your own words so that you could not blame my report for corrupting your logic. Now then, you say, "I simply never stop marveling at the blindness of the many who think that it is a fine feat to collate any work at all with Greek or Hebrew texts, although anyone can infer from the perfidy of the Jews and the various errors of the Greeks that those very texts of theirs must be shockingly corrupt and laden with all sorts of foul errors. Furthermore, from their excessive antiquity it follows that their texts must be more corrupt than our own, not to mention here St. Jerome's testimony that even in his day the Latin texts were less corrupt than the Greek, and the Greek than the Hebrew." I am simply amazed that you never stop marveling at this, since you can easily discern that St. Jerome met with these same objections long ago and completely refuted them. For first of all, he thinks it is foolish for anyone to believe that a whole people would conspire to tamper with all of the books owned by everyone. For not to mention the other difficulties in this scheme, they could have no hope at all of concealing their actions for good, nor could they doubt that as soon as the scheme was revealed they would seem to have lost their case through their own testimony, since it would be clear that the position that they had supported was one they confessed they could defend only by corrupting their texts. But I think even you see that something done publicly by a whole people could not be kept secret. Indeed, I think you also see that, since every day some people defected from the Hebrews to the Christians, and as many from

Hebraeis ad Christianos aliqui nec segnius ad latinos a graecis, falsatio ista librorum illico venisset in lucem. Praeterea quum vtriusque linguae volumina non solum apud infideles essent, sed in manibus etiam versarentur orthodoxorum, aut hos etiam in
5 illorum gratiam necesse est suos deprauasse codices, aut ex veris horum exemplaribus illorum redargutam esse falsitatem. Quid quod his in rebus de quibus nobis est vel cum graecis, vel cum hebraicis controuersia, illorum libri cum latinis consentiunt, nec de littera ferme quaestio fuit vnquam, sed de sensu semper at-
10 que sententia? Qua ex re facile potes iudicare noluisse eos alijs in locis mutare libros, vbi nihil attinebat, quos ibi reliquerunt integ-ros, vbi maxime in rem suam fuerat esse mutatos.

At "nostra exemplaria veriora sunt" inquis "quam graeca." cur igitur suadet Augustinus, vt sicubi dubites de latinis co-
15 dicibus recurras ad graecos? Sed tu libentius adheres Hiero-nymo, qui scribit (vt ais) etiam suo tempore graeca exemplaria veriora fuisse quam hebraica, et latina quam graeca.

Reliqua quae congesseras omnia visa sunt certe facillima. At istud legens, fateor, nonnihil perculsus sum. Nam Hieronymus,
20 apud me nusquam non grauis author, in hac re merito grauissi-mus est, qui si fateretur graecorum libros emendati[L₃v]ores esse, quam hebraeorum et latinos quoque quam graecos, alij fortassis inuenerint aliquam rimam, tamen mihi certe nullum patebat effugium.

25 Caeterum coepi profecto mecum demirari si quid eiusmodi sentiret Hieronymus. Nam hoc sciebam nihil illum posse dicere quod magis aduersaretur ipsius instituto. Locus non occurrebat mihi vbi diceret, quod nusquam potius videretur esse dicturus. Dum pressius ea de re cogito, coepi tandem velut per nebulam
30 recordari eiusmodi olim quippiam me legisse in codice de-

---

1 a] *1520ᵐ*, e *1520ᵃ*; graecis,] graecis: *1520ᵐ*, graecis *1520ᵃ*   3 non solum] *1520ᵃ*, non *1520ᵐ*   6 falsitatem.] *1520ᵃ*, falsitatem *1520ᵐ*   8 controuersia,] *1520ᵃ*, controuersia est *1520ᵐ*   10 sententia?] sententia. *1520*   11 attinebat,] *1520ᵃ*, attinebat *1520ᵐ*   13 At] *No para. 1520;* graeca.] *1520ᵃ*, graeca, *1520ᵐ*   15 graecos?] *1520ᵃ*, graecos. *1520ᵐ*   18 Reliqua] *No para. 1520*   19 legens,] legens *1520;* Hieronymus,] Hieronymus *1520*   25 Caeterum] *No para. 1520;* eiusmodi] *1520ᵐ*, huiusmodi *1520ᵃ*

the Greeks to the Latins, that falsification of books would have been brought to light immediately. Furthermore, since books in both languages were not only in the possession of the unfaithful but also at large in the hands of the orthodox, either the orthodox too would have had to corrupt their own texts as a favor to the unfaithful or else the trustworthy texts of the orthodox would have clearly established the falseness of the others. What of this? On the points we dispute with the Greeks or with the Hebrews, their texts agree with the Latin; the debate never turned on the letter but always on its sense and significance. Thus you can easily conclude that they did not try to alter their books in other passages where it would not matter, since they left them intact even where it would have been most advantageous to alter them.

But "our texts are more trustworthy than Greek ones," you say. Then why does Augustine advise that wherever you have any doubt about the Latin texts you should turn to the Greek? But you would rather side with Jerome, who according to you writes that even in his time the Greek texts were more trustworthy than the Hebrew, and the Latin than the Greek.

The rest of the arguments you had gathered certainly looked very easy to deal with, but I confess that in reading this one I felt somewhat perturbed. For Jerome is an author I always take seriously, and on this point I properly take him most seriously of all. And if he confessed that the books of the Greeks were less corrupt than those of the Hebrews and also that Latin books were less corrupt than the Greek, others might well have found some way out; I myself saw no way to escape.

But then, as I reflected, it started to strike me as perfectly amazing that Jerome should have held such an opinion. For I knew he could not have said anything more opposed to his own undertaking. No passage occurred to me where he said this, and I thought it more likely that he would never have said it anywhere. Thinking harder about it, I finally began to remember, as if through a fog, that I had once read something of the sort in the

cretorum pontificiorum. Corripio librum sperans vt ibi errasse
te deprehenderem. Nam propemodum diuinabam ex illo libro
desumpsisse te, quod perperam accepisse te sperabam.

Vbi locum repperi animo plane concidi, atque omnem pro-
5 pemodum abieci spem, ita eius operis glossema dicere comperio
eadem ipsa quae te. Etenim quanquam non vsqueadeo eius viri,
quisquis fuit, qui prodidit hoc commentum, doctrinam timui,
quin spes esset posse interdum fieri, vt in Hieronymo falleretur,
territus sum tamen diligentia, quam mihi ipsi persuaseram tan-
10 tam esse adhibitam, vt in istud sacrum decretorum volumen,
quod plusquam adamantinas leges toti praescribit orbi, nihil omnino congereret non intellectum. Verum enimuero Hieronymi
prudentiam respiciens trahebar alio, quem plane sciebam ne-
quaquam esse tam stupidum, vt cum graecorum codicum vicia
15 causatus, instrumentum vetus decreuisset ad hebraicam re-
purgare veritatem, ac latinorum sordes, quas in nouo testamento contraxerant, ad graecorum fontes emendare, idem tamen
fateretur exemplaria graeca veriora esse, quam hebraica, et latina quam graeca. Quo quid eius proposito dici potu[L₄]it aut
20 magis confingi contrarium?

Haec reputanti mihi cepit animus eo tandem vergere, vt glossematis potius diligentiam, quam Hieronymi prudentiam suspectam haberem. Itaque verti me ad locum (est enim in fine illius
epistolae quae incipit "Desiderij mei"). Deus bone, quam foede
25 lapsum glossematis autorem video? Nam locus apud Hieronymum sic habet, "Aliud est si contra se postea ab apostolis
vsurpata testimonia probauerunt, et emendatiora sunt exemplaria latina quam graeca, graeca quam hebraica." Quum enim
alijs respondisset obiectionibus, quas aemulos obiecturos puta-
30 bat, ostendit tandem indignos esse responso, si qui tam insigniter
essent stulti, vt exemplaria graeca veriora crederent quam
hebraica, et latina quam graeca. Quam loquendi figuram non

1 pontificiorum] *1520*ᵐ, pontificum *1520*ᵃ   2 deprehenderem.] deprehenderem
*1520*ᵐ, deprehenderem, *1520*ᵃ; illo libro] *1520*ᵐ, illo *1520*ᵃ   3 accepisse te] *1520*ᵐ,
accepisse *1520*ᵃ   4 Vbi] *No para. 1520*   6 viri,] viri *1520*   7 fuit,] *1520*ᵃ, fuit
*1520*ᵐ; commentum,] *1520*ᵃ, commentum *1520*ᵐ   10 volumen,] volumen *1520*
17 contraxerant] *1520*ᵃ, contraxerat *1520*ᵐ   18 graeca] *1520*ᵃ, graeca, *1520*ᵐ   21
Haec] *No para. 1520*   24 mei").] mei. *1520*   25 video?] video. *1520*

book of pontifical decretals. I snatched up the book in the hope I could prove you mistaken, since I was practically sure that that book was the source of your quotation, and I hoped you had got it wrong.

When I found the passage, I simply lost heart, indeed I practically abandoned all hope, since I found that a gloss in that work said the same thing that you do. For although I was not so intimidated by the learning of whoever produced this commentary that I had no hope of his stumbling occasionally in citing Jerome, I was still overawed by the great diligence that I was convinced must have been brought to bear to ensure that that holy volume of decretals, which inexorably lays down the law for the whole world, would not include anything at all that had not been correctly understood. Nonetheless, I was drawn toward a different conclusion by my respect for Jerome's prudence, since I simply knew he could not be so stupid that even after he had noted the faults of the Greek texts and had chosen to correct the Old Testament according to the true Hebrew readings, and even after he had chosen to emend the corruptions that had appeared in Latin texts of the New Testament on the basis of their Greek originals, he would still admit that the Greek texts are more trustworthy than the Hebrew, and the Latin than the Greek. For what could be said or conceived to undermine his own project more thoroughly?

As I thought these things over I eventually started to feel more dubious about the diligence that went into the gloss than about Jerome's prudence. So I turned to the passage, which is at the end of the letter that begins with the words "Desiderij mei." Good lord, what a disgraceful mistake I saw that the author of that gloss had made! For in Jerome the passage reads thus: "It is another matter if as against their own position they have accepted the forms of the text which are subsequently attested by the apostles, and if Latin texts are less corrupt than the Greek and the Greek than the Hebrew." For after anticipating the objections that he thought his opponents would make, he finally indicated that if anyone were so signally foolish as to think the Greek texts more trustworthy than the Hebrew, and the Latin than the Greek, he would not deserve any response. But that author of

intelligens iste, amputatis aliquot verbis, a quibus tota sententiae
pendet vis, reliquum sic adducit, vt quod Hieronymus ex-
istimauit neminem esse tam stultum, qui dicat, id, quod iste,
illum ipsum dicat dixisse Hieronymum. I nunc atque istis crede
5   summularijs, quibus nunc adeo creditur, vt ferme pro super-
uacaneis habeantur illi quorum e spolijs suas isti summas conflauerunt.

     Vbi versionem eius atque annotationes velut acropolim de-
bellasti strenue, iam minora quaelibet opidula veluti praedabun-
10 dus inuadis: Atque in primis insilis in Moriam, amplam quidem
illam, et populo frequentem vrbem, quam tamen, quoniam
muliebri imperio regitur, quae et ipsa non consilio militum, sed
temere atque ex libidine rem consueuit gerere, nullo negocio
speras expugnari posse. Verum heus tu hac in re praedico tibi
15 non esse tam facilem expugnatu quam putas. Nam primum, vt
Salomon ait, "stultorum infinitus est [L₄v] numerus," deinde
quod ingenio deest, supplet audacia. Certe vt in ciuem haud
grauatim admiserint si ambias adscribi, ita victorem nunquam
patientur, parati vel morti deuouere sese citius quam cuiquam
20 pareant.

     Verum omisso ioco, illa ipsa Moria minus habet moriae, plus
etiam pietatis, quam habent eorum pleraque quae vestri
quidam—Sed reprimam me, quanquam illud interim non vere-
bor dicere, quam habent orationes quaedam rithmicae, quibus
25 vestri quidam sese sibi putant omnes deuincire diuos, quoties
eorum laudes tam stultis celebrant naenijs, vt stultioribus non
possit si quis nebulo maxime studet illudere, et tamen harum
nugarum hodie nonnihil irrepsit in templa, tantamque accipit
indies autoritatem, praesertim ab adiuncta musica, vt iam multo

---

1 iste,] *1520*ᵃ, iste *1520*ᵐ   3 dicat, id, quod iste,] dicat id, quod iste *1520*ᵐ, dicat, id iste
*1520*ᵃ   4 I nunc] *1520*ᵐ, Nunc *1520*ᵃ   5 creditur,] *1520*ᵃ, creditur *1520*ᵐ   5–6
pro superuacaneis] *1520*ᵃ, superuacuis *1520*ᵐ   6 quorum e] *1520*ᵐ, e quorum *1520*ᵃ
8 Vbi] *No para. 1520*   10 inuadis:] inuadis *1520;* insilis] *1520*ᵐ, nisi lis *1520*ᵃ; Moriam,] *1520*ᵃ, Moriam *1520*ᵐ   15 primum,] primum *1520*   16 ait,] ait *1520*ᵐ,
ait. *1520*ᵃ   17 audacia.] *1520*ᵃ, audacia *1520*ᵐ   18 ita] *1520*ᵐ, ita ut *1520*ᵃ   19
patientur,] *1520*ᵃ, patientur *1520*ᵐ; parati] *1520*ᵃ, parati, *1520*ᵐ   21 Verum] *No para.*
1520; ioco,] *1520*ᵃ, ioco *1520*ᵐ   23 quidam—] quidam. *1520*ᵐ, quidam, *1520*ᵃ   25
diuos,] *1520*ᵐ, diuos, ut *1520*ᵃ   27 possit] possit, *1520*   28 tantamque] *1520*ᵃ,
tantam *1520*ᵐ

yours, not understanding this figure of speech, lopped off a few words which establish the whole point of the sentence and then cited the rest as a basis for saying that Jerome himself said what he actually thought no one foolish enough to say, namely just what this author of yours says. Now go on and rely on those summary textbooks of yours, on which most now rely so heavily that the authors despoiled by your modern compilers to fill out their summas are regarded as almost superfluous.

Having bravely concluded your siege of his translation and notes—his acropolis, as it were—you attack several of his smaller towns, as if greedy for plunder. You strike hardest of all at his Moria ["Folly"], an ample and populous city, but one which you hope can be taken without difficulty since it has a woman in charge, and since she is not one to defer to her generals but always directs things according to whim and caprice. But listen here, you, I predict that in this undertaking her bastions will not be as easy to take as you think. For first of all, as Solomon says, "The number of fools is infinite," and then what they are lacking in intelligence they make up for in recklessness. Though they would gladly admit you as a citizen if you yearn to become one, they will certainly never agree to have you as a conquerer, for they will fight to the death before they will take orders from anyone.

But joking aside, even Folly herself has less folly to offer, as well as more piety, than some of your—I will restrain myself, and yet I will dare to say this much—than some of the rhythmical prayers with which some of your brethren suppose they put all of the saints in their debt every time that they honor their memory with such foolish jingles that not even a rogue trying his hardest to mock them could muster more foolish ones. And yet some of this trifling stuff has now found a place in our churches, and each day it acquires more authority, particularly when it is provided with a musical accompaniment, so that by now we are

minus erga sobrias ac serias a sanctis olim patribus ordinatas
preces adficiamur, quum nonnihil intersit rei Christianae, vt
pontifices, quod eos aliquando facturos non dubito, omnibus
istiusmodi prorsus interdicant ineptijs, ne callidus hostis efficiat,
5 vt Christi grex, quem ille vt simplicem esse voluit, ita voluit esse
prudentem, paulatim assuescat amplecti pietatis loco stulticiam.
    Moriae patrocinium non suscipiam, quippe quum non sit
opus. Nam et liber iam diu probatus est optimi cuiusque iudicio
et aduersus inuidorum calumnias Erasmi iam olim apologia de-
10 fensus, cum eorum nomine Dorpius vir et prophanis litteris, et
sacris eruditissimus quicquid ab illis excogitari poterat coace-
ruasset, et ne praeuaricari videretur, eloquenter excoluisset
etiam, vt tibi iam difficile fuerit objicere, quod non sit ante reiectum, nisi [M₁] quod vnum prorsus inuenisti nouum, quod in-
15 geras, cum Erasmum dicis in Moria Moscum quendam agere,
quod ego certe conuicium, fateor, non possum refellere, Quippe
qui quid sibi velit, aut quis is fuerit Moscus, prorsus non intelligo,
neque enim tam stulte sum arrogans, vt doctior affectem videri
quam sum. De Momo quodam audiui saepe, cui an cognomen
20 forte Moscus fuerit, ego certe non comperi.
    De Iulij dialogo, neque cuius sit, neque cuiusmodi sit, mihi
vnquam valde libuit quaerere, cum de vtraque re varias audierim sententias. Hoc certe scio, protinus defuncto Iulio, rem
Parisijs ludis actam publicis. Multi sciunt reuerendum patrem
25 Poncherium Parisiensis vrbis antistitem, qui huc legatus venerat,
librum vendicasse Fausto, quod, vt verum fuerit, nihil impedit
Erasmum, cui Faustus non ignotus erat, librum apud se quoque
priusquam excuderetur habuisse. Nam quod ex stilo rem con-
uincis, quem Erasmi suum atque ipsissimum esse confirmas, non
30 possum mihi temperare quin rideam, reputans mecum, quod
cum non permittas Erasmo, vt ex stilo quicquam iudicet in Hi-

1 serias] *1520*ᵃ, serias, *1520*ᵐ   4 istiusmodi] *1520*ᵃ, iustiusmodi *1520*ᵐ   5 grex,]
*1520*ᵃ, grex *1520*ᵐ   7 Moriae] *No para. 1520*   8 iudicio] *1520*ᵃ, iudicio, *1520*ᵐ
12–13 excoluisset etiam,] *1520*ᵃ, excoluisset, etiam *1520*ᵐ   16 conuicium, fateor,]
conuicium fateor *1520*ᵐ, conuicium fateor, *1520*ᵃ; refellere,] refellere. *1520*   17
Moscus,] *1520*ᵃ, Moscus *1520*ᵐ   21 De] *No para. 1520*   22 vnquam] *1520*ᵐ,
nunquam *1520*ᵃ   23 scio,] *1520*ᵃ, scio *1520*ᵐ   25 venerat,] *1520*ᵃ, venerat *1520*ᵐ
26 quod,] quod *1520*   31 permittas] *1520*ᵐ, permittis *1520*ᵃ

much less attentive to the sober and serious prayers holy fathers prescribed long ago. In fact it would be a considerable advantage for Christendom if bishops would utterly ban all such silliness, as I am sure they eventually will, so that our subtle foe cannot cause Christ's flock, whom he meant to be not only simple but prudent as well, to slip gradually into the habit of embracing folly in place of piety.

I will not undertake the defense of the *Folly*, since there is no need. For the book has long had the approval of all the best judges, and it was defended long ago against the aspersions of envious people in Erasmus' apology to Dorp, a man of great learning in both secular and sacred disciplines, who had taken the part of those critics by gathering up every objection that they could contrive and had even gone on to develop them eloquently in an effort to show that he meant what he said, so that you would now be hard pressed to raise any objection that has not been confuted already, though you have found one charge that is utterly new when you say that Erasmus in the *Folly* is acting like someone called Moscus. This reproach I confess I for one cannot answer, since I have no idea what it means, or who that Moscus was, and I am not such an arrogant fool as to make a deliberate pretense of being more learned than I am. I have often heard of someone called Momus, who might have had Moscus as a surname, but I personally cannot confirm it.

I have never been particularly keen to learn who wrote the dialogue *Julius* or what sort of production it is, though I have heard various opinions on both points. I do know that right after Julius' death the affair was the subject of public skits in Paris. Many know that the Reverend Father Poncher, bishop of the city of Paris, declared, when he came here as an ambassador, that the book was by Fausto. But this theory, should it be true, by no means rules out the possibility that Erasmus also had the book in his possession before it was in print, since Fausto is not a complete stranger to him. But when you base your argument on the style, which you claim is distinctly and purely Erasmian, I cannot refrain from a laugh at the thought that, while you will not let Erasmus base any of his judgments concerning the works of

eronymianis operibus, is cui, quod omnibus in confesso est,
omnes orationis virtutes sunt exploratissimae, tu, qui quid sit
stilus aut phrasis explicare non possis, arroges tamen tibi vt ex
stilo discernas Erasmica in tanta litteratorum turba, quorum
5 quisque quoad potest, Erasmicam dictionem conatur imitari.
Iam pone librum illius esse, pone hominem infensum bellis,
iratum turbulentis temporibus, aliquo animi impetu prouectum
latius, quam pacatis post illa rebus, et tranquillatis affectibus
opta[M₁v]uisset. Primum magis hoc erat imputandum ijs, qui
10 librum suo tempore scriptum, tempore non suo vulgauerunt.
Deinde quaeso te, hoccine monachi fuerat, errorem fratris
eruere, cuius officium postulet potius, vt solitarius sedeat, ac sua
peccata defleat, quam vt aliena coarguat? Quod si quem liber
offenderit, apud hos opinor malam inibis gratiam libellum as-
15 serens illi, quando magis eorum e re fuerit, opus vt sit ἀδέσ-
ποτον, quam ab autoris aestimatione commendetur.
  Lutherus qualia scripserit viderint quibus vacat. Erasmus
certe, si quid illi scripsit, non dubito, quin ita scripserit, vt virum
bonum decet, neque tu aliquid habere te certi significas, nec
20 tamen interim quoad habeas potes abstinere conuicijs, credo ne
tantisper voluptate careas illius belli dicterij, "dignum patella
operculum," cuius vnius illecebra videris in Erasmi ac Lutheri
mentionem esse pertractus. Nam mirum est vt vbique affectas
esse facetulus. At ego immodicum istud ocium demiror, quod in
25 schismaticos haereticosque libros tibi liceat, si modo vera dicis,
impendere, nisi tanta bonorum inopia est, vt tempus breue in-
sumere cogaris in pessimos. Nam si boni sunt libelli, cur damnas?
si mali, cur legis? cui cum non ea facultas possit obtingere, vt sis
idoneus qui de refellendis erroribus admoneas mundum, cuius
30 et curam abdicasti, quum temet in claustrum abderes, quid aliud
facis, peruersa legendo, quam discis?

---

1 cui,] cui *1520*   2 tu,] tu *1520*   3 stilus] *1520*ᵃ, stilus, *1520*ᵐ   7 prouectum]
*1520*ᵐ, profectum *1520*ᵃ   8 et] 1520ᵐ, *om. 1520*ᵃ   9 ijs] *1520*ᵐ, his *1520*ᵃ   11 te]
*1520*ᵐ, *om. 1520*ᵃ; fuerat,] *1520*ᵃ, fuerat *1520*ᵐ   13 coarguat?] *1520*ᵃ, coarguat.
*1520*ᵐ   14 gratiam] *1520*ᵃ, gratiam, *1520*ᵐ   15 magis] *1520*ᵃ, plus *1520*ᵐ   15–
16 ἀδέσποτον] ἀδέσποτος *1520*ᵐ, adespoton *1520*ᵃ   17 Lutherus] *No para.*
1520   18 illi] *1520*ᵐ, ille *1520*ᵃ; scripsit,] *1520*ᵃ, scripsit: *1520*ᵐ; scripserit] scripsit
1520   22 operculum] *1520*ᵐ, cooperculum *1520*ᵃ   26 impendere,] *1520*ᵃ, impendere. *1520*ᵐ

Jerome on their style, even though everyone knows that Erasmus is a consummate expert on fine points of language, you yourself are so arrogant that, without even knowing the meaning of style or of diction, you single things out as his work on the basis of style even though there are so many learned people intent upon writing just like him. Now suppose that he did write the book. Suppose that a man who was fed up with war and provoked by the turbulent times did let some passion carry him further than he might have wished after peace was achieved and emotions were soothed. First, most of the blame should then go to the people responsible for the untimely publication of a once timely book. Then I ask you, was this really your job as a monk, to expose a mistake in your brother, when your office enjoins you to sit by yourself and lament your own sins, not denounce other people's? And I think that assigning the book to Erasmus will win you no thanks among those whom it may have offended, since it would be better for them if the work remained anonymous than if it were commended by being ascribed a prestigious author.

Those with leisure to do so may assess Luther's writings for themselves, but I have no doubt at all that if Erasmus has written to Luther he wrote in a way that befits a good man. Nor do you yourself claim to have any real proof, and yet you cannot wait till you do to launch into abuse, doubtless simply in order to get all the pleasure you can from that splendid bon mot, "The pot matches the lid," which appears to have furnished your only incentive for mentioning Erasmus together with Luther. For it is remarkable how you never stop trying to pass for a wit. But what I find amazing is the inordinate quantity of leisure you are free to devote to schismatic and heretical books—if, that is, you are telling the truth—unless a shortage of good ones compels you to spend the short time you do have on the worst ones. For if those books are good, why condemn them? If bad, then why read them? For since you will never be in an appropriate position to lecture the world on combating erroneous beliefs, since you even forswore any care for the world when you entered the cloister, what else do you accomplish by reading false doctrines but to learn them?

Nec satis esse video quod in malos codices bonas horas colloces, nisi plurimum temporis etiam in sermonem [M₂] et confabulationes adhuc deteriores codicibus malis absumas, ita nihil
vsquam gentium esse video rumoris, obtrectationis, infamiae,
5 quod non in cellam recta perferatur ad te. Atqui legimus olim
fuisse monachos, ita penitus mundo subducentes sese, vt ne litteras quidem ab amicis missas legere sustinuerint, ne vel res-
picere cogerentur Sodomam, quam reliquerant. Nunc vero et
haereticos vt video libellos perlegunt, et schismaticos, et immen-
10 sa meris nugis referta volumina. Nunc quicquid audire vereban-
tur in saeculo, et ne audire cogerentur in claustra fugerunt,
callidus hostis ingerit fugientibus, arteque pertrudit in cellas.
Nec aliud illis praestat cultus ille eximius, nisi vt facilius impo-
nant incautis. Nec aliud praestat ocium, nisi vt magis vacet male-
15 dicentiam adornare, nec aliud secessus, nisi vt nihil pudeat ab
hominum oculis semotos, nec aliud occlusae cellulae, nisi vt liberius obtrectent alienae famae. In quas quisquis ingreditur,
primum oratione dominica propiciat deum, vt colloquium illud
sanctum esse ac salutare iubeat. At quid prodest ab oratione
20 dominica imfamatricem ac detractatoriam auspicari fabulam?
Quid est, si hoc non est in vanum sumere nomen dei? Hic multo
nimirum maxime locum habet, quod ex Euangelio citas in Erasmum, Nam certe non omnis qui sic deo dicit, "domine, domine,"
intrabit in regnum coelorum.
25 Itaque quum literas istas tuas intueor, tam plenas obiurga-
tionis, conuicij, detractionis, ac scommatum, menteque rursus
mecum repeto [M₂v] candorem illum, vereque amabilem indolem adolescentiae tuae, quae tam longe tibi ab huiusmodi vicijs
aberat, quam adesse per aetatem tum ac vitae statum poterat
30 excusatius, certe, si reliquos mores tuos ab ista spectarem epis-

1 Nec] *No para. 1520*   2 sermonem] sermonem, *1520ᵐ*, sermones *1520ᵃ*   2–3
confabulationes] confabulationes, *1520ᵐ*, confabulationes etiam *1520ᵃ*   5 perferatur]
praeferatur *1520ᵐ*, proferatur *1520ᵃ (see commentary);* Atqui] *1520ᵐ*, Atque *1520ᵃ*   12
cellas.] *1520ᵃ*, cellas, *1520ᵐ*   15 adornare,] *1520ᵃ*, adornare. *1520ᵐ*   17 famae.]
1520ᵃ, famae, *1520ᵐ*   18 dominica] *1520ᵃ*, dominica, *1520ᵐ*   22–23 Erasmum,]
Erasmum. *1520ᵐ*, ERASMVM *1520ᵃ*   25 Itaque] *No para. 1520*   27 repeto]
1520ᵐ, reputo *1520ᵃ*   30 excusatius,] *1520ᵃ*, excusatius *1520ᵐ*

Nor will you be content, as I see, just to squander good hours on bad books; you must go on to fritter away a great deal of time speaking and chatting on themes even worse than bad books. For I see every rumor and slander and scandal on earth is immediately passed on to you in your cell. And yet we read that once there were monks who withdrew from the world so completely that they would not even read letters from their friends so that they would not have to look back on the Sodom which they had abandoned. Now, however, I see that they read both heretical and schismatic books and vast volumes of absolute rubbish. Now our subtle foe thrusts on the fugitives just the sort of vain talk that they feared among secular people and cloistered themselves to escape, and he artfully thrusts it into their very cells. Nor does their splendid regimen serve any purpose but to help them deceive the unwary, nor does their leisure serve but to give them more time to perfect their disparaging speech, nor does their withdrawal from the world serve but to make them shameless because men cannot see what they do, nor does the narrowness of their little cells serve but to lend freer scope to their slander of others. And yet the first thing that anyone does upon entering those cells is to call on God with the Lord's prayer to ensure that the talk in that place should be holy and wholesome. But what good does it do to say the Lord's prayer at the outset of scandalous and slanderous gossip? If this is not taking God's name in vain, then what is? This is surely the most fitting context of all for that verse from the gospel you cite against Erasmus, for certainly not everyone who says "Lord, Lord" to God in this way will enter into the kingdom of heaven.

Consequently, as I look at this letter of yours, so replete with reproach, abuse, slander, and mockery, and as I think back on the candor and the genuinely amiable nature you had as a youth, when you were as free from these faults as it would have been easy to pardon them in one of that age and condition, if I gauged your whole character on the basis of this letter I would certainly

tola, admonerer haud dubie illius Ouidiani Carminis, quo Di-
anira perstringit Herculem: "Coepisti melius quam desinis,
vltima primis cedunt: dissimiles hic vir et ille puer." Verumenimuero non sum tam iniquus, vt totum te ab vnis aestimem
5 litteris, imo libentius inclinor vt credam, quo tu reliquis morum
tuorum partibus melior es ac sanctior, eo daemonem quempiam
infestius tuis inuidere virtutibus, atque ex insidijs emicantem,
vehementer eniti, alias eius pedicas euitantem te, vna saltem,
eaque insidiosissima, comprehendere atque ad se pertrahere,
10 dum se transformans in angelum lucis, nobis perstringit aciem vt
videntes, non videamus, Sed hallucinantibus oculis atra cande-
fiant, et nigrescant candida, virtus aliena sordeat, nostra nobis
niteant et blandiantur vicia, dum alienam famam incessere, vocatur fraterna monitio: Ira atque inuidia ducitur feruor ac zelus
15 in deum: Inscitia vero, simplex et sancta rusticitas appellatur:
Arrogans ac pertinax animus, fortis et infracta constantia: denique dum aliquo semper pretextu profectus alieni nostris obse-
cundamus affectibus, ijsdemque fere deterrimis, quemadmodum, in his ipsis quas scripsisti litteris, quasi dum me admones,
20 Erasmo detrahis.

    Neque tamen eorum quae in illum tam acerbe conijcis, quic-
quam in illum competit, pleraque vero in tuum caput recta recidunt. Nam stilum carpis vt affectatum, quum tui soloecis[M$_3$]mi
plus oleant olei, quam illius elegantiae. Illius incessis mor-
25 dacitatem, et omnia clamas illum canino dente corrodere, quum
tute his vnis litteris, plus arrodas illum, quam ille vnquam quenquam: Imo si quis libros eius omnes, si quis omnes percurrat
epistolas, si quodcunque vnquam scripti genus emanauit ab illo,
a quo manarunt tam numerosa volumina, atque ex his vndecun-
30 que in vnum congerat cumulum, quicquid vnquam mali scripsit
in quenquam, idque etiam tacitis eorum quos attingebat nomi-

---

2 melius] *1520*^{a}, melius, *1520*^{m} 3 cedunt: dissimiles] cedunt dissimiles, *1520*   4
aestimem] *1520*^{m}, existimem *1520*^{a} 8 te,] te *1520*   9 insidiosissima,] insidiosissima
1520   11 videamus,] *1520*^{a}, videamus. *1520*^{m}; oculis] *1520*^{a}, oculis, *1520*^{m} 11–12
candefiant] *1520*^{m}, candescant *1520*^{a} 14 monitio:] monitio. *1520*   15 deum:]
deum. *1520;* appellatur:] appellatur. *1520*^{m}, appellatur, *1520*^{a} 16 constantia:] constantia, *1520*   18–19 quemadmodum,] quemadmodum *1520*   19 admones,] admones *1520*   20–21 detrahis. Neque] *1520*^{a}, detrahis, neque *1520*^{m} 21 Neque]
No para. 1520   26–27 quenquam:] quenquam, *1520*^{m}, quenquam. *1520*^{a} 29
manarunt] *1520*^{m}, emanarunt *1520*^{a}

be reminded of that poem by Ovid in which Deianira chides Hercules: "Your beginning surpassed your finale; your performance falls short of your promise; the grown man is no match for the boy." But of course I am not so unfair as to judge you entirely on the basis of a single letter. Indeed, I am more willingly inclined to believe that the goodness and holiness of the rest of your character have made some demon especially resentful and envious of your virtues and that, since you are avoiding the rest of his snares, he is insidiously trying his hardest to trap you and draw you to himself with his last and by far most insidious snare, when he transforms himself into an angel of light, dazzling our vision till we see without seeing and to our deranged eyes black looks white and white black, others' virtue seems tarnished, and our own faults impress us as glamorous and appealing. Then we call defamation of character fraternal advice; we regard anger and envy as fervor and zeal to serve God; we name ignorance simple and saintly rusticity, and call arrogant stubbornness bold and invincible constancy; and in sum, we are never without an altruistic pretext for indulging our own passions, and generally the worst passions at that, just as in this very letter, while pretending to give me advice, you disparage Erasmus.

Yet not one of the bitter reproaches you hurl at him actually strikes home, whereas many of them promptly recoil on you. You protest that his style is affected, when your own solecisms are more labored than his refinements. You attack him for his mordant wit and cry out that he sinks his fangs into everything, when you yourself sink more teeth into him in one letter than he ever sank into anyone. In fact, if someone went through all the books of Erasmus, all his letters, every variety of writing he has ever produced in the course of producing such numerous volumes, and if he then gathered in one pile every unkind thing that Erasmus ever wrote about anyone, characteristically withholding the names of the people to whom he referred although

nibus, quum non deessent quoque qui multa essent acerbiora
commeriti, tamen is ipse cumulus multo erit humilior hac tua
mole, qua coaceruandis in illum conuicijs, idque etiam nominatim, videris exsuperare pyramides, quum is te nihil vnquam
5 quicquam offenderit, quum tua studia suis etiam scriptis adiuuerit, teque incompensabili beneficio adfecerit.

Illum vociferaris arrogantem, quod ausus est aliorum errata
taxare, tu tibi nimirum videris esse modestus, dum in illo carpis
quae recta sunt, dum ea reprehendis quae laudant hij, quorum
10 iudicio reclamare non vulgaris est immodestiae, e quibus commemorare tibi multos possem, eosque virtutis et doctrinae gratia
celeberrimos, qui certatim illi vndique gratias agunt quod tantum eius labore profecerint. Verum exteros praetermittam
omnes, quorum, quod tibi sint ignoti, fortassis authoritatem
15 effugies: vnum atque alterum e nostris nominabo, tales vt his
dissentire sit impudens. Nomino, atque adeo honoris causa
nomino, reuerendum in Christo patrem Ioannem ecclesiae
Roffensis antistitem, virum non litteris magis quam virtute nobilem, quibus hodie nemo [M₃v] viuit illustrior. Coletum nomi-
20 no, quo vno viro, neque doctior neque sanctior apud nos aliquot
retro saeculis quisquam fuit. Horum extant litterae, nec ad Erasmum modo scriptae, in quibus aliquid gratiae datum videri possit, ni tales essent illi, qui nulli prorsus mortalium suo mendacio,
in aliorum praesertim damnum, vellent gratificari, sed ad eos
25 datae, quos omnibus inhortantur modis, vt Erasmi versionem
diligenter perlegant, magnum ab ea fructum reportaturi. Dominus Ioannes Longland decanus Salisberiensis, alter, vt eius
laudes vno verbo complectar, Coletus, seu concionantem audias,
seu vitae spectes puritatem, fateri non cessat, ex Erasmicis operi-

---

1 multa] *See commentary.*   3 mole, qua] *1520*ᵐ, mole *1520*ᵃ   3–4 nominatim,] *1520*ᵃ,
nominatim *1520*ᵐ   4 quum is] *1520*ᵐ, cum his *1520*ᵃ   7 Illum] *No para. 1520*
10 immodestiae] *1520*ᵐ, immodestia *1520*ᵃ   10–11 commemorare tibi] *1520*ᵐ, tibi
commemorare *1520*ᵃ   14 quorum,] quorum *1520;* ignoti,] ignoti *1520*   15
effugies:] effugies *1520*ᵐ, effugies, *1520*ᵃ; e] *1520*ᵐ, ex *1520*ᵃ   17 nomino,] nomino
1520; ecclesiae] *1520*ᵃ, ecclesie *1520*ᵐ   20 nos] *1520*ᵃ, nos, *1520*ᵐ   24 damnum,]
damnum *1520*   27 Longland] Landland *1520;* alter,] alter *1520*   28–29
seu . . . seu] *1520*ᵐ, ceu . . . ceu *1520*ᵃ

some deserved much harsher treatment, this whole pile would be dwarfed by the mountainous load of explicitly personal abuse which you heap on Erasmus like a second Great Pyramid, although he never did you the slightest injury, although he even furthered your studies with his writings and thus did you a kindness too great to repay.

You accuse him of arrogance because he dared to challenge the errors of others, and of course you think you are being modest when you find fault with the things he gets right, when you criticize works praised by judges whom only an egregiously immodest man would defy. I could list for you many such men from all over the world, all renowned for their virtue and learning, who vie with each other in thanking Erasmus for all they have gained by his work. But I will omit all his foreign admirers, since you will probably dispute their authority because you do not know who they are. I will name one or two of our countrymen whom it would be outright impudence to contradict. I will name, and most worshipfully I will name, the reverend father in Christ, John the bishop of Rochester, a man as conspicuous for his virtue as he is for his learning and as eminent for both as any man living today. I will name Colet, a man both as learned and as holy as any of our countrymen has been for the last several centuries. Quite apart from the letters that these men have sent to Erasmus, in which they might appear to be flattering him somewhat were it not that such men would never choose to tell anyone flattering lies, and especially lies that might harm someone else, there are letters in which these men exhort other people as strongly as possible to a diligent reading of Erasmus' translation, from which they will learn a great deal. Master John Longland, the dean of Salisbury, whose preaching and pure living would make you suppose he was another Colet (to sum up his praise in a word), never stops testifying that Erasmus' works

bus in testamentum nouum plus sibi lucis accessisse, quam ex
reliquis fere quos habet commentarijs omnibus. Non est cur alios
commemorem, si credas istis: minus etiam, si non credas istis.
Quibus enim credas hac de re, si non credas talibus? Certe
5 multum tibi sumis, quum quam rem isti tantopere laudant, tu
magnifice vituperas.

Quid quod summus pontifex quod tu vituperas bis iam accurate probauit? Quod Christi vicarius, velut diuinae vocis oraculo
pronunciauit vtile, id tu puer propheta altissimi vaticinaris esse
10 damnosum. Quod ex arce religionis summus ille Christiani orbis
princeps suo testimonio cohonestat, id tu monachulus et indoctus et obscurus ex antro cellulae tuae purulenta lingua conspur-
cas. Hic tibi nimirum curandum est, vt facias ipse quod Erasmo
consulis, nempe ne plus sapias quam oportet sapere, sed sapias
15 ad sobrietatem. An non hoc quod facis istuc ipsum est, quod illi
rursus objicis, iusticiam dei [M₄] ignorare, ac tuam velle constituere, cum quod summus Pontifex studiosis omnibus pio totiens
affectu commendauit, id operis ipse non dubitas improbe condemnare?

20 Quam in rem velut fundamentum substernis, Erasmum prorsus esse scripturarum inscium, tu videlicet omniscius, in quas ille
pernoscendas haud multo pauciores insumpsit annos quam tu
vixisti, quem an tu ingenio superas aut diligentia, non excutio.
Hoc certe scio, quod mihi fas est etiam saluo honore tuo dicere,
25 non vsque adeo superas, vt tam longe minore tempore possis
efficere, quod ille tam longe maiore non possit. Et tamen illum
iam in scripturarum studio sensecentem, mirum est quam im-
modeste tu iuuenis αὐτοδίδακτος, imo cui nunquam vacauit discere, γερονταγωγεῖς: mirum est quam tibi videre sciolus, quoties

2 fere] *1520*ᵃ, fere, *1520*ᵐ   3 istis: minus] istis, minus *1520*; etiam,] *1520*ᵃ, etiam
*1520*ᵐ; non credas] *1520*ᵐ, non credis *1520*ᵃ   7 Quid] *No para.* *1520*   8
probauit?] probauit. *1520*ᵐ, probauit, *1520*ᵃ   10 damnosum.] *1520*ᵃ, damnosum
*1520*ᵐ   11 princeps] *1520*ᵃ, princeps, *1520*ᵐ   12 obscurus] *1520*ᵃ, obscurus,
*1520*ᵐ   17 totiens] *1520*ᵐ, toties *1520*ᵃ   18–19 condemnare?] condemnare, *1520*
20 Quam] *No para.* *1520*   23 superas] superas, *1520*   24 est] *1520*ᵃ, est, *1520*ᵐ
27 quam] *1520*ᵐ, quod *1520*ᵃ   28–29 discere, γερονταγωγεῖς:] discere γερονταγωγεῖς
*1520*ᵐ, discere γερονταγωγεῖς, *1520*ᵃ

on the New Testament have done more to enlighten him than virtually all the rest of the commentaries he owns. There is no need to list any others if you will trust these men; there is even less if you will not. For whom will you trust on this point if you will not trust men such as these? Either way you take a great deal on yourself when you attack with such fanfare what those men so earnestly praise.

What of this, that the pope has twice given his explicit sanction to what you attack? Like a boy-prophet of the almighty you proclaim to be harmful what the vicar of Christ, as if with the authority of a divine oracle, has already declared to be useful. What the supreme prince of Christendom honors with his own testimonial from the citadel of our religion you sully with your filthy tongue from the darkness of your little cell, an unlearned, obscure little monk. At this point you yourself should apply the advice that you offer Erasmus: do not be wise beyond your share of wisdom, but be wise with sobriety. Are you not doing precisely what you also charge him with doing, neglecting God's ordinance and setting out to establish your own, when you blithely persist in condemning the very work that the pope has so often recommended with pious goodwill to all scholars?

You take as a basic assumption in this condemnation the thesis that Erasmus is utterly ignorant of scripture—just as you, I suppose, are omniscient—when in fact he has spent almost as many years studying scripture as you have been living. I am not going to dwell on the possibility that you surpass him in intelligence or diligence. I know this much for sure, and can say so without any slight to your honor at all: you do not surpass him by such a wide margin that you could achieve in a much shorter time something he could not in a much longer one. And yet when he is already growing gray in the study of scripture, you yourself, a self-tutored young man—indeed one who has never had time to be tutored—are actually immodest enough to lecture an old man as if he were a schoolboy; you actually think you are being very

talibus agis argumentis quae te manifeste produnt rem non
intelligere.

Sed tum demum praecipue rem te fecisse magnam putas,
quoties e sacris voluminibus corrasis hinc inde centonibus in
5 illum lusitas, et non aliter verbis sacrae scripturae scurraris,
quam in comedijs parasiti solent ludere dicterijs. Qua re vt nihil
est improbius, ita nihil est vsquam facilius: Vsque adeo vt
quidam nebulo mimicus, cum nuper imitaretur habitu, voce,
vultu, gesticulatione, concionantem fratrem, atque in medio ser-
10 mone, quem totum concinnarat e sacris litteris obscenum atque
ridiculum, narrationem quoque de more quibusdam solemni
fratribus insereret, sed impudicam, nempe de fraterculo pro-
cante, ac viciante mulierculam, Is nebulo illam ipsam tam
foedam spurcamque fabulam tamen adeo infarsit centonibus
15 scripturarum, vt neque dum procatur fraterculus, [M₄v] neque
dum conspurcatur adultera, neque dum res superueniente marito deprehenditur, neque dum deprehensus comprehenditur,
neque dum comprehenso vterque testis exsecatur, Interim aliud
verbum vllum, quam e medijs scripturae sacrae codicibus de-
20 prometur, atque ea omnia, quanquam ad rem ex diametro
diuersam, tamen applicata tam commode, vt nemo tam seuerus
esset, qui risum continere possit, cum nemo contra tam esset
ridiculus, qui non indignaretur ad illiusmodi nequitias sacris
illudi litteris. Nec deerant tamen qui dicerent occulta quadam
25 dei dispensatione contingere, vt quando fratres plerique iam diu
verbum dei adulterare consueuerint, existerent aliquando
fratromimi, qui contra fratres fratrissarent, suoque ipsos exemplo confunderent, et velut suo, quod aiunt, gladio iugularent.
Verum si nefas est, vt certe est, abuti sacris litteris ad lasciuiam,
30 aliquanto adhuc magis nefas est, si quis, quod tu facis, in alterius
abutatur infamiam. Quod nihilo facis excusatius, quia mihi

---

3 Sed] *No para. 1520*   4 corrasis] *1520ᵃ*, corrasis, *1520ᵐ*; centonibus] *1520ᵃ*,
centonibus, *1520ᵐ*   6 dicterijs.] *1520ᵃ*, dicterijs *1520ᵐ*   7 facilius:] facilius. *1520ᵐ*,
facilius *1520ᵃ*   8 imitaretur] *1520ᵃ*, imitaretur, *1520ᵐ*   13 mulierculam,] mulierculam. *1520ᵐ*, mulierculam *1520ᵃ*   18 comprehenso] *1520ᵃ*, comprehensus *1520ᵐ*;
exsecatur,] execatur. *1520ᵐ*, execatur, *1520ᵃ*   19 scripturae] *1520ᵃ*, scripture *1520ᵐ*
25 fratres] *1520ᵐ*, fratres et *1520ᵃ*   30 quis,] quis *1520*   31 infamiam.] *1520ᵃ*,
infamiam *1520ᵐ*

clever when you employ arguments which make it quite clear you have just missed the point.

But you think you have done something especially grand every time that you mock him with patchwork citations from various books of the Bible and when you clown around with the words of holy scripture the same way comic parasites play around with their quips. This is not only the most inexcusable game in the world, it is also the easiest. As a case in point, there is a mischievous mimic who recently copied the dress, tone of voice, facial expressions, and gestures of a preaching friar. In the middle of his obscene and ridiculous sermon, which was made up entirely of excerpts from scripture, he also included an anecdote, just as some friars habitually do, but this anecdote was an indecent story of a friar who seduced and corrupted a house-wife. The rogue padded even this disgraceful and sordid tale with so many patchwork citations from scripture that even when the friar was seducing the adulterous wife, and even when she was being polluted, and even when her husband appeared and discovered the matter, and even when upon this discovery the friar was arrested, and even when upon this arrest both his testicles were cut off, not one word was employed that was not taken directly from the text of scripture, and these excerpts were all applied so aptly to this totally incongruous subject matter that no one, no matter how grave, could refrain from a laugh, even as no one, no matter how giddy, did not feel incensed to behold sacred scripture being travestied in this sort of burlesque. And yet there were some present who said it was part of God's own secret plan that, since so many friars had made such an invete-rate habit of adulterating God's word, friar-mimics should final-ly spring up who could outfriar the friars, beat them at their own game, and (as the saying goes) use their own weapons to finish them off. But if it is wrong, and it certainly is, to abuse sacred scripture for bawdy amusement, it is still more wrong to abuse it for slandering some other person as you do. Nor does it mitigate

scribis, quem illi scis amicum esse. Imo tanto peccas impensius.
Etenim si ista praedicasses apud quempiam, cui Erasmus esset
odio, alienasses duntaxat eum, qui iam ante fuisset alienus, nunc
vero quoad per te fieri potest, auulsisti coniunctissimum.

5   Quamobrem, quod ante dicebam, cum adolescentiae tuae mitem illam, ac modestam indolem, animo mecum reuoluerem,
non potui profecto, vt non dolere satis, ita nec satis vsque admirari, nascentem istam tibi, maturioribus annis, in eo vitae statu,
quae tota non humilitatem modo, sed et despectum sui pro-
10   fitetur, (vt ne quid dicam grauius) immodestiam. [N₁] Cuius ego
rei causas dum tacitus atque admirabundus inquiro, praeter
hostem illum communem, cuius occulto suggestu prope vniuersa vicia velut ab impuro fonte promanant, praeterque satellites
eius quosdam, quorum inuidiam video simplicitatem tuam suis
15   infecisse virulentijs, Sentio certe nonnullam huius veneni partem ex affectu quodam suboriri tibi, non nouo quidem illo nec
inusitato mortalibus, Caeterum quo non alius humanas res
grauioribus malis afflixerit. Is est adfectus ille quo quisque fere
occulto quodam fauore sui, sic in suum propendet ordinem, vt
20   eius vicia nec ipse cernere, nec ferre possit indicantem.
        Hoc ipso affectu hallucinatum te zelo quodam video, sed im-
perito stimulari, vt religionum studio de illo dicas male, qui de
religiosis omnibus impendio meretur bene, nec vsquam tamen
impensius, quam quum id ipsum agit, quod tu calumniando
25   conaris in odium atque inuidiam trahere. Nam "quoties
oblatrat," inquis, "contra sacra religionis instituta, contra de-
uotas religiosorum ceremonias, contra vitae asperitatem, contra
sanctam solitudinem, demum contra omnia quae suae vagabundae minime correspondent vitae et conuersationi?" Haec tua
30   verba quum legerem, facile certe deprehendi quod te calcar
extimulet, nempe zelus in religionem tuam. Equidem haud du-

---

5 Quamobrem,] Quamobrem *1520; no para. 1520;* dicebam,] *1520*ᵃ, dicebam *1520*ᵐ
8 tibi,] tibi *1520;* annis,] *1520*ᵃ, annis *1520*ᵐ   9–10 profitetur,] profitetur *1520*   11
causas] causas, *1520;* inquiro,] *1520*ᵃ, inquiro *1520*ᵐ   13 promanant] permanant
*1520*ᵐ, permaneant *1520*ᵃ   14 video] video, *1520*   15 virulentijs,] *1520*ᵃ,
virulentijs. *1520*ᵐ   17 mortalibus,] mortalibus. *1520*   21 Hoc] *No para. 1520*   26
oblatrat,] oblatrat *1520*   26–27 deuotas] *1520*ᵐ, deuotaa *1520*ᵃ   27 vitae] *1520*ᵃ,
vite *1520*ᵐ   29 conuersationi?] conuersationi. *1520*

the offense that you are writing to someone you know is his friend; indeed, that makes it all the worse. For if you had said these things to someone who hated Erasmus you would merely have alienated someone who was alienated already. But in fact you have done all you could to estrange one of his dearest friends.

Thus, as I already said, when I thought back on the mild, modest nature you had as a youth, it gave me no end of grief and amazement to find out that your greater maturity, in a state of life completely committed not just to humility but to self-abnegation as well, could give rise to this sort of immodesty, which could easily be called something worse. As I ponder in silent amazement what caused this distemper, I sense that the blame lies not only with that common foe at whose covert suggestion, as if from a tainted spring, almost all faults arise, and not only with those accomplices of his who have infected your simplicity with the virulence of their envy; at least some of this poison derives from a certain kind of passion which is certainly not new or uncommon to mortals but which has afflicted mankind with more serious evils than any other kind. I refer to that passion of covert self-indulgence which makes almost everyone so partial to his own order of existence that he can neither see its faults by himself nor let anyone else point them out to him.

You were blinded with this very passion, I see, when your misguided zeal and devotion to religious orders goaded you into speaking ill of a man who deserves very well of everyone in those orders, and never better than when he is doing the very thing you are trying to twist into something hateful and invidious. For you say, "How often he clamors against the holy observances of religious orders, against the devout ceremonies of the religious, against austerity of living, against holy solitude, and, in summary, against everything that is not to be reconciled with his vagabond life-style and conduct!" Upon reading these words I could easily tell what sort of spur must be goading you on, namely zeal for your own religious order. I have no doubt at all that there is

bito neminem esse virum vsquam bonum, cui non religiosorum
ordines omnes eximie chari cordique sint, quos et ipse certe non
amaui modo semper verumetiam perquam reuerenter colui,
vtpote suetus praehonorare pauperrimum commendatione vir-
5 tutis, quam si quem vel nobilitent diuitiae, vel natalium splendor
illustret. Verumenimuero [N₁v] quemadmodum cupiam reliquos mortales omnes, vos ac vestros ordines, eximia quadam
charitate prosequi, exigentibus id meritis nimirum vestris,
quorum ego suffragijs huius orbis miseriam nonnihil leuari
10 crediderim (nam si multum valet oratio iusti assidua, quantum
necesse est valeat oratio tam indefessa tot milium?) sic e diuerso
optauerim, ne vos quidem ipsos tam prauo studio vobis indul-
gere, vt si quis res attingat vestras, laboretis aut bene dicta narrando deprauare, aut perperam interpretando bene cogitata
15 corrumpere.

Nescio quid eius verba tuo palato sapiant sic adfecto, verum
hoc certe scio, neminem hactenus repperisse me, qui quae scripsit ille, sic acceperit, tanquam religiosorum reprehendat ceremonias, sed eos potius, qui vel superstitiosius abutuntur, vel
20 innituntur periculosius, ac rem ex se non malam, sua freti stultitia vertunt in perniciem. Qua ex sorte plus satis esse multos tu
quoque opinor, quantumuis in tuos propensus, non inficiabere,
neque enim quicquam est vsquam tam sanctum, quod callidus
hostis non satagat aliqua semper techna viciare, qui vt est deo,
25 omnibus in rebus oppositus, conatur haud aliter ex nostris bonis
operari mala, quam ex malis nostris bona peragit deus. Quam
multos inuenias, qui suae sectae ceremonijs haud paulo plus
quam ipsis dei praeceptionibus incumbunt? An non integros
reperies ordines, qui propter suos ritus cum alijs digladiantur
30 ordinibus, dum semet inuicem student non esse quidem, sed
haberi sanctiores, idque de priuatis vtrinque ceremonijs, ijsdemque crebro non vsquequaque necessarijs, cum de serijs interim

---

2 omnes] *1520*ᵃ, omnes, *1520*ᵐ   7 omnes] *1520*ᵐ, omens *1520*ᵃ   8 prosequi,]
prosequi *1520*   11 milium?)] milium) *1520*ᵐ, milium, *1520*ᵃ   13 vestras, laboretis]
*1520*ᵃ, vestras laboretis, *1520*ᵐ; bene dicta] *1520*ᵐ, benedicta *1520*ᵃ   16 Nescio] *No
para. 1520*   18 acceperit] *1520*ᵐ, acciperet *1520*ᵃ   27 inuenias] *1520*ᵐ, inuenies
*1520*ᵃ   28 incumbunt?] incumbunt. *1520*   29 reperies] *1520*ᵐ, reperias *1520*ᵃ
31 de pruiuatis] *1520*ᵐ, deprauatis *1520*ᵃ   32 serijs] *1520*ᵐ, sociis *1520*ᵃ; interim]
*1520*ᵃ, interim, *1520*ᵐ

no good man anywhere who does not feel a great deal of heartfelt esteem for all religious orders, and certainly I myself have
always regarded them not only with love but also with the utmost
reverence, since it is my custom to honor the poorest man commended by virtue more than anyone distinguished for his riches
or admired for an illustrious birth. But even so, just as I want all
other mortals to be deeply devoted to you and your orders, as
your merits deserve, of course, since I am inclined to believe that
the misery of this world is substantially alleviated by your pleading in its behalf (for if one just man's diligent prayer does a great
deal of good, how much good must be done by the incessant
prayer of so many thousands?), I would similarly hope that not
even you would be so inordinately prejudiced in your own favor
that if anyone aims any remark at your practices you will try to
pervert things well said by the way you report them or to damn
things well thought by the tendentious way you construe them.

I do not know how his words taste to your diseased palate, but
I know this for sure: I have never met anyone yet who interpreted his writings as if he were condemning the devout ceremonies of the religious and not rather those people who abuse
them superstitiously or rely on them too recklessly and thus
foolishly turn to their own peril a practice not bad in itself. I
think not even you will deny that there are too many people of
this sort, no matter how partial you are to your fellows. For
nothing in the world is too holy for our cunning foe to attempt to
corrupt it by some sort of trickery, for since he is God's opposite
in everything, he seeks to produce evil from our good in the
same way that God procures good from our evil. How many you
can find who place far more importance on the ceremonies of
their sect than on God's own commandments! Do you not find
whole orders doing battle with other orders for the sake of their
rituals as each works not to be but to seem holier, each relying on
its own private ceremonies which are frequently less than essential, while they all share a common position on serious, more

magisque ad rem pertinentibus tam omnes [N₂] in commune
consentiant, quam non admodum anxie quidam curant obseruare? In quas factiones, in quot sectas, idem se scindit ordo?
Tum qui tumultus? quae consurgunt tragoediae, vel ob alium
5 colorem, vel ob aliter cinctam vestem, aut aliud quippiam ceremoniolae si non omnino despuendae, at certe non satis dignae
propter quam exulet charitas? Quam multi sunt, quod multo
certe deterrimum est, qui religionis freti fiducia, sic intus cristas
erigunt, vt spatiari sibi videantur in coelis, ac solaribus insidentes
10 radijs humi repentem populum tanquam formicas e sublimi despicere, nec id prophanos modo, verum sacerdotum quoque
quicquid est extra septa illa claustrorum? ita plerisque nihil est
sanctum, nisi quod faciunt ipsi.
   Multum prouidit deus cum omnia institueret communia,
15 multum Christus cum in commune conatus est rursus a priuato
reuocare mortales. Sensit nimirum corruptam mortalitatis naturam non sine communitatis damno deamare priuatum, id quod
res omnibus in rebus docet. Nec enim tantum suum quisque
praedium amat, aut suam quisque pecuniam, nec suo duntaxat
20 generi studet, aut suo quisque collegio, sed vt quicque est quod
aliquo modo vocemus nostrum, ita in se illud affectus nostros a
communium cultu rerum seuocat. Sic nostra quoque ieiunia
publicis anteponimus. Sic vbi diuum quempiam selegimus nobis, pluris illum saepe quam decem potiores facimus, nempe
25 quod ille sit noster, cum reliqui diui sint omnium. Iam si quis
quid taxet huiusmodi, non is plebeculae damnat pietatem, sed
admonet potius ne pietatis praetextu surrepat impietas. Nam vt
nemo gentem aliquam reprehenderit, quae diuum quempiam
nominatim [N₂v] idonea de causa coluerit, ita nonnullis fortasse
30 videbuntur suae pietati plus satis obsecuti quidam, qui in sui diui

---

2 anxie] *1520ᵃ*, anxie, *1520ᵐ*   2–3 obseruare?] obseruare. *1520*   5–6 ceremo-
niolae] ceremoniolae, *1520ᵐ*, ceremoniale, *1520ᵃ*   7 charitas?] charitas. *1520*   10
populum] *1520ᵃ*, populum, *1520ᵐ*   12 septa] *1520ᵃ*, scepta *1520ᵐ*; claustrorum?]
claustrorum, *1520*   14 Multum] *No para. 1520*   15 est] *1520ᵃ*, est, *1520ᵐ*   16
mortalitatis] *1520ᵐ*, mortalitatis nostrae *1520ᵃ*   16–17 naturam] *1520ᵃ*, naturam,
1520ᵐ   20 collegio,] *1520ᵃ*, collegio: *1520ᵐ*   21 vocemus] *1520*, vocamus
1760   23 Sic vbi] *1520ᵐ*, Sicubi *1520ᵃ*   25–26 quis quid] *conj. 1760*, quis *1520*
29 nonnullis] *1520ᵃ*, non nullis *1520ᵐ*

meaningful matters just as surely as some men in orders are not very careful to live by it! Into what a variety of factions and how many sectarian movements one order can split! And then what a commotion, what tragic upheavals ensue on account of a different color, or a differently cinctured robe, or some other trivial ceremony that is possibly not altogether contemptible, but is certainly an unworthy pretext for banishing charity! And worst of all, certainly, how many there are who are encouraged by belonging to a religious order to conceive such a lofty self-image that they think they are walking in the heavens or that they themselves, perched on a sunbeam, look down from the heights on the general populace creeping like ants on the ground, and not only on the laity but also on the whole class of priests who live outside the cloister! So true is it that for many of them, nothing is holy apart from what they do themselves.

God showed great foresight when he instituted all things in common; Christ showed as much when he tried to recall mortals again to what is common from what is private. For he perceived that corrupt mortal nature cannot cherish what is private without detriment to what is common, as experience shows in all aspects of life. For not only does everyone love his own plot of land or his own money, not only does everyone cherish his own family or his own set of colleagues, but to the extent that we call anything our own it absorbs our affections and diverts them from the service of the common good. So, too, we prefer our own fast-days to public ones, and so, after we have selected some saint as our own, we often prize this one more than ten better ones just because he is ours while the other saints belong to everyone. Now if anyone challenges anything of this sort, he is not condemning popular piety but rather warning us not to let impiety creep in under some pious pretext. For, though no one would criticize any nation for fostering the cult of some saint when it had a good reason to do so, some will probably feel that his admirers are carrying their piety too far when as a special

peculiarem gratiam, diuum hosticae gentis praesidem detractum templo proiecerint in coenum. Atqui ritus huiusmodi pri-
uataeque ceremoniae, vt interdum male cedunt apud nos, ita
non semper opinor apud vos cedunt bene, sed apud plerosque vt
5 quicque magis est proprium, ita plurimum habetur in precio.
Hinc pluris multi ceremonias aestimant suas quam cenobij,
cenobij quam ordinis, tum quicquid est ordini proprium, quam
quae sunt omni religioni communia, sed ea tamen quae sunt
religiosorum pluris aliquanto faciunt, quam vilia illa atque hu-
10 milia quae non sint illis vllo modo priuata, sed cum omni prorsus
populo Christiano communia, cuiusmodi sunt virtutes istae
plebeae, fides, spes, charitas, dei timor, humilitas, atque id genus
aliae. Neque nouum est istud, imo iam diu est quod Christus
populo exprobrauit electo, "Quare et vos transgredimini man-
15 data dei propter traditiones vestras?"
    Negabunt ista non dubito etiam ij qui faciunt. Quis enim tam
vecors est vt fateatur pluris se facere ceremonias suas quam
praecepta dei, quibus nisi paruerit, illas ipsas nouit inutiles? Verbis haud dubie si rogentur, recte responderint: factis fidem dic-
20 tis abrogabunt. Mentiri credar nisi sint religiosuli quidam certis
in locis tam obstinati silentij, vt in quadris ambulacris illis magno
conduci non possint, vti vel summisse mussitent, qui pedem
latum in alterutrum subducti latus haud vereantur atrocibus
intonare conuicijs. Non desunt qui metuerent su[N$_3$]peruen-
25 turum daemonem, qui viuos in orcum auferat, si quippiam con-
suetarum demutarent vestium, quos nihil mouet, cum pecuniam
congerunt, aduersantur abbati, ac subinde supplantant. An
paucos esse putas quibus habeatur multis lachrymis expiandum
piaculum, si versiculum omitterent in precibus horarijs, quibus
30 ne scrupulus quidem timoris vllus oritur, cum saepe pessimis
atque infamatricibus impiantur fabulis, ijsdemque longissimis

---

8 sunt omni] *1520*^{m}, sint omni *1520*^{a} 9 aliquanto] *1520*^{a}, aliquando *1520*^{m} 11
istae] *1520*^{a}, iste *1520*^{m} 13 aliae.] *1520*^{a}, aliae *1520*^{m}; Neque] *1520*^{m}, Nec enim
1520^a 14 electo,] electo. *1520*   15 vestras?] *1520*^{a}, vestras, *1520*^{m} 16
Negabunt] *No para.* *1520*; ij] *1520*^{m}, hij *1520*^{a} 19 rogentur,] *1520*^{a}, rogentur
1520^m; responderint:] responderint, *1520*   22 summisse] *1520*^{m}, summissi *1520*^{a}
24–25 superuenturum] *1520*^{a}, susuperuenturum *1520*^{m} 26 demutarent] *1520*^{a},
demutarint *1520*^{m} 30–31 saepe . . . impiantur] *1520*^{m}, sese . . . impiant *1520*^{a}

favor to their own saint they drag the patron saint of an enemy nation from the church and throw him in the mud. But just as rituals of this sort and private ceremonies sometimes work out badly for us, by the same token, I think, they do not always work out well for you; and among many of you, the more exclusively something is yours, the more value you place on it. For this reason many prize their own ceremonies more than those of their religious house, their own house's ceremonies more than those of their order, and whatever is exclusive to their order more than everything that is common to all religious orders, while they prize all that pertains to the religious somewhat more than they do those lowly and humble concerns that are not only not private to them but are common to the whole Christian people, such as those plebeian virtues of faith, hope, charity, fear of God, humility, and others of similar character. Nor is this a new problem: long ago Christ rebuked his chosen people by saying, "Why do even you transgress God's commandments for the sake of your own traditions?"

I am sure that the very people who do such things will deny that they do them. For who is idiotic enough to admit that he prizes his own ceremonies more than God's precepts when he knows that unless he abides by those precepts his own ceremonies are useless? Doubtless they will supply the right answers if asked, but their actions make their words ring false. Put me down for a liar if there are not some wretched fellows in orders at various locations who are so stubborn about keeping silence that you could not pay them enough to make them whisper even discreetly in their cloister walks, while if they are diverted one foot to either side they are not at all coy about thundering out dire abuse. There are some who are afraid that a demon will swoop down and take them directly to hell if they change any item in their customary dress, whereas they feel no qualms about amassing money, opposing their abbot, and often supplanting him. Do you think there are only a few who consider it a foul and extremely lamentable sin if they leave out one line in saying their office, but feel not the least scruple of fear when they often befoul themselves with outrageous and slanderous gossip even

etiam precibus longioribus? Ita nimirum culicem comminuunt, elephantem deglutientes integrum.

  Sane multo sunt plures quam vellem, qui vel ipso religiosi titulo longe supra mortalium sortem sibi videntur ascendere.
5 Sed horum bona pars deliri magis, quam mali, Qui tam suauiter insaniunt, vt quicquid illis amens dictat animus, id protinus sic accipiant, velut inspiretur a deo, et sese credant interim in tercium rapi coelum, cum verius arrepti sint in tercium gradum phrenesis. At illi multo furiunt periculosius, qui vsque adeo su-
10 perbiunt, ac sibi videntur sanctuli, vt non contemnant modo, verum condemnent etiam reliquos mortales omnes prae se, nec alia fere de causa quam quod superstitiose nimium suis inherent ritibus, suis gloriantur obseruantiolis, quibus nonnulli sibi tum quoque videntur tuti, cum talibus fulti patrocinijs quodlibet ar-
15 mantur ad facinus.

  Equidem noui quendam instituto vitae religiosum, idque ex eo genere quod hodie ducitur, et vere ducitur vt ego certe sentio, religiosissimum. Is quum non iam nouicius, sed qui multos annos in regularibus [N₃v] (vt vocant) obseruantijs insumpsisset,
20 eoque promouisset in illis, vt etiam praeficeretur cenobio, dei tamen praeceptorum quam monastici ritus indiligentior e vicio in vicium prolabitur, eo tandem progressus, vt scelus omnium atrocissimum, et supra quam credi possit execrandum des- tinaret animo, Imo non simplex scelus, sed multiplici foecun-
25 dum scelere, vt qui decreuerit addere cedibus et parricidio sacri- legium. Qui cum tot patrandis facinoribus impar sibi solus vi- deretur, aliquot ad se sicarios ac sectores adsciscit. conficiunt fa- cinus omnium quae quidem ego viderim immanissimum. Com-

1 longioribus?] longioribus. *1520*   3 Sane] *No para. 1520*   4 titulo] *1520*ᵃ, titulo, *1520*ᵐ   5 mali, Qui tam] *1520*ᵃ, mali. Quidam *1520*ᵐ   7 accipiant] accipiunt *1520;* deo,] *1520*ᵃ, deo *1520*ᵐ; credant] credunt *1520*   9 furiunt] *1520,* furunt *conj. 1760*   14 patrocinijs] *1520*ᵃ, patrocinijs, *1520*ᵐ   15 facinus.] *1520*ᵃ, facinns, *1520*ᵐ 16 Equidem] *No para. 1520;* religiosum,] religiosum *1520*   17 ducitur vt] duci- tur, vt *1520;* sentio,] sentio *1520*   18 nouicius,] *1520*ᵃ, nouicius: *1520*ᵐ   19 (vt vocant)] vt vocant *1520*   20 illis,] *1520*ᵃ, illis *1520*ᵐ   23–24 destinaret] *1520*ᵐ, destinarat *1520*ᵃ   24 animo,] *1520*ᵃ, animo. *1520*ᵐ   25 cedibus] cedibus, *1520* 26–27 videretur,] *1520*ᵃ, videretur *1520*ᵐ   27 sicarios] *1520*ᵃ, sicarios, *1520*ᵐ; adsciscit.] adsciscit, *1520*   28 viderim] *1520*ᵐ, audierim *1520*ᵃ

longer than their longest prayers? Thus they strain at a gnat as they swallow an elephant whole.

Certainly there are many more than I would wish who suppose that the very title "religious" exalts them far beyond mortal constraints. But a good number of these people are mad without being particularly wicked, the ones who are so pleasantly deranged that they take every product of their addled brain as if it were divinely inspired and think they have been carried up into the third heaven when they have actually been carried away into the third stage of lunacy. But some are mad in a vastly more dangerous way, those who are so insolently assured of their own saintliness that they not only contemn but completely condemn other mortals compared with themselves, and for practically no other reason but that they themselves cling to their own rituals excessively and superstitiously and glory in their own trivial observances, by which some of them think they are protected even when they gird themselves with this sort of defensive equipment for all kinds of crime.

Indeed I know of a man who was formally one of the religious, and in fact he belonged to the order which is currently thought (rightly so, in my personal opinion) to be the most religious of all. Although he was no longer a novice but had already spent many years in what they call regular observances, and had advanced so far in them that he had even been chosen the head of his monastery, through paying less attention to God's precepts than to monastic ritual he slipped from one vice to another, finally sinking so low as to plot the most ghastly and unbelievably heinous crime, and indeed not a single crime but one pregnant with many and various crimes, for he planned to join murder and parricide with sacrilege. But since he did not think himself equal to perpetrating all these crimes by himself he recruited some killers and cutthroats to help him. They committed the most monstrous crime of any I have ever seen. They were arrested

prehensi conijciuntur in vincula. Neque rem tamen explicare decreui, et nominibus abstinebo noxiorum, ne quid obsolescentis inuidiae ordini renouetur innoxio. Verum vt quam ob rem institui narrare persequar, ab illis ego sceleratis audiui sicarijs,

5 cum ad religiosulum illum ventitarent in cubiculum, nunquam ante tractasse de flagitio, quam in priuatum eius introducti sacrarium, diuam virginem, flexis de more poplitibus, angelica salutatione propitiassent: ea re rite peracta, tum demum pure pieque consurgunt ad infandum facinus.

10 Atque vt illud quod dixi facinus multo fuit atrocissimum, ita quod nunc dicam, longe quidem in speciem mitius, ipsa re fortasse nec multo minus nocuit et certe multo nocuit latius. Erat Conuentriae fraterculus ex eo franciscanorum numero, qui nondum ad francisci regulam sunt reformati. Is in vrbe, in sub-

15 urbijs, in finitimis, in circumiectis oppidulis praedicauit, quicunque psalterium beatae virginis oraret cotidie, nunquam posse damnari. Pronis auribus audita res est, et libenter credita, quae viam tam procliuem aperuisset in coelum.

Ibi pastor quidam, homo probus et doctus, etsi stulte dictum

20 esse censebat tamen aliquantisper dissimulat, ra[N₄]tus ex ea re nihil etiam oriturum mali, populum enim, quo effusius in beatae virginis cultum sese daret, eo plus hausturum pietatis. At vbi tandem recognoscens ouile deprehenderit ea scabie vehementer infectum gregem: pessimum quemque in illo psalterio maxime

25 religiosum esse, non alia mente quam quod sponderent sibi quiduis audendi licentiam, neque enim fas habebant quicquam dubitare de coelo, quod tam grauis autor, fraterculus e coelo lapsus, tanta cum fide promiserat: tum vero coepit admonere

---

3 inuidiae] inuidiae, *1520*   4 sceleratis] *1520*ᵃ, seleratis *1520*ᵐ   6 priuatum] *1520*ᵃ, priuatum, *1520*ᵐ   7 virginem,] virginem *1520*; poplitibus,] poplitibus *1520*   8 propitiassent:] propitiassent, *1520*ᵐ, propitiassent. *1520*ᵃ   10 Atque] *No para. 1520*; facinus] *1520*ᵐ, faeinus *1520*ᵃ   11 dicam,] dicam *1520*; speciem] *1520*ᵃ, spetiem *1520*ᵐ   12 nocuit et] *1520*ᵐ, nocuit, *1520*ᵃ; latius] *1520*ᵃ, lacius *1520*ᵐ   14 vrbe,] vrbe *1520*   17 credita,] *1520*ᵃ, credita *1520*ᵐ   18 coelum.] coelum, *1520*   19 Ibi] *No para. 1520*; quidam,] quidam *1520*; doctus,] *1520*ᵃ, doctus *1520*ᵐ   20 censebat] censebat, *1520*   21 enim,] enim *1520*   22 daret,] *1520*ᵃ, daret *1520*ᵐ   23 deprehenderit] *1520*ᵐ, deprehendit *1520*ᵃ   24 gregem:] *1520*ᵃ, gregem *1520*ᵐ   25 sponderent] *1520*ᵃ, sponderent, *1520*ᵐ   27 autor,] autor *1520*   28 lapsus,] *1520*ᵃ, lapsus *1520*ᵐ; promiserat:] promiserat, *1520*ᵐ, promiserat. *1520*ᵃ

and thrown into prison. But I do not plan to unfold the whole incident, and I will withhold the names of the guilty to avoid stirring up any forgotten ill will against their guiltless order. To come to the one point that I had in mind in beginning the story, I heard from these villainous killers that whenever they came to the chamber of that would-be man of religion they never discussed plans for their felony before being ushered into his private chapel to kneel in the approved fashion and pray to the Blessed Virgin with a Hail Mary; it was not until these devotions were rightly concluded that they purely and piously rose to commit their unspeakable crime.

And just as the crime I have mentioned was by far the most ghastly of all, so the one I am now going to mention, though it appears to be much more innocuous, actually may have done little less harm, and the harm that it did was undoubtedly much more widespread. There was a certain friar at Coventry who belonged to that group of Franciscans who have not yet been reformed according to the Rule of St. Francis. This man preached in the city, in the suburbs, and in the neighboring and outlying villages that whoever said the psalter of the Blessed Virgin every day could never be damned. What he said fell upon eager ears and was gladly believed because it opened up such an easy road to heaven.

There was a certain local pastor, a good and learned man, who considered the friar's words to be foolish but nevertheless looked the other way for a while, reasoning that the business would not lead to any real harm, since the more lavish the people's devotion to the cult of the Blessed Virgin the more piety they would imbibe from it. But at length, on inspecting his pastoral fold, he discerned that his flock had been gravely infected with that scabrous error, that the very worst people were those who recited that psalter most religiously, and that they did so precisely in order to secure themselves a license to do anything at all, since they thought it a sin to retain any doubts about heaven when so weighty an authority as that friar had dropped out of heaven to promise it to them with so much conviction. Then the pastor began to admonish the people not to put too much faith in

populum, non nimis esse fidendum si psalterium psallerent, etiam si vno die decies, bene certe facturos, qui bene dicerent, modo non ea dicerent fiducia, qua iam nonnulli ceperant: alioqui, satius esse vti et preces ipsas omitterent, modo et facinora
5 quaedam, quae sub earum patrocinio fidentius committebantur, omitterentur simul.

Haec cum e suggestu diceret, mirum quam indignanter auditur: exsibilatur, exploditur, passimque velut hostis Mariae traducitur. Frater alio die conscendit pulpitum, orditur ab eo the-
10 mate, quo maxime perstringat rectorem, "Dignare me laudare te virgo sacrata, da mihi virtutem contra hostes tuos." Nam eodem themate scotum quendam disputaturum Parrisijs de virginis immaculata conceptione ferunt vsum, qui luteciam in momento delatum, periclitante scilicet alioqui beata virgine, millia
15 passuum plusquam trecenta mentiuntur. Quid multis opus est verbis? facile persuadet volentibus frater, et fatuum et impium esse pastorem.

Dum res flagrabat maxime, fors accidit, ipse vt Conuentriam peterem, visurus ibi sororem. Vix equo descenderam, quum pro-
20 ponitur et mihi quaestio, an qui quotidie precaretur psalterium beatae virginis damnari possit. Irrisi problema ridiculum. Admoneor illico periculose factum, quod sic respon[N₄v]derim: sanctissimum quendam patrem, eundemque doctissimum, contra praedicasse. Contempsi rem totam, vt quae nihil attineret ad
25 me.

Protinus inuitor ad conuiuium, promitto, venio. Ecce intrat frater senex, Silicernium, grauis: puer a tergo sequitur cum co-

---

1 nimis] *1520*ᵐ, minus *1520*ᵃ   3 ceperant:] ceperant, *1520*ᵐ, coeperant, *1520*ᵃ   3–
4 alioqui,] alioqui *1520*   5 committebantur,] *1520*ᵃ, committebantur *1520*ᵐ   7
Haec] *No para. 1520;* indignanter] *1520*ᵃ, indignātur, *1520*ᵐ   7–8 auditur:] *conj.*
1760, aditur, *1520 (see commentary)*   9–10 themate,] *1520*ᵃ, themate *1520*ᵐ   10
rectorem,] rectorem. *1520*ᵐ, pastorem *1520*ᵃ   13 immaculata] *1520*ᵐ, immaculatae
*1520*ᵃ   14 delatum,] *1520*ᵃ, delatum *1520*ᵐ; virgine,] *1520*ᵃ, virgine *1520*ᵐ   18
Dum] *No para. 1520;* maxime,] *1520*ᵃ, maxime: *1520*ᵐ; accidit,] *1520*ᵃ, accidit: *1520*ᵐ
19 sororem.] *1520*ᵃ, sororem, *1520*ᵐ; descenderam,] *1520*ᵃ, descenderam: *1520*ᵐ
21 virginis] virginis, *1520*   22 responderim:] rñderim, *1520*ᵐ, responderim *1520*ᵃ
23 doctissimum,] doctissimum *1520*   25 me.] *1520*ᵃ, me, *1520*ᵐ   26 Protinus]
No para. 1520   27 grauis:] grauis, *1520*ᵐ, grauis, tetricus, *1520*ᵃ

reciting that psalter, even if they did it ten times a day. He said they would certainly be acting virtuously if they said it virtuously and did not say it with that assurance which some had already conceived; otherwise they would do better to omit the prayers themselves if they would only omit along with them the various crimes which were being committed more confidently beneath their protection.

When he spoke these words from his pulpit they fell on completely intolerant ears; he was hissed, shouted down, and reviled on all sides as an enemy of Mary. On another day, the friar ascended the pulpit and took as his text what was obviously a swipe at the rector, "Blessed Virgin, permit me to praise you; give me strength to encounter your foes." For they say that a certain Scotus employed the same theme to begin the debate on the Blessed Virgin's immaculate conception at Paris, to which they falsely claim he was brought in an instant from three hundred miles away, as if she needed Scotus to come to her rescue. What need to say more? The friar easily persuaded his partisan hearers that the minister was both fatuous and impious.

At the most tumultuous stage of the incident I myself happened to set out for Coventry to visit my sister there. I had barely gotten off my horse when the question was put to me, too, whether anyone who said the psalter of the Blessed Virgin every day could be damned. I laughed it off as a laughable problem. I was instantly warned that my answer was rash and that it contradicted the preaching of a certain most holy and most learned father. I scorned the whole business as one which in no way concerned me.

I was promptly invited to dinner, I accepted, I went. Lo and behold, in walked a cadaverous and somber old friar, followed

dicibus. Illico sensi mihi paratas lites, accumbimus, et ne quid
periret temporis, extemplo res proponitur ab hospite. frater,
quod ante praedicarat, idem respondit: ipse tacebam. Neque
enim libenter memet disceptationibus et odiosis et infructuosis
5   immisceo. Tandem rogarunt et quid mihi videretur, qui, cum
tacere non licuit, respondi quod sentiebam, sed paucis et neglectim. Ibi infit frater oratione meditata longaque, et quae binis
ferme concionibus essent satis obblaterabat in coena. Summa
rationum tota pendebat a miraculis, quorum nobis effutiebat
10 iam e Mariali multa, tum quaedam ex alijs eiusdem farinae libellis, quos afferri iubet in mensam quo narrationi maior accedat
autoritas. Quum aliquando tandem perorasset, ego modeste respondi, Primum, nihil esse toto illo sermone dictum quo res
persuadeatur illis, si qui forte quae recensuerat miracula non
15 admitterent, quod fors accidere salua Christi fide possit: Quae
tamen, vt maxime vera sint, ad rem haud quaquam satis habere
momenti. Nam vt facile reperias principem, qui condonet interdum vel hostibus aliquid ad preces matris, ita nullus est vsquam
tam stultus qui promulget legem, qua suorum audaciam in sese
20 prouocet, impunitate promissa proditoribus, quicunque gene-
tricem eius certo demereantur obsequio. Multis vltro citroque
dictis effeci tandem, vt ille tolleretur laudibus, ipse pro stulto
riderer. Quin eo res euasit denique, prauo hominum studio suis
vicijs persona [O₁] pietatis fauentium, vt vix aliquando cohibita
25 sit, adnitente quantis maxime posset viribus episcopo.

---

2 temporis,] *1520*ᵃ, temporis *1520*ᵐ; hospite.] *1520*ᵃ, hospite, *1520*ᵐ; frater,] frater
1520   3 respondit:] respondit, *1520*ᵐ, respondit. *1520*ᵃ   4 disceptationibus et
odiosis] disceptationibus, et odiosis, *1520*   5 rogarunt] rogarunt: *1520*ᵐ, rogarunt,
*1520*ᵃ; qui,] qui *1520*   6 licuit,] *1520*ᵃ, licuit *1520*ᵐ   7 frater] *1520*ᵃ, frater, *1520*ᵐ
8 satis] satis, *1520;* obblaterabat] oblatrabat *1520*ᵐ, eblaterabat *1520*ᵃ (*see commentary*)   9–10 effutiebat iam] *1520*ᵐ, iam effutiebat *1520*ᵃ   10 multa,] multa *1520*ᵐ,
multa: *1520*ᵃ   10–11 libellis,] libellis: *1520*   11 mensam quo narrationi] *1520*ᵃ,
mensam: quo narrationi *1520*ᵐ   12 perorasset,] *1520*ᵃ, perorasset: *1520*ᵐ   12–
13 respondi, Primum,] respondi Primum *1520*ᵐ, respondi, primum *1520*ᵃ   14 illis,]
illis: *1520*   15 admitterent,] *1520*ᵃ, admitterent: *1520*ᵐ; possit:] possit. *1520*   16
tamen,] tamen *1520;* sint,] *1520*ᵃ, sint: *1520*ᵐ   17 principem,] *1520*ᵃ, principem:
*1520*ᵐ   23 euasit denique,] euasit, denique *1520*ᵐ, euasit denique *1520*ᵃ

by a boy carrying books. I knew right then that a fight was in store for me. We sat down, and the host, not wasting any time about it, instantly put the question. The friar responded as he had preached earlier. I myself said nothing. For I take no pleasure in getting involved in vexatious and pointless disputes. They finally asked me what I thought, and since they would not let me keep quiet I said what I thought, but in only a few careless words. Then the friar launched into a long, rehearsed speech, and he blurted out over that dinner enough verbiage for nearly two sermons. The whole gist of his reasoning was dependent on miracles, many of which he rattled off to us from the *Mariale* along with some he had taken from other such books, which he had the boy bring to the table to lend greater authority to his exposition. When he had finished his speech at long last, I modestly answered that, first of all, nothing he had said in that entire sermon would seem really persuasive to anyone who did not accept the miracles that he had reported, a response which would not necessarily contravene Christian faith, and that even if those miracles were true they were hardly an adequate basis for the thesis at hand. For while you might easily find a prince who would sometimes pardon even his enemies at his mother's entreaty, no prince anywhere is foolish enough to promulgate a law which would encourage his own subjects to defy him by promising immunity to every traitor who propitiated his mother with a set form of flattery. After a lengthy exchange, all I finally achieved was that the friar was praised to the skies whereas I was laughed down as a fool. Indeed, through the misguided devotion of people indulging their own vices under a pretext of piety, the affair finally went so far that only the most forceful action on the part of the bishop could put a stop to it at all.

   Non haec eo commemoro, quod vel religionem velim religiosorum quorundam degrauare sceleribus, quum et salutares
herbas et pestiferas eadem terra progerminet, neque quod
eorum ritum improbem, qui subinde diuam salutant virginem,
5 quo nihil potest esse salubrius, Sed quod vsque adeo quidam sibi
fidunt in talibus, vt ab his potissimum securitatem sibi sumant ad
flagitia. Haec sunt atque huiusmodi, quae taxanda censet Erasmus: cui quisquis irascitur, cur non diuo succenset Hieronymo?
cur non alijs item sanctissimis patribus, qui religiosorum vicia et
10 vberius multo commemorant et multo acerbius insectantur? Vt
callidus est antiquus serpens? vt aconita semper oblinit melle, ne
quis reformidet toxicum? vt gustum nobis inficit ac citat nauseam quoties offertur antidotus? Qui nos admirantur et nostra
facta collaudant, qui beatos appellant et sanctos, hoc est qui nos
15 seducunt et ex stultis reddunt insanos, Hi nimirum candidi sunt
et beneuoli: hi vicissim boni pijque vocantur a nobis. At qui
multo magis vtilem nobis impendunt operam, qui vt quales vere
sumus, tales vere nos nobis indicent, Canes illi sunt latratores,
arrosores, maleuolentes, inuidi, et haec audiunt qui nullius vicia
20 perstringunt nominatim, et audiunt ab his qui suis ipsorum sordibus aperte conspergunt alios. Itaque nunc non alibi modo
locum esse video sed ne claustrum quidem dicto clausum esse
comico, "obsequium amicos, veritas odium parit." Hie[O₁v]ro-
nymo quondam veritas opprobrata est a calumniatore Ruffino,
25 cum eam omnes aequi bonique lectores aequi bonique consulerent. Quod Erasmus vero non vere tantum verum etiam
tanta scripsit cum gratia, vt ei per litteras vndique magnae sint
actae gratiae ab ordinis cuiusque religiosis, et praesertim tui, Id

---

1 Non] *No para. 1520*   5 salubrius,] *1520*ᵃ, salubrius. *1520*ᵐ   8 irascitur,] *1520*ᵃ,
irascitur *1520*ᵐ; Hieronymo?] *1520*ᵃ, Hieronymo: *1520*ᵐ   9 patribus,] patribus:
*1520*ᵐ, patribus? *1520*ᵃ   10 commemorant] commemorant: *1520*ᵐ, commemorant,
*1520*ᵃ; acerbius insectantur] *1520*ᵐ, insectantur acerbius *1520*ᵃ   11 melle,] *1520*ᵃ,
melle: *1520*ᵐ   12–13 nauseam] nauseam: *1520*   13 antidotus] *1520*ᵐ, antidotum
*1520*ᵃ   14 collaudant,] *1520*ᵃ, collaudant: *1520*ᵐ   15 seducunt] *1520*ᵃ, seducunt:
*1520*ᵐ; insanos,] *1520*ᵃ, insanos. *1520*ᵐ   16 At qui] *1520*ᵃ, Atqui *1520*ᵐ   18
indicent,] *1520*ᵃ, indicent. *1520*ᵐ   19 audiunt] audiunt, *1520*   20–21 sordibus]
sordibus, *1520*   22 video] video, *1520*   23 amicos,] *1520*ᵃ, amicos *1520*ᵐ   25
lectores] lectores, *1520*   26 tantum] tantum, *1520*   28 gratiae] gratiae, *1520;* tui,]
tui. *1520*

.I do not record these incidents out of any desire to implicate the religious life itself in the offenses committed by some men in religious orders, since the same soil produces both wholesome and noxious herbs, or to criticize the devout practice of those who frequently pray to the Blessed Virgin (for that is a most wholesome devotion), but rather to stress that some people place so much reliance on such rituals that these are precisely what gives them the confidence to commit serious sins. It is this sort of thing that Erasmus believes we should challenge, and if anyone feels angry with him, why not also resent St. Jerome? Why not also resent the other holy fathers who both recorded the faults of the religious at much greater length and attacked them with much greater bitterness? How cunning is that ancient serpent! How he always flavors his toxins with honey so that no one will balk at the poison! How he sickens our taste and arouses our nausea every time we are offered an antidote! Those who admire us and praise what we do, those who hail us as blessed and saintly, in other words those who seduce us and turn us from fools into madmen, these are obviously candid, benevolent fellows, and these we call good, pious men in return. But those who work to do something much more useful for us, to make us see ourselves as we really are, those men are barking dogs, snappish, malicious, and envious, and those words are used against them even when they never attack the vices of anybody by name and when those who describe them this way openly smear their own filth upon others. And so I see that now there is no place where that comic saying does not apply, since not even the cloister is closed to it: "Flattery is the way to make friends, truthfulness to make enemies." Jerome's truthfulness was once held against him by the slanderer Rufinus even though every fair, virtuous reader construed it in a fair, virtuous way. But you take what Erasmus has written not only truthfully but also so very graciously that he has received from all sides written expressions of deep gratitude

nunc tandem satis insulse superbeque calumnijs et conuicijs op-
pugnatur abs te, cuius professio tota fundamentis humilitatis
innititur, qua videlicet humilitate tu non tuam tantum sectam
magnificis effers laudibus, nempe sacris institutis, sancta soli-
5 tudine, deuotis ceremonijs, vigilijs, asperitate vitae, ieiunijs, sed
illum quoque pedibus tanquam canem calcas, dum latrantem
facis, et vagabundae conuersationis. Quae verba cum lego tam
religioso perscripta calamo, videor mihi propemodum humiles
illas sancti pharisaei preces audire, "Gratias tibi ago domine,
10 quia non sum sicut caeteri hominum, sicut et publicanus iste."
   Tametsi paulo sanctius esse putem in bonorum laude virorum
quam criminatione versari, non est tamen in praesente consilium vt Erasmi scribam encomium. Nam et nostrae vires tanto
sunt operi impares, et vbique gentium optimi atque doctissimi
15 pro sua quisque virili certatim faciunt: quibus alioqui tacentibus,
sua illum benefacta, cunctis fructuosa mortalibus, vt viuum com-
mendant bonis, ita sublata cum fatis inuidia, quod sero precor
obtingat, vita functum commendabunt omnibus, facientque vt
aliquando desideretur etiam his, quorum nunc liuore lippientes
20 oculi velut illustri fulgore perstricti contra tueri non sustinent.
Ego [O$_2$] certe, quandoquidem apud bonos laudatione non indiget, ita temperabo mihi, ne vel eorum per me turgescat inuidia,
quorum tam improbum est ingenium vt et quibuslibet alantur
obtrectationibus et bonorum laudibus intabescant: Quibus ipsis
25 inoffensis, puto, fas est hoc saltem dicere. Si quis diligenter ex-
penderit, quam assidue, quam magna, quam multa, quam bona

---

1 nunc] *1520*ᵃ, non *1520*ᵐ; calumnijs] calumnijs, *1520*   3 tu] tu, *1520*   4 institutis,]
*1520*ᵃ, institutis *1520*ᵐ   5 ieiunijs,] ieiunijs: *1520*ᵐ, ieiunijs. *1520*ᵃ   8
propemodum] *1520*ᵐ, propemodnm *1520*ᵃ   9 audire,] *1520*ᵃ, audire. *1520*ᵐ   11
Tametsi] *No para. 1520;* putem] *1520*ᵃ, putem, *1520*ᵐ; virorum] virorum, *1520*   12
praesente] *1520*ᵐ, praesenti *1520*ᵃ   13 Erasmi] *1520*ᵃ, Erasmo *1520*ᵐ; encomium]
*1520*ᵐ, encomion *1520*ᵃ   14 optimi] *1520*ᵃ, optimi, *1520*ᵐ; doctissimi] doctissimi,
*1520*ᵐ, doctissimi. *1520*ᵃ   15 faciunt:] faciunt, *1520*   16 benefacta,] benefacta
1520   19 his,] *1520*ᵃ, his: *1520*ᵐ   20 oculi] *1520*ᵃ, oculi, *1520*ᵐ; tueri] *1520*ᵃ, con-
tueri *1520*ᵐ   23 ingenium] ingenium, *1520*   24 obtrectationibus] obtrectationibus,
1520; intabescant:] intabescant. *1520*   25 inoffensis, puto,] in offensis puto *1520*ᵐ,
inoffensis puto *1520*ᵃ; est] *1520*ᵃ, est, *1520*ᵐ

from members of every religious order, especially your own, and now, of all times, you tastelessly and arrogantly attack it with slander and abuse. Your whole profession rests on humility as its foundation, and in this spirit of humility you not only exalt your own sect with extravagant praise for its sacred traditions, holy solitude, devout ceremonies, vigils, austere living, and fasts, but you kick him around like a dog while you speak of his bark and his vagabond life-style. When I read these words flowing from so religious a pen, I almost imagine I am hearing the humble prayer spoken by that holy pharisee: "Lord, I thank you that I am not as other men are, even as this publican."

Even though I think it a bit closer to holiness to dwell on the praise of good men than to slander them, I have no intention at present of writing an encomium of Erasmus. For my own powers are unequal to so great a task, and everywhere on earth the best and most learned men are each vying to do it as well as they possibly can. And even if they remained silent, his own rich benefactions to all mortal men, which commend him to virtuous men now, will commend him to all when his death puts an end to their envy (though I pray it will not happen soon), when at last he will be missed even by those people whose jaundiced, bleared eyes, as if dazzled with his intense brightness, cannot stand to look straight at him now. Since he has no shortage of praise among virtuous judges, I myself will refrain from fueling the envy even of those who have such perverse minds that they feed on all kinds of detraction and pine away at the praises of virtuous men. But without any offense even to them, I think, I may say this at least. If anyone carefully considers the steady stream of massive, excellent, and numerous volumes that Erasmus has

volumina vnus aedat Erasmus, quibus vel exscribendis tantum
non vnus satis fuisse videretur, is opinor perpendet facile, etiamsi non totus esset in virtutibus, non multum certe superesse temporis, quod impendatur in vicia. Iam si quis aequos oculos ad-
5 moueat propius, atque operum pensitet fructum, ad haec eorum
attestationes aestimet, quorum vel studijs lux est addita vel feruor accessit affectibus, huic ego certe reor non admodum fore
probabile, pectus illud, vnde velut ignis quidam pietatis exsiliens
aliorum animos inflammat, ipsum in semet vsquequaque
10 frigescere.

Has opinor laudes, non ad inuidiam vsque benignas, nemo est
adeo malignus, vt abnuat, quibus ego tamen ipsis abstinuissem,
nisi quod tua me petulantia ne sic quidem sinit sistere, verum
necessario tecum longius aliquanto prouehit. Nam quis tam pa-
15 tientes aures habet, vt te tam petulanter insultantem ferat, cum
vagabundi nomine insectaris, quod aliquando sedem (quod nunquam fere facit, nisi quum publici boni poscit ratio) demutet?
Perinde quasi desidere perpetuo, atque ostreorum in morem,
aut spongiae, eidem semper affigi saxo, ea demum sit absoluta
20 sanctitas: quod si verum est, haud satis recte institutus est ordo
Minoritarum, quo (nisi me fallit opinio) nullus est ordo sanctior,
quorum plerique tamen idoneis de causis totum peruagantur
orbem: [O₂v] Non recte fecit Hieronymus, qui quod Romam
atque Hierusalem interiacet viae permensus est: Multo intra ves-
25 tram sanctitatem sanctissimi fuerunt apostoli, qui sedentibus
vobis, imo nondum sedentibus, totam vndique terram per-
agrarunt. Nec istud eo dico, quod eis Erasmum comparem, ne
quis id cauilletur ad calumniam, sed vt ostendam tibi, quemadmodum loci mutatio saepe sine vicio contingit, ita non esse
30 praecipuam in sedendo semper sitam sanctimoniam.

1 exscribendis] *1520*ᵃ, ex scribendis *1520*ᵐ; tantum] tantum, *1520*   6 addita] addita,
1520   7 reor] *1520*ᵃ, reor, *1520*ᵐ   8 illud,] *1520*ᵃ, illud *1520*ᵐ; exsiliens] exiliens,
1520   11 Has] *no para. 1520;* laudes,] laudes *1520*   13 sistere,] *1520*ᵃ, sistere
*1520*ᵐ   16–17 sedem (quod . . . ratio)] sedem, quod . . . ratio *1520*ᵐ, sedem,
quod . . . ratio, *1520*ᵃ   20 sanctitas:] sanctitas, *1520*ᵐ, sanctitas *1520*ᵃ   21
Minoritarum,] *1520*ᵃ, Minoritarum *1520*ᵐ; (nisi . . . opinio)] *1520*ᵃ, nisi . . . opinio,
*1520*ᵐ   22 causis] causis, *1520*   23 orbem:] orbem. *1520*   24 viae] viae, *1520;*
permensus est:] permensus est. *1520*ᵐ, permensus. *1520*ᵃ   26 vobis] *1520*ᵃ, nobis
*1520*ᵐ

produced single-handedly, so many that you would think that one man would not even be equal to copying them all out, he will readily conclude that even if Erasmus were not totally preoccupied with virtue he would certainly have little time left to devote to vice. Now if you look even closer with an unbiased eye, first considering the fruitfulness of his works and then appraising the testimony of those who have derived from his works either illumination in their studies or fervor in their affections, I for one think you will not find it at all likely that the heart from which such sparks of piety leap forth to kindle the spirits of others is utterly cold in itself.

Such praises are not, I think, generous enough to stir up any envy, nor is anyone grudging enough to deny it. Yet I would have withheld even this except that your impudence keeps me from drawing the line even there, and compels me to push well beyond it to catch up with you. For whose ears are long-suffering enough to endure your shameless insults when you twit Erasmus with being a vagabond just because he occasionally changes his residence, something he rarely does except when his concern for the good of the public directs him to do so? As if it were the essence of holiness to stagnate forever and stay glued to one rock all the time like an oyster or sponge! But if that is so, then the Franciscan order was quite ill conceived, though no order (unless I am mistaken) is holier than this one; and yet many of its members, with perfectly good reasons, go wandering all over the world. Jerome did something wrong when he traveled all the way from Rome to Jerusalem. The most holy apostles were much beneath your sort of holiness when they journeyed all over the earth while you people sat still, indeed even before you sat still. Nor am I saying this as a way of placing Erasmus on a level with them, so that no one will captiously charge me with meaning to do so, but rather to show you that just as there is often nothing wrong about moving around so there is no special holiness seated in always sitting still.

Etenim vt ad Erasmum veniam, quoquo pacto sese habeant
caetera, quae sese habent optime, vagationem interim, quam tu
tam procaciter inuadis in illo, profecto non dubitauerim cuiquam vestrarum parti virtutum, quacunque vobis maxime
5 placetis, anteferre. Neque enim quenquam hodie esse vsquam
puto, qui quidem suum curet genium ac laborem horreat, quin is
vobiscum sessitare malit, quam vagari cum illo. Qui, seu spectetur labor, plus nonnunquam in vno laborat die, quam vos in
multis mensibus: seu laboris aestimetur vtilitas, plus in vno men-
10 se nonnunquam ecclesiae toti profuit, quam vos in annis plurimis, nisi cuiuspiam vel ieiunia putes vel preculas tantum et tam
late conducere, quam tot egregia volumina, e quibus totus
eruditur orbis ad iusticiam, aut nisi deliciari videtur is, qui maris
hyemes, saeuiciam coeli, labores omnes in terra, dum prosit in
15 commune, contemnit. An non delicata quaedam res est e nauiga-
tione nausea, e iactatione cruciatus, e tempestate periculum,
morsque ac naufragium semper obuersans oculis? Quum toties
per syluas horridas, per inculta nemora, per crepidines asperas,
per montes perreptaret praecipites et vias obsessas latronibus,
20 cum quassus [O₃] ventis, conspersus luto, complutus ac
madidus, a via fessus, a labore lassus, malo subinde acceptus
hospitio, vestrum cubile, vestrum cibum desideret, An non vo-
luptuari videtur, praesertim cum haec tot mala, quae virentem
quoque ac robustum iuuenem facile defatigent, obeat atque sus-
25 tineat senescente iam et studijs ac laboribus fathiscente corpusculo, vt sit pene perspicuum iam olim necessario fuisse tot
malis succubiturum, ni deus eum, qui solem suum facit oriri
super bonos et malos, etiam in ingratorum commoda conseruasset? Nam vndecunque reuertitur, caeteris omnibus
30 egregios affert secum itinerum suorum fructus, sibi vero nihil

1 Etenim] *No para. 1520*   5 placetis,] placetis *1520*   7 Qui,] Qui *1520*   8 labor,]
1520ᵃ, labor *1520ᵐ*   9 vtilitas] *1520ᵃ*, vtiltas *1520ᵐ*   11 putes] putes, *1520;*
preculas] *1520ᵃ*, preculas, *1520ᵐ*   13–14 maris hyemes,] *1520ᵃ*, maris, hyemis, *1520ᵐ*
15 contemnit.] *1520ᵃ*, contemnit? *1520ᵐ*; est] *1520ᵃ*, est, *1520ᵐ*   16 iactatione]
1520ᵐ, iactione *1520ᵃ*   19 praecipites] praecipites, *1520*   22 vestrum cubile, vestrum cibum] *1520ᵐ*, uestrum cibum, uestrum cubile *1520ᵃ*; desideret,] desideret. *1520ᵐ*,
desiderat, *1520ᵃ*   27 eum,] eum *1520*   28–29 conseruasset?] conseruasset.
1520

For to come to Erasmus, whatever the character of the rest of his conduct, which is actually quite irreproachable, I would certainly not hesitate to prefer his kind of wandering, which you run down so shamelessly, to any part of your virtues, however proud you all may be of it. For I think there is not a man living today who loves ease and hates work who would not rather sit still with you than go wandering with him. For if you consider work, he sometimes does more in one day than you do in many months, and if you consider the usefulness of the work, he sometimes does more fruitful work for the Church in one month than you do in several years, unless you think that anyone's fasts or perfunctory prayers do as much or do such widespread good as so many great volumes, through which the whole world is instructed in righteousness, or unless you suppose he is out for sheer fun when he makes light of turbulent seas, inclement skies, and all sorts of trials in order to work for the common good. What a fine sort of fun, to get seasick from being on a ship, to be battered around by its tossing, to be threatened by storms, and to have death and shipwreck continually before one's eyes! When he crawls so often through rugged forests and wild groves, over rough slopes and precipitous mountains, along roads beset with bandits, when he is buffeted by the wind, splashed with mud, drenched with rain, worn out by his travels, and exhausted by overwork, when he frequently lodges in a miserable inn and wishes that he had your bed and board, what a hedonist's life he appears to be leading! Especially since all these hardships, which could easily wear down a vigorous and sturdy young man, are confronted and borne by Erasmus' old body, which is already breaking down with the strain of his study and work, so that it is practically obvious that he must have succumbed long ago to so many hardships if God, who makes his sun rise on both good men and bad, had not protected him for the benefit even of ingrates. For from each of his voyages he brings home the splendid fruits of his travels for others but for himself nothing more

vnquam quicquam nisi detritam valetudinem et suis beneficijs
excitata maledicta pessimorum. Quamobrem tales ille profec-
tiones tam gratas habet, vt nisi studiorum causa postularet, hoc
est publicum omnium commodum, quod ille priuato toties in-
5 commodo redimit, perquam libenter omitteret: Interim vero
non nisi cum hijs versatur, quos et doctrina commendet, et vita,
Semper aliquid parturiens, quod post in illis (quae tu sic incessis)
itineribus non absque publico studiorum fructu pariat, quem si
posthabuisset ille suis ipsius commodis, cum corpus haberet
10 hodie minus aliquanto fractum, tum vero, multo magis vberem
locupletemque fortunam, Principibus omnibus, omnibus fere
magnatibus, eximia conditione certatim illum ad sese pellicen-
tibus. Quanquam certe par ac iustum fuerat, vti quemadmodum
ab illo, vbiubi viuat, eximius fructus in omnes orbis partes velut e
15 sole radij diffunduntur, sic [O₃v] ab omni parte vicissim commoda refunderentur ad illum.

Quamobrem quando ille sese totum alienis vtilitatibus impar-
titur, nec emolumenti quicquam sibi deposcit in terris, dubitare
certe non debeo, quin ei deus illic benignissimus, vbi satius erit
20 accepisse, retribuat: Eoque, cum illum abs te contemptum tecum
comparo, et vtriusque merita compono simul, quantum videlicet
humana fas est coniectura consequi, spes indubitata suboritur,
cum vtrique tandem illa dies affulserit, qua vestris virtutibus
suum reddetur praemium, quanquam vt tuum permagnum fore
25 spero, sic opto fore quam maximum, tamen expensor aequus
vtriusque deus, quod sine tuo damno atque (vt tum affectus eris)
etiam te libente fecerit, non vagationes eius tantum praeferet
sessitationi tuae, sed quoniam bonis omnia cooperantur in
bonum, loquentiam eius anteferet tuo silentio, silentium eius

---

1 vnquam] *1520ᵐ*, usquam *1520ᵃ*; quicquam] *1520ᵃ*, quicquam, *1520ᵐ*; valetudinem]
1520ᵃ, valetudinem, *1520ᵐ*   5 omitteret:] omitteret. *1520*   6 vita,] *1520ᵃ*, vita.
1520ᵐ   7 illis (quae . . . incessis)] illis, quae . . . incessis *1520ᵐ*, illis, quae . . . incessis,
1520ᵃ   10 hodie] *1520ᵃ*, hodie, *1520ᵐ*; vberem] *1520ᵃ*, vberem, *1520ᵐ*   12
magnatibus,] magnatibus *1520*   14 vbiubi] vbi vbi *1520;* partes] partes, *1520*   16
illum.] *1520ᵃ*, illum *1520ᵐ*   17 Quamobrem] *No para. 1520*   19 illic] *1520ᵃ*, ille
1520ᵐ   20 retribuat: Eoque,] retribuet. Eoque *1520ᵐ*, retribuet, eoque *1520ᵃ*   26
damno] damno, *1520;* (vt . . . eris)] vt . . . eris, *1520*   27 libente] *1520ᵐ*, libenter
1520ᵃ; praeferet] praeferat *1520*

than poor health and the ill words that his good deeds provoke from the worst sort of men. Thus he takes so much pleasure in those expeditions that if they were not required for the sake of his studies, that is, for the public benefit of everyone (something he often buys at the cost of some private disadvantage), he would be very glad to forgo them. But in the meantime he associates only with people who are respected for both learning and character, and he is constantly gestating some new idea which he later brings forth, not without public intellectual profit, during those travels which you so malign. But if he had paid less attention to that public profit and more to his own advantages, he would have today not only a much less debilitated body but also a much richer and more opulent fortune, since all princes and almost all great nobles are vying to draw him to them on the most generous terms. And yet it would surely have been fair and just that Erasmus, who, wherever he lives, spreads his great bounty all over the world as the sun spreads its rays, should receive benefits from all over the world in return.

Thus, since he is devoted entirely to the welfare of others and asks for no reward whatsoever on earth, I certainly ought not to doubt that God will reward him most generously there where it is better to get one's reward. And for this reason, though I anticipate that your own reward will be very great and I wish for it to be as great as possible, when I compare you with the man you despise and I consider your merits side by side, insofar as I can judge on the basis of human conjecture, I firmly expect that when the day finally dawns on you both when your virtues will get their reward, on that day, without any injury to you and indeed with your cheerful assent as your feelings will stand then, God, the impartial assessor of both of you, will not only prefer his wandering to your sitting still, but since all things work together for good in good men, God will also prefer his eloquence to your silence, his silence to your prayers, his food to your

tuis praeponet precibus, cibos eius tuis ieiunijs, et somnum tuis
vigilijs, ac denique quicquid in illo tam superbe despicis, pluris
omnino faciet illis omnibus, quaecunque in tua tibi vita tam
suauiter adblandiuntur.

5   Nam haud dubie, quanquam fateri pudor impediat, nunquam
tamen potuisset accidere, quenquam vt tam arroganter impeteres, ni mira persuasione sanctitatis impense placeres tibi, qua
vna re nihil est vsquam religioni periculosius, aut a qua longius
abesse te pro meo in te amore cupio. Etenim mihi meique simi-
10 libus, qui misero fluctuamur orbe, vos profuerit velut inferne
suspicere vestraque instituta non aliter atque angelicae vitae
exemplar admirari, quo quasi stupore quodam virtutis alienae
nostra nobis vita vilescat impensius. At vobis [O₄] contra non
admodum fuerit vtile, aliorum vitam contemnere, et condem-
15 nare prae vestra nonnunquam etiam meliorem. Verum as-
suescas potius in alijs vel inferiora suspicere, de tuis vero non
modo sentire modestius, verum omnia suspectare quoque, trepidumque semper viuere, Et quanquam in bona spe, tamen omnino sollicitum, non tantum ne posthac aliquando corruas, iuxta
20 id quod dicitur, "Qui stat videat ne cadat," Sed ne iam olim
cecideris, ac tum potissimum, quum tibi maxime videbaris ascendere, nempe cum religionem ingredereris.

    Nec istud eo dico, quod quicquam dubitem, quin meliorem
partem delegerit sibi Maria. Sed quoniam "omnis iusticia mor-
25 talium velut pannus est menstruatae," eoque etiam bona sua
cuique merito debent esse suspecta, tibi fortasse non insalubre
fuerit addubitare, timereque tecum, ne tu vel in Mariae parte
non sis, vel Mariae partem perperam delegeris, dum eius

---

2 vigilijs,] *1520*ᵃ, vigilijs *1520*ᵐ   3 quaecunque] *1520*ᵃ, quecunque *1520*ᵐ; in tua tibi
vita] *1520*ᵐ, uita in tua tibi *1520*ᵃ   5 Nam] *No para. 1520;* dubie,] dubie *1520;*
impediat,] *1520*ᵃ, impediat *1520*ᵐ   7 sanctitatis] *1520*ᵃ, sanctitatis, *1520*ᵐ   8 re]
*1520*ᵃ, re, *1520*ᵐ   9 te pro] te, pro *1520*   11 instituta] *1520*ᵃ, instituta, *1520*ᵐ
12 alienae] *1520*ᵃ, alienae, *1520*ᵐ   13 vobis] *1520*ᵃ, nobis *1520*ᵐ   15 vestra] vestra,
1520   16 alijs] alijs, *1520*   18 viuere,] *1520*ᵃ, viuere *1520*ᵐ   20 dicitur,] dicitur.
1520; cadat,] *1520*ᵃ, cadat. *1520*ᵐ   23 Nec] *No para. 1520*   24 Maria.] Maria,
1520   24–25 mortalium] *1520*ᵃ, mortalium, *1520*ᵐ   25 menstruatae] *1520*ᵃ,
menstruate *1520*ᵐ   27 fuerit addubitare,] *1520*ᵃ, fuerit, addubitare *1520*ᵐ   28
delegeris,] *1520*ᵃ, delegeris: *1520*ᵐ; dum] dum aut *1520*

fasting, and his sleep to your vigils, and in summary, God will prize all that you so proudly despise in Erasmus above all that you so dearly esteem in your own way of life.

For undoubtedly, though you might be ashamed to admit it, you could never have attacked anyone so arrogantly unless you grossly flattered yourself with an amazing assurance of your own holiness. There is absolutely nothing more dangerous than this to the religious life, and nothing that I, for the love that I bear you, want you to avoid more completely. For it could benefit me and those like me, who drift here and there in a miserable world, to look up to you from below, so to speak, and to admire your observances as we would a pattern of angelic life, so that we could be prompted as if by our awe at the virtue of others to hold our own lives in more perfect disdain. But it could do you, on the other hand, no good at all to contemn and condemn others' lives, sometimes even superior ones, in comparison with your own. You should make it your habit instead to look up even to inferior attainments in others and not only to think more modestly of your own attainments but also to hold them all suspect, and live not without hope but yet always in fear, not just of falling hereafter (for which there is the saying, "He who stands, let him take heed of falling"), but of having fallen long before now, in particular when you yourself thought that you were ascending most rapidly, namely when you entered the religious life.

I am not saying this because I doubt in the least that the portion Mary chose was the better one. But since "All mortal justice is as the rag of a menstruating woman," so that everyone has good reason to hold even his own good qualities suspect, it would probably be not unwholesome for you to feel inwardly doubtful and fearful lest either you do not share Mary's portion or you have chosen Mary's portion mistakenly, since you rank her func-

munus, cui Christus Marthae postposuit officium, tu apostolorum officio anteponis, aut ne, tibi visus, dum leuiter temet
examinas, in sanctam fugiens solitudinem noxijs te subducere
voluptatibus, in dei secretiore conspectu, qui nos multo penitius
5   introspicit, qui corda nostra profundius quam nos ipsi rimatur,
cuius oculis imperfecta nostra videntur, deprehendaris fortasse
negocia detrectasse, et te subtraxisse laboribus, et pietatis vmbra
quaesiuisse voluptatem quietis, et molestiarum fugam appetisse,
talentumque tibi creditum inuoluisse sudario, quod ne foras
10 emitteres, [O₄v] intus perderes.

    Huiusmodi cogitationibus hoc saltem facies lucri, quod sug-
geretur occasio ne, quo nihil est perniciosius, de tua tecum secta
superbias, neue in priuatis nimium confidas obseruantijs, spem-
que vt in religione colloces potius Christiana, quam tua, nec
15 innitaris in illis quae per te facere potes, sed quae nisi per deum
non potes. Ieiunare potes ex te, vigilare potes ex te, precari potes
ex te, quin potes et ex diabolo. Caeterum vere Christiana fides,
qua Christus Iesus vere dicitur in spiritu: vere Christiana spes,
quae de suis desperans meritis in vna dei benignitate confidit:
20 Vere Christiana charitas, quae non inflatur, non irascitur, non
suam querit gloriam, nulli prorsus nisi sola dei gratia et gratuito
fauore contingunt. Quo plus fiduciae posueris in communibus
istis Christianismi virtutibus, eo minus assuesces fidere priuatis

---

1 munus,] *1520*ᵃ, munus *1520*ᵐ; officium,] *1520*ᵃ, officium: *1520*ᵐ   2 anteponis,]
*1520*ᵃ, anteponis: *1520*ᵐ; ne,] ne *1520;* visus,] *1520*ᵃ, visus: *1520*ᵐ   3 examinas,]
exanimas: *1520*ᵐ, exanimas, *1520*ᵃ; solitudinem] solitudinem: *1520*ᵐ, solitudinem,
*1520*ᵃ   4 voluptatibus,] *1520*ᵃ, voluptatibus: *1520*ᵐ; conspectu,] *1520*ᵃ, conspectu:
*1520*ᵐ   5 introspicit,] *1520*ᵃ, introspicit: *1520*ᵐ; rimatur,] *1520*ᵃ, rimatur: *1520*ᵐ
6 videntur,] *1520*ᵃ, videntur: *1520*ᵐ; deprehendaris] *1520*ᵃ, deprehendaris: *1520*ᵐ
7 detrectasse,] *1520*ᵃ, detrectasse: *1520*ᵐ; laboribus,] *1520*ᵃ, laboribus *1520*ᵐ   8
quietis,] *1520*ᵃ, quietis *1520*ᵐ; appetisse,] *1520*ᵃ, appetisse: *1520*ᵐ   9 sudario,] *1520*ᵃ,
sudario: *1520*ᵐ   10 emitteres,] *1520*ᵃ, emitteres: *1520*ᵐ   11 Huiusmodi] *No para.*
1520; lucri,] *1520*ᵃ, lucri: *1520*ᵐ   12 occasio ne,] occasio: ne *1520*ᵐ, occasio, ne *1520*ᵃ
15 innitaris] *1520*ᵃ, inuitaris *1520*ᵐ; in] 1520ᵐ, *om. 1520*ᵃ   16 potes. Ieiunare] *1520*ᵃ,
potes, ieiunare *1520*ᵐ   18 Christus] *1520*ᵐ, Chrisus *1520*ᵃ; spiritu:] spiritu, *1520*
19 meritis] meritis, *1520;* confidit:] confidit. *1520*   21 gratia] gratia, *1520*   22 con-
tingunt] *1520*, contingit *conj. 1947*

tion not merely above Martha's office, as Christ did, but even above that of the apostles. You should be afraid that, when you view yourself, too indulgently, as one who has retreated into holy solitude to escape harmful pleasures, the deeper scrutiny of God, who observes us with more penetration, who explores our own hearts more profoundly than we do, and whose eyes discern our imperfections, may find that what you have been doing is avoiding responsibility, dodging work, cultivating the pleasure of repose in the shadow of piety, looking for a way out of life's troubles, and wrapping your talent up in a napkin, thus wasting it inside for fear of losing it out-of-doors.

You will gain at least this much by such meditations: they will stop you from using your sect to fuel personal pride, the most dangerous habit there is, and from putting too much faith in private ceremonies, while they will encourage you to place more hope in the Christian religion than you do in your own religious order and to trust less in the things you can do by yourself than in the things you cannot do except with God's help. You can fast by yourself; you can watch by yourself; you can pray by yourself; why, you can even do all this by the devil. But a truly Christian faith, through which Christ Jesus' name is truly uttered in the spirit; a truly Christian hope, which despairs of its own merits and puts all its faith in the generosity of God; and a truly Christian charity, which is not puffed up, which does not become angry, which does not seek its own glory, are not to be had by anyone except through God's grace and gratuitous favor alone. The more confidence you place in these common virtues of Christianity the less faith you will come to place in your own

ceremonijs vel ordinis tui vel tuis, in quibus quo minus fides, eo
tibi magis conferent. Nam tum demum deus te fidelem seruum
ducet, quum tu te duces inutilem. Quod merito certe poterimus,
etiam si fecerimus omnia quaecunque possumus, quod ego
5 deum precor, vterque vt aliquando faciamus, et ERASMVS
etiam, nec faciamus tantum, sed, vel multo potius si multa fecisse
contingat, nihil vt nos omnino fecisse censeamus. nam ea via
potissimum eo conscenditur, vbi neque nos quicquam virtus aliena torquebit, neque lachrymam vllam lippientibus oculis ex-
10 cutiet aliena claritas. [O_5]

Quod in calce tandem scribis, meae fore modestiae, ne tuas
litteras cuiquam ostendam, non video qui id pertineat admodum
ad modestiam meam. Fuisset haud dubie tuae vel modestiae, vel
certe prudentiae, ostendisse paucioribus: Modestiae, si quales
15 tibi videntur, tales essent: Prudentiae, si quales vere sunt, tales
etiam tibi viderentur. Nunc vero noua est ista modestia, exigere
a me silentium, quasi vel tua tibi non placeret epistola vel declinares laudem, ac temet illico, cum te gloriolae pruritus incenderet, quaerere quosdam simili titillatos scabie, vt iucundo frictu
20 pariter et scabereris et scaberes. A quibus cum audirem passim
esse iactatum, tuis elegantissimis et a spiritu sancto dictatis epistolis ita mutatum me, vt Erasmica scripta reiecerim, arbitratus
sum conuenire mihi, meam sententiam litteris vt testatam redderem, eorumque vel stultitiam, si credidere, vel maliciam, si
25 confinxere, conuincerem. Etenim iudicare non possum quonam

---

1 ceremonijs] ceremonijs, *1520*ᵐ, ceremonijs. *1520*ᵃ; tui] tui, *1520;* tuis,] tuis *1520*   2
demum] *1520*ᵃ, demun *1520*ᵐ   5 faciamus,] *1520*ᵃ, faciamus *1520*ᵐ   6 sed,] sed
1520; potius] potius, *1520*   7 censeamus.] *1520*ᵃ, censeamus, *1520*ᵐ   10 claritas]
*1520*ᵐ, charitas *1520*ᵃ   11 Quod] *No para. 1520*ᵃ; scribis,] scribis *1520;* modestiae,]
modestiae *1520*ᵐ, modestiae. *1520*ᵃ   13 Fuisset] *1520*ᵐ, fuisse *1520*ᵃ   14
prudentiae,] prudentiae *1520;* paucioribus:] paucioribus. *1520*   16 modestia,] *1520*ᵃ,
modestia: *1520*ᵐ   17 silentium,] *1520*ᵃ, silentium: *1520*ᵐ; epistola] epistola: *1520*ᵐ,
epistola, *1520*ᵃ   18 laudem,] *1520*ᵃ, laudem: *1520*ᵐ; illico,] illico *1520*   18–19
incenderet,] incenderet: *1520*   19 scabie,] *1520*ᵃ, scabie: *1520*ᵐ; frictu] *1520*ᵐ, fructu
*1520*ᵃ   20 scabereris] *1520*ᵃ, scabereris: *1520*ᵐ   21 iactatum,] iactatum *1520;*
elegantissimis] elegantissimis: *1520*ᵐ, elegantissimis, *1520*ᵃ   22 me,] *1520*ᵃ, me:
*1520*ᵐ; reiecerim,] *1520*ᵃ, reiecerim: *1520*ᵐ   23 mihi,] mihi: *1520*ᵐ, mihi *1520*ᵃ
23–24 redderem,] redderem: *1520*ᵐ, redderem *1520*ᵃ   24 stultitiam, si credidere,]
*1520*ᵃ, stultitiam si credidere: *1520*ᵐ; maliciam,] maliciam *1520*   25 quonam] *1520*ᵐ,
quo nam *1520*ᵃ

private ceremonies or in those of your order; and the less faith you have in such things, the more good they will do you. For it is when you consider yourself a useless servant that God will consider you a faithful one. And we can certainly find good cause to see ourselves as useless even when we have done all we can, which I pray to God that both of us, and Erasmus as well, will eventually do, yet not only that we will do all we can, but (especially if it turns out we have done a good deal) that we reckon ourselves to have done really nothing at all. For this way is the surest of all to aspire to the place in which neither the virtue of others will cause us distress nor the brilliance of others will draw any tear from our own bleary eyes.

At the end of your letter you write that my modesty ought to prevent me from showing your letter to anyone. I do not see how that can pertain to my modesty at all. Your own modesty, or at least your own prudence, should certainly have stopped you from showing your letter to as many as you did: modesty if your letter had been what you deem it to be; prudence if you had deemed it to be what it is. But in view of the facts, your own notion of modesty is novel indeed: even as you insist on my silence, as if you were either displeased with your letter or loath to accept any praise for it, you yourself, the moment that you start to burn with a prickling desire for ephemeral glory, go out looking for others provoked by the same scabby itch, so that you can scratch each other's backs in a pleasurable medley of chafing. Having heard how those fellows were boasting wherever they went that your elegant letters, dictated by the Holy Spirit, had changed my opinions enough to make me reject Erasmus' writings, I thought it best to declare my position in a letter in order to show up their folly, if they actually believed what they said, or their malice, if they made it up. For I cannot judge how

pacto litterae tuae affecerint illos, quando asinino palato pla-
centes cardui locum etiam fecerunt adagio. Mihi certe nihil in eis
visum est vsque adeo splendidum, vt nobis oculorum sic per-
stringeret aciem, quin quod album esset album etiamnum vid-
5 eretur. Hunc itaque meum animum cum propter vanissimam
siue tuam siue tuorum iactantiam declarandum esse censuissem,
hactenus tamen statui habere semper famae tuae rationem, vt
neque nomen tuum, alioqui mihi percharum, meis litteris insererem, et e tuis ipsius (quae quidem in mea manu essent) ex-
10 pungerem: "Hoc vereor, ne paulo videri possit inuerecundius
dictum." Atque istoc pacto fiet, vt quicquid hoc de facto tuo vel
dicent vel sentient homines (de quo boni doctique sentient di-
centque omnes pro[O₅v]cul dubio pessime), nihil te tamen
pudoris ac ruboris attingat.
15   Illud mihi vehementer placet, quod vbi satis debacchatus es,
redditus tandem tibi, factus es in fine placatior, insinuata spe
irae in Erasmum conditione non admodum difficili componen-
dae. Nam hunc in modum scribis: "Nec tamen vsqueadeo inimi-
cus sum Erasmo, quin facile cum eo in gratiam redeam, si ille sua
20 correxerit erratula." Papae, beasti hominem, qui alioqui periculum erat ne moerore misere maceraret sese, si spes omnis
prorsus adempta esset, fore vt aliquando te, tanto videlicet viro,
magis vteretur propitio. Verum nunc, quandoquidem tam facilem pacem offers, in qua tam aequa postulas, haud dubie pa-
25 rebit auide, corrigetque protinus, simul atque tu errores eius
ostenderis. Nam hactenus tantum ostendisti tuos. Quanquam ea
ipsa quae tu vocas erratula, nempe "verriculum" pro "sagena,"

---

1 affecerint] *1520*ᵃ, affecerunt *1520*ᵐ; illos,] *1520*ᵃ, illos: *1520*ᵐ   2 cardui] cardui:
*1520*ᵐ, cardui, *1520*ᵃ   3 splendidum,] *1520*ᵃ, splendidum: *1520*ᵐ   4 aciem,]
*1520*ᵃ, aciem: *1520*ᵐ, esset] esset: *1520*ᵐ, esset, *1520*ᵃ   5 animum] *1520*ᵃ, animum:
*1520*ᵐ   6 tuam] tuam, *1520*; declarandum] *conj. 1760*, declarandam *1520*; censuissem,] *1520*ᵃ, censuissem: *1520*ᵐ   7 rationem,] *1520*ᵃ, rationem: *1520*ᵐ   8 tuum,]
tuum *1520*; percharum,] percharum *1520*   8-9 insererem,] *1520*ᵃ, insererem: *1520*ᵐ
9-11 expungerem: "Hoc vereor, ne . . . dictum." Atque] expungerem. Hoc vereor
ne . . . dictum. Atque *1520*ᵐ, expungerem. Atque *1520*ᵃ   11 fiet,] *1520*ᵃ, fiet: *1520*ᵐ;
hoc de] *1520*ᵐ, hoc *1520*ᵃ; tuo] tuo: *1520*ᵐ, tuo, *1520*ᵃ   13 pessime),] pessime)
1520   15 Illud] *No para. 1520*   16 spe] *1520*ᵃ, spe, *1520*ᵐ   18 scribis:] scribis.
1520   20 Papae] *1520*ᵃ, Pape *1520*ᵐ   21 erat] erat, *1520*

THE MONK FINALLY BECOMES LESS IMPLACABLE

307

your letter struck them, since an ass's penchant for thistles has
even given rise to an adage. I, at any rate, found nothing in it
sufficiently splendid or dazzling to make us stop seeing white as
white. Thus although I felt I had to state my own views on
account of the unfounded boasting which you or your friends
have been doing, thus far I have decided to continue to safeguard your own reputation: I have not only not mentioned your
name in my letter (a name which I otherwise hold very dear); I
have also erased it in yours, or at any rate in the one copy I have
("I am afraid that what I have to say may appear somewhat
brash . . ."). These steps will ensure that no matter how men
speak or think of your action—and all good, learned men will
undoubtedly think and speak ill of it—you yourself will be
spared the least blush of embarrassment.

It pleases me greatly that once you have finished your raving
you finally return to your senses and grow less implacable, even
hinting that you may be willing to settle your feud with Erasmus
on quite easy terms. For you write the following: "Even so, I am
not such an enemy of Erasmus that I would refuse to make up
with him if he would correct his minor mistakes." My word, you
have crowned the man's bliss! For without this assurance the
poor fellow might well have wasted away from sheer grief had he
lost every hope of eventually gaining your favor, great man that
you are. But now that you offer him peace with such easy conditions, making such fair demands, I am sure he will rush to oblige,
and correct his mistakes just as soon as you point any out; for
thus far you have pointed out only your own. And yet even those
readings that you call his minor mistakes, where he alters "sage-

et "remitte" pro "dimitte," et "discumbentibus" pro "discumbentium," atque eiusdem generis alia, sicubi latinum vocabulum
pro barbaro supposuit, aut sermonem purum pro soloeco, aut
perspicuum pro ambiguo, Sicubi vel interpretis errorem correx-
5   it, vel scriptoris lapsum restituit, vel graecitatis idioma Romanae
linguae figuris enunciauit, Haec inquam ipsa, potius quam te
inimicum habeat, immutabit omnia, ac barbarismos omnes,
omnes soloecismos, quicquid vsquam fuit obscurum, quicquid
aut dormitanter versum, aut inemendate transscriptum, Eras-
10 mus hunc thesaurum omnem, quandoquidem non furtum tantum (vt video) sed sacrilegium quoque, dum haec auferret e
templo, commiserat, in san[O₆]ctuarium rursus bona cum fide
reponet, Nihil eo deterritus, quod bonos doctosque omnes ab se
alienare videbitur, quos illo officio deuinxerat, quando illorum
15 vice omnium te tandem atque apologastrum illum, hoc est, populi vice primarios quosdam principes ac veluti litteratorum omnium duumuiros conciliabit sibi.

Sed omisso ioco, hoc vnum certe, sicuti abs te probe pieque
factum est, ita ego quoque vere atque ex animo laudo, quod dum
20 erratula tantum fateris esse quae sunt corrigenda, fateris interim
verecunde quidem pro tua modestia, sed vere tamen, quo te
mendacio liberares tam scelesto: confiteris, inquam, falsa fictaque esse omnia, quae de haeresi, de schismate, deque Antichristi
praeconio initio praeferuidus obieceras. Neque enim vsque adeo
25 mihi deploratus es, quin melius de te sentiam, quam vt haeresim,
schismata, atque Antichristi praeconium, quorum atrocitatem

---

1 dimitte,] *1520ᵃ*, dimitte: *1520ᵐ*; discumbentibus] discumbentibus, *1520*   2
eiusdem] *1520ᵐ*, eius *1520ᵃ*; alia,] *1520ᵃ*, alia: *1520ᵐ*   3 supposuit,] *1520ᵃ*, supposuit:
1520ᵐ; soloeco,] *1520ᵃ*, soloeco: *1520ᵐ*   4 ambiguo,] *1520ᵃ*, ambiguo: *1520ᵐ*   4–
5 correxit,] *1520ᵃ*, correxit: *1520ᵐ*   5 restituit,] *1520ᵃ*, restituit: *1520ᵐ*   6
enunciauit,] enunciauit. *1520;* ipsa,] ipsa *1520*   7 habeat,] *1520ᵃ*, habeat: *1520ᵐ*;
omnia,] *1520ᵃ*, omnia *1520ᵐ*; omnes,] *1520ᵃ*, omnes: *1520ᵐ*   8 soloecismos,] *1520ᵃ*,
soloecismos: *1520ᵐ*; obscurum,] *1520ᵃ*, obscurum: *1520ᵐ*   9 versum,] *1520ᵃ*,
versum: *1520ᵐ*; transscriptum,] transscriptum: *1520ᵐ*, transcriptum. *1520ᵃ*   10
omnem,] omnem *1520;* furtum] *1520ᵃ*, furtim *1520ᵐ*   11 quoque,] quoque: *1520ᵐ*,
quoque *1520ᵃ*   12 templo, commiserat,] templo: commiserat: *1520ᵐ*, templo commiserat, *1520ᵃ*   13 reponet,] reponet. *1520;* deterritus,] *1520ᵃ*, deterritus: *1520ᵐ*
14 videbitur,] *1520ᵃ*, videbitur: *1520ᵐ*; deuinxerat,] *1520ᵃ*, deuinxerat: *1520ᵐ*   15
est,] est *1520*   16 vice] *1520ᵃ*, vice, *1520ᵐ*; principes] principes, *1520*   18 Sed] *No
para. 1520;* ioco] *1520ᵃ*, iocc *1520ᵐ*; certe,] certe *1520*   20 sunt] *1520ᵐ*, sint *1520ᵃ*
22 liberares] *1520ᵐ*, liberes *1520ᵃ*; scelesto: confiteris, inquam,] scelesto, confiteris inquam *1520*

na" to "verriculum," "dimitte" to "remitte," "discumbentium" to "discumbentibus," and so on, wherever he replaces a barbarous word with a Latin one, a solecism with a grammatical phrase, or an ambiguous phrase with a clear one, wherever he either corrects a mistake of the translator or redresses the lapse of a scribe, even these I repeat, he will change for the worse, one and all, to avoid having you as an enemy, and since (as I see) it was sacrilege, not simple theft, for Erasmus to remove all this treasure from the temple, he will retrieve every barbarism, every solecism, each and every obscurity, each careless rendering or faulty transcription, and faithfully put it all back in the sanctuary, not deterred in the least by the thought that this action will look like a quite unforgivable insult to all of the good, learned men he won over with that other service. For at last, by dispensing with all of them—with the mere rank and file—he will be making friends with the mightiest potentates and paired prefects of literacy, namely you and that paltry apologist.

But joking aside, I sincerely and wholly approve of the decent and pious intentions you showed here, at least, in confessing that all that needs to be corrected are some minor mistakes. For thereby you confessed (somewhat bashfully, in keeping with your modesty, but still truthfully enough to disburden yourself of such a criminal lie), you confessed, I repeat, that all the intemperate charges with which you began about heresy, schism, and the heralding of Antichrist were all pure fabrications. For I still do not think you so totally hopeless that you could regard heresy, schism, and the heralding of Antichrist, three crimes which no

scelerum nulla malorum moles exaequarit, pro leuiculis habeas
erratulis. Quamobrem, cum te videam quicquid erat graue recantasse, non est animus de leuibus tecum contendere, Vt vtrinque pariter quae dicta sunt habeantur indicta omnia, tumultus-
5 que omnis, vt de nihilo natus est, ita in nihilum vicissim desinat,
atque haec tragoedia tandem exeat in comoediam. Vale. Et si
claustro nolis frustra claudi, quieti potius spirituali, quam istiusmodi rixis indulge.

FINIS

---

1 scelerum] scelerum, *1520;* exaequarit] *1520*[m], exaequat *1520*[a]   2 Quamobrem,]
Quamobrem *1520;* videam] *1520*[a], videam, *1520*[m]   3 contendere,] contendere.
1520   3–4 vtrinque] *1520*[m], vtrunque *1520*[a]   4 sunt] *1520*[a], sunt, *1520*[m]   5
omnis,] *1520*[a], omnis *1520*[m]

mass of evils could rival, as minor mistakes. Therefore, since I see you have recanted all your really serious charges, I am not going to argue with you over trifles, so that we can both simply forget what was said, let the whole uproar, which sprang out of nothing, dissolve at long last into nothing again, and thus finish this tragedy as a comedy. Farewell; and if you hope to reap any benefit from secluding yourself in a cloister, find contentment in spiritual repose, not in this sort of quarreling.

THE END

HISTORIA RICHARDI TERTII
TEXT AND TRANSLATION

Historia Richardi·iij·regis Angliae
Thoma Moro authore./

Eduardus Rex eius nominis quartus / actis vitae annis quin-
quaginta tribus / mensibus septem / diebus sex / quum annum ab
5 regno cepto secundum et vicesimum numeraret / concessit fatis
anno post Christum natum quadringentesimo tertio et oc-
tuagesimo supra millesimum / superstitibus masculi sexus liberis
duobus femellis quinque / Eduardo videlicet rege designato /
annorum circiter tredecim / Richardo Eboraci Duce / qui biennio
10 minor erat / Elisabetha / quae postea / ducentibus fatis / Henrici
septimi coniux fuit et octaui mater / regina specie atque indole
egregia / Cecilia / non perinde fortunata quam formosa /
[Brigitta / virtutem eius cuius nominis erat repraesentante / pro-
fessa / et vitam religiosam ducente in monasterio monialium
15 inclusarum apud Dertfordiam / Anna / postea honorifice nupta
Thomae / tunc temporis Domino Havvardo / et postea Comiti de
Surre /] Catherina / quae sortem subinde variam experta / interdum placidam / sepius improsperam / postremo / si hec postrema
est (nam adhuc viuit) pietate nepotis Henrici Regis octaui pros-
20 perimam ac se plane dignam consecuta est. /

1–2 Historia . . . authore] *title added by another hand in* P, HISTORIA RICHARDI REGIS
ANGLIAE EIVS NOMINIS TERTII, PER THOMAM MORVM, LONDINENSIS
CIVITATIS IAM TVM VICECOMITEM CONSCRIPTA, ANNVM CIRCITER M.D.
XIII. Quam propriae exercitationis gratia, nec ita magno studio conscriptam, neque
absolutam haud vnquam postea emendauit, vt minime mireris, si cum alijs eius Latinis
operibus quoad sermonis elegantiam non conferenda sit. Hoc opus nunc primum Latine
in lucem aeditum est. Nam ante complures annos Britannice ab eodem authore quam
elegantissime conscriptum, in manus hominum prodierat: quod in eius Anglicorum
operum volumine insertum inuenies. *1565, no title* H A   4 sex /] sex. P   5 fatis] fatis /
(*apparently corrected from* famae A) P   8 femellis] femellae P H, femelle A, foeminei
1565 (see notes); quinque] A H, quatuor *1565* P, *changed to* quinque Pᵃ; quinque /] quinque./ P   9 tredecim] *1565*, vndecim P A H, (*cf.* thirtene *1557*); Duce /] Duce, P   10
erat / Elisabetha / quae] erat, Elisabetha que P; postea / ducentibus fatis /] postea ducentibus fatis´ P   11 mater /] mater./ P   12 egregia /] egregia P; Cecilia /] Cecilia P;
formosa /] formosa./ P   12–17 formosa / Brigitta . . . Surre / Catherina] formosa /
Catherina P A H, formosa. Et Brigitta . . . Surre. Et Catherina *1565*, *probably interpolated
from the English of 1557 (see introduction, p. 0000). For consistency's sake in this excerpt virgules
have been substituted for periods and commas.*   17 Catherina /] Catherina P   18
placidam /] placidam P   20–316/1 est. Is] *eight-line gap P, seven-line gap A, almost no gap
H*

The History of Richard III, King of England
Written by Thomas More

KING EDWARD, the fourth of that name, having lived fifty-three years, seven months, and six days, succumbed to fate as he was numbering the twenty-second year of his reign, in the fourteen hundred and eighty-third year after the birth of Christ, leaving as his survivors two male children and five girls: Edward, the heir-apparent, about thirteen years old; Richard, Duke of York, two years his junior; Elizabeth, who later by the guidance of fate became the consort of Henry VII and the mother of Henry VIII, a queen of remarkable beauty and character; Cecily, not as fortunate as she was fair; [Bridget, who imitated the virtue of her namesake, took vows, and led the life of a religious in a convent of cloistered nuns at Dartford; Anne, later honorably married to Thomas, at that time Lord Howard and afterwards Earl of Surrey;] Catherine, who experienced many changes of fortune, occasionally benign but more often unfavorable, and who at last, if this change be the last (for she is still alive), gained the generous favor of fortune she eminently deserved through the pious goodwill of her nephew, King Henry VIII.

Is rex / quem dico / quum in palatio obijsset quod est apud
Benedictinorum coenobium ad occidentem solem / circiter mille
passus ab Londino / magnifico inde funere delatus [208v] est
Vindesoram ibique multis cum lachrimis sepultus / nempe prin-
5 ceps tam benignus ac mitis dum pax erat (nam bello necesse erat
partes mutuo esse infestas) vt neque alius quisquam in Anglia
regnarit vnquam patribus populoque charior / neque is ipse alia
vitae parte eque charus atque ea quae illi postrema fuit. At eam
ipsam tamen charitatem desideriumque eius sequentis tem-
[4/1] 10 pestatis crudelitas / immanis inuisusque parricidae principatus
intendit. Etenim quo tempore vita functus est / inuidia omnis
depositi Regis Henrici ·vi· / quae diu apud eius fautores flagrauerat / tandem consopita resederat atque extincta est / tam multis
eorum in plusquam viginti annis imperij sui / magna mortalis
15 aeui parte / defunctis / alijs interea in gratiam atque amicitiam
adscitis / in quam conciliandam obuius ac pronus ferebatur./
Erat corpore procero / specie vere regia / multum animi nec
minus consilij inerat. Aduersis rebus imperterritus / prosperis
letus magis quam elatus / equus in pace clemensque / militiae
20 acer et ferox / in aggrediendis periculis promptus / nec vltra
tamen quam posceret ratio praeceps / cuius res bellicas quisquis
recte estimet / is profecto non minus prudentiam eius admi-
rabitur sicubi cessit / quam laudabit audaciam vbi vicit./ Os et
vultus erat quem videre velles / corpus amplum ac magno
25 robore / strictis artubus / quanquam liberiore victu corporisque
indulgentia paulo tandem habitior est factus / nec tamen indecorus. [209] Ceterum genio ac libidini ab ineunte statim aetate

---

1 obijsset] obijsset, *P*   4 sepultus /] sepultus. *P*   4–5 princeps] *inserted in margin P*
7 charior /] charior./ *P*   8 vitae] vite *P*   9 ipsam] *A H 1565, changed to* ipsius *P*
9–10 sequentis . . . principatus] *P A H,* inuisus parricidae sequentis principatus
1565   11 est /] est *P*   12 .vi. /] . vi. *P*   12–13 flagrauerat /] flagrauerat *P*   13
tam] *P A H,* iam *1565,* i *interl. above* t *of* tam *P*ˢ   14 sui /] sui *P*   15 parte /] parte
P   16 adscitis /] adscitis *P*   19 militiae] militie *P*   20 periculis] periculis / *P*   21
praeceps /] praeceps./ *P*   26–27 indecorus.] indecorus *P*   27 ineunte] *P A H*ˢ *1565,*
iuuentute *H;* statim] *interl. P*

When the king I am speaking of died in the palace which is located next to the Benedictine abbey about a mile toward the setting sun from London, he was borne to Windsor in a magnificent funeral procession and there interred amid great lamentation; for he was a prince so kindhearted and gentle in peacetime (for in the war it was inevitable that the factions should be bitter enemies) that no other ruler of England was ever dearer to the nobles and the people, nor was he himself ever as dear as he was in the last part of his life. And yet even this esteem and regret for his absence were enhanced by the cruelty of the following period, the dire and detestable rule of a parricide. For by the time of his death, all the ill will which he had provoked by deposing King Henry VI, which had long smoldered among his supporters, had finally been smothered and snuffed out; for a great many of Henry's supporters had died in the more than twenty years of Edward's reign, a large fraction of a mortal existence, whereas others had meanwhile been drawn to partake of his favor and friendship, in the fostering of which he was reputed to be open and accommodating. He was a man tall in stature, truly regal in appearance; he had great courage and no less discretion. Undaunted by hardship, cheerful rather than arrogant in prosperity, fair and merciful in peace, keen and ferocious in battle, prompt to face danger, and yet no more impetuous than reason required, so that whoever rightly assesses his conduct in war will have no less admiration for his prudence whenever he retreated than praise for his boldness when he won victories. His face and expression were pleasing to view, his build ample, exceedingly powerful and well-muscled, though his rather loose living and fleshly indulgence eventually rendered him somewhat too portly; but yet not unseemly. Even so, from early youth throughout

per omnem vitam quatinus eum res gerendae non auocabant
admodum dedebatur / more hominum fere omnium / nam valentibus egre persuaseris modum in magna fortunae licentia. Id
vitium eius non admodum fuit molestum populo / quod neque
5   vnius voluptas viri diffundere se tam late sufficiebat vt omnibus
fieret graue / et ille vel precio quod libuit emercari solebat / vel
precibus eblandiri / nusquam grassatus violentia / flexu preterea
etatis effectus (vt fit) postremis diebus moderatior / in quibus
regnum eius quietissimum et rerum statu florentium fuit. Bel-
10   lum neque aderat vllum neque vllum imminebat nisi quod nemo
expectabat / quippe externus metus omnis aberat / domi vulgo
quies et inter purpuratos ab Rege conciliata concordia. Regi ipsi
omnes haud vi sed sua sponte obediebant veriusque reuereban-
[5/1]   tur eum quam metuebant./ A pecunijs exigendis (que res vna
15   fere mentes Anglorum disiungit a principe) iam pridem prorsus
destiterat neque decreuerat quidquam secum vnde nasceretur
occasio./ Tributorum vectigal e Gallia iam olim obtinuerat./ Bar-
uici anno ante mortem vno armis potitus fuerat./

Hic rex quanquam per omne tempus imperij tanta comitate
20   fuit in quoslibet vt nulla pars morum eius magis estimaretur / ea
tamen progressu temporis (quo plerosque principes diu confir-
mata potentia vertit in superbiam) [209v] mirum in modum
creuit atque inaucta est / nempe ea estate quae illi suprema fuit /
Vindesorae versatus / prefectum Londini atque aliquot e se-
25   natoribus accersit ad se / haud alia de causa quam vt venatione
secum delectarentur. Ibi eis non tam magnificum ac sublimem
quam amicum ac popularem vultum exhibuit / ferinamque tam
affluenter inde misit in vrbem vt haud temere inuenias aliud /
quod ei aut plurium aut maiorem beneuolentiam conciliauerit
30   apud populum / cui plerumque res exigua facta comiter magnis
beneficijs preponderat / ac pro maioris in se amoris argumento
ducitur./

---

5 vnius] *interl. P*   6 graue /] graue *P*   7 eblandiri] *H 1565*, eblandire *P A*; flexu] *A H
1565*, fluxu *P*   9 rerum statu florentium] *P A H*, rerum status florentissimus *1565*
12 concordia.] concordia *P*   23 est /] est *P*; quae] que *P*; fuit /] fuit *P*   24 versatus /]
versatus *P*   26 magnificum] *H 1565*, magnificem *P A*   29 plurium] *H*, plurimum *A
1565*, plurimam *P*

his life, whenever business did not call him away, he was particularly given to dissipation and wantonness, like virtually everyone
else; for you will hardly persuade anyone in good health to
restrain himself when his fortune permits great extravagance.
This fault of his was not particularly irksome to the people, since
one man's pleasures could scarcely be extravagant enough to be
burdensome to everyone, and since he used to procure what he
wanted with presents or wheedle it out with entreaties, never
resorting to violence. Besides, after passing the midpoint of life,
he—like most people—became less immoderate in his final
days, when his kingdom was perfectly calm and its affairs in a
flourishing state. No war was at hand, and none threatened,
except for the one war that no one expected: there was no fear
from abroad, and at home there was calm among the commons
and concord among the great nobles secured by the king. All the
people obeyed the king himself not by constraint but of their
own free will, and did not so much fear as revere him. He had
long ago totally given up the exacting of money (which is virtually the only thing which alienates the minds of the English
from a prince), nor had he made any plans which would give him
occasion to exact it. He had long since obtained tribute from
France; one year before his death, he captured Berwick.

Although throughout his reign this king treated everyone
with such courtesy that no part of his virtues was more esteemed,
with the passage of time (when a long-confirmed sovereignty
makes many princes turn haughty) his courtesy was enhanced
and extended remarkably. In the last summer of his life, while
the king was at Windsor, he invited the mayor and several aldermen of London to visit him simply in order to join him in the
pleasure of a hunt. There he received them in a manner less
stately and lofty than friendly and popular, and he sent such an
abundance of game from there back to the city that you could
scarcely find anything else which secured him such widespread
and hearty goodwill with the people, in whose judgment a small
courtesy often outweighs great favors and is reckoned a token of
greater affection.

Ita princeps iste tum obijt mortem quum vita eius maxime
cupiretur / cuius tam egregia apud suos gratia liberis eius /
quibus etiam ipsis tam eximiae naturae dotes et illustria re-
giarum virtutum signa conspiciebantur quam capere eorum
5   aetas poterat / mirum haud dubie firmamentum fuisset ad principatum si non eos amicorum inter se diuisio exarmasset atque
execrabilis imperandi sitis ad eorum perniciem incitasset illum /
qui si aut natura valere quicquam / aut fides / aut gratitudo
[6/1]   potuisset / suum corpus hostibus pro ipsorum obijcere debuisset:
10   quippe Richardus Glocestriae Dux / natura patruus / nomine
tutor / beneficijs deuinctus / obstrictus sacramento / ruptis omnibus humanae societatis vinculis / contra ius ac fas / nepotibus
suis orphanis ac sibi creditis auferre vitam regnumque in se
transferre decreuit./
15   Ceterum quoniam huius viri facta materiam fere presentis
operis implent / haud ab re [210] fuerit mores eius ostendere /
quo fiat illustrius cuiusmodi vir ille fuerit qui tantum animo
scelus sustinuit concipere./ Richardus Eboraci Dux / nobilis /
factiosus / potens / cum Rege de regno non armis hostiliter sed
20   ciuili more legibus in senatu disceptauit: tantum aut causa aut
gratia valuit / quum Rex innocentior esset quam sapientior / vt ex
senatusconsulto Parlamenti / cuius apud Anglos summa atque
absoluta potestas est / successor Henrico Regi / repudiata ipsius
sobole (quanquam egregie principe) / designaretur / regnum sibi
25   posterisque suis perpetuum protinus ab Henrici morte auspicaturus / quam ille non moratus / dum ciuilium pretextu dissentionum conatur legitimum regnandi tempus anticipare viuo-
que adhuc Henrico sceptrum sibi asserere / in Vacensi prelio
cum multis vna purpuratis occubuit / relinquens liberos tres /

2 cupiretur /] cupiretur P; eius /] eius P   7 illum /] illum./ P   8 aut gratitudo] om.
1565   9 potuisset /] potuisset P; debuisset:] debuisset P   10 Glocestriae] Glocestrie
P; patruus /] patruus P   12 vinculis /] vinculis P; fas /] fas P   18 Dux /] dux P;
nobilis /] nobilis P   20 disceptauit:] disceptauit P   21 valuit /] valuit P; sapientior] P
A 1565, prudentior H   22 Parlamenti /] Parlamenti P   23 Regi /] regi P   24
egregie] P A, egregio H 1565; principe) /] principe) P; designaretur /] designaretur P
25 perpetuum] perpetuum / P   25–26 auspicaturus /] auspicaturus P   26
moratus /] moratus P   28 asserere /] asserere P; Vacensi] A H 1565, Vaclusi P   29
occubuit /] occubuit P

Thus that prince's death occurred just when his life was most cherished; and his extraordinary popularity among his subjects would undoubtedly have provided a firm foundation for the reign of his children (who themselves showed all the natural distinctions and all the illustrious tokens of kingly virtue that their youth could accommodate) had they not been disarmed by dissension among their supporters and if an odious craving for power had not egged one man on to destroy them even though every prompting of either nature, fidelity, or gratitude should have moved him to lay down his own life to thwart any enemy of theirs. This man, Richard, Duke of Gloucester, their natural uncle, their titular guardian, tied to them by kindnesses, bound to them by an oath, ruptured all bonds of human society; in defiance of man's law and God's, he determined to take away the lives of his own orphaned nephews and wards and to take over their throne for himself.

But since this man's deeds furnish most of the contents of this work, it will not be out of place to delineate his character, so that it will be clearer what sort of man he was who was able to conceive such a terrible crime. Richard, Duke of York, a noble, factious, and powerful man, quarreled over the throne with the king, letting civil litigation in parliament take the place of armed conflict. Either his case or his popularity carried sufficient weight (since the king's innocence exceeded his prudence) that a decree passed by parliament, whose authority in England is supreme and absolute, declared him King Henry's successor, and disowned the king's offspring through it was exceedingly princely. Richard was to assume the kingship for himself and his heirs in perpetuity upon Henry's death; but instead of delaying, he tried, under the pretext of civil disturbances, to anticipate the legitimate inception of his reign and appropriate the throne while Henry was still alive. In the battle of Wakefield he perished together with many of the nobility. He was survived by three

Eduardum quem diximus / Georgium / ac Ricardum hunc / qui
vt erant omnes illustri loco nati / sic animo etiam vasto ac sublimi
fuere / auidi potentiae / neque superiorum neque parium satis
patientes. Eduardus patris mortem vltus Henricum bello victum
[7/1] 5 regno exuit ac se suffecit./ Georgius Clarentiae Dux procerus
elegansque vndique fortunatus videri potuit si non aut ipsum
regnandi cupiditas in fratrem aut inimicorum calumnia fratrem
incitasset in illum. Nam siue ei Reginae factio struxit insidias /
quam inter ac Regis consanguineos acre odium flagrabat (vt
10 mulieres non malicia quidem sed natura [210v] inuisos fere semper habent quicunque sunt maritis chari) / siue etiam Dux suapte
superbia viam affectabat ad regnum / certe proditio obiecta est /
cuius siue insons erat siue noxius / frequens eum senatus acer-
bissimo supplicio adiudicauit. Sed Rex atrocitatem penae sus-
15 tulit: mortem tulit: qua vt leuissime defungeretur / in vini Cre-
tensis dolium immerso capite respirare prohibitus expirauit:
cuius necem / idem qui iussit / vbi resciuit patratam miser
deplorauit./
      Ricardus hic de quo sermo praesens instituitur / ingenio atque
20 animi robore alterutri fratrum par / forma probitateque vtrique
fuit inferior / inequalibus atque informibus membris / extanti
dorso / alteroque humero erectior / os inamabile / toruum / ac
plane eiusmodi quale bellicosum in purpuratis ac martium appellari / in alijs aliter solet / versipellis iracundus inuidus semper-
25 que etiam ante partum prauus / quippe quem fama est haud
aliter aluo materna eximi quam obstetricante ferro potuisse:
quin agrippam etiam natum eum pedibusque prelatis exijsse
ferunt / preterea nec indentatum / siue aliquid astruxit vero /
odio natus rumor / siue natura futuri prescia prepostere multa in

---

3 fuere] *corr. from* fuerunt P; fuere / auidi potentiae /] fuere auidi potentie P   4
patientes.] patientes / P   5 Clarentiae] Clarentie P   6 elegansque] P H *1565,* atque
elegansque A   8 Reginae] Regine P; insidias /] insidias P   11 chari) /] chari) P
12 est /] est P   13 noxius /] noxius P   14 penae] pene P   14–15 sustulit:] sustulit
P   15 tulit:] tulit P; qua vt] vt P, *changed to* qua vt P^b; leuissime] H, leuissima P A *1565;*
defungeretur /] defungeretur P   16–17 expirauit:] expirauit / P   17 necem /]
necem P; iussit] iussit ⟨mortem tulit⟩ P; iussit /] iussit P   21 inferior /] inferior. P;
membris /] membris P   22 toruum /] toruum P   26 potuisse:] potuisse P   28
ferunt /] ferunt P; indentatum /] indentatum P; vero /] vero P

sons, namely Edward, whom we have mentioned, George, and this Richard; all three were of high rank by birth, and all three were insatiably ambitious, hungry for power, and too quick to resent both superiors and equals. Avenging his father's death, Edward defeated Henry in battle, deprived him of his kingdom, and took his place as king. George, Duke of Clarence, tall and distinguished, might have seemed fortunate in every respect if either his own greed for power had not turned him against his own brother or his enemies' slander had not turned his brother against him. For whether the queen's faction laid a trap for him (for the queen's partisans and the king's kinsmen were bitterest enemies, as women by nature and not out of malice almost always hate those who are dearest to their husbands) or the duke's own insolence made him aspire to the throne, in any case he was indicted for treason, and innocent or guilty, he was condemned by a full parliament to the most grievous punishment. But the king withheld the severity of his punishment even as he upheld the death penalty; to make his death as easy as possible, his head was immersed in a barrel of Cretan wine and his breathing was cut off until he expired; and the very man who had ordered his execution lamented it bitterly when he heard it had been carried out.

This Richard, about whom the following discourse is written, was a match for either one of his brothers in intelligence and fortitude but was inferior to both in appearance and character. His limbs were ill matched and misshapen, his back hunched, one shoulder higher than the other, his face forbidding and cruel, of the sort that is called warlike and soldierly in great nobles but described otherwise in other men. He was crafty, irascible, envious, and always perverse, even in the womb; for it is said that a knife was the midwife which drew him from his mother's belly, and that he was born an Agrippa, feet first, and even that he was born with his teeth, whether a rumor begotten of hatred has added a bit to the truth, or a prescient nature performed many details perversely at the birth of one who in life

[8/1]

eius ortu fecit qui multa fuit in vita contra naturae fas desig-
naturus./ Ceterum bello haud instrenuus dux est habitus / cui
quam ad pacem natura fuit appositior: sepe vicit / interim etiam
victus / quam rem ne emulorum [211] quidem quisquam ipsius
5 vnquam aut inscitiae aut ignorantiae vertit vitio. Supra facultates
largitiosus / ne materia deficeret / ex alijs exhaurire cogebatur
quod in alios effunderet: his artibus factum / vt amorem infirmum / constans odium pareret. Consilia sua non alijs vnquam
credere quam per quos exequi necesse fuit / at ne ijs ipsis quidem
10 aut ante aut amplius quam res vrgebat. Personam quamlibet
induere gerereque et tueri gnauiter / hylarem / seueram /
grauem / remissam / prout sumere aut ponere suasit commodum. In vultu modestia / in animo fastus impotens / ingens /
immanis / verbis adblandiens his quos intus impense oderat / nec
15 eorum abstinens complexibus quos destinabat occidere. Crudelis atque immitis / haud ob iram semper / sed ambitionis ergo
sepius / dum vel augendae fortunae suae vel firmandae studet /
quippe amici inimicique aequa ratio fuit comparati cum commodis / neque cuiusquam morte abstinuit vnquam cuius vita
20 videretur consilijs suis obstare. Constans fama est Henricum /vj/
dum exutus regno in arce Londinensi captiuus adseruaretur ab
isto crudeliter adacto sub costas pugione confossum ac trucidatum / idque nec iubente nec opinante Rege / qui si maxime
decreuisset amoliri quem fortassis e commodo magis ducebat
25 suo viuum in sua manu esse / alium tamen haud dubie tam dirae
carnificinae fuerat prefecturus quam germanum fratrem.

---

1 naturae] nature P; fas] ⟨phas⟩ fas P   2 habitus /] habitus P   3 appositior:] appositior P   5 inscitiae aut ignorantiae] inscitie aut ignorantie P; vitio] P A 1565, in vitio
A; vitio.] vitio / P   6 largitiosus /] largitiosus P; deficeret /] deficeret P   7
effunderet:] effunderet / P; factum] 1565, factus P A H; factum /] factus P   7–8
infirmum /] infirmum, P   8 pareret.] pareret / P   9 ijs] 1565, changed from hijs P,
hijs A H   10 vrgebat.] vrgebat / P   11 gnauiter] A 1565, grauiter P H   12
remissam /] remissam P   12–13 commodum.] commodum / P   13 modestia /]
modestia P; fastus] fastus / P   15 occidere.] occidere / P   16 immitis /] immitis P;
semper /] semper P   17 studet /] studet./ P   18–19 commodis /] commodis P
20 /vj/] P, sextum A H 1565   22–23 trucidatum /] trucidatum P   24 amoliri] P A
1565, eum amoliri H;   26 fratrem.] ⟨frrem⟩ fratrem P

would do much which would flout nature's law. In any case, he was considered a skillful commander in warfare, for which he was naturally better adapted than for peace; he often won, and occasionally he lost—something which not even any of his enemies ever imputed to blundering or ignorance. Lavish beyond his means, to maintain his resources he was forced to squeeze money from one group only to squander it on another; by such tactics he made fickle friends and firm enemies. He never confided his own plans to anyone but those who were needed to carry them out, and not even to them any earlier or any further than the business required. He could adopt any role, then play it out to perfection, whether cheerful or stern, whether sober or relaxed, just as expediency urged him to sustain or abandon it. There was modesty in his countenance when in his heart there was arrogance, uncontrollable, boundless, and monstrous. He would speak flatteringly to those whom he inwardly loathed, and would not hesitate to embrace those whom he had decided to kill. He was cruel and inexorable, not always from anger, but more often because of ambition, as he sought to augment or secure his own fortune; he had equal regard for a friend and for an enemy in comparison with his own advantage, and never hesitated to kill anyone whose life seemed to stand in the way of his plans. It is constantly rumored that when Henry VI had been stripped of the crown and was being held captive in the Tower of London, he was cruelly stabbed and slaughtered by Richard with a dagger thrust under his ribs, all this happening without the king's order or knowledge; for even if he had decided to kill one whom he may have considered it better to keep alive as his prisoner, without doubt he would still have entrusted such a grim execution to someone else besides his own full brother.

    Sunt qui suspicantur istius etiam tecta et callide occultata con-
silia in fratris [211v] Clarentiae Ducis perniciem non defuisse /
quanquam resisteret ac reniteretur aperte / ceterum (vt rem
estimantibus visum est) aliquanto languidius quam is facturus
5 putabatur qui sibi serio statuisset ad salutem germani fratris
incumbendum./ Quibus hoc verum videtur / hi nimirum persuasum habent Ricardum iam olim / viuente adhuc Eduardo /
hoc apud se consilium de asserendo sibi aliquando regno agi-
tasse si qua forte / vti accidit / frater immaturis ad regnum liberis
[9/1] 10 decessisset: cuius rei spem commessatio frequens atque intem-
perans Regis fecit victus./ Eam igitur ob causam Ricardum putant Clarentiae Ducis mortem appetisse / quum ipsius proposito
illius vita non satis opportuna videbatur / quippe quem siue in
fide nepotis manentem / siue aspirantem ad regnum hostem sese
15 vidit exitialiter habiturum. Sed hac de re asserere nihil certe
possum / suspitiones duntaxat hominum coniecturasque secutus: quibus vestigijs / vt aliquando venitur ad verum / ita frequenter erratur: quamquam hoc ipse iam olim fideli relatione
comperi / Mistelbrocum quemdam protinus Eduardo functo ad
20 Potieri domum / qui Ricardo familiaris erat / curriculo contendisse / pulsatoque inciuiliter hostio multo ante lucem / quum et
violenta et intempestiua pulsatio magni ac subitarij negocij
fidem faceret / propere intromissum / Regem eadem hora extinctum nunciasse / ad quam vocem Potierus velut exultabun-
25 dus / "Non est ergo dubium" (inquit) "quin meus herus
Glocestriae Dux illico sit futurus rex" / siue consiliorum eius

1 suspicantur] P, suspicentur A H 1565; callide] callidae P   2 Clarentiae] Clarentie P;
defuisse /] defuisse P   3 aperte /] aperte./ P   3–4 (vt . . . est)] vt . . . est P   6
videtur /] videtur P   7 olim /] olim P; Eduardo /] Eduardo P   9 forte /] forte P
10 decessisset:] decessisset./ P   11 fecit victus] P, victus fecit A H 1565   12
Clarentiae] Clarentie P   13 videbatur /] videbatur./ P   15 hac de] A H 1565, de hac
P   16 possum /] possum P   16–17 secutus:] secutus / P   17 vestigijs / vt . . . verum /] vestigijs vt . . . verum P   18 erratur:] erratur / P; relatione] A H 1565, ratione
P   19 comperi /] comperi P   20 domum /] domum P; erat /] erat P   20–21
contendisse /] contendisse P   21 hostio] hostio / P; lucem /] lucem P   22 magni]
magni / P   23 intromissum /] intromissum P   24 quam] A H 1565, quem P   26
Glocestriae] Glocestrie P

There are also some who suspect that Richard's secret and cunningly hidden plans also played a part in the destruction of his brother, the Duke of Clarence, though he openly repined and opposed it—a little too feebly, as it seemed to careful observers, for one who could be thought to be seriously committed to saving his own brother. Those who think that this story is true naturally suppose that before Edward's death Richard had already conceived his plan of ultimately claiming the throne for himself if his brother should happen to die (as he actually did) leaving children not old enough to rule, a hope strengthened by the king's frequent feasts and immoderate eating. And so they think that on this account Richard sought the Duke of Clarence's death, since his life seemed to be inconvenient for Richard's designs; for he saw that whether the duke remained loyal to his nephews or aspired to the crown, he was going to be Richard's mortal enemy. But of this matter I can state nothing for certain; I am going on nothing but people's suspicions and conjectures, a route which occasionally leads to the truth but more often away from it. And yet I personally learned this much long ago by trustworthy report. Just after Edward's death, a certain Mistlebrook ran to the house of Potter, a servant of Richard's, and knocked importunately at the door well before dawn, and since his violent and untimely knocking testified to the seriousness and urgency of his business, he was hastily admitted. He announced that the king had died that very hour, to which Potter responded exultantly, "Then there is no doubt that my master the Duke of Gloucester will promptly be king," whether he knew of his plans or some portent alerted him to what was in store; for

peritus fuit siue aliquo signo quod erat [212] futurum presensit
(nam temere dictum haud existimo): quem ego sermonem ab eo
memini / qui colloquentes auscultauerat / iam tum patri meo
renuntiatum cum adhuc nulla proditionis eius suspicio habe-
5   retur./

Ceterum vt reuertar ad hystoriam / seu Ricardus olim secum
animo regnum inuaserat / seu consilium ex nepotum etatis opor-
tunitate ceperat / quae res plerunque segnes etiam et quietos
impellit ad facinus / certum est decreuisse eum / vita pueris
10 adempta / regno velut sceleris precio potiri. Gnarus itaque veterum factionum quibus inter aulicos laborabatur (quas quoad
eius erat / sedulo etiam aluerat) / Regis Eduardi cognatis Reginae
sanguini tantum authoritatis opumque inuidentibus contraque
non minus ijsdem de rebus inuisis / eam rem suis consilijs magno
[10/1]   15 putauit adminiculo fore si partium pretextu / velut offensas veteres vlturus / suum occulte negotium ageret / iraque et ignoratione factionis alterius ad alterius perniciem abuteretur / tum ex
ea quae superesset paulatim quos posset commodum in suam
sententiam perductis / si quos parum oportunos offenderet / eos
20 per insidias incautos nec mali quicquam veritos opprimeret./
Nam hoc certum animo proposuit / si qua rima consilium eius
immaturius efflueret confestim fore vti inter dissidentes factiones ipsius sanguine fedus sanciretur./

Hae diuisiones amicorum quanquam nonnihil erant ipsi Ed-
25 uardo molestae tamen dum erat incolumis eo negligentius eas
habuit quod vtramque partem cognouit frenare se quum vellet
pro suo arbitratu posse./ Ceterum vbi postrema egritudine de-
cumbens vires labascere sensit / et deploratam medicis salutem
suam / etatem liberorum animo reputans / quanquam nihil for-

1–2 presensit (nam . . . existimo):] presensit / nam . . . existimo / P   3 memini /]
memini P; auscultauerat /] auscultauerat P   8 ceperat / quae] ceperat que P   9
eum /] eum P   10 potiri.] potiri / P; Gnarus] A H 1565, Ignarus P   12 erat /] erat P;
aluerat) /] aluerat) P   13 contraque] contraque, P   14 inuisis /] inuisis P   15
adminiculo] P, adiumento A H 1565; pretextu /] pretextu P   16 vlturus /] vlturus P;
ageret /] ageret./ P   16–17 ignoratione] ⟨ignorantie⟩ ignoratione P   17 alterius ad]
alterius / ad P; abuteretur /] abuteretur P; tum] A H 1565, tamen P   19 perductis /]
perductis P; offenderet /] offenderet P   20 veritos] P H, ⟨suspicantes⟩ veritos A,
suspicantes Psa As 1565   21 proposuit] P A H, presumpsit Ps As; proposuit /] proposuit
P   23 sanciretur] 1565, sanxiretur P A H   24 Hae] He P; nonnihil] non nihil P
28 sensit /] sensit, P   29 reputans /] reputans P

I doubt that he said it capriciously. I remember that this conversation was reported to my father by a man who had heard them conversing, well before there was any suspicion of this treachery.

But to return to the history, whether Richard had first thought of seizing the throne long before or his plan was suggested by the opportune circumstance of his nephews' age—for opportunity will often make even the lazy and peaceful do wrong—it is certain that he decided to take the boys' lives and seize the throne as a reward for his crime. And so, well aware of the old vying factions at court (factions which he had even done all that he could to foment), with the king's relatives envying the queen's kindred for all their authority and wealth and being envied for the same things in turn, he supposed it would further his plans a great deal if he secretly served his own interests under a pretext of partisanship, as if he were going to avenge previous injuries, and exploited the anger and ignorance of one faction to wipe out the other; and then when he had gradually won over all he conveniently could from the remaining faction, if he found some unlikely to help him he would use treacherous means to destroy them when they were off guard, not expecting any trouble. For he knew for a certainty that if somehow his plan leaked out prematurely the quarreling factions would promptly make peace with each other by spilling his blood.

Even though these divisions among his supporters caused Edward himself some distress, for as long as he stayed in good health he did little about them, since he knew he could restrain either party whenever he pleased. But in the grip of his last illness, when he perceived that his own strength was failing and that the doctors despaired of his recovery, he began to consider his children's tender age; and though he feared nothing less

midabat minus quam id quod euenit / prospiciens tamen multa
illis mala nasci ex [212v] amicorum dissentione posse / quando
etas eorum per se imbecilla atque improuida / consilijs amicorum / quibus fulciri solis poterat / nudaretur / qui dum se
5   discessione ac discordia disiungerent / partibus et studijs intenti
minus verum quod esset curarent / sepeque / quo suam quisque
factionem in Principis gratiam promoueat / placitura magis
omnes quam profutura consulerent / hec atque huiuscemodi
cum animo voluens multos e purpuratis accersi iubet / nomi-
10   natim Marquesium Dorsettum Reginae ex priore marito filium
atque Ricardum Hastingum virum nobilem cubicularium suum /
[11/1]   qui insigniter inter se inimicitias exercuerant / item alios vtriusque factionis qui tum in aula fuerunt atque haberi poterant./
Hos vbi Rex adesse vidit / leuatus paululum et suffultus puluinis
15   sic / vti fertur / alloquutus est:

   "Viri clarissimi ijdemque cognati mihi affinesque charissimi /
mea quo loco vita sit et vos videtis et ego sentio / quae res facit vti
quo minus diu futurum me vobiscum reputo / tanto impensior
animum sollicitudo subeat / quo animorum affectos habitu vos
20   relinquam. Enimuero qualescunque a me relinquemini tales li-
beri mei vos excipiant necesse est: qui si (quod superi prohibeant) discordantes inuenerint / ipsi nimirum partibus accessuri
nouasque ante lites inter se moturi videantur quam in id peritiae
maturuerint qua vos compositis vestris reponant in concordiam.
25   Teneram eorum aetatem cernitis / cuius ego presidium vnicum

2 illis] *interl. P*   3–4 amicorum /] amicorum *P*   4 poterat /] poterat *P*   6 curarent /] curarent *P*   6–8 curarent / sepeque . . . consulerent] *H*, cernerent curarent sepeque . . . consulerent *P A, changed to* cernerent curarentque sepe . . . consulere *by another*
hand P, cernerent, aut curarent: saepeque . . . consulerent *1565*   6 sepeque /] sepeque *P*   7 gratiam] ⟨f⟩ gratiam *P*   8 consulerent /] consulerent *P*   9 cum animo
voluens] *P A H* secum reuoluens *1565 (see notes)*   10 Reginae] Regine *P*   11 suum /]
suum *P*   12 inimicitias] *P A H 1565*, simultates *P*ˢᵃ *A*ˢ   13 tum] *changed from* tamen
*P*ᵇ   15 sic / vti fertur /] sic vti fertur *P; *est:] est./ *P*   16 cognati mihi] cognati / mihi / *P*
17 sentio /] sentio *P; *quae] que *P*   19 subeat] ⟨subleuat⟩ subeat *P; *subeat /] subeat
*P; *affectos habitu] *P H*, affectos *A*   20 relinquam.] relinquam / *P*   21 est:] est / *P*
22 inuenerint /] inuenerint *P; *accessuri] accessuri / *P*   23 peritiae] peritie ⟨pernitie⟩
P   24 concordiam.] concordiam / *P*

than what actually happened, he foresaw that the dissension of
their supporters could do them great harm, since their naturally
frail and improvident youth would be stripped of its one source
of strength, their supporters' advice. For when dissension and
discord polarized the supporters, they would pay more attention
to partisan interests than to stating the truth, and would often
advise what was pleasant, and not what was profitable, in order
to advance their own faction in the favor of the prince. Bearing
in mind these and similar possibilities, he summoned many of
the great nobles before him, in particular the Marquess of Dor-
set, the queen's son by her previous husband, and Richard Hastings, a nobleman and his own chamberlain (for these two had
feuded with particular ferocity), as well as other members of
each faction who were then in the court and within the king's
reach. When the king saw that they had arrived, he first raised
himself slightly, and then, when he was propped up on pillows, it
is reported that he addressed them as follows:

"Illustrious gentlemen, my dear kinsmen by blood and by
marriage, you see and I feel where my own life now stands; so
that the shorter the time I expect to be staying with you, the more
troubled I feel about what state of mind I am leaving you in. For
my children must take you however you are when I leave you,
and if (heaven forbid) you are at variance when they first encounter you, they are apt to join factions themselves and begin
further quarrels with each other before they gain sufficient experience and discretion to settle your quarrels and restore you to
concord. You see their tender age, and I judge that your concord

censeo in vestra concordia situm esse / siquidem haud satis firma
res est vestra in illos charitas si vobis inuicem odio sitis./ Virilis
etatis robori vestra fortasse sufficiat fides / at puerilis authoritate
regenda est / [213] adolescens fulcienda consilijs / quas res neque
5 illi aliunde poterunt consequi nisi vos dederitis / neque vos concedere si dissenseritis. Etenim vbi mutuo infensi diuersa sentiunt
et alter alterius consilium odio consulentis eludit / ibi necesse est
bene consulta male pereant / quippe quae rata esse nisi consensu
non possunt. Preterea / dum suam quisque factionem studet
10 insinuare principi / fiat nimirum vti ad gratiam plura quam ex
vero atque vtili suadeantur: ita prauis adulationibus imbutus
adolescentiae animus tener / praeceps in vicia voluitur ac regnum secum in perniciem trahit / nisi si quid Deus inspiret
melius./ Quod si eueniat vt resipiscat princeps atque ad frugem
15 redeat / tum vero hi quorum primae partes apud eum fuerant /
longissime ab fauore excident. Ita gratia male parta cito perit:
quae vero bonis artibus inita est / ea demum stabilis firmaque
perdurat./
    "Diu iam inter vos magna odia exarsere / haud magnis sepe de
20 causis: rem enim plerunque non male factam / aut male narran-
tis deprauat oratio / aut per se exiguam durius interpretando
audientis affectus exaggerat. Vnum hoc scio / haud quaquam
pares vobis irarum causas et amoris esse./ Nam quod homines
sumus / quod in Christi verba iurauimus qui vnum atque vnicum
25 charitatis symbolum suis militibus dedit / concionatoribus com-
memoranda pretereo / quanquam haud scio an cuiusquam verba
concionatoris magis vos commouere debeant quam mea / qui
protinus hinc ad ea loca demigro de quibus illi tam multa predi-

---

2–4 Virilis . . . adolescens] *P A H,* Quod si viri essent, minus fortasse desideraretur fides.
At vero pueritia . . . adolescentia *1565*   3 puerilis] puerilis / *P*   5 dederitis /] dederitis *P*   6 dissenseritis.] dissenseritis *P;* Etenim] *A H 1565,* Etiam *P*   7 eludit /]
eludit *P*   8 pereant /] pereant. *P;* quae] que *P*   9 Possunt.] possunt *P;* Preterea /]
preterea *P*   10 principi /] principi *P*   11 suadeantur:] suadeantur *P*   12
praeceps] *H,* ⟨princeps⟩ praeceps *P,* princeps *A 1565*   15 redeat /] redeat *P*   16
excident] *A H 1565,* excedent *P;* excident.] excedent / *P;* perit:] perit./ *P*   17 quae] que
P   19 exarsere /] exarsere *P*   20 causis:] causis *P*   22 affectus] *A H 1565,* animus
P; exaggerat.] exaggerat *P;* scio /] scio *P;* haud] *interl. P;* quaquam] qua⟨n⟩quam *P*   24
vnum atque vnicum] *P 1565,* viuum atque vnicum *H,* vnum *A*   26 pretereo /] pretereo
P

provides its sole safeguard, since your love for them is a feeble defense if you hate one another. If they were grown men, your good faith might suffice them, but their childhood must be ruled with authority and their youth reinforced with advice, things which no one can furnish unless you provide them and which you cannot furnish if you are at odds. For where mutual enemies hold different opinions and one makes a mockery of the other's advice out of hatred for the adviser, good advice turns out badly, perforce; for without a consensus, it cannot turn out well. In addition, when everyone tries to ingratiate his own faction with the prince, the result is that his favor, more than truth and expediency, determines how people advise him; and thus steeped in perverse adulation, the impressionable soul of a minor will fall head over heels into vice and drag the kingdom to ruin along with him, unless God should inspire him to think better of it. But if the prince does return to his senses and go back to the path of virtue, then the very people who influenced him most will fall furthest from favor. Thus ill-gotten goodwill is soon lost, whereas that which is earned the right way remains stable and durable.

"For some years great feuds have been raging among you, often touched off by quite trivial injuries. For a hostile witness often makes something innocently done appear sinister or a prejudiced hearer makes a minor offense into a major one. I am certain of this much: your reasons for hate are outnumbered by reasons for love. As for our common humanity and our sworn allegiance to Christ, who gave his soldiers one and only one watchword, that of charity, I leave these points for preachers to handle, though I am not sure that any preacher's words ought to affect you more deeply than mine, since I am going hence so soon to those places about which they have so much to say. But I

cant./ At istud tantum a me rogabimini vti vobiscum reputetis /
alteram harum factionum partem cognatos mihi / [213v] alteram
affines esse / vosque ipsos inuicem aut sanguinis vinculo / aut
affinitatis coniungi: quae necessitudo / iuncta sacramento con-
5 iugij / si Christi instituta tantum haberent ponderis quantum
apud Christianos habere deberent / atque vtinam habeant / certe
non minus momenti ad conciliandos animos quam ipsa sanguinis ratio contineret: tantum prohibeant superi ne id ipsum in
causa sit quo minus concordetis quod maxime ad concordiam
10 deberet incitare.

    "Equidem nescio quo malo fato sic videmus accidere vt inimi-
citia nusquam exerceatur infestius quam apud hos quos potissimum aut naturae fas aut legum debeat ab omni simultate deterrere./ Tam execrabilis bellua superbia est et precellendi
15 cupiditas / quae quum semel generosis illustrium virorum pectoribus irrepserit / non ante desinit contentione proserpere
quam cedibus omnia et sanguine permiscuerit / dum quisque
primum summo proximus esse / mox equare / postremo super-
[13/1]   gredi ac precellere conatur. Qui tam improbus ardor gloriae hoc
20 in regno intra paucos annos proximos quantum suscitauerit incendij / quantum stragis ediderit / vtinam tam facile Deus obli-
uisci velit quam nos reminiscimur: cuius mala si priuato mihi tam
animo praecipere et precogitare licuisset quam re ipsa postea
maiore meo dolore quam voluptate sum expertus / dispeream si
25 flexis poplitibus exhibitum honorem tam multis hominum capitibus comparassem. Sed quando facta quae sunt infecta esse
non queunt / qua ex re ante tam multum damni acceptum
nouimus / ea ne porro accidat / danda sedulo [214] opera est./

    "Omnia iam pacata sunt et spes est perfore prospera sub libe-
30 ris meis / cognatis vestris / si neque illos vita destituat neque vos

---

2 mihi /] mihi *P*   4 coniungi:] coniungi *P;* quae] que *P;* necessitudo /] necessitudo
P   4–5 coniugij /] coniugij *P*   6 habeant /] habeant *P*   7 conciliandos] *1565,*
consiliandos *P A H*   8 contineret:] contineret / *P;* id] id ⟨quod⟩ *P*   13 naturae]
nature *P*   15 quae] que *P*   19 precellere] *P A 1565,* precurrere *P*sa *A*s *H;* conatur.]
conatur *P;* gloriae] glorie *P*   20 suscitauerit] *1565,* suscitauit *P A H*   20–21 incendij /] incendij *P*   22 reminiscimur:] reminiscimur / *P*   23 praecipere] *inserted P*b;
re ipsa] *1565,* re ipsa / ⟨re⟩ *P H,* re ipsa re *A*   24 expertus /] expertus./ *P*   27
queunt] *P A,* possunt *P*sa *A*s *H 1565*   28 nouimus] *corr. from* non minus *P*b; nouimus /]
nouimus *P;* accidat /] accidat *P*   30 meis / cognatis vestris /] meis cognatis vestris *P*

will ask you this: just remember that one of these factions is my kindred by blood and the other my kindred by marriage, and that you yourselves are related by ties either of blood or of marital affinity; and if we took Christ's precepts as seriously as Christian men ought to (and would that we did), the latter bond, joined by the sacrament of marriage, would certainly be no less effective in joining men's hearts than an actual blood-tie; God forbid, then, that the very thing which ought to make you most desirous of harmony should give rise to discord.

"And yet, by some evil influence, we see that as a rule none feud more bitterly than those whom either natural or human law should deter most completely from all enmity. Such an odious monster is pride and the lust for supremacy; and once it has crept into illustrious noblemen's hearts, it never ceases to creep forth in contentiousness until it has drenched all in slaughter and bloodshed, as every man tries first of all to be next to the greatest, then to equal him, and at last to excel and surpass him. Would that God would as readily forget as we personally remember what a great conflagration this wicked ardor for glory has ignited and how much slaughter it has provoked in this kingdom within these last few years; and if I as a private citizen had been able to foresee and anticipate its ill effects as distinctly in thought as I later experienced them in deed, with less pleasure than pain, on my life I would never have sacrificed so many men's heads to see men on their knees doing me honor. But since what is done cannot be undone, we must take great pains to ensure that the same thing which we know has caused such great harm heretofore will not happen again.

"All is peaceful at present, and my hope is that all will remain prosperous under my children if their lives and your concord

concordia: quarum si prorsus alterutra sit carendum / profecto
in illis minus iacturae fuerit: quibus si quid communis hominum
sors attulerit / Anglia tamen facile inueniet reges nulla fortassis
parte deteriores./ Verum si vos in pueri regno discordia oc-
5 cupet / multi nimirum viri boni atque egregij videntur ante perituri / nec Principe interim tuto et vobis ipsis imprimis periculo
obnoxijs / quam populus intestina semel seditione seuiens in
pacem rursus et concordiam redeat./ Vos igitur oratione hac
quam hodie vobiscum postremam mihi videor habiturus hortor
10 obtestorque per amorem illum quem ego semper hactenus erga
vos / quem vos vicissim erga me / quem Deus erga nos omnes
habuit / ex hoc tempore / condonatis et remissis offensis omnibus / vos amore mutuo complectamini / quod ego vos profecto
facturos confido / si vos respectus vllus aut Dei / aut Principis /
15 cognationis / patriae / aut vestrae denique ipsorum salutis
habeat."

Hec vbi Rex locutus est / haud diutius sustinens sese in dexterum latus recubuit / facie ad proceres versa / quorum nemo
erat qui lachrimis temperare potuerit. Ceterum verbis eum
20 quantum quisque poterat consolati / tum de re quae placitura
sentiebant respondentes / velut icto federe in morientis gratiam
Regis manus inter se iunxerunt / quum (vti paulo post apparuit)
animis [214v] longe disiungerentur./

[14/1] Defuncto Rege / filius natu maior Londinum / vtpote regiam
25 vrbem / petere maturat / qui viuo patre Ludloi vixit in Vallia./
Nam ea deinceps primogenitis regum / viuis adhuc parentibus /
propria ditio est / quae quum ab Rege porro sita eo negligentius
habita in morem prope siluestrem cepta est efferari / improbis

---

1 concordia:] concordia / P; carendum /] carendum P   2 iacturae fuerit:] iacture
fuerit P   3 attulerit /] attulerit./ P   3–4 occupet /] occupet P   5–6 perituri] P H,
perituri et (vt *1565*) pariter ipsi A *1565;* perituri /] perituri P   6 tuto] ⟨tuto⟩ tuto P
7 obnoxijs /] obnoxijs P   10 hactenus erga] hactenus er⟨a⟩ga P   12 tempore /]
tempore P; omnibus /] omnibus P   13 complectamini /] complectamini P   15
cognationis / patriae /] cognationis patrie P; vestrae] vestre P   16 habeat.] habeat./ P
17–18 dexterum] ⟨dexterum⟩ dexterum P   19 potuerit.] potuerit / P   20
consolati /] consolati P   22 iunxerunt /] iunxerunt P; (vti . . . apparuit)] vti . . . apparuit P   24 Londinum /] Londinum P   25 vrbem /] vrbem P; maturat /] maturat P
26 regum / viuis . . . parentibus /] regum viuis . . . parentibus P   27 quae] que P;
porro sita] P A H, prout sita est *1565*   28 efferari /] efferari P

endure; though if you had to do without one or the other, the loss of my children would be the less serious. For if they meet with mankind's common fate, England will easily find other kings who perhaps are in no wise inferior; but if you fall at variance in the reign of a child, many good and excellent men are likely to perish, with the prince threatened and you in most danger of all, before a nation which has once broken out in internal sedition will be restored to tranquility and harmony. And so in this, the last speech I am likely to make to you, I entreat and beseech you, in the name of that love I have always shown you, which you have always shown me in return, and which God has always shown all of us, that from this moment you will forgive and forget all your injuries and embrace one another in mutual love, as I am confident that you will if you have any regard for either God, your prince, your relations, your nation, or finally your own safety."

Having spoken, the king promptly sank down and lay on his right side, his face turned toward the nobles, of whom not one could keep back his tears. But after each of them gave him whatever verbal consolation he could and said what he thought the king wanted to hear in response to his plea, they joined hands as if making a truce for the dying king's sake, though in spirit (as it soon became clear) they were not joined at all.

When the king had died, his older son quickly set out toward London, the regal metropolis, from Ludlow in Wales, where he lived during his father's lifetime. For that region is the proper domain of successive kings' firstborn sons while their parents are still living; and since that country was far from the king and thus carelessly governed, so that it had begun to revert into a sort of

hominibus latrocinijs ac cede licenter impuneque grassantibus /
Eduardus filius eo cum imperio missus est / vti presentis authoritate Principis facinorosorum audacia refrenaretur. Moderator
pueritiae datus est Anthonius Vodeuilus / cognomento ex di-
5 tione Riuerus / Reginae frater / vir haud facile discernas manune
an consilio prestantior / tum adhibiti in consilium alij / vt quisque
puero proximus materno genere fuit.

Eam rem / ab Regina curatam quo suae factionis opes ab tene-
ris statim Principis annis confirmaret / frustratus tantam eius
10 spem / Ricardus pretextum sibi ad eos euertendos initiumque ad
reliquum inceptum suum conficiendum fecit./ Nam quorum in
illos odium maxime implacatum nouit animosque in se bene-
uolos eos partim coram / alios per epistolam ac nuncios explora-
tae fidei compellens admonet / rem neutiquam ferendam Prin-
15 cipem amisso patre iuuenem ipsis cognatum in custodia et
manibus esse agnatorum / ablegatis propemodum ipsis qui neque minus certa in eum fide et longe honoratior pars regij generis fuit quam sanguis eius maternus / qui / nisi libidini patris
visum aliter esset / perquam erat indignus qui cum eius atque
20 ipsorum sanguine [215] misceretur / quos nunc non primos
apud Regem esse neque illi honorificum neque sibi tutum / vt
quorum permagni referat haud quaquam pati emulorum
[15/1] suorum potentiam gratia et fauoribus adolescere apud Principem puerum / natura facilem / etatis vitio credulum nec satis
25 callentem aduersus delatorum calumnias./

"Meminisse vos" (inquit) "opinor patrem eius quamquam
annis et rerum vsu maturum tamen eius factionis suasu impulsuque quouis circumactum / longe profecto magis quam aut ex

---

4 pueritiae] pueritie P; Vodeuilus /] Vodeuilus P   5 Riuerus /] Riuerus P; Reginae
frater /] Regine frater P; manune] A H 1565, manuve P   6 prestantior /] prestantior./
P; alij /] alij P   7 fuit] P A H 1565 but perhaps we should read esset; fuit.] fuit P   8
rem /] rem P; suae] sue P   10 spem /] spem P   13–14 exploratae] explorate P
16 agnatorum] H 1565, agnitorum P (reading uncertain), agnotorum A; agnatorum /]
agnitorum P   18 qui /] qui P   19 esset /] esset P   21 Regem] A H 1565, Regnum
P; tutum /] tutum P   22 permagni] per magni P; quaquam] qua⟨n⟩quam P   24
puerum /] puerum P; facilem /] facilem P   25 callentem] P A 1565, cauentem H; ca-
lumnias] ⟨insidias⟩ calumnias P   28 circumáctum /] circumactum P

wild savagery, with evil men freely and safely engaging in robbery and murder, the younger Edward was sent there with a military command so that the authority of the prince's presence would check the audacity of wrongdoers. The man assigned as the young prince's governor was Anthony Woodville, entitled Lord Rivers, the queen's brother, a man as distinguished in battle as in counsel, and various others were chosen as counsellors, all the prince's closest relatives on his mother's side.

This arrangement of the queen's, by means of which she intended to strengthen her faction's position from the earliest years of the prince, was embraced as a pretext by Richard for thwarting her ambitious hopes and overthrowing her partisans as a groundwork for the rest of his own enterprise. For of those whom he knew to be implacable enemies of the queen's party and friends of his own he warned some openly and others by letter and by messengers of proven loyalty that it was intolerable that, after his father's death, the young prince—their own kinsman—should be left in the custody and control of half-kinsmen, whereas they themselves should be virtually banished although they were no less assuredly loyal to the prince and a far more distinguished branch of the king's family than his mother's kindred, whose blood (though it seemed otherwise to the wantonness of the father) was not at all worthy of being mixed with his blood and their own, whose subordinate role in the king's entourage was dishonorable for him and unsafe for themselves; for it was crucial for them not to allow their rivals to augment their own power by lavishing indulgence and favors on a boy prince who was naturally accommodating, gullible on account of his age, and too susceptible to the slanders of backbiters.

"I think you remember," he said, "how his father, though ripe in both age and experience, was easily swayed at the urging and whim of that faction, far more easily than was compatible with

ipsius honore aut re cuiusquam fuerit preterquam illorum immoderatam [praepotentiam] qui suane bona an mala nostra
auidius appetierunt in incerto est./ Itaque si non quorundam
nostrum gratia magis apud Regem quam vlla cognationis ratio
5 valuisset / paulum certe abfuerat quo minus aliquot nostrum
circumuentos insidijs oppressissent / tam hercle facile quam op-
presserunt eum qui Regis sanguine haud minus prope aberat./
Verum fauentibus superis eo periculo defuncti sumus / sic tamen vt vel maius impendeat si Principis affectus patimur
10 quocunque inimicis nostris libebit impelli / quibus haud difficile
sit vel ignorantis iussum ad perniciem nostram pretexere nisi
Deus vel vestra vigilantia malitiam eorum in ipsos auertat. Qua
in re nemo nostrum magis segniter gerat se ob male sartam
paulo ante concordiam / quam qui inierunt / ne dubitari queat
15 quam sincera sit / Regis potius affectibus sunt obsequuti quam
suis: neque quemquam nostrum tam vecordem arbitror vt
multum sibi putet ei confidendum qui ex inimico vetere amicum
nuperum se profiteatur / nisi quis forte existimet vna hora subito
coactam pacem ac ne toto quidem adhuc mense [215v] coalitam
20 altius eorum pectoribus insedisse quam tot annis altam ac radi-
catam inuidiam."

His atque huiusmodi verbis literisque homines ex se ardentes
vehementer incendit /.sed precipue duos / Eduardum Bukyngamiae Ducem et Ricardum Hastyngum / ambos fama clara /
25 magnis opibus / sed Dux natalibus illustrior: alteri ex munere
quod gerebat multum authoritatis adcreuerat / siquidem pre-

1 preterquam] P A H 1565 (used as an equivalent of praeter)   1–2 illorum immoderatam praepotentiam] illorum immoderatam followed by a six- to ten-letter gap P A H,
auauncement inserted in margin Pᵃ (cf. the immoderate aduancement of them selfe 1557),
illorum 1565 (for the conjecture praepotentiam see notes)   10 inimicis nostris] P, nostris
inimicis A H 1565   11 vel] P, vt A, et H 1565   12 auertat] A H 1565, auertant P;
auertat.] auertant P   13 nemo . . . se] P A H, non est quod quisquam nostrum negligentius se gerat 1565; gerat] changed from gerit H, gerit P A; sartam] A H 1565, factam
P   14 inierunt /] inierunt P; dubitari queat] H, dubitare queat A, dubitari queant P
15 obsequuti] P Aˢ H 1565, oblati A; suis:] suis./ P   20 altam] A H, alitam P, alte
actam 1565   23 incendit /] incendit P; duos /] duos P   23–24 Bukyngamiae]
Buykngamie P   24 Ducem] ⟨du⟩ Ducem P; Hastyngum /] Hastyngum P; clara /] clara
P   25 illustrior:] illustrior P   26 adcreuerat /] adcreuerat P

his own honor or anyone's interests besides the immoderate [advancement] of those who were as eager to hurt us as to benefit themselves. And so if the personal influence of some of our number had not carried more weight with the king than any considerations of kinship, they might quite easily have trapped and destroyed some of us, every bit as easily as they destroyed someone else just as closely related to the king. And yet with heaven's help we have lived through that danger; yet an even greater one is in store for us if we let the king's affections be steered in whichever direction seems best to our enemies, who would have little trouble producing an order for our destruction even without the king's knowledge unless God or your vigilance ensures that their malice recoils on them. Nor should anyone be less energetic in this undertaking on account of the peace botched together a short time ago. Have no doubt about just how sincere it is: those who accepted it did so to suit the king's humor rather than their own. For I doubt that any of us is mad enough to place very much trust in an old enemy who professes himself a new friend, unless perhaps anyone thinks that a peace hastily contracted in a single hour and still not a month old has sunk more deeply into their hearts than an enmity deeply rooted for so many years."

With these words and letters, and others like them, he greatly inflamed people already smoldering, two of them in particular: Edward, Duke of Buckingham, and Richard Hastings. Both were men of great fame and wealth; the duke was of nobler birth, but Hastings had gained great authority through the posi-

fecerat eum Rex cubiculo suo / quod est apud Anglos perquam
honorificum. Hi / quum non tam sibi mutuo bene vellent quam
Reginae partibus pariter cuperent male / hactenus facile cum
Ricardo conspirarunt vt suorum inimicorum pretextu maternos
5   amicos Principis amolirentur./

Ea re decreta / cum illos accepissent tanta manu Regem deduc-
turos vt nihil in eos auderi tuto queat ab inermibus / sin ipsi
contra parent copias / ad manus rem venturam / cuius et semper
dubius euentus sit et quum ab aduersa parte Princeps esset /
10 suam proditionis nomen ac speciem subituram / ingenio illos
exarmandos statuunt. Itaque curauerunt vti per viros idoneos
Reginae persuaderetur / multum esse periculi in eo consilio
quod depellendi periculi causa inibatur / nam pacatis rebus /
proceribus reductis in concordiam / animisque omnium intentis
15 ad excipiendum Regem ac diademate insigniendum / si amici
Reginae cogant multitudinem / iniecturos haud dubie metum his
quibus aliquando simultas cum illis intercesserat / ne non tutandi
Regis causa / cui nemo discrimen intentet / sed inuadendi sui
congregetur / recrudescente discordia / atque hoc pacto fore
20 [216] vti hi vicissim suas compellerent copias: deinde / velut vim
repellerent / illaturos / quorum opes (quod illa nosceret) late
paterent / qua ex re totum regnum in armis et tumultu futurum:
tum eius damnum omne / quod et immensum expectabatur et
magna pars in eos fortasse casura a quibus illa maxime vellet
25 auerti / omnes ei vni forent atque amicis eius acceptum relaturi /
vtpote quos causarentur priuati odij respectu conturbasse rempublicam / violata per iniuriam concordia cuius maritus ipsius

---

2 honorificum.] honorificum /] P; Hi /] Hi P   6 decreta /] decreta P   8 parent] A^s
1565, corr. from. parant P H, parant A; copias] ⟨insidias⟩ copias P; copias /] copias P;
venturam /] venturam P   10 subituram /] subituram P   12 persuaderetur /] persuaderetur P   13 inibatur /] inibatur P   14 concordiam /] concordiam P   16
Reginae] Regine P; multitudinem /] multitudinem P   17–19 non tutandi . . . discordia] P A H, non tantummodo regis causa, cui nemo discrimen intentet,
inuadendi: sin congregetur, discordia 1565   18 causa /] causa P; inuadendi] written
over some other word P   19 congregetur] ⟨cogeretur⟩ congregetur P; discordia /] discordia./ P   20 copias:] copias / P; deinde /] deinde P   21 repellerent / illaturos /]
repellerent illaturos P   22 paterent /] paterent P; futurum:] futurum / P   23 tum]
corr. from tamen P^b; omne /] omne P   25 auerti /] auerti P; relaturi /] relaturi, P
26–27 rempublicam /] rempublicam P

tion he occupied, for the king had appointed him keeper of the king's chamber, which is a very honorable office in England. Though these men shared less mutual goodwill than ill will for the queen's faction, they readily joined Richard in conspiring to exterminate the prince's maternal supporters on the pretext that they were their enemies.

Having reached that decision, they learned that the queen's friends were about to accompany the king with such a large retinue that no safe attempt could be made on the party except by an armed band; on the other hand, if they raised troops of their own, the affair would come down to a battle, with the outcome as always uncertain, the king on the other side, and their own faction accordingly sure to assume both the name and appearance of treason; and so they resolved to disarm them by cunning. Through suitable intermediaries they persuaded the queen that the measures being planned as a safeguard were actually a source of great danger; for in the new state of peace, with the nobility restored to accord, and with everyone intent on the reception and crowning of the king, if the queen's friends summoned up a large force, they would undoubtedly make their former enemies afraid that the force was being gathered not for the protection of the king, who was in no danger, but for an assault on themselves, as the feud was renewed; they, in turn, would call up their own forces, and then mount an offensive as if they were defending themselves; as she knew, their resources were vast, and the mobilization would have the whole realm up in arms and confusion; and then the whole cost of the conflict, which was apt to be huge and to fall in large part on the very group she most desired to protect, would be blamed by everyone wholly on her and her friends, who would be charged with disrupting the commonwealth for the sake of a private feud and unjustly destroying the accord that her own dying husband was

[17/1]   moriens author sanciendae fuisset. His rationibus adducta Re-
            gina sic apud Vodeuilum fratrem filiumque Ricardum Graium
            egit / qui tum in aula Principis primi erant / vt illi / repudiato
            priore consilio / presidio supersedentes / Regem comitatu mo-
      5   dico Londinum versus producerent.
                 Erat in itinere Regis Hamptona quae quanquam in vmbilico
            prope regni sita tamen alteri eiusdem nominis oppido quod
            obiacet australi freto comparata / Borealis vocatur./ Hanc eodem
            die quo Rex inde digressus est / Gloucestriae ac Bokyngamiae
     10   Duces intrant / ac forte accidit vt Vodeuilus Reginae frater quem
            diximus ibidem restiterit / postero mane Stratfordiam iturus ad
            Regem vbi eam noctem transegit [·xi·] ab Hamptona millibus.
            Igitur Vodeuilus officiose Ducibus occurrens ac summa gratula-
            tione vicissim exceptus / vbi quantum temporis visum est ser-
     15   mone atque epulis produxere / dimittitur / ita delinitus humani-
            tate Ducum vt optima spe plenus / hilaris / atque animi securus
            iret cubitum.
                 Sed illi / qui longe diuersum agitabant [216v] animo quam
            vultu pre se tulerant / reliquis omnibus facessere iussis / Ricar-
     20   dum Ratcliffum equitem ac   qui talibus erant consilijs intimi
            retinuerunt / ac discumbentes ad mensam de suis inceptis in
            adultam noctem deliberant. Rebus consultis adsurgentes mit-
            tunt qui nullo tumultu comites suos admoneant vti parent sese /
            nempe Duces tantum non in equis esse. Hoc nuncio excitatus
     25   ipsorum comitatus presto aderat / quum Vodeuili adhuc ministri
            sterterent. Ad hec effecerant vti omnibus exitibus oppidi ob-

---

1 sanciendae] *1565*, sanctiendae *P A H;* fuisset.] fuisset / *P*   2 Graium] ⟨graium⟩
Graium *P*   3 egit /] egit *P;* tum] ⟨tamen⟩ tum *P;* illi /] illi *P*   4 consilio /] consilio *P*
5 producerent] *last word in H;* producerent.] producerent *P*   6 quae] que *P*   9
Gloucestriae] Gloucestrie *P*   10 Reginae] Regine *P*   11 restiterit /] restiterit. *P*
12 transegit] *P A,* traduxit *P*sa *A*s *1565;* transegit .xi.] transegit *followed by four-letter gap A,*
transegit *P (numeral also om. 1557; first supplied by the editor Lumby in 1884);* millibus.]
millibus *P*   13 occurrens] *P 1565,* concurrens *A*   14 exceptus /] exceptus *P*   15
produxere / dimittitur /] produxere dimittitur *P*   17 cubitum.] cubitum *P*   18 illi /]
illi *P*   19 tulerant /] tulerant *P;* facessere] *written over some other word P,* secessere *A,*
secedere *1565;* iussis /] iussis *P*   20 ac] *followed by four-letter gap in A but not in P,* ac alios
1565   22 deliberant.] deliberant / *P*   23 sese /] sese *P*   25 comitatus] commitatus
P; aderat] *1565,* aderant *P A;* aderat /] aderant, *P*   26 sterterent.] sterterent / *P*

responsible for ratifying. Convinced by this reasoning, the queen brought her brother Woodville and her son Richard Grey (then the dominant men at the court of the prince) to give up their earlier plan, dispense with a bodyguard, and conduct the king toward London with only a modest escort.

On the king's route there was a town, Hampton, which although it lies virtually in the center of the realm is called Northampton to distinguish it from another town of the same name which is located on the south coast. The Dukes of Gloucester and Buckingham entered this town the same day the king left, and it happened that Woodville, the queen's brother whom we have mentioned, remained there, intending to join the king the next morning at [Stony] Stratford, where he had spent the night, [eleven] miles from Northampton. And so Woodville went out politely to welcome the dukes; he was given their heartiest greetings, in turn; and after passing as much time as they saw fit in conversation and dining, they gave him permission to go, leaving him so gratified with their cordial behavior that he went to bed full of hope and good cheer, feeling quite secure.

But the two dukes, whose thoughts and expressions were wholly at odds, dismissed everyone else besides Sir Richard Radcliff and some others who were aware of their plans, and they sat at the table until late in the night planning their strategy. After settling their plans they got up and dispatched discreet messengers to bid their retainers make ready, for the dukes would be mounting very shortly. Roused by this message, their retinue stood ready while Woodville's servants were still fast asleep. They also blocked all the gates of the town so that no one

[18/1]

sessis nemo sineretur exire: tum paulo ab oppido longius qua
parte Stratfordiam itur disposuerant equites qui si quos forte
deprehenderent fefellisse custodiam in Hamptonam rursus repellerent. Pretexunt causam quod quasi Duces constituerint /
5 videlicet officium suum approbaturi / ipsi eo die omnium primi
salutare Principem./

At Vodeuilus vbi accepit clausos vndique exitus / facultatem
vero eundi neque suis neque sibi fieri / rem tam atrocem et non
temere et se inscio ceptam / facta eorum presentia cum proximae
10 noctis vultu verbisque conferens paucarum horarum interuentu
tam magna rerum mutatione anxius erat./ Ceterum quum neque discedere liceret et continendo se nihil assequuturus erat
aliud quam vt latebras quesiuisse videretur / quod cur opus factu
esset nullius culpae sibi conscius erat / adire Duces statuit et
15 causas huius moliminis conscientiae suae fiducia sciscitari: quem
vt primum in conspectu habuerunt / queri illicet vltro atque
[217] accusare ceperunt quod discordias inter proceres sereret
animumque Regis niteretur ab se alienare perdereque per insidias moliretur / quas ipsi deprehensas merito sint in authorem
20 regesturi. Mirantem hanc orationem ac se purgare conantem /
quum ratione causaque deficerentur / ad vim conuersi com-
prehendunt atque in antro clausum adhibitis custodibus
relinquunt./

Mox conscensis equis Stratfordiam contendunt ac Regem re-
25 periunt parantem iam tum discedere / ideo / vti fertur / vt oppidum vniuersis angustum liberum illis relinqueret. Dimissis igitur equis / preeunte longa stipatorum serie / vbi ad Regem
propius ventum est / scindente se in partes comitatu / per medios

[19/1]

ordines perrexerunt ac se dimittentes in genua / Principem re-

1 exire:] exire./ P; tum] A 1565, tamen P   2 Stratfordiam] Strafordiam P   3–4
repellerent.] repellerent P   4 constituerint /] constituerint P   5 approbaturi /] approbaturi, P   7–8 facultatem vero] 1565, vero facultatem P A   8 eundi] corr. from
eunque Pb; fieri /] fieri P   9 ceptam /] ceptam, P; proximae] proxime P   13
videretur /] videretur P   14 erat /] erat P   15 suae] sue P; sciscitari:] sciscitari, P
16 habuerunt /] habuerunt P   20 regesturi.] regesturi / P; conantem /] conantem P
21 deficerentur /] deficerentur P   22 clausum] corr. from clauso P   25 discedere /
ideo /] discedere ideo P; fertur /] fertur P   26 relinqueret.] relinqueret / P   27
equis /] equis P   28 comitatu /] comitatu P

was able to leave, and a bit farther from the town in the direction of [Stony] Stratford they stationed horsemen to force back to Northampton anyone who they found had eluded the guard. They used the pretext that the dukes, to display their devotion, of course, had decided to be earliest of all in saluting the king that day.

But when Woodville found that all exists were closed, that he and his men were prevented from leaving, and that this shocking move undertaken without his own knowledge could not be for nothing, as he compared the dukes' present deeds with the expressions and words of the previous night, he was deeply disturbed by the radical change which had taken place in the interval of just a few hours. But since he was not free to depart, and by staying inside he would not achieve anything but to give the appearance of trying to hide (and he knew of no guilt on his part which might give him a reason for hiding), he decided to go to the dukes and on the strength of his own conscience ask what was the meaning of their conduct. As soon as they saw him, they instantly began to complain and accuse him of sowing discord among the nobility and of trying to prejudice the king's mind against them and destroy them by treachery, which they now had exposed and intended, quite rightly, to turn back against the traitor. As he was marveling at this speech and trying to clear himself, they ran out of arguments and causes, and so turned to force, seizing him and leaving him locked under guard in a cellar.

They soon mounted and hastened to [Stony] Stratford, where they found the king just then preparing to depart, reportedly in order to leave the town free for the dukes since it was too small to accommodate everyone. And so leaving their horses and following a large troop of retainers which split into two companies not far from the king, they passed through the ranks and respectfully saluted the king on their knees. He in turn extended

uerenter salutarunt / quos ille contra porrecta manu de terra
leuatos amabiliter complexus est / nihil etiam mali aut resciscens
aut suspicans: quum illi nihil cunctati aut eius reueriti presen-
tiam Ricardo Graio fratri eius vterino mouere litem occipiunt
5 calumniantes illum ac germanum eius Marquesium cum auun-
culo Vodeuilo coniurasse aduersus suum sanguinem / decreuisseque / circumuentis ac sublatis fraude nobilibus / Regis
pariter ac regni sibi regimen arrogare / atque eam ob rem protinus ab defuncto Rege Marquesium arcem Londinensem irru-
10 pisse atque expilato Regis aerario stipendium in milites elar-
gitum quos in classem ad confirmandas illius factionis opes
coegisset./ Ita rem quam gnari erant communi consilio decretam
Regisque plurimum reique publicae retulisse vt [217v] fieret / illi
per calumniam inuerterant / ne nihil esset quod dicerent.
15   At Princeps Graium parantem respondere preueniens "Quid
fecerit" (inquit) "Marquesius / quamquam nihil mali spero / tamen quoniam nobiscum non fuit certo non queo scire./ Verum
quod ad fratrem attinet Graium / atque auunculum Vodeuilum /
innocentes hercle illos facile prestare possum / vt qui non vs-
20 quam a nobis iam diu sint digressi." "Non dubium est eos" inquit
Gloucestriae Dux "tam sceleratum propositum / optime Princeps / sedulo te celasse" / nec plura locutus manus iniecit in
Graium ac Thomam Vaughanum equitem / Reginae cognatum./
Graius vt erat et animo generoso et non improcero corpore /
25 commotus presenti periculo / manum ad capulum tulit: tum
increpatus a quopiam admonente serum esse conatum / concidens animo / manum retulit et se capiendum dedit./ Ergo Regem retro agunt Hamptonam vbi de integro consultant./ Ibi

---

1 salutarunt /] salutarunt P   3 suspicans:] suspicans / P   4 vterino] ⟨vltimo⟩ vterino
P; mouere] *changed from* monuere P^b   6–7 sanguinem / decreuisseque /] sanguinem
decreuisseque P   7 ac] *interl.* P^b, *om.* A, atque *1565;* nobilibus /] nobilibus P   8
arrogare /] arrogare./ P   10 aerario] aerario, P   12 gnari erant] *corr. from some other*
word P^b   13 fieret /] fieret P   14 inuerterant /] inuerterant P; dicerent.] dicerent P
16 Marquesius /] Marquesius P; spero /] spero P   18 Vodeuilum /] Vodeuilum P
19 possum /] possum. P   21–22 propositum / optime Princeps /] propositum optime
Princeps P   23 Reginae] Regine P   24 corpore /] corpore P   25 periculo /] periculo P; tulit:] tulit P; tum] A *1565,* tamen P   26 increpatus] P, increpitus A *1565*
26–27 conatum / concidens animo /] conatum concidens amino P   27 animo] *corr. from*
non P^b

his hand, raised the dukes from the ground, and embraced them affectionately, still unaware and unafraid of any trouble. Without any delay and without any respect for his presence, they started a quarrel with Richard Grey, the king's half-brother, falsely charging that he and his brother the marquess along with his uncle Woodville had conspired against their family, fully intending first to circumvent and eliminate the nobles by trickery and then to seize control both of king and of kingdom; and for that purpose, just after the king's death, the marquess had broken into the Tower of London and plundered the king's treasury to pay wages to the soldiers whom he had assembled for a fleet to consolidate the power of his faction. In this way they misrepresented an action which had been ordered by common consent and which was very much in the interest of both king and commonwealth, lest they should have nothing at all to say.

But when Grey was about to defend himself the prince spoke first, saying, "As for the marquess, though I hope he has done nothing wrong, I cannot know for certain, since he was not with us. But when it comes to my brother Grey and my uncle Woodville, I can, by heaven, easily establish their innocence, since they have not left my side for some time now." "Without any doubt, my good liege, they took care to conceal their insidious plot from you," said the Duke of Gloucester, and without more ado he laid hands on Grey and Sir Thomas Vaughan, the queen's kinsman. Grey, a man both stouthearted and powerfully built, was provoked by the immediate danger to reach for his sword-hilt; but when someone rebuked him and said the attempt came too late, he lost heart, and withdrawing his hand, he surrendered. Then they took the king back to Northampton, where they con-

[20/1]   quos volunt e ministris Regis exauthorant substituuntque quos
ipsis magis quam illi lubeat / quibus rebus grauiter offensus /
quum prohibere non posset / quod solum potuit / illachrimauit./
    In prandio Gloucestriae Dux e suis ferculis vnum Vodeuilo
5   misit iusso dapifero vti solaretur eum iuberetque Ducis nomine
vt bono esset animo neu dubitaret huius tumultus mitem et cle-
mentem exitum fore. Ille gratijs actis orat ministrum / idem
ferculum ad nepotem ferret Graium eumque tali nuntio recrearet / quem vt fortunae aduersae insuetum eoque minus fer-
10 entem magis egere consolationis arbitrabatur / sibi vero sepius
vtramque experto turbidam minus nouam videri. Ceterum
Glaucestrie Dux post tam ciuilem con[218]solationem captiuos
omnes alium alio ablegauit in carcerem atque inde haud multo
post in vnum oppidum cui Pons Fractus vocabulum est adductos
15 capite detruncauit./
    Sed nocte quae eum diem sequebatur / quo hec Stratfordiae
gesta sunt / trepidus ad Reginam nuncius venit ad occidentale
coenobium tristia omnia atque atrocia denuncians: captum a
patruo Principem retroque vi abductum: Vodeuilum fratrem ac
20 Ricardum Graium / tum alios amicos eius / comprehensos atque
ablegatos incertum quo / tractandos incertum quomodo: muta-
tam rerum summam: euersa concidisse omnia: proinde occu-
pandum ipsi tempus / ac sibi reliquisque suis fortunis dum liceret
consulendum / ne propere accurrentes inimici reliquias inter-
25 ciperent. Hoc nuncio exanimata Regina calamitatem tam insignem / tantam / tam insperatam filiorum / amicorum / ac suam
ipsius ingemiscens / ad hec damnans ac detestans consilium
suum quae Principis dimittendum presidium suaserat / pauida

---

2 lubeat] *P*, lubebat *A 1565*   2–3 offensus / quum . . . posset /] offensus
quum . . . posset *P*   3 potuit /] potuit *P;* illachrimauit] *P*, lachrimauit *A,* fleuit
1565   4 Gloucestriae] Gloucestrie *P*   7 fore.] fore / *P;* ministrum /] ministrum
P   8–9 recrearet /] recrearet *P*   9 aduersae] aduerse *P*   10 arbitrabatur /] arbitrabatur *P*   11 videri.] videri / *P*   14 vnum] *P A,* quoddam *1565*   16 quae]
que *P;* sequebatur /] sequebatur *P;* Stratfordiae] Stratfordie *P*   17 sunt /] sunt *P*
18 denuncians:] denuncians *P*   19 abductum:] abductum *P*   20 Graium /]
Graium *P;* eius /] eius *P*   21 quomodo:] quomodo. *P*   22 summam:] summam *P;*
omnia:] omnia *P*   22–23 occupandum] occuppandum *P*   24 consulendum /] consulendum *P*   26 filiorum / amicorum /] filiorum amicorum *P*   27 ingemiscens /]
ingemiscens *P*   28 quae] que *P;* suaserat /] suaserat *P*

sulted again. There they dismissed the king's servants at will and replaced them with men they liked better than he did; and gravely offended at these measures, since he could not prevent them, he did all that he could: he wept over them.

At lunch the Duke of Gloucester sent one of his dishes to Woodville, ordering the servant to console him and bid him to be of good cheer in the name of the duke, and assure him that this storm would end gently and mercifully. After thanking the servant Woodville begged him to take the same dish to his nephew Grey and console him with a similar message, for he thought that since Grey was unused to ill fortune and therefore less able to bear it he had greater need to be solaced than Woodville, who had had more experience of good and bad fortune and thus found the latter less startling. At any rate, after this courteous reassurance the Duke of Gloucester sent all the captives off in different directions to prison, and shortly thereafter he assembled them in a town known as Pontefract and had them beheaded.

But the night after the day when these events happened at [Stony] Stratford, a frightened messenger came to the queen at Westminster full of grim and terrible tidings of how the prince had been taken and forcibly abducted by his uncle, how her brother Woodville, Richard Grey, and other friends of hers had been arrested and sent off to unknown destinations to face unknown punishment, how everything was topsy turvy and her world overthrown and in ruins, and how she should hurry to save herself and the remnants of her fortune while there was still time, before her enemies could rush in and snatch up the rest. Devastated by the news, the queen groaned at this awesome, immense, unexpected disaster for her sons, for her friends, and for herself, and she cursed and deplored her poor judgment in urging that the prince's bodyguard be dismissed. Anxious and

[21/1]   ac trepida e palatio se in coenobium proripit: erat enim asylum
            illud edibus palatinis contiguum./ Ibi se ac minorem filium et
            filias quatuor in Abbatis domum cum familia sua conijcit./
            Missus est eadem nocte minister ab Hastyngo cubiculario ad
5   Eboracensem Archiepiscopum / qui et ipse haud longe ab occi-
            dentali coenobio habitabat / qui ministris Episcopi narrauit / sibi
            ab hero mandatum ne quieti presulis parceret / tanti esse mo-
            menti quod afferebat./ Illi magnitudinem negocij ex festinatione
            mensi / soporem domini haud cunctanter interrumpunt./ Is in-
10   tromisso ad puluinar nuncio quum auersum retro Principem et
            captiuos eius cognatos accepisset / immani tantae [218v] rei
            atrocitate perculsus obstipuit. Tum nuncius "Iubet te" inquit
            "herus meus / reuerende pater / animo bono esse / ac tibi pol-
            licetur omnia tamen bene fore." "Abi" inquit ille "ac renuntia /
15   quantumuis bene futura sint / nunquam tamen tam bona fore
            quam fuerunt."
            Tum eo dimisso protinus excitat familiam et stipatus suis /
            appenso ad collum sigillo regio (erat enim Cancellarius) / recta
            contendit ad Reginam./ Ibi plena reperit consternationis luctus
20   pauoris ac tumultus omnia / trepidari / festinari / conuehi in
            asylum e palatio cistas / clitellas / sarcinas / ociosum neminem /
            imponentes alios / alios deponentes onera / alios depositis quae
            pertulerant noua petere / effringere alios parietem medium / qui
            solus ab asylo palatium discriminabat / vti viae compendium
25   fieret: nec deerant (vt accidere fere in tali tumultu solet) qui alio
            quaedam quam quo destinabantur efferrent./ Reginam videt
            humi sedentem / solam / tristem atque attonitam / complicatis
            digitis suam suorumque fortunam complorantem. Solatur eam
            Episcopus / ne presentibus rebus animum deijciat desperatione
30   meliorum / sibi factam spem / rem haud perinde attrociter ces-

---

1 proripit:] proripit / P   11 accepisset /] accepisset P   11–12 immani tantae rei
atrocitate] *1565*, immanitate rei [et *interl.* P^b] atrocitate P A   13 meus / reuerende
pater /] meus reuerende pater P   14 tamen] P A *but perhaps we should read* tandem;
fore.] fore / P; renuntia /] renuntia P   15 bona] P *1565*, bene A   16 fuerunt.]
fuerunt./ P   18 regio] regio / P; Cancellarius) /] Cancellarius) P   20 omnia /] omnia, P   22 alios / alios] alios alios P; quae] que P   23 medium /] medium P   24
discriminabat /] discriminabat P; viae] vie P   25 fieret:] fieret / P   26 quaedam]
quedam P; efferrent] A *1565*, efferent P   27 solam /] solam P; attonitam /] attonitam
P   29 animum deijciat] P, deijciat animum A *1565*   29–30 desperatione
meliorum /] *1565* desperatione / meliorem P A   30 spem /] spem P

frightened, she fled from the palace into Westminster Abbey, for that sanctuary was adjacent to the walls of the palace, and there she betook herself with her younger son, her four daughters, and their attendants to the house of the abbot.

That same night, a servant was sent by the chamberlain, Lord Hastings, to the archbishop of York, who also lived not far from Westminster Abbey. This servant told the bishop's servants that his master had ordered him not to wait for the prelate to finish his rest, he was bearing a message of such great importance. Gauging the importance of the message by the messenger's haste, they did not hesitate to interrupt their master's slumber. He admitted the messenger to his bedchamber, and when he learned that the prince had been turned back from London and that his kinsmen were captives, he was appalled by the gravity of the outrage. Then the messenger said, "My master bids you to be of good cheer, reverend father, and he promises you that all will be well even so." "Go tell your master," he said, "that no matter how well all will be, it will never be as well as it has been."

Then, dismissing the messenger, he quickly roused his own servants, and surrounded with his own men and wearing the king's seal around his neck (for he was the chancellor), he hastened straight to the queen. There he found a scene full of distress, sorrow, fear, and confusion, full of panic and haste; boxes, saddlebags, and bundles were being conveyed from the palace to the sanctuary; no one was idle, some loading, some unloading parcels, some going to get more after putting down what they had brought, others breaking down the wall which was all that divided the palace from the sanctuary and thus making a shortcut, and still others (as some generally do in this sort of confusion) carting off some things where they did not belong. He saw the queen sitting on the ground by herself, sad and dazed, wringing her hands and lamenting her own and her family's misfortune. The bishop consoled her, exhorting her not to let present conditions dismay her or make her despair of recovery; he had been given reason to hope that the outlook was not

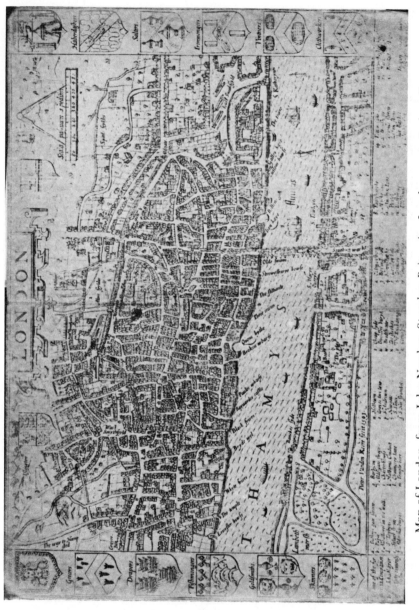

Map of London, from John Norden, *Speculum Britanniae*, London, 1593 (reduced)

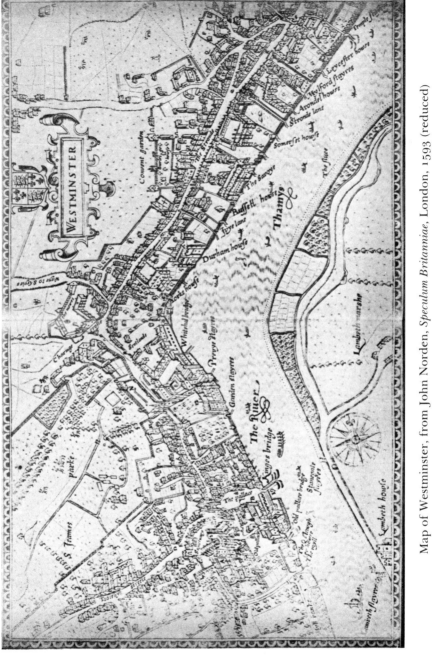

Map of Westminster, from John Norden, *Speculum Britanniae*, London, 1593 (reduced)

suram ac sibi fingeret iniquus rerum interpres timor./ Addit /
quo magis eam confirmaret / authorem esse spei suae / nuncio ad
se misso / cubicularium. "Ah pereat" inquit illa. "Is enim signifer
est eorum qui odio implacabili in sanguinis mei perniciem gras-
5 santur." Tum ille "Regina" inquit / "erige animum. In hanc rem
fidem hic tibi astringo meam / quo die alium quemquam illi in
regem vnxerint quam filium illum tuum quem habent secum /
nos postridie istum alterum quem hic [219] tecum habes hoc ipso
in loco dyademate insigniemus: quod quo minus dubites / en hoc
10 sigillum / quod meae fidei Princeps illustrissimus credidit maritus tuus / in vestrae sobolis vsum tibi iam nunc resigno" / et simul
hec dicens sigillum Reginae reddidit et priusquam illuxit abijt
domum: quum iam e fenestra despiciens vnde illi prospectus
erat in Thamesin / persultari totum fluuium cymbis videt /
15 asylum videlicet obsidente Ducis Gloucestriae satellicio ne quis
eo per aquam transfugeret aut inexcussus preterueheretur./
    Iam continuo res dispargi / toti populo in ore esse / stupore
omnes / ira / metu / ac merore compleri / conglobari alij alibi in
armis / turmatim volitare diuersi atque inuicem minitantes prout
20 quosque partium studium aut periculi formido copulauerat./ Ad
hec vt odio quisque aut fauore ferebatur / ita lenire alij verbis
inuidiam facti / pars intendere oratione nitebatur. Tum ne quid
Londinum subitae calamitatis acciperet / excubari ab ciuibus
ceptum / quum proceres iam quicunque aut in vrbe erant aut
25 non longe aberant de hiis rumoribus ac tumultu consultant. Sed
Eboracensis Episcopus veritus ne leuis ac precipitis consilij videretur iniussu Regis sigillum resignasse Reginae / priusquam in
consilium iret / quo factum tegeret / sigillum ab ea receperat.

1 Addit /] Addit P   2 confirmaret /] confirmaret P; suae] sue P   2–3 suae / nuncio . . . misso /] sue nuncio . . . misso P   3 cubicularium] A 1565, cubilarium P   4–5
grassantur.] grassantur./ P   5 animum.] animum / P   6 meam /] meam P   7
vnxerint] P A (easily mistaken for vinxerint), creauerint 1565   9 insigniemus:] insigniemus P   10 sigillum /] sigillum P; meae] mee P   11 tuus /] tuus P; vestrae] vestre
P   12 Reginae] Regine P   13 domum:] domum / P   14 videt /] videt P   15
Gloucestriae] Gloucestrie P   16 inexcussus] in excussus P   17 dispargi /] dispargi
P; stupore] P stupere A 1565   18 omnes /] omnes P; metu /] metu P   19 armis /]
armis P   20 studium] changed from studia P   21 ferebatur /] ferebatur P   22 facti /] facti P; nitebatur.] nitebatur P   23 subitae] subite P; acciperet /] acciperet P
24 ceptum /] ceptum P   25 consultant.] consultant P   26 precipitis] precepitis
P   27 Reginae /] Reginae P   28 iret /] iret P; tegeret /] tegeret P; receperat.]
receperat P

nearly as terrible as fear, that poor judge of events, made it out to be. To hearten her further, he added that the source of his hope was a message sent to him by the lord chamberlain. "Ah, fie on him!" said the queen. "He is the standard-bearer of those ruthless enemies intent on destroying my family. "Your majesty, take heart," he replied. "I here give you my word that the day they anoint anyone to be king but that son of yours whom they have with them, the next day we will crown this other one whom you have here with you, on this very spot. Lest you have any doubt of it, here is the seal which that noble prince your husband entrusted to me, which I now resign to you for the use of your son," and with these words he handed the seal to the queen and went home before daybreak. By that time, as he surveyed the scene from a window overlooking the Thames, he saw that the whole river was teeming with boats, and in them the Duke of Gloucester's men were blockading the sanctuary so that no one could get there over the water or pass by unsearched.

Now the news quickly spread; everyone was talking about it; they were all overwhelmed with amazement and rage, fear and sadness; various armed bands assembled in various quarters, and the different bands rushed about here and there, exchanging defiances according to the factional zeal or the fear which had brought each together. And as each was inclined by a positive or negative bias, so some speakers attempted to minimize the gravity of the deed while another group sought to exaggerate it. Then the citizens of London began to stand watch to guard the city from sudden disaster, while all the nobles in the city or its vicinity consulted about these reports and the general upheaval. But the bishop of York, who was afraid that his having delivered the seal to the queen without the orders of the king would be viewed as a capricious and precipitate gesture, retrieved the seal from her before he went to the council, hoping to conceal the deed.

Ibi factum illud Ducum plerisque incessentibus atque odiose interpretantibus tanquam priuatae simultates structis in Principem insidijs pretexerentur / Hastingus contra (quem nesciebatur huius facti conscium esse) suam fidem / quam indubiam
5 habuerunt omnes / pro Ducibus obstringere / nihil aduersus Regem cogitatum / positos ab his in custodiam eos a quibus sua salus impetita credebatur: [219v] "Verone contra / vestrum erit iudicium" inquit "quorum examini reseruant eos hii / qui nihil merentes se tamen lesos ab illis esse conqueruntur. Ceterum eam
10 litem vos aut iudicabitis vestro arbitratu / aut componetis: tantum ne re incognita statuatis et / priuatas controuersias in publicam seditionem atque intestina bella vertentes / eo rem deducatis vt irritatis animis / interturbata coronatione Principis / quem huc eadem causa comitantur / componi res et redintegrari
15 non possit./ In quo certamine / si cetera paria essent / tamen ius et authoritas maior in illis castris sit necesse est in quibus Princeps erit."

Hec oratio ob creditam viri fidem magnam habuit vim ad commouendum / sed multo maxime tumultuantes animos com-
20 pressit imminens aduentus Regis / quem comitatu magnifico Duces admodum reuerenter habitum Londinum versus producebant. Ceterum quacumque ibant rumorem disseminari curauerunt / molitos qui in vinculis erant primum se / deinde alios e proceribus per vim opprimere / atque ita sibimet viam struere
[24/1] 25 qua Regem pariter ac regnum regerent./ Cuius commenti quo fides plebeculae fieret / aurigae atque alij Ducum ministri qui presidio impedimenta sequebantur ostentabant vndique inter

---

2 priuatae] priuate *P*   3 pretexerentur /] pretexerentur./ *P*   3–4 (quem . . . esse)] quem . . . esse *P*   4 fidem /] fidem *P*   5 omnes /] omnes *P*; obstringere /] obstringere *P*   6 cogitatum /] cogitatum *P*   7 credebatur:] credebatur *P*; Verone contra /] Vero ne contra *P A*, Rectene an secus *1565*   8 hii /] hii *P*   9 conqueruntur.] conqueruntur *P*   10 componetis:] componetis / *P*   11 ne . . . statuatis] *corr. from* ve . . . statuetis *P*b; et /] et *P*   13 irritatis] *corr. from* veritatis *P*b; animis /] animis *P*   13 Principis /] Principis *P*   14 comitantur /] comitantur *P*   15 certamine /] certamine *P*; essent /] essent *P*   17 erit.] erit./ *P*   20 Regis /] Regis *P*   21–22 producebant.] producebant *P*   22–23 curauerunt /] curauerunt *P*   23 in] *interl. P, om. A*; erant] erant / *P*; se /] se *P*   26 plebeculae] plebecule *P*; aurigae] aurige *P*   27 sequebantur] ⟨erant⟩ sequebantur *P*

There many criticized the dukes' action, condemning it as if private conflicts were merely being used as a pretext for a plot against the king. Hastings, however, whose own part in the plot was unknown, offered his word of honor (which everyone trusted completely) that the dukes had no intention of injuring the king and that those they had placed in custody were suspected of plotting their downfall. "Whether they actually did, on the other hand," Hastings proceeded, "is a question for you to decide; for the dukes are detaining those persons for you to examine who they complain did them an injury without provocation. But that quarrel is one you will judge or resolve at your pleasure; but beware of deciding the matter before learning the facts and of turning private controversies into public insurrection and civil strife, pushing matters so far by inflaming men's tempers and disrupting the king's coronation, whom they are accompanying hither for that ceremony, that you cannot restore proper order again. And even if all else were equal in this confrontation, better title and greater authority necessarily fall to the camp where the king dwells."

This speech had a considerable influence because of the speaker's honorable reputation, but a far greater calming effect was exerted by the imminent arrival of the prince, whom the dukes were conducting most worshipfully toward London with a magnificent escort. And wherever they went they took care to spread the rumor that their prisoners had plotted to destroy first the dukes and then other members of the nobility and thus clear the way for themselves to control both the king and the kingdom. To substantiate this fiction in the eyes of the common folk, the wagoners and the dukes' other servants who were guarding the baggage displayed everywhere among the equipment they

captiuam suppellectilem vasa quaedam armis impleta / quae dominis / quum transferretur aula Principis / necesse fuit auferre
secum / nisi vellent abijcere: quod / quamquam satis scirent /
tamen per malitiam dissimulantes / quum ea passim tanquam
5 manifestarij criminis argumentum ostentarent / inclamauerunt /
"En arma ipsa quae proditores isti in vasa clam abdiderant / vt
Duces atque omnes nobiles per insidias obtruncarent." Hoc commentum / [220] tametsi pendentibus rem suspectiorem reddidit /
facile coniectantibus eos / qui tale facinus animo destinassent /
10 corporibus potius arma fuisse gesturos quam vincta atque im-
pedita congesturos in dolia / simplici tamen ac rudi populo
mirum quam satisfecerit / adeo conspectis armis velut certa atque explorata proditione salus vndique Ducibus suspendium
captiuis acclamatum est./
15   Quum Rex aduentare propius nunciaretur / senatus vrbis cum
magno ciuium numero progressi obuiam / quatuor ab vrbe millibus occurrerunt. Ita Princeps honorifice exceptus / procerum ac
ciuium celebri pompa ciuitatem est inuectus quarto die Maij
anno regni sui primo eodemque vltimo./ Sed hac honoris magni-
20 fica specie vultuque in obseruantiam Principis composito
Glocestriae Dux e summa inuidia ac suspicione quibus paulo
ante flagrabat in tantam subito charitatem omnium tantamque
integritatis opinionem venit vt vnus omnium Protector Regis
regnique eius consensu procerum renunciaretur./ Itaque siue id
25 inscitia factum siue accidit fato / agnus certe consulto in lupi
fidem creditus. Mox Eboracensis Episcopus acriter increpatus
[25/1]   quod sigillum Reginae tradiderat administratione priuatus est:

---

1 quaedam] quedam P; impleta /] impleta P; quae] que P   1–2 dominis] P, dm̄s A, ipsis
1565; dominis /] dominis P   2 transferretur] A *1565,* transferetur P; Principis /]
Principis P   3 secum /] secum P; abijcere:] abijcere P; quod /] quod P; scirent /] scirent
P   4 dissimulantes /] dissimulantes P   5 ostentarent / inclamauerunt /] ostentarent,
inclamauerunt. P   6 quae] que P; abdiderant /] abdiderant, P   7 obtruncarent.]
obtruncarent./ P   7–8 commentum / tametsi] commentum tam et si P   8 reddidit /]
reddidit P   9 coniectantibus] A *1565,* concertantibus P; eos /] eos P   11 dolia /]
dolia. P; populo] *changed from* popello A   12 satisfecerit /] satisfecerit, P   16
numero] ⟨apparat⟩ numero P   19 eodemque] eodem que P   20 composito] A *1565,*
compositio P   21 Glocestriae] Glocestrie P   26 increpatus] P, increpitus A
1565   27 Reginae] Regine P; est:] est P

had captured certain vessels full of weaponry, which the lords clearly had to take with them when the prince moved his court unless they wished to throw them away; but the dukes' servants maliciously dissembled this fact, although they knew it perfectly well, constantly displaying these weapons as if they furnished manifest proof of the crime, and exclaiming, "See the very weapons which those traitors had secretly hidden in these vessels in order to cut down the dukes and the rest of the nobles by treachery." Though this fiction made the charges more dubious to anyone weighing it carefully (it was easy enough to infer that anyone who had planned such a crime would carry his weapons about on his person, not pack them away out of reach in a barrel), it was remarkable how thoroughly it convinced simple and ignorant people; as if seeing the arms were the same thing as proving the matter conclusively, people everywhere cried out long life for the dukes and the gallows for the prisoners.

When it was announced that the king was drawing closer to London, the city council and a large number of citizens went out to meet him four miles away. After this honorable reception he was conveyed into the city by a solemn procession of nobles and citizens the fourth day of May in the first year of his reign and the last. But with this magnificent show of honor and with his studied pose of concern for the prince, the Duke of Gloucester, who had quite recently been the object of burning hatred and suspicion, gained so much love and such a reputation for honesty that he was chosen over everyone as the sole protector of the king and his kingdom by the unanimous consent of the nobles. And thus, whether it came about through poor judgment or was fated to happen, what is certain is that the lamb was deliberately entrusted to the wolf. Soon the bishop of York, reprimanded severely for giving the seal to the queen, was de-

eo munere inauthoratus est Russellus Episcopus Lincolniensis
vir et vsu rerum / et vitae probitate singulari / tum in litteris haud
dubie sua tempestate primarius./

    Igitur vbi Protector effectus est / quanquam omnis ei dies anno
5 longior videretur / qui gestientem ac morae impatientem impet-
um eius moraretur auidumque quam primum re ipsa vsurpandi
regni quod animo iam ante inuaserat / tamen haud temere quicquam censuit [220v] ante tentandum quam reliquam predae
partem in nassam pellexerat / haud ignarus fore vt si alterum
10 fratrem priuaret imperio / in alterum protinus euehendum
vniuersa studia incumberent / siue permaneret in asylo / siue
(quod multo metuebat magis) extra Britaniam aliquo transmit-
teretur in tutum. Ergo in proximo conuentu procerum grauiter
incusat Reginam / odiose ab ea factum / quae sacrosanctae maies-
15 tati Principi vnicum et charissimum germanum fratrem distinere audeat / tanquam vtrique inuideat dulcia illa mutuae con-
suetudinis oblectamenta / in illum vel magis impia cuius
potissimum curam pre se fert / quippe quem libertati subductum
ab luce ac splendore clarissimae fortunae suae detractum in
20 asylum misere velut in tenebras et squalorem abstrudat: nec
horum quicquam alia causa patratum quam vti nobilibus qui
[26/1] Regi a consilio sunt acris apud populum concitaretur inuidia./
Adeo ei odio esse eos vt vel cum liberorum suorum dispendio /
quod de Medea ferunt fabulae / vlcisci quos odit ardeat.

25   "Alioquin enim quorsum in asylo puerum" inquit "nisi quod
videri vult popello vos aut parum fideliter aut non sat sapienter
prospexisse Principi si periculum sit eius mihi fratrem credere /
cuius ipsum corpus mihi vos alendum tuendumque credidistis?

---

2 vitae] vite *P;* singulari /] singulari, *P;* tum] *corr. from* tamen *P*b   4 est /] est *P*   5
videretur /] videretur, *P;* morae] more *P*   7 inuaserat /] inuaserat *P*   8 predae]
prede *P*   9 nassam pellexerat] ⟨nassam⟩ nassam pellexerat *written with a different pen P;*
pellexerat /] pellexerat *P*   10 imperio /] imperio *P*   12 (quod . . . magis)]
quod . . . magis *P*   14 Reginam /] Reginam *P;* factum / quae] factum que *P;*
sacrosanctae] sacrosancte *P*   15–16 distinere] distinere / *P*   16 mutuae] mutue *P*
17 oblectamenta /] oblectamenta *P*   19 clarissimae fortunae suae] clarissime fortune
sue *P*   20 abstrudat:] abstrudat *P*   23 dispendio /] dispendio *P*   24 fabulae /]
fabule *P*   25 in] *A 1565,* iam *P*   26 popello] *A,* populo *P 1565*   28 credidistis?]
credidistis *P*

prived of his office and replaced by Bishop Russell of Lincoln, a man of remarkable virtue and practical wisdom, and undoubtedly the most learned man of his time.

After gaining the title of Protector, though to him days seemed longer than years while he had to restrain his unruly and impetuous appetite, keenly impatient to seize the same throne in reality which he had already usurped in his thoughts, he knew he must try nothing rash before luring the rest of his prey into his snare; for he knew that if he removed one brother from the throne, everyone would at once turn his thoughts to enthroning the other, whether he remained in the sanctuary or was sent somewhere safe outside Britain, a prospect the duke feared even more. And so in the next meeting of the nobles he sharply criticized the queen, saying that out of pure spite she had dared to keep his sacred majesty the prince and his only dear brother apart, as if she begrudged both of them those sweet pleasures of mutual companionship, showing even more cruelty to the brother for whom she ostensibly felt most concern, since she had deprived him of his freedom, dragged him away from the brightness and splendor of his fortune, and hidden him away in a wretched sanctuary, in darkness and filth as it were, simply in order to stir up bitterness and ill will among the people against the noblemen of the king's council, whom she hated so much that like the poets' Medea, she would even sacrifice her own children to take vengeance on those whom she hated.

"For why else take the boy into sanctuary," he asked, "but to give the rabble the impression that you must have been either disloyal or foolish in making provision for the prince if it is risky to entrust the brother to me, to whom you have entrusted the prince's own person to keep and protect? But his good health

Cuius incolumitas haud mihi certe fulciri satis vlla victus cura
videtur nisi ludi quoque voluptas accesserit / quae mirum in
modum pueriles spiritus reficit vegetatque./ Nec eam potest
mollis puerorum etas ab senibus capere: blandus adhiberi col-
5 lusor debet qui neque annos eius superet neque nimis infra sit /
tum qui ad eius nobilitatem accedat proxime: ita simul [221]
etatis habebitur simul maiestatis ratio. Quis igitur omnibus partibus appositior quam germanus frater / quem nunc deterior
nouerca mater abstinet? Si quis hec leuicula sentiat / quod ego
10 certe nemini visum iri puto cui salus Principis curae fuerit / is sic
habeto / maximas interdum machinas consistere nisi minorum
adminiculo non posse. Ad hec quam istud nobilibus inhonestum
nobis / quam ipsi Regi inuidiosum / omnium per ora non in hoc
regno tantum sed apud exteras etiam gentes iactari (vt cito per-
15 uolat malus rumor) / fratrem eius eo necessitatis adactum / vt
florentibus illius rebus ipse in asylo delitescat? Neque enim temere credetur quisquam in antrum sese abdere cui citra periculum liceat in luce ac libertate viuere. Hec persuasio vbi semel
animis insederit haud facile euellas postea / maiusque in malum
20 crescet denique quam diuinare quisquam in procliui queat.

    "Huic igitur pesti quo propere eatur obuiam / virum aliquem
etate grauem atque authoritate pollentem mittendum ad matrem censeo / eumque cui et Regis honor et ordinis huius fama
curae sit / tum cui apud eam sit et amoris nonnihil et fidei: quibus
25 omnibus de causis / nemo circumspicienti mihi magis occurrit
idoneus quam reuerendissimus iste pater" (aderat enim) "Cardinalis qui solus mihi sua prudentia videtur rem effectam red-
[27/1]   diturus / modo ne laborem recuset. Non recusaturum autem

---

1 fulciri] *corr. from* fulturi *P*b   2 quae] que *P*   2–3 in modum] *A 1565*, immodum *P*
4 capere:] capere / *P*   5 nimis] *corr. from* minus *P*b   6 tum] *1565*, tamen *P A;*
proxime:] proxime *P*   9 Si] *P 1565*, Quod, si *A;* sentiat /] sentiat *P*   10 curae fuerit /]
cure fuerit *P*   11 habeto /] habeto *P*   12 adminiculo] ⟨adminculo⟩ adminiculo *P;*
posse.] posse / *P;* quam] *1565, corr. from* quod *P*b, quod *A*   13 nobis /] nobis *P;*
inuidiosum /] inuidiosum *P*   14 apud exteras . . . gentes] *P A 1565*, foras *in margin*
*P*a   14–15 iactari (vt . . . rumor) /] iactari, vt . . . rumor, *P*   15 adactum /] adactum
P   16 delitescat?] delitescat *P*   17 credetur quisquam] *P*, quisquam credetur quisquam *A*, quisquam credetur *1565;* sese] se se *P*   19 euellas postea /] euellas / postea *P*
20 queat.] queat *P*   21 obuiam /] obuiam *P*   24 curae] cure *P;* nonnihil] non
nihil *P;* fidei:] fidei *P*   25 causis /] causis *P*   26 enim] *A 1565*, nimirum *P;* enim)]
nimirum *P*

cannot be completely ensured by good diet alone; he also needs
the enjoyment of play, which is an excellent restorative and tonic
for growing boys' spirits. Nor can a boy's tender age get that sort
of enjoyment from old people; we ought to provide a congenial
playmate neither older nor very much younger than the prince,
and as nearly as possible his equal in rank. Thus we will take into
account simultaneously his age and his majesty. And so who
could be better suited in every respect than his very own brother,
whom his mother, even worse than a stepmother, is now keeping
away from him? If anyone views these as trivial issues (and I
think no one will who has the welfare of the prince at heart), let
him reflect that the greatest devices are often dependent on
lesser ones. And besides, how dishonorable it is for us noblemen,
how invidious for the king himself, not only here but also in
foreign countries (for bad news travels fast), to have everyone
talking about how the king's brother has been driven to languish
in a sanctuary while his brother is prospering! For they are not
going to believe that anyone arbitrarily shuts himself up in a cell
if he can safely live outside at liberty. Once this opinion takes
root in people's minds you will have a hard time ever uprooting
it, and it will ultimately grow into a greater evil than anyone can
readily foresee.

"To nip this menace in the bud, I think we should send some
venerable and influential emissary to the mother, someone who
cares about the king's honor and the reputation of our order but
who also commands some affection and trust from the queen;
taking all these considerations into account, I see no one more
suitable as I look around me than that reverend father" (he was
actually present) "the cardinal; with his great discretion, he looks
to me like the only man likely to gain our objective, provided he
does not refuse the assignment. But I hope that he will not refuse

spero vel Regis causa vel nostra vel ipsius Ducis nepotis mei
secundum Principem ipsum charissimi / quibus omnibus si / id
quod spero / Reginae recta persuaserit / non facile dictu fuerit
quantum adimet molestiae./ Ceterum [221v] ea si incepto prauo
5   muliebri pertinacia sic institerit / vt ab libidine animi ad verum
flecti nulla tanti patris neque authoritate neque consilio neque
fide possit / ego certe author fuerim ex edicto regio e coenobio
eximendi eius ducendique in felicissimum Regis contubernium /
cuius perpetua consuetudine tam honorifice habebitur / vt orbi
10 toti pro nobis et contra matrem eius testatum reddi possit / eam
quum filium in asilum clauderet vel maliciam a consilio vel stultitiam habuisse. Hec mea est hac de re sententia / nisi vestrum
quisquam contra sentiat./ Neque enim vnquam vsqueadeo mea
mihi ratio blandietur vt non paratus sim cuiuis vestrum rectiora
15 consulenti parere."

Huic orationi nobiles fere quotquot aderant suffragabantur.
Cardinalis atque episcopi reliqui cetera adsensi tantum inuita
matre nihil audendum censebant / neque vi grassandum si forte
verbis minus obtemperetur: rem enim videri superis hominibus-
20 que inuisam / tantae vetustatis asylum tam religiosum temerari /
[28/1]   quod reges ac pontifices tam boni instituerant / tam multi ratum
sanctumque habuerant / atque ei loco inferre contumeliam
quem locum Petrus ipse Princeps Apostolorum magno supero-
rum choro comitatus olim tam peculiariter Deo sibique dedica-
25 uit / vt per tot retro secula neque rex tam audax fuerit quisquam
qui non sit veritus violare / neque tam religiosus episcopus qui sit
ausus consecrare./

"Nullo ergo pacto me authore" Cardinalis inquit "eius sanctuarij imminuetur immunitas quod tam multis misere alioqui peri-
30 turis tam [222] sepe fuit presidio. Sed neque necesse erit spero /
verum quantumuis etiam necesse fuerit / non faciendum censeo.

2–3 si / id quod spero / Reginae] si id quod spero Regine P   3 persuaserit /] persuaserit
P   4 molestiae] molestie P   7 possit /] possit P   8 contubernium /] contubernium P   17 adsensi] *1565*, adcensi P A   19 obtemperetur:] obtemperetur./ P;
superis] superis / P   20 inuisam / tantae] inuisam tante P   21 instituerant /] instituerant P   23 magno] *1565*, magne P A   24 Deo] A *1565*, dei P   24–25 dedicauit /] dedicauit P   29 imminuetur] A *1565*, minuetur P   31 fuerit /] fuerit P;
censeo.] censeo P

it, whether for the king's sake or for ours, or indeed for the sake of the duke, of my own dearest nephew apart from the prince; for if the cardinal succeeds in persuading the queen to be reasonable, it would be hard to express just how much trouble he will be saving everyone I have mentioned. But if she in her feminine stubbornness is so set on her own perverse plan that she cannot be moved to abandon her wanton designs and to do the right thing by either the authority or the counsel or the good faith of that worthy father, I personally would advocate using a royal edict to get the boy out of the abbey and into the cheerful society of the king, where he will be treated so honorably in their constant intimacy that the whole world will give its judgment in our favor and against the duke's mother, bearing witness that when she closed him up in a sanctuary she did so out of deliberate malice or folly. There you have my opinion on the matter, unless any of you holds a different one. For I have never been so firmly wedded to my own point of view that I would not be prepared to defer to any of you who can offer better advice."

Virtually all the nobility present approved of this speech. The cardinal and the other bishops accepted the other points but maintained that nothing should be done against the mother's will, and that they should not resort to force even if she did not listen to their words; for it would outrage saints and men if they violated such a holy and ancient sanctuary, one established by such virtuous kings and bishops and held sacred and unalterable by so many others, or if they did violence to a place which St. Peter himself, the prince of apostles, accompanied by a large choir of saints, long ago dedicated to God and himself so distinctively that for many centuries past no king, not even the most reckless, had been brash enough to violate it and no bishop, not even the most scrupulous, had been bold enough to consecrate it.

"Therefore, under no circumstances," said the cardinal, "would I undertake to impair the immunity of that sanctuary, which has so often protected so many who would otherwise have suffered a miserable death. I hope it will not even be necessary, but no matter how necessary it might be I do not think that it ought to be done. For I hope that the queen is going to listen to

Equidem spes est Reginam audientem rationi fore / quod si
minus succedat e sententia / tamen ipse tam sedulo conabor vt
facile omnes intelligant / non meam industriam defuisse negotio / sed maternam indulgentiam ac muliebrem potius metum
5   obstetisse."

"Muliebrem [metum]" inquit Dux Bukyngamiae / "Imo peruicaciam mulieris inuictam. Nam hoc ego certe vel anima pignore contenderim / nihil illam prorsus vel filio timere vel sibi.
Quis enim bellum sibi sumat cum femina? quod si mares quoque
10 sanguinis eius aliquot feminae essent melius profecto sese res
haberent: quanquam nec illis quidem Reginae sanguis fraudi est
sed ipsorum comparatus ad seditionem animus. Ceterum vt
maxime nobis ipsa foret cognatioque eius inuisa / non posset
tamen charus non esse frater Principis nempe cui nos ipsi cog-
15 nati sumus. Cuius vere conseruandi si tanto studio duceretur
quantum vel sua libido vel nostri inuidia cordi est / eum ex illo
claustro festinaret emittere: haud minus egre ferret illic filium
condi quam nunc abdere ac vincire satagit. Nam si quid habet
ingenij (vt habet haud dubie pro muliere non contemnendum)
[29/2]   20 haud quaquam sibimet prouidentiae tribuit amplius quam
quibusdam nobis / idque ijs de quorum fide non dubitat / sed
vere persuasum habet / filij sui salutem non minus eis cordi esse
quam sibi: cui quo magis bene volunt / eo minus esse eum apud
[222v] illam volunt / si fixum illi animo sedeat in asylo deli-
25 tescere: contraque nemini non placere arbitror vel Principem
ipsum a parente curari modo inducat animum ibi viuere / in quo
versari neutri sit indecorum. Quamobrem si in reddendo libertati filio eorum consilia aspernetur sequi / quorum neque du-

---

1 fore /] fore *P*   2 sententia /] sententia *P*   5 obstetisse.] obstetisse / *P*   6
Muliebrem metum] *1565*, muliebrem *P A;* Bukyngamiae] Bukyngamie *P*   6–7
peruicaciam] *1565*, peruicatiam *P A*   7 Nam hoc] *A 1565*, Nam *P*   9 femina?]
femina. *P*   10 feminae] femine *P;* sese] se se *P*   11 haberent:] haberent *P*   13
foret] *P 1565*, est forer *A*   16 est /] est *P*   17 emittere:] emittere / *P*   19
vt . . . contemnendum] *om. 1565*   20 prouidentiae] prouidentie *P*   21 dubitat /]
dubitat *P*   22 habet /] habet *P*   23 sibi:] sibi. *P;* volunt /] volunt *P*   24–25
delitescere] *P A*, degere *P*sa *A*s, continere *1565;* delitescere:] delitescere *P*   27 neutri
sit indecorum] *P A 1565*, ex honore vtriusque sit *P*sa   28 aspernetur] *P A 1565*, recuset
*P*sa *A*s   28–368/1 dubitabilis] *P A*, ambigua *P*sa *1565*

reason, and even if it turns out otherwise, I will attempt the task so energetically that it will be quite evident to everyone that the real stumbling block was not my lack of diligence but rather maternal indulgence and womanly fear."

"Womanly fear?" said the Duke of Buckingham. "No; the woman's invincible stubbornness. For I for one would bet my life on it that she is not a bit frightened—no, not for her son or herself. For who goes to war with a woman? And if some of the men of her family were women, too, it would be better for all of us; though the queen's blood is not what has gotten even them into trouble, but rather their taste for sedition. But even if she and her kinsmen were our mortal enemies, the prince's brother could never be anything but dear to us, seeing that we are his kinsmen as well. And if her zeal for his welfare were really as great as her willfulness and her hostility toward us, she would be rushing to get him out of the cloister; she would be as reluctant to have him confined there as she is now eager to lock him away. For if she has any sense (and she has quite a bit, for a woman), she surely does not suppose she has more foresight than any of us, in particular those whose good faith she has no cause to question, since she rightly believes that they care as much about her son's welfare as she does; and the more good they wish him, the less they wish to see him remaining with her if she stubbornly insists on languishing in a sanctuary. On the other hand, I think there is no one who would not like to see her taking care of the prince too, if only she would make up her mind to reside in a place which would not be unseemly for either of them. Now, then, if she rejects the advice to release her son, advice offered by men of

bitabilis prudentia est neque incerta fides / quis non intelligat
facile / tam improbi causam propositi maliciam magis quam
metum esse?

5   "Quod si adeo meticulosa sit vt ex animo metuat quod nusquam est / vere metuat: quis enim prohibere queat ne vel
vmbram horreat suam? Certe quo ea magis filium nobis timet
credere / eo nobis contra iustius timendum est puerum illi relinquere. Etenim si tam vanos metus figurat animo vt filio periculum esse fingat / profecto / vt est metuentium solicitus animus /
10   ne asylo quidem satis fidet: facile certe secum cogitabit / si quis
adeo immani feritate sit / vt puero innocenti nocere studeat /
animo tam impio ac scelerato vt neque superum timor neque
hominum pudor ab flagitio reuocet / asyli nomen ei leue ac
vanum fore./ Itaque falsa suspicione periculi subigetur animus
15   munimentum aliquod firmius extra regnum querere. Quin
nunc quoque / quanquam nihil tale metuentem / haud dubio
tamen hoc ipsum tam illam animo agitare vt faciat quam nos
contra ne faciat. Quae si tam improbum consilium [223]
muliebri temeritate patrauerit (patrabit enim facile oscitantibus
20   nobis) omnes vbique mortales predicabunt dignos scilicet nos qui
Principi a consilio simus / cuius germanum fratrem per vecor-
diam sub oculis nostris perire patiamur. Ego igitur illustrissimum Ducem dum licet vel inuita matre censeo eximendum po-
[30/1]   tiusquam tantisper ibi dimittendum quoad eum mulieris mala
25   mens obtentu metus emittat in periculum.

"Nec asyli tamen immunitatem vllo pacto violari velim./ Quae
quum vires ab vetustate cepit / non ego is sum qui suadeam
infringendam / contraque si integra esset res non suaserim instituendam. Neque tamen inficior bene factum ac misericorditer vt

---

1 fides /] fides P; intelligat] ⟨facile⟩ intelligat P   2 facile /] facile P; improbi] P A, incepti
Psa As (del. P); propositi] P A, facinoris Psa   3 esse?] esse P   5 est /] est P; vere
metuat] om. 1565; metuat:] metuat P   6 suam?] suam / P   7–8 relinquere.] relinquere P   9 profecto /] profecto P; solicitus] P As 1565, inquietus Psa A; animus /]
animus P   10 fidet:] fidet P; certe] interl. P; cogitabit /] cogitabit P   11 studeat /]
studeat P   13 reuocet /] reuocet P   15 aliquod] A 1565, aliquot P; querere.]
querere P; Quin] ⟨Quis⟩ Quin P   16 quoque /] quoque P; metuentem /] metuentem P;
dubito] dubito / P   18 faciat. Quae] faciat Que P   20 dignos] P A 1565, changed to
indignos Pb   21 simus /] simus P   22 patiamur.] patiamur P   26 Quae] Que
P   28–29 instituendam.] instituendam / P

sure prudence and undoubted loyalty, who fails to see that the source of her obstinate determination is malice, not fear?

"But if she is so fearful that she really fears an imaginary danger, let her fear in good earnest; who can stop her from dreading her own shadow? But the more frightened she is of entrusting her son to us, the more reason we have to be frightened of leaving the boy in her hands. For if her irrational fears even extend to imagining that her son is in danger, then (as is the way of those afflicted by fear) she will not even have confidence in the sanctuary; she will very readily reach the conclusion that if anyone is monstrous or savage enough to want to injure an innocent child and so wicked and hardened that no fear before heaven nor shame before men can deter him from wrongdoing, the term 'sanctuary' will be empty and meaningless to him. And so her false premonition of danger will drive her to look for some more secure refuge abroad; indeed I have no doubt that though she actually fears nothing of the sort, she is even now planning her flight just as surely as we are planning to prevent it. For if with a woman's rashness she carries out her outrageous design (and she easily will if we are caught napping), people everywhere will pronounce us worthy indeed to be counseling a prince when we let his own brother be lost before our very eyes through stupidity. And so I think we should bring forth his highness the duke while we still can, even against his mother's will, instead of leaving him there until female perversity sends him away into danger on a pretext of fearfulness.

"And yet by no means would I want to see anyone violate the immunity of sanctuary. Since it is based on a venerable tradition, I am not one to advocate infringing it, though if it were to do over again I would not advocate ever establishing it. And yet I concede it was virtuous and merciful to have some haven left

quos naufragium aut male expuncta nomina / aliave quaepiam
fortunae vis aduersa fecit inopes / hijs aliquis aperiatur portus
qui corpora saltem integra prestet ab creditorum seuicia./ Ad
hec si regni titulus (quod non semel accidit) in questionem ven-
5   iat / dum armis de iure decernitur atque alteri alteros habent
proditorum loco / non displicet aliquem locum esse ad quem
vtrique confugiant vbi dubijs aut afflictis rebus inuicem alter-
nante victoria sint in tuto. Ceterum furibus ac latronibus / quis ea
loca plena sunt / quique semel eiuscemodi flagitijs imbuti nun-
10 quam resipiscunt postea / facinus est profecto asylum vllum presidio esse / multoque magis homicidis / quos ab aris ipsis auelli
mactarique iussit deus / modo ad crimen accesserit industria. At
nisi sedulo peccatum est / nec opus [223v] quidem apud nos asylo
est. Nam si quem in alterius necem aut necessitas armauit aut
15 impegit casus / eius delicti aut veniam lex aut princeps gratiam
facit. Numeret aliquis nunc quam raros in asylo comperiat quos
illuc fauorabilis vlla necessitudo compulit: contra / quanta illic
turba scaturiat perditorum / quos alea / luxus / ac libido vastauerunt: preterea latronum / sicariorum / sectorum / homi-
20 cidarum / atque immanium proditorum / quam tetra atque hor-
renda colluuies in asylum velut in pestilentissimam sentinam
confluxerit: idque potissimum in duo / e quibus alterum ad manum est vrbi / alterum in ipsis vrbis visceribus collocatum est./
Ausim profecto confirmare / quisquis asylorum commoda com-
[31/1] 25 paret cum incommodis / eum pronunciaturum / potius quam tot
incommoda perpetienda sint / multo fore commodius ipsis etiam
commodis caruisse./
     "Atque hec affirmo sic habere se / vt non accedant alia / quibus

---

1–2 quaepiam fortunae] quepiam fortune *P*   4 (quod . . . accidit)] quod . . . accidit
P   4–5 veniat] *P 1565*, eueniat *A*   5 decernitur] decernitur / *P*   6 loco /] loco *P*
8 latronibus /] latronibus *P*   9 sunt /] sunt *P*   10 resipiscunt] resipiscunt / *P*   15
impegit] *corr. from* impunxit *P*b; impegit] impegit / *P*   17 illuc] illic *P A 1565 (cf.* thyther
1557); compulit: contra /] compulit / contra, *P*   18–19 vastauerunt:] vastauerunt /
P   19–20 sectorum / homicidarum /] sectorum homicidarum *P*   20 proditorum /]
proditorum *P*   22 confluxerit:] confluxerit *P*   23 vrbi] vrbi⟨s⟩ *P*   24 confirmare /] confirmare *P*   25 incommodis /] incommodis *P;* pronunciaturum /] pronunciaturum *P*   28 se /] se *P;* quibus] *P A,* in quibus *1565*

open for people impoverished by shipwreck, or faulty accounting, or some other misfortune, where they could shelter their
bodies, at least, from the cruelty of their creditors. And if (as has
happened a number of times) someone's right to the throne is
disputed, when the title is determined by warfare and each side
treats the other as traitors, it makes sense to have some place
where each side can be safe in uncertain or threatening circumstances as victory swings from one side to the other. But as for
the thieves and robbers who swarm in those places, and who
never reform once they are steeped in that sort of crime, it is
simply criminal for any sanctuary to protect them, let alone killers, who God ordered should be torn from the very altar and
slain if the crime was deliberate. But with us, unless the offense is
intentional, sanctuary is not even necessary. For if a killing was
unavoidable or accidental, then either the law will excuse it or
the prince will pardon it. Let anyone today count how few he can
find in sanctuary with any good excuse for having to be there,
and on the other hand, what a great crowd of degenerates
abounds there, destroyed by dice, luxury, and wantonness; and
then what a vile, loathsome scum of footpads and marauders,
cutthroats and killers and abominable traitors, has poured into
sanctuary as if into the foulest of sewers; and of the two main
receptacles, one is located near at hand by the city and the other
in its very bowels. I would venture to assert that anyone who
compared the advantages with the disadvantages of sanctuaries
would find it much more advantageous to do without the benefits than to put up with so many detriments.

"And I say that these things are true even without taking into
account other ways in which criminal rogues are abusing the

ad perniciem bonorum homines flagitiosissimi indies magis ac
magis abutuntur asylorum licentia. Nam nunc iuuentas improba
non alia causa liberius quam horum locorum fiducia profundit
perdit abligurit. Quin ditiores aliquot eo prouolant cum tenu-
5 iorum bonis: ibi edificant / oblectant sese / et creditoribus mandant laqueum./ Illuc vxores fugiunt cum suppellectile mari-
torum / duriciem eorum libidini suae pretexentes./ Illuc fures
conuehunt quae furto sustulere / ibique inde viuunt ac triumphant: ibi noua latrocinia machinantur: inde quauis nocte
10 prorepunt / furantur / [224] occidunt / et commisso facinore
reuertuntur tanquam loci reuerentia non tueretur modo eorum
vitam in penitentiam ante actorum scelerum / sed noua quoque
designandi licentiam indulgeret./ Quanquam si viri prudentes
adniterentur bona pars huius mali facile tolli posset / idque cum
15 bona Diui Petri gratia./ Reliquum quum nescio quis pontifex ac
princeps misericordes magis quam prudentes instituerunt / ac
ceteri deinceps religioso metu pertulere / nos feramus censeo
quatenus feret ratio / quae non eousque suffragatur asylo vt nos
prohibeat illustrissimum inde Ducem ipsius bono producere /
20 cuius loci priuilegium nullum in eo locum habet.

   "Ego certe hunc asylorum verum ac natiuum vsum esse semper sum arbitratus / vt eorum corpora tuerentur quos alioquin
maneret malum tum magnum tum imprimis meritum./ Nam vt
declinetur immeritum / non est cur implores peculiare cuiusuis
[32/1] 25 loci priuilegium./ Etenim ne cuiquam vsquam inferatur iniuria /
eam immunitatem leges / mores / natura cuique loco ex equo
tribuunt: nisi quis aliquem nouit locum in quo maleficia fas est
perpetrare. At vbi ab ipsa lege periculum est / ibi vero presidium

---

2 licentia.] licentia *P*   3 locorum fiducia] *P A*, fiducia locorum *P*sa *A*s *1565*   4 perdit]
corr. from perardit *P*b, perardit *A*; abligurit.] abligurit / *P*   5 bonis:] bonis / *P*; edificant /
oblectant sese /] edificant oblectant se se *P*   7 suae] sue *P*   8 quae] que *P*; viuunt]
viuut *P*   8–9 triumphant:] triumphant / *P*   9 machinantur:] machinantur *P*   10
furantur /] furantur *P*; occidunt / et] occidunt et *repeated as catchwords P*   12 in
penitentiam] *A*, impenitentiam *changed to* impenitentem *P*, ad poenitentiam *1565*   13
licentiam] licentiam ⟨si viri prudentes adniterentur⟩ *P*   13–14 si . . . adniterentur]
*interl. P*b   14 posset /] posset *P*   18 ratio / quae] ratio que *P*   19 producere /]
producere *P*   22 arbitratus /] arbitratus *P*; tuerentur] *1565*, tueretur *P A*; quos] *A*s
1565, ⟨quibus⟩ quos *P*, quibus *A*   24 immeritum /] immeritum *P*; implores] implores /
P; cuiusuis] cuius *P A*, cuiusque *1565*   25 iniuria /] iniuria *P*   27 tribuunt:] tribuunt
P

license of sanctuary to hurt virtuous people more and more every day. For now their reliance on sanctuaries gives prodigal young people their main incentive for squandering, wasting, and spending extravagantly. Indeed, some who are better off flee into sanctuary with the property of those who are poorer; there they build and enjoy themselves, thumbing their noses at their creditors. Wives flee there with their husbands' goods, citing mistreatment to mask their own wantonness. Thieves take their loot there, and there they live on it in triumph; there they plan their next robberies; from there they slink forth every night, steal, kill, and return after committing their crimes, as if the reverence accorded to that place not only protected their lives so that they could repent their past crimes, but also gave them a license to commit others. And yet if sensible men put their minds to it a large part of this mischief could be easily eliminated, with St. Peter's approval, at that. As for the rest, since some bishop or other and some prince with more mercy than prudence established it, and since their successors retained it out of a kind of religious fear, I think that we ought to endure it, but only within the limits of reason; and reason is not so very partial to sanctuary as to stop us from bringing forth his highness the duke from that place for his own good, when in his case the privilege of that place has no place at all.

"I for one have always supposed that the true and original function of sanctuaries is to protect the persons of those who would otherwise face some harm both great and (above all) deserved. For to avoid undeserved harm there is no need to appeal to a privilege belonging exclusively to any one place. For that immunity which protects anyone against unjust harm is accorded to every place alike, by law, custom, and nature, unless anyone knows of a place where it is legal to do wrong. But it is when the source of the danger is the law itself that one has to

a priuilegio petendum est / indeque ego natum altumque
asylorum vsum putem: a qua necessitate illustrissimus iste Dux
abest procul / cuius fidem erga Principem sanguinis necessitudo
probat / cuius erga reliquos omnes innocentiam tenera declarat
5 infantia / ne quis illi opus asylo putet / in quod ascribi nec potest
quidem. Neque enim ad asylum sic quemadmodum ad baptisma
confugitur vt susceptorum compatrumque vicaria voce bene-
ficium impetretur / sed cuius [224v] bono datur / ipse supplex
flagitet ac precetur oportet: idque adeo merito / cum competit
10 nemini preterquam ei cuius mens facinoris conscia indigum
egentemque talis auxilij facit. Quam ergo voluntatem habet ille
puerulus qua sibi inutile munimentum ab asylo postulet qui / si
eo proueheretur etatis vt vsum eius loci posset intelligere / profecto non parum irasceretur his qui illic manendum ei
15 suaderent? Vnde nunc eximere non repugnantem / vsque adeo
nihil mihi videtur formidandum / vt in eos quoque quibus vere
asyli ope opus est aliquanto tamen magis audendum quam sol-
emus censeam. Nam si quis eo subducat se cum alienis bonis /
quid ni regi liceat ea fugitiuo direpta domino reddere sine vllo
20 priuilegij preiudicio?" Verba fere qui e clero aderant / siue assen-
tabantur Duci siue ita vere sentiebant / confirmauere / sic diuino
iure cautum vti oberatorum bona in asyla confluentium dispar-
tiantur creditoribus / relicta tantum libertate corporibus quorum
labore victum queritent. "Credo vos" inquit ille "verum dicere:
25 quod si mulier eo transfugiat pertesa mariti sed tanquam perter-
[33/1]   rita / mihi certe videtur inoffenso Diuo Petro maritus e medio
Petri templo coniugem iniecta manu protracturus. Alioqui / si
nemo inde deduci potest qui sese dixerit manere velle / certe

---

1 est / indeque] est. Indeque *P*   2 putem:] putem *P*   3 procul /] procul. *P*   4
innocentiam] innocentiam / *P*   5 infantia /] infantia./ *P;* putet /] putet *P*   8 impetretur /] impetretur. *P;* datur /] datur *P*   9 oportet:] oportet. *P;* merito /] merito *P*
11 facit] *interl. P*   12 qui /] qui *P*   13 intelligere /] intelligere *P*   15 suaderent?]
suaderent *P;* eximere non repugnantem /] ex imere non repugnantem *P*   16
formidandum /] formidandum *P*   18 bonis /] bonis. *P*   19 direpta] ⟨ea⟩ direpta *P*
20 preiudicio?] preiudicio. *P;* Verba] *P A,* Ea verba *1565 but neither reading appears
quite correct (cf.* And with that diuers of the clergy yᵗ were present *1557);* aderant /]
aderant *P*   20–21 assentabantur] *corr. from* assentibantur *P*   21 confirmauere /]
confirmauere./ *P*   22 iure] *1565,* in rem *P A*   23 creditoribus /] creditoribus *P*
24 queritent.] queritent *P;* dicere:] dicere *P*   25–26 perterrita /] perterrita *P*   27
protracturus.] protracturus *P;* Alioqui /] Alioqui *P̣*   28 sese] se se *P*

resort to a privilege for protection; and I believe it is from this necessity that the custom of sanctuaries arose and grew up. But this sort of necessity has no bearing at all on his highness the duke; for his loyalty to the prince is demonstrated by their blood-relationship, and his innocence of injury to anyone else is established by his tender youth, unless somebody thinks that he has need of sanctuary when he is not even eligible to obtain it. For one cannot obtain the benefit of sanctuary like the benefit of baptism, at the vicarious request of his sponsors and godparents; rather, the suppliant who stands to benefit from the privilege must ask for it and pray for it himself—rightly so, in that it applies only to people whose own guilty consciences make them need and require such assistance. Now what desire does that little boy have to ask the useless protection of a sanctuary? And if he were mature enough to understand the purpose of that place, he would certainly be not a little angry at those who urged him to remain there. In fact, I think there is so little to fear if we remove him when he has no objection to leaving that in my view we should be somewhat bolder then we generally are with the people who do have need of sanctuary. For if someone makes off there with another person's property, is the king not at liberty to take it away from the fugitive and restore it to its owner without any infringement of the privilege?" Whether they were playing up to the duke or they actually thought so, almost all of the clergy who were present confirmed his words, saying that according to canon law the property of debtors who gather in sanctuary is to be divided up among their creditors, leaving only their bodies at liberty so that they can work for a living. "I believe you are right," he went on. "And if a woman flees there out of weariness with her husband but claims to be scared of him, I for one think that with no offense to St. Peter her husband can take hold of his wife and drag her from the very midst of Peter's church. Otherwise, if no one can be taken from sanctuary who says that he wants to

puer quispiam qui preceptori diffugerit ibi relinquendus est:
quod exemplum quanquam leue / vt est / videri possit / tamen hec
nostra causa est aliquanto leuior./ Nam illic quanquam puerilis
metus est / est tamen aliquis / at hic omnino nullus est / et profec-
5   to antehac sepe viros asylanos audiui sed pueros [225] nunc
primum audio.

"Quamobrem / vt aliquando finiam / quisquis id facinoris admiserit vt opus ei asili ope sit / is ibi maneto. Sed hic illustrissimus
dux ibi dimittendus non est / qui neque etatem habet qua possit
10 istud petere / neque maliciam qua possit indigere / cuius neque
vita neque libertas venire in discrimen vllo iure potest / per iniuriam vero prope minus potest / fratre rerum summa potiente /
ipse opibus potens / amicis etiam potentior / quippe patruo clarissimo nobisque omnibus ad salutem atque incolumitatem eius
15 incumbentibus. Postremo / qui ex asylo quempiam ipsius bono
commodoque protraxerint / etiam si vim fecerint / hos ego tamen
asylo vim fecisse pernego."

Huic Ducis orationi cum laici quotquot aderant / tum vero
clericorum plerique / nihil etiam mali suspicantes adsensere /
20 eoque discessum denique vt ni redderetur vltro / vi deducendus
ex asylo videretur./ Ceterum verbis ante visum est quam vi expe-
riendum./ Cardinalis ergo e consilio in asylum recta contendit
vnaque aliquot e nobilibus / siue dignitatis eius viri habita ratio
est / siue Protector huc respexit vti ex tot presentia procerum
25 Regina colligeret non ex vnius esse hominis sententia quod tum
agebatur / siue ne ausus quidem est tantam rem vni credere./
[34/1]   Quanquam suspicantur aliqui / si Regina (quod expectabatur)
filium obstinate pernegare pergeret / demandatum seorsum

---

1 est:] est./ P   2 leue / vt est /] leue vt est P; possit /] possit P   4 est / est] A 1565, est P;
et] ⟨et⟩ et P   6 audio.] audio / P   7 Quamobrem /] Quamobrem P; finiam /] finiam P
8 maneto.] maneto P   13 potens /] potens P   15 incumbentibus. Postremo /] incumbentibus Postremo P   16 protraxerint /] protraxerint P; fecerint /] fecerint P
17 pernego.] pernego./ P   18 aderant /] aderant P   19 plerique /] plerique P
20 discessum] A 1565, dicessum P; ni] corr. from vi P[b], ne A, in 1565; vltro /] vltro P
23 nobilibus /] nobilibus P   25 colligeret] colligeret / P   26 agebatur /] agebatur P
27 aliqui /] aliqui P; (quod expectabatur)] quod expectabatur P   28 pergerent /]
pergeret P

remain there, we will certainly have to let every schoolboy remain there who has run away from his schoolmaster. Even
though this example may seem frivolous—it is—our own case is
a good deal more frivolous still. For though the fear in that
instance is childish, it is at least fear of a sort; in this case there is
no fear at all. And indeed, I have often heard references to
sanctuary-men in the past, but this is the first I have heard of a
sanctuary-boy.

"Now, then, to conclude at long last, let anyone who has committed a crime such that he needs the benefit of sanctuary remain there. But his highne¯ʿ the duke ought not to be left there,
since he is too young to request it and too innocent to need it;
neither his life nor his liberty is in any danger from the law, and
against the law they can be threatened even less, so to speak,
since his brother is the highest authority and he himself is rich in
resources and even richer in his friends, what with his illustrious
uncle and all the nobility looking out for his health and well-
being. And finally, if people remove someone from a sanctuary
in his own best interests, even if they use force, I deny that they
violate the sanctuary."

Still not thinking he meant any harm, all the laity present and
most of the clergy agreed with the duke's speech, and it was
finally conceded that if the boy was not freely returned he
should be forcibly taken from the sanctuary. But they thought it
best to try verbal persuasion before using force. So the cardinal
hastened straight from the council to the sanctuary escorted by
several of the nobles, whether out of respect for his dignity or
because the Protector intended the queen to infer from the presence of so many lords that their mission was not all one man's
doing or because he did not dare to trust such an important
errand to a single individual, even though some suspect that
secret orders had been given to some of the company that if the
queen—as they thought she would—stubbornly persisted in
withholding her son, they should forcibly take him immediately

fuisse quibusdam e comitibus / illicet vt inuitae per vim eriperent
neu tempus amandandi darent / cuius rei consilium post eum
sermonem habitum agitatura videbatur modo suppeteret
spacium./ [225v]

5   Igitur vbi mutuo in conspectum venere Cardinalis exponit
rem atrocem videri nobilibus / vnicum Regis fratrem ab eo
seiunctum ab illa velut in carcere adseruari / quo ex facto / vt nihil
super ipsorum infamiam queratur / consequi tamen et conflari
apud exteras omnes gentes inuidiam ipsi nimirum Principi /
10 cuius vnicus germanus narretur in asylo delitescere / ne patria
quidem interim exempta calumniae / tanquam populum tam
immanem gignat [ac] efferum / vt fratri etiam ab fratre sit periculum: proin se ad eam ab Rege proceribusque missum vti pro
sua in eam fide atque amore recta et conductura consuleret / eius
15 generis imprimis esse vt Ducem emissum ex illis latebrarum angustijs augustissimae Principis aulae / iucundissimo fratris contubernio redderet: id si ita fecisset / et regni rebus publice / et
amicorum communiter / et priuatim suis recte consulturam / sed
Regi in primis atque ipsi etiam Duci egregie gratificaturam /
20 quibus maxime commodum sit maxime simul viuere./

   Ad hec Regina "Haud equidem negauerim" inquit "hono-
rande pater / optandam filio huic meo conditionem esse quam
affers / vti videlicet perpetuo cum Rege versetur et conuiuat
fratre. Ceterum contra quoque rem ego neutri parum com-
25 modam censuerim si ambos aliquot adhuc annos tueretur atque
educaret mater / estimata vtriusuis etatula sed huius presertim
minoris / cui preter teneros annos infantiae quae et ipsa curae
non oscitantis indiget / febris etiam neutiquam leuis accessit / qua

[35/1]

1 comitibus /] comitibus *1565*, commitibus *P A;* inuitae] inuite *P*   2 neu] *A 1565*, ne *P;*
darent /] darent *P*   7 facto /] facto *P*   8 queratur /] queratur *P*   9 Principi /]
Principi *P*   10 vnicus germanus] *P*, germanus vnicus *A 1565;* delitescere /] delitescere
P   11 calumniae /] calumnie *P*   12 gignat ac] *1565* gignat *P A*   12–13 periculum:] periculum / *P*   16 augustissimae . . . aulae /] augustissime . . . aule *P*   17
redderet:] redderet *P;* fecisset /] fecisset *P*   18 communiter /] communiter *P;*
consulturam /] consulturam *P*   19 egregie gratificaturam] *P A*, perquam rem gratam
facturam *1565*   20 maxime commodum] *A 1565*, maximum commodum *P*   21
Regina] Regina. *P*   22 pater /] pater *P*   23 affers /] affers *P;* vti] vti ⟨per⟩ *P*   24–
25 commodam] ⟨in⟩commodam *P*, incommodam *A 1565*   26 mater /] mater *P*   27
infantiae quae . . . curae] infantie que . . . cure *P;* indiget /] indiget *P*

without her consent and not give her time to send him away, a plan she would be likely to put into action after her conversation with them if they gave her the time.

And so when the queen and the lords came together, the cardinal explained that the nobles considered it outrageous for her to keep the king's only brother shut away from him as if in a prison, an act which might simply be meant to insult the nobles but which would also disgrace the prince himself in the eyes of all foreign nations, when it was reported that his only brother was lurking in sanctuary; nor would England herself escape slanderous comments, as if she produced a race so monstrous and savage that not even brothers were safe from each other. And so he had been sent to her by the king and his nobles to offer her sound and useful advice as her trustworthy and loving friend, and especially to urge her to set the duke free from those confining recesses and send him to the prince's splendid court and to his brother's sweet fellowship, for in doing so she would be serving both the realm's public interests, her friends' mutual interests, and her own private interests, and would also be performing a particular service for the king and the duke himself, for whom it would be most advantageous to live in the most perfect intimacy.

"Reverend father," the queen answered, "I certainly would not deny that what you are proposing would be very desirable for my son, that is, spending all his time with the king and enjoying life together with his brother. But on the other hand I would also suggest that it would be more than a little advantageous for both of them to be sheltered and brought up for several more years by their mother, given their immaturity, and especially that of the younger one whom I have here. For quite apart from the tender years of his infancy, which itself requires diligent care, he has also been subject to quite a serious fever, from which

diu conflictatus / adeo nuper potius remissius egrotare cepit
quam reualuit vt ego nemini mortalium omnium eum audeam
preterquam vni mihi credere / quandoquidem et medicarum
rerum periti aiunt / quod vel tacentibus illis cotidiana probant
5 pericula / neminem in morbum nisi duplicato periculo recidere /
opinor quod priore conflictu fatigata [226] natura minus re-
centes vires ad secundos congressus adfert. Neque diffido tamen
inueniri posse qui sint ad salutem eius partes suas diligenter
obituri./ Sed neminem esse vsquam reor cui aut penitius
10 exploratum sit quid eius corpus ferat postuletque quam ego /
quae ei tam diu quam continenter adsueui / neque qui minus
remisse vel magis indulgenter puerum sit curaturus quam
mater."
　　Ad hec Cardinalis "Nemo ibit inficias / Regina clarissima /
15 neminem vsquam esse / qui vna te sit appositior tuorum vitae
liberorum istac presertim etatula moderandae / neque procerum quisquam est omnium qui non ambos optet in tua manu
oculoque potissimum enutriri / modo animum possis inducere
vti in ea prodeas loca quae neque dignationem tuam neque il-
20 lorum maiestatem dedeceant: sin tibi ipsa persuaseris in hoc
asylo delitescendum / communi omnium sententia iudicatum
est / longe magis e re esse Ducis cum Rege liberum in dignitate ac
splendore viuere / vtriusque bono et commodo / quam cum alterius damno / alterius inuidia / certe amborum dolore / miseram
25 tecum vitam in latebris et squalore ducere./ Neque enim vsque
quaque adeo necesse est puerum educari a matre vt non interdum incidat occasio qua alibi eum ali prestet: nam et quum olim
charissimus filius tuus tunc designatus rex profecturus esset in
Valliam / sui patriaeque commodi causa procul abs te victurus /

1 conflictatus /] conflictatus P; remissius] 1565, corr. from remissus P, remissus A　3
credere /] credere./ P　　5 pericula /] pericula P　　7 adfert.] adfert / P　　9 penitius]
penitius P A 1565　　10 corpus] P A, natura Psa As 1565; ego] we would normally expect
mihi; ego / quae] ego que P　　11 adsueui /] adsueui P　　13 mater.] mater./P　　14
Ad] New para. P; inficias / Regina clarissima /] inficias regina clarissima P　　15 vitae]
vite P　　16 moderandae] moderande P　　19 quae] que P; dignationem] ⟨dignitatem⟩
dignationem P　　20 dedeceant:] dedeceant P　　21 delitescendum /] delitescendum
P　　22 est /] est P　　23 commodo /] commodo P　　24 damno / alterius inuidia /]
damno alterius inuidia P; dolore /] dolore P　　27 prestet:] prestet P　　28 profecturus
esset] 1565, profecturus est A, profecturus P　　29 Valliam / sui patriaeque] Valliam sui
patrieque P

he has recovered, or rather gained a respite, so recently after a long struggle that I would not dare to entrust him to anyone other than myself; for, as medical authorities attest (and as daily experience proves even without them to testify), no one suffers a relapse without doubling the danger, I suppose since the invalid's constitution, worn out by the first struggle, brings less strength to the second encounter. And yet I have no doubt that you could find someone who would diligently do his best to keep him in good health. But I do not think that there is anyone anywhere who has deeper experience than I do (since I have been with him so constantly for such a long time) of his body's capacities and needs, nor will anyone look after a boy less perfunctorily or more lovingly than his mother."

To this the cardinal replied, "Noble queen, no one is going to deny that no one anywhere is better qualified than you yourself to bring up your own children, especially at their present tender age; all of the nobles would be glad to have both of them brought up in your hands and under your supervision, if you can bring yourself to move to a place not unseemly for either your dignity or their majesty. But if you are determined to lurk in this sanctuary, a general consensus has determined that it is much more in the duke's interest to live at large with the king to their mutual benefit and advantage in conditions of dignity and splendor than for him to lead a wretched existence in a squalid lair with you, to the deprivation of the one, to the disgrace of the other, and certainly to the sorrow of both. For it is not so completely essential for a child to be reared by his mother that nothing which happens can ever make it preferable for him to be raised somewhere else; for some time ago, when your own dearest son, the heir-apparent, was about to set off for Wales to live apart from you in his own and the nation's best interests, I remember

memini eam rem pro egregia prudentia tua te quoque ipsa approbante fieri."

"Non admodum approbante" inquit illa "neque tamen [226v]
hec causa simile quicquam habet cum illa / quum et alter tunc

[36/1]   5   esset incolumis et alter nunc infirma valetudine. Quo in statu cur
tam auide conetur eum Protector ad se trahere nequeo edepol
satis demirari. In quo si puer (absit omen verbo) citra vllam eius
culpam periret fato / facile tamen posset in suspicionem fraudis
incidere. Iam quod rem neque per se inhonestam / etiam si

10   abesset necessitas / et nunc tam necessariam vt veniam facile
mereretur etiam si paulum ab honestate deflecteret / ille (quod
cuique proclive est) orationis atrocitate deprauat / dum piam
hanc meam pro filio solicitudinem tristibus verbis inuadit /
metumque meum interpretatur maliciam / neque mihi natoque

15   salutem sed sibi ac proceribus inuidiam queri: hec ego certe non
admodum inique fero: vtinam non maioribus erumnis dis-
tringerer quam vt vacaret verbis commouerier. Neque tamen
satis video quomodo ipse secum constet./ Nam qui incolumia
mihi simulat esse omnia / idem egre me retinere sustinet vel

20   filium / et qui vbiuis tutam me esse fingit / is ne ibi quidem sinit /
vbi et latrones tuti sunt / quiescere./ Nam quid iniqui habet / me /
si modo libera sum / vbi mihi libet viuere? aut cur inuidiosum
fuerit puerulum manere cum matre? Nam quod sibi istud in-
honorum clamitat / tum proceribus omnibus / tum ipsi denique

25   Principi / ego certe contra censeo nemini esse non honorificum
ibi Ducem relinquere potissimum vbi sit credibile haberi exactis-
simam salutis suae rationem / quam hoc habendam loco / me hic
manente / nemo opinor dubitat: e quo non est consilium adhuc
exire meque in discrimen post reliquos necessarios meos inij-

30   cere / [227] qui vtinam hic mecum essent in tuto potius quam
ipsa cum illis foris in vitae versarer periculo."

Sub hec verba / "Ergo" inquit quidam ex nobilibus qui comes

---

2 fieri.] fieri./ P   5 valetudine.] valetudine P   8 facile] fcile P   9 quod] *1565*,
quam P A; inhonestam /] inhonestam P   11–12 (quod . . . est)] quod . . . est P   15
queri:] queri. P   16 fero:] fero P   20 sinit /] sinit P   21–22 me / si . . . sum /] me
si . . . sum P   24 clamitat /] clamitat P   27 suae] sue P   28 manente /] manente
P; dubitat:] dubitat. P   29–30 inijcere /] inijcere./ P   31 vitae] vite P; periculo.]
periculo./ P   32 verba /] verba. P

that you too approved of the plan in accordance with your singular prudence."

"I approved? Not particularly," she responded, "nor does this case bear any resemblance to that one: at that time the one son was safe, while at present the other is sickly. And in view of his feeble condition I can never stop wondering for the life of me why the Protector is trying so desperately to get hold of him; for if the boy (God forbid) should die naturally in his custody through no fault of his own, he could still readily come under suspicion of treachery. Now as for his misrepresenting with sinister language (as anyone can easily do) an act which would not be dishonorable even if it were not a matter of necessity and which is in reality so necessary that it would readily deserve pardon even if it did stray from honor a bit, and as for his grim invective against my devoted concern for my son and his move to interpret my fear as malice, as if my real aim were not safety for me and my child but notoriety for the Protector and the nobles, these slurs do not bother me very much at all. I only wish I were not too distracted by more serious troubles to find time to be upset by words. But I still fail to see any consistency in what he is saying; for the same man who pretends that everything I have is quite safe is unwilling to let me keep even my son, and the same man who maintains I am safe anywhere will not leave me in peace even where robbers find safety. For if I am a free woman, what harm does it do if I live where I like? Why should it bring disgrace on anyone if a little boy stays with his mother? For though he cries out that it brings dishonor on him, on the nobles in general, and finally on the prince himself, I for one hold on the contrary that it is perfectly honorable for everyone to leave the duke in the very place where it is likely the most care will be taken for his welfare; I think no one doubts this is that place for as long as I stay here, and I have no intention of leaving as yet and imperiling myself along with the rest of my relatives. For I would much rather that they were here with me in safety than that I were out there with them in the same mortal danger."

At these words a noble who had come there in the cardinal's

eo venerat Cardinali "nostin aliquid / Regina / cur eorum cuiquam debeat imminere periculum?" "Non cur debeat" inquit
illa / "vt ne cur in carcerem quidem trudi / in quod truduntur
tamen./ Quamobrem non est quod mirere si metuam ne qui
5 immerentes in vincula coniecerunt / ijdem ad innocentium perniciem sint incubituri."

Tum Cardinalis nutu linguacem illum admonens vt con-
ticesceret / neque eam cordam tam inconcinne tangeret amplius /
mox Reginam super amicorum casum solabatur / nempe excussa
10 et cognita causa nihil fore discriminis / de se ipsa vero vanis-
simum esse quod metuat / quippe cui neque mali impendeat
[37/1] quicquam neque intentari queat.

"At istud qui confidam?" inquit "Num innocentiae conscientia? Quasi vero illi nocentes sint? An quod illorum inimicis sim
15 fortasse minus inuisa / quibus illi vel maxime propter me inuisi
sunt? An securam prestet sanguinis hec necessitudo cum Principe? Sed quoto cognationis gradu absunt illi / quibus iam vides
quam nihil prodest cognatio? Quae ne exitialiter obsit etiam / id
mihi etiam in votis est. Quamobrem et ipsa me intra hec septa
20 continere statui nec filium hinc emittere donec salubriora com-
perero./ Nam illum / quo magis impense quosdam laborare video / vt inanium pretextu rerum in suam potestatem redigant / eo
nimirum ipsa vehementius quoque horreo a me amittere."

"At contra" inquit ille "quo tu / Regina / magis pertimescis ami-
25 cis eum tam propinquis credere / eo vicissim alij magis metuunt
apud te relinquere / [227v] ne muliebris iste frustra conceptus
timor in mentem tibi subigat vt aliquo eum ableges longius. Sunt
qui negant etiam fratrem posse te Regi distinere / quum nihil ad

1 Cardinali] *1565*, cardinalis *P A;* aliquid / Regina /] aliquid Regina *P*   2 periculum?]
periculum. *P*   5 coniecerunt /] coniecerunt *P*   6 incubituri.] incubituri./ *P*   8
amplius /] amplius. *P*   9 casum] *P, changed from* casu *A,* casu *1565;* solabatur /] solabatur *P*   10 discriminis /] discriminis./ *P*   13 confidam?" inquit] confidam inquit?
P; Num] *A 1565,* Non *P;* innocentiae] innocentie *P*   15 inuisa /] inuisa? *P*   16
sunt?] sunt. *P*   17 quoto] *A 1565,* quanto *P*   18 Quae] que *P;* etiam / id] etiam id
interl. P   20–21 comperero] *P,* comperio *A*   21 illum /] illum *P;* impense quosdam]
A 1565, impense *P;* laborare] *P A,* hoc agere *1565*   23 horreo] ⟨hereo⟩ horreo *P*   24
tu / Regina /] tu Regina *P*   26 relinquere /] relinquere *P*   27 ableges] *corr. from*
ablegas *P;* longius.] longius *P*   28 distinere /] distinere *P*

escort said, "Well then, queen, do you know of some reason why any of them should be in danger?" "Not why they should be," she answered, "any more than why they should be thrown into prison, into which they are thrown nonetheless. And so you should not be surprised if I fear that the same people who have put guiltless men in chains may intend the destruction of innocents."

Then the cardinal, first nodding a warning to that loose-tongued fellow that he should be quiet and stop harping on that jangling chord, promptly comforted the queen about her friends' misfortune, telling her that once the matter had been thoroughly sifted and cleared up they would be out of danger, and that her fear for herself had no basis at all, since no trouble was threatening her nor would anyone be able to cause any.

"But how can I be sure of that?" she responded. "In the certainty of my innocence? As if they had done anything wrong! Or perhaps because I am less hated by their enemies, when they are hated primarily on my account? Or would my blood kinship with the prince guarantee my safety? But how distant is their kinship with him? And you see that their kinship helped them not at all; I even pray it will not harm them fatally. Therefore I have resolved both to stay within these walls myself and not to let my son leave until I see that our prospects are healthier. For the more frantically I see some people working to get him into their power on some frivolous pretext the more vehemently abhorrent I find the idea of sending him away from me."

"But on the other hand, my queen," he replied, "the more frightened you are to entrust him to such closely related friends, the more others in turn fear to leave him with you, lest this groundless womanly fear of yours put it into your head to send him somewhere farther away. Some deny that you even have the right to keep his brother apart from the king, since the boy's

asyli sortem faciat simplex atque innocens etas pueri / qui neque
iudicio preditus sit / quo possit implorare / et malicia careat / qua
possit indigere: itaque nec infringi quidem censent huius loci
priuilegium si inuitae quoque eum tibi hinc ereptum eant / quod
5   te obstinate commodis tuorum refragante fortasse facturi sunt:
adeo anxius est Protector amantissimus eius patruus ne tu / dum
vanos tibi metus figuras animo / in certam perniciem aliquo
emittas puerum."

    "Itane?" inquit illa "adeon efflictim filium amat meum vt nihil
10 eque vereatur ac ne elabatur aliqua manusque eius euadat?
Timet scilicet ne emittam hinc longius eum quem / sic adfectum /
nec possum quidem citra salutis dispendium / quam non libenter
periclitari me / quidam non libenter vident: hinc ne eum emitterem / credo vt in dispositos ex itinere casses immitterem. Liceat
15 edepol / quod ad hanc rem attinet / in vtramuis aurem vt dormiat. Nam vbi ego illum sperem tutum si hic desperem? Estne
vllus vsquam locus hoc vno sanctior / cuius immunitatem nec
tyrannus quisquam hactenus inuentus est tam impius qui non sit
[38/1]   veritus violare? Atque ego certe confido Diui Petri sanctissimi
20 huius asili presidis numen non minus potentem vindicem aduersus sanctuarij sui violatores hodieque fore quam fuit olim. Sed
puerilis etas priuilegium non capit: pulchre scilicet / vt quo
latrones indemnes sunt / eo deficiatur [228] innoxius./ Nam
quod argutatur asyli beneficio non indigere puerulum / vtinam
25 non egeret / nec egeret certe si per se tuta esset aduersus
sceleratos innocentia.

    "Adeon me Protector (qui superos precor vt protectorem [se]
probet) adeon me stupidam arbitratur vt quorsum eius pha-
lerata tendat oratio non sentiam? Asyli latibulum Principis

---

2 sit /] sit P; careat /] careat P   3 possit] corr. from posset P; indigere:] indigere./ P   4
inuitae] inuite P; eant /] eant P   5 sunt:] sunt. P   6 tu /] tu P   7 animo /] animo
P   8 puerum.] puerum./ P   9 Itane?] Ita ne P   10 euadat?] euadat / P   11
quem / sic adfectum /] quem sic adfectum P   12 dispendium /] dispendium P   13
me /] me P; vident:] vident P   13–14 emitterem /] emitterem P   14 Liceat] P 1565,
licet A   15 edepol /] edepol P; attinet /] attinet P   15–16 dormiat.] dormiat / P
16 Estne] est ne P   17 sanctior /] sanctior P   20 presidis] 1565, presidi P, presidij A
21 fuit olim] olim fuit A 1565 (written as catchwords at the beginning of a large lacuna in A);
olim.] olim P   22 capit:] capit P; scilicet /] scilicet P   23 sunt /] sunt P   25 egeret /]
egeret P   26 innocentia.] innocentia P   27 protectorem se] 1565, protectorem P

simple and innocent age has nothing to do with the character of a sanctuary, and since he has neither the judgment to ask for admission nor the wickedness to need it; and so they hold that the privilege of this place would not even be infringed if they came to take him away even without your consent. And they probably will if you stubbornly go on obstructing your own children's interests; that is how much it worries the Protector, his most loving uncle, lest your empty and fanciful fears should provoke you to send the boy off to sure ruin somewhere else."

"Is that so?" she retorted. "Is the Protector so madly in love with my son that he fears nothing more than that he may make off somehow and give him the slip? Of course, he is afraid I might send my son somewhere farther away, though in his feeble state I could not even do so without risking his life (and my unwillingness to endanger his life is precisely what some are unwilling to tolerate); he is afraid I might send him away—oh, yes, to send him straight into the traps laid for him on the way! On my word, he does not need to lose any sleep over that possibility. For where can I hope he will be safe if I despair of his being safe here? Is there any place in the world holier than this one, the immunity of which no tyrant has ever before now been impious enough to violate? And I for one have no doubt that the spirit of St. Peter, holy guardian of this sanctuary, has no less power to take vengeance upon violators of his sanctuary today than he had in the past. But supposedly the boy's age is incapable of claiming the privilege; a wonderful argument, so that the privilege which protects brigands cannot help an innocent! Now, as for his claim that the boy does not need the benefit of sanctuary, would that he did not; and he certainly would not if innocence in and of itself were safe against wrongdoers.

"Does the Protector—and I pray to heaven that he actually lives up to his title—does the Protector think I am too stupid to see where his pretty oration is leading? The recesses of a sanctu-

maiestatem dedecorat: concitat infamiam proceribus / inuidiam
Principi: vtrique benefactum fratri / ne diuersi habitent / maxime quum Princeps egeat collusoris: quod ego superos omnes
obtestor / vtrique vt collusor obtingat felicior quam is qui callidis
5 consilijs pretexit tam grandibus verbis personatas ineptias / tanquam nusquam reperiri posset qui iocetur cum Principe (si
modo hoc ipsi vacat) nisi frater / cui per valetudinem non libet
ludere / ex asylo / id est extra munitiones suas / velut lusurus
eliceretur: perinde ac pueri tantam habeant rationem maiestatis
10 vt abstenturi ioco sint potius quam admittant impares / aut tanquam ludere nisi cum fratribus suis non possint / quibus id etatis
minus plerunque oblectantur quam alienis./
   "Sed puer hic petendo loci beneficio non sufficit scilicet. Quid
si petentem audiat? Sed finge non posse / finge non velle / imo
15 recusare putetur et egressum conari / tamen quisquis illum vel
volentem inuitae mihi abstulerit / eum ego plane contendo sanctum hoc asylum temerare / nisi putemus vnde sacrilegium sit
equum mihi abducere / inde fas esse abstrahi filium. Quin nisi
me periti fallunt / filium cui nullum hereditate [228v] predium
[39/1] 20 obuenit operae cuiquam militaris obnoxium / Angliae iura matri
tuendum credunt / et quisquam hinc mihi pupillum abstrahet
meum inoffensa libertate sanctuarij? Quod si neque meum ius
eum tueri posset neque ille suum petere / tamen cum tutela eius
ad me pertineat quis me non videt petere eius vice posse? Nisi
25 forte lex bonorum tantum haberi tutelam velit / nulla corporis
habita cura / cuius vnius gratia curat lex salua vt pupillo bona
sint./
   "Quod si quid ad obtinendum puero priuilegium exempla
valent / haud longe petitis indigeo./ Nempe hic ipse locus in quo

---

1 dedecorat:] dedecorat / *P*; proceribus /] proceribus *P*   2 Principi:] Principi / *P*;
vtrique . . . habitent] *P*, ex vtriusque commodo esse vt coniunctim habitent *1565;* fratri /]
fratri *P*; habitent /] habitent./ *P*   3 collusoris:] collusoris / *P*   4 obtestor /] obtestor *P*
5 ineptias /] ineptias *P*   6 nusquam] *corr. from* vsquam *P*b   7 frater /] frater *P*
8 ludere /] ludere *P*; asylo / id . . . suas /] asylo id . . . suas *P*   9 eliceretur] eliceatur
P, eliciatur *1565;* eliceretur:] eliceatur./ *P*   10 impares /] impares *P*   11 possint /]
possint *P*   16 volentem] *P*a *(in margin) 1565,* voluntate *interl. and deleted P*; abstulerit /]
abstulerit *P*   18 abducere /] abducere *P*   19 fallunt /] fallunt *P*   20 operae]
opere *P*; Angliae] Anglie *P*   21 credunt /] credunt./ *P*; et] ⟨Quod⟩ et *P*   25
bonorum] ⟨ta⟩ bonorum *P*   26 cura /] cura *P*   29 valent /] valent *P*

ary are a disgrace to the prince's majesty; they dishonor the nobles and stir up ill will toward the prince; it would be to each brother's advantage for them to stop living apart, especially since the prince needs a playmate; but I beseech all the saints to give each of them a better playmate than this uncle who invokes such grandiloquently fatuous pretexts for such cunning schemes, as though no one could be found anywhere who would play with the prince (if he is actually at leisure to play) unless his brother, who is in no condition for playing, were enticed from his sanctuary (that is, from his defenses) in order to play with him; as if boys care enough about majesty that they will give up play before they will accept an inferior as a playmate, or as though they cannot play with anyone besides their own brothers, though at that age they generally prefer strangers.

"But the boy, to be sure, is incompetent to ask for the benefit of this place. What if his uncle heard him asking for it? But suppose that he cannot; suppose that he will not; imagine that he even rejects it and tries to escape; I myself still contend that anyone who removes him against my will, even with his consent, will be violating this sanctuary, unless we are to think that abducting my son is permissible in a place where to take away my horse would be sacrilege. Why, indeed, if the experts inform me correctly, when the estate which a son has inherited includes no obligations of knight's service, English law makes his mother his guardian; and can anyone abduct my ward from this place without infringing the liberty of sanctuary? But even if my rights could not shelter him and he could not apply for his own, who does not see that as his legal guardian I can apply for them on his behalf? Unless maybe the law only means for me to take care of his property, taking no thought at all for his person, though it is only for the sake of his person that the law seeks to safeguard his property.

"But if precedents will help to secure the boy's privilege, I will hardly need to look very far for them. For the very place in which

nunc stamus / qui nunc an puero esse vsui possit disputatur /
alterum olim filium meum / videlicet ipsum Principem / et nascentem excepit et vagientem texit et prosperiori fortunae / quae
nunc precor vt ei sit perpetua / conseruauit. Neque enim / quod
5   omnes intelligitis / asyli nunc primum incola sum: eiecto quondam e regni solio atque exulante marito meo / grauida huc con-
fugi / hic Regem peperi / hinc reduci ac victori marito gra-
tulatura prodij / hinc infantem filium primis parentis
amplexibus obtuli: cui nunc regnanti vtinam tam tutum pala-
10 tium sit quam hic locus olim regnantis hosti fuit.

"Quo ex loco alterum etiam filium mittere non decreui / neque
vni cuiquam vtrumque credere / illi presertim cui deficientibus
ambobus patriae leges regnum destinant./ Nemo timores meos
excutiat: maternae sollicitudini fas est etiam vana metuere:
15 quanquam ego nihil in hac re sum publica lege cautior / quae / si
periti vera narrant / neminem vnquam admittit tutorem eius
cuius interitu sit hereditatem aliquanto minorem etiam regno
lucraturus. [229] Aduersus quae pericula certissimum ac prope
[40/1]   vnicum est in huius immunitate loci presidium / e quo is quem
20 habeo me volente non exibit. Quod si quis inuitae / quod non
opinor / abstraxerit / ac sanctissimam asyli religionem duxerit
violandam / tum ego superos eius presides obtestor / idem vt asyli
propediem immunitate egeat / careat facultate / interceptus pre-
occupatusque omnium sacrorum sedium prohibeatur aditu:
25 nam ingressum extrahi / ne inimicum quidem vellem."

Cardinalis vbi vidit sese multum vrgendo nihil promouere /
sed illam / magis magisque incensam / posteriora quaeque du-

---

1 stamus /] stamus *P*   2 meum /] meum *P;* Principem /] Principem *P*   3 fortunae /
quae] fortune que *P*   4 perpetua / conseruauit.] perpetua conseruauit / *P*   4–5
enim / quod . . . intelligitis /] enim quod . . . intelligitis *P*   5 sum:] sum *P*   6 meo /]
meo *P*   9 obtuli:] obtuli / *P*   10 regnantis hosti] *P,* regnante hoste *1565 (cf.* And I
praye God y[t] my sonnes palace may be as great sauegard to him now rayning, as thys
place was sometime to the kinges enemye. *1557*[L]*);* fuit.] fuit *P*   12 credere /] credere
P   13 patriae] patrie *P*   14 excutiat: maternae] excutiat / materne *P;* metuere:]
metuere *P*   15 cautior / quae /] cautior que *P*   16 narrant /] narrant *P*   18
lucraturus.] lucraturus / *P;* quae] que *P*   20 exibit] *corr. from* exiet P[b]; exibit.] exibit *P;*
inuitae / quod] inuite quod *P*   21 opinor / abstraxerit /] opinor abstraxerit *P*   22
obtestor /] obtestor *P*   23 egeat / careat facultate /] egeat, careat facultate, *P*   24
aditu:] aditu *P*   25 extrahi /] extrahi *P*   27 illam /] illam *P;* incensam /] incensam *P;*
quaeque] queque *P*

we are now standing and debating about whether a boy can enjoy its immunities was at one point the birthplace of my other son—namely, the prince—his protection as a wailing baby and his preservation for better times to follow, better times which I now pray will last for him. For as you all know, this is not the first time I have lived in a sanctuary; when my husband was driven from his throne and in exile some time ago, I sought refuge here during my pregnancy; I gave birth to the king here; from here I went forth to congratulate my husband upon his victorious return; from here I took our infant son for his father's first embrace; and may he be as safe in the palace now that he is king as he was in this place at the time when he was the king's enemy.

"I have made up my mind not to send forth my second son from this place as well as the first, or to entrust any one man with both of them, especially the man whom the nation's laws designate the heir to their throne if both perish. No one should pry into my reasons for worrying; maternal devotion is allowed even groundless anxieties, though in this instance, if the experts are telling the truth, I am being no more cautious than the common law, which allows no one to become guardian of a person on whose death he would stand to inherit much less than a kingdom. Against these risks the surest and practically the only protection is in the immunity which this place affords, and the son I have with me will not leave it with my consent. But if anyone removes him without my consent and deliberately violates this most holy sanctuary, as I think no one will, then I call on its guardian saints to ordain that that man will soon need its immunity without any means to obtain it, cut off, circumvented, and barred from access to all holy places; for I would not pray that even an enemy should be dragged out once he has gained entry."

When the cardinal saw that his long arguments were getting him nowhere and that she was growing more and more heated,

riora iacere / tristibusque verbis fidem Protectoris inuadere /
quam ille / quum integram crederet / grauatim audit insimulari /
denique respondit haud diutius rem disputaturum: si Regina
puerum vellet credere / fidem ipsos suam in eius incolumitatem
5 obstricturos / sin retinere certum esset / discessuros illico / nec
verbum addituros amplius in ea re in qua vel prudentiam eorum
suspectam illa / vel fidem habeat / prudentiam si alienae per-
fidiae creduli / fidem si prudentes ministri putarentur./
    Sub hec Regina longius deliberabunda conticuit: cui / quum
10 Cardinalis ad abitum accinctior quam quidam e comitatu suo
videretur et Protector ipse in palatio adesset cum satellitum
globo / subire animum cepit haud palam seruari filium in asylo
posse / celandi vero spem non esse / subducendo illinc nil non
inoportunum / neque tempus suppetere / neque quo mitteretur
15 prouisum / comites adhuc incertos / imparata omnia / adeo securam nuntius hic oppresserat nihil minus cogitantem quam
asylo [229v] inferendam vim / quod nunc obsessum etiam reputabat / nec vllum puero exitum nisi in insidias dari. Aliquando
contra / vt perditissimis rebus intermicat interim spes / cogitabat
20 non esse fors tam inclementem patrui in nepotes animum quam
ipsa concepisset: denique / si non vanus eius timor esset / certe
serum fore. Preterea Cardinalis animum satis exploratum
habuit / nec minus compertam nobilium aliquorum qui simul
venerant fidem / quos vt verebatur ne falli possent / ita sibi per-
25 suaserat non potuisse corrumpi. Igitur si filium omnino di-
missura sit / prestare censuit / sponte vt illum tradere quam
inuita videretur / rata fore vti id nonnihil in conseruandum puerum curam atque industriam eorum quibus iam tradebatur

[41/1]

---

1 iacere /] iacere P; inuadere /] inuadere P   2 ille / quum . . . crederet /] ille
quum . . . crederet P; insimulari /] insimulari P   3 disputaturum:] disputaturum P
5 esset /] esset P   7–8 alienae perfidiae] aliene perfidie P   9 conticuit: cui /] conticuit / cui P   11 videretur] videretur / P; adesset] 1565, accessit P   12 globo /]
globo P   13–14 nil non inoportunum] nil non oportunum P, nihil oportunum
1565   14 inoportunum /] oportunum P   15 prouisum /] prouisum P; prouisum /
comites . . . incertos / imparata] prouisum esset imparata 1565; adhuc] apparently corr.
from ad hec P   17 vim /] vim P   17–18 reputabat /] reputabat P   18 dari.] dari P
19 contra /] contra P; spes /] spes P   21 concepisset:] concepisset P; denique /] denique P   22 fore.] fore / P   23 habuit /] habuit P   24 possent /] possent P
26 sit /] sit P; censuit /] censuit P; tradere] 1565, tradere or credere P   27 nonnihil]
non nihil P

using harsher expressions the longer she argued and grimly assailing the Protector's good faith, which the cardinal did not like to hear questioned because he believed it was genuine, he finally responded that he was not going to debate the matter any longer; if she wanted to entrust the boy to them, they would give her their word for his safety, but if she was determined to keep him, they would leave right away without saying another word about it, since she seemed to doubt either their prudence or good faith in the matter, their prudence if she thought they were dupes of another man's perfidy, their good faith if she thought they were knowing accessories.

Upon these words the queen entered into a long, thoughtful silence. Since it seemed that the cardinal was more bent on leaving than some of his escort and since the Protector himself was on hand in the palace with a band of retainers, it began to occur to her that she could not openly keep her son in the sanctuary, but that she could not hope to conceal him; that circumstances could not be more awkward for slipping away with him; that there was neither enough time, nor a planned destination; that no escort had so far been chosen, and nothing was ready; so thoroughly had this emissary caught her by surprise, expecting nothing less that that anyone might violate the sanctuary, although she now considered that it was surrounded, as well, and that any way out for her son would lead straight to a trap. But since there is occasionally a glimmer of hope in the gloomiest circumstances, at length she had the thought that their uncle's intentions toward his nephews might not be as ruthless as she had supposed; and in any event, if her fear of him was not groundless, it would certainly be too late to help. Besides, she was assured of the cardinal's good intentions and had no reason to doubt the good faith of several of the nobles in his escort, and though she feared that they might be deceived, she was convinced they could not be corrupted. And so if she was going to send her son away at all, she thought it would be better if she seemed to be giving him up freely instead of unwillingly, since she reasoned it would quicken the interest and diligence of those who received him in guarding

incenderet si ipsa sua manu filium velut in tutelam fidemque
committeret.

Producto igitur et constituto in presentia puero / "Viri" inquit
"clarissimi / neque adeo imprudens ipsa sum vestrae vt pruden-
5 tiae diffidam neque adeo suspiciosa vt de fide dubitem / cuius
meae fiduciae id documentum hodie dabo quod si alterutra desideretur in vobis / eternum sit mihique reique publicae vulnus
inflicturum." Simul manu puerum apprehendens / "En hic
quem vultis" inquit "meum atque Eduardi charissimi olim regis
10 vestri filium / quem ego me non ambigo / nisi vobis eum credere
statuissem / huius loci posse sancta religione tueri. Tamen istud
etiam minus ambigo / esse aliquos meo sanguini tam exitialiter
infestos vt si quid eius scirent sanguinis in ipsorum corporibus
conditum non cunctarentur exhaurire. Ad hec periculo di-
15 dicimus quam facile cognationis adfectum omnem execranda
regni sitis [230] obimbibet: frater fratrem amolitur / sobolesque
per ipsum parentis corpus proruit ad imperium / et nepos de
patruo securus est? Meorum certe liberorum alter alterius presidium est dum distinentur: mutuo sese animant: vteruis in-
20 columis vtrumque seruat: eoque nihil ancipitius quam ambos vni
credere / mercator siquidem parum cautus haberi solet quisquis
in vna rate sortem semel vniuersam periclitatur. Tamen hunc
vobis in manus do / fratremque simul in illo: vtrumque vestrae
committo fidei / ab ijsdem vtrumque rursus coram dijs atque
[42/1]   25 hominibus repetitura. Prudentiae vobis multum inesse scio /
fidei plurimum: opes ac potentia supersunt / nec deerunt qui hac

1 incenderet] intenderet *P*, accenderet *1565*   2 committeret.] committeret / *P*   3
puero /] puero./ *P*   4 clarissimi /] clarissimi *P*   4–5 vestrae vt prudentiae] vestre vt
prudentie *P*   5 suspiciosa . . . dubitem] *P 1565*, formidolosa vt formidem fidem
*P*sa   6 fiduciae] fiducie *P*   6–7 desideretur] *1565*, desideraretur *P*   7 vobis /]
vobis *P*   8 inflicturum.] inflicturum *P*   10 filium /] filium *P;* ambigo /] ambigo *P*
11 statuissem /] statuissem *P;* tueri.] tueri *P*   12 ambigo /] ambigo *P*   13 si
quid] siquid *P*   16 obimbibet] *P*, extinguat *1565;* obimbibet:] obimbibet / *P*   17
imperium /] imperium *P*   19 distinentur:] distinentur / *P*   19 mutuo sese animant]
om. 1565; animant:] animant *P*   20 seruat:] seruat *P*   21 credere /] credere. *P*
22 periclitatur.] periclitatur / *P*   23 do /] do *P;* illo:] illo / *P;* vestrae] vestre *P*   25
repetitura. Prudentiae] repetitura / prudentie *P;* scio /] scio *P*   26 plurimum:] plurimum / *P*

his life if she personally handed him over as though she was entrusting him to them for safekeeping.

So, then, bringing the boy out to stand him in their presence, she said to them, "Noble sirs, I am not so imprudent as to lack faith in your prudence, nor am I so suspicious as to doubt your good faith; and today I shall give you such a token of my confidence that if you are lacking in either it will inflict an incurable wound on both me and the commonwealth." At the same time she took the boy by the hand and said, "Here is the boy that you want, my son and Edward's, your dear former king; I have no doubt that if I had not chosen to entrust him to you, I could protect him with the hallowed immunity of this sanctuary. But I have even less doubt that some people are such mortal enemies of my blood that if they knew that there was a drop of it hidden in their bodies they would not hesitate to spill it. Furthermore we have learned by experience how easily the detestable thirst for dominion swallows up any feelings of kinship; when brother slays brother and a child forces his way to the throne over his parent's dead body, will a nephew be safe from his uncle? My own children, at any rate, safeguard each other by being kept apart; they give each other life; each one's safety depends on the other's; and so there could be nothing more hazardous than to entrust both of them to one man, just as it is a very rash merchant, in most people's view, who will risk his whole fortune in one ship. Nevertheless, I give this son into your hands, and in him I also give you his brother; I entrust them both to your loyalty, and from you, before God and men, I will ask for them back again. I know you have a great deal of prudence and even more good faith; you have power and resources to spare, nor will

in causa sese libenter adiungent. Vnum tantum per vestram
fidem perque mariti mei memoriam / per meam de filijs sollicitudinem vobisque fiduciam / vos obtestor vti quam ego vobis
nimium timere videor / tam vos vicissim nimium ne confidatis."
5 Statimque in puerulum versa / "Vale charissime" inquit "filj /
superi tibi curatores adhibeant / immo ipsi curam habeant. Matrem semel saltem amplectere atque exosculare digrediens / incertus an idem vnquam licebit denuo." Simul os admouit ori /
cruce eum lustrata auertit sese / lachrimansque a plorante di-
10 cessit./ Quem Cardinalis comitesque eius exceptum recta in palatium / vbi Protector cum proceribus eorum reditum opperiebatur / per dispositos tota via satellitum ordines adduxerunt.
Adductum Protector amplexus atque in vlnas e terra sub-
uehens / "aduenisti / charissime nepos" inquit "ac domine /
15 gratus nimirum omnibus / mihi longe profecto gratissimus."
Tum inde continuo Londinum itur ad Principem [230v] (diuersabatur is in Episcopi palatio) vnde protinus ambo mediam per
vrbem celebri pompa faustis vndique proclamationibus et clam-
antium vota frustraturis arcem ingressi sunt / vnde nunquam
20 pedem retulisse creduntur./
    Igitur vbi Protector vtrumque puerum nactus est / maiore
fiducia cum alijs aliquot / tum precipue Duci Bukyngamiae /
aperit sese: quanquam non ignoro multis visum totius eum consilij iam inde ab initio participem: Protectoris amici quidam au-
[43/1] 25 thorem etiam eum incipiendae rei tradunt / vltro ad Glocestren-
sem misso protinus ab Eduardi morte clandestino nuncio. Sed
alij quibus exploratius est callidum Protectoris ingenium negant

1 libenter] P, libenter vobis *1565;* adiungent.] adiungent P   3 fiduciam /] fiduciam P;
vobis] ⟨vbis⟩ vobis P   4 videor /] videor P; confidatis.] confidatis P   5 charissime] P,
dulcissime *1565;* filj] ⟨filij⟩ filj P   6 adhibeant /] adhibeant P   6–7 habeant. Ma-
trem] habeant matrem / P   7 digrediens /] digrediens P   8 vnquam] ⟨licebit⟩ vnquam P; ori /] ori P   9 sese /] se se P; lachrimansque] P, ploransque *1565*   10–11
palatium /] palatium P   11–12 opperiebatur] operiebatur P *1565;* opperiebatur /]
operiebatur P   14 aduenisti /] aduenisti P; domine /] domine P   15 omnibus /]
omnibus P; gratissimus.] gratissimus./ P   16–17 (diuersabatur . . . palatio)] diuersabatur . . . palatio P   18 proclamationibus] P, acclamationibus *1565*   19 ingressi]
1565, iniecti P; nunquam] P, nunquam eos *1565*   20 creduntur] P, constat *1565*
21 est /] est P   22 aliquot /] aliquot P; Bukyngamiae /] Bukyngamie P   23 sese:]
sese / P   24 participem:] participem / P   25 incipiendae] incipiende P; tradunt /]
tradunt P   27 nuncio.] nuncio / P

there be any shortage of people who will gladly support you in this cause. But in the name of your faith and my late husband's memory, in the name of my care for my children and my trust in you, I beg one thing only: just as I seem to you to be overly fearful, so on your part do not be overconfident." Then, immediately turning to her little boy, she said, "Goodbye, my dear son; may the saints provide someone to care for you, or rather, may they care for you themselves. Hug your mother and kiss her one last time at least as you go, without knowing whether you will ever get the chance again." And with this, touching her lips to his and making the sign of the cross over him, she turned away tearfully, leaving the little boy weeping. The cardinal and his escort received him and led him directly to the palace between rows of retainers which lined the whole route to where the Protector and the nobles were awaiting their return. When the boy was brought to him, the Protector hugged him, lifting him off the ground in his arms, and said, "My dearest nephew and liege, you are a welcome arrival to everyone, and especially welcome to me." Then they went from there straight to the prince, who was living in London in the bishop's palace, and from there, escorted through the middle of the city by a large retinue, attended on all sides by cheers which would frustrate the hopes of the cheerers, both brothers immediately entered the Tower, outside which it is thought that they never set foot again.

And so when the Protector had gotten both boys, he grew more trusting and opened his mind to a number of other people and especially the Duke of Buckingham, though I am not unaware of the widespread opinion that he was privy to the whole scheme from the outset; some adherents of the Protector even maintain that the duke instigated the business by sending a secret messenger on his own initiative to Gloucester just after Edward's death. But others who are better acquainted with the

ante communicata postrema quam priora patrauerat / ceterum
coniectis in carcere necessarijs Reginae et vtroque filio in suas
manus perducto / reliqua minus timide quibus res postulare
videbatur aperuisse: Ducique potissimum / cuius accessione di-
5 midio suas vires auctas [fore] intelligebat / per homines astutos et
tractandarum rerum artifices rem insinuat. Proponitur ei cog-
natorum causa Princeps iratus et / si quando licuerit / futurus
vltor / qui / seu dimittantur / instigarent: hesuram etenim semper
carceris et vinculorum memoriam: sin trucidentur / haud am-
10 bigue mortem illorum ei curae fore quorum carcer dolori fuit.
Ad hec penitendo nihil profici. Redimendae beneficijs offensae
non relictum locum. Nam suas spes procliuius corrupturum
quam profuturum Principi / quem cum fratre vna cognatisque
eo iam iniectum videat vbi Protector omnes posset vno nutu
15 tollere / nec dubium sit / si quid [231] noui moliminis intentaretur / ausurum. Quem vt erat credibile occultum sibi presidium / ita Duci exploratores struxisse et / si aduersaretur /
insidias: idque fors ex his quos minime suspectaret: eum namque rerum statum / eos animorum habitus esse / vt cui confidas /
20 quem pauescas statuere certo non possis. Talia suggerendo
fatigatum Ducis animum eo perpulere vti qua iam ingressum
[via] penitebat / eadem pergeret / et quando semel ceperat /
gnauiter vsque insisteret. Itaque scelestissimo consilio / quod
depelli non posse credebat / fautorem sese sociumque adiunxit /

1–2 patrauerat /] patrauerat. *P*   2 Reginae] Reginae / *P*   3 perducto /] perducto *P*
4 aperuisse:] aperuisse *P*; potissimum /] potissimum *P*   5 auctas fore] auctas *P*, auc-
tum iri *P*sa, auctiores fere (*for* fore?) *1565*; intelligebat /] intelligebat *P*   6 insinuat.]
insinuat / *P*   7 et /] et *P*; licuerit /] licuerit *P*   8 vltor /] vltor *P*; qui /] qui *P*;
dimittantur /] dimittantur *P*; instigarent:] instigarent / *P*   9 memoriam:] memoriam /
P; trucidentur /] trucidentur *P*   10 curae] cure *P*   11 Redimendae] Redimende *P*;
offensae] offense *P*   12 locum.] locum *P*   12–13 suas . . . Principi] *P*, sese nempe
facilius perditurum quam seruaturum Principem *P*sa, at esse facilius . . . Principem *1565*
(*cf.* but he should soner distroy himself than saue the king *1557*L)   13 Principi /]
Principi *P*   15 tollere /] tollere · *P*; dubium] *corr. from* dubie *P*b; sit /] sit *P*   15–16
intentaretur /] intentaretur *P*   16 ausurum.] ausurum *P*; credibile] credibile /
P   16–17 presidium /] presidium *P*   17–18 et / si aduersaretur / insidias:] et si
aduersaretur insidias *P*   18 fors] foris *P*, sors *1565*; suspectaret:] suspectaret /
P   19 statum /] statum *P*; esse /] esse *P*; confidas /] confidas *P*   20 possis.] possis
P   21–22 qua iam ingressum via] qua iam ingressum *P*, quam viam ingressum iam
sese esse *1565*   22 penitebat / eadem pergeret /] penitebat eadem pergeret *P*;
ceperat /] ceperat *P*   23 gnauiter] *1565*, grauiter *P*; consilio /] consilio *P*   24 credebat /] credebat *P*

Protector's cunning deny that he shared the last steps in his plan before he had completed the earlier ones; they maintain that when he had imprisoned the queen's relatives and had both of her sons in his hands he was less cautious about opening his other designs to all those whose assistance he thought he would need, and since he saw that his strength would be doubled by enlisting the duke, he was particularly diligent in broaching the matter to him through astute, diplomatic intermediaries. They faced him with the prospect of a prince who was angry for the sake of his kinsmen, and apt to avenge them when he got the chance; for if they were released, they would incite him (for the memory of prison and fetters would never abandon them), and if they were killed off, he would certainly take their deaths to heart if he felt sorrow about their imprisonment. Nor was anything to be gained by repenting; there was no longer any possibility of compensating for the injury with good deeds; for he was likelier to ruin his own hopes than to rescue the prince, whom he saw the Protector now had in his power so completely along with his brother and kinsmen that he could kill all of them with a nod, and would certainly dare to do so if anyone tried to rebel. It was also quite possible that he had developed not only his own secret bodyguard but also a network to spy on the duke and a trap to destroy him if he should resist, one which might well be laid by the people whom he least suspected, at that; for the state of affairs and the nature of people's intentions were such that you could not tell for certain whom you should rely on and whom you should fear. Wearing down the duke's spirit with suggestions like these, they induced him to follow out a course he already regretted initiating and to persevere vigorously once he had started. And so, since he believed he could not beat the nefarious conspiracy, he joined it as a partner and ally, and

malumque publicum statuit / quando nequiret corrigi / quam
maxime posset in suum bonum vertere./

[44/1]   Conuentum est vt Protector / opera Ducis in regnum vsus /
natum quem habebat vnum legitimum cum illius filia con-
5 iungeret: ad hec / Herfordiae conuentum / quem Dux velut
hereditarium vendicabat neque Eduardo superstite potuit obtinere / perempta lite concederet: his illius postulatis Protector
magnam vltro thesauri vim regiaeque supellectilis adiecit / nisi
falsa discordanti post exprobrauit velut tantis ipsius beneficijs
10 ingrato. Igitur vbi inter eos conuenit / principatus auspicatio /
quam in rem dictus appetebat dies / magnifico apparatu in speciem / ne noctu quidem intermisso labore / multis operantibus
adornabatur / inque eam celebritatem / quo magis ab suis consilijs oculos animosque hominum auerterent alio / proceres ex
15 omni regni parte euocati frequentes aderant. Ceterum Protector
ac Dux / vbi Cardinalem atque Cancellarium cum Eboracensi
Archiepiscopo Comiteque Darabiae atque Eliensi Presule nec
non Hastyngo Camerario multisque alijs nobilibus collocauerant
de ordine [231v] ritu ac solemnibus insigniendi Regis ceremonijs
20 locuturos / ipsi interim subducentes sese cum his quos sui propositi participes habebant alio in loco longe diuersa tractabant: cui
consilio quanquam pauci adhibebantur ijdemque minime
futiles / spargi tamen suspicio cepit àc mussitare populus tan-

---

1 statuit / quando . . . corrigi /] statuit quando . . . corrigi *P*   3 Conuentum] *New para.*
P; ends lacuna in A; Protector /] Protector *P;* vsus /] vsus *P*   4 natum] *P,* filium *P*sa *1565,*
filium natum *A*   4–5 coniungeret] *1565,* coniugeret *P A;* coniungeret: ad hec /] coniugeret / ad hec *P*   5 conuentum] comentum *P A,* comitatum *1565 (cf. 406/11);*
conuentum /] comentum *P*   6 vendicabat] *P A,* petebat *P*sa, apetebat *A*s *1565 (cf.* he
claimed as his enheritance *1557*L)   6–7 obtinere /] obtinere *P*   7 concederet:] concederet *P*   8 regiaeque] regieque *P;* adiecit /] adiecit *P*   8–10 nisi . . . ingrato] *P A,*
*om. 1565 1557*L   10 ingrato.] ingrato *P;* conuenit /] conuenit *P;* auspicatio /] auspicatio *P*   11 quam . . . dies] *P A, om. 1565 1557*L; dies /] dies *P*   11–12 speciem /]
speciem *P*   12 intermisso] intermisso ⟨a⟩ *P,* intermisso a *A 1565;* labore /] labore *P*
13 adornabatur /] adornabatur *P;* celebritatem /] celebritatem *P*   16 Dux /] Dux
P   16–17 Cardinalem atque Cancellarium cum Eboracensi Archiepiscopo] *P A 1565,*
the Lord Cardinall, the Archebishoppe of Yorke than lorde Chancellour *1557*L   17
Darabiae] Darabie *P*   18 Camerario] *P A*s, cubiculario *P*s *A 1565*   21 tractabant:]
tractabant / *P*   22 ijdemque] *A 1565,* ijdem *P*

decided that since he could not remedy the public evil he would turn it as much as he could to his private advantage.

It was agreed that in exchange for the duke's help in gaining the throne the Protector would marry his only legitimate son to the duke's daughter and would also concede to him without any further litigation the county of Hereford, which the duke claimed as a hereditary possession but could not secure in the lifetime of Edward; beyond these stipulated rewards the Protector voluntarily added a large sum of treasure and regal property, unless Gloucester falsely reproached him with this, as if he were ungrateful for such immense favors, when he opposed him later on. And so when they reached an agreement, preparations of specious magnificence were carried out by many workers around the clock as the date appointed for the coronation approached; and the better to distract people's eyes and attention from their own designs they had summoned large numbers of nobles who arrived from every part of the realm to be present at that ceremony. But when the Protector and the duke had assembled the cardinal and the chancellor along with the archbishop of York, the Earl of Derby, the prelate of Ely, Hastings the lord chamberlain, and many other noblemen to talk over the program, the ritual, and the solemnities of the king's coronation, they themselves slipped off meanwhile with their henchmen to discuss very different things elsewhere. Though few were admitted to their confidence, none of them indiscreet, the suspicion still started to spread and the people to murmur that mat-

quam rebus haud diu bene futuris / cum neque sciret quisquam
aut quam ob causam aut quo authore metueret / siue animis
ingentia mala secretiore naturae vi presagientibus / pelagi in
morem sponte sua exestuantis aduersus instantem procellam /
5   siue vnus quispiam aliquid odoratus multos suspitione impleuerat: quanquam nonnihil ipsa res etiam quantumuis dissimulata cogitationes hominum excitauit / siquidem paulatim
quisque ab arce regia dilabi / in domo Protectoris aula esse / ibi
frequentia celebritasque versari / silentium ac solitudo vasta circa
[45/1]   10   Principem / plerisque eo divertentibus vnde negotiorum expedi-
tio sperabatur / quibusdam etiam admonitis incaute Regem fre-
quentaturos quibus nihil necessarij negotij esset.
      Sic vbi multa signa concurrere partim casu / quaedam indus-
tria / ad vltimum effecere vti non plebs modo / quae temere
15   quouis agitatur / sed prudentes quoque atque aliquot etiam proceres expergiscerentur ac rem notarent / hactenus tamen vt dis-
putarent potius quam diffiderent./ Ceterum Darabiae Comes
qui multarum vsu rerum senuerat / prouidenter illa suspectans /
Hastyngo (quod erant mutuo sibi secretorum conscij) com-
20   pellato / "Nae bina hec mihi haud placent" inquit "seorsum habita consilia / nempe dum nos in altero communem rem simpliciter et aperte tractamus / qui scias illi quibus de rebus in altero
clandestine mussitent?" "Tace" inquit Hastyngus "et pignore
mea vita confide / dum quidem illic aderit qui nunquam abest /
25   ne verbum [232] vnquam dubium sic dici posse vt non citius ad
me perferatur quam loquenti excidat."
      Hec ille de Catesbio innuebat / quo valde familiariter vtebatur /

1 futuris] *P A*, mansuris *P*ˢ *A*ˢ, permansuris *1565*; futuris /] futuris *P*; cum neque] *corr.
from* neque cum *P*ᵇ, neque cum *A*, cum nec *1565*   3 naturae] nature *P*;
presagientibus /] presagientibus *P*   5–6 impleuerat:] impleuerat *P*   6 nonnihil]
non nihil *P*   7 excitauit /] excitauit *P*   10 Principem /] Principem *P*   11 sperabatur /] sperabatur *P*; incaute] *P A*, intute *P*ˢ *A*ˢ, parum tuto *1565*   12 esset.] esset *P*
13–14 quaedam industria /] quedam industria *P*   14 modo / quae] modo que *P*
16 notarent /] notarent *P*   17 potius] *P A*, verius *P*ˢ *A*ˢ *1565*; Darabiae] Darabie *P*;
Comes] ⟨Dux⟩ Comes *P*   18 suspectans /] suspectans *P*   19 (quod . . . conscij)]
quod . . . conscij *P*   19–20 compellato /] compellato *P*   21 consilia /] consilia *P*
22 tractamus /] tractamus *P*   23 mussitent?] mussitent./ *P*   24 confide /] confide *P*;
quidem] *P*, quidam *A*, vnus quidam *1565*; abest /] abest *P*   25 verbum] *P A*, verbum
quidem *1565*; dici] *P A*, efferri *1565*   26 excidat.] excidat *P*   27 Catesbio] *A 1565*,
Calesbio *P*; innuebat /] innuebat *P*; vtebatur /] vtebatur *P*

ters would soon take a turn for the worse, even though no one knew what or who actually prompted his fear, whether they had a foreboding of great troubles through some secret instinct of nature, as the sea with no apparent reason becomes turbulent in the face of an oncoming storm, or whether one of them got wind of something and then fueled the suspicions of many. And yet the facts themselves, however carefully dissembled, still gave people at least some food for thought as everyone gradually drifted away from the royal seat in the Tower and court came to be held in the Protector's house, as crowds and activity filled that place while silence and solitude surrounded the prince, what with most people resorting where they hoped that their business would be expedited, some even being warned that if they had no urgent business with the king they would be unwise to linger in his company.

Thus, the concurrence of many signs, some accidental and others intentional, eventually caused not only the common folk, who are easily provoked to all sorts of snap judgments, but also the judicious and even a few of the nobles to wake up and consider the state of affairs, and yet less as a cause for alarm than as something to debate about. But the Earl of Derby, old in years and in the experience of many things, felt a prescient mistrust of these circumstances, and speaking to Hastings (for they were in each other's confidence) he said to him, "I do not like these two separate councils a bit! For while we are handling public business forthrightly and openly in this one, how do you know what they are stealthily whispering about in the other?" "Say no more," Hastings said, "for upon my life you can be sure that whenever one person is present at those meetings—and he never misses them—not one dubious word will ever be spoken without being reported to me before the speaker himself finishes saying it."

He was alluding to Catesby in making this claim, a man with

neque tantum sibi de cuiusquam in se amore fideque promittebat / vt cui perinde sese ratus est charum ac deuinctum sibi
illum sentiebat / nempe quem opibus admodum atque authoritate prouexerat: et erat qui prouehi haud difficulter posset.
5 Nam preter egregiam Britanicarum legum peritiam accessit corporis amplitudo et non ingrata visendo species / vt idoneus non
ad agendas modo causas sed ad magnas etiam res gerendas
haberetur / ingenij vero tanti quantum homini tam pusilla fide
non optasses / quippe cuius vnius dissimulatione tota hec ma-
10 lorum moles stetit: alioquin Hastingi Comitisque Darbiae
[46/1]   multorumque suae partis nobilium coactae vires tempestiue ma- ·
turauissent haud dubie in hoc discedere / si non istius fiducia
securus Hastingus iturientes reliquos continuisset / quoad is inopine / ceteri cunctantes / pariter omnes oppressi / perfidiam
15 tum demum senserant quum tantum damnare / non vitare /·
possent.
    Sed et Protector quoque et Dux Hastingum mira / ne quid
suspicaretur / amicitiae simulatione lactabant / quanquam illi
creditur ex animo amatus / huic inuisus / neutri ad hec consilia

---

1 cuiusquam] *A 1565*, cuiusque *P*   1–2 promittebat /] promittebat *P*   2 sese] se se *P*
3 sentiebat] *P A*, intelligebat *P*sa *A*s *1565*; sentiebat /] sentiebat *P*   4 prouexerat] *P A*,
promouerat *P*s *A*s *1565*; prouexerat:] prouexerat *P*; posset.] posset / *P*   5 preter
egregiam] *P A 1565*, super eximiam *P*s *A*s   6 non ingrata visendo] non ingrata visenda
P A; visenda *might also be an alternative reading for* non ingrata, *or perhaps we should read* non
ingrate visenda; species /] species *P*   8 haberetur /] haberetur *P*; tam pusilla fide] *P A*,
tam nullius fidei *1565*   9–14 quippe . . . ceteri] *P A*, quippe cuius vnius dissimulatio
totam eam quae illam consecuta est malorum pestem conflauit. Cuius fidem nisi secutus
fuisset Hastyngus, Standlaeus, comesque Darbiae, caeterique earum partium nobiles, ad
primam statim fraudis suspitionem discessissent, et discessu suo omnia eorum clan-
destina, et nepharia consilia turbassent. Caeterum Hastyngus dum nimium illius vnius
fide nititur, caeteri *1565 (cf.* For his dissimulacion onelye, kepte all that mischyefe vppe.
In whome if the lord Hastinges had not put so special trust, the lord Stanley and he had
departed with diuerse other lordes, and broken all the daunce, for many il signes that hee
sawe *1557)*   10 stetit:] stetit / *P*   10–11 Darbiae . . . suae] Darbie . . . sue *P*   11
coactae vires] *P*sb, coactis viribus *P A*   12 discedere /] discedere *P*   13 continuisset /]
continuisset *P*   13–14 inopine /] inopine *P*   14 cunctantes /] cunctantes *P*;
oppressi /] oppressi *P*   15–16 damnare / non vitare / possent.] damnare non vitare
possent *P*   17 Dux] *interl. P*   17–18 mira / ne . . . suspicaretur / amicitiae] mira
ne . . . suspicaretur amicitie *P*   18 lactabant /] lactabant *P*   19 amatus /] amatus *P*;
inuisus /] inuisus *P*

whom he was on very close terms; nor was there anyone else whose devotion and loyalty he considered to be so completely assured, since he thought he was no less dear to Catesby than he knew that Catesby was indebted to him. He had advanced Catesby greatly in personal wealth and authority; nor was he a man it would ever be hard to advance. For besides his great mastery of British law, he possessed an imposing physique and a face that was fair to behold, so that his competence seemed to extend beyond pleading in court to performing great deeds; his intelligence was so great that one might have wished it were less in a person of such little faith. For this whole mass of troubles was based on this one man's dissembling; for otherwise Hastings, the Earl of Derby, and many other noblemen of their party would doubtless have gathered their forces and withdrawn in time to confront this threat had not Hastings been lulled by his confidence in Catesby so as to detain all the rest, who were ready to leave, until Hastings himself was taken by surprise, the others were caught dawdling, and all were alike overthrown, not detecting the perfidy of Catesby until they could only condemn it instead of escaping it.

But the Protector and the duke also led Hastings on with a remarkable show of feigned friendship to keep him from suspecting anything, although people believe that the Protector was genuinely fond of him, the duke detested him, and both found

commodus./ Fertur Catesbius / a Protectore iussus vt animo eius
callide pertentato experiretur an pertrahi quoquo pacto hominem posse ad suam partem speraret / aspera omnia et contraria
retulisse. Pessime etiam cesserat quod Hastyngus huic / in fami-
5 liari colloquio / iactantia suae fiduciae / aliorum formidines aperuerat. Veritus ergo Catesbius ne multi contra suam simula-
tionem [232v] mouendo ac fatigando proficerent / neu consilia
quae iam prorepere videbantur cuncta erumperent / censet ma-
turandum facinus / occupandos dum dubitant / illum / quia flecti
10 non posset / amoliendum: quod eo suasit auidius quum Hastyngi
potentia quae tum valida erat in Lecestrensi conuentu sibi des-
tinabatur / cuius rei detestabilis ambitio Catesbium in execrandi
sceleris societatem compegerat./
       Igitur consultantibus paulo post in arce proceribus quo eos
[47/5] 15 Protector conuocauerat / ipse serius veniens in consilium excusat
tarditatem / increpita festiuiter somnolentia: tum hylaris ac prope ludibundus accubuit / protinusque in Eliensem versus Episcopum / "Pater" inquit "fragra tibi in hortis audio insignia
mitescere. Non grauatim scio ferculum vnum tot nobilibus in
20 prandium velut symbolum tuum conferes." "Vtinam" inquit ille
"maius aliquid tam facile possim quam hoc libenter faciam" simulque ministrum qui adferret emittit. At Protector velut nescio
quid necessariae rei in proximo facturus cubiculo / statimque in
consilium rediturus / egreditur / proceribus interim tantam eius
25 festiuitatem gaudentibus / quantam haud temere ante in illo
viderant / simulque humanitatem benignitatemque animi certatim laudantibus. Ille non diu moratus reuertitur / sed mirum
quam totus ab illo mutatus qui modo tam letus exierat / nempe

---

1 Catesbius /] Catesbius *P*   3 speraret /] speraret *P*   4 retulisse.] retulisse / *P;* huic /]
huic *P*   5 colloquio / iactantia suae fiduciae /] colloquio iactantia sue fiducie *P*   5–6
aperuerat.] aperuerat / *P*   7 proficerent /] proficerent *P*   8 quae] que *P*   9
facinus /] facinus *P;* dubitant / illum /] dubitant illum *P*   10 posset /] posset *P;*
amoliendum:] amoliendum *P*   11 quae] que *P;* tum] *corr. from* tamen *P*[b]; Lecestrensi]
Laucestrensi *P,* lancestrensi *A,* Lancastrensi *1565 (cf.* the county of Leceter *1557)*   15
conuocauerat /] conuocauerat *P*   16 tarditatem /] tarditatem *P;* somnolentia:] somnolentia / *P*   20 conferes.] conferes / *P*   22 adferret] *corr. from* adferet *P*[b]   23
necessariae] necessarie *P;* cubiculo /] cubiculo *P*   24 rediturus /] rediturus *P*   25
gaudentibus /] gaudentibus *P*   26 viderant] ⟨viderent⟩ viderant *P*   27 laudantibus.]
laudantibus *P;* reuertitur /] reuertitur *P*   28 quam] *A 1565,* quod *P;* exierat /] exierat
P

him intractable for their purposes. It is reported that Catesby
was ordered to probe him discreetly and to explore every possible means which might give cause to hope they could draw the
man into their faction, but that Catesby brought back only bad
and discouraging news. It was also very unfortunate that in a
private conversation with him Hastings chose to show off his
own confidence by revealing the fears of the others. And so
Catesby, afraid that the pushing and persistence of many were
making headway against his dissembling and that the plans
which appeared to be creeping abroad would get out all at once,
urged that they should strike quickly, catch them while they were
still unprepared, and crush Hastings since they could not bend
him. He urged this the more keenly since he expected to be given
Hastings' power, which was then very considerable in the county
of Leicester; that detestable ambition it was which originally
made Catesby enlist as a party to this execrable crime.

    And so shortly thereafter, as the lords were consulting in the
Tower where the Protector had summoned them, he arrived
somewhat late, begging pardon for his tardiness and merrily
blaming his sleepiness; then exuberantly and indeed almost
playfully he took his seat, turning at once to the bishop of Ely and
saying to him, "Father, I hear you have some very fine strawber-
ries ripening in your garden. I know you will not mind presenting one bowl of them to so many nobles as your contribution to
lunch." "I wish I could as easily do something bigger as I will be
glad to do this much," he answered, and at once sent a servant to
fetch them. But the Protector stepped out as if he had some
pressing business to do in the neighboring room and would
promptly return to the council, while the lords took delight in
how cheerful he was—they had scarcely ever seen him so cheerful—and vied in applauding his courteous and generous spirit.
He returned before long, but amazingly and totally transformed
from the man who departed so jovially a short time before; now,

nunc contra tristis / toruus / obducto supercilio / corrugata
fronte / admorso labro / minabundus / astupentibus vniuersis
quae illum intemperies tam de repente corripuisset./

   Hoc vultu se in sellam conijciens / vbi paulum tristi silentio
5 pauidos [233] expectantium animos suspendisset / hoc pacto
prorupit: "Quae supplicia excogitentur illorum digna sceleribus
qui me / non sanguine modo tam propinquum Principi / sed eius
regnique huius Protectorem / impijs artibus machinantur tollere?" Ad hec verba qui aderant omnes / attoniti atrocitate rei /
10 conticescere / voluentes tacite secum quis tanti flagitij conscius
esset cuius quisque eorum sibi insons erat. Sed Hastyngus / cui
presumptus in se Protectoris fauor animos loquendi fecit / vltima
meritos exempla respondit / quicunque essent. "At huius" inquit
ille "sceleris machinatrix est fratris vxor." Innuebat Reginam:
15 cui qui fauebant ad eam vocem miro pauore defigebantur.

   Sed Hastyngus / cui vni cedes imminebat / cepit recreari quum
id malum quod amicorum cuipiam pertimuerat deriuari ad ini-

[48/1] micam cerneret. Ceterum animo nonnihil anxio requirebat secum / cur se Protector hanc rem celasset quem conscius esset ab
20 oprimenda Regina non abhorrere / nec rationem inire poterat
cur hoc dissimulatum oportuerit apud se / cuius conscientia Protector fuerat vsus in captiuos Reginae cognatos ea ipsa die in quo
adseruabantur oppido trucidandos / videlicet haud opinantis in
eandem propemodum horam sibi vicissim alio clanculario con-
25 silio constitutam necem.

   Interim Protector "Videbitis" inquit "vt hec scelesta mihi cum
vxore Shori atque alijs prestigiatricibus fascinatum corpus magicis veneficijs exhauserit." Simul subducta in cubitum manica

---

1 contra] contra / P; supercilio] 1565, supersilio P A   2 quae] que P   4 conijciens /]
conijciens P   5 suspendisset] P A 1565, suspendit Ps; suspendisset /] suspendisset P
6 prorupit: "Quae] prorupit / Que P; excogitentur] P 1565, excogitentur inquit A
7 me /] me P   8 Protectorem /] protectorem P   9 omnes /] omnes P; rei /] rei P
10 flagitij] P A 1565, facinoris Ps As   11 Hastyngus /] Hastyngus P   12 fecit] A
1565, corr. from facit P, dabat Ps As   13 respondit /] respondit P; essent.] essent./ P
14 vxor.] vxor P; Reginam:] Reginam P   15 defigebantur.] defigebantur P   16
Hastyngus / cui . . . imminebat /] Hastyngus cui . . . imminebat P   17 ad] P A 1565, in
Ps   18 cerneret.] cerneret / P; nonnihil] non nihil P   18–19 secum /] secum P
19 celasset] P A 1565, celauerit Ps   20 oprimenda] P A 1565, oppugnanda Ps; abhorrere /] abhorrere P   21 se /] se P   22 Reginae] Regine P   23 trucidandos /]
trucidandos P

to the contrary, he was grim and dour, knitting his eyebrows, wrinkling his forehead, and biting his lip threateningly, leaving everyone mystified at the rage which had seized him so suddenly.

With this expression he threw himself down in his chair, and after a few moments of grim silence to heighten the suspense for his frightened listeners, he broke out as follows: "What fitting punishment can you imagine for the crimes of those who are plotting and wickedly scheming to kill me—me the close relative of the prince and protector of him and this kingdom?" At these words all those present remained silent, astounded by the gravity of the outrage and inwardly wondering who could be party to such a crime, since each of them knew himself to be innocent. But Hastings, emboldened to speak by his presumption of the Protector's goodwill toward him, responded that they deserved capital and exemplary punishment, whoever they were. "But the chief plotter," the Protector continued, "is my brother's wife." By this he meant the queen; and at that phrase her partisans were transfixed with terror.

But Hastings, the one person with death hanging over his head, began to recover his spirits when he saw that the trouble which he had feared might touch one of his allies was deflected toward his enemy. Still, he asked himself somewhat uneasily why the Protector had kept this matter secret from him, even though he knew that he had no aversion to crushing the queen, nor could he think of any reason why this stratagem had been kept from him, since the Protector had had his complicity in the beheading of the queen's kinsmen on that very day in the town where they were being held; for he had not the slightest idea that by another secret plan his own death had been set for almost the same hour.

Meanwhile the Protector declared, "You shall see how this villainess with Shore's wife and other enchantresses has cast a spell on my body and withered it with their magic potions," and pulling up his sleeve he exposed an arm which was indeed very

brachium profert / admodum haud dubie miserum / sed quale
tamen ab initio fuerat. Tum vero merito preter conscios cuncti
pauescere / reputantes occasionem tantum rixae primum, deinde cedis apertae [233v] captari./ Nam brachium illud miserum
5 probe nouerant / Reginam ab magicis prestigijs longe abesse /
nec si maxime statuisset incumbere / Shori vxorem vnquam sociam sibi lecturam / mulierem libidinis haud magiae famosam /
tum sibi maxime omnium inuisam / vt pellicem olim suam omnium gratissimam Regi.
10   Igitur iam Hastyngus amicae commemoratione perculsus
(nam eam deamare ferebatur) "Si talia" inquit "ausae sunt /
merito certe sunt puniendae." Ad hec ille "Quid tu mihi" inquit
" 'si'? Ego tibi fecisse aio / idque si deffendas / duello tecum /
proditor / approbauero" / manumque fortiter velut iratus in-
15 cussit in mensam. Iamque ad ostium "Proditio" clamabatur /
simulque ad hoc intenti signum satellites introrumpentes armis
totum locum compleuere. Protector illico manu in Hastyngum
iniecta "Ego te sisto / proditor" inquit. "Mene" inquit "o Protector?" "Te" inquit "ipsum / o proditor" / statimque Mideltonus
[49/1] 20 quidam in Darbiae Comitem quanquam tabula media securim
sic vibrauit vt nisi propere sub mensam elusisset ictum / ad dentes vsque caput fuerit diuisurus / quippe quem sic quoque celeri
lapsu declinantem extrema tamen acies consecuta / vertici im-
pacto vulnere / totum cruore perfuderit. Comitem inter et per-
25 cussorem hunc lis de predijs olim atque hinc inimicitia vetus
intercesserat. / Nam Comes eum de possessione / vine an iure

---

1 miserum] P A, macilentum 1565; miserum /] miserum P   2 cuncti] A 1565, amoti
P   3 pauescere /] pauescere P; rixae] rixe P   4 apertae] aperte P; miserum] P A,
macilentum 1565   5 nouerant /] nouerant P   6 nec si] A, changed to et si Pᵇ, etsi
1565; incumbere /] incumbere P; vnquam] A, nunquam P 1565   6–7 sociam] A,
serciam P   7 lecturam /] lecturam P; magiae] magie P   8 suam] Perhaps we should
read eam or suarum   8–9 suam . . . Regi] P A, nam et regi in primis charam 1565;
gratissimam] gratissimam / P   11 ausae] ause P   12 puniendae] puniende P   13
aio /] aio P; deffendas / duello tecum /] deffendas duello tecum P   14 proditor /]
proditor P   15 mensam.] mensam P   17 compleuere.] compleuere P   18 sisto /]
sisto P; inquit.] inquit / P; Mene] me ne P   18–19 Protector?] Protector / P   19
ipsum /] ipsum P   20 Darbiae] Darbie P   21 vibrauit] P A, librauit Pˢ¹ Aˢ 1565,
distrinxit (for destrinxit?) Pˢ²; elusisset] P A, euitasset Pˢ Aˢ 1565; ictum /] ictum P   22
diuisurus /] diuisurus P   23 consecuta /] consecuta P   23–24 impacto] 1565, in
pacto A P   24 vulnere /] vulnere P   26 possessione /] possessione P; vine] vi ne P

puny—just as it had been from the beginning. But then everyone but the Protector's accomplices had good reason to be terrified, judging that he was simply in search of a pretext for
wrangling, to start with, and then open slaughter. For they knew
very well that that arm was puny, that the queen had nothing to
do with magical enchantments, and that even if she did choose to
practice them she would never choose Shore's wife for a partner,
a woman notorious for wantonness, not magic, and a woman
particularly hated by the queen for once being the king's favorite
out of all of his mistresses.

Unnerved by the mention of his beloved (for reputedly he was
in love with her), Hastings then answered, "If they have dared to
do such things, they certainly deserve to be punished." To this he
retorted, "What do you mean saying 'if' to me? I tell you they
did, and if you deny it, you traitor, I will prove it in armed
combat with you"; then as if out of anger he forcefully struck the
table with his hand. And then at the door someone cried "treason," and at the same time the retainers awaiting the signal burst
in and filled the whole chamber with weapons. The Protector
immediately seized Hastings and said, "I arrest you, you traitor."
"Me, Protector?" he said. "Yes, you indeed, traitor," he answered; and then suddenly a certain Middleton swung an axe
across the table at the Earl of Derby so accurately that if he had
not dodged the blow under the table it would have split his head
down to the teeth; for even as he evaded it by dropping down
quickly, the edge of the blade, making contact and wounding the
crown of his skull, left him covered with blood. The earl and this
assassin had once had a quarrel about land holdings, which gave
rise to a long-standing enmity. For the earl had ejected him from
occupancy, it is not certain whether by violence or by legal action,

incertum / inuitum certe deiecerat: ita is contra nunc plus quam demandabatur ausus / in alieno tumultu suo dolori obsequebatur.

Iam reliqui proceres episcopique comprehendebantur et / ne
5 mutuo consultarent / in antra diuersa coniecti sunt. Sed Hastyngum Protector iussit ad mortem vt se accingeret ac si quid cum sacerdote vellet / adproperaret / "Nam ita Diuum" [234] inquit "Paulum / cui peculiariter seruio / propitium habeam / vt non ante cibi quicquam gustabo quam tibi caput amputatum
10 videam." Ergo ille / cum nihil profuisset causam querere / tacitus ac mestus presbitero qui non in hoc aderat confessionem qualemcunque fecit / nam longiorem haud licuit / ne Protector non satis tempestiue pranderet / cui non erat fas ante discumbere quam ille occubuisset / videlicet homo pius ne peieraret.
15 Quamobrem / vrgente Bukyngamiae Duce (quem ille suppliciter intuens vt sui misereretur obsecrabat) / mors festinabatur / productusque in planiciem quae menibus arcis ambitur / caput in oblongum tignum qui destinatus edificio iacebat reclinare iussus / securi decutitur. Corpus amici cum capite Vindesoram
20 vectum haud procul ab Eduardi charissimi sibi principis ossibus humauere./

---

1 incertum /] incertum P; deiecerat:] deiecerat. P   2 alieno tumultu] P A, aliena causa 1565; tumultu] P A, negotio Ps As   2–3 obsequebatur] P A, morem gessit Ps As, seruiebat 1565; obsequebatur.] obsequebatur / P   4 et] A 1565, vt P; et /] vt P 5 consultarent /] consultarent P; sunt.] sunt / P   6 accingeret] P A, apararet Ps As, corr. from apparuit Ps, componeret 1565   7 vellet / adproperaret /] vellet adproperaret./ P   7–8 Diuum" inquit] A 1565, Diuum P   8 Paulum /] Paulum P; Paulum / cui peculiariter seruio / propitium] Paulum cui ⟨me⟩ peculiariter seruio (deuoui Ps As) propitium P A (me uncanceled A), Paulum propitium 1565; seruio /] seruio P; habeam /] habeam P   9 amputatum] corr. from amputandum Pb   10 videam.] videam / P; ille /] ille P; ille . . . querere] P A, Ille facile cernens nil profuturum si causam quereret Ps, ille nihil se reluctando profecturum sciens 1565; querere /] querere P 10–11 tacitus . . . aderat] P A adducto quem locus ille offerebat sacerdoti 1565   12 fecit /] fecit P   12–14 nam . . . peieraret] P A, nam prolixiorem temporis breuitas non admittebat, protectore iam ad prandium composito, et vt caput illi praecisum esse audiret intento 1565   13 pranderet /] pranderet P   14–15 peieraret. Quamobrem /] peieraret Quamobrem P   15 Bukyngamiae] Bukyngamie P   16 obsecrabat) /] obsecrabat) P   16–17 obsecrabat) / mors festinabatur / productusque] P A, obsecrabat) vix temere facta confessione, producitur 1565   17 quae] que P, ambitur /] ambitur P 18 qui destinatus] P A where we expect quod destinatum (but see Livy 44.54)   19 iussus /] iussus P; decutitur] Ps As, decussum est P A, where the sense really calls for percutitur; decutitur.] decutitur / P

but in any case against the man's will; so now he in his turn dared to go beyond his orders and indulge his own grudge in another man's quarrel.

Now the rest of the nobles and bishops were seized and imprisoned in separate cells so that they could not consult together. As for Hastings, the Protector told him to prepare for his death and to hurry if he had any business to do with a priest; "As St. Paul, to whom I have a special devotion, is my patron, I will not take another bite of food before seeing you beheaded." And so, since it would have been futile to ask for a reason, he stood silent and sorrowful and hastily made his confession as best he could to a priest who was on hand for some other purpose; there was no time for a longer confession, since the Protector did not want to be late for lunch and could not take his seat until Hastings had gone to the block; pious man, he did not want to violate his oath. And so at the Duke of Buckingham's urging, whom Hastings with looks of entreaty implored to be merciful, his death was ordered at once; led out into the open space which runs around the walls of the Tower and instructed to lay his head on an oblong piece of timber lying there to be used for construction, his head was struck off with an ax. His friends took the body and the head to Windsor and buried them close to the bones of his beloved prince Edward.

Operae precium est cognoscere quae somnia mortem eius au-
guriaque antecesserint / siue monitus talia putanda sint / vt pre-
caueantur insidiae / siue ineluctabilis fati preuia signa / siue mortalium in rebus aut ludificet demon / casusue aut fortuna
5 colludat / aut anima / futuri presaga / sopitis somno sensibus /
imminentia fata confusis ymaginibus adumbrans / effectum pre-
monstrat corpori. Iam primum eius medio noctis quam letalis ei
dies sequebatur / ab Stanleo minister anhelus / heri sui verbis /
hortatur vt protinus exurgens festinaret aufugere / nam domino
10 oblatam nocturno sopore terribilem magnique mali speciem et
vtrique ipsorum nisi fuga preueniretur exiciosi: visum enim aprum prostratos ambos impetere dentibus / Hastyngum repente
confectum / ipsi viuo sic lancinatum caput [234v] vt sanguis vber-
tim in sinus efflueret: hanc imaginem animo eius tam altum
15 impressisse terrorem / quum aprum recordetur Protectoris esse
gestamen / vt plane decreuerit nihil cunctari diutius modo ille
itineris comes accedat: plus adhuc viae / priusquam desiderarentur / emensuros quam vt consequi eos si qui persequerentur
possent./ "Vah" inquit Hastyngus "adeone meticulosus est vti ad
20 vana somniorum figmenta pauescat quae vel ipsius bilis animo
figurat vel diurna cogitatio reddit dormienti? Superstitio est
nimirum propeque adeo impietas inania isthec nugamenta cura-
re / quae si futurorum omnino signa putet / cur non cogitat rata
posse etiam fugiendo fieri / vel multo certe potius si retractos ex
25 itinere (vt fugientibus nihil est fidum) iure nos aper inuaserit
tanquam sceleris conscientia fugitiuos? Quare aut nihil est vs-

1 Operae] Opere P; quae] que P   1–2 auguriaque] A, auguria quoque P, praesagiata
1565   2 antecesserint /] antecesserint P; sint] sint a deo missa 1565; sint /] sint P   3
insidiae] insidie P; signa / siue] A, signa P   3–5 siue mortalium . . . colludat] om. 1565
4 casusue] casus ne A P   5 anima /] anima P; sensibus /] sensibus P   6 ymaginibus
adumbrans / effectum] ymaginibus / adumbrans effectum / P   7 corpori.] corpori / P;
ei] ⟨illi⟩ ei P   8 sequebatur /] sequebatur P; anhelus /] anhelus P; verbis /] verbis P
9 aufugere /] aufugere P   10 et] interl. Pᵇ, om. A 1565   11 exiciosi:] exiciosi / P   12
dentibus /] dentibus P   14 efflueret:] efflueret P   16 gestamen] P A, insigne Pˢ
1565; gestamen /] gestamen P; diutius] diutius / P   17 accedat:] accedat P; viae /] vie P
17–18 desiderarentur /] desiderarentur P   19 adeone] adeo ne P   20 figmenta pauescat] P A, deliramenta contremiscat Pˢ Aˢ 1565; quae] que P   21 dormienti?] dormienti P   22 propeque] prope que P   23 quae] que P; putet /] putet P   24 fieri /] fieri P   25 (vt . . . fidum)] vt . . . fidum P   26 fugitiuos?]
fugitiuos / P

It is worth knowing what dreams and omens preceded his death, whether they should be thought of as warnings to guard against dangers to come or as foretokens of an inevitable destiny, or whether some demon is mockingly meddling in mortal existence, or either chance or fortune is mocking us, too, or the soul becomes prescient of the future when the senses are deadened by sleep and intimates the approach of doom in a confusion of images which foretell the result to the body. First of all, in the middle of the night which preceded the day of his death, he was urged by a breathless messenger from Stanley, in his master's words, to get up immediately and flee, for that night his master had seen in his sleep a terrible image of great evil which would mean the destruction of both of them unless they forestalled it by fleeing. He had seen them both prostrate being mauled by a boar with his tusks; Hastings had been killed at once, while a wound to his own head had left him alive but with blood pouring down over his chest; when he recalled that the boar was the Protector's insignia, the image in his dream had stricken him with such mortal terror that he was completely determined to flee without further delay if only Hastings would go along with him; they could still cover so much ground before they were missed that no one who pursued them could catch them. "Bah!" said Hastings. "Is he actually timid enough to be frightened by the vain specters of dreams which his own bile projects into his mind or the thoughts of the day raise again in his sleep? It is pure superstition and almost impiety to worry about those empty trifles; and if he really thinks they foretoken the future, does it not occur to him that they may be borne out even by our fleeing, all the more so, indeed, if we are taken en route and brought back (for no haven is trustworthy for fugitives) and the boar has good reason to assail us, as if we were fleeing because of our own guilty

quam periculi / nec certe est / aut illic etiam amplius: quod si
omnino esset / malo tamen aliena vt perfidia cedidisse quam vel
culpa vel ignauia nostra videamur. Proin abi ac manendum re-
nuncia / nam ego virum illum quem nouit tam certum fidumque
5 mihi quam dextram hanc meam habeo." "Faxint" inquit ille "superi verum istud vt euentu comprobes" atque ita discessit / cuius
nuncio manente Stanleo / horas intra decem proximas correpti
ambo neglecto fidem somnio fecere. Certum est / quum iam in
arcem tenderet / paulum abfuisse quo minus ter intra breue
10 spatium toties collapso equo prouolueretur in terram / quae res /
etsi nullo die non accidat vel equi vicio vel insidentis incuria /
tamen [235] vetusta superstitione sic est obseruata tanquam no-
tabiliter precedat infortunium.

Iam quod sequitur haud perinde monitio atque inimici lu-
[51/1]   15 dibrium fuit. Eques ad eum quidam / tum perquam tenuis / nunc
inter purpuratorum primos / adhuc dormientem venit / officij
simulatione comitaturus ad arcem / ceterum iussu Protectoris et
gnarus exicii vt acceleraret aduentum. Is restitantem in via et
cum noto sibi sacerdote qui forte occurrerat colloquentem /
20 quasi per iocum interpellans / "Quid nunc tam multa cum sacerdote?" inquit "Nondum enim sacerdote tibi opus est" / tecte
insultans breui fore.

Sed quiduis potius quam humanae mentis vanissimam et exi-
tio iam contiguam securitatem preterierim. In ipso arcis intro-
25 itu / tam prope locum in quo tam cito caput eius erat amputandum / forte caduceator offertur gentilicio sibi nomine. Eius

---

1 periculi /] periculi P; est /] est P; amplius:] amplius P   2 esset] P A, sit Ps 1565; esset /]
esset P   3 videamur.] videamur P   5 habeo.] habeo / P   7 Stanleo /] Stanleo P;
intra] 1565, ⟨intr⟩ inter P, inter A   8 fecere] P A 1565, impleuere Ps As; fecere.] fecere /
P; est /] est P   9 tenderet /] tenderet P   10 collapso] P A, corruente Ps1 As, bante
(meant to be combined with the colla of collapso) Ps2, offendente 1565; terram] P A 1565,
lutum Ps As; quae res /] que res P   11 etsi] et si P; vicio] ⟨vitio⟩ vicio P   13
infortunium.] infortunium P   15 fuit.] fuit / P; tenuis /] tenuis P   17 ad] P A 1565,
in Ps; ceterum] P A, re vera Ps As, re autem ipsa 1565; iussu Protectoris] P, missu
protectoris A, a protectore missus 1565   18 acceleraret aduentum] P A 1565,
festinaret venturum Ps As; aduentum.] aduentum / P   19 sacerdote] A 1565, changed to
sacerdoti P; colloquentem] P A 1565, habentem sermonem Ps As; colloquentem /] colloquentem P   20–21 sacerdote?] sacerdote P   22 breui] P A 1565, statim Ps As; fore.]
fore P   23 humanae] humane P   24 preterierim.] preterierim / P   25
amputandum /] amputandum P   26 gentilicio] A 1565, gentilico P; nomine.] nomine
P

consciences? So either we are in no danger anywhere (and we certainly are not) or else we are in even more danger there; and even if we were in danger, I would rather appear to have fallen by another man's treachery than for any guilt or cowardice on my part. Go, then, and tell him to stay; for I consider that man (he will know who I mean) as reliable and faithful to me as this very right hand of mine." "May the saints make it prove so indeed," said the servant, departing. Upon his report, Stanley remained; and within the next ten hours the arrest of both men made them believe the disregarded dream. It is certain that on his way to the Tower, three times in a short interval he was nearly thrown to earth by his stumbling horse; and even though this is something which happens every day through the fault of the horse or the carelessness of the rider, an old superstition regards it as a notable omen of misfortune.

Now what follows was far less a warning than an enemy's mockery. A certain knight, quite insignificant then, and now one of the highest nobility, came to Hastings while he was still sleeping, ostensibly to escort him to the Tower as a gesture of respect, but in fact under orders from the Protector, and privy to the execution of Hastings, to hasten his coming. As Hastings paused on the way to converse with a priest he knew who had happened to run into them, the knight interrupted and asked jokingly, "Why speak so long now with a priest? You do not need a priest yet," a mocking hint that he would need one shortly.

But I would rather overlook anything than pass over the human mind's illusion of security even on the very brink of destruction. In the very entrance to the Tower, so very close to the place in which he would so soon be beheaded, he happened on a certain herald who shared his last name. Upon meeting

occursu subijt animum temporis alterius recordatio / quo tempore eidem eodem in loco similiter occurrenti dolorem ac
metum suum communicauerat. Fuerat enim tum reus apud Eduardum factus accusante Riuero germano Reginae tanquam agi-
5 tauisset consilium de prodendo Gallis Caleto / cuius presidij prefectus erat / quae tametsi (quod paulo post inclaruit) mera esset
calumnia / indignante Riuero sibi illum in eo magistratu pre-
latum / quem velut destinatum ac promissum ipse sperauerat /
tamen accusatoris dolo et nocturna Reginae oratione preoc-
10 cupatis Regis auribus / initio sibi magno in periculo versari videbatur. Igitur ingens eum libido nunc incessit ibi cum illo de
discrimine preterito iam atque euitato colloquendi vbi aliquando
[52/1]   [235v] presens impertiuerat. "Ecquid Hastynge" inquit (nam id
erat etiam caduceatori nomen) "meministi quibus de rebus olim
15 hoc ipso in loco sermonem conseruimus?" "Memini" inquit ille
"admodumque certe gratulor ab inuidis intentas insidias / ipsis
male tibique bene cessisse." "Quanto magis" inquit "istud sentias
si ea scires quae sunt adhuc mihi paucisque cognita / quae tu
quoque paulo audies posterius." Hoc de perimendis eo die quos
20 ante captos ostendimus Reginae cognatos intelligebat / haud
quaquam gnarus quam prope ceruicibus idem fatum imminebat
suis. "Quin superis" inquit "habeo gratias / vt nunquam eque
mihi dubiae res ac tum fuere / ita vicissim nunquam perinde
certae confirmataeque quam nunc." O densam mortalitatis cal-
25 iginem: metuenti nihil impendebat mali: securus intra duas

1 occursu] occursu⟨m⟩ P   3 communicauerat.] communicauerat / P   4 Reginae]
Regine P   4 agitauisset] P A, habuisset Pˢ Aˢ 1565   6 erat / quae] erat que P;
(quod . . . inclaruit)] quod . . . inclaruit P   7 calumnia /] calumnia P   8 sperauerat /] sperauerat P   9 tamen] tñ P, tum A 1565   9 Reginae] Regine P   9–10
preoccupatis] preoccupa⟨n⟩tis P   10 magno] ⟨in⟩ magno P   10–11 videbatur.] videbatur P   12 colloquendi] P A 1565, tum recogitandi Pˢ Aˢ   12–13
vbi . . . impertiuerat] om. 1565; impertiuerat.] impertiuerat P   15 conseruimus?] conseruimus / P   16 ipsis] A 1565, illis P   17 male] P A 1565, secus Pˢ Aˢ; cessisse.]
cessisse./ P   18 quae . . . quae] que . . . que P; cognita /] cognita P   19 audies] corr.
from audis P   20 Reginae] Regine P; intelligebat /] intelligebat P   21 fatum]
fa⟨c⟩tum P   22 gratias /] gratias P   23 dubiae] dubie P; fuere /] fuere P   24
nunc.] nunc./ P   24–25 caliginem:] caliginem P   25 metuenti . . . mali:] om. 1565;
mali:] mali P

him, Hastings remembered another occasion when he had similarly happened to meet the same man in the same place and had
shared his grief and fear with him, for he then stood indicted
before Edward, on a charge leveled by the queen's brother, Lord
Rivers, as if he had been plotting to hand over Calais, of which he
was captain, to the French. Even though, as it soon became obvious, the charge was pure slander, caused by Rivers' resentment
at losing an office to Hastings which he thought had been definitely intended for him, it still seemed to Hastings initially that,
what with the guile of his accuser and the queen's nightly
speeches to prejudice the king, he was in serious danger. And so
he now had a powerful impulse to talk to the same man about
danger now past and eluded where he once had described it as a
present danger. "Hastings," he said to him (for that was the
herald's name, too), "do you happen to remember the matters
we spoke of in this place a long time ago?" "I remember," he said,
"and I am very glad indeed that the traps which were set by your
enemies turned out badly for them and well for you." "How
much more you would think so if you knew certain things only I
and a few others know but which you will soon hear about." He
was referring to the execution that day of the queen's kinsmen
whose arrest we have described; he had no idea of how close to
his own neck the same fate impended. "Yes, indeed," he went
on, "I thank the saints above, just as my fortunes have never
been as uncertain as they were at that time, so they have never
been as securely and firmly established as they are today." The
dense blindness of mortal existence! When he was afraid, he was
in no real danger; when he felt secure, he was less than two hours

horas perijt misere: vir haud obscuris natalibus / nempe equitum
vetusto genere / sed cui nobilitas ab ipso accessit / bello impiger
nec imperitus / vitae non admodum seuerae / sed comitate
multum popularis gratiae meruerat / Regi ob fidem egregie
5 charus / preterea non iniucundus vel societate vel conscientia
voluptatum / insidiantibus facile obnoxius / vtpote ob innatam
animo audaciam minus prouidens / satisque fidus et fidens
nimium.

　　Cedis huius fama repente per vrbem primum / inde qua-
10 quauersum prouolauit. Sed Protector illico ab facinore patrato /
quo suam culpam aliquo velaret pallio / prefectum vrbis ac sena-
tores aliquot accersit in arcem. Vbi venere / ostendit sibi Ducique
structas in eum diem insidias / quas ipsi quum nihil minus opinati
paulo ante prandium deprehendissent [236] in ipso conatu /
[53/1] 15 coactos arma subito qualiacunque corripere (id quo verius dicere
videretur / stabant armis incincti tam sordidis vt nec infimus ea
quisquam e gregarijs militibus nisi vrgenti periculo putetur induturus) / ceterum gnauiter ac strenue depulso periculo plu-
ribusque coniurantium captis / ipsorum tamen benignitatem
20 vnius Hastyngi / quod is immedicabilis esset inuidiae / supplicio
contentam / reliquos omnes servasse paenitentiae. Ad hec illi /
tanquam crederent / extollere fortitudinem / laudare clemen-

---

1 misere:] misere. *P*   1–8 vir . . . nimium] *P A,* Vir celebri apud suos loco, vtpote
equestris ordinis, illustri et antiqua familia natus, familiae gloriam a maioribus acceptam
ipse rerum belli domique gestarum laude cumulauit. Vitae fuit paulo remissioris, populo
ob comitatem gratiosus, regi ob fidem in primis charus, artibus et insidijs malitiosorum
hominum expositus propter generosam quandam animi simplicitatem sibi praefi-
dentem, et a dolo maxime alienam. Insidiantibus facile obnoxius, vtpote ob innatam
animo audaciam. *1565 (cf.* this honorable man, a good knight and a gentle, of gret
aucthorite w[t] his prince, of living somewhat desolate, plaine and open to his enemy, and
secret to his friend: eth to beguile, as he that of good hart and corage forestudied no
perilles. A louing man, and passing well beloued. Very faithful, and trusty enough,
trusting too much. *1557)*   1 natalibus/] natalibus *P*   3 seuerae /] seuerae *P*   4
meruerat] *P A,* meritus *P*s   5 iniucundus] *reading uncertain* (iniurandus?) *P A*   6
voluptatum /] voluptatum *P;* obnoxius /] obnoxius *P*   7 audaciam] audatiam *P A;*
prouidens /] prouidens *P*   9 primum /] primum *P*   10 prouolauit.] prouolauit *P;*
illico] *P A 1565;* illicet *P*s *A*s; patrato /] patrato *P*   11 pallio /] pallio *P*   12 venere /]
venere *P*   13 quas ipsi] *P A 1565 where* seque eas *would be neater*   15 corripere (Id]
corripere. Id *P*   16 videretur /] videretur *P*   17–18 induturus) /] induturus *P*
19 captis /] captis *P*   20 Hastyngi /] Hastyngi *P;* inuidiae /] inuidie *P*   21
paenitentiae] *P*sb *A*s *1565,* penitere *P A;* paenitentiae.] penitere *P;* illi /] illi *P;*
fortitudinem /] fortitudinem *P*

from a miserable death. He was a gentleman of no obscure origins, for he came from an old knightly family, but for which he himself gained nobility, a hardy and not inexperienced warrior, a man of somewhat loose living, but whose jovial nature had gained him much popular favor, especially dear to the king on account of his trustworthiness, and not unentertaining as a partner or confidant in his pleasures, an easy target for treacherous enemies, since his natural boldness made him too incautious; a man trusty enough, trusting too much.

The news of this killing flew rapidly, first through the city, then in every direction. But right after the crime was committed, the Protector summoned the mayor and some of the aldermen to the Tower in an effort to palliate his guilt. When they arrived, he reported that there had been a conspiracy planned against himself and the duke, to be executed on that very day, and that when they themselves, who had never suspected a thing, learned about it a short time before lunch when it was already under way, they were forced to snatch up any armor they could on the spur of the moment—to lend these words some appearance of truth they stood there wearing armor so shabby that not even the lowest footsoldier would be likely to put it on except in an emergency—but that after repelling the threat gravely and vigorously and capturing many of the plotters, they had generously chosen to content themselves with the punishment of Hastings alone (since his malice was incorrigible) and to spare all the rest for repentance. Upon these words, as if they believed them, the city officials applauded their fortitude, praised their for-

tiam / et incolumitatem gratulari / quum tacite interim secum
crucem vtrique precarentur.

　　Protector etiam eodem commento ratus leniendum populum /
caduceatorem interea cum edicto iam olim in id parato miserat /
5　e quo ad tubae sonum conuocata plebe locis maxime celebribus
eadem fere preconis voce pronunciarentur. Sed addebantur in
Hastyngum quo nex eius equius audiretur / tanquam preter
noxam eam flagitiosi multa consilij / conatu punitum ne quam
forte turbam eius liberandi causa perditi et proditionis conscien-
10　tia stimulati parricidae concitarent / quorum nunc spe merito
[54/1]　illius supplicio prouidenter oppressa / nihil restare periculi quo
minus omnes boni sub optimo principe quietissime sint victuri.
Iam hoc edictum / quod intra horas duas ab eius nece pronunciabatur / et longius erat quam vt vel temere dictatum interea
15　potuerit scribi et tam ambitiose compositum depictumque mem-
brana tam sedulo vt ne dupplicato quidem temporis interuallo
parari quiuerit./ Ita quiuis puer facile sensit falsi tam laborate
commenti conspicuam vanitatem / nempe quam rem videri vole-
bant [236v] modo primum repente comperisse / eius rei penam
20　deprehendebantur antea meditati. Itaque magister ludi quidam
(nisi quod res atrocior erat quam quae ioculares facetias admitteret) haud irridicule tam solertem edicti stulticiam illuserat /
nam vt turbae immixtus auscultabat legentem / temporis angustias cum longitudine scriptorum et cura comparans protinus
25　Terentiani dicti admonitus / "Haud satis commode diuisa sunt
temporibus / Daue / hec tibi" inquit./

1 incolumitatem] *1565*, incolumitate *P*, incolumitat *A;* gratulari /] gratulari *P*　　3
populum /] populum *P*　　4 miserat /] miserat *P*　　5 tubae] tube *P*　　6
pronunciarentur.] pronunciarentur *P;* addebantur] *P A*, addita *Ps As 1565*　　7 nex] *P*
A, supplicium *Ps As 1565;* audiretur /] audiretur *P;* tanquam] *P A*, velut *Ps As 1565*　　10
parricidae concitarent /] parricide concitarent *P*　　12 victuri.] victuri / *P*　　13
edictum /] edictum *P;* quod intra horas duas] *P 1565*, intra duas quod horas *A*　　13–14
pronunciabatur /] pronunciabatur *P*　　15 ambitiose compositum] *A 1565*, ambitiose *P;*
depictumque] depictum que *P*, descriptum *interl. above* depictum *Ps As*, descriptum *1565*
17–18 sensit falsi tam laborate commenti conspicuam vanitatem] sensit falsi tam laborati
commenti conspicuam vanitatem *P A*, persensit elaborati commenti perspicuam vanitatem *1565*　　20–26 Itaque ... inquit] *om. 1565*　　21 quae] que *P*　　23–24 legentem
/ temporis ... comparans protinus] *A*, legentem / protinus *P*　　23–24 angustias] an-
gustiã *A*　　24 longitudine] longitudinem *A*　　26 temporibus / Daue /] temporibus
Dauae *P*

bearance, and gave thanks for their safety, whereas everyone secretly wished each of them on the gallows.

The Protector, who thought they should use the same fiction to mollify the people, had meanwhile sent a herald with an edict, prepared long before for that purpose, from which virtually the same claims would be read aloud by the crier when the commons had been gathered by the sound of a trumpet at the principal points of assembly. But allegations were added against Hastings so that the news of his death would be taken more calmly, as if, quite apart from the main offense, it were a penalty for giving evil counsel, and that he had been punished during the very attempt lest degenerate and traitorous parricides, goaded on by their own guilt, might stir up a mob to free him, but that now that their hopes had been prudently dashed by his well-deserved punishment there was no further danger, and all good citizens would live peacefully and quietly under their excellent prince. Now this edict, which was read aloud within two hours of his death, was too long to have been written down even from casual dictation in that length of time and was too ceremoniously phrased and too carefully limned on the parchment to have been prepared even in double the time. Thus every child quickly sensed the transparent frivolity of such an elaborate fiction, since they were seen to have thought out the punishment in advance for a crime which they claimed they had learned about only just now. And so, if the matter were not too atrocious to be a fit subject for witticisms, the joke that a certain schoolmaster directed at the crafty stupidity of the edict would certainly have been not unamusing. For as he stood in the crowd listening to the man who was reading the edict and as he compared the shortness of the time with the length and meticulousness of the writing, he was promptly reminded of a saying from Terence and commented, "You have not spaced these episodes very well, Davus."

Sed inde protinus in Shorae domum irruitur / extrahitur ipsa
et truditur in carcerem / direpta bona per iram scilicet atque ad
Protectorem comportata velut in multam veneficij / cuius /
vtpote vanissimi / quum nullum in illam signum posset herere /
5 ne per iniuriam afflictam faterentur / tandem in id descenditur
crimen quod nec ipsa poterat negare / quippe quod populus tam
sciuit verum quam nemo tum demum tam atrociter obiectum ei
non risit / Nempe quod esset meretrix. Sed Protector / vt pius
purusque princeps e celo in miserum hunc delapsus orbem cor-
10 rigendis mortalium moribus / adegit / vti in Diui Pauli templo
magna celebritate senatu Londinensi prodeunte supplicatum /
ipsa nudipes et gestato cereo insignis (qui mos est illic publice
penitentium) crucem et psallentium chorum anteiret. Ceterum
illa vultu gressuque tam composito incedebat et quanquam ne-
15 glecto horridoque cultu / facie tamen adeo venusta / presertim
cum decentissimam in candidas eius genas rubedinem pudor
adfunderet / vt ingens illud dedecus haud parum ei laudis gratiaeque pepererit apud magis appetentes corporis quam animae
curiosos / quanquam boni quoque et quibus vitia inuisa [237]
20 erant / miserebantur tamen eius opprobrium potiusquam gaudebant / reputantes a Protectore id simulatis et corruptis affectibus / nullo honesti studio procuratum.

Hec mulier Londini bonis prognata parentibus / bene pudice-
que educata / copulata est matrimonio cetera feliciter nisi quod
25 nimium festinato. Nam quum virum haberet honestum / elegantem / opulentum / iuuenem / tamen quod immatura nupsit /

[55/1]

---

1 Shorae] Shore P; extrahitur] *1565*, ⟨xtrahitur⟩ extrahitur P, extraditur A   3
veneficij] P A, proditionis P^s1 A^s, maleficij magici P^s2 *1565;* veneficij /] veneficij P   3–
4 cuius / vtpote vanissimi /] cuius vtpote vanissimi P   4 herere /] herere P   5
faterentur /] faterentur P   6 negare] P A *1565*, inficiari P^s; negare /] negare P   8
risit /] risit P; meretrix.] meretrix P   8–10 Sed Protector / vt . . . moribus / adegit / vti]
P A, vnde effecit protector, vt *1565*   8 Protector /] Protector P   10 moribus] P A,
flagitijs P^s; adegit /] adegit. P   11 prodeunte] P *1565*, prodente A   12–13
(qui . . . penitentium)] qui . . . penitentium P   13 anteiret] P A, preiret P^s,
praecederet *1565;* anteiret.] anteiret / P   15 cultu /] cultu P; venusta /] venusta P
17 adfunderet /] adfunderet P   17–18 gratiaeque pepererit] gratieque pepererit / P
18 animae] anime P   20–21 gaudebant /] gaudebant P   21–22 affectibus /]
affectibus P   22 nullo] *1565*, nulli P A; procuratum.] procuratum / P   23 bonis] P A
1565, ditibus P^s; parentibus /] parentibus P   24 educata] *corr. from* educta P; educata /] educata P; copulata] P A, coniuncta P^s *1565*   25 festinato.] A *1565*, festinate P
26 iuuenem /] iuuenem P; nupsit /] nupsit P

But immediately thereafter they broke into the house of Shore's wife, dragged her out, and threw her into jail, seizing her property, ostensibly out of anger, and transferring it to the Protector as if this were her punishment for brewing potions. But since it was impossible to make such a frivolous charge stick, to keep from admitting that they were persecuting her unjustly, they were reduced to the one charge that not even she could deny, since the whole populace was as certain that it was the truth as that it was ridiculous at that point for anyone to make such a terrible crime of it, namely, that she was a harlot. But the Protector, like a pious, pure prince dropped from heaven to this wretched earth to correct human morals, decreed that in St. Paul's Cathedral, before a great crowd, with the council of London coming forth to worship, she should walk barefoot, marked out by bearing a candle, in front of the cross and the choir singing psalms, in the manner of all those who do public penance there. But her expression and gait were so decorous as she stepped forward, and despite her disheveled and unkempt appearance her face was so lovely, especially when shame sent a most fetching blush into her snowy cheeks, that this great dishonor won her no little measure of praise and goodwill from all those more desirous of her body than concerned for her soul, although even good people who hated her faults pitied her disgrace rather than joying in it, since they considered that it had been arranged by the Protector not out of any real interest in decency but out of hypocrisy and malice.

This woman, born into a good London family and given a good, modest upbringing, was joined in a marriage which was otherwise promising enough but contracted too early. For though her husband was honorable, fashionable, prosperous, and youthful, since she married before she was ready she never

haud vnquam admodum dilexit eum quo prius est potita quam
adfectauit / eoque auersus olim ab marito animus procliuiter in
procantem eam regem ferebatur. Et alioqui tanti proci splendor
et respectus insolens viri ceteris metuendi / sibi blandientis ac
5 supplicis / ad hec spes apparatus et mundi muliebris conspicui /
denique ocij / luxus / voluptatum / facile poterant mollem puellae
animum vellicare. Sed eam vbi resciuit coniunx rem habuisse
cum Rege / vt erat homo modestus / haud se tanto honore dignatus / principalem vt concubinam attingeret / in totum eam
10 Regi cessit: quanto ciuilior alijs quibus haud quaquam equum in
illam ius erat. Defuncto Rege sucessit Hastyngus / quam etsi viuo
illo adamauerat / abstinuisse tamen ferebatur / siue reuerentia
siue sodalicia quadam fide.
    Erat hec cute candida / totius oris egregia specie / sed oculis
15 presertim mirae illecebrae inerant / reliquo corpori nihil quod
mutari velles / nisi quis forte optasset altiorem. Nam bella fuit
magis quam procera: quod ipsum fere longissimo cuique maxime cordi. Sic illam narrant qui videre florentem / plerisque
hodie inspectantium (nam etiam adhuc viuit) haud credentibus /
20 quippe qui preteritam figuram ex presenti estimantes nunquam
fuisse venustam censent. Quorum [237v] mihi iudicium propemodum perinde videtur / ac si quis formam olim defunctae
virginis ex effossa sepulchro calua coniectet: siquidem nunc sep-
tuagenaria vetula / rugosa / flaccida / macilenta / cadauerosa /
25 prope euanuit / nulla pristini illius tam laudati corporis parte

1 dilexit] P A, amare potuit Ps; quo prius] P A, cuius ante Ps   2 adfectauit /] adfectauit
P   3 procantem] P A, ambientem Ps As 1565; ferebatur.] ferebatur / P; splendor]
splendor / P   4 metuendi /] metuendi P   6 ocij / luxus / voluptatum /] ocij luxus
voluptatum P; mollem] P A, mobilem 1565; puellae] puelle P   7 vellicare] P A,
peruellere (for impellere?) Ps, impellere As 1565; vellicare.] vellicare / P   8 Rege /]
rege P; modestus /] modestus P   8–9 dignatus] A 1565, dignus P; dignatus /] dignus P
9 attingeret /] attingeret P; totum] A 1565, totam P   10 cessit:] cessit / P   11 erat.]
erat / P; Hastyngus /] Hastyngus P; etsi] et si P   12 adamauerat /] adamauerat P
14 hec] P A, illa Ps As 1565; candida /] candida P; specie /] specie P   15 inerant /]
inerant P   17 procera:] procera P   17–428/11 procera . . . Rex] drastically shortened
in 1565   17–18 quod . . . cordi] om. 1557 1565   18 cordi.] cordi / P   19 credentibus /] credentibus P   20 quippe . . . estimantes] om. 1557 1565   21 censent.]
censent P   22 videtur] P A, valet Ps; defunctae] defuncte P   23 effossa] corr. from
effosso P; coniectet:] coniectet P   24 vetula] ⟨est⟩ vetula P; flaccida / macilenta / cadauerosa /] flaccida macilenta cadauerosa P

cherished her husband at all, having gotten him before she desired him, so that her heart, long averse to her husband, was
easily drawn to the king when he courted her. Even had it been
otherwise, the glamor of such a great suitor and the heady spec-
tacle of a man feared by others deferring to her and imploring
her favor, as well as the prospect of finery, a lavish feminine
wardrobe, and furthermore leisure, extravagance, and pleasure, could easily make an impression in the girl's tender heart.
But when he learned about her affair with the king, her spouse,
being a modest man, felt he did not deserve the great honor of
sharing the king's concubine and so gave her up to him totally, a
good deal more courteously than certain other men who had far
less legitimate claims on her. When the king had died, Hastings
succeeded him; for even though he loved her while the king was
still living, it was said he restrained himself, whether out of respect or some feeling of comradely loyalty.

Her complexion was fair, and her whole face was strikingly
beautiful, though her eyes were especially alluring; there was
not one feature in the rest of her body that you would have
wanted to change, unless one might have wished she were taller.
For she was pretty rather than statuesque, something which is
especially attractive to every tall man. So she is described by the
people who saw her in her prime, although many who look at her
today (for she is still alive) cannot believe it, for they gauge her
past features by her present ones and conclude she could never
have been beautiful. To me their judgment seems almost like
guessing the beauty of a long-deceased maiden from a bald pate
dug up from the grave; for now she is a little old woman of
seventy, wrinkled, rivelled, emaciated, and cadaverous, rapidly
withering away, leaving no trace of that much-esteemed body

reliqua preterquam arida cute contecta ossa. Tamen sic quoque
penitius intuenti vultum / subire possit / quae partes / quem ad
modum resarsitae ac reparatae / formosam redderent faciem.

[56/1]   Nec tamen pulchritudine quemquam eque atque comitate
5   quadam et dextra illicibili suauitate conuiuendi capiebat / vtpote
lepido ac festiuo ingenio / docta hactenus vt legere suam linguam
et scribere vtcunque posset / serendi colloquij haud rudis / neque
silentio rustico nec immodica loquacitate notabilis / nemo appositior exhillarando conuiuio / seu commode interuertendis
10 tristibus seu proferendo letiora / ludens interim salibus et facetijs
citra dolorem cuiusquam / nec sine risu./ Rex siquidem hylarior
interdum solebat predicare meretriculas se habere tres diuersis
quamque dotibus insignem / vnam letissimam / alteram as-
tutissimam / tertiam porro meretricum quae vsquam essent om-
15 nium sanctissimam / vt quae grauatim vnquam e templo quoquam preterquam in eius lectum diuerteret./ Reliquae haud sat
compertum habeo quae fuerint: laetissimam hanc esse constat
quam dicimus / eo nomine Regi charissimam / qui quum alias
haberet / vnam hanc adamauit / nulla super libidinem noxa.
20 Nam et vxorem magno amplectebatur adfectu et honorifice
tractauit.

    Quin hec muliercula (facinus enim sit calumniari caco-
demonem) tantam defuit vt fauore Principis in cuiusquam
[238] abuteretur malum / vt plurimis etiam bono fuerit. Nam et
25 offensum Regis animum plerumque mitigabat: inuisis gratiam /
delinquentibus veniam impetrabat: denique multis magnis in
rebus suis vsui erat / mercede plerumque vel nulla vel perex-
igua / eaque specie magis quam precio spectanda / siue satis sibi
habebat facti sui conscientiam / seu beneficijs ostentare placuit
30 quantum posset apud Principem / seu puella presente fortuna

---

1 ossa.] ossa / P   2 penitius] A, penitus P, pressius Pˢ Aˢ; possit / quae partes /] possit
que partes P   3 resarsitae] resarsite P; reparatae /] reparate P; faciem.] faciem P   5
capiebat / vtpote] capiebat vt pote P   7 posset /] posset P   8–10 nemo . . . letiora]
om. 1557 1565   11 cuiusquam /] cuiusque P   14–15 quae . . . quae] que . . . que
P   15 sanctissimam /] sanctissimam P; quae] ⟨que⟩ que P   17 quae fuerint:] que
fuerint / P   18 dicimus /] dicimus P   19 haberet /] haberet P   19–22
nulla . . . tractauit.] om. 1557 1565   19 noxa.] noxa P   21 tractauit] P A, habuit Pˢ
Aˢ; tractauit.] tractauit P   22–23 (facinus . . . cacodemonem)] om. 1565   24 malum /] malum P   25 mitigabat:] mitigabat /] P; gratiam /] gratiam, P   26 impetrabat:] impetrabat / P   28 spectanda] P A 1565, estimanda Pˢ Aˢ   29 conscientiam /]
conscientiam P   29–430/2 seu . . . inhiabat] om. 1565

besides dry skin and bones. And yet even as she is, if one looks at
her face more attentively, one can conjecture which features
restored and repaired in a particular manner would make her
face fair again.

And yet her greatest charm was not beauty, but rather a certain gracious manner and a winning air of convivial urbanity, for
she had a quick, sprightly wit, with enough education to read her
own language and write in it, after a fashion; she was a skilled
conversationalist, conspicuous neither for tongue-tied rusticity
nor for immoderate talkativeness; there was no one more adept
at enlivening a banquet, whether by tactfully interrupting a grim
conversation or by starting a more cheerful one, sometimes en-
tertaining the feasters with witty expressions and jests which
raised laughter without hurting anyone's feelings. For the king
in a merry mood used to maintain that he had three fine harlots,
each one with her own special distinction, one of them the most
cheerful, another the most astute, and the third the most saintly
of all the world's harlots, since she scarcely ever left church but to
come to his bed. I am not sure who the other two were, but the
one we are describing was without any doubt the most cheerful,
and for that very reason most dear to the king; for while he had
other mistresses, he loved only this one, with no harm done apart
from their wantonness. For he cherished his wife with great
affection and treated her honorably.

Indeed, this little woman—for it would be a crime to slander
the devil—was so far from abusing the prince's favor to hurt
anyone that she actually helped many people. For she frequently
soothed the king's temper, won indulgence for enemies and
pardon for offenders, and finally assisted many people in their
great transactions, usually for no reward or a token one, something worth having for its appearance instead of its price,
whether she considered her actions their own reward or she
wanted to show by good deeds how much power she had over the
prince or whether a girl reveling in her present good fortune

lasciuiens nec de futuro sollicita non vsque quaque diuitijs inhiabat. Certum est adeo extra inuidiam fuisse vt preterquam vni
Reginae vtrique factioni reliquae sibi infestae pariter amaretur /
[57/3] haud temere cuiquam illorum authoritate gratiaque inferior /
5   qui diuersis etatibus apud suos quique principes valentes sola
scelerum fama posteris inclarescunt / eo diuturniore memoria
quo deteriore / vt beneficia puluere / mali si quid patimur /
marmori insculpimus. At eadem tam olim celebris / amicis nunc
notisque fere omnibus superstes / annisque velut in alterum pro-
10 gressa seculum / deleta propemodum etiam sibi longis malis
pristini luxus memoria / miseram hodie vitam egre mendicando
sustinet / viuentibus tamen ac dissimulantibus quibusdam qui
nunc ei fuissent aduersae fortunae consortes nisi res illis in-
columes ipsa aliquando conseruasset./
15   Sed vti supra tetigimus / eadem hora qua Londini truncatus est
Hastyngus / Anthonius interim Vodeuilus / Reginae frater / [et]
Ricardus Graius quos Hamptoniae ac Stratforiae comprehensos diximus in oppido Pontis Fracti capite plectebantur / curante
cedem Ricardo Ratcliffo equite / cuius ministerio Protector in
20 eiusmodi tyrannica facinora plurimum vtebatur / vtpote valde
taciturni et multarum experti rerum / [238v] ingenij magni malique: sermone rudis erat / habitu rusticus / nunquam ad scelera
timidus: neque miserebatur homines neque superos reuereba-
tur./ Is e carcere productos criminatusque apud circumfusam
25 eos turbam proditionis / ac respondere prohibitos ne cognita
eorum innocentia Protectori conflaret inuidiam / indempnatos /

1 nec . . . sollicita] P, et incuriosa futuri Ps A   1–2 inhiabat.] inhiabat / P   3 Reginae
vtrique] A, Regine P; reliquae . . . infestae] relique . . . infeste P; amaretur] P A 1565,
foueretur Ps As; amaretur /] amaretur./ P   7 puluere /] puluere P; patimur /] patimur
P   9 superstes /] superstes P   10 seculum /] seculum P; propemodum] prope
modum P   13 aduersae fortunae] aduerse fortune P   15 tetigimus /] tetigimus P
16 Hastyngus /] Hastyngus P; Vodeuilus / Reginae frater /] Vodeuilus Regine frater P;
frater   /   et] frater   P   A   1565   17   Hamptoniae . . . Stratfordiae]
Hamptonie . . . Stratfordie P   18 in oppido] Ps As, apud P A, ad oppidulum 1565;
plectebantur /] plectebantur P   19 equite /] equite P   20 vtebatur /] vtebatur P
21 rerum /] rerum P   21–22 malique:] malique / P   22 rusticus /] rusticus P   23
timidus] P A, cunctator Ps As; timidus:] timidus P   23–24 miserebatur homines . . . superos reuerebatur] P A (verebatur A), misertor hominum . . . superum cultor
Ps As, ab omni aut erga homines misericordia, aut erga superos reuerentia alienissimus
1565   24–25 criminatusque . . . proditionis] om. 1565   26 indempnatos /] indempnatos P

and having small thought for the future felt no greed for gold. She was certainly so far from being resented that (with the sole exception of the queen) the two factions, who hated each other, both loved her alike; she was little inferior in authority and influence to any of those who at various periods had great power with their princes but who are known to posterity only for their crimes, the more scandalous their memory, the more lasting, as we record good deeds done to us in dust but the wrongs we have suffered in marble. But this very woman, so famous once, who has now outlived virtually all of her friends and acquaintances and who with the years has passed on in effect to an alien century, her memory of that early luxury almost effaced by her long years of hardship, today ekes out a wretched existence by begging, although some are still living and pretending not to know her who would now be her partners in adversity had she not once salvaged their fortunes.

But as we briefly mentioned above, at the very hour at which Hastings was decapitated in London, Anthony Woodville, the queen's brother, and Richard Grey (seized, as we said, in Northampton and [Stony] Stratford) were beheaded in Pontefract. Their execution was managed by Sir Richard Radcliff, whose help the Protector employed very frequently in tyrannical actions of this sort, since he was exceedingly tight-lipped and widely experienced, a man of great and malignant intelligence; he was coarse in speech, churlish in manner, and never timid about committing a crime; he neither pitied man nor feared heaven. After bringing them forth from their cells, charging them with treason before the surrounding crowd, and denying them a chance to respond lest the knowledge of their innocence should stir up rancor against the Protector, he had them quickly killed,

[58/1] inauditos / atque adeo nec accusatos quidem / celeriter necandos
curauit / nulla alia culpa quam quod boni erant aut vel nimis
propinqui Reginae vel nimis fideles Principi./

Igitur patratis rebus his / et nobilium quos maxime aduer-
5 saturos putabat necatis / alijs adhuc captiuis / tum reliquis fere
Londini agentibus procul ab suis cuiusque viribus / denique at-
tonitis et perculsis omnibus / quum neque sciret quisquam quorsum res euaderet aut cui consilia crederet / Protector capiendam
occasionem ratus est et occupato pauore dubitantium in posses-
10 sionem regni ponendum sese priusquam cogitatis et perpensis
suis consilijs in diuersa discedendi spacium firmatis partium
copijs esset. Ceterum in hoc herebatur / quinam color rei de se
inuisae pretexeretur quo leniretur inuidia.

Huic consultationi plures adhibebant quos aliqua de causa
15 facile ad se traductos vsui fore sperabant vel virium opibus vel
ingenij / in his Edmundum Shaum Londini prefectum / velut
ingentium premiorum spe / quae homini talium famelico pro-
dige promittebantur ciues ex illorum sententia tractaturum./ E
clero delecti quibus apud plebem authoritas concionando
20 quesita fuerat / nec animi ad superstitionem vsque pij / potissimum vero Iohannes Shaus prefecti frater / ac Pinkerus Au-
gustiniensium fratrum in Anglia prouincialis / ambo sacrarum
professione [239] literarum insignes / ambo contionum gloria
celebrati / ceterum vtrique doctrina tam infra famam quam vir-
25 tus infra doctrinam./ Hi sermones e suggestu accuratissimos in
[59/1] Protectoris laudem alter antequam esset rex / alter post regnum
initum habuere plenos adulationis intolerandae. Pinkerus in

1 inauditos /] inauditos P; quidem /] quidem P   2 curauit /] curauit P; quam] quam-
⟨quam⟩ P   3 Reginae] Regine P   5 necatis /] necatis P; captiuis /] captiuis P   7
omnibus /] omnibus P   8 cui consilia crederet] P A 1565, que tacita vellet tacenda (or
fatenda) Pˢ; crederet /] crederet P   12 esset.] esset P; herebatur] P A 1565, scrupulus
erat Pˢ Aˢ; herebatur /] herebatur P; quinam] qui nam P   12–13 de se inuisae] de se
inuise P A, tam scelerate Pˢ Aˢ 1565   13 pretexeretur] P, pretexi posset Pˢ A 1565
(pretexti Pˢ); inuidia.] inuidia P   16 ingenij /] ingenij P; prefectum /] prefectum P
17 spe /] spe P; quae] que P   17–18 prodige] P, large Pˢ A   13 tractaturum] P Aˢ,
formaturum Pˢ A (where we expect a dative participle)   20 quesita] P 1565, parata Pˢ,
perta A; pij /] pij P   22 prouincialis] P, rector / primas Pˢ, rector primas A, Praeses
1565 (cf. prouincial 1557)   24 celebrati /] celebrati P   24–25 virtus infra doc-
trinam] P A 1565, infra doctrinam virtus Pˢᵃ   27 intolerandae.] intolerande P

unconvicted, unheard, and not even accused, guilty of nothing but of being too closely akin to the queen or too loyal to the prince.

And so when these deeds had been perpetrated and those nobles he thought would be most opposed to him had been slain, while other nobles were still in captivity and almost all the rest were residing in London far away from their centers of power, and while everyone was dismayed and unnerved by uncertainty as to where all this was leading and whom one could trust, the Protector decided that he ought to seize the occasion, take advantage of their fear and uncertainty, and put himself in possession of the throne before giving them time to elaborate and think through their plans and withdraw to their various bases with their forces consolidated. But he was at a loss for a suitable pretext with which to disguise an inherently odious business and thus mitigate the ensuing indignation.

They invited many to their consultations who they hoped might be easily won over, one way or another, and who might then assist them with either their power or their intellect. Edward Shaw, mayor of London, was among them; he was wooed with the hope of great profits, which they promised extravagantly to this man, who was ravenous for prizes of that sort, if he managed the citizens to their liking. From the clergy men were chosen who had gained some authority as popular preachers and whose minds were not pious to the point of superstition, and especially John Shaw, the mayor's brother, and Penker, the provincial of the English Augustinian friars; although both were celebrated for their exposition of sacred scripture and renowned for the brilliance of their sermons, the learning of each of them was as far below his reputation as his virtue was below his learning. From the pulpit they delivered extremely elaborate sermons in praise of the Protector, the former before he became king and the latter after his coronation, both full of intolerable

medio orationis cursu destitutus voce descendit / auditorio rem
in superos referente velut sacrilegae palpationis vltores. Shaus
omnem honesti famam perdidit / haud multo post et vitam tedio
solitudinis in quam sese pudore publici conspectus abdiderat / at
5 frater perfrictissimae frontis / vt e qua sepe inter disputandum
sputa deterserat / olim ad infamiam obtorpuerat.

   Sunt et qui Pynkerum negant initio propositi conscium / sed re
peracta / vulgato more / gratiam aucupatum apud ieiunum
laudis principem. Ceterum vt de illo ambigitur / ita Shao constat
10 vsque adeo communicatum consilium / vt ei primae etiam partes
insinuandae populo rei demandarentur./ Nam ea commodis-
sima incipiendi negocij visa est via / si is concione solemni / propo-
sita re et tractata concinne / labefactatos plebis animos ab Rege
ad Protectorem pertrahat. Ceterum totus labor in excogitanda
15 mutandi regis causa versabatur ne tam impium consilium / impudenter expositum / protinus exploderetur. In eam rem alijs
alia conferentibus / huc denique summa recidit / vt persuaderetur populo et Eduardum ipsum et eius omnem sobolem
illegitimo esse coitu natam / ita nec illum vnquam iuste regnasse
20 nec hos ei rite successuros: ea ratione restare Protectorem vnum
regni capacem / vt vnicum Eboraci Ducis legitimum filium. Sed
obiectum Eduardo ipsi natalium vicium / id quidem aperte matrem Protectoris [239v] erat infamaturum vtpote ei cum Eduardo communem / nec ideo tamen censuit abstinendum / sed eum
25 locum obliquo ingrediendum ductu atque arte tractandum
veluti timide / sic vt cum dicantur omnia multa tamen supprimi

---

1 descendit /] descendit *P*   2 sacrilegae] sacrilege *P*   4 abdiderat /] abdiderat *P*
4–6 at . . . obtorpuerat] *om. 1565*   5 perfrictissimae frontis /] perfrictissime frontis
P   6 deterserat /] deterserat *P; obtorpuerat.*] obtorpuerat *P*   8 peracta /] peracta *P;*
more /] more *P*   9 principem.] principem *P; ambigitur /]* ambigitur *P*   10 primae]
prime *P*   11 insinuandae] insinuande *P*   12 solemni /] solemni *P*   13 concinne /]
concinne *P*   14 pertrahat] *P A*ˢ, pelliceat *P*ˢ *A*, pelliceret *1565;* pertrahat.] pertrahat
P   15 consilium /] consilium *P*   16 expositum /] expositum *P;* exploderetur.] exploderetur *P*   17 conferentibus] *P 1565,* comminiscentibus *P*ˢ *A;* conferentibus /]
conferentibus *P;* recidit /] recidit *P*   20 successuros:] successuros / *P*   21 filium.]
filium *P*   22 vicium /] vicium *P*   24 abstinendum /] abstinendum *P*   25 ductu] *A
1565,* dictu *P*   26 veluti] *P,* velutique *A;* veluti timide] *om. 1565;* timide /] timide *P*

flattery. Penker lost his voice and stepped down in the middle of a statement, with his hearers ascribing this event to the saints as the punishers of blasphemous adulation. Shaw lost all reputation for honesty and, shortly thereafter, his life, out of weariness with the solitude into which he retreated for shame of being looked at in public; but the friar, who had wiped out his own sense of shame as he wiped off the spit of his many disputations, had long been impervious to infamy.

There are also some who say Penker was initially not in on the plot but that he curried favor after the fact (as men commonly do) with a prince who was hungry for praise. But though that is debated, it is certain that Shaw was so deeply involved in the plot that he was even assigned the main role in coaxing the people to accept the plan. For they decided that the best way to begin the business was for him first to weaken the hearts of the common people by proposing and elaborating the matter in a solemn sermon so as to draw them away from the king to the Protector. But all their efforts were directed to thinking up a reason for replacing the king, lest such an impious plot shamelessly expounded would be shouted down at once. After various people made various suggestions on that score, it all finally came down to a plan of convincing the people that Edward himself and all his offspring were the products of an illegitimate union, so that he never had any right to be king nor could his children rightly succeed him; therefore only the Protector remained eligible for the throne as the Duke of York's only legitimate son. But the bastardy alleged against Edward would clearly dishonor the Protector's own mother, since she gave birth to them both; and yet he chose not to exclude the topic but told the preacher to introduce it obliquely and develop it artfully, as if he were afraid, so that though everything would be said it would still seem that

viderentur / scilicet ne ipsius animus in matrem pius offenderetur. At illud alterum de filijs Eduardi pro spurijs habendis
[60/1]   recta atque aperte agi / et quam maxime posset intendi volebat:
cuius rei / quam falsam et olim reuictam reiectamque calumniam
5   reuocarit melius cognoscetur si quaedam altius ab Eduardi coniugio facta repetemus. /

    Eduardus Henrico deposito potitus regno Comitem Varuici /
virum ditione potentem neque bellica fama neque populari
gratia cedentem cuiquam / legauerat in Hyspaniam tractaturum
10   de capienda in reginam sibi Regis Hyspani filia. Sed interea forte
ad eum venit Elizabetha Graia / paulo post vxor eius / tum vero
vidua / fortunae perquam tenuis / at materno genere nobilitatis
magnae vetustaeque / paterno impari sed non obscuro. Ipsa
quum in aula versaretur Henrici / Reginae obsequens nupserat
15   Graio / eleganti quidem ac strenuo sed honesto magis quam claro
diuitive / nempe nullo adhuc pacis bellive gradu insigni. Sed eum
Henricus postea prelium initurus aduersus Eduardum equitem
fecerat / quo ille honore haud biduum gauisus / eodem in prelio
occubuit. Ergo vxor eius vt dixi amisso viro / Henrico victo capto-
20   que / ipsa bonis reiecta / relatis videlicet in Eduardi fiscum quod
maritus eius ab aduersa parte steterat cedideratque (vtrobique vt
victi vocantur [240] proditores) / habitu miserabili ac aduoluta
pedibus Eduardi supplicium porrigit: tum in se conuersum ac
restitantem videns audituro similem / causam verbis proponit
25   atque addit preces vti predia quaedam haud magni census ob

---

1 viderentur /] viderentur *P*   1–2 offenderetur.] offenderetur *P*   3 volebat:] volebat / *P*   4 reuictam] *interl. P;* reiectamque] *P A 1565,* atque antiquatam *P*sa   5
reuocarit] *P*sa *A,* pretexuit *P 1565;* quaedam] quedam *P*   7 Varuici /] Varuici *P*   8
potentem] potentem, *P*   9 cuiquam /] cuiquam, *P*   10 capienda] *P,* copulanda *P*sa *A*
11 Graia /] Graia *P;* eius /] eius *P*   12–13 fortunae . . . magnae vetustaeque] fortune . . . magne vetusteque *P*   12 tenuis /] tenuis *P;* at] *A 1565,* et *P*   13 obscuro.]
obscuro *P*   14 versaretur] *P A*s *1565,* versabatur *A;* Henrici /] Henrici, *P;* Reginae]
Regine *P*   16 diuitive /] diuiti ve *P;* bellive] belli ve *P;* insigni.] insigni *P*
17–18 equitem fecerat] *P*sa *A 1565,* ad equm rescripserat *P (cf. Livy 9.10)*   18 biduum]
⟨dubium⟩ biduum *P;* gauisus /] gauisus *P*   19 victo] victo / *P*   20 reiecta /] reiecta *P*
21–22 cedideratque (vtrobique . . . proditores) /] cedideratque / vtrobique . . . proditores
P; vtrobique . . . proditores] *P A, om. 1557 1565*   22 proditores] *written twice, once as*
catchword in P; miserabili] *P,* lugubri *P*sa *A,* lugubri et miserabili *1565*
23 porrigit:] porrigit / *P;* conuersum] *P A*s *1565,* reiectum *P*s *A (cf. Terence, Andria*
136)   24 restitantem] restitantem / *P;* similem /] similem *P*   25 quaedam] quedam
P; haud magni census] *P 1565,* exigui redditus *P*sa, haud exigui redditus *A,* magni sensus
*A*s *(cf. such smal landes 1557)*

much was left unsaid, ostensibly to avoid any affront to the Protector's devotion to his mother. But he wanted the other suggestion about treating Edward's children as bastards to be presented directly and openly and to be stated as emphatically as possible; but in order to demonstrate clearly what a false, long-disproven and discredited slander he recalled for that purpose we will recapitulate certain earlier events from the time of Edward's marriage.

After deposing Henry and taking the throne, Edward sent the Earl of Warwick, a powerful lord unsurpassed for his martial renown and for popular favor, on an embassy to Spain to negotiate for Edward to be given the king of Spain's daughter as his queen. But in the meantime it happened that Edward was approached by Elizabeth Grey, who would soon be his wife but who then was a widow, a woman of very mean fortune but of lofty and ancient noble lineage on her mother's side, on her father's of less noble lineage but yet not obscure. While living in the court of Henry she obeyed the queen's wishes and married one Grey, a fashionable and energetic man but respectable without being distinguished or wealthy, since he did not yet possess any title whether civil or military. But afterwards Henry made him a knight on the eve of a battle, a distinction which he enjoyed barely two days before falling on that very battlefield. Consequently his wife, as I said, after the loss of her husband, the defeat and imprisonment of Henry, and the forfeiture of her own property (for it had been confiscated for Edward because her husband had stood and fallen with Edward's opponents, since on either side the losers are called traitors), went to Edward in mourning attire as a suppliant and threw herself down at his feet, and then when she perceived he had turned to her and stopped, seeming ready to listen, she explained her case verbally

[61/1]   nuptias ei pridem ab marito donata reddi sibi iuberet / neque
           enim / quae sua iam erant facta / vllo viri sui crimine cadere in
           commissum potuisse / vt modo detur crimen esse / apud quem
           sacramentum dixerat / in eius fide regis ad mortem vsque man-
     5   sisse / nec minus firmum / si fata seruassent incolumem / nouo
           regi victoria deciso iure futurum./
               Rex in loquentis vultu defixus animi presentiam cum tanta
           modestia [coniunctam] mirabatur / et orationi gratiam dupli-
           cante forma non misereri modo supplicem suam sed amare quo-
    10   que incipit et in presens placide respondens / bene sperare iubet /
           breui enim se de re cogniturum / sed paulo post reuocatam / de
           negotio pauca prefatus / facilem se ostentat fore modo illa sese
           non difficilem prebeat / quin vltro plura daturum si ea vicissim
           paululum ei quiddam gratifficaretur. Illa / quam diu per am-
    15   biguam Regis orationem licuit / dissimulare scire se quid ille
           vellet: interim respondere benigne et circumspecte omnia / nec
           absque honesti cautione promittere: sed vbi remotis ambagibus
           inhonesti appellata est / tum vero aperte resistere / verum sic
           temperato sermone / vt desiderium eius incenderet: quod vbi
    20   validius animaduertit accensum / quam vt facile posset extingui /
           modo infamiam / modo culpae [240v] conscientiam pretendens /
           orabat vti frustra niti desisteret: ipsam enim / vt longe abesset ab
           ea superbia qua dignam sese illius coniugio censeat / ita non adeo
           esse abiectam vt non maioris estimet sese quam cui per flagitium
    25   libido eius illuderet./ Regi haudquaquam ante sueto tam obsti-

---

1 ab] P A, a Ps 1565   1–2 iuberet / neque enim / quae] iuberet neque enim que P;
facta /] facta P   3 potuisse /] potuisse P; esse /] esse P   4 dixerat /] dixerat P   4–5
mansisse /] mansisse P   5 nec] P A 1565 but non would be neater; firmum /] firmum P;
incolumem /] incolumen P   7–8 cum tanta modestia coniunctam mirabatur] cum
tanta modestia mirabatur (contemplatur Psa) P, cum tanta modestia contemplata A, tanta
cum modestia coniunctam mirabatur 1565   8 orationi] P A, orationis 1565   10
respondens /] respondens P   11 reuocatam /] reuocatam P   12 prefatus /] prefatus
P   13 vltro] A 1565, vltra P   14 gratifficaretur. Illa /] gratifficaretur Illa P   15
licuit /] licuit P; dissimulare scire] A 1565, dissimulare P   16 vellet:] vellet P; omnia /]
omnia P   17 promittere:] promittere P   18 est /] est P   19 sermone /] sermone
P; incenderet] 1565, intenderet P A; incenderet:] intenderet P   20 accensum /] accensum P   21 infamiam /] infamiam P; modo culpae] 1565, mod culpe P A; pretendens /]
pretendens P   22 desisteret:] desisteret./ P; enim /] enim P   23 sese] se se P;
censeat /] censeat P   24 vt non maioris] P, quin pluris Ps A; sese] se se P   25
haudquaquam] haud quanquam P

and added a plea that by his command some estates which produced little income and which she had been given as a jointure
long before by her husband should be given back to her, since
what had already become her own property could not be rendered forfeit by any misdeed of her husband, even it were conceded that it was a crime to remain true until death to the king to
whom he had sworn fealty, whereas he would rightly have been
no less faithful to the new king if the fates had preserved him
until one had been chosen by a victory.

His eyes fixed on the face of the speaker, he admired such
great presence of mind complemented by such modesty, and as
her beauty doubled the charm of her speech he began not only to
pity his supplicant but to love her, as well. For the time being he
calmly replied she should hope for the best, for he would shortly
look into the matter, but before long he summoned her back,
opened with a few words about her petition, and then indicated
that he would be accommodating if she would, and that indeed
he would willingly give her even more if she would repay him
with one little kindness. As long as the king's ambivalent language permitted, she pretended not to know what he wanted,
answering everything politely and cautiously, promising to do
anything within the bounds of her honor. But when he proposi-
tioned her outright without mincing words for dishonor, only
then did she openly resist, and yet tempered her speech in a way
which inflamed his desire; and when she saw it was burning too
hot to be easily quenched, citing as her excuse now the scandal
and now guilty conscience, she begged him to stop urging in
vain, for though she was by no means so vain as to think herself
worthy of being his wife, neither was she so base that she thought
she deserved nothing better than to be made the plaything of his
wicked wantonness. To the king, who was not at all used to being

nate repelli / noua illa constantia fuit admirationi: quin tam
raram castitatem cum eximia venustate coniunctam maximarum
opum loco ponens / et amorem consulens suum / celeriter eam
ducere statuit: iamque certus facere / cum amicis consultat / sed
5 ita / facile vt scire possent / quisquis contra suasurus esset / operam esse lusurum: ergo futurum quod videbant / certatim
approbant./

[62/1]   Ceterum mater eius adeo rem egre tulit vt dissuadendo vix
temperaret iurgijs: honorificentius illum vtiliusque rebus con-
10 sulturum suis haud satis adhuc domi pacatis si externum sibi
regem affinitate conglutinet: inde non presidium tantum sta-
biliendo regno / sed augendae preterea ditionis spes. "Nam istud" inquit "coniugium / haudquaquam sane regium / fuerit vt si
quispiam paulo ditior ancillam depereat suam sibique adsciscat
15 in sociam / quod quoties accidit / etiam qui puellae gratulantur
irrident herum / quanquam haud ita longe supra conditionem
virginis quam huius humilitas viduae infra tuae maiestatis emi-
nentiam subsidit: in cuius corpore indoleve animi / vt nihil improbo / ita nihil tam eximium esse contenderem / idem vt non
20 alijs etiam supersit quae tibi multis preterea modis congruerent
magis./ Incommode certe iunguntur imparia / nec vnquam co-
alescunt [241] bene quae valde dissident. Manca sunt et imperfecta semper disparibus nata parentibus. Sustinere potes vt huic
florentissimo quod obtines regno progeneres ibridas ac de-
25 generes reges / et tuus sanguis Graij filijs vt fratres det? Certe si
illa te alioqui conueniret maxime / qua nunc nihil conuenit
minus / tamen sacrosanctam maiestatem principis / quem eque

1 repelli /] repelli P; admirationi:] admirationi P   2 coniunctam] P A 1565, raro (haud
sepe Ps²) coalescentem Ps¹   3 ponens /] ponens P; suum /] suum P   4 statuit:]
statuit P; consultat] P, deliberat Ps A 1565   4–5 consultat / sed ita /] consultat sed ita
P   5 scire] P A, sentire Ps; esset /] esset P   6 lusurum:] lusurum / P; videbant] P,
preuident Ps A; videbant /] videbant P   9 iurgijs:] iurgijs P   11 conglutinet:] conglutinet / P   12 regno /] regno P; augendae] augende P; spes.] spes P   13
coniugium /] coniugium P; haudquaquam] haudquanquam P; regium /] regium P
15 sociam /] sociam P; puellae] puelle P   17 viduae] vidue P; tuae] tue P   18
subsidit:] subsidit / P; animi /] animi P; vt] interl. P   18–19 improbo /] improbo P
19 contenderem /] contenderem P   20 quae] que P   21 imparia /] imparia P   23
disparibus nata parentibus] P 1565, disparium animalculorum faetus Ps A (cf. Aristotle,
De gen. an. 2.8); parentibus.] parentibus / P   25 reges] P A, regulos Ps As 1565   26
maxime /] maxime P; conuenit] 1565, venit P A   27 principis /] principis P

held off so stubbornly, that new constancy of hers appeared marvelous. Indeed, setting such chastity conjoined with such beauty on a par with the greatest of riches and letting his love guide his actions, he quickly decided to marry her, and with his mind already made up he consulted his friends. But the way that he did so made it very clear to them that anyone who opposed his decision would be wasting his time; and so, since they perceived that the marriage was inevitable, they vied in applauding it.

On the other hand, his mother was so bitterly opposed to the match that in trying to dissuade him she could scarcely refrain from abusiveness, saying that he would be making a more honorable and practical provision for his own domestic estate, which was still far from tranquil, if he would establish a marriage alliance with some foreign king, who would furnish not only protection to strengthen his throne but also a chance to enlarge his dominions. "For that marriage of yours, which could scarcely be called regal, would be as if some fairly prosperous fellow who doted on his serving-maid asked her to marry him; and whenever that happens, even those who are glad for the girl think the master ridiculous, although he is not nearly as far above the condition of the maiden as this widow's humble condition falls below the preeminence of your own majesty; and even though I see nothing wrong with her person or character, I would contend that there is nothing so special about them that you could not find even more of it in other women who would be better suited for you in many other ways. Unequal matches are certainly unhappy ones, nor do extreme opposites ever blend well together. The offspring of two unlike parents is always ill formed and defective. Can you bear to spawn mongrel, degenerate kings for this flourishing realm which you rule, or to have your own blood beget brothers for the children of Grey? Certainly even if she were suitable in other respects (and no one could actually be less suitable), I assuredly do not think that the sacrosanct majesty of a prince, who should rival a priest in purity

deceat sacerdotem puritate contingere ac dignitate proxime accedit / haud quaquam censeam statim primo coniugio indelebili
bigamiae labe polluendam. Quid quod tractando alibi matrimonio longius progressus es quam vnde regredi non inhoneste
5 queas / fortasse nec tuto quidem / quippe legato in id Varuici
Comite / totius regni tui secundum te potentissimo / qui ne frus-
trari labores suos et eludi quae firmauit indoleat / non satis es-
timare te video quam valde tuarum rerum interfuerit."

[63/1]   At Rex quanquam libenter optabat / quam ipse delegisset /
10 matri quoque probari / tamen vtvt illa rem caperet ipse propositi
sui firmus / multa serio quedam ioco respondit / vt qui solutum
sese materna tutela meminisset. "Tametsi matrimonium diuina
quaedam res" inquit "virtutis ergo contrahi / non opulentiae
debeat / Deo videlicet amorem fidemque mutuam inspirante
15 coniugibus / quod ego certe nobis contigisse confido / tamen hoc
meum coniugium si quis vel crasse estimet / vulgato more hominum sanctis vtilia preferentium / is ipse ni fallor inueniet illud
non tam vehementer incommodum. Nam ego [241v] certe nullius amorem populi potiorem duco mihi quam mei / cui haud
20 paulo chariorem ita me spero fore / si coniugium videar non
aspernari suum. Externorum vero necessitudines principum
quas maternus adfectus tuus potissimum censet ambiendas /
vnde nos malorum sepe flumen erupisse vidimus / tamen licebit
adiungere / minore cum damno meo / si qui meorum forte susti-
25 neant cum incognitis copulari./ Nam ipse certe nec ducere possum quam non amo / nec adamare quam non video / nec sat
consultum arbitror / futuri incrementi spe / quod promittunt

1–2 accedit /] accedit *P*   2 indelebili] *1565*, ⟨uidebili⟩ indelebili *P*, ineluibili *A*   3
bigamiae] bigamie *P*   5 queas /] queas *P;* Varuici] Varuice *P A*, Varnice *1565*   6
Comite /] Comite *P*   7 eludi] *A 1565, changed from* illudi *P;* quae] que *P;* indoleat /]
indoleat *P*   9 optabat /] optabat *P*   9–10 optabat . . . probari] *P A 1565* (propari *A*),
dilectum suum valde cupiebat approbare matrem *P*sa *A*s (probare *A,* matri *P*); *superscript
starts above* quam *in both mss.*   9 delegisset /] delegisset *P*   10 vtvt] *1565,* vt *P A;*
propositi] *P A,* animi sententiae *P*sa   11 firmus] *P A,* certus / constans / tenax *P*sa;
firmus /] firmus *P;* respondit /] respondit./ *P*   12 tutela] *P A,* curatione *P*s *1565;*
meminisset.] meminisset *P*   13 quaedam] quedam *P;* ergo] *interl. P;* contrahi /] contrahi *P;* opulentiae] opulentie *P*   15 coniugibus /] coniugibus *P;* confido /] confido *P*
16 crasse] *P A,* crassius *1565;* estimet /] estimet *P*   18 incommodum.] incommodum *P*
19 mei /] mei *P*   20 fore /] fore *P*   21 suum.] suum *P*   22 ambiendas /] ambiendas *P*   24 adiungere /] adiungere *P;* meo /] meo *P*   26 amo /] amo *P;* video /] video
P   27 arbitror /] arbitror *P*   27 spe /] spe *P*

just as he is almost his equal in dignity, ought to be tainted with the indelible blot of the twice-married condition from the moment he marries the first time. What of this, that you have already proceeded too far with marriage negotiations elsewhere to be able to back out with honor, perhaps even with safety, since your ambassador for that purpose is the Earl of Warwick, the most powerful man in your realm besides you; for I see that you fail to appreciate sufficiently how much in your interest it is to ensure he does not have to grieve to see his efforts wasted and the match he arranged made a mockery."

But though the king wished that his mother, too, would approve of the mate he had chosen, he was resolved to go through with it no matter how she reacted, and so he answered many points in earnest and several in jest, since he recalled he had outgrown his mother's authority as his guardian. "Holy sacrament that it is, marriage ought to be contracted in the interests of virtue, not wealth—when, that is, God inspires mutual love and fidelity in both partners, as I am sure that he has in our own case. And yet, even if someone applied even a crass standard to my marriage, joining most men in paying more attention to profit than to sanctity, unless I am mistaken even he will not find it to be so outrageously disadvantageous. For I certainly consider that no people's love matters more to me than the love of my own, and I hope it will endear me to them not a little when I seem not to be spurning a match with them. As for familial connections with foreign princes, which your motherly affection represents as supremely desirable, but which we have seen often give rise to a torrent of troubles, they can still be established, with less hardship for me, if it happens that some of my kinsmen can bear to be wedded to strangers. For I for one can neither marry a woman without loving her, nor love her without seeing her, nor do I think it very judicious to be induced by the hope of future gain (something promised more often than furnished by these for-

quam prestant sepius externa matrimonia / presentium bonorum fructum corrumpere / quorum quis esse sensus potest
eam habenti perpetuam vitae sociam / quam non libenter videat?
Quin accedere mihi vxoris nomine in vlteriore ditione nouos
5   titulos ne velim quidem / quippe cui iam nunc eius generis tantum terrae marisque debetur quantum adserere fideliter tueri-
que satis nimirum vnicuipiam superque fuerit. At sunt vbique
nonnullae quae huic meae nulla dote cesserint / multis ex-
superant etiam. Istud ego neque hercle inficior / neque prohibeo
10 sane quo minus eas hi quibus sic videntur habeant: eoque contra /
iniurium est egre cuiquam esse / meo me quoque genio obsequi.
Nec Varuici Comitem / quem vel vtcunque animatum non tam
valde formido / tamen haud tam aduerso in me animo reor / id
illi vt doleat quod mihi sentit lubere / neque tam iniquum vt
15 postulet in delegenda coniuge eius me potius oculis regi quam
meis / perinde [242] ac pupillus adhuc sim cui requiratur tutoris
[64/1]   authoritas: quin disperearm ni priuatus esse liber quam rex hac
seruitute vellem / vxor vt inuito mihi alieno arbitratu
obtruderetur. Iam bigamiae labes illa quam tu / charissima
20 mater / inuadis / non me tam multum valde territat: objiciat hanc
mihi patiar pontificulus ambienti forte sacerdotium / nam ad-
ministrando (quantum memini) regno non officit. Denique
quod habet ex priore matrimonio liberos / id ego per gratias
etiam in lucro pono: quin mihi quoque celebi adhuc non desunt
25 aliquot./ Ita mutuo probamentum dedimus nuptias nobis non
steriles fore. Quamobrem coniugium hoc quod ipse mihi superis

1 matrimonia /] matrimonia *P*   3 vitae sociam /] vite sociam *P;* videat] *P A,* aspiciat *P*ˢ
1565; videat?] videat *P*   5 velim] *P,* optem *P*ˢ¹, optarim *P*ˢ² *1565,* vellem *A*   6
terrae] terre *P;* quantum adserere] *A,* quantum adferre *1565,* quantum *P*   8
nonnullae quae huic meae] nonnulle que huic mee *P*   8–9 exsuperant] exuperant *P A*
1565   9 etiam.] etiam *P*   9 inficior /] inficior *P;* prohibeo] *P A 1565,* impedio
intercedo *P*ˢ   10 habeant] *P A,* accipiant ducant *P*ˢ, fruantur *1565;* habeant; eoque
contra /] habeant eoque contra *P*   11 esse /] esse *P;* obsequi.] obsequi / *P*   12
Varuici Comitem /] Varuici / comitem *P*   13 reor /] reor *P*   16 cui] *P,* cuius coniugio *P*ˢ *A 1565*   17 authoritas:] authoritas *P;* ni priuatus] *P A,* in priuatis *1565*   18
vellem] *P A 1565 but the sense calls for* mallem   19 obtruderetur.] obtruderetur *P;*
bigamiae] bigamie *P;* tu /] tu *P*   20 mater / inuadis /] mater inuadis *P;* multum valde] *P*
A, valde multum *1565* (valde *may be simply an alternative reading for* multum); territat:]
territat / *P*   21 sacerdotium /] sacerdotium *P*   22 (quantum memini)] quantum
memini *P;* officit.] officit *P*   23 liberos /] liberos *P;* gratias] gatias *P*   24 pono:]
pono *P*   26 steriles] *P A,* infecundas *P*ˢᵃ *1565;* fore.] fore / *P*

eign marriages) to spoil the enjoyment of one's present prosperity; for what sense of that can a man have who is mated for
life with a woman he cannot bear to look at? Indeed, I would not
even want any new titles in a distant domain to accrue to me in
my wife's name, since on those terms so much land and sea is
already supposed to belong to me that it would be more than
enough for any one ruler to claim and defend it all faithfully.
But there are some women everywhere who have every advantage that mine does and many others that she does not. On my
word, I am certainly not denying it, nor am I stopping anyone
who sees those women that way from marrying one of them, but
by the same token it is unjust for anyone to take it ill if I too suit
myself. As for the Earl of Warwick, I do not feel so very afraid of
him no matter how he is disposed, but I doubt that he feels so
completely at odds with me that he is bound to resent anything
that he knows gives me pleasure, and I doubt he is unfair enough
to demand that in choosing a wife I should be governed by his
eyes instead of my own, as if I were still a mere minor who
needed his guardian's authority; on my soul, I would rather be a
free private citizen than a king in a state of such servitude that a
wife should be forced on me at another's discretion without my
consent. Now, then, my darling mother, that blot of the twice-
married state you inveigh against does not have me particularly
terrified; I would willingly let some underprelate reproach me
with it if I ever aspire to the priesthood, for to the best of my
memory it is no obstacle to ruling a kingdom. Finally, as for her
having children from her previous marriage, by heaven I even
regard that as a gain; indeed, I too have several without ever
having been married. In this way we have both furnished proof
that our marriage will not be a barren one. And so, my sweet

aspirantibus delegi / tu quoque / dulcissima genitrix / approba /
idemque nobis vt feliciter cedat faustis comprecationibus tuis
adiuua / quae si pergas in presens aduersari / nascetur hinc breui
nepotulus tibi qui nobis te blandicijs suis conciliet tamen."

5   Mater vbi regis animum vidit inflexibilem / ipsa contra offirmatior / nec ita perinde iam humilitate nurus ac dolore spreti
consilij sui succensa / nouam ingreditur viam ad disturbandas
nuptias. Erat Elizabetha quaedam gentilicio nomine Lucia /
puella nec ignobilis et perquam pulchra. Eam forte virginem
10   Rex deuirginauerat. Igitur vbi nuptiarum appetebat dies / et pro
more populus admoneretur ne / si quis obicem sciret / eludi
sacramentum pateretur / mater eius / velut exsolutura sese pol-
lutorum religione sacrorum / defert Luciam filio vere vxorem
esse / data fide et firmata concubitu. Igitur seu non [242v] ausis
15   progredi pontificibus siue nolente Rege nuptias suas aduerso
rumore conspergi cui materna pietas authoritatem pondusque
tribueret / interea restitum est quoad cognita re falsitas eius
famae reuinceretur. Accersita Lucia / quanquam occultis subor-
nata et subnixa consilijs / ostentata spe vxorem se Regi fore modo
[65/1] 20   fidem datam adsereret / tamen vbi semel adiurata est vera dicturam / fatetur nullo coniugij promisso obstrictum Regem /
ceterum amoris prae se tulisse tantum vt ipsa suum obsequium
sperauerit consecuturas nuptias: alioqui nunquam fuisse con-
cubitum eius passuram. Comperta ergo et denunciata falsitate
25   commenti matrimonij / eluto demum eo scrupulo / Elizabetham

---

1 delegi /] delegi P; quoque /] quoque P; genitrix /] genitrix P   3 adiuua] P A, adnitere
Ps As 1565; quae] que P; aduersari /] aduersari P   4 tamen.] tamen / P   5–6
offirmatior] P, obfirmat sese Pa (in margin), A, fit obstinatior 1565; offirmatior /]
offirmatior P   6–7 nec . . . succensa] P A, ac dolore spreti consilij sui magis succensa
1565   6 nurus] P, mirus A; spreti] A 1565, sperni P   7 succensa /] succensa P   8
nuptias.] nuptias P; quaedam] quedam P; gentilicio] A, gentilico P 1565; Lucia /] Lucia
P   9 perquam pulchra] P, egregia forma Ps A 1565; pulchra.] pulchra P   10
deuirginauerat] P A, corrupit 1565; deuirginauerat.] deuirginauerat P   11 ne /] ne P;
sciret /] sciret P   12 pateretur /] pateretur. P; eius /] eius P   13 sacrorum /] sacrorum P   14 concubitu.] concubitu P   16 conspergi] conspergi / P   17 quoad] quo
ad P; falsitas] falcitas P   18 famae] fame P; Lucia /] Lucia P   19 consilijs /] consilijs
P   20 adsereret] P, constanter affirmet Ps A 1565; adsereret /] adsereret P; adiurata]
ad iurata P   20–21 dicturam /] dicturam P   21 Regem /] Regem P   22 prae] pre
P   23 nuptias:] nuptias P   25 commenti] P A 1565, putati Ps; matrimonij /] matrimonij P; scrupulo /] scrupulo P

parent, give your approval for this marriage on which I have settled with heaven's encouragement, and help us with your auspicious prayers for a prosperous future. But even if you continue opposing it now, a little grandson will be born to you before long whose endearments will win you over anyway."

When his mother saw that the king's mind was made up, she herself grew more obstinate, angered now not so much by the lowly estate of her daughter-in-law as by her resentment at having her counsel disregarded, and began a new scheme for disrupting the marriage. There was a certain Elizabeth, surnamed Lucy, a girl not ignoble and remarkably beautiful. As it happened, the king had divested that maiden of her maidenhead. And so when the day of the wedding approached and according to custom the people were told that if they knew of any impediment they should not let the sacrament be made a mockery, his mother came forward, as if to disburden herself of her scruples against dishonoring the sacrament, and reported that Lucy was his son's true wife, since they had plighted their troth and confirmed it by intercourse. At that point, whether the bishops did not dare to proceed or the king did not want his marriage to be tainted by a sinister rumor which gained weight and authority from his mother's piety, matters came to a halt until the case was examined and the falsity of that rumor was proven. Lucy was summoned and, although she had been both suborned and encouraged in secret discussions with the hope of becoming the king's consort if she would assert he had plighted his troth, nevertheless she had no sooner sworn to tell the truth than she confessed that the king had been bound by no promise of marriage but that he had displayed so much love that she thought that their marriage would follow her yielding; otherwise she would never have consented to sleep with him. Once the falsity of the fictitious marriage had been confirmed and proclaimed and that scruple was finally eliminated, the king wedded Elizabeth Grey and took her as his queen who was lately the wife of

Graiam ducit Rex / sibique in reginam sociat hostis paulo prius
uxorem / quae vota sepe contra eius salutem fecerat / charior
superis quam vt malo exaudiretur suo./

    Sed Comes Varuici reuersus adeo egre tulit illusam lega-
5 tionem suam / vt coacta manu Regem in exilium expulerit / e
carcere restituto in regem Henrico / quem Eduardus ipsius ope
Varuici deposuerat. Tantus ille vir fuit et reliquis opibus et
populari gratia vt a qua parte staret is / in eam regnum vergeret /
potens et sibi sumere nisi honorificentius duxisset reges facere
10 quam regnare. Sed immodica potentia raro perpetua: siquidem
Eduardus / quum biennium abfuisset / Regina interea in asylo
memorato enixa Principem / haudquaquam pari manu cum
[66/3]   Varuico congressus apud Bernettum decem ab Londino milibus / capto rursus Henrico / Comiteque magna vtriusque [243]
15 strage partis occiso / regnum in sua domo sic constabiliuit vt
concuti nisi domestico dissidio et intestina fraude non posset./

    Hec vt fors narrata verbosius / ita pretermitti prorsus haud
decuerat / ne Protector ignoraretur / Eduardi filijs natalium
vicium obiecturus / nihil reperisse quod illius matrimonio im-
20 pingeret preter excussam olim et antiquatam calumniam./
Ceterum id commentum / vtvt frigidum / illi placuit cui satis erat
tantum aliquid dici / nimirum securo certoque probationes ab se
non exigendas./ Igitur postquam initium insinuandae populo
rei Shao decretum est / hactenus vt Eduardo fratreque eius Clar-
25 entiae totaque Eduardi sobole spurijs declaratis Protectoris ad
regnum ius ostenderet / taceret voluntatem / is e suggestu do-

---

1 Rex /] Rex P   2 quae] que P   4 Sed] *New para.* P   5 expulerit /] expulerit P
6 Henrico /] Henrico P   8 a qua parte staret] P, ab vtra parte stetisset P^{sa} A *1565* (ab
om. A); is /] is P; regnum] P A, nimirum corona sceptra P^{sa}, nimirum regni gubernacula
1565; vergeret] P A, ent (*meant to be combined with the* verger *of* vergeret) P^{sa}, inclinarent
1565; vergeret /] vergeret P   9 nisi honorificentius] P A *1565,* si non in rem magis
superbam P^{sa} 10 perpetua:] perpetua / P   11 Eduardus /] Eduardus P   12
Principem] P A *1565,* filium P^s; Principem /] Principem P; haudquaquam] haud quanquam P   17 verbosius /] verbosius P   18 ignoraretur /] ignoraretur P   19
obiecturus /] obiecturus P   21 commentum / vtvt frigidum /] commentum vtvt frigidum P   22–23 ab se non exigendas] P^{sa} A *1565,* non exigendum se P (*for such
constructions see Aulus Gellius 15.14)*   23 insinuandae] insinuande P   24 est /] est
P   24–25 Clarentiae] Clarentie P   26 ostenderet /] ostenderet P; voluntatem /]
voluntatem P

his enemy and had frequently prayed for his downfall; she was too dear to heaven for her prayers to be granted against her best interests.

But upon his return the Earl of Warwick was so angry about having his mission made pointless that he gathered an army and drove the king into exile, returning Henry from prison to the throne although Edward had had Warwick's help in deposing him. That man was so mighty in other resources and in popular favor that the crown leaned to whichever side he stood on; he was powerful enough to have claimed it himself if he had not considered it more honorable to make kings than to be one. But extreme power is rarely long-lasting; for after an absence of two years during which the queen, as we have mentioned, gave birth to the prince in the sanctuary, Edward leading a much smaller army met Warwick at Barnet ten miles outside London, recapturing Henry and killing the earl with great losses on both sides, and thus settled the throne in his house so securely that it could not be shaken except by domestic dissension and internal treachery.

Though this account of those happenings may have been overly wordy, it would certainly not have been right to pass over them completely, thus leaving it unclear that when the Protector was preparing to charge Edward's children with bastardy he could find no other grounds for impeaching his marriage but a long-exposed and outdated slander. But that fiction, however incompetent, was quite good enough for a man content merely to say something, since he knew very well that he would not be required to give any proof of it. And so after Shaw was assigned the initial move in presenting the matter tactfully to the people—he was to go so far as to declare Edward, his brother Clarence, and all Edward's offspring to be bastards and then to indicate the Protector's right to the throne without mentioning his

minico die proximo ad aedem Pauli / frequentissimo auditorio
quod eius fama viri contraxerat / hoc themate sermonem exor-
sus est: "Spuria vitulamina non agent radices altas." Inde prefatus infundi atque inspirari semper contracto rite matrimonio
5 propriam quandam et peculiarem gratiam quae in sobolem
sancte conceptam deriuetur / qua plerumque deficerentur hi qui
vago vel adulterino concubitu nati parentium crimen prauitate
sua testentur et infelicitate castigent / vsque adeo vt si qui mater-
[67/1]   na fraude celato originis vicio / supplantatis veris heredibus /
10 alieni patris fortunas inuaserit atque occuparit ad tempus / ita
tamen / rem disponente Deo / erumpente breui aliqua rima veritate / restitui legitimos successores et genuinos reddi suae terrae
surculos deprehenso ac reuulso vitulamine spurio priusquam
altius agat radices / [243v] hec vbi vetustis aliquot confirmasset
15 exemplis / protinus in laudes diuertit Richardi nuper Eboraci
Ducis / obiter eum sepe vocans patrem Protectoris: tum admoni-
to populo successionem regni perpetuam / senatus consulto ac
scito plebis / eius vnius deinceps stirpi decretam / ostendit Eduardum contra ius ac fas Reginae copulatum / superstite Lucia vera
20 eius et indubitata coniuge / etenim contracto cum ea virgine
matrimonio / tum suscepta etiam sobole confirmato / superue-
nientis forma viduae transuersum actum / fidem post voluptatem habuisse: sic nullum eius sobolem regni capacem esse.
Hunc locum egit magna contentione non signis modo et suspi-
25 cionibus sed nominatis etiam falso testibus. Addit non ignarum
se quanto cum periculo dicat / sed ex eo loco loquentibus in quo

---

1 Pauli /] Pauli *P*   2 contraxerat] *P 1565*, consciuerat *Ps A;* contraxerat /] contraxerat.
P   3 est:] est. *P*   5 quae] que *P*   8 testentur] *corr. from* detestantur *P;* et infelicitate castigent] *om.* 1565; castigent] *P A*, vlciscantur puniant *Psa*; castigent /] castigent *P*
9 vicio /] vicio *P;* heredibus] *1565*, heres *P*, herus *A;* heredibus /] heres *P*   11 tamen] tñ
P A, tum *1565*   11–12 veritate /] veritate *P*   11–13 veritate / restitui legitimos
successores et . . . surculos] *1565*, veritate et . . . surculos *P A*, restitui legitimos successores *Psa*   12 genuinos] *P*, geminos *A 1565;* suae terrae] sue terre *P*   14 radices /] radices *P*   15 exemplis /] exemplis *P;* diuertit] *P A 1565*, descendit, erupit *Psa*;
Richardi] *1565*, .R. *P*, R *A*   16 Ducis /] Ducis *P;* sepe] *P A*, subinde *Ps 1565;*
Protectoris:] Protectoris / *P*   17 perpetuam /] perpetuam *P*   18 plebis /] plebis *P;*
decretam / ostendit] decretam ostendit. *P*   19 Reginae] Regine *P*   21 matrimonio /]
matrimonio *P;* confirmato] *P*, firmato absoluto *Psa*, consummato *A 1565;* confirmato /]
confirmato *P*   22 transuersum actum] *P A 1565*, correptum *Ps*; actum /] actum *P*
23 habuisse:] habuisse / *P*   24 magna] *1565*, magnaque *P A where a word may have been
overlooked, e.g.,* [multa] magnaque

wish for it—from the pulpit of St. Paul's on the following Sunday, before a great audience attracted by his reputation, Shaw introduced a sermon with the following text: "Bastard slips shall never take deep root." Then he opened by saying that rightly contracted marriages are always imbued and inspired with a certain characteristic and singular grace which is passed on to legitimate offspring but is generally lacking in those born of promiscuous or adulterous unions, who attest to their parents' crime by their perversity and punish it by their ill fortune, to the point that if a mother lies and hides the illicit origin of her offspring, and if he supplants the true heirs and temporarily appropriates the fortune of someone else's father, even so, by divine dispensation, the truth soon finds some outlet, the legitimate heirs are restored, and the genuine shoots are returned to their soil, while the bastard slip is discovered and torn up before it takes deep root; after supporting these statements with various ancient examples, he immediately turned away into a eulogy of Richard, the late Duke of York, often casually calling him the father of the Protector; then, reminding the people that by parliamentary decree and by the will of the people the succession to the throne had been settled in perpetuity exclusively on the Duke of York's line, he said that Edward's union with the queen was unlawful and impious, since Lucy, his true and unquestionable spouse, was still living; for after contracting a marriage with that maiden and even confirming it by begetting a child, he was seduced by the beauty of a widow who happened on the scene and brought him to put pleasure before fealty; thus none of his children were eligible for the throne. He elaborated this topic with great assertiveness, not only with probable signs and suspicions but also with falsely named witnesses. He added that he was not unaware of how dangerous it was for him to be giving that

ipse stabat veritatem habendam vita quoque ipsa potiorem: sibi
Iohannem Baptistam authorem esse contempnendae necis dum
illicita regum coniugia redarguat: nec tamen admodum mirari
se Eduardo nihil habitum pensi / rectos aut spurios relinqueret /
5 quippe nec ipsum nec fratrem item eius Clarentiae Ducem satis
certo habitos patre / vt qui notos quosdam ac notatos homines e
familiaribus Eboraci Ducis magis representarent quam ipsum
Ducem: a cuius etiam generosa indole dicebat Eduardum longe
degenerasse: ceterum Protectorem / virum omnium quos sus-
10 tineret terra clarissimum / non vita modo sed vultu quoque ipso
patrem referre. "Hic est" inquit "vnus atque vnicus Eboraci
Ducis verus et indubitatus filius / hec illius viri nota facies / hec
certa forma atque ipsa charissimi Ducis pectoribus adhuc vestris
[244] obuersantis effigies."
15   Sed antea iam conuenerat vt dum hec verba dicebantur / Pro-

tector offerret sese: ita tali oratione cum superuentu ipsius competente / fore vt putetur eam concionator haud humano consilio
sed diuino quopiam adflatus numine protulisse / tum vt ea re
permotus populus Ricardum regem illicet inclamaret: sic visum
20 iri posteris diuinitus in regem illum quasique miraculo delec-
tum. Verum id consilium siue negligentia Protectoris siue nimia
concionatoris diligentia corruptum ridicule vertit. Nam dum
vterque metuit ne superuentus eius illa verba / in quae debebat
incidere / preueniret / altero moras in via nectente / alter ita
25 dicendo festinauerat vt eo loco toto perorato in alias res neque
similes neque adfines ei descendisset quum iam Protector intraret. At concionator vbi conspicatur ingressum / relicta ea re

---

1 potiorem:] potiorem *P*   2 contempnendae] contempnende *P*   3 redarguat:] redarguat *P;* tamen] *changed to* tum *P,* tum *A 1565*   4 pensi] *1565,* pense *P A;* pensi /]
pense *P;* spurios] *P A 1565,* vernas *P*s   5 Clarentiae] Clarentie *P*   8 Ducem:]
Ducem *P*   8–9 a . . . degenerasse] *inserted in margin P*   9 degenerasse:] degenerasse / *P;* Protectorem /] Protectorem *P*   10 clarissimum /] clarissimum *P*   12 filius /]
filius *P*   14 effigies.] effiges *P*   15 dicebantur /] dicebantur *P*   16 sese:] sese *P*
16–17 competente /] competente *P*   18 adflatus] ⟨afflatu⟩ adflatus *P;* numine] *A*
1565, minime *P;* protulisse] *P 1565,* reddidisse *P*s *A;* protulisse /] protulisse *P*   19
inclamaret] inclamare⟨n⟩t *P,* inclamarent *A,* ingeminare⟨n⟩t *P*sa, ingeminaret *1565;*
inclamaret:] inclamaret *P*   22 vertit.] vertit *P*   23 verba /] verba *P;* quae] que *P*
24 incidere /] incidere *P;* preueniret /] preueniret *P;* nectente /] nectente *P*   26
descendisset] descenderat *P A,* descenderit *1565*   26–27 intraret.] intraret *P*   27
ingressum /] ingressum *P;* ea] *interl. P*

speech, but for people speaking from the place where he stood truth should be held to be more important than even life itself; he had a model in John the Baptist for scorning death while condemning the unlawful marriages of kings. Nor yet did he feel at all surprised that Edward did not care whether he left legitimate children or bastards, since neither he nor his brother the Duke of Clarence was considered to be of entirely sure paternity; for they bore a closer resemblance to certain known and notorious dependents of the Duke of York than they did to the duke himself. He also said that Edward's degeneracy was a far cry from the duke's noble nature, but that the Protector, the most splendid man on the face of the earth, recalled his father not only in his mode of living but even in his very appearance. "Here," he said, "is the one and only true and indubitable son of the Duke of York; here is that man's well-known face; here is the definitive figure and the very image of that dearest duke who still lives in your hearts."

But it had been agreed previously that while these words were being spoken the Protector would make his appearance, so that the concurrence of that sort of speech with his arrival would make the audience think that the preacher had delivered it not through any human device but rather by some sort of divine inspiration, the people would be moved by that thought to acclaim Richard king then and there, and thus it would appear to posterity that he had been chosen by divine guidance and almost by a miracle. But that plan went ridiculously awry, whether by the negligence of the Protector or the excessive diligence of the preacher; for while both feared that the Protector's arrival would anticipate those words of the preacher on which he was intended to enter, he dawdled en route while the preacher spoke so quickly that he had finished with the topic completely and moved on to other matters which had nothing to do with it by the time the Protector finally entered. But on seeing him enter, the preacher abandoned the subject at hand, and abruptly, as if he

quam tum habebat in manibus / repente velut attonitus / nullo
ductu ordineve sed ineptissimo recursu / illa verba repetit denuo: "Hic est vnus atque vnicus Eboraci Ducis verus et indubitatus filius" et quae sequuntur / inter quae verba Protector

5 commitante Bukyngamiae Duce ad locum in quo reliquum sermonem audiret per medium incedebat populum. Sed illi tam
longe aberant ab inclamando in regem illo vt propemodum versi
in saxa viderentur stupore tam pudendae concionis: cuius author postea / quum amicum quendam rogasset quidnam de se

10 sentirent ac loquerentur homines / quanquam satis e sua conscientia intelligebat nihil boni / tamen vbi omnia sinistra accepit /
ita perculsus est vt paucis post diebus moerore contabuerit.

    Sed quoniam quod tam aperte iam ceptum erat vrgendum

[69/1] videbatur / vno tantum die post eum sermonem interposito

15 Bukyngamiae [244v] Dux nobilium atque equitum non exiguo
comitatu / plurium fortasse quam quid afferrent scirent / Londini in forum venit / locum et elegantem et maximae turbae capacem: tum conuocato in curiam populo Dux ex editiore loco /
septus nobilibus et senatu Londinensi / paulum promouens sese /

20 vt erat neque prorsus illiteratus et suapte natura facundus / huiuscemodi verba fertur habuisse./

    "Amor vestri / viri Londinenses / effecit vti nos (quales enim
sumus cognoscitis) huc veniamus ad vos de re in primis magna
relaturi / nec magis magna quam in publicum vtili / neque cui-

25 quam vtiliore quam vobis. Etenim quam rem diu maximis votis
optastis / quam longe petituri magnoque redempturi fueritis /

1 habebat in manibus] P A, tractabat Psa¹, tractare ceperat Psa² 1565; manibus] P A, ore
Ps; attonitus /] attonitus P   2 recursu /] recursu P   2–3 denuo:] denuo. P   4
quae . . . quae] que . . . que P   5 Bukyngamiae] Bukyngamie P; in quo] ⟨vbi⟩ in quo A
8 pudendae concionis:] pudende concionis P   9 postea /] postea P; quidnam] quid
nam P   10 homines /] homines P   11 tamen] tñ A, tum P 1565; accepit /] accepit P
12 contabuerit.] contabuerit / P   14 videbatur /] videbatur P   16 comitatu /]
comitatu P; afferrent] A, afferret⟨ur⟩ P, ageretur 1565; scirent] P A, sciretur 1565;
scirent /] scirent P   17 forum] P, curiam Ps A 1565   17–18 maximae turbae capacem /] maxime turbe capacem: P   19 promouens] A 1565, permouens P; sese /] sese
P   20 facundus /] facundus P   22 Amor] New para. P; vestri / viri Londinenses /]
vestri viri Londinenses P   22–23 (quales . . . cognoscitis)] quales . . . cognoscitis P A
1565, qualescunque sumus Psa   23 huc] ⟨ve⟩ huc P; veniamus] P A, veniremus Ps
1565   24 in publicum] P A, omnibus Ps 1565   25 vobis.] vobis / P   26 optastis /]
optastis P; fueritis /] fueritis P

were stupefied, with no preparation or orderly transition but rather in an utterly tactless reversal, he repeated the words, "Here is the one and only true and indubitable son of the Duke of York," and so on; and at these words the Protector, accompanied by the Duke of Buckingham, went to his place through the midst of the people to hear out the sermon. But they were so far from acclaiming him king that they seemed almost petrified with amazement at so shameful a sermon. Later on, when its author asked a friend what people thought of it and were saying about it, though his own conscience told him to expect nothing good, when he heard nothing but bad it distressed him so terribly that he pined away from grief a few days later.

But since it seemed best to push forward with what they had so obviously begun, allowing an interval of only one day after that sermon, the Duke of Buckingham came with a sizable escort of noblemen and knights—more, perhaps, than knew what they were there to deliver—to the great forum in London, an elegant place which is spacious enough for huge crowds, and then when the people had been summoned into the hall, the duke, who was standing on a platform surrounded by nobles and the aldermen of London, stepped forward a bit, and being a man not completely unlearned and naturally eloquent, he is reported to have spoken words such as these:

"Citizens of London, you know who we are; it is our love for you which has brought us here to address you concerning a matter of the utmost importance, no less advantageous for the public than it is important, and no more advantageous for anyone than it is for you. It is something you have long hoped and prayed for intently, something for which you would go to great lengths and pay large sums of money, and now we are bringing it

eam nunc vltro vobis nos afferimus / nullo discrimine vestro /
labore nullo / nec vllo prorsus impendio. Queritis ea quae sit?
Corporum certe vestrorum securitas / vxorum filiarumque inop-
pugnata pudicicia / bonaque vestra certa vobis atque ab insidijs
5   tuta: quorum omnium quid iam diu fuit quod vocare suum quisquam certo poterat / tot intentatis laqueis atque exstructis exci-
pulis / exactis preterea tam multis magnisque nullo non anno
tributis / quorum ne tum quidem finis erat etiam cum opus non
erat? Quod ipsum cum luxu magis prodigendoque euenit quam
10   bona aliqua atque honesta causa. Sic bonis indies abradebatur vt
effunderetur in improbos: quae calamitas eo processerat / vt iam
ne consuetae quidem tributorum formae sufficerent / sed bene-

[70/1]   uolentiae placidum ac mite nomen meris rapinis obtendebatur.
Nam questores a quoque non quantum ille sponte sua dedisset
15   sed quantum ipsis collibuisset auferebant / tanquam populus in
concedendo tributo vocabulum beneuolentiae ad [245] ipsius
voluntatem Regis non ad suam cuiusque bonam retulisset. At ille
nunquam mediocre contentus / omnem corradendi pretextum
ad summum vsque auxerat. Itaque delicta non sua vi sed diuitijs
20   peccantis estimata sunt: sic minimis quibusque offensis maximae
indictae mulctae: quin linguae lapsus interdum totis locupletum
fortunis redimebatur / aut quo res irae [magis] quam auaritiae

---

2 impendio.] impendio / P; quae] que P   4 pudicicia /] pudicicia P   5 tuta:] tuta P
5–6 quid . . . poterat] P A 1565, quid iam diu fuit cuius non ambigua fuit possessio in
margin Pa   5–6 quisquam certo] P 1565, quisquam A   6 poterat] P A 1565, potuit /
posset Psa   6 exstructis] extructis P A 1565   6–7 excipulis] P A, decipulis 1565
8 tributis /] tributis P   8–10 erat etiam . . . causa. Sic] P A, erat, cum nec regi qua de re
exigeret causa, vel populo vnde exolueret facultatum quicquam relictum esset. Sic 1565
9 erat?] erat / P   10 causa.] causa P   11 effunderetur] P A 1565, prodideretur (for
perdideretur?) Ps; improbos:] improbos / P; calamitas] P A 1565, res Ps; processerat /]
processerat P   12 consuetae . . . formae] consuete . . . forme P   12–13 beneuolen-
tiae] beneuolentie P   13 obtendebatur] P A, obtrudebatur 1565   15 auferebant /]
auferebant P   16 beneuolentiae] beneuolentie P   17 non ad suam] written twice,
once as catchwords in A; retulisset.] retulisset P   18 contentus /] contentus P   19
auxerat] P A, intenderat Ps 1565; auxerat.] auxerat P; diuitijs] P A, opibus Ps1 1565,
facultate Ps2   20 sunt:] sunt P; maximae] maxime P   21 indictae mulctae . . . lin-
guae] indicte mulcte . . . lingue P; mulctae:] mulcte P   22 redimebatur /] redimebatur
P; irae magis] 1565 irae P A; auaritiae] 1565, auratie P, aueritie A

to you for free, with no risk on your part, no effort, and absolutely no cost. Do you ask what it is? Why, the safety of your
persons, the inviolate chastity of your wives and daughters, and
the assurance that your property is protected against trickery;
for what part of his property could any man long since call truly
his own, what with all the pitfalls and traps which were laid for it,
and the many great taxes exacted each year, of which there was
no end even when there was no need? And what need there was
stemmed more from luxury and extravagance than from any
good cause. Thus more was extorted from good men day after
day to be thrown away on scoundrels; and this disaster had
gotten so bad that not even the standard forms of taxation were
sufficient any longer, but the bland, harmless-sounding term
'benevolence' was used to cloak pure highway robbery. For the
tax agents took not the sum that each person would willingly
have given but the sum that they wanted to take, as if the people
in granting that tax had intended 'benevolence' to refer to the
king's personal pleasure and not to each citizen's goodwill. But
never content with a moderate sum, he exploited every excuse
for extortion to the limit. And so crimes were assessed not according to their seriousness but according to the wealth of the
offender. Thus immense fines were levied for petty offenses;
indeed, sometimes a slip of the tongue cost the whole fortunes of
rich men, or else earned them the death penalty and, so as to
make the motive seem to be anger rather than greed, an act

data videretur / luebatur morte / dum rei neutiquam de se
letiferae pretenditur lesae maiestatis atrox nomen.

"Quarum rerum nemo est (opinor) vestrum a me qui exempla
exigat / tanquam vobis Burdeti nomen exciderit / hominis op-
5 timi / atque ob solum verbum quod inter pocula temere exciderat / trucidati crudeliter / abusu legum in libidinem Principis /
non minore Markami gloria / qui iudicum primus quum esset /
adempto ob idipsum magistratu / restitit / quam eterno illorum
dedecore iudicum qui restabant et / metu vel adulatione cor-
10 rupti / innocentem hominem ipsorum fidei religionique creditum praua legum deriuatione iugularent. Quid de Thoma Coco
loquar / equite ciueque vestro / sed qualem rarae ciuitates habent /
qui omnes apud vos honores et ordine rite consecutus est et
magnifice gessit: qui vestrum est aut tam rerum negligens om-
15 nium vt non cognouerit / aut tam obliuiosus vt non meminerit /
aut tam durus vt non ingemiscat eius viri damno / quid damnum
dico? calamitati / spolijs / atque ex tantis opibus non egestati
modo sed nuditati quoque / non aliam ob causam quam quod
eum amari contigit ab illis quibus Rex infensus erat?

20 "Sed quis finis erit si viritim recenseam / quum nemo sit ex hac
tanta frequentia qui non aut suorum periculo sit expertus / aut
suo / familias totas in vltimum [245v] discrimen adductas / causa
plerumque nulla / interdum humili coturnatis subnixa nomi-
[71/1] nibus? Quin nullum erat crimen tantum in cuius calumniam
25 deesse argumentum poterat. Nam cum Rex / preueniens legi-

---

1 videretur] *P A 1565*, videbatur *interl. subscript P*a; videretur /] videretur *P;* morte /]
morte· *P*   2 letiferae] letifere *P;* lesae maiestatis] *P A 1565* (lese *P*), proditionis *P*sa;
nomen.] nomen / *P*   3 (opinor)] opinor *P*   4 exigat /] exigat *P;* exciderit /] exciderit
P   4–5 hominis optimi] *corr. from* trucidati crudeliter *P;* optimi /] optimi *P*   5
solum] *P 1565*, ⟨soru⟩ vnum *A*, vnum *P*s   5–6 exciderat /] exciderat *P*   6 crudeliter /] crudeliter *P;* Principis /] Principis *P*   7 gloria /] gloria *P;* esset /] esset *P*   8
idipsum] *1565*, idipsum e *P A;* magistratu / restitit /] magistratu restitit *P*   9 et /] et *P*
9–10 corrupti /] corrupti *P*   10–11 creditum] *P A,* commissum *P*s *1565*   11 deriua-
tione] *P A,* interpretatione *1565;* iugularent] *P A 1565,* confoderent *P*s; iugularent.]
iugularent *P*   12 loquar /] loquar *P;* vestro /] vestro *P;* rarae] rare *P;* habent /] habent
P   13 omnes] *interl. P;* ordine] *P A,* ordines *1565*   14 gessit:] gessit *P*   15
meminerit] *P A 1565,* recordetur *P*s   16 ingemiscat] *P A 1565,* indoleat ingemuerit
*P*s   17 dico?] dico *P;* calamitati / spolijs /] calamitati spolijs *P*   18 quoque /] quoque
P   19 erat?] erat *P*   20 viritim] viritim ⟨reser⟩ *P;* recenseam /] recenseam *P*   21
expertus /] expertus *P*   22 adductas /] aductas *P*   23 nulla /] nulla *P*   23–24
nominibus?] nominibus. / *P*   25 argumentum] *P A,* pretextus color *P*s; poterat.] poterat *P;* Rex /] Rex *P;* preueniens] *P A 1565,* anticipato *P*s

which was by no means inherently a capital crime was alleged to
fall under the horrendous title of lèse majesté.

"I think none of you will press me for examples of such unjust
verdicts, as if Burdet's name had escaped you, an excellent man,
cruelly slain for one word which he carelessly let slip over a
drink, while the law was abused for the prince's wanton pleasure,
albeit no less to the glory of Markham, the chief judge, who
resisted the verdict and so lost his office, than to the eternal
disgrace of the remaining judges, who, corrupted by fear or
obsequiousness, slaughtered an innocent man by deliberately
twisting the law when his life depended on their honor and
integrity. Why do I even mention Sir Thomas Cook, your fellow
citizen, but a citizen the likes of whom few other cities can boast,
who duly obtained all your honorable offices one after the other,
and administered them splendidly? Is any of you so heedless that
he has not heard about, or so forgetful that he does not remember, or so heartless that he does not groan over the man's
loss—why do I say merely loss?—over his ruin, devastation, and
not only poverty but total destitution after being a man of such
wealth, all because, as it happened, he was dear to some people
the king hated?

"But will I ever finish if I mention each case by name, since
there is no one in this great assembly who does not know by his
own or his own friends' experience of whole families reduced to
the utmost extremity, frequently for no reason, sometimes for a
petty one bolstered with grand-sounding pretexts? In fact, no
crime was too great to furnish a pretext for false accusation. For
since the king anticipated the lawful inception of his reign, win-

timum regnandi tempus / sceptrum vendicaret bello / habendum
erat argumentum proditionis in diuite / cognatum / affinem /
necessarium / amicum / familiarem / vel notum fere cuiquam
vnquam fuisse quem Rex aliquando pro hoste habuerit / cui
5 diuersis temporibus aduersum plus quam dimidium populi fuit.
Hoc pacto dum bonis vestris tendebantur insidiae / corpora simul in periculum trahebantur / atque in pace hec / preter tot
erumnas bellicas: e quo quum velut e fonte malorum torrens
omnium promanat / nunquam tamen exundat infestior quam
10 sicvbi intestina seditione laboretur / nec id maiore cum pernicie
vsquam accidit gentium quam vbi semel exisset in hac nostra
Britania / neque in ea ipsa vel tam pertinacibus vnquam studijs
discordatum est neque acerbiosius certatum / neque tam longo
bello conflictatum / neque tam crebris prelijs neque tam cruentis
15 depugnatum est neque summa rerum prope in vltimam vnquam
perducta perniciem quam eius vnius principatu fuit / qui dum
init regnum / dum tuetur / dum eijcitur / dum redit ac recuperat
rursus / dum depulsores suos vlsciscitur / tantum sanguinis ex-
haustum est Angli quanto non olim stetit bis subiugata Gallia. Ita
20 populus imminutus aut oppressus est: nobilium procerum verum quota pars relicta? Denique alterius dum pecunia petebatur / alterius formidabatur potentia / neutra pars tuta aut
quieta fuit. Et quem non suspectabat ille cui [246] formidolosus
erat etiam frater / cui pepercisset qui germanum sustulit / aut
25 quis amare potuisset eum si istud potuit ne frater quidem?
    Iam quis hoc ferat / quod nemo tamen ignorat / vxorem Shori /

---

1 tempus /] temps *P;* bello /] bello *P*   3 familiarem /] familiarem *P*   4 habuerit /]
habuerit *P*   5 fuit.] fuit / *P*   6 tendebantur] *A 1565,* trudebantur *P;* insidiae] insidie
P   7 trahebantur] *P A,* veniebant *P*s *1565;* trahebantur /] trahebantur *P*   9
promanat /] promanat *P;* exundat] *corr. from* exundauit *P*   10 sicvbi] sic vbi *P;*
intestina] *P A,* ciuili *P*s; laboretur /] laboretur *P*   12 Britania /] Britania *P*   13
acerbiosius] *P A,* acerbius *1565 (the traditionally correct form);* certatum] *P A 1565,*
laboratum *P*s   14 conflictatum /] conflictatum *P*   15 prope] *perhaps we should read
tam prope*   17 init] ⟨inijt⟩ init *P;* eijcitur /] eijcitur *P*   18 rursus /] rursus *P*   18
vlciscitur /] vlciscitur *P*   18–19 exhaustum] exahaustum *P*   19 Gallia.] Gallia / *P*
20 est: nobilium procerum] est nobilium procerum / *P;* nobilium procerum] *P A,*
nobilium vero ac procerum *1565* (procerum *may be merely an alternative reading for*
nobilium)   21–22 petebatur /] petebatur *P*   22 potentia /] potentia *P*   23 fuit.]
fuit *P*   24 pepercisset] pepersisset *P;* sustulit /] sustulit *P*   25 quidem?] quidem
P   26 ferat /] ferat *P;* ignorat /] ignorat *P;* Shori /] Shori *P*

ning the scepter in battle, a pretext could be found for charging a rich man with treason if he had ever had a relative by blood or by marriage, a close associate, a friend, a member of his household, or virtually even a casual acquaintance whom the king ever saw as his enemy, though at various times more than half of the populace was against him. In this way, while traps were being laid for your property, your bodies were endangered as well; and all this was in peacetime, besides all your trials while he was at war. For though war, like a wellspring, gives rise to a torrent of all sorts of evil, this torrent is never more deadly than when a nation is suffering from internal strife, nor has it ever brought about more destruction in any nation than it did when it once broke out in this Britain of ours, nor in Britain itself was there ever such stubborn factional rivalry nor such bitter conflict nor such protracted warfare nor such numerous and bloody battles nor such near-universal and total destruction as there was in this one man's reign; for in winning his throne, in defending it, in being deposed, in returning to win it again, and in taking vengeance on those who deposed him, he spilled more English blood than it formerly cost us to conquer France twice. Thus the people were decimated or destroyed; and how little of the nobility has been left alive! Finally, while he coveted the money of the former and feared the power of the latter, neither element was safe or secure. And whom did he not suspect, since he was even afraid of his brother? Whom would he have spared, since he did his own brother to death? Or who could have loved him if not even his own brother could?

"And then, who can stand it—though everyone knows of it—

tam vile scortum / plus apud Principem quam omnes regni sui
nobiles valuisse plusque vnam in promouendis ambitam quam
proceres vniuersos / quin ex ipsis quosdam magnis in rebus suis
[72/1]   vsos meretriculae necessario magis quam honesto patrocinio?
5   Quanquam ea muliercula haud quaquam ferebatur impura /
quoad improba libido Principis viro eam suo abstulisset / ciuj
nimirum vestro neque inopi et indolis ac spei bonae. Ceterum
hac in re / de qua libentius in defuncti reuerentiam super-
sederem dicere nisi frustra taceretur quod omnes norunt / adeo
10 insatiabilis ardor inerat vt nulla pars morum eius minus ferenda
videretur. Neque enim vlla fuit vnquam neque tam humilis neque tam potens virgo / matrona / vidua in quam semel oculum
coniecisset quae modo forma / vultu / voce / gestu / denique vlla
dote placuisset ei / quam non ille statim / nullo dei metu / nulla
15 retardatus infamia / persequeretur / vrgeret / oprimeret / irre-
parabili damno multarum ipsarum / nec minore cum luctu et
dolore virorum / parentum / et quicquid cuique erat amicorum
reliqui / qui cum suapte sint honesti / tam charam habent vxorum
castitatem honestatemque familiae vt talem contumeliam non
20 illatam quauis libenter velint suarum fortunarum iactura
decidere.

"At licet his atque alijs talibus / vndique regnum mire premebatur / vos tamen semper precipue / ciues urbis huius / cum

1 scortum /] scortum P   2 plusque] plus que P   2–3 plusque . . . vniuersos] om.
1565   3 vniuersos /] vniuersos P   4 meretriculae] meretricule P; honesto] P A
1565, decente decoro Pˢ; patrocinio?] patrocinio P A   5 haud . . . impura] P A, nihil
certe quicquam audiebat mali in margin Pᵃ, satis pudice vixisse fertur 1565   6
abstulisset /] abstulisset P   7 bonae.] bone / P; Ceterum] P A, sed Pˢ   8 re /] re P
8–9 supersederem] se upersederem P   9 norunt /] norunt P   10
insatiabilis . . . inerat] P A, insatiabili cupiditate flagrauit Pᵃ (margin), 1565   10–11
ferenda videretur] P A 1565, ferri posset Pˢ   11 vnquam] vnquam ⟨et⟩ P   12
potens] P A 1565, superba Pˢ; matrona /] matrona P   13 quae] que P; forma / vultu /
voce / gestu /] forma vultu voce gestu P   14 ei /] ei P; statim /] statim P; metu /] metu
P   15 retardatus] P A 1565, remoratus Pˢ; infamia / persequeretur / vrgeret /
oprimerit /] infamia persequeretur vrgeret oprimeret P   17 virorum / parentum /]
virorum parentum P; erat] P A 1565, est Pˢ   18 reliqui /] reliqui P; honesti /] honesti P
19 honestatemque] 1565, honestatumque A, honestumque P; familiae] familie P
19–21 vt . . . decidere] P, vt quamuis potius iacturam ferre (pati Pˢᵃ) quam talem
contumeliam queant Pᵃ (margin), A 1565   22 talibus /] talibus P   22–23
premebatur] P A, grauabatur Pˢᵃ, premeretur 1565; premebatur /] premebatur P   23
precipue /] precipue P; huius /] huius P

that Shore's wife, a contemptible whore, had more influence over the prince than all the nobles in his realm, and that she alone was more sought after for help in promoting petitions than all of the lords put together, and that indeed some of them used the harlot's patronage, indispensable rather than honorable, in ordering their own great affairs? And yet that little woman had a perfectly clean reputation until the prince's wanton lust stole her away from her husband, your own fellow citizen, a prosperous man of good character and prospects. But then in this matter, about which I would rather keep silent out of reverence for the deceased but that it makes no sense to suppress something everyone knows, he was driven by such an insatiable passion that no aspect of his character appeared more intolerable. For any time he laid eyes on a woman—no matter how lowly or how powerful, whether a maiden, a wife, or a widow—whom he found appealing for her beauty, figure, face, voice, gestures, or in sum, any feature at all, unrestrained by any fear of God, or by any thought for scandal, he would pursue her, coerce her, and ruin her, causing irreparable harm to many women and no less sorrow and grief to their husbands, their parents, and any other friends they might have left; for since they are naturally honorable people, they hold the chastity of their wives and the honor of their family so dear that they would gladly pay out any sum to keep such an affront off the books.

"But even though the entire realm was astoundingly victimized in these ways and others much like them, you, the cit-

quod non alibi tam copiose exuberat iniuriarum materia / tum
quod [246v] eratis plurimum proximi. Maximam enim anni partem haud longe discedebat ab vrbe. Et tamen vos estis hi quos vt
precipue foueret egregiae suberant causae / non ideo modo
5 (quanquam ideo quoque) quod ab hac ciuitate / maxime totius
regni famigerata / multum apud exteros omnes inclitae famae
accedit principi / sed quod magno cum impendio periculoque
vestro in rebus eius prosperis aduersisque omnibus amicissimos
animos / eximiam fidem / singularem semper operam prebuistis.
10   "Cui tam pio affectui vestro in Eboracensem domum / quum is
qui maxime debebat minime sese gratum gessit / restat nunc
saltem qui superis annuentibus faciat diligentius: quod ipsum ne
nesciretis / ea demum totius huius nostri ad vos negotij causa est.
Quam dum exponimus / queso / vt cepistis / attendite. Non est
15 opus / satis scio / eadem vt ipse recenseam denuo quae tam nuper
doctor Shauus exposuit e suggestu vobis / vir vt longe facundior /
sic author longe certe quam sum ego grauior. Neque enim mihi
tantum ipsi arrogo vt mea perinde valere verba postulem atque
eius qui ipsum Dei verbum predicat populo / presertim tam
20 prudentis vt melius nemo quid sit dicendum intelligat / porro
tam religiosi vt certum sit nihil eum contra suasurum quam sentiat / ex eo presertim loco quem nemo bonus vnquam mentiturus
ascendit. Igitur ab hoc tali viro vos tanto predicatore didicistis /
huius administrandi regni ius Ricardo Glocestriae Duci poten-
25 tissimo atque omni virtutum genere florentissimo deberi /
nempe quum patri suo clarissimo Duci / cuius sanguine lata lege

[73/1]

---

1 materia /] materia *P*   3 vrbe.] vrbe *P*   4 egregiae . . . causae /] egregie . . . cause *P*
5 ciuitate /] ciuitate *P*   6 famigerata /] famigerata *P;* inclitae famae] inclite fame *P*
10 domum /] domum *P*   11 sese] se se *P;* gratum gessit] *P A,* parem exhibuit *P*s,
gratum gesserit *1565;* gessit /] gessit *P*   12 diligentius:] diligentius *P*   13
nesciretis /] nesciretis *P;* totius huius] *1565,* totius *P A,* huius *P*s   14 exponimus /]
exponimus *P;* queso / vt cepistis /] queso vt cepistis *P*   15 opus / satis scio /] opus satis
scio *P;* recenseam] *P A 1565,* repetam commemorem *P*s; quae] que *P*   16 longe] *P A
1565,* multo *P*s; facundior /] facundior *P*   18 arrogo] *1565,* arorgo *P,* arago *A*   20
intelligat /] intelligat *P*   21–22 sentiat /] sentiat *P*   23 ascendit.] ascendit *P*   23
ab hoc tali viro vos tanto predicatore] ab tali (tanto *P*s) viro vos tanto predicatione *P,* ab
hoc tali viro vos tanto predicatione *A,* ab hoc tali ac tanto viro *1565 but the right way to read
More's own manuscript at this point may well have been* ab ⟨hoc tali ⟨tanto *X* s⟩ viro⟩ hoc tanto
predicatore (*cf.* which honorable preacher *1557)*   24 Glocestriae] Glocestrie *P*   25
deberi /] deberi *P*   26 Duci /] Duci *P*

izens of this town, were always the principal sufferers, first because nowhere else was there such a great wealth of occasions for wrongdoing and second because you were generally the nearest victims. For during much of the year he was not far from the city. And yet there were always very good reasons why he should have favored you especially, not only (though partly, to be sure) because this city, the most celebrated in the realm, wins its prince a great deal of illustrious renown among all foreign peoples, but also because at great cost and great risk to yourselves you provided Edward, in times of prosperity and adversity alike, with most loving friends, exceptional loyalty, and singular effort on his behalf.

"Though the man who by rights should have shown the most gratitude for your loyal devotion to the house of York has behaved like an ingrate, there is at least someone else who will behave more considerately, heaven willing; and the whole point of our business with you today is to make sure you know this very thing. We shall presently explain what we mean; please continue to listen attentively. I am quite aware that I do not need to repeat all that Dr. Shaw has so recently explained from the pulpit, a man far more eloquent than I am and a far more reliable authority. Nor am I arrogant enough to expect that my own words should carry as much weight as those of a man who is speaking the very word of God to the people, especially when that man is so prudent that no one knows better what needs to be said and so pious that we can be certain he will never try to persuade us of anything that he does not believe, especially from the pulpit, where no virtuous person is ever going to tell lies. And so from this fine man and great preacher you have learned that the right to the rule of this kingdom belongs to Richard, the mighty and in every way excellent Duke of Gloucester, since he is the only heir left who can legitimately succeed to his father, the illustrious duke, on whose line the succession was settled by law, both be-

regnum firmatum est / is nunc supersit vnus qui rite queat succedere / cum ob illegitimas Eduardi [247] nuptias / quibus nullam potuit sobolem nisi spuriam gignere / tum aliam ob causam
quam vt ille significauit potius quam explanauit ita nec a me
5   dicetur / quippe qua nemo non libenter abstinet pudore ac reuerentia Protectoris / adeo pium in matrem etiam talem retinen-
tis adfectum vt grauatim in eam sinistri quidquam ferat etiam
suo cum bono dici.

[74/3]   "Eas res ergo nobiles bonaque ex parte populus quum per-
10   pendissent et simul animaduertissent non bellicas modo virtutes
sed omnes preterea moderando imperio appositas artes in vnum
hunc virum ita competisse diuinitus vt solus ad regnum natus
videri possit / haud ferentes amplius vitulamine spurio regi sese
nec tam acerba mala diutius inueterascere / magno decreuere
15   consensu cum supplicijs adire Protectorem atque eius obsecrare
clementiam / ne ipsorum respuat preces neve in se recuset onus
administrandi regni suscipere / quod non e iure magis suo quam
publico fecerit bono. Sed eam rem dubio procul haud libenter
accipiet / qui gnarus pro sapientia sua perpendat facile quanto
20   plus curarum quam commodi secum ferat imperium / presertim
ei qui sic decernat gerere quo modo illum sat scio gesturum si
ceperit. Quod ego munus predico vobis haud quaquam puerilis
esse ludi: idque ipsum certe sensit sapiens ille qui dixit / 'Veh
regno cuius rex puer est': eoque magis et vestrae fortunae gra-
25   tulandum et superis habenda est gratia quorum benignitate prouisum est vt is quem ipsi [247v] regno destinauerunt / non etatis
modo maturae sit / verum admirabilem quoque prudentiam

---

1 est /] est *P*   1–2 succedere /] succedere *P*   2 nuptias /] nuptias *P*   3 gignere /]
gignere *P*   4 significauit] *P A 1565*, indicauit *P*s1 *A*s, intimauit *P*s2; explanauit] *P A*
1565, declarauit *P*s1 *A*s, exposuit *P*s2   5 dicetur /] dicetur *P*   6 Protectoris /] Protectoris *P*   8 suo cum bono dici] *P A, followed by ten-letter gap A,* cum bono publico dici *1565*
9 nobiles] nobiles / *P*   13 possit /] possit *P;* ferentes] *P A 1565,* volentes *P*s   14
inueterascere /] inueterascere *P;* decreuere] ⟨decreuere⟩ decreuere *P*   15
Protectorem] Protectorem / *P*   16 clementiam /] clementiam *P;* preces] *interl. P;* onus]
changed from huius *P*   17 suscipere /] suscipere *P*   18 bono.] bono *P*   19 accipiet]
P A, admittet *P*s *1565;* accipiet /] accipiet *P*   20 commodi] *1565,* comodi *P A*   21
quo modo] *P A,* quemadmodum *P*s *1565*   22 ceperit.] ceperit *P;* munus] *changed from*
minus *P;* quaquam] *A 1565,* quanquam *P*   23 ludi] *P A,* ingenij *1565;* ludi:] ludi / *P*
24 est:] est / *P;* vestrae fortunae] vestre fortune *P*   27 maturae] mature *P;* pruden-
tiam] ⟨pudentiam⟩ prudentiam *P*

cause of Edward's unlawful marriage, in which he could en-
gender only bastards, and for another reason which Dr. Shaw
hinted at rather than stated and which I too will avoid mentioning expressly, since it is a subject that anyone would gladly avoid
out of modesty and respect for the Protector, so devoted to his
mother even such as she is that he hates to hear anything disparaging said about her even when it is to his advantage.

"After weighing these things and simultaneously perceiving
that all martial virtues and all princely arts coincided in this
single man so miraculously that he alone might seem born for
the throne, the nobility and large part of the populace, unwilling to be ruled by a bastard slip any longer or to let such grievous
ills become even more deep-seated, resolved in a mighty consensus to approach the Protector as his suppliants and appeal to his
clemency not to reject their entreaties or refuse to take over the
burden of ruling this kingdom, for in doing so he would be
serving the public interest no less than asserting his rights. But
he will doubtless be loath to accept that proposal, since in his
sagacity and wisdom he can easily recognize how much more
care than advantage dominion brings with it, especially for a
man who intends to administer it as I know he will if he accepts it.
For I assure you that that office is not child's play, as that wise
man surely perceived who said, "Woe to that kingdom which is
ruled by a child"; and so you have all the more reason to rejoice
in your fortune and to thank heaven for kindly providing that
the man it has destined to rule is not only mature in his age but
has also combined admirable prudence with great practical ex-

magno cum rerum vsu ac summa domi forisque parta virtute
gloria coniunxerit.

"Qui tametsi tantum onus / vt dixi / grauatim sit in se sumpturus / tamen (speramus) haud paulo minus aduersaturus vi-
5 detur si vos quoque ciues honestissimi ciuitatis huius regni longe
clarissimae statueritis nostris in hac re supplicijs vestras preces
adiungere./ Quod vos vt faciatis / quamquam pro sapientia vestra non exiguam spem concepimus / tamen etiam vehementer
oramus / idque eo certe confidentius quod preter has nostras
10 preces / quas ipsas quoque pro nostro in vos adfectu nonnihil
habituras momenti credimus / non toti modo in publicum regno
profueritis tali deligendo principe / sed vobis quoque seorsum
ipsis precipue procurabitis commoda / quorum ille officijs haud
aliter ac si dedissetis imperium semper fert acceptum."

[75/1] 15   Hec Dux quum dixisset expectauit protinus vt manibus pedibusque applauderetur / vtique Ricardus vna omnium voce rex
inclamaretur: ita prefectum preformasse populum sperauerat.
Sed contra tantam suam spem quum altum vndecunque silentium animaduerteret / propius insusurrans prefecto / "Quid hic
20 sibi vult habitus?" inquit. "Opinor" inquit ille "non satis exau-
ditam illis orationem tuam." "Id quidem" inquit Dux "corrigetur
facile" / statimque aliquanto quam ante audibilius eadem alijs
verbis / alio rursus ordine / repetebat / verum adeo dilucide
ornateque / voce / vultu / gestu tam accommodo / vt quisquis
25 aderat fateretur facile [248] nunquam ante audisse se tam malam causam peroratam tam bene. Ceterum siue admiratione siue

---

2 gloria] *interl.* P; coniunxerit.] coniunxerit P   3 onus / vt dixi /] onus vt dixi P   3–4
sumpturus /] sumpturus P   4 (speramus)] speramus P   6 clarissimae] clarissime P
7 faciatis / quamquam] *1565* faciatis quam P, faciatis ⟨p⟩ A   8 concepimus /] concepimus P   9 oramus /] oramus P   10 preces /] preces P; nonnihil] non nihil P
11 credimus /] credimus P   12 profueritis tali] ⟨profuturis⟩ profueritis ⟨talis⟩ tali P
13 precipue] P A, egregie Pˢ *1565*   14 acceptum.] acceptum / P   15 expectauit] P
1565, expectauitque A   16 applauderetur /] applauderetur. P   17 inclamaretur:]
inclamaretur P; ita . . . sperauerat] *om.* A *1565*; prefectum] *changed from* perfectum P;
preformasse] performasse P (*cf.* the people whome he hoped yᵗ the Mayor had framed
before *1557*); sperauerat.] sperauerat / P   19 propius] *1565*, prop⟨r⟩ius P, proprius A
20 habitus?" inquit.] habitus inquit / P   21 tuam.] tuam./ P   23 verbis /] verbis P;
ordine /] ordine P   24 ornateque /] ornateque P; vultu /] vultu P; accommodo /]
accommodo P   25 ante] *interl.* P   26 bene.] bene / P

perience and unsurpassed glory achieved by his virtue at home and abroad.

"But even if, as I said, he is reluctant to take such a great burden upon himself, nonetheless, as we hope, it seems likely that he will put up not a little less resistance if you, too, the most honorable citizens of what is by far the most illustrious city in the kingdom, decide to add your prayers to our supplications. And though, in view of your wisdom, we have already conceived no mean hope you will do so, we still vehemently beg you to do so, as well, and we certainly beg you all the more confidently because (quite apart from our prayers, which in view of the love that we bear you we think will have some small effect) by choosing such a prince you will not only be publicly benefiting the realm as a whole, you will also be gaining certain private advantages for yourselves, for whose efforts he will always consider himself as indebted as if you had given him the kingship."

When the duke had said this, he expected that there would immediately be enthusiastic applause and that Richard would be unanimously proclaimed king; so well he hoped that the mayor had already conditioned the populace. But despite his high hopes, when the duke noticed the perfect silence everywhere, he drew close to the mayor and asked in a whisper, "What is the meaning of this conduct?" He answered, "Perhaps they had trouble understanding your speech." "That is easily mended," said the duke, and immediately repeated in a slightly more audible voice than before the same points in different words and in a different order, speaking so clearly and elegantly with such decorous intonation, demeanor, and gestures that anyone who was present would readily admit that he had never before heard such a bad cause propounded so well. But whether speechless

metu attoniti / seu quod alium quisque loquendi ducem sequi
quam ipse preire malebat / omnes ex equo tacebant. Prefectus
igitur ea re nonnihil et ipse perturbatus in orbem se cum Duce et
conscijs quibusdam colligens negauit moris esse quidquam pro-
5 poni ciuibus alterius quam recordatoris voce: inde natam fortasse taciturnitatem / ne quid suas consuetudines immutare viderentur. Appellant recordatorem Londinenses ibi eum qui
prefecti assessor est / eruditus patrijs legibus / ne quid in redden-
dis iudicijs imperitia peccetur. Id munus recens inierat
10 Vihelmides quidam / vir honestus et grauis / quem quum haud
vnquam adhuc allocutus populum fuerat male vrebat tam inaus-
picatum initium. Ceterum iussus dicere / malum sibi metuens si
recusaret / eadem etiam ipse proposuit denuo / sed ita sermonem
temperans vt Ducis omnia verbis acciperentur dicta non suis./
15 Sed nihilo secius durabat idem populi status / non aliter quam
sileri concubia nocte solet obticentis / vultuque adeo immobili /
nullo vt signo prorsus vllum animi sui sensum pre se ferrent.
   At Dux / nonnihil offensus quod eius orationem tam aduersis
auribus animisque excepissent / auersus in prefectum "Que-
20 rant" inquit "isti qui ferat silentium istud tam contumax" statim-
[76/1]   que versus ad turbam / "Viri [248v] Londinenses" inquit "nos ea
de re ad vos relaturi venimus quam in rem neque auxilio admodum vestro neque consilio egebamus. Poteramus enim proceres [et] reliquus regni populus suffecisse deligendo principi /
25 nisi noster in vos amor suasisset ne vos ab eius tractatu rei segre-
garemus / in quam adscitos ac socios esse / vestrarum tam valde
rerum vt nullius eque retulerit./ Hunc animum nostrum vos aut
parum cernere aut parui pendere videmini / quem ne responso

---

1 attoniti /] attoniti *P*   2 preire] *changed from* perire *P*   3 nonnihil] non nihil *P*;
orbem] *P A*, globum *P*ˢ *A*ˢ, vnum *1565*   5 voce:] voce / *P*   6 taciturnitatem /]
taciturnitatem *P*   6–7 viderentur.] viderentur / *P*   9 imperitia] *A 1565*, imperita *P*;
peccetur.] peccetur / *P*   10 Vihelmides] Williamsonus *1565*; quidam] *A 1565*, quidem
P; quidam /] quidem *P*   12 initium.] initium *P*; dicere /] dicere *P*   13 recusaret] *P A*
1565, detrectaret *P*ˢ; denuo /] denuo *P*   16 obticentis /] obticentis *P*; immobili /]
immobili *P*   18 Dux / nonnihil] Dux non nihil *P*   21 turbam /] turbam./ *P*   22
auxilio] *corr. from* auxilium *P*   23 vestro neque] *1565*, vestro ne *A*, vestro ve *P*;
egebamus.] egebamus *P*   23–24 proceres et] *1565*, proceres *P A*   26 ac] *A 1565*, a
P; esse /] esse *P*   28 responso] *1565*, responsum *P A*

with admiration or with fear, or whether each man would rather let someone else open the talking than begin it himself, all alike remained silent. And so the mayor, who himself was a little perturbed by that turn of events, formed a circle with the duke and a few of their cohorts and told him that it was not the custom for any proposal to be put to the citizens in any other voice besides the recorder's; perhaps that was the reason for their silence, lest they should seem to be changing their customs. The Londoners use the title "recorder" for a mayoral assistant well trained in the laws of his country who prevents any erroneous judgments from being given through ignorance of the law. A certain Fitzwilliam had recently succeeded to that office, an honorable and dignified man; having never addressed the populace before, he felt bitterly vexed to be making such an ill-starred beginning. But being ordered to speak and afraid of reprisals if he should refuse, he proposed the same points yet again; but by qualifying his language he indicated that everything should be taken as the duke's words and not as his own. But the people's demeanor remained altogether unchanged, keeping silence as deep as the quiet which generally holds late at night, and with such an impassive expression that they furnished no indication at all of their actual thoughts.

But the duke, quite offended to see them receiving his speech with such closed ears and minds, turned aside to the mayor and said "Let them find someone else to put up with their insolent silence," and then turning at once to the crowd he said, "Citizens of London, we came to address you concerning a matter in which we had no particular need for either your help or your counsel. For we nobles and the rest of the people in the kingdom could have chosen a prince by ourselves if our love for you had not induced us not to exclude you from taking part in a matter in which you stood to benefit more richly than anyone else by being active participants. It appears that you either mistake or scorn our good intentions, since you have not even dignified them with

quidem dignum censuistis./ Quin vno saltem verbo respondeatis / potentissimum Glocestriae Ducem / quem ceteri alioquin
omnes proceres populusque delecturi sunt / vosne in regem
adscisci vultis an non. Responso namque in vtramuis partem
5   dato discedemus / haud amplius molesti vobis hac de re futuri."
Ad hunc sermonem excitatus aliquantum populus / mussitare
inter se / et audiri sonus magis quam verba / qualis ex alueo
redditur migraturis apibus / quoad ex vltima parte curiae / qua se
ministri quidam Nashefeldi huius consilij participes con-
10 globauerant / a tergo repente clamor tollitur "Richarde Rex"
ingeminantium. Ciues retro ceruices admirabundi flectere./ Sed
clamantibus adiungunt sese famuli quidam / nulla Ricardi cura
(vt in turba fit) / ac pueri leti nouandis quomodocumque rebus /
et iam bireta pileosque sursum eiaculabantur in signum gaudij.
15 Sed Dux tametsi displicebat illud / quod nullum honestum
ciuem in ea parte videbat / factum tamen commode pro se vertens / indicto rursus silentio / iucundissimum illum clamorem
dicit animi in designandum regem alacris adeoque [249] in
vnum consentientis vt ne vnus quidem sit auditus qui contra
20 dixerit: "Quem tam eximium adfectum vestrum / nos quum erit
oportunum / sic faciemus vt audiat / idem vt vobis haud dubie in
magnum aliquando bonum vertat. Sed interim vos oramus vt
crastina die simul omnes eius maiestatem adeamus rogaturi /
quod vos ei tanto cum consensu detulistis / idem vt suo consensu
[77/1] 25 faciat ratum." His dictis descendit ipse / ceteri discedunt / pars
aperte moesti / multi simulata leticia / nec deerant ex ipsis ducis
comitibus qui / quum premere mestitudinem / quam non aude-

---

2 Glocestriae Ducem /] Glocestrie Ducem *P*   3 vosne] vos ne *P*   5 discedemus /]
discedemus *P;* futuri.] futuri./ *P*   6 populus /] populus *P*   7 audiri] ⟨ex⟩audiri
P   8 apibus /] apibus *P;* curiae /] curie *P*   9 participes] *P A,* periti *P*s, participis
1565   10 tollitur] tollitur. *P*   11 ingeminantium.] ingeminantium / *P*   12
quidam /] quidam *P*   13 (vt . . . fit)] vt . . . fit *P;* rebus /] rebus *P*   14 et . . . gaudij]
om. 1565; gaudij.] gaudij *P*   15 tametsi] tam etsi *P;* illud /] illud *P*   16–17 vertens /]
vertens *P*   17 silentio /] silentio *P*   18 alacris adeoque] adeoque alacris *P A 1565*
20 dixerit:] dixerit *P*   21 oportunum /] oportunum *P*   22 vertat.] vertat / *P*
23 simul] *P,* pariter *P*s *A 1565;* adeamus rogaturi /] adeamus / rogaturi *P*   24
detulistis /] detulistis *P*   26 moesti /] moesti *P*   27 qui /] qui *P;* mestitudinem /]
mestitudinem *P*

a response. Come now! Answer with one word at least, whether you do or do not want the mighty Duke of Gloucester to be chosen as king, whom the rest of the nobility and the people are going to elect anyway. For as soon as you give us your answer one way or the other, we shall take our leave, never to trouble you about this matter further."

Somewhat roused by this speech, the people began to murmur among themselves, and a sound was heard rather than words, like the sound that bees make when abandoning their hive, until from the farthest part of the council-house, where the servants of a certain Nashfield who were in on the plot had assembled, a sudden shout of men calling "King Richard" again and again was sent up from the rear. The citizens turned their heads and looked back in amazement. But those shouting were joined by a few apprentices, without any real interest in Richard (as it often happens in a crowd), and by schoolboys delighted with any kind of change, who were throwing their caps and hats in the air as a sign of their pleasure.

But though the duke was unhappy that he could not see any honorable citizens in that party, he still made the most of what had happened, first calling for silence again and then hailing that shouting as a most pleasant display of enthusiasm in select-ing their king and of such perfect unanimity that not even one voice of dissent had been heard. "And," he said, "when the moment is right we shall ensure that he hears about your great affection, so that he will undoubtedly turn it at some point to your great advantage. But meanwhile we beg you to join us in going to his majesty tomorrow and asking him to ratify with his consent the nomination which you have tendered to him with such perfect consensus." With these words he stepped down, and the others departed, some of them grieving openly, others feigning delight; and even in the duke's company there were several who were unable to hold in the grief which they dared

bant ostendere / non poterant / vertere in parietem vultus coacti
sunt dum pectoris dolor per oculos erumperet./

Igitur postridie nobiles ciuesque magna frequentia adeunt
Protectorem (diuersabatur ibidem Londini). Missus intro nun-
5 cius ait proceres omnes senatum populumque Londinensem pro
foribus esse qui eius expetant expectentque colloquium. Sed is
primo dubitat progredi / incertus quid moliatur ea turba quae sic
superueniret inopinanti. Hanc Protectoris cunctationem Dux ad
se allatam ostentat reliquis vti scirent quam longe adhuc abesset
10 Protector ab huius cogitatione propositi. Ceterum remisso nuncio magnis obsecrant precibus admitti: adferre ea quae nisi apud
ipsum proferent non sunt prolaturi. Prodit ergo tandem / nec
adhuc tamen plane se credit / verum ex ambulacro superne
despiciens accipit redditque sermonem. Tacentibus igitur
15 vniuersis Dux ex equo insignis primum petit vti liceret ipsis quae
vellent libere citra vllam eius offensam proloqui / [249v] quanquam enim nihil meditarentur vnde non et illi decus et regno
[78/2]   commodum proueniret / tamen quum incertum sit quam in partem illius serenitas esset acceptura nihil ipsos nisi impetrata ven-
20 ia locuturos. Ad hec Protector / vt erat in tali re perquam benignus atque adfabilis / tum cui mirus ardor inerat cognoscendi

---

1 ostendere /] ostendere *P*   2 pectoris dolor] *P A*, animi dolorem *P*ˢ *1565;* per oculos
erumperet] *P A*, per lachrymas egererent *1565 (cf.* while the doloure of their heart braste
oute at theyr eyen *1557);* erumperet] *P A*, gererent *P*ˢ   3 Igitur] *New para. P;* nobiles]
A 1565, nobile *P*   4 Protectorem (diuersabatur . . . Londini).] Protectorem / diuersabatur . . . Londini / *P*   5 senatum populumque] *1565,* senatumque populum *P,*
senatumque *A (where the scribe may have omitted* populum *as a mere variant reading for*
senatum)   7 progredi /] progredi *P;* incertus] *P A 1565,* nescius *P*ˢ; moliatur] *P A,*
vellet / afferat *P*ˢ, sibi vellet *1565;* ea] ⟨illa⟩ ea *P;* quae] que *P*   7–8 sic superueniret
inopinanti] *P A 1565,* se inopinante superueniat *P*ˢ   9 ostentat] *P 1565, changed to*
ostendit *A;* reliquis] *P A,* ceteris *P*ˢ *1565*   10 propositi] *P A 1565,* consilij *P*ˢ   11
admitti:] admitti / *P;* quae] que *P*   12 proferent] *P A, om. 1565;* prolaturi] *P A 1565,*
proferenda *P*ˢ; prolaturi.] prolaturi / *P;* tandem /] tandem *P*   13 adhuc] *interl. P;*
credit /] credit *P*   14 redditque] *A,* reddit *P,* ac reddit *1565;* sermonem.] sermonem *P*
15 vniuersis] *P A 1565,* omnibus *P*ˢ; ex equo insignis] *P,* ex equo insegnis *A,* ab equo
sublimis *1565;* insignis] *last word in A;* primum] *P 1565;* imprimis *P*ˢ; quae] que *P*   16
proloqui] *P 1565,* proponere *P*ˢ   18 proueniret] *P 1565,* esset prouenturum *P*ˢ;
quum] *P 1565,* quia *P*ˢ   20 locuturos.] locuturos, *P;* Protector /] Protector *P*   21
atque adfabilis] *P 1565,* et comis *P*ˢ; adfabilis /] adfabilis *P*

not display, and who had to turn aside, face to the wall, while their eyes burst forth with their heart's sorrow.

Then the next day, a large throng of nobles and citizens went to see the Protector, who was dwelling there in London. They sent a messenger in to announce that all the lords and the council and people of London were outside eagerly awaiting an interview. But at first he was hesitant to go out, wondering what that crowd meant by coming to him so unexpectedly. Upon hearing of the Protector's hesitation, the duke told the others about it to show them how far the Protector still was from any thought of what they were intending. But they sent back the messenger, begging fervently to be granted admission, for they were not going to reveal what they had come for unless they could reveal it to him personally. And so he finally came out, but even then he did not altogether entrust himself to them, but instead he received their proposal and responded to it looking down on them from a gallery above. And then when everyone was quiet, the duke, in an equally prominent position, first asked that they might be permitted to speak their minds freely without giving him any offense, for although they had nothing in mind that would not serve both his honor and the good of the kingdom, since they did not know how his serenity would react to their words they would say nothing before getting his pardon. To this the Protector consented, being a very indulgent and affable man when it came to such things and feeling very curious to know

quid vellent / annuit / atque hortatur ne dubitent quicquid decreuissent edicere / sibi vero animi in eos sui conscientia persuasum / nihil in se quemquam cogitare quod non gratia magis
quam venia dignum./

5   Igitur Dux ea demum Protectoris oratione securus ausus est
rem cum suis causis exponere / tandemque immensam eius implorare clementiam / ne regnum tam diu tot intolerandis malis
afflictum negligeret / proceres populumque ipsius aduolutum
pedibus pro consueta eius benignitate respiceret / procumbenti
10 in se vnum patriae subijceret humeros / rempublicam prope
dirutam ac proculcatam erigeret / manus sceptro tandem velut
temoni nauis diu sine perito gubernatore fluitantis admoueret /
caputque illud venerandum pateretur onerari diademate / neque adeo dominationis tempestates horreret neque delectetur
15 immodesta modestia / vt suae quietis causa cum neglectu publicae regnum sibi humano more debitum / ab superis destinatum
rem curantibus Britanicam / refugeret / e quo tanto plus honoris
ferret ac minus sollicitudinis / quod nullus vnquam rex tam li-
bentibus imperauit populis quam ille suus arderet ipsius auspi-
20 cijs regi./

    Protector vbi verba Ducis accepit / vultu haudquaquam an-
nuente respondit [250] quod nec ipse nesciret vera esse quae ille
retulisset: se tamen eo fuisse affectu in fratrem / eo in liberos eius
esse / ad hec tantam habere honoris sui rationem / quam tribus
25 etiam coronis anteferret / vt inducere non posset animum illorum petitioni concedere: nempe exteras gentes / quibus res

---

1 vellent /] vellent *P*   1–2 quicquid decreuissent edicere] *P 1565*, quicquid habent in
animo dicere *P*sa; decrevissent] *P 1565*, concepissent / cogita⟨ssent⟩ sponte *P*s   2–3
persuasum /] persuasum *P*   3 magis] *P*, magis sit *1565*   6 exponere /] exponere
P   7 clementiam /] clementiam *P*   10 patriae] patrie *P*; humeros /] humeros *P*
12 admoueret] *P*, apponeret *P*s *1565*; admoueret /] admoueret *P*   13 diademate /]
diademate *P*   14 delectetur] *perhaps we should read* delectaretur   15 suae] sue *P*
15–16 publicae] publice *P*   16 destinatum] destinatum / *P*   17 Britanicam /] Britanicam *P*   18 sollicitudinis /] sollicitudinis *P*; quod] *changed from* quam *P*b   21
haudquaquam] haud quanquam *P*   21–22 annuente] *1565*, annuante *P*, approbante
*P*s   22 quae] que *P*   23 retulisset:] retulisset *P*   26 concedere:] concederet *P*,
satisfacere *1565*; gentes /] gentes *P*

what they wanted, and urged them not to hesitate to say everything they had planned to say, since his knowledge of how he felt
about them convinced him that none of them would have any
thought about him which was not more deserving of thanks than
of pardon.

Then the duke, finally reassured by the Protector's remarks,
dared to explain their whole purpose together with its causes,
and then to call upon his immense clemency not to neglect a
realm plagued for so long with so many intolerable evils, to look
with his usual indulgence upon the lords and the people prostrate at his feet, to take on his shoulders a country which was
wholly dependent on him, to rebuild a commonwealth which
was virtually crushed and downtrodden, to take the scepter in
hand as if it were the helm of a ship which had long been adrift
without any skilled steersman, to let his worshipful head bear the
weight of a diadem, and not to let fear of the tempests of kingship or love of an immoderate modesty make him serve his own
ease and abandon the public's by shunning the crown which was
owed him according to human custom, destined for him by the
heavenly guardians of Britain, and which would bring him all
the more honor and less trouble because no king had ever
reigned over more willing subjects than his in their eagerness to
serve under his auspices.

After hearing the duke's words, the Protector, with a look of
strong disapproval, responded that he, too, was not unaware
that the things which the duke had reported were true, but that
he felt such affection for his brother and his brother's children,
and he had so much regard for his own honor, which he would
not give up even for three crowns, that he could not bring himself to comply with their request; for foreign peoples with less

quo pacto gereretur minus compertum foret / ex aliorum cupiditate se quoque estimaturas / ita suam famam venturam in periculum / quae non respuisset quae vltro obtulisset de regno. Haud
grauatim posse se suo iure cedere / quod semper aloes plus
5 adferre quam mellis vidisset ei qui sic institueret regere /
quomodo / qui non vellet / non est vt posset ei permittendum /
[79/2] sed tamen se non modo eorum postulatis ignoscere / verum
etiam voluntatibus egregie in se propensis habere habiturumque
gratias. Ceterum orare / vel sua causa / quem in se animum
10 gererent / eum totum consignarent Principi / cui ipse parere
quam regnare malit: nec tamen operam consiliumque suum /
quatenus Regi libuerit vti / defuturum vnquam rei publicae /
quam etiam nonnihil exiguo suae procurationis tempore (quod
Deo non sibi referebat acceptum) subleuasset / vel eo precipue
15 quod improbos quorundam conatus qui eam perturbassent antea / agitabantque vt vexarent de integro / ipse sua partim industria sed plurimum diuina prouidentia compressisset.

   Tum Dux habito paulisper cum suis colloquio rursus ostendit
rem eiusmodi esse quam incepissent / vt etiam si [250v] esset
20 integra tamen vellent eam magnis de causis aggredi: nunc vero
longius progressos quam vnde sit regrediendum./ Denique patribus populoque certum / non passuros amplius spurijs Eduardi
liberis regnari se. Proin si delatum vltro non aspernetur impe-

2–3 suam . . . regno] suam famam venturam in periculum que vltro obtulisset de regno
P (que non ⟨respexisset⟩ respuisset P^{sa1}), periclitaturum ne ambiuisse videretur P^{sa2},
suam famam venturam in periculum quasi regnum non iure debitum per iniuriam
occuparet 1565   3–6 Haud . . . permittendum] om. 1565   4 cedere /] cedere P
4–5 aloes . . . mellis] P, incommodi . . . commodi P^s   5 adferre] adfert P; quam]
quum P; institueret] institueret⟨ur⟩ P   5–6 regere / quomodo / qui non vellet /] regere
quomodo qui non vellet P   6 est] P^s, sit P; permittendum /] permittendum P   7
ignoscere /] ignoscere P   9 gratias.] gratias P; orare /] orare P; causa /] causa P   10
gererent /] gererent P; Principi /] Principi P   11 malit:] malit P; suum /] suum P
12 vti /] vti P; vnquam] nunquam P 1565; publicae /] publice P   13 nonnihil] non nihil
P; suae] sue P   14 subleuasset /] subleuasset P; eo] 1565 ea P   15–16 antea /] antea
P   17 compressisset.] compressisset P   19 incepissent /] incepissent P   20
aggredi:] aggredi P   22 certum /] certum P   23 se.] se / P   23 480/1
imperium /] imperium P

knowledge of how the matter had been done would judge him by the standard of others' cupidity, and thus his reputation would be compromised for not rejecting what the duke freely offered concerning the kingship. He could cheerfully waive his own rights to the throne, having seen that it always brought more gall than honey to anyone who intended to rule in such a way that anyone who did not wish to rule so should not be allowed to rule; nonetheless, he not only excused their petition, he thanked them and would continue to thank them for their great devotion to him. But he begged them for his sake to transfer their affection for him to the prince, whom he would rather obey than be king; and yet insofar as the prince wished to use them, he would never withhold his own help and advice from the commonwealth, which he had already helped a good deal (for which he gave the credit to God, not himself) in the brief period of his protectorate, especially by crushing (partly by his own industry but more by the help of God's providence) the villainous schemes of some parties who had upset the commonwealth before and were plotting to trouble it again.

Then after a brief talk with his cohorts, the duke again stated that, their business being what it was, even if they had it to do over they would still undertake it, with very good reason; but in fact they had already proceeded too far to turn back. In sum, the nobles and people had made up their minds not to be ruled any longer by Edward's bastard children; and so if he did not spurn

rium / vnum esse ipsum omnibus votis expetitum principem: sin
omnino precise respondeat se non suscepturum / facile ipsos
inuenturos quempiam cui respublica curae sit./

Hec verba Ricardi animum tam valde abhorrentem sola flex-
5 ere / cogitantem si recusaret ipse / nepotem nihilo tamen magis
regnaturum. Igitur "Ego / vt" inquit "doleo animo tam obfirmato decretum vobis / regem hunc non ferre diutius / sic inuitos
a quoquam regi neque posse video neque fas esse sentio. Certe
quod ad me attinet / quanquam alium neminem esse scio cui
[80/1]   10 regnum hereditate iure debeatur / pluris tamen has voluntates
vestras quam omnes leges / quarum vis omnis a vobis pendet /
existimo: quorum quoniam tam solidum in me consensum perspicio / ne vel parum fortis videar in capescenda republica vel
vestram in me beneuolentiam non agnoscere / en hic in me
15 hodierno die moderamen vtriusque regni Angliae Galliaeque
suscipio / alterum vt tuear atque inaugeam / alterum vt illi sub-
ijciam atque in ditionem vestram audiens esse quibus parere
debet redigam: nempe administrationem eorum duntaxat
meam duco / ius vero [251] fructumque ac proprietatem vtrius-
20 que omnem vestrum haud dubie publicam. Quem ego animum
quo die habere desiero / eo die precor vt superi mihi non regnum
hoc vestrum modo / quod improbe conarer auertere / sed vitam
quoque ipsam / vt indignam quae retineatur / eripiant."

Hanc orationem eius alacris excepit clamor "Ricarde Rex"
25 ingeminantium. Proceres cum Rege (sic enim ab ea vocabatur

---

1 principem:] principem / P   2 suscepturum /] suscepturum P   3 inuenturos]
1565, inuenturum P   3 curae] cure P   5 cogitantem] P, reputantem Pˢ, cogitantis
1565; tamen] *interl.* P   6 regnaturum.] regnaturum / P   7 vobis /] vobis P; diutius /]
diutius P   8 quoquam] *1565*, quoque P   9 attinet /] attinet P   10 debeatur /]
debeatur P   11 leges /] leges P; pendet /] pendet P   12 existimo] P, facio Pˢ
1565; existimo:] existimo / P   12–13 perspicio /] perspicio P   13 ne vel . . . re-
publica] P *1565*, ne vel videar rempublicam animo parum prompto capescere Pˢᵃ;
republica] republica / P   14 agnoscere /] agnoscere. P   15 moderamen] P, regimen
Pˢ, procurationem *1565*; Angliae Galliaeque] Anglie Gallieque P   17–18
audiens . . . debet] *om. 1565*   17 parere] P, obedere Pˢ   18 redigam:] redigam P
20 publicam.] publicam P   21 habere] P *1565*, retinere Pˢ   22 modo /] modo
P; quod . . . auertere] *om. 1565*; auertere /] auertere P   23 ipsam /] ipsam P; quae] que
P; retineatur /] retineatur P; eripiant.] eripiant. / P   25 ingeminantium.] ingeminantium P   25–482/1 (sic . . . hora)] sic . . . hora P   25 vocabatur] P, vocatus est Pˢ,
vocari coepit *1565*

the kingship which they freely offered him, he was their only unanimous choice as their prince; but if he flatly responded that he would not accept, they could easily find some other candidate who cared for the commonwealth.

These words alone conquered Richard's great reluctance by making him consider that even if he refused them, his nephew would still lose the throne. And so he declared, "Though I personally regret your unbending resolve not to tolerate this king any longer, I consider it to be neither possible nor proper for anyone to rule unwilling subjects. For my own part, at least, though I know that there is no other to whom the crown rightly belongs by inheritance, I consider your desires more important than any number of laws, which derive all their efficacy from you; and since I see that your solid consensus supports me, lest I should seem either timid about laboring for the commonweal or unmindful of your goodwill toward me, here on this day I take upon myself the government of the two realms of England and France, the one to protect and extend and the other to subdue for England, bringing it back into your power and making it submit to those it should obey; for I regard only the management of these realms as my own, but the title and the profit and the ownership as totally your own—as a genuine commonwealth. And the day I stop thinking this way, I pray heaven to deprive me not only of this realm of yours, which I would have wickedly tried to subvert, but of my very life, which would no longer be worth the keeping."

This speech was received with loud and enthusiastic cries of "King Richard" repeated again and again. The lords passed

hora) concedunt intro: populus discedit domum varie adfectus /
multaque super ea re secum disserens. Sed plurimis in ore erat
impudens illa simulatio sic agentium loquentiumque tanquam
Protector de eo quod agebatur nunquam neque audisset neque
5 cogitasset antea / quum interim nec ipsi quidem dubitarent
neminem esse tam stupidum vt haberet dubium / tantam rem de
composito geri. Sed alij morem causabantur et receptam in
rebus humanis consuetudinem / qua sic oporteat maximas quas-
que res legitimis quibusdam perfici ceremonijs: quin rustice
10 nonnulla tractari si non et qui gerunt simulent aliqua / et eadem
spectatores dissimulent. Nam et eum qui creatur episcopus bis
rogari num velit / bis perquam sancte negare / tertio vix adduci
posse vt dicat nolentem velle / quum interim / vt nihil soluat
principi / tamen ambitum pene declarant emptae Pontificis bul-
[81/1] 15 lae. Iam qui imperatorem ludat in tragaedia / populusne ignorat
forsitan esse cerdonem? Tamen adeo inscitia est illic scire quae
scias vt si quis eum vocet qui vere est / non qui falso fingitur /
veniat [251v] in periculum ne ab simulatis satellitibus malo ioco
bene vapulet / vel merito / qui totam fabulam sit aggressus intem-
20 pestiua veritate turbare. Sic quae modo spectassent ipsi / tragicos
esse ludos regum: populum in id vocari vt spectet tantum / et
spectaturum tantum qui sapiat: quosdam quibus impetus fuit
prodire in proscenium et gregi semet immiscere scenico / per
imperitiam turbata fabula / magna in semet concitasse pericula./
25 Sequente die magno cum comitatu venit in forum / non illud
Londinense / sed maius atque augustius quod est in palatio proximum occidentale coenobium vbi ab omni parte regni promiscue
aguntur causae. Ibi quum in ea sede collocasset se quae regia ob
id vocatur / quod iudicia sic in ea feruntur curia tanquam ipsius

---

1 intro:] intro / P   2 disserens.] disserens / P; plurimis] *1565*, plurimus P   3
impudens] imp⟨r⟩udens P   4 nunquam] *changed from* vnquam P   6 dubium /] dubium P; tantam] P, omnem *1565*   7 composito] P *1565*, compacto Pˢ; geri.] geri / P
9 ceremonijs:] ceremonijs / P   9–11 quin . . . dissimulent] *om. 1565*   10 simulent]
simulen P   13 velle /] velle? P; interim /] interim P   14 principi /] principi P
14–15 emptae . . . bullae] empte . . . bulle P   15 populusne] populus ne P   16
quae] que P   17 est /] est P   20 turbare] P *1565*, corrumpere Pˢ; turbare.] turbare
P   20–24 Sic . . . pericula] *om. 1565*   20 quae] que P; ipsi /] ipsi P   21 regum:]
regum P; tantum /] tantum P   22 sapiat:] sapiat P   23 scenico /] scenico P   24
fabula /] fabula P; magna] magnum P   25 Sequente] *New para.* P; forum /] forum
P   26 Londinense /] Londinense P   26–27 proximum] P, apud Pˢ *1565*   28
causae] cause P; quae] que P   29 vocatur /] vocatur P

inside with the king (for so he was called from that hour), and the people departed for home with mixed feelings, exchanging many views on what had happened. But they had most to say about that shameless pretense in which people acted and talked as if the Protector had never before heard a word or dreamed a thing about what they were doing, when they themselves knew perfectly well that no one was stupid enough not to know that this momentous business was all prearranged. But others appealed to tradition and the standard conventions of human behavior, according to which all great affairs must be executed with some sort of legitimate ceremony; indeed, some things would be boorishly done if the performers did not indulge in some pretenses and the spectators did not pretend not to notice them. For when someone is ordained a bishop, he is twice asked if he would be willing, and twice he denies it devoutly, and the third time he is barely induced to say he would be willing in spite of himself, whereas even supposing he has not paid the prince any money, the bulls he has bought from the pope show how he has been angling for the title. And when someone plays an emperor in a tragedy, are the people unaware he might be a mere craftsman? But in such circumstances it shows such ignorance to know what you know that if anyone calls him what he really is, not what he is falsely supposed to be, he risks getting a good beating for a bad joke from that man's make-believe retainers, and quite rightly, since he went about to disrupt the whole drama with his untimely truth. In the same way, what they had just watched was a regal tragicomedy; the people had been summoned merely to watch, and a sensible person would do nothing else; certain people who had followed an impulse to get onstage and step in among the theatrical company had disrupted the drama through their inexperience and thus landed themselves in great danger.

On the following day, with a large escort, he arrived at the forum, not the one situated in London but a larger and grander one located in the palace right next to Westminster Abbey, where all types of cases are argued from every part of the realm. There he took the seat called the King's Bench because the judg-

ore regis proferantur / pro concione rursus ostendit ex eo loco
potissimum possessionem sese regni capere vnde regis ore populo iura redduntur / quod ideo faciendum censuisset quum sic
sentiret / leges exequi earumque ministrum agere / id sit demum
5 regem esse./ Deinde proceres / mercatores / artifices / denique
omne genus hominum / sed ea collegia nominatim quae Bri-
tanicis student legibus / oratione quam maxime potuit blanda
conciliat./ Postremo ne cuiquam inuisum eum faceret metus /
simul vt beneuolentiam pareret insidiosa [252] clementia / mala
10 dissentionum prefatus et concordiae bona / edicit omnes inimicitias ex animo delere / omnes omnium in se offensas condonare publice / cuius rei quo specimen edat / iubet ad se accer-
siri Foggum / quem diu capitaliter oderat. Adducto ex asylo
proximo / nam illuc timore eius perfugerat / in populi conspectu
15 dat manum. Rem vulgo acceptam ac iactatam laudibus / prudentes pro vana habuere. Inter remigrandum / vt quemque
[82/1]   habuit in via obuium / ita [semper adblandiri / nam] semper ad
seruilem prope adulationem animus iacet admissi conscius / nec
sic quidem securus esse aut / quibus blandiebatur / confidere /
20 manum a capulo non referre / et circumspectare vndique velut
repercussurus.
        Cum ludicra illa electione die [·xxvi·] Iunij regnare cepisset /
mensis tempore coronatus est / eaque celebritas magna parte illo
ipso apparatu peracta qui nepoti eius coronando fuerat
25 destinatus./

---

3 redduntur /] redduntur *P;* censuisset] ⟨censuit⟩ censuisset *P*   4 sentiret /] sentiret *P;*
earumque ministrum agere] earumque ministrum id agere *P,* easque administrare *1565*
6 hominum /] hominum *P;* ea] *1565,* ⟨eam⟩ enim *P (possibly a misreading of* iuris*);* quae]
que *P*   7 blanda] *P,* populari *1565*   8 metus /] metus *P*   10 concordiae] concor-
die *P*   11 delere /] delere *P*   12 ad se] *interl. P*   12–13 Foggum /] Foggum *P*
13 oderat.] oderat / *P*   14 proximo /] proximo *P*   15 manum.] manum / *P;* laudibus /] laudibus./ *P*   16 habuere.] habuere / *P;* remigrandum /] remigrandum *P*   17
obuium /] obuium *P*   17–18 ita semper adblandiri / nam semper ad . . . conscius] ita
semper ad . . . conscius *P,* ita semper illis ad seruilem prope adulationem se demisit,
admissi conscius *1565; cf.* In his returne homewarde, whom so euer he met he saluted.
For a mind that knoweth it self giltye, is in a manner dejected to a seruile flattery *1557*[L]
(see introduction, pp. ooo–oo)   19 aut /] aut *P;* blandiebatur / confidere /] blandiebatur
confidere· *P*   21 repercussurus.] repercussurus *P*   22 ludicra . . . Iunij] *P,* post
ludicram illam electionem *1565;* xxvi.] *eight-letter blank space in P 1557 (date interpolated
from CW₂)*   23 mensis tempore] *P, om. 1565,* the   day of Iuly *1557*[L]

ments of that court have the same force as if they came straight
from the king's mouth, and for his speech there he stated that he
was taking possession of the throne from that place in particular
where the voice of the king gives the people its verdicts because
he felt that to carry out the laws and to act as their servant was the
essence of kingship. Then with the most flattering language he
could muster he tried to win over the lords, the merchants, the
artisans, and in short every order of men, but in particular the
colleges for the study of English law. Finally, to keep anyone
from turning against him through fear and to curry goodwill
with insidious clemency, he first spoke of the evils of dissension
and the blessings of concord and then proclaimed that he would
forget all his grudges and publicly forgive anyone who had ever
offended him; and to illustrate the point, he ordered one Fogg
to be brought to him, a man he had long hated with a deadly
passion. When Fogg was brought from the neighboring sanctuary, where he had taken refuge out of fear of Richard, he publicly gave him his hand. This gesture was commonly praised and
applauded, but prudent judges considered it empty. In returning to London, he fawned on whomever he met, for a mind
knowing itself to be guilty always stoops to a near-servile flattery,
and yet even then he did not feel secure or trust those whom he
fawned on, never taking his hand from the hilt of his dagger and
constantly looking around like one ready to strike back.

Having started his reign with that ludicrous election on the
[twenty-sixth] day of June, he was crowned a month later, that
solemnity being supplied for the most part with the very provisions which had been intended for the crowning of his nephew.

COMMENTARY

The following bibliography includes works and abbreviations cited frequently in the Introductions and the Commentary. The titles of works mentioned only once or in two widely separated references are given in full as they occur. Unless otherwise noted, references to the Bible and Latin quotations from it are from the Clementine Vulgate. Wherever possible, and unless otherwise noted, quotations of classical authors are taken from the readily available texts of the Loeb Library, which are cited with the permission of the Harvard University Press.

BIBLIOGRAPHY AND SHORT TITLES

Adagia. See Erasmus, *Opera omnia.*

Alberigo, Giuseppe, et al., eds. *Conciliorum oecumenicorum decreta*, 3rd ed., Bologna, 1973. Cited as "Alberigo."

Allen. *See* Erasmus.

ASD. See Erasmus.

Blaise, Albert. *Lexicon latinitatis medii aevi* . . . , Turnhout, 1975. Cited as "Blaise."

Boyle, Marjorie O'Rourke. *Erasmus on Language and Method in Theology*, Toronto and Buffalo, 1977. Cited as "Boyle."

Brann, Noel L. *The Abbot Trithemius (1462–1516): The Renaissance of Monastic Humanism*, Leiden, 1981. Cited as "Brann."

Buridan, John. *Sophisms on Meaning and Truth*, trans. T. K. Scott, New York, 1966. Cited as "Buridan."

Camporeale, Salvatore I. "Da Lorenzo Valla a Tommaso Moro: Lo statuto umanistico della teologia," *Memorie domenicane*, New Series, *4* (1973), 9–102. Cited as "Camporeale, 'Da Lorenzo Valla a Tommaso Moro.'"

———. *Lorenzo Valla: Umanesimo e teologia*, Florence, 1972. Cited as "Camporeale, *Lorenzo Valla.*"

CHLMP. The Cambridge History of Later Medieval Philosophy, from the Rediscovery of Aristotle to the Disintegration of Scholasticism, 1100–1600. ed. Norman Kretzman et al., Cambridge, 1982.

Chomarat, Jacques. *Grammaire et rhétorique chez Erasme*, 2 vols., Paris, 1981. Cited as "Chomarat."

Chrimes, S. B. *Henry VII*, London, 1972.

CIC. Corpus iuris canonici, ed. Emil Ludwig Richter and Emil Albert Friedberg, 2 vols., Leipzig, 1879–81; reprint, Graz, 1959.

Courcelle, Pierre. *Late Latin Writers and Their Greek Sources*, trans. Harry E. Wedeck, Cambridge, Mass., 1969. Cited as "Courcelle."

CW. See More.

CWE. See Erasmus.

De Vocht, Henry. *Monumenta Humanistica Lovaniensia: Texts and Studies about Louvain Humanists in the First Half of the Sixteenth Century*, Louvain, 1934. Cited as "De Vocht, *Monumenta.*"

DNB. Dictionary of National Biography, 63 vols., London, 1885–1900.

DTC. Dictionnaire de théologie catholique, 15 vols., Paris, 1908–50.

Du Cange, Charles du Fresne. *Glossarium mediae et infimae latinitatis, editio nova,* ed. Léopold Favre, 10 vols., Niort, 1883–87; reprint, Graz, 1954. Cited as "Du Cange."

EETS. Early English Text Society.

Epistolae obscurorum virorum, ed. Francis G. Stokes, London, 1925.

Erasmus, *Apologia qua respondet invectivis Lei* [1520], in *Erasmi opuscula,* ed. Wallace K. Ferguson, The Hague, 1933, pp. 224–303.

———. *Ausgewählte Werke,* ed. Hajo Holborn and Annemarie Holborn, Munich, 1933. Cited as "Holborn."

———. *Collected Works of Erasmus,* trans. Roger A. B. Mynors and Douglas F. S. Thomson and annot. Peter G. Bietenholz, Wallace K. Ferguson, and James K. McConica, 8 vols., Toronto, 1974–. Cited as *CWE.*

———. *Opera omnia,* ed. Johannes Clericus (Jean LeClerc), 10 vols., Leiden, 1703–06. Cited as "*Opera omnia.*"

———. *Opera omnia Desiderii Erasmi Roterodami,* ed. Jan H. Waszink et al., 10 vols., Amsterdam, 1969–. Cited as *ASD.*

———. *Erasmi opuscula: A Supplement to the Opera omnia,* ed. Wallace K. Ferguson, The Hague, 1933. Cited as "Ferguson."

———. *Opus epistolarum Des. Erasmi Roterodami,* ed. Percy S. Allen et al., 12 vols., Oxford, 1906–58. Cited as "Allen."

Essential Articles. See Sylvester, Richard S., and Germain P. Marc'hadour.

The Essential Thomas More. See Greene, James J., and John P. Dolan.

EW. See More.

Ferguson. *See* Erasmus.

Flesseman-Van Leer, E. "The Controversy about Scripture and Tradition between Thomas More and William Tyndale," *Nederlands Archief voor Kerkgeschiednis,* n. s. *43* (1959), 143–64. Cited as "Flesseman-Van Leer."

Fox, Alistair. *Thomas More: History and Providence,* New Haven and London, 1982. Cited as "Fox, *Thomas More.*"

Garin, Eugenio, ed. *Prosatori latini del Quattrocento,* Milan, 1952. Cited as "Garin."

Gibaud, Henri. "Thomas More: Réponse à un moine anti-Erasmien," unpublished Mémoire pour le diplome d'études supérieures, University of Tours, 1967. Cited as "Gibaud, 'Réponse.'"

Gibson, Reginald W., and John Max Patrick. *St. Thomas More: A Preliminary Bibliography of His Works and of Moreana to the Year 1750,* New Haven and London, 1961. Cited as "Gibson."

Gilman, Sander. *The Parodic Sermon in European Perspective,* Wiesbaden, 1974. Cited as "Gilman."

Gogan, Brian. *The Common Corps of Christendom: Ecclesiological Themes in the Writings of Sir Thomas More,* Leiden, 1982. Cited as "Gogan."

Gray, Hanna H. "Valla's Encomium of St. Thomas Aquinas and the Humanist Conception of Christian Antiquity," in *Essays in History and Literature Presented . . . to Stanley Pargellis,* ed. Heinz Bluhm, Chicago, 1965. Cited as "Gray."

Greenblatt, Stephen. *Renaissance Self-Fashioning: From More to Shakespeare,* Chicago and London, 1980. Cited as "Greenblatt."

Greene, James J., and John P. Dolan, eds. *The Essential Thomas More,* New York, 1967. Cited as "*The Essential Thomas More.*"

Hanham, Alison. *Richard III and His Early Historians, 1483–1535,* Oxford, 1975. Cited as "Hanham."

Harpsfield, Nicholas. *The Life and Death of Sir Thomas Moore,* ed. E. V. Hitchcock, EETS, Original Series no. 186, London, 1932. Cited as "Harpsfield."

Heath, Terrence. "Logical Grammar, Grammatical Logic, and Humanism in Three German Universities," *Studies in the Renaissance, 18* (1971), 9–64. Cited as "Heath."

Herford–Simpson. *See* Jonson, Ben.

Holborn, *See* Erasmus.

Inventaire chronologique. See Moreau, Brigitte.

Jonson, Ben. [*Works*], ed. Charles H. Herford, Percy Simpson, and Evelyn Simpson, 11 vols., Oxford, 1925–52. Cited as "Herford–Simpson."

Kinney, Daniel. "Erasmus' *Adagia:* Midwife to the Rebirth of Learning," *Journal of Medieval and Renaissance Studies, 11* (1981), 169–92. Cited as "Kinney, 'Erasmus' *Adagia.*'"

―――. "More's *Letter to Dorp:* Remapping the Trivium," *Renaissance Quarterly, 34* (1981), 179–210. Cited as "Kinney, 'More's *Letter to Dorp.*'"

Knowles, Dom David. *The Religious Orders in England,* 3 vols., Cambridge, 1948–59. Cited as "Knowles."

Kühner, Raphael, ed. *Ausführliche Grammatik der lateinischen Sprache,* rev. Carl Stegmann, 2 vols. in 3, Hanover, 1912–14. Cited as "Kühner–Stegmann."

Latham, Ronald. *Revised Medieval Latin Word-List from British and Irish Sources,* London, 1965. Cited as "Latham."

Leader, Damian R. "Professorships and Academic Reform at Cambridge: 1488–1520," *The Sixteenth Century Journal, 14* (1983), 215–27. Cited as "Leader."

Leclercq, Jean, O. S. B. *The Love of Learning and the Desire for God: A Study of Monastic Culture*, trans. Catharine Misrahi, New York, 1961. Cited as "Leclercq, *Love of Learning*."

Lee, Edward. *Annotationes in Annotationes Novi Testamenti Desiderii Erasmi*, Paris, [1520]. Cited as "Lee, *Annotationes*."

Levi, Anthony. *Pagan Virtue and the Humanism of the Northern Renaissance*, The Society for Renaissance Studies Occasional Papers 2, London, 1974. Cited as "Levi."

LP. *Letters and Papers, Foreign and Domestic, of the Reign of Henry VIII*, ed. John S. Brewer, James Gairdner, and R. H. Brodie, 21 vols., London, 1862–1932; reprint, Vaduz, 1965.

Luther, Martin. *D. Martin Luthers Werke*, 60 vols., Weimar, 1883–1980. Cited as *WA*.

McConica, James K. *English Humanists and Reformation Politics under Henry VIII and Edward VI*, Oxford, 1965. Cited as "McConica, *English Humanists*."

———. "Erasmus and the Grammar of Consent," in *Scrinium Erasmianum*, ed. Joseph Coppens, 2 vols, Leiden, 1969, 2, 77–99. Cited as "McConica, 'Erasmus.'"

———. "The Patrimony of Thomas More," in *History and Imagination: Essays in Honour of Hugh Trevor-Roper*, ed. Hugh Lloyd-Jones et al., London, 1981, pp. 56–71. Cited as "McConica, 'Patrimony.'"

Marc'hadour, Germain. *The Bible in the Works of St. Thomas More: A Repertory*, 5 vols., Nieuwkoop, 1969–72. Cited as "Marc'hadour, *The Bible*."

Marius, Richard C. "Thomas More and the Early Church Fathers," *Traditio, 24* (1968), 379–407. Cited as "Marius."

Minnis, A. J. *Medieval Theory of Authorship*, London, 1984. Cited as "Minnis."

Missale Sarum. Missale ad usum . . . ecclesiae Sarum, ed. Francis H. Dickinson, Burntisland, 1861–83.

Mone, Franz Joseph, ed. *Hymni latini medii aevi*, 3 vols., Freiburg im Breisgau, 1853–55. Cited as "Mone."

Monsuez, R. "Le Latin de Thomas More dans *Utopia*," *Annales publiées par la Faculté des lettres et sciences humaines de Toulouse*, new series 2/1 (1966), *Caliban 3*, 35–78. Cited as "Monsuez."

More, Thomas. *The Yale Edition of the Complete Works of St. Thomas More* (cited as *CW*): *CW 2, The History of King Richard III*, ed. R. S. Sylvester; *CW 3*, Part 1, *Translations of Lucian*, ed. C. R. Thompson; *CW 3*, Part 2, *The Latin Poems*, eds. C. H. Miller, Leicester Bradner, C. H. Lynch, and R. P. Oliver; *CW 4, Utopia*, ed. Edward L. Surtz, S. J., and J. H. Hexter; *CW 5, Responsio ad Lutherum*, ed. J. M. Headley, trans. Sister

Scholastica Mandeville; *CW 6, A Dialogue Concerning Heresies,* ed. T. M. C. Lawler, G. Marc'hadour, and R. C. Marius; *CW 8, The Confutation of Tyndale's Answer,* ed. L. A. Schuster, R. C. Marius, J. P. Lusardi, and R. J. Schoeck; *CW 9, The Apology,* ed. J. B. Trapp; *CW 11, The Answer to a Poisoned Book,* ed. Stephen M. Foley and Clarence H. Miller; *CW 12, A Dialogue of Comfort,* ed. L. L. Martz and F. Manley; *CW 13, Treatise on the Passion,* etc., ed. G. Haupt; *CW 14, De Tristitia Christi,* ed. C. H. Miller; New Haven and London, 1963–.

―――. *The Correspondence of Sir Thomas More,* ed. Elizabeth F. Rogers, Princeton, 1947. Cited as "Rogers."

―――. *Selected Letters,* ed. Elizabeth F. Rogers, trans. Marcus Haworth, S. J., et al., New Haven and London, 1961. Cited as *SL.*

―――. *The Workes . . . in the Englysh tonge,* London, 1557. Cited as *EW.*

Moreau, Brigitte. *Inventaire chronologique des éditions parisiennes du seizième siècle,* 2 vols., Paris, 1972–. Cited as *"Inventaire chronologique."*

Nijhoff, Wouter, and Maria E. Kronenberg. *Nederlandsche bibliographie van 1500 tot 1540,* 2 vols. and supplements, The Hague, 1923–71. Cited as "Nijhoff–Kronenberg."

OED. Oxford English Dictionary, 13 vols, Oxford, 1933.

Ong, Walter J. *Ramus: Method, and the Decay of Dialogue,* Cambridge, Mass., 1958. Cited as "Ong."

Otto, August. *Die Sprichwörter und sprichwörtlichen Redensarten der Römer,* Leipzig, 1890. Cited as "Otto."

Owst, Gerald R. *Preaching in Medieval England,* Cambridge, 1926. Cited as "Owst."

Peter of Spain. *Tractatus, called afterwards Summule Logicales,* ed. Lambertus M. de Rijk, Assen, 1972. Cited as *"Tractatus."*

PG. Patrologiae Cursus Completus: Series Graeca, ed. J.-P. Migne, 161 vols., Paris, 1857–66.

PL. Patrologiae Cursus Completus: Series Latina, ed. J.-P. Migne, 221 vols., Paris, 1844–64.

Polydore Vergil. *Anglica historia, 1485–1537,* ed. and trans. Denys Hays, London, 1950. Cited as "Polydore Vergil."

Porphyry. *Isagoge,* ed. Adolf Busse, in *Commentaria in Aristotelem Graeca,* 23 vols., Berlin, 1882–1909, 4/1, 1–51. Cited as "Porphyry."

Rashdall, Hastings. *The Universities of Europe in the Middle Ages,* rev. ed. Frederick M. Powicke and Alfred B. Emden, 3 vols., Oxford, 1936. Cited as "Rashdall."

Reuchlin, Johann. *Defensio . . . contra calumniatores suos Colonienses,* Tübingen, T. Anselm, 1514. Cited as "Reuchlin, *Defensio.*"

Rice, Eugene F., Jr., ed. *The Prefatory Epistles of Jacques Lefèvre d'Etaples and Related Texts,* New York and London, 1972. Cited as "Rice."

Rizzo, Silvia. *Il lessico filologico degli umanisti,* Rome, 1973. Cited as "Rizzo."

Rogers. *See* More.

Roper, William. *The Lyfe of Sir Thomas Moore, knighte,* ed. Elsie V. Hitchcock, EETS, Original Series no. 197, London, 1935. Cited as "Roper."

Ross, Charles. *Edward IV,* London, 1974.

——. *Richard III,* Berkeley and Los Angeles, 1981.

Santinello, Giovanni. "Teologia e linguaggio in Tommaso Moro," *Studia Patavina: Rivista di scienze religiose,* 24 (1977), 617–29. Cited as "Santinello."

Schoeck, Richard J. *The Achievement of Thomas More: Aspects of His Life and Works,* Victoria, British Columbia, Canada, 1976. Cited as "Schoeck."

Schwarz, Werner. *Principles and Problems of Biblical Translation: Some Reformation Controversies and Their Background,* Cambridge, 1955. Cited as "Schwarz."

Seigel, Jerrold E. *Rhetoric and Philosophy in Renaissance Humanism: The Union of Eloquence and Wisdom, Petrarch to Valla,* Princeton, 1968. Cited as "Seigel."

SL. *See* More.

Souter, Alexander. *A Glossary of Later Latin to 600 A.D.,* Oxford, 1949. Cited as "Souter."

Stapleton, Thomas. *Tres Thomae . . . ,* Douai, 1588. Cited as "Stapleton."

STC. *A Short-Title Catalogue of Books Printed in England, Scotland, and Ireland . . . 1475–1640,* comp. Alfred W. Pollard and Gilbert R. Redgrave, London, 1926.

Surtz, Edward L., S. J. *The Praise of Pleasure: Philosophy, Education, and Communism in More's Utopia,* Cambridge, Mass., 1957. Cited as "Surtz, *Praise of Pleasure.*"

——. *The Praise of Wisdom: A Commentary on the Religious and Moral Problems and Backgrounds of St. Thomas More's Utopia,* Chicago, 1957. Cited as "Surtz, *Praise of Wisdom.*"

Sylvester, Richard S., and Germain P. Marc'hadour, eds. *Essential Articles for the Study of Thomas More,* Hamden, Conn., 1977. Cited as "Essential Articles."

Thompson, Craig R. "The Humanism of More Reappraised," *Thought,* 52 (1977), 231–48. Cited as "Thompson."

Thomson, Douglas F. S. "The Latinity of Erasmus," in *Erasmus,* ed. Thomas A. Dorey, London, 1970, pp. 115–37. Cited as "Thomson."

Tilley, Morris P. *A Dictionary of the Proverbs in England in the Sixteenth and Seventeenth Centuries*, Ann Arbor, 1950.

TLL. Thesaurus Linguae Latinae, 9 vols., Leipzig, 1900–.

Tracy, James D. *Erasmus: The Growth of a Mind*, Geneva, 1972. Cited as "Tracy, *Erasmus*."

Tractatus. See Peter of Spain.

Tshibangu, Tharcisse. *Théologie positive et théologie spéculative: Position traditionelle et nouvelle problématique*, Louvain and Paris, 1965. Cited as "Tshibangu."

Valla, Lorenzo. *Opera omnia*, Basel, 1540; reprinted as *Opera omnia*, vol. 1, Turin, 1962. Cited as "Valla, *Opera omnia*."

Vives, Juan Luis. *Juan Luis Vives against the Pseudodialecticians: A Humanist Attack on Medieval Logic*, ed. and trans. Rita Guerlac, Dordrecht, Boston, and London, 1979. Cited as "Vives, *Epistola*."

———. *Opera omnia*, ed. Gregorius Majansius, 6 vols., Valencia, 1745; reprint, London, 1964. Cited as "Vives, *Opera omnia*."

WA. See Luther, Martin.

Walther, Hans. *Proverbia sententiaeque latinitatis medii aevi*, 6 vols., Göttingen, 1963–69. Cited as "Walther."

Whiting, Bartlett J. and Helen W. *Proverbs, Sentences, and Proverbial Phrases from English Writings Mainly before 1500*, Cambridge, Mass., 1968. Cited as "Whiting."

Witt, Ronald. "Medieval 'Ars Dictaminis' and the Beginnings of Humanism: A New Construction of the Problem," *Renaissance Quarterly*, 35 (1982), 1–35. Cited as "Witt."

2/1–2 **Viro ... Louanij.** These words are written on the outermost sheet of *P* as one would write an address, parallel to the long side of the page. At the top of the page another hand has written the seventeenth-century Bibliothèque Royale catalogue number for this manuscript, along with the following title: "Thomae Mori Defensio Moriae Erasmi ad Martinum Dorpium." On fol. 2 in *P* another hand has written: "Habetur impressa inter Epistolas in Lucubrationibus Mori pag. 367." The title on fol. 1 of *P* is probably derived from the title assigned to the letter in *1563:* "Apologia pro Moria Erasmi, qua etiam docetur quam necessaria sit linguae Graecae cognitio." The more accurate title of *1625* reads as follows:

> Thomae Mori | v. c. | Dissertatio Epistolica | De aliquot sui temporis Theologastrorum ineptijs, | Deque correctione translatio | nis vulgatae N. testamenti | Ad Martinum Dorpium theo | logum Louaniensem

Since the title of *1563* is inadequate and somewhat misleading, and since there is no basis in *P* for the title of *1625* (although that text almost certainly derives from *P*), it is likely that none of these titles originates with More. Several words at the lower left corner of fol. 1 in *P* have been thoroughly crossed out.

2/7–8 **committo litteris.** Cf. Cicero, *Epistolae ad Atticum* 4.1.8: "Praeterea sunt quaedam domestica, quae litteris non committo." At 6/12-8/3 More reports someone else's harsh censure of Dorp for entrusting his criticisms of Erasmus to letters instead of discussing such sensitive points with Erasmus in private.

2/9–10 **praesens praesente.** Cf. Terence, *Adelphoe 668.*

2/14 **apud ... predicet.** Cf. Col. 2:5.

2/16–18 **conatur ... conglutinet.** More represents Erasmian *amicitia* as an exemplary expression of Christian *caritas.* Cf. 1 Cor. 12:12–27; Gal. 3:28; and Erasmus, *Moriae encomium, ASD 4/3,* 192, lines 220–23: "Repraesentatur autem [*sc.* in synaxi] mors Christi, quam domitis, extinctis, quasique sepultis corporis affectibus exprimere mortales oportet, vt in nouitatem vitae resurgant vtque vnum cum illo, vnum item inter sese fieri queant." The connection between *amicitia* and *caritas* in the *Letter to Dorp* is also discussed in Germain Marc'hadour, "Thomas More convertit Martin Dorp à l'humanisme érasmien," in *Thomas More 1477–1977,* Travaux de l'Institut interuniversitaire pour l'étude de la Renaissance et de l'humanisme 6 (Brussels, 1980), pp. 13–25.

4/1–3 **animi ... eluxit.** More refers to the "stilus imago animi" *topos* dating back to Socrates (see Cicero, *Disputationes Tusculanae* 5.47) and formulated at length by Seneca (*Epistolae morales* 114). Cf. Allen, *4,* 260, commentary at line 7; *Moriae encomium, ASD 4/3,* 74, line 68; and

Adagia 550 (*Opera omnia*, 2, 242E–243B). Since Dorp's two rash attacks on Erasmus reflect none too well on Dorp's character, More's professed admiration for the character which is reflected in all of Dorp's works soon takes on the sharp edge of ironic reproach.

4/4–11 **Itaque ... alligauit.** For details of More's service as one of several English ambassadors who went to the Low Countries in 1515 see Rogers, p. 16, and *CW 4*, 573–76. More arrived in Bruges in mid-May and remained there with few interruptions until mid-October.

4/10–11 **oratoribus.** More's choice of the term *oratores* to refer to the diplomats representing Dorp's monarch in Bruges links the world of affairs with the world of intellectual endeavor: a true orator, like More or Erasmus, is equally at home in both. Other sixteenth-century writers exploited the fact that *orator* conventionally meant "diplomat" to suggest that rhetorical skill is essential for civilized diplomacy; see Richard Pace, *De fructu qui ex doctrina percipitur*, ed. and trans. Frank Manley and Richard S. Sylvester (New York, 1967), p. 22; and Sir Thomas Elyot, *The Boke Named the Gouernour*, ed. H. H. S. Croft, 2 vols. (London, 1883), *1*, note on 119.

4/16 **quosdam.** More may actually have learned of Dorp's letters to Erasmus through Dorp's long-standing patron Jerome Busleyden, who would also have been able to furnish More with the many other *opuscula* by Dorp to which More refers in the course of this letter (De Vocht, *Monumenta*, pp. 366–68). According to Erasmus (Allen, *9*, 35–36), both Busleyden and More wrote "acerrime" against Dorp for attacking Erasmus. More met Busleyden in Mechelin in 1515, and Busleyden subsequently obliged More by contributing a commendatory letter to *Utopia;* see *CW 4*, Commentary at 20/11.

4/24 **litteras ... ternas.** For these letters see Allen, 2, 10–16, 90–114, and 126–36. The manuscript version of Erasmus' letter to which More and Dorp both refer must have been somewhat different from the printed version; see notes on 4/31-6/3 and 38/24-40/6 and Allen, 2, 91.

4/25–31 **ille ... dissuadeas.** Cf. Erasmus in Allen, 2, 91, lines 1–4.

4/31-6/3 **Alterae ... esset.** Though the first part of this sentence paraphrases Erasmus in Allen, *2*, 91, lines 20–22, the second part seems to refer to a promise included in the manuscript version of Erasmus' letter (cf. notes on 78/19–20 and 104/16–18) but deliberately dropped in the printed version. Dorp refers to the same promise in Allen, 2, 126–27, lines 8–9. It may be that Erasmus considered a lengthier version of his first letter to amount to the "fuller response" which his first letter promised.

6/10–11 **ab amicissimo pectore profectum.** This is a direct echo of Dorp's letters (Allen, 2, 11, line 11; 16, line 148; 136, line 351).

6/12–8/3 **At . . . omnes.** For More's shifting of the accuser's role onto an unnamed third party, cf. Dorp's similar tactics in Allen, 2, 12.

6/13–17 **si . . . senibus.** Cf. Erasmus' less forceful expression of this claim in Allen, 2, 100, lines 360–64.

6/16–17 **morosissimis . . . senibus.** Cf. *Moriae encomium, ASD 4/3,* 82–85; *Adagia* 436 (*Opera omnia,* 2, 195B). Cf. also *Moriae encomium, ASD 4/3,* 96, line 451: "pro facundo infans"; and Isa. 65:20.

6/17–18 **quos . . . rident.** See note on 16/2.

6/22–23 **Dorpius . . . solus.** Cf. Dorp in Allen, 2, 11, lines 7–8.

6/24 **praesentem, praesens.** See note on 2/9–10.

6/25–26 **cur . . . uia.** Cf. Terence, *Andria* 490–91.

6/27–29 **quae . . . acceperit?** Cf. Jerome to Augustine, *Epistolae* 105.1 (*PL* 22, 835); "satis mirari nequeo, quomodo ipsa [*sc.* tua] epistola et Romae et in Italia haberi a plerisque dicatur, et ad me solum non pervenerit, cui soli missa est."

8/4–9 **Hec . . . possim.** Cf. Dorp in Allen, 2, 12, lines 35–37.

8/13 **secundas . . . secunde.** Cf. *CW 8,* 147/18–19 and 264/24–25.

8/19–20 **neclectim.** More is remarkably fond of this rare adverb, which is normally spelled thus (not "neglectim") in the autograph manuscript of More's *De Tristitia Christi;* see 288/6–7; variant at 66/18; *CW 4,* 48/19, 132/30; *CW 14,* 125/6, 131/4, 133/5. For related forms similarly spelled see *CW 14,* 115/5, 119/7, 125/4, 145/1, 203/1, 327/6, 597/7, 691/11, 13, 17; and Rogers, p. 560, line 17. The only authority for *neglectim* ever cited by the lexicons is an epigram, sometimes attributed to Petronius, which first appeared in a seventeenth-century anthology. Cf. also the pun cited in the note on 214/23–24.

8/24 **parcius . . . salsius.** Cf. Suetonius, *Claudius* 16.

8/25 **Moriam insectaris.** Cf. Dorp in Allen, 2, 127, lines 17–47. Dorp had treated the same theme in Allen, 2, 12–14, lines 15–79.

8/25 **in Poetas inueheris.** Cf. Dorp in Allen, 2, 127, lines 34–43; 128, lines 51–56; 129–30, lines 98–150; 133, lines 243–45.

8/26 **Grammaticos omnes subsannas.** Cf. Dorp in Allen, 2, 128–29, lines 57–92; 130–31, lines 151–68; 133, lines 246–53.

8/26–27 **Annotationes in scripturam parum probas.** Cf. Dorp in Allen, 2, 131–33, lines 169–237. Dorp had treated the same theme in Allen, 2, 14–15, lines 86–146.

8/27–28 **graecarum . . . censes.** Cf. Dorp in Allen, 2, 131, lines 174–88; 132, lines 205–08; 133, lines 233–37; 135–36, lines 337–49. Dorp had briefly treated the same theme in Allen, 2, 15, lines 111–31.

10/4–8 **tantum . . . communiendi.** Cf. Dorp in Allen, 2, 126–27, lines 6–12.

10/12 **e sublimi derideas.** Cf. *Adagia* 180 (*Opera omnia*, 2, 101A). See 200/12–13, 278/10–11.

10/13 **patruus.** Cf. *Adagia* 1339 (*Opera omnia*, 2, 535D–E).

10/14–15 **uerbis . . . concites.** Cf. Dorp in Allen, 2, 127, lines 43–47; 129, lines 93–104; 133, lines 238–45; 134, lines 274–75.

10/15 **uniuersitates (quas uocant).** Erasmus, too, had some reservations about using the term *universitas.* Cf. Allen, *4,* 82, commentary at line 115; and *De pronuntiatione, ASD 1/4,* 24, lines 357–58: "publicis scholis, quas ambitioso vocabulo, vt dixi, nunc appellant Vniuersitates, quasi nihil absit bonae disciplinae." The original meaning of the term *universitas* was simply "a gathering of masters and students."

10/16 **Nec . . . uolo.** For the wording cf. Tacitus, *Dialogus de oratoribus* 10: "neque hunc meum sermonem sic accipi volo. . . ."

10/18–19 **ego . . . illum.** For the wording cf. Terence, *Eunuchus* 770. Erasmus formally entrusted the defense of the *Folly* to More in the dedication of *Moriae encomium, ASD 4/3,* 70, lines 65–67; cf. 104/13.

10/22 **ansam apprehendunt.** Cf. *Adagia* 304 (*Opera omnia*, 2, 152C–F). See also 180/18, 212/5.

10/23 **cycneus . . . candor.** Cf. Vergil, *Eclogae* 7.38.

10/25–27 **Aeneas . . . spectauit.** See Vergil, *Aeneid* 1.439–40, 488–89, where we read that Aeneas saw his deeds carved in stone. More himself may be thinking of tapestries depicting Troy's fall; for one such group of tapestries (once housed in the palace at Richmond) see Gordon Kipling, *The Triumph of Honor: Burgundian Origins of the Elizabethan Renaissance* (Leiden, 1977), pp. 60–61.

10/27–28 **utinam . . . posses.** Cf. Cicero on Gyges, *De officiis* 3.9.38: ". . . a nullo videbatur, ipse autem omnia videbat." Cf. also Lucian, *Somnium sive Gallus* 28.

12/4–5 **coram . . . clam.** Cf. Erasmus' letter to Antonio Ammonio about Dorp himself, written October 6, 1516 (Allen, 2, 355, lines 21–22): "Blanditur coram, mordet absens."

12/8 **per cancellos.** Cf. *Adagia* 2049 (*Opera omnia*, 2, 728AB): "per transennam inspicere"; and Cant. 2:9. In this context *cancellus* refers to a screen or a window-lattice.

12/10–11 **Theologos . . . uestros.** Cf. especially Dorp's words in Allen, 2, 128, lines 77–81.

12/12 **grammaticulos.** This diminutive is attested in Albert Blaise, *Lexicon latinitatis medii aevi . . .* (Turnhout, 1975; hereafter cited as

"Blaise"), p. 424; and in R. E. Latham, *Revised Medieval Latin Word-List from British and Irish Sources* (London, 1965; hereafter cited as "Latham"), p. 214. Relying on two instances of the word in documents of 1515 and 1520, Latham defines *grammaticulus* as "elementary pupil." But the diminutive *grammaticellus* was used to refer to inferior teachers of grammar; see Charles du Fresne du Cange, *Glossarium mediae et infimae latinitatis, editio nova,* ed. Léopold Favre, 10 vols. (Niort, 1883–87; reprint, Graz, 1954; hereafter cited as "Du Cange"), *4,* 96.

12/13–14 **sedes . . . praesides.** Cf. Cicero, *Epistolae ad familiares* 1.6.1 and 1.8.1 ("interfuit . . . praefuit"); and *CW 4,* 142/25–26.

12/14–15 **Nec . . . depellendus.** Cf. Erasmus, *Vita Hieronymi,* Ferguson, p. 179, lines 1215–20: "An ideo theologus non erit [*sc.* Hieronymus], quia nobiscum non balbutiat, ne dicam ineptiat? An ideo grammaticis annumerabitur, et Scotistis in sublimi cathedra tonantibus, Hieronymus ad horum pedes in imis sedebit subsellis, quod diuina maluit dicere quam hominum somnia; quod inter vernantia scripturarum prata versari maluit, quam inter horum spineta luctari. . . ?"

12/19–21 **Grammaticum . . . effundit.** Cf. Suetonius, *De grammaticis* 4: ". . . grammatic[i] . . . initio litterati vocabantur. . . . sunt qui litteratum a litteratore distinguant, ut Graeci grammaticum a grammatista, et illum quidem absolute, hunc mediocriter doctum existiment." In his *Praelectio in priora Aristotelis analytica, cui titulus Lamia,* Angelo Poliziano develops Suetonius' distinction in much the same way that More does; see *Omnia opera Angeli Politiani* (Venice, Aldus, 1498), sig. Y₇v. The pertinent passage is also to be found in Aldo Scaglione, "The Humanist as Scholar and Politian's Conception of the *Grammaticus,*" *Studies in the Renaissance, 8* (1961), 61–62. See also note on 138/20–21.

12/24–25 **litteratus . . . debet.** Cf. Cicero, *De oratore* 1.6.20: "mea quidem sententia nemo poterit esse omni laude cumulatus orator, nisi erit omnium rerum magnarum atque artium scientiam consecutus."

12/28-14/3 **ferulas . . . structuram.** Cf. Dorp in Allen, 2, 131, lines 159–62. See 18/21-20/10, where the passage is quoted at length and verbatim. Erasmus appears to be borrowing from Dorp's phrasing here in *De conscribendis epistolis, ASD 1/2,* 259, lines 16–19. Cf. also *Moriae encomium, ASD 4/3,* 138, lines 250–55. For *regnare* see note on 30/14. Erasmus elaborates a similar comparison between *rex* and *grammaticus,* but without irony, in *De pronuntiatione, ASD 1/4,* 20, lines 217–23.

14/1 **plagoso.** More quotes Dorp quoting Horace; see Horace, *Epistolae* 2.1.70–71, an unflattering sketch of another grammarian, Orbilius.

14/1 **philautia ac Moria stultiores.** Cf. August Otto, *Die sprichwörter und sprichwörtlichen Redensarten der Römer* (Leipzig, 1890; hereafter cited as "Otto"), no. 1699; Hans Walther, *Proverbia sententiaeque latinitatis medii aevi*, 6 vols. (Göttingen, 1963–69; hereafter cited as "Walther"), nos. 30404–04a; and *Moriae encomium, ASD 4/3*, 94, line 434: "stultior stulticia." Philautia or Self-Love is a favorite attendant of Folly; she is first introduced in *Moriae encomium* at *ASD 4/3*, 78, line 127.

14/7–8 **quanquam . . . dissimulamus.** Cf. *Moriae encomium, ASD 4/3*, 82, line 179.

14/10–11 **perplexum . . . labyrinthum.** Cf. *CW* 5, 114/24, 180/2, 582/31; *Moriae encomium, ASD 4/3*, 144, line 376; and 148, line 417; Erasmus in Allen, 2, 101, lines 414–15; and *Adagia* 1951 (*Opera omnia*, 2, 696B).

14/15–16 **bonarum . . . quoque.** Cf. 62/8–9 and note, as well as Erasmus in Allen, 2, 100, lines 350–51: "Ego tantum tribuo theologicis literis vt eas solas soleam appellare litteras." In Allen, 2, 13, lines 64–65, Dorp himself hints that *litterae sacrae* have a greater affinity with philosophy than with the *bonae litterae* espoused by the humanists (cf. Allen, 2, 128, lines 59–65).

14/17–18 **eiusdem . . . notae.** Cf. *Adagia* 2444 (*Opera omnia*, 2, 839E).

14/18 **Si . . . uideris.** Dorp in Allen, 2, 132, lines 212–13. The *Epistolae decretales*, a collection of definitive papal pronouncements, is a standard text of canon law; see note on 50/20–21.

14/21–22 **Aquam . . . descenditur.** More is condensing Dorp's comments in Allen, 2, 133, lines 240–43. Dorp himself states that the proverb "Ardeae omnem aquam esse perturbatam, ideoque aquam culpare ardeam" appears in Erasmus' *Adagia*. It actually occurs not in the *Adagiorum chiliades* but in a much smaller and earlier collection; see *Collectanea adagiorum veterum Desiderii Erasmi Roterodami* (Sélestat, M. Schürer, 1512), sigs. H₂v–H₂. The *Collectanea* was first printed in 1500; see Allen, *1*, 289–97.

14/23–24 **Non . . . ignores.** Cf. Dorp's words in Allen, 2, 134, lines 300–02, responding to Erasmus in Allen, 2, 101, lines 413–14.

14/25–26 **Nisi . . . dialectici.** Dorp in Allen, 2, 135, lines 311–13.

16/2 **quae . . . omnes.** Cf. *Adagia* 1042 (*Opera omnia*, 2, 422C): "Et puero perspicuum est."

16/3–4 **At . . . concedes.** Cf. Dorp in Allen, 2, 127, lines 12–16.

16/5–10 **recte . . . obruitque.** The opposition of the palm and the fist was readily available in Cicero (*Orator* 32.113–14, *De finibus* 2.6, *Brutus*

309; cf. Quintilian 2.20.7); the dagger point and the overwhelming mass appear to be More's own additions. Cf. Erasmus, *Apologia adversus Petrum Sutorem* (*Opera omnia, 9,* 810C).

16/24 **animaduertit? Tantum.** Between these two words *S* and *1563* add a passage which may be translated as follows:

> For I think no one doubts that if Erasmus ever wishes to do so, he will discuss these very problems so ably in writing, or else in a sober and serious debate (not, I grant, in those wrangling encounters where clamor wins out over reason, where everyone spits on the rest and is spat on in turn, for Erasmus' modesty and restraint cannot countenance that sort of behavior), that he will prove to be not only not inferior to all of them but either equal or superior to even the best.

For "ubi rationem clamor uincit" cf. Lucian, *Bis accusatus* 11, a passage quite similar to this one. The wordplay in the phrase "conspuentes . . . consputique" is derived from Jerome, *Epistolae* 50.4 (*PL* 22, 515), where Jerome asks with regard to an unmannerly monkish critic, "quoties conspuit, et consputus abscessit?" More's punning association of *conspuo* with *disputo,* however, is probably original. Cf. *Historia Richardi Tertii,* 434/4–6 below, on "Freer Penker prouincial of the Augustine freers": ". . . at frater perfrictissimae frontis / vt e qua sepe inter disputandum sputa deterserat / olim ad infamiam obtorpuerat." Cf. Erasmus, *De libero arbitrio, Opera omnia, 9,* 1215E: ". . . quis ex huiusmodi disputationibus fructus, nisi ut uterque ab altero consputus discedat?" Ben Jonson seems to borrow the conceit from Erasmus in *Timber or Discoveries* (*Ben Jonson,* ed. C. H. Herford, Percy Simpson, and Evelyn Simpson, 11 vols., Oxford, 1925–52, *8,* 596; hereafter cited as Herford–Simpson): "Such Controversies, or Disputations . . . are odious. . . . And the fruit of their fight is; that they spit one upon another, and are both defil'd."

18/2 **uentiletur.** Cf. 72/23 and 140/17. The verb *ventilo* was used transitively with the meaning "to discuss" or "to dispute" from the second century onward. See Alexander Souter, *A Glossary of Later Latin to 600 A.D.* (Oxford, 1949; hereafter cited as "Souter"), p. 438.

18/3 **Hieronymi Hussitae.** See note on 20/6–9.

18/3 **Cresconijque grammatici.** This is a reference, not to the seventh-century ecclesiastic mentioned by Rogers (p. 34, commentary at line 222), but to a minor Donatist opponent of Augustine; see Allen, *2,* 135, lines 313–16, 321–23; and Augustine's reply to Cresconius (*PL 43,* 445–594).

18/9–10 **inque . . . abutaris?** Cf. Erasmus in Allen, *2,* 102–03, lines 451–65, on Dorp's habitual misrepresentation of Erasmus' own meaning. See also note on 40/24–27.

18/11–15 **quum . . . damnauerant.** Cf. Erasmus in Allen, 2, 108, lines 665–70.

18/12–13 **excitare Tragoedias.** Cf. 174/26 and *Adagia* 1791 (*Opera omnia*, 2, 660F–661A). This disparaging use of *tragoediae* is more characteristic of Erasmus than of More; see P. Bietenholz, *History and Biography in the Works of Erasmus of Rotterdam* (Geneva, 1966), pp. 26–28.

18/16–17 **Noua . . . probabunt.** Dorp in Allen, 2, 130, line 153.

18/17–20 **quasi . . . eximantur.** Cf. Erasmus in Allen, 2, 97–98, lines 264–77; 100, lines 345–50; and 102, lines 443–45. See also note on 76/21-78/4.

18/21-20/10 **Age . . . graece.** Dorp in Allen, 2, 130–31, lines 153–68.

18/23–24 **falcem . . . messi?** Cf. Walther, no. 873, *Adagia* 341 (*Opera omnia*, 2, 167E–168A), and Deut. 23:25.

18/26–27 **parturiant . . . mure.** Cf. Horace, *Ars poetica* 139.

18/27 **nec metus est.** Allen, 2, 131, lines 158–59, prefers the reading of the sole manuscript which preserves the entirety of Dorp's second letter, namely *metus est*. But the next sentence, which suggests that grammarians *already* hold sway with a tyrant's authority, clearly calls for the sarcasm of *nec metus est:* there is *no* fear that scholars will challenge the grammarians' primacy. See also note on 12/28-14/3.

20/1–4 **Sceptra . . . structuram.** See notes on 12/28-14/3 and 14/1.

20/5 **Schola Zoulensis aut dauentriana.** The schools of Zwolle and Deventer, both associated with the Brethren of the Common Life, were then regarded as the best in the Low Countries. Erasmus received much of his elementary education at Deventer; see Albert Hyma, *The Youth of Erasmus* (Ann Arbor, 1930), pp. 81–87.

20/6–9 **magni . . . Constantiensi.** Jerome of Prague (ca. 1365–1416), a major disciple of John Hus, was burned at the stake in Constance for maintaining the doctrines of Wyclif and Hus; see R. R. Betts, "Jerome of Prague," *University of Birmingham Historical Journal*, *1* (1947–48), 51–91. The article mentioned by Dorp was actually the twenty-ninth article of Wyclif condemned by the Council of Constance (1414–1418) in its Eighth Session (May 4, 1415); see Alberigo, pp. 412–13. Dorp's main incentive for linking the article with Jerome of Prague was probably the fact that the humanist Poggio Bracciolini, who was an eyewitness of Jerome's trial and execution in Constance, wrote an admiring account of Jerome's conduct there, representing him as a kind of new Socrates; see Poggio's letter to Bruni (May 29, 1416), *Poggii epistolae*, ed. T. de Tonelli, 3 vols. (Florence, 1832–61, reprint, Turin, 1964), *1*,

11–20; tr. R. N. Watkins, *Speculum, 42* (1967), 120–29. Cf. also C. B. Schmitt, "A Fifteenth-Century Translation . . ." *ARG, 58* (1967), 5–6.

20/10 **amusum.** *Adagia* 1518 (*Opera omnia,* 2, 588D–589B). Cf. 116/2 and *Moriae encomium, ASD 4/3,* 67, line 3.

20/10 **ignorauerit graece.** The phrase *ignoro graece* is a postclassical equivalent of *nescio graece;* see Isidore Hispalensis, *Etymologiae* 8.11.14 (*PL 82,* 315): "Latini ignorantes Graece."

20/12–13 **Sed . . . Dorpi.** Cf. 306/15; *CW 8,* 634/28; and Terence, *Adelphoe* 184: "si satis iam debacchatus es, leno, audi si vis nunc iam."

20/17 **extra controuersiam.** See *Adagia* 1147 (*Opera omnia,* 2, 464A): "Lucianus ἐξαγώνια vocat, quae ad causam non pertinent." In Lucian the word appears both in *Anacharsis* 19 and in *Pro imaginibus* 18. In *Hyperaspistes I* (*Opera omnia, 10,* 1302F), Erasmus uses *extra controuersiam* the same way that More does.

20/18–19 **quo in uniuersitates affectu.** Cf. More's own defense of the universities in *CW 5,* 256, 404. Many humanists were at least somewhat hostile to these bastions of the medieval intellectual establishment, and Erasmus himself blamed them for disrupting liberal studies as he understood them (*De pronuntiatione,* 1528, *ASD 1/4,* 24). See further M. A. Nauwelaerts, "Erasmus en de universiteiten van zijn tijd," *Tijdschrift voor Geschiedenis, 85* (1972), 374–89.

20/23 **parisijs.** For Erasmus' mixed experience as a student in Paris see Allen, *1,* 145–46.

20/24 **fuit, Tum.** Between these words *S* and *1563* insert "tum Patauiae" ("and then in Padua"). For Erasmus' casual contacts with Paduan academics see Allen, *1,* 447.

20/24 **Bononiae.** For Erasmus' casual contacts with Bolognese academics see Allen, *1,* 55, 426, 437, and 443.

20/24–26 **Rhoma . . . duco?** This is high praise indeed for a university which "at no period of the Middle Ages was . . . of much importance from an educational point of view" (Hastings Rashdall, *The Universities of Europe in the Middle Ages,* new edition by F. M. Powicke and A. B. Emden, 3 vols., Oxford, 1936, 2, 39; hereafter cited as "Rashdall"). But according to Rashdall, 2, 30 and 39, the university at Rome was packed with fine professors, chiefly humanists, during Erasmus' stay in Italy, and the papal *studium* had long been a center for Greek studies. See also Deno Geanakoplos, *Greek Scholars in Venice* (Cambridge, Mass., 1962), pp. 251–52. The Greek humanist Janus Lascaris, greatly admired by More (Rogers, p. 134), took charge of Greek studies in the papal *studium* in 1513; see Allen, *1,* 523. For Erasmus' contacts with prestigious men of learning in Rome see Allen, *1,* 61–62, 568.

20/26–29 **Iam . . . est.** For Erasmus' stay in Oxford and Cambridge see Allen, *1*, 241–73; 473, commentary on line 8; and 569. Erasmus spent only a short time in Oxford but some years in Cambridge; see H. C. Porter, ed., and D. F. S. Thomson, trans., *Erasmus and Cambridge: The Cambridge Letters of Erasmus* (Toronto, 1963; reprint, 1970).

20/30–31 **eo . . . insignitus.** Erasmus received his doctorate in theology on September 4, 1506, from the University of Turin; see Allen, *1*, 432, and L. Firpo, "Erasmo da Rotterdam a Torino," *Studi Piemontesi, 10* (1981), 239–59.

22/3–5 **Ais . . . seculis.** Cf. Dorp in Allen, *2*, 134, lines 302–04.

22/6 **Ego . . . septennium.** This is the only clear record of More's 1508 trip to the Continent. See R. W. Chambers, *Thomas More* (Westminster, Md., [1936]), pp. 97–98, where it is suggested that More may have gone to the Continent in preparation for a voluntary exile when he was in danger from Henry VII. Allen (*1*, 266) notes a passage from Erasmus' *Colloquiorum formulae* (1518) which suggests that More also visited Paris on his way to Germany as early as 1500.

22/15–17 **Iacobo . . . Aristotelicae.** See Rice, pp. 86–90 and 106–07; these are the prefaces for parts 1 and 3 of Lefèvre d'Etaples' reformed Latin *Organon* (Paris, 1501, 1503). This humanist theologian also published a reformed elementary textbook for students of "neoteric" dialectic or supposition theory (Rice, pp. 38–41, 53–55, and 78–85) as well as improved Latin versions of most other principal Aristotelian texts. A valuable bibliography of works by and about Lefèvre d'Etaples appears in Charles H. Lohr, "Renaissance Latin Aristotle Commentaries: Authors D–F," *Renaissance Quarterly, 29* (1976), 726–32. See More's similar tribute to his scholarship in Allen, *4*, 228, lines 448–61. For Dorp's criticisms of Lefèvre d'Etaples see p. xxii, n. 1, above.

22/19–23 **gratiam . . . retulerit.** More refers, not to Johannes Duns Scotus' Parisian lectureship, but to the supposed role of the great English pedagogue Alcuin, Charlemagne's mentor, in founding the University of Paris itself. See R. Gaguin, *Compendium super Francorum gestis* (Paris, G. Wolf and T. Kerver, 1500–01), fol. 28v:

> alcuinus . . . soli . . . gallici benignitate delectatus apud carolum mansit. Quo autore parisiensis schola (quam vniuersitatem vocant) hac occasione coepit. . . . Hoc initium habuit parisiensis schola celebre mox philosophis atque theologis gymnasium.

Other editions of this work were titled *Annales*. Cf. Robert Gaguin, *Epistole et orationes*, ed. Louis Thuasne, 2 vols. (Paris, 1903; reprinted in 1 vol., Geneva, 1977), *2*, 20. Erasmus wrote an enthusiastic commendatory letter for the first edition of Gaguin's history. See Allen, *1*, 148–52. For a brief biographical sketch of Gaguin see Allen, *1*, 146.

22/22–23 **nec . . . nostrae.** Cf. Livy 34.15.9, "Cato ipse haud sane detrectator laudum suarum"; for "buccinator nostrae [laudis]" cf. *Moriae encomium, ASD 4/3,* 72, lines 32–33.

24/1–4 **Miror . . . affectent.** The University of Louvain was firmly committed to the *via antiqua* of the realists; the University of Paris was generally regarded as the cradle of nominalism. More exaggerates the polarization of these universities. See Rashdall, *1,* 561–65, and 2, 268 and 287; and Astrik L. Gabriel, "Intellectual Relations between the University of Louvain and the University of Paris in the Fifteenth Century," in *The Universities in the Late Middle Ages,* ed. Jozef IJsewijn and Jacques Paquet, Medievalia Lovaniensia 1/6 (Louvain, 1978), pp. 117–27.

24/4-16 **si . . . digladiari.** For a similar polemical tactic directed against pagan philosophers see the note on 70/19–20.

24/16–19 **digladiari . . . dimicatur.** Cf. *Moriae encomium, ASD 4/3,* 144, line 369; and Erasmus in Allen, 2, 95, lines 152–54: "rixosas et frigidissimas quaestiones commenti, de nugacissimis nugis perinde ac pro focis ac aris inter se digladiantur." On "velut pro aris focisque" see Otto, no. 147.

24/18 **illam.** This reading may be a mistake for *illarum.*

24/22–23 **et ipse . . . intelligere.** For this traditional partition of grammar see Eugene Vinaver, *The Rise of Romance* (New York and Oxford, 1971), pp. 19–20. See also the notes on 12/19–21, 138/20–21.

24/24 **litterasque . . . insenescere.** Cf. Quintilian 12.11.15–16. For the placement of "inter" cf. Vergil, *Aeneid* 2.632 and 681. The reading *consenescere* of S and *1563* is slightly preferable to the *insenescere* of *P* and *1625,* a reading which More may have borrowed from a similar passage in Quintilian 10.3.11.

24/24-26/9 **itidem . . . abstinuit.** This passage was later appropriated with minor changes by both Dorp and Juan Luis Vives; see Dorp's *Apology to Meinard Man,* De Vocht, *Monumenta,* p. 88, lines 387–410; and Vives, *Epistola,* p. 78. Cf. also Cicero, *Orator* 32.115.

24/26–28 **Dialecticam . . . accommodare.** More's stress on the practical applications of dialectic relies partly on the primary sense of the Greek term *organon* ("tool" or "instrument") generally used to describe Aristotle's whole logical corpus.

24/29-26/4 **decem . . . absoluit.** Vives, *Epistola,* p. 78, actually names the six treatises by Aristotle to which More is alluding: " . . . dictionum videlicet natura quae docetur in libris *Categoriarum,* Enuntiationum viribus quae in *Perihermenias,* tum formulis collectionum quae in *prioribus Analyticis,* adjectis, et quae demonstrant in *posterioribus,* et quae probabili suadent ratione, quaeque ad inventionem faciunt, in *topicis*, et quae astute cavillantur, in *elenchis*. . . ."

26/4–6 **Ad haec . . . adiecit.** More is referring to Porphyry's *Isagoge* or "Introduction." Porphyry's Greek text and Boethius' Latin translation have been edited by Adolf Busse, *Commentaria in Aristotelem Graeca*, 23 vols. (Berlin, 1882–1909), *4/1*, 1–51 (hereafter cited as "Porphyry").

26/8–9 **Porphirius . . . abstinuit.** See Porphyry, p. 1, lines 8–16.

26/10 **portenta.** More again uses this word to refer to wrongheaded scholastics at 224/11.

26/13–14 **Alexandrum.** Alexander de Villa Dei (fl. 1200) was the author of a popular Latin grammar in verse, the *Doctrinale;* for a modern edition see Dietrich Reichling, ed., *Das Doctrinale des Alexander von Villa Dei* (Berlin, 1893). Erasmus frequently attacked Alexander's grammar along with many other medieval grammatical treatises, but in *De pueris instituendis* (1529), in a passage very reminiscent of More's comments in the *Letter to Dorp*, he declared, "Alexandrum inter tolerabiles numerandum arbitror" (*ASD 1/2*, 77, lines 15–16). For his earlier strictures, see M. A. Nauwelaerts, "*Grammatici, summularii* et autres auteurs réprouvés: Érasme et ses contemporains à la remorque de Valla," *Paedagogica Historica, 13* (1973), 471–85; *De conscribendis epistolis, ASD 1/2*, 257, 283, 285; *Colloquia, ASD 1/3*, 747; and Allen, 2, 99, lines 312–14, and 328, lines 228–34.

26/15–22 **Albertus . . . assequutus.** More refers, not to Albert of Saxony's *Tractatus* on logic (as Rogers suggests, p. 38, commentary at line 344), but to the Modist grammatical treatise (now attributed to Thomas of Erfurt) which was variously known in More's time as *Grammatica speculativa* and *De modis significandi*. More mockingly associates it with Luther and Tyndale (*CW 5*, 584/19–20, and *CW 8*, 212/30–32) along with the gynecological treatise *De secretis mulierum*, which in More's day was generally attributed to Albertus Magnus. The grammatical treatise in question was printed twice in England and twice in the Low Countries before the end of 1515 under the titles *Alberti Modi significandi* and *Alberti Liber modorum significandi* (*A Short-Title Catalogue of Books Printed in England . . . 1475–1640*, comp. A. W. Pollard and G. R. Redgrave, London, 1926, nos. 268 and 278; hereafter cited as *STC;* M. F. A. G. Campbell, *Annales de la typographie néerlandaise au XVe siècle*, The Hague, 1874, nos. 73 and 74). Its subtitle ("sine quibus grammatice notitia haberi nullo pacto potest") makes it clear that this treatise, rather than the less influential *Alberti Quaestiones de modis significandi* (*STC*, nos. 270–71), is foremost in More's mind here; cf. his wording at 26/20–22. The *Quaestiones* is also available in a modern edition; see Pseudo–Albertus Magnus, *Quaestiones Alberti de Modis Significandi*, ed. L. G. Kelly, Amsterdam Studies in the Theory and History of Linguistic Science, 3rd Series, no. 15 (Amsterdam, 1977). The Modists went much further than Alexander in laying down a priori rules for what constitutes good grammar. For more information on the Modist grammars see Thomas of Erfurt, *Grammatica speculativa*, ed. and trans. G. L. Bursill-Hall (London, 1972); G. A. Padley, *Grammatical Theory in Western Europe 1500–1700* (Cambridge, 1976), with bibliographies; and Jan Pinborg, "Speculative Grammar," *CHLMP*, pp. 254–69.

26/17 **mera deliria.** Cf. *Moriae encomium*, *ASD 4/3*, 138, line 256 (in a passage concerning grammarians): "mera deliramenta."

26/18 **nugacissimae nugae.** See note on 24/16–19.

26/22–24 **Tantum . . . persuasio.** Cf. Erasmus in Allen, 2, 55, lines 1–4; 56, lines 61–62.

28/2 **nisi.** Though More is trying to make the diction of this arrogant dialectician seem as barbarous as possible, *nisi* may be simply a scribal mistake for *non nisi*. The same mistake evidently occurred in the source-text of *S* and *1563* at 106/5. The dialectician's whole speech is written in gothic script in *P*, as is the speech of the aged theologian at 68/13–16.

28/3 **paruis Logicalibus.** While there were several neoteric treatises on logic entitled *Parva logicalia*, the fact that Vives in his closely related *Epistola in pseudodialecticos* speaks only against Peter of Spain's *Parva logicalia* (pp. 70–79), the most famous of them all, suggests that More, too, alludes only to Peter of Spain's work. See also the Introduction, p. liii, above.

28/3 **tam mirabiliter fundati.** Cf. *Epistolae obscurorum vivorum*, ed. Francis G. Stokes (London, 1925), p. 68, line 77: "bene fundatus in Theologia."

28/4–5 **resurrexeret.** A barbarous equivalent of *resurgeret*.

28/5 **illi bene concluderent eum.** Cf. *Epistolae obscurorum virorum*, p. 238, lines 57–59: " . . . saltem irent [*sc.* theologi] in Boemiā concludentes Illam gentem cum Argumentis et Syllogismis suis."

28/9 **paruorum logicalium.** See note on 28/3.

28/10-32/25 **In suppositionibus . . . ministrasse.** On this section of the letter see the Introduction, pp. liv–lvii.

28/13 **praeceptiunculas.** This contemptuous diminutive is attested in Latham, p. 364, from documents of 1515 and 1520. The word also appears in Erasmus, *Methodus* (1516), Holborn, pp. 154 and 159.

28/19 **Logistas.** The Latin form of λογιστής normally refers to a civic administrator. Aristophanes uses the phrase λεπτὸς λογιστής to refer

humorously to a hypersubtle reasoner in *Aves* 318. But when More uses *logista* in this sense he is probably mocking the scholastics' own fondness for academic titles concluding with *–ista;* see notes on 62/22, 96/17, and 106/16. The verb *logiso* is attested in Latham, p. 281, from a document of ca. 1365.

30/1–5 **hec . . . uapulent.** There is a similar joke based on the sophism "You beat your father" in Plato, *Euthydemus* 298C–299A.

30/10 **Sortes.** This word is a scholastic abbreviation for Socrates and is expanded accordingly in *1625*.

30/14 **regnant.** Cf. 14/1; *CW 8,* 808/16; and Terence, *Phormio* 405.

30/15 **ampliatiua.** This barbarous word is attested in Blaise, p. 43.

30/15–16 **pomeria . . . proferunt.** On the *pomeria* or "city limits" of Rome see Tacitus, *Annales* 12.23, where it is reported that whoever extends the boundaries of the Roman empire is entitled to extend the boundaries of the city itself. Cf. also *Moriae encomium, ASD 4/3,* 112, line 758; and *Adagia* 2546 (*Opera omnia,* 2, 858C). For "ultra ipsas naturae fines" cf. Horace, *Satirae* 1.1.49–50: "intra | naturae fines viventi," "a man living within nature's bounds."

32/7 **amatiuus.** This barbarous word is attested in Blaise, p. 39.

32/18–19 **Poetae . . . loquuntur.** Cf. Plutarch's title for one of the essays comprised in *Moralia* (1057C–1058E): "Stoicos absurdiora poetis dicere." This passage is almost as close as More comes to defending the poets against the scholastics' aspersions (cf. 8/25, 48/11–12, 114/3–23).

32/23 **doctoribus tam irrefragabilibus.** More is mocking the ambitious epithets ("subtilissimus," "seraphicus," and so on) which were commonly used to distinguish the most influential scholastic theologians; cf. Erasmus, *Antibarbari, ASD 1/1,* 90, lines 8–9; and *Moriae encomium, ASD 4/3,* 166, lines 636–38, and commentary. "Doctor irrefragabilis" was the epithet of the English theologian Alexander of Hales (d. 1245), whose most celebrated work is a *Summa universae theologiae.*

32/26–27 **Hyeronymus . . . Augustinus?** This answers a passage in Dorp's second letter (Allen, 2 133, lines 261–64).

32/27–28 **Non . . . Orestes.** See Persius 3.118 and *CW 3/2,* 604/23–24.

34/3–5 **Nec . . . est.** More is stressing the fact that the words which are used in these sophisms, unlike the *dialecticorum verba* which Cicero sanctions (*Academica* 1.7.25), are not "terms of art": dialecticians cannot change the meanings of everyday words as they please. Cf. Quintilian 1.6.3: " . . . utendumque plane sermone ut nummo cui publica forma

est." Cf. also *Moriae encomium, ASD 4/3*, 158, lines 517–19: "Mira vero maiestas theologorum, si solis illis fas est mendose loqui, quanquam hoc ipsum habent cum multis cerdonibus commune."

34/9 **malum.** This interjection is common in angry rhetorical questions (see Terence, *Heauton timoroumenos* 318; *Eunuchus* 780; *Phormio* 723, 948; *Adelphoe* 544, 557).

34/9 **in angulo.** *Adagia* 3467 (*Opera omnia*, 2, 1069CD). In his later works More is constantly accusing the heretics of plotting "in corners"; for a list of examples see *CW 12*, Commentary at 11/10.

34/11–14 **Grammatica . . . admonet.** Cf. Quintilian 1.6.16: "Non enim, cum primum fingerentur homines, analogia demissa caelo formam loquendi dedit, sed inventa est postquam loquebantur. . . . Itaque non ratione nititur, sed exemplo, nec lex est loquendi sed observatio, ut ipsam analogiam nulla res alia fecerit quam consuetudo."

34/18 **barbara.** On the various moods of the syllogism, *barbara* in particular, see *CW 8*, 1578–79. *S* adds the words "vel caterua," probably an indication of some uncertainty as to which mood of the syllogism this example in fact represents.

36/5–6 **Nummum non habeo.** Cf. Plautus, *Pseudolus* 356: "nummum non habes," where a sophist might claim that the sense, namely "You haven't got a penny," requires "non habes nummum."

36/7 **transpositiones.** This postclassical word (equivalent to μετάθεσις) is attested in Souter, p. 427, from a document of the early Christian era.

36/8–9 **Bibas . . . bibas.** The same example is used in *CW 6*, 324/24. More may well be thinking of the adage "Aut bibat aut abeat"; see *Adagia* 947 (*Opera omnia*, 2, 381). The reading of *S* and *1563* means "'Drink before you eat' and 'Eat before you drink.'"

36/14–18 **Nam . . . accipere.** Cf. *Moriae encomium, ASD 4/3*, 158, lines 514–16: " . . . cumque adeo balbutiunt vt a nemine nisi balbo possint intelligi, acumen appellant quod vulgus non assequatur."

36/14–15 **hebetissimum acumen.** Cf. *CW 3/2*, 636/31–32, *CW 8*, 719/27, and *Debellation, EW*, sig. O₇v ("such bloont subtil trifles").

36/17–18 **contra . . . sensum.** There seems to be some reminiscence of Folly's philosopher par excellence here, who "communium rerum sit imperitus et a populari opinione vulgaribusque institutis longe lateque discrepet" (*ASD 4/3*, 100, lines 524–25; cf. 111, lines 742–43). See also 48/13–16. In the *Responsio, CW 5*, 554/24–29, More accepts Luther's association of the dictates of grammar with the dictates of common sense but proceeds to suggest that Luther's own notion of grammar shows him to have no common sense at all. Cf. also *CW 5*, 564/13–14, and especially 618/30–620/2, where More suggests that the upshot of Luther's teaching is simply "[ut] interpretetur e suo quisque sensu scripturam sacram: et sibi, quam libeat, fidem formet nouam."

36/25–27 **nisi . . . uoluptatem.** Cf. *CW 8*, 135/18–19.

38/12–13 **theologos . . . designari.** Cf. Dorp in Allen, 2, 133, line 238.

38/14 **huius . . . furfuris.** Cf. *Adagia* 2444 (*Opera omnia*, 2, 839DE): "Nostrae farinae." For "istius furfuris" cf. *CW 3/2*, 616/27, and *CW 5*, 18/6.

38/24-40/6 **Nonne . . . religionem.** Allen, 2, 134, lines 272–82. Dorp cites Matt. 5:22 and Jerome's commentary on Matthew, *PL 26*, 37A. The description "qui nil habent mentis" that Dorp cites from Erasmus' letter does not occur in the printed version, but cf. Allen, 2, 99, lines 310–19.

40/12–13 **me miseret . . . quod.** The impersonal form *miseret* does not normally appear with a relative clause. For *poenitet* with a relative clause see Cicero, *Epistolae ad Atticum* 7.3.

40/14–19 **Nam . . . numerus.** There is a very similar passage in *The Debellation of Salem and Bizance, EW*, sig. O₈v. More cites the Vulgate translation of Eccles. 1:15; the author of this book is conventionally thought to be Solomon. Cf. 258/15–16 and *Moriae encomium, ASD 4/3*, 180, lines 919–22.

40/24–27 **nullius . . . inflectere.** Cf. Erasmus in Allen, 2, 102–03, lines 454–65; and Terence, *Phormio* 696–98:

> nil est, Antipho,
> Quin male narrando possit depravarier:
> tu id quod boni est excerpis, dicis quod malist.

Cf. also Plautus, *Epidicus* 513–14. More makes the same charge in almost the same words against the monk Batmanson (276/13–15) and Luther (*CW 5*, 212/27–28).

42/4–6 **epistola . . . traiecto.** This letter of 1515 dedicating Adrian's *Quaestiones quodlibeticae* to Abbot Meinard Man is reprinted with an introduction in De Vocht, *Monumenta*, pp. 112–20. Adrian of Utrecht was the future Pope Adrian VI (see *CW 5*, 878–79).

42/8–9 **interpres paulo malignior.** Cf. Martial 1 pref.: "malignus interpres."

42/9 **altera . . . lapidem.** Cf. *Adagia* 729 (*Opera omnia*, 2, 309CD) and Matt. 7:9.

42/12 **opplorationibus.** This derivative of the rare verb *opploro* (pseudo-Cicero, *Rhetorica ad Herennium* 4.52.65) is attested in Latham,

p. 323, probably drawing on *Utopia, CW 4,* 82/2–3. Dorp uses the form *opplorauerunt* in the dedicatory letter (De Vocht, *Monumenta,* p. 116).

42/16–21 **Ioannes Athensis . . . interdiu.** John Briart of Ath (d. 1520) was one of the most influential of the Louvain theology professors. He was frequently in conflict with Erasmus, who unflatteringly labeled him "Noxus," a Latin approximation of ἄτη ("perdition"). It has been noted that Briart may have been the main instigator of Dorp's first attack on Erasmus (Allen, 2, 100, commentary at line 373), which would account for More's rather irreverent reference here. Dorp's own reference to Briart in the dedicatory letter (De Vocht, *Monumenta,* p. 117) omits the comparison of Briart to an overworked midwife. On Briart, see also Henry de Vocht, "Anecdota humanistica Lovaniensia: John Briart of Ath," *Sacris Erudiri,* 7 (1955), 335–66.

42/21–24 **Quid . . . flexibilem?** Cf. De Vocht, *Monumenta,* p. 119: "quis aequitatis (vt ita dicam) Lesbiae perspicacior [*sc.* Hadriano]?" For the *lesbia regula* see *CW 6,* Commentary at 129/11; Aristotle, *Ethica Nicomachea* 5.10.7; and *Adagia* 493 (*Opera omnia,* 2, 217CD). Contrast the "inflexibilem ueritatis regulam" of the "uiuum euangelium fidei" at 88/2-6.

44/2–3 **in . . . perfectum.** Cf. Pliny, *Epistolae* 4.14.7, a warning against comparing dissimilar works and disparaging "quod est in suo genere perfectum."

44/10–12 **cottidie . . . addidicerunt.** See note on 38/24–40/6.

44/14–18 **Quamobrem . . . uestris.** For similarly intricate syntax see 206/27–29 and note.

44/14–16 **Porro . . . uia.** Dorp in Allen, 2, 133, lines 265–66.

44/16 **tota erras uia.** Cf. *Moriae encomium, ASD 4/3,* 116, line 865; *Adagia* 48 (*Opera omnia,* 2, 47F–48A); and Erasmus in Allen, 2, 107, line 627.

44/22–23 **Dic . . . euoluenda?** Dorp in Allen, 2, 133, lines 266–68.

44/24-46/1 **aliqui . . . inspicere.** Cf. *Moriae encomium, ASD 4/3,* 154, lines 485–87.

46/2–6 **Proferam . . . rhetorissant.** Dorp in Allen, 2, 133–34, lines 268–72.

46/4–5 **Endimionis somnum dormire.** *Adagia* 863 (*Opera omnia,* 2, 357D–F).

46/11 **Moriae ui.** Erasmus' Moria is expert in distorting scriptural texts (*ASD 4/3,* 182–84).

46/13–15 **qui . . . intelligant.** Augustine recommends memorization of scripture, even by those who do not understand it, in *De doctrina christiana* 2.9.14 (*PL 34*, 42). In his *Ratio verae theologiae* (1519), Holborn, p. 293, Erasmus qualifies Augustine's recommendation in much the same way that More does here.

46/18–19 **in Theologorum albo . . . collocandos.** Cf. *Adagia* 634 (*Opera omnia*, 2, 275E–276A).

46/26 **Theologiae huic disputatrici.** The phrase *disputatrix theologia* is also used by Erasmus (Allen, *3*, 381, line 55; *4*, 319, line 13; and 336, line 72). Quintilian introduces the adjective *disputatrix* at 2.20.7 and 12.2.13 as an equivalent for *dialectice.*

48/3 **positiua.** See André Prévost, *Thomas More et la crise de la pensée européenne* (Paris, 1969), pp. 363–70. According to Prévost, who points out the parallel usage in the *Letter to Oxford* (140/15), this is the earliest surviving document in which "positive" is used to describe patristic (as opposed to scholastic) theology. But the *Dictionnaire de théologie catholique*, 15 vols. (Paris, 1908–50; hereafter cited as *DTC*), *15*, 426–28, and Tshibangu, pp. 195–99, note an instance of the opposition *positiva–scholastica* from the year 1509, and More's wording in both letters actually seems to refer to a commonplace distinction between philological and "speculative" approaches to the discipline of theology. For the parallel contrast between historical or "positive" grammar and theoretical or "speculative" grammar see Terence Heath, "Logical Grammar, Grammatical Logic, and Humanism in Three German Universities," *Studies in the Renaissance, 18* (1971), 13 and 49 (hereafter cited as "Heath"). Since More elsewhere in this letter upholds the former sort of grammar against the latter (24/21–24, 26/13–22), he himself probably wants us to recognize the parallel between positive grammar and positive theology. See also notes on 68/17–22 and 68/17–70/3.

48/4–5 **neque . . . suos.** Cf. Terence, *Eunuchus* 312.

48/18–24 **omnium . . . interpretentur.** Cf. Cicero, *De oratore* 2.4.18, 2.18.76.

48/19–20 **quicquam . . . uiderint.** In Allen, *1*, 412, lines 185–89, Erasmus stresses the importance of seeing a text "with one's own eyes"—that is, reading a text for oneself in its original language and form—before jumping to conclusions about its meaning.

48/22–24 **se . . . interpretentur.** Cf. *Moriae encomium, ASD 4/3*, 184, lines 5–9; and Erasmus, *Ecclesiastes, Opera omnia, 5*, 1026A. More later transfers this charge from the scholastics to heretics (cf. *CW 8*, 688/30, and note on 36/17–18, above). Tyndale assigned no less importance to contextual reading than More did; for an account of the different ways in which Tyndale and More qualified the validity of this method, see Flesseman-Van Leer, pp. 157, 159–60. Erasmus develops his own program for contextual interpretation of scripture in *Ratio verae theologiae*, Holborn, pp. 196–201.

50/1-54/13 **Cenaui . . . periere.** In 1517–18 Erasmus inserted into the *Adagia* a similar tale of a ludicrous dispute involving Henry Standish and a continental theologian (*Adagia* 1498, *Opera omnia*, 2, 581A–583C; cf. Allen, *3*, 296).

50/1–2 **Italum . . . ditissimus.** This may be a reference to More's friend Antonio Bonvisi (1487–1558); see Rogers, pp. 87–88; and Elizabeth McCutcheon, " 'The Apple of My Eye': Thomas More to Antonio Bonvisi, A Reading and Translation," *Moreana*, 71–72 (1981), 39–44. Harpsfield, pp. 138–39, mentions Bonvisi as his source for a very similar anecdote in which More gets the better of a foreign theologian.

50/20–21 **De . . . factae.** Usury, tithes, and confessions heard by friars in parishes where the bishop had not granted them faculties were topics of lively discussion among medieval theologians and canon lawyers. On usury see *Decretales Gregorii IX*, 5.19 (*Corpus iuris canonici*, ed. Emil Ludwig Richter and Emil Albert Friedberg, 2 vols., Leipzig, 1879–81, reprint, Graz, 1959 [hereafter cited as *CIC*], 2, 811–16); *Sexti Decretales*, 5.5 (*CIC* 2, 1081–82); *Clementinae*, 5.5 (*CIC* 2, 1184); and John T. Noonan, Jr., *The Scholastic Analysis of Usury* (Cambridge, Mass., 1957). On tithes see *Decretales Gregorii IX*, 3.30 (*CIC* 2, 555–69); *Sexti Decretales*, 3.13 (*CIC* 2, 1048–50); *Clementinae*, 3.8 (*CIC* 2, 1164–65); *Extravagantes communes*, 3.7 (*CIC* 2, 1273–77); and C. E. Boyd, *Tithes and Parishes in Medieval Italy* (Ithaca, 1952). On the protracted struggle between friars and parish clergy over who was entitled to preach and hear confessions in any given parish see G. R. Owst, *Preaching in Medieval England* (Cambridge, 1926; hereafter cited as "Owst"), pp. 71–73.

50/25–27 **sermonem . . . discurrere.** On *clerici concubinarii* see *Decretales Gregorii IX*, 3.2 (*CIC* 2, 454–57).

52/2 **limpidissimi.** Here, too, More is mocking the scholastics' devotion to pretentious epithets; see note on 32/23.

52/3–4 **Directorium concubinariorum.** The actual title of this anonymous work, first printed in Cologne in 1508, is *Directorium concubinariorum saluberrimum quo quedam stupenda et ob tanti sceleris impunem tolerantiam quasi inaudita pericula resoluuntur.* . . . See H. M. Adams, *Catalogue of Books Printed on the Continent of Europe, 1501–1600, in Cambridge Libraries*, 2 vols. (Cambridge, 1967), *1*, 359, where three editions of this work are mentioned.

52/9 **olfecisset.** For this proverbial metaphor see note on 208/20.

52/27 **loco . . . turpissimum.** Cf. Ovid, *Ex Ponto* 2.6.21; *Adagia* 1625 (*Opera omnia*, 2, 619CD); and the note on 258/19–20, below.

52/28 **proteus.** Cf. *Adagia* 1174 (*Opera omnia*, 2, 473BC): "Proteo mutabilior." More applies the same epithet to Luther in *CW 5*, sidenote at 636/10. Cf. also *Moriae encomium, ASD 4/3,* 146, lines 392–93.

54/8 **afferebat.** This reading may be a mistake for *asserebat.*

54/8–9 **iurabat . . . credere.** Cf. Terence, *Hecyra* 60–61, and 482/12, below.

54/9 **Nicolaum de Lyra.** See note on 216/10.

54/10–12 **plusquam . . . poculis.** Cf. Erasmus in Allen, *1,* 268, lines 20–21: "His ordinibus ita digestis statim bellum oritur inter pocula, non tamen ex poculis neque poculentum." For "inter pocula" cf. *Adagia* 601 and 3870 (*Opera omnia*, 2, 262A–F and 1158F–1159A).

54/12 **terrigenae.** Cf. Ovid, *Metamorphoses* 3.102–03, 115–25. The same image appears with more sinister effect in *CW 5*, 690/32–692/1: "populus [*sc.* Lutheri] . . . uelut terrigenae illi fratres, mutuo se confodiet." Cf. also *CW 14,* 445/9–447/5, and the note on 70/19–20, below.

54/14–16 **sacrarum . . . distentos.** Cf. Augustine, *De doctrina christiana* 2.13.20 (*PL 34,* 44–45), cited by Dorp in Allen, 2, 133, lines 251–53: " . . . eo sunt [*sc.* homines] infirmiores quo doctiores videri volunt, non rerum scientia qua edificamur, sed signorum qua non inflari difficile est." Augustine in turn is alluding to 1 Cor. 8:1: "Scientia inflat, caritas vero aedificat."

54/18–56/8 **Non . . . periclitari.** Dorp in Allen, 2, 135, lines 323–36.

54/22 **pro quo mortuus est Christus.** Cf. Rom. 14:15.

54/23–24 **ut . . . formae.** While the scholastics recast the discussion of the sacraments by invoking Aristotle's distinction between matter and form, their distinction between matter and form in the sacraments closely corresponds to the distinction between *res sacramenti* and *verba sacramenti* which had been current in the Church since the patristic era. See the article "Matière et forme dans les sacrements," *DTC 10,* 335–55.

54/24–56/1 **quando . . . reijciendus.** Peter Lombard and others discussed the conditions that must be fulfilled before penitents may be given absolution. See Paul Anciaux, *La théologie du sacrement de pénitence au XIIᵉ siècle* (Louvain and Gembloux, 1949), pp. 253–54; and Peter Lombard, *Sententiae* 4.18.7 (*PL 192,* 888).

56/1–2 **quid . . . possit.** Restitution of unlawful gains is discussed in *Decretales Gregorii IX*, 2.13 (*CIC* 2, 279–91); *Sexti Decretales*, 2.5 (*CIC* 2, 999); and *DTC 13*, 2466–2501.

56/14 **culice . . . Elephantem.** Cf. Matt. 23:24; *Adagia* 2027 (*Opera omnia*, 2, 723DE): "Culicem elephanti conferre"; and *Adagia* 869 (*Opera omnia*, 2, 359AB). See also 282/1–2, above.

56/17–18 **nodum . . . in scirpo.** *Adagia* 1376 (*Opera omnia*, 2, 546F–547A).

56/18–19 **in . . . luto herendum.** Cf. *CW* 5, 268/13, 490/1; and *Adagia* 399 (*Opera omnia*, 2, 180D).

56/20 **amoenissimum . . . pratum.** See note on 12/14–15. St. Ambrose employs similar images for scripture in *Epistolae* 49.3 (*PL 16*, 1154) and *In psalmum David 118 expositio* 14.2 (*PL 15*, 1390). Cf also Jerome, *Epistolae* 115, *PL* 22, 935 (criticized by Augustine in *Epistolae* 116, *PL* 22, 936–37), and Erasmus in Allen, 2, 106, lines 597–99; *4*, 73, lines 21–23; 151, lines 499–508; 158, lines 29–30.

56/20–21 **a capite . . . calcem.** *Adagia* 137 (*Opera omnia*, 2, 84A–D).

56/26 **stipites.** Otto, no. 1695. Cf. *Moriae encomium*, *ASD 4/3*, 100, line 522, and *CW 3/2*, 686.

56/26 **pistillo . . . obtusiore.** *Adagia* 2521 (*Opera omnia*, 2, 854A), based on Jerome, *Epistolae* 69.4 (*PL* 22, 657).

56/27 **promouerint.** More frequently uses *promoveo* in an intransitive sense; cf. 64/22, 160/5, and 282/20. Cf. Erasmus, *Paraclesis*, Holborn, p. 141, line 31; and Gerardus Listrius in Allen, 2, 414, line 5. This usage seems to have evolved from such idiomatic expressions as *nil promoves*, "You are getting nowhere" (Terence, *Eunuchus* 913; cf. *Andria* 640, *Hecyra* 703, and *CW 4*, 80/17). The first distinctly intransitive use of *promoveo* occurs in Aulus Gellius 5.10.7: "Postea cum diutule auditor adsectatorque Protagorae fuisset et in studio quidem facundiae abunde promovisset. . . ."

58/2 **equis . . . albis.** *Adagia* 321 (*Opera omnia*, 2, 159C–160A); cf. *Moriae encomium*, *ASD 4/3*, 132, line 142.

58/2–5 **quouis . . . pudor.** Cf. Otto, no. 853; *Moriae encomium*, *ASD 4/3*, 102–04, lines 566–76; and *Adagia* 3454 (*Opera omnia*, 2, 1066DE).

58/6-60/23 **Est . . . patefecerit.** More appears to touch on the difficulty of scripture on all four traditional levels of interpretation, moral (58/21-60/2), literal (60/2–10), allegorical (60/15–18), and anagogical (60/18–23). In *CW* 5, 126/5–18, More grants that the literal sense is almost always the only one effective for proving anything but insists on the value of alternative levels of interpretation for reconciling obscure texts with clear ones. Thus More may assign somewhat more value to the figural senses of scripture than Erasmus does in his later works (see *Moriae encomium, ASD 4/3,* commentary at 166, line 643), but there is certainly nothing reactionary about stressing the value of the figural senses the way More does here. In the *Enchiridion* (1503), Holborn, pp. 33–35, 71–73, Erasmus faults the scholastics in general for not paying *more* attention to the figural senses.

58/6–12 **Est . . . aperit.** Cf. James 1:17, Rev. 5:1–6, and Isa. 22:22; the third passage refers to the key of the house of David.

58/13–20 **Hieronimo . . . torpescerent.** Cf. Jerome, *Epistolae* 49.4, 53, 105.5 (*PL* 22, 512, 540–49, 836); Augustine, *De doctrina christiana* 2.6.7 (*PL 34,* 38); *CW 8,* Commentary at 331/5–10; and *CW 14,* Commentary 2 at 13/7–15/1. For "impenetrabilem," cf. Augustine on Genesis (*PL 34,* 223). Cf. also Erasmus, *Hyperaspistes I* (*Opera omnia, 10,* 1301E).

58/17 **obstrusum.** The odd word *obstrusa* is a variant reading in Seneca, *Epistolae* 68.4, to which More is probably alluding: "multi aperta transeunt, condita et abstrusa rimantur. . . ."

58/21–25 **Iam . . . uideantur.** For an example of the tactful allegoresis that More is commending see *CW 13,* 57/25–59/4. But here More is primarily concerned with the moralization of seemingly immoral texts like the story of Lot's daughters (Gen. 19:30–38) and of the concubine chosen for the elderly King David (3 Kings 1:1–4; cf. *CW 8,* 637/15–32 and Commentary).

58/26–27 **quum . . . perduxerint.** Cf. *Moriae encomium, ASD 4/3,* 154–56, lines 490–91, on the scholastics' handling of scripture in general, and Listrius' commentary in *Opera omnia, 4,* 469C: "Notat [sc. Erasmus] eos qui non accommodant suas sententias ad mentem scripturarum, sed scripturas ad suam mentem trahunt." For a striking example of an inept "moralization," see Allen, *4,* 571–72.

58/27–60/1 **quum . . . frigescat.** Cf. Erasmus, *Enchiridion,* Holborn, p. 71, lines 31–32: "non potest non frigere mysterium, quod non eloquentiae viribus ac dicendi lepore quodam condiatur."

60/1 **moralisatio.** This word, meaning "a moral interpretation," is attested in Latham, pp. 304–05, and Blaise, p. 600; see also *The Oxford English Dictionary,* 13 vols. (Oxford, 1933; hereafter cited as *OED*), 6, 655.

60/2–4 **ipsum litteralem sensum . . . possit.** Cf. *CW 8,* 635/35–37: "And somtyme he [*sc.* God] endyghted it [*sc.* scripture], & our sauyour hym self somtyme spake his wordes in such wyse, that the letter had none other sense then mysteryes & allegoryes. . . ."

60/4–10 **Neque . . . aperuit.** Ps. 109:1; cf. Matt. 22:41–46; Mark 12:35–37; Luke 20:41–44. Cf. also Erasmus, *Hyperaspistes I* (*Opera omnia, 10,* 1300F): "An ibi [*sc.* in vetere testamento] nihil erat de Christo

COMMENTARY

praedictum, quod non omnibus esset clarissimum, modo scirent Hebraice? Imo nec discipuli Domini post tot sermones auditos, post tot visa miracula, post tot notas et indicia, quae de Christo prophetae praedixerant, intelligunt Scripturas, donec Christus illis aperiret sensum, ut intelligerent Scripturas."

60/11–12 **neque . . . unquam.** Cf. *Moriae encomium, ASD 4/3,* 154, lines 460–61.

60/12–23 **Non . . . patefecerit.** This passage is paraphrased with a number of small but significant alterations in *CW 8,* 337/24–33. Cf. also *CW 6,* 146, and *CW 14,* 441–43.

60/22–23 **temporibus . . . prouidentiae.** Cf. Matt. 24:36, Acts 1:7. Erasmus appeals to the same texts to establish the obscurity of some parts of scripture in *De libero arbitrio (Opera omnia, 9,* 1217A). Cf. also 1216D: "Multa servantur ei tempori, cum jam non videbimus per speculum & in aenigmate, sed revelata facie Domini, gloriam contemplabimur." In *CW 14,* 587, More suggests that the identity of the young man who according to Mark 14:51–52 ran away naked from Christ's persecutors will remain unconfirmed until it is revealed in heaven.

60/26–27 **saltare . . . faciunt.** Cf. *Adagia* 3680 (*Opera omnia, 2,* 1117EF): "diserte saltare."

60/27 **saltatriculi quidam ac circulatores.** There are several difficulties with the reading at this point in the text. *P* and *1625* read "saltatriculi quidam circulatores," while *S* and *1563* read "saltatriculae quidem ac circulatores." The masculine form *saltatriculus* is not attested in any of the lexicons, and since the feminine form *saltatricula* is a diminutive of the feminine noun *saltatrix* the masculine variant form found in *P* and *1625* is a startling innovation, to say the least. On the other hand, the reading of *S* and *1563* ("saltatriculae quidem") looks suspiciously like a misguided editorial emendation in which the masculine adjective *quidam* has been replaced by the superfluous adverb *quidem* ("indeed" or "at least") to permit the replacement of the masculine noun "saltatriculi" by its more common feminine equivalent. The reading of *P* and *1625* is also problematic because it omits a conjunction between "quidam" and "circulatores" and thus requires us to take "saltatriculi" as an adjective rather than a noun. Possibly in the copy-text of *P* the noun "circulatores" appeared as an interlineated authorial variant for *saltatriculi quidam,* while in the copy-text of *S* and *1563* More decided to add a conjunction and thus integrate the variant in the text.

62/8–9 **Bibliae . . . reginae.** Cf. 14/15–16. More's description of the Bible as the "holy queen of all genres of literature" is probably a polemical variation on the commonplace medieval description of theology as the "queen of all disciplines" (see note on 140/9–10).

62/9 **confers . . . prefers.** For the wording cf. 172/23–24 and note.

62/11–12 **Abite . . . fugitiuae.** Cf. Terence, *Phormio* 930–32:

> In hinc malam rem cum istac magnificentia,
> Fugitiue? etiam nunc credis te ignorarier
> Aut tua facta adeo?

S and *1563* add an adaptation of Terence's second sentence, translated as follows: "Do you really think we do not know about you or your doings?"

62/14–17 **tanquam . . . incumbat.** Cf. Buckingham's hypocritical petition to the usurper in *Historia Richardi Tertii*, 476/9–10: "[ut] procumbenti in se vnum patriae subijceret humeros."

62/14–15 **in Atlantis humeros.** Cf. *Adagia* 67 and 3493 (*Opera omnia, 2,* 52E and 1074F); Erasmus in Allen, 2, 111, line 807; and *Moriae encomium, ASD 4/3,* 154, lines 488–90.

62/16–17 **arundinem . . . incumbat.** Cf. *CW 12,* 5/2; *Adagia* 1570 (*Opera omnia, 2,* 605DE); 4 Kings 18:21; Isa. 36:6; Ezek. 29:6–7. For "inclinata incumbat" cf. also Vergil, *Aeneid* 12.59.

62/17–18 **collaberetur in cineres.** Cf. *Debellation, EW,* sig. Q₇, where More uses the phrase "to fall into the fire" to refer to the consequences of heresy.

62/18–21 **alioqui . . . possit?** Dorp in Allen, 2, lines 327–30.

62/22 **questionistas.** This word is attested in Latham, p. 388, from a document of 1250; cf. *OED 8,* 49.

64/1–6 **Ergo . . . habuit.** Cf. Erasmus, *Vita Hieronymi,* Ferguson, p. 179, lines 1198–99: "O calamitatem orbis Christiani, qui plus mille annos absque theologis steterit!" Erasmus, like More, treats scholastic presumption sarcastically.

64/3–4 **Petri Lombardi . . . sententijs.** Peter Lombard (ca. 1100–1160), bishop of Paris (1158), wrote the basic textbook of scholastic theology, *Sententiarum libri quatuor.*

64/3–4 **sententijs . . . Troiano.** For the conceit equating an influential teacher with a Trojan horse, see Cicero, *De oratore* 2.22.94, on the orator Isocrates. Cf. also *Adagia* 3101 (*Opera omnia, 2,* 992A–E).

64/10–12 **Zacheus . . . est.** Cf. Luke 19:2–10; *CW 12,* 176/7–178/15; and *CW 13,* 203/16–204/14.

64/15–16 **illorum . . . diligentiam.** Terence, *Andria* 18–21, where Terence is suggesting that it is better to err with authors like Naevius, Plautus, and Ennius than to be as punctilious as Terence's critics. Erasmus invokes the same verse in *De pronuntiatione, ASD 1/4*, 99, as a sanction for the sort of *docta negligentia* that is frequently called *sprezzatura;* see note on 218/26–27.

64/18–19 **non . . . accedere.** Cf. *Debellation, EW*, sig. P$_6$v.

64/21–23 **citra . . . promoueat.** More is apparently using "citra" and "ultra" adverbially; "mille passus" and "latum unguem" are almost certainly simple accusatives of extent of space. For *promoveo* used in an intransitive sense see note on 56/27.

64/22 **latum . . . unguem.** *Adagia* 406 (*Opera omnia*, 2, 184E–185B).

64/25-66/2 **quaecunque . . . tradita.** For the same formula of hand-to-hand transmission applied to the Church's authority and oral traditions see *CW 5*, 90/21–25. The formula "per manus tradita" is proverbial (*Adagia* 3428, *Opera omnia*, 2, 1060E–1061B).

66/6–13 **At . . . porrigere.** Cf. Peter Lombard, *Sententiae 1, prologus* (*PL 192*, 522), and more generally Richard H. Rouse and Mary A. Rouse, "*Statim invenire:* Schools, Preachers, and New Attitudes to the Page," in *Renaissance and Renewal in the Twelfth Century*, ed. Robert L. Benson et al. (Cambridge, Mass., 1982), pp. 201–25.

66/7 **in numerato.** Cf. *Adagia* 3282 (*Opera omnia*, 2, 1021AB).

66/14–16 **hoc . . . caruisse.** Very similar passages occur at 370/24–27 and in *CW 12*, 221/14–16. Cf. also Erasmus, *Institutio christiani matrimonii, Opera omnia*, 5, 672B.

66/16-70/3 **Neque . . . Theologum.** Cf. 258/4–7 and Erasmus in Allen, 2, 213–14, lines 83–87. Many humanists felt a particular animosity toward medieval *summularii* or compilers, who had effectively conspired to prevent ready access to the *fontes* of pagan and Christian antiquity; see M. A. Nauwelaerts, "*Grammatici, summularii,* et autres auteurs réprouvés: Érasme et ses contemporains à la remorque de Valla," *Paedagogica Historica, 13* (1973), 471–85. Humanists often presented their own compilations as strictly provisional surveys of their subject matter and encouraged their readers to improve on them; Erasmus' *Adagia* and *Apophthegmata* are two prime examples.

66/18 **neclectui.** For More's idiosyncratic spelling of the forms and derivatives of *negligere* see note on 8/19–20. He employs the same noun in *CW 14*, 125/4.

66/25–26 **alterum . . . sepulchro.** Cf. *Adagia* 1052 (*Opera omnia*, 2, 427BD) and *Moriae encomium, ASD 4/3*, 108.

66/27–28 **beatum Augustinum . . . corporeas.** Augustine, *De divinatione daemonum* 4 (*PL 40*, 584–86); cf. *Supplementum ad opera Sancti Augustini* (*PL 47*, 686–88).

68/1–2 **supercilium . . . compescere.** Cf. *Adagia* 748 and 2471 (*Opera omnia*, 2, 316F–317A and 844AB).

68/3–4 **Homo . . . potuit.** For various other Latin expressions of the proverbial sentiment "To err is human," see Otto, no. 821. For More's own wording cf. Erasmus, Allen, *3*, 574, line 19: "Homo tamen sum, labi possum"; *Ratio verae theologiae*, Holborn, p. 183: "homo erat [*sc.* Hieronymus], et falli potuit et fallere." Cf. also Luther, *De servo arbitrio*, *D. Martin Luthers Werke*, 60 vols. (Weimar, 1883–1980; hereafter cited as *WA*), *18*, 657–58: " . . . nemo est qui non malit nosse quam discere videri; quamvis apud nos id proverbii omnes . . . passim in ore versent: Opto discere; paratus sum doceri et monitus meliora sequi; Homo sum, errare possum."

68/8 **Me . . . protelasset.** Cf. Terence, *Phormio* 213.

68/9 **elenchus.** More appears to be using this word (derived from ἔλεγχος) with the meaning "refutation." The first definite precedents for the use of *elenchus* with this meaning in Latin occur in Boethius' translations of Aristotle. Renaissance authors also employed the word to refer to an index or catalogue. The readings in *S* and *1563* both suggest that More may have originally written ἔλεγχος.

68/13 **admirabundus.** This late equivalent of *mirabundus* is attested in Latham, p. 8, from a document of 1537. See also 274/11 and 472/11.

68/15 **magistro sententiarum.** Since his main work was entitled *Sententiarum libri quatuor*, Peter Lombard was also known as "Magister sententiarum"; see note on 64/3–4.

68/15 **magistralis.** This adjective, which also appears in *Epistolae obscurorum virorum*, p. 79, is distinctly postclassical. Listrius criticizes the adverb *magistraliter* in his commentary on *Moriae encomium*, ASD *4/3*, 182, line 990.

68/17–22 **Qui . . . ediscere.** Cf. Allen, 2, 99, lines 313–18. For Alexander de Villa Dei see note on 26/13–14. Niccolo Perotti (1430–1480) was an important humanist grammarian. His *Cornucopiae* (1489) is a huge, rambling compilation of linguistic and miscellaneous information which was begun as a commentary on Martial; it was one of the principal precedents for Erasmus' *Adagia*. Erasmus recommends Perotti's *Rudimenta grammatices* (1473) in *De ratione studii*, ASD *1/2*, 114–15, lines 14–16; More praises the same grammar in an epigram of about 1500 (*CW 3/2*, 274/16). Ambrogio Calepino (1430–1510) wrote an important Latin lexicon, first published without title in Reggio nell'Emilia, Italy, 1502, which evolved into a massive polyglot lexicon published more than 200 times before 1779; see Albert Labarre, *Bibliographie du Dictionarium d'Ambrogio Calepino (1502–1779)* (Baden-

Baden, 1975). For More's warning against an excessive reliance on grammars and glossaries cf. Quintilian 1.6.27: "mihi non invenuste dici videtur, aliud esse Latine aliud grammatice loqui."

68/17-70/3 **Qui . . . Theologum.** In *CW 8*, 806/35–807/22, More criticizes Tyndale for making a similar comparison between a return to the sources in the study of grammar and a return to the sources in the study of articles of faith. More's conclusion amounts to a virtual reversal of his own earlier stress on returning to scriptural sources:

> And therefore syth grammar in the laten tong is a thyng that may fayle / & the trewe fayth is a thynge by the spyrite of god accordynge to Crystes promyse perpetually taught vnto hys chyrche, and therfore canne neuer fayle no not though all the bokes in the worlde sholde fayle: therfore hys symylytude of grammar lykened vnto fayth, is no more lyke then an apple to an oyster.

70/6–7 **Disputando . . . uenditare.** On disputing against heretics cf. *Moriae encomium, ASD 4/3*, 154, lines 465–70, and 185, lines 50–51. For the phrasing cf. 104, line 578.

70/13 **eum . . . putant.** Cf. *Moriae encomium, ASD 4/3*, 128–30, lines 59–75, on the *philautia* of various nations; for the example of the French language, cf. Dorp in Allen, 2, 128, lines 76–81.

70/16–18 **ex . . . materia.** Cf. *CW 5*, 112/34–114/1, where More predicts that from Luther's rejection of every religious injunction not clearly attested in scripture "inexhausta suggeretur fidei oppugnandae materia."

70/19–20 **nudis . . . habeat.** Cf. *Adagia* 196 (*Opera omnia*, 2, 104F–105A): "Inter lapides pugnabant, nec lapidem tollere poterant"; and Seneca, *Epistolae morales* 7.3, speaking of gladiators: "Nihil habent quo tegantur, ad ictum totis corporibus expositi nunquam frustra manum mittunt." But the most telling parallel is probably the following passage from Lactantius, *Divinae institutiones* 3.4 (*PL 6*, 358A) on the disagreements of pagan philosophers: "Pereunt igitur universi hoc modo, et tamquam sparti illi poetarum, sic se invicem iugulant, ut nemo ex omnibus restet: quod eo fit, quia gladium habent, scutum non habent." For the mythical "Sparti" ("sown men," "earth-born brothers") see the note on 54/12; for a valuable study of an earlier humanist polemic and its debt to Lactantius see Letizia A. Panizza, "Lorenzo Valla's *De vero falsoque bono*, Lactantius, and Oratorical Skepticism," *Journal of the Warburg and Courtauld Institutes, 41* (1978), 76–107.

70/22–24 **quasdam . . . irridere.** Folly lists several ridiculous theological problems of this sort in *ASD 4/3*, 146–48.

70/28 **in eodem docti ludo.** *Adagia* 1750 (*Opera omnia*, 2, 650E).

70/29–31 **si ... pertimescerent.** More is probably referring not so much to the practice of burning intransigent heretics as to the practice of forcing even abjured heretics to submit to the humiliation of bearing a bundle of faggots in public; see *CW 9*, Commentary at 130/3. This interpretation of More's words is strengthened by the fact that the verb *vereor* is associated with feelings of shame as well as with feelings of fear. When Erasmus develops the contrast between argumentation and physical coercion as rival approaches to silencing heretics, it is almost invariably to the distinct disadvantage of the latter approach; see *Moriae encomium, ASD 4/3*, 185–86; *Vita Hieronymi*, Ferguson, p. 179, lines 1201–02; *Responsio ad Albertum Pium (Opera omnia, 9, 1168E);* and, more generally, *Supputatio errorum in censuris Beddae (Opera omnia, 9, 580C–583F); Declarationes ad censuras Lutetiae vulgatas (Opera omnia, 9, 904F–910F);* and *Apologia adversus monachos quosdam hispanos (Opera omnia, 9, 1054B–1060C).* On the other hand, in *Methodus* (1516), Holborn, p. 162, and again in *Ratio verae theologiae* (1519), Holborn, p. 304, Erasmus, like More, clearly takes the position that bundles of faggots are more useful weapons than syllogisms in combating heretics. In *Moriae encomium, ASD 4/3*, 154, lines 462–64, Erasmus also notes that the Church fathers, unlike the scholastics, confuted the infidels "vita magis ac miraculis quam syllogismis."

72/2 **Bouem ad ceroma.** Cf. *Adagia* 362 *(Opera omnia, 2, 172BC);* Otto nos. 264, 1284; and *Moriae encomium, ASD 4/3*, 90, line 337–38.

72/2–4 **quum ... idoneae.** Erasmus criticizes scholastic preachers for padding their sermons with esoteric quibbles in Allen, *3, 612*; and *Ratio verae theologiae*, Holborn, p. 301. He later directs a similar charge against Luther; see Allen, *4, 487–88*.

72/5–6 **Sermonibus ... SECVRE.** The *Sermones discipuli de temporibus et sanctis* was a collection of sermons prepared for the benefit of other, less industrious preachers by the fifteenth-century Dominican Johannes Herolt and printed many times before 1515; see Johannes Herolt, *Miracles of the Blessed Virgin Mary*, trans. C. C. Swinton Bland (London, 1928), pp. 1–3. The *Sermones Dormi Secure dominicales et de sanctis* was a similarly popular collection, now attributed to either Johannes de Verdena or Ricardus de Maidstone. Owst (p. 238) notes that there is at least one other collection of sermons with the title *Dormi secure.* The generic title *Veni mecum* is not specifically associated with any early collection of sermons in any of the better-known catalogues.

72/8–9 **ex ... declamet.** Cf. Jeromes's prologue to his translation of Origen's sermons on Luke *(PL 26, 219):* "molestam rem et tormento similem, alieno, ut ait Tullius, stomacho et non suo scribere." Jerome is apparently alluding to Cicero, *Epistolae ad familiares* 7.1.2: "ludi apparatissimi, sed non tui stomachi; coniecturam enim facio de meo." More himself may intend a comparison between these unoriginal speakers and ventriloquists' dummies, a very apt image for this context.

72/14 **domi suae est.** Cf. *Adagia* 650 and 3775 (*Opera omnia*, 2, 282E and 1139F–1140A).

72/14 **cristas erigit.** Cf. *Adagia* 769 (*Opera omnia*, 2, 324CD); *Moriae encomium*, *ASD 4/3*, 72, line 39; and Erasmus in Allen, 2, 99, line 318.

72/14–15 **gallus . . . superbit.** Cf. *CW 5*, 44/22, and *Adagia* 3325 (*Opera omnia*, 2, 1030AB).

72/16–17 **tenebras . . . offundit.** For a discussion of this phrase and related phrases in *Moriae encomium* see *ASD 4/3*, 104, commentary at lines 573–74.

72/21 **illas ipsas questiones.** Both this reading and that of *S* and *1563* ("illas ipsas captiunculas") retain the accusative case where the syntax of the rest of the sentence calls for the nominative.

72/23 **uentilantur.** For this sense of the verb *ventilare* see note on 18/2.

72/25 **nullo . . . pondere.** Cf. Aulus Gellius 1.15.1, where idle talkers are described as "nullo rerum pondere innixi."

74/1–2 **de anima . . . rasa.** See Aristotle, *De anima* 3.4.14.

74/7–8 **Stentore . . . pisce.** Cf. *Moriae encomium*, *ASD 4/3*, 144, line 360; and *Adagia* 1237 (*Opera omnia*, 2, 496BC). For "taciturnior pisce," see *Adagia* 429 (*Opera omnia*, 2, 192D–193B) and *CW 5*, 340/23, 350/18.

74/9 **caput sine lingua.** *Adagia* 979 (*Opera omnia*, 2, 390EF).

74/10 **personae . . . Hermae.** Cf. *Adagia* 978, 1910, and 3299 (*Opera omnia*, 2, 390DE, 687C, and 1024C–E), and note the paradox of a mute god of eloquence. The truncated statue is a typical "herm," lacking both arms and legs to begin with. The words "truncoque simillimus Hermae" are borrowed from Juvenal 8.53. Both the reading of *P* and *1625* and the reading of *S* and *1563* complement the words borrowed from Juvenal to produce a complete hexameter line; therefore both readings are probably authorial. Since More is obviously trying to thrust as many proverbial allusions as he can into these mocking lines, it would seem that the reading of *P* and *1625*, which links two rather different proverbial motifs in its closing hexameter, is a more refined reading than that found in *S* and *1563*, where the closing hexameter merely refers to the same motif twice. Perhaps More left both readings in his autograph text and the scribe who copied out the source-text of *S* and *1563* arbitrarily retained the less refined reading. More refers to this very phenomenon in the *Letter to Brixius*, *CW 3/2*, 626/25–27.

74/20 **suo . . . metiantur.** Cf. *Adagia* 589 (*Opera omnia*, 2, 255F–256B).

74/20–21 **neque ... anteferant.** For the wording cf. 172/23–24 and note.

74/23 **quibus ... ingenia.** More uses virtually the same terms in a later defense of scholastic disputation; see the *Letter to Bugenhagen*, Rogers, p. 335, line 360.

76/15–19 **Istos ... eiurandum.** This pronouncement is extraordinarily bold in both political and theological terms. The appeal to the constitutional practice of the Roman republic suggests that not only theologians but all secular and ecclesiastical "magistrates" may be held accountable for their misconduct in the same way that the senators of Rome were. More appears to maintain an opposing position in his later works; see especially *CW 8*, 590–92, which emphasizes that only the most heinous and persistent misconduct is grounds for impeachment and that even truthful criticism of both secular and ecclesiastical magistrates is rightly discouraged by law. More's pronouncement about the impeachment of bad theologians appears only in *P* and the printed texts which are derived from it, and in view of his later position it is tempting to think he himself was responsible for deleting this passage from the source-text of *S* and *1563*. But the passage is needed to complete an ambitious chiastic rhetorical structure intended to sum up More's views on the right way to practice theology (74/11-76/19), and it is hard to believe he would delete the most emphatic part of his summary without even attempting to patch the resulting rhetorical gap. The most plausible view is that More personally intended to let the pronouncement remain in the letter and that someone more cautious (Erasmus, perhaps) struck More's bold, hyperbolic suggestion from the source-text of *S* and *1563*.

76/16–17 **apud Rhomanos ... muneribus.** More is probably thinking of the extensive powers of impeachment exercised by the censors of republican Rome. Cf. *Moriae encomium, ASD 4/3*, 156, line 493; Listrius' commentary in *Opera omnia, 4*, 469D; and *The Oxford Classical Dictionary* (Oxford, 1949), pp. 178–79.

76/17–18 **non tam re quam uocabulo Theologos.** Cf. Cicero, *De officiis* 1.30.105: "homines non re, sed nomine"; and Johann Reuchlin, *Defensio ... contra calumniatores suos Colonienses* (Tübingen, T. Anselm, 1514; hereafter cited as "Reuchlin, *Defensio*"), sig. c₂: "alteros re, alteros opinione sola dicendos esse theologos." Cf. also *CW 14*, 373/9–375/9, where More maintains that an undeserved title is a permanent reproach to its bearer, as well as 18/19–20, above.

76/21-78/4 **Nam ... imminuit.** The same argument used here to sanction general criticism of faulty theologians, or "magistrates," figures prominently in the *Responsio* (*CW 5*, 80/21–82/30) as a rhetorical device for defending the magistracy of the papacy despite any misconduct imputed to various unspecified popes. Similar arguments appear frequently in the works of Erasmus; see note on 18/17–20 and *Encomium medicinae, ASD 1/4,* commentary on 184–85. From a twentieth-century perspective it is hard to see how anyone could deny that either widespread misconduct or even the imputation of widespread misconduct in any profession reflects on the profession itself. We are more prone to agree with Erasmus' conservative critic, Alberto Pio: "quia neminem nominas, gravius offendis totum ordinem" (cited by Erasmus in *Responsio ad Albertum Pium, Opera omnia, 9,* 1179A). But our notions of particular institutions are also more flexible than those of the sixteenth century: we do not have to condemn an institution altogether in order to judge that it needs to be changed. Only in his Utopian disguise could More venture to criticize institutions themselves; otherwise he was forced to restrict his attention to persons (anonymous persons in the case of the bad theologians) or forswear criticism entirely. Cf. also Suetonius, *Augustus* 35, for the expulsion of unworthy men who had bought membership in the Senate.

76/26–27 **fuerunt . . . aequabant.** "The Roman Senate seems to be an assembly of many kings" (Cineas to Pyrrhus in Plutarch's *Pyrrhus* 19).

76/27–28 **erant . . . perierint.** See Suetonius, *Divus Iulius* 40.4, an account of how two senators and a sizable number of other people were accidentally crushed in the crowd that had come to watch various spectacles commissioned by the new despot Julius Caesar.

78/10–12 **quem si . . . futurum.** Cf. Cicero, *De oratore* 2.3.14.

78/12–14 **Neque . . . iussurum.** For the wording cf. 364/12–15 and 480/6–7.

78/15 **hec hactenus.** This elliptical phrase is quite common in classical Latin; see Cicero, *De officiis* 1.26.91, 1.39.140, 1.45.160, and Horace, *Satirae* 1.4.63. See also *Moriae encomium, ASD 4/3,* 76, line 87; and Listrius' commentary in *Opera omnia, 4,* 409E. Listrius points out that "et haec quidem haec" is the meaning of καὶ ταῦτα δὴ μὲν ταῦτα, used by More in Rogers, p. 310.

78/19–20 **se . . . scripturum.** See 4/31-6/3 and note.

78/21–23 **Diuus . . . pronunciauerit.** See Jerome's polemical prefaces to the books of the Bible in *PL 28* and *29* and note on 88/22-90/22, below.

80/1–10 **translationibus . . . curatum.** This is a summary of several passages in Dorp's second letter (Allen, 2, 132, lines 202–05, 210–12, 226–28; 133, lines 235–36).

80/17–18 **Augustino adhortante.** Augustine praised Jerome's project of correcting the Vulgate translation of the New Testament from the Greek but at first disapproved very strongly of Jerome's plan to translate the Old Testament directly from the Hebrew (Augustine to Jerome in Jerome's *Epistolae* 56.3, 104.4; *PL 22*, 566, 834). When Augustine finally accepted Jerome's plan to retranslate the Old Testament, it was only because he believed Jerome's actual intention was to expose how the Jews had corrupted the Hebrew (Augustine to Jerome in Jerome's *Epistolae* 116.31, *PL 22, 952*). Had the Greeks been considered schismatic in Augistine's own era he might well have opposed Jerome's project of correcting the New Testament according to the Greek just as strongly as he opposed Jerome's other plan to retranslate the Old Testament from the Hebrew.

80/18–19 **Mutauit . . . graeco.** Cf. Jerome's preface to the New Testament (*PL 29, 528*): "Quae [*sc.* scripturae] ne multum a lectionis Latinae consuetudine discreparent, ita calamo temperavimus, ut his tantum quae sensum videbantur mutare, correctis, reliqua manere pateremur ut fuerant."

80/20–24 **ea . . . admoneat.** Cf. Dorp in Allen, 2, 14, lines 94–96; 15, lines 121–24 and 143–46; 131–32, lines 190–200.

80/27–30 **Sed . . . fore.** Cf. Dorp in Allen, 2, 131–32, lines 192–98.

82/5–6 **Ergo . . . erit?** Dorp never explicitly raises this particular objection in the two letters to which More is responding, but he does hint that translations of scripture would never stop multiplying if the Church had not given its particular sanction to the Vulgate; see Allen, 2, 132, lines 221–28. More responds to the same objection in a different way at 248/29-250/13.

82/11–13 **quod . . . uacillarent.** Cf. Dorp in Allen, 2, 132, lines 226–28.

82/17 **canendam.** The manuscript reading here is supported by 228/10 ("in templis canitur").

82/19–21 **quemadmodum . . . notitiam.** More refers here and at 88/1 to the exegetical method of comparing various similar passages to establish the true meaning of an ambiguous one; see Augustine, *De doctrina christiana* 2.6.8, 2.9.14, 3.26.37, 3.28.39 (*PL 34*, 39, 42, 79, 80); and Erasmus, *Ratio verae theologiae*, Holborn, pp. 292–95, as well as Rogers, p. 335, lines 358–65. This method, generally known as *collatio locorum*, was highly congenial to the philologically-minded humanists as well as to figures like Luther and Tyndale; see *CW 6*, Commentary at 117/5. Nevertheless, as early as the *Letter to Dorp*, More subordinates *collatio locorum* to the "inflexibilem ueritatis regulam" of the "living gospel" inscribed in the hearts of the faithful, in other words to the unwritten tradition of the Catholic church (see 88/2–6).

82/21 **ita in.** This reading, which appears in both *P* and *1625*, may be a copyist's error for *ita tum*, which More may have abbreviated *ita tū*. The reading of *S* and *1563* ("ita tum ex") may result from another scribe's hasty attempt to improve on More's syntax.

82/23 **Amphibologia.** This form, frequently found as a variant of *amphibolia* in manuscripts of classical Latin authors, is now generally dismissed as a spurious compound. Erasmus uses it in his *Apologia,* Holborn, p. 173, and in *Ratio verae theologiae,* Holborn, p. 272.

82/24–26 **Quod . . . docuit.** For Augustine's recommendation see *De doctrina christiana* 2.12.17–18, 2.14.21 (*PL 34,* 43, 45–46). Origen's *Hexapla* was a collection of four Greek translations of the Old Testament along with the Hebrew original and a transliteration of the Hebrew in Greek letters; see Rice, p. 201. For Lefèvre d'Etaples' edition of the *Quincuplex psalterium* with commentary (first printed in 1509 and again in 1513 and 1515), see Rice, pp. 192–201; Guy Bedouelle, *Le Quincuplex psalterium de Lefèvre d'Etaples: Un guide de lecture* (Geneva, 1979); and Jacques Lefévre d'Etaples, *Quincuplex psalterium: Facsimile de l'édition de 1513* (Geneva, 1979).

84/2–4 **non . . . colligeret.** Cf. Deut. 24:19, an injunction to leave to the needy any grain that was missed the first time that the harvesters passed through a field. A more elaborate literary application of this passage occurs in Giovanni Pico della Mirandola's proem to the *Heptaplus* (*De hominis dignitate, Heptaplus, De ente et uno,* ed. Eugenio Garin, Florence, 1942, p. 178).

84/6–7 **ne uestigia quidem.** Cf. *Adagia* 3832 (*Opera omnia,* 2, 1151B–E).

84/8 **in confesso.** Cf. *Moriae encomium, ASD 4/3,* 106, line 625, and Listrius' commentary in *Opera omnia, 4,* 429F.

84/9–16 **Nam . . . contingit?** Cf. Dorp in Allen, 2, 132–33, lines 203–05, 232–37. For a few such divergences see the note on 228/11–13.

84/26 **ecclesia . . . comprobauit.** More is referring back to his own summary of Dorp's arguments at 80/3–5.

86/2–4 **Augustinus . . . Authoritas.** Cf. Augustine, *Contra Faustum Manichaeum* 5 (*PL 42,* 176); this is More's favorite patristic text. For a full discussion see *CW 5,* 742–43. Dorp cites the text from Augustine at Allen, 2, 132, lines 231–32.

86/11 **archetypo.** For the various meanings expressed by this term in the philological discussions of More's day see Rizzo, pp. 308–17, and Chomarat, *1,* 485–86.

86/13–15 **in . . . potuisse.** Cf. 216/10–13 for Augustine's own careful distinction between fallible human authorities and the authority of Scripture itself.

86/18–21 **Apostoli ... scriberent?** See notes on 88/22-90/22 and 254/14-258/4. The apostles' Old Testament citations sometimes correspond more closely to the Hebrew text and sometimes more closely to the Greek of the Septuagint translation; see Augustine, *De civitate dei* 15.14.2 (*PL 41*, 455), and Erasmus, *Apologia*, Holborn, p. 169.

88/1 **ex ... expiscentur.** See note on 82/19–21.

88/2–5 **ad uiuum ... est.** Cf. 2 Cor. 3:2–6, where Paul speaks about his epistle "inscribed in the hearts" of the Corinthians. Paul's discussion, which concludes with the assertion "The letter kills, but the spirit gives life," supports the reading of *P* and *1625* ("uiuum") against that of *S* and *1563* ("unius"). Cf. also 64/24–66/2, above, and *CW 6*, 149/33–36 and 152/3–8.

88/6 **inflexibilem ... regulam.** Cf. Tertullian, *De virginibus velandis* 1.5,7 (*PL 2*, 937–38):

> Regula quidem fidei una omnino est, sola immobilis, et irreformabilis ... Quae est ergo Paracleti administratio nisi haec, quod disciplina dirigitur, quod Scripturae revelantur, quod intellectus reformatur, quod ad meliora proficitur? ... Hunc qui receperunt, veritatem consuetudini anteponunt.

On this theme in Tertullian and the later church fathers see Gerhart B. Ladner, *The Idea of Reform*, Rev. ed. (New York, Evanston, and London, 1967), pp. 137–39.

88/6–8 **ad quam ... dubitant.** See note on 216/10–13, Rogers, p. 335, lines 366–72, *CW 6*, 127/13–33, and *CW 8*, 677/17–30.

88/10–11 **a fonte ... repetendam.** Cf. *Adagia* 4137 (*Opera omnia*, 2, 1209EF): "a fonte ducere."

88/13–22 **Verum ... sit.** Cf. Dorp in Allen, 2, 15, lines 111–16 and 128–31; 131, lines 179–80.

88/22–90/22 **Hec ... uoluissent?** In the *Letter to a Monk* (252/16-254/12) More reproduces this argument and attributes it directly to Jerome, even though there is no trace of such an argument in the polemical prefaces to the books of the Bible included in *PL 28* and 29. From the remarks introducing the argument in the *Letter to Dorp* it seems likely that More is adapting an argument used by Jerome to defend Hebrew scriptures alone against charges of tampering. The text More has in mind is probably the following passage in Jerome's commentary on Isaiah (*PL 24*, col. 99):

> Quod si aliquis dixerit, Hebraeos libros postea [*sc.* post translationem LXX interpretum] a Judaeis esse falsatos, audiat Origenem quid in octavo volumine Explanationum Isaiae huic respondeat quaestiunculae, quod nunquam Dominus, et Apostoli,

qui caetera crimina arguunt in Scribis et Pharisaeis, de hoc crimi-
ne, quod erat maximum, reticuissent. Sin autem dixerint post ad-
ventum Domini Salvatoris, et praedicationem Apostolorum libros
Hebraeos fuisse falsatos, cachinnum tenere non potero, ut Sal-
vator, et Evangelistae, et Apostoli ita testimonia protulerint, ut
Judaei postea falsaturi erant.

More's second argument stressing the agreement of Greek and Latin
texts in those passages whose sense is a source of disagreement between Greeks and Latins owes much to Jerome's second argument (cf.
also Allen, 2, 110). For Jerome's first, historical argument More substitutes a weak psychological argument; More himself later notes that
most heretics have no qualms at all about tampering with the text of
scripture (*CW 8*, 684–88). By the time More reproduces these arguments in the *Letter to a Monk* he has forgotten how different they are
from the arguments of Jerome which inspired them. Cf. p. 583 below.

90/14 **his . . . controuersia.** In a similar passage in Allen, 2, 110, lines
752–57, Erasmus maintains that the only points which are disputed
between the Latin and Greek churches are the terms *hypostasis*, the
procession of the Holy Spirit, the ceremonies of consecration, the poverty of priests, and the power of the pope. The Greeks generally held
that the Trinity consists of three distinct *hypostases;* since *hypostasis* generally means "substance," the Latins rejected this formulation and instead chose to speak of the Trinity as a union composed of three
persons. The controversy regarding the Holy Spirit bore on whether
the Holy Spirit proceeds from the Father and the Son or exclusively
from the Father. For the argument itself, cf. 254/7–12. In *CW 9*,
28/33–36, More refers to disputes with heretics in much the same
fashion that he here refers to disputes with the Greeks.

90/25-92/1 **Possem . . . latinos.** See note on 254/14-258/4.

92/9–13 **Hoc . . . obseruanda.** Cf. Dorp's words in Allen, 2, 131, lines
180–83, responding to Erasmus in Allen, 2, 110, lines 763–67.

92/14–15 **ibi . . . proponam.** Cf. *CW 8*, 459/31–35, and *Adagia* 2499
(*Opera omnia*, 2, 850A).

92/16–19 **in planicie . . . descendamus.** More applies the same imag-
ery to a distinction between two modes of faith at 200/5–9.

92/21–22 **ipsa securitate labatur.** Cf. Walther, no. 27794b: "Securitas
initium calamitatis." Cf. 300/17–21 and note.

92/27–94/3 **quum . . . ducemus?** For doctrinal issues at stake in this
parallel see pp. lxvi–lxvii above.

94/4–8 **quaeris . . . castigatiores.** Cf. Dorp in Allen, 2, 131, lines 185–
88.

94/12–14 **quum . . . sit.** Though the Greek New Testament was not actually published before it appeared in Erasmus' *editio princeps* of February 1, 1516 (Allen, 2, 181–87), another edition supervised by Cardinal Francisco Ximenes de Cisneros of Spain had already been printed by January 10, 1514. This edition, included in volume 5 of the Complutensian Polyglot, was not actually released until 1522. See Bruce M. Metzger, *The Text of the New Testament* (New York and Oxford, 1968), pp. 96–97.

94/21–22 **Aldus . . . Basiliensis.** Aldus Manutius (1450–1515), the most renowned humanist printer of Italy, produced many elegant and scholarly editions of many Greek and Latin classics. Though Aldus was actually from Bassiano near Velletri, he regularly styled himself "Romanus" in his later years; see Allen, *1*, 437. Erasmus worked closely with Aldus in Venice in 1507–08, and the Aldine press published the first edition of Erasmus' *Adagiorum chiliades* in September 1508; see Allen, *1*, 443–47. Johann Froben (ca. 1460–1527), a renowned humanist printer of Basel, was responsible for printing subsequent editions of the *Chiliades* as well as first and later editions of Erasmus' New Testament and many other Erasmian works. Both printers are praised in the long adage-essay "festina lente" (*Adagia* 1001, *Opera omnia*, 2, 402E–406A).

96/4–9 **id quod . . . desino.** Cf. Erasmus in Allen, 2, 106–07, lines 609–11, 628–30.

96/9–10 **optare . . . depono.** More is fond of opposing the notion of "wishing" to the notion of "hoping," which implies somewhat more confidence of actual success; cf. 298/25 and *CW 4*, 246/2 and Commentary. Lorenzo Valla expounds the distinction between the two notions in *Antidoti in Pogium libri quatuor* (*editio princeps* Siena, 1490), *Opera omnia*, sig. V₂v.

96/10–11 **nec . . . post.** For the wording cf. *CW 14*, 9/3: "non ita multo post."

96/17 **graecistas.** More sarcastically applies to all students of Greek a rather barbarous term which was rarely if ever applied to anyone but the pretentious medieval grammarian Eberard of Bethune. Eberard wrote a Latin verse grammar, *Graecismus*, professing to explain Latin words on the basis of Greek roots. See Erasmus, *Antibarbari, ASD 1/1*, 61, commentary at line 16. Borrowing from Plautus, *Menaechmi* 11, Dorp uses the verb *graecisso*, "to speak like a Greek," in Allen, 2, 15, line 125.

96/18 **suis . . . confodias.** Cf. 272/28; *Adagia* 51 (*Opera omnia*, 2, 48D–49A); and *CW 5*, 46/8–9, sidenote at 112/16, sidenote at 310/26.

98/2–4 **unaquaeque . . . contineat.** Cf. Dorp in Allen, 2, 128, lines 70–71: "Quatenus ergo hac vel illa lingua traditae sunt disciplinae, eatenus prestat."

98/7–8 **nouum testamentum fere totum.** Jerome thought that the Gospel of Matthew was originally written in Hebrew (*De viris illustribus* 2–3; *PL 23*, 611–13); others speculated that the letter to the Hebrews was originally written in Hebrew (*De viris illustribus* 5; *PL 23*, 617–19).

98/11–12 **in illa oratione commemoras.** More refers to Dorp's *Oratio in laudem Aristotelis* (1510). For a summary of its contents see De Vocht, *Monumenta*, p. 318. The oration is printed on sigs. C₃–C₆ of *Martini Dorpij Naldiceni Sacrae theologiae licenciati Concio de diue virginis deiparae in coelum assumptione dicta Louanij anno millesimo quingentesimo decimo* (Louvain, T. Martens, 1513); Dorp's catalogue of Aristotelian commentators appears on sig. C₅.

98/12–13 **siue . . . Aristotelem.** Dorp presents his encomium of Aristotle as an indignant rejoinder to Lorenzo Valla (1406–1457), who had ventured to criticize Aristotle in his *Dialecticae disputationes* (written between 1435 and 1439; *editio princeps* not later than 1499; found in Valla, *Opera omnia*, sigs Ss₂–qq₅ [pp. 643–761]). In Allen, 2, 14, 15, 128, and 135, Dorp also disparages Valla's *Annotationes* on the New Testament and his *Elegantiae linguae latinae.*

98/14–21 **Alexandro . . . intelligatur.** Although only a few of the commentators More mentions had been published in Latin by 1515, a large number of their works had been translated by the great thirteenth-century translator William of Moerbeke. Moerbeke's versions (among others) are now being published in the *Corpus latinum commentariorum in Aristotelem graecorum,* 5 vols. (Louvain and Paris, 1957–), and the following works are already available: Themistius (fl. A.D. 350), *Paraphrasis eorum quae de anima Aristotelis, CLCAG 1* (1957); Ammonius Hermiae (fl. ca. A.D. 490), *In librum Peri hermenias Aristotelis recordatio, CLCAG 2* (1961); Joannes Philoponos, also known as "Joannes grammaticus" (fl. ca. A.D. 530), *Commentum super capitulum de intellectu in libro tertio Aristotelis De anima, CLCAG 3* (1966); Alexander of Aphrodisias (fl. ca. A.D. 200), *Expositio libri Meteorologicorum Aristotelis, CLCAG 4* (1968); and Simplicius (fl. ca. A.D. 535), *Scolia in Praedicamenta Aristotelis, CLCAG 5* (1971). Themistius' commentaries had already been published in a humanist translation by Ermolao Barbaro (Venice, 1480), as had the *Problemata* falsely ascribed to Alexander of Aphrodisias (trans. Teodoro Gaza, Giorgio Valla, and Angelo Poliziano [three distinct versions], Venice, 1503–04, Venice, 1488, Venice, 1498). Book 1 of Alexander's commentary on Aristotle's *De anima* (trans. Hieronimo Donato, Brescia, 1495), Ammonius' commentary on Porphyry (trans. Pomponio Guarico, Venice, 1494), and possibly Simplicius' commentary on Aristotle's *Categoriae* (trans. William of Moerbeke, perhaps published 1500; see *CLCAG 5*, xlix) had also been published by 1515. The commentary of Olympiodorus (fl. ca. A.D. 550) on Aristotle's *Meteorologica* was first printed with Joannes Philoponus' commentary on the same work (trans. J. B. Camotio, Venice, 1551). For more information on Latin translations of Alexander and Olympiodorus see P. O. Kristeller and F. E. Cranz, eds., *Catalogus translationum et commentariorum: Medieval and Renaissance Latin Translations and Commentaries*, 3 vols. (Washington, D.C., 1960–), *1*, 77–135, and *2*, 199–204.

100/1 **Ioannes Grammaticus.** *Grammaticus* was one of the sobriquets of Joannes Philoponos (fl. ca. A.D. 530); see note on 98/14–21.

100/4 **Grammaticus cum Grammaticis.** Cf. Dorp in Allen, *2*, 135, lines 313–14: "Cresconius gramaticus cum suis, hereticus videlicet cum hereticis."

100/5 **propicius.** The word normally refers to divinities; cf. *Moriae encomium*, *ASD 4/3*, 146, line 385 and commentary.

100/5–8 **At . . . subuersi.** Cf. 142/22–27 and notes.

100/11–13 **Hic . . . innotescere.** More is answering Dorp's comments in Allen, *2*, 136, lines 346–49.

100/13–15 **nihil . . . potentius.** Cf. Jerome, *Epistolae* 53.2 (*PL* 22, 541): "Habet nescio quid latentis energiae viva vox; et in aures discipuli de auctoris ore transfusa fortius sonat." Erasmus cites the same passage in *Adagia* 117 (*Opera omnia*, *2*, 76E–77A). More also exploits the analogy between reading an author in his original language and hearing him speak *viva voce* at 100/2–5 and 142/27–29.

100/17–18 **habent . . . non habeant.** Cf. 1 Cor. 7:29; *Moriae encomium*, *ASD 4/3*, 190, lines 190–91; and *Apologia adversus Petrum Sutorem* (*Opera omnia*, *9*, 755C): "Etenim habere Scripturam, quam non intelligas, perinde est ac si non habeas." See also the note on 214/23–24, below.

100/19 **Metheorologicorum opus.** For More's interest in meteorology see *CW 4*, 160/6 and Commentary. Since he selects Aristotle's *Meteorologica* as a prime example of a Greek work that is still inaccessible to readers of Latin, it seems unlikely that More knew of Lefèvre d'Etaples' Latin paraphrase of this work included in *Totius Aristotelis philosophiae naturalis paraphrases* (1492), even though this entire collection was reprinted in 1504 and the paraphrase of the *Meteorologica* was reprinted separately in 1512. See Rice, pp. 1–3, 126–28, and 257–61. A word-for-word medieval version of the *Meteorologica* by William of Moerbeke was included in *Aristotelis opera latine, cum commentariis Averrois* (Venice, 1483) and was reprinted with other works by Aristotle several times before 1520. There also existed partial translations by a number of other medieval scholars and an unpublished translation by the humanist Mattia Palmieri. A new humanist translation by François Vatables (ca. 1493–1547) was published alongside the translation of William of

Moerbeke in Paris in 1518; this translation was apparently polished enough to make Linacre's version unnecessary. See Rice, pp. 249–50, 406–10; F. H. Fobes, "Textual Problems in Aristotle's *Meteorology*," *Classical Philology, 10* (1915), 188–214; Lorenzo Minio-Paluello, "Henri Aristippe, Guillaume de Moerbeke et les traductions médiévales des 'Météorologiques' et du 'De generatione et corruptione' d'Aristote," *Revue philosophique de Louvain*, 45 (1947), 206–35 (reprinted in his *Opuscula: The Latin Aristotle*, Amsterdam, 1972, pp. 57–86); Eugenio Garin, "Traduzioni umanistiche di Aristotele," *Atti e memorie dell' Accademia Fiorentina di scienze morali "la colombaria,"* New Series, 2 (1947–50), 55–104; and more generally Bernard G. Dod, "Aristoteles Latinus," *CHLMP*, pp. 45–79, and Charles B. Schmitt, *Aristotle and the Renaissance* (Cambridge, Mass., and London, 1983).

100/25 **hoc opus . . . Linacro.** Linacre's version of the *Meteorologica* with the commentary of Alexander was never published and perhaps never even completed; see "Editors' Introduction," in *Essays on the Life and Work of Thomas Linacre, c. 1460–1524*, ed. Francis R. Maddison, Margaret Pelling, and Charles Webster (Oxford, 1977), pp. xli and xlvi. For a full history of Linacre's relations with More see Rogers, pp. 8–9, and Germain Marc'hadour, "Thomas More et Thomas Linacre," *Moreana, 13* (1967), 63–67. Linacre's translation of Galen's *De sanitate tuenda*, praised by Budé (*CW 4*, 4/7–18), was first published in Paris in 1517; Linacre also translated Galen's *Methodus medendi* (Paris, 1519), *De temperamentis* and *De inaequali temperie* (Cambridge, 1521), *De pulsuum usu* (London, 1522[?]), *De naturalibus facultatibus* (London, 1523), *De symptomatum differentiis* and *De symptomatum causis* (London, 1524). See further R. J. Durling, "Linacre and Medical Humanism," in *Essays on the Life and Work of Thomas Linacre*, pp. 76–106. As Aldus Manutius indicates in his preface to the *Sphaera* of Proclus in Julius Firmicus Maternus, *Astronomicorum libri octo . . .* (Venice, 1499), Linacre had begun his translation of Alexander's commentary on the *Meteorologica* by 1499. Aldus' letter is translated in Ambrose Firmin Didot, *Alde Manuce et l'hellénisme à Venise* (Paris, 1875), pp. 129–31. The first published Latin version of Alexander's work (trans. Alessandro Piccolomini) appeared in Venice in 1540; the *editio princeps* of the Greek text appeared in Venice in 1527. More apparently heard Linacre lecture on the *Meteorologica* in London after Linacre's return from Italy in 1499; see Allen, 4, 294, and C. B. Schmitt, "Thomas Linacre and Italy," in *Essays on the Life and Work of Thomas Linacre*, p. 45, n. 1.

102/4 **nec incomitatus.** Cf. Ovid, *Tristia* 2.480; Apuleius, *Metamorphoses* 2.18.

102/13 **uulgatam etiam translationem.** See note on 100/19.

102/14–16 **eiusdem . . . sint.** The statement attributed to Aristotle appears in a probably spurious letter to Alexander the Great which is preserved in Aulus Gellius 20.5. The letter itself does not limit the reference of the statement to Aristotle's *Physics,* but cf. Aulus Gellius 20.5.3. In the late Middle Ages and Renaissance the statement was used as a sanction for the obscure or deliberately enigmatic style of scholastics and other philosophers; see Leo Hebraeus, *Dialoghi d'amore,* ed. Santino Caramella (Bari, 1929), p. 102; and Philip Melanchthon, "Oratio de vita Aristotelis" and "Oratio de Aristotele," in *Melanchthons Werke in Auswahl,* ed. Robert Stupperich, 7 vols. (Gütersloh, 1951–75), *3,* 103–04, 130–31.

102/20–24 **albertus . . . diuersa.** More is referring to one of the Aristotelian paraphrases by Albertus Magnus (ca. 1200–1280), the teacher of Thomas Aquinas. For an annotated bibliography of Albert's works see Charles H. Lohr, S.J., "Medieval Latin Aristotle Commentaries: Authors A–F," *Traditio, 23* (1967), 338–45. The term *periphrastes* was rarely if ever applied to Albertus Magnus, nor is it attested in any of the better-known lexicons of Latin or Greek. More appears to have adopted the term as a neutral alternative to the term *paraphrastes* construed in a negative or pejorative sense. To explain the intended distinction between *periphrasis* and *paraphrasis* he would probably have claimed that *periphrasis* applies equally well to all forms of restatement while *paraphrasis* often suggests a distinctly inaccurate form. Ambrogio Calepino, [*Dictionarium*] (Venice, P. Liechtensteyn, 1506), sig. E₂v, notes two meanings for the term *paraphrastes:* "Paraphrastes dicitur interpres qui non litteram ex littera sed sensum e sensu transfert. quasi iuxta ponens. Et pro peruerso et deprauatore ponitur. . . ." His authority for the second, pejorative meaning is Jerome's preface to his translation of Kings (*PL 28,* 557B): "Et cum intellexeris quod antea nesciebas, vel interpretem me aestimato, si gratus es, vel παραφραστὴν, si ingratus." Calepino and More both appear to believe that *paraphrastes* can be glossed in two quite distinct senses, both as *iuxta loquens* and as *contra loquens.* There is actually no need to construe *paraphrastes* as *contra loquens* to explain the restricted pejorative meaning Jerome makes it bear: if a rigorous translation is what we require, then we may well disdain a mere paraphrase, even one which is basically correct. Erasmus is forced to defend his New Testament paraphrases against similar mockery based on the pejorative meaning of *paraphrastes* in his *Appendix respondens ad Antapologiam Petri Sutoris (Opera omnia, 9,* 811B–D).

102/22 **paraphrastes uerius.** The reading of *S* and *1563* is "paraphrastes uerius uero," "a paraphrast more truly than true." The emphatic hyperbole "uerius uero" (*Adagia* 3802, *Opera omnia, 2,* 1145AB) is used here with an ironic twist: Albertus Magnus is too paraphrastic to be truthful.

102/24 **ex diametro diuersa.** Cf. *Adagia* 945 (*Opera omnia, 2,* 380EF).

102/24-104/3 **Gaitanus . . . progreditur?** More is almost certainly referring to a volume entitled *Libri metheororum Aristotelis . . . cum commen-*

tarijs . . . Gaietani de Thienis . . . Quaestiones perspicacissimi philosophi Thimonis super quattuor libros Metheororum (Venice, heredes O. Scoti, 1507). On sig. AA₅ of this volume Thimo goes into a lengthy description of how a handful of earth yields 10 handfuls of water, how 10 handfuls of water yield 100 handfuls of air, and how 100 handfuls of air yield 1,000 handfuls of fire. Speculation of this sort may be marginally relevant to Aristotle's *De coelo* and *De generatione et corruptione*, but it is almost completely irrelevant to the *Meteorologica*. It would seem that the similar appearance of "Thienis" and "Thimonis" on the Gothic title page of this volume has led More to confuse the Paduan scholar Gaetano da Thiene (1387–1465) with the Parisian scholar Themo (or Thimo) Iudaei de Monasterio (fl. 1355). For a helpful bibliography of Gaetano da Thiene see Charles H. Lohr, "Medieval Latin Aristotle Commentaries: Authors A–F," *Traditio, 23* (1967), 390–92; for Themo Iudaei, see Lohr, "Medieval Latin Aristotle Commentaries: Authors Robertus to Wilgelmus," *Traditio, 29* (1973), 152–53. Gaetano's commentary appeared separately in 1476 and 1491. He is not to be confused with Tommaso de Vio, or Cajetan.

104/3–4 **immensurabiles mensuras metitur.** Cf. *Adagia* 344 (*Opera omnia, 2,* 168F–169A) and *Moriae encomium, ASD 4/3,* 144, lines 362–64.

104/4 **ne Gry quidem.** *Adagia* 703 (*Opera omnia, 2,* 304AB); see 136/26. The expression οὐδὲ γρῦ means "not a whit."

104/7 **ipsam doctrinae arcem.** Cf. *Moriae encomium, ASD 4/3,* 106, lines 623–24; Allen, *2,* 99, lines 322–23; *Adagia* 3831 (*Opera omnia, 2,* 1151AB). See 200/11–12.

104/9 **sudantes atque anhelantes.** Cf. Lucian, *Hermotimus 5* and *Rhetorum praeceptor* 10.

104/12 **te . . . superabis.** Cf. *Adagia* (158 (*Opera omnia, 2,* 93B).

104/13 **meo patrocinio.** Cf. *Moriae encomium, ASD 4/3,* 68, lines 21–22; 70, lines 65–67.

104/15–16 **res . . . facilior.** Cf. *Adagia* 1295 (*Opera omnia, 2,* 521CD).

104/16–18 **ille . . . debent.** See 4/31-6/3 and note.

104/20–21 **Ecce . . . omnia.** Cf. Allen, *2,* 13, lines 53–54, where Dorp is alluding to Terence, *Andria* 601 and 663–67. Davus is the name of a mischievous slave in that comedy.

104/23–24 **plus . . . uersata.** Cf. Erasmus' letter to Dorp of late May 1515, Allen, *2,* 94, lines 140–41: "intra pauculos menses plus septies fuerit typis stanneis propagatus, indque diuersis in locis." The first edition of the *Moria* appeared in Paris in 1511; seven known editions had appeared by May 1515 (*ASD 4/3,* 15, n. 9). In declaring that the

Moria has been circulating for more than seven years More is clearly referring to the date of composition rather than the date of publication, but it appears that the *Moria* was actually written in the autumn of 1509, only six years before More wrote to Dorp; see *Moriae encomium, ASD 4/3,* 14–15.

106/2 **ex fece uulgi.** Cf. *Moriae encomium, ASD 4/3,* 96, line 475, Lucian, *Iupiter tragoedus* 53, and Otto, no. 633. More also uses the phrase in *CW 14,* 371/4.

106/2–4 **neque . . . scaturit.** For the wording and sentiment cf. Erasmus in Allen, *4,* 190, lines 84–86.

106/13–14 **Asperae . . . relinquunt.** Cf. Allen, 2, 13, lines 50–51: "Aspere facetiae, eciam vbi multum est veri admixtum, acrem sui relinquunt memoriam." Dorp is alluding to Tacitus, *Annales* 15.68.4.

106/16 **Theologistae.** Cf. Leonard Priccard in Allen, *3,* 598, line 22. Johann Reuchlin popularized this term as a title for false theologians in his *Defensio,* sigs. C₁v–C₂. It appears once in an English-Latin glossary of 1483 (*Catholicon anglicum,* ed. Sidney J. H. Herrtage, EETS, Original Series no. 75, London, 1881, p. 102) as a neutral term for a theologian or a "divine."

106/21–22 **cui . . . blandiantur.** Cf. Dorp in Allen, 2, 13, lines 58–59; and *Adagia* 3032 (*Opera omnia,* 2, 978AB).

106/24–25 **Gerardus . . . Nouiomagus.** Gerard Geldenhouwer of Nijmegen (ca. 1482–1542) enjoyed the close friendship of Dorp and another correspondent of More, Herman van Cranevelt. He had a hand in publishing many books written by other humanists, including More's *Utopia* (see *CW 4,* 30, 276–77). Although Geldenhouwer had belonged to the religious order of the Crucigeri since 1501, in the mid-1520s he defected to join the reformers; see Allen, 2, 379. Geldenhouwer's *Satyrae octo* were printed in Louvain in June 1515; they have been reprinted in Jacob Prinsen, ed., *Collectanea van Gerardus Geldenhauer Noviomagus* (Amsterdam, 1901), pp. 151–76. The satires are prefaced by a letter from Dorp dated January 24, 1512, in which Dorp declares, "Satyrae igitur tuae mihi quidem omni ex parte perplacent, neque offendere quivi, quod mutatum velim" (Prinsen, p. 151). Since Geldenhouwer strikes out at scholastic theologians as well as corrupt monks and friars (see especially Prinsen, p. 160), Dorp probably found the 1515 publication a considerable embarrassment.

106/26–27 **sumpta . . . iocatur.** Cf. Erasmus in Allen, 2, 95, lines 155–56.

106/27-108/1 **Palinodiam cani.** *Adagia* 859 (*Opera omnia,* 2, 356A–D), where Erasmus associates the phrase closely with Augustine's critique of Jerome (see 212/20-214/7 and notes). Since *P* and *S* are in basic agreement at this point in the text, it is likely that the Greek reading in *1563* is an editorial refinement.

108/1–2 **in Satyris . . . uelles.** See note on 106/24–25.

108/14–15 **atque . . . etiam.** See note on 106/24–25.

108/19 **memorata epistola tua.** See note on 42/4–6. The passage to which More here refers is reprinted in De Vocht, *Monumenta,* pp. 118–19.

110/1 **humi repere.** Cf. *Adagia* 1988 (*Opera omnia,* 2, 704C–E).

110/9 **sua . . . ratio.** Cf. *CW* 2, 27/13; *Moriae encomium, ASD 4/3,* 94, line 407 and Commentary; 96, line 452; and *Adagia* 2902 (*Opera omnia,* 2, 935F–936A).

110/10 **bene . . . olet.** *Adagia* 2302 (*Opera omnia,* 2, 806BC).

110/10–11 **frontem contrahimus.** See note on 68/1–2.

110/18–19 **nemo . . . ferat.** Cf. *Moriae encomium, ASD 4/3,* 116, lines 841–44; and Erasmus in Allen, 2, 96, lines 224–25, alluding to Suetonius, *Divus Iulius* 73.

110/20–22 **facile . . . deplorare.** Cf. Plautus, *Amphitruo* 53–55, in which Mercury is speaking: "deus sum, commutavero. eandem hanc, si voltis, faciam ex tragoedia comoedia ut sit omnibus isdem vorsibus."

110/22–23 **neque . . . sint.** Cf. Lucian, *De sacrificiis* 15, where Lucian exploits a proverbial contrast between the "weeping" and "laughing" philosophers, Heraclitus and Democritus.

112/1–7 **Miraris . . . paucitas.** Allen, 2, 127, lines 22–27, Dorp's rejoinder to Erasmus' comments in Allen, 2, 100, lines 366–71.

112/7–9 **quum . . . perfundis.** Cf. *Moriae encomium, ASD 4/3,* 68, lines 50–51.

112/11–12 **Theologos . . . esse.** Cf. Dorp in Allen, 2, 127, lines 44–45.

112/13–16 **episcopi . . . locum.** The doctrine that bishops are direct successors of the apostles is at least as old as the early Church martyr Irenaeus (*Contra haereses* 3.3; *PG* 7, 848–55); see *DTC 1,* 1658–60; and cf. *CW 8,* 614/8–10; *CW 14,* 259/10 and 451/1. Cf. also *Epistolae obscurorum virorum,* p. 69: "Quia magistri sunt in loco apostolorum."

114/1 **Pyrgopolinicen.** The swaggering captain Pyrgopolynices is the leading character in Plautus' *Miles gloriosus.*

114/3–5 **eorum . . . congeris.** Cf. Dorp's comments in Allen, 2, 129–30, lines 116–32, drawn from Augustine, *Confessiones* 1.16.26. More's ad hominem defense of theatrical literature may owe something to Lucian's *De saltatione* 5.

114/19–21 **Quid . . . adiecisti.** For Dorp's Plautine supplements see note on 116/6-118/2.

116/2 **amusos.** See note on 20/10.

116/6-118/2 **Primum . . . Virginis.** The verses More cites from Dorp's prologue to Plautus' *Miles gloriosus* appear in *Martini Dorpij sacrae theologiae licenciati Dialogus in quo Venus et Cupido omnes adhibent versutias* . . . (Louvain, T. Martens [1514]), sig. E₃v. The text of this edition corresponds very closely to that cited in *P.* Dorp's prologue is also included in Jozef IJsewijn, "Theatrum Belgo-Latinum: Het Neolatijns Toneel in de Nederlanden," *Academiae Analecta: Mededelingen van de Koninklijke Academie voor Wetenschappen, Letteren en Schone Kunsten van België, Klasse der Letteren, 43/1* (1981), 106–09. For the publishing history of Dorp's Plautine supplements see De Vocht, *Monumenta*, pp. 326–28. De Vocht holds that the first edition of the supplements, an edition of which no known copy survives, must have come out in late 1513. In his dedication of the second edition to Jerome Busleyden (summarized in De Vocht, *Monumenta*, p. 366), Dorp endeavors to distance himself from his poetic efforts by stressing that five years have passed since he turned his attention from literature to theology. More subverts this disclaimer by noting that Dorp would not have published his verses in 1514 if he did not still approve of them and that by 1510, when he delivered his sermon on the Virgin, he was already an avowed theologian. For the title of Dorp's published sermon, in which both the date 1510 and Dorp's status as a *theologus* are mentioned expressly, see note on 98/11–12. For the dates of Dorp's various promotions as a theologian see the Introduction, p. xxi.

116/8 **maximam malam crucem.** Plautus, *Casina* 611, *Menaechmi* 66.

116/11 **ampullosis.** This late adjective formed from *ampulla* is attested in Blaise, p. 43.

116/12 **effunditare.** This iterative form of *effundere* is not attested in any of the lexicons.

116/14 **carniuoracibus.** The postclassical form *carnivorax* first appears in Fulgentius Ruspensis, *Sermones* 22 (*PL 65*, 889B).

116/17 **agrarij.** This word normally lacks a pejorative sense and means simply "agrarian" or "agricultural." A substantive use of *agrarius* with the meaning "a peasant" is attested in Blaise, p. 30.

116/20 **graxint.** Though this verb is not attested in any modern lexicon, it does appear in early printed versions of Plautus, *Asinaria* 5; for example, see Plautus, *Viginti comoediae* (Milan, V. Scinzenzeler, [1497]), sig. e₆. Older lexicons associate this reading with the Greek verb "to croak." Dorp apparently regarded the form *graxis* as a future perfect indicative or perfect subjunctive corresponding to the early form *faxis* and wrote *graxint* to correspond to the third person plural form *faxint*.

116/20 **minatust fore ulmeos.** Cf. Plautus, *Asinaria* 363: "mihi tibique interminatust nos futuros ulmeos."

116/23 **suis coloribus depinxisti.** Cf. *Adagia* 306 (*Opera omnia*, 2, 153CD). See 180/15–16.

116/25 **sesquiannus.** This late coinage is also employed by Erasmus in Allen, *4*, 198, line 2. Latham notes its occurrence in no text earlier than 1570. Cf. *sesquihora* (Pliny, *Epistolae* 4.9.9) and *sesquimensis* (Varro, *De re rustica* 1.27.1).

118/3–4 **comprobaueris? Ergo.** Between these words *S* and *1563* add a passage translated as follows: "Or rather, it does make a difference. For we often write purely on impulse; when we review works laid aside for a while, we apply careful judgment."

118/15 **uix homines.** Dorp accuses Erasmus of regarding every un-cultured theologian as "vix homo" in Allen, *2*, 128, line 84. The phrase "vix hominis" occurs in Cicero, *De officiis* 2.14.50. Cf. Ovid, *Tristia* 5.7.45.

118/19–20 **Hieronimi . . . querere.** Cf. Allen, *2*, 12, line 22, where Dorp cites this *sententia* without mentioning its source. In *S* and *1563* "Hieronimi" is replaced by "Sallustij." While the *sententia* does ulti-mately derive from Sallust, *Bellum Iugurthinum* 3.3, it also occurs in Jerome's preface to his Latin translation of Ezra (*PL 28*, 1403).

118/20–22 **Cornelij . . . relinquere.** See note on 106/13–14.

118/22–23 **Epicteti . . . dictu.** Cf. Dorp's comment in Allen, *2*, 127, lines 32–34, drawn from Epictetus, *Enchiridion* 33.14.

120/3–4 **Reuclinum (Deus bone, quem uirum?).** Johann Reuchlin, or Capnio, of Pforzheim (1455–1522) was one of the leading Hebrew scholars of the Renaissance. More's countrymen John Colet and John Fisher almost venerated Reuchlin, and Fisher compared him to Giovanni Pico della Mirandola, for whom More, too, had great admira-tion; see Allen, *2*, *4*, 49–50, 269, 330, and especially 350. His opposi-tion to an anti-Hebrew faction in Cologne led to a bitter quarrel with the theologians of Cologne and Mainz, in the course of which Reuchlin printed a German polemic, *Augenspiegel* (1511), and a Latin apology, *Defensio . . . contra calumniatores suos Colonienses* (Tübingen, T. Anselm, 1514); see Allen, *1*, 555–56; Ludwig Geiger, *Renaissance und Human-ismus in Italien und Deutschland* (Berlin, 1882), pp. 504–25; and Charles G. Nauert, Jr., "The Clash of Humanists and Scholastics: An Ap-proach to Pre-Reformation Controversies," *The Sixteenth Century Jour-nal, 4/1* (1973), 1–18. The incidents to which More refers probably occurred in connection with Reuchlin's *Defensio* (see note on 120/4–6).

Reuchlin also published a collection of letters from his well-known humanist friends, the *Clarorum virorum epistolae* (Tübingen, T. Anselm, 1514), which was designed to show their solidarity in the cause of the New Learning; a year later (ca. October 1515) Reuchlin's friends also published the famous travesty *Epistolae obscurorum virorum*, which was ostensibly intended as a similar show of support by scholastics for Reuchlin's leading opponent, Ortwin Gratius (see Allen, 2, 3, 152; *3*, 44). While Erasmus officially disapproved of the *Epistolae obscurorum virorum* and repeatedly attempted to distance himself from the Reuchlin affair, More had nothing but praise for the travesty; see Allen, 2, 372, and *3*, 44–45. On the satirical strategies in the *Epistolae,* see Reinhard P. Becker, *A War of Fools: the Letters of Obscure Men: A Study of the Satire and the Satirized* (Bern, Frankfurt, and Las Vegas, 1981), especially chapters 2, 4, and 5. By comparing Reuchlin to Erasmus, More may also be hinting that Dorp is in danger of getting the same kind of treatment as Ortwin Gratius, who was also regarded by some as a traitor to the humanist cause; see James V. Mehl, "Ortwin Gratius' *Orationes quodlibeticae:* Humanist Apology in Scholastic Form," *Journal of Medieval and Renaissance Studies, 11* (1981), 57–69. Certainly there was no lack of humanists who were ready to treat Dorp like Gratius (Allen, *3*, 162; *4*, 3; *5*, 367; *9*, 35), and the *Epistolae eruditorum virorum,* assembled and published in May 1520 against Dorp's Louvain colleague Edward Lee, was quite probably modeled on Reuchlin's original collection. Erasmus compares Lee to Gratius in Allen, *4*, 145. More's defense of Reuchlin's outspokenness should be contrasted with Erasmus' own scrupulous protestations of polemical restraint; see Allen, 2, 92–93, and especially 2, 4, and *3*, 589, where Erasmus condemns the outspokenness of the very apology that More is applauding.

120/4–6 **in emulos . . . integerrimus.** Cf. Reuchlin, *Defensio,* sig. A₂:
   Vehementer grata mihi est quae sese obtulit imperator Maxiaemiliane caesar Auguste, apud te post omnium rerum conditorem unum mundi dominum contra pacis inimicos, apud principem iustissimum contra iniurios, grauissimum contra leues, aequissimum contra iniquos, denique ueritatis amantissimum contra falsos delatores, sperata diu et exoptata, illa ipsa, uitae meae innocentiam quae a nocentibus nocens insimulatur, integritatemque fidei quae a nugatoribus labefactata garritur, et Christianam simplicitatem in qua sum ab infantia enutritus defendendi occasio. . . .

120/6–8 **ab ijsdem . . . uideretur.** In *Defensio,* sig. A₃, Reuchlin claims to be driven to use violent language by the violence with which his detractors assail his own character: "[eorum] leuitatem et improbitatem crimina et scelera ostendere palam omnibus necessarium erit, ut delatorum meorum dictis nulla fides adhibeatur, et non aliam ob causam." Cf. *Epistolae obscurorum virorum,* p. 145.

120/14–17 **Ergo . . . quoquam?** In these lines More is simply anticipating what is likely to be Dorp's response to the preceding paragraphs.

120/20 **tibi . . . uerteris.** *Adagia* 2833 (*Opera omnia*, 2, 926C).

122/5–8 **Sapiunt . . . laudati?** Cf. *Moriae encomium, ASD 4/3*, 69, lines 62–64: "Tum si quis est, quem nec ista placare possunt, is saltem illud meminerit, pulchrum esse a stulticia vituperari"; 176, lines 857–58: ". . . neue quis existimet bonos principes a me taxari, dum malos laudo"; and Listrius' commentary on this second passage, "Mira facetia inuertit, malos vocat, quos laudauit, hoc est, vituperauit hactenus. Nam a stulticia laudari, vituperari est." Cf. also Cicero, *Epistolae ad familiares* 5.12.7: "laetus sum laudari a laudato viro."

122/8–10 **Preterea . . . redderet.** Cf. Erasmus in Allen, 2, 107, lines 655–57.

122/10 **uelit nolit.** *Adagia* 245 (*Opera omnia*, 2, 130EF).

122/12 **Moriae mystas.** Cf. 208/28 and *Moriae encomium, ASD 4/3*, 76, line 89; 194, line 276 and commentary.

122/14–15 **Hec . . . reuocat.** On October 24, 1515, Richard Pace encountered More on the highway between Calais and Antwerp, presumably en route back to England; see *Letters and Papers, Foreign and Domestic, of the Reign of Henry VIII*, ed. J. S. Brewer, James Gairdner, and R. H. Brodie, 21 vols. (London, 1862–1932; reprinted Vaduz, 1965; hereafter cited as *LP*), 2, no. 1067.

122/15 **scripturientem.** This odd verb first appears in Sidonius, *Epistolae* 7.18.1, 8.11.8. Erasmus uses the equally odd form *lecturientem* in Allen, *3*, 554, line 21. For the related verb *iturio* ("to wish to go"), attested in Latham, p. 261, from a document of ca. 1520, see *Historia Richardi Tertii*, 404/13, below.

122/17–19 **quae . . . increscere.** The apologetic device of comparing an inordinately long letter to a leisurely conversation is fairly conventional; see Cicero, *Epistolae ad Quintum fratrem* 1.1.16.45; and Augustine to Jerome in Jerome's *Epistolae* 104.6 (*PL* 22, 834): "Brevem putabam futuram hanc epistolam: sed nescio quomodo ita mihi dulce factum est in ea progredi, ac si tecum loquerer."

122/17–18 **scriptus . . . Orestes.** Juvenal 1.6.

122/19 **increscere. Verum.** Between these words *S* and *1563* add a sizable passage responding to Dorp's comments in Allen, 2, 12, lines 15–30. Both these texts of the passage contain several corruptions (see variants), but together they tend to corroborate the following restored version:

> Quanquam iam nunc opinor nihil intactum reliquimus: certe quod sciam nihil per dissimulationem pretermisimus. Neque enim

istud reor expectaturum quenquam ut Moriam a βλασφη-
miarum atque impietatis etiam suspicione defenderem, tanquam
ab ea Christi religio male audierit. Nam hoc et in prioribus tuis
litteris ita posuisti, ut plane te ostenderes contra animi tui sensum
alienam referre sententiam, et in hac epistola posteriore, quum
cetera omnia, quanquam illa quoque magna ex parte non tua,
tamen in quibus herere aliquis potuit color pro hoc ingenio atque
hac doctrina tua, magnifice atque ampliter excolueris, hanc tamen
de Impietate calumniam consulto uelut impiam ipsam, sacrilegam, ac non manifestariam modo uerum futilem quoque atque
ineptam prorsus omisisti. Ea ergo de re nihil erat mihi dicendum,
de ceteris dixisse me puto. Nihil ergo restabat de quo tractare
uolueram. Sed nisi principis me interpellassent litterae scripturus
fortasse fui ijsdem de rebus plenius.

The passage may be translated as follows:

Yet I do not think I have overlooked anything, and so far as I know
I have definitely not glossed over anything. For I do not think
anyone will expect me to defend Folly from that charge of blas-
phemy and impiety, as well, as if she had defamed the religion of
Christ; for even in your first letter you presented this charge in a
way that would show you were stating someone else's opinion, with
which you yourself disagreed, and in this second letter, while you
magnificently and copiously elaborated all of those other charges
(although these too were largely not yours) on which all your
intelligence and learning could impose some appearance of
cogency, by choice you completely omitted this slanderous charge
of impiety as one which was impious in itself, sacrilegious, and not
merely blatantly false but both futile and pointless, as well. Thus
there was nothing else that I wished to discuss, but if my prince's
letter had not interrupted me I might well have written more fully
on my previous points.

The unusual number of corruptions and variant readings in S and
1563 at this point in the text suggests that this passage was unusually
illegible in their source-text; like many passages in the De Tristitia Christi
(CW 14), this passage was probably introduced as a marginal addition,
written not in a large, precise "texte hande" but "in a small ragged
hande, wherin a yonge begynner can scante perceyue one letter from
an other" (CW 8, 492/4–5). Since the passage disrupts the rhetorical
flow of the paragraph to which it was added, and since it repeats in an
otiose way what More says at 124/19–20, it was probably added in haste
as an afterthought to be integrated more fully at some later date.

124/3–4 **sub incudem reuocare.** Cf. Adagia 492 (Opera omnia, 2,
217BC).

124/4–5 **rudem . . . refingere.** Cf. Donatus, Vita Vergilii 22, and Erasmus, Parabolae sive similia (1514), ASD 1/5, 284: "Vrsus informes gignit

catulos, eos lambendo format; ita rudem ingenii foetum diutina cura expoliri conuenit." Erasmus' own source is Pliny, *Historia naturalis* 8.126.

124/6–7 **cui . . . cupio.** Cf. Erasmus in Allen, 2, 91, line 17.

124/10 **nec . . . fuit.** Cf. Ovid, *Tristia* 5.12.53–54.

124/14–15 **mihi . . . imposuit.** See 120/1–3, 13–14, and note on 68/3–4; *Moriae encomium, ASD 4/3*, 68, lines 44–45; *Adagia* 292 (*Opera omnia*, 2, 147C); Cicero, *Epistolae ad Atticum* 13.21.5, "possum falli, ut homo"; and Pliny, *Epistolae* 5.12.1.

124/16 **culpam . . . meam.** Cf. Vergil, *Aeneid* 3.188: "moniti meliora sequamur," and the note on 68/3–4.

124/17–18 **Nempe . . . gaudeo.** Cf. *CW 8*, 198/6–10, and Seneca, *De ira* 3.36.4: "admoneri bonus gaudet: pessimus quisque correctorem asperrime patitur." More is hinting that Dorp should be equally ready to admit his mistakes.

124/19–20 **Neque . . . pertulisse.** Cf. Dorp in Allen, 2, 136, lines 353–55; for the phrasing, see note on 72/8–9.

124/21–22 **illis . . . tibi.** More seems to refer to a larger audience here; this is an additional sign that he seriously intended to publish the *Letter to Dorp*.

126/4 **toto diuisos orbe Britannos.** Vergil, *Eclogae* 1.66; cf. *CW 5*, 694/3, "extremis Britannis"; and *CW 3/2*, 143/192–93, "ultimam . . . Britanniam," an allusion to Catullus 29.4. Vergil's phrase is also cited in *Adagia* 297 (*Opera omnia*, 2, 105D): "in alio mundo."

130/2–4 **Commissario . . . Oxoniensium.** For the titles and duties assigned to the various officials of Oxford University in the fifteenth and sixteenth centuries see Charles E. Mallett, *A History of the University of Oxford*, 3 vols. (London, 1924–27), *1*, 26, 34–35, 170; *2*, 86, 499.

130/9–14 **homuncio . . . consulat.** Cf. Chaucer, *Canterbury Tales*, General Prologue 573–85, on the Manciple.

130/17–19 **sicuti . . . consilium.** See notes on 58/2–5, 124/17–18, and 138/3–7.

130/22–24 **laudem . . . pectore.** Cf. Cicero, *De officiis* 2.9.32: "Ac primum de . . . benevolentiae praecepta videamus, quae quidem capitur beneficiis maxime; secundo autem loco voluntate benefica benevolentia movetur, etiam si res forte non suppetit."

130/25–27 **hanc . . . retuli.** Cardinal John Morton sent the young More to Oxford in approximately 1492; More apparently studied there for only two years. Although one tradition reports that More studied in St. Mary's College, a more generally accepted tradition assigns him to the Benedictine foundation of Canterbury College, which was later absorbed into Christ Church. See Harpsfield, p. 12 and commentary.

130/26 **secundum Deum.** Cicero uses the phrase "secundum deos" in the sense of "next after the gods" in *De officiis* 2.3.11.

130/27–29 **videtur . . . censeam.** Cf. Cicero, *De officiis* 3.12.53, where Cicero cites the proposition "non, quicquid tibi audire utile est, id mihi dicere necesse est," only to refute it at length in 3.12.53–3.13.57.

132/9 **vestra grauitate.** For this title of respect see pseudo-Quintilian, *Declamationes* 4.13, 14.1; and Ulpian, *Digesta* 40.12.27.

132/15 **senior quam sapientior.** Cf. 320/21, "quum Rex [*sc.* Henricus sextus] innocentior esset quam sapientior"; and Bartlett J. and Helen W. Whiting, *Proverbs, Sentences, and Proverbial Phrases from English Writings Mainly before 1500* (Cambridge, Mass., 1968; hereafter cited as "Whiting"), H23, "Long hair and short wit."

132/22 **digito notetur.** Cf. Otto, no. 550.

132/26 **Sero . . . Phryges.** *Adagia* 28 (*Opera omnia*, 2, 37F–38A). The saying refers to the stubbornness of the Trojans in refusing to hand over Helen.

134/2–4 **nunquam . . . essent.** See note on 76/21-78/4 and *Adagia* 1329 (*Opera omnia*, 2, 532B–D): "Nemo mortalium omnibus horis sapit."

134/5 **Abingdoniam . . . comitatus.** Henry's court retired to Abingdon in the spring of 1518 to escape the sweating sickness which was ravaging London. Henry's retinue remained there from early March to April 16; see *LP* 2, nos. 3985, 4089.

134/6–7 **ineptias . . . procedere.** Cf. *Moriae encomium*, *ASD* 4/3, 68, lines 46–48; and Horace, *Epistolae* 2.1.145–50.

134/7–9 **hominem . . . insanum.** Cf. Cicero, *In Verrem* 2.4.1: "Venio nunc ad istius, quem ad modum ipse appellat, studium, ut amici eius, morbum et insaniam, ut Siculi, latrocinium . . ."

134/10 **hoc . . . publicis.** More is referring to the series of sermons traditionally delivered at Lent. See note on 134/25–31.

134/11 **politiem.** The rare noun *polities*, a synonym for the more common *politio*, is cited from a postclassical glossary by Egidio Forcellini, *Totius latinitatis lexicon*, ed. Giuseppe Furlanetto, 6 vols. (Prato, 1858–75), 4, 719. Another variant spelling, *politia*, is attested in Du Cange, 6, 395.

134/13–14 **neu . . . capite.** Cf. Juvenal 10.356.

134/14–16 **neque . . . inoleuit.** On choosing the texts (*themata*) of one's sermons from scripture see Erasmus, *Ecclesiastes* (*Opera omnia*, 5, 862D–863F). For the technical meaning of *themata* and for the overall structure of a medieval sermon see Sander L. Gilman, *The Parodic Sermon in European Perspective* (Wiesbaden, 1974; hereafter cited as "Gilman"), pp. 4–6.

134/17 **anilia proverbia.** Cf. 1 Tim. 4:7 and *Adagia* 2616 (*Opera omnia*, 2, 887F–888A). Tendentious or captious applications of proverbial lore played an important part in mock-sermons; see Gilman, pp. 19, 25, 27, 29.

134/21 **qui . . . scintillam habet.** Cf. Plautus, *Trinummus* 678; and *Adagia* 2675 (*Opera omnia*, 2, 902D).

134/23 **quod . . . lucrifacit.** Cf. 1 Cor. 9:18–19.

134/25–31 **In . . . naenias?** In referring to Lent as the holiest season of the year More is thinking of Lent in connection with Easter. The "quadrigesimal sermons" of Lent (daily sermons delivered in all churches) were among the most solemn of the year; see Owst, pp. 146–48. On mock-sermons see note on 272/5–28. It would seem that real preachers in the later Middle Ages resorted to levity quite frequently to hold the attention of their audiences; see Allen, *4*, 282, and *CW 12*, 84.

134/29–30 **in venerabilis Christi corporis conspectu.** The Host played an especially prominent part in Palm Sunday and Holy Thursday services; see *New Catholic Encyclopedia*, 16 vols. (New York and St. Louis, 1967), 7, 105–07; *10*, 934. On the exposition of the Host, generally in a pyx over the altar, see C. W. Dugmore, *The Mass and the English Reformers* (London and New York, 1958), pp. 65–72.

134/30–31 **bacchanales . . . naenias.** Cf. *Adagia* 545 (*Opera omnia*, 2, 241D).

134/31-136/6 **Quo . . . infamatum?** Erasmus may be echoing this passage in Allen, *4*, 471–72, lines 369–74.

134/31 **stetisse.** Though many English churches acquired pews in the fifteenth and sixteenth centuries it was still not uncommon for sermons to be delivered to a standing audience; see J. Charles Cox and Alfred Harvey, *English Church Furniture* (New York, 1907), pp. 261–63; and Charles H. Smyth, *The Art of Preaching: A Practical Survey of Preaching in the Church of England 747–1939* (London, 1940), p. 17.

136/1–3 **gesticulantem . . . morem.** Cf. *Adagia* 2479 (*Opera omnia*, 2, 846BC) and *Moriae encomium, ASD 4/3*, 75, commentary at line 71. More himself owned a monkey for amusement; see Allen, *4*, 17, line 133 and commentary.

136/3 **verba vitae.** John 6:69.

136/7–16 **At . . . inscitiam.** Cf. Erasmus in Allen, 2, 106–07, lines 619–24; and *Antibarbari, ASD 1/1*, 76.

136/8 **heremo.** The Latin form of ἔϱημος, from which we derive the word "hermit" ("desert-dweller"), is normally spelled *eremus*.

136/10–11 **hac . . . petant.** Cf. Vergil, *Aeneid* 9.641: "sic itur ad astra," and pseudo-Seneca, *Octavia* 476, "petitur hac caelum via."

136/15 **benigni.** The manuscript reading may be a mistake for *benigne* (to match "grauissime" in line 16).

136/17–18 **paenulatum . . . literatum.** More's vague terms could refer to several different items of academic dress. Fur and sheepskin were used to trim and line both gowns and hoods in late medieval Oxford; see L. H. Dudley Buxton and Strickland Gibson, *Oxford University Ceremonies* (Oxford, 1935), pp. 21, 24. More's expression "humeris instratum velleribus" probably refers to the *caputium* or medieval hood, "a kind of cape worn over the shoulders and reaching to the elbows" (Buxton and Gibson, p. 24, n. 3); "paenulatum" probably refers to the long gown called *cappa*, the main outer garment of a scholar in formal dress.

136/26 **οὐδὲ γϱὺ.** See note on 104/4.

136/28 **septem . . . idonea.** Preaching on the seven deadly sins was especially common in Lent; see Morton W. Bloomfield, *The Seven Deadly Sins* ([East Lansing], Michigan State University Press, 1952; reprint, 1967), p. 119. Cf. also *Epistolae obscurorum virorum*, pp. 47–48: "Aesticampianus . . . dixit quod magistri artium non sunt magistri in septem artibus liberalibus, sed potius in septem peccatis mortalibus. . . ."

136/29-138/7 **qui . . . superbia?** There is a similar catalogue in *CW 8*, 726/23–26. Erasmus accuses the "barbari" of the same three deadly sins, in the same order, in *Antibarbari, ASD 1/1*, 69, line 6.

136/30–31 **quicquid . . . discere.** Cf. Jerome's prefaces to his biblical translations (*PL 29*, 403): "Optima enim quaeque, ut ait Plinius, malunt contemnere et invidere plerique quam discere." Jerome expresses the same notion at *PL 28*, 1125–26, and *29*, 120. I have not been able to find the text attributed to Pliny by Jerome. Cf. also *Adagia* 2006 (*Opera omnia*, 2, 718B).

136/31-138/3 **quum . . . est?** Cf. Erasmus, *Antibarbari, ASD 1/1*, 74–76, a chapter titled "Invidum esse, haud religiosum, odisse literas, quas nescias."

138/3–7 **quum . . . superbia?** Cf. Erasmus in Allen, 2, 111, lines 797–98; and *Antibarbari, ASD 1/1*, 87–93, a chapter titled "Ignorantiam esse superbiae matrem, eruditionem contra modestiam parere"; see also above, note on 130/17–19.

138/10–11 **doctrina ... praeparat.** Cf. More's letter to Gonnell, Rogers, pp. 121–22; Erasmus, *Antibarbari, ASD 1/1*, 87–93, 98; and Seneca, *Epistolae morales* 88.20: "Quare ergo liberalibus studiis filios erudimus? Non quia virtutem dare possunt, sed quia animum ad accipiendam virtutem praeparant." More's words neatly sum up the message of Saint Basil's *Sermo de legendis libris gentilium (Patrologiae Cursus Completus: Series Graeca*, ed. J.-P. Migne, 161 vols., Paris, 1857–66, *31*, 563–90; hereafter cited as *PG*). Basil's sermon or treatise, first published in Leonardo Bruni's Latin translation (Venice, 1470/71), was a favorite patristic authority for humanist defenders of secular learning; see C. L. Stinger, *Humanism and the Church Fathers: Ambrogio Traversari (1386–1439) and Christian Antiquity in the Italian Renaissance* (Albany, 1977), pp. 11, 233.

138/17–21 **rerum ... hauriatur.** The assumption that literary studies afford privileged insights into human nature is implicit in the conventional description of literary studies, along with history, as *studia humanitatis* or "humanities." See *CW 6,* 132; Erasmus, *De conscribendis epistolis, ASD 1/2,* 242; Isocrates, *Antidosis* 253–92; and Rudolf Pfeiffer, *Humanitas Erasmiana* (Leipzig and Berlin, 1931). While the reading "historicis" of *1633* is attractive, the reading "historijs" has far better textual authority.

138/18–19 **sibi ... canere.** Cf. *Adagia* 1030 and 2480 (*Opera omnia,* 2, 417C–E and 846CD).

138/19–20 **inepte sit cantaturus.** Cf. *Adagia* 388 (*Opera omnia,* 2, 178EF).

138/20–21 **Quae ... hauriatur.** The three types of writing More mentions in this passage were the foremost concerns of traditional grammar conceived as an *ars enarrandi auctores*. See Marius Victorinus, *Ars grammatica* 1 (in *Grammatici latini,* ed. Heinrich Keil, 7 vols., Leipzig, 1855–80, *6,* 4): " ... ut Varroni placet, ars grammatica, quae a nobis litteratura dicitur, scientia est ⟨rerum⟩ quae a poetis historicis oratoribusque dicuntur. ..." More is effectively claiming that philology and not dialectic is the cardinal human science. See also notes on 12/19–21, 24/22–23.

138/22–25 **cognitionem ... theologiam.** Cf. Erasmus, *Antibarbari, ASD 1/1,* 128, lines 32–35, based on Augustine, *Retractationes* 1.6 (*PL 32,* 591), where Augustine refers to the books he began on the liberal arts, "per corporalia cupiens ad incorporalia quibusdam quasi passibus certis vel pervenire vel ducere." Cf. also Rom. 1:20.

138/24–25 **liberales ... damnat.** Cf. Erasmus, *Antibarbari, ASD 1/1,*

72, lines 11–12: " . . . literae seculares (sic enim vos appellare soletis, quicquid non didicistis)."

138/25-140/1 **spoliatis . . . cultum.** Cf. Exod. 3:22, 11:2, 12:36. More uses the same *topos* in *A Dialogue Concerning Heresies;* see *CW 6,* Commentary at 132/10–22. Erasmus develops the *topos* at considerable length in *Antibarbari, ASD 1/1,* 116–18, mainly drawing on Augustine, *De doctrina christiana* 2.40.60 (*PL 34,* 63). For the commonplace medieval description of theology as the "queen of all disciplines," see note on 140/9–10.

140/6–7 **intra septum . . . quaestionum.** Cf. *Adagia* 993 (*Opera omnia,* 2, 394F–395B).

140/9–10 **coeli reginam theologiam.** For this description of theology cf. 62/8–9 and 138/25–140/1 as well as Erasmus in Allen, *1,* 247 and 410. For an early defense of theology's claim to be "queen of all disciplines" see Jean Leclercq, ed., "Un témoinage du XIIIe siècle sur la nature de la théologie," *Archives d'histoire doctrinale et littéraire du Moyen Age, 17* (1942), 316; cf. Minnis, p. 257, n. 145. The epithet "regina coeli" is normally reserved for the Virgin Mary.

140/9–12 **theologiam . . . peregrinetur.** Cf. the pilgrimages of learning described in Erasmus, *Antibarbari, ASD 1/1,* 91–93. Erasmus is drawing on Jerome, *Epistolae* 53.1–2 (*PL 22,* 540–41). See also Erasmus, *Vita Hieronymi,* Ferguson, p. 144.

140/15 **positiua scribentibus.** See note on 48/3.

140/16–17 **plus . . . quaestiunculae.** Cf. 64/1–6 and notes.

140/17 **uentilantur.** See note on 18/2.

140/17–20 **Quorum . . . credant.** Cf. Erasmus in Allen, 2, 107, lines 624–27.

140/25–142/1 **Neque . . . subsisterent.** Cf. 220/25–26.

142/3–4 **quicunque . . . haereticos.** The same charge is mentioned in the 1520 version of the *Antibarbari, ASD 1/1,* 56, lines 18–19. For further examples see Schwarz, p. 93.

142/7–8 **diaboli . . . quendam.** This is almost certainly a reference to Erasmus. Cf. Erasmus, *Colloquia, ASD 1/3,* 655, lines 76–77, where another conservative preacher is said to have called Erasmus a *diabolus.*

142/10–12 **uerum . . . amentiae.** Cf. *Moriae encomium, ASD 4/3,* 162, lines 583–85.

142/14 **Prudentias vestras.** Cf. 144/4–5 and 148/1. The respectful title *prudentia vestra,* first occurring in documents of the fourth century

A.D., is recorded in Souter, p. 331 (cf. Latham, p. 380). More may also be thinking of the English honorific "your wisdoms," often used in addressing the members of a deliberative body like Parliament (*OED 13*, 192).

142/16–18 **cui . . . Graecos?** Cf. 98/1–8.

142/18–21 **Nam . . . est.** Cf. 220/13–14. Hythloday says the same thing in *Utopia, CW 4*, 48/32–50/3. Such a statement indirectly denies both the originality and the importance of scholastic philosophy in general. Like most humanists, More was less interested in the metaphysical speculations of medieval philosophers than in the ethical teachings of the ancients; see More's letter to Gonnell, Rogers, pp. 120–23.

142/21–22 **nouum . . . graece.** See note on 98/7–8.

142/22–24 **vetustissimos . . . scripsisse.** Cf. 100/5–8 and 220/11–12. Erasmus, too, ranked the Greeks above the Latins in theology; see *De ratione studii, ASD 1/2*, 120–21; and *Ecclesiastes, Opera omnia, 5*, 1026A. There were a number of reasons for this preference. The Greek fathers were not as remote from the *fontes* of the Christian religion either temporally or linguistically as most of the Latins were; under the influence of Origen, the Greek fathers were also better philologists than many of the Latins, and often more at home with the legacy of the classical past. In Allen, *3*, 334, lines 164–65, Erasmus also suggests that the Greek fathers were not only more learned than most of the Latins but also less quick to define their positions dogmatically; cf. above, 174/2–3. See further Robert Peters, "Erasmus and the Fathers: Their Practical Value," *Church History, 36* (1967), 254–61; and Robert Peters, ed., *Desiderius Erasmus: Prefaces to the Fathers, the New Testament, On Study* (Menston, England, 1970).

142/26–27 **neque . . . est.** Many works of the Greek fathers remained untranslated in 1518. For patristic works readily available in Greek or Latin in the early sixteenth century see Hughes H. Old, *The Patristic Roots of Reformed Worship*, Zürcher Beiträge zur Reformationsgeschichte 5 (Zurich, 1975), pp. 156–79; cf. also *CW 11*, xlvii–lxi.

142/27–29 **neque . . . efficacius.** Cf. 100/13–15 and note.

142/130–31 **Hieronymus, Augustinus, Beda.** For Jerome's dedication to the study of Greek see Pierre Courcelle, *Late Latin Writers and Their Classical Sources*, trans. Harry E. Wedeck (Cambridge, Mass., 1969; hereafter cited as "Courcelle"), pp. 48–127. Augustine had little taste for Greek studies when he was a youth, but in his later years he acquired enough Greek to compare various translations of scripture and to debate with Pelagians who were learned in Greek; see Courcelle, pp. 153–65. For Bede's knowledge of Greek see Claude Jenkins, "Bede as

Exegete and Theologian," in *Bede: His Life, Times, and Writings,* ed. A. Hamilton Thompson (Oxford, 1935), pp. 157–65.

144/2–3 **posteris . . . facerent.** See Augustine, *De doctrina christiana* 2.11.16 (*PL 34,* 42–43). For Jerome on the necessity of Greek, see note on 254/14-258/4 and Jerome, *Epistolae* 39.1 and 85.3 (*PL 22,* 465 and 753). There is a spirited exhortation to the study of Greek in a work which was traditionally attributed to Bede but which many now consider to be spurious, a short treatise *De linguis gentium* (*PL 90,* 1179D).

144/4–5 **Prudentias vestras.** See note on 142/14.

144/8–9 **quam . . . esse.** The twenty-fourth decree of the Council of Vienne (1311–12) acknowledges the importance of language instruction for both scriptural studies and missionary work; furthermore, it explicitly provides for instruction in Hebrew, Arabic, and Chaldean at each of the great universities of early fourteenth-century Europe (Alberigo, pp. 379–80). Some texts of this decree also explicitly name Greek; see the variants for the *Constitutiones* of Pope Clement V (usually called "*Clementinae*") 5.1.1, "De magistris" (*CIC 2,* 1180). The provisions of this decree were reaffirmed with a special emphasis on Greek by the Council of Basel (1431–1445) in its nineteenth session (September 7, 1434; Alberigo, p. 483). Erasmus appeals to the same conciliar directives in Allen, *1,* 353, 481; and *3,* 315.

144/14–17 **multos . . . graecam.** More is mainly referring to the 1516 foundation of Corpus Christi College, Oxford, by Richard Foxe, bishop of Winchester, in conjunction with Wolsey; see Allen, *3,* 584, 588. Foxe provided for three public readers in Greek, Latin, and theology.

144/19–23 **Cantabrigiae . . . contribuunt.** The University of Cambridge solicited such a contribution from William Blount, Baron Mountjoy, in 1511 or 1513, when Erasmus was lecturing in Greek there; see Allen, *1,* 473, 613–14. For the progress of Greek studies in Cambridge in 1515–1517 see Erasmus in Allen, *2,* 313, 328; and *3,* 546.

144/29 **peior . . . excrescere.** Cf. *Adagia* 529 (*Opera omnia, 2,* 233D).

146/1–3 **Reuerendissimus . . . Cancellarius.** William Warham (ca. 1450–1532) became archbishop of Canterbury in 1503. He was lord chancellor of England from 1504 until 1515, when he was replaced in that office by Wolsey, and he was chancellor of Oxford University from 1506 until his death. He was one of Erasmus' most loyal and most cherished patrons; see Allen, *1,* 417–18, and More's epigram to Warham commending Erasmus' New Testament, *CW 3/2,* no. 257.

146/7–8 **reuerendissimus . . . Eboracensis.** Thomas Wolsey (1472/73-1530), a graduate of Magdalen College, Oxford, became archbishop of York in 1514 and lord chancellor and cardinal in 1515. See More's epigram to Wolsey recommending Erasmus' New Testament, *CW 3/2*, no. 256.

146/11 **sciolos.** See note on 270/29.

146/16–17 **tantum . . . nemo.** For a brief sketch of Henry VIII's intellectual attainments, see J. J. Scarisbrick, *Henry VIII* (Berkeley and Los Angeles, 1968), pp. 5–6, 14–15.

146/18–19 **bonarum . . . studijs.** Cf. *CW 4*, 130/18: "inertes artes."

146/19–21 **eo . . . statuerunt.** In More's day it was generally believed that the University of Oxford and University College had been founded by the Saxon king Alfred in the ninth century; see Charles E. Mallett, *A History of the University of Oxford*, 3 vols. (London, 1924–27), *1*, 2, 89–90. For a study of the many royal privileges accorded to the University of Oxford after its actual inception in the thirteenth century see James F. Willard, *The Royal Authority and the Early English Universities* (Philadelphia, 1902).

148/1 **Prudentias vestras.** See note on 142/14.

148/9–10 **hac . . . duxi.** More's words seem to imply that the copy of the letter which was actually sent to the University of Oxford was written in More's own hand; cf. 1 Cor. 16:21; Gal. 6:11; Col. 4:18; 2 Thess. 3:17; and Philem. 19. On the other hand, "hac mea manu" may be a simple metonymy for *mihi*.

152/3–4 **fratre . . . adolescente.** Lee's brother Wilfred actually sided with Erasmus in this controversy: see Allen, *4*, 143, commentary at line 130; and 309, line 6; as well as Erasmus, *Apologia qua respondet*, Ferguson, p. 267, commentary at line 717. For Lee's family see further the Introduction, p. xxxi, n. 6, above.

152/4–6 **litteras . . . die.** These letters are apparently no longer extant.

152/13–14 **ne . . . faceres.** *Adagia* 706 (*Opera omnia*, 2, 304E).

152/15–16 **habenas dolori permitteres.** Cf. *Adagia* 147 (*Opera omnia*, 2, 89C).

152/17–18 **in astra laudibus vexeris.** Cf. *Adagia* 500 (*Opera omnia*, 2, 220E).

152/18–21 **tibi . . . sententiam.** Erasmus makes a similar appeal to the reader in the preface to the New Testament (Allen, 2, 172).

154/5–6 **istam . . . superatus.** Cf. Lee, *Annotationes*, sigs. AA$_2$–AA$_2$v; and Allen, *4*, 160, lines 51–53; answered by Erasmus in *Apologia qua respondet*, Ferguson, pp. 242, 260.

154/7 **minutias ac nugamenta.** For the charge that Erasmus rejected Lee's notes as "hairsplitting trifles" (*minutiae ac nugae*) see Allen, *3*, 424 and 471; *4*, 199; Lee, *Annotationes,* sig. AA₄; Erasmus, *Apologia qua respondet,* Ferguson, pp. 246–47. The rare form *nugamenta* first appears in Apuleius, *Metamorphoses* 1.25.3; cf. 414/22, above.

154/8–10 **a scriba . . . melius.** See note on 182/26–27.

154/9 **excerpsisse.** Perhaps we should read *excerpserit.*

154/17–18 **reuerendum . . . Roffensem.** Erasmus and Lee had agreed to let John Fisher (1459–1535), bishop of Rochester since 1504, arbitrate their dispute. Lee repeatedly claimed to have taken the initiative in suggesting that Fisher should arbitrate (see 178/5–8; 178/23–24; Lee to Erasmus, Allen, *4*, 177, lines 693–94; and Lee, *Annotationes,* sig. BB₃), and Erasmus referred to Lee's claim at least twice without contradicting it directly (see *Apologia qua respondet,* Ferguson, pp. 247, 267). It seems more likely, however, that Lee felt compelled to ask Fisher to arbitrate after Fisher had sent him a letter in March 1519, urging him to give up his attack on Erasmus altogether (see 178/29-180/2 and Erasmus to Fisher, April 2, 1518, Allen, *3*, 524–25, lines 89–91; for the date of Lee's offer, again see Lee's letter to Erasmus, Allen, *4*, 177, lines 693–94). For Fisher's biography see especially Edward Surtz, S.J., *The Works and Days of John Fisher* (Cambridge, Mass., 1967); for Fisher's admiration for Erasmus' New Testament see note on 268/21–22.

154/20 **aequa lance.** Cf. *Adagia* 1482 (*Opera omnia,* 2, 575EF).

154/30-156/1 **adesse . . . praesumpseris.** Cf. Erasmus to Fisher, Allen, *4*, 94, lines 36–38.

156/9–10 **in sua contra Latomum apologia . . . vomuerit.** Erasmus, *Apologia in dialogum Iacobi Latomi* (March 28, 1519), *Opera omnia,* 9, 106A. In Allen, *4*, 1–2, lines 34–43, Erasmus somewhat unconvincingly denies that the target of this passage was Lee.

158/8 **iurata styge.** In Greek mythology the Styx is an infernal river by which the gods swear their most solemn, inviolable oaths; see Homer, *Iliad,* 15.37; and Ovid, *Metamorphoses* 1.188–89; 2.45–46, 101.

158/11–12 **feras . . . potest.** Cf. *Adagia* 214 (*Opera omnia,* 2, 117DE).

158/16 **deierare liquet.** Cf. Terence, *Eunuchus* 331.

158/17 **ex animo.** *Adagia* 946 (*Opera omnia,* 2, 381AB).

158/28–29 **fratrem vtrumque charissimum.** For Lee's family see the Introduction, p. xxxi, n. 6.

160/5 **promouerint.** For *promoueo* used in an intransitive sense see note on 56/27.

160/6–8 **tibi . . . retulisti.** Cf. Erasmus, *Apologia qua respondet,* Ferguson, p. 280, lines 1039–43. For More's phrasing see note on 162/11–12.

160/10–11 **parentum . . . coniunctio.** For the probable character of the relations between More's family and Lee's see the Introduction, p. xxxii, n. 1.

160/12 **annis . . . prouectior.** More was probably born in 1477 or 1478 (Harpsfield, commentary on p. 9); Lee is generally supposed to have been born ca. 1482. More's remark puts Lee's birth five years later.

160/15–16 **diuersa . . . institutum.** Apart from Lee's protracted university studies there was nothing distinctive in his mode of life which could have kept Lee and More from becoming close friends. See further the Introduction, p. xxxi, n. 6.

160/17–24 **eximium . . . industria.** Cf. Cicero, *Oratio pro Caelio* 31.76, cited in *Adagia* 3899 (*Opera omnia*, 2, 1164B):

> Sed ego non loquor de sapientia, quae non cadit in hanc aetatem; de impetu animi loquor, de cupiditate vincendi, de ardore mentis ad gloriam, quae studia in his iam aetatibus nostris contractiora esse debent, in adulescentia vero tanquam in herbis significant quae virtutis maturitas et quantae fruges industriae sint futurae.

There is a much less flattering sketch by Erasmus of virtually the same aspects of Lee's character in Allen, *4,* 336, lines 55–59.

162/6–12 **huius . . . coelo.** Cf. 298/17-300/4.

162/11–12 **fructum . . . retulerunt.** For More's phrasing here see 160/7–8 and *CW 3/2,* Commentary at 654/16. Cf. also the parable of the sower in Luke 8:14, where the Latin of the Vulgate reads "non referunt fructum" and the English of the King James version reads "they . . . bring no fruit to perfection." More also uses the phrase *referre gratiam* with the unusual meaning "to receive thanks" in Allen, *4,* 234, line 27; cf. Erasmus in Allen, *2,* 218, line 252, and *In epistolam de delectu ciborum scholia, ASD 9/1,* 66, line 57.

162/19 **aliorum . . . calculis.** Cf. *Adagia* 455 (*Opera omnia,* 2, 203DE), and Erasmus, *Apologia adversus Petrum Sutorem* (*Opera omnia, 9,* 753D): "Stultus fuissem, si Lei iudicium tot eruditorum calculis praetulissem."

162/21 **vno celeumate.** Cf. 200/21 and *Adagia* 817 (*Opera omnia,* 2, 340F): "Vno ore." A κέλευσμα or κέλευμα was a shout of command or encouragement, especially the shout of a chief sailor setting the pace for the oarsmen; see Daniel J. Sheerin, "'Celuma' in Christian Latin: Lexical and Literary Notes," *Traditio, 38* (1982), 45–73.

162/26-164/1 **Cui . . . resistere.** Cf. *Apologia adversus Petrum Sutorem* (*Opera omnia, 9,* 753E): "Quod si sensissent [*sc.* eruditi] esse verum quod constantissime vociferatur *Sutor,* aut egregie stulti sunt, aut insigniter impii, qui passi sunt tale opus toties excudi."

164/1–2 **Dauid . . . Israhel.** See 1 Kings (A. V. 1 Sam.) 17:4–7.

164/3–4 **recta . . . tendere.** Lee writes similarly in *Annotationes,* sig. DD₁v; cf. Erasmus, *Apologia qua respondet,* Ferguson, p. 278.

164/5 **quam.** Perhaps we should read *quam vt.*

164/8–10 **quisquis . . . accedere.** Cf. Vergil, *Aeneid* 5.320, "proximus huic, longo sed proximus intervallo"; and *Adagia* 1282 (*Opera omnia, 2,* 516D), "multis parasangis praecurrere."

164/13–14 **obblaterantes.** This rare and postclassical verb appears with the direct object "affanias" ("cavils') in some editions of Apuleius at *Metamorphoses* 9.10 (other editions read "blaterantes" or "adblaterantes"). More's spelling both here and at 288/8 suggests that a connection is intended between *obblaterare* and *oblatrare* ("to bark at"), though the latter verb takes only personal objects (for example, "cur me oblatras?").

164/16–17 **Caesareus . . . Romae.** Caesar's saying is quoted in Plutarch, *Iulius* 11.2 (*Vitae* 712F) and *Moralia* 206B (cf. Erasmus, *Apophthegmata, Opera omnia, 4,* 213EF). The saying itself does not mention "Mutina" (modern-day Modena in Italy), nor could Plutarch have spoken of ancient Modena, a thriving provincial city, as a "miserable little hamlet" in the Alps. More may have intended a play on the similarity in sound between *Mutina* and *mutiny* or its equivalent in some other language; the word *mutin* ("mutineer") was already current in early sixteenth-century French.

164/17–18 **vt . . . superbia.** See note on 138/3–7.

164/24 **albine . . . nescimus.** *Adagia* 599 (*Opera omnia, 2,* 261C–E).

164/25 **nimisquam.** Plautus, *Mostellaria* 511.

164/25–26 **vt . . . aemulatio.** See note on 124/14–15.

166/5 **Christi . . . praepediant.** Cf. *CW 8,* 911/20–21, on the heretics who "vnder pretexte of techynge the trewe fayth, labour to destroye the trewe fayth"; and *CW 14,* 509/7, "pretextu pietatis oppugnabant pietatem."

166/6 **Sycophantijs.** See note on 210/8.

166/8 **promptuario.** Cf. 210/24. Though this word is not common in classical authors, it appears in a similar context in Ps. 143:13.

166/10 **in transuersum agunt.** Cf. *Adagia* 1792 (*Opera omnia, 2,* 661AB).

166/11–13 **aliquos . . . committant.** This may be a reference to Martin Lypsius; cf. Allen, *4,* 169, lines 403–05; and *Apologia qua respondet,* Ferguson, p. 263.

166/19 **Sed.** Perhaps we should read *Sed vt.*

166/19 **adeo contorqueas machinam.** Cf. *Adagia* 3472 (*Opera omnia*, 2, 1070A) and *Moriae encomium*, *ASD 4/3*, 113, lines 791–92 and commentary.

166/24-168/6 **ipso . . . vtilem.** More suggests that Pope Leo X formally approved both the first and second editions of Erasmus' New Testament. Actually Leo, to whom both editions were dedicated, formally acknowledged only the second (Allen, *3*, 387–88); in the other epistle to which More refers (Allen, *2*, 114–15), the words thanking Erasmus for planning to dedicate his *editio princeps* to Leo are apparently an unauthorized interpolation. Though Erasmus appears to have juggled the facts more than once in his eagerness to place his New Testament under Leo's official protection (see Allen, *3*, 305, line 13 and commentary), both this humanist pope and his curia do seem to have looked very sympathetically on Erasmus and most of his projects. See also 200/21–22, 270/7–19, and Leo in Allen, *2*, 436–38.

168/1–2 **rem . . . perfecit.** Perhaps we should read *rem cum . . . perfecerit*, thus retaining the verb form attested in *1520*ᵐ.

168/11–12 **ad me non peruenerat.** In his letter to Erasmus of February 1, 1520, Lee claimed that More did get a chance to read Lee's *Annotationes* at some point (see Allen, *4*, 160, lines 61–62; and 179, lines 797–803 and commentary).

168/15–17 **ad te . . . supersederes.** More's omission of *ut* in a substantive clause after *scribere* is unusual but not unprecedented. Cf. Caesar, *De bello gallico* 5.46: "scribit Labieno, si rei publicae commodo facere posset, cum legione ad fines Nerviorum veniat" ("He wrote instructions to Labienus to come with his legion as far as the borders of the Nervii, if he could do so without damage to the public interest").

168/22–23 **Ne . . . crepidam.** *Adagia* 516 (*Opera omnia*, 2, 228AB).

168/28 **ex vngue . . . leonem.** *Adagia* 834 (*Opera omnia*, 2, 347D–F). More is probably punning on *Leus* and *leo*. Cf. Erasmus in Allen, *4*, 76, line 5.

170/4–16 **Nam . . . commemorasti.** More similarly opposes a priori linguistics by appealing to common usage at 34/11-36/18. More and Lee both appeal to the explanation of *proprium* (τὸ ἴδιον) given by Porphyry, p. 12, lines 13–22. Lee appears to have canceled his remarks about *proprium* before publishing the rest of his notes on Erasmus' New Testament in early 1520.

170/4 **adamantinis vinculis.** Cf. *Adagia* 643 and 1241 (*Opera omnia*, 2, 279A–280A and 497D).

170/19–20 **Erasmeos.** Lee uses the same term in *Annotationes*, sigs. AA₄–AA₄v, and Allen, *4*, 177, line 727. The more common adjective is *Erasmicus;* see 16/18, 152/7, 152/22, and 262/4–5.

170/24–25 **vt id . . . desumas.** More's elliptical phrasing is somewhat obscure. It would also be possible to punctuate "vt id (quod vnum) sic Erasmo tribuis, vt praeterea nihil ipsi tibi desumas," which would mean, "how you attribute the blame to Erasmus (and it is the only thing you attribute to him) in such a way that you take none of the blame yourself." But that reading is somewhat more complex syntactically and even more obscure than the reading adopted in this text. More uses "nihil praeterea" elliptically in a similar fashion at 44/13–14. Lee repeatedly claims that Erasmus' prestige stems primarily from his power to beguile other people with his dazzling rhetoric; see Lee's open letter to Erasmus, Allen, *4*, 160, lines 37–39; 176, lines 647–51; and Erasmus, *Apologia qua respondet,* Ferguson, pp. 237, 265. Cf. also Dorp in Allen, *2*, 127, lines 12–16.

170/25–27 **rhetoris . . . exaggerans.** Cf. Quintilian 4.1.15: "Neque haec dicere sat est . . . pleraque augenda aut minuenda, ut expediet. Hoc enim oratoris est, illa causae." Erasmus, too emphasizes Lee's rhetorical exaggerations in *Apologia qua respondet,* Ferguson, pp. 237, 260.

170/26 **cumulatim.** This rare work first appears in Prudentius, *Liber apotheosis* 717, 739.

170/27 **detracta mole.** Cf. 16/5–10, where More opposes the daggerlike point of dialectic to the ponderous cogency of rhetoric.

170/29 **capitaliter offensus.** Cf. Pliny, *Epistolae* 1.5.4, where the phrase "capitaliter lacessere" is used the same way.

172/7 **se . . . edoctum.** In *Apologia qua respondet,* Ferguson, pp. 260–61, Erasmus explicitly states that he did not mention Lee in the second edition of his notes on the New Testament, though at one point he did offer to give Lee full credit for any accepted corrections in exchange for a chance to examine Lee's own *Annotationes* in manuscript; see Allen, *4*, 142, lines 91–94; 556–57, lines 84–90; and *Apologia qua respondet,* Ferguson, p. 247. Elsewhere Erasmus repeatedly stated that only "two or three" of Lee's notes had been of even the slightest use to him; see Allen, *3*, 424; *4*, 199; and *Apologia qua respondet,* Ferguson, p. 246.

172/21–32 **Caeterum . . . litteras.** Cf. 270/20–26.

172/23–24 **conferat . . . praeferat.** For the phrasing cf. 62/9 and 74/20–21. Augustine plays on the same words in *De doctrina christiana* 2.15.22 (*PL 34*, 46).

172/24–25 **a puero.** Cf. *Adagia* 653 (*Opera omnia,* 2, 283BC).

174/2–3 **Quis . . . fortiter?** Cf. *CW 4*, 226/15–17: "Nihil enim sollicitius observant [sc. Utopienses], quam ne temere quicquam ulla de religione pronuncient." Folly mocks the presumption of scholastic theologians in presenting their own biased views as if they were definitive in *ASD 4/3*, 154, lines 480–84. Cf. Listrius' commentary in *Opera omnia, 4*, 467F–468F; Erasmus, *Antibarbari, ASD 1/1*, 90; and especially Erasmus' long note on Matt. 11:30, "Iugum enim meum suave est," *Opera omnia, 6*, 63F: " . . . saepenumero fit, ut quod semel utcunque prodidit definiendi temeritas, confirmet et augeat tuendi pertinacia." See also 200/22–25.

174/4–5 **sibi stetur.** For the phrasing cf. Mic. 1:11 and Rom. 14:4.

174/9 **hominem . . . subterfugere.** See Erasmus, *Apologia,* Holborn, p. 165; Allen, 2, 171; and above, note on 124/14–15.

174/12 **harenam tuam.** Cf. *Adagia* 883 and 2562 (*Opera omnia, 2*, 361EF and 860F–861A).

174/18–19 **quum . . . admoneri.** See note on 124/17–18; Allen, *4*, 202, commentary at line 6; and Allen, 5, 517–18, commentary at line 89.

174/20–24 **epistolis . . . senserunt.** Few letters of precisely this character are extant in Erasmus' pre-1519 correspondence, but see, for example, Erasmus to Budé, Allen, 2, 281–82.

174/25 **quum . . . didicissent.** Cf. Otto, no. 563: "Homines dum docent, discunt."

174/26 **tragoedias mouerit.** See note on 18/12–13.

176/3 **ea Apologia . . . palam.** More is referring to Erasmus' open letter to Dorp, Allen, 2, 90–114.

176/7–8 **praesertim lacessitus.** More emphasizes that Dorp was the first to offend, so that Erasmus would have had every right to respond with like harshness. In his *Letter to Brixius* More is very concerned with the question of who struck the first blow. See Adagia 3126 (*Opera omnia, 2*, 996D).

176/11–13 **illam epistolam . . . meam.** Allen (2, 126) takes these words as referring to a second and harsher response by Erasmus to Dorp which Erasmus suppressed. Allen's interpretation does not suit More's context, since More's aim is to show that Erasmus consistently and characteristically treated Dorp's charges more generously than they deserved, so that Dorp ought to feel nothing but gratitude for the way that Erasmus responded to his admonitions. Furthermore, it is hard to see why More should have suppressed his response to Dorp's charges "vicissim" ("in turn") after Erasmus suppressed his own harsher response: there is no quid pro quo in a pact such as this between allies, while "vicissim" invites us to seek one. Finally, since there is only one extant manuscript of Dorp's second letter (Allen, 2, 126–36), which Dorp never published, and since this single manuscript appears to derive from a copy belonging to More (Allen, 2, 126, 197, and 496), it seems perfectly likely that Dorp did agree to suppress his second letter and that this is the agreement to which More refers. Cf. Erasmus' catalogue of his critics in his *Compendium vitae* (1524), Allen, *1*, 52: "Nam Dorpiana orsa suppressa sunt."

176/16–17 **tibi . . . petituro.** Lee matriculated in the University of Louvain on August 25, 1516; see Henry De Vocht, "Excerpts from the Register of Louvain University from 1485 to 1527," *English Historical Review*, *37* (1922), 98. By July 1517, Lee was busily studying Greek; see Erasmus in Allen, *3*, 20.

176/20–21 **tu . . . cognouimus.** Cf. 186/19–24. For other passages suggesting that Lee actually planned an attack on Erasmus' New Testament even before Lee arrived in Louvain to learn Greek see Erasmus in Allen, *3*, 599, and *4*, 151, 198; and *Apologia qua respondet,* Ferguson, p. 241. There may be another reference to Lee's premature condemnation of Erasmus' New Testament in Allen, *3*, 325, lines 484–90, where Lee is probably the "paraclete" or instigator that Erasmus attacks indirectly.

176/26 **regestis . . . maledictis.** Cf. 1 Pet. 2:23 and Plautus, *Menaechmi* 945.

176/27–29 **locis . . . euomuerint.** Cf. 142/7–8 and note. In addressing this comment to Lee, More is probably thinking of Jacob Latomus; see Erasmus in Allen, *3*, 519 and 523, and the note on 156/9–10, above.

176/33 **immodesta modestia.** Cf. Gerardus Listrius in Allen, *2*, 408, line 23. More uses this phrase with the same sense at 476/15, above. In Erasmus the phrase seems to refer strictly to false moderation or false modesty; see Allen, *3*, 523, lines 41–42; and *Antibarbari, ASD I/I*, 93, lines 5–6.

178/1–2 **tot . . . repullulent.** Cf. *Adagia* 909 (*Opera omnia*, 2, 370DE).

178/15 **toto pectore.** *Adagia* 326 (*Opera omnia*, 2, 160E–161A).

178/27 **prior . . . librum.** Fisher acknowledged receipt of a gift copy of Erasmus' New Testament in a letter of mid-1516 (Allen, 2, 268, lines 3–5).

178/29-180/2 **Tu . . . iudicem.** See note on 154/17–18. Fisher's letter to Lee counseling him to give up his attack is apparently not extant.

180/2–4 **ita . . . cognouerit.** Lee's suggestion that Fisher should arbitrate was apparently made in late March; his abortive decision to publish at once in response to Erasmus' *Apologia in dialogum Iacobi Latomi* was made in mid-April. See 152/4–6, 154/17–18, 156/9–10 and notes.

180/15–16 **non . . . coloribus.** See note on 116/23.

180/18 **ansa.** See note on 10/22.

180/19–20 **vestigia ... perueniatur.** Cf. *Adagia* 3118 (*Opera omnia*, 2, 995AB).

182/26–27 **tuis ... didicisse.** Cf. 154/8–9; Lee, *Annotationes*, sig. BB₁; and Allen, *4*, 161, lines 76–78; 169, lines 401–07; 179, lines 795–97; answered by Erasmus in *Apologia qua respondet*, Ferguson, pp. 262–63; and Allen, *4*, 200, lines 102–08.

184/20–21 **dum ... obficere.** Cf. Terence, *Andria* 625–28 and *CW 4*, 164/17–18: "eadem [*sc.* natura] te nimirum iubet etiam atque etiam obseruare, ne sic tuis commodis obsecundes: ut aliorum procures incommoda." See also Cicero, *De legibus* 1.18.49.

184/21–22 **vt nunc sunt mores.** Terence, *Phormio* 55.

184/22–23 **tibi ... alteri.** Cf. *Adagia* 291 (*Opera omnia*, 2, 147AB).

184/26-186/7 **si ... temperantius.** See note on 186/14–15.

186/11 **rumigeruli.** This word is used similarly by Jerome; see *Epistolae* 50.1 (*PL* 22, 512, 959).

186/14–15 **litteras ... scio.** Erasmus had certainly begun to attack Lee obliquely in his letters to other people by April 1519; see especially Erasmus' letter to Budé of December 22, 1518, Allen, *3*, 459–60, lines 448–66, and commentary.

186/16–17 **tuas ... αὐτογράφους.** These letters are apparently no longer extant.

186/19–20 **praeiudicium ... attuleris.** Cf. Quintilian 4.5.4 and *Adagia* 1206 (*Opera omnia*, 2, 486C–E), where Erasmus cites Plutarch for τὴν οἴκοθεν κρίσιν ("a judgment brought from home"). According to Erasmus, such proverbs have two almost contradictory senses: on the one hand, one's conscience is always the most trustworthy judge; on the other, one's personal bias is always the least trustworthy witness.

186/20–24 **sementem ... promitterent.** Cf. *Adagia* 3899 (*Opera omnia*, 2, 1164B).

186/26 **oporteat.** In preclassical Latin (especially in Plautus) the present subjunctive was used in contrary-to-fact conditional clauses; Raphael Kühner, *Ausführliche Grammatik der lateinischen Sprache*, rev. Carl Stegmann, 2 vols. in 3 (Hanover, 1912–14; hereafter cited as Kühner–Stegmann), 2/2, 399–400.

186/27–28 **dum ... permisceas.** Cf. *Adagia* 967 (*Opera omnia*, 2, 385CD).

188/4 **adhuc ... lis.** Horace, *Ars poetica* 78.

188/6 **nouas conficias tabulas.** The phrase *novae tabulae* normally refers to an official cancellation of debts (Cicero, *De officiis* 2.23.84); here it suggests that Lee plans to appropriate everything that is held to Erasmus' credit.

188/9–10 **mutum . . . aduersarium.** Cf. *Adagia* 118 and 2475 (*Opera omnia*, 2, 77E and 845B).

188/14–15 **non . . . auditurus.** Cf. *Adagia* 27 (*Opera omnia*, 2, 36F–37F): "Qui quae vult dicit, quae non vult audiet."

188/22 **reum . . . ridicule.** More's phrasing is probably elliptical: "reum etiam aget insolentiae, eiusque rei valde ridicule [reum]." The reading "ridiculae" in *1520*ᵃ does not clarify the meaning.

188/23 Ἐπιμηθεὺς μετὰ τὰ πράγματα. Cf. *Adagia* 31 (*Opera omnia*, 2, 39DE), where Erasmus quotes the comic fragment, Κλέων Προμηθεύς ἐστι μετὰ τὰ πράγματα; and Erasmus in Allen, *3*, 224, lines 108–09: "An, vt Epimetheus quispiam, iam peracto negocio mones ne suscipiatur negocium. . . ?" Prometheus was the wily Titan who stole fire for the good of mankind; Epimetheus was his stupid brother who found out too late that Zeus' gift of Pandora was more of a curse than a blessing. "Prometheus" and "Epimetheus" are significant names meaning "Foresight" and "Hindsight."

188/25 **lacunas . . . complanatae.** Cf. *Adagia* 3928 (*Opera omnia*, 2, 1169AB).

190/2–3 **quos . . . abiecerint.** Cf. 124/4–5 and note.

190/6–7 **vertet . . . vela.** *Adagia* 860 (*Opera omnia*, 2, 356DE); cf. *CW 4*, 88/21.

190/10–11 **tacere nefas.** Cf. *Adagia* 1604 (*Opera omnia*, 2, 613F–614B).

190/13 **funditus.** *Adagia* 3722 (*Opera omnia*, 2, 1127C–F).

190/13–14 **id . . . scilicet.** Terence, *Andria* 185.

190/15 **tuam . . . retaliet.** Cf. *Adagia* 35 (*Opera omnia*, 2, 41A–E).

190/21 **reculas.** This diminutive of *res* appears in a fragment of Plautus cited by Priscian (*Institutiones grammaticae* 3.6.33) and in Apuleius, *Metamorphoses* 4.12. More seems to intend a punning connection with "parum recte" in the following line.

190/24–25 **quasi . . . tractauerit.** Cf. *Adagia* 855 (*Opera omnia*, 2, 354C–355C).

190/27 **sibi.** Perhaps we should read *tibi*.

190/27 **suum . . . persequatur.** Cf. Terence, *Adelphoe* 163, 493.

192/4–5 **euentus iudicet.** Cf. Publilius Syrus 163, cited in Otto, no. 614: "Extrema semper de ante factis iudicant." The reading "euentus

562 COMMENTARY

indicet" would make equally good sense; cf. *Adagia* 2349 (*Opera omnia*, 2, 815C–E): "Res indicabit."

192/6–8 **suae . . . computent.** Cf. *The Debellation of Salem and Bizance, EW*, sig. R₄; and Whiting H550.

192/13 **sanctissimum . . . amicitiae.** Cf. Ovid, *Tristia* 1.8.15, "Illud amicitiae sanctum et venerabile nomen."

192/14–15 **Sic . . . vt habeam.** For the syntax of this adjuration cf. Ovid, *Metamorphoses* 8.866–67, and Kühner–Stegmann, 2/1, 190–91.

192/20 **prouinciam suscipere.** Cf. *Adagia* 1341 (*Opera omnia*, 2, 535F).

192/22 **tunica molesta.** Cf. *Adagia* 1988 (*Opera omnia*, 2, 706C–707B): "ardens vestis." A *tunica molesta* was a combustible straitjacket used to torture very serious offenders in Rome; cf. Juvenal 8.235, Martial 10.25. More may also be thinking of Hercules' burning on Oeta.

192/27–194/5 **feliciorem . . . deo.** Apart from a lost commentary on the Pentateuch Lee wrote nothing else of great importance. See the list of his works in *DNB 32*, 349.

194/9–10 **ne . . . lapidem.** *Adagia* 408 (*Opera omnia*, 2, 185CD).

194/14–15 **a quo limite . . . deliret.** The verb *delirare* properly means "to veer away from a straight line in plowing"; a *sulcus* is the furrow that is cut by a plow; a *limes* is the straight boundary of the field to which each furrow ought to run parallel. For various medieval metaphors which link writing with plowing see Ernst R. Curtius, *European Literature and the Latin Middle Ages*, trans. Willard K. Trask (Princeton, 1973), pp. 313–14.

194/15–16 **liber . . . commititur.** Cf. Allen, *4*, 151, lines 490–92.

194/20 **splendorem . . . obducere.** Cf. *Adagia* 330 (*Opera omnia*, 2, 1031BC).

194/25 **tam . . . gloriae.** See note on 160/17–24.

194/26 **genuinum frangere.** *Adagia* 1159 (*Opera omnia*, 2, 467EF); cf. More in Allen, *4*, 230, line 532.

198/1–7 **ERVDITISSIMA . . . etc.** The shortened form of this title in *1520*ᵃ makes no mention of Erasmus' translation "In principio erat sermo," probably because *1520*ᵃ was issued along with an expanded version of Erasmus' own *apologia* for this translation. The phrase "rabiosa maledicentia" found in the title of *1520*ᵃ also occurs in Erasmus' *Enchiridion*, Holborn, p. 80.

198/5–7 **Erasmus . . . sermo.** See note on 236/3–6.

198/8–12 **Perlatae . . . pertimescas?** More seems to pattern his opening on that of a letter in which Jerome indirectly responds to another monkish critic. See Jerome, *Epistolae* 50.1 (*PL* 22, 512): "Litterae tuae et amorem pariter sonant, et querelam. Amorem tuum, quo sedulo monens, etiam quae tuta sunt in nobis pertimescis: querelam eorum, qui non amant. . . ." The phrase *tuta pertimescis* is proverbial; see *Adagia* 1280 (*Opera omnia*, 2, 515EF).

198/14 **noua . . . doctrina.** Cf. Mark 1:27 and Erasmus in Allen, *8*, xlvi, line 59.

198/16 **totis . . . habenis.** See note on 152/15–16.

198/18 **tantum non.** Cf. *Moriae encomium, ASD, 4/3,* 122, line 968; and Listrius' commentary in *Opera omnia, 4,* 444C.

198/19–20 **Corrumpunt . . . praua.** 1 Cor. 15:33; *Adagia* 974 (*Opera omnia*, 2, 388E–389D). More himself cites the verse against heretics in *The Debellation of Salem and Bizance, EW,* sig. P₄v; *The Answer to the First Part of the Poisoned Book, EW,* sig. U₂; and *The Confutation of Tyndale's Answer, CW 8,* 151/4-8.

198/21 **qui . . . subclaudicare.** *Adagia* 973 (*Opera omnia*, 2, 387E–388D).

198/22–23 **vt facias . . . triadem.** Erasmus refers to the practice of arranging religious themes in *terniones* ("groups of three") in Allen, *4,* 522, lines 507–08; and in *Ecclesiastes, Opera omnia, 5,* 862D. Though such an arrangement is clearly related to the tricolon of classical rhetoric, its primary function in religious applications is presumably to serve as a reminder of the Trinity. The humanists generally preferred the term *Trias* for the Trinity over the late coinage *Trinitas;* see Erasmus, *Moriae economium, ASD 4/3,* 164, commentary at line 599; *Explanatio symboli (Opera omnia, 5,* 1145E); and *Precationes (Opera omnia, 5,* 1199E and 1210E). In *Christiani hominis institutum (Opera omnia, 5,* 158F), Erasmus even refers to the Trinity as "hic Ternio Sanctus."

198/23 **dum . . . ipsi.** Ovid, *Remedia amoris* 615.

200/5–9 **posteaquam . . . corruas.** Cf. 92/16–19; More's letter to Gonnell, Rogers, p. 122, lines 49–51; and Horace, *Satirae* 2.3.51–62.

200/10–11 **locum . . . docuero.** Cf. Ovid, *Tristia* 2.301–02: "omnia perversas possunt corrumpere mentes; | stant tamen illa suis omnia tuta locis." See also Vergil *Aeneid* 1.583, 4.298.

200/11–12 **arcem istam tuam.** See note on 104/7.

200/12–13 **e sublimi . . . despicis.** See note on 10/12.

200/21 **vna voce.** See note on 162/21.

200/21–22 quos pontifex maximus ... studiosis? See note on 166/24-168/6.

200/22–25 Quomodo ... lectori? See Erasmus in Allen, *3*, 324, lines 468–70; and cf. 174/2–3, 216/10–13, and notes.

200/27–28 nec ... iuratus. Cf. Horace, *Epistolae* 1.1.14.

202/7–8 quod ... venenum. Cf. *CW 5*, 132/31–32; and *CW 8*, 162/19–20 and 179/4–8. Underlying More's figure of speech is the proverbial representation of the spider as a creature who turns everything it consumes into poison. Cf. *Enchiridion*, Holborn, p. 109; Allen, *3*, 327; *Apologia contra Stunicam* (*Opera omnia, 9*, 388A).

202/11 conuicia velut e plaustro. Cf. *Adagia* 673 and 674 (*Opera omnia, 2*, 290F–291D).

202/13 pseudotheologum. This word, borrowed from Greek, is attested in Latham (p. 381) from a document of ca. 1400.

202/15 praeconem ... Antichristi. In later life More himself often made the same charge against heretics; see *CW 8*, Commentary at 271/11 and 1338.

202/16 praemollias. For the rhetorical practice of "softening" or cushioning a potentially jarring expression see Quintilian 4.3.10 and 6.5.9, as well as Erasmus' introduction to *Adagia* (*Opera omnia, 2*, 13DE).

202/18 amice ... charissime. More again refers to his long-standing acquaintance with the monk at 264/26–28 and 274/5–6. If the identification of the monk as the Carthusian John Batmanson is correct, More's acquaintance with him probably dates from More's four years of residence as a lay brother in the Charterhouse of London; see Roper, p. 6.

202/24–26 Antichristi ... asseruerit? In Allen, *4*, 453–54 and 528, Erasmus mentions a report that a Parisian Carmelite (described as a *monachus* in the second of these passages) has identified Erasmus, an Italian Minorite, Lefèvre d'Etaples, and Reuchlin as the "praecursores" of Antichrist; see also Allen, *2*, 374, commentary at line 26; *4*, 453, commentary at lines 25–26; and the second part of *Epistolae obscurorum virorum*, pp. 241–42. In the *Letter to Botzheim* (Allen, *1*, 23) Erasmus declares that monks in London, Paris, and Brussels launched a concerted attack on his translation "In principio erat sermo" in about 1519; it may be that the monk to whom More is responding and the Carmelite preacher in Paris both drew on the same "revelation." For Batmanson's parallel attack on Lefèvre d'Etaples see Erasmus in Allen, *4*, 287.

202/26–27 Parco ... de me. Cf. 2 Cor. 12:6, where the reading at the end of the sentence is "ex me."

202/27–28 **Proh . . . fidem.** Cf. *Adagia* 3776 (*Opera omnia*, 2, 1140AB).

204/4–5 **detrectationem, opus plane diaboli.** Erasmus, too, stresses the etymological connection between *diabolus* and διαβάλλεσθαι, "to slander"; see *Institutio christiani matrimonii* (*Opera omnia*, 5, 622A); *Annotationes in Novum Testamentum* (*Opera omnia*, 6, 22E–F); and *Responsio ad Adnotationes Lei* (*Opera omnia*, 9, 284AB).

204/10–11 **quam . . . credidissem.** Cf. *Adagia* 3461 (*Opera omnia*, 2, 1068AB).

204/11–12 **ne . . . crederes.** Cf. 1 John 4:1.

204/11–14 **suasissem . . . prodidisset.** Cf. 2 Cor. 11:14. This passage, like 266/3–20, is closely related to the passage on the testing of spirits in *A Dialogue of Comfort, CW 12*, 132/24–134/9. Each of these passages is significantly indebted to John Gerson's *De probatione spirituum;* see *CW 12*, Commentary at 132/25–133/1 and 133/30–134/3, where the references to Gerson's *Opera omnia* should read *1*, 37–43 and *1*, 43–59.

204/15 **occinere.** This verb, generally meaning "to croak" or "to sing inauspiciously," has both here and in *CW 14*, 375/8, the additional sense, "to chant loudly to silence another."

204/15–18 **In nouissimis temporibus . . . conscientiam.** 1 Tim. 4:1–2. The Vulgate has "suam conscientiam."

204/18–20 **Nemo . . . carnis.** Col. 2:18. The Vulgate has "ambulans" and "carnis suae."

204/20–22 **Haec . . . apostolo.** See note on 202/26–27 and cf. the *Letter to Bugenhagen*, Rogers, p. 326, lines 33–35: ". . . fecisse modestius videreris, si mores Apostoli potius esses imitatus, quam si tibi arrogasses Apostolicum stylum."

204/27 **energumeno . . . genius.** More returns to the notion that some evil genius accounts for some fantasies in *De Tristitia Christi;* cf. *CW 14*, 139/5–7 and Commentary. Erasmus represents slanderers as *energumeni* in *Lingua, ASD 4/1*, 363, lines 565–69. The word *energumenus*, borrowed from Greek, was the standard ecclesiastical term for a victim of demon possession; see *Documenta iuris canonici veteris* (*PL 56*, 885C).

204/28–29 **Non . . . te.** Erasmus employs similar rhetoric in Allen, *3*, 325, lines 484–90; 326, lines 516–17; and 327, line 577, where the "suggestor spiritus" is probably Lee; see note on 176/20–21.

204/28 **orgijs.** The word *orgia* properly refers to the nocturnal rituals of Bacchus and more generally to any disreputable ritual at all; cf. Juvenal 2.91.

204/28-206/6 **is . . . Leum.** In his note on this passage Gibaud identifies this nameless apologist with Lee despite More's explicit denial that

Lee is intended. A similar but likelier candidate is the Franciscan Henry Standish, bishop of St. Asaph, who according to Erasmus was a principal instigator of Batmanson's bitter attack on him (Allen, *4*, 286–87). The description "secundum saeculi dignitatem honorabilem" (206/13–14) fits a bishop much better than it fits a theology student like Lee, and Standish, unlike Lee, would have been vulnerable to the argument at 210/8–14, which presumes that the apologist never talked with Erasmus outside England. For More's defense of Erasmus against Standish's oral attacks in this period see Erasmus in Allen, *4*, 310–12, and *8*, xlv–xlvi. One of Standish's principal grievances was Erasmus' translation "In principio erat sermo," and More used some of the same arguments against Standish's oral attacks that he uses against the monk's written attack (see 236/3–248/28). John Bale, *Scriptorum illustrium maioris Brytanniae* . . . 2 vols. (Basel, 1557–59), *1*, sigs. Vu₁v–Vu₂, attributes to Standish a book *Contra versiones Erasmi*. Lucas Wadding refers to what is probably the same work, for which he gives the title *Contra versionem novi testamenti factam per Erasmum, liber unus*, in *Scriptores ordinis minorum* . . . (Rome, 1650), p. 167.

206/7–8 **eo . . . regredi.** Cf. *Historia Richardi Tertii*, 478/21 and note.

206/22 **quibusdam . . . interuallis.** Cf. *OED 6*, 485: "The Latin phrase 'non est compos mentis, sed gaudet lucidis intervallis' is common in English legal documents from the 13th to the 15th centuries; so also in the medieval Latin commentators on Justinian's *Institutes*."

206/27–29 **excutiamus . . . habeas.** For similarly intricate syntax see 44/14–18 and the *Letter to Bugenhagen*, Rogers, p. 333, lines 290–91. For a similar play on the various meanings of "faith" see the emblem of the "Maye" eclogue in Edmund Spenser's *The Shepheardes Calender:* "Πᾶς μὲν ἄπιστος ἀπιστεῖ. τίς δ'ἄρα πίστις ἀπίστῳ; This hexameter has not been traced. Cf. Baptista Mantuanus, *Eclogae* 4.15: "Qui non credit, inops fidei." In *A Dialogue Concerning Heresies, CW 6*, 261/8–9, the Messenger declares it outrageous that in heresy trials canon law should "admytte and receyue a person infamed / and giue faythe and credence to an infidel. . . ." More responds by defending the same sort of testimony he assails more or less categorically in the *Letter to a Monk*.

208/1–3 **Vt . . . produnt.** Cf. *CW 8*, 902/18–20: " . . . so stronge a thynge is trouth, and so feble a thynge is falsshed, and so hard to be borne out and defended." Cf. also *CW 4*, 220/16–17 and Commentary; *CW 6*, 88–90; Erasmus' introduction to *Adagia* (*Opera omnia*, 2, 8A); *Adagia* 1317 (*Opera omnia*, 2, 528E); and Erasmus in Allen, *3*, 599, lines 11–12. For a shrewd general comment on the humanists' optimistic assumption that truth would invariably win out over falsehood if both sides were given a hearing, see *CW 5*, Introduction, 808–09.

208/2–3 **ipsi . . . produnt.** Cf. Otto, no. 1676, and *Adagia* 265 (*Opera omnia*, 2, 137C): "Suo ipsius indicio periit sorex." Erasmus explains that the shrew-mouse betrays itself by squeaking louder than ordinary mice or by making more noise when it gnaws on scraps.

208/3–8 **Quid . . . haereticum?** In the absence of *compurgatores* who would bear witness to a suspect's good character, the testimony of any two hostile witnesses would suffice to convict him of heresy; see *CW 6*, 261/1–3 and Commentary; and *CW 9*, lx–lxi and Commentary at 136/6–7.

208/7 **solitum [eum].** The pronoun "eum" is needed to clarify the syntax of the words following "quam." It could have been omitted after "solitum" through haplography.

208/10 **Coletum.** John Colet (ca. 1466–1519), dean of St. Paul's Cathedral in London from 1504, was an important spiritual influence on both More and Erasmus. More hailed him as his spiritual adviser in 1504 (Rogers, pp. 8–9); Erasmus wrote an inspiring short biography of him in 1521 (Allen, *4*, 514–27). Colet stressed the importance of preaching and took a great interest in "ancient theology," including the writings of the Platonists; see Sears Jayne, *John Colet and Marsilio Ficino* (Oxford, 1963). For Colet's influence on Erasmus see James D. Tracy, *Erasmus: The Growth of a Mind* (Geneva, 1972; hereafter cited as "Tracy, *Erasmus*"), pp. 84–85. Erasmus frequently visited Colet at Oxford in 1499 and made a pilgrimage to Canterbury with him in 1514; see Erasmus in Allen, *1*, 268–70, and *4*, 517, commentary at line 327. Colet applauded Erasmus' New Testament; see below, note on 268/21–22. For further details of Colet's biography see Rogers, pp. 5–6, and J. H. Lupton, *A Life of John Colet* (London, 1887).

208/10–11 **Reuerendum . . . episcopum.** John Fisher, bishop of Rochester since 1504; see notes on 154/17–18 and 268/21–22. Erasmus stayed with Fisher for ten days at Rochester in 1516; see Erasmus in Allen, 2, 317.

208/11–12 **Reuerendissimum . . . pontificem.** William Warham, archbishop of Canterbury from 1503; see note on 146/1–3.

208/13 **Monioium.** William Blount, Lord Mountjoy (1478–1534), Erasmus' first great English patron, was responsible for bringing Erasmus to England for the first time in 1499. Erasmus lived with Mountjoy as his personal tutor for several months in 1499 and stayed with him again in 1505, 1515, and 1516; see Allen, *1*, 207; and 2, 68 and 243.

208/13 **Tunstallum.** Cuthbert Tunstall (1474–1559), bishop of London 1522–29/30, bishop of Durham from 1529/30, was a learned and steadfast defender of orthodox Catholicism. In March 1527/28 he commissioned More to write against heretics; see Rogers, p. 387. Though he supported the royal supremacy under Henry he was deprived of his bishopric under Edward VI and Elizabeth for advocating a return to the old order. He spent most of the winter of 1516 enjoying Erasmus' company in Brussels; see Allen, 2, 278, 355–56. At that time Tunstall made a significant contribution to preparing the second edition of Erasmus' New Testament (*Apologia qua respondet*, Ferguson, pp. 239–41). For further details of Tunstall's biography see Rogers, p. 16, and for his later attitude toward Erasmus see *CW 6*, 460–61.

208/13 **Paceum.** Richard Pace (ca. 1483–1536) was a close friend of both More and Erasmus and an important servant of Henry VIII. In 1516 More wrote to Erasmus: "Ego interim videor mihi dimidio mei carere, dum abest ille [*sc.* Paceus]; altero dimidio dum tu" (Allen, 2, 193, lines 12–13). Erasmus was impressed with Pace's learning but dismayed by his lack of discretion; see Erasmus in Allen, *1*, 445, and *3*, 218, 251, and 254–55, where Erasmus deplores the publication of Pace's main work, *De fructu qui ex doctrina percipitur* (Basel, 1517). Although Pace suffered a mental collapse in 1526, he was entrusted with many important diplomatic missions in earlier life and was rewarded with a number of ecclesiastical benefices, including the deanery of St. Paul's (October 1519; see Allen, *4*, 87). He wrote a letter to Dorp (now lost) in defense of Erasmus and played an important role in mediating between Erasmus and Lee; see Erasmus in Allen, *3*, 162, and *4*, 256 and 262. For further details of Pace's biography see Richard Pace, *De fructu qui ex doctrina percipitur*, ed. and trans. Franz Manley and Richard S. Sylvester (New York, 1967), pp. ix–xii.

208/13 **Grocinum.** William Grocyn (ca. 1446–1519), fellow of New College, Oxford, was one of the first to teach Greek at Oxford. Between 1488 and 1490 he studied Greek in Italy with Poliziano and Chalcondyles; he was More's Greek instructor in London in 1501 (Rogers, p. 4). Erasmus enjoyed Grocyn's hospitality in London in 1511, but by 1515 their friendship had apparently cooled; see Allen, *1*, 485, and 2, 139. For further details of Grocyn's biography see Rogers, p. 4.

208/14–16 **de . . . posse.** Cf. *CW 4*, 46/15–20.

208/20 **subodorati.** Cf. *Adagia* 581 (*Opera omnia*, 2, 253B). Erasmus goes on to establish that almost all metaphors derived from the senses and parts of the body can be used with the force of a proverb.

208/23 **intimius.** This late coinage, a comparative adverb formed from a word which is already a superlative, occurs in Latham, p. 257.

208/28 **mysten.** See note on 122/12.

210/8 **Sycophanta.** *Adagia* 1281 (*Opera omnia*, 2, 515F–516C).

210/11 **Erasmus . . . abfuit.** Erasmus had departed from England for the last time in late April 1517; see Allen, 2, 553; and 3, 578–79.

210/14–15 **in libris . . . eruerint.** Cf. *Debellation, EW,* sig. N₆: "For the wordes once red: the trouth should shewe it selfe."

210/16–17 **praestigiaturis.** The late coinage *praestigiatura* ("magic," "illusion") is attested by Latham (p. 370), who assigns it to a text of ca. 1115.

210/18 **suopte indicio reo.** See note on 208/2–3.

210/24 **promptuarium.** See note on 166/8.

210/24-212/2 **Nec . . . reddere.** Cf. Erasmus' *Enarratio Psalmi 38* (1532), *Opera omnia,* 5, 435F. Ɔr the custom of requiring a person suspected of heresy to declare his own creed see F. J. Badcock, *The History of the Creeds,* (New York, 1930), pp. 78–79, 89–93. Jerome answers a challenge to declare his own creed in *Epistolae* 17 (*PL 22,* 359–61). Cf. 1 Pet. 3:15 as paraphrased in *CW 6,* 23/3–6.

210/26 **tam . . . machina.** See note on 166/19.

212/4–5 **per . . . somnia.** Cf. Homer, *Odyssey* 19.562–67, imitated by Vergil in *Aeneid* 6.893–96. More sarcastically assigns the hallucinations of Batmanson's inspired informant to the gate of horn, through which only true visions pass; false dreams pass through the gate of ivory.

212/5 **ansam . . . arripuisti.** See note on 10/22.

212/14 **lapsos esse alicubi.** These words, missing in *1520*ᵐ, are supplied in *1520*ᵃ, presumably from 212/15.

212/19-214/21 **Age . . . desciuit.** There is a similar catalogue of patristic errors, introduced with a similar polemical intent, in Erasmus' *Enarratio Psalmi 38* (1532), *Opera omnia,* 5, 432B–435E. Cf. also Minnis, pp. 59–60, on Abelard's similar remarks in the *Sic et non* prologue.

212/20–21 **cum . . . factum.** See Augustine to Jerome and Jerome to Augustine in Jerome's *Epistolae* 104.4–5 and 112.21–22 (*PL 22,* 833–34 and 929–31). Erasmus recounts this particular exchange in Allen, *3,* 313–14; and *Annotationes in Novum Testamentum* (*Opera omnia, 6,* 336C).

212/22–24 **Quum . . . contendat.** Cf. Augustine, *De doctrina christiana* 2.15.22 (*PL 34,* 46) and *De civitate dei* 15.14.2 and 18.43 (*PL 41,* 455 and 603–04); Jerome, *Praefatio in Pentateuchum* (*PL 28,* 150; later incorporated into Jerome's *Apologia adversus libros Rufini* 2.25; *PL 23,* 449).

212/24-214/1 **Cum . . . derideat.** Cf. Augustine, *De doctrina christiana* 2.15.22 (*PL 34,* 46); *De civitate dei* 18.42 (*PL 41,* 602–03) and commentary; Jerome, *Praefatio in Pentateuchum* (*PL 28,* 150; later incorporated into Jerome's *Apologia adversus libros Rufini* 2.25; *PL 23*, 449). Erasmus refers to this disagreement in a similar way in Allen, 2, 57, lines 77–82; and *3*, 321, lines 336–41.

214/1–2 **quum ... ex diametro diuersa.** *Adagia* 945 (*Opera omnia*, 2, 380EF). The punctuation of *1520*ᵃ links this clause with the following sentence. It is hard to decide which punctuation is correct; both the preceding and the following sentence refer to disputes in which Augustine and Jerome held diametrically opposite views.

214/2–4 **Quum ... neget.** The main texts for this quarrel about Gal. 2:11 are included in Jerome's correspondence with Augustine; see Jerome, *Epistolae* 56.3–4, 67.3–7, 112.4–17, and 116.4–30 (*PL 22*, 566–67, 648–50, 917–27, and 937–50). Cf. also Erasmus' discussion in *Annotationes in Novum Testamentum* (*Opera omnia*, 6, 807B–810B).

214/4–5 **Quum ... placeant.** Cf. Jerome, *Epistolae* 105.5 and 112.20 (*PL 22*, 836–37 and 928–29).

214/6–7 **Quum ... laudet.** For this disagreement, closely connected with Augustine's critique of Jerome's way of reading Galatians, see *CW 12*, Commentary at 132/17–21. More perhaps overstates Jerome's willingness to sanction a well-meaning lie.

214/7–9 **Quum ... confirmet.** See Matt. 5:32, 19:9; Mark 10:11; Luke 16:18; and 1 Cor. 7:11–15. Augustine declares his position in *De sermone Domini in monte* 1.14 (*PL 34*, 1248–49) and *De coniugiis adulterinis* 1.1 (*PL 40*, 451); Ambrose gives the opposite position in *Commentaria in epistolam ad Corinthios primam* 7 (*PL 17*, 218BC). The authorship of this work is disputed by many modern scholars.

214/10–12 **Hieronymus ... errasse.** See Jerome, *Epistolae* 69 (*PL 22*, 653–59). Men who had been married twice were explicitly barred from the priesthood in the sixteenth constitution of the Council of Lyons (1274); see Alberigo, p. 322. More refers to the same prohibition at 440/27–442/3 and 444/19–22; cf. *CW 6*, 53/10–11, and *CW 9*, 47/2–4.

214/12–13 **Augustinus ... corporeas.** See note on 66/28.

214/14–15 **Asserit ... torquendos.** For Augustine's actual position on the fate which awaits unbaptized infants see *Sermones* 294.2–3 (*PL 38*, 1336–37); *Enchiridion* 93 (*PL 40*, 275); *De peccatorum meritis et remissione* 1.16 (*PL 44*, 120–21); and *Opus imperfectum contra Iulianum* 2.117 and 3.199 (*PL 45*, 1191 and 1333); cf. also *Supplementum ad opera Sancti Augustini* (*PL 47*, 630–70). By far the most categorical assertion that unbaptized infants are damned to eternal bodily torment occurs in *Liber de fide ad Petrum* (*PL 40*, 774), a work which Erasmus suspected was not by Augustine (*Enarratio Psalmi 38*, *Opera omnia*, 5, 434B) and which moderns assign to Fulgentius. More also takes up the question of infant damnation in *A Treatise upon the Passion*, *CW 13*, 30–36.

214/16–17 **Lutherus . . . instaurare?** For Luther's actual position on the salvation of unbaptized infants see *CW 5*, Introduction, 781, n. 4. While he does not maintain that unbaptized infants are damned to eternal torment, there are passages in his early *Sermon von dem Sakrament der Taufe* (*WA 2*, 727–37) which do stress the quite orthodox notion that the unbaptized are "children of wrath"; such passages could quite easily by misrepresented by hearsay to make Luther appear to be reaffirming Augustine's extreme view. The phrase "mordicus tenens" is proverbial; cf. *Moriae encomium, ASD 4/3*, 130, line 72; and *Adagia* 322 (*Opera omnia, 2*, 160AB).

214/17–21 **Quotus . . . desciuit.** More again refers to the controversy concerning the immaculate conception of the Virgin Mary at 286/10–15. The doctrine of the immaculate conception was declared to be an article of faith by Pope Pius IX in 1854 in the bull *Ineffabilis Deus*. Margaret Roper describes More's later attitude to the doctrine of the immaculate conception in Rogers, pp. 525–26. In Margaret's account More does not treat the immaculate conception as an example of a general article of "faith growen by the workynge of God vniuersally thorow all Christian nacions," although his words are interpreted this way in the Introduction to *CW 6*, 484. To the contrary, More adduces the doctrine as an example of a belief which may not yet be altogether universal and thus not altogether obligatory, explicitly stating, "whether it be yet decided and determined by any generall counsaile, I remember not" (Rogers, p. 525, lines 428–30). Certainly the Dominicans of More's day resisted the treatment of the Virgin's immaculate conception as an article of faith; see Allen, *4*, 423 and commentary. More's treatment of the doctrine in the *Letter to a Monk* suggests that he felt at least some reservations about accepting it as an article of faith; he expresses unmistakable reservations about its main champion, Scotus (see note on 286/12–15). Both More and Erasmus apparently regard the debate on the immaculate conception as partly a pretext for feuding between rival scholastics; see *Moriae encomium, ASD 4/3*, 150–52, lines 432–34 and commentary.

214/23–24 **quorum . . . intelligas.** Cf. Cato, *Disticha*, pref.: "legere enim et non intelligere neglegere est."

216/1 **qua fronte.** Cf. Rogers, p. 330, line 165; and *Adagia* 747 (*Opera omnia, 2*, 316C).

216/8–9 **coelum terrae permisces.** *Adagia* 281 (*Opera omnia, 2*, 142AB).

216/9 **Carrensem.** Cardinal Hugh of St. Cher (1200–1263), a Dominican, was the author of a biblical *Concordantia* frequently criticized by Erasmus; see Erasmus, *Annotationes in Novum Testamentum* (*Opera omnia, 6*, 50F, 100DF, 236C, 317C, 358DE, 371F, 411F, and 528C); and Allen, *3*, 326, lines 533–40. Cf. 252/2 and note.

216/10 **Lyranum.** Nicolas de Lyra (1270–1340), a Franciscan, was the author of *Postillae perpetuae in universam Sacram Scripturam,* a diligent and thorough exposition of the literal sense of the Bible. According to Stapleton, Lyra's comments, which were printed in the margins of folio Bibles in More's day, were read in More's household at mealtimes; see *CW 8,* Commentary at 233/16–18. Though Lyra's commentary reveals a good deal of sound learning and even some knowledge of Hebrew, he too was a favorite target of Erasmian criticism; see *Annotationes in Novum Testamentum (Opera omnia,* 6, 67D, 83D, 219F–220A, 236C, 317C, 411F, and 655A–656A). In later life More himself bitterly attacked Tyndale for voicing the common taunt "Lyra delirat"; see *CW 8,* 233/16–18, 273/8, and Commentary.

216/10–13 **Augustinus . . . docere.** Cf. Augustine, *Contra Faustum Manichaeum* 11.5 *(PL 42,* 249):

> Ibi [*sc.* in canonicis libris Veteris et Novi Testamenti] si quid velut absurdum moverit, non licet dicere, Auctor huius libri non tenuit veritatem: sed, aut codex mendosus est, aut interpres erravit, aut tu non intelligis. In opusculis autem posteriorum . . . etiam in quibuscunque eorum invenitur eadem veritas, longe tamen est impar auctoritas. Itaque in eis, si qua forte propterea dissonare putantur a vero, quia non ut dicta sunt intelliguntur, tamen liberum ibi habet lector auditorve iudicium, quo vel approbet quod placuerit, vel improbet quod offenderit: et ideo cuncta eiusmodi nisi vel certa ratione, vel ex illa canonica auctoritate defendantur, ut demonstretur sive omnino ita esse, sive fieri potuisse quod vel disputatum ibi est, vel narratum; si cui displicuerit, aut credere noluerit, non reprehenditur.

A very similar passage occurs in a letter from Augustine to Jerome; see Jerome's *Epistolae* 116.3 *(PL 22,* 937), also cited (though somewhat corruptly) in Gratian's *Decretum* 1.9.5 *(CIC 1,* 17). Cf. also *Decretum* 1.9.8–11 *(CIC 1,* 17–18). Luther regarded such passages as an important precedent for his own principle of *sola scriptura (Antwort auf Sprüche, so man führet, Menschenlehre zu Stärken,* 1524; *WA 10/2,* 89), even though R. H. Popkin regards Luther's principle of *sola scriptura* as a "critical step" which "presented a radically different criterion of religious knowledge" from the orthodox Catholic criterion of the "rule of faith of the Church" *(A History of Scepticism from Erasmus to Spinoza,* 2nd ed., Berkeley and Los Angeles, 1979, p. 2). More is certainly not trying to assert the autonomy of the individual judgment as categorically as Luther does, but More's appeal to Augustine in this passage does suggest that in 1519 More had a considerably less rigid conception of the "rule of faith of the Church" than he came to embrace somewhat later. Cf. 200/25–28 and 250/17–27.

216/15 **importunum istud studium.** Cf. Rom. 10:2, translated thus by Erasmus: "studium Dei habent, sed non iuxta scientiam." See also note on 274/21–22.

216/16–18 **quorum charitas . . . alios.** Cf. Erasmus in Allen, 2, 325: "Ostendo locis aliquot lapsum esse Hilarium, lapsum Augustinum, lapsum Thomam: idque facio, sicut oportet, reuerenter citraque contumeliam: adeo vt si viuerent ipsi, mihi qualicunque sic admonenti gratiam habituri sint."

216/23–24 **in illo . . . permiscet.** Erasmus responds to the same objection in Allen, 4, 353–54, and *Apologia adversus febricitantis libellum* (*Opera omnia, 10,* 1677BC). Cicero himself disapproved of the practice when carried to excess; see *De officiis* 1.31.111. For a more detailed account of this practice in Erasmus' own letters, see Erika Rummel, "The Use of Greek in Erasmus' Letters," *Humanistica Lovaniensia, 30* (1981), 55–92.

216/26 **velis nolis.** See note on 122/10.

216/26–27 **ipse . . . graeca.** Many of the Greek words which appear in Jerome's Latin works have been noted and classified in Courcelle, pp. 51–52.

216/27–29 **quaedam . . . intelligant.** Cf. 224/4–6. See also Rogers, p. 122, lines 75–82. More is referring to Jerome's many writings addressed to Marcella and her circle, a group of Roman women committed to voluntary celibacy. Other prominent members of the circle were Paula and her daughter Julia Eustochium, who both followed Jerome to Palestine. See F. A. Wright, ed., *Select Letters of St. Jerome* (Cambridge, Mass., and London, 1963), app. 1, pp. 483–97.

218/4–5 **nimiam . . . reprehendere?** See Budé in Allen, 2, 396–401; and Erasmus' response in Allen, 2, 464–70.

218/6–8 **isti . . . nouum.** Cf. Erasmus in Allen, 3, 327, lines 586–89.

218/9–10 **morigeratus . . . identitas.** While a better Latinist than the monk would have written simply *morigerus* instead of "morigeratus," "morigeratus" ("accommodating" or "obliging") is a legitimate participle of the classical verb *morigerari,* "to accommodate." The words *identitas* and *tenebrositas* are typical postclassical abstractions first appearing in works of the fourth and fifth centuries; see Marius Victorinus, *Adversus Arium* 1.48, 52, 53, 57, 59 (*PL 8,* 1078A, 1080C, 1081B, 1084A, and 1085A); and Arnobius the Younger, *Commentarii in Psalmos* 103 (*PL 53,* 477A). The phrase "vagabunda conuersatio" is perhaps rather clumsy as a whole, but *conuersatio* is reasonably classical, and *vagabundus* occurs twice in Augustine's *Confessiones* 5.6.10 and 13.5.6 (*PL 32,* 710 and 847).

218/19 **cum . . . male grammaticus.** The future participle "marcessuris" is a barbarous coinage loosely based on *marcescere,* "to wither," which lacks a future participle. A better Latinist would have written simply *marcentibus.* More may also be upset by the monk's use of "expendunt" where we would normally expect something like *impendunt,* though the monk's use of *expendere* with the dative or ablative is not wholly unprecedented; see Symmachus, *Epistolae* 1.31.3, 1.53.1, and 1.76.

218/24–27 **cum .. elegantiam.** More draws a careful distinction between *eloquentia* (the object of rhetoric) and *elegantia* (the object of grammar); cf. Erasmus, *De copia* (*Opera omnia, 1,* 7C) and Allen, *3,* 315, lines 105–11.

218/26–27 **olim . . . elegantiam.** Cf. 220/21–22 and note. As the overall context of this passage suggests, humanist *sprezzatura* has religious as well as secular motives. See also Erasmus, *Antibarbari, ASD 1/1,* 78; *Ciceronianus, ASD 1/2,* 618–19, 625, and 633; and *De pronuntiatione, ASD 1/4,* 99. Harry Caplan records many important examples of the maxim "caput est artis dissimulare artem" in his edition of the pseudo-Ciceronian *Rhetorica ad Herennium* (Cambridge, Mass., and London, 1954), p. 250, *ad* 4.7.10.

220/4–5 **Hieronymus . . . venustatem.** Jerome, *Commentarii in Aggaeum 2* (*PL 25,* 1416): "Obsecro te, lector, ut ignoscas celeri sermone dictanti, nec requiras eloquii venustatem, quam multo tempore Hebraeae linguae studio perdidi." Jerome says much the same thing in *Epistolae* 29.7 (*PL 22,* 441).

220/9–10 **nouum . . . antecellit.** Cf. *CW 8,* 719/36–37; John 1:17; and Col. 2:16–17.

220/11–12 **sacrarum . . . graece.** See note on 142/22–24.

220/13–14 **artes . . . nihil.** See note on 142/18–21.

220/21–22 **vbique . . . inaccersita.** Cf. Augustine, *De doctrina christiana* 4.6.10 (*PL 34,* 93), on the unostentatious eloquence of the apostles: "quasi sapientiam de domo sua, id est, pectore sapientis procedere intelligas, et tanquam inseparabilem famulam etiam non vocatam sequi eloquentiam." See also above, note on 218/26–27.

220/25–26 **quasi . . . subsistitur.** Cf. 140/25-142/1.

220/27 **obuijs . . . vlnis.** *Adagia* 1854 (*Opera omnia, 2,* 675D).

220/28 **tragicis clamoribus.** Cf. *Adagia* 1439 (*Opera omnia, 2,* 564E–565A).

222/1–3 **qui . . . contaminent.** Cf. *Moriae encomium, ASD 4/3,* 154, lines 483–84; 158, lines 513–19; and Listrius' commentary in *Opera omnia, 4,* 470F: "Hoc, quod ait, nimis verum est in multis, qui nihil existimant eruditum, nihil acutum, quod non sit barbaris ac spurcis dictum verbis: quicquid elegans, id ut Grammaticum aspernantur. Simplicitas sermonis probe decet theologum, spurcities minime, quae veritatem non nudam, ut ipsi iactant, obstendit, sed oblitam et sordidatum."

222/12 **epiphonemate.** See Quintilian 8.5.11: "Est enim epiphonema rei narratae vel probatae summa acclamatio." Erasmus discusses *epiphonemata* in *De copia* (*Opera omnia, 1,* 97C–E). More sarcastically praises the monk's rhetoric as the monk is attempting to attack rhetoric. See also Rhenanus' discussion, *CW 3/2,* 74/29–30.

222/12 **Vetus melius est.** Luke 5:39.

222/14–17 **Augustinus . . . etiam.** On the unique eloquence of the apostles see *De doctrina christiana* 4.6.9 (*PL 34,* 92–93); on rhetorical figures in the apostles see *De doctrina christiana* 3.29.40 and 4.7.11–13 (*PL 34,* 80–81, 93–96).

222/20–22 **Eloquentia . . . dilucidus.** Aristotle, *Rhetorica* 3.4 (1404b1–3). Augustine discourages other writers from imitating the apostles' obscurity in *De doctrina christiana* 4.8.22 (*PL 34,* 98–99). The phrase "officit orationis luci" suggests competition or even upstaging; cf. Rogers, p. 329, lines 135–36; and *Adagia* 3508 (*Opera omnia, 2,* 1077EF).

224/1 **luceat etiam caecis.** Cf. *CW 12,* 72/27; and *Adagia* 793 (*Opera omnia, 2,* 331BC): "vel caeco appareat." In this case More negates the traditional hyperbole.

224/4–6 **quae . . . virgunculae.** See note on 216/27–29. "Magister noster" was the standard title for a doctor of divinity; cf. Erasmus, *Moriae encomium, ASD 4/3,* 158, lines 519–23 and commentary; *Enchiridion,* Holborn, p. 107, lines 8–14; and Allen, 2, 109, line 709.

224/13 **latinogotthica.** More probably coined this term himself to refer to dog Latin. The similar term *latinobarbarus* is attested in Latham (p. 270) from a document of 1520.

224/14–17 **centona . . . centonam.** The monk uses the barbarous word *centona* for the masculine noun *cento* or "patchwork." His word may actually be a revealing conflation of *catena* and *cento.*

224/18 **in tuum caput . . . retortum.** Cf. *Adagia* 3588 (*Opera omnia, 2,* 1096AB).

224/19 **Eiusdem farinae.** See note on 38/14.

224/19 **facetulus.** This diminutive, which also appears at 262/24, is not recorded in any of the lexicons. More's frequent employment of diminutives in this letter gives it a particularly Erasmian tone; for Erasmus' devotion to diminutives see Erasmus, *Declamatio de pueris statim ac liberaliter instituendis,* ed. J.-C. Margolin (Geneva, 1966), app. 3, pp. 618–19.

224/19–20 **labores . . . perstringis.** Erasmus' edition of Jerome was similarly criticized by Henry Standish and an unnamed defender of

Standish; see Erasmus in Allen, 2, 108, lines 676–84; and 3, 21 and
326–27.

224/20–21 **perdidisti . . . aqua.** *Adagia* 1196 (*Opera omnia,* 2, 481F–
482C).

224/23–24 **Cur . . . integrum?** Cf. Jerome's answer to Augustine when
the latter had criticized his new translation of the Old Testament:
"Bibat vinum vetus cum suavitate, et nostra musta contemnat" (*Epistolae* 112.20, *PL* 22, 929). A secular application of the proverb occurs in
Adagia 2002 (*Opera omnia,* 2, 717D). More completely reverses the
thrust of this sarcasm in *CW 8,* 39/9–13.

224/26 **digito quoque monstratas.** Otto, no. 550; cf. *CW 4,* 158/28–29.

226/6–8 **Hillarius . . . veritatem.** For Hilary on the Septuagint see
Tractatus in II Psalmum 2 (*PL 9,* 262–63); for Augustine see above, note
on 212/22–24.

226/21 **translationes in nouum testamentum.** It is not technically correct to say "translations on the New Testament." More was probably
thinking of phrases like *commentaria in nouum testamentum* ("commentaries on the New Testament").

226/23–25 **quanquam . . . vtilem.** See note on 82/24–26.

226/25–27 **hodie . . . aliam.** A Latin New Testament by the fifteenth-
century humanist Gianozzo Manetti existed in Italy in a few scattered
manuscripts; see Jerry H. Bentley, *Humanists and Holy Writ: New Testament Scholarship in the Renaissance* (Princeton, 1983), pp. 10, 58–59. For
later Latin versions see the note on 250/10–13, below.

226/27–30 **Adnotauit . . . testamentum.** Cf. Erasmus in Allen, 2, 112–
13, lines 858–62. Erasmus published Valla's *Annotationes* in 1505; see
Erasmus' introduction in Allen, *1,* 406–12. Jacques Lefèvre d'Etaples'
Latin translation of the Pauline epistles first appeared in 1512 and was
reprinted in 1515. The volume included the Vulgate translation with
the corrected translation in parallel columns, along with an apology for
revising the Vulgate and a long commentary on the letters themselves.
See Rice, pp. 295–302.

228/5–7 **id . . . intelligat.** For this letter, Jerome's preface to the New
Testament, see *PL 29,* 525–30, and especially the passage cited above,
note on 80/18–19.

228/10–11 **nullum . . . vestigium.** See note on 84/6–7.

228/11–13 **illas . . . annotauit.** See, for example, Erasmus, *Annotationes in Novum Testamentum, Opera omnia, 6,* 10C, 419C, 678E, 834F,
and 850C.

230/3 **propugnatrices.** This late word is attested in Blaise (p. 744) from
a document of the ninth century.

230/3–4 **Hilarij atque Augustini sententias.** See note on 226/6–8.

230/4–5 **Quid . . . vertam?** Cf. Terence, *Hecyra* 516.

230/20–21 **eos . . . natum.** According to legend, the Septuagint translation of the Old Testament into Greek was prepared by either seventy or seventy-two Jewish scholars (Septuagint means "seventy" in Greek) at the request of the Egyptian king Ptolemy II (Philadelphus, third century B.C.) for his library at Alexandria.

230/27–28 **totos quaternos.** "Quaternos" ("four each") is a barbarous error for *quaterniones* ("groups of four leaves"). See Rizzo, p. 45.

230/29–30 **displiceat . . . velit.** See Erasmus' note on Matt. 13:47 in *Opera omnia, 6,* 76E.

230/31–232/1 **Non . . . praeclare.** Cf. the *Letter to Bugenhagen,* Rogers, p. 340, lines 565–66.

232/13–15 **Neque . . . homines.** Cf. the grammarian M. Pomponius Marcellus' remark to Tiberius in Suetonius, *De grammaticis* 22: "tu enim Caesar civitatem dare potes hominibus, verbis non potes."

232/16 **quanquam Cicero . . . est.** Cicero, *Oratio pro L. Flacco* 6.15, 7.17, 8.19, 10.23.

232/17–18 **Hieronymus . . . est.** Jerome, *Epistolae* 53.2 (*PL* 22, 541) and *Dialogus contra Pelagianos* 1.8 (*PL 23,* 524C). For additional information concerning Greek words in Jerome's Latin works see note on 216/26–27, above.

232/25–27 **parum latine . . . discumbentibus.** See Erasmus' note on Matt. 22:10 in *Opera omnia, 6,* 114F.

232/28 **Calepinum.** See note on 68/17–22 and Ambrogio Calepino, [*Dictionarium*] (Venice, P. Leichtensteyn, 1506), sig. t₆: "Impleo. es. Construitur cum ablatiuo vel genitiuo. Virgilius. Impleuitque mero pateram. Idem implentur veterisque Bacchi pinguisque ferinae. Quandoque additur praepositio dicimus Impleui nauem de omni genere frumenti. Lactantius. libro iiii. et in super duodecim cophini de residuis fragminibus impleti. Huius compositum est adimpleo."

234/8–9 **Matthaei vi. . . . dimitte.** See Erasmus' note on Matt. 6:12 in *Opera omnia, 6,* 35C–E. As his note shows, Erasmus was frequently criticized for attempting to change the Lord's prayer. One of his critics was Nicholas Egmondanus; see the *Letter to Botzheim* (1523), Allen, *1,* 24.

234/14–16 **dimitto . . . sensui?** The monk is mistaken in thinking that *dimittere* ("to give up," "to dismiss") can express the same meaning as *dare* ("to give"). Nonetheless it seems that *dimittere,* like *remittere,* can in fact sometimes have the same meaning as *condonare* ("to remit," "to forgo for the sake of"). Cf. Caesar, *De bello civili* 1.8, "studium et iracundiam reipublicae dimittere"; Tacitus, *Historiae* 3.55, "his [*sc.* populis vectigalibus] tributa dimittere." More here seizes upon the monk's error concerning the meaning of *dare* to distract us from the meaning of *dimittere.* Cf. Matt. 5:40 for *dimitte/remitte pallium.*

234/25 **non . . . mederi.** Cf. *Adagia* 990 (*Opera omnia*, 2, 394C).

234/31-236/2 **Cyprianum . . . dimitte.** Cyprian, *De oratione dominica* 22–23 (*PL 4,* 552–53).

236/3–6 **contra . . . apponens.** See Erasmus' note on John 1:1–4 in *Opera omnia*, 6, 335A–336D; and cf. the changed wording in Erasmus' revised dedication to Leo X, Allen, 2, 185, lines 46–47. In the first edition of his New Testament Erasmus cautiously refrained from substituting *sermo* for *verbum* in his own translation; he introduced this change into his printed text in the second edition (Basel, March 1519). For a discussion of the relation between More's own defense of Erasmus' translation and Erasmus' *Apologia de In principio erat sermo* (February and August 1520) see the Introduction, p. xlv, n. 1. Camporeale (*Lorenzo Valla*, p. 297) claims that Valla anticipated Erasmus in altering *verbum* to *sermo,* but this claim seems unsupported by the passage in Valla's *Annotationes* to which Camporeale refers (*Opera omnia*, sig. CC_4 [p. 839]). Every mass concluded with the recitation of John 1:1–14, a fact which helps to explain why Erasmus' conservative critics placed so much stress on this change; see Francis H. Dickinson, ed., *Missale ad usum . . . ecclesiae Sarum,* 2 vols. (Burntisland, 1861–67; hereafter cited as "*Missale Sarum*"), *1*, 61–62, 629; and the note on *Canterbury Tales,* "General Prologue" 254, in *The Works of Geoffrey Chaucer,* ed. F. N. Robinson, 2nd ed. (Boston, 1961), p. 657. See also Morton W. Bloomfield, "The Magic of *In Principio*," *Modern Language Notes, 70* (1955), 559–65.

236/8–9 **Hieronymum . . . dei.** Jerome, *Epistolae* 53.4 (*PL 22,* 543).

236/9–10 **id . . . filium.** See Gregory of Nazianzus, *Orationes* 30.20 (*PG 36,* 130).

236/12–13 **significata** τοῦ λόγου. See note on 238/18.

236/17–18 **κύριε ἐλέησον . . . Osanna.** Cf. Augustine, *De doctrina christiana* 2.11.16 (*PL 34,* 42–43). For κύριε ἐλέησον, a chant which forms an integral part of the Latin mass, cf. the Greek text of Matt. 20:30–31.

236/20–21 **quam cui praeferas.** Cf. Vergil, *Aeneid* 4.371: "quae quibus anteferam?"

238/18 **λόγου significatum.** This reading, if correct, makes it necessary to treat "significatum" as a substantive term, though it never appears as a substantive in classical Latin. The unsatisfactory reading of *1520*[m], "λόγομυ significatum," could conceivably be a corruption of "λόγῳ significatum." If this were the case, "significatum" would be construed as an ordinary participle, while the dative of λόγος would express the same meaning as an instrumental ablative in Latin. The translation of this clause would then read, "λόγος was used to mean 'sermo' much more often than 'verbum.'" But More clearly employs *significatum* as a substantive at 236/12–13 and 248/25, and Augustine employs both *significatum* and *significatus* as substantives in *De magistro* 4.8 (*PL 32*, 1199).

238/20–30 **Nam ... verbum.** Cf. Erasmus in Allen, *8*, xlv; and Augustine, *De trinitate* 15.11.20 (*PL 42*, 1071–72):

> ... verbum, quod foris sonat, signum est verbi quod intus lucet, cui magis verbi competit nomen. Nam illud quod voce profertur carnis ore, vox verbi est: verbumque et ipsum dicitur, propter illud a quo ut foris appareret assumptum est.... Quapropter quicumque cupit ad qualemcumque similitudinem Verbi Dei, quamvis per multa dissimilem, pervenire, non intueatur verbum nostrum quod sonat in auribus, nec quando voce profertur, nec quando silentio cogitatur.... Perveniendum est ergo ad illud verbum hominis ... quod neque prolativum est in sono, neque cogitativum in similitudine soni ... sed quod omnia quibus significatur signa praecedit, et gignitur de scientia quae manet in animo, quando eadem scientia intus dicitur, sicuti est.

Augustine makes much the same point in his commentary on John (*PL 35*, 1383 and 1671–72; cf. *De doctrina christiana* 1.13.12, *PL 34*, 24); in the second of these passages the casual opposition *Verbum Dei–usus sermocinationis tuae* corresponds at least vaguely to the monk's opposition between *verbum* and *sermo*. But in *De trinitate* 15.10.18 (*PL 42*, 1070), Augustine defines *cogitationes* as *locutiones cordis*, as internal propositions which, like other propositions, involve true or false predication; these *locutiones cordis* must therefore be organized in much the same way as the sentences of discursive *sermo*. Cf. Erasmus, *Apologia de In principio erat sermo, Opera omnia, 9*, 120C: "... ut est verbum mentis, ita est sermo mentis. Etenim qui cogitat, sibi quodammodo loquitur." Remarkably, Erasmus later espouses the description of the divine Word as a *tacitus mentis conceptus;* see *Explanatio symboli* 2 (*Opera omnia, 5*, 1143D). For thinking as unspoken discourse see also Plato, *Theaetetus* 189E, 206D; and *Sophist* 263E.

238/31–32 **sentiant ... deductum.** This etymology is rejected in Quintilian 1.6.35 but accepted in Priscian, *Institutiones grammaticae* 8.1.1. More puns on *verbum* and *verber* in *CW 14*, 559/7–8.

240/10–11 **ille ... recubuit.** More is referring to St. John the Evangelist; see John 13:23–25, 21:20.

240/15–18 **dum ... venit.** More is referring to an introit based on Sap. 18:15 and sung on the sixth day after Christmas; see *Missale Sarum, 1*,

73. Both the missal and modern editions of the Vulgate omit the word *exsiliens*, though several manuscripts of More's own day included it (*Biblia sacra iuxta latinam vulgatam versionem ad codicum fidem . . .*, 16 vols. [Rome, 1926–], *12*, 97). On the various forms and uses of this verse see Allen Cabaniss, *Liturgy and Literature: Selected Essays* (University, Tuscaloosa, Alabama, 1970), p. 146, notes 1–5.

240/19–21 **nos . . . sunt.** Augustine, *Enarratio in Psalmum 32* (*PL 36*, 286), citing Ps. 32:6.

240/22-242/3 **Ambrosius . . . est.** Ambrose, *De fide orthodoxa contra Arianos* 2 (*PL 17*, 554). The authorship of this work is disputed by many modern scholars.

242/3–5 **Hilarius . . . aeternus.** Hilary, *De trinitate* 2.15 (*PL 10*, 61).

242/6–11 **Lactantius . . . 'rationem.' "** Lactantius, *Divinae institutiones* 4.8, 9 (*PL 6*, 467, 469).

242/12–29 **Cyprianus . . . dei.' "** Cyprian, *Testimonia adversus Iudaeos* 2.3 (*PL 4*, 726).

242/29-244/5 **Augustinus . . . dei.** See note on 240/19–21.

244/5–13 **ad Hebraeos quarto . . . exponit.** More's point is borne out by the commentaries on Heb. 4:12 included in *Biblia latina cum glosa ordinaria et expositione lyre literali et morali*, 6 vols. (Basel, J. Peter and J. Froben, 1498). The *Glossa ordinaria* is traditionally assigned to Walafrid Strabo (d. 849) and the *Glossa interlinearis* to Anselm of Laon (d. 1117), who in fact helped with both. Lyra's *Postillae* were intended as a lucid expression of the literal sense of the Bible. See also note on 216/10.

244/12 **litteraliter.** This late word is attested by Latham (p. 279), who cites documents dating from the eighth to fifteenth centuries.

244/27 **sapuisses.** The more common spellings of this verb form are *sapiisses* and *sapiuisses*.

246/1 **in sinu patris.** John 1:18.

246/5–11 **Cyprianus . . . sermo.** Cyprian, *Testimonia adversus Iudaeos* 2.3, 2.5 (*PL 4*, 726, 730).

246/12 **nouatorem . . . verborum.** The same phrase is used in Aulus Gellius 1.15.18 as a description of Sallust.

246/13 **athletam Christi.** Erasmus refers to Cyprian as a *Christianae pietatis athleta* in a prefatory letter to Cyprian's *Opera* (1519; Allen, *4*, 27, line 115).

246/15–17 **Qua in re . . . subscribit.** Augustine, *In Iohannis evangelium tractatus* 108.3 (*PL 35*, 1915–16), mentioned by Erasmus in *Annotationes in Novum Testamentum* (*Opera omnia*, 6, 335D).

246/23 **quum . . . reprehendit.** Erasmus seems to echo this argument in the second version of his *Apologia de In principio erat sermo* (August, 1520). See *Opera omnia, 9,* 113E: ". . . ita praeferam sermonem, ut verbum non reijciam."

248/2-5 **Quis . . . coniugem?** Erasmus replaced *coniunx* with *uxor* in Matt. 1:20 and 1:24; see *Annotationes in Novum Testamentum* (*Opera omnia, 6,* 8EF).

248/8-24 **Ille . . . schismatis.** Cf. Erasmus, *Apologia qua respondet,* Ferguson, p. 275, lines 930-38.

248/9-10 **simplicem . . . cogitatura.** More may well have underestimated the average layman's resistance to any divergence at all from the Vulgate translation of John 1:1-14. See notes on 236/3-6 and 248/17-18.

248/10-13 **velut alter Chain . . . occidere.** Cf. Gen. 4:4-8 and 1 John 3:12.

248/17-21 **si . . . possunt.** Cf. Erasmus in Allen, *3,* 324, lines 450-56; and Reuchlin, *Defensio,* sig. B₃:

> Iam enim miseri peperiphrones cruciabantur, nullis hactenus scriptis ualuisse celebrem famam meam labefactare, quare dolo malo inuenerunt occasionem, ut sub colore praedicationis absentem me et tales insidias ne cogitantem quidem lacerare et infamare, nomenque meum denigrantes in commune odium deferre possent, ut quod literis nequeant, id uerbis et ore suo me non audiente attentent.

248/17-18 **quod . . . doctis.** Erasmus frequently stresses that his new translation is intended as an aid to private scriptural studies and not as a rival to the Vulgate translation recited in churches. See especially the *Apologia* which accompanied the first edition of Erasmus' New Testament (Holborn, p. 168).

248/27-28 **Ambrosio . . . sensu.** Ambrose, *Expositio evangelii secundum Lucam* 2.42 (*PL 15,* 1568).

248/29-30 **At . . . aeditiones.** Cf. 82/5-6 and note.

248/30-250/2 **haud . . . superiores.** Erasmus responds to a similar claim in Allen, *3,* 314, lines 74-80.

250/10-13 **neque . . . operaeprecium.** Other Latin translations of the New Testament were published by the Dominican Santi Pagnini (1528) and the protestants Sebastian Castellio (1551) and Theodore Beza (1557); see P. R. Ackroyd et al., eds., *The Cambridge History of the Bible,* 3 vols. (Cambridge, 1963-70), *3,* 62, 69-72.

250/15-22 **Diuus Augustinus . . . elicere.** See note on 82/24-26. More's paraphrase of Augustine in this passage closely resembles Erasmus' paraphrase in Allen, *3,* 313, lines 45-48.

250/19 **stipes.** See note on 56/26.

250/26-27 **et tamen . . . occasionem.** Cf. Erasmus, *Ecclesiastes* (*Opera omnia,* 5, 1026F): "horum [*sc.* patrum] commentationes etiam cum ambigunt aut errant, praebent occasionem aliquid exactius inveniendi."

250/27-29 **Denique . . . declarant.** See note on 82/24-26.

252/2 **viennensis . . . commenta.** More is apparently referring to some undistinguished biblical commentary, perhaps limited in scope to the Psalms. He is certainly not referring to the decrees of the Council of Vienne (1311–12; Alberigo, pp. 333–401), where no special attention was given to the actual exposition of scripture. Cardinal Hugh of St. Cher, mentioned earlier (at 216/9), was also called Hugh of Vienne (*de Vienna*), since the French town St. Cher was quite clost to Vienne; See T. Käppeli, *Scriptores ordinis Praedicatorum Medii Aevi,* 3 vols. (Rome, 1970–), 2, 269–81. More may well be referring to Hugh's own *Postilla in Psalmos,* part of his longer Biblical commentary.

252/3 **Omiseram . . . quiddam.** Cf. Quintilian 4.5.4 on the figure of "afterthought" ("adiectio").

252/4 **vno flatu possit euerti.** Cf. *CW 3/2,* 630/18–19 and Plautus, *Miles gloriosus* 17.

252/16-254/12 **Quod . . . mutatos.** See note on 88/22-90/22.

252/24 **cecidisse causa.** The phrase *cadere causa* is a legal formula meaning "to lose one's case"; see Cicero, *De oratore* 1.36.166–67.

254/14-258/4 **cur . . . Hieronymum.** Erasmus, too, mocks the glossator of Gratian's *Decretum* who misrepresents Jerome as maintaining that the Latin texts of scripture are more reliable than the Greek and the Greek than the Hebrew; see Erasmus' preface to Valla's *Annotationes,* Allen, *1,* 411. Ironically, while both More and Erasmus make fun of the glossator for misconstruing one text from Jerome, they both seem to accept the mistaken ascription to Augustine of another text taken from Jerome which the glossator holds that the misconstrued text contradicts. Though Augustine himself often stresses the authority of Greek texts (see notes on 80/17–18 and 212/22–24), only Jerome unconditionally endorses a return to the Hebrew and Greek *fontes* to establish the text of the Bible in Latin. Here is the passage, supposedly by Augustine but actually by Jerome (*PL 22,* 671–72), which is cited by Gratian (*Decretum* 1.9.6, *CIC 1,* 17) as an authority for the thesis that Latin translations should be checked against their Greek and Hebrew originals: "Vt ueterum librorum fides de ebreis uoluminibus examinanda est, ita nouorum graeci sermonis normam desiderat." The gloss which opposes this misascribed text with a misconstrued excerpt from the letter to Desiderius introducing Jerome's Latin Pentateuch (*PL 28,*

152) reads as follows in *Decretum Gratiani cum Glossis domini Ioannis theutonici prepositi alberstatensis* . . . (Venice, L. Giunta, 1514), sig. B₂:

> Hieronymus in secundo prologo biblie contra ait dicens quod emendatiora sunt exemplaria latina quam greca: et greca quam hebrea. Sed Augustinus ad primitiuam ecclesiam respicit: quando exemplaria greca et hebrea non erant corrupta. Sed procedente tempore cum populus christianus multum esset auctus: et hereses multe essent facte inter grecos: ob inuidiam christianorum iudei et greci sua exemplaria corruperunt: et sic factum est quod exemplaria eorum magis corrupta sunt quam latinorum: ad quod tempus respicit Hieronymus. . . . Vel dic quod in hoc magis credendus est Hieronymus quam Augustinus quod inter istos tres Augustinum Hieronymum et Gregorium Augustinus magis credendus est in disputationibus. Hieronymus in historijs et translationibus. Gregorius in moralibus proponitur.

See also the passages listed by A. Landgraf, "Zur Methode der biblischen Textkritik im 12. Jahrhundert," *Biblica, 10* (1929), 449–52. In the second edition (1531) of *A Dialogue Concerning Heresies* More inserted a similar anecdote about how the heretics rashly cite Gratian and the glosses on Gratian out of context; see *CW 6*, 355/28-359/31, and Introduction, 530–33. In *The Answer to the First Part of the Poisoned Book, EW*, sigs. CC₃v–CC₄, there is another anecdote telling of how an unscrupulous heretic deliberately misquoted More's own arguments from another of his works against heretics.

254/23 **inuenerint . . . rimam.** *Adagia* 2175 (*Opera omnia, 2,* 764CD).

254/29 **per nebulam.** *Adagia* 263 (*Opera omnia, 2,* 136CD).

256/11 **adamantinas leges.** See note on 170/4.

256/26–28 **Aliud . . . hebraica.** The first part of this excerpt from the letter to Desiderius introducing Jerome's Latin Pentateuch (*PL 28,* 152) is unusually obscure; the editor of the text in *PL* would prefer to read *reprobaverunt* for the manuscript reading *probaverunt*. In either case, Jerome seems to be arguing that his Hebrew critics defeat their own cause by objecting to his literal rendering of the Hebrew Old Testament.

258/4–7 **I nunc . . . conflauerunt.** Cf. 66/16-70/3 and note.

258/8–20 **Vbi . . . pareant.** For this comic siege-imagery cf. *CW 3/2,* 622/4–10 and Commentary, and the *Letter to Bugenhagen,* Rogers, p. 348, lines 854–55.

258/8 **acropolim.** See note on 104/7 and *Adagia* 1061 (*Opera omnia, 2,* 429E–430A).

258/10–11 **Moriam . . . vrbem.** Here More fashions out of Erasmus'
Moria an imaginary realm which is almost the perfect antithesis of the
commonwealth sketched in *Utopia,* a commonwealth ruled by the wise
for the wise. The eponymous founder of the Utopian republic is
named, not Utopia, but Utopus; by analogy the founder and sovereign
of Moria should be named, not Moria, but Morus—that is, Thomas
More. In this elegant topographical conceit there may be an obscure
reminiscence of Erasmus' original letter praising More as a fit patron
for Erasmus' ingenious pageant in honor of Folly (*ASD 4/3,*
67/10-68/21). More toyed with the fantasy of being crowned king of
Utopia itself (Allen, 2, 414). Here, at last, with this masterly display of
wise foolery, More appears to be pressing his claim to preside in the
neighboring fools' paradise, as well; neighboring not because it is located at the ends of the earth, like Utopia, but rather because, as King
Solomon notes, it is not far from anyone's doorstep. For a similar
topographical conceit (towns transformed into characters in books), cf.
Debellation, EW, sig. N$_5$.

258/12 **muliebri imperio.** *Adagia* 1481 (*Opera omnia,* 2, 575CD).

258/14–15 **hac . . . putas.** Cf. *Adagia* 3434 (*Opera omnia,* 2, 1061F–
1062A).

258/15–16 **vt Salomon ait . . . numerus.** See note on 40/14–19.

258/17 **quod . . . audacia.** See Rogers, p. 519, lines 181–82; *Moriae
encomium, ASD 4/3,* 96, lines 470–71; and above, note on 58/2–5.

258/19–20 **parati . . . pareant.** Cf. Plautus, *Amphitruo* 240, "animam
omittunt priusquam loco demigrent"; *Adagia* 2410 (*Opera omnia,* 2,
830AB); and note on 52/27, above. While the subjects of Moria are
totally unreceptive to new or different ideas, the citizens of Utopia,
according to Hythloday, owe most of their successes to the way in which
they have acknowledged their own limitations and then wisely borrowed from others (*CW 4,* 108/13–19).

258/21–23 **ipsa Moria . . . quidam.** Cf. *Moriae encomium, ASD 4/3,* 68,
lines 37–39. For "ipsa Moria minus habet moriae" see note on 14/1.

258/24 **orationes quaedam rithmicae.** Erasmus mounts similar attacks
on such rhythmical prayers in *Ratio verae theologiae,* Holborn, p. 189;
and in *Annotationes in Novum Testamentum* (*Opera omnia,* 6, 36B–C,
731C–732C, and 768E–769A). Most of the "sequences" (Latin prayers
set to music) which were current in the medieval church were suppressed by the Council of Trent; see Alberigo, p. 737 (Twenty-second
Session, September 17, 1562); and Surtz, *Praise of Wisdom,* p. 216.

258/25–27 **vestri . . . illudere.** For the wording cf. *Moriae encomium,
ASD 4/3,* 160, lines 531–33.

260/4 **callidus hostis.** See 290/10–11 and note.

260/5–6 **quem . . . prudentem.** Cf. Matt. 10:16 and Erasmus' note in *Opera omnia, 6,* 55C; Erasmus, *Antibarbari, ASD 1/1,* 118, lines 20–21; and Germain Marc'hadour, "Symbolisme de la colombe et du serpent," *Moreana, 1* (1963), 47–63. Of Peter Giles More asserts in *Utopia* (*CW 4,* 48/9–10): "nulli simplicitas inest prudentior." Cf. also *CW 6,* 22/3–4.

260/11–13 **quicquid . . . etiam.** See note on 122/19.

260/15 **Moscum.** More clearly thinks that the monk was hunting for the name "Momus," a proverbial term for a faultfinder; see *Adagia* 474 (*Opera omnia, 2,* 210B–211A). Neither More nor the monk could have been thinking of Moschus the bucolic poet or Moschus the rhetorician of Pergamum, but the monk may have confused Momus the fault-finder with a tactless musician named Moschus, who is mentioned in *Adagia* 2276 (*Opera omnia, 2,* 798F), "Moschus canens Boeoticum." Erasmus himself says of this proverb, "Quadrabit in multiloquos, sed tamen inepte loquaces [cf. Homer, *Iliad* 2.213, on Thersites]."

260/21 **Iulij dialogo.** The dialogue *Iulius exclusus e coelo,* a bitter, anonymous attack on the warlike Pope Julius II, is now generally accepted as the work of Erasmus, even though the work's marked pro-French bias has left some lingering doubts as to whether Erasmus composed the whole satire. See Allen, 2, 42–43; Ferguson, pp. 43–48; J. K. Mc-Conica, C.S.B., "Erasmus and the 'Julius': A Humanist Reflects on the Church," in *The Pursuit of Holiness in Late Medieval and Renaissance Religion,* ed. C. E. Trinkaus and H. A. Oberman (Leiden, 1974), pp. 444–71; and J. D. Tracy, *The Politics of Erasmus* (Toronto, 1978), pp. 26–30, 142–45. The work has been edited in Ferguson, pp. 65–124. Since much of the evidence for Erasmus' authorship is found in Erasmus' correspondence with More it seems certain that More himself knew that Erasmus had written the satire; in fact, even as More tries to dismiss the monk's arguments for Erasmian authorship he avoids making any explicit denial. Erasmus himself was afraid to acknowledge the work, which was roundly condemned by Louvain theologians and cherished by reformers like Luther.

260/23–24 **protinus . . . publicis.** Cf. Allen, *3,* 45, 58, and 574, where Allen suggests that the French play associated with the *Iulius* is a morality play by Pierre Gringore, the actual title of which is *Le jeu de prince des sotz,* in which Julius II figures as the principal character under the name "l'homme obstiné"; see Pierre Gringore, *Oeuvres complètes,* 2 vols. (Paris, 1858), *1,* 198–286. This play was staged in Paris in February 1512, when Julius II was still living.

260/25–26 **Poncherium . . . Fausto.** Etienne Poncher (d. 1525) was created bishop of Paris in 1502/03; see Allen, 2, 454. His ambassadorial mission to England to negotiate the transfer of Tournai lasted from September until December 1517; see Allen, *3*, 173. One of the earliest editions, probably printed in Paris, assigned the *Iulius* to the Italian poet Fausto Andrelini of Forli (ca. 1462–1518), who had long been a resident of Paris, and this published attribution may have furnished Poncher's only basis for assigning the dialogue to Fausto. See Ferguson, pp. 46, 55, 63; and Allen, *2*, 419, and *3*, 575; for additional details of Fausto's biography see Allen, *1*, 220–21.

260/26–28 **quod . . . habuisse.** There is an alternative way of construing these words: to take the clause "Erasmum . . . habuisse" as the subject of "impedit" and the clause "vt verum fuerit" as its object. According to this interpretation, the sentence means: "The fact that Erasmus, who was an acquaintance of Fausto, had a copy of his book in his possession even before it was published does not contradict that ascription." This reading requires us to take the abnormal construction *impedit vt* as equivalent to *impedit ne* or *impedit quin.*

260/26–28 **nihil . . . habuisse.** These words seem to imply that the monk must have heard of a manuscript text of the *Iulius* which had definitely belonged to Erasmus, perhaps written in Erasmus' own hand. One such copy undoubtedly existed, as More himself indicated in a private letter to Erasmus of December 1516, and as Erasmus came close to admitting in a letter to Bucer of 1532 (see Allen, *2*, 419). But More's *Letter to a Monk* is the earliest clear indication of a general rumor concerning Erasmus' possession of the *Iulius* before it was printed. Cf. Allen, *2*, 575 and 592, where Erasmus admits to having glanced over the *Iulius* in approximately 1514.

260/28-262/5 **Nam . . . imitari.** Cf. Erasmus in Allen, *3*, 575, lines 44–48; and 592, lines 172–76.

262/6 **infensum bellis.** For Erasmus' self-characterization as an "enemy of war" see Allen, *4*, 543, commentary at line 41.

262/9–10 **Primum . . . vulgauerunt.** Cf. Erasmus in Allen, *3*, 575, lines 43–44. The *Iulius* was probably written in 1513 or 1514, soon after Julius's death; the first reference to a printed version dates from 1517. The argument "Other times, other manners" is proverbial; see *CW 8*, 923/13–14 and Commentary.

262/12–13 **solitarius . . . defleat.** Cf. Lam. 3:28: "sedebit solitarius, et tacebit." In *De Tristitia Christi, CW 14*, 263/7, More cites the words, "sedebam solitarius et gemebam." Mary Basset's Tudor translation of the *De Tristitia, CW 14*, 1113, refers these words to Lam. 3 in a sidenote but translates them "I sate alone and wepte," where "wepte" is a puzzling equivalent for "gemebam" and an even more puzzling equivalent for "tacebit." Perhaps More is conflating Lam. 3:28 with Ps. 136:1: "super flumina Babylonis illic sedimus et flevimus." Cf. also Lam. 3:39: "Quid murmuravit homo vivens, vir pro peccatis suis?" As Listrius points out in his commentary on *Moriae encomium, ASD 4/3*, 158, lines 524–25, "solitarius" is the Latin equivalent of μόναχος ("monk").

262/19–20 **nec . . . conuicijs.** For the wording cf. *CW 4*, 82/25–26.

262/21–22 **dignum patella operculum.** *Adagia* 972 (*Opera omnia*, 2, 387CD). For the letters in question see p. xli, n. 2.

262/24 **facetulus.** See note on 224/19.

262/26 **tempus breue.** Cf. 1 Cor. 7:29.

262/30–31 **quid . . . discis?** For three similar applications of the maxim "lectio cibus animi" see Erasmus, *Institutio principis christiani, ASD 4/1*, 179–80; and *Ratio verae theologiae*, Holborn, pp. 180, 296–97.

264/1–2 **in . . . colloces.** Cf. Martial 1.113.3.

264/5 **perferatur.** This word, unlike the readings of *1520* ("praeferatur" and "proferatur"), has the requisite meaning "is delivered." The three prefixes were similarly abbreviated and thus often confused.

264/5–7 **Atqui . . . sustinuerint.** See John Cassian, *De coenobiorum institutis* 5.32 ("De epistolis, priusquam legerentur, incensis," *PL 49*, 248–49). Chapter 54 of the Rule of St. Benedict (*PL 66*, 767–68) forbids monks to receive or send letters without the permission of their abbot. For similar restrictions imposed somewhat later see Witt, p. 14, n. 31.

264/7–8 **ne . . . reliquerant.** Cf. Gen. 19:17, similarly invoked by Jerome in *Epistolae* 22.1–2 (*PL 22*, 395).

264/17–20 **In . . . fabulam?** Cf. J. Leclercq, "La récréation et le colloque dans la tradition monastique," *Revue d'ascetique et de mystique, 169* (1967), 10–18, and Erasmus, *Lingua, ASD 4/1*, 320, lines 975–79.

264/20 **infamatricem.** Cf. 280/31. This word is attested—as a noun, not an adjective—in Latham (p. 247), from a text of ca. 1325.

264/20 **detractatoriam.** More seems to have coined this adjective from the noun *detractator* (see 22/22 and note).

264/21 **in vanum sumere nomen dei.** Cf. the second commandment, Exod. 20:7.

264/23–24 **non . . . coelorum.** Cf. Matt. 7:21.

264/26–28 **menteque . . . tuae.** See note on 202/18.

266/2–3 **Coepisti . . . puer.** Ovid, *Heroides* 9.23–24.

266/10 **se transformans . . . lucis.** See note on 204/11–14.

266/11 **videntes, non videamus.** Cf. Isa. 6:9, to which Christ often refers while explaining why he speaks in parables. See especially Matt. 13:13–18.

266/11–13 **atra . . . vicia.** Cf. Isa. 5:20; Ovid, *Metamorphoses* 11.314; Juvenal 3.30; *CW 5*, 260/26; *CW 8*, 137/34, 653/15–21; *CW 12*, 33/25. See further *Adagia* 116 (*Opera omnia*, *2*, 75A–C), "Suum cuique pulchrum," which includes an attack much like More's on self-love or *philautia*.

266/13–16 **alienam . . . constantia.** Cf. especially Thucydides 3.82 on the degeneration of moral vocabulary in a time of extreme factional strife. Such seductive, self-serving misnomers for vice are a major concern of traditional Christian moralists and a virtually ubiquitous feature of allegorical morality drama; see Bernard Spivack, *Shakespeare and the Allegory of Evil: The History of a Metaphor in Relation to his Major Villains* (New York and London, 1958), pp. 155–61. Cf. also *CW 4*, 166/13–15, Erasmus, *Antibarbari*, *ASD 1/1*, 75, lines 16–20, and *Enchiridion*, Holborn, pp. 46, 76.

266/22–23 **in tuum caput recta recidunt.** See note on 224/18.

266/24 **plus oleant olei.** Cf. *Adagia* 671 (*Opera omnia*, *2*, 290D).

266/25 **canino dente corrodere.** Cf. Otto, no. 317. The phrase "canino dente rodere" appears in Jerome, *Epistolae* 50.1 (*PL 22*, 513).

268/1 **multa.** This reading may be a mistake for *multo*.

268/4 **pyramides.** Cf. Horace, *Odae* 3.30.2 and Propertius 3.1.57 (3.2.19 in modern editions).

268/17–19 **reuerendum . . . Coletum.** On John Fisher and John Colet see notes on 154/17–18 and 208/10.

268/21–22 **litterae . . . scriptae.** For the letters of Fisher and Colet addressed to Erasmus in which they applaud his New Testament see Allen, *2*, 257–58, 268, and 598. Their letters recommending Erasmus' New Testament to others apparently no longer survive. Erasmus also refers to Fisher's appreciation for his New Testament in Allen, *6*, 67–69; and *Apologia qua respondet*, Ferguson, p. 271.

268/27 **Ioannes Longland.** Joannes Longland (1473–1543) was the dean of Salisbury from 1514 until 1521, when he was appointed bishop of Lincoln. He zealously opposed English heretics but supported the Act of Supremacy. His life and preaching are discussed at length in J. W. Blench, *Preaching in England in the Late Fifteenth and Sixteenth Centuries* (Oxford, 1964), pp. 20–28 and passim. For Longland's friendly relations with Erasmus see Allen, *6*, 1–2.

268/29-270/2 **fateri . . . omnibus.** For the wording cf. Allen, 2, 112, lines 833–34.

270/7–19 **Quid . . . condemnare?** Cf. 166/24-168/6 and note.

270/8 **velut diuinae vocis oraculo.** Cf. *Adagia* 3980 (*Opera omnia*, 2, 1178BC).

270/9 **puer propheta altissimi.** Luke 1:76.

270/10 **ex arce religionis.** See note on 104/7.

270/11–12 **monachulus . . . tuae.** These two phrases elaborate a pun based on a similarity in sound between *monachulus* ("little monk") and *monoculus* ("one-eyed" or "Cyclops"). In Greek mythology, Cyclopes live in caves and show total contempt for the laws others live by (Homer, *Odyssey* 9; and *Adagia* 969 and 3470, *Opera omnia*, 2, 385F–386C and 1132D). Petrarch develops the pun very similarly in *Carmen bucolicum* 1, using the epithet "one-eyed" to hint at the blindness of monks to the realities of everyday life. The diminutive *monachulus* is attested in Blaise (p. 597) from a document of the sixth century. Jerome arraigns arrogant monks in the following words in *Epistolae* 17.2 (*PL* 22, 360): "Pudet dicere: de cavernis cellarum damnamus orbem. In sacco et cinere volutati, de Episcopis sententiam ferimus." Cf. also Erasmus, *Enchiridion*, Holborn, p. 86, lines 25–27.

270/14–15 **ne . . . sobrietatem.** Cf. Rom. 12:3.

270/16–17 **iusticiam . . . constituere.** Cf. Rom. 10:3.

270/20–26 **Quam . . . possit.** Cf. 172/21–32.

270/26–29 **illum . . . γεϱονταγωγεῖς.** Cf. *Adagia* 160 (*Opera omnia*, 2, 93DE). The true meaning of the word αὐτοδίδαϰτος is somewhere between "self-taught" and "inspired"; see Homer, *Odyssey* 22.347, and Aeschylus, *Agamemnon* 991. Jerome sarcastically applies the word to an arrogant monkish critic of his own in *Epistolae* 50.2 (*PL* 22, 513); cf. *CW 14*, 445 and Commentary. The word γεϱονταγωγεῖς is from Aristophanes, *Equites* 1099.

270/29 **sciolus.** This postclassical word generally means either "a know-it-all" or "a smatterer." Cf. Jerome, *Epistolae* 50.5 (*PL* 22, 516), where Jerome is referring to an insolent monkish critic of his own: "Inter mulierculas sciolus sibi et eloquens videbatur."

272/3–5 **Sed . . . lusitas.** Erasmus similarly criticizes impertinent citations from scripture in *Ratio verae theologiae*, Holborn, p. 287.

272/5–28 **non . . . iugularent.** There is a surviving parodic *exemplum* very much like the one More describes; see Paul Lehmann, *Die Parodie im Mittelalter*, 2nd ed. (Stuttgart, 1963), pp. 224–31 (text), 121–23 (discussion). For two other instances of scriptural citation with a ribald

intent see *CW 6*, 87/30–88/3 and 297/13–19. On mock-sermons see
CW 8, 42/9–43/9, and Commentary, as well as Gilman, *The Parodic
Sermon*. Clarence H. Miller notes an affinity between *Moriae encomium*
and parodic sermons in *ASD 4/3*, 22–23.

272/20–21 **ex diametro diversam.** See the Commentary at 102/24.

272/25–26 **fratres . . . consueuerint.** Cf. Erasmus' *Annotationes in
Novum Testamentum, Opera omnia, 6*, 851BC.

272/26 **verbum dei adulterare.** 2 Cor. 2:17, 4:2.

272/27 **fratromimi . . . fratrissarent.** These words appear to be coinages of More's own. Cf. "rhetorissant" at 46/6. More also appears to
have coined the verb "frere" with the meaning "to play the friar"; see
"A mery gest," line 234 (St. Thomas More, *The History of King Richard
III and Selections from the English and Latin Poems*, ed. Richard S. Sylvester, New Haven and London, 1976, p. 106), and *OED*, "friar," *v*.

272/28 **suo . . . iugularent.** See note on 96/18.

274/5–6 **adolescentiae . . . reuoluerem.** See note on 202/18.

274/11 **admirabundus.** See note on 68/13.

274/13 **velut ab impuro fonte.** Cf. 460/8 and *Adagia* 56 (*Opera omnia, 2,*
49F).

274/18–20 **adfectus . . . indicantem.** More is referring to self-love or
philautia; cf. *Moriae encomium, ASD 4/3*, 96, lines 455–59. For the wording of More's final clause cf. Livy's *praefatio:* "haec tempora, quibus nec
vitia nostra nec remedia pati possumus."

274/21–22 **zelo quodam . . . sed imperito.** More is alluding to Rom.
10:2: ζῆλον θεοῦ ἔχουσιν, ἀλλ᾽ οὐ κατ᾽ ἐπίγνωσιν. Neither the Vulgate
nor Erasmus' translation retains the Greek word *zelus*, but cf. Jerome's
commentary on Matthew (*PL 26*, 168): "quae habent quidem zelum
dei, sed non iuxta scientiam." Erasmus cites the verse similarly in *Enchiridion*, Holborn, pp. 88 and 134.

274/30–31 **quod te calcar extimulet.** Cf. *Adagia* 147 (*Opera omnia, 2,*
89B–D).

276/4–6 **suetus . . . illustret.** Cf. Walther, no. 14341b.

276/10 **multum . . . assidua.** James 5:16. For "oratio" the Vulgate and
Erasmus both read "deprecatio."

276/10–11 **quantum . . . milium.** Cf. John Fisher, *English Works*, ed.
John E. B. Major, EETS Extra series no. 27 (London, 1876), p. 273.

276/13–15 **bene . . . corrumpere.** See note on 40/24–27.

276/16 **Nescio . . . adfecto.** Cf. 224/23–24 and note.

276/23–24 **callidus hostis.** See note on 290/10–11.

276/25–26 **conatur . . . deus.** Cf. *CW 8*, 527/21–23: "And all thys doth god for the beste, vsyng our euyll to goodnes as we vse his goodnes to euyll." Cf. also Erasmus, *Enarratio in primum psalmum* (1515), *Opera omnia*, 5, 192C–E, where a similar thesis is stated on the basis of Rom. 8:28, and *De praeparatione ad mortem* (1534), *Opera omnia*, 5, 1301AB.

278/3–7 **In quas . . . charitas?** Cf. Erasmus, *Enchiridion*, Holborn, p. 101; and *Moriae encomium, ASD 4/3*, 160, lines 544–52.

278/5–6 **ceremoniolae.** This contemptuous diminutive is not attested in any of the lexicons. Erasmus employs it in *Enchiridion* (Holborn, p. 77) and *Ratio verae theologiae* (Holborn, p. 258).

278/8–11 **religionis . . . despicere.** More seems especially fond of describing the giddy extremity of pride in this way (cf. Isa. 14:14). There is an extremely similar passage in *CW 12*, 158/8–13; and cf. Roper, p. 35. All three passages owe some debt to Folly's remarks on stuck-up theologians, who, "felices sua philautia, perinde quasi ipsi tertium incolant coelum, ita reliquos mortaleis omneis, vt humi reptantes pecudes, e sublimi despiciunt ac prope commiserantur" (*ASD 4/3*, 146, lines 387–90). But remarkably enough, More's main debt seems to be to Chrysostom's *Homilia 16 in Epistolam ad Hebraeos*, which is actually an exhortation to high-minded sanctimony of the sort More considers to be dangerously close to intolerable pride. In the Latin of the *editio princeps* (Basel, 1517), here is the most pertinent passage from Chrysostom (*PG 63*, 343–44; for the Greek see *PG 63*, 126):

> Efficiamur itaque caelum, ascendamus in altitudinem illam, et ita videbimus homines, ut putemus a formicis nihil differre: non pauperes dico tantum neque plurimos; sed etiam si magistratus, si imperator sit, non videbimus Imperatorem, neque privatum agnoscemus . . . cuncta tanquam muscas videbimus, si in illa altitudine sederimus. . . . Paulum dico et eius similes [an allusion to 2 Cor. 12:2], qui in terra constituti, in coelo conversabantur.

For More's "cristas erigunt," see note on 72/14; for "spatiari . . . caelis," cf. *Adagia* 500 (*Opera omnia*, 2, 220C–E) and Aristophanes, *Nubes* 225 (Ἀεροβατῶ καὶ περιφρονῶ τὴν ἥλιον); for "solaribus insidentes radijs" ("sit[ting] on the rayne bow" in *CW 12*, 158), cf. Whiting R21; for "humi repentem," see note on 110/1; for "tanquam formicas," cf. Aeschylus, *Prometheus* 452–53, and Lucian, *Hermotimus* 5 and *Icaromenippus* 6.19, from which Chrysostom may derive the comparison; and for "e sublimi despicere," see note on 10/12.

278/12 **septa illa claustrorum.** See note on 140/6–7.

278/12–13 **plerisque . . . ipsi.** Cf. *Adagia* 3616 (*Opera omnia*, 2, 1101F–1102A) and Terence, *Adelphoe* 98–99. Erasmus adduces the same lines from Terence in *Enchiridion,* Holborn, p. 77, lines 20–23; and p. 78, line 36–p. 79, line 1.

278/14–16 **Multum . . . mortales.** Cf. Lev. 19:18; John 13:34–35, 15:12–13; Acts 2:44–46, 4:32–35. Erasmus, Budé, and More drew an especially close connection between Christ's "sole precept of charity" and the communal or cenobitic regimen embraced by the early church generally and described in the book of Acts; see Erasmus, *Enchiridion,* Holborn, pp. 99–102; *Ratio verae theologiae,* Holborn, pp. 238–39, 243, 249; *CW 4,* Commentary at 8/25–26 and 218/5–6; and Surtz, *Praise of Pleasure,* pp. 160–91.

278/16–22 **Sensit . . . seuocat.** Cf. *CW 4,* 104/6–10, and contrast Cicero, *De officiis* 1.16.50, 1.17.53–54:

> Optime autem societas hominum coniunctioque servabitur, si, ut quisque erit coniunctissimus, ita in eum benignitatis plurimum conferetur. . . . Gradus autem plures sunt societatis hominum. Ut enim ab illa infinita discedatur, propior est eiusdem gentis, nationis, linguae, qua maxime homines coniunguntur; interius etiam est eiudem esse civitatis. . . . Artior vero colligatio est societatis propinquorum: ab illa enim immensa societate humani generis in exiguum angustumque concluditur. . . . prima societas in ipso coniugio est, proxima in liberis, deinde una domus, communia omnia.

Cicero is torn between his desire to defend the institution of private property (whence the stress that he places on familial and personal loyalties) and his desire to present civil loyalties as paramount (whence the stress that he places on the thesis that familial and personal loyalties are the seedbed of civic ones). At 1.45.160, reversing himself, he even claims that duty to country takes natural precedence over duty to family. In this letter More seems to reiterate the Utopian thesis that private and public loyalties can never be adequately reconciled until the communal spirit of family relations prevails throughout the whole state; see *CW 4,* 102/7-104/10, 148/2–3.

278/25–27 **Iam . . . impietas.** Erasmus offers a similar defense in Allen, *3,* 372, and *Enchiridion,* Holborn, p. 67.

278/27–280/2 **Nam . . . coenum.** Erasmus criticizes excessive devotion to national patron saints in *Enchiridion,* Holborn, p. 66; *Moriae encomium, ASD 4/3,* 124, lines 990–91; and *Ecclesiastes, Opera omnia, 5,* 885B.

280/14–15 **Quare . . . vestras?** Matt. 15:3. The Vulgate reads "mandatum" and "traditionem vestram."

280/19–20 **factis . . . abrogabunt.** Cf. Cicero, *De finibus* 2.30.96, "facta eius cum dictis discrepa[nt]"; and Plautus, *Pseudolus* 108, "dictis facta suppetant."

280/20 **religiosuli.** This contemptuous diminutive occurs in Jerome, *Apologia adversus libros Rufini* 3.7 (*PL 23*, 463B); see also Erasmus, *Antibarbari, ASD 1/1*, 86, line 1 and commentary. Erasmus also employs this word in Allen, *3*, 373, and *Enchiridion*, Holborn, p. 66.

280/22–23 **pedem latum.** See note on 64/22.

280/31 **infamatricibus.** See note on 264/20.

282/1–2 **culicem . . . integrum.** Cf. Matt. 23:24 and 56/14, above.

282/3–9 **Sane . . . periculosius.** For a similar contrast between benign and malignant insanity see *Moriae encomium, ASD 4/3*, 116–18, lines 866–80. For "Qui tam suauiter insaniunt" cf. *CW 4*, 168/6, and *Moriae encomium, ASD 4/3*, 144, line 362: "Quam vero suauiter delirant. . . ."

282/5 **deliri magis, quam mali.** Cf. Plautus, *Bacchides* 1139: "stultae atque haud malae videntur."

282/7–9 **sese . . . phrenesis.** Cf. 2 Cor. 12:2 and note on 278/8–11.

282/10 **sanctuli.** This contemptuous diminutive occurs in Jerome, *Apologia adversus libros Rufini* 3.7 (*PL 23*, 463B). Erasmus repeatedly applies it to Lee; see Allen, *3*, 523, line 33; and *4*, 11, line 52. See also the *Letter to Bugenhagen*, Rogers, p. 353, lines 1042–43.

282/13 **obseruantiolis.** This contemptuous diminutive is not attested in any of the lexicons. Erasmus employs *observatiunculae* in *Enchiridion*, Holborn, pp. 83–84.

282/16–284/9 **Equidem . . . facinus.** More is intentionally vague in reporting this incident, and it is impossible to identify it with any real certainty. Nonetheless, it is hard to believe that the "most monstrous crime" More had ever seen left no trace in contemporary histories. It is possible that More is referring to the "Evil May Day" incident of 1517 in which London apprentices, egged on by a "Chanon in sayncte Mary spittell, a doctor in Deuinitie, called doctor Bele," rampaged through London beating foreigners and looting their business establishments; see Edward Hall, *Chronicle,* ed. Sir Henry Ellis (London, 1809), pp. 586–91; and Polydore Vergil, *Anglica historia,* ed. and trans. Denys Hay (London, 1950; hereafter cited as "Polydore Vergil"), pp. 242–46. According to Hall, p. 589, Wolsey was driven to fortify his own residence against the rioters, who presumably resented his role as a major defender of the foreigners' interests in England. This threat to Wolsey's personal safety may account for More's statement that the criminal cleric whom he is describing contemplated not only murder but "parricide and sacrilege" as well. More himself played a principal part in suppressing these riots; see Hall, pp. 588–89, and *CW 9*, Commentary at 156/9. Both Hall and Polydore Vergil report that Dr. Bele was thrown into prison for his part in provoking the riots and that a number of rioters were executed. Cf. also *CW 9*, 49/20–34.

282/20 **promouisset.** For *promoveo* used in an intransitive sense see note on 56/27.

282/21–22 **e vicio in vicium prolabitur.** Cf. Erasmus, *Enchiridion*, Holborn, p. 58: "An nescis negotium e negotio seri? Vitium vitio invitari?"

284/5–9 **nunquam . . . facinus.** Cf. *A Dialogue Concerning Heresies, CW* 6, 236/33–36, where More speaks of brigands in Ireland and Wales who pray for God's help and protection before they set out on a robbery; cf. also J. C. Holt, *Robin Hood* (London, 1982), pp. 17–35.

284/12–288/25 **Erat . . . episcopo.** It appears that no other report of this incident at Coventry survives, though some additional information might be gleaned from episcopal records for the old diocese of Coventry and Lichfield. The approximate date of the incident is fixed by More's statement at 286/18–19 that he journeyed to Coventry to visit his sister. Elizabeth More married John Rastell by 1504 and spent her first years of marriage at Coventry; see A. W. Reed, *Early Tudor Drama* (London, 1926), pp. 2–3, who further notes a bequest for the saying of Our Lady's Psalter in a Coventry testament of 1507. Coventry was actually more troubled by Lollardy in this period than by excessive devotion to the cult of the Virgin Mary. See Reed, p. 3; John Fines, "Heresy Trials in the Diocese of Coventry and Lichfield, 1511–12," *Journal of Ecclesiastical History, 14* (1963), 160–74; and Imogen Luxton, "The Lichfield Court Book: A Postscript," *Bulletin of the Institute of Historical Research, 44* (1971), 120–25.

284/13 **Conuentriae.** While the name of the city of Coventry is actually a product of two words which mean "Cofa's tree," the alternative derivation from *convent* is widely attested. The latter derivation, the one emphasized by More's spelling ("Conuentriae"), is certainly a good deal more suggestive than the former in a tale of a friar run amok.

284/13–14 **fraterculus . . . reformati.** More's friar belongs to the Conventual Franciscans rather than to the Observants.

284/15–17 **quicunque . . . damnari.** Folly mocks the extravagant claims made for other special prayers and devotions in *Moriae encomium, ASD 4/3,* 122–24.

284/16 **psalterium beatae virginis.** This title, like the English phrase "Our Lady's Psalter," was often used to refer to the rosary, and More is probably referring to the rosary here. But the title was also used for several different medieval collections of devotional poems honoring the Virgin; see F. J. Mone, *Hymni Latini Medii Aevi,* 3 vols. (Freiburg in Breisgau, 1855), 2, 233–60. The devotional collections generally include 150 short poems just as the complete rosary includes 150 Hail Marys; since the actual psalter includes 150 psalms, it is not hard to see why these other devotional texts were called psalters, as well. J. B. Trapp emphasizes the simplicity and popularity of the rosary in arguing that More is referring to the rosary itself in this passage; see "A Double *Mise au Point*," *Moreana, 11* (1966), 47–50, with additional remarks by W. J. Anderson in *Moreana, 12* (1966), 90–92; and *CW 9*, Commentary at 9/20. A collection of 150 short poems to the Virgin was sometimes called a *Psalterium minus beatae virginis* to distinguish it from the odd form of the actual psalter, falsely ascribed to St. Bonaventure, in which the word *Dominus* is consistently replaced with the word *Domina*. It is this form of the psalter to which John Day relates More's anecdote in *Day's Descant on Davids Psalmes* . . . (Oxford, 1620), sig. D₃v. But extravagant claims were occasionally advanced for the redemptive effectiveness of "Our Lady's [ ]lter" in each of these senses.

284/17 **Pronis auribus.** Tacitus, *Historiae* 1.1 and *CW 4*, 90/21–22; cf. *Adagia* 2156 (*Opera omnia*, 2, 760CD).

284/17–18 **libenter . . . coelum.** See note on 286/16, as well as the *Letter to Bugenhagen*, Rogers, p. 334, lines 306–13; p. 349, lines 900–05.

284/23–24 **ea scabie . . . gregem.** Otto, no. 1598. Cf. *Debellation, EW*, sig. O₁v.

284/27–28 **e coelo lapsus.** Cf. *Adagia* 500 and 786 (*Opera omnia*, 2, 220D and 329BC); Otto, nos. 287 and 516.

286/2 **vno die decies.** Cf. Plautus, *Aulularia* 70: "decies die uno."

286/2 **bene certe . . . dicerent.** Cf. 1 Tim. 1:8.

286/7–8 **auditur.** This conjecture of *1760* makes considerably more sense than the 1520 reading "aditur." The two verbs are easily confused; Erasmus records two instances in which a form of *audire* supplanted *adire* in the New Testament (*Opera omnia*, 6, 263E, 500C).

286/8 **exsibilatur, exploditur.** Cicero, *Paradoxa stoicorum* 3.26.

286/10–11 **Dignare . . . tuos.** These words appear at the beginning of a prayer to the Virgin by St. Anselm of Canterbury (*PL 158*, 962) and in many breviaries as an antiphon for the octave of the Assumption of the Blessed Virgin (August 22); see W. H. Freere and L. E. G. Brown, eds., *The Hereford Breviary*, 3 vols., The Henry Bradshaw Society 26, 40, 46 (London, 1904–13), 2, 305. In the Bridgettine monastery at Sion these words were used to begin matins every day; see A. J. Collins, ed., *The Bridgettine Breviary of Syon Abbey*, The Henry Bradshaw Society 96 (London, 1969), p. 13. In Rogers, p. 526, More mentions St. Anselm as one of the most vigorous champions of the Virgin's immaculate conception.

286/12–15 **eodem . . . mentiuntur.** More refers to two of the legends surrounding the disputation conducted by Johannes Duns Scotus in

Paris, ca. 1305, in defense of the Virgin's immaculate conception. According to one of these legends (cf. *CW 6*, 71,80), Christ himself instantaneously transported Scotus to Paris to uphold the honor of the Virgin; see Carl Balić, ed., *Ioannis Duns Scoti, doctoris mariani, theologiae marianae elementa* (Šibenik, Yugoslavia, 1933), p. civ. Balić suggests that the first written account of this legend appears in the *Mariale* of Bernardo de' Busti; see "officium de conceptione beatae mariae, lectio quarta," in *Bernardi de Bustis Mariale . . .* (Strasbourg, 1498), sig. f₇v; and below, note on 288/10. According to another legend, on his way to the disputation Scotus saluted a statue of the Virgin with the verse which More cites, and the statue miraculously nodded to show its approval; see Balić, p. cxix; and Henri Lemaître, "La statue miraculeuse de la Sainte-Chapelle," *Le Moyen Age*, 2nd Series, *16* (1912), 65–76. Neither author mentions any authority for this legend from before 1520. For More's own position on the Virgin's immaculate conception see note on 214/17–21. While More eventually became an outspoken defender of scholastics like Thomas Aquinas, he declined to defend Scotus against Tyndale; see *CW 8*, 713/1–4 and Commentary.

286/15–16 **Quid . . . verbis?** Cf. Plautus, *Menaechmi* 484: "quid multis verbis opust?"

286/16 **facile persuadet volentibus.** See Caesar, *De bello gallico* 3.18.6: "libenter homines id quod volunt credunt." Cf. also Erasmus, *Adagia* 112 and 1290 (*Opera omnia*, 2, 72DE and 518EF); and 284/17–18, above.

286/18–19 **Conuentriam . . . sororem.** See note on 284/12–288/25.

286/27 **Silicernium.** *Adagia* 1052 (*Opera omnia*, 2, 427D). See *CW 3/2*, 646/29.

288/1 **paratas lites.** Terence, *Phormio* 133, *Adelphoe* 792.

288/6–7 **neglectim.** See note on 8/19–20.

288/8 **obblaterabat.** See note on 164/13–14.

288/10 **Mariali.** *Mariale* was used as a title for several books honoring the Virgin. More is probably referring to one of the following:

> Bernardo de' Busti, *Mariale de singulis festivitatibus beatae virginis per modum sermonum tractans* (Milan, 1492; reprints 1493, 1496, 1498, 1500, 1502, 1503, 1515)
> *Opus insigne de laudibus beatae mariae virginis, alias Mariale appellatum* (Strasbourg, 1493)

288/14–15 **si qui . . . possit.** Cf. Listrius' commentary on *Moriae encomium* at *ASD 4/3*, 122, lines 959–60.

288/17–21 **Nam . . . obsequio.** Cf. *CW 8*, 451/5–9: "For yf a prynce wolde promyse euery man a perdon byfore hand, yᵗ wold so surely truste vpon his promyse, as what so euer he shold do he wolde not let to come & aske it / no man dowteth I suppose what plenty thys promyse wold make of all kynde of vnthryftes." Cf. also Listrius' commentary on *Moriae encomium* at *ASD 4/3*, 124, line 996.

288/21 **obsequio.** In *Annotationes in Novum Testamentum* (*Opera omnia*, 6, 610B), Erasmus objects to the Vulgate's rendering of λατρεία at Rom. 9:4 as "obsequium" rather than "cultus" or "religio": "*Obsequium* enim dicitur morem gerentis alienae voluntati, quod frequenter sonat in malam partem."

288/21 **vltro citroque.** *Adagia* 284 (*Opera omnia*, 2, 142F–143A).

288/25 **episcopo.** More must be referring to Geoffrey Blythe (d. 1530), bishop of Coventry and Lichfield from 1503 until his death.

290/2–3 **et salutares . . . progerminet.** Cf. Ovid, *Remedia amoris* 45–46: "Terra salutares herbas eademque nocentes | Nutrit." More may also be thinking of the parable of the wheat and the tares in Matt. 13:25–30.

290/8 **cur . . . Hieronymo?** On this aspect of Jerome's work see David S. Wiesen, *St. Jerome as a Satirist: A Study in Christian Latin Thought and Letters* (Ithaca, 1964); and J. N. D. Kelly, *Jerome: His Life, Writings, and Controversies* (London, 1975), pp. 108–09.

290/10–11 **Vt . . . serpens?** Cf. Gen. 3:1.

290/11 **aconita . . . melle.** Cf. Rogers, p. 337, lines 433–35; *CW 8*, 187/34; Whiting H433 and P289; and Ovid, *Amores* 1.8.103, of a perfidious woman: "Impia sub dulci melle venena latent."

290/12–13 **vt . . . antidotus?** Cf. Erasmus, *Enchiridion*, Holborn, p. 26, lines 16–19; and *Ratio verae theologiae*, Holborn, p. 165, lines 2–5. On the proverbial usage of *antidotus* see Otto, no. 118.

290/13–19 **Qui . . . inuidi.** Cf. the fable of the ape and the flatterer ("Simius tyrannus") in *Aesopica*, ed. Ben E. Perry, 2 vols. (Urbana, 1952), *1*, 613.

290/15 **ex stultis reddunt insanos.** Cf. *CW 8*, 302/16; *CW 12*, 216/25–26; and Terence, *Eunuchus* 254.

290/23 **obsequium . . . parit.** Terence, *Andria* 68; *Adagia* 1853 (*Opera omnia*, 2, 675A–C).

290/23–24 **Hieronymo . . . Ruffino.** See Rufinus' criticisms in *Apologia contra Hieronymum* 2.5 (*PL 21*, 576) and Jerome's answer in *Apologia adversus libros Rufini* 1.30 (*PL 23*, 421).

290/27–28 **ei . . . tui.** Erasmus twice mentions the enthusiastic reaction of Gregory Reisch, prior of the Carthusians at Freiburg, to Erasmus'

New Testament; see Allen, 2, 244, 326–27. Reisch also approved of Erasmus' intention to edit Jerome's letters; see Allen, 2, 29. For another tribute to Erasmus by a Carthusian, see Allen, 2, 537–38.

292/2–3 **cuius . . . innititur.** Cf. *De Tristitia Christi, CW 14*, 113/3–4, where More describes humility as the foundation of all the virtues.

292/6 **tanquam canem calcas.** Cf. Plautus, *Amphitruo* 680: "eum salutat magis haud quicquam quam canem."

292/9–10 **Gratias . . . iste.** Luke 18:11.

292/15–20 **quibus . . . sustinent.** Cf. Luke 19:40, Horace, *Carmina* 3.24.31–32 ("virtutem incolumem odimus, sublatam ex oculis quaerimus invidi"), and *Adagia* 1611 (*Opera omnia, 2*, 615A–616A). More appears to be punning again on Erasmus' first name, Desiderius.

292/19–20 **liuore lippientes . . . sustinent.** Cf. *Parabolae sive similia, ASD 1/5*, 196, lines 564–66; and *Antibarbari, ASD 1/1*, 86, lines 4–5: "Iniquissimum autem fuerit, si lippus solem accuset, cuius luce offenditur."

292/22–24 **turgescat . . . intabescant.** Cf. Ovid's description of Envy in *Metamorphoses* 2.768–71, 775–81.

292/26–294/2 **quam multa . . . videretur.** Cf. Erasmus, *Apologia ad Iacobum Fabrum Stapulensem* (*Opera omnia, 9*, 53E): "Mirabantur illi [*sc.* impressores] me tantum potuisse scribere quantum vel legisse laboriosum fuisset."

294/4–10 **Iam . . . frigescere.** Cf. Lorenzo Valla, *De voluptate, ac de vero bono* 3 proemium (*Opera omnia*, sig. LL$_2$): "Demus tamen, ut possit quis [*sc.* theologus] bene loqui cum male uiuat, numquid hic persuadebit alijs, quod non persuaserit sibi? An audientes ad iram misericordiamque commouebit, nisi prius eisdem [eiusdem *in copy-text*] se affectibus permouerit? Fieri non potest. Ita nemo amorem diuinorum in aliorum mentibus incendet, qui ab eo ipso amore frigescat."

294/8–9 **ignis . . . inflammat.** Cf. Luke 12:49.

294/14–298/8 **quis . . . pariat.** Despite the disclaimer at 294/27–28, More's description of Erasmus' wanderings is quite reminiscent of 2 Cor. 11:23–30, where Paul recounts the hardships that he has endured in his travels for the good of all Christians. Erasmus' continual wanderings are also represented as an unending pilgrimage of learning; see note on 140/9–12. More's defense of Erasmus' wanderings has significant precedents in Erasmus, Allen, *1*, 568, and *3*, 266–68.

294/16–17 **sedem . . . demutet.** More's dignified phrase may be meant to recall Virgil's *Aeneid* 3.161: "mutandae sedes."

294/18 **ostreorum in morem.** *Adagia* 3745 (*Opera omnia*, 2, 1133CD), first said of an old man refusing to part with a young lover.

294/19 **spongiae . . . saxo.** Cf. *Moriae encomium, ASD 4/3*, 162, line 567; and Erasmus in Allen, *3*, 267, lines 137–39.

294/20–23 **quod . . . orbem.** Erasmus, too, appeals to the example of wandering friars in Allen, *3*, 266, but whereas More's tone is almost reverential Erasmus suggests that unlike wandering scholars, such friars are generally up to no good. For early Franciscan missions to China and the New World, see John L. Phelan, *The Millennial Kingdom of the Franciscans in the New World,* 2nd ed. (Berkeley and Los Angeles, 1970), especially pp. 17–21 and notes.

294/24–25 **intra vestram sanctitatem.** The preposition *intra* is frequently used in comparisons to express the same meaning as *infra* ("beneath"); see *TLL, 7/2*, 37–38.

294/29–30 **non . . . sanctimoniam.** There is an alternative way of construing these words: to link "semper" with "sitam" instead of with "sedendo." According to this alternative construction the clause means, "there is not always some special holiness seated in sitting still." The parallel phrases "desidere perpetuo" and "eidem semper affigi saxo" in lines 18–19 both support the construction which links "semper" with "sedendo."

296/2–5 **vagationem . . . anteferre.** Here More suddenly shifts from a first person singular mode of address to a first person plural, thus embracing all monks in an unusually outspoken criticism of monastic repose for its own sake.

296/6 **suum curet genium.** Cf. *Adagia* 1374 (*Opera omnia*, 2, 546DE).

296/11–13 **nisi . . . iusticiam.** Cf. Erasmus, *Antibarbari, ASD 1/1*, 103, lines 11–28; and Dan. 12:3. See also Allen, *1*, 62, lines 227–36; 326, lines 34–42. Cicero similarly ranks eloquence above contemplation in *De officiis* 1.44.156. Although More probably intends "preculas" to be taken as simply a contemptuous diminutive, it can also mean "rosary beads"; see *Moriae encomium, ASD 4/3*, 162, line 572 and commentary. The word also appears in Erasmus, *Enchiridion*, Holborn, pp. 55, 66, 80, 82; *Methodus*, Holborn, p. 158; and *Ratio verae theologiae*, Holborn, pp. 258 and 285.

296/13 **deliciari.** This medieval coinage is attested in Du Cange, *3*, 52.

296/15–17 **An . . . oculis?** See Erasmus' own vivid account of the terrors of seafaring in the colloquy *Naufragium, ASD 1/3*, 325–32.

296/23–26 **haec . . . corpusculo.** Cf. Erasmus in Allen, *3*, 401, 426, 427, 429, 431.

296/27–29 **solem . . . conseruasset?** Cf. Matt. 5:45; Luke 6:35; and Seneca, *De beneficiis* 3.25.

296/29-298/2 **Nam . . . pessimorum.** Erasmus develops the image of the Christian scholar as an *audax mercator* in *Enchiridion*, Holborn, p. 64.

298/7–11 **Semper . . . fortunam.** Cf. Erasmus in Allen, *2*, 257, lines 16–18.

298/14–15 **ab illo . . . diffunduntur.** See note on 296/11–13 and Matt. 13:43: "iusti fulgebunt sicut sol."

298/17–20 **Quamobrem . . . retribuat.** Cf. Matt. 6:2–4.

298/17-300/4 **Quamobrem . . . adblandiuntur.** Cf. 162/11–12.

298/23-300/4 **cum . . . adblandiuntur.** Cf. *Moriae encomium, ASD 4/3*, 162, lines 557–76.

298/25 **spero . . . opto.** See note on 96/9–10.

298/28 **sessitationi.** This noun, derived from the iterative verb *sessito* (Cicero, *Brutus* 15), is not attested in any of the lexicons.

298/28–29 **bonis . . . bonum.** Cf. Rom. 8:28. The Vulgate has "diligentibus Deum" where More here and at *CW 12*, 248/27, has "bonis." More is probably conflating the verse with the secular proverb "Omnia bonos viros decent" (*Adagia* 1860, *Opera omnia, 2,* 676C). Cf. *Adagia* 1162 (*Opera omnia, 2,* 468D–F): "Homines frugi omnia recte faciunt," where Erasmus explicitly notes the concurrence of secular and biblical precepts. For a fuller discussion of the various forms in which More cites Rom. 8:28 see *CW 6*, Introduction, 506–07.

300/9–17 **Etenim . . . quoque.** Cf. More's letter to Gonnell, Rogers, p. 121, lines 35–44.

300/11–12 **angelicae vitae exemplar.** For the commonplace comparison of monastic existence and the *vita angelica* see Leclercq, *Love of Learning*, pp. 71–72.

300/17–21 **trepidumque . . . cecideris.** Cf. Prov. 28:14: "Beatus homo, qui semper est pavidus: qui vero mentis est durae, corruet in malum." See also 92/16–22 and notes.

300/18–19 **quanquam . . . sollicitum.** Cf. *Ludus Coventriae*, "The Prologue of John the Baptist," lines 36–37: "For hope withouten dread . is manner of presumption | And dread withouten hope . is manner of desperation."

300/20 **Qui . . . cadat.** Cf. 1 Cor. 10:12: "qui se existimat stare, videat ne cadat." More cites the verse in the same variant form in *CW 12*, 162/5. According to Germain Marc'hadour, "Saint Bernard et saint Thomas More," *Collectanea Cisterciensia, 44* (1982), 33, St. Bernard also cites the verse in this shortened proverbial form; see also Fisher, *English Works*, p. 286, lines 24–25.

300/20–22 **ne . . . ascendere.** Cf. *Glossa ordinaria* (*PL 113*, 890) on Ps. 32:17: " . . . quanto in eo [*sc.* saeculo] altius erigeris, tanto gravius cades." This passage, a paraphrase of Augustine's *Enarrationes in Psalmos,* is discussed by Marius, pp. 382–83.

300/23–24 **meliorem . . . Maria.** Cf. Luke 10:42 and *Moriae encomium, ASD 4/3,* 193, lines 256–57 and commentary. Traditionally Mary was taken to stand for the contemplative life and Martha for the active life.

300/24–25 **omnis . . . menstruatae.** Isa. 64:6, cited according to the Vulgate.

302/4–6 **in . . . videntur.** Cf. Ps. 138:1–24.

302/7–8 **pietatis vmbra . . . voluptatem quietis.** Cf. Erasmus, *De pronuntiatione, ASD 1/4,* 22, line 264 and commentary, which notes close parallels in *Antibarbari, ASD 1/1,* 46, lines 37–39; and in *Colloquia, ASD 1/3,* 532, line 1371. The phrase "pietatis vmbra" also occurs in Ovid, *Metamorphoses* 9.460, but the way in which More and Erasmus employ it relates it more closely to pastoral indolence; cf. Vergil, *Eclogae* 1.1. For a more sympathetic account of monastic *otium* see Leclercq, *Love of Learning,* pp. 24, 84–85, 355.

302/8 **molestiarum fugam.** Cf. Cicero, *De finibus* 1.10.33: "simili sunt in culpa, qui officia deserunt mollitia animi, id est laborum et dolorum fuga"; and Erasmus, *Antibarbari, ASD 1/1,* 97, lines 5–7.

302/9 **talentumque . . . sudario.** Cf. Luke 19:20. Erasmus makes similar use of this parable in *Antibarbari, ASD 1/1,* 105, lines 5–11.

302/11-304/10 **Huiusmodi . . . claritas.** Cf. Erasmus in Allen, 3, 376–77.

302/16–17 **Ieiunare . . . diabolo.** Cf. Hos. 13:9.

302/17–18 **fides, qua . . . spiritu.** Cf. 1 Cor. 12:3.

302/18–19 **spes, quae . . . confidit.** Cf. Rogers, p. 545, lines 45–47; and Rom. 4:18, where Paul speaks of Abraham's trust in God's promises and represents him as an exemplary believer "qui contra spem in spem credidit." More's definition of hope differs significantly from that of Peter Lombard in *Sententiae* 3.26 (*PL 192,* 811): "Est enim spes certa expectatio futurae beatitudinis, veniens ex Dei gratia et meritis praecedentibus, vel ipsam spem, quam natura praeit charitas, vel rem speratam, id est, beatitudinem aeternam. Sine meritis enim aliquid sperare, non spes, sed praesumptio dici potest." On the other hand, Aquinas had already modified Peter's position by declaring that "spes non praesupponit merita in actu, sed in proposito" (*Commentum in*

602   COMMENTARY

quatuor libros sententiarum lib. III, dist. 26, art. 3, q. 2). For More's
definition cf. Erasmus, *In quartum psalmum concio* (1525), *Opera omnia*,
5, 252D: "Qui diffidunt operibus ac meritis, et viribus suis, sed toti
pendent a gratia Dei, sperant in Domino." Cf. also Erasmus, *Enchiridion*, Holborn, p. 58, lines 22–24 and the *Letter to Volz* (1518), Allen, *3*,
377, lines 585–88.

302/20–21 **charitas, quae . . . gloriam.** Cf. 1 Cor. 13:4–8.

302/21–22 **sola dei gratia et gratuito fauore.** This formulation sounds
a good deal like Luther's "sola fides"; the crucial difference between
the two formulas is that More and the humanists generally continued
to stress the unity of faith, hope, and charity, emphasizing the moral
dimension of a truly Christian existence, whereas Luther placed primary emphasis on *fides* alone—on the soteriological dimension. Cf. the
Letter to Bugenhagen, Rogers, p. 352, lines 1003–13, and p. 353, lines
1072–74; and see Lewis Spitz, *The Religious Renaissance of the German
Humanists* (Cambridge, Mass., 1963), pp. 265, 285–87, and 290–91, for
a strongly pro-Lutheran discussion of this crucial difference.

304/2–3 **tum . . . inutilem.** Cf. *CW 12*, 39/12–13; Matt. 25:21, 23;
Luke 17:9–10.

304/3–10 **Quod . . . claritas.** Cf. Erasmus, *Ratio verae theologiae*,
Holborn, p. 231, lines 30–32.

304/9–10 **neque . . . claritas.** See note on 292/19–20, and for "claritas" cf. 1 Cor. 15:41–42.

304/11 **in calce.** *Adagia* 137 (*Opera omnia*, 2, 84D).

304/19–20 **quaerere . . . scaberes.** Cf. *Adagia* 699 (*Opera omnia*, 2,
300F–301A), "Fricantem refrica"; and *Adagia* 696 (*Opera omnia*, 2,
300A–D), "Mutuum muli scabunt"; Erasmus in Allen, *3*, 330, lines
677–78; and *Moriae encomium, ASD 4/3*, 120, lines 957–58.

304/20–25 **A quibus . . . conuincerem.** Cf. the *Letter to Bugenhagen*,
Rogers, p. 325, lines 24–28.

304/21 **a spiritu sancto dictatis.** Cf. *CW 14*, 15/2–3, where More uses
almost the same phrase in a serious sense to refer to the Bible.

306/1–2 **asinino . . . adagio.** Cf. *Adagia* 971 (*Opera omnia* 2, 386D–
387C).

306/3–5 **oculorum . . . videretur.** Cf. 266/11–13 and note.

306/10–11 **Hoc . . . dictum.** This clause, omitted in *1520*ᵃ, can be ac-
counted for in *1520*ᵐ only if we assume it is the *incipit* of Batmanson's
letter to More. For similar citations of an *incipit* see 228/5–6 and
256/24. Carthusians in general were expected to exhibit an uncommon
degree of modesty; see Erasmus, *Apologia adversus Petrum Sutorem* (*Opera omnia, 9*, 777E).

306/15 **satis debacchatus es.** Cf. 20/12–13 and note.

306/20 **erratula.** This diminutive is not attested in any of the lexicons.

306/20 **Papae, beasti hominem.** Cf. Terence, *Eunuchus* 279.

306/23 **propitio.** See note on 100/5.

308/9 **dormitanter.** This adverbial derivative of *dormito* (Horace, *Ars poetica* 359) is not attested in any of the lexicons.

308/10–12 **non . . . commiserat.** According to Quintilian 3.6.38 a theft of unconsecrated property within the confines of a temple could be classed as a simple theft, *furtum; sacrilegium,* the theft of consecrated property, was a vastly more serious offense. Cf. 374/21–24, 388/17–18, and notes

308/15 **apologastrum.** This contemptuous term, meaning "a driveling apologist" (see 204/28-206/6), is apparently original with More; it is formed on the analogy of terms like *philosophaster,* employed by Augustine in *De civitate dei* 2.27 (*PL 41,* 76). But the root word *apologus* means simply "a fable."

308/18 **omisso ioco.** Cf. Pliny, *Epistolae* 1.21: "omissis iocis."

308/19 **ex animo.** See note on 158/17.

308/22–23 **falsa fictaque.** See *CW 3/2,* Commentary at 620/28.

310/2–3 **recantasse.** This verb is the precise Latin equivalent of the Greek παλινωδεῖν; see Horace, *Carmina* 1.16.27, and note on 106/27-108/1 above.

310/4 **dicta . . . indicta.** Cf. Terence, *Phormio* 951.

310/4–5 **tumultusque . . . desinat.** For the maxim "ex nihilo nihil fit" see Lucretius 1.205 and Persius 3.84. For a still closer parallel to More's words see Maximianus, *Elegiae* 1.272–73: "Ortus cuncta suos repetunt matremque requirunt, / Et redit ad nihilum, quod fuit ante nihil." In the *editio princeps* of these elegies (Venice, Pomponio Gaurico, 1501) and in most other early editions the poems were ascribed to Cornelius Gallus.

310/5 **ita . . . desinat.** In both *1520*^m and *1520*^a the text tapers down to the end in an inverted pyramid.

310/6 **haec tragoedia . . . comoediam.** Cf. *Adagia* 3240 (*Opera omnia,* 2, 1014CD); Germanus Brixius in Allen, *4,* 130, lines 85–86; and notes on 18/13–14 and 110/20–22 above.

310/6–8 **Vale . . . indulge.** Cf. Erasmus in Allen, *3,* 330, lines 680–84.

HISTORIA RICHARDI TERTII
A Supplementary Commentary

For a more detailed historical commentary elucidating both the English and Latin versions of More's *Richard III*, the reader should consult Richard S. Sylvester's parallel critical edition of the texts in *CW 2*. The scope of this commentary is generally limited to recording the stylistic and interpretive debts and affinities of More's Latin history. For the abbreviations and bibliographical conventions employed in this commentary see the headnote to the commentary on the humanist letters (p. 487, above).

314/3–4 **actis ... sex.** Perhaps following some obscure (and apocryphal) chronicle, More overstates Edward's age by almost thirteen years in both English and Latin; see *CW* 2, Commentary at 3/1. It seems highly unlikely that Cardinal Morton, already a bishop under Edward, could be guilty of such flagrant misreckoning; if More was relying on a lost written source at this point, it was probably not written by Morton.

314/4–20 **quum ... est.** This part of the opening paragraph in *P, A,* and *H* bears a very close resemblance to a passage in Robert Fabyan's *New Chronicles of England and France* [1516], ed. Henry Ellis (London, 1811), p. 667, cited by Judith H. Anderson, *Biographical Truth: The Representation of Historical Persons in Tudor-Stuart Writing* (New Haven and London, 1984), p. 80. Both Fabyan's English and the Latin of More's manuscripts omit any mention of Bridget and Anne.

314/7–20 **superstitibus ... est.** For Edward's children and the textual problems in More's list of them see *CW* 2, Commentary at 3/5–14, and p. cxlv above. The manuscript reading "superstitibus masculi sexus liberis duobus femellae ⟨quatuor⟩ quinque" is odd Latin at best. I have treated "femellae" as a misreading of "femellis," quite an easy mistake in a manuscript like *P;* we might also conjecture that the phrase is imperfectly assimilated from a source where it appeared in the nominative.

314/8 **femellis.** The only instance of this diminutive in classical Latin is in Catullus 55.7.

316/5–8 **tam ... fuit.** Cf. 318/19–31 and notes, below.

316/8–11 **eam ... intendit.** Cf. Suetonius, *Caligula* 6, and Erasmus, *Institutio principis christiani, ASD 4/1,* 138, lines 67–68: "Foedissima commendatio est, quoties deterior succedens facit, vt superior dum viueret intolerabilis, iam vt probus ac salutaris desyderetur." Cf. *CW* 3/2, no. 113.

316/10 **parricidae.** If we acknowledge that Edward himself probably ordered the murder of Henry VI (see the Commentary at 324/20–25 below), the term "parricida" (a loose synonym for "traitor" or "regicide") fits Edward as well as his brother. More just twice (at 320/7–14 and 328/9–10) charges Richard explicitly with plotting the death of his nephews; these proleptic indictments allow More to get on with the drama of factional conflict which constitutes the real substance of his Latin history.

316/11–16 **Etenim ... ferebatur.** For More's pregnant allusions to Tacitus, *Annales* 1.3, in this passage, see *CW* 2, xciii. Tacitus' passage is not only a tribute to the relative calm of Augustus' reign but also a lament for the republican liberties which Augustus himself gradually undermined. More's apparent allusion is also significant for dating the *Historia;* see the note on 344/6–346/23.

316/14–15 **in plusquam . . . parte.** Cf. Tacitus, *Agricola* 3: "per quin-
decim annos, grande mortalis aeui spatium . . ."

316/18–19 **Aduersis . . . elatus.** Cf. Horace, *Carmina* 2.10.21–24.

316/20–23 **in aggrediendis . . . vicit.** On princes' wisdom as a mean
between temerity and timidity see Erasmus, *Institutio principis christiani,*
ASD 4/1, 170–71, lines 125–31, and cf. 136, lines 8–11; all three passages may be treated as restatements of the principle "Festina lente."

316/27 **ab ineunte . . . aetate.** Cicero, *De oratore* 1.21.97.

318/2–3 **valentibus . . . licentia.** Cf. Terence, *Andria* 78, Vergil, *Aeneid*
10.501–02, Seneca, *Hippolytus* 205–08, *Oedipus* 691–92, Erasmus, *Institutio principis christiani, ASD 4/1,* 136, line 9, and *CW 3/2,* no. 19/90.

318/3–8 **Id . . . moderatior.** Cf. Erasmus, *Institutio principis christiani,*
ASD 4/1, 187, lines 668–71:

> Alioqui tolerabilior est reipublicae status, vbi princeps ipse malus
> est, quam vbi principis amici mali. Vnum tyrannum vtcumque
> ferimus. Quandoquidem vnius auariciam facile populus explet,
> vnius libidini non magno negocio fit satis, vnius saeuiciam satiare
> licet. At tot tyrannos explere grauissimum est.

More's defense of the king may be intentionally feeble; cf. 462/7–16
and *CW 2,* Commentary at 4/20. In any event, the defensive appeal to
one man's limitations reminds us that all the main characters in More's
Historia were to some extent *partners* in Edward's self-indulgence.

318/7–8 **flexu . . . etatis.** Cf. Cicero, *De oratore* 1.1.1, *Pro Caelio* 31.75.

318/9–11 **Bellum . . . expectabat.** Cf. Sallust, *Bellum Iugurthinum* 41.2.

318/14–17 **A pecunijs . . . occasio.** This claim is rightly contradicted
by Buckingham at 456/4–9, below; for Edward's continuing exactions
near the end of his life see *CW 2,* Commentary at 5/1, and Charles Ross,
Edward IV (London, 1974; hereafter cited as "Ross, *Edward IV*"), pp.
248, 380. If regal avarice is itself a tyrannical tendency, the late Edward
and Richard may well have been equally serious offenders (despite
More's remarks at 324/5–6 Richard's own greed is virtually undocu-
mented), but an even more obvious villain was Henry VII. Cf. Ross, p.
380: "Even in his later years, however, Edward proved far less grasp-
ing in such matters [sc., keeping any estates which had happened to fall
under royal control] than Henry Tudor was to be."

318/21–22 **progressu . . . superbiam.** Cf. Sallust, *Bellum Iugurthinum*
40.5, Tacitus, *Annales* 12.29, and *CW 3/2,* no. 198. Although Edward
was famed for his affable nature, at least some of his contemporaries
felt that he grew *more* despotic with age; see Ross, *Edward IV,* p. 245.

318/26–27 **Ibi . . . exhibuit.** See 484/8–16 for a hostile description of
Richard's own parallel efforts to curry popular favor, and cf. Erasmus,

Institutio principis christiani, ASD 4/1, 165, lines 923–24 (based on Suetonius, *Augustus* 53): "Octauius Augustus, quamuis scelere occuparat imperium, contumeliae loco ducebat uocari dominum . . ."

318/30–31 **populum . . . preponderat.** For the popular appeal of gracious informality see Cicero, *De officiis* 2.14.48, and Erasmus, *Institutio principis christiani, ASD 4/1,* 186, lines 625–27.

320/7 **execrabilis imperandi sitis.** See the note on 334/14–15.

320/7–14 **ad eorum . . . decreuit.** See the note on 316/10.

320/10–11 **natura . . . deuinctus.** Cf. Sallust, *Bellum Iugurthinum* 10.3.

320/12–14 **contra . . . decreuit.** Cf. the verses cited in *CW 2,* Commentary at 8/13–14.

320/15–16 **materiam . . . implent.** For this phrasing cf. Lactantius, *Divinae institutiones* 5.4 (*PL 6,* 563A).

320/18 **Richardus Eboraci Dux.** The promised description of Richard of Gloucester momentarily becomes, or appears to become, a description of his factious father, Richard of York. For the merits of York's claim to the throne see *CW 2,* Commentary at 6/10, and for another passage suggesting an especially intimate resemblance between Richard of Gloucester and his father see 452/9–14, below.

320/18–21 **nobilis . . . valuit.** Cf. Sallust, *Bellum Iugurthinum* 15.4, 21.4.

320/21 **innocentior quam sapientior.** Cf. 372/16, below, and *Utopia, CW 4,* 226/11–12.

320/22–23 **Parlamenti . . . est.** See *CW 2,* Commentary at 6/14, and Tacitus, *Historiae* 1.84, for a similar overstatement of the Senate's importance in imperial Rome.

320/29-322/4 **relinquens . . . patientes.** Cf. Lucan 1.85, 92–93, 125–26.

322/6–14 **si non . . . adiudicauit.** On the circumstances of Clarence's execution see *CW 2,* Commentary at 7/1–9, and most recently Charles Ross, *Richard III* (Berkeley and Los Angeles, 1981; hereafter cited as "Ross, *Richard III*"), pp. 32–34.

322/10–11 **mulieres . . . chari.** Cf. Euripides, *Andromache* 181–82, Whiting W540, and Walther, no. 15360a.

322/17–18 **cuius . . . deplorauit.** Cf. Seneca, *Hippolytus* 1118, and the unusually Machiavellian advice of Erasmus, *Institutio principis christiani, ASD 4/1,* 186, lines 656–57: ". . . ita sumendum supplicium, vt appareat principem huc inuitum descendisse."

322/21–24 **inequalibus . . . inuidus.** Most of these details, along with some others, are listed in virtually the same way by Polydore Vergil; see

CW 2, Commentary at 7/16. One important exception is Richard's hunchback; see *CW* 2, Commentary at 7/20.

322/25–28 **fama . . . indentatum.** For an earlier, still more grotesque version of this rumor and for a 1514 Erasmian use of "Agrippa" as a term for a breech baby see *CW* 2, Commentary at 7/20–21 and 7/23.

322/29-324/2 **natura . . . designaturus.** Cf. Lucan 2.2–4: "legesque et foedera rerum | Praescia monstrifero vertit natura tumultu | Indixitque nefas."

324/2 **haud instrenuus dux.** Cf. Suetonius, *Vespasianus* 4, "non instrenuo duce."

324/5–7 **Supra . . . effunderet.** Cf. Aristotle, *Ethica nicomachea* 4.1.33, Cicero, *De officiis* 2.15.54, and Sallust, *Catilina* 38.2, 52.11. For the truthfulness of this allegation about Richard see the note on 318/14–17, above; *CW* 2, Commentary at 8/4–6; and Ross, *Richard III*, pp. 177–80. More may have borrowed several details of his characterization of Richard from Sallust's description of Catiline.

324/7–8 **his artibus . . . pareret.** Cf. Cicero, *De officiis* 2.15.54: ". . . non tanta studia assequuntur eorum, quibus dederunt, quanta odia eorum, quibus ademerunt."

324/10–15 **Personam . . . occidere.** Cf. Lucian, *De calumnia* 24.

324/13–14 **In vultu . . . immanis.** Cf. Tacitus, *Annales* 4.1, on Sejanus: "iuxta adulatio et superbia: palam compositus pudor, intus summa apiscendi libido . . ."

324/14–15 **nec . . . occidere.** These words may contain an allusion to Judas' betrayal of Christ with a kiss. Cf. *CW 14*, 407, and Tacitus, *Annales* 14.56 (on the same sort of behavior in Nero).

324/19–20 **neque cuiusquam . . . obstare.** Cf. Lucan 1.149–50.

324/20 **Constans fama.** Suetonius, *Iulius* 6.

324/20–23 **Constans . . . trucidatum.** For one of the earliest versions of this rumor see the verses cited in *CW* 2, Commentary at 8/13–14. Cf. Seneca, *Troades* 44–48, on the killing of Priam.

324/20–26 **Henricum . . . fratrem.** For the (dubious) truthfulness of this allegation about Richard see *CW* 2, Commentary at 8/13–14; and Ross, *Edward IV*, p. 175, and *Richard III*, p. 22. For this rather feeble defense of King Edward cf. Tacitus, *Annales* 1.6.

326/1–6 **Sunt . . . incumbendum.** See the note on 322/6–14.

326/15–18 **Sed . . . erratur.** Similar malicious reports are accompanied by similar disclaimers in Sallust, *Catilina* 14.7 and 22.3. Cf. also Vergil's description of *Fama* in *Aeneid* 4.188 as "tam ficti pravique tenax, quam nuntia veri."

328/6–7 **olim . . . inuaserat.** Cf. Sallust, *Bellum Iugurthinum* 20.6.

328/7–9 **opportunitate . . . facinus.** Cf. Sallust, *Bellum Iugurthinum* 6.3.

328/9–10 **certum . . . potiri.** Here More seems to assert that the princes were dead by the time Richard started to reign; for a similar, much earlier assertion see the verses cited in *CW 2*, Commentary at 8/13–14, and contrast *CW 2*, 83/7–14.

328/10 **regno . . . precio.** Cf. Sallust, *Bellum Iugurthinum* 14.11.

328/10–17 **Gnarus . . . abuteretur.** Cf. Erasmus, *Institutio principis christiani*, *ASD 4/1*, 156, lines 604–06 (loosely based on Aristotle, *Politics* 5.1313b17–18): "Tyrannus gaudet inter ciues factiones ac dissidia serere et simultates forte fortuna obortas diligenter alit ac prouehit atque his rebus ad suae tyrannidis communitionem abutitur."

328/24–336/23 **Hae diuisiones . . . disiungerentur.** Cf. Sallust, *Bellum Iugurthinum* 9.4-11.1. For the historicity of Edward's peacemaking effort see *CW 2*, Commentary at 10/14.

330/4–8 **qui . . . consulerent.** Cf. Erasmus, *Institutio principis christiani*, *ASD 4/1*, 176, lines 327–29: "Nam proceres, quoniam fere studiis inter se dissentiunt, certatim omnes principis fauorem ambiunt vel quo premant aduersarium, vel ne quam ansam nocendi ministrent inimico."

330/9 **cum animo voluens.** Cf. Sallust, *Bellum Iugurthinum* 6.2.

330/12 **inter se inimicitias exercuerant.** Cf. Sallust, *Catilina* 49.

330/25-332/2 **cuius . . . sitis.** Cf. Sallust, *Bellum Iugurthinum* 10.4–5.

332/8 **bene . . . pereant.** Cf. *Bellum Iugurthinum* 42.4.

332/8–9 **rata . . . possunt.** Cf. Pseudo-Seneca, *Octavia* 460 ("[Nero:] Statuam ipse. [Seneca:] Quae consensus efficiat rata") and Publilius Syrus, *Sententiae* 4 ("Auxilia humilia firma consensus facit").

332/11–16 **ita . . . excident.** Cf. Erasmus, *Institutio principis christiani*, *ASD 4/1*, 141–42, lines 178–82.

332/16 **gratia . . . perit.** Cf. Plautus, *Poenulus* 844, and contrast 430/7–8, below.

332/20–21 **rem . . . oratio.** See the *Letter to Dorp*, note on 40/24–27.

332/24–26 **quod . . . pretereo.** Cf. John 13:35 and Erasmus, *Institutio principis christiani*, *ASD 4/1*, 218, lines 585–86, 592–93, 601–03.

334/1 **rogabimini.** For More's taste for unusual passive constructions like this one see *CW 3/2*, Commentary at 137/1–3.

334/11–14 **inimicitia . . . deterrere.** Cf. Tacitus, *Historiae* 4.70.

334/14–17 **Tam . . . permiscuerit.** Cf. Walther, no. 36399; *CW 4*, 242/24–26; Sallust, *Bellum Iugurthinum* 5.1–2; and Augustine, *De civitate dei* preface (*PL 41*, 13), on the governing drive in the *civitas terrena* or City of Man, *dominandi libido.*

334/21–22 **vtinam . . . reminiscimur.** Cf. Cicero, *De finibus* 2.32.104 ("Memini etiam quae nolo; oblivisci non possum quae volo") and *De oratore* 2.74.299.

334/24–26 **dispeream . . . comparassem.** Cf. Erasmus, *Instutio principis christiani, ASD 4/1*, 162, lines 820–22 (based on Seneca, *De clementia* 1.9.5): ". . . Augustus . . . negauit tanti esse viuere, vt omnibus inuisus incolumitatem suam tot ciuium sanguine tueretur."

334/26–27 **facta . . . queunt.** Cf. Plautus, *Aulularia* 741.

334/29–30 **Omnia . . . meis.** For the wording of the first part of this sentence cf. Tacitus, *Annales* 15.36, a hypocritical farewell missive from Nero. For the general sentiment cf. Sallust, *Bellum Iugurthinum* 10.6.

334/29 **perfore.** This extremely rare form is attested along with other compound forms incorporating the future infinitive of "sum" in Niccolo Perotti, *Cornucopiae* (Venice, Aldus, 1499), sig. b₁v.

336/4–5 **vos . . . occupet.** Cf. Is. 3:4–5, Eccles. 10:16.

336/9–16 **hortor . . . habeat.** Cf. Sallust, *Bellum Iugurthinum* 10.3.

336/19–23 **Ceterum . . . disiungerentur.** Cf. Sallust, *Bellum Iugurthinum* 11.1.

338/16 **agnatorum.** This word normally refers to paternal kinsmen, though here Richard (or More) clearly wants it to mean much the same thing as "his mothers kinred," the reading of *1557*. Perhaps More tried to take the a-prefix as privative or intended a pun on *ignoti.*

338/24–25 **puerum . . . calumnias.** Cf. Erasmus, *Institutio principis christiani, ASD 4/1*, 175/267–70: "Iam ipsa aetatis simplicitas huic malo [sc., adulationi] praecipue patet, partim quod naturae propensione blandis magis gaudeat quam veris, partim quod ob rerum imperitiam, quo minus suspicatur insidias, hoc minus cauere nouit."

340/2 **praepotentiam.** All three manuscripts leave a space here large enough for an accurate equivalent of More's term in English, "advancement" (see the variants at 340/1–2). Though "potentiam" by itself would make adequate sense here, it is hard to see why any scribe would omit it; More may have been looking for an even more accurate equivalent, or his scribes may have had trouble deciphering the short form of the noun proposed here (p̄potentiā).

340/2–3 **suane . . . est.** Cf. Sallust, *Bellum Iugurthinum* 46.8.

340/7 **eum . . . aberat.** A reference to Clarence's death; see the note on 322/6–14.

340/12 **malitiam . . . auertat.** See Tacitus, *Annales* 2.20, and the note on 346/18–20.

340/17–18 **ex inimico . . . profiteatur.** See Whiting F662 and contrast Tilley F686.

340/22–23 **ardentes . . . incendit.** Cf. Tacitus, *Historiae* 1.24.

342/2–3 **non . . . male.** Cf. Sallust, *Bellum Iugurthinum* 40.3.

342/6–11 **cum . . . statuunt.** Cf. Cornelius Nepos, *Hannibal* 10.4: "Dolo erat pugnandum, quum par non esset armis."

342/8–9 **cuius . . . sit.** Cf. Seneca, *Phoenissae* 629, "Fortuna belli semper ancipiti in loco est."

342/9–10 **quum . . . subituram.** Cf. Tacitus, *Historiae* 1.84: ". . . senatus nobiscum est: sic fit ut hinc res publica, inde hostes rei publicae constiterint."

342/12–13 **multum . . . inibatur.** For the thought cf. the *Letter to Lee*, 186/25–28, above. Queen Elizabeth actually restricted the size of the Prince of Wales' escort under strong direct pressure from Hastings; see *CW 2*, Commentary at 16/8–9.

344/6-346/23 **Erat . . . relinquunt.** For this episode cf. Tacitus, *Annales* 2.65; there is another parallel with this Tacitean passage at 356/7–11. Since Books 1–6 of Tacitus' *Annales* were first published in 1515, these two parallels may be significant for dating More's history.

344/6–7 **in vmbilico . . . sita.** For the phrasing cf. *CW 4*, 112/25–26, on the city of Amaurotum.

344/15–17 **dimittitur . . . cubitum.** For a similar description of ill-founded confidence in similar circumstances see Suetonius, *Domitian* 11.

344/18–19 **longe . . . tulerant.** Cf. Sallust, *Bellum Iugurthinum* 11.1.

344/25–26 **ipsorum . . . sterterent.** For the contrast cf. *CW 14*, 35/3–4.

346/18–20 **perdereque . . . regesturi.** Cf. 340/12; Prov. 26:27, Ovid, *Ars amatoria* 1.645–46, 655–56, and *CW 3/2*, no. 19/98–99.

346/21 **quum . . . conuersi.** The rhetorical relation between theoretical legitimacy and brute force is extremely unstable in More's *Historia;* cf. 348/13–14, 370/5–6, 376/21–22, 436/21–22, 438/6, 448/21–23. Heroes and traitors can instantaneously and even repeatedly exchange titles according to the variable fortunes of war; what makes Richard III's coup d'etat illegitimate use of coercion but Henry

VII's coup d'etat providential and lawful reform? The question was especially crucial for the more thoughtful subjects of Henry VII, since the first Tudor not only maintained his own right to the throne *iure belli* but also insisted that Parliament declare Richard's loyal lieutenants to be outlaws and traitors *ex post facto,* as if it were a crime not to know in advance how God planned to receive Henry's challenge to the then-reigning monarch at Bosworth (see S. B. Chrimes, *Henry VII*, London, 1972, hereafter cited as "Chrimes," pp. 62–63, and Mortimer Levine, *Tudor Dynastic Problems 1460–1571*, London and New York, 1973, pp. 34–36). A primary effect of More's unstable treatment of force in relation to theoretical legitimacy is to show just how hard it is to avoid the equation "might is right" in evaluating secular history. For a trenchant pre-Machiavellian statement of the problem see Seneca, *Hercules furens* 251–53: "Prosperum ac felix scelus | Virtus vocatur; sontibus parent boni; | Ius est in armis, opprimit leges timor." See also Erasmus, *Adagia* 528 (misnumbered 529) and 3650, *Opera omnia*, 2, 233F–234B, 1108D–1109A.

352/19–25 **Ibi . . . fieret.** Cf. Sallust, *Bellum Iugurthinum* 12.5.

352/26–28 **Reginam . . . complorantem.** Cf. Lam. 1:1.

354/1 **iniquus . . . timor.** For the thought cf. Seneca, *Hercules furens* 316, and Statius, *Thebais* 3.564; for the wording, cf. Seneca, *Troades* 545–46 ("Est quidem iniustus dolor rerum aestimator").

354/5–6 **In . . . meam.** For the wording cf. Terence, *Eunuchus* 102.

354/17-356/17 **Iam . . . erit.** For the historicity of these confrontations and debates see *CW* 2, Commentary at 22/16–17, 23/2–3.

356/2–3 **structis . . . insidijs.** The idiom "insidias struere alicui" is quite common in classical Latin; for "in alios odium struere" see Cicero, *De Oratore* 2.51.208.

356/7–11 **Verone . . . statuatis.** For a Tacitean parallel see the note on 344/6-346/23.

356/15–17 **ius . . . erit.** See the note on 342/9–10.

356/26–358/7 **aurigae . . . obtruncarent.** For an earlier mention of this detail see *CW* 2, Commentary at 24/3.

358/25–26 **agnus . . . creditus.** For an earlier application of this image to Richard see *CW* 2, Commentary at 24/30-25/1.

358/26–27 **Mox . . . priuatus est.** For the accuracy of this statement see *CW* 2, Commentary at 25/1.

360/4–7 **omnis . . . inuaserat.** Cf. Sallust, *Bellum Iugurthinum* 20.6, 64.6. Cf. also Erasmus, *Panegyricus, ASD 4/1,* 34, lines 279–80: "votis impatientibus nulla non lenta [est] festinatio."

360/5 **morae impatientem.** Cf. Seneca, *Phaedra* 583 ("impatiens morae").

360/13-364/15 **Ergo . . . parere.** For other reports of this speech see *CW 2*, Commentary at 25/19.

360/20 **velut . . . squalorem.** Cf. Vergil, *Aeneid* 2.92.

360/23–24 **Adeo . . . ardeat.** Cf. Seneca, *Medea* 580–83.

360/26 **popello.** Erasmus uses the same contemptuous diminutive in *Institutio principis christiani, ASD 4/1*, 170, line 114.

362/8–9 **deterior nouerca mater.** Cf. Ovid, *Heroides* 6.127 ("Medeam timui: plus est Medea noverca") and Seneca, *Hippolytus* 1191–92, where Phaedra addresses Theseus as "pater peior noverca." Cf. *CW 3/2*, no. 258/9–10 and Commentary at no. 224/12.

362/11–12 **maximas . . . posse.** Cf. Horace, *Epistolae* 1.1.25, and Livy 27.9.

362/14–15 **cito . . . rumor.** Cf. Whiting S619 and Ovid, *Fasti* 6.527.

362/18–19 **Hec . . . postea.** Cf. Whiting T23 and More's *Debellation, EW*, sig. N₈v: "And so a rumour ones begonne & spread abrode, is not after soone remoued."

362/21 **Huic . . . obuiam.** Cf. Persius 3.64.

362/21–24 **Huic . . . fidei.** For the Council's peaceful overtures to Elizabeth see *CW 2*, Commentary at 26/25–26 and 33/23–26.

364/5 **muliebri pertinacia.** Cf. Terence, *Hecyra* 202–03, and Whiting W519 and 549.

364/12–15 **Hec . . . parere.** Cf. More's *Letter to Dorp,* 78/9–15.

364/19–27 **rem . . . consecrare.** For the legendary consecration of Westminster Abbey and for the longstanding controversy in England about fugitives' right of sanctuary see *CW 2*, Commentary at 27/32-28/6 and 28/19. Sanctuary is also an issue in Tacitus, *Annales,* 3.36, 3.60.

366/4 **maternam . . . metum.** For these phrases see Pliny, *Epistolae* 8.11.1 and Velleius Paterculus 2.87.1, and cf. Livy 1.13.1, 2.40.1.

366/6–376/17 **Muliebrem . . . pernego.** For the intellectual background of Buckingham's attack on sanctuaries see *CW 2*, Commentary at 28/19. Rhetorically the speech bears an intriguing resemblance to More's *Letter to a Monk,* just as Buckingham's second speech bears an intriguing resemblance to the *Letter to Oxford;* see the note on 454/22–468/14.

366/6–7 **peruicaciam mulieris.** Cf. Tacitus, *Historiae* 3.77.

366/20 **providentiae . . . amplius.** For other uses of *amplius* with the genitive see Plautus, *Cistellaria* 777, Cicero, *In Catilinam* 4.5.9, and Caesar, *De bello gallico,* 6.9.

368/1 **prudentia . . . fides.** For the relative importance of prudence and loyalty (or more generally, justice or honesty) in earning others' confidence see Cicero, *De officiis* 2.9.33. The uneasy relationship between prudence and loyalty in an era of factional strife is a primary theme of More's *Historia;* see also 330/1-332/11, 360/25–26, 362/21– 27, 364/5–7, 366/20–21, 392/5–8, 392/22–394/8, 394/25–26, and 420/6–8.

368/4–5 **meticulosa . . . est.** Cf. Publilius Syrus 500, "Pericla timidus etiam quae non sunt videt"; for "quod nusquam est" cf. Plautus, *Miles gloriosus* 315, *Curculio* 144–45, *Pseudolus* 395–408, and Ovid, *Metamorphoses* 3.433.

368/6 **vmbram horreat suam.** Cf. Whiting S177 and Ovid, *Epistolae ex Ponto* 2.7.14.

368/12–13 **neque superum . . . pudor.** Cf. Pseudo-Seneca, *Octavia* 90, on Nero: "spernit superos hominesque simul."

368/19 **muliebri temeritate.** Cf. Seneca, *Hippolytus* 824: "Quid sinat inausum feminae praeceps furor?"

368/27 **vires . . . cepit.** Cf. Cicero, *De inventione* 1.2.3: "consuetud[o] . . . quae praesertim iam naturae vim obtineret propter vetustatem."

370/1 **male expuncta nomina.** For the phrasing cf. Plautus, *Cistellaria* 189.

370/5 **dum . . . decernitur.** See the note on 346/21.

370/5–6 **alteri . . . loco.** See the note on 436/21–22.

370/6–8 **non displicet . . . tuto.** See the note on 390/6–9.

370/8–9 **furibus . . . sunt.** For the prevalence of this opinion see *CW* 2, Commentary at 30/14–15.

370/8–11 **furibus . . . homicidis.** Cf. Pietro Carmeliano's obsequious tribute to Richard (letter published by A. Modigliani, "Un nuovo manoscritto di Pietro Carmeliano," *Humanistica Lovaniensia,* 33 [1984], 102): "Cui magis furta, latrocinia, stupra, adulteria, homicidia, fenus heresisque . . . exosa sunt, quam sibi [*sc.* Richardo]?"

370/11–16 **homicidis . . . facit.** Cf. Exod. 21:14 and Num. 35:27–31.

370/17–22 **quanta . . . confluxerit.** For the phrasing cf. Sallust, *Catilina* 37.5–6, and *CW 4,* 208/12–13.

370/22–23 **alterum . . . alterum.** Westminster and St. Martin le Grand; see *CW 2*, Commentary at 30/30.

370/24–27 **Ausim . . . caruisse.** Cf. the *Letter to Dorp*, 66/14–66, and note.

372/3–4 **profundit perdit abligurit.** Cf. Terence, *Adelphoe* 134.

372/4–5 **mandant laqueum.** Cf. Juvenal 10.53.

374/21–24 **sic . . . queritent.** Cf. Gratian, *Decretum* lib. II causa 17 quest. 4 cap. 6 (*CIC, 1,* 816), which exempts the possessions of *publici latrones* from the immunities afforded by sanctuary; this "causa" includes several other teachings on sanctuary which are relevant to Buckingham's discussion.

376/21 **verbis . . . vi.** See the note on 346/21.

378/10–13 **patria . . . periculum.** Cf. Ovid, *Metamorphoses* 3.115–25, a mythic anecdote in which Ovid explicitly likens earthborn brothers' reciprocal slaughter to ruthless civil war. For other allusions to this passage see the Letter to Dorp, 54/12, *CW 5*, 690/32-692/1, *CW 14*, 445/9-447/5. See also Lucan 1.97, on the feuding of Romulus and Remus: "Exiguum dominos commisit asylum."

378/15–16 **ex illis . . . aulae.** For the word-play cf. the *Letter to Oxford,* 140/9.

378/21-390/25 **Haud . . . vellem.** Cf. Sallust, *Bellum Iugurthinum* 14.

380/5 **neminem . . . recidere.** The notion that a relapse would probably be worse than the initial attack of an illness was already proverbial in classical times; see Livy 24.29.

382/8–9 **in suspicionem fraudis incidere.** Cf. Cicero, *Pro Milone* 27.72.

382/11–12 **(quod . . . deprauat.** See the note on 332/20–21.

382/21–22 **me . . . viuere?** Cf. Persius 5.83–84: "An quisquam est alius liber, nisi ducere vitam | Cui licet ut libuit?"

384/5–6 **innocentium perniciem.** This phrase would naturally be referred by More's readers to the two little princes; for the "slayer of innocents" theme in early anti-Ricardian propaganda see C. A. J. Armstrong, "An Italian Astronomer at the Court of Henry VII," in Italian *Renaissance Studies,* ed. E. F. Jacob (London, 1960), pp. 447–50. Tacitus (*Annales* 4.33) mentions "perniciem innocentium" as a disgraceful but commonplace theme in imperial Roman history.

384/8 **neque . . . amplius.** Cf. Horace, *Ars poetica* 355–56.

384/19 **etiam . . . est.** Cf. Horace, *Sermones* 2.6.1.

386/14–16 **Liceat . . . dormiat.** Cf. Terence, *Heauton timoroumenos* 342, and More's *Debellation, EW*, sig. O₃: "The good man may take his rest I warrant hym, & shal not nede to break his slepe therfore."

386/25–26 **nec . . . innocentia.** Cf. Sallust, *Bellum Iugurthinum* 14.4.

386/27–29 **Adeon . . . oratio.** Cf. Terence, *Phormio* 499–500.

388/17–18 **nisi . . . filium.** For the argument *a fortiori* cf. *CW 6*, 415/22–26; for the pertinent definition of "sacrilege" see the *Letter to a Monk*, note on 308/10–12, and 374/21–24, above.

388/19–21 **filium . . . credunt.** For the force of this argument based on "knight's service" see CW 2, Commentary at 38/29–30. The queen's understanding of the common law on wardship is supported both here and at 390/15–18 by Bracton, *De legibus et consuetudinibus Angliae*, ed. George E. Woodstock, tr. Samuel E. Thorne, 3 vols. (Cambridge, Mass., 1968–77), 2, 226, 254 (F.77, F.88).

390/6–9 **grauida . . . obtuli.** Cf. 370/5–9 and Seneca, *Thyestes* 657–58, on the solemn and sheltered royal grove ("nemus," "penetrale regni") where the main crime of the tragedy occurs: "Hinc auspicari regna Tantalidae solent. | Hinc petere lapsis rebus ac dubiis opem." Cf. also Cicero on Leto, who found shelter and gave birth on Delos; Verres made off with her children's effigies (*signa*), which all others held sacred (*In Verrem* 2.1.17.48).

390/14 **maternae . . . metuere.** For the proverbial extravagance of motherly worry cf. Ovid, *Fasti* 4.558.

390/15–18 **quae . . . lucraturus.** For this appeal to common law see the note on 388/19–21.

390/20–25 **Quod . . . vellem.** Cf. Dido's imprecation against Aeneas in Vergil, *Aeneid* 4.612–21, and Agrippina's curse on Nero in pseudo-Seneca, *Octavia* 619–31. This and one other prophetic curse uttered by Richard himself (480/20–23) provide a kind of elliptical closure for More's open-ended exemplum.

390/26 **multum . . . promouere.** Cf. *CW 9*, 9/8.

392/9 **Sub hec . . . conticuit.** For a similar earlier account of the Queen's deliberations at this juncture see *CW 2*, Commentary at 40/24.

392/13–18 **subducendo . . . dari.** Cf. *CW 4*, 78/16–19.

392/19 **perditissimis . . . spes.** Cf. Tibullus 2.6.19–20.

392/21–22 **si . . . fore.** Cf. Seneca, *Thyestes* 965–66, "vel sine causa, vel sero times."

392/27-394/2 **rata . . . committeret.** Cf. Livy 22.22.14: "Habita fides ipsam plerumque obligat fidem."

394/12–14 **esse . . . exhaurire.** Cf. Seneca, *Medea* 1112–13: "In matre si quod pignus etiamnunc latet, | Scrutabor ense viscera, et ferro extraham."

394/16 **obimbibet.** This word is apparently More's coinage.

394/16–17 **frater . . . imperium.** Cf. Seneca, *Thyestes* 40–41: "Fratrem expavescat frater, et natum parens | natusque patrem . . ." The historical basis for Elizabeth Woodville's first statement is presumably the execution of Clarence by Edward IV; for the second, presumably the deposition of Edward II by the murderous partisans of his son, Edward III. See also 334/14–17, and note.

394/18–20 **alter . . . seruat.** Cf. Aeneas' comment to his father Anchises in Vergil, *Aeneid* 2.709–10: "Quo res cumque cadent, unum et commune periclum, Una salus ambobus erit." Also pertinent in view of More's parallel English ("eche of their liues lieth in the others body," *CW 2*, 41/29) is Aristotle's definition of friendship as "a single soul dwelling in two bodies" (Diogenes Laertius 5.20). Either allusion is somewhat ironic, since they stress wholesome togetherness while More emphasizes cautionary separation. Cf. *Macbeth* 2.3.140–43.

394/21–22 **mercator . . . periclitatur.** Cf. Walther, no. 32193.

396/5–10 **Statimque . . . dicessit.** Cf. Chaucer, "Clerk's Tale," *Canterbury Tales*, IV 551–60. For *dicessit* we could read *discessit* or *decessit*.

396/9 **lachrimansque a plorante.** Cf. Cicero, *Ad Quintum Fratrem* 1.3.1 ("flens flentem . . . dimiseras") and Ovid, *Tristia* 1.3.17.

396/10–20 **Quem . . . creduntur.** For several earlier accounts of this episode see *CW 2*, Commentary at 42/14, 42/20, and 42/22–23.

398/6 **tractandarum rerum artifices.** Cf. the *Letter to Lee*, 188/11–12, where More compliments Erasmus' rhetoric by calling him "cuiusuis tractandae rei mirificus artifex."

398/11–12 **Redimendae . . . locum.** Cf. Erasmus, *Institutio principis christiani*, *ASD 4/1*, 186, lines 623–24.

398/14–15 **omnes . . . tollere.** Cf. Suetonius, *Caligula* 32, and 2 Mach. 8:18, cited in *CW 14*, Commentary 1 at 59/7.

398/16–17 **Quem . . . struxisse.** Another reminder of Henry VII; for his bodyguard see Chrimes, p. 68, and cf. *CW 3/2*, no. 19/132–33.

398/18–20 **eum . . . possis.** Cf. Erasmus, *Institutio principis christiani*, *ASD 4/1*, 156, lines 617–18, 622–24.

398/21–23 **qua . . . insisteret.** Cf. the note on 478/21 and Seneca, *Hippolytus* 721–22: "Scelere velandum est scelus. | Tutissimum est inferre, cum timeas, gradum."

400/1–2 **malumque . . . vertere.** Cf. the *Letter to Lee,* 184/20–21 and note; Erasmus, *Institutio principis christiani, ASD 4/1,* 153, lines 537–38, 174, lines 232–35, 176, lines 334–35.

400/5 **conuentum.** In *CW 4,* 134/32, More uses the word *conuentus* to refer to the territory surrounding a particular Utopian city. For additional instances of *conuentus* employed to mean "county" (and possibly "earldom") see Polydore Vergil, *Anglica historia,* ed. Denys Hay (London, 1950), p. 80, line 18, and p. 108, lines 20–21.

400/23-402/4 **spargi . . . procellam.** Cf. Seneca, *Thyestes:*
> Causam timoris, ipse quam ignoro, exigis.
> Nihil timendum video; sed timeo tamen. (434–35)
> Mittit luctus signa futuri
> Mens, ante sui praesaga mali.
> Instat nautis fera tempestas,
> Cum sine vento tranquilla tument. (957–60)

For Shakespeare's echo of the second Senecan passage in *Richard III* (2.3.42–44), see *CW 2,* Commentary at 44/22–23. In *Macbeth* 4.2.18–22 Shakespeare appears to be echoing More's own adaptation of Seneca.

402/5 **odoratus.** For the proverbial force of such metaphors see the *Letter to a Monk,* note on 208/20.

402/11–12 **admonitis . . . esset.** Cf. Tacitus, *Annales* 2.42.

402/14–15 **plebs . . . agitatur.** Cf. Chaucer, "The Clerk's Tale," *Canterbury Tales,* IV 995–96, and Petrarch, *Il Trionfo di Tempo* 132–34, for the weathervane inconstancy of the people; see also Horace, *Carmina* 1.1.7, "mobilium turba Quiritium."

406/1–2 **animo . . . pertentato.** Cf. Tacitus, *Historiae* 1.29.

406/8–9 **maturandum . . . dubitant.** Cf. 432/9–12 and Lucan 1.279–80: "Dum trepidant nullo firmatae robore partes, | Tolle moras; semper nocuit differre paratis." More is almost undoubtedly wrong to date Hastings' demise after the Duke of York was extracted from sanctuary; see *CW 2,* Commentary at 44/9 and 45/3-4, and Ross, *Richard III,* pp. 83–84.

406/14-412/7 **Igitur . . . adproperaret.** For other similar accounts of the Tower episode and Richard's charges see *CW 2,* Commentary at 46/27–47/1, 47/29, and 49/1. Though More denies that Elizabeth Woodville could have possibly conspired with Jane Shore, he himself notes one instance of two rivals banding together to quell a third party; see 342/2–5. The queen later joined forces with a rival "queen mother," Lady Margaret Beaufort; see Chrimes, p. 22.

406/20 **symbolum.** we would normally expect "symbolam." Cf. Prov. 23:21.

406/28 **quam totus ab illo mutatus.** Cf. Vergil, *Aeneid* 2.274, on Aeneas' vision of the dead Hector.

408/1–2 **toruus . . . minabundus.** Cf. Seneca, *Troades* 467, also on Hector, "fronte sic torva minax . . ." We would normally expect *minitabundus*.

408/1–2 **obducto . . . fronte.** Cf. Erasmus, *Adagia* 748–49, *Opera omnia*, 2, 316F–317B.

408/2 **admorso labro.** See *CW 2*, Commentary at 47/17 and cf. Prov. 16:30.

408/2–3 **astupentibus . . . corripuisset.** Cf. Plautus, *Miles gloriosus* 434, *Epidicus* 475, *Aulularia* 71.

408/9–11 **Ad hec verba . . . erat.** Cf. Vergil, *Aeneid* 2.119–21.

408/14 **sceleris machinatrix.** For the phrasing cf. Seneca, *Medea* 266.

408/16–18 **cepit . . . cerneret.** Cf. Vergil, *Aeneid* 2.130–31.

408/22 **ea ipsa die.** More seems to link the two executions for purely dramatic reasons. For Hastings' death (June 13) see the note on 406/8–9; for the death of the Queen's kinsmen at Pomfret (June 25) see *CW 2*, Commentary at 20/13–14 and 57/21.

408/27 **vxore Shori.** On "Shore's wife" (Elizabeth, not Jane) see *CW 2* (third printing), 314.

408/27 **praestigiatricibus.** Plautus, *Amphitruo* 782, *Truculentus* 134.

410/3–4 **occasionem . . . captari.** Cf. Tacitus, *Historae* 2.52.

412/7–10 **ita . . . videam.** Cf. Acts 23:12, where several Jews swear that they will neither eat nor drink until they have killed Paul. Paul himself was decapitated.

414/1-416/8 **Operae . . . fecere.** Though debates about how dreams are caused and what they might portend may have been quite as common in the Renaissance as they were in the Middle Ages, the discussion of dreams in More's *Historia* bears a strong family resemblance to several medieval, specifically Chaucerian instances; see *The House of Fame* 1.52, "The Nun's Priest's Tale," *Canterbury Tales*, VII 2881–3148 (especially 3067–3109), *Troilus and Criseyde* 5.358–85, 1233–53 (all with precedents in Macrobius and Avicenna). Pandarus in *Troilus and Criseyde*, 5.358–74, offers basically the same alternative explanations as Hastings for a "natural dream" (*somnium naturale*); Troilus' ultimate nightmare, like the Earl of Derby's, involves a tusked boar (Derby's Richard III, Troilus' Diomede); and both dreams may be equally fictional. For the "bile" mentioned at 414/20 cf. "malencolie" (*Troilus and Criseyde* 5.360) and "rede colera" ("Nun's Priest's Tale" 2928).

414/3–5 **siue ineluctabilis . . . colludat.** Cf. Lucan 2.7–13.

414/8 **Stanleo.** Thomas Stanley, Earl of Derby; see 402/17-404/16 and *CW* 2, Commentary at 44/17.

414/23–24 **rata . . . fieri.** Cf. Livy 8.24: "ferme fugiendo in media fata ruitur."

414/25 **vt fugientibus . . . fidum.** Cf. Sallust, *Bellum Iugurthinum* 24.4.

414/25–26 **iure . . . fugitiuos?** Cf. Publilius Syrus, *Sententiae* 204: "Fatetur facinus is, qui iudicium fugit."

416/2–3 **malo . . . videamur.** Cf. Seneca, *Phoenissae* 493–94, "Quoties necesse est fallere aut falli a suis, | Patiare potius ipse, quam facias, scelus."

416/4–5 **tam . . . habeo.** Cf. Whiting H76.

416/8 **fidem somnio fecere.** Cf. *CW 4*, 80/28, "fidem adagio facerent."

416/8–10 **Certum . . . terram.** Cf. Vergil, *Aeneid* 2.242–43.

418/9–10 **Reginae . . . auribus.** Cf. Lucian, *De calumnia* 8.

418/19–22 **Hoc . . . suis.** Cf. *CW 14*, 457/5–8, on Judas' blindness in the face of destruction, Tacitus, *Historiae* 2.70 ("tam propinquae sortis ignarus"), and Cicero, *Disputationes tusculanae* 5.21.62, on the sword of Damocles. For an earlier reference to Hastings' deluded elation see *CW* 2, Commentary at 49/25–26.

418/24–420/1 **densam . . . misere.** Cf. Lucian, *De calumnia* 1; Vergil, *Aeneid* 10.501–02; *CW 3/2*, no. 56; and *CW 14*, 459/1–4.

420/19–21 **ipsorum . . . paenitentiae.** Cf. Erasmus, *Institutio principis christiani*, *ASD 4/1*, 154, lines 563/65, on the good king "apud quem praemia parata sint bonis omnibus, malis venia, si modo sese ad frugem meliorem referant."

420/21-422/2 **Ad hec . . . precarentur.** Cf. Erasmus, *Institutio principis christiani*, *ASD 4/1*, 160, lines 735–37.

422/8 **flagitiosi . . . consilij.** Erasmus himself advocates using the death penalty to make an example of bad counsellors; see *Institutio principis christiani*, *ASD 4/1*, 176, lines 297/311.

422/21–22 **nisi . . . admitteret.** Cf. the *Letter to Dorp*, 36/25–27, 110/20–24, and notes; see also 424/6–8, below. For transgressions too serious for mockery see Cicero, *De oratore* 2.59.238, and the *Letter to Brixius, CW 3/2*, 598/10–11.

422/25–26 **Haud . . . tibi.** Terence, *Andria* 476.

424/1 **Shorae.** For "Shore's wife" see note on 408/27; for an earlier account of her punishment see *CW* 2, Commentary at 54/14.

424/8–10 **vt . . . moribus.** Cf. Tacitus, *Annales* 2.33, on Tiberius the selfstyled reformer, and Chaucer, "Clerk's Tale," *Canterbury Tales*, IV

440–41, on the supposed providential accession of Griselda. Cf. also Erasmus, *Adagia* 786, *Opera omnia*, 2, 329BC, and *Moriae Encomium*, *ASD 4/3*, 104, line 604.

424/11–18 **magna . . . pepererit.** Cf. Chaucer, "Clerk's Tale," *Canterbury Tales*, IV 894–900.

424/13–19 **Ceterum . . . curiosos.** Cf. Seneca, *Troades* 1137–46.

424/19–22 **quanquam . . . procuratum.** Cf. Tacitus, *Annales* 15.44, on Nero's outrageous treatment of Christians charged with plotting to burn Rome: ". . . unde quanquam adversus sontes et novissima exempla meritos miseratio oriebatur, tamquam non utilitate publica, sed in saevitiam unius absumerentur."

424/23-430/14 **Hec . . . conservasset.** More's portrait of "Jane" Shore includes various ironic affinities with Augustine's exemplary portrait of his sainted mother (*Confessions* 9.9.19–9.11.27); the gaunt, humbled "Jane" Shore also bears some resemblance to the traditional penitent Magdalen (see Marjorie M. Malvern, *Venus in Sackcloth: The Magdalene's Origins and Metamorphoses*, Carbondale and Edwardsville, 1975, esp. pp. 76–79). The convergence of St. Monica, Mary Magdalene, Cressida, and Griselda in one feminine figure betokens her singular importance as a foil for More's Richard.

426/8–9 **haud . . . dignatus.** An ironic echo of Vergil, *Aeneid* 1.335.

426/21-428/1 **Quorum . . . ossa.** Cf. 430/8–14 below and note. See also Plautus, *Captivi* 135.

428/4–8 **Nec . . . notabilis.** Cf. *CW 3/2*, 143/97–101, Chaucer, "Clerk's Tale," *Canterbury Tales*, IV 407–13, as well as Sallust's description of the courtesan Sempronia (*Catilina* 25.5).

428/19–21 **nulla . . . tractauit.** Cf. Tacitus, *Annales* 13.2, where the subject is Nero.

428/22–27 **hec muliercula . . . erat.** Cf. Chaucer, "Clerk's Tale," *Canterbury Tales*, IV 428–36.

428/22–23 **facinus . . . cacodemonem.** Cf. Tilley S470.

428/28–29 **siue . . . conscientiam.** Cf. Tacitus, *Annales* 2.22.

430/2–3 **adeo . . . amaretur.** Cf. Erasmus, *Panegyricus, ASD 4/1*, 55, lines 924–25.

430/6 **scelerum . . . inclarescunt.** Cf. Plautus, *Rudens* 619.

430/7–8 **beneficia . . . insculpimus.** Cf. Seneca, *Epistolae* 81.23, and contrast 332/16, above.

430/8–14 **At eadem . . . conseruasset.** Cf. 426/21–428/1, above; Tacitus, *Agricola* 3; and Lucian, *Timon* 5, 8, on the closely linked themes of oblivion and ingratitude. For a strikingly similar vision of a destitute woman of pleasure see Robert Henryson, "The Testament of Cresseid," especially lines 495–504; but More's stress on the thanklessness of Jane Shore's own former dependents has no ready parallel in Henryson.

430/15 **eadem hora.** For the actual dates see the note on 408/22.

432/2–3 **nulla . . . Principi.** Contrast 338/6–11 and 418/3–11, above.

432/9–12 **occupato . . . esset.** See the note on 406/8–9, above.

434/5–6 **frater . . . deterserat.** See the *Letter to Dorp*, note on 16/24. For "perfrictissimae frontis" see Erasmus, *Adagia* 747, *Opera omnia*, 2, 316A.

434/17–21 **huc . . . filium.** For the actual proclamations and sermons advancing these claims see *CW* 2, Commentary at 58/27.

434/21–24 **Sed . . . abstinendum.** In her anger over Edward's engagement to Elizabeth Woodville, his own mother reportedly threatened to declare him a bastard; see *CW* 2, Commentary at 59/25.

434/25 **obliquo . . . ductu.** See *CW* 4, Commentary at 98/30.

436/9 **Hyspaniam.** More here confuses two different proposals; see *CW* 2, Commentary at 60/7.

436/12–13 **materno . . . obscuro.** See *CW* 2, Commentary at 60/15–17; for the phrasing cf. Tacitus, *Historiae* 2.50.

436/21–22 **vtrobique . . . proditores.** Cf. 370/5–6; for an earlier expression of much the same notion see *Scriptores historiae augustae*, Pescenninus Niger 1.1. More's remark recalls Henry VII's retroactive impeachment of Richard's supporters as traitors (see the note on 346/21 above) and reminds us that objective history of factional conflicts like this one is almost impossible.

438/6 **victoria deciso iure.** See the note on 346/21.

438/8–9 **orationi . . . forma.** Cf. Publilius Syrus, *Sententiae* 199: "Formosa facies muta commendatio est."

438/17–18 **remotis . . . est.** Cf. Ovid, *Metamorphoses* 10.19, "falsi positis ambagibus oris"; for *appellare* meaning "to proposition" see Seneca, *Controversiae* 2.7(15).7.

438/18–20 **tum . . . extingui.** Cf. Sir Thomas Malory, *Works*, ed. E. Vinaver, 3 vols. (Oxford, 1947), 2, 918, of an enchantress enticing Sir Perceval: "Than she refused hym in a maner when he requyred her, for cause he sholde be the more ardente on hir. . . . And whan she saw hym well enchaffed, than she seyde . . . ," and Vergil, *Aeneid* 5.344.

438/22–25 **ipsam . . . illuderet.** See the passages cited in the note on 440/12–18 below.

440/1–4 **tam ... statuit.** Cf. Chaucer, "Clerk's Tale," *Canterbury Tales*, IV 239–45. For "amorem consulens suum" cf. Livy 30.12.19 and the reading of *1565*.

440/4–6 **certus ... lusurum.** Cf. Chaucer, "The Merchant's Tale," *Canterbury Tales*, IV 1606–16.

440/12–18 **istud ... subsidit.** Cf. Chaucer, "Clerk's Tale," *Canterbury Tales*, IV 814–24, and the Latin version by Petrarch which Chaucer adapted (*Sources and Analogues of Chaucer's Canterbury's Tales*, ed. W. F. Bryan and Germaine Dempster, Chicago, 1941, p. 320): ". . . semper scivi inter magnitudinem tuam et humilitatem meam nullam esse proporcionem; meque nunquam tuo, non dicam coniugio, sed servicio dignam duxi, inque hac domo, in qua tu me dominam fecisti, Deum testor, animo semper ancilla permansi." Cf. also *Adagia* 3457, *Opera omnia*, 2, 1067C, and Tacitus, *Annales* 13.13. There is probably an ironic allusion to Griselda's second self-deprecating assertion in Elizabeth Woodville's remarks at 438/22–25 above. For other references to Griselda's lowly origins see Chaucer, "Clerk's Tale," *Canterbury Tales*, IV 479–83, 631–34, 722–25, 792–801, 988–91.

440/21–22 **Incommode ... dissident.** Cf. Walther, no. 20638.

440/25 **tuus ... det?** Cf. Seneca, *Medea* 508: "Meis Creusa liberis fratres dabit?"

442/3 **bigamiae labe.** On the "stain of a second marriage" see Gratian, *Decretum*, lib. I. dist. 34 cap. 13 (*CIC*, 1, 129), and *CW 2*, Commentary at 62/25; on English dislike for their kings' marrying widows see *CW 2*, Commentary at 62/23–24.

442/4–5 **longius ... quidem.** See the note on 478/21.

442/9–11 **At rex ... respondit.** This may be an ironic variation on Aeneas' rebuff of Dido in Vergil, *Aeneid* 4.393–96.

442/10–11 **propositi sui firmus.** We would expect rather "proposito suo firmus" (cf. Velleius 2.63.3); for "propositi tenax," one of the possible variant phrasings in *P*, see Ovid, *Metamorphoses* 10.405.

442/12 **materna tutela.** Cf. Horace, *Epistolae* 1.1.21–22.

442/12–14 **matrimonium ... debeat.** Cf. Chaucer, "Clerk's Tale," *Canterbury Tales*, IV 792–95.

442/18–23 **Nam ... vidimus.** Cf. Erasmus, *Institutio principis christiani*, *ASD 4/1*, 208–09, lines 302–27.

442/27-444/1 **promittunt ... sepius.** Cf. Livy 43.18.11.

444/5–7 **iam ... fuerit.** Cf. *CW 4*, 88/22–23, 90/20–21.

444/17–19 **priuatus . . . obtruderetur.** Cf. Chaucer, "Clerk's Tale," *Canterbury Tales*, IV 171–73, 796–98. For "vxor . . . obtruderetur" see Terence, *Hecyra* 295, *Andria* 250.

446/3–4 **nascetur . . . tamen.** Cf. Lucian, *Toxaris* 26.

446/6–7 **dolore spreti consilij.** Cf. Vergil, *Aeneid* 1.27, on Juno's wrath, which was aroused by "Iudicium Paridis spretaeque iniuria formae."

446/8 **Elizabetha . . . Lucia.** For More's confusion of Elizabeth Lucy and Eleanor Butler see *CW* 2, Commentary at 64/24–25, and Ross, *Richard III*, pp. 89–90.

446/16 **materna pietas.** Cf. C. A. J. Armstrong, "The Piety of Cicely, Duchess of York: A Study in Late Medieval Culture," in *For Hilaire Belloc: Essays in Honor of his 71st Birthday*, ed. Douglas Woodruff (London, 1942), pp. 68–91.

448/2–3 **charior . . . suo.** Cf. Juvenal 10.350, on the gods' resistance to prayers which are actually harmful: "Carior est illis [sc., numinibus] homo, quam sibi." In view of the violent consequences of Elizabeth Woodville's marriage with Edward, More's remark here is highly ironic.

448/7–8 **Tantus . . . vergeret.** Cf. Justinus 5.4, a remark about Alcibiades' role in the Peloponnesian war: "Enimvero tantum in uno viro fuisse momenti, ut . . . unde stetisset, eo se victoria transferret." Polydore Vergil makes a very similar statement about Warwick in *Anglica historia* (Basel: J. Bebel, 1534), sig. T_4, and the manuscript version of this passage (Vatican MS. urb. lat. 498 [II], dated 1514, fols. 183–83v) is worth quoting at length:

> Praeterea animi magnitudo / cum paribus corporis uiribus / eandem [*sc.*, Varuici] gratiam augebat / quibus populus fictus [*for* fisus?] persuasum habebat / nullam esse tam grandem rerum molem: quae ipsi Ricardo / tuto committi non posset. Qua propter quo se ille inclinabat: eo quoque maioris partis populi fauor sese uertebat. Quo demum factum est: ut hic solus uir pulso Henrico: Regnum Edwardo praebuerit: illique mox (ut suus edocebit locus) ademerit: atque Henrico restituerit: quem ab iniuria perpetuo deinceps defendisset: si diutius uixisset.

In the *Anglica historia* this passage heads up a discussion of Warwick's initial alliance with Richard, Duke of York, under Henry VI; in the 1534 published version the passage omits the last sentence, clearly parallel with More's previous statement at 448/5–7. More's *staret* or *stetisset* suggests that his echo of Justin is fairly direct; Polydore's rather intrusive comment on Edward's much later contentions with Warwick may indicate that Polydore is drawing on More's terse synopsis, not vice versa (cf. *CW 2*, lxxv–lxxvii). At any rate, this remarkable parallel between the two manuscript histories suggests that the relation of More's work to Polydore's *manuscript* history of Richard III's rise to power deserves much closer study.

448/10 immodica . . . perpetua. Cf. Tacitus, *Annales* 3.30, "fato potentiae raro sempiternae," Lucan 1.70–71, "summisque negatum | Stare diu."

448/21–23 cui . . . exigendas. See the note on 346/21.

450/3 Spuria . . . altas. Sap. 4:3.

450/11–12 erumpente . . . veritate. Cf. the *Letter to a Monk*, 208/1–3, and note.

452/2–3 Iohannem . . . redarguat. Matt. 14:3–12, Mark 6:14–28. For this form of adulation cf. Tacitus, *Annales* 1.8.

452/9–10 virum . . . clarissimum. An ironic reversal of Sallust, *Bellum Iugurthinum* 14.2: "[Iugurtha] homo omnium quos terra sustinet sceleratissimus."

452/17–18 haud . . . numine. Cf. Cicero, *In Verrem* 1.1.1.

454/22-468/14 Amor . . . acceptum. The beginning and ending of this speech bear some resemblance to the beginning and ending of More's *Letter to Oxford.* For the phrasing of Buckingham's first two sentences cf. also Demosthenes 1.1–2, cited in Lucian, *Jupiter tragoedus* 15. For various other reports of Buckingham's oration see *CW 2*, Commentary at 69/2.

456/10–11 bonis . . . improbos. Cf. *CW 4*, 102/24–25, and Erasmus, *Institutio principis christiani, ASD 4/1*, 156/598–99: "Tyrannus hoc agit, vt ciuium opes ad paucos eosque pessimos conferantur . . ." For Edward's continuing exactions in the last years of his life see the note on 318/14–17 above.

456/12–17 beneuolentiae . . . retulisset. For a similar attack on "benevolences" see *CW 2*, Commentary at 69/27-70/1.

456/14–15 non . . . auferebant. Cf. Cicero, *In Verrem* 2.3.114.35.

456/19–20 delicta . . . sunt. Cf. Erasmus, *Institutio principis christiani, ASD 4/1*, 199–200, lines 10–11. This claim would almost certainly have reminded More's readers of Henry VII's rapacity, a good deal more notorious than Edward's or Richard's; see *CW 3/2*, no. 19/36–41, and Commentary.

456/22 irae . . . auaritiae. Cf. More's English at *CW 2*, 54/14.

458/1–6 rei . . . Principis. Cf. Erasmus, *Institutio principis christiani, ASD 4/1*, 202, lines 91–93.

458/3–19 **Quarum . . . erat?** For Edward's self-serving judicial attacks on Thomas Burdett and Thomas Cook see Ross, *Edward IV*, 99–101, 240–41.

458/11–14 **Quid . . . gessit.** Cf. Cicero, *In Verrem* 2.2.46.112.

458/13-16 **qui . . . damno.** Cf. the *Letter to Lee*, 162/29–164/1, the *Letter to Brixius*, *CW 3/2*, 646/5–8, and Erasmus, *Panegyricus*, *ASD 4/1*, 28, lines 76–78.

458/23–24 **coturnatis . . . nominibus.** Cf. Macrobius, *Saturnalia* 5.7.

458/24- 460/5 **Quin . . . fuit.** Cf. Erasmus, *Institutio principis christiani*, *ASD 4/1*, 156, lines 600–01: "Tyrannus hoc agit, vt omnes sibi legibus aut delationibus habeat obnoxios . . ." Though it is clearly ironic for a partisan of Richard III to be making a charge of this sort against Edward, the irony is two-edged; an even worse offender in the matter of judicial blackmail was Henry VII. See the note on 346/21, *CW 3/2*, no. 19/32–33, 42–45, and Commentary; for a comparison of all three kings' coercive use of bonds and recognizances see Ross, *Richard III*, pp. 180–81.

460/8–9 **e quo . . . promanat.** Cf. Erasmus, *Institutio principis christiani*, *ASD 4/1*, 156, lines 611–12.

460/20–21 **nobilium . . . relicta?** Cf. Seneca, *Hercules furens* 383.

460/23–25 **quem . . . quidem?** Cf. Sallust, *Bellum Iugurthinum* 10.5. For the wording cf. also Terence, *Heauton timoroumenos* 202.

462/1–4 **scortum . . . patrocinio?** Cf. Cicero, *In Verrem* 2.5.13.34. Cf. the feeble defense of Edward's sexual conduct at 318/3–8, above.

462/4 **necessario . . . patrocinio.** Cf. Tacitus, *Historiae* 2.60: "necessariis magis defensionibus quam honestis."

462/9–15 **adeo . . . oprimeret.** Cf. Cicero, *In Verrem* 2.4.45.101: "tu tantam cupiditatem concepisti, ut eam non metus, non religio, non deorum vis, non hominum existimatio contineret."

462/18–21 **tam . . . decidere.** Cf. Cicero, *In Verrem* 2.1.27.68.

464/8–9 **in rebus . . . prebuistis.** Cf. Cicero, *In Verrem* 2.5.46.124.

464/14 **Quam . . . attendite.** Cf. Erasmus, *Panegyricus*, *ASD 4/1*, 28, lines 79–81; Cicero, *In Verrem* 2.5.17.42.

464/19–23 **tam . . . ascendit.** Cf. Erasmus, *Panegyricus*, *ASD 4/1*, 61, lines 115–18.

466/19–22 **qui . . . ceperit.** On the virtuous wise man's reluctance to govern see Plato, *Republic* 7.521AB, and Erasmus, *Institutio principis christiani*, *ASD 4/1*, 152/511–15:

Cum principatum suscipis, ne cogita, quantum accipias honoris,
sed quantum oneris ac sollicitudinis neque censum ac vectigalium
modum expende, sed curam, nec arbitreris tibi praedam obtigisse,
sed administrationem.

Nullus imperio gerendo censetur idoneus authore Platone, nisi
qui coactus et inuitus suscipit imperium. . . .

Richard's echo of Buckingham's statement at 478/3–6 makes a total
mockery of the pretense that Richard had no part in Buckingham's
own machinations as king-maker; see also 482/3–7 and cf. Tiberius'
hypocritical disclaimers in Tacitus, *Annales* 1.11.

466/22–23 **Quod . . . ludi.** Cf. Walther, no. 9245: "Femina subtilis non
est ludus puerilis."

466/23–24 **Veh . . . est.** Eccl. 10:16. Cf. 336/4–5, above.

468/15–16 **manibus pedibusque.** Terence, *Andria* 161. Erasmus,
Adagia 315 and 2868, *Opera omnia*, 2, 157B and 931A; Otto 1034.

468/25–26 **nunquam . . . bene.** Cf. Terence, *Phormio* 278, quoted by
More in Allen, *4*, 219, lines 80–81: "Ni nossem causam, crederem vera
hunc loqui." On the common sophistic ambition to "make the worse
argument the better" see Aristotle, *Rhetorica* 2.24.11, Quintilian
2.17.17., and Diogenes Laertius 2.20.

472/1–2 **vno . . . respondeatis.** Cf. Terence, *Andria* 45.

472/5 **haud . . . futuri.** Cf. the *Letter to Brixius*, *CW 3/2*, 620/29–30, and
Debellation, *EW*, sig. O₃: "we shall for this matter trouble you no
longer."

472/13 **pueri . . . rebus.** Cf. Chaucer, "Clerk's Tale," *Canterbury Tales*,
IV 1004.

472/14 **bireta.** On this word see *CW 3/2*, Commentary at 95/12.

474/5 **senatum populumque Londinensem.** This phrase almost certainly alludes to the common description of the Roman state in antiquity as *Senatus populusque Romanus* (S.P.Q.R.).

474/21-476/1 **cui . . . vellent.** An ironic echo of Vergil, *Aeneid* 3.298–
99.

476/6–13 **immensam . . . diademate.** Cf. the ceremonious rhetoric of
More's tribute to Henry VIII in the *Letter to Brixius*, *CW 3/2*, 640/12–
23.

476/9–10 **procumbenti . . . humeros.** Cf. Vergil, *Aeneid* 12.59, and
Erasmus, *Adagia* 3493 (*Opera omnia*, 2, 1074F).

476/11–12 **manus . . . admoueret.** Cf. Plato, *Republic* 6.488A–D, Seneca, *Epistolae* 85.33, and Cicero, *Pro Sestio* 20.46, as well as *CW 4*, Commentary at 98/27.

476/12 **temoni . . . fluitantis.** For a similar use of this metaphor see ps.-Plato, *Second Alcibiades* 147a.

476/14 **dominationis tempestates.** Cf. Erasmus, *Institutio principis christiani, ASD 4/1,* 182, line 517: "At regno nunquam deest tempestas."

476/15 **immodesta modestia.** See the *Letter to Lee,* note on 176/33.

476/16–17 **ab superis . . . Britanicam.** Cf. Erasmus, *Institutio principis christiani, ASD 4/1,* 154, lines 559–60.

478/1–2 **ex . . . estimaturas.** Cf. Plautus, *Persa* 212,681, and *Trinummus* 1048–49.

478/3–6 **Haud . . . permittendum.** See the note on 466/19–22 and Erasmus, *Adagia* 766, *Opera omnia,* 2, 323 D–F.

478/10–11 **Principi . . . malit.** Cf. Plautus, *Miles gloriosus* 1356–57: "tibi servire malui multo quam alii libertus esse."

478/21 **longius . . . regrediendum.** Cf. 206/7–8, 398/21–23, 442/4–5, and Tacitus, *Historiae* 3.69: "longius iam progressus erat, quam ut regredi posset."

480/17–18 **audiens . . . redigam.** Such constructions are somewhat unusual in Latin but common in English and Greek; for the closest parallels in classical Latin see Kühner-Stegmann, 2, 501–03.

480/18–20 **administrationem . . . publicam.** See the note on 466/19–22.

480/20–23 **Quem . . . eripiant.** See the note on 390/20–25.

482/3–7 **impudens . . . geri.** See the note on 466/19–22.

482/12–13 **bis . . . velle.** For this ritual coyness or modesty cf. Gratian, *Decretum,* lib. II causa 8 quest. 1 caps. 9, 11 (*CIC,* 1, 592–94). In adapting these lines, Shakespeare (*Richard III* 3.7.51) conflates this ritual coyness with the ritual coyness of courtship: "Play the maid's part, still answer nay, and take it." Cf. also Tacitus, *Annales* 1.3 ("specie recusantis flagrantissime cupiverat") and 1.13 ("flexit [sc. Tiberius] paulatim, non ut fateretur suscipi a se imperium, sed ut negare et rogari desineret").

482/15–24 **Iam . . . pericula.** For More's use of this Lucianic stage-metaphor both here and elsewhere, see *CW 2,* Commentary at 81/1, and *CW 4,* Commentary at 98/12, 14–15, 17, and 18. Also pertinent are Erasmus, *Moriae encomium, ASD 4/3,* 104, lines 591–603, and Henry Medwall, *Fulgens and Lucrece* 1.360–68; for More's possible connection with this play (written for More's patron Morton) see *The Plays of Henry Medwall,* ed. Alan H. Nelson (Cambridge and Totowa, N.J., 1980), p. 17. More may well be obliquely referring to just such an interlude, though a craftsman might be likelier to appear in the role of a monarch (perhaps Herod or Pharaoh) in one of the cycle plays; cf. *CW 2*, Commentary at 81/2, and Till Eulenspiegel's outrageous prank of unmasking an Easter play angel as a priest's concubine (*Howleglass* [?1528], in *A Hundred Merry Tales and Other English Jestbooks of the Fifteenth and Sixteenth Centuries*, ed. P. M. Zall, Lincoln, Nebraska, 1963, p. 166).

482/15–21 **imperatorem ... regum.** In *Utopia, CW 4*, 98/14–22, where life is likened to comedy and not tragedy, More actually uses the word *tragicomoedia* to refer to the effect of disrupting a basically lighthearted play with the rhetoric of serious dialogue. In the *Historia Richardi Tertii*, on the other hand, More suggestively offsets the notion of merely playing an emperor in a tragedy with the "tragic play-acts" of real kings; in these terms, the stage-play of life is invariably tragicomic, and the only consistent and stable role is not that of the decorously purposeful activist but rather that of the disengaged ironic spectator. It may be significant that the last lines of this passage were omitted in the Louvain edition of More's Latin works, an edition which emphasized his performance as a Catholic activist and martyr.

482/16–17 **inscitia ... scias.** Cf. Plautus, *Miles gloriosus* 572, Terence, *Heauton timoroumenos* 748 and *Eunuchus* 721, and Publilius Syrus, *Sententiae* 234; see also Tacitus, *Annales* 1.11, on a similar group of spectators, "quibus unus metus, si intellegere viderentur."

482/26–27 **proximum ... coenobium.** For this prepositional usage cf. Sallust, *Bellum Iugurthinum* 19.4, "proxime Hispaniam Mauri sunt."

484/1–5 **ex eo loco ... esse.** Cf. Erasmus, *Institutio principis christiani, ASD 4/1*, 210–11, lines 375–86.

484/17 **semper ... nam.** See Introduction, p. cxxxix, above.

484/17–18 **nam ... conscius.** Cf. Plautus, *Bacchides* 1024.

484/18–21 **nec ... repercussurus.** Cf. Sallust, *Bellum Iugurthinum* 72.2; "circumspectare ... repercussurus" has an even closer precedent in Homer, *Odyssey* 11.608, an unsettlingly lively description of Hercules' specter in Hades. Cf. also Spenser's endlessly errant Blatant Beast (*Faerie Queene* 6.12.38–41).

INDEX

INDEX

Abelard, Peter, 569
Abingdon, xxx–xxxi, 135, 149
Abraham, 601
Absolution, 55–57, 63, 515
Ackroyd, P. R., 581
Acts, xlvi n., 592, 621
Adams, H. M., 514
Ad hominem arguments, lxx–lxxi, xcvi–xcvii, c–ci
Adrian VI, pope. *See* Floriszoon, Adriaan
Adultery, 215, 273, 429, 435, 451
Aemilius, Paulus, c n.
Aeneas, 11, 499, 618–20, 625
Aeschylus, 589, 591
Aesop, xxii n., 597
Agricola, Rodolphus, xxi, lxiii–lxiv
Agrippa, Marcus Postumus, 323
Agrippina, 618
Alard of Amsterdam, xxiv
Alberigo, Giuseppe, lxxxii n., 489, 503, 570, 584
Albert of Saxony, 507
Albertus Magnus, 27, 103, 507, 535
Alcibiades, 626
Alcuin, 505
Alexander of Aphrodisias, 99, 103, 532–34
Alexander of Hales, 509
Alexander of Ville-Dieu, 27, 69, 507, 521
Alexander the Great, 103, 534
Alexandria, 577
Alfred, Saxon king, 552
Allen, P. S., xx n., xxii–xlv nn., xlviii n., xlix n., liii n., lxvii n., lxix n., lxxiii n., lxxiv n., lxxvi n., lxxvii n., lxxix n., lxxxi n., lxxxv n., lxxxvii n., lxxxix n., cxi n., xcii n., cxix, cxxviii n., clii n., 490, 497–506, 508–09, 511–13, 515–17, 520–24, 526–28, 530–31, 533–34, 536–38, 540–42, 544, 546–73, 575–78, 580–81, 584–89, 592–93, 598–99, 602–03, 629
Allusions, recurrent. *See* Metaphors and allusions, recurrent

Altman, Janet G., xciii
Ambition, 11, 19, 31, 35, 47–51, 75, 97, 161, 165, 181, 189, 193, 219, 259, 305, 321–25, 329, 335, 349, 357, 395, 407, 441–49, 483, 612. *See also* Factional strife
Ammonio, Andrea, xxv, 499
Ammonius, 99, 532
Amorbach, Boniface, cxx
Ampliations, liv–lv, lx, lxv, 29–37
Anciaux, Paul, 515
Anderson, Judith H., 607
Anderson, W. J., 595
Andrelini, Fausto, 261, 586
Anecdotes and "merry tales," xxix–xxx, 27–28, 49–55, 67–69, 253–59, 273, 282–89. *See also* Eyewitness testimony
Anne of York, daughter of Edward IV, 315, 607
Antichrist, xliii n., 31–33, 203, 309, 564. *See also* Satan
Antwerp, xxii–xxiii, xxiv n., xxxv n., xxxvi, cxxvii, 542
Apostles, 87–89, 113, 217, 223, 295, 303, 365, 529, 538, 565, 575
Apostolic succession, 538
Appellations, liv–lvi, lx, 29–31, 37
Apuleius, 534, 553, 555
Aquinas. *See* St. Thomas Aquinas
Arabic (language), 95, 551
Aristarchus, lvii, lxii, 15
Aristippus, Henricus, 534
Aristophanes, 508, 589, 591
Aristotle: commentaries and translations, 99–101, 532–33; his dialectic, li n., lii n., liv, lix–lxi, lxiv, lxxi; his *Meteorologica*, 101–05; realists and nominalists, 25–27. Mentioned, 43, 75, 103, 494, 500, 505–07, 512, 515, 521, 524, 532–36, 575, 610–11, 629
Armstrong, C. A. J., 617, 626
Arnobius the Younger, 573
Ashworth, E. J., liv n., lv n.

635

ADDENDA AND CORRIGENDA
TO VOLUMES 3 (part II) 4, 5, 9, 11, AND 12

ADDENDA AND CORRIGENDA

TO VOLUMES 3 (PART II) 4, 5, 9, 11, AND 12

Volume 3, Part 2, *Latin Poems*

Pages 65 and 67, running heads. Change "IN" to "ON"
Page 132, no. 59, line 4. Change "anino" to "animo"
Page 175, middle of no. 132. Change "thoughlessly" to "thoughtlessly"
Page 207, no. 167, fourth line up. For "if read" if
Pages 320–21, note on Rhen. Pref./74–78. Add: and *CW 4*, sidenote at 130/5.
Page 328, note on 19/32–33. Change "delcaration" to "declaration"
Page 416, note on 269/12. Change "friged" to "fringed"
Page 421, note on 275/1. Add: and Giles Barber, "Thomas Linacre: A Bibliographical Survey of his Works" in *Essays on the Life and Work of Thomas Linacre,* ed. Francis Maddison, Margaret Pelling, and Charles Webster, (Oxford, 1977), pp. 292–95.
Pages 612–13. Move top line of page 613 to the bottom of page 612
Page 667. Change "64/28" to 604/28"

Volume 4, *Utopia*

Page 84, line 30, and page 86, line 4. Change "Raphäel" to "Raphaël"
Page 121, line 13. Change "nothing is private property" to "there is no private property"
Page 548, note on 230/8. Add: Cf. Vergil, *Aeneid* 1.93 and *CW 3/2*, page 665, note on 602/22.

Volume 5, *Responsio ad Lutherum*

Page 902. Add a note on 180/13 ("meientes mulae"): Cf. Catullus 97.8.

Volume 6, *A Dialogue concerning Heresies*

Page 701, note on 354/3-8. Change "Schwermgeister, 1529" to "Schwermgeister, 1527"; "October 1527" to "October 1529"

Volume 9, *The Apology*

Page 379, note on 131/32. Change "where he claims . . . Council." to "where he claims that since the canon *Excommunicamus* had been approved by the fourth Lateran Council of 1215 and the canon *Ad abolendam* in the same title contains identical phrases, the canon *Ad abolendam* could also be said to have been approved by the Council."

Page 381, note on 138/11-12. Change "chap. 23" to "chap. 18"

Volume 11, *The Answer to a Poisoned Book*

Page xviii, note 1. Change "L'Eucharistic" to "L'Eucharistie"; "réele" to "réelle"; "*age*" to "*âge*"

Page lv, fifth line from bottom. Change "farago" to "farrago"

Page lv, note 3. Change "Ende der" to "Ende des"; "luterischen" to "lutherischen"

Page lvii, note 1. Change "*de XVIe*" to "*du XVIe*"

Page 417. Change "Bareille, G. il" to "Bareille, G. xlix"

Volume 12, *A Dialogue of Comfort against Tribulation*

Page 437, note on 299/19-27. Change "indicii" to "iudicii"; "institiam" to "iustitiam"

Page 487, 2nd last line of Latin poem. Change "tota" to "totam"